September 30–October 4, 2013,
Miami, Florida, USA

Association for
Computing Machinery

*Advancing Computing as a Science & Profession*

# MobiCom'13

## Proceedings of the 19th Annual International Conference on
# Mobile Computing & Networking

*Sponsored by:*

**ACM SIGMOBILE**

*Supported by:*

**NSF, Microsoft Research, Google, IBM, and the University of Florida**

Association for
Computing Machinery

*Advancing Computing as a Science & Profession*

**The Association for Computing Machinery**
**2 Penn Plaza, Suite 701**
**New York, New York 10121-0701**



**ISBN:** 978-1-4503-1999-7 (Digital)

**ISBN:** 978-1-4503-2610-0 (Print)

Additional copies may be ordered prepaid from:

**ACM Order Department**
PO Box 30777
New York, NY 10087-0777, USA

Phone: 1-800-342-6626 (USA and Canada)
+1-212-626-0500 (Global)
Fax: +1-212-944-1318
E-mail: acmhelp@acm.org
Hours of Operation: 8:30 am – 4:30 pm ET

Printed in the USA

# General Chair's Welcome Message

It is my great pleasure to welcome you to Miami, Florida, and to the 19th Annual International Conference on Mobile Computing and Networking – *MobiCom'13*. This year the program is packed with exciting and high quality sessions, including nine paper sessions, seven workshops on emerging research/technologies, four keynotes from highly recognized researchers and visionary leaders in the industry, two hot panels, and a joint demos and posters session along with an associated one-minute-madness preview show. Additionally, and new this year, are the industry paper session addressing emerging trends and the mobile app competition. The latter, which I co-chaired with Wendong, has attracted over 50 mobile app submissions from 20 countries, utilizing Android (and Google Glass), iOS, Windows Phone, and HTML5 platforms.

In addition to the technical program, an exciting social program has been planned for all registrants. A welcome reception will kick start our social program. A Gala dinner will follow offering banquet food and entertainment. An Afro-Cuban band from the Miami area known for its unique rhythms influenced by Jazz, Blues, Brazilian and Soul music will hopefully please, entertain, and energize the *MobiCom* crowd after two intense conference days.

Putting together *MobiCom'13* has been a team effort. I would like to first thank the authors for submitting their best work and providing the content of the program in terms of papers, demos and posters. I would also like to thank the workshop organizers, the panelists, and the four keynote speakers for their contributions. I am grateful to the organization committee and its dedication in making *MobiCom'13* a success. Victor provided invaluable guidance which was very helpful throughout the process. Ranveer and Robin did an excellent job in assembling a world-class program committee for soliciting and reviewing the main track papers. Paolo and Tamer N., and Yongguang and Tamer E. have also done an excellent job in organizing an exciting joint posters and demo session. Sasu and Lili, with help from Marco and Thyaga, pulled two panels on very hot de jour topics. The panels will spice up our program and for that we are thankful to them. I am very grateful to Christine Julien for handling the tricky Publications Chair role so professionally and attending to many details carefully. Moustafa and Raja have done an awesome job in attracting and selecting interesting workshops and handling many details to meet the individual needs of each workshop. My Thai sat up RegOnline and handled registration smoothly and professionally – many thanks to My. Ahmed kept an eye on the conference finances and to him I am grateful. Many thanks go to Wendong who has put significant effort in getting the mobile app competition off the ground. Maria also did her share of carefully attending to details and running the NSF student travel grants competition. Souvik kindly stepped up to take care of the SRC competition. The publicity campaign and the timely messaging orchestrated by Pei were no doubt vital in reaching out to the broadest audience, and for that I am thankful to Pei. Last but not least, Jung Wook Park, our Web Chair, has done a herculean job in managing the MobiCom web site content and meticulously keeping it up to date. I am truly appreciative of all his efforts.

Now we cannot forget to thank our sponsor, ACM SIGMOBILE, and our generous government, academic and corporate supporters: the National Science Foundation (Platinum), Microsoft Research (Gold), Google and IBM Research (Silver), and the University of Florida (Bronze). Their sponsorship and support were vital to the successful organization of this conference.

I wish you all a pleasant stay in Miami, and a memorable and rich experience in *MobiCom*.

**Sumi Helal**
*MobiCom'13* General Chair

# Message from the Technical Program Chairs

Welcome to ACM MobiCom 2013, the 19th Annual International Conference on Mobile Computing and Networking. Over the years, MobiCom has established itself as a premier forum for publishing and presenting cutting-edge research in mobile systems and wireless networks, and this year's final program continues this wonderful tradition.

The high quality and success of MobiCom can be credited to two groups. First and foremost is the authors of all of the submitted papers who submitted their very best research ideas and results. The 28 accepted papers represent leading-edge, and sometimes bleeding-edge, advances in a large variety of important mobile computing topics – from traditional yet still very important topics, such as improving the efficiency of cellular and Wi-Fi networks, to topics focusing on the use of new wireless technologies in new mobile environments, such as enabling gesture recognition, managing indoor white space networks, and deploying performance improving femto cells. However, the hidden strength of MobiCom comes from the hard work of a very dedicated program committee, which consisted of 41 members from academia, government and industry spread across 7 different countries with expertise in many areas relevant to wireless networking and mobile computing.

As Program Committee (PC) chairs, it was our task to keep MobiCom fresh and grow it to keep up with all the new challenges of the wireless and mobile community. This year, we introduced several new initiatives to further enhance the reach and quality of the conference. To increase MobiCom's visibility in industry, we included five PC members from product teams of Cisco, Google, Qualcomm and Broadcom. To ensure the strength and breadth, but most importantly the vision, of the PC, one-sixth of the PC were new members who had previously not served on the MobiCom PC. This year's MobiCom also has an invited industry session, in which speakers from Broadcom, Alcatel-Lucent, Google, and Microsoft will present the latest results and research challenges from industry in an effort to bridge the gap between academic research and how it is, or maybe isn't, relevant to industry.

This year's call for papers attracted 207 submissions from five continents: Asia, Europe, Africa, North America and South America. We used HotCRP for handling the paper submission and reviewing, which was done in three phases. In the first phase, each paper was reviewed by at least three PC members, and the top 98 papers were selected for the next round. In the second phase, each paper was reviewed by at least two more PC members. In some cases when the paper was at the intersection of new topics, such as RADAR or robotics, additional expert opinions were solicited. The final phase was the PC meeting held on May 30th and 31st in Redmond, WA. A total of 34 members attended the PC meeting in-person, while 5 members attended the meeting on Skype. Over one and a half days, the PC extensively discussed the merits and flaws of the 60 top-rated papers and ultimately accepted 28 papers for final publication in the conferences' proceedings. Across the three phases, each PC member reviewed about 25 papers, such that most round two papers had an average of 6 reviews (a high number for any top-tier conference). To ensure fairness and preserve the anonymity of all authors and reviewers, papers authored by PC chairs were mixed with a random selection of other papers and handled out-of-band by Alex Snoeren, who was the PC co-chair for MobiCom 2012.

All of this would not have happened without the time and effort of several people. We would like to thank Alex Snoeren and Geoff Voelker for hosting the HotCRP site in UCSD and ensuring that it had no downtime throughout the review process. We are also grateful to Kirstie Magness and the Microsoft Research A/V team for ensuring a smooth, glitch-free PC meeting in Redmond, WA. Finally, we would like to thank all of the PC members for the hard work in ensuring such a high-quality conference program.

The final success of MobiCom is now up to you, the participants. We put it to you to read the papers, attend the talks and participate in the wonderful technical discussion and professional networking that go on during and between the sessions. We hope that you will find this program interesting and look forward to meeting you in Miami.

**Ranveer Chandra**
*Microsoft Research*

**Robin Kravets**
*University of Illinois*

# Table of Contents

## Posters Session

# MobiCom 2013 Conference Organization

**General Chair:** Sumi Helal *(University of Florida, USA)*

**Program Co-Chairs:** Ranveer Chandra *(Microsoft, USA)*
Robin Kravets *(University of Illinois, Urbana-Champaign, USA)*

**Workshops Co-Chairs:** Raja Bose *(Microsoft, USA)*
Moustafa Youssef *(Egypt-Japan Univ. of Science & Technology, Egypt)*

**Demos Co-Chairs:** Tamer ElBatt *(Cairo University and Nile University, Egypt)*
Yongguang Zhang *(Microsoft Research, Beijing, China)*

**Posters Co-Chairs:** Paolo Bellavesta *(University of Bologna, Italy)*
Tamer Nadeem *(Old Dominion University, USA)*

**Panels Co-Chairs:** Lili Qiu *(University of Texas at Austin, USA)*
Sasu Tarkoma *(University of Helsinki, Finland)*

**Web Chair:** Jung Wook Park *(LG Electronics, Korea)*

**Publications Chair:** Christine Julien *(University of Texas at Austin, USA)*

**Publicity Chair:** Pei Zhang *(Carnegie Mellon University, USA)*

**Publicity Co-Chairs:** Sunghyun Choi *(Seoul National University, Korea)*
Lin Zhang *(Tsinghua University, China)*

**Registration Chair:** My T. Thai *(University of Florida, USA)*

**Mobile App Competition Co-Chairs:** Wendong Li *(Nokia, USA)*
Sumi Helal *(University of Florida, USA)*

**Finance Chair:** Ahmed Helmy *(University of Florida, USA)*

**SRC Chair:** Souvik Sen *(HP Labs, USA)*

**Student Travel Grants Chair:** Maria Papadopouli *(University of Crete and FORTH, Greece)*

**Steering Committee Chair:** Victor Bahl *(Microsoft Research, USA)*

**Steering Committee:** Suman Banerjee *(University of Wisconsin-Madison, USA)*
Ramesh Govindan *(University of Southern California, USA)*
David B. Johnson *(Rice University, USA)*
Kang Shin *(University of Michigan, USA)*

**Program Committee:** Aditya Akella *(University of Wisconsin, USA)*
Alex Snoeren *(University of California San Diego, USA)*
Ashu Sabharwal *(Rice University, USA)*
Ben Greenstein *(Google, USA)*
Cecilia Mascolo *(University of Cambridge, UK)*
Cong Shen *(Qualcomm, USA)*
Debojyoti Dutta *(Cisco, USA)*
Dina Papagiannaki *(Telefonica I and D, Spain)*
Douglas Chan *(Cisco, USA)*
Edward Knightly *(Rice University, USA)*
Elizabeth Belding *(University of California Santa Barbara, USA)*
Eric Rozner *(AT&T Labs, USA)*
Li Erran Li *(Lucent Bell Laboratories, USA)*
Heather Zheng *(University of California Santa Barbara. USA)*
Jason Nieh *(Columbia University, USA)*
Kannan Srinivasan *(Ohio State University, USA)*
Krishna Sekar *(Broadcom, USA)*
Kun Tan *(Microsoft Research, China)*
Kyle Jamieson *(University College London, UK)*
Lakshmi Subramanian *(New York University, USA)*
Lili Qiu *(University of Texas Austin, USA)*
Lin Zhong *(Rice University, USA)*
Marco Gruteser *(Rutgers University, USA)*
Mingyan Liu *(University of Michigan, USA)*
Moustafa Youssef *(Egypt-Japan Univ. of Science and Technology, Egypt)*
Prabal Dutta *(University of Michigan, USA)*
Shyam Gollakota *(University of Washington, USA)*
Sneha Kasera *(University of Utah, USA)*
Songwu Lu *(University of California Los Angeles, USA)*
Srdjan Capkun *(ETH Zurich, Switzerland)*
Srikanth Krishnamurthy *(University of California, Riverside, USA)*
Sunghyun Choi *(Seoul National University, Korea)*
Thomas Moscibroda *(Microsoft Research, USA)*
Thyaga Nandagopal *(National Science Foundation, USA)*
Victor Bahl *(Microsoft Research, USA)*
Vikram Srinivasan *(Alcatel-Lucent, India)*
Vishnu Navda *(Microsoft Research, India)*
Yih-Chun Hu *(University of Illinois, USA)*
Z Morley Mao *(University of Michigan, USA)*

# MobiCom 2013 Sponsors & Supporters

**Sponsor:** acm sigmobile

**Platinum Supporter:** NSF

**Gold Supporter:** Microsoft Research

**Silver Supporters:** Google IBM Research

**Bronze Supporter:** UF UNIVERSITY of FLORIDA

# The Evolution of Mobility and Wireless Technologies in the Age of the Internet of Things

Flavio Bonomi
Cisco Systems
170 West Tasman Drive,
San Jose', California, 95134, USA
email: flavio@cisco.com

## ABSTRACT

This keynote presentation will focus on the challenges and opportunities imposed on mobility and wireless communications technologies by the emerging and explosive needs of the future Internet of Things. As traditional (wireless) networking meets the "real world", with its highly mobile requirements, its noisy and lossy environments, its need to optimize communications across multiple, non-homogeneous wireless technologies, with often intermittent connectivity, its requirements for more deterministic exchanges, the urgent need of innovation and accelerated research into a number of relevant and exiting domains become apparent.

We will describe the ICT Infrastructure developments needed to support these new requirements, and identify broad open mobility and wireless research topics, which may help catalyze innovation affecting our industry.

In particular, among other topics, we will deal with the issue of IP mobility, and will discuss technologies responding to these requirements (LISP among them). We will then consider the need to support and manage non-homogeneous, multi-homed, highly lossy wireless connectivity, and will highlight the potential roles of Distributed Computing and of Network Coding in this domain. Finally, we will detail the deterministic networking requirements arising in a number of Internet of Things verticals, and highlight progress towards the definition and standardization of techniques enabling more predictable exchanges even in wireless networks.

## Categories and Subject Descriptors

**C.2.4 [Distributed Computing]**: Cloud Computing, Ubiquitous Computing

**H.4 [Information Systems Applications]:** Miscellaneous

## Keywords

Distributed Computing, Network Coding, Deterministic Networking, LISP, Multi-homing, Internet of Things.

## BIOGRAPHY

Flavio Bonomi is a Cisco Fellow, and is heading the Advanced Architecture and Research Organization at Cisco Systems, in San Jose', California.

He is co-leading (with JP Vasseur) the vision and technology direction for Cisco's Internet of Things initiative. This broad, Cisco-wide initiative encompasses major verticals, including Energy, Connected Vehicle and Transportation, Connected Cities. In this role, with the support of his team, he is shaping a number of Research and innovation efforts relating to mobility, security, communications acceleration, distributed computing and data management.

Before joining Cisco in 1999, Flavio Bonomi was at AT&T Bell Labs, between 1985 and 1995, and then was Principal Architect at two Silicon Valley startups, ZeitNet and Stratum One.

Flavio Bonomi received a PhD Electrical Engineering in 1985, and a Master or Electrical Engineering in 1981 from Cornell University in Ithaca, New York.

He received his Electrical Engineering Degree from Pavia University, in Italy.

## ACKNOWLEDGMENTS

I sincerely acknowledge the entire Cisco Advanced Architecture and Research Team for their precious contributions to the work presented here.


*MobiCom'13*, September 30–October 4, 2013, Miami, FL, USA.
ACM 978-1-4503-1999-7/13/09.
http://dx.doi.org/10.1145/2500423.2500455

# RF-Compass: Robot Object Manipulation Using RFIDs

Jue Wang Fadel Adib Ross Knepper Dina Katabi Daniela Rus
Computer Science and Artificial Intelligence Laboratory
Massachusetts Institute of Technology
{jue_w, fadel, rak, dk, rus}@mit.edu

## ABSTRACT

Modern robots have to interact with their environment, search for objects, and move them around. Yet, for a robot to pick up an object, it needs to identify the object's orientation and locate it to within centimeter-scale accuracy. Existing systems that provide such information are either very expensive (e.g., the VICON motion capture system valued at hundreds of thousands of dollars) and/or suffer from occlusion and narrow field of view (e.g., computer vision approaches).

This paper presents RF-Compass, an RFID-based system for robot navigation and object manipulation. RFIDs are low-cost and work in non-line-of-sight scenarios, allowing them to address the limitations of existing solutions. Given an RFID-tagged object, RF-Compass accurately navigates a robot equipped with RFIDs toward the object. Further, it locates the center of the object to within a few centimeters and identifies its orientation so that the robot may pick it up. RF-Compass's key innovation is an iterative algorithm formulated as a convex optimization problem. The algorithm uses the RFID signals to partition the space and keeps refining the partitions based on the robot's consecutive moves. We have implemented RF-Compass using USRP software radios and evaluated it with commercial RFIDs and a KUKA youBot robot. For the task of furniture assembly, RF-Compass can locate furniture parts to a median of 1.28 cm, and identify their orientation to a median of 3.3 degrees.

**Categories and Subject Descriptors** C.2 [**Computer Systems Organization**]: Computer-Communications Networks

**General Terms** Algorithms, Design, Performance, Theory

**Keywords** Robot Mobile Manipulation, RFID, RF Localization, Optimization

## 1. INTRODUCTION

Today's robots routinely replace human labor in assembly tasks [34, 43]. However, the substantial cost and complexity involved restrict their use to large factories with high-volume production lines. There, the robots are typically bolted to a bench at a known location, and one type of parts is repeatedly presented to them, one item at a time with a fixed positioning and orientation. Such highly specialized assembly robots are cost-effective only in the presence of economies of scale. This leaves small to medium size factories and manufacturers unable to leverage robot operations to automate their production. Hence, it has been of a great interest in both the robotics academic community and industry to enable robots to perform more flexible and complex tasks, such as assembling products [26], fetching and delivering items [7], and collaborating with other robots [31]. For example, it is desirable to have a robot automatically fetch the various components of IKEA furniture and assemble them. In contrast to robots on large-volume assembly lines, such a robot could be deployed to assemble different types of furniture in a store.

Such more capable, adaptive robots must interact with their environment in the presence of uncertainty. They need to search for a desired object, pick it up, and move it around. These tasks require locating the object to centimeter-scale accuracy and identifying its orientation to within a few degrees so that the robot may grasp it. Currently, these functions rely on technologies that are expensive and/or error-prone. For instance, recent research demonstrating robots assembling an IKEA table [31] relies on the infrared VICON motion capture system, which costs hundreds of thousands of dollars [47]. Other solutions based on computer vision [52] and depth-imaging [38] require learning visual models of the desired objects and can fail in distinguishing visually similar objects or partially occluded objects [52]. Further, all existing technologies, whether infrared or vision-based, fail in the absence of a line-of-sight to the object, e.g., furniture part covered by other parts.

In comparison to infrared and vision-based approaches, emerging RF-based localization systems [50, 41, 6] offer an appealing alternative, with the advantages of being cost-effective and applicable to occluded and non-line-of-sight objects. Further, the wireless signal can encode the object ID, enabling the robot to easily identify a desired object without complex machine learning algorithms based on object shape and color. There are two main challenges, however, in using RF localization in robot navigation and object manipulation tasks. First, although many robots today already have WiFi connectivity, it is impractical to also place WiFi nodes on every object the robot needs to interact with. Second, the accuracy achieved by current RF localization techniques is not sufficient for object manipulation and grasping. For example, fetching the correct IKEA table leg without knowing its placement in the environment a priori requires an accuracy of position and orientation on the order of a few centimeters and degrees, respectively.


*MobiCom'13,* September 30–October 4, Miami, FL, USA.

ACM 978-1-4503-1999-7/13/09 ...$15.00.
http://dx.doi.org/10.1145/2500423.2500451

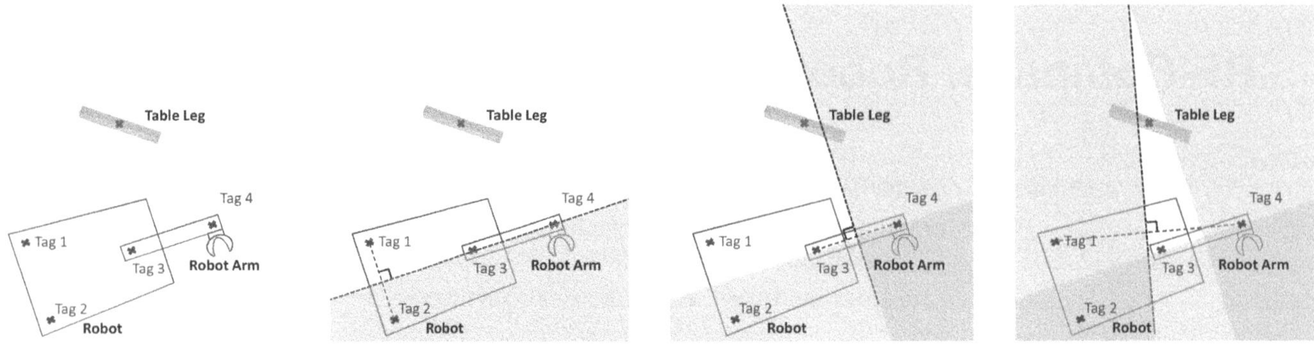


(a) **Setup** (b) **Partition by tags 1 and 2** (c) **Partition by tags 3 and 4** (d) **Partition by tags 1 and 4**

**Figure 1—Illustration of RF-Compass's partitioning algorithm:** By comparing the distances from the red RFID to a pair of blue RFIDs on the robot, we can partition the space into two regions, one of which contains the furniture part. Overlaying these partitions narrows down the candidate region. Further, the motion of the robot naturally leads to different ways of partitioning the space, which when combined iteratively refine the candidate region as the robot navigates.

This paper introduces RF-Compass, an RFID-based system that navigates and adjusts the actions of the robot to centimeter accuracy. In RF-Compass, ultra-low power, low cost RFIDs are placed on both the robot and the objects it needs to work on. In contrast to WiFi nodes, RFIDs (5–10 cents each) can be easily embedded into physical objects, as articulated in the vision of the Internet of Things [3]. In fact, many industries are already rapidly deploying RFIDs on their products as a replacement to barcodes, which do not work in non-line-of-sight settings [19, 18, 46].

RF-Compass's key innovation is a new algorithm capable of leveraging the robot's consecutive moves to iteratively refine its location and orientation estimates. Our algorithm uses pairwise comparison of RFID signals to partition the space into regions according to their distances to the desired object. Suppose we have four tags on the robot and one tag on the object as in Fig. 1(a). By comparing whether the object is closer to tag 1 than to tag 2, we can partition the space into two regions; one of them contains the desired object, as shown in Fig. 1(b). We can repeat this process to check if tag 3 or tag 4 is closer to the RFID on the object. This will generate a second partition, which when laid on top of the first partition, adds specificity to the solution, as in Fig. 1(c) and then 1(d). Mathematically, each relation between a pair of tags on the robot and the tag on the object translates into a linear constraint. We can incorporate these constraints into an optimization problem that bounds the region where the object is located.

Comparing its distances to a few RFIDs on the robot may not bound the object into a centimeter-scale region. The strength of the algorithm comes from that every move of the robot gives us new partitions, which we can lay over the old partitions to obtain a finer region for the desired object. As the robot gets close, it can maneuver its arm above the object to calibrate the size of the region to the desired accuracy. Furthermore, by having more than one RFID on the object itself, we can apply the same partitioning algorithm to each of the tags on the object to discover the orientation of the object and pinpoint its center.

An important feature of this algorithm is robustness to potential errors in estimating the RFIDs' pairwise distances. Specifically, the optimization returns the region that is consistent with the maximum number of pairwise constraints and ignores inconsistent constraints. Correct pairwise distances are consistent with each other because they all reflect the actual layout of the RFIDs. In contrast, errors are typically random and inconsistent with each other, and hence can be overcome by optimizing for consistency.

**Summary of Results:** We built a prototype of RF-Compass using software radios and commercial UHF RFIDs. We integrated the system with ROS, the Robot Operating System [40] which has support for robot navigation and path planning. We used our prototype to navigate a KUKA youBot robot [32] and direct its actions in grasping an IKEA table leg in both line-of-sight and occluded scenarios. We compared RF-Compass with the VICON motion capture system used in past work on robot furniture assembly [31]. VICON is a highly accurate system that provides millimeter positioning information [47], but costs hundreds of thousands of dollars and works only in instrumented rooms where the whole ceiling is fitted with infrared cameras and the robot and objects are equipped with intrusive infrared-reflective markers.

Our experiments lead to the following findings:

- Across experiments, the length of the path traversed by an RF-Compass-guided robot to reach the object (an IKEA table leg) is on average only 6% longer than the optimal path, and at most 16% longer than the optimal path.
- Using two RFIDs on the object, RF-Compass's median accuracy of estimating the center position and orientation is 2.76 cm and 5.77°. Increasing the number of RFIDs on the object to four, RF-Compass can pinpoint its center and orientation to a median of 1.28 cm and 3.3°. These results enable commercial robots with a variety of hand gripper sizes to grasp an object, while leaving a sufficient margin for error, which we validated via trace-driven simulations.
- The VICON infrared system cannot locate the furniture part in occluded settings (e.g., the part is under a chair). Hence, it fails to navigate the robot in these cases. In contrast, RF-Compass's performance is consistent in both line-of-sight and non-line-of-sight.

**Contributions:** This paper makes the following contributions:

- RF-Compass is the first RF localization system that supports robot object manipulation and grasping. It enables robots to leverage RF signals to locate an object to within a few centimeters and identify its orientation to within a few degrees so that the robot may grasp it. As such, RF-Compass bridges robotics with RF localization and solves a real problem for the robotics community, who needs localization solutions that are highly accurate, cost-effective, and capable of dealing with occlusion.

- RF-Compass introduces a new RF localization algorithm formulated as a space partitioning optimization problem. The new algorithm has three features: 1) it can leverage the robot's consecutive moves to refine the accuracy of its estimates; 2) it is robust to potential errors in pairwise comparisons of RFID distances; and 3) it estimates the object's orientation in addition to its location.
- Finally, RF-Compass is implemented and evaluated in a testbed of RFIDs and robots, demonstrating the practicality of the design.

## 2. RELATED WORK

Enabling robots to navigate to objects in their environment and grasp them is a fundamental problem in robotics, commonly referred to as mobile manipulation. In this context, RF-Compass facilitates two operations: object detection and centimeter-scale localization. Past works that address these problems may be divided into two categories. The first category requires significant instrumentation of the environment. In particular, the VICON motion capture system [47], widely used in robotics [31, 35], requires the deployment of many infrared cameras (costing hundreds of thousands of dollars) on the ceiling of the room of operation. It also requires adding intrusive infrared-reflective markers to the objects as well as the robot. The output of this system, however, is highly accurate to the millimeter scale.

The second category of work requires no major modification of the environment and mainly relies on optical cameras [42, 13] or depth imaging (e.g., Kinect, LIDAR) [38, 12]. These systems must solve the object detection problem using machine vision algorithms. Thus, they typically require prior training to recognize specific objects [42, 38]. When successful at detecting an object, they can locate it with an error of a few centimeters to tens of centimeters, depending on the amount of clutter and the system capability [28, 15]. The challenge in these systems is that variations in background, lighting, scene structure, and object orientation exacerbate an already difficult computer vision problem, and can cause these systems to miss the desired object [21, 15].

In comparison to the above systems, RF-Compass is relatively cheap and does not require heavy instrumentation of the environment. It naturally solves the object detection problem by leveraging the unique EPC [16] IDs of the deployed RFIDs, and hence eliminates the need for complex computer vision software. Also, since RF signals propagate in non-line-of-sight, it can address the occlusion problem which is common to all of the above approaches, including VICON.

Prior papers have used RF signals, both WiFi and RFID, for localization and robot navigation [6, 22, 29, 30, 5, 45, 14, 41, 50, 27] but not for grasping objects. The typical accuracy of these systems is a fraction of a meter to a few meters. Although they are adequate for fuzzier localization tasks like detecting which room a robot is in, they cannot support high-precision tasks like object grasping and manipulation.

Several past proposals can achieve higher localization accuracy at the cost of covering the whole floor with a dense, surveyed grid of RFID tags that are spaced at a few to tens of centimeters [39, 23, 44, 11, 49]. Among these proposals, the closest to our work is PinIt [49], which employs dynamic time warping (DTW) to compare RF signals in order to map a tagged object to its nearest neighbor among the deployed reference RFIDs. RF-Compass builds on this past work but differs from all proposals in this category along four major axes: First, RF-Compass does not require a deployment of reference RFIDs in the environment. Second, RF-Compass introduces a novel RF localization algorithm formulated as a space partitioning optimization that leverages the robot's consecutive moves to iteratively refine the accuracy of the optimization. Third, RF-Compass has built-in robustness to errors in identifying the nearest neighbor based on comparing RF signals. Finally, RF-Compass is significantly more accurate than past work and can localize an object to within a couple of centimeters and identify its orientation to within a few degrees, hence enabling robotic object manipulation and grasping.

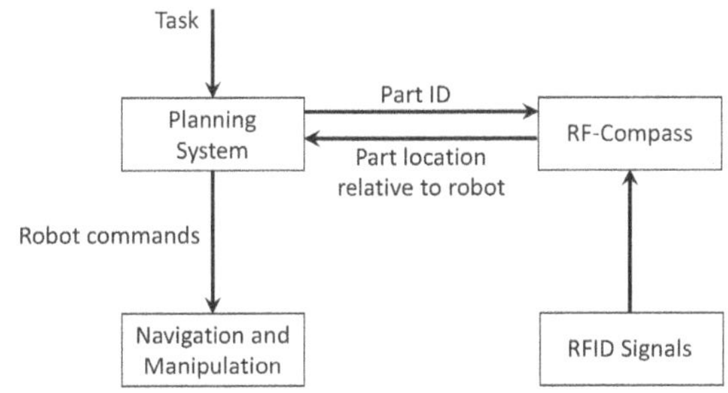


**Figure 2—System Architecture:** A task planning system directs the robot to perform various actions in order to accomplish a higher-level goal, such as fetching all parts of a piece of furniture and assembling it. RF-Compass interfaces with the task planning system to estimate the location of individual parts needed by the system.

## 3. OVERVIEW

RF-Compass is an RFID-based solution for enabling robots to navigate towards an object of interest and manipulate it. Although we present the system in the context of the furniture assembly task, RF-Compass's technique applies to a variety of robotic applications, including other assembly tasks, fetching and delivery, and robot collaboration.

### 3.1 Scope

Robot mobile manipulation tasks, e.g., delivery and assembly, involve multiple modules that work together to complete the task. These modules include: 1) a task *planner* that has a blueprint of a sequence of actions to be performed by the robot in order to complete the task; 2) a *navigator* that controls and commands the robot's wheels and hand to move towards a specified destination; and 3) an *object detection and positioning* system that locates the desired object and computes its orientation so that the robot may navigate towards it and grasp it. Each of these modules on its own spans a research area. RF-Compass focuses on the last module, i.e., it provides a centimeter-scale solution for object detection and localization. It is easy to integrate with standard task planners and navigators. For our empirical evaluation, we have leveraged the planner and navigator functions available in ROS, the Robot Operating System [40].

RF-Compass's design assumes that one can attach UHF RFIDs to the body and hand of the robot, as well as the objects of interest. We believe this assumption is reasonable since UHF RFIDs are cheap and naturally designed to be adhered to products. We also assume that the RFIDs on the robot and the furniture parts are within the reading range of the RFID reader. Today's UHF RFIDs have an operating range of around 10 m [53, 48]. Thus, the assumption is

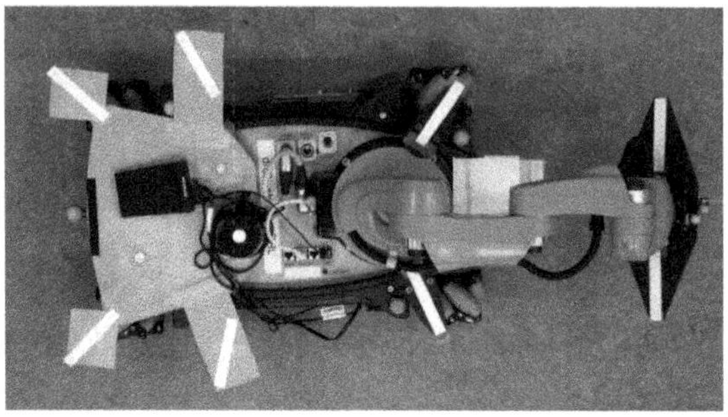

**Figure 3—The manipulator robot:** In our experiments, the KUKA youBot has 9 UHF RFIDs deployed on its hand and base.

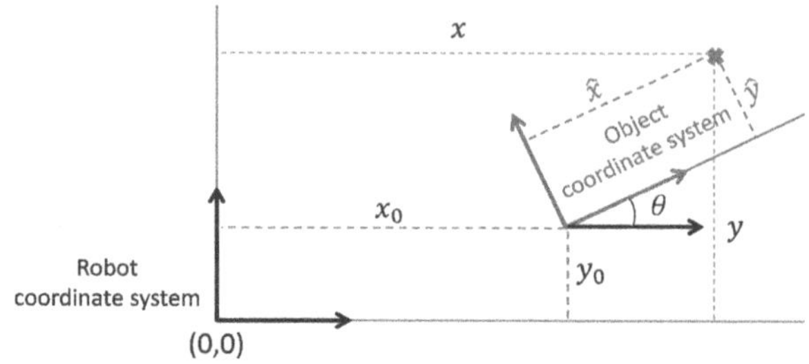


**Figure 4—Robot's and object's coordinate systems:** The robot and the object of interest each have their own coordinate systems. The origin of the object coordinate system is represented as $(x_0, y_0)$ in the robot's coordinate system, and its orientation is $\theta$. The position of an RFID tag can be expressed in the robot's coordinate system as $(x, y)$, or in the object's coordinate system as $(\hat{x}, \hat{y})$.

satisfied in common cases where the delivery and assembly task is performed in a confined space.

### 3.2 System Architecture

We provide a brief overview of how RF-Compass fits within a standard robot mobile manipulation framework, illustrating the components in our system and their interaction. A diagram of the system architecture is shown in Fig. 2. The input to the system is a high-level task, such as "fetch all parts and tools needed for table assembly". A task planner receives this input and constructs a sequence of actions to be performed by the robot, such as "fetch table leg 3". It then queries RF-Compass about a particular object "table_leg_3".

Given the part identifier ("table_leg_3") from the task planner, RF-Compass looks up in its database the RFID tags on the part and their positions within the part itself. Then, RF-Compass queries both the RFIDs deployed on the robot and the ones on the part. Based on the RFID signals collected, RF-Compass estimates the center position and the orientation of the part with respect to the robot.

RF-Compass returns to the task planner its estimate of the part's relative location to the robot as a tuple (direction $\phi$, distance $D$, orientation $\theta$).[1] Based on this relative location, the planner calculates the robot motion needed. The planner issues instructions to the navigation and manipulation component, which commands the robot to move accordingly.

The task planner, the navigator, and RF-Compass reside on one computer, and communicate with the robot over a WiFi link, a setup commonly used in modern robots [40].

## 4. RF-COMPASS

In RF-Compass, we deploy a set of RFIDs on the manipulator robot. For example, for the youBot which has a base of 0.58 m by 0.38 m and an arm of length 0.65 m, we deploy a total of 9 RFIDs, as shown in Fig. 3. We also attach several (e.g., 1–4) RFIDs to each of the manipulated objects.

RF-Compass uses an iterative algorithm, where each iteration involves the following steps:

1 *Measuring relative proximity:* RF-Compass queries the RFIDs on the robot and the manipulated object. It uses the RFID signals to learn, for each tag on the object, whether it is closer to tag $i$ or tag $j$ on the robot.
2 *Localization by partitioning:* RF-Compass feeds this pairwise relative proximity information as constraints to a convex optimization problem that partitions the space into regions according to the relative proximity information.
3 *Refinement:* The partitions are overlaid over previously learned partitions to keep refining the resolution. The algorithm stops when RF-Compass can identify the object's center and orientation with sufficient precision. Otherwise, the robot moves towards the partition that contains the object, and the algorithm proceeds to the next iteration.

Below we describe these steps in detail.

### 4.1 Measuring Relative Proximity

RF-Compass bootstraps its algorithm with questions of the form: given a pair of RFID tags on the robot, which of the two tags is closer to a particular RFID tag on the object? The answers to these questions provide a list of inequalities of the form $d_{T_k^P,T_i^R} \leq d_{T_k^P,T_j^R}$, where $T_i^R$ and $T_j^R$ are two RFIDs on the robot, $T_k^P$ is an RFID on the object, and $d_{T_k^P,T_i^R}$ is the distance between tag $T_k^P$ and tag $T_i^R$. RF-Compass then uses these inequalities as constraints in an iterative space-partitioning algorithm that estimates the location of the desired object to within a couple of centimeters and its orientation to within a few degrees.

The literature has multiple proposals that RF-Compass may leverage for obtaining such bootstrapping information. They estimate the relative distance between pairs of RF sources by comparing the RSSI [36], angle of arrival (AoA) [37, 4], or the multipath profile of their signals [49]. In RF-Compass, we use the approach in [49], which has been shown to be more robust to multipath effects and non-line-of-sight propagation. To do so, we use an antenna array on the RFID reader to receive the RFID signals. Such an antenna array can be implemented cheaply using a single sliding antenna by employing the technique of synthetic aperture radar (SAR) [17, 49]. We then estimate a measure of similarity between the signals of two RFIDs using dynamic time warping (DTW). Higher DTW-similarity between two signals is associated with a shorter distance.

We note that RF-Compass can deal with potential errors in the above relative proximity information. Specifically, RF-Compass obtains a large number of pairwise comparisons in the form of $d_{T_k^P,T_i^R} \leq d_{T_k^P,T_j^R}$, creating a highly over-constrained partitioning problem. The valid constraints are coherent, i.e., they agree on a common region for the tag on the object, while the outliers tend to be random and inconsistent with each other. In §4.3.A, we explain

[1]RF-Compass's estimate of the orientation $\theta$ is only meaningful after the part is within a short distance from the robot, which is needed for the final steps of positioning the robot hand for grasping.

| Term | Definition |
|---|---|
| $(x_0, y_0)$ | the origin of object coordinate system (center of object) expressed in robot coordinate system |
| $\theta$ | the orientation of the object coordinate system in the robot coordinate system |
| $T_1^R, ..., T_N^R$ | the $N$ RFIDs deployed on the robot |
| $(x_1^R, y_1^R), ..., (x_N^R, y_N^R)$ | positions of $T_1^R, ..., T_N^R$ expressed in the robot coordinate system |
| $T^P$ | the RFID at the object center, whose position is $(x_0, y_0)$ in the robot coordinate system |
| $T_1^P, ..., T_K^P$ | the $K$ RFIDs deployed on object |
| $(\hat{x}_1^P, \hat{y}_1^P), ..., (\hat{x}_K^P, \hat{y}_K^P)$ | positions of $T_1^P, ..., T_K^P$ expressed in the object coordinate system |
| $(x_1^P, y_1^P), ..., (x_K^P, y_K^P)$ | positions of $T_1^P, ..., T_K^P$ expressed in the robot coordinate system |
| $d_{T_k^P, T_i^R}$ | Euclidean distance between RFIDs $T_k^P$ and $T_i^R$ |
| $\varepsilon$ | a confidence threshold used in outlier rejection |
| $\mathbf{z}$ | the vector to be estimated in basic optimization with a single RFID on the object $\mathbf{z} = [x_0, y_0]^T$ |
| $\mathbf{z}'$ | the vector to be estimated in optimization using multiple RFIDs on object $\mathbf{z}' = [x_0, y_0, \cos\theta, \sin\theta]^T$ |
| $(x_0^{new}, y_0^{new})$ | the origin of object coordinate system expressed in the new robot coordinate system |
| $\theta^{new}$ | the orientation of the object coordinate system in the new robot coordinate system |
| $(x_m, y_m)$ | the origin of the new robot coordinate system expressed in the old robot coordinate system |
| $\theta_m$ | the orientation of the new robot coordinate system expressed in the old robot coordinate system |

**Table 1—Terms used in the description of RF-Compass.**

how RF-Compass performs outlier rejection by seeking the solution that agrees with the largest number of constraints.

## 4.2 Localization by Space Partitioning

The relative proximity information provides constraints on the distances between the tags on the robot and those on the object. We feed these constraints to a convex optimization solver that locates the object via iterative space partitioning. Before we describe the partitioning algorithm, we discuss the coordinate systems used in expressing locations. For reference, all terms used in our algorithm are defined in Table 1.

### 4.2.A Coordinate Systems

RF-Compass locates objects from the perspective of the robot – i.e., it expresses locations in a Cartesian coordinate system whose origin is at the center of the robot, and the three axes are oriented according to the robot's front-back, left-right, and up-down lines. For clarity, we will omit the up-down coordinates and describe the system in two dimensions.

RF-Compass exploits the fact that it knows the placement of the RFIDs deployed on the robot, e.g. two RFIDs are placed on the left and right of the robot's hand. It likewise knows the placement of the tags deployed on the object with respect to the object itself. For example, IKEA may deploy two RFIDs at the two ends of the table leg during manufacturing, and provide this information as input to RF-Compass. Given this information, RF-Compass estimates the position and the orientation of the object in the robot's coordinate system. Note that the placement of the RFIDs on the object is typically provided with respect to the object itself, such as one tag at each end of a table leg. Thus, we need a transform to convert from the object's coordinate system to the robot's coordinate system.

Fig. 4 illustrates the relation between these two coordinate systems. The origin of the object's coordinate system is at position $(x_0, y_0)$ in the robot's coordinate system, i.e., as perceived by the robot. The object's coordinate system is rotated by $\theta$ relative to the robot's coordinate system.

We denote the coordinates of an RFID in the robot's coordinate system as $(x, y)$, and its coordinates expressed in the object's system as $(\hat{x}, \hat{y})$. Given $(x_0, y_0)$ and $\theta$, one can convert between the two coordinate systems as follows:

$$\begin{aligned} x &= x_0 + \hat{x}\cos\theta - \hat{y}\sin\theta \\ y &= y_0 + \hat{x}\sin\theta + \hat{y}\cos\theta \end{aligned} \tag{1}$$

In RF-Compass, we define the origin of the object's coordinate system to be the center of the object. For any tag $T_k^P, k \in \{1, ..., K\}$ deployed on the object, we know its position in the object's coordinate system $(\hat{x}_k^P, \hat{y}_k^P)$, but do not know its coordinates from the perspective of the robot $(x_k^P, y_k^P)$. For any tag $T_i^R, i \in \{1, ..., N\}$ deployed on the robot, we know its position $(x_i, y_i)$ in the robot's coordinate system. Based on this set of information and the pairwise relative proximity information discussed in §4.1, RF-Compass estimates the center of the object $(x_0, y_0)$ and its orientation $\theta$ in the robot's coordinate system as explained below.

### 4.2.B Convex Optimization for a Single Robot Position and a Single Tag on the Object

Although our algorithm is iterative, this section considers a single iteration with a fixed robot location. We focus our discussion on the basic case where one RFID $T^P$ is deployed at the center of the object and $N$ RFIDs $T_1^R, ..., T_N^R$ are deployed at $(x_1, y_1), ..., (x_N, y_N)$ on the robot.

Recall that $d_{T^P, T_i^R}$ is the Euclidean distance between object tag $T^P$ and robot tag $T_i^R$. RF-Compass uses the relative proximity information from §4.1:

$$d_{T^P, T_i^R} \leq d_{T^P, T_j^R}$$

$$(x_0 - x_i)^2 + (y_0 - y_i)^2 \leq (x_0 - x_j)^2 + (y_0 - y_j)^2$$

$$[2(x_j - x_i) \quad 2(y_j - y_i)] \cdot \begin{bmatrix} x_0 \\ y_0 \end{bmatrix} \leq x_j^2 + y_j^2 - x_i^2 - y_i^2 \tag{2}$$

The right side of the inequality and the row vector on its left side are both known, since we know the placement of the tags on the robot. The unknown variables are $[x_0, y_0]^T$, which RF-Compass aims to estimate.

Given $N$ tags on the robot, we have $\frac{N(N-1)}{2}$ equations similar to Eq. 2, which form a matrix inequality

$$\mathbf{A}\mathbf{z} \leq \mathbf{b}, \tag{3}$$

where $\mathbf{z} = [x_0, y_0]^T$. $\mathbf{A}$ is a matrix of size $\frac{N(N-1)}{2} \times 2$, each row of which is $\left[2(x_j - x_i) \quad 2(y_j - y_i)\right]$ for different pairs of $i$ and $j$. $\mathbf{b}$ is a

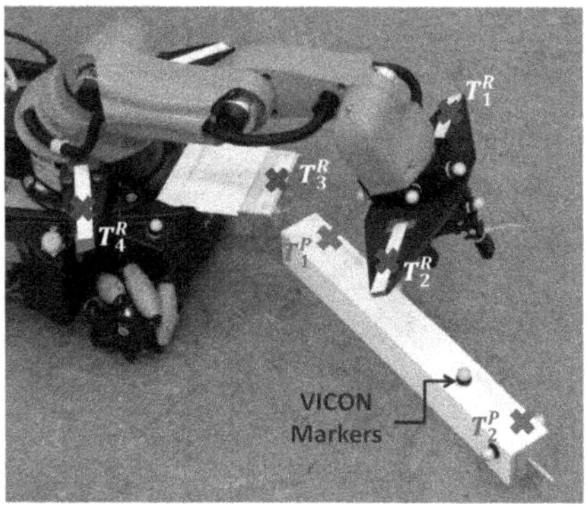


**Figure 5—Robot arm and object:** The figure shows the robot arm and hand equipped with RFIDs marked in blue, and the IKEA table leg with RFIDs marked in red. The silver balls on the robot and the table leg are the VICON infrared-reflective markers (VICON is used as a baseline).

column vector, where each element is $x_j^2 + y_j^2 - x_i^2 - y_i^2$ for different pairs of $i$ and $j$.

Eq. 3 defines a linear feasibility problem, which can be rewritten in the following convex optimization formulation:[2]

$$\begin{aligned} \underset{\mathbf{z}}{\text{minimize}} \quad & 0 \\ \text{subject to} \quad & \mathbf{Az} \leq \mathbf{b} \end{aligned} \tag{4}$$

Many efficient methods exist to solve for $\mathbf{z}$ given $\mathbf{A}$ and $\mathbf{b}$. In our implementation, we use a solver based on the interior-point method [20]. The solver uses logarithmic barrier functions to approximate linear inequality constraints and returns the center of the feasible region. In this basic formulation, RF-Compass can use the returned $\mathbf{z} = [x_0, y_0]^T$ to navigate the robot in the direction of $\phi = \arctan \frac{y_0}{x_0}$. At the end of each iteration, RF-Compass has an estimate of the distance to the object $D = \sqrt{x_0^2 + y_0^2}$. The robot conservatively moves by $\frac{D}{2}$ in each iteration, until the object is within its reach, which can be decided by comparing the average distance between the robot tags themselves and their distances to the object tag.

### 4.2.C Generalizing to Multiple Tags on the Object

Aside from navigating towards the object, the robot also needs to know the exact center position and the orientation of the object so as to perform manipulation tasks such as grasping a particular part of the object. In order to estimate the orientation and pinpoint the center, we deploy $K > 1$ RFIDs $T_1^P, ..., T_K^P$ at $(\hat{x}_1^P, \hat{y}_1^P), ..., (\hat{x}_K^P, \hat{y}_K^P)$ on the object. In our evaluation, we experiment with $K = 2$ to 4 tags in estimating the object orientation.

Since the long arm of the robot extends outside its base as Fig. 5 shows, once the object is within 0.6 m of the robot's body center, the tags installed on the robot's hand and the ones on its base will start to appear at different sides of the object. Fig. 6(a) shows the topology of the same RFIDs as in Fig. 5 when viewed from above, where $T_1^R$ and $T_2^R$ are the two tags next to the robot's hand and $T_3^R$ and $T_4^R$ are two tags at the front of its base. The IKEA table leg has two RFIDs deployed at its two ends.

Taking the object tag $T_1^P$ alone, we can determine that it is in the white partition in Fig. 6(a), using the basic optimization in *4.2.B*.

[2]It is standard to formulate a feasibility problem as an optimization by specifying a constant objective function [8].

Similarly, taking $T_2^P$, we can identify that it is in the white partition in Fig. 6(b). Overlaying the two figures together produces Fig. 6(c). Since we know the dimensions of the IKEA table leg and that $T_1^P$ and $T_2^P$ are at the two ends of it, we can leverage the relationship between the two tags to jointly solve an optimization problem. In Fig. 6(c), imposing the constraints based on the distance between $T_1^P$ and $T_2^P$ allows us to better confine the orientation and center position of the object. Next we explain how to incorporate such constraints into our optimization problem.

Using the coordinate transform in Eq. 1, we have

$$\begin{aligned} x_k^P &= x_0 + \hat{x}_k^P \cos\theta - \hat{y}_k^P \sin\theta \\ y_k^P &= y_0 + \hat{x}_k^P \sin\theta + \hat{y}_k^P \cos\theta \end{aligned} \tag{5}$$

For each tag on the object $T_k^P$, RF-Compass evaluates its relative proximity to each pair of robot tags $T_i^R$ and $T_j^R$:

$$d_{T_k^P, T_i^R} \leq d_{T_k^P, T_j^R}$$

$$(x_k^P - x_i)^2 + (y_k^P - y_i)^2 \leq (x_k^P - x_j)^2 + (y_k^P - y_j)^2$$

Replacing $x_k^P$ and $y_k^P$ using Eq. 5 leads to:

$$\begin{bmatrix} 2(x_j - x_i) \\ 2(y_j - y_i) \\ 2(x_j - x_i)\hat{x}_k^P + 2(y_j - y_i)\hat{y}_k^P \\ 2(y_j - y_i)\hat{x}_k^P - 2(x_j - x_i)\hat{y}_k^P \end{bmatrix}^T \begin{bmatrix} x_0 \\ y_0 \\ \cos\theta \\ \sin\theta \end{bmatrix} \leq x_j^2 + y_j^2 - x_i^2 - y_i^2 \tag{6}$$

Note that we know all elements in the row vector on the leftmost in Eq. 6, since the placement of the robot tags is known and the placement of the tags on the object with respect to the object's center is known. Similarly, we also know the right side of the inequality. The unknown variables are now $x_0$, $y_0$ and $\theta$, the center position and the orientation of the object in the robot's coordinate system.

Given $K$ tags on the object and $N$ on the robot, we have $\frac{KN(N-1)}{2}$ equations as Eq. 6, which form a matrix inequality:

$$\mathbf{A}'\mathbf{z}' \leq \mathbf{b}, \tag{7}$$

where $\mathbf{z}' = [x_0, y_0, \cos\theta, \sin\theta]^T$. $\mathbf{A}'$ is a matrix of size $\frac{KN(N-1)}{2} \times 4$, each row of which is the row vector in Eq. 6 for different $k$, $i$, and $j$. $\mathbf{b}$ is the same column vector as in the basic formulation before.

$\mathbf{A}'$ and $\mathbf{b}$ are known to RF-Compass. If we consider $\cos\theta$ and $\sin\theta$ as two variables, then Eq. 3 defines a feasibility problem linear in $\mathbf{z}'$. In order to leverage the relationship between various tags on the object, we introduce another constraint $\cos^2\theta + \sin^2\theta \leq 1$,[3] and the formulation becomes:

$$\begin{aligned} \underset{\mathbf{z}'}{\text{minimize}} \quad & 0 \\ \text{subject to} \quad & \mathbf{A}'\mathbf{z}' \leq \mathbf{b} \\ & \|z'(3)\|^2 + \|z'(4)\|^2 \leq 1 \end{aligned} \tag{8}$$

Eq. 8 is still a convex optimization problem and can be solved using the same interior-point method as before. In fact, when the robot is fairly far away from the tag, Eq. 8 reduces to the basic formulation in Eq. 4. This is because all the tags on the object will lie in one partition defined by the robot tags. As a result, the interior-point method will estimate their positions to be the same, and hence the orientation of the object $\theta$ cannot be decided. In other words, the $\cos\theta$ and $\sin\theta$ estimated in $\mathbf{z}'$ via Eq. 8 are not meaningful when the object is far away. Once the object is within a certain distance to the robot, different tags on the object will lie in different regions. In this case, the joint optimization based on their relationship will lead to a solution that best fits the position and orientation of the object.

[3]Note that we cannot impose the constraint as $\cos^2\theta + \sin^2\theta = 1$, because such an equality is non-convex.

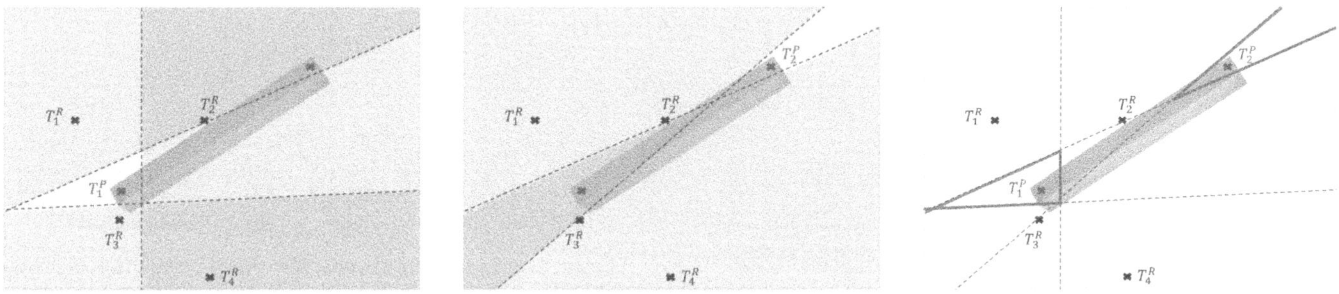

(a) **Partition for $T_1^P$** (b) **Partition for $T_2^P$** (c) **Constraining the center and orientation**

**Figure 6—Utilizing multiple tags on object:** (a) and (b) show the partitions obtained by individually locating $T_1^P$ and $T_2^P$ using the basic optimization in Eq. 4. Leveraging the knowledge about the relationship between their positions, RF-Compass formulates a joint convex optimization problem, pinpointing the orientation and center position of the object.

### 4.3 Iterative Refining and Outlier Rejection

RF-Compass leverages the motion of the robot to iteratively refine the resolution of partitioning. Specifically, each motion of the robot (e.g., moving its base or adjusting its hand) is an iteration. Each location of the robot will result in a different set of partitions. By overlaying these partitions, we can obtain a larger number of smaller regions, i.e., a higher resolution of the space.

Translating this idea into an iterative algorithm, we formulate a larger convex optimization problem by integrating the constraints derived from several consecutive moves of the robot. Note, however, that as the robot moves, its own coordinate system changes. Since RF-Compass knows the motion of the robot, we can transform the different coordinate systems in different iterations to a unified one. Yet, due to minor wheel slips of the robot, odometry error accumulates as the robot moves more and more, which means the coordinate transforms will be less and less accurate. Hence, RF-Compass only combines the partitioning constraints created in three consecutive motions of the robot and across at most 2 m.

Without loss of generality we describe how to formulate a larger convex optimization problem by integrating over two iterations, i.e, two consecutive locations of the robot. Let us still use Eq. 6 to represent the linear constraints created at the first location. Now let us consider the linear constraints at the second location:

$$\begin{bmatrix} 2(x_j-x_i)\\ 2(y_j-y_i) \\ 2(x_j-x_i)\hat{x}_k^P + 2(y_j-y_i)\hat{y}_k^P \\ 2(y_j-y_i)\hat{x}_k^P - 2(x_j-x_i)\hat{y}_k^P \end{bmatrix}^T \begin{bmatrix} x_0^{new}\\ y_0^{new}\\ \cos\theta^{new}\\ \sin\theta^{new}\end{bmatrix} \le x_j^2+y_j^2-x_i^2-y_i^2$$

Since the robot has moved, the position and the orientation of the object with respect to the robot has changed: $\mathbf{z}'^{new} = [x_0^{new}, y_0^{new}, \cos\theta^{new}, \sin\theta^{new}]^T$ is different from $\mathbf{z}' = [x_0, y_0, \cos\theta, \sin\theta]^T$. However, the placement of the RFIDs on the robot with respect to the robot itself does not change; nor does the placement of the RFIDs on the object with respect to the center of the object. As a result, the right side of the inequality and the row vector on the leftmost are known, and can be calculated similarly as at the first location: $\mathbf{A}'^{new}\mathbf{z}'^{new} \le \mathbf{b}^{new}$.[4]

We use $x_m$, $y_m$ and $\theta_m$ to denote the origin and orientation of the coordinate system at the second robot location in the first coordinate system, i.e., the one defined in the first iteration. RF-Compass knows $x_m$, $y_m$ and $\theta_m$ because we know the exact movement the robot performed. We can derive the following equation using the coordinate transform in Eq. 1:

$$\mathbf{z}' = \mathbf{U}\cdot\mathbf{z}'^{new} + \mathbf{V}, \tag{9}$$

where

$$\mathbf{U} = \begin{bmatrix} \cos\theta_m & -\sin\theta_m & 0 & 0 \\ \sin\theta_m & \cos\theta_m & 0 & 0 \\ 0 & 0 & \cos\theta_m & -\sin\theta_m \\ 0 & 0 & \sin\theta_m & \cos\theta_m \end{bmatrix} \tag{10}$$

and

$$\mathbf{V} = [x_m, y_m, 0, 0]^T \tag{11}$$

Since we have $\mathbf{z}'^{new} = \mathbf{U}^{-1}\cdot(\mathbf{z}'-\mathbf{V})$, we can rewrite $\mathbf{A}'^{new}\mathbf{z}'^{new} \le \mathbf{b}^{new}$ as

$$\mathbf{A}'^{new}\mathbf{U}^{-1}\cdot(\mathbf{z}'-\mathbf{V}) \le \mathbf{b}^{new} \tag{12}$$

$\mathbf{A}'^{new}$, $\mathbf{U}, \mathbf{V}$ and $\mathbf{b}^{new}$ are known, hence by now we have transformed the partitions created in the second iteration into linear constraints in the first iteration's coordinate system, with the same variable $\mathbf{z}'$. Thus, we can combine these linear constraints with the ones in the first iteration and solve them jointly. The resulting optimization has the same form as Eq. 7 except with more rows, and can be solved similarly.

Feasibility problems in the form of Eq. 12 are solved using linear programming and have a complexity of $O(rn^{2.5})$, where $n$ is the number of linear constraints and $r$ is the rank of the matrix $\mathbf{A}'^{new}\mathbf{U}^{-1}$ [51]. In our implementation, we use the CVX [20] MATLAB package to solve the convex optimization problem. While it is possible to reduce the running time by optimizing the code, the MATLAB code on a 64-bit laptop with Intel Core i5 processor takes on average 0.6 seconds, which is insignificant compared to the mechanical process of moving the robot.

#### 4.3.A Outlier Rejection

The RF propagation environment can result in outliers in RF-Compass's relative proximity measurements, i.e., the optimization takes the constraint $d_{T_k^P,T_i^R} \le d_{T_k^P,T_j^R}$ while tag $T_k^P$ is in fact closer to tag $T_j^R$ than to tag $T_i^R$. RF-Compass's outlier rejection works as below. On a high level, since the iterative algorithm is formulated as an over-constrained system with a large number of relative proximity constraints, the optimization problem will turn out to be infeasible due to the outliers. However, the majority of the relative proximity constraints are correct and will coherently converge. Thus, we can leverage this to reject the inconsistent outliers by seeking a solution that agrees with most of the constraints.

[4]Note that $\mathbf{A}'^{new}$, $\mathbf{b}^{new}$ are different from $\mathbf{A}'$, $\mathbf{b}$ because the relative proximity information changes as the robot moves.

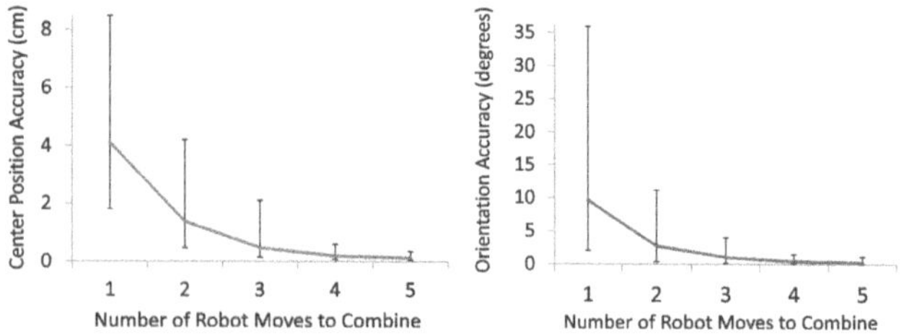


(a) **Center position accuracy** (b) **Orientation accuracy**

**Figure 7—Iterative refining by combining multiple moves of robot:** This figure shows the median, $10^{th}$, and $90^{th}$ percentile accuracy of RF-Compass's joint optimization, as we vary the number of robot moves combined. The median accuracy is around 4 cm when using a single location of the robot to partition the space. The accuracy quickly improves to within a fraction of a centimeter as the algorithm overlays the partitions obtained from consecutive moves of the robot.

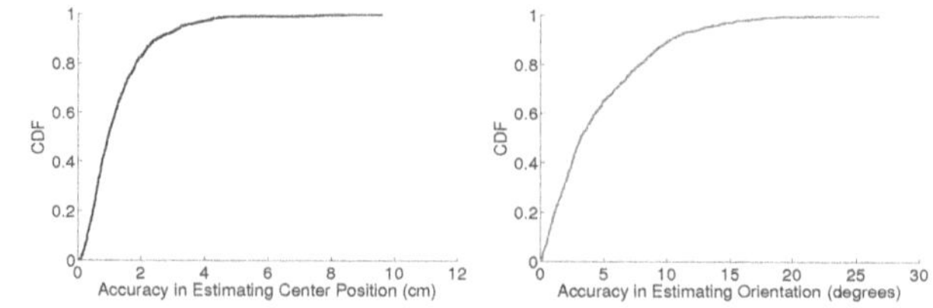


(a) **Center position accuracy** (b) **Orientation accuracy**

**Figure 8—Simulation results for the partitioning algorithm with 10% errors in the relative proximity information:** Despite that 10% of the distance constraints are flipped randomly, the partitioning algorithm still achieves a centimeter scale location accuracy and can identify the orientation to within a few degrees.

In particular, since outliers are more likely to occur when the pair of distances being compared have a small difference, RF-Compass sets a predefined threshold $\varepsilon$ and decides that tag $T_k^P$ is closer to tag $T_i^R$ than to $T_j^R$ only if $m_{T_k^P,T_i^R} \leq (1-\varepsilon) \cdot m_{T_k^P,T_j^R}$, where $m_{T_k^P,T_i^R}$ is the DTW distances measured between tags $T_k^P$ and $T_i^R$ [49]. The larger $\varepsilon$ is, the more constraints we are ruling out from the optimization, and the more confident RF-Compass is about the remaining constraints. RF-Compass initializes the confidence threshold $\varepsilon = 0$, and increases it by 0.05 each time if the optimization problem is infeasible, until finding a solution. In our experiments, with 9 RFIDs on the robot and 2–4 RFIDs on the object, typically increasing $\varepsilon$ to 0.05 or 0.1 is sufficient to solve the optimization and reject the outliers.

Using the above techniques to refine the estimation and reject outliers, RF-Compass directs the robot step by step to reach the object of interest and grasp it. RF-Compass decides that the robot's hand is well-positioned for grasping the object, when the proximity metric between the tags installed on the left and right of the hand and their counterparts on the object is below a threshold. At this point, RF-Compass's iterative partitioning algorithm terminates and lets the robot grasp the object.

### 4.4 Simulation Results

To understand the resolution that can be achieved using our optimization formulation of the partitioning algorithm, we perform a simulation with six RFIDs on the robot including the two next to its hand as in Fig. 5, and two RFIDs on the object. We focus on the accuracy of estimating the center position and the orientation of the object in the final steps of the algorithm. Hence, we assume the object is already within reach, e.g., 25 cm of the robot's hand, and check whether the algorithm can pinpoint the object's location to within a few centimeters and its orientation to within a few degrees, so that the robot may grasp it. In each trial, we randomly generate a location and orientation for the object. We derive the relative proximity constraints based on the positions of the RFIDs on the robot and the RFIDs on the object.

**Impact of combining partitions across consecutive moves of the robot:** We investigate the impact of iterative refinement on the performance of RF-Compass. We plot in Fig. 7 the center position and orientation accuracy of the iterative partitioning algorithm when it utilizes different numbers of consecutive robot moves to form the joint optimization. Fig. 7 shows the median accuracy as well as the $10^{th}$ and $90^{th}$ percentiles (error bars) for 1000 runs. As we can see, the error of the center position estimate rapidly decreases as the number of combined robot moves increases. The median position accuracy is around 4 cm when using a single location of the robot, and quickly improves to within a fraction of a centimeter as we overlay the partitions obtained from multiple moves of the robot. This behavior is expected because every time we add a new location of the robot (i.e., a new iteration), the granularity of partitioning becomes finer. Similarly, the orientation accuracy also quickly improves as we combine partitions obtained from consecutive moves of the robot.

We note however that the simulation assumes no noise in odometry measurements. In practice, odometry errors accumulate as the robot moves. In order to limit this effect on the performance of RF-Compass's iterative algorithm, we only combine up to three moves of the robot.

**Robustness to potential errors in relative proximity constraints:** We investigate RF-Compass's outlier rejection. We flip 10% of the relative proximity constraints so that they are wrong. We then run the partitioning algorithm identifying the region that is consistent with the maximum number of pairwise constraints and plot in Fig. 8 the CDFs of the error in estimating the center and the orientation of the object. The CDFs are taken over 1000 runs.

Fig. 8(a) and 8(b) show that the median error in center position is 0.96 cm, and its $90^{th}$ percentile is 2.5 cm. The median error in orientation estimation is only $3.1^\circ$ and its $90^{th}$ percentile is $10^\circ$. These results verify that the partitioning algorithm is both accurate, and robust to potential errors in the relative proximity information. This robustness is due to that we are dealing with an over-constrained optimization. Errors tend to make the optimization infeasible, whereas all of the correct constraints have a consistent solution. Hence, eliminating the constraints that make the optimization infeasible tends to eliminate the errors.

## 5. IMPLEMENTATION

We built a prototype of RF-Compass using USRP software radios [25] and the Alien Squiggle RFIDs [2]. We used the prototype to direct the actions of a KUKA youBot [32] in reaching and grasping furniture parts, as detailed below.

**Robot and Manipulated Objects:** We use a KUKA youBot robot, which has four separately-controlled wheels and is capable of moving with arbitrary linear and angular velocity up to approximately 80 cm/sec and 1 rad/sec. The robot has a manipulator arm, which consists a serial chain of five links 65.5 cm in total length and five joints. The combination of the arm and the wheels is capable of performing essentially arbitrary motions in all dimensions.

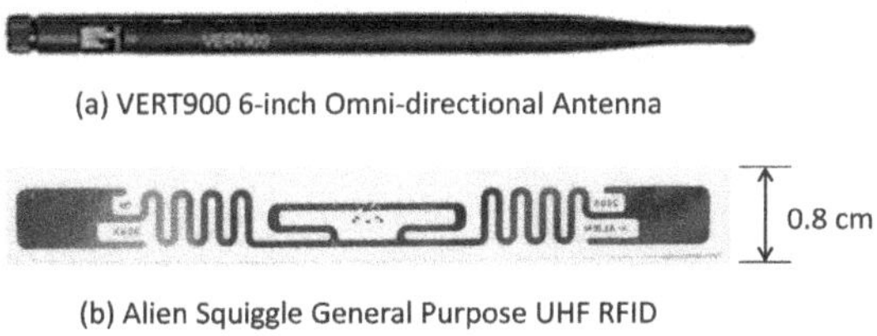


**Figure 9—Antenna and commercial UHF RFID used in experiments:** (a) We move the VERT900 6-inch vertical antenna in a straight line to emulate a linear antenna array. (b) the Alien Squiggle General Purpose UHF RFID Tags. The sizes of (a) and (b) are not proportional to the real sizes of the devices.

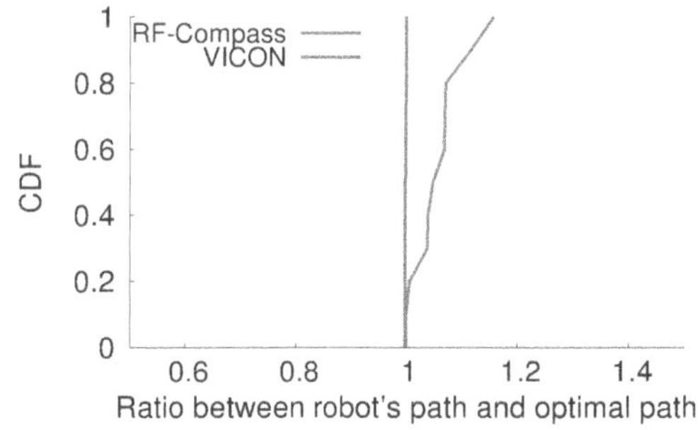


**Figure 10—Ratio between the length of path traversed by the robot and the length of optimal path in line-of-sight:** When directed by RF-Compass, the path traversed by the robot is on average only 6% longer than the optimal path, and at most 16% longer.

The arm can lift a payload of 0.5 kg, which is sufficient to assemble many products from IKEA. The youBot hand's maximum aperture (finger tip-to-tip distance) is 7.5 cm. In these experiments, the robot's goal is to grasp table legs measuring 5 cm wide, leaving a 2.5 cm margin of error tolerance.[5] The furniture parts are the legs of the IKEA Lack table [24]. The dimensions of the table legs are 40 cm×5 cm×5 cm.

**RFIDs:** We deploy the Alien Squiggle RFIDs [2] on both the robot and the furniture part. The Alien Squiggle Inlay shown in Fig. 9(b) is a commercial off-the-shelf passive UHF RFID widely used in supply chains, logistics and asset tracking operations. Each tag costs 5–10 cents. 9 RFIDs are placed on the robot and 1–4 RFIDs are placed on the table leg. Note that each RFID has a unique 96-bit EPC ID [16], and as a result we can easily distinguish different objects in a pile based on the unique IDs of the RFIDs attached to them.

**RFID Reader and Antenna Array:** We adopt a USRP implementation of an EPC Gen-2 RFID reader developed in [9] to query the RFIDs. We use RFX900 daughterboards and Cushcraft 900 MHz RFID reader antennas [33], and run all experiments at a carrier frequency of 920 MHz.

As mentioned in §4.1, we extract relative proximity information using the approach in [49]. Similarly to the work in that paper, we implement an antenna array on the RFID reader by using a single sliding antenna and post-processing the received signal with the SAR algorithm [17]. Specifically, one option for building an antenna array is to use multiple USRPs, synchronize them via an external clock, and have each of them act as one antenna in the array. This approach, however, will unnecessarily limit the array to a handful of antenna elements. Alternatively, and since we are working with robots, we can leverage motion to build an array with many antenna elements using a technique known as SAR (Synthetic Aperture Radar) [17, 49, 1]. To implement SAR, we mount a USRP RFID reader equipped with an omni-directional VERT900 antenna (shown in Fig. 9(a)) on a second robot, which moves with a constant speed in a straight line. As it moves, the antenna acts as if it were a different antenna situated at that point in space. Thus, this moving receive antenna emulates in time an array of antennas spaced along a line. One can then process the signal received by the moving antenna at different points in time as if it were the output of a spatial array of antennas, and apply standard antenna array equations (see [49] for more details on SAR).

The reader repeatedly queries the tags and uses the moving antenna to collect the response signals. We use these signals to extract pairwise relative proximity information as explained in §4.1, which is fed to the partitioning algorithm.

[5]In comparison, Baxter [42], like most commercial robots designed for manipulating objects, has more joints (seven), longer arms (104 cm), larger hands (>15 cm) and higher payload (2.3 kg) than the youBot, and thus can pick up a wider variety of objects.

**Navigation and Manipulation:** ROS [40] provides software stacks for navigation and manipulation. The navigation stack delivers real-time obstacle avoidance and the object manipulation stack provides control of a manipulator arm for picking up and moving objects.

**Baseline:** In [31], the VICON motion capture system is used to demonstrate letting a youBot fetch and deliver the same type of IKEA table legs. Thus, we use VICON as a baseline. We place both the robot and the table legs inside the VICON room and vary their initial distance in a range of 2–6 meters. The choice of the range is mainly dictated by the size of our VICON deployment where the maximum area reliably covered by the infrared cameras is 6×5 $m^2$.[6] VICON requires placing infrared-reflective markers on both the robot and the object of interest. Thus, we place 10 such markers on the robot and 4 markers on the table leg.

## 6. EVALUATION

RF-Compass is applicable to many mobile manipulation tasks, such as tool delivery, collecting wastes, collaborating with other robots, etc. Here, we evaluate it in a task related to furniture assembly. Specifically, the IKEA furniture assembly application in [31] involves robot collaboration where the delivery robots retrieve various furniture parts and hand them off to the assembly robots for installation. In our evaluation, we focus on the job of the delivery robot.

We study RF-Compass's performance in three phases:

- **Navigation:** In this phase, RF-Compass should detect the needed part and navigate the delivery robot towards it. By the end of this phase, the object is within the reach of the robot's hand. RF-Compass can determine that the furniture part is within reach when the RFIDs next to the robot's hand are closer to the RFIDs on the part than to the RFIDs at the end of the robot's base, as described in §4.1. For this phase, we evaluate the length of the navigation path traversed by the robot.
- **Localization:** The second phase is preparation for manipulation. For this phase, we evaluate whether RF-Compass can accurately identify the center of the part and its orientation to enable the robot to grasp it.
- **Object Manipulation:** The third phase is grasping. We evaluate the impact of RF-Compass's accuracy on the number of trials the robot needs before it can successfully grasp the part.

[6]This deployment of VICON costs a few hundred thousand dollars.

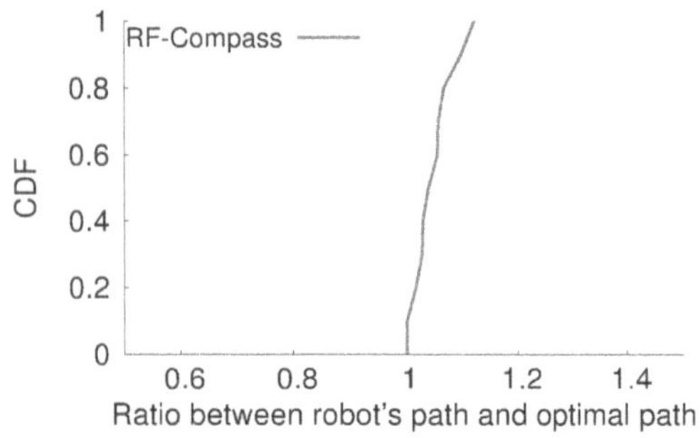


**Figure 11—Ratio between the length of path taken by the robot and the length of the optimal path in non-line-of-sight:** When directed by RF-Compass, the path traversed by the robot is on average 5% longer than the optimal path, and at most 12% longer.

## 6.1 Efficiency of RF-Compass in Robot Navigation

We conduct 10 experiments in line-of-sight and another 10 experiments in non-line-of-sight, comparing using RF-Compass and VICON to navigate the robot towards the part. In each experiment, the robot and the furniture part are placed at different random initial locations and their initial distance is in a range of 2–6 meters. We compare the paths traversed by the robot using RF-Compass versus using VICON, for the same sets of initial locations. RF-Compass uses 2 RFIDs on the furniture part and 9 RFIDs on the robot, while the VICON system uses 4 infrared-reflective markers on the furniture part and 10 such markers on the robot.

**Line-of-Sight Evaluation:** In these experiment, we keep the emulated antenna array, the furniture part, and the robot all in direct line-of-sight of each other. We also ensure that both the robot and the part are within the reliable detection region of the VICON motion capture system and there is no occlusion of the VICON markers on the robot or the part.

Fig. 10 shows the CDF of the ratio between the length of the path traversed by the robot to that of the optimal path, for both RF-Compass and VICON. The optimal path has a length equal to the Euclidean distance between the robot's initial position and its destination. In this case, the VICON system can locate both the furniture part and the robot to millimeter accuracy, since there is no occlusion or clutter of the infrared-reflective makers. Hence, it always finds the optimal path. The path traversed by the robot as directed by RF-Compass is on average 6% longer than the optimal and at most 16% longer than the optimal path.

**Non-Line-of-Sight Evaluation:** In these experiments, we put up a 1.5 m×2.2 m solid wooden board supported by metal structures to block the line-of-sight for RF-Compass's emulated antenna array. We also create occlusion of the furniture part by placing it under an office chair. We further use desks, chairs, and other objects to introduce obstructions. In each experiment, we vary the placement of the obstructions.

Fig. 11 shows the CDF of the ratio between the length of the path traversed by the robot to that of the optimal path. Since the object is occluded from the sight of the infrared cameras, the VICON system cannot locate it and hence fails to provide an estimate of where the robot should move. This behavior is common in existing localization systems for object manipulation, including vision-based systems as well as infrared systems like VICON, LIDAR, and Kinect. In contrast, RFID signals can penetrate obstacles and reach the RFID reader even when the object is occluded. Thus, as in the line-of-sight experiments, with non-line-sight and occlusions, the path in RF-Compass is close to optimal.

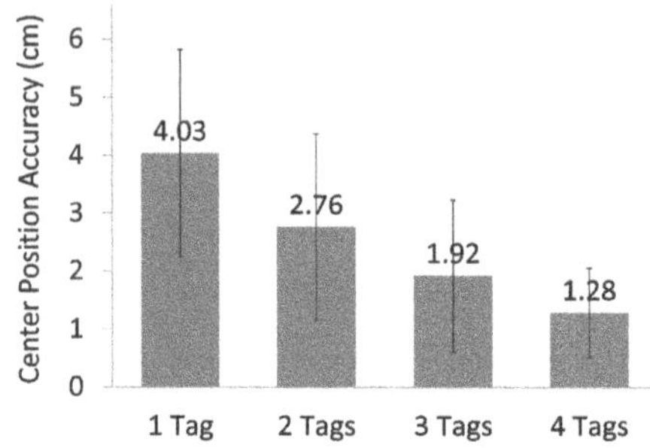


**Figure 12—RF-Compass's accuracy in estimating center position:** With 1 tag on the part, the error in RF-Compass's estimation has a median of around 4 cm. Leveraging 4 tags on the part, RF-Compass's median error reduces to 1.28 cm.

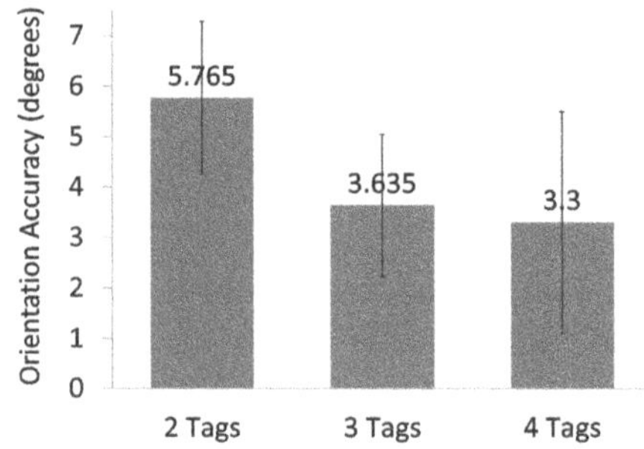


**Figure 13—RF-Compass's accuracy in estimating object orientation:** With two tags on the part, RF-Compass's median accuracy of the orientation estimate is around 6°, and further decreases to around 3° when 4 tags are used.

## 6.2 Accuracy of RF-Compass in Estimating Center Position and Orientation

Next, we evaluate RF-Compass's performance in mobile manipulation. At this stage, the object is already within the reach of the robot, e.g., 0.25 m from its hand. Thus, we focus on the accuracy RF-Compass can achieve in identifying the center of the part and its orientation. We experiment with 1–4 tags deployed on the IKEA table leg.

**Center Position Accuracy:** Fig. 12 shows the distance between RF-Compass's estimate of the center of the table leg and the ground truth captured by the VICON system.[7] With one tag at the center of the table leg, RF-Compass's median error in estimating the position is 4.03 cm, with a standard deviation of 1.8 cm. The accuracy improves to 2.76 cm when two tags are placed at the two ends of table leg, and further improves to 1.28 cm when four evenly spaced tags on the part are used in the partitioning algorithm.

**Orientation Accuracy:** In order to determine the orientation of an object, at least two RFIDs need to be placed on the object. Fig. 13 shows the difference between RF-Compass's estimate of the table leg's orientation and the ground truth. RF-Compass has a median orientation error of around 6° when two tags on the table leg are used. This error further decreases to around 3° when all four tags are used in the optimization.

[7]When the robot arm is above the part, sometimes it prevents the VICON cameras from seeing the infrared-reflective markers. To make sure our ground truth measurement of the part is accurate, after RF-Compass's iterative algorithm terminates, we move the robot away without moving the part, and let VICON record its position.

### 6.3 Number of Attempts in Grasping Furniture Part

Finally, we investigate the impact of RF-Compass's accuracy on the robot's ability to grasp objects. Specifically, we compute the number of attempts before the robot succeeds in grasping the leg of the IKEA table. Given the location and orientation of the object, the planner commands the robot to position its hand. The robot moves and lowers its hand to grasp the part. If it fails, the robot assumes that it accidentally bumped and moved the part, and it must therefore take another set of measurements and try again until it successfully grasps the part.

In practice, several factors affect the robot's grasping performance besides the accuracy of the localization system. In particular, the gripper's quality is highly important [10]. Grippers of different materials trade off between ease of grasping and stability of holding a part. Firmer surfaces provide rigid control, but may fail to pick up the part due to inadequate friction between the grippers and the part. The size of the gripper is another determining factor. Today's commercial manipulator robots have a typical hand size of >10 cm [42]. The KUKA youBot designed for educational and research use has a slightly smaller hand (its gripper aperture is 7.5 cm).

In order to isolate the impact of RF-Compass on the grasping task, we perform this evaluation using trace-driven simulations. We simulate the IKEA leg grasping procedure by feeding to the simulator the empirical results in §6.2, which measure RF-Compass's error in locating the center of the table leg and identifying its orientation. For each grasp attempt, we draw the position and orientation error uniformly at random from the empirical results of our experiments. We repeat the simulation for different robot hand sizes.

Fig. 14 shows the results for the case where two tags on the part are used. Each CDF contains 1000 runs of the grasping task where the part width is 5 cm. We vary the gripper size among 7.5 cm, 8.5 cm and 10 cm. If the robot's gripper is 7.5 cm wide, and the IKEA part has only two RFID tags, the robot needs to try on average 9 times to grasp the part. If the robot's gripper is 8.5 cm wide, the average number of trials decreases to 5. With a hand size of 10 cm, the robot can grasp the part on the first try in over 80% of the time.

Fig. 15 shows the equivalent CDFs for the case where four tags are deployed on the IKEA part. Now, even with a small 7.5 cm gripper like that of the KUKA youBot, the robot can immediately grasp the object almost 90% of the time.

In conclusion, the accuracy achieved by RF-Compass can enable a commercial manipulator robot with a typical hand size of >10 cm to reliably grasp the furniture part with 2 RFIDs. Robots with a smaller gripper, e.g., a 7.5 cm wide gripper, can also be supported if four RFID tags are placed on the target object.

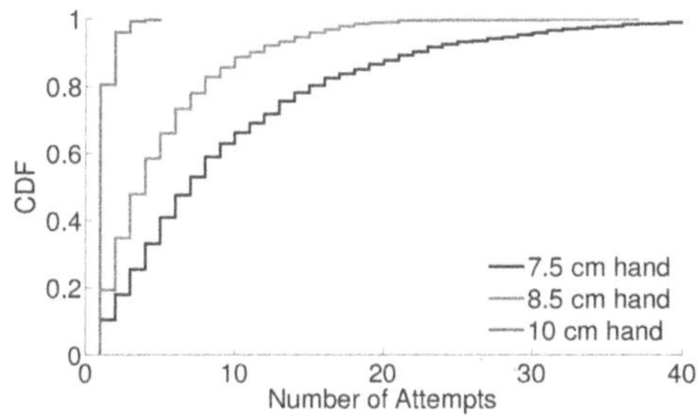


**Figure 14—CDF of the number of attempts made by the robot before succeeding at grasping the part with 2 RFIDs:** With 2 tags on the furniture part, a commercial manipulator robot with a typical hand size of >10 cm can grasp the part successfully upon the first try in over 80% of the cases.

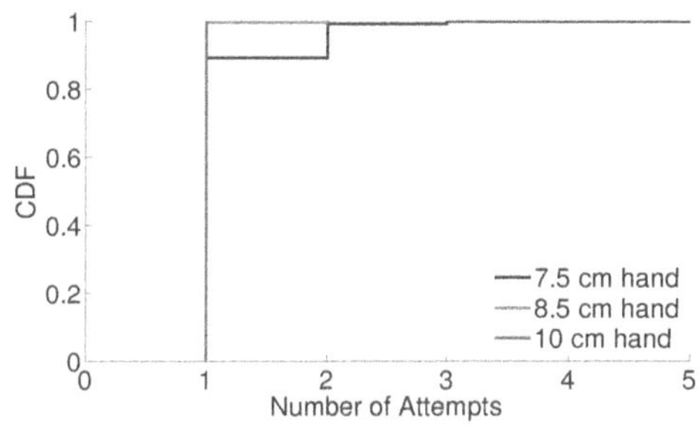


**Figure 15—CDF of the number of attempts made by the robot before succeeding at grasping the part with 4 RFIDs:** With 4 tags on the furniture part, robots with a small hand 7.5 cm such as the youBot can retrieve the part successfully upon the first try in almost 90% of the cases.

## 7. Conclusion

This paper presents RF-Compass, an RFID-based system for robot object manipulation. RF-Compass's key innovation is an iterative localization algorithm that leverages the robot's consecutive moves to iteratively refine its estimates of the desired object's location and orientation. It can pinpoint the center position and the orientation to an accuracy of a few centimeters and degrees respectively, providing the necessary precision for object grasping and manipulation using a purely RF-based solution.

By bridging robotics and advances in wireless signal processing, RF-Compass delivers a highly accurate robot object manipulation scheme which opens up a wide range of exciting opportunities. We believe future systems can leverage the techniques in this paper to enable new features in robotic applications such as picking up an object from a pile, grasping objects with arbitrary shapes, complex assembly tasks, robot collaboration, and many others.

**Acknowledgments:** We thank Haitham Hassanieh, Nate Kushman, Lixin Shi, Omid Abari, Zack Kabelac, Jonathan Perry, Peter Iannucci, the reviewers, and our shepherd, Eric Rozner, for their insightful comments. This research is supported by NSF. We thank members of the MIT Center for Wireless Networks and Mobile Computing: Amazon.com, Cisco, Google, Intel, Mediatek, Microsoft, ST Microelectronics, and Telefonica for their interest and support.

## 8. References

[1] F. Adib and D. Katabi. See through walls with Wi-Fi! In *ACM SIGCOMM*, 2013.

[2] Alien Technology Inc. ALN-9640 Squiggle Inlay. www.alientechnology.com.

[3] L. Atzori, A. Icra, and G. Morabito. The internet of things: A survey. *Computer Networks*, 2010.

[4] S. Azzouzi et al. New measurement results for the localization of UHF RFID transponders using an Angle of Arrival (AoA) approach. In *IEEE RFID*, 2011.

[5] P. Bahl and V. Padmanabhan. RADAR: an in-building RF-based user location and tracking system . In *IEEE INFOCOM*, 2000.

[6] J. Biswas and M. Veloso. Wifi localization and navigation for autonomous indoor mobile robots. In *IEEE ICRA*, 2010.

[7] M. Bonert, L. Shu, and B. Benhabib. Motion planning for multi-robot assembly systems. *International Journal of Computer Integrated Manufacturing*, 2000.

[8] S. Boyd and L. Vandenberghe. *Convex Optimization*. Cambridge University Press, 2004.

[9] M. Buettner and D. Wetherall. A software radio-based uhf rfid reader for phy/mac experimentation. *IEEE RFID*, 2011.

[10] I. Bullock, R. Ma, and A. Dollar. A hand-centric classification of human and robot dexterous manipulation. *IEEE Trans. on Haptics*, 2013.

[11] H. Chae and K. Han. Combination of RFID and vision for mobile robot localization. In *IEEE ICSSINP*, 2005.

[12] G. Champleboux, S. Lavallee, R. Szeliski, and L. Brunie. From accurate range imaging sensor calibration to accurate model-based 3d object localization. In *IEEE CVPR*, 1992.

[13] R. T. Chin and C. R. Dyer. Model-based recognition in robot vision. *ACM Computing Surveys (CSUR)*, 1986.

[14] K. Chintalapudi, A. Padmanabha Iyer, and V. N. Padmanabhan. Indoor localization without the pain. In *ACM MobiCom*, 2010.

[15] A. Collet, D. Berenson, S. S. Srinivasa, and D. Ferguson. Object recognition and full pose registration from a single image for robotic manipulation. In *IEEE ICRA*, 2009.

[16] EPCglobal Inc. EPCglobal Class 1 Generation 2.

[17] J. Fitch. Synthetic aperture radar. 1988.

[18] Frost & Sullivan. Global RFID healthcare and pharmaceutical market. Industry Report, 2011.

[19] Frost & Sullivan. Global RFID market. Industry Report, 2011.

[20] M. Grant, S. Boyd, and Y. Ye. CVX: Matlab software for disciplined convex programming. http://cvxr.com/cvx.

[21] W. E. L. Grimson and D. Huttenlocher. On the verification of hypothesized matches in model-based recognition. *Computer Vision - ECCV*, 1990.

[22] D. Hahnel, W. Burgard, D. Fox, K. Fishkin, and M. Philipose. Mapping and localization with RFID technology. In *IEEE ICRA*, 2004.

[23] S. Han, H. Lim, and J. Lee. An efficient localization scheme for a differential-driving mobile robot based on RFID system. *IEEE Trans. Industrial Electronics*, 2007.

[24] Ikea lack table. `www.ikea.com/us/en/catalog/products/20011413`.

[25] E. Inc. Universal software radio peripheral. http://ettus.com.

[26] S. Jorg, J. Langwald, J. Stelter, G. Hirzinger, and C. Natale. Flexible robot-assembly using a multi-sensory approach. In *IEEE ICRA*, 2000.

[27] K. Joshi, S. Hong, and S. Katti. Pinpoint: Localizing interfering radios. In *Usenix NSDI*, 2013.

[28] K. Khoshelham and S. O. Elberink. Accuracy and resolution of kinect depth data for indoor mapping applications. *Sensors*, 2012.

[29] M. Kim and N. Y. Chong. Rfid-based mobile robot guidance to a stationary target. *Mechatronics*, 2007.

[30] M. Kim and N. Y. Chong. Direction sensing RFID reader for mobile robot navigation. *IEEE Trans. Automation Science and Engineering*, 2009.

[31] R. A. Knepper, T. Layton, J. Romanishin, and D. Rus. Ikeabot: An autonomous multi-robot coordinated furniture assembly system. In *IEEE ICRA*, 2013.

[32] KUKA, youBot specification sheet. `youbot-store.com/downloads/ProductFlyer_KUKA_youBot_2pages.pdf`.

[33] Laird Technologies. Crushcraft S9028PCRW RFID antenna.

[34] M. T. Mason. Creation myths: The beginnings of robotics research. *IEEE Robotics Automation Magazine*, 2012.

[35] N. Michael, D. Mellinger, Q. Lindsey, and V. Kumar. The GRASP multiple micro-UAV testbed. *IEEE Robotics & Automation Magazine*, 2010.

[36] L. M. Ni et al. Landmarc: indoor location sensing using active rfid. *Wirel. Netw.*, 2004.

[37] P. Nikitin et al. Phase based spatial identification of uhf rfid tags. In *IEEE RFID*, 2010.

[38] S. Nirjon and J. Stankovic. Kinsight: Localizing and tracking household objects using depth-camera sensors. In *IEEE DCOSS*, 2012.

[39] S. Park and S. Hashimoto. Autonomous mobile robot navigation using passive RFID in indoor environment. *IEEE Trans. Industrial Electronics*, 2009.

[40] M. Quigley, B. Gerkey, K. Conley, J. Faust, T. Foote, J. Leibs, E. Berger, R. Wheeler, and A. Ng. ROS: an open-source robot operating system. In *IEEE ICRA Workshop on Open Source Robotics*, 2009.

[41] A. Rai, K. K. Chintalapudi, V. N. Padmanabhan, and R. Sen. Zee: zero-effort crowdsourcing for indoor localization. In *ACM Mobicom*, 2012.

[42] Rethink robotics, Baxter specification sheet. `www.rethinkrobotics.com/files/8513/4792/6562/ProductBrochure_WebDownload.pdf`.

[43] J. Rifkin and E. Kruger. *The end of work*. 1996.

[44] S. Schneegans, P. Vorst, and A. Zell. Using RFID snapshots for mobile robot self-localization. In *ECMR*, 2007.

[45] A. Smith et al. Tracking Moving Devices with the Cricket Location System. In *ACM MobiSys*, 2004.

[46] ThingMagic. Why Use RFID. www.thingmagic.com/.

[47] VICON T-Series. `www.vicon.com/products/documents/Tseries.pdf`.

[48] J. Wang, H. Hassanieh, D. Katabi, and P. Indyk. Efficient and Reliable Low-Power Backscatter Networks. In *ACM SIGCOMM*, 2012.

[49] J. Wang and D. Katabi. Dude, Where's my card? RFID Positioning That Works with Multipath and Non-Line of Sight. In *ACM SIGCOMM*, 2013.

[50] J. Xiong and K. Jamieson. Arraytrack: A fine-grained indoor location system. In *Usenix NSDI*, 2013.

[51] Y. Ye. Improved complexity results on solving real-number linear feasibility problems. *Math. Program.*, 2006.

[52] A. Yilmaz, O. Javed, and M. Shah. Object tracking: A survey. *ACM Comput. Surv.*, 2006.

[53] T. Zimmerman. Assessing the capabilities of RFID technologies. Gartner, 2009.

# LightSync: Unsynchronized Visual Communication over Screen-Camera Links

Wenjun Hu
Microsoft Research Asia
wenjun@microsoft.com

Hao Gu*
Microsoft Research Asia and USTC
v-haogu@microsoft.com

Qifan Pu*
University of Washington and USTC
qp@cs.washington.edu

## ABSTRACT

A key challenge for smartphone based visual communication over screen-camera links is imperfect frame synchronization. The difficulty arises from frame rate diversity and variability due to camera capability, lighting conditions, and system factors. On the 4 smartphone cameras we tested, the frame rate varies between 8 and 30 frames per second. If the transmit frame rate is too high, the receiver might lose original frames or capture mixed frames, which are normally not decodable. Previous systems simply reduce the effective screen frame rate to be half the camera frame capture rate, to guarantee receiving a decodable frame every other frame. This under-utilizes the transmitter side capacity and is inefficient.

We achieve frame synchronization with LightSync, which features in-frame color tracking to decode imperfect frames and a linear erasure code across frames to recover lost frames. LightSync allows smooth communication between the screen and the camera at any combination of the transmit and receive frame rates, as long as the receive rate is at least half the transmit rate. This means that each receiver can scale the decoding performance with its own camera capability. Across several phones, our system can more than double the average throughput compared to previous approaches.

## Categories and Subject Descriptors

C.2.1 [**Network Architecture and Design**]: Wireless Communication

## Keywords

Screen-camera links, unsynchronized communication, per-line tracking, inter-frame erasure coding

## 1. INTRODUCTION

Smartphone possession is rising quickly, fostering growing interest in and efforts to enrich smartphone based user interaction and experience. Perhaps one of the most common scenarios is acquiring information via the phone, e.g., in retail and tourism. For example, QR codes are now widely adopted for advertising, because many smartphones ship with a built-in 2D barcode scanner or can be installed with such an app easily. Many brochures often come with one QR code per product[6]. There are even initiatives like Gibraltar targeting tourists with Wikipedia QR codes[1], where a QR code is placed next to each point of interest, and scanning the code will take the user to the corresponding Wikipedia page. In China, for example, it is increasingly common for websites to show several QR codes on a page and even TV adverts include QR codes. Mary Meeker's latest predictions on mobile Internet trends report 4 times more QR codes being scanned in March 2013 than a year before[4].

However, the capacity of a single, static 2D barcode is very limited. Indeed, existing QR codes often encode a single URL, and require cellular or WiFi connectivity for access to additional information. On the other hand, public displays are also widely available, and, when combined with smartphone cameras, form communication links that can complement RF wireless connectivity, as suggested in previous works[10, 15]. Therefore, we can imagine embedding not only a web link, but also the full information on the linked page, in a video of 2D barcodes. Screen-camera links enjoy several advantages compared to traditional RF wireless connectivity. They are free, directional, and free of interference. There is no overhead in link setup and management, and therefore it is well suited to one-time transfer of a small amount of information. Consider the Gibraltar initiative again. The text in the entire Wikipedia page for Gibraltar can be stored in a `.txt` file of 37.8 KB, while the text for Gibraltarian cuisine is only 4.6 KB in size. Transferring either text represents a suitable workload for the screen-camera link. We can envision a display playing the barcode video continuously or on-demand, and recording the video on the smartphone will download the Wikipedia page directly.

To achieve a high capacity, real screen-camera communication systems must address such challenges as imperfect frame synchronization, image distortion, and computational complexity. While previous research often focused on reducing image quality distortion to increase the per-frame capacity, we aim to solve the basic synchronization problem in such a system to push the frame rate. This is orthogonal to per-frame improvement. In other words, we consider temporal domain coding, compared to spatial domain coding in most previous works.

Frame synchronization is a prerequisite for effective communication. The camera must be able to detect the displayed frames from individual captured video frames. In a Gibraltar like scenario, there is an additional requirement that the same video playback rate should work with any

*Part of the work was performed while Hao Gu and Qifan Pu were research interns at Microsoft Research Asia.


*MobiCom'13,* September 30–October 4, Miami, FL, USA.

http://dx.doi.org/10.1145/2500423.2500437 ...$15.00.

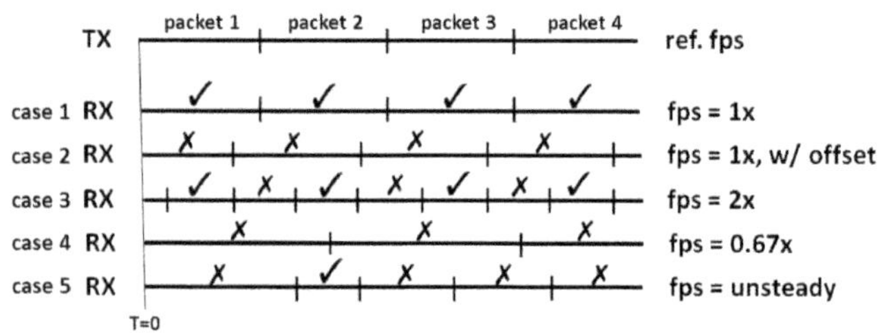


**Figure 1: Mismatched frame rates between TX-RX pairs. "|" marks the boundary between two consecutive frames. ✗: "mixed" frames, ✓: "clean" frames. Inter-frame intervals are omitted.**

phone camera that wishes to record the video. Implicitly, this is a broadcast system.

Lack of synchronization is mainly caused by mismatched frame rates and a phase offset between the screen and the camera. Figure 1 shows several examples. Typically, only frames staying within the period of one transmission are *clean* (marked "✓"), and thus decodable. If a captured frame spans different TX frames, it becomes a *mixed* frame (marked "✗"). Worse, smartphone camera sensors typically employ a *rolling shutter*, which scans a scene one line at a time. This makes the frame mixing vary on a per-line basis. Such a frame has to be dropped usually. We might also lose frames due to discrete shutter sampling, if the screen's display frame rate is higher than the camera's capture rate. Only after receiving all the transmitted frames 'cleanly' can a receiver successfully decode the original message (cases 1 and 3).

The difficulty in frame synchronization arises from frame rate diversity and variability. With a traditional coding scheme, a receiver should capture frames at a rate at least twice the transmitter's display frame rate, to guarantee receiving all frames cleanly (case 3). Unfortunately, in terms of rate capability the opposite often happens in practice. Modern LCD or AMOLED screens usually have a 60 fps rate or at least 30 fps, while cameras have lower and more diverse frame rates of up to 30 fps. For example, HTC One X[2] and Nokia Lumia 920[5] support video recording at up to 24 and 30 fps respectively. Worse, many smartphone cameras exhibit unsteady frame rates due to hardware design, firmware settings, and API constraints. Our tests on several phones (Section 2.3) show that the camera will automatically adjust its frame rate according to the perceived lighting conditions. We observe heterogeneous frame rates for the same phone across videos, and for the same video across phones. Therefore, it is neither desirable nor possible to control the frame rate at the application level.

To achieve frame synchronization, previous systems like PixNet [15] and COBRA [9] simply reduce the screen frame rate in the hope that the receiver can pick out a good frame every other frame. Langlotz et al [12] embed 2D barcodes into time-multiplexed 4D barcodes by repeating frames on multiple, orthogonal color channels, essentially limiting the transmitter's frame rate.

However, there are several fundamental drawbacks with these approaches. First, these approaches are inefficient. The transmitter side capacity is under-utilized, while the receiver drops a large number of mixed frames that actually contain much information. Second, they assume an initial sender setup based on receiver capability, which in practice requires feedback and needs to tailor to individual receivers. Third, these approaches are still unreliable in the face of a fluctuating receive rate, which makes it difficult to work with a general purpose phone camera. For COBRA, the authors fixed the receive rate via a firmware change.

Instead, we argue that the display rate could be higher. The key to displaying frames more quickly is to decode imperfect frames and recover any lost frames on the camera.

We design LightSync to achieve faster and more flexible frame synchronization. LightSync allows each phone to receive at its own capacity. Across links, this avoids the system being bottlenecked by the least capable smartphone camera.

LightSync features two main components. First, it adopts in-frame per-line color tracking to decode heterogeneous frame mixes due to the rolling shutter. Second, it employs inter-frame erasure coding and frame-based tracking to recover lost frames and guard against incorrectly decoded frames. This provides reliable information transfer. Our design also takes into account the computational capability of typical smartphones to enable real-time decoding. In our system, all captured frames contain useful information and can contribute to the overall frame recovery. Note that our design mainly addresses frame synchronization, and therefore could be viewed as an outer code over a base 2D barcode per frame. In that sense, our scheme is orthogonal to existing 2D barcodes like QR codes, PixNet, and COBRA. Furthermore, the notions of per-line tracking and inter-frame coding are generically applicable to screen-smartphone links, even though our current design targets the one-way transfer scenario.

We implement LightSync as a frame generator for the display and an Android phone app to decode the frames in real time. Our system works with off-the-shelf devices and existing general-purpose APIs.

To compare more broadly, we also capture the test barcode video on more phones, and run an offline decoder on the desktop. We find that our test phones can decode the video irrespective of the display frame rate. This means that the screen can display at a high rate so that each phone can get the best performance in line with its capability. Compared to the base line, we achieve up to 2.3× the average throughput across phones.

To summarize, we make the following contributions:

First, we characterize frame rate variability on several smartphones and the challenges to frame synchronization for successful decoding. We address the above challenges with an inter-frame erasure code.

Second, we use efficient in-frame per-line color tracking to resolve artifacts caused by the rolling shutter, which enables us to decode mixed frames. As a result, any received frame is decodable and useful.

Third, with the per-line tracking and the inter-frame code, the screen-camera communication can proceed smoothly at any combination of the transmit and receive frame rates, provided the receive rate is at least half the transmit rate. Since our one-way communication scenario is implicitly a broadcast system, our techniques allow each receiver to scale the performance with its own camera capability and avoid being bottlenecked by the least capable device.

# 2. SYNCHRONIZATION CHALLENGES

We start with an overview of the typical screen-camera communication process and discuss the main challenges for unsynchronized communication. Although we motivated such communication with a one-way transfer scenario, the issues discussed in this section are broadly applicable to these links.

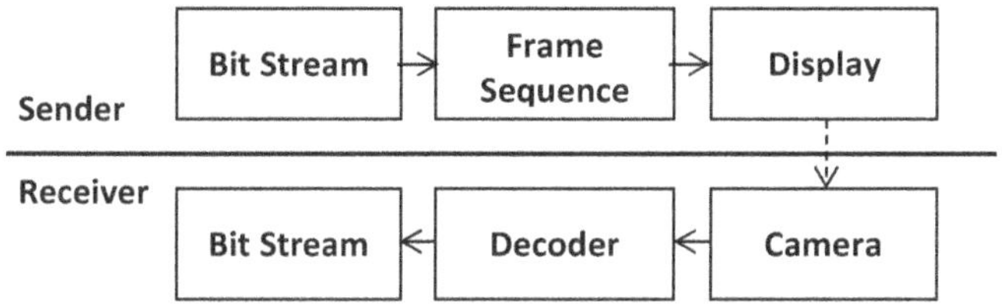


**Figure 2: Screen-camera communication.**

## 2.1 Screen-camera communication overview

With the screen acting as the transmitter and the camera the receiver, a pair of screen and camera forms a communication channel.

Figure 2 shows the typical encoding and decoding processes of such a system. This resembles the typical process in RF communication, although specific techniques differ when mapping bits to signals, generating and sampling signals. Hence we can reason about many issues in the same way. For example, we need mechanisms for frame detection and channel compensation. An immediate issue is the frame rate at the transmitter and the receiver respectively, measured in frames per second (fps). Naturally, they need to match in order for both sides to synchronize on the same frames. In particular, conventional decoding mechanisms require a distinct displayed frame to be detected within a captured video frame to ensure successful decoding.

## 2.2 Display (Transmit) frame rates

Modern LCD or AMOLED screens can typically display content at 30 fps or 60 for high definition videos, although there could be minor variances. With pre-generated video frames, the main cause to the variance is the interplay between when a new frame is written to the LCD's frame buffer and the LCD rendering the current frame. Generating the video frames on the fly, for example from a compressed format, would further add to the variation.

Given the typical video configurations, however, it is more common for videos to be played at 24 or 30 fps, in line with the human visual perception capability. Although this is not a hard limit for our system, off-the-shelf screens and cameras are normally designed with this in mind.

## 2.3 Capture (Receive) frame rates

**Variability and unsteady inter-frame intervals.** Compared to the transmit side, the received frame rate exhibits more variability for several reasons, and such variability affects the captured image quality.

The camera needs sufficient light exposure to capture legible frames. The time it takes to harvest sufficient light depends on the sensor hardware sensitivity and the lighting conditions, in particular, the contrast and intensity levels. Therefore, it is necessary to adopt a different frame rate given specific contrast and intensity levels, and cameras normally adjust this rate automatically to ensure the visual quality for the captured video.

When saving captured frames to the storage, we can also run into system factors. This is specific to cameras fitted on smartphones and tablets. There might be interruptions due to background processes. On our Huawei phone, we sometimes observe an inter-frame interval twice the usual length. There are also artifacts due to the API. For example, our HTC One X camera appears to record videos at close to 24 fps, but the camera callback API can only support sav-

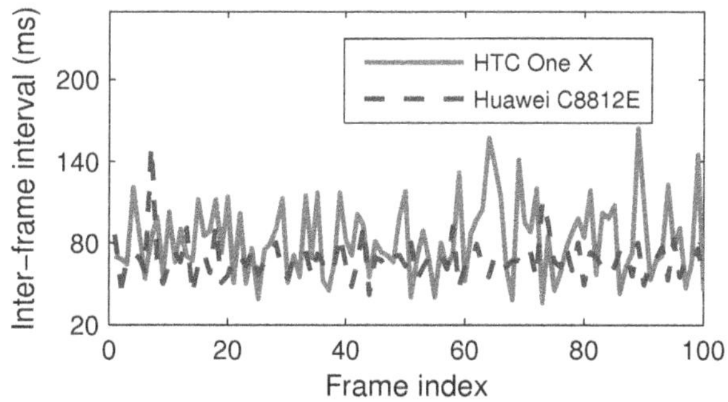


**Figure 3: Example inter-frame intervals.**

ing the frames at 15 to 20 fps. Further, the callback slows down on the One X when there is insufficient memory available in the system. The frame rate on the Samsung Galaxy S III[7] is only stable if we lock the CPU to its maximum frequency with its `setCPU` app. Otherwise, it fluctuates hugely between 21 to 29 for an entirely white foreground, averaging around 25 fps. Even when the frame rate appears steady, the inter-frame interval still varies. Figure 3 shows examples of inter-frame intervals on two phones. The intervals measured on the One X oscillate significantly, which can also introduce arbitrary phase offsets between the transmit and receive sides. Although these issues are artificial and could be addressed with API or firmware fixes, they highlight the complexity of working with off-the-shelf devices.

As exposure time increases with decreasing frame rate, there are several implications on the recorded image quality. While one might expect some minimum average intensity, the effect is non-uniform across each image, depending on the dynamic range of the camera sensor. For example, the probability of over-exposure in some part of the image increases. Moreover, the image becomes more susceptible to blur due to any camera motion during prolonged exposure.

**Operation range and diversity across devices.** The maximum frame rate is determined by the hardware quality, for example, the sensor quality and the amount of heat the device can handle. Table 1 lists the specification of several smartphones. A Nokia Lumia 920, which boasts of great camera quality, can support up to 30 fps, whereas a Huawei Ascend C8812E[3] can only support up to 15 fps. At the low end, the minimum frame rate depends on how much light can be captured in the focal area. Both phones support at least 8 fps, though not for the same images.

Since it is typical to have a certain barcode pattern, we perform a simple experiment to assess the achievable frame rate in practice. We make four test barcode videos (Figure 4), display them on a Dell LCD (2007WFP) turned to the lowest brightness, and record the videos on several phones, placing the phone at a distance to capture the entire video frame[1]. In each video frame, we set the code area of the barcode to black, gray, or white, and the surrounding color to white or black. This changes the average intensity of each video frame, and the camera automatically compensates for that by adjusting the frame rate. Table 2 summarizes the results. We calculate the *effective frame rate* by counting how many camera API callback function calls can be made per second. There are two interesting high-level findings. First, the Lumia 920 can achieve 30 fps even for the darkest video.

[1]We have verified that brightness beyond the focal area does not affect the results.

Table 1: **The smartphones used in the experiments and their specifications.**

| Model | Display size | Video camera | OS | CPU |
|---|---|---|---|---|
| Ascend C8812E | 480 x 800, 4 in | 720p, 15fps | Android 4.0.4 | 1 GHz |
| HTC One X | 720 x 1280, 4.7 in | 1080p, 24fps | Android 4.0.3 | Quad-core 1.5 GHz |
| Galaxy S III | 720 x 1280, 4.8 in | 1080p, 30fps | Android 4.0.4 | Quad-core 1.4 GHz, ARM Cortex-A9 |
| Lumia 920 | 768 x 1280, 4.5 in | 1080p, 30fps | Windows 8 | Dual-core 1.5 GHz Krait |

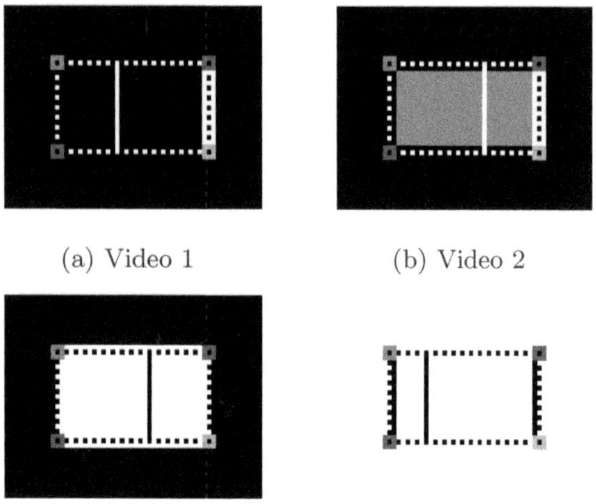

(a) Video 1 (b) Video 2

(c) Video 3 (d) Video 4

**Figure 4: Snapshots of test videos for receive frame rates. The column in the center area moves to the right by one block per frame. Barcodes in Video 4 are surrounded by some white space.**

**Table 2: Recording frame rates per second.**

| Video | 1 | 2 | 3 | 4 |
|---|---|---|---|---|
| Ascend C8812 | 8 | 10 | 15 | 15 |
| HTC One X | 13 | 15 | 15 | 15 |
| Galaxy SIII | 17 | 26 | 30 | 30 |
| Lumia 920 | 30 | 27 | 30 | 29 |

Second, we can ensure a minimum rate even on the low-end phone. The latter is helpful, since frames captured at a very low frame rate are more susceptible to blur or over-exposure, and are harder to decode correctly. Note that the results for Lumia 920 exactly show frame rates are not steady.

To conclude, we observe heterogeneous frame rates for the same phone across videos, and for the same videos across phones. By adopting certain contrast features in the barcode design, we have some control for each phone, although we still need to deal with a range of different frame rates across phones even for the same raw video.

In previous works[15, 9], the frame rate on the receiving phone was fixed to 30 through firmware hacking. The above result clearly shows that a fixed rate may be undesirable, for breaking the camera's adaptive lighting compensation algorithm and potentially producing low-quality images.

**Sensitivity.** We next assess the sensitivity of the frame capture rate and the generality of the above observations. Our findings are summarized below:

1. As long as the intensity of the focal area is stable, the frame rate hardly changes. Within each camera's operating frame rate range, the camera may only support a few rates.
2. Screen brightness has little effect, since even the minimum brightness on our test LCD is bright enough given an average intensity of the focal area.
3. The distance between the screen and the phone only matters to the extent of the average intensity of the focal area.
4. Different environments, such as outdoor, shopping mall, and office, mainly feature different ambient light settings. The typical displays we can find in these environments are bright enough to stabilize the frame rate, although the image quality differs.

## 2.4 Frame synchronization

**Received frame patterns.** Given various potential combinations of the transmit and receive frame rates, we perform a simple experiment to study the received frame pattern. We play Video 4 at several playback rates, and record the video with the Ascend phone. Note that the inter-frame intervals on the receiver side essentially introduce random phase offsets between the two sides.

Figure 5 shows the received frame pattern. For each received frame, i.e., a captured image on the camera, we can detect which originally displayed frames are present[2], and plot a circle for each detected frame. When two or more detected frame indices correspond to the same received frame index, this captured frame is a mixture of two or more displayed frames. Any gap indicates a missed frame, i.e., neither of the consecutive received frames captured the displayed frames corresponding to the gap.

At 7 fps (slightly less than $\frac{15}{2}$), we capture at least one complete frame every other frame. The 'other frame' normally has split original frames due to a phase offset.

When the transmit rate approaches 15 fps, the receive rate, almost every frame is a mix of two frames, but there are occasional missed lines. Split frames are common, and the component frames at the top and bottom might differ.

As the transmit rate increases further, we start to capture 3-frame mixes and miss frames at times. However, consecutive losses or 3-frame mixes are very rare. Missing lines or frames are caused by discrete shutter sampling or delayed return from the camera callback function. In a 3-frame mix, the middle frame is present in its entirety.

Since the Ascend records videos at 15 fps, detecting the same number of displayed frames requires receiving far more frames at a low transmit rate. Therefore, the scales of the vertical axis are different across the subfigures of Figure 5.

**Rolling shutter.** If we examine the mixed frames more closely, we see that the extent of overlap can vary by line, even when the same component frames are present at both the top and the bottom. This is caused by a *rolling shutter*, meaning that the sensor scans the scene line by line to synthesize the complete image. This is specific to CMOS camera sensors, which are the norm for smartphone cameras due to their low energy footprint. Newer smartphone models try to reduce the shutter lag to mitigate this effect. In contrast, CCD sensors, typically used for high-end cameras, capture the whole image at a time.

**Frame synchronization.** Conventionally, only completely clear frames can be decoded, and therefore the goal of frame

[2]This is part of the LightSync decoding process, detailed in Section 3.3.

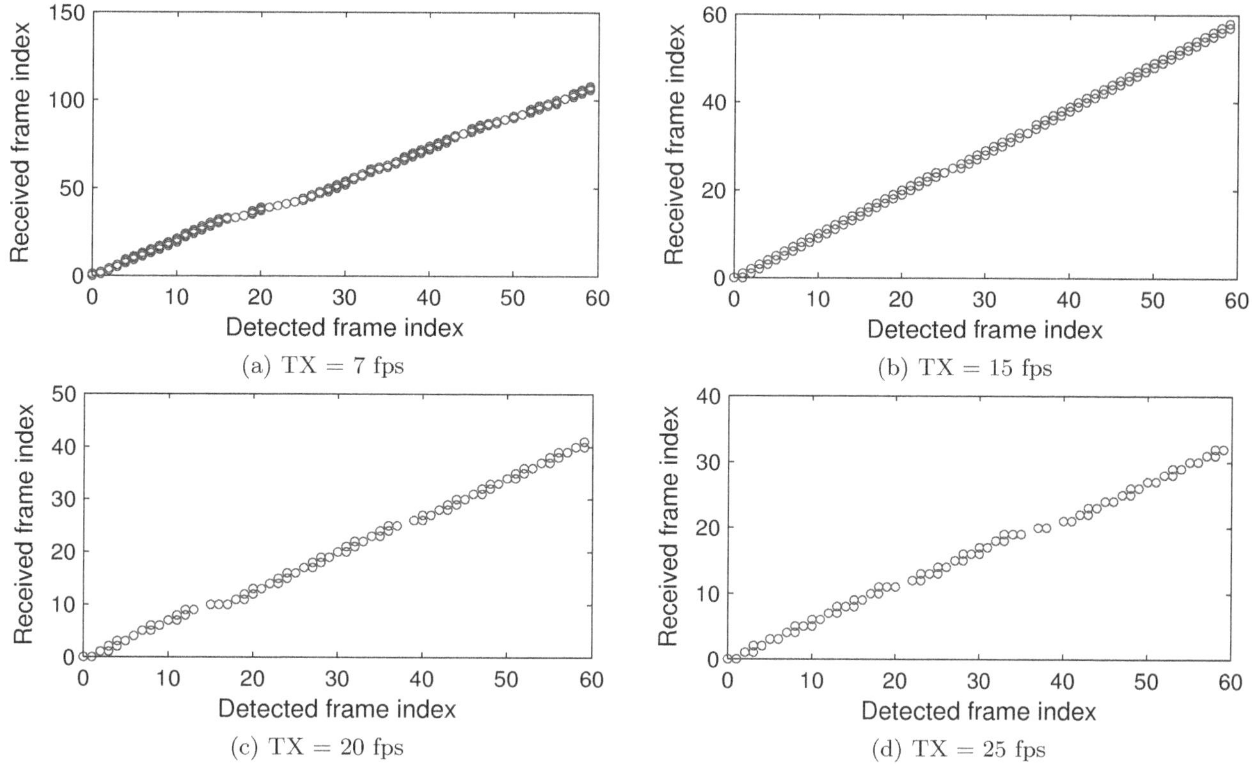


**Figure 5: Received frame patterns on the Ascend.**

synchronization is to adjust the frame rates on both sides to capture enough such frames to decode all original information. In the light of the above received frame patterns, the typical frame synchronization approach is to have the receive capture frames twice as fast as the display, in the hope of ensuring a good frame every other frame. This also appears to fit in with the Nyquist sampling requirement.

However, this approach is wasteful, since a large number of imperfect frames are dropped, which could provide useful information. Further, since each frame is a discrete sample already, in theory we could have equal frame rates on both sides. The key to achieving this is to decode imperfect frames and recover lost frames. The latter can be easily addressed with erasure coding across the original frames, which can also help recover incorrectly decoded frames. The former is complicated by inherent image quality issues.

## 2.5 Challenges in decoding imperfect frames

**Heterogeneous mixes.** If each frame was *homogeneous*, then we would only need a per-frame tracker to record the proportion of each component frame.

Unfortunately, there are two practical issues. First, we often obtain mixtures between different frames in the same captured frame, e.g., the top half is from original frames 1 and 2, while the bottom half is from 2 and 3.

Second, given the rolling shutter, we need to track the proportion of mixture variation per line even for the same component frames.

**Inherent image quality issues.** Image quality is generally lower for smartphone cameras than for regular cameras due to form factor and cost constraints. This is reflected in such issues as color distortion around the focus within an image and the dynamic range of the color spectrum. Compensating for these issues becomes more challenging for mixed frames.

When mixing colors, there is a tradeoff between being able to distinguish all mixtures and ensuring the result color stays within the dynamic range. Most notably, having too many white blocks mix will cause over-exposure at the mixed position. Therefore, designing for many-component mixed frame is near impossible.

The main solution is to discretize the color levels used, i.e., use *sparse* colors so that we can disambiguate their combinations. This means we cannot expect much 'soft information' between the discrete levels.

# 3. LightSync DESIGN

LightSync achieves fast frame synchronization by making it possible to decode imperfect frames. Specifically, we address rolling shutter with multiple tracking bars and per-line tracking within each frame. We adopt a linear erasure code across the original frames to recover lost frames and leverage partial or mixed frames. In some sense, frames are synchronized by default in LightSync. Practically, synchronization (or resynchronization) is achieved as long as we can identify the component frames of each received frame.

## 3.1 Line-based overlap tracking

With the rolling shutter effect, frame mixes vary by proportion at different lines, sometimes involving different frames. We resolve these with standard color bars, which form an implicit encoding pattern.

**Encoding pattern.** Generally, we need to insert tracking bars in each frame in the shutter rolling direction (perpendicular to the scanning direction). These can track the percentage overlap at each line by showing the reference colors. Our current design is based on findings from the experiments in the previous section. We target a frame capture rate that is at least half of the display rate.

To recap, we only need to resolve mixed frames with up to 3 component frames, i.e., each block may have contributions from up to 3 blocks. In such a mixed frame, the middle frame always takes up 50% of the mixture, whereas the re-

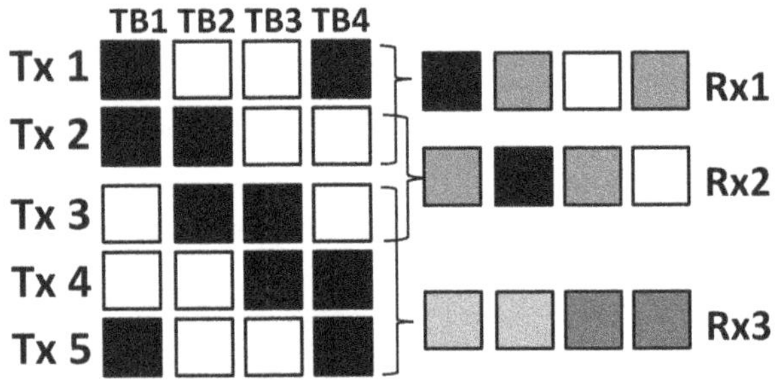


**Figure 6: Per-frame tracking bar pattern.**

maining 50% is split between the first and the third frames. Further, color distortion on the Huawei phone only allows us to reliably use two grayscale levels as the base color blocks, i.e., black and white. Thus, there are only 8 possible color combinations at each block. All white and all black are easy to detect and do not vary by line. White-black-white and black-white-black will both produce 50% gray at any line, and therefore are two further trivial cases. The remaining four combinations may produce varying results depending on the color composition and need to be tracked.

With this in mind, we place four bars in each sent frame, two white and two black. Figure 6 illustrates the color pattern. Each vertical line represents a tracking bar, while each horizontal line represents the color pattern of a line in a frame. The color pattern shifts by one bar in each successive displayed frame, and the overall pattern across frames repeats every four frames. As a result, all four combinations are present in any received frame, and the four blocks in each line serve as reference colors for per-frame decoding. They are analogous to training sequences in traditional RF wireless communication.

**Decoding mixed frames.** For any block in a mixed frame, the decoding algorithm proceeds in two stages.

First, we determine the exact displayed frames present at this block. This is needed if the top and bottom frame indices differ or one of the frame index blocks is too dim, and only needs to be done once per line. Given the tracking bar encoding pattern, if the first or the last frame is missing, one of the bars will be completely black, and another completely white. Further, the positions of these two depend on which frame is missing. Consider the first three frames in Figure 6, if the first frame is missing (Rx 2), TB4 will be white, and TB2 will be black. If the third frame is missing (Rx 1), TB1 will be black, and TB3 will be black. This process implicitly detects lost lines from the displayed frames, because blocks from those lines will remain unknown after per-frame decoding. By identifying the component frames per line, we are also able to handle practically any phase offset between the displayed and the captured frames.

Second, we compare the code block color with the reference colors to determine the code block sequence in the original frames concerned. There are three known colors, white, black, and 50% gray, and four tracking block colors. If the code block is matched to only one reference color except the gray, the block sequence can be unambiguously decoded. Otherwise, we look up the block at the same position in the previous captured frame to help resolve the ambiguity. If that still fails, we mark this block unknown, and leave it to the cross-frame correction stage, combined with undoing the erasure code.

We determine a color match if the code block and the reference colors are within a small range of each other. Given color distortion due to the lens, readings for the same color at the center and at the edge of the image might differ by 5 to 10%. Therefore, for any two-component mix, the range is set to 10%. We can decode a 3-component mix with less than 10% contribution from the third frame as if a two-component mix. To allow for this slight additional error, we relax the range by a further 5% for 3-component mixes. Relaxing the range too much would cause too much unnecessary ambiguity, and hence we keep it tight.

In theory, we can calculate the exact percentage mixture from the tracking bars. However, color distortion makes this generally impossible. Instead, the inference based approach is simpler, and allows us to decode multiple displayed frames from a single mixed frame captured.

**Implicit cross-frame error correction.** The tracking bar pattern embeds error correction capability, and we leverage this to ensure correct decoding. The color thresholds are set such that if the code block color matches that of only one tracking block, the original blocks concerned are guaranteed to follow the pattern of the matched tracking bar and can be decoded correctly. Further inference based on already decoded blocks is then guaranteed to yield correct decoding results. Extending this further, the decoding results from decoding the inter-frame erasure code are also guaranteed correct. This resembles hard-decision decoding.

## 3.2 Inter-frame erasure coding

**Erasure coding in LightSync.** One of the key ideas of LightSync is to apply erasure coding across the original frames, so that each sent frame may contain information from multiple original frames. This also means that any partial or mixed frame is just a version of coded frame and can be decoded as long as we keep track of the coding coefficients. Therefore, once we receive enough linearly independent frames, we should be able to recover all original frames. This makes it easy to recover lost frames.

Ideally, each encoded frame should be a linear combination of all original frames, while linearly independent of any other encoded frame. This would allow us to recover all $N$ original frames from any $N$ encoded frames. However, recovering the original frames requires solving a simultaneous linear system, and the computational complexity increases quickly with $N$. Therefore, we opt for a simpler, suboptimal coding scheme.

Our previous study shows that frame losses are rare, and there are no more than two consecutive losses given the typical frame rate range on our phones. Furthermore, we expect the capture rate to be at least half the display rate, which means that we expect to receive all frames after the transmitter 'repeats' all frames once. Therefore, we only need a very simple form of erasure coding to recover such losses with low computational overhead.

For our purposes, each frame can simply be treated as a stream of bits, and our erasure coding process produces a coded bit stream of the same length. Therefore, the inter-frame coding is independent of the base code per frame, and can be viewed as an outer code over a 2D barcode. The coded bits within a frame can then be mapped to colored blocks and the blocks arranged in some pattern following the per-frame base code. Optimizations for the base code, such as the blur-aware color ordering in COBRA, can equally apply here. We might even be able to apply such techniques in the temporal domain, although we leave this to future work.

**Low-complexity coding.** We use a sparse and deterministic coding matrix for low complexity recovery.

First, we simply transmit the original frames verbatim as the first half of our frame sequence. Second, we generate encoded frames to complete the second half. We divide all original frames to groups of three consecutive frames. This is because we expect no more than one frame loss per three frames, and coding together few frames will speed up decoding. For each group of original frames $F_1$, $F_2$, and $F_3$, the coded frames are $F_1 \oplus F_2$, $F_2 \oplus F_3$, and $F_1 \oplus F_3$.

Our coding matrix is quite suboptimal in guarding against linear dependency, since the second half of the sequence is generated from the original frames in the first place. However, we trade off suboptimal coding for low-complexity decoding. Further, even seemingly linearly dependent later frames are still helpful when per-frame decoding did not succeed 100%. We will show examples in Section 5.

We apply the matrix to bits at the same position of the frames within each coding group, which implies no coding within or across lines. Coding within or across lines of a frame offers little additional redundancy in the event of a lost frame, since the entire frame is lost anyway[3].

**Stopping criteria.** For our main scenario, the display simply plays the entire code frame sequence in a looping fashion. The phone client stops recording the video once enough frames have been successfully decoded.

Having the original frames first is helpful if the video is played on-demand, because a high-rate phone is less likely to lose the first few frames, and would need to target a shorter decoding delay. Later iterations can be viewed as auxiliary transmissions to provide incremental redundancy.

If we had a unicast scenario and a duplex communication channel, the receiver could acknowledge receipt of all frames to stop further transmissions.

**Frame tracking and on-demand decoding.** We insert a few fields in each frame to keep track of the sent frames. First, each frame carries a frame sequence length, which is twice the total frame count. This gives an indication of how many frames need to be captured, although the exact number of frames needed might deviate from this total depending on the decoding performance. Second, each frame carries the sent frame indices within the sequence of all coded frames, from which we can determine the component original frames.

Once we have the coded frames and the rows of the coding matrix these correspond to, decoding is straightforward. For our coding scheme, we only need a few XORs to recover the original frames. Since we often lose only part of a frame, we perform decoding only for the lines with missing information.

Note that we are effectively encoding and decoding in a line-by-line fashion within each frame. Therefore, the current design is suboptimal, because we still transmit whole frames. In future, we can extend the design to mimic transmitting and receiving per line, analogous to partial packet recovery in wireless networks[11].

## 3.3 End-to-end system flow

**Frame format.** Our techniques are not related to the per-frame layout, so we can mostly follow existing designs, e.g., that for COBRA, since COBRA includes optimizations for fast code block extraction[4]. Figure 7 shows an example frame. The corners and borders are basically the same as in COBRA, except that we alter the vertical border pattern slightly. Our border blocks per line have different colors, which aids color calibration. Although not apparent in Figure 7(b), we do surround each barcode with some white space to ensure the average light intensity of the frame. This follows the observations in Table 2.

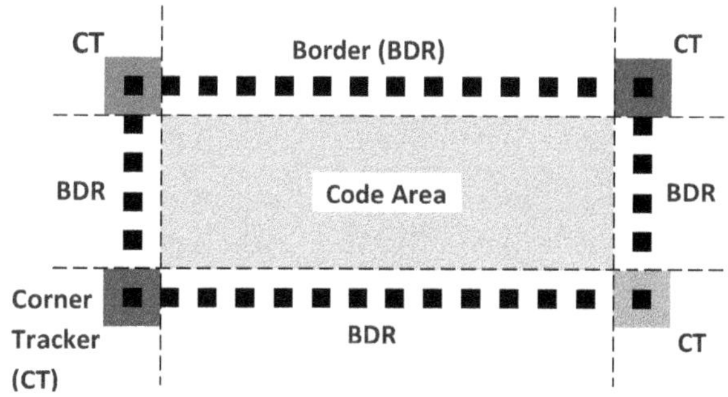


(a) Corner and border design in COBRA

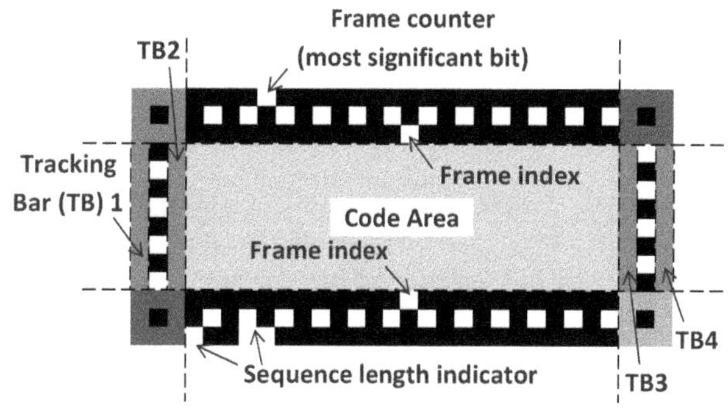


(b) Additional fields for LightSync

**Figure 7: Frame layout.**

Generally speaking, the tracking bars need to be perpendicular to the scanning direction (i.e., in the shutter rolling direction), whereas the frame tracking fields should be in bars parallel to the scanning direction. We currently arrange the code block in a landscape orientation, and hence the shutter scanning direction is horizontal.

We fit the frame tracking fields and the tracking bars in the spare space around the border blocks to avoid additional overhead. The four tracking bars are placed to the left and right of the two vertical border bars.

There are four frame-tracking fields in the bars around the top and bottom border bars. These index the sent frame within the entire coded frame sequence. They reset when the frame sequence is repeated. We use white block on black bars, since the camera is more receptive to white and better preserves the frame information this way.

The *coded frame sequence length* is represented in *binary* in the space below the bottom border bar, and is the same in all frames. This is twice the number of the original frames. The bar above the top border shows *the most significant bits of the frame index.* It is represented in *unary* to be distinguishable even in a mixed frame. The bar immediately below the top border bar shows in *unary* the *frame index modulo the bar length.* A mixed frame will have multiple blocks set in this bar to indicate the component frames. The

[3]They can provide more protection against perspective distortion, but this is beyond the focus of the current work.

[4]We will discuss how to improve the layout in Section 5.

bar immediately above the bottom border bar shows the same information. This is because the mixture components can change within a frame.

**Encoding and transmission.** We start with a bit stream divided into frames, and generate an erasure coded bit stream. Frames are then generated following some bit-to-block mapping, such as that for COBRA or data matrix. Any applicable code block optimizations can be added too. This is our base code. We then add frame tracking fields and the line-based tracking bars to each encoded frame. Finally, these frames are turned into a video and played in a looping fashion at a given frame rate.

**Reception and decoding.** Decoding bootstraps by identifying where in the coded sequence the first frame is. Note that part of the first received frame may need to be discarded, since there might be insufficient information of the previous frames. We start with per-frame decoding and then invoke cross-frame correction after receiving half a sequence.

Per-frame decoding proceeds in two stages. For each captured frame, we first detect the corners and the borders, and calculate all code block positions following the block localization algorithms in COBRA. We then extract the color values at these locations. Note that each position corresponds to a single pixel, but we average the color readings of a $3 \times 3$ square centered at this position as the reading for the block. This can reduce errors due to color distortion.

In the second stage, we find the frame tracking blocks to record the component frame index information. If we determine that the received frame contains information of any original frames that have not been fully decoded, we decode the code blocks in this newly received frame line by line. At the start of each line, we first calibrate the data block by comparing its reading to the black and white border blocks in the same line, and then decode the block by comparing its color to those of the tracking blocks.

Once the decoder detects a second half of the video sequence in the received frame, we start cross-frame correction after decoding each new frame by undoing the erasure code and filling in any missing blocks at the relevant positions if possible. Frame capture and decoding both terminate if all original frames have been decoded. The blocks are then mapped to bits to output a bit stream.

**API.** LightSync can serve as a piece of middleware, taking a bit stream as input at the transmitter, and producing a decoded bit stream as output at the receiver. An application written on top of LightSync just needs to generate and interpret the bit stream accordingly.

## 3.4 Discussion

In signal processing terms, unsynchronized communication in our scenario is essentially a form of *undersampling*, where the sampling rate is lower than the Nyquist rate. Mixed frames correspond to *aliasing*. The reason and condition for being able to resolve such aliasing in our setting is that our raw signals, the blocks taking on black or white, are *sparse* in the available color spectrum. This ensures a small number of possibilities when aliasing occurs, such that we can still disambiguate many raw signal combinations that produce the aliases.

The use of tracking bars and linear erasure codes is generic, although our current design takes into account the particular challenges and requirements of the current system. In theory, the design would scale to apply directly over orthogonal color channels. We will explore this in future work.

As technology improves, we might expect to adopt a simpler design yet capable of higher performance. For example, if we had CCD camera sensors employing *global shutters*, the per-line tracking could be significantly simplified. The frame counters can almost fully determine the component frames, and the vertical tracking bars only need to detect the transition across frames.

Given we focus on resolving frames temporally, we assume a reasonable image quality for each received frame so that we can extract the code blocks per frame. In other words, we expect the afore-mentioned first stage of per-frame decoding to succeed[5]. Mechanisms to guard against poor image quality, possibly caused by motion-induced blur or poor lens focus, would also improve the robustness of our scheme, though they are orthogonal to our main focus.

# 4. LightSync IMPLEMENTATION

We implement LightSync to work with a standard LCD and an Android phone app.

**Encoder.** For the transmitter part of the system, we write a frame generator in Matlab. It takes a given bit stream, and produces encoded frames following a pre-specified bit-to-block mapping (default is 0 to black and 1 to white) and the frame layout described in the previous section. The frames are then turned into a video, to be played at a specified frame rate and displayed on the screen.

**Decoder.** The decoder is implemented in Java as a phone app using Android SDK 2.3.3 and Android development tools. The app runs two threads. One thread obtains the recorded frames using the camera callback API, and puts them in a queue to be processed. The other thread takes the frame at the front of the queue and decodes it in real time without saving the image. Decoding results for the frame are saved, which may involve code blocks in up to 3 original frames, even if there are unresolved blocks at this stage. Both threads are stopped when all original frames have been decoded completely.

As we explained earlier, the output of LightSync can be piped into an actual application that will interpret the bit stream decoded in a meaningful way. For our experiments, however, we simply make the decoder a standalone app.

Changing the interfaces slightly, we also turn the online app into an offline desktop decoder that can take timestamped captured video frames and decode them. This helps us analyze the captured frames and the decoding results.

**Optimizations for real-time processing.** Our design for the erasure coding and the tracking bars have already taken into account the real-time processing requirements. In addition, we take three measures to achieve real-time decoding.

First, we minimize the number of pixels to process. Specifically, we limit the initial search area for the corners. Once the corners are located, we calculate the central pixel locations of the remaining blocks, including borders, tracking blocks, and data blocks. For each block, we only process the 9 pixels centered around the calculated location to extract the color value. From the second frame onwards, we

[5]Otherwise, the received frame will simply be dropped and the corresponding component frames considered missing. Although LightSync can handle such situations, it is not optimized for them.

also use locations from the previous frame as initial references. For example, we use the previous corner locations, and only briefly search around these to confirm or re-locate the corners. The number of border blocks on each side is only counted when processing the first frame.

Second, we avoid using any large high-dimensional array in processing the images, since Java does not provide efficient operations with such arrays.

Third, we use a single thread to complete all decoding operations[6]. This avoids unnecessary context switches.

Since our current implementation already meets the real-time target, we do not explore further optimizations, even though some operations could be sped up more.

# 5. EVALUATION

## 5.1 Experiment setup

**Hardware.** We use a Dell LCD (2007WFP) as the display and several smartphones. Table 1 lists the phones and their specifications. Note that the published specifications describe video capture frame rates in the recording mode, with the video saved directly to a compressed format. In contrast, our app runs in the preview mode to access the color information of the individual pixels in the raw images, and so might see a different capture rate.

**Workload.** Our workload is a file transfer that can be encoded into a 30-frame barcode video. Once erasure coding is applied, this turns into a 60-frame sequence played repeatedly. This means that the phone camera would only need to record for 1 to 2 seconds, which is a reasonable duration to expect the user to hold the camera for. Furthermore, the total of 60 frames in a sequence is a suitable lowest common denominator for our cross-phone experiments later in the section, so that we can capture a few rounds of the video given the available memory on each phone.

We play the video at 10 to 27 fps with `mplayer`. All phones try to recover the file from recorded video frames. The playback rates of 28 to 30 fps cannot be precisely controlled and are hence omitted. All the video players we tried use rounding when trying to achieve a certain playback rate. For 27 fps, the inter-frame gap is almost exactly 37 ms, and fairly steady. For 30 fps, the gaps should be 33.3 ms, but more variable in practice. These cause the display to sometimes skip (part of) a frame, which cannot be recovered on the receiving side. Although our erasure code can handle this to some extent, the frame skipping cannot be controlled and causes too much randomness across experiment runs.

Unless otherwise stated, we use a data area of 36×20 blocks per frame, 10×10 pixels per block. Including the borders and corners, each frame has 38×26 blocks. The phone is placed around 10 cm from the Dell LCD, though the exact distance varies slightly by the phone based on their individual display sizes. Note that these parameters are not hard operating constraints for LightSync, but do affect the image quality. In a real scenario, we can support larger distances by using much larger code blocks and displaying much larger barcodes to achieve acceptable image quality.

36×20 is much smaller a code area size than was considered in PixNet or COBRA. While our techniques scale with the code area size, the image quality does not. We experimented with such sizes as 60×40 and 48×26, and each

[6]A small number of threads may also be fine.

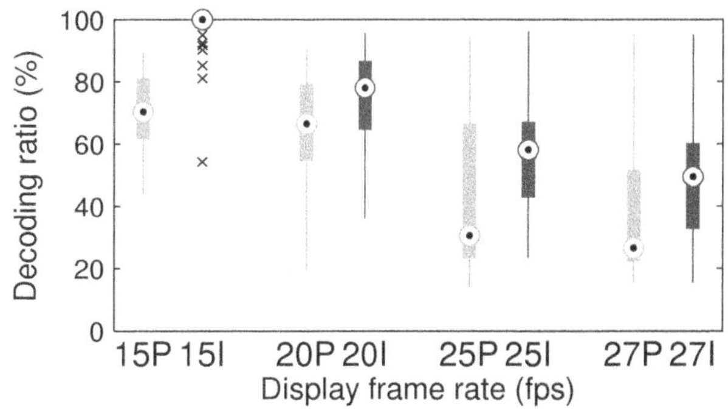


**Figure 8: Per-frame decoding performance.**

suited a specific phone. When more blocks are packed, the block size decreases quickly in the captured frame, and we find that corner detection fails easily in the face of various lens effects (for example, color distortion on the Ascend and moiré pattern on the HTC One X). Larger corner and border blocks would be needed to offset such distortions. Since frame layout optimization is beyond the scope of this work and we assume a reasonable image quality, we stick to the small code area size for most experiments.

**Metric.** The main metric is the effective frame rate, seen in the transfer completion time. Minimizing the completion time can improve user experience, in that the user only needs to hold the camera for a shorter time. This would also reduce the chance of capturing blurred images due to hand motion. We will also calculate the equivalent throughput.

Since our implementation goal is to have the client application operate in real time, we time individual operations to assess their computational complexity.

## 5.2 LightSync microbenchmarks

We first evaluate the individual performance of the in-frame tracking and erasure coding as much as possible. We will also time each stage in the decoding process. These microbenchmarks are performed on the Ascend unless otherwise stated, which represents a low-end phone with an average quality camera. The CPU and memory are also at the low end among currently available smartphones.

**Performance without erasure coding.** In this experiment, we assess how well we can identify the component blocks of any received block by comparing its color to those of the corresponding tracking blocks. We collect 150 received frames for each setting on the One X, and calculate the per-frame decoding ratio (Figure 8). There are two boxplots per frame rate setting, one for *only* using tracking bars within a frame (suffixed with 'P'), and the other for additionally using the previous frame to resolve some ambiguous block combinations (suffixed with 'I'). Since we cannot control the frame mixing patterns, the received frames are composed from mixtures of different original frames and block patterns, and therefore large variances are seen for all these boxplots. Not surprisingly, decoding becomes more challenging with increasing display rate, due to more missing and 3-component mixed frames. Cross-frame disambiguation and correction are essential to decode the remaining blocks.

**Efficiency of the erasure code.** Our code is strictly sub-optimal in guarding against linear dependency between received frames, so we evaluate its efficiency by considering the performance variation with the received frame pattern.

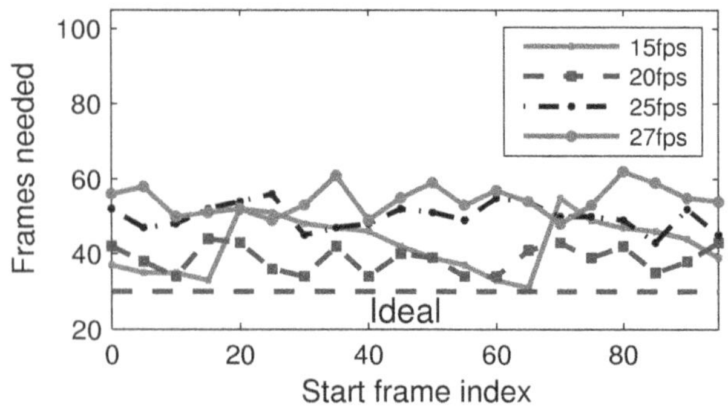


**Figure 9: Efficiency of the inter-frame code.**

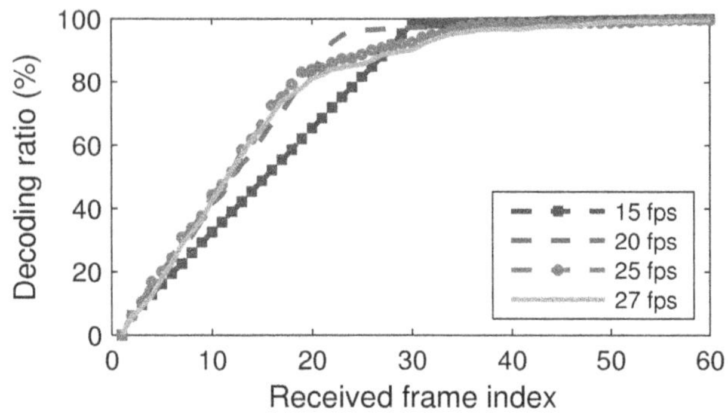


**Figure 10: Decoding progress as frames are received.**

We collect more than 100 frames for display rates at 15, 20, 25, and 27 fps, and start decoding from different points in the received sequence. Figure 9 plots the number of frames needed for successful decoding.

Recall the Ascend phone supports 15 fps, and therefore the received frame patterns are different at these display rates. Ideally, decoding should complete when we receive 30 frames. When the display frame rate is 15, the phone only occasionally misses a frame, and per-frame decoding often succeeds completely. Therefore, how many extra frames are needed depends on the position of the missing frame, and it is uniformly distributed between 1 and 30. As the display rate increases, per-frame decoding becomes more challenging and the decoding ratio drops. This is reflected in many more frames are needed, sometimes to complete a few blocks. However, the variance also decreases compared to that at 15-fps video playback, since most frames contribute at least a few lines of information.

Although the exact lines look different for a different phone, the general observation still holds. Figure 10 shows the decoding ratio of the blocks *in the 30 original frames* as more frames are received for a comparable run on the One X across display frame rates. We assume decoding only starts when the first original frame in the video is detected in a received frame. Initially the higher the display rate, the faster the growth rate of the decoding ratio. This is because a received frame is more likely to contain more component frames at a high display rate, and decoding a received block means several original video blocks are successfully decoded. Once the erasure code frames are detected, the decoding ratio grows more slowly for all display rates, because the decoder is now only filling in missing blocks.

**Computational complexity and memory usage.** Our target is to decode each frame within 33 ms to support 30 fps, the highest receive frame rate observed so far. Table 3 lists the time taken for each operation. The first frame takes longer because corner detection is the slowest part of the whole process. Later frames can build on the corner positions identified in the first frame, and only slight adjustment is needed. Border detection is essentially a no-op from the second frame onwards.

**Table 3: Processing time breakdown in ms.**

| Operation | 1st frame | Later |
|---|---|---|
| Corner detection | 27 | 4 |
| Border block count | 6 | 1 |
| Block extraction | 9 | 10 |
| Per-frame decoding | 8 | 10 |
| Linear decoding per frame | No-op | 1 |
| Per-frame total | 50 | 26 |

The client app decodes the captured frames on-the-fly without saving the frames. Therefore, the memory requirement mainly includes caching the raw frame being processed and storing information for the frames already decoded. The former is about 200 KB for the Ascend (and 1 MB for the HTC One X). For the latter, each frame contains $36\times20$ data blocks, each mapping to 1 or 2 bits. If per-frame decoding is not successful, we mark the block 'unknown'. In all we only need 1 bit of state information per block after decoding, and therefore around 720 bits per frame. This is at most double the amount of raw bits carried in each video frame.

**Sensitivity to distortion.** The linear coding part of LightSync is entirely independent of the common distortions applicable to screen-camera communication.

Due to following the frame layout in COBRA, we cannot effectively assess how such distortions affect the tracking bars. This is because if the corners and borders are not sufficiently affected, neither will the tracking bars. Conversely, decoding cannot even start without successfully identifying the corner and border locations. In this sense, however, the current corner and border design acts as a natural guard to ensure the resilience of decoding using tracking bars.

Generally speaking, ambient light or screen brightness has little effect provided the border blocks used for calibration can be identified. The tracking bars can be affected by perspective distortion if a data block cannot locate its reference tracking blocks in the same line. However, we can extend the inter-frame coding to code across lines for further in-frame protection, and we will explore this in future work.

## 5.3 Performance comparison

**Performance across phones.** For this set of experiments, we capture all frames and decode offline. This allows us to analyze the images in more detail and to compare image quality across devices. Decoding stops when all 30 original frames have been successfully recovered. We calculate the effective frame capture rate as the number of frames needed to complete decoding over the time taken to capture these frames. Since we have previously shown that the processing is fast enough, we simply calculate the throughput from the effective frame rate and the per-frame capacity. We also run the app on all the Android phones to verify that the offline performance results match the real-time performance.

Figure 11 shows the effective frame capture rates achieved by each phone. The phone's actual capture rate is marked in the legend. All phones can achieve a decent frame rate at any display rate, which meets our initial goal of unsynchronized communication. Not surprisingly, the highest effective rate is

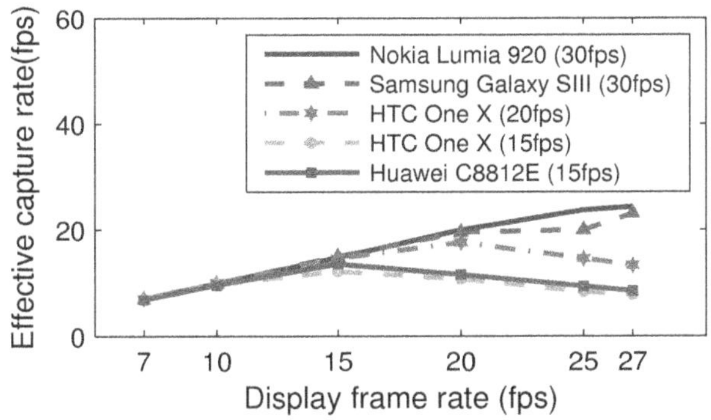


**Figure 11: Effective capture rates on each phone.**

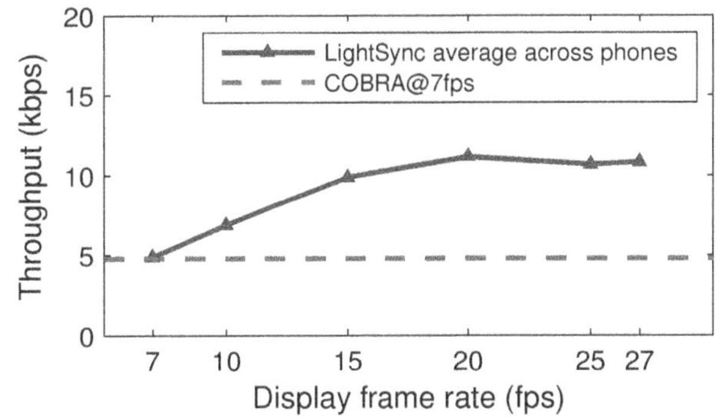


**Figure 12: Average throughput across phones.**

achieved when the display rate is comparable to the phone's actual frame rate. This is because per-frame decoding performance degrades and frame loss occurs for higher display rates. It takes extra frames and time to recover even a few undecoded blocks, due to either per-frame decoding failure or even a single lost frame. Note that we are interested in the shapes of the lines rather than the relative heights of them. The former shows how LightSync scales with increasing disparity between the display and capture frames rates, whereas the latter is determined by the hardware quality.

**Alternative schemes.** We next compare LightSync against COBRA and a simplified version of Unsynchronized 4D barcodes (4D barcodes for short). We omit PixNet in the comparison, since it was shown to be too computationally expensive for current smartphones[9].

COBRA is essentially our base code. The original proposal includes code optimizations based on color ordering and sender motion. We skip these since they do not matter in our setting. Note, however, that COBRA uses 4 colors, whereas LightSync is only in monochrome now, and therefore COBRA has twice the per-frame capacity as LightSync.

For this comparison, we assess the average rate across phones at the same display rate, emulating our broadcast scenario. The decoding algorithm in COBRA means it can only decode frames captured at a rate at least double that of the display rate. Therefore, when the lowest-quality phones can only capture at 15 fps, the video playback rate can be no higher than 7 fps. For a higher display rate, the low-fps phones capturing a COBRA-coded video will simply see a sequence of mixed frames and unable to decode much, unless the blocks at the same positions in consecutive frames happen to have the same color. This cannot be resolved simply by caching captured frames and decoding offline, and means that COBRA can only be run for the 7 fps screen rate for all phones. Figure 12 shows that the average throughput across phones LightSync can support is up to 2.3× that for COBRA. In terms of decoding time, the main additional decoding step in LightSync is undoing the inter-frame coding, which takes negligible time.

The basic idea of 4D barcode is to repeat frames on multiple, orthogonal color channels. Since the original design cannot support real-time processing[9], we adapt it to be based on COBRA like frame layout but encoding data in colored blocks in the original spirit. However, we observe that it cannot be decoded even when displayed at 7 fps.

4D barcode performs poorly for three reasons. First, red, green, and blue are not orthogonal in practice. Decoding is practically impossible when the patterns on different color channels interfere, and different color distortion behavior across phones makes it nearly impossible to correct for the colors generically. This could in theory be corrected in software if the colors are calibrated precisely per device. However, it is not practical for the type of scenarios we are targeting. The original design included color rectification and specific block patterns that could alleviate the color interference. Second, even when the colors can be differentiated, the frames can only be decoded if the display frame rate is no more than $\frac{3}{2}$ of the frame capture rate. The original paper evaluated their system with animated `.gif`, whose rate is 10 fps. At a higher display rate, we face the same issue with mixed frames as for COBRA, which cannot be decoded using the conventional approach. Third, the throughput of 4D barcode even in the ideal case is equivalent to using a monochrome channel at the same frame capture rate.

# 6. RELATED WORK

**Visible Light Communications (VLC).** Our work falls within Visible Light Communication. The technology was first explored by VLCC (Visible Light Communication Consortium) in Japan[13]. Since then, there have been many efforts exploring various hardware and techniques (e.g., [11, 8]). However, they generally involve LEDs as transmitters and photodiodes as receivers, and a significant focus is on modulation via pulses. [10] uses pixelated wireless optical channels, though. In comparison, we use general-purpose LCDs and smartphone cameras for communication. Furthermore, our encoding mechanism mainly involves operating over groups of pixels spatially, but the pixels can also take on different colors to encode bits.

**Screen-camera links.** As a specific type of VLC, LCD-camera communication tends to be one-way, involving showing a video to transmit information. We already referred to PixNet, COBRA, and 4D barcode. Building on building on [10], PixNet is designed for LCDs and high-end cameras, and proposes a high-throughput 2D barcode per frame modulated using 2D OFDM. COBRA is for phone-to-phone optical streaming. The authors design a color barcode with a layout optimized for low-complexity processing and mobility-aware adaptive code block arrangement to be blur-resilient. To draw an analogy with traditional RF propagation based wireless communications, PixNet is analogous to designing an OFDM-based modulation scheme over BPSK for individual frames, whereas COBRA optimizes the frame format while using a simpler bit-to-waveform mapping as the modulation scheme over the entire channel.

LightSync is orthogonal, in that we address frame synchronization and aim to increase the frame rate. The analogous task in traditional wireless is to decode undersampled frames, e.g., when consecutive frames are sent on 20 MHz channels, but sampled at less than 40 MHz and received as a single frame. 4D barcode targets the same issue by extending a 2D barcode across time on orthogonal color channels. We have explained in Section 5 that the design is suboptimal.

VRCodes[18] follows a further orthogonal avenue by exploring unobtrusive barcode design that is imperceptible to human eyes. The authors leverage rolling shutter to mimic a high frequency change of selected colors, such that human eyes would only perceive the mixture of both colors at all times. The idea could be combined with LightSync, if we replace black and white with suitable colors.

Note that the encoding and decoding goals and mechanisms for communication over screen-camera pairs are substantially different from conventional video coding and computer vision work. Video coding and transmission aims to use a small number of bits to describe and convey the original scene information, in the hope of reconstructing the scenes with little or acceptable quality degradation. Vision work tries to interpret the captured images, which is an open-ended process. In contrast, all the screen-camera communication work modulates a bit stream to well-defined colored pixel blocks, which are then demodulated accordingly to retrieve the original bit stream. This is simply software-defined radio in the visible light frequency bands.

**Visual interactions.** There has long been interest in enabling visual interactions with phone cameras[16, 17], including to assist local communication, e.g., by obtaining a security token with the camera. Although we share the same ultimate goal of enriching visual interaction, we aim to enhance the visual communication capability.

There are many 2D barcodes, such as QR code or data matrix. These codes can be printed on any surface, but is static. In comparison, our scenario requires a screen, but can display dynamic content.

Optical Character Recognition (OCR) could be another alternative to 2D barcodes, although current OCR technologies can only recognize simple patterns.

**Short-range RF wireless technologies.** Latest smartphones typically support Bluetooth and Near Field Communication (NFC), and can communicate with another device fitted with the needed chips. These can power such applications as file transfer and contact-less payment.

We view screen-camera based visual communication as complementary to NFC, because we are adding communication capability to devices that may not be NFC-capable. Visual links can sometimes be more efficient than NFC due to non-interference with similar wireless devices.

# 7. CONCLUSION

In this work, we show how to achieve unsynchronized communication in real time between LCDs and phone cameras with LightSync. Our techniques mainly include in-frame per-line color tracking to decode mixed frames and inter-frame erasure coding to recover lost frames. Our implementation works with off-the-shelf screens and smartphones without any OS or firmware changes. It also work with other 'auto' settings of the smartphone camera as much as possible, to allow the user to seamlessly switch between normal camera usage and such visual communication. The frame rate can also adjust automatically based on the average intensity of each frame without breaking the system.

With LightSync, we are able to decode information even when the display frame rate is higher than the camera frame capture rate. This shifts the performance bottleneck to the individual receiving camera's hardware capability, instead of the display frame rates. As a result, when the same content is displayed to a range of phones, the average throughput across phones can more than double and is not constrained by the least capable phone, unlike in previous approaches. Techniques like LightSync provide primitives for more sophisticated visual communication scenarios.

## Acknowledgments

We are very grateful to Heran Lin for helping with the experiments during the revision of the paper and to the anonymous reviewers for very insightful comments that helped improve the paper.

# 8. REFERENCES

[1] Gibraltar targets tourists with Wikipedia QR codes. http://www.bbc.co.uk/news/technology-19544299.

[2] HTC One X specification. http://www.gsmarena.com/htc_one_x-4320.php.

[3] Huawei Ascend C8812E specification. http://pdadb.net/index.php?m=specs&id=3532&c=huawei_ascend_c8812.

[4] Mary Meeker's 2013 Internet Trends Report. http://allthingsd.com/20130529/mary-meekers-internet-trends-report-is-back-at-d11-slides/.

[5] Nokia Lumia 920 specification. http://www.gsmarena.com/nokia_lumia_920-4967.php.

[6] QR codes improve shopping experience. http://www.iogear.com/blog/2011/03/15/qr-codes-improve-shopping-experience/.

[7] Samsung Galaxy S III specification. http://www.phonearena.com/phones/Samsung-Galaxy-S-III_id6330.

[8] A. Ashok, M. Gruteser, N. Mandayam, J. Silva, M. Varga, and K. Dana. Challenge: Mobile optical networks through visual MIMO. In *Proceedings of MobiCom*, 2010.

[9] T. Hao, R. Zhou, and G. Xing. COBRA: Color Barcode Streaming for Smartphone Systems. In *Proceedings of MobiSys*, 2012.

[10] S. Hranilovic and F. R. Kschischang. A Pixelated MIMO Wireless Optical Communication System. *IEEE Journal of Selected Topics in Quantum Electronics*, 2006.

[11] K. Jamieson and H. Balakrishnan. PPR: Partial packet recovery for wireless networks. In *ACM SIGCOMM*, 2007.

[12] T. Langlotz and O. Bimber. Unsynchronized 4D Barcodes Coding and Decoding Time-Multiplexed 2D Colorcodes. In *Proceedings of the International Symposium on Visual Computing*, 2007.

[13] M. Nakagawa. The world of visible optical communication - It opens with LED — Light Communications. *Kogyo Chosakai Publishing, Inc.*

[14] G. Pang, T. Kwan, H. Liu, and C. Chan. LED Wireless. *IEEE Industry Applications Magazine*, 2002.

[15] S. D. Perli, N. Ahmed, and D. Katabi. PixNet: LCD-camera pairs as communication links. In *Proceedings of MobiCom*, 2010.

[16] M. Rohs. Real-world Interaction with Camera-Phones. In *Proceedings of the International Symposium on Ubiquitous Computing Systems*, 2004.

[17] P. Vartiainen, S. Chande, and K. Rämö. Mobile Visual Interaction: Enhancing Local communication and Collaboration with Visual Interaction. In *Proceedings of the International Conference on Mobile and Ubiquitous Multimedia*, 2006.

[18] G. Woo, A. Lippman, and R. Raskar. VRCodes: Unobtrusive and Active Visual Codes for Interaction by Exploiting Rolling Shutter. In *IEEE International Symposium on Mixed and Augmented Reality*, 2012.

# Whole-Home Gesture Recognition Using Wireless Signals

Qifan Pu, Sidhant Gupta, Shyamnath Gollakota, and Shwetak Patel
University of Washington
{qp, sidhant, gshyam, shwetak}@cs.washington.edu

**Abstract** – This paper presents WiSee, a novel gesture recognition system that leverages wireless signals (e.g., Wi-Fi) to enable whole-home sensing and recognition of human gestures. Since wireless signals do not require line-of-sight and can traverse through walls, WiSee can enable whole-home gesture recognition using few wireless sources. Further, it achieves this goal without requiring instrumentation of the human body with sensing devices. We implement a proof-of-concept prototype of WiSee using USRP-N210s and evaluate it in both an office environment and a two-bedroom apartment. Our results show that WiSee can identify and classify a set of nine gestures with an average accuracy of 94%.

## Categories and Subject Descriptors

C.2.1 [**Network Architecture and Design**]: Wireless Communication

## Keywords

Gesture Recognition, Wireless Sensing

## 1. Introduction

As computing moves increasingly away from the desktop, there is a growing need for new ways to interact with computer interfaces. The Xbox Kinect is an example of a commercially available input sensor that enables gesture-based interaction using depth sensing and computer vision. The commercial success of these kinds of devices has spurred interest in developing new user interfaces that remove the need for a traditional keyboard and mouse. Gestures enable a whole new set of interaction techniques for always-available computing embedded in the environment. For example, using a swipe hand motion in-air, a user could control the music volume while showering, or change the song playing on a music system installed in the living room while cooking, or turn up the thermostat while in bed. Such a capability can enable applications in diverse domains including home-automation, elderly health care, and gaming. However, the burden of installation and cost make most vision-based sensing devices hard to deploy at scale, for example, throughout an entire home or building. Given these limitations, researchers have explored ways to move some of the sensing onto the body and reduce the need for environmental sensors [8, 14, 13]. However, even on-body approaches are limited to what people are willing to constantly carry or wear, and may be infeasible in many scenarios (e.g., in a shower).


*MobiCom'13,* September 30–October 4, Miami, FL, USA.

ACM 978-1-4503-1999-7/13/09 ...$15.00.
10.1145/2500423.2500436

This paper presents WiSee, the first whole-home gesture recognition system that requires neither user instrumentation nor an infrastructure of cameras. WiSee achieves this by leveraging wireless signals (e.g. Wi-Fi) in an environment. Since these signals do not require line-of-sight and can traverse through walls, very few signal sources need to be present in the space (e.g., a Wi-Fi AP and a few mobile devices in the living room). WiSee works by looking at the minute Doppler shifts and multi-path distortions that occur with these wireless signals from human motion in the environment.

To this end, we address the following two challenges:

*(a) How do we capture information about gestures from wireless signals?* WiSee leverages the property of Doppler shift [12, 3], which is the frequency change of a wave as its source moves relative to the observer. The canonical example is the change in the pitch of a train's whistle as it approaches and departs from a listener. In the context of wireless signals, if we consider the multi-path reflections from the human body as waves from a source, then a human performing a gesture, results in a pattern of Doppler shifts at the wireless receiver. Thus, a user moving her hand away from the receiver results in a negative Doppler shift, while moving the hand towards the receiver results in a positive Doppler shift.

The challenge, however, is that human hand gestures result in very small Doppler shifts that can be hard to detect from typical wireless transmissions (e.g., Wi-Fi). Specifically, since wireless signals are electromagnetic waves that propagate at the speed of light ($c$ m/sec), a human moving at a speed of $v$ m/sec, results in a maximum Doppler shift of $\frac{2f}{c}v$, where $f$ is the frequency of the wireless transmission [3]. Thus, a 0.5 m/sec gesture results in a 17 Hz Doppler shift on a 5 GHz Wi-Fi transmission. Typical wireless transmissions have orders of magnitude higher bandwidth (20 MHz for Wi-Fi). Thus, for gesture recognition, we need to detect Doppler shifts of a few Hertz from the 20 MHz Wi-Fi signal.

At a high level, WiSee addresses this problem by transforming the received signal into a narrowband pulse with a bandwidth of a few Hertz. The WiSee receiver (which can be implemented on a Wi-Fi AP) then tracks the frequency of this narrowband pulse to detect the small Doppler shifts resulting from human gestures. In §3, we describe our algorithm in more detail and show how to make it applicable to existing 802.11 frames.

*(b) How can we deal with other humans in the environment?* A typical home may have multiple people who can affect the wireless signals at the same time. WiSee uses the MIMO capability that is inherent to 802.11n, to focus on gestures from a particular user. MIMO provides throughput gains by enabling multiple transmitters to concurrently send packets to a MIMO receiver. If we consider the wireless reflections from each human as signals from a wireless transmitter, then they can be separated using a MIMO receiver.

Traditional MIMO decoding, however, relies on estimating the channel between the transmitter and receiver antennas. These channels are typically estimated by sending a distinct known preamble from each transmitter. Such a known signal structure is not available in our system since the human body reflects the same 802.11 transmitter's signals.

Our solution to this problem is inspired by the trigger approach taken by many multi-user games that use Xbox Kinect, in which a user gains control of the interface by performing a specific gesture pattern. In WiSee the target human performs a repetitive gesture, which we use as that person's preamble. A WiSee receiver leverages this preamble to estimate the MIMO channel that maximizes the energy of the reflections from the user. Once the receiver locks on to this channel, the user performs normal (non-repetitive) gestures that the receiver classifies using the Doppler shifts. In §3.3, we explore this idea further and show how to extract the preamble without requiring the human to perform gestures at a pre-determined speed.

The WiSee proof-of-concept is implemented in GNURadio using the USRP-N210 hardware. We classify the gestures from the Doppler shifts using a simple pattern-matching algorithm described in §3.2. We evaluated WiSee with a total of five users in both an office environment and a two-bedroom apartment whose layout is shown in Fig. 7. We performed gestures in a number of scenarios including line-of-sight, non-line-of-sight, and through-the-wall scenarios where the person is in a different room from the wireless transmitter and the receiver. The users perform a total of 900 gestures across the locations.

Our findings are as follows:

- WiSee can classify the nine whole-body gestures shown in Fig. 1, with an average accuracy of 94%. This is promising, given that the accuracy for random guesses is 11.1%.
- Using a 4-antenna receiver and a single-antenna transmitter placed in the living room, WiSee can achieve the above classification accuracy in 60% of the home locations. Adding an additional single-antenna transmitter to the living room achieves the above accuracy in locations across all the rooms. Thus, with a WiSee-enabled Wi-Fi AP acting as a receiver and a couple of mobile devices acting as transmitters, WiSee can enable whole-home gesture recognition.
- Over a 24-hour period, WiSee's average false positive rate—events that detect a gesture in the absence of the target human—is 2.63 events per hour when using a preamble with two gesture repetitions. This goes down to 0.07 events per hour, when the number of repetitions is increased to four.
- Using a 5-antenna receiver and a single-antenna transmitter, WiSee can successfully perform gesture classification, in the presence of three other users performing random gestures. However, the classification accuracy reduces as we further increase the number of interfering users. This is a limitation of WiSee: Given a fixed number of transmitters and receiver antennas, the accuracy reduces with the number of users. However, since typical home scenarios do not have a large number of users in a single room, WiSee can enable a large set of interaction applications for always-available computing in home environments.

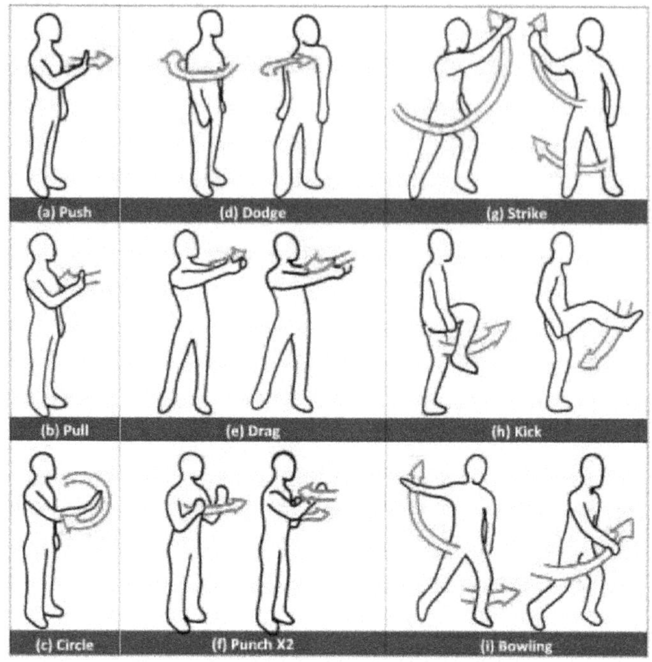


**Figure 1—Gesture sketches:** WiSee can detect and classify these nine gestures in line-of-sight, non-line-of-sight, and through-the-wall scenarios with an average accuracy of 94%.

**Contributions:** We make the following contributions:

- We introduce the first wireless system that enables gesture recognition in line-of-sight, non-line-of-sight, and through-the-wall scenarios.
- We present algorithms to extract gesture information from communication-based wireless signals. Specifically, we show how to extract minute Doppler shifts from wideband OFDM transmissions that are typical to most modern communication systems including Wi-Fi.
- Finally, using a proof-of-concept prototype, we demonstrate that our system can detect a set of nine whole-body gestures in typical environments.

This paper takes the first step towards leveraging existing wireless networks to enable novel human-computer interaction mechanisms such as whole-home gesture recognition. We hope that this line of work would open up a number of research opportunities at the intersection of wireless networking and HCI, and bridge the two communities.

## 2. Related Work

Our work is related to prior art in both wireless systems and in-air gesture recognition systems.

**(a) Wireless Systems:** One can classify the related work in this domain into three main categories: wireless localization, wireless tomography, and through-the-wall radar systems. Prior work on localization use a variety of techniques to localize wireless devices, including, RSSI [6], fine-grained OFDM channel information [21], and multiple antennas [26]. There has also been recent interest in device-free localization of humans [28, 20] using the RSSI information from wireless devices. WiSee builds on this foundational work but is complementary to it in that it focuses on achieving human gesture recognition using wireless signals.

WiSee is also related to work on wireless tomography that aims to localize humans by deploying a network of sensors throughout the environment [29, 25, 24]. These systems typically use the RSSI value observed at each sensor to localize humans. WiSee builds on this work but significantly differs from it in that it extracts Doppler shifts from wireless signals to perform human gesture recognition. Further, we demonstrate that one can perform whole-home gesture recognition without requiring wireless devices in every room.

Finally, WiSee is related to work on through-the-wall radar systems [4, 18, 3] that can identify objects such as metal pins behind a wall. These systems use expensive ultra-wideband transceivers that use bandwidths on the order of 1 GHz [4]. In contrast, WiSee focuses on gesture recognition and shows how to extract gesture information from wireless transmissions. The closest to our work in this domain is recent work [5] that demonstrates the feasibility of using Wi-Fi signals to detect running in through-the-wall scenarios. However, to the best of our knowledge, none of the prior radar systems have been designed to work for gesture recognition. In contrast, WiSee introduces mechanisms that enable it to go beyond coarse human motion such as running and walking, and delivers the first wireless system that can identify finer-grained human motion such as gestures in LOS, NLOS, and through-the-wall scenarios.

**(b) In-Air Gesture Recognition Systems:** The commercial success of products like the Xbox Kinect has popularized the use of gestures to control computer systems [22]. Increasingly, in-air gesture recognition is being incorporated into consumer electronics and mobile devices, including laptops [2], smartphones [9, 12], and GPS devices [19]. The related work in this domain use four main techniques: computer vision, ultra-sonic, electric field, and inertial sensing.

Vision-based systems extract gesture information using advances in the hybrid camera technology like pixel-mixed devices (PMDs) [22]. Likewise, ultra-sonic systems leverage Doppler shifts on sound waves to perform gesture recognition [12]. Both these systems, however, require a line-of-sight channel between the sensing device and the human. In contrast, WiSee leverages wireless signals that can operate in non-line-of-sight scenarios and can go through wooden walls and obstacles like curtains and furniture.

Electric Field sensing systems like Magic Carpet [17] instrument the floor with multiple sensors to perform human localization and gesture recognition. However, this imposes heavy instrumentation of the environment and is not practical. Inertial sensing and other on-body sensing methods on the other hand, require the users to wear multiple sensors or carry a device such as a wristband [8, 14, 13]. While attractive, in many instances, such an approach can be inconvenient (for instance, while showering). In contrast, WiSee enables whole-home gesture recognition without the need to instrument the human body.

Finally, prior work has leveraged Doppler shifts to perform gesture recognition in line-of-sight scenarios [12, 15]. In this paper, we present algorithms that allow us to extract Doppler shifts in line-of-sight, non-line-of-sight and through-the-wall scenarios; thus enabling gesture recognition without the need for sensing devices in every room. Further, we introduce algorithms to extract minute Doppler shifts from wide-band OFDM signals that are typically used in communication technologies including Wi-Fi.

# 3. WiSee

WiSee is a wireless system that enables whole-home gesture recognition. Since wireless signals can typically propagate through walls, and do not require a line of sight channel, WiSee can enable gesture recognition independent of the user's location. To achieve this, we need to answer three main questions: First, how does WiSee extract Doppler shifts from conventional wireless signals like Wi-Fi? Second, how does it map the Doppler shifts to the gestures performed by the user? Third, how does it enable gesture recognition in the presence of other humans in the environment? In the rest of this section, we address each of these questions.

## 3.1 Extracting Doppler shifts from Wireless Signals

Doppler shift is the change in the observed frequency as the transmitter and the receiver move relative to each other. In our context, an object reflecting the signals from the transmitter can be thought of as a virtual transmitter that generates the reflected signals. Now, as the object (virtual transmitter) moves towards the receiver, the crests and troughs of the reflected signals arrive at the receiver at a faster rate. Similarly, as an object moves away from the receiver, the crests and troughs arrive at a slower rate. More generally, a point object moving at a speed of $v$ at an angle of $\theta$ from the receiver, results in a Doppler shift [3] given by:

$$\Delta f \propto \frac{2vcos(\theta)}{c} f \qquad (1)$$

where $c$ is the speed of light in the medium and $f$ is the transmitter's center frequency. We note the following:

- The observed Doppler shift depends on the direction of motion with respect to the receiver. For instance, a point object moving orthogonal to the direction of the receiver results in no Doppler shift, while a point object moving towards the receiver maximizes the Doppler shift. Since human gestures typically involve multiple point objects moving along different directions, the set of Doppler shifts seen by a receiver can, in principle, be used to classify different gestures.
- Higher transmission frequencies result in a higher Doppler shift for the same motion. Thus, a Wi-Fi transmission at 5 GHz results in twice the Doppler shift as a Wi-Fi transmission at 2.5 GHz. We note, however, that much higher frequencies (e.g., at 60 GHz) may not be suitable for whole-home gesture recognition since they are more directional and typically not suitable for NLOS scenarios.
- Faster speeds result in larger Doppler shifts, while slower speeds result in smaller Doppler shifts. Thus, it is easier to detect a human running towards the receiver than to detect a human walking slowly. Further, gestures involving full-body motion (e.g. walking towards or away from the receiver) are easier to capture than gestures involving only parts of the body (e.g., hand motion towards or away from the receiver). This is because a full-body motion involves

many more point object moving at the same time. Thus, it creates Doppler signals with much larger energy than when the human uses only parts of her body.

**Challenge:** Human motion results in a very small Doppler shift that can be hard to detect from a typical wireless transmission (e.g., Wi-Fi, WiMax, LTE, etc.). For instance, consider a user moving her hand towards the receiver at 0.5 m/sec. From Eq. 1, this results in a Doppler shift of about 17 Hertz for a Wi-Fi signal transmitted at 5 GHz ($\theta = 0$). Since the bandwidth of Wi-Fi's transmissions is at least 20 MHz, the resulting Doppler shift is orders of magnitude smaller than Wi-Fi's bandwidth. Identifying such small Doppler shifts from these transmissions can be challenging.

**Our Solution:** WiSee presents a receiver design that can identify Doppler shifts at the resolution of a few Hertz from Wi-Fi signals. The basic idea underlying WiSee is to transform the received Wi-Fi signal into a narrowband pulse with the bandwidth of a few Hertz. The receiver then tracks the frequency of this narrowband pulse to detect the small Doppler shifts.

WiSee is designed for OFDM-based systems – OFDM is the modulation of choice for most modern wireless systems including 802.11 a/g/n, WiMAX, and LTE. OFDM divides the used RF bandwidth into multiple sub-channels and modulates data in each sub-channel. For instance, Wi-Fi typically divides the 20 MHz channel into 64 sub-channels each with a bandwidth of 312.5 KHz. The time-domain OFDM symbol is generated at the transmitter by taking an FFT over a sequence of modulated bits transmitted in each OFDM sub-channel. Specifically, the transmitter takes blocks of $N$ modulated bits ($N = 64$ in 802.11), and applies an $N$-point Inverse Fast Fourier Transform (IFFT),

$$\mathbf{x}_k = \sum_{n=1}^{N} \mathbf{X}_n e^{i2\pi kn/N}$$

where $\mathbf{X}_n$ is the modulated bit sent in the $n^{th}$ OFDM sub-channel. Each block of $\mathbf{x}_1, \cdots \mathbf{x}_N$ forms a time-domain OFDM symbol that the receiver decodes by performing the FFT operation, i.e.,

$$\mathbf{X}_n = \sum_{k=1}^{N} \mathbf{x}_k e^{-i2\pi kn/N} \tag{2}$$

To demonstrate how WiSee's receiver works on these OFDM signals, we first consider the scenario where the transmitter repeatedly sends the same OFDM symbol. We then generalize our approach to arbitrary OFDM symbols, making the scheme applicable to existing 802.11 frames.

**Case 1: Transmitter sends the same OFDM symbol.** In this case, instead of performing an FFT over each OFDM symbol, WiSee's receiver performs a large FFT over $M$ consecutive OFDM symbols. As a consequence of this operation, the bandwidth of each OFDM sub-channel is reduced by a factor of $M$. To see this, say the receiver performs a $2N$-point FFT over two consecutive, identical OFDM symbols. The output of the FFT can be written as,[1]

$$\mathbf{X}_n = \sum_{k=1}^{N} \mathbf{x}_k e^{-i2\pi kn/2N} + \sum_{k=N+1}^{2N} \mathbf{x}_k e^{-i2\pi kn/2N}$$

[1]For simplicity, we ignore the noise term in the above equation. However, as with standard OFDM decoding, these linear equations hold even in the presence of noise.

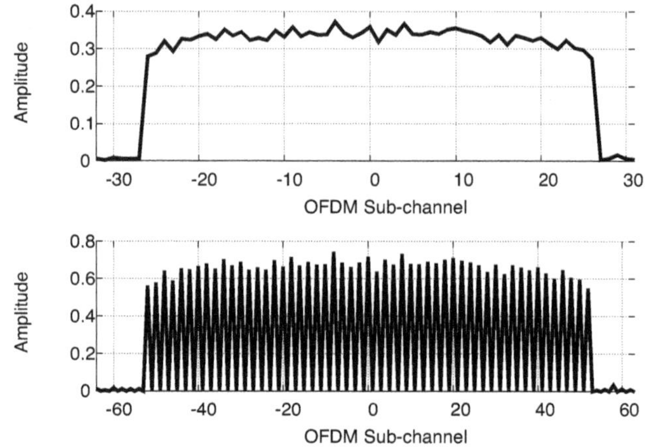


**Figure 2—Creating a narrowband signal using WiSee:** The first subplot shows the output of an FFT taken over an OFDM symbol. The second subplot shows the output of an FFT taken over two identical OFDM symbols. They show that taking a larger FFT over identical OFDM symbols, reduces each subchannel's bandwidth.

Since the first $N$ transmitted samples are identical to the last $N$ samples, i.e., $\mathbf{x}_k = \mathbf{x}_{k+N}$, for $k = 1$ to $N$, we can re-write the above equation as,

$$\mathbf{X}_n = \sum_{k=1}^{N} \mathbf{x}_k e^{-i2\pi kn/2N} + \sum_{k=1}^{N} \mathbf{x}_k e^{-i2\pi(k+N)n/2N}$$

After simplification, we get:

$$\mathbf{X}_n = \sum_{k=1}^{N} \mathbf{x}_k e^{-i2\pi kn/2N}(1 + e^{-i\pi n})$$

Now, when $n$ is an even number, $(1+e^{-i\pi n}) = 2$, but when $n$ is an odd number, $(1+e^{-i\pi n}) = 0$. Thus, the above equation can be re-written as,

$$\mathbf{X}_{2l} = 2\sum_{k=1}^{N} \mathbf{x}_k e^{-i2\pi kl/N}, \quad \mathbf{X}_{2l+1} = 0$$

Thus, as shown in Fig. 2, the odd sub-channels are zero and the even sub-channels capture the output (Eq. 2) of an $N$-point FFT on a single OFDM symbol. Intuitively, this happens because in each sub-channel, the same modulated information is transmitted in both the OFDM symbols. Thus, the bandwidth used by each sub-channel effectively halves. More generally, when the receiver performs an $MN$-point FFT over an OFDM symbol that is repeated $M$ times, the bandwidth of each sub-channel is reduced by a factor of $M$. Thus, WiSee can create multiple narrowband signals centered at each sub-channel by repeating an OFDM symbol and performing a large FFT operation.

Now, by performing a large FFT over an one-second duration, the WiSee receiver can create a one-Hertz wide narrowband signal. The WiSee receiver tracks this narrowband signal to capture the Doppler shift (see §3.2). Note that one can average the Doppler shifts observed across all the OFDM sub-channels to significantly reduce the noise in the Doppler measurements.

**Case 2: Transmitter sends arbitrary OFDM symbols.** Our description so far assumes that the transmitter repeatedly sends the same OFDM symbol. Typical 802.11 transmitters however send different data across symbols. We

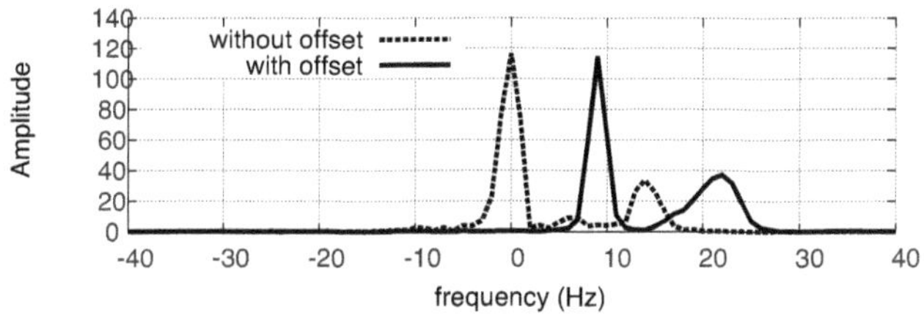


**Figure 3—Dealing with Residual Frequency offset:** The figure plots the frequency profile of the narrowband signal centered at one of the subchannels. It shows the profile in the presence of a gesture, both with and without residual offsets. WiSee accounts for the residual offset by tracking the peak with the maximum energy (the other peaks correspond to Doppler shifts).

show how to extract Doppler shifts from such transmissions. At a high level, WiSee achieves this by designing a *data-equalizing re-encoder* at the receiver that transforms each received OFDM symbol into the same symbol. To do this, the receiver first decodes the symbols using the standard 802.11 decoder. Specifically, the receiver performs an FFT on each time-domain OFDM symbol and transforms it into the frequency-domain. The receiver, then, decodes the modulated bits in each sub-channel, passes the modulated bits through the demodulator and the convolutional/Viterbi decoder to get the transmitted bits.[2]

Now that the WiSee receiver knows the modulated bits, it transforms every received symbol into the first OFDM symbol. Say $\mathbf{X}_n^i$ denotes the modulated bit in the $n^{th}$ sub-channel of the $i^{th}$ OFDM symbol. The WiSee receiver equalizes the $i^{th}$ OFDM symbol with the first symbol. In particular, it multiplies the $n^{th}$ frequency sub-channel in the $i^{th}$ symbol with $\frac{\mathbf{X}_n^1}{\mathbf{X}_n^i}$.

Now that all the received symbols are data-equalized to the first symbol, the receiver performs an IFFT on each of these equalized symbols to get the corresponding time-domain samples. Since these data-equalization operations only modify the data in each sub-channel, it does not change either the wireless channel or the Doppler shift information. Now, the receiver effectively has repeated OFDM symbols and we are back to Case 1.

We note that human gestures change the phase and amplitude of the received symbols. A traditional decoder accounts for these changes by using the pilot bits that are present in every OFDM symbol. In particular, the receiver decodes by removing these phase and amplitude changes that encode the gesture information. To avoid this, during the re-encoding phase before computing the IFFT, the WiSee receiver re-introduces the phase and amplitude changes that were removed by the decoder. This ensures that the gesture information is not lost in decoding.

### *3.1.1 Practical Issues*

We answer the following questions:

*(a) How does WiSee deal with frequency offsets?* A frequency offset between the transmitter and the receiver creates a shift in the center frequency, which can be confused for a Doppler shift. To address this issue, a WiSee receiver takes a two-pronged approach. First, it leverages prior work [23, 16] to get a coarse estimate of the frequency offset using the preamble at the beginning of the transmission; it compensates the estimated frequency offset in the rest of the transmission. Second, to account for any residual frequency offset, WiSee leverages the fact that in the absence of residual offsets, the energy in the DC frequency (center frequency of each OFDM sub-channel) corresponds to the paths from the transmitter to the receiver that do not involve the human. This shows up as the large peak in Fig. 3 (dotted line). However, with residual offsets, both the DC and the Doppler frequencies are shifted by the same amount (the solid line in the figure). Since the DC energy (i.e., the energy from the transmitter to the receiver minus the human reflections) is typically much higher than the Doppler energy (reflections from the human), the WiSee receiver tracks the frequency corresponding to the maximum energy and corrects for the residual frequency offset.

[2]For the reasons described in §3.1.1, discarding occasional erroneous packets does not significantly affect Doppler shift computation.

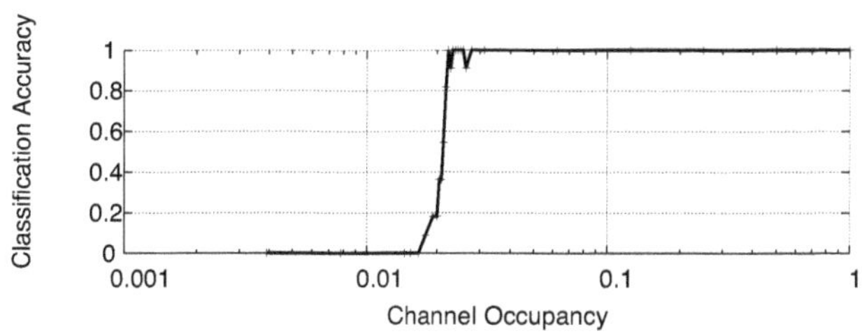


**Figure 4—Classification accuracy versus transmitter occupancy:** The accuracy of distinguishing between two gestures is high even when the transmitter transmits only 3% of the time.

*(b) Does the transmitter have to continuously transmit on the wireless medium?* So far, we assume that the transmitter transmits continuously and the receiver uses the signal to compute the Doppler shifts. This is, however, not feasible since 802.11 packets are typically less than a few milliseconds. Further, while transmitting continuously might be feasible in an un-utilized network, it can significantly affect the throughput of other devices in a busy network. WiSee instead performs the following procedure: it linearly interpolates the received OFDM symbols to fill the time slots where no transmission happens. The interpolation is done per sub-channel after the OFDM symbols are transformed into the frequency domain. After interpolation, the receiver transforms all OFDM symbols, both original and interpolated, back to the time domain and forms a synthesized time-continuous trace. The underlying assumption here is that during the short time-period between two transmissions, the user's motion does not dis-continuously change the wireless channel. To see the effects of this interpolation, we perform an experiment where the user performs two simple gestures—either move her arm towards the receiver or away from the receiver. The user is ten feet away from the receiver. We apply our gesture classification algorithm, which we describe in the next section. Fig. 4 shows the results with the transmissions evenly spread out in time. The plot shows that the classification accuracy is high even when the transmission occupancy is as low as 3%.

*(c) What about the cyclic prefix?* The above discussion assumes that the transmitter sends the OFDM symbols back-to-back. However, an 802.11 transmitter sends a cyclic prefix (CP) between every two OFDM symbols to prevent inter-symbol interference. The CP is created by taking the last $k$ samples from each OFDM symbol. We consider the CP

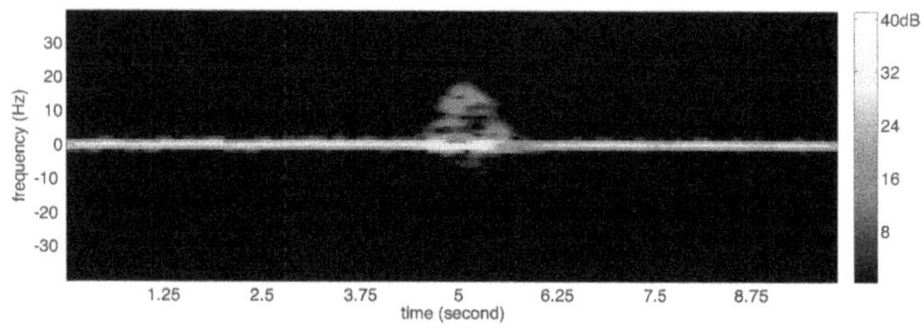


**Figure 5—Frequency-time Doppler profile of an example gesture.** The user moves her hand towards the receiver.

to be a specific kind of discontinuity between the OFDM symbols. Thus, we can perform interpolation between the OFDM symbols as described earlier. We note, however, that since all the CPs have a fixed length, such an interpolation is equivalent to resampling the OFDM symbols at a constant rate given by $\frac{Symbol\_length+CP\_length}{Symbol\_length}$, where $Symbol\_length$ and $CP\_length$ denote the length of the OFDM symbol and CP respectively. Since such resampling of the symbols does not change the doppler pattern, in practice we simply skip the CPs to reduce the computation.

### 3.2 Mapping Doppler Shifts to Gestures

So far we described how to transform the wideband 802.11 transmissions into a narrowband signal at the receiver. In this section, we show how to extract the Doppler information and map it to the gestures. Specifically, we describe the following three steps: (1) Doppler extraction which computes the Doppler shifts from the narrowband signals, (2) Segmentation which identifies a set of segments that correspond to a gesture, and (3) Classification which determines the most likely gesture amongst a set of gestures. We describe how WiSee performs each of these steps. We focus on the single user case; in §3.3, we extend our design to work in the presence of other users.

**(1) Doppler Extraction:** WiSee extracts the Doppler information by computing the frequency-time Doppler profile of the narrowband signal. To do this, the receiver computes a sequence of FFTs taken over time. Specifically, it computes an FFT over samples in the first half-a-second interval. Such an FFT give a Doppler resolution of 2 Hertz. The receiver then moves forward by a 5 ms interval and computes another FFT over the next overlapping half-a-second interval. It repeats this process to get a frequency-time profile.

Fig. 5 plots the frequency-time Doppler profile (in dB) of a user moving her hand towards the receiver. The plot shows that, at the beginning of the gesture most of the energy is concentrated in the DC (zero) frequency. This corresponds to the signal energy between the transmitter and the receiver, on paths that do not include the human. However, as the user starts moving her hand towards the receiver, we first see increasing positive Doppler frequencies (corresponding to hand acceleration) and then decreasing positive Doppler frequencies (corresponding to hand deceleration).

We note that the WiSee receiver is only interested in the Doppler shifts produced by human gestures. Since the speeds at which a human can typically perform gestures are between 0.25 m/sec and 4 m/sec [12], the Doppler shift of interest at 5 GHz is between 8 Hz and 134 Hz. Thus, the WiSee receiver reduces its computational complexity by analyzing the FFT output corresponding to only these frequencies.

**(2) Segmentation:** To do this, WiSee leverages the structure of the Doppler profiles, shown in Fig. 6. These correspond to the gestures in Fig 1. The plots show that the profiles are a combination of positive and negative Doppler shifts. Further, each gesture comprises of a set of segments that have positive and negative Doppler shifts. For example, the profile in Fig. 6(a) has just one segment with positive Doppler shift. However, Fig. 6(b) has two segments each of which has a positive and a negative Doppler shift. Further, within each segment, the Doppler energy first increases and then decreases (which correspond to acceleration and deceleration of human body parts).

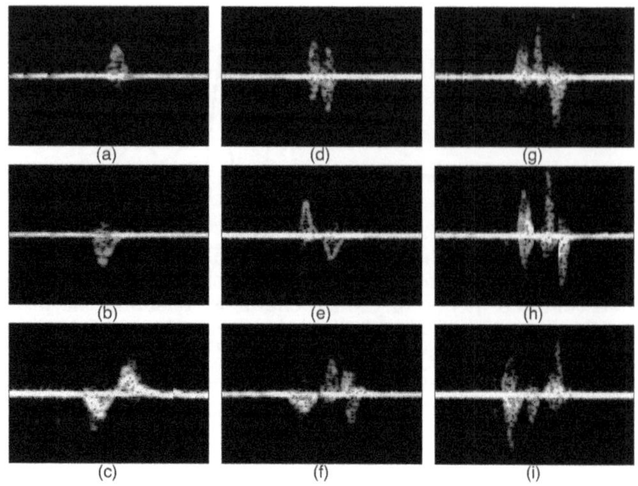


**Figure 6—Frequency-time Doppler profiles of the gestures in Fig. 1.** WiSee segments the profiles into sequences of positive and negative Doppler shifts, which uniquely identify each gesture.

A WiSee receiver leverages these properties to first find segments and then cluster segments into a gesture. Our process of finding segments is intuitively similar to packet detection in wireless communication systems. In communication, to detect the beginning of a packet, the receiver computes the average received energy over a small duration. If the ratio between this energy and noise level is greater than a threshold, then the receiver detects the beginning of a packet. Similarly, if this ratio falls below a threshold, the receiver detects the end of the packet. Likewise, in our system, the energy in each segment first increases and then decreases. So the WiSee receiver computes the average energy in the positive and negative Doppler frequencies (other than the DC and the four frequency bins around it). If the ratio between this average energy and the noise level is greater than 3 dB, the receiver detects the beginning of a segment. When this ratio falls below 3 dB, the receiver detects the end of the segment.[3] To cluster segments into a single gesture, WiSee's receiver uses a simple algorithm: if two segments are separated by less than one second, we cluster them into a single gesture.

**(3) Gestures Classification:** As described earlier, the Doppler profiles in Fig. 6 can be considered as a sequence of positive and negative Doppler shifts. Further, from the plots, we see that the patterns are unique and different across the nine gestures. Thus, the receiver can classify gestures by matching the pattern of positive and negative Doppler shifts. Specifically, there are three types of segments: segments with only positive Doppler shifts, segments with only

[3]The noise level is calibrated at the receiver by computing the energy in the non-DC frequencies, in the absence of gestures.

negative Doppler shifts, and segments with both positive and negative Doppler shifts. These can be represented as three numbers, '1', '-1', and '2'. Each gesture in Fig. 6 can now be written as a unique sequence of these three numbers. Now, gesture classification can be performed by comparing and matching the received number sequence with the set of pre-determined sequences. We note that our classification algorithm works with different users performing gestures at different speeds. This is because, different speeds only change the duration of each segment and the specific Doppler frequencies that have energy, but do not change the pattern of positive and negative shifts. Thus, the gestures performed at different speeds result in the same pattern of numbers and hence can be classified.

We briefly comment on the selection of the gestures in Fig. 1. In this paper, we picked gestures that can be encoded by a sequence of positive and negative Doppler shifts. As shown in Fig. 1, this covers a variety of interesting gesture patterns. In principle, one can imagine extending WiSee to more general gesture patterns by modeling the human body motion and leveraging additional features from the signal; this, however, is not in the scope of this paper.

We note that it is unlikely that random gestures such as eating, stretching, etc. would be confused with the specific gestures used to control devices. This is because, as we describe in the next section, a user gains control of the system by performing a special, hard-to-confuse gesture sequence that acts as a preamble. We also note that one can leverage techniques like Hidden Markov Models (HMMs) and Dynamic Time Warping (DTW) to increase the gesture space. Exploring these algorithms however is not in the scope of this paper.

## 3.3 Multiple Humans

WiSee leverages MIMO to improve the accuracy and robustness of the system, and to enable it to work in the presence of multiple humans. However, as described in §1, MIMO decoding requires a known preamble to compute the MIMO channel of the target user. WiSee uses a repetitive gesture as a preamble. Specifically, the user pushes her hand towards and away from the receiver, and repeats this gesture to form the preamble. This creates a sequence of alternating positive (+1) and negative (-1) Doppler shifts, i.e., an alternating sequence of +1 and -1 symbols. The WiSee receiver uses this sequence to correlate and detect the presence of a target human. Note that, similar to communication systems [11], this correlation works even in the presence of interfering users, since their motion is uncorrelated with the preamble's alternating sequence of positive and negative Doppler shifts. Next, WiSee finds the MIMO channel that maximizes the Doppler energy from the target user. At a high level, it runs an iterative algorithm (similar to [10]) on each segment of the preamble gesture to find the MIMO direction that maximizes the Doppler energy. It then averages the MIMO direction across segments to improve the estimation accuracy. Using this estimated MIMO direction, a WiSee receiver mitigates interference from other users and locks onto the target user by projecting the received signal on the desired direction.[4]

[4]Prior AoA algorithms [27] typically require fine-grained calibration of the MIMO systems, including measuring the distance between antennas, and tracking phase offset. Our system, however, avoids such calibration since we are not interested in the physical direction of the signal, but the MIMO direction that maximizes the Doppler energy.

Specifically, say the WiSee receiver has $N$ antennas and the preamble gesture has $M$ segments. Our objective is to find complex weights, $\mathbf{W}_n$, for each of the antennas, such that the Doppler energy for each of the segments is maximized. Specifically, if $\mathbf{D}_m$ is the Doppler energy in the $m$th segment, then we want to find the set of directions, $\mathbf{W}_n$, $n = 1, \cdots, N$, that maximizes:

$$\mathbf{D}_m = \sum_{n=1}^{N} \mathbf{W}_n \mathbf{D}_{nm},$$

for all $n = 1, 2, 3...N$, where $\mathbf{D}_{nm}$ is the Doppler energy corresponding to the $m$th segment on the $n$th antenna.

WiSee applies gradient descent that iterates over the amplitudes and phases of all $\mathbf{W}_n$s to find a optimal set of weights. Note that while the phases can span values between 0 and $2\pi$, the dynamic range of amplitudes is primarily determined by the antenna gains and the different receive gains on the radios (in our implementation this range is 6 dB).

We note the following: Firstly, the iterative algorithm occasionally gets stuck in local minima where the Doppler energy does not considerably increase with iterations. To mitigate this problem, we select multiple initial points that are evenly spaced and repeat the algorithm starting from these points. Secondly, since WiSee's receiver uses up to five antennas, the search space significantly increases with the number of receive antennas. To minimize complexity, we run the iterative algorithm pair-wise on each antenna with respect to the first antenna. Specifically, we run the iteration algorithm to find the weights on the N-1 antennas independently where the weights are computed with respect to the first antenna.

Finally, using the repetitive gesture in the preamble, the receiver can improve the estimation accuracy by averaging across gestures. WiSee further improves this accuracy by tracking this channel as the user performs gestures. Specifically, the WiSee receiver applies the iterative algorithm on every gesture performed by the target user. This allows it to adapts the MIMO direction as different users interfere with the target user.[5] Our results in §4.3 show that, in the presence of three other interfering users, WiSee can classify the first two gestures in Fig. 1 with an average accuracy of 90% using a 5-antenna receiver.

We note that WiSee not only enables a user to perform gestures in presence of other humans, but also enables multiple users to concurrently interact with the system. Specifically, the WiSee receiver can track the MIMO direction of each user to classify the gestures from multiple users.

### 3.3.1 Further Discussion

We discuss how one may augment WiSee's current design to make it more robust and secure.

*(1) Tracking a mobile target user:* Our description and evaluation assume that the target user performs gestures from a fixed location and that she performs the repetitive motion (preamble) when she moves to a new location. However, in principle, one can reduce the need for repeating the pattern by tracking the user as she moves in the environment.

[5]As the interfering users change, the optimal MIMO direction that maximizes the Doppler energy also changes. By applying the iterative algorithm on every gesture, WiSee can track these changes.

Specifically, human motion (e.g., walking and running) creates significant Doppler shifts, which as explained in §3 have a higher energy than human gestures. Thus, the receiver can, in principle, track the MIMO channel as the target user moves, reducing the need to perform the repetitive gesture again.

*(2) Providing security:* One of the risks of using a whole-home gesture recognition system is enabling an unauthorized user outside the home to control the devices within. To address this problem, one may use a secret pattern of gestures as a secret key to get access to the system. Once the access is granted, the receiver can track the authorized user and perform the required gestures. Evaluating the potential of such an approach, however, is outside the scope of this paper.

### 3.4 Addressing Multi-path Effects

So far we assumed that the reflected signals from the human body arrive at the wireless receiver along a single direction. In practice, however, the reflections, like typical wireless signals, arrive at the receiver along multiple paths.

Extracting general Doppler profiles in the presence of multi path is challenging. However, the use of only the positive and negative Doppler shifts for gesture classification simplifies our problems. Specifically, we have to address two main problems: First, due to multi-path, a user performing a gesture in the direction of the receiver from an adjacent room, can create both positive and negative Doppler shifts at the receiver. Second, strong reflectors like metallic surfaces can flip the positive and negative Doppler shifts. For example, the receiver can observe stronger negative Doppler shifts from a user moving her hand towards the receiver, if the user is standing close to a metallic surface behind her.

The iterative algorithm used by WiSee intrinsically addresses the first problem. Specifically, as shown in recent work on Angle-of-Arrival (AoA) systems [27], multiple antennas can be used to separate multi-paths by adjusting the phase on each antenna. Since WiSee's iteration algorithm can adapt both the amplitude and the phase to maximize either the positive or the negative Doppler energy, it automatically finds a MIMO direction that can focus on multi paths that result in similar Doppler shifts. We note however that unlike AoA systems, computing Doppler shifts does not require distinguishing between the multi-paths in the system. Instead WiSee only needs to distinguish between sets of paths that all create either a positive or a negative Doppler shift. Thus, one can perform gesture recognition using a lower number of antennas than is required in AoA systems.

To address the flipping problem between positive and negative Doppler shifts, WiSee leverages the preamble. Specifically, since the repetitive gesture in the preamble always starts with the user moving her hand towards the receiver, the receiver can calibrate the sign of the subsequent Doppler shifts. Specifically, if it sees a negative Doppler shift when it expects a positive shift, the receiver flips the sign of the Doppler shift. This allows WiSee to perform gesture recognition independent of the user location.

## 4. Evaluation

We implement a prototype of WiSee on the software radio platform and evaluate it on the USRP-N210 hardware. Each USRP is equipped with a XCVR2450 daughterboard, and communicates on a 10 MHz channel at 5 GHz. Since USRP-N210 boards cannot support multiple daughterboards, we built a MIMO receiver by combining multiple USRP-N210s using an external clock [1]. In our evaluation, we use MIMO receivers that have up to five antennas. We use single-antenna USRP-N210s as transmitters.[6]

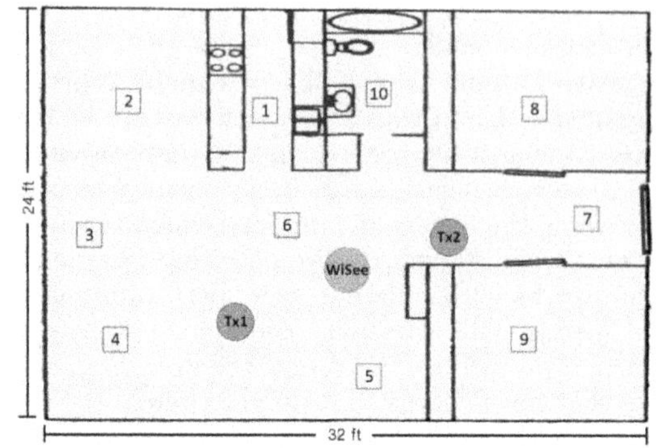


**Figure 7—Floor plan of the two-bedroom apartment:** The WiSee receiver, Tx1, and Tx2 are placed in the living room. The layout has 4 LOS, 4 NLOS, and 2 through-the-wall scenarios.

The transmitter and the receiver are not connected to the same clock. We build on the UHD code base to continuously transmit OFDM symbols over a 10 MHz wide channel. The transmitter uses different 802.11 modulations (BPSK, 4QAM, 16QAM, and 64QAM) and coding rates. The transmit power we use in our implementation is 10 mW which is lower than the maximum power allowed by USRP-N210s (and Wi-Fi devices). This is because USRP-N210s exhibit significant non-linearities at higher transmit powers, which limits the ability to decode OFDM signals. We note, however, that, with higher transmission powers, one can in principle perform gesture recognition at larger distances.

We evaluate our prototype design in two environments:

- *An office building.* The UW CSE building has an external structure that is primarily metal and concrete. We run the experiments in offices that are separated by double sheet-rock (plus insulation) walls with a thickness of approximately 5.7 inches. The building has a number of other Wi-Fi access points and devices operating in the frequency of interest.
- *A two-bedroom apartment.* The layout of the apartment is shown in Fig. 7. It consists of a living room connected to the kitchen and dining area, and two bedrooms and a bathroom. The walls are hollow and have a thickness of 5.5 inches; the doors are made of wood and have a thickness of 1.4 inches.

We run our experiments with a total of five users. In addition to evaluating WiSee's ability to achieve whole-home gesture recognition, we extensively evaluate it in the six different scenarios, shown in Fig. 8.

*(a) LOS-txrxcloseby:* Here a receiver and a transmitter are placed next to each other in a room. The user performs gestures in line-of-sight to the receiver.

*(b) LOS-txrxwall:* Here a receiver and a transmitter are placed in adjacent rooms separated by a wall. The user performs the gestures in the room with the transmitter.

[6]Our implementation does not use off-the-shelf Wi-Fi transmitters since we don't have a configuration that will allow current USRPs to reliably operate at a bandwidth of 20 MHz.

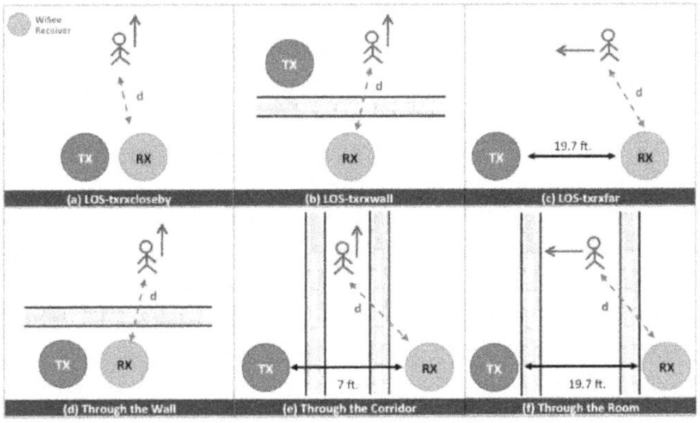


**Figure 8—Scenario layouts.**

*(c) LOS-txrxfar:* Here a receiver and a transmitter are placed 19.7 feet away from each other. The user performs gestures in line-of-sight to the receiver.

*(d) Through-the-Wall:* Here a receiver and a transmitter are placed next to each other close to a wall. The user performs gestures in the room adjacent to the wall.

*(e) Through-the-Corridor:* Here a receiver and a transmitter are placed in different rooms separated by a corridor. The user performs the gestures in the corridor.

*(f) Through-the-Room:* Here a receiver and a transmitter are placed in different rooms separated by a room. The user performs the gestures in the middle room.

In scenarios (b), (c), (e), and (f) both the transmitter and the receiver use omnidirectional antennas. However, in scenarios (a) and (d) where the transmitter and the receiver are placed next to each other, to prevent the transmitter's signal from overwhelming the receiver's hardware, the transmitter uses a Ettus LP0965 directional antenna that is placed in a direction orthogonal to the receive antennas. The receiver, however, still uses omnidirectional antennas. In principle, we can further reduce the transmitter's interference in these two scenarios by leveraging techniques like full-duplex [7] and interference nulling [16]. However, this is not in the scope of this paper.

In the rest of this section, we first evaluate the feasibility of gesture recognition using wireless signals in these six scenarios. We then evaluate WiSee's performance in a whole-home scenario. Finally, we demonstrate WiSee's ability to work in the presence of other humans.

## 4.1 Feasibility of Wireless Gesture Detection

We start by evaluating the feasibility of gesture detection using wireless signals in various scenarios.

*Experiments:* We run experiments in the six scenarios depicted in Fig. 8. We pick the office building to run these experiments since it has more rooms and also allows us to evaluate the system at larger distances than in our two-bedroom apartment. To evaluate how well WiSee can detect the presence of a gesture, we compute the Doppler SNR from the frequency-time Doppler profile. Specifically, Doppler SNR is the ratio between the average energy in the non-DC frequencies in the profile, with and without the gesture. We ask the user to move her hand towards the receiver, i.e., the first gesture in Fig. 1. The user performs the gesture in the general direction of the receiver independent of its location. Our intuition behind this choice is that the user would naturally gesture in the direction of the device she wants to control. We compute the average Doppler SNR at each location by having each user repeat the gesture ten times.

*Results:* Figs. 9(a)-(f) plot the average Doppler SNR as a function of distance, for the six scenarios. The plots show the results for different number of antennas at the receiver. They show the following:

**(a) Versus distance:** In scenarios (a), (b), (d), and (e), as the distance between the user and the receiver increases, the average Doppler SNR reduces. This is expected because the strength of the signal reflections from the human body reduces with distance. However, the received Doppler SNR is still about 3 dB at 12 feet, which is sufficient to identify gestures. In scenarios (c) and (f), however, the Doppler SNR does not significantly reduce with the distance from the receiver. This is because in both these scenarios, as the user moves away from the receiver, she gets closer to the transmitter. Thus, while the human reflections get weaker as the user moves away from the receiver; since the user moves closer to the transmitter, the transmitted signals arrive at the user with a higher power, thus, increasing the energy in the reflected signals. As a result, the Doppler SNR is as high as 15 dB at distances of about 25 feet.

**(b) Versus number of antennas:** Across all the scenarios, using more antennas at the WiSee receiver increases the Doppler SNR. This is expected because additional antennas provide diversity gains that are particularly helpful in the low SNR regime. Further the gains in the Doppler SNR are higher at large distances, and through-the-* scenarios—the gains are as high as 10 dB in some locations. Also note that in scenarios (d) and (f), the Doppler SNR at a single-antenna receiver is as low as 1 dB across many positions; such low SNRs are not sufficient to classify gestures. Additional antennas significantly increase the Doppler SNR, enabling gesture detection in these scenarios. As described in §3.4, this is because of the wireless multi-path effects. In line-of-sight scenarios there is a strong direct path between the human body and the WiSee receiver or the transmitter. However, the through-the-* scenarios experience significant multi-path that effectively adds additional interference at the receiver. With more antennas at the receiver, the algorithm in §3.2 can reduce the multi-path interference and hence can significantly improve the Doppler SNR. We note that across all the scenarios, using 3-4 antennas at the receiver is sufficient to achieve most of the MIMO benefits.

*Summary:* The key takeaways from the above results are: First, using 3-4 antennas at the WiSee receiver is sufficient to achieve gesture detection in all the above scenarios. Second, gesture detection is feasible as long as the user is in the "range" of the receiver. This range can, however, be increased by spatially separating the transmitter and the receiver. Another option that we explore in the next section, is to leverage multiple transmitters (e.g., mobile phone in the living room, and laptop in the kitchen) to increase this range.

## 4.2 Gesture Recognition in Whole-Home Scenario

Next, we evaluate WiSee in a whole-home scenario.

*Experiments:* We run experiments in the two-bedroom apartment shown in Fig. 7. We use a 4-antenna WiSee receiver to compute the frequency-time Doppler profile using the al-

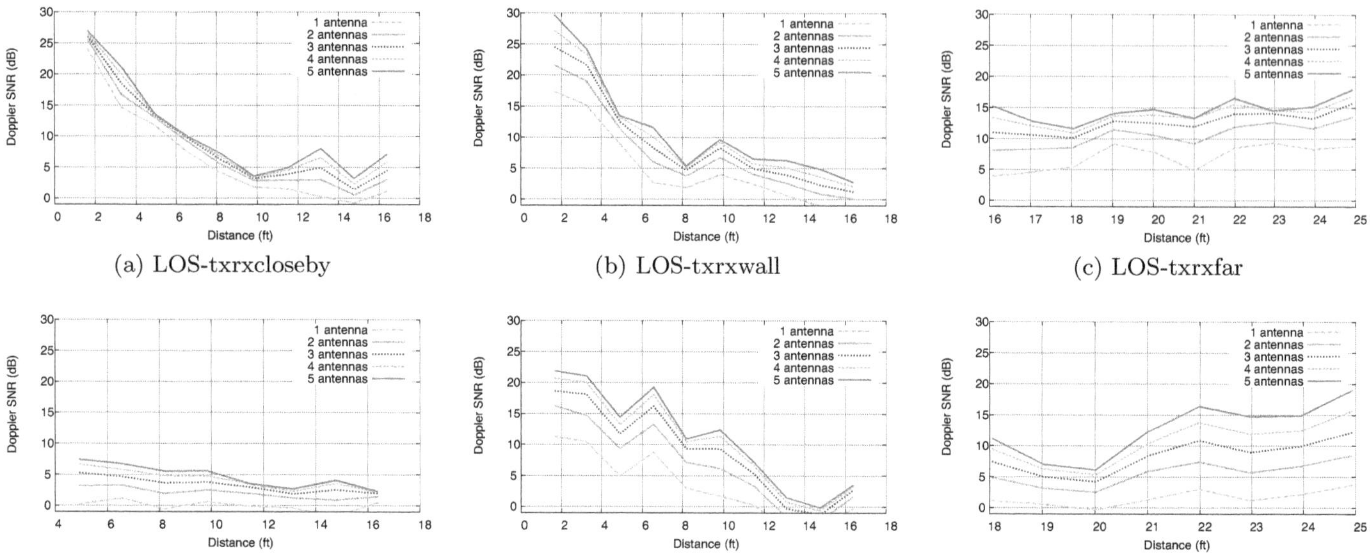


(a) LOS-txrxcloseby (b) LOS-txrxwall (c) LOS-txrxfar

(d) Through-the-Wall (e) Through-the-Corridor (f) Through-the-Room

**Figure 9—Doppler SNR versus distance from the receiver.** The plots show the Doppler SNR in various scenarios as a function of both distance and the number of receiver antennas.

gorithm described in §3.2. We then map the profile to the gestures using our pattern-mapping algorithm. We use two single-antenna transmitters, as shown in Fig. 7, to maximize the range of our system. The transmitter and receiver use omni-directional antennas in our experiments. Since it is difficult to implement carrier sense on software radios, the two transmitters time-share the medium every 10 ms. The receiver and the two transmitters are all placed in the living room, with all the doors closed. We note that performing gesture recognition with the doors closed is more challenging since the signal has to traverse through the doors and walls and hence experiences significant attenuation. We pick ten locations (marked in the layout) spanning all the rooms in the apartment. These locations include line-of-sight, non-line-of-sight, and through-the-wall settings. In each location,the users perform the nine gestures shown in Fig. 1 in the direction of the receiver, at a speed that was not predetermined. Before each experiment, the users were shown how to perform each gesture. The users were also able to check the gesture sketches (Fig. 1) during the experiment. Each gesture is performed a total of 100 times across all the locations.

*Results:* Fig. 10 plots the confusion matrix for the ten gestures across all the locations. Each row denotes the actual gesture performed by the user and each column the gestures it was classified into. The last column counts the fraction of gestures that were not detected at the receiver. Each element in the matrix corresponds to the fraction of gestures in the row that were classified as the gesture in the column. The table shows the following:

- The average accuracy is 94% with a standard deviation of 4.6% when classifying between our nine gestures. This is in comparison to a random guess, which has an accuracy of 11.1% for nine gestures. This shows that one can extract rich information about gestures from wireless signals. We note that despite wireless signals typically being noisy, since Doppler shifts are detected over the duration that is of the order of a second, WiSee achieves the above high accuracy by averaging across time. Further, the multiple antennas also provide spatial diversity that also increases the accuracy.
- Only 2% of all the gestures (18 out of 900) were not detected at the receiver. Further investigation revealed that these mis-detections occurred when the user was in the kitchen and one of the bedrooms. In these locations, the reflected signals are weak and hence the Doppler SNR for these specific gestures was close to 0 dB.

We note that when only tx1 was used to perform gesture recognition, the accuracy was greater than 90% only in six of the ten considered locations. This shows that each transmitter provides a limited range for gesture recognition. Adding more transmitters increases this effective range. We, however, note that the two-bedroom apartment scenario only required two transmitters placed in the living room to successfully classify gestures across all the locations.

## 4.3 Gestures in the Presence of Other Humans

Finally, we evaluate WiSee in the presence of other humans. We first measure the false detection rate in the absence of the target human. Then, we compute the accuracy of gesture recognition for the target human, in the presence of other humans. Finally, we stress test WiSee to see where it fails.

*False detection rate in the presence of other humans:* As described in §3.3, WiSee detects the target human by using a repetitive gesture as a preamble. The repetitive gesture provides a protection against confusing other humans for the target user. We compute the average number of false detection events, i.e., when the WiSee receiver detects the target user (repetitive gesture), in her absence. To do this, we place our WiSee receiver and transmitter in the middle of an office room (with dimensions 32 feet by 30 feet) occupied by 12 people, over a 24-hour period. The receiver looks for a repetitive gesture where the user moves her hand towards and away from the receiver; thus, each repetition results in a positive Doppler shift followed by a negative Doppler shift.

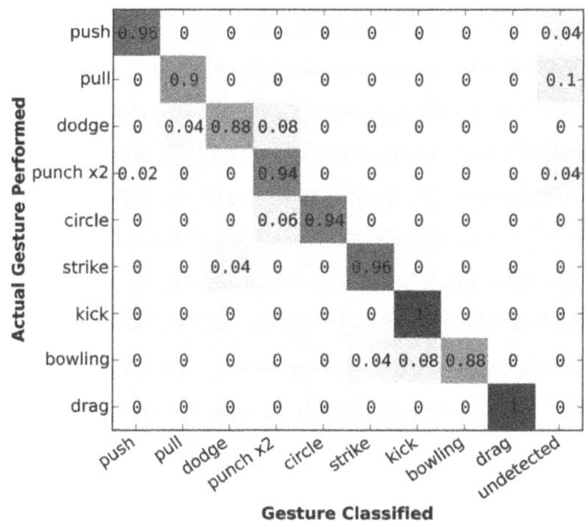


**Figure 10—Confusion matrix for gestures in the home scenario:** The figure shows that the average detection and classification accuracy is 94% across the nine gestures. In contrast, random guesses have an accuracy of 11.1%. This shows that WiSee can extract rich information about gestures from wireless signals.

The occupants move about and have meetings and lunches in the office as usual. We believe that, given the higher density of people, the office room is a worse scenario compared to our two-bedroom apartment. We note that there are other scenarios in which WiSee can be evaluated, which are, however, not in the scope of this paper.

Fig. 11 plots the number of false detection events per hour as a function of time. The figure shows results for different number of repetitions in the preamble. The plot shows that when the receiver uses a preamble with only one repetition (i.e., perform the gesture once), the number of false events is, on the average, 15.62 per hour. While this is low, it is expected because typical human gestures do not frequently result in a positive Doppler shift followed by a negative Doppler shift. For example, in our experiments, walking caused a continuous monotone Doppler shift that was not confused with alternating positive and negative Doppler shifts. Also, as the number of repetitions in the preamble increases, the false detection rate significantly reduces. Specifically, with three repetitions, the average false detection rate reduces to 0.13 events per hour; with more than four repetitions, the false detection rate is zero. This is expected because it is unlikely that typical human motion would produce a repetitive pattern of positive and negative Doppler shifts. Further, since the WiSee receiver requires repetitive positive and negative Doppler shifts to occur at a particular range of speeds (0.25 m/s to 4 m/s), it is unlikely that even typical environmental and mechanical variations would produce them.

*Classifying the target human gestures in the presence of other humans:* As described in §3.3, WiSee computes the MIMO channel for the target user that minimizes the interference from the other humans. We would like to evaluate the use of MIMO in classifying a target user's gestures, in the presence of other moving humans. We run experiments in a 13 feet by 19 feet room with our WiSee receiver and transmitter. We have the target user perform the two gestures in Fig. 1(a) and Fig. 1(b). Our experiments have up to four interfering users in random locations in the room. The users were asked to perform arbitrary gestures using their arms.

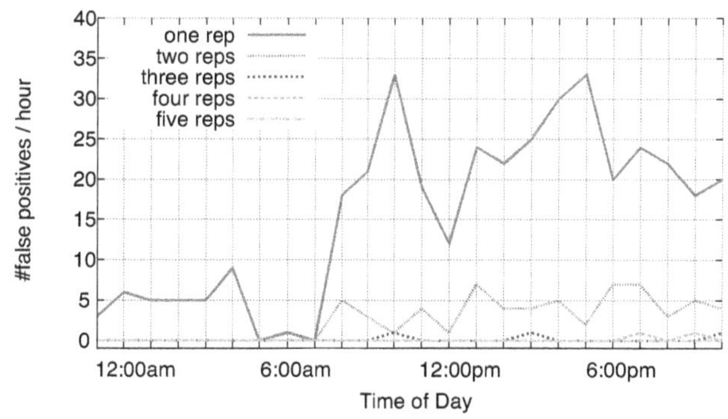


**Figure 11—False Detection Rate from a 24-Hour Trace:** The figure plots the false detection rate in an office room with 12 people over a 24-hour period on a weekday.

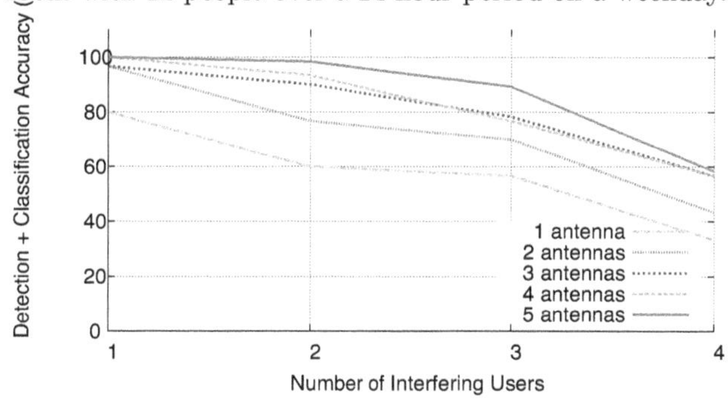


**Figure 12—WiSee in the presence of other interfering users:** The figure plots the detection and classification accuracy of the target user in the presence of other users in a $13 \times 19$ sq. feet room. The plots show that, given a fixed number of antennas, as the number of interfering users increases, the accuracy decreases. However, with three interfering users, the accuracy is still as high as 90% with a five-antenna receiver.

Fig. 12 plots the average recognition accuracy of the target user's gestures as a function of the number of interfering users. The figure shows results for different number of antennas at the WiSee receiver. The plots show that using a five-antenna receiver, the accuracy is as high as 90% with three interfering users in the room. Further, using additional antennas significantly improves this accuracy in the presence of multiple interfering users. We note however, that for a fixed number of transmitters and antennas at the receiver, the classification accuracy degrades with the number of users (e.g., a conference room setting or a party scenario). For example, in our experiments, the accuracy is less than 60% with four interfering users. However, since typical home scenarios do not have a large number of users in a room, WiSee can enable a significant set of interaction applications for always-available computing embedded in the environment.

*Stress-testing WiSee:* Since WiSee leverages MIMO to cancel the signal from the interfering human, it suffers from the near-far problem that is typical to interference cancellation systems. Specifically, reflections from an interfering user closer to the receiver, can have a much higher power than that of the target user. To evaluate WiSee's classification accuracy in this scenario, we run the following experiment: We fix the location of the target user six feet away from the WiSee receiver. We then change the interfering user's location between three feet and ten feet from the receiver. The target user performs the two gestures shown in Fig. 1(a) and

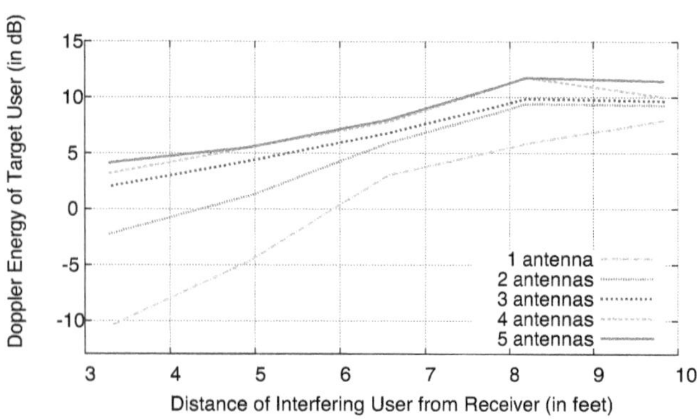


**Figure 13—Stress testing WiSee in a near-far scenario:** The figure plots the Doppler energy of a target user in the presence of another interfering user at various distances. The target user is fixed 6 feet away from the receiver. The plot shows that adding antennas at the receiver helps address the near-far problem.

Fig. 1(b). In each experiment, the interfering user adversarially performs the opposite gesture to the one performed by the target user. The WiSee receiver computes the MIMO channel for the target user using her preamble.

Fig. 13 plots the target user's Doppler SNR at the WiSee receiver as a function of the distance between the interfering user and the receiver. The figure shows multiple plots corresponding to different number of antennas at the receiver. The plots show that, smaller the distance between the interfering user and the receiver, lower the Doppler SNR. Specifically, the Doppler SNR is as low as -10 dB when the interfering user is about 3.4 feet from the receiver. However, the figure also shows that adding antennas at the receiver significantly improves the Doppler SNR. Specifically, with four-antennas, the Doppler SNR increases from -10 dB to 4.7 dB; which is sufficient to classify gestures. Thus, we conclude that adding additional receive antennas can help mitigate the near-far problem.

## 5. Conclusion

In this paper, we take the first step towards transforming Wi-Fi into a gesture-recognition sensor. We present WiSee, a novel gesture recognition system that leverages wireless signals to enable whole-home sensing and recognition of human gestures. Since wireless signals do not require line-of-sight and can traverse through walls, WiSee can enable whole-home gesture recognition using few signal sources. Our results in a 2-bedroom apartment show that WiSee can extract a rich set of gesture information from wireless signals and enable whole-home gesture recognition using only two wireless sources placed in the living room.

**Acknowledgements:** We thank the members of the UW Networks and Wireless group, our shepherd Moustafa Youssef, and the anonymous MOBICOM reviewers for their helpful comments and Lilian de Greef for help with the gesture sketches in Fig. 1.

## 6. References


[1] ACQUITEK Inc. Fury GPS Disciplined Frequency Standard.

[2] R. Block. Toshiba Qosmio G55 features SpursEngine, Visual Gesture Controls.

[3] W. Carrara, R. Goodman, and R. Majewski. Spotlight Synthetic Aperture Radar: Signal Processing Algorithms. Artech House, 1995.

[4] G. Charvat, L. Kempel, E. Rothwell, C. Coleman, and E. Mokole. A Through-dielectric Radar Imaging System. In Trans. Antennas and Propagation, 2010.

[5] K. Chetty, G. Smith, and K. Woodbridge. Through-the-wall Sensing of Personnel Using Passive Bistatic WiFi Radar at Standoff Distances. In Trans. Geoscience and Remote Sensing, 2012.

[6] K. Chintalapudi, A. Iyer, and V. Padmanaban. Indoor Localization without the Pain. In NSDI, 2011.

[7] J. Choi, M. Jain, K. Srinivasan, P. Levis, and S. Katti. Achieving single channel full duplex wireless communication. In Mobicom, 2010.

[8] G. Cohn, D. Morris, S. Patel, and D. Tan. Humantenna: using the body as an antenna for real-time whole-body interaction. In CHI 2012.

[9] M. Fisher. Sweet Moves: Gestures and Motion-Based Controls on the Galaxy S III.

[10] S. Gollakota, F. Adib, D. Katabi, and S. Seshan. Clearing the RF Smog: Making 802.11 Robust to Cross-Technology Interference. In SIGCOMM,2011.

[11] S. Gollakota and D. Katabi. Zigzag decoding: combating hidden terminals in wireless networks. In ACM SIGCOMM, 2008.

[12] S. Gupta, D. Morris, S. Patel, and D. Tan. Soundwave: using the doppler effect to sense gestures. In HCI 2012.

[13] C. Harrison, D. Tan, and D. Morris. Skinput: appropriating the body as an input surface. In CHI 2010.

[14] D. Kim, O. Hilliges, S. Izadi, A. D. Butler, J. Chen, I. Oikonomidis, and P. Olivier. Digits: freehand 3d interactions anywhere using a wrist-worn gloveless sensor. In UIST 2012.

[15] Y. Kim and H. Ling. Human Activity Classification Based on Micro-Doppler Signatures Using a Support Vector Machine. In Trans. Geoscience and Remote Sensing, 2012.

[16] K. Lin, S. Gollakota, and D. Katabi. Random Access Heterogeneous MIMO Networks. In SIGCOMM, 2011.

[17] J. Paradiso, C. Abler, K.-y. Hsiao, and M. Reynolds. The magic carpet: physical sensing for immersive environments. In CHI, 1997.

[18] T. Ralston, G. Charvat, and J. Peabody. Real-time through-wall imaging using an ultrawideband MIMO phased array radar system. In Array, 2010.

[19] A. Santos. Pioneer's latest Raku Navi GPS units take commands from hand gestures.

[20] M. Scholz, S. Sigg, H. R. Schmidkte, and M. Beigl. Challenges for device-free radio-based activity recognition. In CoSDEO workshop, 2007.

[21] S. Sen, B. Radunovic, R. R. Choudhury, and T. Minka. Spot localization using PHY layer information . In Mobisys, 2012.

[22] J. Shotton, A. Fitzgibbon, M. Cook, T. Sharp, M. Finocchio, R. Moore, A. Kipman, and A. Blake. Real-time human pose recognition in parts from single depth images. In CVPR, 2011.

[23] K. Tan, J. Fang, Y. Zhang, S. Chen, L. Shi, J. Zhang, and Y. Zhang. Fine-grained Channel Access in Wireles LAN. In SIGCOMM, 2010.

[24] J. Wilson and N. Patwari. Radio Tomographic Imaging with Wireless Networks. In Trans. Mobile Computing, 2009.

[25] J. Wilson and N. Patwari. Through-Wall Motion Tracking Using Variance-Based Radio Tomography Networks. In ARXIV, 2009.

[26] J. Xiong and K. Jamieson. Towards fine-grained radio-based indoor location. In HotMobile, 2012.

[27] J. Xiong and K. Jamieson. ArrayTrack: A Fine-Grained Indoor Location System. In NSDI, 2013.

[28] M. Youssef, M. Mah, and A. Agrawala. Challenges: Device-free passive localization for wireless environments. In Mobicom, 2007.

[29] Y. Zhao and N. Patwari. Robust Estimators for Variance-Based Device-Free Localization and Tracking. In ARXIV, 2011.

# Secure Unlocking of Mobile Touch Screen Devices by Simple Gestures – You can see it but you can not do it

Muhammad Shahzad, Alex X. Liu
Michigan State University
East Lansing, Michigan, USA
{shahzadm, alexliu}@cse.msu.edu

Arjmand Samuel
Microsoft Research
Redmond, WA, USA
arjmands@microsoft.com

## ABSTRACT

With the rich functionalities and enhanced computing capabilities available on mobile computing devices with touch screens, users not only store sensitive information (such as credit card numbers) but also use privacy sensitive applications (such as online banking) on these devices, which make them hot targets for hackers and thieves. To protect private information, such devices typically lock themselves after a few minutes of inactivity and prompt a password/PIN/pattern screen when reactivated. Passwords/PINs/patterns based schemes are inherently vulnerable to shoulder surfing attacks and smudge attacks. Furthermore, passwords/PINs/patterns are inconvenient for users to enter frequently. In this paper, we propose GEAT, a gesture based user authentication scheme for the secure unlocking of touch screen devices. Unlike existing authentication schemes for touch screen devices, which use *what* user inputs as the authentication secret, GEAT authenticates users mainly based on *how* they input, using distinguishing features such as finger velocity, device acceleration, and stroke time. Even if attackers see what gesture a user performs, they cannot reproduce the behavior of the user doing gestures through shoulder surfing or smudge attacks. We implemented GEAT on Samsung Focus running Windows, collected 15009 gesture samples from 50 volunteers, and conducted real-world experiments to evaluate GEAT's performance. Experimental results show that our scheme achieves an average equal error rate of 0.5% with 3 gestures using only 25 training samples.

## Categories and Subject Descriptors

D.4.6 [**Security and Protection**]: Authentication

## Keywords

Authentication; Locking/Unlocking; Mobile Touch Screen Devices; Gesture


*MobiCom'13,* September 30–October 4, Miami, FL, USA.
Copyright 2013 ACM 978-1-4503-1999-7/13/09 ...$15.00.
http://dx.doi.org/10.1145/2500423.2500434.

## 1. INTRODUCTION

### 1.1 Motivation

Touch screens have revolutionized and dominated the user input technologies for mobile computing devices (such as smart phones and tablets) because of high flexibility and good usability. Mobile devices equipped with touch screens have become prevalent in our lives with increasingly rich functionalities, enhanced computing power, and more storage capacity. Many applications (such as email and banking) that we used to run on desktop computers are now also being widely run on such devices. These devices therefore often contain privacy sensitive information such as personal photos, email, credit card numbers, passwords, corporate data, and even business secrets. Losing a smart phone with such private information could be a nightmare for the owner. Numerous cases of celebrities losing their phones with private photos and secret information have been reported on news [1]. Recently, security firm Symantec conducted a real-life experiment in five major cities in North America by leaving 50 smart phones in streets without any password/PIN protection [2]. The results showed that 96% of finders accessed the phone with 86% of them going through personal information, 83% reading corporate information, 60% accessing social networking and personal emails, 50% running remote admin, and 43% accessing online bank accounts.

Safeguarding the private information on such mobile devices with touch screens therefore becomes crucial. The widely adopted solution is that a device locks itself after a few minutes of inactivity and prompts a password/PIN/pattern screen when reactivated. For example, iPhones use a 4-digit PIN and Android phones use a geometric pattern on a grid of points, where both the PIN and the pattern are secrets that users should configure on their phones. These password/PIN/pattern based unlocking schemes have three major weaknesses. First, they are susceptible to shoulder surfing attacks. Mobile devices are often used in public settings (such as subway stations, schools, and cafeterias) where shoulder surfing often happens either purposely or inadvertently, and passwords/PIN/patterns are easy to spy [15, 18]. Second, they are susceptible to smudge attacks, where imposters extract sensitive information from recent user input by using the smudges left by fingers on touch screens. Recent studies have shown that finger smudges (*i.e.*, oily residues) of a legitimate user left on touch screens can be used to infer password/PIN/pattern [3]. Third, passwords/PINs/patterns are inconvenient for users to input frequently, so many people disable them leaving their devices vulnerable.

## 1.2 Proposed Approach

In this paper, we propose GEAT, a gesture based authentication scheme for the secure unlocking of touch screen devices. A gesture is a brief interaction of a user's fingers with the touch screen such as swiping or pinching with fingers. Figure 1 shows two simple gestures on smart phones. Rather than authenticating users based on *what* they input (such as a password/PIN/pattern), which are inherently subjective to shoulder surfing and smudge attacks, GEAT authenticates users mainly based on *how* they input. Specifically, GEAT first asks a user to perform a gesture on touch screens for about 15 to 25 times to obtain training samples, then extracts and selects behavior features from those sample gestures, and finally builds models that can classify each gesture input as legitimate or illegitimate using machine learning techniques. The key insight behind GEAT is that people have consistent and distinguishing behavior of performing gestures on touch screens. We implemented GEAT on Samsung Focus, a Windows based phone, as seen in Figure 1 and evaluated it using 15009 gesture samples that we collected from 50 volunteers. Experimental results show that GEAT achieves an average Equal Error Rate (EER) of 0.5% with 3 gestures using only 25 training samples.

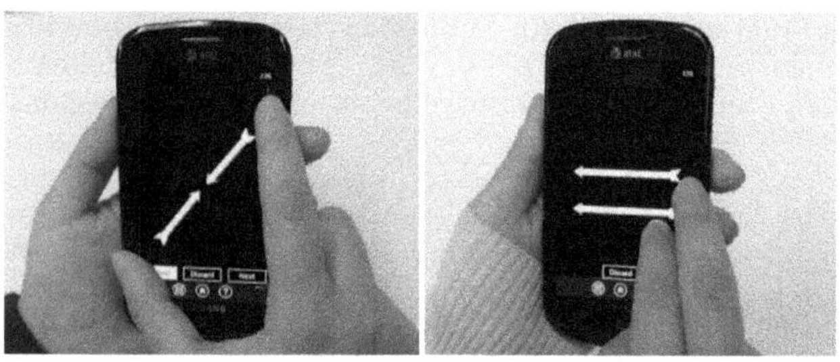

**Figure 1: GEAT implemented on Windows Phone 7**

Compared to current secure unlocking schemes for touch screen devices, GEAT is significantly more difficult to compromise because it is nearly impossible for an imposter to reproduce the behavior of others doing gestures through shoulder surfing or smudge attacks. Unlike password/PIN/pattern based authentication schemes, GEAT allows users to securely unlock their touch screen devices even when imposters are spying on them. GEAT actually displays the gesture that the user needs to perform on the screen for unlocking. Compared with biometrics (such as fingerprint, face, iris, hand, and ear) based authentication schemes, GEAT has two key advantages on touch screen devices. First, GEAT is secure against smudge attacks whereas some biometrics, such as fingerprint, are subject to such attacks as they can be copied. Second, GEAT does not require additional hardware for touch screen devices whereas biometrics based authentication schemes often require special hardware such as a fingerprint reader.

For practical deployment, we propose to use password/PIN/pattern based authentication schemes to help GEAT to obtain the training samples from a user. In the first few days of using a device with GEAT enabled, in each unlocking, the device first prompts the user to do a gesture and then prompts with the password/PIN/pattern login screen. If the user successfully logged in based on his password/PIN/pattern input, then the information that GEAT recorded during the user performing the gesture is stored as a training sample; otherwise, that gesture is discarded. Of course, if the user prefers not to set up a password/PIN/pattern, then the password/PIN/pattern login screen will not be prompted and the gesture input will be automatically stored as a training sample. During these few days of training data gathering, users should specially guard their password/PIN/pattern input from shoulder surfing and smudge attacks. In reality, even if an imposter compromises the device by shoulder surfing or smudge attacks on the password/PIN/pattern input, the private information stored on the device during the initial few days of using a new device is typically minimal. Plus, the user can easily shorten this training period to be less than a day by unlocking his device more frequently. We only need to obtain about 15 to 25 training samples for each gesture. After the training phase, the password/PIN/pattern based unlocking scheme is automatically disabled and GEAT is automatically enabled. It is possible that a user's behavior of doing the gesture evolve over time. Such evolution can be handled by adapting the scheme proposed by Monrose *et al.* [13].

## 1.3 Technical Challenges and Solutions

The first challenge is to choose features that can model *how* a gesture is performed. In this work, we extract the following seven types of features: velocity magnitude, device acceleration, stroke time, inter-stroke time, stroke displacement magnitude, stroke displacement direction, and velocity direction. The first five feature types capture the dynamics of performing gestures while the remaining two capture the static shapes of gestures. (1) *Velocity Magnitude:* the speed of finger motion at different time instants. (2) *Device Acceleration:* the acceleration of touch screen device movement along the three perpendicular axes of the device. (3) *Stroke Time:* the time duration that the user takes to complete each stroke. (4) *Inter-stroke Time:* the time duration between the starting time of two consecutive strokes for multi-finger gestures. (5) *Stroke Displacement Magnitude:* the Euclidean distance between the centers of the bounding boxes of two strokes for multi-finger gestures, where the bounding box of a stroke is the smallest rectangle that completely contains that stroke. (6) *Stroke Displacement Direction:* the direction of the line connecting the centers of the bounding boxes of two strokes for multi-finger gestures. (7) *Velocity Direction:* the direction of finger motion at different time instants.

The second challenge is to segment each stroke into sub-strokes for a user so that the user has consistent and distinguishing behavior for the sub-strokes. It is challenging to determine the number of sub-strokes that a stroke should be segmented into, the starting point of each sub-stroke, and the time duration of each sub-stroke. On one hand, if the time duration of a sub-stroke is too short, then the user may not have consistent behavior for that sub-stroke when performing each gesture. On the other hand, if the time duration of a sub-stroke is too large, then the distinctive information from the features is too much averaged out to be useful for authentication. The time duration of different sub-strokes should not be all equal because at different locations of a gesture a user may have consistent behaviors that last different amounts of time. In this work, we propose an algorithm that automatically segments each stroke into sub-strokes of appropriate time duration where for each sub-stroke the user has consistent and distinguishing behavior. We use coefficient of variation to quantify consistency.

The third challenge is to learn multiple behaviors from the training samples of a gesture because people exhibit different behaviors when they perform the same gesture in different postures such as sitting and lying down. In this work, we distinguish the training samples that a user made under different postures by making least number of *minimum variance partitions*, where the coefficient of variation for each partition is below a threshold, so that each partition represents a distinct behavior.

The fourth challenge is to remove the high frequency noise in the time series of coordinate values of touch points. This noise is introduced due to the limited touch resolution of capacitive touch screens. In this work, we pass each time series of coordinate values through a low pass filter to remove high frequency noise.

The fifth challenge is to design effective gestures. Not all gestures are equally effective for authentication purposes. In our study, we designed 39 simple gestures that are easy to perform and collected data from our volunteers for these gestures. After comprehensive evaluation and comparison, we finally chose 10 most effective gestures shown in Figure 2. The number of unconnected arrows in each gesture represents the number of fingers a user should use to perform the gesture. Accordingly we can categorize gestures into single-finger gestures and multi-finger gestures.

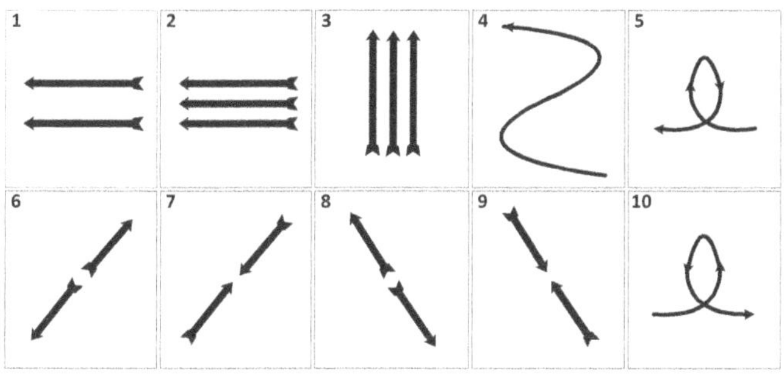

**Figure 2: The 10 gestures that GEAT uses**

The sixth challenge is to identify gestures for a given user that result in low false positive and false negative rates. In our scheme, we first ask a user to provide training samples for as many gestures from our 10 gestures as possible. For each gesture, we develop models of user behaviors. We then perform elastic deformations on the training gestures so that they stop representing legitimate user's behavior. We classify these deformed samples and calculate EER for a given user for each gesture and rank the gestures based on their EERs. Then we use the top $n$ gestures for authentication using majority voting where $n$ is selected by the user. Although larger $n$ is, higher accuracy GEAT has, for practical purposes such as unlocking smart phone screens, $n = 1$ (or 3 at most) gives high enough accuracy.

## 1.4 Threat Model

During the training phase of a GEAT enabled touch screen device, we assume imposters cannot have physical access to it. After the training phase, we assume imposters have the following three capabilities. First, imposters have physical access to the device. Such physical access can be gained in ways such as thieves stealing a device, finders finding a lost device, and roommates temporarily holding a device when the owner is taking a shower. Second, imposters can launch shoulder surfing attacks by spying the owner when he performs gestures. Third, imposters have necessary equipment and technologies to launch smudge attacks.

## 1.5 Key Contributions

In this paper, we make following five key contributions.

1. We proposed, implemented, and evaluated a gesture based authentication scheme for the secure unlocking of touch screen devices.
2. We identified a set of effective features that capture the behavioral information of performing gestures on touch screens.
3. We proposed an algorithm that automatically segments each stroke into sub-strokes of different time duration where for each sub-stroke the user has consistent and distinguishing behavior.
4. We proposed an algorithm to extract multiple behaviors from the training samples of a given gesture.
5. We collected a comprehensive data set containing 15009 training samples from 50 users and evaluated the performance of GEAT on this data set.

# 2. RELATED WORK

## 2.1 Gesture Based Authentication on Phones

A work parallel to ours is that Luca *et al.* proposed to use the timing of drawing the password pattern on Android based touch screen phones for authentication [9]. Their work has following two major technical limitations compared to our work. First, unlike ours, their scheme has low accuracy. They feed the time series of raw coordinates of the touch points of a gesture to the dynamic time wrapping signal processing algorithm. They do not extract any behavioral features from user's gestures. Their scheme achieves an accuracy of 55%; in comparison, ours achieves an accuracy of 99.5%. Second, unlike ours, they can not handle the multiple behaviors of doing the same gesture for the same user.

Another work parallel to ours is that Sae-Bae *et al.* proposed to use the timing of performing five-finger gestures on multi-touch capable devices for authentication [14]. Their work has following four major technical limitations compared to our work. First, their scheme requires users to use all five fingers of a hand to perform the gestures, which is very inconvenient on small touch screens of smart phones. Second, they also feed the time series of raw coordinates of the touch points to the dynamic time wrapping signal processing algorithm and do not extract any behavioral features from user's gestures. Third, they can not handle the multiple behaviors of doing the same gesture for the same user. Fourth, they have not evaluated their scheme in real world attack scenarios such as resilience to shoulder surfing.

## 2.2 Phone Usage Based Authentication

Another type of authentication schemes leverages the behavior in using several features on the smart phones such as making calls, sending text messages, and using camera

[5, 17]. Such schemes were primarily developed for continuously monitoring smart phone users for their authenticity. These schemes take a significant amount of time (often more than a day) to determine the legitimacy of the user and are not suitable for instantaneous authentication, which is the focus of this paper.

## 2.3 Keystrokes Based Authentication

Some work has been done to authenticate users based on their typing behavior [13, 19]. Such schemes have mostly been proposed for devices with physical keyboards and have low accuracy [10]. It is inherently difficult to model typing behavior on touch screens because most people use the same finger(s) for typing all keys on the keyboard displayed on a screen. Zheng *et al.* [20] reported the only work in this direction in a technical report, where they did a preliminary study to check the feasibility of using tapping behavior for authentication.

## 2.4 Gait Based Authentication

Some schemes have been proposed that utilize accelerometer in smart phones to authenticate users based upon their gaits [6, 11, 12]. Such schemes have low true positive rates because gaits of people are different on different types of surfaces such as grass, road, snow, wet surface, and slippery surface.

# 3. DATA COLLECTION AND ANALYSIS

In this section, we first describe our data collection process for gesture samples from our volunteers. Second, we extract the seven types of features from our data and validate our hypothesis that people have consistent and distinguishing behaviors of performing gestures on touch screens.

## 3.1 Data Collection

We developed a gesture collection program on Samsung Focus, a Windows based phone. During the process of a user performing a gesture, our program records the coordinates of each touch point and the accelerometer values and time stamps associated with each touch point. The duration between consecutive touch points provided by the Windows API on our device is 18ms. To track movement of multiple fingers, our program ascribes each touch point to its corresponding finger.

We found 50 volunteers with age ranging from 19 to 55 and jobs ranging from students, faculty, to corporate employees. We gave a phone to each volunteer for a period of 7 to 10 days and asked them to perform gestures over this period. Our data collection process consists of two phases. In the first phase, we chose 20 of the volunteers to collect data for the 39 gestures that we designed and each volunteer performed each gesture for at least 30 times. We conducted experiments to evaluate the classification accuracy of each gesture. An interesting finding is that different gestures have different average classification accuracies. We finally choose 10 gestures that have the highest average classification accuracies and discarded the remaining 29 gestures. These 10 gestures are shown in Figure 2. In the second phase, we collected data on these 10 gestures from the remaining 30 volunteers, where each volunteer performed each gesture for at least 30 times. Finally, we obtained a total of 15009 samples for these 10 gestures. The whole data collection took about 5 months.

## 3.2 Data Analysis

We extract the following seven types of features from each gesture sample: velocity magnitude, device acceleration, stroke time, inter-stroke time, stroke displacement magnitude, stroke displacement direction, and velocity direction.

• **Velocity and Acceleration Magnitude:** From our data set, we observe that people have consistent and distinguishing patterns of velocity magnitudes and device accelerations along its three perpendicular axes while doing gestures. For example, Figure 3(a) shows the time series of velocity magnitudes of two samples of gesture 4 in Figure 2 performed by a volunteer. Figure 3(b) shows the same for another volunteer. Similarly Figures 4(a) and 4(b) show the time series of acceleration along the x-axis in two samples of gesture 4 by two volunteers. We observe that the samples from same user are similar and at the same time different from samples from another user.

To quantify the similarity between any two time series, $f_1$ with $m_1$ values and $f_2$ with $m_2$ values, where $m_1 \leq m_2$, we calculate the root mean squared (RMS) value of the time series obtained by subtracting the normalized values of $f_1$ from the normalized values of $f_2$. Normalized time series $\hat{f}_i$ of a time series $f_i$ is calculated as below, where $f_i[q]$ is the $q^{\text{th}}$ value in $f_i$.

$$\hat{f}_i[q] = \frac{f_i[q] - \min(f_i)}{\max\big(f_i - \min(f_i)\big)} \quad \forall q \in [1, m_i] \tag{1}$$

Normalizing the time series brings all its values in the range of [0, 1]. We do not use metrics such as correlation to measure similarity between two time series because their values are not bounded.

To subtract one time series from the other, the number of elements in the two need to be equal; however, this often does not hold. Thus, before subtracting, we re-sample $f_2$ at a sampling rate of $m_1/m_2$ to make $f_2$ and $f_1$ equal in number of elements. The RMS value of a time series $f$ containing $\mathcal{N}$ elements, represented by $P_f$, is calculated as:

$$P_f = \sqrt{\frac{1}{\mathcal{N}} \sum_{m=1}^{\mathcal{N}} f^2[m]} \tag{2}$$

Normalizing the two time series before subtracting them to obtain $f$ ensures that each value in $f$ lies in the range of $[-1, 1]$ and consequently the RMS value lies in the range of $[0, 1]$. An RMS value closer to 0 implies that the two time series are highly alike while an RMS value closer to 1 implies that the two time series are very different. For example, the RMS value between the two time series from the volunteer in Figure 3(a) is 0.119 and that between the two time series of the volunteer in Figure 3(b) is 0.087, whereas the RMS value between a time series in Figure 3(a) and another in Figure 3(b) is 0.347. Similarly, the RMS values between the two time series of each volunteer in Figures 4(a) and 4(b) are 0.159 and 0.144, respectively, whereas the RMS value between one time series in Figure 4(a) and another in Figure 4(b) is 0.362.

• **Stroke Time, Inter-stroke Time, and Stroke Displacement Magnitude:** From our data set, we observe that people take consistent and distinguishing amount of time to complete each stroke in a gesture. For multi-finger gestures, people have consistent and distinguishing time duration between the starting times of two consecutive strokes

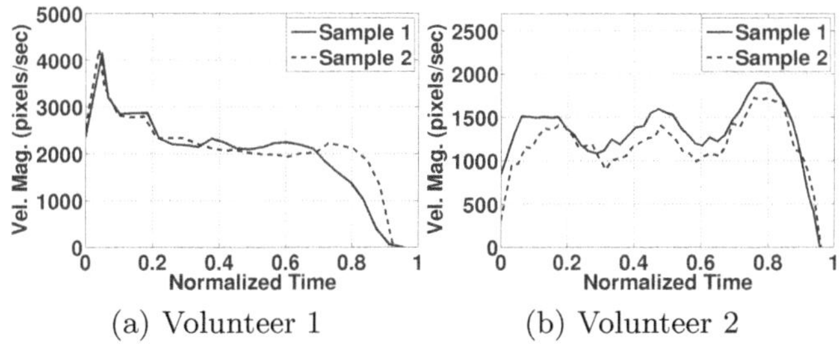


(a) Volunteer 1 (b) Volunteer 2

**Figure 3: Velocity magnitudes of gesture 4**

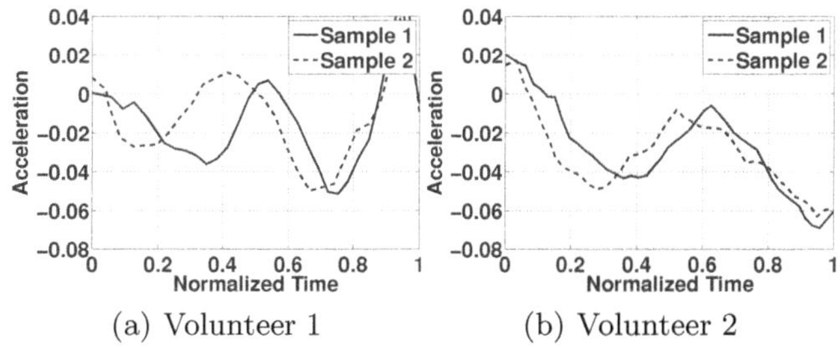


(a) Volunteer 1 (b) Volunteer 2

**Figure 4: Device acceleration of gesture 4**

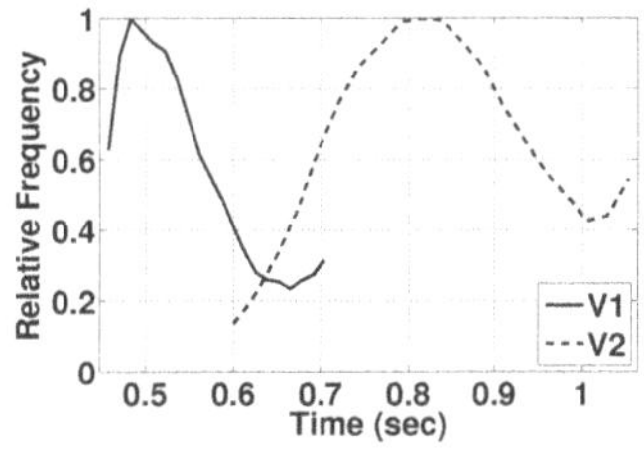


**Figure 5: Distributions of stroke time**

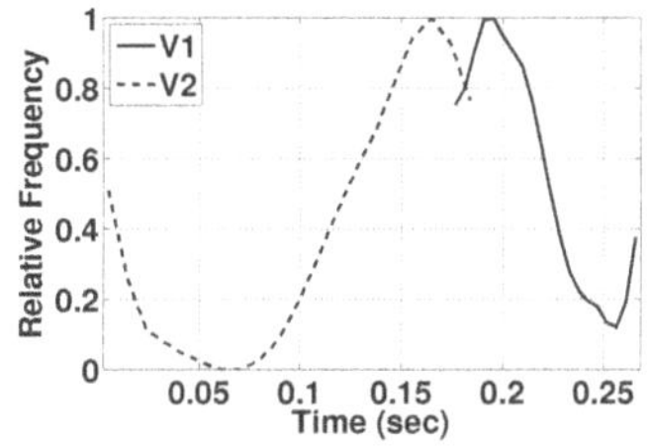


**Figure 6: Distributions of inter-stroke time**

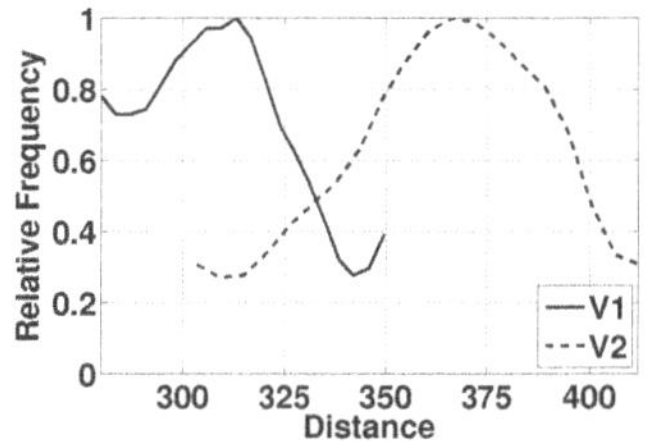


**Figure 7: Distributions of stroke disp. mag.**

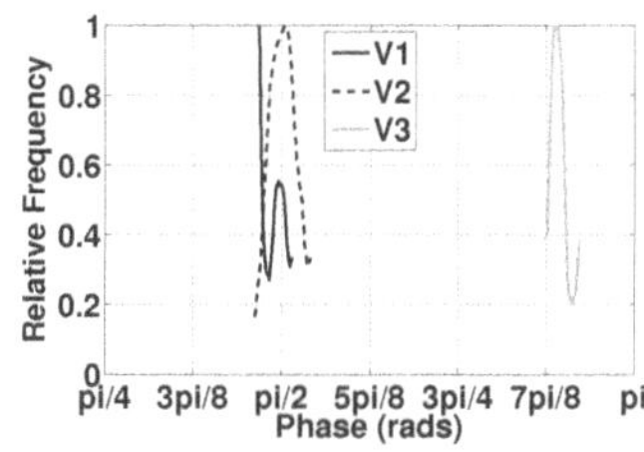


**Figure 8: Distributions of stroke disp. direction**

in a gesture and have consistent and distinguishing magnitudes of displacement between the centers of any two strokes. The distributions of stroke times of different users are centered at different means and the overlap is usually small, which becomes insignificant when the feature is used with other features. Same is the case for inter-stroke times and stroke displacement magnitudes. Figures 5, 6, and 7 plot the distribution of stroke time of gesture 4, inter-stroke time of gesture 6, and stroke displacement magnitude of gestures 7, respectively, for different volunteers. The figures show that the overlap in distributions for different users is small and are centered at different means.

• **Stroke Displacement and Velocity Directions** From our data set, we observe that people have consistent, but not always distinguishing, patterns of velocity and stroke displacement directions because different people may produce gestures of similar shapes. For example, Figure 8 plots the distributions of the displacement direction of gesture 1 for three volunteers. Figure 9 shows the time series of velocity directions of gesture 10 for three volunteers. Volunteers V1 and V2 produced similar shapes of gesture 1 as well as gesture 10, so they have overlapping distributions and time series. Volunteer V3 produced shapes of the two gestures different from the corresponding shapes produced by volunteers V1 and V2, and thus has a non-overlapping distribution and time series.

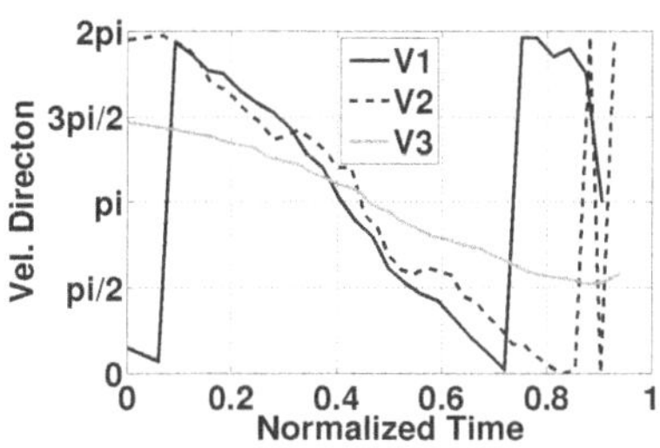


**Figure 9: Velocity direction of gesture 10**

## 4. GEAT OVERVIEW

To authenticate a user based on his behavior of preforming a gesture, GEAT needs to have a model of the legitimate user's behaviors of preforming that gesture. Given the training samples of the gesture performed by the legitimate user, GEAT builds this model using Support Vector Distribution Estimation (SVDE) in the following five steps.

The first step is *noise removal*, where GEAT passes the time series of touch point coordinates in each gesture sample through a filter to remove high frequency noise.

The second step is *feature extraction*, where GEAT extracts the values of the seven types of features from the gesture samples and concatenates these values to form a feature vector. To extract feature values of velocity magnitude, velocity direction, and device accelerations, GEAT segments each stroke in a gesture sample into sub-strokes at multiple time resolutions and extracts values from these sub-strokes. We call these three types of features *sub-stroke based features*. For the remaining four types of features, GEAT extracts values from the entire strokes in each gesture. We call these four types of features *stroke based features*.

The third step is *feature selection*. For each feature element, GEAT first partition all its $N$ values, where $N$ is the total number of training samples, into the least number of minimum variance partitions, where the coefficient of variation for each partition is below a threshold. If the number of minimum variance partitions is less than or equal to the number of postures in which the legitimate user provided the training samples, then we select this feature element; otherwise, we discard it. For this purpose, ideally the user should inform GEAT the number of postures in which he performed the training gestures. However, if the user does not provide this information, the classification accuracy of GEAT decreases, but only very slightly, as shown in our experimental results in Section 9.

The fourth step is *classifier training*. GEAT first partitions all $N$ feature vectors into the minimum number of groups so that within each group, all feature vectors belong to the same minimum variance partition for any feature element. We call each group a *consistent training group*. Then, for each group of feature vectors, GEAT builds a model in the form of an ensemble of SVDE classifiers trained using these vectors. Note that we do not use any gestures from imposters in training GEAT because in the real-world deployment of authentication systems, training samples are typically available only from the legitimate user.

The fifth step is *gesture ranking*. For each gesture, GEAT repeats the above four steps and then ranks the gestures based on their EERs. A user can pick $1 \le n \le 10$ gestures to be used in each user authentication. Although the larger $n$ is, the higher accuracy GEAT has, for practical purposes such as unlocking smart phone screens, $n = 1$ (or 3 at most) gives us high enough accuracy. To calculate the EER of a gesture, GEAT needs the true positive rates (TPR) and false positive rates (FPR) for that gesture. TPRs for each gesture are calculated using 10 fold cross validation on legitimate user's samples of the gesture. To calculate FPRs, GEAT needs imposter samples, which are not available in real world deployment at the time of training. Therefore, GEAT generates synthetic imposter samples by elastically deforming the samples of legitimate user using cubic B-splines and calculates the FPRs using these synthetic imposter samples. Note that the synthetic imposter samples are used only in ranking gestures, the performance evaluation of GEAT that we present in Section 9 is done entirely on real world imposter samples. These synthetic imposter samples are not used in classifier training either.

When a user tries to login on a touch screen device with GEAT enabled, the device displays the $n$ top ranked gestures for the user to perform. Then authentication process behind the scene works as follows. First, for each gesture, GEAT extracts the values of all the feature elements selected earlier by the corresponding classification model for this gesture. Second, GEAT feeds the feature vector consisting these values to the ensemble of SVDE classifiers of each consistent training group and gets a classification decision. If the classification decision of any ensemble is positive, which means that the gesture has almost the same behavior as one of the consistent training groups that we identified from the training samples of the legitimate user, then GEAT accepts that gesture input to be legitimate. Third, after GEAT makes the decision for each of the $n$ gestures, GEAT makes the final decision on whether to accept the user as legitimate based on the majority voting on the $n$ decisions.

Table 1 summarizes the symbols used in this paper.

## 5. NOISE REMOVAL

The time series of $x$ and $y$ coordinates of the touch points of each stroke contain high frequency noise as we can see from the time series of $x$ coordinates for a sample gesture in Figure 10(a). There are two major contributors to this noise. First, the touch resolution of capacitive touch screens is limited. Second, because capacitive touch screens determine the coordinates of each touch point by calculating the coordinates of the centroid of the area on the screen touched by a finger, when a finger moves on the screen, its contact area varies and the centroid changes at each time instant, resulting in high frequency noise. Such noise should be removed because it affects velocity magnitude and direction values.

**Table 1: Symbols used in the paper**

| Symbol | Description |
|---|---|
| $f_i$ | Time series of values |
| $\hat{f}_i$ | Normalized time series of $f_i$ |
| $m_i$ | # of values in time series $f_i$ |
| $f_i[q]$ | $q^{\text{th}}$ value in time series $f_i$ |
| $P_f$ | RMS value of time series $f$ |
| $\mathcal{N}$ | # of elements in time series $f$ |
| $n$ | # of gestures used when authenticating |
| $\alpha$ | # of points used in SMA for averaging |
| $N$ | # of training samples |
| $b$ | # of postures user provided training samples |
| $k$ | # of minimum variance partitions |
| $\mathcal{P}_k$ | Partitioning of $N$ values into $k$ partitions |
| $\mathcal{Q}_k$ | Partitioning of $N$ values into $k$ partitions |
| $\sigma_i^2(\mathcal{P}_k)$ | Variance in partition $i$ of partitioning $\mathcal{P}_k$ |
| t | time duration of a stroke |
| $p$ | time duration to segment strokes into sub-strokes |
| $c$ | # of sub-strokes with consistent behavior |
| $s$ | # of sub-strokes in a stroke |
| $\gamma$ | Parameter of RBF kernel |
| $\nu$ | Parameter of SVDE |
| $z$ | # of classifiers in an ensemble |

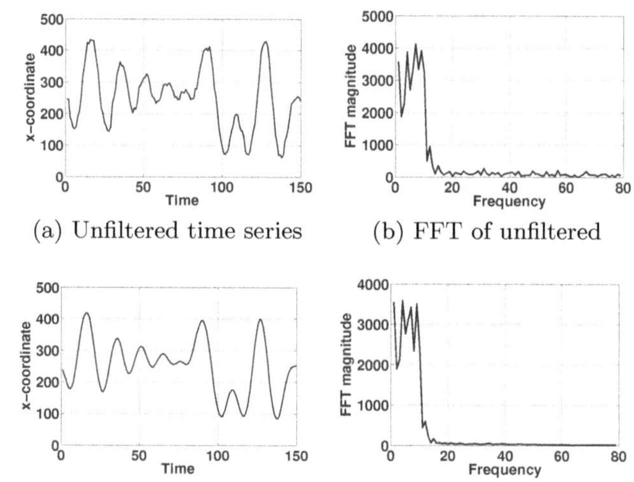


(a) Unfiltered time series (b) FFT of unfiltered

(c) Filtered time series (d) FFT of filtered

**Figure 10: Unfiltered and filtered time series**

We remove such high frequency noise by passing the time series of $x$ and $y$ coordinates of touch points through a low pass filter. We consider frequencies above 20Hz as high frequencies because the time series of touch points contain most of their energy in frequencies lower than 20Hz, as we can see from the magnitude of the fourier transform of this time series in Figure 10(b). In this work, we use a simple moving average (SMA) filter, which is the unweighted mean of previous $\alpha$ data points. We choose the value of $\alpha$ to be 10. Figure 10(c) shows the time series of Figure 10(a) after passing through the SMA filter. We can see that the filtered time series is much smoother compared to the unfiltered time series. Figure 10(d) shows the magnitude of fourier transform of the filtered time series. We observe from this figure that the magnitudes of frequency components above 20Hz are negligible.

## 6. FEATURE EXTRACTION & SELECTION

In this section, we describe the feature extraction and selection process in GEAT. We categorize the seven types of features into *stroke based features*, which include stroke time, inter-stroke time, stroke displacement magnitude, and stroke displacement direction, and *sub-stroke based features*, which include velocity magnitude, velocity direction, and device acceleration.

### 6.1 Stroke Based Features

#### 6.1.1 Extraction

To extract the stroke time of each stroke, we calculate the time duration between the time of the first touch point and that of the last touch point of the stroke. To extract the inter-stroke time between two consecutive strokes in a gesture, we calculate the time duration between the time of the first touch point of the first stroke and that of the second stroke. To extract the stroke displacement magnitude between any two strokes in a gesture, we calculate the Euclidean distance between the centers of the two bounding boxes of the two strokes. To extract stroke displacement direction between any two strokes in a gesture, we calculate the arc-tangent of the ratio of the magnitudes of the vertical component and the horizontal component of the stroke displacement vector directed from the center of one bounding box to the center of the other bounding box. We calculate inter-stroke time and stroke displacement magnitude and direction from all pairs of strokes in a gesture.

#### 6.1.2 Selection

Given $N$ training samples, for each feature element, we first partition all its $N$ values into the least number of minimum variance partitions (MVPs) where the coefficient of variation ($cv$) for each partition is below a threshold. Let $\mathcal{P}_k$ and $\mathcal{Q}_k$ represent two different partitionings of $N$ values, each containing $k$ partitions. Let $\sigma_i^2(\mathcal{P}_k)$ and $\sigma_i^2(\mathcal{Q}_k)$ represent the variance of values in partition $i$ ($1 \leq i \leq k$) of partitioning $\mathcal{P}_k$ and $\mathcal{Q}_k$, respectively. Partitioning $\mathcal{P}_k$ is the MVP if for any $\mathcal{Q}_k$, $\max_i\left(\sigma_i^2(\mathcal{P}_k)\right) \leq \max_i(\sigma_i^2(\mathcal{Q}_k))$. We empirically determined the threshold of the $cv$ to be 0.1. The detailed empirical evaluation of this threshold is given in Section 9.

To find the least number of MVPs, we start by increasing the number of MVPs from one until $cv$ of all partitions is below the threshold. To obtain MVPs, we use agglomerative hierarchical clustering with Ward's method [7]. Ward's method allows us to make any number of partitions by cutting the dendrogram built by agglomerative hierarchical clustering at an appropriate level. Figure 11 shows dendrograms made through hierarchical clustering with Ward's method form the values of stroke time of two volunteers for gesture 5. A dendrogram visually illustrates the presence and arrangement of clusters in data. The dendrogram in Figure 11(a) is for a volunteer who performed gestures in two postures, sitting and laying down. The dendrogram in Figure 11(b) is for a volunteer who performed gestures in one posture. We make two MVPs for Figure 11(a) and one for Figure 11(b).

After we find the least number of MVPs, where the $cv$ for each partition is below the threshold, we decide whether to select this feature element. If the number of partitions in these MVPs is less than or equal to the number of postures

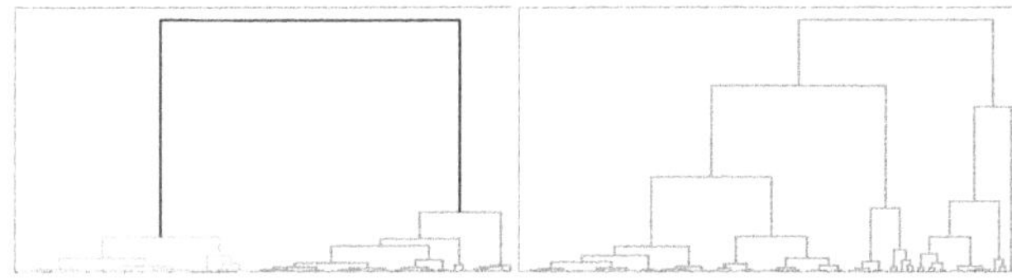

(a) Two behaviors (b) One behavior

**Figure 11: Dendrograms for feature values with one and two behaviors**

in which the training samples are performed, then we select this feature element; otherwise, we discard it. We ask the user to enter the number of postures in which he performed training samples. If the user does not provide this input, we assume the number of postures to be 1.

### 6.2 Sub-stroke Based Features

Sub-stroke based features include velocity magnitude, velocity direction, and device acceleration. To extract values for these features, GEAT needs to segment each stroke into sub-strokes because of two major reasons. First, at different segments of a stroke, the finger often has different moving speed and direction. Second, at different segments of a stroke, the device often has different acceleration. If we measure the feature values from the entire stroke, we will only utilize the information measured at the starting and ending points of the stroke, by which we will miss the distinguishing information of velocity magnitude, velocity direction, and device acceleration at different segments of the stroke.

Our goal is to segment a stroke into sub-strokes so that the velocity magnitude, velocity direction, and device acceleration information measured at each sub-stroke characterizes the distinguishing behaviors of the user who made the stroke. There are three key technical challenges to this goal. The first technical challenge is how we should segment $N$ stroke samples of different time durations assuming that we are given an appropriate time duration as the segmentation guideline. The second technical challenge is how to find the appropriate time duration as the segmentation guideline. The third technical challenge is how to select sub-strokes whose velocity magnitude, velocity direction, and device acceleration information will be included in the feature vector used by GEAT for training. Next, we present our solutions to these three technical challenges.

#### 6.2.1 Stroke Segmentation and Feature Extraction

Given $N$ strokes performed by one user and the appropriate time duration $p$ as the segmentation guideline, we need to segment each stroke into the same number of segments so that for each stroke we obtain the same number of feature elements. However, because different strokes have different time durations, segmenting each stroke into sub-strokes of time duration $p$ will not give us the same number of segments for different strokes. To address this issue, we first calculate $\lceil \frac{t}{p} \rceil$ for each stroke where t is the time duration of the stroke. From the resulting $N$ values, we use the most frequent value, denoted $s$, to be the number of sub-strokes that each stroke should be segmented into. Finally, we segment each stroke into $s$ sub-strokes where each sub-stroke within a stroke has the same time duration.

After segmenting all strokes into sub-strokes, we extract velocity magnitude, velocity direction, and device acceleration from each sub-stroke. To calculate velocity magnitude and direction, we first obtain the coordinates of the starting and ending points of the sub-stroke. The starting and ending points of a sub-stroke, which is segmented from a stroke based on time duration, often do not lie exactly on touch points reported by the touch screen device. For any end point that lies between two consecutive touch points reported by the touch screen device, we calculate its coordinates by interpolating between these two touch points. Let $(x_i, y_i)$ be the coordinates of a touch point with time stamp $t_i$ and $(x_{i+1}, y_{i+i})$ be the coordinates of the adjacent touch point with time stamp $t_{i+1}$. Suppose the time stamp of an end point is $t$ where $t_i < t < t_{i+1}$. Then, we calculate the coordinates $(x, y)$ of this end point based on the straight line between $(x_i, y_i)$ and $(x_{i+1}, y_{i+i})$ as follows:

$$x = \frac{(t - t_i)}{(t_{i+1} - t_i)} \times (x_{i+1} - x_i) + x_i \quad (3)$$

$$y = \frac{(t - t_i)}{(t_{i+1} - t_i)} \times (y_{i+1} - y_i) + y_i \quad (4)$$

We extract the velocity magnitude of each sub-stroke by calculating the Euclidean distance between the starting and ending points of the sub-stroke divided by the time duration of the sub-stroke. We extract the velocity direction of each sub-stroke by calculating the arc-tangent of the ratio of the magnitudes of the vertical and horizontal components of the velocity vector directed from the starting point to the ending point of the sub-stroke. We extract the device acceleration during each sub-stroke by averaging the device acceleration values reported by the touch screen device at each touch point in that sub-stroke in all three directions.

### 6.2.2 Sub-stroke Time Duration

Next, we investigate how to find the appropriate sub-stroke time duration. On one hand, when the sub-stroke time duration is too small, the behavior information extracted from each sub-stroke of the same user may become inconsistent because when feature values become instantaneous, they are unlikely to be consistent for the same user. For example, from Figure 12, which shows the *cv* for the velocity magnitude values extracted from the first sub-stroke from all samples of a gesture performed by a random volunteer in our data set, when we vary the sub-stroke time duration from 5ms to 100ms, we observe that the *cv* is too large to be usable when the sub-stroke time duration is too small and the *cv* decreases as we increase sub-stroke time duration. On the other hand, when the sub-stroke time duration is too large, the behavior information extracted from each sub-stroke of different users may become similar because all unique dynamics of individual users are too averaged out to be distinguishable. For example, treating all the samples of a gesture performed by all our volunteers as if they are all performed by the same person, Figure 13 shows that when the sub-stroke time duration is 80ms, over 60% of feature elements of velocity magnitude are consistent, which means that they do not have any distinguishing power among different users. It is therefore challenging to trade off between consistency and distinguishability in choosing the appropriate time duration for sub-strokes.

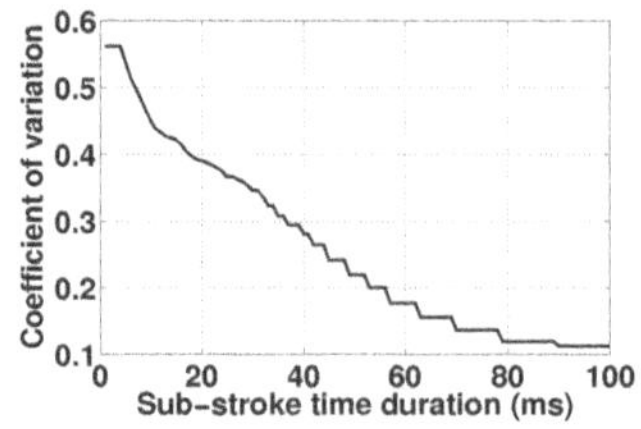


**Figure 12: *cv* vs. time periods**

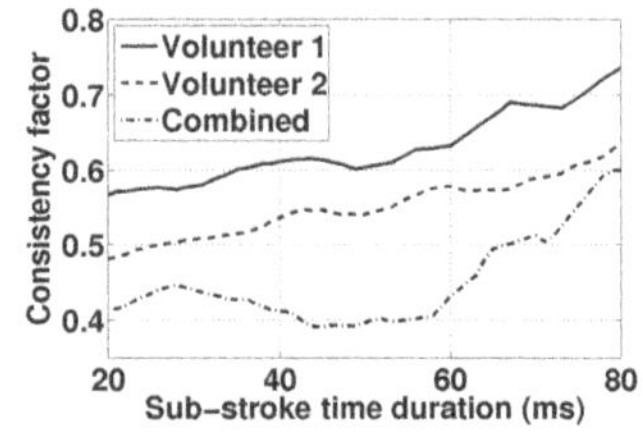


**Figure 13: Consistency factor**

Next, we present the way that we achieve this tradeoff and find the appropriate time duration for sub-strokes. We first define a metric called *consistency factor*. Given a set of samples of the same stroke, which are segmented using time duration $p$ as the guideline, let $s$ be the number of sub-strokes, $c$ be the number of sub-strokes that have the consistent behavior for a particular feature, we define the consistency factor of this set of samples under time duration $p$ to be $\frac{c}{s}$. For simplicity, we use *combined consistency factor* to mean the consistency factor of the set of all samples of the same stroke from all volunteers, and *individual consistency factor* to mean the consistency factor of the set of all samples of the same stroke from the same volunteer. Figure 13 shows the combined consistency factor plot and two individual consistency factor plots of an example gesture. We have two important observations from this figure. First, the individual consistency factors mostly keep increasing as we increase sub-stroke time duration $p$. Second, the combined consistency factor has a significant dip when $p$ is in the range from 30ms to 60ms. We conducted the similar measurement for other strokes from other gestures for velocity magnitude, velocity direction, and device acceleration and made the same two observations. This means that when sub-stroke time duration is between 30ms to 60ms, people have distinguishing behavior for the features of velocity magnitude, velocity direction, and device acceleration. Therefore, we choose time duration $p$ to be between 30ms to 60ms.

### 6.2.3 Sub-stroke Selection at Appropriate Resolutions

So far we have assumed that all sub-strokes segmented from a stroke have the same time duration. However, in reality, people have consistent and distinguishing behavior for sub-strokes of different time durations. Next, we discuss how we find such sub-strokes of different durations. For each type of sub-stroke based features, we represent the entire time duration of a stroke as a line with the initial color of white. Given a set of samples of a stroke performed by one user under $b$ postures, we first segment the stroke with the time duration $p = 60$ms and the number of MVPs $k = 1$. For each resulting sub-stroke, we measure *cv* of the feature values extracted from the sub-stroke. If it is lower than the threshold, then we choose this sub-stroke with $k$ MVPs as a feature element and color this sub-stroke in the line as black. After this round of segmentation, if any white sub-stroke is left, we move to the next round of segmentation on the entire stroke with $p = 55$ms and the number of MVPs $k$ still being 1. In this round, for any sub-stroke whose color is completely white, we measure its *cv*; if it is lower than the threshold, then we choose this sub-stroke with $k$ MVPs as a feature element and color this sub-stroke in the line as black. We continue this process, decrementing the time duration $p$ by

5ms in each round until either there is no white region of length greater than or equal to 30ms left in the line or $p$ is decremented to 30. If $p$ is decremented to 30 but there are still white regions of length greater than or equal to 30ms, we increase $k$ by 1, reset $p$ to be 60ms, and repeat the above process again. The last possible round is the one with $k = b$ and $p =$ 30ms. The process also terminates whenever there is no white region of length greater than or equal to 30ms.

# 7. CLASSIFIER TRAINING

In this section, we explain the internal details of GEAT on training its classifiers. After feature extraction and selection, we obtain one feature vector for each training sample of a gesture. For a single-finger gesture, the feature vector contains the values of the selected feature elements such as stroke time and the velocity magnitude, velocity direction, and device acceleration from selected sub-strokes. For a multi-finger gesture, the feature vector additionally contains the selected feature elements such as inter-stroke time, displacement magnitude, and direction between all pairs of strokes.

## 7.1 Partitioning the Training Sample

Before we use these $N$ feature vectors to train our classifiers, we partition them into consistent training groups so that the user has the consistent behavior for each group for any feature element. Recall that for each feature element, we have already partitioned the $N$ feature vectors into the least number of MVPs. For different feature elements, we may have partitioned the $N$ feature vectors differently. Thus, we partition the $N$ feature vectors into the least number of consistent training groups so that for each feature element, all feature vectors within a training group belong to one minimum variance partition. If the number of feature vectors in a resulting consistent training group is below a threshold, then it is not used to train classifiers.

## 7.2 Training the SVDE Classifiers

In real world deployment of authentication schemes, training samples are often all from the legitimate user. When training data is only from one class (*i.e.*, the legitimate user in our scenario) while test samples can come from two classes (*i.e.*, both the legitimate user and imposters), Support Vector Distribution Estimation (SVDE) with the Radial Basis Function (RBF) kernel is effective and efficient [8, 16]. We use the open source implementation of SVDE in libSVM [4].

We build an ensemble of classifiers for each consistent training group. First, for each feature element, we normalize its $N$ values to be in the range of $[0, 1]$; otherwise feature elements with larger values will dominate the classifier training. Second, we empirically find the appropriate values for $\gamma$, a parameter for RBF kernel, and $\nu$, a parameter for SVDE, by performing a grid search on the ranges $2^{-17} \leq \gamma \leq 2^{0}$ and $2^{-10} \leq \nu \leq 2^{0}$ with 10-fold cross validation on each training group. As the training samples are only from one class (*i.e.*, the legitimate user), cross validation during grid search only measures the true positive rate (TPR). Figure 14(a) plots a surface of TPR resulting from cross validation during the grid search for a training group of a gesture for one volunteer. We see that TPR values are different for different parameter values and there is a region where the TPR values are particularly high. The downside of selecting parameter values with higher TPR is that it increases the false positive rate (FPR). While selecting parameter values with lower TPR decreases the FPR, it is inconvenient for the legitimate user if he cannot successfully authenticate in several attempts. Therefore, we need to tradeoff between usability and security in selecting parameter values. In this paper, we choose the highest value of TPR such that 1−TPR equals FPR, which results in the lowest EER. To calculate FPRs, GEAT needs imposter samples, which are not available in real world deployment at the time of training. Therefore, GEAT generates synthetic imposter samples by elastically deforming the samples of legitimate user using cubic B-splines and calculates the FPRs using these synthetic imposter samples. Note that these synthetic imposter samples are not used in classifier training.

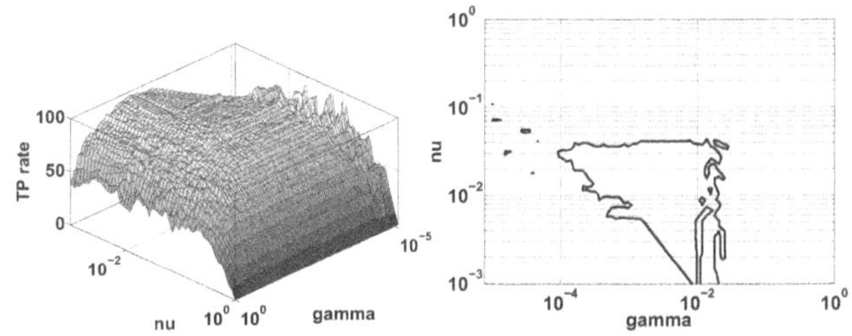

(a) TPR surface plot (b) 95% TPR contour

**Figure 14: Parameter selection**

Once we decide on TPR, we obtain the coordinates of the points on the contour of that TPR from the surface formed by the grid search. Figure 14(b) shows the 95% TPR contour on the surface in Figure 14(a). From the points on this contour, we randomly select $z$ (say $z = 10$) points, where each point provides us with the parameter values of $\gamma$ and $\nu$. For each of the $z$ pairs of parameter values of $\gamma$ and $\nu$, GEAT trains an SVDE classifier on a consistent training group. Thus, for each consistent training group, we get an ensemble of $z$ classifiers for modeling the behavior of the legitimate user. This ensemble can now be used to classify any test sample. The decision of this ensemble of classifiers for a test sample is based on the majority voting on the decision of the $z$ classifiers in the ensemble. Larger value of $z$ increases the probability of achieving the TPR at which the contour was made, however, the computation required to perform authentication also increases. Therefore, we need to tradeoff between classification reliability and efficiency in choosing the value of $z$. We choose $z = 10$ in our experiments.

## 7.3 Classifying the Test Samples

Given a test sample of a gesture on a touch screen device, we first extract values from this test sample for the selected feature elements of the legitimate user of this device and form a feature vector. Then, we feed this feature vector to all ensembles of classifiers. If any ensemble of classifiers accepts this feature vector as legitimate, which means that this test sample gesture is similar to one of the identified behavior of the legitimate user, we accept this test sample as legitimate and skip the remaining ensembles of classifiers. If no ensemble accepts this test sample as legitimate, then this test sample is deemed as illegitimate.

# 8. RANKING AND CLASSIFICATION

For each gesture, GEAT repeats the above three steps given in Sections 5, 6, and 7 and then ranks the gestures based on their EERs. The user chooses the value of $n$, the number of gestures with lowest EERs that the user needs to do in each authentication attempt. Although larger $n$ is, higher accuracy GEAT has, for practical purposes, $n = 1$ (or 3 at most) gives high enough accuracy.

When a user tries to unlock, the device displays the $n$ top ranked gestures for the user to perform. GEAT classifies each gesture input as discussed in Section 7.3, and uses majority voting on the $n$ decisions to make the final decision about the legitimacy of the user.

# 9. EXPERIMENTAL RESULTS

In this section, we present the results from our evaluation of GEAT. First, we report EERs from Matlab simulations on gestures in our data set. Second, we study the impact of the number of training samples on the EER of GEAT. Third, we study the impact of the threshold of $cv$ on the EER of GEAT and justify our choice of using 0.1 as the threshold. Fourth, we report the results from real world evaluation of GEAT implemented on Windows smart phones. Last, we compare the performance of GEAT with the scheme proposed in [9]. We report our results in terms of equal error rates (EER), true positive rates (TPR), false negative rates (FNR), and false positive rates (FPR). EER is the error rate when the classifier parameters are selected such that FNR equals FPR.

## 9.1 Accuracy Evaluation

First, we present our error rates when the number of postures $b$ is equal to 1, which means that GEAT only looks for a single consistent behavior among all training samples. Second, we present the error rates of GEAT when $b > 1$, which means that GEAT looks for multiple consistent behaviors in training samples. We present these error rates for $n = 1$ and $n = 3$ where $n$ is the number of gestures that the user needs to do for authentication. Recall that GEAT allows a user to choose the $n$ top ranked gestures. Third, we present the average error rates for each of the 10 gestures. We calculated the average error rates by treating each volunteer as a legitimate user once and treating the remaining as imposters for the current legitimate user. To train SVDE classifiers on legitimate user for a given gesture, we used a set of 15 samples of that gesture from that legitimate user. For testing, we used remaining samples from the legitimate user and 5 randomly chosen samples of that gesture from each imposter. We repeated this process of training and testing on the samples of the given gesture for 10 times, each time choosing a different set of training samples. We did not use imposter samples in training.

For the training samples of a gesture performed by a user, ideally, we would like to know the number of postures $b$ in which the user performed the gesture. Knowing the value of $b$ helps us to achieve higher classification accuracy. However, in real deployment, the value of $b$ may not be available. In such scenarios, actually our classification accuracy is still very high. Next, we first present the evaluation results if we do not know the value of $b$. In such cases, we treat all training samples to be from the same posture by setting $b = 1$. Then, we present the evaluation results if we know the value of $b$.

### 9.1.1 Single Behavior Results

In this case, we assume $b = 1$. Figure 15(a) plots the cumulative distribution functions (CDFs) of the EERs of GEAT with and without accelerometers, and the FNR of GEAT when FPR is less than 0.1%, for $n = 1$. Similarly, Figure 15(b) shows the corresponding plots for $n = 3$. We make following two observations when device acceleration features are used in training and testing. First, the average EER of users in our data set for $n = 1$ and $n = 3$ is 4.8% and 1.7%, respectively. Second, over 80% of users have their EERs less than 4.9% and 3.4% for $n = 1$ and $n = 3$, respectively. We make following two observations when device acceleration features are not available. First, the average EER of users in our data set for $n = 1$ and $n = 3$ is 6.8% and 3.7%, respectively. That is, EER increases by 2% for both $n = 1$ and $n = 3$ when accelerometers are not available. This shows that even when accelerometers are not available, GEAT still has high classification accuracy. Second, over 80% of users have their EERs less than 6.7% and 5.2% for $n = 1$ and $n = 3$, respectively. We also observe that the average FNR is less than 14.4% and 9.2% for $n = 1$ and $n = 3$, respectively when FPR is taken to be negligibly small (*i.e.* FPR $< 0.1\%$). These CDFs show that if the parameters of the classifiers in GEAT are selected such that the legitimate user is rejected only once in 10 attempts *i.e.*, for TPR$\approx$ 90%, an imposter will almost never be accepted *i.e.* FPR$\approx$ 0%.

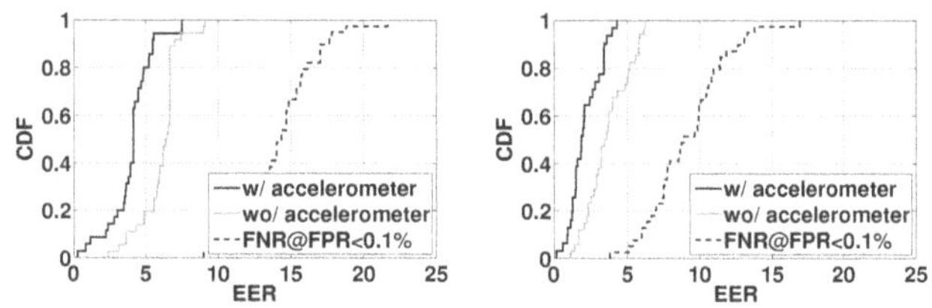


(a) $n = 1$ (b) $n = 3$

**Figure 15: EERs with and without accelerometer and FNR at FPR $< 0.1\%$**

### 9.1.2 Multiple Behaviors

Among our volunteers, we requested ten volunteers to do each of the 10 gestures in 2 postures (*i.e.*, sitting and laying down). In this case, $b = 2$. Figure 16(a) shows the EER for these ten volunteers for $b = 1$, 2, and 3. We see that the EER is minimum when $b = 2$ for these ten volunteers because these volunteers provided training samples of gestures in two postures. Figure 16(a) shows that the use of $b < 2$ results in a larger EER because it renders most of the sub-strokes inconsistent, which leaves lesser consistent information to train the classifiers. Figure 16(a) shows that the use of $b > 2$ results in a larger EER as well because dividing the training samples made under $b$ postures into more than $b$ consistent training groups reduces the training samples in each group, resulting in increased EER.

### 9.1.3 Individual Gestures

The FPR of each gesture averaged over all users is always below 5% for a TPR of 90% and decreases with the decrease in TPR. Figures 17(a) and 17(b) show the plots of FPRs vs. TPRs for each of the 10 gestures, averaged over all users. Table 2 shows AUC, the area under the receiver operating characteristic (ROC) curve, of all gestures for both filtered and unfiltered samples. Unfiltered samples are the samples before the noise is removed. We see that the AUC values are greater than 0.95 for most gestures. Note that an ideal classification scheme that never misclassifies any samples has AUC=1. We also see from Table 2 that AUC values for unfiltered gestures are slightly lower compared to AUC values for filtered gestures showing that filtering before

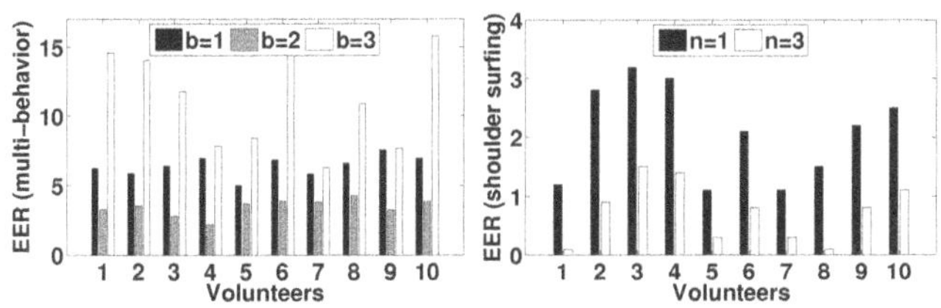


(a) EER w.r.t $b$ (b) Shoulder surfing attack

**Figure 16: EER under different scenarios**

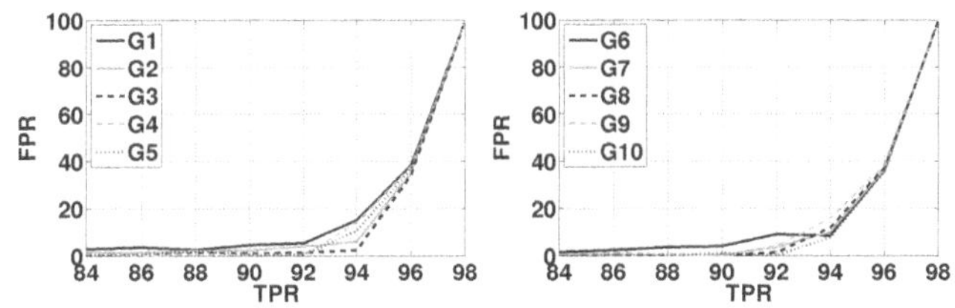


(a) Gestures 1 to 5 (b) Gestures 6 to 10

**Figure 17: Average FPR vs. TPR for all gestures**

feature extraction improves classification accuracy. We have presented both FPR and TPR for all gestures individually only to show how individual gestures perform. In real world implementation, a user will only perform $n$ top ranked gestures, resulting in much lower FPR at much higher TPR as shown by the small values of EER in 15(b).

**Table 2: AUC for filtered and unfiltered gestures**

| Filtered | | | | | | | | | |
|---|---|---|---|---|---|---|---|---|---|
| G1 | G2 | G3 | G4 | G5 | G6 | G7 | G8 | G9 | G10 |
| 0.94 | 0.96 | 0.95 | 0.95 | 0.95 | 0.96 | 0.96 | 0.96 | 0.96 | 0.96 |
| Unfiltered | | | | | | | | | |
| G1 | G2 | G3 | G4 | G5 | G6 | G7 | G8 | G9 | G10 |
| 0.92 | 0.95 | 0.94 | 0.93 | 0.94 | 0.95 | 0.94 | 0.95 | 0.95 | 0.94 |

## 9.2 Impact of Training Samples Size

The EER decreases with the increase in the number of training samples. Figure 18(a) plots the EERs averaged over all users for $n = 1$ and $n = 3$ for the increasing number of training samples. For $n = 1$ and $n = 3$, average EER falls to 3.2% and 0.5%, respectively, with just 25 training samples. An EER of 0.5% means TPR=99.5% and FPR=0.5%, which are very good results for classification schemes. A user can achieve these rates by providing only 25 training samples for each gesture. Providing more training samples over time further lowers the EER.

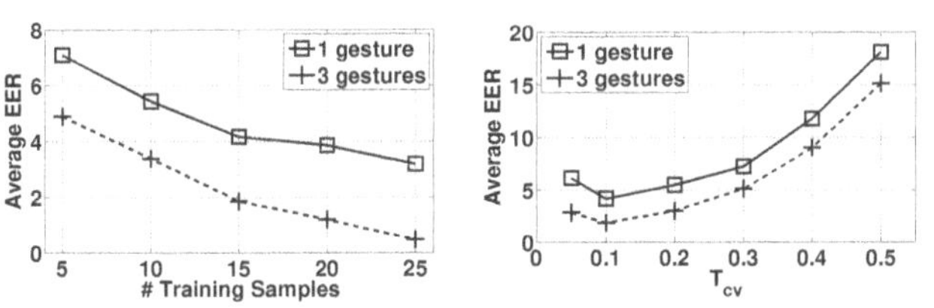


(a) # of training samples (b) Effect of $T_{cv}$

**Figure 18: Effect of system parameters on EER**

## 9.3 Determining Threshold for cv

The average EER is a convex function in terms of the threshold of $cv$, denoted by $T_{cv}$. On one hand, if $T_{cv}$ is too small, then it is difficult to find sub-strokes in which the user has consistent behavior, which gives us less information for classifier training. On the other hand, if $T_{cv}$ is too large, then the feature elements with less consistent behavior will be selected, which adds noise in the user behavior models. Figure 18(b) shows the average EER for $n = 1$ and $n = 3$. We see that the average EER is the smallest for $T_{cv} = 0.1$.

## 9.4 Real-world Evaluation

We evaluated GEAT on two sets of 10 volunteers each in real-world settings by implementing it on Samsung Focus running Windows. We used the first set to evaluate GEAT's resilience to attacks by imposters that have not observed the legitimate users while doing the gestures. We used the second set to evaluate GEAT's resilience to shoulder surfing attack, where imposters have observed the legitimate users while doing the gestures.

### 9.4.1 *Non-shoulder Surfing Attack*

In this case, our implementation requests the user to provide training samples for all gestures and trains GEAT on those samples. We asked each volunteer in the first set to provide at least 15 training samples for each gesture. GEAT also asks the user to select a value of $n$. We used $n = 1$ and 3 in our experiments. Once trained, we asked the legitimate user to do his $n$ top ranked gestures ten times and recorded the authentication decisions to calculate TPR. After this, we randomly picked 5 out of 9 remaining volunteers to act as imposters and did not show them how the legitimate user does the gestures. We asked each imposer to do the same top $n$ ranked gestures, and recorded the authentication decisions to calculate FPR. We repeated this process for each volunteer by asking him to act as the legitimate user once. Furthermore, we repeated this entire process for all ten volunteers five times on five different days. The average (TPR, FPR) over all volunteers for $n = 1$ and $n = 3$ turned out to be (94.6%, 4.02%) and (98.2%, 1.1%), respectively. Figures 19(a) and 19(b) show the bar plots of TPR and FPR of each of the 10 volunteers for $n = 1$ and 3, respectively.

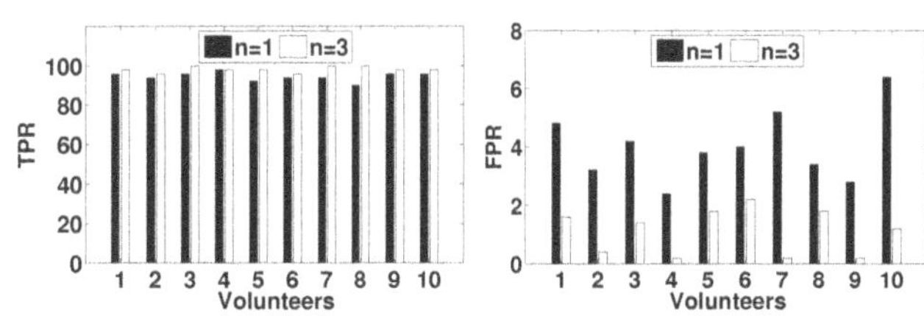


(a) TPR for $n = 1, 3$ (b) FPR for $n = 1, 3$

**Figure 19: Real world results of GEAT**

### 9.4.2 *Shoulder Surfing Attack*

For this scenario, we made a video of a legitimate user doing all gestures on the touch screen of our Samsung Focus phone and showed this video to each of the 10 volunteers in the second set. The volunteers were allowed to watch the video as many times as they wanted and then requested them to perform each gesture ten times. The average FPR over all 10 volunteers turned out to be 0% for $n = 1$ as well as

$n = 3$ when we set the TPR at 80%. The average EER over all volunteers for $n = 1$ and $n = 3$ turned out to be only 2.1% and 0.7%, respectively. These results show that GEAT is very resilient to shoulder surfing attack. Figure 16(b) shows the bar plots of EER for each of the 10 volunteers in the second set for $n = 1$ and $n = 3$.

### 9.5 Comparison with Existing Schemes

We compared the performance of GEAT with the only work in this direction reported in [9] where Luca *et al.* used the following four gestures: swipe left with one finger, swipe down with one finger, swipe down with two fingers, and swipe diagonally up from bottom left of the screen to top right. The highest FPR, when TPR= 93%, that they achieved is 43%, which is way higher than our average FPR of 4.77% at TPR of 95.23%. For a fair comparison, we also collected data for these 4 gestures from 45 volunteers and calculated the value of FPR at the TPRs reported in [9]. Table 3 reports the FPR achieved by GEAT and the scheme in [9]. We see that the FPRs of GEAT on these gestures are at least 4.66 times lesser than the corresponding FPRs in [9] for the TPRs used in [9]. We do not use these 4 gestures because their average EERs are larger compared to the average EERs of the 10 gestures we have proposed in this paper.

**Table 3: Comparison of GEAT with [9]**

| | TPR | FPR | |
|---|---|---|---|
| | | Luca *et al.* [9] | GEAT |
| Swipe left | 85.11 | 48 | 5.12 |
| Swipe down–1 finger | 95.71 | 50 | 10.71 |
| Swipe down–2 fingers | 89.58 | 63 | 8.12 |
| Swipe diagonal | 90.71 | 43 | 8.01 |

## 10. CONCLUSIONS

In this paper, we propose a gesture based user authentication scheme for the secure unlocking of touch screen devices. Compared with existing passwords/PINs/ patterns based schemes, GEAT improves both the security and usability of such devices because it is not vulnerable to shoulder surfing attacks and smudge attacks and at the same time gestures are easier to input than passwords and PINs. Our scheme GEAT builds single-class classifiers using only training samples from legitimate users. We identified seven types of features (namely velocity magnitude, device acceleration, stroke time, inter-stroke time, stroke displacement magnitude, stroke displacement direction, and velocity direction). We proposed algorithms to model multiple behaviors of a user in performing each gesture. We implemented GEAT on real smart phones and conducted real-world experiments. Experimental results show that GEAT achieves an average equal error rate of 0.5% with 3 gestures using only 25 training samples.

## 11. REFERENCES


[1] "25 leaked celebrity cell phone pics," `http://www.holytaco.com/25-leaked-celebrity-cell-phone-pics`.

[2] "The symantec smartphone honey stick project,"

[3] A. J. Aviv, K. Gibson, E. Mossop, M. Blaze, and J. M. Smith, "Smudge attacks on smartphone touch screens," in *Proc. 4th USENIX Conf. on Offensive technologies*, 2010, pp. 1–10.

[4] C.-C. Chang and C.-J. Lin, "LIBSVM: a library for support vector machines," *ACM Transactions on Intelligent Systems and Technology*, vol. 2, no. 3, pp. 27:1–27, 2011.

[5] M. Conti, I. Zachia-Zlatea, and B. Crispo, "Mind how you answer me!: transparently authenticating the user of a smartphone when answering or placing a call," in *Proc. ACM Symposium on Information, Computer and Communications Security*, 2011, pp. 249–259.

[6] D. Gafurov, K. Helkala, and T. Søndrol, "Biometric gait authentication using accelerometer sensor," *Journal of computers*, vol. 1, no. 7, pp. 51–59, 2006.

[7] J. Joe H. Ward, "Hierarchical grouping to optimize an objective function," *Journal of the American statistical association*, vol. 58, no. 301, pp. 236–244, 1963.

[8] S. S. Keerthi and C.-J. Lin, "Asymptotic behaviors of support vector machines with gaussian kernel," *Neural computation*, vol. 15, no. 7, pp. 1667–1689, 2003.

[9] A. D. Luca, A. Hang, F. Brudy, C. Lindner, and H. Hussmann, "Touch me once and I know it's you!: implicit authentication based on touch screen patterns," in *Proc. ACM (SIGCHI)*, 2012.

[10] K. Killourhy and R. Maxion, "Why did my detector do that?!" in *Proc. RAID*, 2010.

[11] J. Kwapisz, G. Weiss, and S. Moore, "Cell phone-based biometric identification," in *Proc. IEEE Int. Conf. on Biometrics: Theory Applications and Systems*, 2010, pp. 1–7.

[12] J. Mantyjarvi, M. Lindholm, E. Vildjiounaite, S. Makela, and H. Ailisto, "Identifying users of portable devices from gait pattern with accelerometers," in *Proc. IEEE Int. Conf. on Acoustics, Speech, and Signal Processing*, 2005.

[13] F. Monrose, M. K. Reiter, and S. Wetzel. Password hardening based on keystroke dynamics. In *Proc. ACM CCS*, pages 73 – 82, 1999.

[14] N. Sae-Bae, K. Ahmed, K. Isbister, and N. Memon. Biometric-rich gestures: a novel approach to authentication on multi-touch device. In *Proc. ACM SIGCHI*, 2012.

[15] F. Schaub, R. Deyhle, and M. Weber, "Password entry usability and shoulder surfing susceptibility on different smartphone platforms," in *Proc. Mobile & Ubiquitous Multimedia*, 2012.

[16] B. Schölkopf, J. C. Platt, J. Shawe-Taylor, A. J. Smola, and R. C. Williamson, "Estimating the support of a high-dimensional distribution," *Neural computation*, vol. 13, no. 7, 2001.

[17] M. Shahzad, S. Zahid, and M. Farroq, "A hybrid GA-PSO fuzzy system for user identification on smart phones," in *Proc. GECCO*, 2009, pp. 1617–1624.

[18] F. Tari, A. Ozok, and S. Holden, "A comparison of perceived and real shoulder-surfing risks between alphanumeric and graphical passwords," in *Proc. SOUPS*, 2006, pp. 56–66.

[19] S. Zahid, M. Shahzad, S. A. Khayam, and M. Farooq, "Keystroke-based user identification on smart phones," in *Proc. RAID*, 2009.

[20] N. Zheng, K. Bai, H. Huang, and H. Wang. You are how you touch: User verification on smartphones via tapping behaviors. Technical report, College of William and Mary, 2012.

# CorLayer: A Transparent Link Correlation Layer for Energy Efficient Broadcast


Shuai Wang
University of Minnesota
Minneapolis, MN, USA
shuaiw@cs.umn.edu

Song Min Kim
University of Minnesota
Minneapolis, MN, USA
ksong@cs.umn.edu

Yunhuai Liu
Third Research Institute of
the Ministry of Public Security
Shanghai, China
yunhuai.liu@gmail.com

Guang Tan
SIAT
Chinese Academy of Sciences
Shenzhen, China
guang.tan@siat.ac.cn

Tian He
University of Minnesota
Minneapolis, MN, USA
tianhe@cs.umn.edu


## ABSTRACT


Wireless communication essentially occurs in a broadcast medium with concurrent receptions. Recent works [34,41] have shown clear evidence that wireless links are not independent and that transmissions from a transmitter to multiple receivers are correlated, a phenomenon that has profound implications for the performance of network protocols such as broadcast, multi-cast, opportunistic forwarding and network coding. In this paper, we show how link correlation can significantly impact broadcast. We present the design and implementation of CorLayer, a general supporting layer for energy efficient reliable broadcast that carefully blacklists certain poorly correlated wireless links. This method uses only one-hop information, which makes it work in a fully distributed manner and introduces minimal communication overhead. The highlight of our work is CorLayer's broad applicability and effectiveness. Our system effort is indeed significant. We integrate CorLayer transparently with sixteen state-of-the-art broadcast protocols specified in thirteen publications [1, 3, 18, 19, 23, 25–27, 32, 36, 38–40] on three physical testbeds running TelosB, MICAz, and GreenOrbs nodes, respectively. The experimental results show that CorLayer remarkably improves energy efficiency across a wide spectrum of broadcast protocols and that the total number of packet transmissions can be reduced consistently by 47% on average.


## Categories and Subject Descriptors

C.2.1 [**Network Architecture and Design**]: Wireless communications

## General Terms

Design, Experimentation, Algorithms, Performance



*MobiCom'13*, September 30–October 4, Miami, FL, USA.
Copyright 2013 ACM 978-1-4503-1999-7/13/09 ...$15.00.
http://dx.doi.org/10.1145/2500423.2500425.



## Keywords

Energy Efficiency, IEEE 802.15.4, Wireless, Protocol


## 1. INTRODUCTION

Link correlation refers to the phenomenon in which packet receptions from a transmitter to multiple receivers may be correlated. As recently highlighted by Srinivasan et al. [34] and Zhu et al. [41], link correlation challenges the widely made assumption that wireless transmissions are independent (i.e., the reception probability of a receiver is solely governed by that link's quality measure). The finding of link correlation brings in a more realistic radio model for wireless network design, opening up new opportunities for network performance optimization.

For example, suppose two receivers have a high correlation, and thus a reception acknowledgement from the first receiver strongly implies that the second one receives the packet as well. Statistically, the second acknowledgement is not quite necessary. This insight has been successfully used by Zhu et al. [41]. They proposed a concept called collective ACKs which solves the ACK storm problem [30] by inferring the success of a transmission to a receiver based on the ACKs from other neighboring receivers. More generally, link correlation has a broad impact on network protocols that utilize concurrent wireless links, which include but are not limited to (i) traditional network protocols such as broadcast [27, 32], multi-cast [12, 16], and multi-path routing [13], or (ii) diversity-based protocols such as opportunistic forwarding [5, 7, 10], collaborative forwarding [6], and network coding [2, 21, 25].

In this paper, we focus on how to exploit link correlation to improve the energy efficiency of *reliable broadcast protocols* that try to guarantee every node in the network receives packets. Reliable broadcast is a fundamental operation in wireless network design and plays a critical role in many other operations such as code dissemination (e.g., Deluge [17] and MNP [22]), content delivery (e.g., Cabernet [11]), and routing discoveries (e.g., ODRMP [24] and OLSR [8]).

In reliable broadcast designs, we essentially need to select a set of forwarding nodes that cover all the other nodes, called the dominating set. Once nodes in this set are connected, we call it a connected dominating set (CDS). For energy efficiency, the broadcast algorithms should seek a CDS with a minimal size. Based on different approaches of finding the CDS, existing reliable broadcast algorithms can be classified as (i) tree-based (e.g., ZigBee [9]);

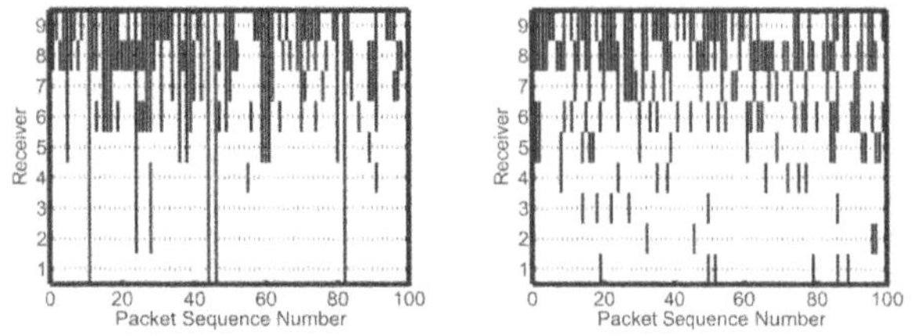

(a) Empirical Trace (b) Synthetic Independent Trace

**Figure 1: Packet receptions at 9 receivers when a single transmitter broadcasts 100 packets; (a) empirical trace from the testbed in UMN on channel 16. (b) Synthetic trace with the independent links under the same packet reception ratio. Packet losses are marked by black bends. Compared with synthetic independent trace, empirical trace has many more long vertical black bands, indicating that the empirical links have more correlated losses.**

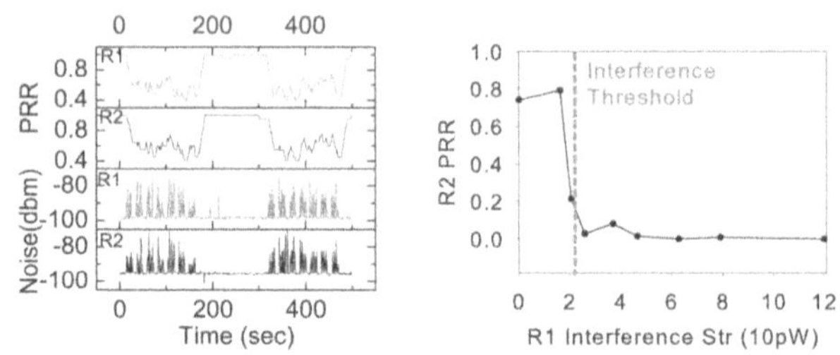

(a) PRR & Noise RSSI (b) R2's PRR vs. R1's Interference

**Figure 2: Cross-network interference; (a) two receivers' PRR and the corresponding noise level. Both receivers' PRR decreases when the noise is introduced by the microwave oven. (b) R2's PRR under R1's interference strength. We can tell R2's PRR from R1's interference strength – R2's PRR decreases when R1's interference is above a certain level.**

(ii) cluster-based (e.g., passive clustering [23]); (iii) multi-point relays (e.g., OLSR [8]); (iv) pruning-based (e.g., RNG relay subset [18] and partial dominating pruning [27]), (v) location-based (e.g., curved convex hall [38]). Prior efforts on reliable broadcast focus mainly on how to select the optimal set of forwarding nodes (e.g.,with the minimum size). Though the research along this line has been comprehensive, all of the designs implicitly or explicitly assume independent wireless links and do not yet take link correlation into consideration.

Instead of coming up with yet another broadcast protocol or modification to existing protocols, we attempt to improve a wide range of existing broadcast protocols by designing a general supporting layer, called *CorLayer*. Taking link correlation into account, we blacklist links that are poorly correlated with adjacent links. With the CorLayer, broadcast algorithms will naturally form clusters with higher link correlations, which means that a forwarder needs fewer transmissions to deliver a packet to all of its covered members. Specifically, our contributions are as follows:

- Although the phenomenon of link correlation has been mentioned in the literature [34, 41], we provide the first extensive study to exploit the root cause of link correlation. We reveal the impact of link correlation on broadcast efficiency and demonstrate experimentally and theoretically why link correlation matters in wireless broadcasting.
- We design a supporting layer by blacklisting certain links in the original wireless network. Sitting between the MAC and routing layers, CorLayer presents a reduced network topology that can be transparently utilized by broadcast protocols, requiring no modification of broadcast protocols.
- We evaluate our design on three real-world multi-hop testbeds: a network with 36 MICAz nodes in University of Minnesota, U.S., a network with 30 TelosB nodes in SIAT, Chinese Academy of Sciences, China, and a network with 20 GreenOrbs nodes in the Third Research Institute of Ministry of Public Security (TRIMPS), China. The results are very encouraging, as with CorLayer we are able to broadly improve the performance of sixteen state-of-the-art broadcast protocols specified in thirteen publications [1, 3, 18, 19, 23, 25–27, 32, 36, 38–40], ranging from 20% $\sim$ 64%.

The rest of our paper is organized as follows. Section 2 presents the motivation of our design. The main design is presented in Section 3. Sections 4 and 5 report testbed and simulation experiments. In Section 6, we review related work. Finally, Section 7 concludes the paper.

## 2. MOTIVATION

In this section, we present empirical studies to demonstrate the existence of link correlation. Then, we demonstrate theoretically that the performance of network protocols can be improved by exploiting link correlation. Finally, we show the impact of link blacklisting on broadcasting.

### 2.1 Existence of Link Correlation

To verify the existence of link correlation, we conducted a small experiment on an 802.15.4 testbed in UMN. In this testbed, ten MICAz nodes are deployed to form a single-hop network. A randomly selected node serves as the transmitter and broadcasts 100 messages to the others under channel 16, and the other 9 nodes act as receivers (i.e., a star topology). Each packet is identified by a sequence number. All the receivers report their reception results to a sink node.

Figure 1(a) shows the packet receptions at different receivers from empirical measurements. Successful packet receptions are marked by white bands. Long vertical black bands indicate that packets are lost at multiple receivers, and vice versa for the white bands. As a comparison, Figure 1(b) shows the reception of packets in synthetically generated traces with independent wireless links. In the latter, we observe few multiple simultaneous receptions and losses. This comparison indicates that the packet receptions of different links in Figure 1(a) are indeed correlated. We note that this experiment reaffirms the empirical study reported in recent works [34, 41].

**Cause of link correlation:** We now move further to show the underlying causes of link correlation: (i) cross-network interference under shared medium; and (ii) correlated fading introduced by highly dynamic environments.

- Cross-Network Interference: With the increasing popularity of wireless network technologies, the wireless spectrum now often becomes crowded. For example, 802.11b, 802.11g, and 802.15.4 all use the 2.4 GHz ISM band, leading to possible cross-network interference. Traffic from high-power wireless networks (e.g., Wi-Fi) could introduce destructive noise in other low-power networks (e.g., ZigBee), causing correlated packet loss in multiple links simultaneously. Non-network appliances such as microwave ovens can also introduce high-power interference in this unlicensed band and we succeed in reproducing the effect with a controlled experiment in which microwave is toggled on and off with a period of 2.5 minutes. This simple experiment consists of three MicaZ nodes.

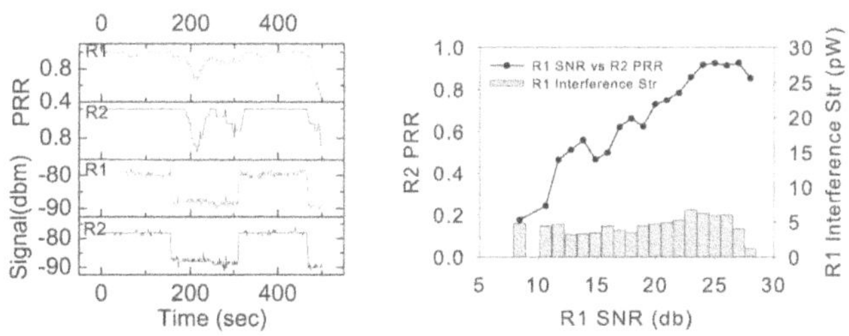


(a) PRR & Signal RSSI (b) R2's PRR vs. R1's SNR

**Figure 3: Correlated fading; (a) two receivers' PRR and signal RSSI. Both receivers' PRR decreases when signal RSSI decreases because of shadow fading. (b) R2's PRR under R1's SNR. There exists a near-linear relationship between R2's PRR and R1's SNR when R1' interference is under threshold.**

A sender node transmits packets at a fixed rate of one packet per second. In between transmissions, the two receivers record RSSI values, indicating noise level. Note that channel assessment (CCA) function of the sender is turned off so that transmission could take place regardless of the channel noise. The upper two figures in Figure 2(a) show the PRR of the two receivers, while the lower two show the noise levels. Similar peaks in the noise levels are observed in both receivers when microwave is left on. Such high-power noise corrupts packets at both receivers simultaneously, leading to highly correlated packet losses in the upper two figures. Figure 2(b) shows PRR of R2 relative to interference power observed at R1. From the figure, we see that R2's PRR faces a steep decrease when interference at R1 is above a certain level, which we call interference threshold (indicated by the dashed line), where almost no reception can be made on R2 upon crossing it.

• Correlated Shadow Fading: In reality, wireless signals suffer shadow fading caused by the presence of obstacles in the propagation path of the radio waves, leading to correlated reception performance among receivers that are closely located. Figure 3(a) plots two receivers' PRR and the corresponding signal RSSI with the introduction of shadow fading by object blocking with a period of 2.5 minutes in every 5 minutes. From Figure 3(a), we can find that both PRR and RSSI are in similar patterns at these two receivers, which means that the packet losses caused by object blocking (i.e., fading) are correlated. Figure 3(b) shows the case when interference is under the threshold. This is part where the fading correlation comes into play. Under threshold, there exists a near-linear relationship between R1's SNR and R2's PRR, as shown in Figure 3(b). In other words, fading correlation induces approximately linear relationship between the quality of R1's link and reception probability of R2. The bar graph (Figure 3(b)), which represents interference power, indicates that interference does not affect the relationship between R1's SNR and R2's PRR when it is under threshold.

## 2.2 How Link Correlation Affects Broadcast

This section theoretically analyzes the impact of link correlation upon the energy efficiency of broadcasting. Table 1 summarizes some notations that will be used in this paper. We demonstrate that a node incurs *fewer* transmissions when the packet receptions of its one-hop neighbors have a *higher* correlation. Figure 4 shows two simple 3-node clusters where $S$ is the source node and $A$ and $B$ are two receivers. If link quality is the only factor to be considered, intuitively we could deduce that, node $S$ in Figure 4(a) should have fewer transmissions because the link quality (80%) in this cluster is higher than that in Figure 4(b) (70%). If link correlation is considered, however, this intuition no longer holds, as is evident from the following analysis: We use $p(e_i) \in (0, 1]$ to denote the probability that a source node can directly deliver a packet via link $e_i$. Let $p(e_1)$ and $p(e_2)$ denote the link qualities for the two children respectively. Corresponding packet loss probabilities are denoted as $p(\bar{e_1}) = 1 - p(e_1)$ and $p(\bar{e_2}) = 1 - p(e_2)$. Let $p(\bar{e_1} \cap \bar{e_2})$ denote the probability that a broadcasting packet from a parent is not received by either child. For an arbitrary positive integer threshold $k$, we denote $\epsilon$ as the number of transmissions a parent node needs to deliver the packet to its two children. The probability that $\epsilon$ exceeds the threshold $k$ satisfies the following equation:

$$Pr(\epsilon > k) = p(\bar{e_1})^k + p(\bar{e_2})^k - p(\bar{e_1} \cap \bar{e_2})^k$$

Taking the difference yields

$$Pr(\epsilon = k) = Pr(\epsilon > k - 1) - Pr(\epsilon > k)$$

Then the expected number of transmissions $\mathrm{E}[\epsilon]$ to cover two children nodes can be calculated as

$$\begin{aligned} \mathrm{E}[\epsilon] &= \sum_{k=1}^{+\infty} k \cdot Pr(\epsilon = k) \\ &= \sum_{i=1}^{2} \frac{1}{p(e_i)} - \frac{1}{1 - p(\bar{e_1} \cap \bar{e_2})} \end{aligned} \quad (1)$$

We note that $p(\bar{e_1} \cap \bar{e_2})$ obtains its maximum value when links $e_1$ and $e_2$ are perfectly positive correlated while it gets a minimum value when links $e_1$ and $e_2$ are perfectly negative correlated. Let us revisit the two clusters in Figure 4. For the cluster in Figure 4(a), the expected number of transmissions $\mathrm{E}[\epsilon]$ is 1.5 based on Eq.(1),

| Notation | Description |
|---|---|
| $e = \{u, v\}$ | A link or transmission event from node $u$ to $v$ |
| $p(e)$ | Link quality, measured by the transmission successful probability |
| $N(u)$ | Node $u$'s one-hop neighbor set, $N(u, v) = N(u) \cap N(v)$ is the common neighbor set of $u$ and $v$ |
| $K_i(u)$ | A subset of $i$ nodes among $u$'s neighbors with the highest link quality |
| $p(K(u))$ | Joint Packet Reception Probability (JPRP), a joint probability of links from $u$ to $k(u)$ nodes |
| $Pr(v\|K(u))$ | Set link probability, a conditional probability |
| $\epsilon(u)$ | The expected transmission count for $u$ to reliably broadcast one packet |

**Table 1: Notations used in this paper**

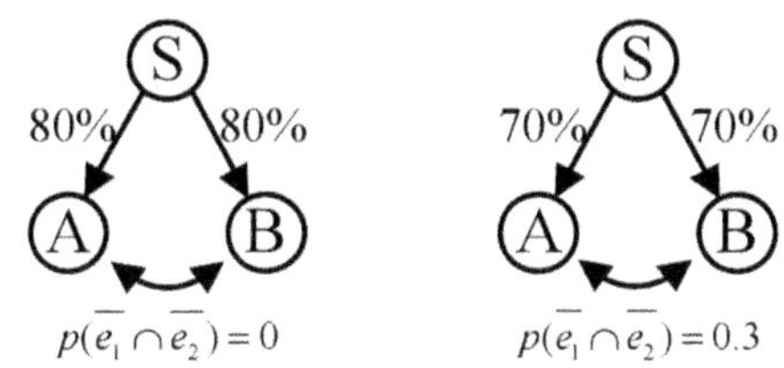


**(a) Negative correlated** **(b) Positive correlated**

**Figure 4: Impact of link correlation on broadcast. The expected number of transmissions to cover two receivers is (a) 1.5, and (b) 1.43. Because of the high link correlation, case (b) needs less transmissions although its link quality is worse than case (a).**

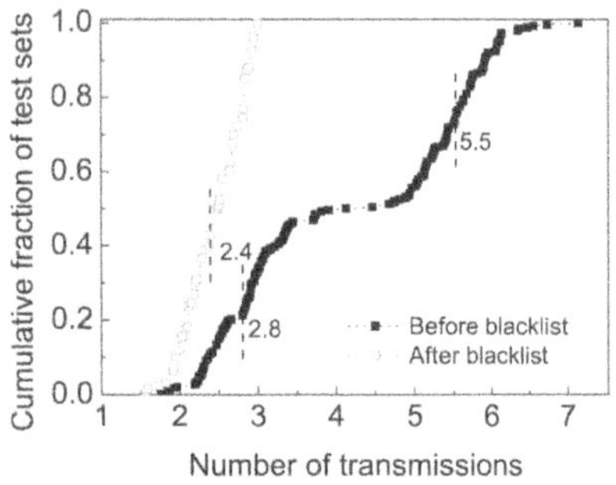


**Figure 5: The effect of blacklisting on transmissions. The average number of transmissions before blacklisting is mainly concentrated around 2.8 and 5.5 while it's 2.4 after blacklisting. Blacklisting leads to a significant reduction in transmission.**

given that $p(\bar{e}_1 \cap \bar{e}_2) = 0$ since $SA$ and $SB$ are perfectly negative correlated. In Figure 4(b), however, since $SA$ and $SB$ are perfectly positive correlated, it is not difficult to get that $p(\bar{e}_1 \cap \bar{e}_2)$ is 0.3. As a result, $\mathrm{E}[\epsilon]$ is 1.43 which is less than the cluster in Figure 4(a) even though it has better links. This suggests that we need to take link correlation into consideration in energy efficient broadcast and if we can manage to increase the link correlation within each cluster, then the number of transmissions can be significantly reduced. This can be done without modifying the broadcast algorithms at all – we simply *blacklist* certain links in the original network topology when they are found to be poorly correlated with others. By doing so, the upper layer broadcast protocols automatically avoid using them, thereby forming better-correlated clusters.

## 2.3 Link Blacklisting for Better Correlation

For the sake of clarity, we explained the impact of link correlation using a hypothetical example in the previous section. In this section, we present statistical evidence obtained from a physical setting. In the experiment, a sender is placed in the center, and the other 10 nodes are randomly deployed as single-hop receivers to receive 100 packets (i.e., a star topology).

In a practical broadcast protocol, some of the forwarder's neighbors may be dominated by other forwarders. In this experiment, we let the sender cover only five out of the ten nodes and measured the average number of transmissions to guarantee the successful reception of a single packet by the selected five nodes. There are $\binom{10}{5} = 252$ different combinations of such five nodes (out of ten). Then, we manually blacklist one negatively correlated link from the ten links and conduct the experiments again. Figure 5 shows the transmission CDF before and after blacklisting. From Figure 5, we find that the average number of transmissions before blacklisting varies from 1.76 to 7.13 and is mainly concentrated around 2.8 and 5.5. The results after blacklisting show that the average number of transmissions for covering arbitrary five nodes (out of the nine receivers) is around 2.4. In other words, in this particular experiment a simple blacklisting of one link improves the link correlation, leading to a significantly reduction in the number of transmissions.

# 3. THE DESIGN OF CORLAYER

Since a wireless network has a much more complex structure than a star topology as we describe in Section 2.3, it is not practical to manually blacklist wireless links and an advanced design is needed. This section presents CorLayer, which handles link blacklisting automatically and transparently in an arbitrary topology. CorLayer is a supporting layer above the network topology, such as neighbor discovery and transmission power control, and beneath the network communication layer in which the broadcast protocol resides. In what follows, the design principles and core ideas of CorLayer are presented in Section 3.1. We then introduce the basis of CorLayer – the expected transmission count of broadcast – in Section 3.2. To support efficient calculation, we propose a heuristic to reduce computational cost in Section 3.3. The general design is presented in Section 3.4.

## 3.1 Design Insight and Principles

Generally, broadcast algorithms work as follows. Given the network topology, they select a subset of nodes as forwarders (in a centralized or distributed manner). These forwarders, called dominators, should be connected so that they alone can forward packets. Though different broadcast algorithms differ in their way of selecting the forwarder nodes, they share the common feature that every dominator is responsible for covering its one-hop non-dominators (called dominatees), and every dominatee must be covered by at least one of its one-hop dominators. This feature provides the key insights we used to exploit link correlation when building CorLayer.

Recalling the example in Figure 4, roughly speaking, a dominator needs fewer transmissions when its covered dominatees have a higher link correlation. In other words, we can safely blacklist a wireless link and provide a better network topology to upper layer protocols if we can ensure that (i) the link correlation is increased by blacklisting the link and; (ii) the whole network is still connected.

The blacklisting procedure involves several key challenges that are addressed in this section. First, we need an efficient algorithm to assess the cost of covering one-hop neighbors, taking link correlation into consideration. Second, we need a low-cost method to deal with changes of link dynamics and maintain fresh values over time. Third, we need a localized light-weight algorithm for connectivity check. It is worth noting that CorLayer is constructed in a fully distributed manner where only one-hop neighbor information is needed. For the sake of description, we first assume that the link correlation between links within one-hop is known, and explain how to efficiently obtain the link correlation in Section 3.3.

## 3.2 Expected Transmission Count

In this section, we present the model by which a node assesses its cost to cover the one-hop neighbors in the presence of link correlation. With such assessments, we derive the relation between node cost and the link correlation, which provides an essential guideline for CorLayer design.

We assess the cost of a node' covering its neighbors using the expected transmission count $\epsilon(u)$, i.e., an expectation of how many transmissions $u$ needs to successfully transmit a packet to all its neighbors. The total cost of a reliable broadcast is thus $\xi = \sum \epsilon(u)$ where $u$ is a dominator.

From the theoretical analysis in Section 2.2, we know that to get $\epsilon(u)$ with two covered nodes, we need to compute $\binom{2}{1} + \binom{2}{2} = 3$ polynomial terms. Indeed, for more general cases of $M$ covered nodes, the computational complexity of $\epsilon(u)$ is on the order of obtaining all possible logical combinations, i.e., $2^M - 1$. Although in wireless networks, the number of covered nodes $M$ is relatively small, the exponential growth of complexity with $M$ shall be avoided when possible. In the following section, we present a novel approach to exploiting conditional probability in concurrent receptions to simplify the calculation.

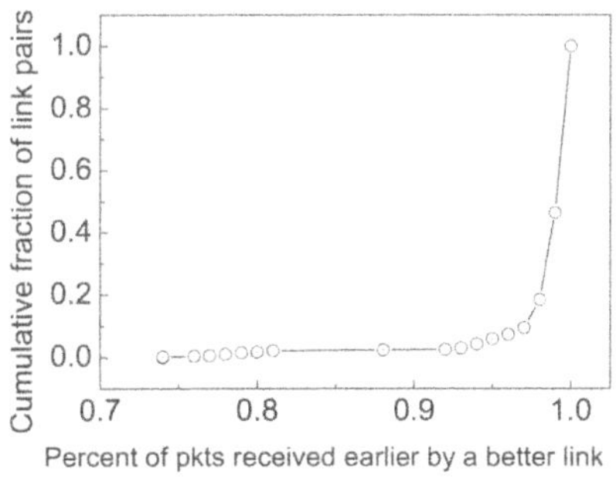


**Figure 6: Statistics of receiving probability. The node with a better link receives about 98% of the packets earlier or at the same time than the node with a worse link.**

## 3.3 Transmission Count Approximation

Concerning the cost of computing $\epsilon(u)$, we seek a more efficient algorithm to approximate $\epsilon(u)$ with lower computational complexity. It is noted that in wireless broadcast, the nodes with a higher link quality usually receive the broadcast packet before those with a lower link quality [41]. To further confirm this observation, we deploy 31 nodes near a sender $u$, which broadcasts a packet every 0.2s. The total number of packet broadcasts is 1000. The receivers keep the packet sequence number and time stamp. After collecting the packet reception trace, for each packet, we compare the reception between each link pair (there are $\binom{31}{2} = 465$ such pairs). Figure 6 shows that the node with a better link from $u$ receives about 98% of the packets earlier (or at the same time) than the node with a worse link from $u$.

Based on this observation, we propose a heuristic algorithm to approximate $\epsilon(u)$ denoted as $\hat{\epsilon}(u)$. For a given node $u$, we use $N(u)$ to denote $u$'s one-hop neighbor set and $|N(u)|$ is $u$'s out-degree. We define

DEFINITION 1. ***(Joint Packet Reception Probability)*** *Suppose $u$ is transmitting a packet to a nonempty neighbor set $K(u) \subset N(u)$. We define $u$'s Joint Packet Reception Probability (JPRP) as the probability that all the nodes in $K(u)$ successfully receive a packet, denoted as $p(K(u))$*

When $|K(u)| = 1$, i.e., $u$ has only one neighbor, JPRP equals to the quality of the link from $u$ to this neighbor. Without loss of generality, assume the link qualities of the $M$ covered nodes satisfy $p(e_1) \geq p(e_2) \geq \ldots \geq p(e_M)$, and the set of the first $m \leq M$ covered nodes is $K_m(u) = \{v_1, v_2, \ldots, v_m\}$.

DEFINITION 2. ***(Set Link Correlation)*** *Given a source node $u$, a non-empty neighbor set $K(u) \subset N(u)$ and a receiver $v$ that is not in set $K(u)$ (i.e., $v \in N(u) - K(u)$), the set link correlation $Pr(v|K(u))$ between $K(u)$ and $v$ is the conditional probability that $v$ successfully receives the packet under the condition that all the nodes in $K(u)$ receive the packet, i.e.,*

$$Pr(v|K(u)) = \frac{p(K(u) \cap v)}{p(K(u))}. \quad (2)$$

We note that our set link correlation more generically characterizes correlations among links. When $|K(u)| = 1$, the set link correlation reduces the traditional pair link correlation defined before [34, 41]. With these concepts, we are able to approximate the cost that a node delivers a message to its one-hop neighbors.

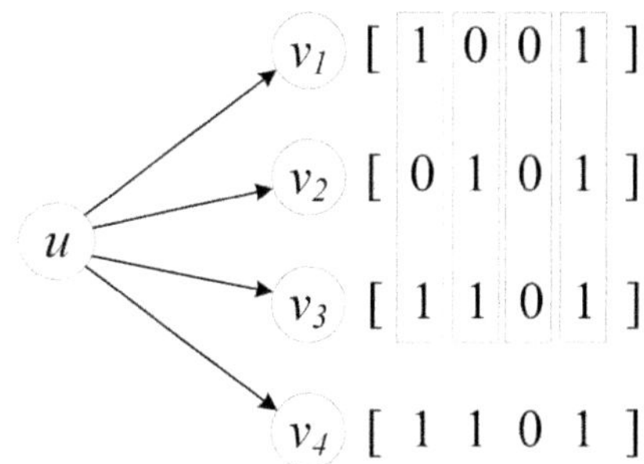


**Figure 7: Example of Calculating u's JPRP for $\{v_1, v_2, v_3\}$**

LEMMA 3.1. ***(Approximation of $\epsilon(u)$)*** *Assuming nodes with higher link quality receive the broadcast packet earlier than those with lower link quality, u's expected transmission count with $M$ covered nodes is approximated by*

$$\hat{\epsilon}(u) = \sum_{i=1}^{M} \frac{1}{p(e_i)} - \sum_{i=2}^{M} \frac{1}{p(e_i)} \cdot \frac{p(K_i(u))}{p(K_{i-1}(u))} \quad (3)$$

PROOF.

$$\begin{aligned}\hat{\epsilon}(u) &= \frac{1}{p(e_1)} + \frac{\Pr(\bar{e_2}|p(e_1))}{p(e_2)} + \ldots + \frac{\Pr(\bar{e_M}|\bigcap_{i=1}^{M-1} p(e_i))}{p(e_M)} \\ &= \frac{1}{p(e_1)} + \frac{p(K_1(u)) - p(K_2(u))}{p(e_1)\cdot p(e_2)} + \ldots \\ &\quad + \frac{p(K_{M-1}(u)) - p(K_M(u))}{p(K_{M-1}(u))p(e_M)} \\ &= \sum_{i=1}^{M} \frac{1}{p(e_i)} - \sum_{i=2}^{M} \frac{1}{p(e_i)} \cdot \frac{p(K_i(u))}{p(K_{i-1}(u))}\end{aligned}$$

□

**Special Case:** Note that Eq.(3) includes the special case that the links are independent. When links are all independent, we have

$$p(K_i(u)) = p(e_i) \cdot p(K_{i-1}(u))$$

And $\hat{\epsilon}(u)$ reduces to

$$\hat{\epsilon}(u) = \sum_{i=1}^{M} \frac{1}{p(e_i)} - M + 1. \quad (4)$$

THEOREM 3.2. *The higher the set link correlation, the smaller the expected number of transmissions $\hat{\epsilon}(u)$.*

PROOF. From Eq.(3), we find that the expected number of transmissions is composed of two parts: $\sum_{i=1}^{M} \frac{1}{p(e_i)}$ and $\sum_{i=2}^{M} \frac{1}{p(e_i)} \cdot \frac{p(K_i(u))}{p(K_{i-1}(u))}$. The first part is involved with the quality of each outgoing link and the second part is introduced by the link correlation. As the second part is always positive, the higher the set link correlation, the smaller the expected transmission count. □

**Implementation:** To calculate $\hat{\epsilon}(u)$, we need to get every link's quality $p(e)$ and $p(K_i(u))$ for $\forall i = 2, \ldots, M$. Suppose each node maintains a packet reception bitmap (e.g., [1001]) recording the reception status of a fixed number (e.g., 4) of most recent packets. The link quality is given simply by the number of 1s in the bitmap divided by the bitmap length. The calculation of JPRP deserves a little more explanation.

In our design, every node broadcasts a probe packet to its neighbors at an adaptive time interval, the length of which is adjusted based on the link's stability. Every probe message is identified by

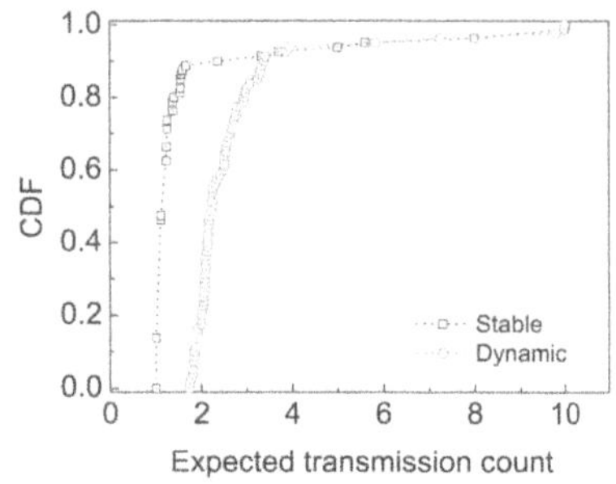


**Figure 8: CDF of the expected transmission count – $\epsilon$ in stable and dynamic scenarios.**

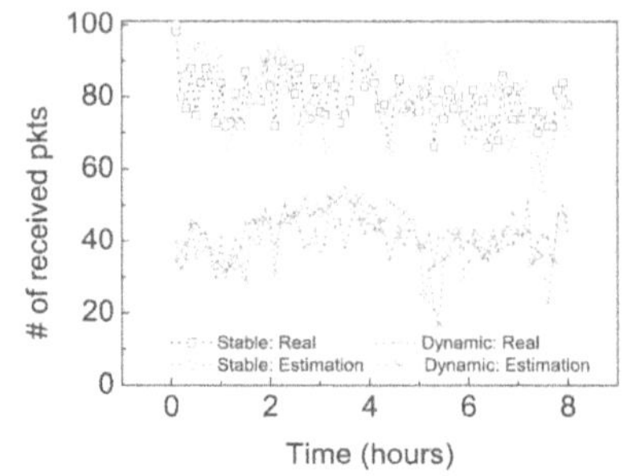


**Figure 9: Received pkts vs. Estimation**

the node ID and a packet sequence number. It is used not only for neighbor discovery, but also for updating the link quality and JPRP. Each node exchanges its reception bitmap with its neighbors. Assume the bitmap length is $W$, we have

$$p(K_i(u)) = \frac{1}{W}\sum_{k=1}^{W} B_{v_1}(k)\&B_{v_2}(k)\&\ldots\&B_{v_i}(k), \quad (5)$$

where $B_{v_i}(k)$ is a bit representing the neighbor $v_i$'s reception status of the $k$th probe packet. $B_{v_i}(k) = 1$ if node $B_{v_i}(k)$ receives the packet, otherwise $B_{v_i}(k) = 0$. For example, in Figure 7, node $u$ has 4 neighbors. We calculate $u$'s JPRP for $\{v_1, v_2, v_3\}$. Suppose the bitmap of node $v_1$ is [1001], which indicates that $v_1$ receives the 1st and 4th packets and misses the 2nd and 3rd packets. When node $u$ receives the bitmaps from all its neighbors, it can use Eq.(5) to calculate the corresponding JPRP $p(K_3(u)) = (1\&0\&1 + 0\&1\&1 + 0\&0\&0 + 1\&1\&1)/4 = 25\%$.

**Overhead under Link Dynamics:** In dynamic network environments, both link quality and set link correlation change over time. The nature question is that how much overhead is required to maintain these values fresh? To answer it, we conduct a set of experiments, in which the source node keeps broadcasting packets to ten receivers in every 3s while the probe packet is sent in every 32s. The main overhead of our design comes from two sources. First, we need to broadcast probe packets. The energy cost of this part is about 3.5% of the total energy in our setting. Note that periodically sending probe packets has been already required by other protocols [4, 14] to measure link quality or to improve the robustness of routing structure. We argue such cost is not introduced solely by our design, hence it should be amortized. Second, we need to exchange packet reception bitmaps among one-hop neighbors in order to calculate the values of set link correlation, which is exclusively introduced by our blacklisting algorithm. Fortunately, binary bitmaps are small and are much less frequently exchanged, therefore the overhead occupies a tiny fraction (0.9%) of the total energy cost according to our measurements.

**Estimation Accuracy under Link Dynamics:** We run our experiments under both stable and dynamic scenarios in a period of eight hours, during which probe packets (3.5% overhead) and bitmap exchange (0.9% overhead) are used to fresh link quality and correlation values. As shown in Figure 8 and 9, we maintain the estimation of expected number of transmission $\epsilon$ accurately over time. Specifically, Figure 8 shows the CDF of $\epsilon$, from which we can see that the metric $\epsilon$ is stable. Figure 9 shows the number of received packets (during a time period of 5 minutes) closely follows the number of sent packets (i.e., 100) divided by $\epsilon$.

## 3.4 The Process of Link Blacklisting

As mentioned before, the objective of link blacklisting is to increase link correlation among neighbors of a dominating node (say $u$) by disabling a subset of its links, so that we can statistically reduce the number of transmissions $\epsilon(u)$. To achieve this goal, we implement the design of link blacklisting as a transparent layer – CorLayer. There are two key steps in our design. One is a connectivity check: a network should not be partitioned because of blacklisting. The other is a blacklisting efficiency check: blacklisting should not increase the number of transmissions to cover neighbors via alternative paths. We explain how we address these two issues in Section 3.5 and Section 3.6.

## 3.5 Connectivity Check

Clearly, when blacklisting a link, CorLayer must not disconnect a network. Otherwise, the broadcast protocols running above CorLayer will not function correctly. Furthermore, we need to guarantee connectivity in a distributed fashion, in which a node needs only one-hop information and blacklist links asynchronously. Our design is simple yet effective. A link between node $u$ and $v$ can be blacklisted from the network only when at least a common neighbor (say $w$) of both $u$ and $v$ exists. In other words, eliminating a link requires the existence of an alternative path through at least a common neighbor. A similar idea has been used to guarantee connectivity when GPRS [20] constructs a reduced planar RNG graph.

Since blacklisting is performed asynchronously, we need to avoid a race condition. This is achieved by traditional two-phase locking. A node $u$ that attempts to blacklist a link $u \rightarrow v$ first sends a lock messages to both $v$ and their common neighbor $w$ to "lock" them, requiring that $v$ and $w$ cannot perform link blacklisting at the same time as $u$. Only when $u$ has received confirmation from both $v$ and $w$ can $u$ start to blacklist its link to $v$. If $u$ does not receive confirmation as expected or experiences a timeout (we assume a certain timeout period), $u$ gives up the blacklisting. In either case, $u$ will send a message to "unlock" $v$ and $w$. $v$ and $w$ also start a timer when receiving a "lock" message, and release the lock when they receive an unlock message or the timer expires (for fault-tolerate purpose). This lock/unlock mechanism is very lightweight as it involves only one-hop neighbors and requires maintaining little state information (lock/unlock state and a timer), and so incurs negligible overhead.

## 3.6 Efficient Link Blacklisting Rule

In addition to ensure network connectively, more importantly, we need to make sure network efficiency improves using the CorLayer. Specifically, blacklisting needs to ensure that all neighboring nodes of a dominating node $u$ can be covered with a *reduced* expected

| Protocol Name | Reference | Network Info. | Probe Msg | Broadcast Msg | Category |
|---|---|---|---|---|---|
| Spanning Tree (S-Tree) | [19] | One-hop | ID | Msg only | Tree-based |
| Cluster Tree (C-Tree) | [3] | Quazi-Global | Global | Msg only | Tree and Cluster-based |
| Forwarding Node Cluster (Cluster) | [40] | Local | ID | Covered set | Tree and Cluster-based |
| Intermediate | [39] | Two-hop/One-hop | One-hop/Position | Msg only | Cluster-based |
| Clustering | [36] | Quazi-Local | Degree | Msg only | Cluster-based |
| Passive Clustering (P-Clustering) | [23] | Two-hop | None | Msg + 2 bits | Cluster-based |
| Multi-Point Relay (MPR) | [32] | Two-hop | One-hop | Msg + Covered set | Multi-point relay |
| Mini-id MPR | [1] | Two-hop | One-hop | Msg only | Multi-point relay |
| MPR-CDS | [1] | Two-hop | One-hop | Msg only | Multi-point relay |
| Self Pruning (SP) | [26] | One-hop | One-hop | Msg + Covered set | Pruning-based |
| Dominating Pruning (DP) | [26] | Two-hop | One-hop | Msg + Covered set | Pruning-based |
| Pruning | [27] | Two-hop | One-hop | Msg + Covered set | Pruning-based |
| TDP | [27] | Two-hop | One-hop | Msg + Covered set | Pruning-based |
| RNG Relay Subset (RNG) | [18] | Two-hop | One-hop | Msg only | Pruning-based |
| Curved Convex Hull (CCH) | [38] | One-hop | One-hop + Position | Msg only | Location-based |
| CODEB | [25] | Two-hop | One-hop | Msg + Covered set | Pruning-based+NC |

**Table 2: Sixteen state-of-the-art protocols supported through CorLayer embedding**

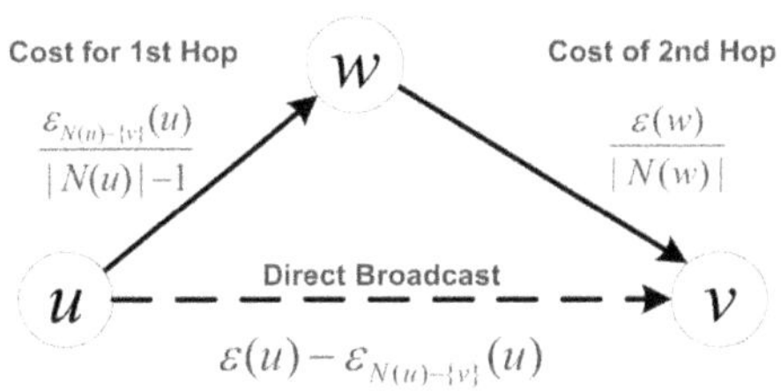


**Figure 10: Triangular Blacklist Rule**

number of transmissions after a link is blacklisted. As shown in Figure 10, the key idea is to blacklist a link from $u \to v$ if the source node $u$ could take fewer transmissions to broadcast a packet to $v$ via intermediate nodes (two-hop broadcast) than broadcasting the packet directly to $v$.

Let a link from the transmitter to the receiver be $u \to v$, and the common neighbor set of nodes $u$ and $v$ be $N(u, v)$. Recall that in the process of connectivity checking, our algorithm guarantees that there exists at least one common neighbor (say $w$) of $u$ and $v$, that is, $|N(u, v)| \geq 1$. Let $\epsilon_{N(u)-\{v\}}(u)$ be the expected number of transmissions for node $u$ to broadcast a packet to all of its neighbors except node $v$. The efficient blacklist rule for the link $u \to v$ is:

$$\epsilon(u) - \epsilon_{N(u)-\{v\}}(u) > \frac{\epsilon_{N(u)-\{v\}}(u)}{|N(u)|-1} + \frac{\epsilon(w)}{|N(w)|} \qquad (6)$$

The left-hand part of Eq.(6), $\epsilon(u) - \epsilon_{N(u)-\{v\}}(u)$, is the additional number of transmissions for node $u$ to cover node $v$ directly through broadcast, compared with covering only the neighbor set $N(u) - \{v\}$ (denoted as directed broadcast cost in Figure 10).

Intuitively, the link $u \to v$ is worth eliminating if node $u$ could take fewer transmissions to broadcast the packet to $v$ via the intermediate node $w$, a cost calculated by the right-hand part of the Eq.(6). Specifically, the right-hand part of the Eq.(6) is the sum of per-link two-hop broadcast: (i) $\frac{\epsilon_{N(u)-\{v\}}(u)}{|N(u)|-1}$ is the per-link cost for the first-hop broadcast between $u$ and $w$, after the link $u \to v$ has been blacklisted (Note $|N(u)| - 1$ is the size of node $u$'s neighbor set without considering node $v$). (ii) $\frac{\epsilon(w)}{|N(w)|}$ represents the per-link cost for the second hop broadcast between $w$ and $v$. These two costs are shown in Figure 10 as "cost for 1st hop" and "cost for 2nd hop".

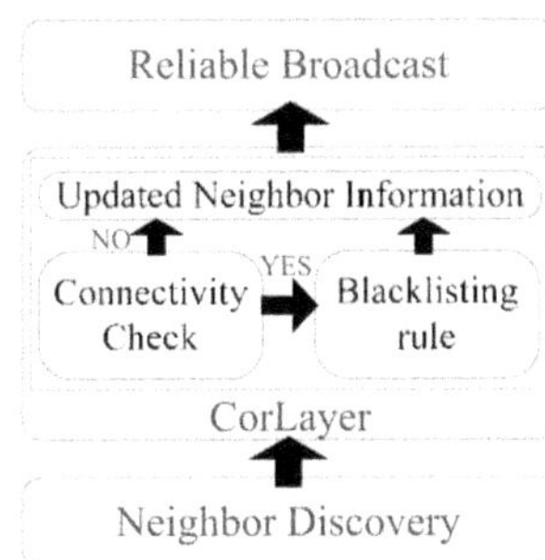


**Figure 11: CorLayer in the protocol stack**

In summary, Eq.6 presents a *Triangular Blacklist Rule* shown in Figure 10: When it takes fewer transmissions to deliver a packet via alternative two-hop broadcast paths than broadcasting the packet to $v$ directly, we blacklist the link. We note that more aggressive blacklist rules could be tailored for particular broadcast designs; our design conservatively eliminates links that are clearly detrimental to broadcast performance. Such a general design ensures that CorLayer, as a middleware, can improve a wide range of broadcast protocols.

We note when $|N(u, v)| > 1$, multiple alternative paths exist. In this case, we shall model the average cost of these alternative paths among $|N(u, v)|$ paths. Accordingly Eq.6 shall be revised to a more generic one, which is used in our final design.

$$\epsilon(u) - \epsilon_{N(u)-\{v\}}(u) > \frac{\sum \frac{\epsilon_{N(u)-\{v\}}(u)}{|N(u)|-1} + \frac{\epsilon(w_i)}{|N(w_i)|}}{|N(u, v)|} \qquad (7)$$

## 3.7 CorLayer Embedding

CorLayer is designed as a generic middleware to assist a wide range of broadcast protocols and be compatible with other energy efficient MAC layers such as low power listening (LPL) [31]. To do that, we insert CorLayer beneath the broadcast protocol and above the MAC layer. As shown in Figure 11, CorLayer provides a reduced topology to the upper layer broadcast protocols in a transparent manner.

We classify the existing reliable broadcast algorithms into tree-based [9, 19], cluster-based [3, 23, 36, 39, 40], multi-point relays [1, 8, 32], pruning-based [18, 26, 27], and location based [38]. Recently, network coding (NC) has been adapted to support broadcast appli-

(a) Testbed in UMN

(b) Testbed in SIAT

(c) Testbed in TRIMPS

**Figure 12: Testbed experiment**

| Platform | Location | Environment | Nodes/APs |
|---|---|---|---|
| MICAz | UMN | Lab | 36/5 |
| TelosB | SIAT | Office | 30/8 |
| GreenOrbs | TRIMPS | Outdoor | 20/0 |
| Physical Size | Degree | Channel | Power |
| $8m \times 2.5m$ | $7 \sim 23$ | Ch16 | -25dBm |
| $18m \times$ 13m | $6 \sim 21$ | Ch16, Ch26 | -25dBm |
| $15m \times 5m$ | $4 \sim 13$ | Ch16 | -25, -19.2dBm |

**Table 3: Testbed settings and topology properties**

cations in wireless networks, e.g., COPE [21] and CODEB [25]. CorLayer also supports these network coding schemes and helps them save transmissions. Besides, in low-duty-cycle networks, a common wake-up time unit is assigned to nodes sharing common senders. CorLayer may improve the energy efficiency of low-duty-cycle protocols by helping them form clusters with higher correlation thus the nodes in the same cluster receive broadcasting packets simultaneously. Thus far, we have successfully implemented sixteen classical algorithms and embedded CorLayer with them. The basic information of these protocols is shown in Table 2.

# 4. TESTBED EXPERIMENTATION

Packet reception patterns vary significantly across network environments, as they are affected by environmental noise and external interference. We evaluate CorLayer on three testbeds, whose basic information is shown in Table 3. The first testbed is in a dedicated lab environment, in which a total of 36 MICAz nodes are randomly deployed on a $8m \times 2.5m$ wall, as shown in Figure 12(a). The second testbed consists of 30 TelosB nodes deployed in an $18m \times 13m$ open office environment following a grid pattern; see Figure 12(b). The third testbed is an outdoor environment (Figure 12(c)), in which 20 GreenOrbs nodes were deployed on the grass-covered curb along a river.

In all three testbeds, the default transmission power is set at -25dBm so that the nodes form multi-hop networks. The default channel is 16. After deployment all nodes are synchronized and start the neighbor discovery by sending out probe packets, based on which we get the link quality and set link correlation information about their one-hop neighbors. For broadcast without blacklisting, two nodes are considered as neighbors when the link quality between them is greater than 0.2. With CorLayer, it updates the one-hop neighbor information based on the Link Blacklist Rule (in Section 3.6). Based on the one-hop neighbor information, forwarders and their corresponding covered nodes are determined by using sixteen existing reliable broadcast protocols. In the experiment, each protocol sends out 20 data packets with a time interval of 2 seconds. For performance analysis purposes, each packet includes information – time stamp, hop count, and previous hop's node ID. Upon receiving the data packets, the intermediate node records the number of transmissions for each data packet.

## 4.1 Performance Metrics

We use the total number of transmissions needed to deliver one packet to all the nodes in the network as the metric for evaluating the energy efficiency of a broadcast protocol either with or without CorLayer. Furthermore, energy gain is defined as the percentage of saved transmissions.

## 4.2 Main Performance Results

The experimental results of the sixteen classical reliable broadcast protocols are shown in Figure 13. The upper parts of the bars (in gray) represent the proportion of transmissions reduced by our blacklisting method. For example, for the MPR algorithm, the nodes need 21.1 transmissions on average to guarantee that every node in the network receives one packet, while the number is 7.6 after blacklisting, achieving a reduction of 64%. The average transmission of different protocols before and after blacklisting is 17.8 and 9.4, respectively. Compared with the schemes without using network coding, CODEB saves 41.2% transmissions. Our design makes a further 39.3% improvement upon CODEB. On average, our blacklist design reduces transmissions by 47.2%. The reason why our design has better performance is as follows: Low link correlation may cause the nodes in a cluster losing different packets. The source node of a lower correlated cluster needs to retransmit more packets. By blacklisting those low correlated links, the upper layer broadcast protocols automatically avoid using them, thereby forming clusters with high correlation. Besides, in high correlated clusters, a transmission can recover the lost packet for multiple receivers.

Although we have collected results for all the sixteen protocols, space constraints do not allow presenting all of them here. Therefore, we choose four representative broadcast algorithms, namely Multi-Point Relay [32] (MPR for short), Forwarder Node Cluster [40] (Cluster for short), Partial Dominating Pruning [27] (Pruning for short), and CODE-B [25] for the rest of the experiments.

## 4.3 Impact of Blacklisting Rules

In this section, we consider alternative link blacklisting rules, including random blacklisting ("R_B" for short), worst link blacklisting ("WL_B"), AVG blacklisting ("AVG_B"), MIN blacklisting ("MIN_B"), and MAX blacklisting ("MAX_B"); see Table 4 for a

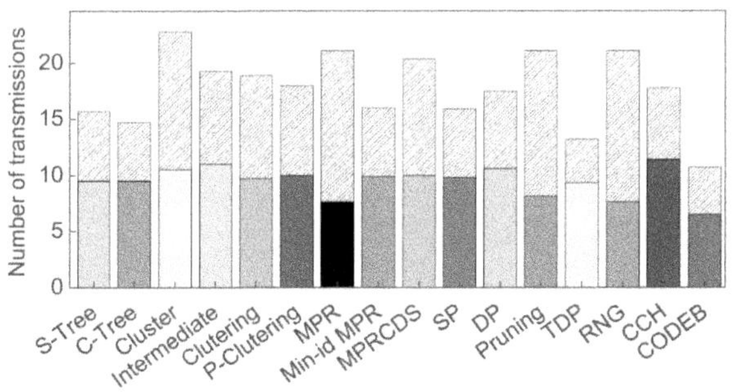

Figure 13: Improvements over 16 protocols

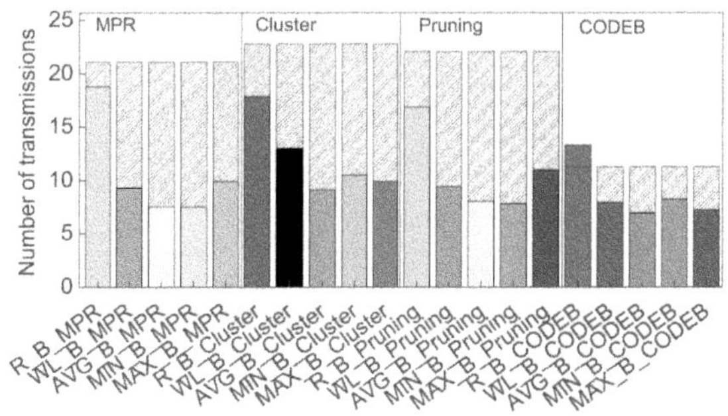

Figure 14: Impact of blacklist rules

| Method | Blacklist Rule |
|---|---|
| Random Blacklist (R_B) | Each node blacklists $x\%$ of links ($x = 10$ in our experiment). |
| Worst Link Blacklist (WL_B) | Each node blacklists the worst $x\%$ of links ($x = 10$ in our experiment). |
| AVG Blacklist (AVG_B) | Our design, please refer to Eq.(7). |
| MIN Blacklist (MIN_B) | A link is blacklisted when there exists one alternative path with lower cost. |
| MAX Blacklist (MAX_B) | A link is blacklisted when its broadcast cost is higher than all alternative paths. |

Table 4: Different link blacklisting strategies.

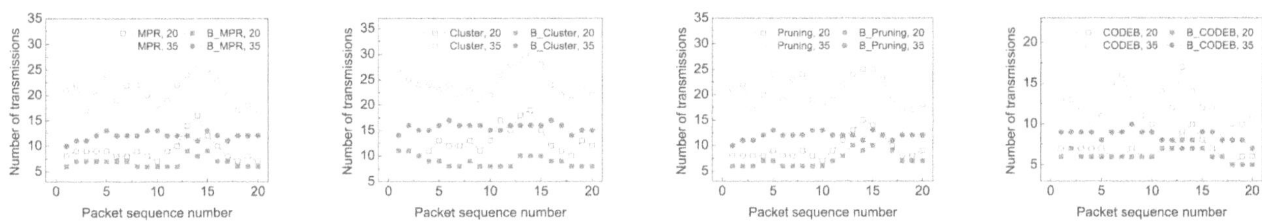

(a) Multi-point relays (b) Cluster based broadcast (c) Pruning based broadcast (d) Network coding

Figure 15: Impact of network sizes

brief description. We shall use "link blacklisting strategy_broadcast algorithm name" to represent a specified algorithm configuration. For example, WL_B_MPR means MPR with the worst link blacklisting strategy.

Figure 14 shows the energy consumption of the four broadcast strategies with the five different blacklisting rules. On average, our design reduces the number of packet transmissions by 55.8%. The "MIN blacklisting" rule blacklists links when there exists an alternative path with a lower broadcast cost. This rule may blacklist too many links, and it is possible that the upper layer broadcast protocols do not select low-cost paths. For example, the energy consumption of "MIN blacklisting" with the pruning algorithm is 7.8, which is lower than that of our design. Yet, in the cluster algorithm, the energy consumption of "MIN blacklisting" is 10.5, while our design has an energy consumption of 9.1. The "MAX blacklisting" rule blacklists links when the broadcast cost of the link is greater than all the alternative paths. This rule guarantees that the upper layer protocols can always obtain energy gain from the blacklist strategy. It is too conservative, however, to obtain a further energy gain – many black sheep (the high cost broadcast links) failed to be blacklisted. From Figure 14, we see that the average energy gain of the "MAX blacklisting" rule is 48.9%. The worst link blacklisting produces an average energy gain of 45.7%. This strategy, however, faces two problems: (i) a threshold is required to blacklist $x\%$ of the worst links, but the threshold usually depends on the network environment, and (ii) it may remove some good quality links since it always blacklists $x\%$ worst links, which may well contain a good quality link. For the removed neighbors, there may exist no alternative paths with a lower message cost, so the removal can only reduce energy efficiency. The random blacklisting algorithm is a blind method, with an energy gain of only 18.6%. The negative effect of random blacklisting is understandable since some high-quality links may be removed.

## 4.4 Impact of Network Size

In this experiment, we use the data from the testbed in UMN. Figure 15 shows the total number of packets transmitted for each packet with 20 and 35 MICAz nodes. In the figure, the protocol $x$ using blacklisting is labeled "$B\_x$". It can be seen that without link blacklisting, the transmission count ranges from 5 to 30, while with link blacklisting, it ranges from 5 to 17. On average, our design obtains an energy gain of 31.3%. From Figure 15, we can also see that the trend of energy gain with increasing network sizes is quite stable, suggesting that our design scales well with large networks.

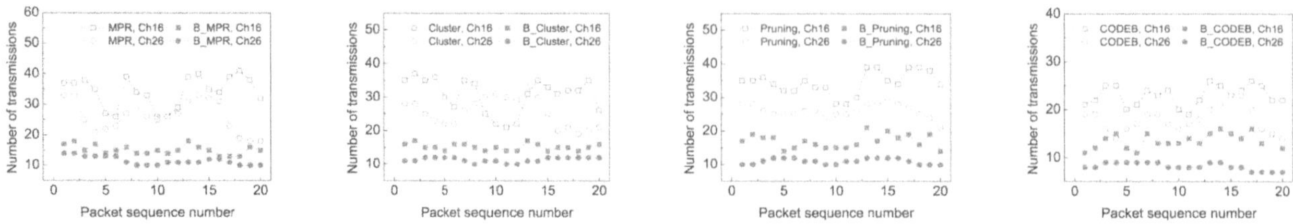


(a) Multi-point relays (b) Cluster based broadcast (c) Pruning based broadcast (d) Network coding

**Figure 16: Impact of channels**

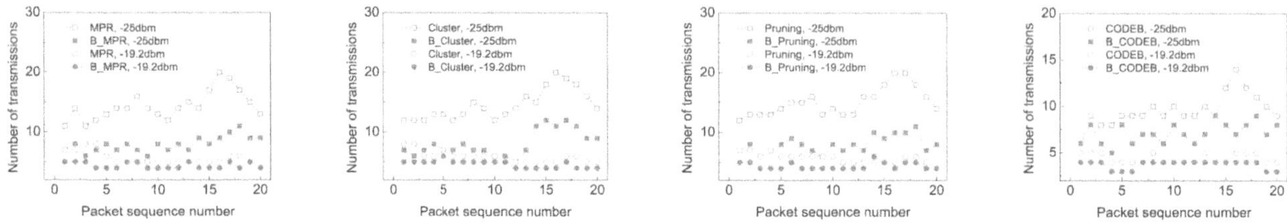


(a) Multi-point relays (b) Cluster based broadcast (c) Pruning based broadcast (d) Network coding

**Figure 17: Impact of power levels**

## 4.5 Impact of Different Channels

In this experiment, we explore the impact of channels on our design. We use the data from the testbed in SIAT that is in an open office environment that includes total of 8 access points. Note that channel 16 overlaps with a co-habiting access point's 802.11 channel and that channel 26 is free of Wi-Fi interference. We ran the experiments during normal office time. The power level for transmission is set to -25dBm. Figure 16 shows the energy consumption of the eight broadcast strategies for networks using two different channels – channels 16 and 26. From Figure 16, we can see that the broadcast protocols need more transmissions to finish the same task in channel 16. This is because the overlapped channel causes more packet losses. Besides, we find that the average gain of our design under the four broadcast algorithms is 56% using channel 26, and 50% using channel 16. This result shows that our design performs better using channel 26, the interference-free channel, because the interference of Wi-Fi signals makes the transmissions using channel 16 better correlated, a phenomenon consistent with the observation by Srinivasan et al. [34]. The better correlation thus leaves us less room to improve the energy efficiency since the gain relies on the improvement of link correlation.

## 4.6 Impact of Power Level

We conducted this experiment in an outdoor scenario where we can control the range among nodes freely; see Figure 12(c). The power level for transmission is set from -25dBm to -19.2dBm to form a multi-hop network. Figure 17 shows the transmissions of the four broadcast algorithms with and without link blacklisting for networks with different power levels. Again, we find that the link blacklisting greatly reduces transmissions for reliable broadcasting. Here we use the pruning algorithm as an example, although similar results have been observed with the other three algorithms. Under power level -25dBm, the transmission count for the pruning algorithm is 13.4 on average, while it is 7.8 after link blacklisting, providing a reduction of 42%. Under power level -19.2dBm, fewer transmissions are needed for broadcasting because a higher power level leads to better link quality. In this case, our link blacklisting layer still reduces transmissions by 20.1%.

# 5. SIMULATION EVALUATION

Adjusting the power level actually affects two things: link quality and network density (average node degree). Because both factors cannot be set directly on the testbed, we use simulations to study the performance trend. The following simulation results are the average values of 100 rounds over the same network settings.

## 5.1 Impact of Link Quality

First, let us consider the energy gain of the four link blacklisting strategies for networks with different link qualities. Since it is impossible to simply set a quality for each link on the testbed, it is necessary to vary link quality in a controlled way and look at each strategy's performance in different cases. In the experiment, we first collect the packet reception trace from the testbed (a 20-node scenario). Then, we introduce losses to each receiver using a link correlation packet loss model [28] that makes the one-hop receivers drop packets in a link correlated way with a controlled loss rate. The results are shown in Figure 18, where we can see that the transmission of our design varies from 19.8 to 2.8 when the average link quality varies from 0.31 to 0.95. The Cluster algorithm without link blacklisting, for example, needs 47.5 transmissions to finish the broadcast task when the average link quality is 0.31. Under the same condition, our design saves 58% of transmissions in this poor link quality scenario. For an increased average link quality of 0.95, our energy gain reduces to 25%, suggesting that the energy gain of our design decreases as link quality increases.

## 5.2 Impact of Network Density

In this experiment, we consider both uniform and non-uniform node distribution. The network size is 64, and the field size is $800m \times 800m$ with a communication range of 160m. The average link quality is about 0.5. Figures 19 shows the transmission counts of the eight broadcast strategies for networks with different

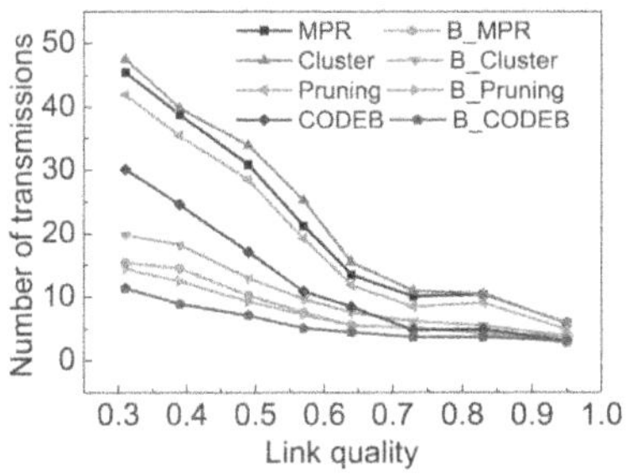


**Figure 18: Impact of ink qualities**

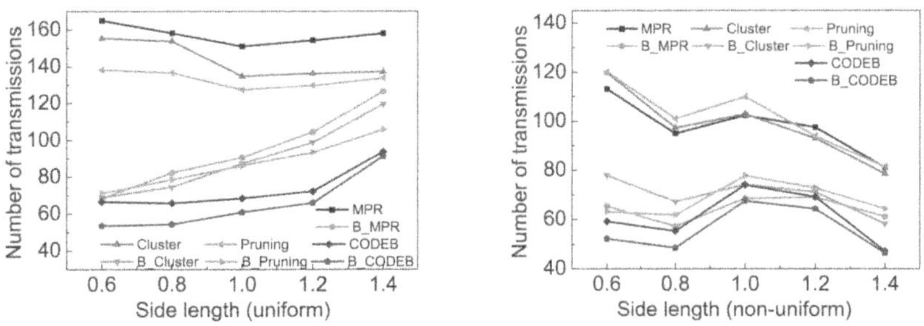


**Figure 19: Impact of densities**

densities. The average node degrees for side lengths (of the simulated square sensing field) 0.6, 0.8, 1, 1.2, 1.4 are, respectively, 20.2, 13.0, 8.4, 5.9, and 3.9. From Figures 19, we can see that with variation in density, the transmission count does *not* change monotonically. This is because with the increase of network density, a forwarder needs more transmissions to make sure all its covered nodes receive the packet, but the number of forwarders decreases in a fixed size (i.e., 64) network. In Figures 19, the energy gain of our design decreases as the side length increases (and thus the density decreases). For example, in uniform case, the energy gain of our design under the MPR algorithm is 58.6% at an average node degree of 20.2, and it drops to 19.9% when the average node degree is only 3.9. As the network becomes denser, a forwarder tends to cover more nodes. This increases the possibility that links with poor link correlations are put into the same cluster, thus giving our algorithm more opportunities to improve the link correlation within the cluster. This explains the increasing energy gain when the node density grows.

# 6. STATE OF THE ART

Our design leverages a recently discovered phenomenon, link correlation, to improve the performance of reliable broadcasting. In the following, we briefly review related work.

As a primitive of wireless network communications, broadcasting has been extensively studied in the literature. A major problem in broadcast is that many intermediate nodes unnecessarily forward a message. Nodes often hear the same packet multiple times. This is known as the *broadcast storm* problem [30]. The existing methods that address this problem can be divided into two categories: probabilistic and deterministic [37]. In probabilistic methods [15, 35], each node rebroadcasts the packet to its neighbors with a given forwarding probability. The deterministic approaches predetermine a set of forwarders to relay the broadcast packet. In this paper, we design CorLayer for deterministic protocols. Generally, deterministic reliable broadcast algorithms can be classified into five types, namely tree-based, cluster-based, multi-point relays, pruning-based, or location-based.

• **Tree-based:** In [19], the authors present a fully distributed, online, and asynchronous method to maintain a spanning tree, along which the broadcast is performed. Ding et al. [9] present a tree-based reliable broadcast for IEEE 802.15.4 and ZigBee networks.
• **Cluster-based:** The authors in [3] construct a CDS using a cluster tree method. They first apply a distributed leader election algorithm to construct a rooted spanning tree. Then a maximum independent set (MIS) is calculated based on the tree level. The nodes in the MIS are then spanned by a *dominating tree*. Wu and Li [39] introduce the concept of intermediate node to calculate a CDS for reliable broadcast.
• **Multi-Point Relays:** In MPR [32], the set of relays is an optimal subset of a node's direct neighbors whose collective neighborhood entirely covers the node's two-hop neighbors. The authors in [1] propose two modified MPR algorithms, named Min-id MPR and MPR CDS, which compute multi-point relays without using the last-hop knowledge.
• **Pruning-based:** In [26], the authors propose two algorithms called self-pruning (SP) and dominant pruning (DP), using one-hop and two-hop neighbor information, respectively, to reduce redundant transmissions. Based on [26], Lou et al. further propose two extended algorithms: total dominating pruning (TDP) and partial dominant pruning (PDP) [27], which generate a smaller relay node set than the DP and SP algorithms do.
• **Location-based:** The authors in [38] propose a location based broadcast algorithm by calculating the curved convex hull.
• **Network coding:** On top of all these protocols, network coding schemes such as COPE [21] and CODEB [25] can deduce the broadcast transmission by retransmitting several lost packets with one coded packet.

Previous studies on wireless links focus on packet receptions of individual receivers [4, 29]. The phenomenon of link correlation has recently been experimentally studied in [33, 41]. Zhu et al. [41] propose a probabilistic flooding algorithm to reduce energy consumption in transmission by using implicit ACKs inferred from link correlation. In [34], the authors explore a metric called $\kappa$ that captures the degree of packet reception correlation on different links. The $\kappa$ value of a network can be used to help network designers decide which protocol should be used for the network. As a generic correlation-aware middleware, our work is different from the aforementioned works.

# 7. CONCLUSION

We have presented CorLayer, a link correlation-based layer that enhances the energy efficiency of reliable broadcasting. This layer blacklists links with low correlation by following a triangular blacklisting rule, using only one-hop information. It is transparent to upper layer broadcast protocols, which can obtain significant gains without modifications. To test CorLayer's broad applicability and effectiveness, we integrated CorLayer transparently with sixteen state-of-the-art broadcast algorithms and evaluated the design on three real-world multi-hop testbeds: a network with 36 MICAz nodes, a network with 30 TelosB nodes, and a network with 20 GreenOrbs nodes. The results indicate that with CorLayer, reliable broadcast avoids unnecessary transmissions caused by wireless links that are less positively correlated.

## 8. ACKNOWLEDGMENTS

This work was supported in part by National Science Foundation grants CNS-0917097. We also received partial support from McKnight Land-Grant Professorship. We thank our shepherd Dr. Prabal Dutta and the reviewers for their valuable comments.

## 9. REFERENCES


[1] C. Adjih, P. Jacquet, and L. Viennot. Computing connected dominated sets with multipoint relays. In *Technical Report 4597, INRIA-Rapport de recherche*, October 2002.

[2] R. Ahlswede, N. Cai, S.-Y. Li, and R. Yeung. Network information flow. *IEEE Transactions on Information Theory*, 2000.

[3] K. Alzoubi, P. Wan, and O. Frieder. New distributed algorithm for connected dominating set in wireless ad hoc networks. In *Hawaii Int. Conf. System Sciences*, 2002.

[4] N. Baccour, A. Koubaa, L. Mottola, M. Zuniga, H. Youssef, C. Boano, and M. Alves. Radio link quality estimation in wireless sensor networks: a survey. *ACM TOSN*, 2012.

[5] S. Biswas and R. Morris. Exor: Opportunistic multi-hop routing for wireless networks. In *SIGCOMM*, 2005.

[6] Q. Cao, T. Abdelzaher, T. He, and R. Kravets. Cluster-based forwarding for reliable end-to-end delivery in wireless sensor networks. In *INFOCOM*, 2007.

[7] S. Chachulski, M. Jennings, S. Katti, and D. Katabi. Trading structure for randomness in wireless opportunistic routing. In *SIGCOMM*, 2007.

[8] T. Clausen, C. Dearlove, and P. Jacquet. The optimized link state routing protocol version 2. In *MANET Working Group*, 2008.

[9] G. Ding, Z. Sahinoglu, P. Orlik, J. Zhang, and B. Bhargava. Tree-based data broadcast in ieee 802.15.4 and zigbee networks. *IEEE Transactions on Mobile Computing*, 2006.

[10] J. Du, H. Liu, and P. Chen. Omr: An opportunistic multi-path reliable routing protocol in wireless sensor networks. In *ICPPW*, 2007.

[11] J. Eriksson, H. Balakrishnan, and S. Madden. Cabernet: vehicular content delivery using wifi. In *MOBICOM*, 2008.

[12] A. Forster and A. Murphy. Froms: A failure tolerant and mobility enabled multicast routing paradigm with reinforcement learning for wsns. *Elsevier Ad Hoc Networks*, 2011.

[13] D. Ganesan, R. Govindan, S. Shenker, and D. Estrin. Highly-resilient, energy-efficient multipath routing in wireless sensor networks. *SIGMOBILE*, 5, 2001.

[14] O. Gnawali, R. Fonseca, K. Jamieson, D. Moss, and P. Levis. Collection tree protocol. In *SENSYS*, 2009.

[15] Z. Haas, J. Halpern, and L. Li. Gossip-based ad hoc routing. In *INFOCOM*, 2002.

[16] Q. Huang, C. Lu, and G. C. Roman. Spatiotemporal multicast in sensor networks. In *SENSYS*, 2003.

[17] J. Hui and D. Culler. The dynamic behavior of a data dissemination protocol for network programming at scale. In *SENSYS*, 2004.

[18] J.Cartigny, F. Ingelrest, and D. Simplot. Rng relay subset flooding protocols in mobile ad hoc networks. *International Journal of Foundations of Computer Science*, 2003.

[19] A. Juttner and A. Magi. Tree based broadcast in ad hoc networks. *Mobile Networks and Applications*, 10(5), 2005.

[20] B. Karp and H. T. Kung. Gpsr: greedy perimeter stateless routing for wireless networks. In *MOBICOM*, 2000.

[21] S. Katti, H. Rahul, W. Hu, D. Katabi, M. Medard, and J. Crowcroft. Xors in the air: Practical wireless network coding. *IEEE/ACM Transactions on Networking*, 2008.

[22] S. Kulkarni and L. Wang. Mnp: Multihop network reprogramming service for sensor networks. In *ICDCS*, 2005.

[23] T. J. Kwon and M. Gerla. Efficient flooding with passive clustering (pc) in ad hoc networks. In *SIGCOMM Computer Communication Review*, January 2002.

[24] S. J. Lee, W. Su, and M. Gerla. On-demand multicast routing protocol in multihop wireless mobile networks. In *ACM/Kluwer MONET*, 2002.

[25] E. L. Li, R. Ramjee, M. M. Buddhikot, and S. C. Miller. Network coding-based broadcast in mobile ad-hoc networks. In *Proceedings of IEEE INFOCOM*, 2007.

[26] H. Lim and C. Kim. Flooding in wireless ad hoc networks. In *Computer Communications Journal*, 2001.

[27] W. Lou and J. Wu. On reducing broadcast redundancy in ad hoc wireless networks. *IEEE Transactions on Mobile Computing*, 2002.

[28] J. Macke, P. Berens, A. Ecker, A. Tolias, and M. Bethge. Generating spike trains with specified correlation coefficients. *Neural Computation*, 2009.

[29] E. Miluzzo, X. Zheng, K. Fodor, and A. T. Campbell. Radio characterization of 802.15.4 and its impact on the design of mobile sensor networks. In *EWSN*, 2008.

[30] S. Ni, Y. T. Y. Chen, and J. Sheu. The broadcast storm problem in a mobile ad hoc network. In *MOBICOM*, 1999.

[31] J. Polastre, J. Hill, and D. Culler. Versatile low power media access for wireless sensor networks. In *SENSYS*, 2004.

[32] A. Qayyum, L. Viennot, and A. Laouiti. Multipoint relaying for flooding broadcast messages in mobile wireless networks. In *HICSS*, 2002.

[33] K. Srinivasan, P. Dutta, A. Tavakoli, and P. Levis. An empirical study of low power wireless. In *SING Technical Report*, 2008.

[34] K. Srinivasan, M. Jain, J. I. Choi, T. Azim, E. S. Kim, P. Levis, and B. Krishnamachari. The $\kappa$-factor: Inferring protocol performance using inter-link reception correlation. In *MOBICOM*, 2010.

[35] F. Stann, J. Heidemann, R. Shroff, and M. Z. Murtaza. Rbp: Robust broadcast propagation in wireless networks. In *SENSYS*, 2006.

[36] I. Stojmenovic, M. Seddigh, and J. Zunic. Dominating sets and neighbor elimination based broadcasting algorithms in wireless networks. *IEEE TPDS*, 2002.

[37] I. Stojmenovic and J. Wu. Broadcasting and activity scheduling in ad hoc networks. *Mobile Ad Hoc Networking*, 2004.

[38] M. T. Sun, X. Ma, C. Y. Yi, C. K. Yang, and T. H. Lai. Computing optimal local cover set for broadcasting in ad hoc networks. *Computer Science - Networking and Mobile Computing*, 2005.

[39] J. Wu and H. Li. A dominating set based routing scheme in ad hoc wireless networks. *Telecommunication Systems*, 2001.

[40] J. Wu and W. Lou. Forward-node-set-based broadcast in clustered mobile ad hoc networks. In *Wireless Communication and Mobile Computing*, 2003.

[41] T. Zhu, Z. Zhong, T. He, and Z.-L. Zhang. Exploring link correlation for efficient flooding in wireless sensor networks. In *NSDI*, 2010.

# Coordinating Cellular Background Transfers using LoadSense

Abhijnan Chakraborty, Vishnu Navda,
Venkata N. Padmanabhan, Ramachandran Ramjee
Microsoft Research India

## ABSTRACT

To minimize battery drain due to background communication in cellular-connected devices such as smartphones, the duration for which the cellular radio is kept active should be minimized. This, in turn, calls for scheduling the background communication so as to maximize the throughput. It has been recognized in prior work that a key determinant of throughput is the wireless link quality. However, as we show here, another key factor is the load in the cell, arising from the communication of other nodes. Unlike link quality, the only way, thus far, for a cellular client to obtain a measure of load has been to perform active probing, which defeats the goal of minimizing the active duration of the radio.

In this paper, we address the above dilemma by making the following contributions. First, we show experimentally that to obtain good throughput, considering link quality alone is insufficient, and that cellular load must also be factored in. Second, we present a novel technique called *LoadSense* for a cellular client to obtain a measure of the cellular load, locally and passively, that allows the client to determine the ideal times for communication when available throughput to the client is likely to be high. Finally, we present the *Peek-n-Sneak* protocol, which enables a cellular client to "peek" into the channel and "sneak" in with its background communication when the conditions are suitable. When multiple clients in a cell perform Peen-n-Sneak, it enables them to coordinate their communications, implicitly and in an entirely distributed manner, akin to CSMA in wireless LANs, helping improve throughput (and reduce energy drain) for all. Our experimental evaluation shows overall device energy savings of 20-60% even when Peek-n-Sneak is deployed incrementally.

## Categories and Subject Descriptors

C.2.1 [**Computer Communications Networks**]: Network Architecture and Design—*Wireless communication*; C.4 [**Performance of Systems**]: Design Studies, Performance Attributes

## General Terms

Algorithms, Design, Measurement, Experimentation, Performance


*MobiCom'13,* September 30–October 4, Miami, FL, USA.

http://dx.doi.org/10.1145/2500423.2500447 .

## Keywords

Cellular, Load, 3G, LTE, 4G, Energy Saving, Background Transfers

## 1. INTRODUCTION

Background communication on cellular devices such as smartphones has been growing in importance [5], due to applications such as social networking and software updates. Users want gratification (e.g., the Facebook photos posted by a friend) sooner rather than later, and are typically unwilling to accept a long delay, e.g., several hours. Also, despite its prevalence, WiFi is often not usable, because of sign-in or payment requirements, vehicular mobility, etc. So the cellular link becomes the only means of communication in many situation.

However, the battery drain due to background cellular communication has been a matter of concern. Indeed, there has been much research on quantifying the energy costs, both due to transmission and reception [15] and signaling-induced radio-tail periods [14]. For these reasons, many mobile platforms (e.g., Apple iOS, Microsoft Windows Phone) restrict background communication.

Battery drain due to communication is lower when the throughput is higher, because the cellular radio remains in the active state (DCH state in 3G parlance) for a shorter duration. A key determinant of throughput is the link quality, which is quantified by the strength of the base station's pilot signal, as recorded at the receiver. Prior work on energy-efficient scheduling [15] has suggested preferentially communicating while the link quality is good.

However, link quality does not yield the full picture. *As our first contribution, we show experimentally that cellular load also matters.* The load is caused by the communication of other clients in the cell and also interference due to the neighboring cells (the latter in cell-edge locations), and fluctuates over time scales of several seconds, even when a client is stationary. The higher the load, the more the channel resources get divided, and so the lower the throughput obtained by any one client.

In view of the above, we would ideally want to schedule background communication by factoring in the load as well as the link quality. However, unlike the link quality, which can be measured passively by a cellular client, estimating load has hitherto required active measurements such as a trial download or packet-pair probes. This is because the closed nature of the cellular network does not allow a client to listen in on the communication of other clients, and the network does not share load information with the clients. However, active measurements defeat the goal of saving energy since even a single-packet probe would cause the radio to remain in a high-energy state for several seconds, even with optimization such as fast dormancy [14].

*Our second contribution is a novel technique called LoadSense that allows a client to obtain a measure of cellular load, locally and passively*, i.e., while keeping the radio in the idle state. LoadSense is based on sensing the total power in the cellular channel and comparing it with the power of the pilot signal transmitted by the base station. We compute the ratio of the pilot power to the total power as the power ratio. When the cellular load is nil, the total power would equal the pilot power, so the power ratio would be 0dB. However, in the presence of load due to other clients, the total power would be greater than the pilot power, since the measurement interval would span both the pilot phase and the subsequent communication with other clients in the cell. So the power ratio would be lower, as low as -10dB when the full power of a fully-loaded channel is used, assuming typical allocation of 10% of total power to the pilot channel. In practice, the power ratio could be even lower because of inter-cell interference at cell-edge locations.

We show experimentally that, while extreme values of link quality and the power ratio can, individually, help predict low or high throughput, there is a wide range in the middle where neither metric, by itself, enables accurate prediction. Therefore, LoadSense uses a support vector machine generated classifier that works with a set of readily-available features, including link quality, power ratio, and the observed variation in the power ratio, to make a binary prediction of the availability of low or high throughput for the cellular client. We show that our classifier is efficient to compute on the client, utilizes only three seconds of passive measurements to make its prediction and achieves accuracy levels of 80-90% across a range of network conditions and operators.

Armed with the above, we present *our final contribution — the Peek-n-Sneak protocol — which allows cellular clients to "peek" into the channel cheaply and "sneak" in with their communication when the conditions are suitable*, i.e., when high throughput is predicted. Peek-n-Sneak is *incrementally deployable*, i.e., beneficial even to a single client that uses it. Furthermore, with wider adoption, *Peek-n-Sneak allows the set of participating clients in a cell to coordinate their communications, implicitly and in a fully distributed manner, with no support from the network operator.* By avoiding "stepping on each other's toes", each client is able to enjoy higher throughput, and complete its communication and go back to the idle state more quickly. In a sense, the coordination enabled by Peek-n-Sneak is akin to (though not the same as) that enabled by the widely-used carrier sense multiple access (CSMA) protocol in wireless LANs.

Our experimental evaluation of Peek-n-Sneak spans three network operators in two countries and includes both 3G and LTE networks. We find that a single stationary client employing Peek-n-Sneak for background downloads can save 20-60% of total energy consumed by a client that does not employ Peek-n-Sneak. The benefits grows as more clients adopt Peek-n-Sneak until the cell load is saturated. Further, we show that a mobile client employing Peek-n-Sneak can save on average up to 40% of total energy compared to not using Peek-n-Sneak. Finally, we show that a wider adoption of Peek-n-Sneak would also benefit foreground communication, by helping streamline and thereby reducing contention due to background communication.

## 2. CELLULAR LOAD DYNAMICS

We have performed extensive measurements spanning a period of four months, downloading 100+ GB of data over 100+ hours to characterize the dynamics of cellular load and its impact on mobile device energy consumption. We used TCP for all our experiments since operators have been known to treat UDP traffic differently (e.g., subject them to throttling, etc.). Our experiments were conducted on the following operator networks and locations:

- Airtel: 3G and LTE in Bangalore, India
- AT&T: LTE in Seattle, US
- BSNL: 3G in Bangalore, India

Since we do not have the ground truth on the cellular load, i.e., the total volume of data traffic due to the active users in the cell, we perform active throughput measurements to sense load. A higher throughput for our active download implies a lower cellular load due to other users, and vice versa. We postulate that any throughput variation is largely due to contention in the wireless channel, and not in the wired part of the operator network. In Section 3, we present evidence to corroborate this presumption. Note that in all cases, throughput was measured by downloading from a server located in the same geographic region as the cellular client, to avoid wide-area network bottlenecks.

To get a more detailed look at the dynamics of cellular load, we present the throughput measurements from a long, continuous TCP download of 1 GB on AT&T's LTE network in Seattle during peak hour (Figure 1a) and lean hour (Figure 1b), and 500 MB on BSNL's 3G network in Bangalore during peak hour (Figure 1c). The throughput samples were computed over 1-second intervals. The peak hour downloads were performed during a busy hour (mid-day) in downtown locations, when the cell can be expected to have many other active users. The figures show that throughput fluctuates considerably, with several periods of low throughput but also sustained periods (tens of seconds) of good throughput, despite it being a busy period. This suggests that there is considerable scope for benefiting from optimal scheduling over relatively short timescales.

To analyze these results further, in Figure 2a, we show the autocorrelation of the throughput values for lags ranging from 0 to 50 seconds. The figure shows that, although the autocorrelation drops rapidly with increasing lag (which points to the fluctuating nature of cellular load and hence throughput), there is a modest degree of correlation over short time scales; for example, the autocorrelation exceeds 0.5 for about the first 10 seconds. This suggests that, even during peak hours, if we are somehow able to identify a good throughput period, then the chances are that we will continue to enjoy good throughput for next several seconds, enabling high-throughput and hence energy-efficient transfer of a few megabytes of data (e.g., a throughput of 1.5 Mbps over 10 seconds would amount to almost 2 MB of data).

Can signal quality serve as a predictor of good throughput periods? Figure 2b answers this question in the negative, showing that there is minimal correlation between link quality and throughput in a busy cell. This finding highlights the importance of devising a way to sense cellular load, so that there is hope of predicting good throughput periods.

Finally, assuming we are able to accurately predict throughput, with low overhead, and thereby schedule background communication optimally, how much of battery energy savings can we expect? To answer this question, we compare the naive approach of downloading immediately, with an oracular approach of picking the optimal starting time for the download assuming perfect knowledge of future throughput. We used a workload comprising one 5MB download performed by a stationary device every 15 minutes. We treated 15 minutes as the "deadline" for completion of the download, thus giving the oracle some room to play with scheduling. Given the modest size of the individual downloads (5 MB), we assume that once the download starts, it runs to completion; this helps

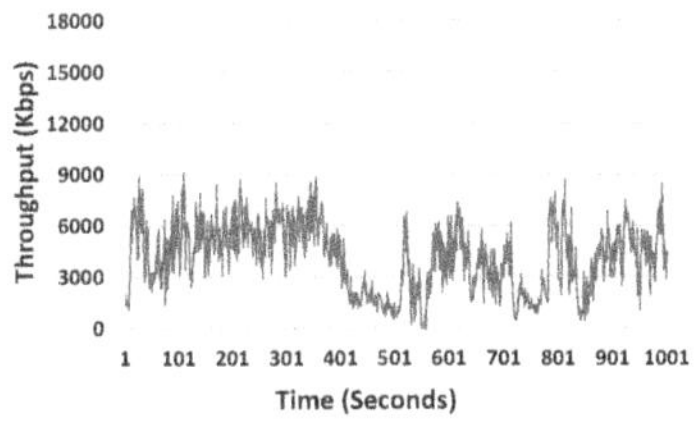


(a) Throughput on AT&T LTE network during peak hour

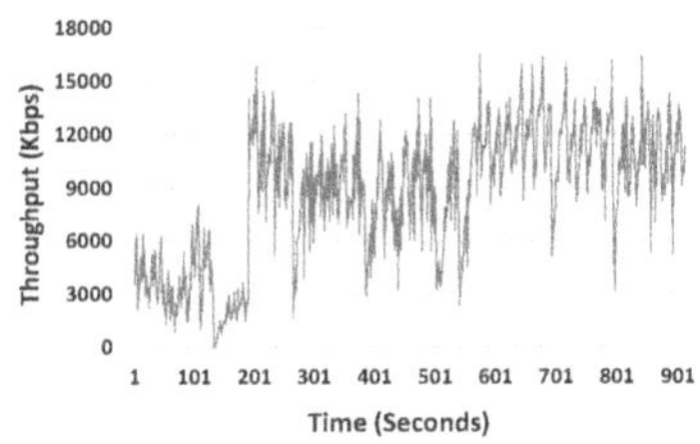


(b) Throughput on AT&T LTE network during lean hour

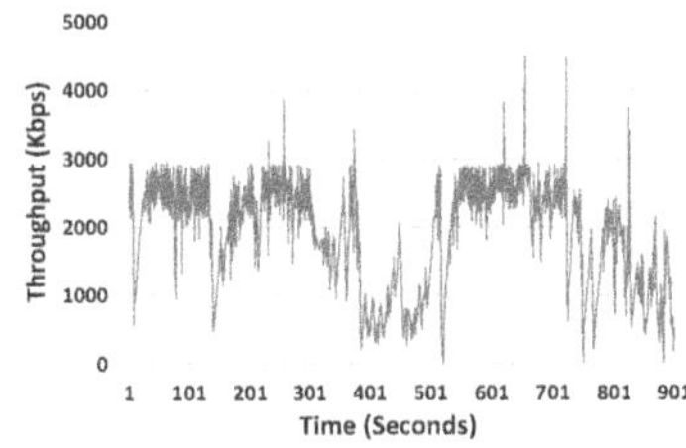


(c) Throughput on BSNL 3G network during peak hour

Figure 1: TCP download throughput over cellular networks

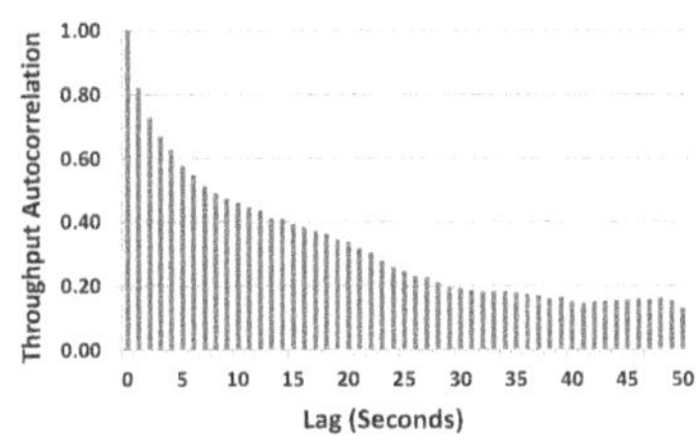


(a) Autocorrelation of throughput on AT&T LTE during peak hour

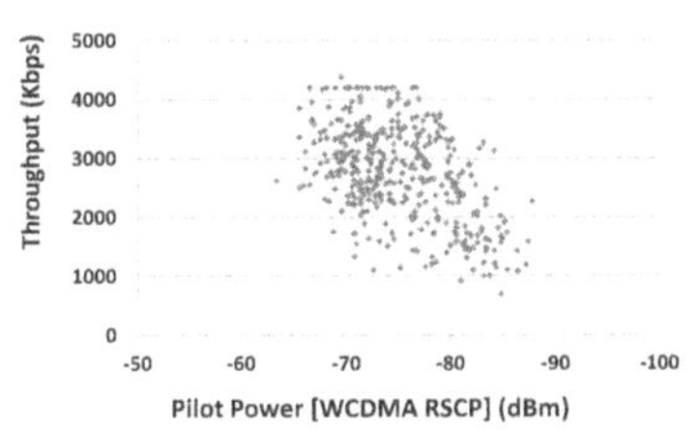


(b) Throughput vs Signal for BSNL 3G download

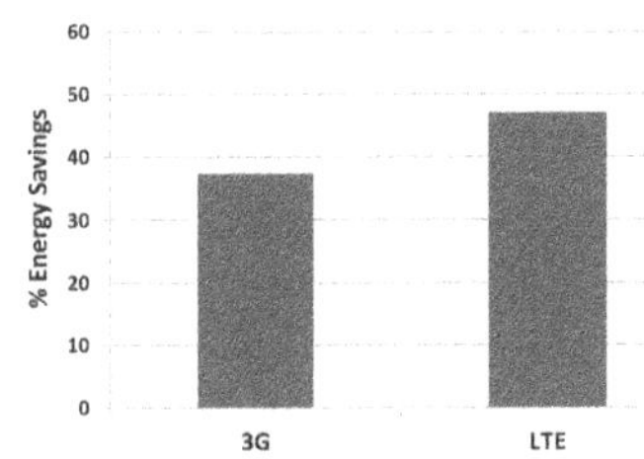


(c) Energy savings for an oracular approach

Figure 2: Analysis of cellular download throughput

avoid the overhead of radio "tails" [14]. Based on the throughput attained by these 5 MB downloads, we estimate the corresponding energy cost for the whole device (not just the radio).

Figure 2c shows the average energy savings of the oracular scheme relative to the naive scheme for BSNL's 3G network during peak hour in a busy downtown location in Bangalore as well as for peak hour traffic using AT&T's LTE network in Seattle. In both cases, we see significant energy savings of 37-47%.

The above findings clearly indicate that an effective throughput prediction scheme can be very beneficial. Note, however, that such a predictor is not sufficient, since multiple clients with background workloads could use the same predictor and start their downloads at the same time, to everyone's detriment. So, in our work, we develop low-overhead techniques for both cellular throughput prediction (LoadSense) and distributed coordination (Peek-n-Sneak).

# 3. LOADSENSE: SENSING CELLULAR LOAD

We now consider the problem of sensing cellular load in a way that imposes a low energy overhead on the mobile device and works without assistance from the network. The energy overhead requirement rules out performing active network measurements or even transitioning the radio to the high-power, active state. The lack of network assistance reflects the reality of cellular networks being closed, operator-controlled entities. Furthermore, unlike in the case of wireless LANs, the cellular interface on mobile devices does not support carrier sensing. Even snooping on background data traffic is not possible, as cellular modems do not decode data destined for other clients.

We look at how we can achieve carrier sensing like functionality for cellular interfaces, despite the challenges listed above. The basic intuition of our approach is that, as the number of active clients in a cell increases, the volume of downlink transmissions from the base station would likely also increase. As a result, the raw power in the downlink channel is likely to increase. This phenomenon would occur in both WCDMA (3G) and LTE networks, and points to how a client could sense the cellular load.

One issue is that we need to know the base power level, before we can determine whether there is an increase in power level due to load. To obtain the base power level, we can leverage pilot signals that are transmitted in cellular networks. Each cell tower periodically broadcasts pilot signals, to enable clients to detect the presence of the tower. Clients use pilot information for a number of purposes, such as cell reselection, handoff decisions, and synchronization. For instance, cell reselection is a procedure whereby clients can passively evaluate which tower to connect to in case there is a data transmission in the near future. This procedure is performed continuously, even when the radio is in the low-power, idle state.

The pilot power is a measure of how good the link is (i.e., the link quality) between the base station and the device. The link quality, as indicated by the pilot power, is an indicator of the download data rate that can be expected, in absence of background traffic. The closer the client is to the cell tower, the higher the pilot power it sees and the higher the modulation rate that can be used. On the other hand, the farther the device is from the tower, the lower the pilot power it measures and the lower the usable modulation rate.

However, the pilot power can sometimes give a conservative estimate of the achievable data rate, since it ignores transmit power control that is typically employed by cell towers while transmitting to individual clients. Depending on the power budget available at the base station, different amounts of power can be allocated for transmissions to different clients. If there are few other active clients in a cell, the base station can devote more of its power budget to serving a particular client. Thus, sometimes even when a

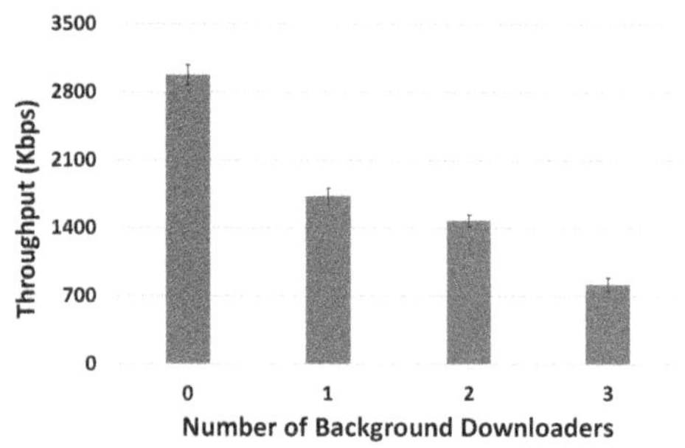


Figure 3: Throughput vs Number of Background downloaders (3G)

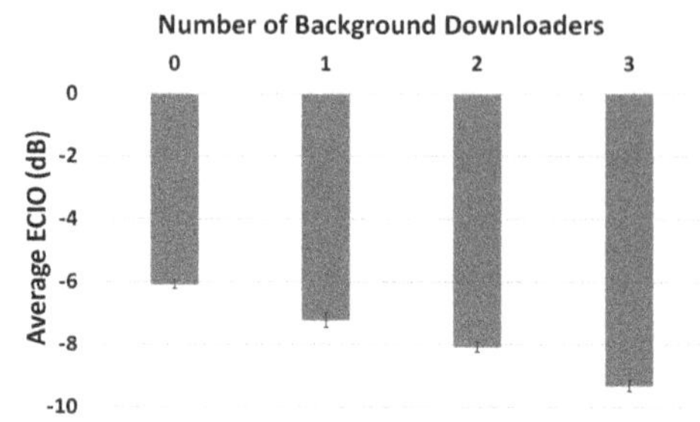


Figure 4: ECIO vs Number of Background downloaders (3G)

client is far away from the base station, it might still enjoy a high data rate if there are not many other active clients in the cell.

In addition to measuring the pilot power, mobile devices, in both WCDMA (3G) and LTE networks, measure the total, or raw, power in the channel. The raw power comprises the accumulation of the pilot power and the power due to data transmissions to other clients. The ratio of the pilot power to the raw (total) power in the channel turns out to be a a good indicator of cellular load. Thus, we define:

$$PowerRatio = \frac{PilotPower}{TotalRawPower}$$

In WCDMA (3G), the particular parameters that correspond to the pilot power and the power ratio are Received Signal Code Power (RSCP) and Received Energy per chip and Interference level (ECIO), respectively. In LTE, these are called Reference Signal Received Power (RSRP) and Reference Signal Received Quality (RSRQ), respectively. These parameters are typically exposed by most cellular devices through applications such as field test [2] [1]. We used a specific tool from Qualcomm, called QXDM, to obtain these parameters from a Windows Phone device. We can obtain around 3 samples a second from the cellular modem for each of these parameters.

When there are no transmissions, the power ratio is very close to 0 dB, since the raw power in the channel is equal to the pilot power observed, assuming that ambient noise is negligible.

With increased transmissions, the power ratio value drops, as the raw power in the channel is more than just that of the pilots in the carrier. There are couple of contributors to the increased raw power: (a) increased transmissions in the same cell, and (b) interference from neighboring cells, typically at locations near the cell edge. In either case, the expected throughput for the client device goes down. When there is a large number of active clients in the same cell, the proportional scheduler allocates fewer resource blocks to the individual clients due to increased contention, resulting in lower throughput per client. With increased interference from neighboring cells, the modulation rates have to be lowered to ensure successful communication, and thus the achievable bitrate for the client drops.

To validate point (a) above, we performed the following controlled experiment, which was done at a late night hour, to make it likely that the cell was unloaded. We had a test client measure the ECIO on a WCDMA channel for 20 seconds and then perform a 20-second download to measure throughput. Alongside this, we had 0 to 3 background clients, under our control and in the same cell, perform continuous downloads. Figure 3 shows that the throughput seen by the test client falls from 3 Mbps to under 1 Mbps, as the number of background downloads grows from 0 to 3. Correspondingly, the ECIO seen by the test client also drops (Figure 4) as the background load increases.

This controlled experiment shows that ECIO (or the power ratio, in general) is indicative of the load in the cell and hence the throughput that can be expected. However, both the link quality (as indicated by the pilot power) and the cellular load plus interference (as indicated by the power ratio) have an impact on the achievable data rate and hence the throughput for clients, as we discuss next.

To understand the relationship between the pilot power, power ratio, and observed throughput, we performed a large number of experiments, wherein we measured the RSCP and ECIO values on a 3G network while the device was in a disconnected state, and then initiated a data transfer immediately thereafter to measure throughput.

Figure 5 shows a 3D plot of throughput achieved at different locations and at different times of the day, corresponding to a range of measured values of RSCP and ECIO. We find that there is a wide range of throughput for each RSCP level, which indicates that congestion due to cellular load is a significant factor that impacts throughput.

For the purposes of throughput prediction, we confine ourselves to predicting one of two throughput classes — High or Low — where the threshold of 1.5 Mbps is used to separate the classes in 3G networks (7 Mbps in LTE networks). Figure 6 shows the RSCP and ECIO values for data points corresponding to the High and Low classes. It is clear that whenever RSCP is very low (<-90dBm) and/or ECIO is very low (<-10dB), we can predict with high accuracy (90+%) that a low throughput is to be expected. Similarly, when RSCP is very high and ECIO is low, we can predict with (90+%) accuracy that throughput is going to be high. However, we find that there is a significant intermediate region where the throughput could be high or low.

We observe similar behavior for LTE devices. Figure 7 show data points for the high and low throughput classes, and the corresponding pilot power (RSRP) and power ratio (RSRQ) values. The patterns are similar to those in 3G, with there again being an intermediate region where it is difficult to predict the high and low throughput classes.

It turns out that the power ratio (ECIO in WCDMA) exhibits high variation over time. The reason is the bursty nature of data traffic. At one instant, when lots of transmissions are occurring, ECIO would be low, and in the next instant, if there is a relative lull in transmissions, ECIO would go up again. Figure 8 shows a time series plot of ECIO measured at one client, where we had a separate client initiating short bursts of data transfer periodically, so create background traffic. We notice that ECIO variations are high whenever there is data transfer activity in the background.

This experiment clearly highlights the fact that there are temporal signatures in the ECIO (and also RSCP) parameters that could

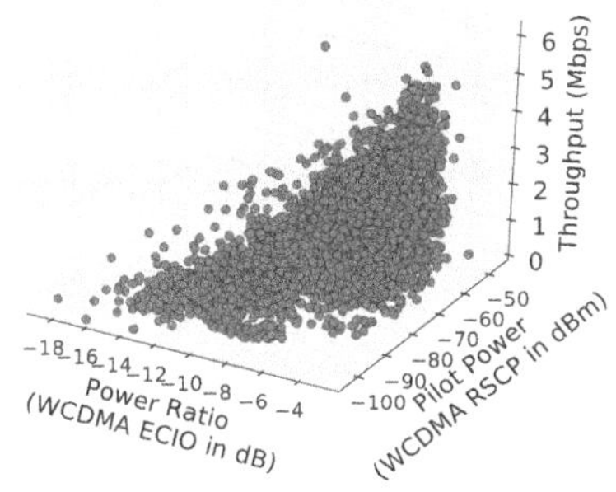


Figure 5: 3G Pilot Power vs Power Ratio vs Observed Throughput

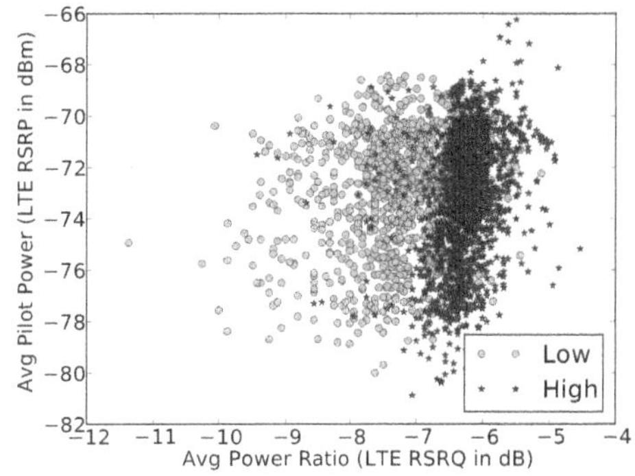


Figure 7: LTE Pilot Power vs Power Ratio for two throughput classes (many High points overlap with Low points)

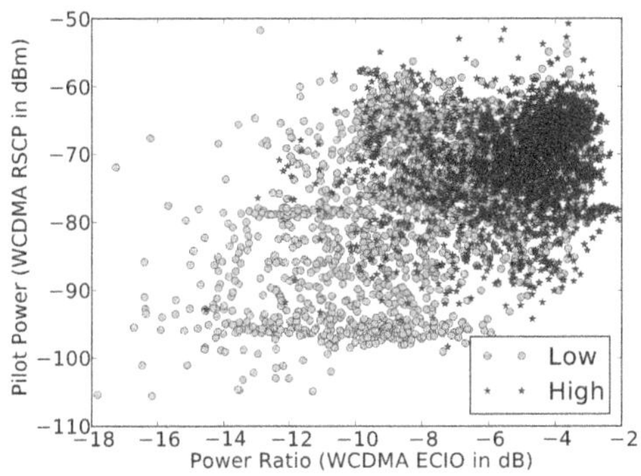


Figure 6: 3G Pilot Power vs Power Ratio for two throughput classes

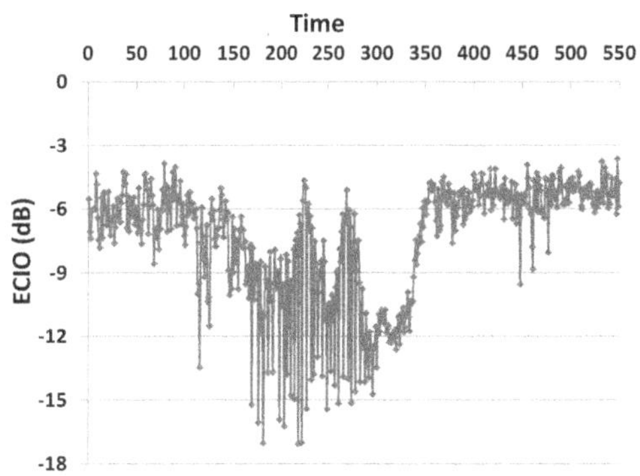


Figure 8: Temporal variation in ECIO with background traffic

be used to predict the throughput class better. To this end, we trained an empirical, Support Vector Machine (SVM) based classifier that is able to predict the occurrence of high or low throughput values, using the RSCP and ECIO measurements made by the client while it is idle, immediately preceding the download. We used the default Radial Basis Function (RBF) kernel for SVM. We trained using various features that capture temporal variations in ECIO and RSCP to determine which set of features enables the best prediction.

For evaluation, we tested each candidate empirical model with a dataset comprising equal numbers of high and low throughput observations, to avoid any bias. Accuracy for High (Low) period is computed as the fraction of actual High (Low) observations that we correctly predict as High (Low). Figure 9 shows the overall detection accuracy, and the accuracy for the individual classes, when various features are used as ingredients in the empirical model. By including as features the standard deviation, min, and max values of RSCP and ECIO over a short period (typically 3 seconds, although in Section 6 we evaluate other window sizes), the prediction accuracy is around 85% for predicting whether we will see good throughput. In other words, when we predict good throughput, we are right 85% of the time. However, we achieve a lower accuracy of 68% when predicting low throughput; in other words, when we predict low throughput, we in fact see high throughput 32% of the time. The reason for the lower accuracy is that our predictor is conservative, tuned to reduce misprediction of the high throughput class. This is important, since mispredictions of high throughput can cause the radio to be woken up and data transfer performed at an inappropriate time, leading to low throughput and wasted energy. On the other hand, mispredicting an actual high throughput period as low only leads to missed opportunities for downloading and hence increased delay, which is often less critical for background communication.

The predictions of high and low throughput based on the empirical model discussed above is what we term as *LoadSense*. We use LoadSense to make predictions of throughput class, and thereby infer the load conditions in a cell at runtime. Low throughput implies that the network is congested (Busy) and high throughput implies lightly loaded cell (Idle).

# 4. PEEK-N-SNEAK DESIGN

In this section, we describe the Peek-n-Sneak protocol that enables a large number of mobile devices that are connected to the same cell tower to coordinate their data transfers, without using any explicit message exchange.

Lack of support or visibility from the operator is a key challenge. One workaround might be to coordinate data transfers across different nodes using a central "controller" in the cloud. However, there are significant energy costs of doing so. Devices would need to continuously inform the controller of the current load conditions in their respective cells as well as keep the controller updated with their background transfer needs and deadlines. This will incur significant energy consumption on the client device for every such update, since the radio has to transition to high power active state (CELL_DCH state) before the device can communicate, even with the controller. Also, there would be a significant radio-tail energy cost, before the radio transitions back to the idle state.

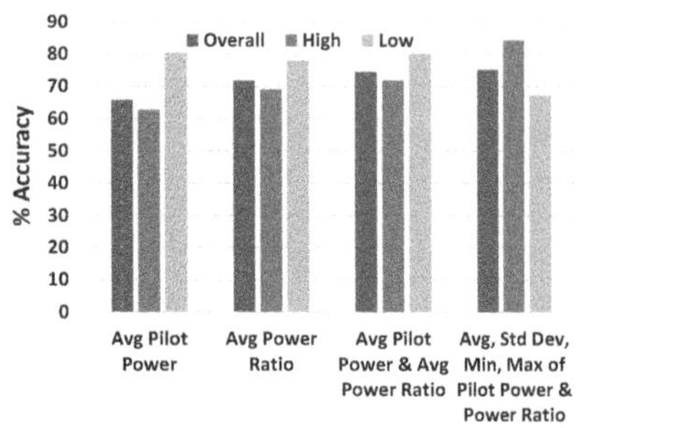


Figure 9: Predicting throughput using different features (3G)

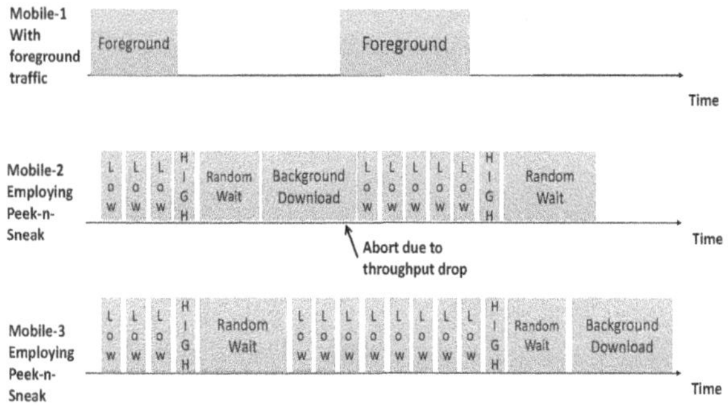


Figure 10: Peek-n-Sneak Protocol Illustration

Instead, the Peek-n-Sneak protocol operates by implicit distributed coordination among the clients attached to a cell, thereby avoiding the energy costs of a centralized solution. The Peek-n-Sneak protocol operation is illustrated through an example in Figure 10. At a high level, the design is similar to the CSMA protocol used in WiFi. However, Peek-n-Sneak operates at much coarser timescales compared to packet-level coordination used in WiFi. For example, slot duration for sensing the channel using LoadSense is 3 seconds in Peek-n-Sneak compared to 9 $\mu$seconds used in WiFi. The second difference is that clients with user initiated foreground communication access the channel immediately and do not follow the Peek-n-Sneak protocol.

Whenever there is some data to be downloaded from the Internet but the download can be delayed (e.g., background updates to social networking applications), the request is sent to the background transfer service running locally on the mobile device. The client then performs LoadSense to determine whether the channel is idle or busy. When the channel is sensed as idle, the client starts a random backoff timer. Whenever a client is counting down idle slots, if the channel becomes busy due to either foreground communication or due to some other background client winning the random backoff contention, the counter is frozen as in WiFi. Finally, to ensure fairness and avoid starvation of other clients, after acquiring the channel for background transmission, each client voluntarily stops its transfer after it has transferred a maximum transfer unit (MTU) worth of data.

**Collisions:** Unlike WiFi, where only one client transmits at a time in a cell, cellular networks allows multiple clients to communicate simultaneously. For example, in LTE, time-frequency resource blocks are allocated to clients. When there are no other clients in the network, all resources can be allocated to one user. This is a case where link quality is what determines achievable throughput. However, with an increasing number of clients, the scheduler multiplexes available resources among the active clients. When two or more clients start downloading at the same time, each may experience a lower throughput than what it would have got if it were the only client operating in the cell. Thus, "collision" in Peek-n-Sneak merely implies sharing of the channel that results in lower throughput, rather than the total loss of throughput as is typical in WiFi collisions.

However, we still would like to avoid the lower throughput due to sharing. So, during download, Peek-n-Sneak at a client continues to monitor the throughput that the client receives. If the client detects that its throughput is lower than predicted (say, because of another client initiating a foreground transfer or collisions among background clients), it has the option to suspend its background transfer. Before doing so, the client estimates the energy consumption for the ongoing data transfer, if the download were continued to completion at the current throughput, and compares it with the energy cost of suspending the transfer (thereby incurring the radio-tail energy cost) and resuming it at a later point in time when the expected throughput is higher. If the energy savings is higher than a certain threshold for the suspend-and-resume option, the client pauses the download and goes back into sensing mode to determine when it should resume.

Finally, Peek-n-Sneak not only coordinates background clients, it also ensures that background traffic does not overlap with foreground traffic. Thus, foreground communication also enjoys better performance since they have to contend with fewer clients for resources. One exception to this conservative policy is that when there is already a background transfer that is active at the point when one or more foreground clients start downloading, the background transfer continues unless it experiences a significant drop in throughput because of (significant) contention with the foreground communication.

# 5. IMPLEMENTATION DETAILS

We describe two engineering challenges we faced while implementing our system. First, from an energy efficiency viewpoint, LoadSense should ideally be implemented inside the cellular modem as it would avoid the energy cost of waking up the CPU periodically to poll the radio for obtaining channel measurements. The cellular modem can perform an asynchronous callback to the CPU whenever the channel is idle. However, since current cellular modems do not support such a callback feature, our implementation uses CPU-based polling to query the modem. Second, the frequency of polling the channel parameters impacts how quickly and accurately LoadSense can estimate channel load. We explored two ways to poll the modem, each of which entails a different polling frequency.

Our first version of the system was completely built on the mobile client. We used the Radio Interface Layer (RIL) API calls to query the modem to obtain pilot power and power ratio values. However, the current RIL API does not provide fine-grained samples, and we observed that, irrespective of how frequently we invoke the API, the values only changed every two to three seconds. We evaluated LoadSense using this setup (see section 6), and observed that the accuracy is quite low (<70%). To address this issue we employed a different setup to measure pilot power and power ratio using a desktop tool provided by the modem vendor. For both 3G and LTE equipped client devices, we used a Windows Desktop tool called QXDM from Qualcomm. Our 3G experiment setup consisted of multiple phones running the Windows Phone 7.5 OS, each tethered to a separate Windows laptop running the QXDM tool. For LTE, since there are no LTE capable phones currently supported in the LTE network in India because of a mismatch in spectrum band, we used multiple LTE USB dongles for the experiments. We can read the power ratio and pilot power values for both 3G and LTE interfaces in realtime at a high frequency ( 5 per second in the radio idle state).

We also implemented a background transfer service (BTS) app that takes requests for downloading data with an optional deadline parameter. When a new background request is in the queue, the BTS app employs the Peek-n-Sneak protocol to determine when to initiate the data transfer. To perform LoadSense, the BTS app requests the desktop application for pilot power and power ratio values for a certain period of time and then predicts whether the channel is busy or idle based on the expected throughput class.

# 6. EVALUATION

In this section, we evaluate the LoadSense primitive and the Peek-n-Sneak coordination protocol. All experiments are conducted over commercial cellular networks in Bangalore (BSNL 3G Network and Airtel LTE network). We use the HTC Maaza phone running the Windows Phone 7.5 OS for the 3G experiments and the Huawei E392 USB dongle for the LTE experiments.

We first start with micro-benchmarks to evaluate the accuracy of our LoadSense technique. We then demonstrate the effectiveness of Peek-n-Sneak through several experiments in both static and mobile settings, over both 3G and LTE networks.

## 6.1 Micro-benchmark

In order to evaluate the accuracy of LoadSense, we need to compare the LoadSense prediction (high/low) with the observed cellular throughput at a given mobile. However, since LoadSense works when the radio is in RRC disconnected state, we don't know the exact cellular throughput available when the radio is passively estimating load. Therefore, as soon as the LoadSense technique comes up with a prediction, we perform an active TCP download (for 20 seconds) immediately after the prediction and measure the actual throughput achieved and use this as our ground truth. While the ground truth could change between the prediction and measurement intervals, this is mitigated in our experiments since 1) as we discuss below, our prediction interval is fairly short (3 seconds) and 2) the autocorrelation findings in Section 2 indicate that the available throughput typically remain stable over ten seconds or more.

We classify measured cellular throughput below a certain threshold (unless specified otherwise, we used throughput of 1.5 Mbps in our 3G experiments and 7 Mbps in our LTE experiments) as low, and as high otherwise. Similarly, LoadSense also makes a low or high prediction based on its observations. As mentioned earlier, the detection accuracy of LoadSense is computed as the fraction of measured throughput values classified as High (Low) that are predicted accurately by LoadSense as being High (Low) and use this as our metric for evaluating the effectiveness of LoadSense.

Finally, note that signal quality (pilot power) is also automatically taken into account in our load estimation. LoadSense predicts the throughput available as being low when the pilot power at the mobile radio is poor and/or when there is high amount of congestion due to competing mobile traffic.

### 6.1.1 *Detection time*

We first evaluate how long a client needs to observe the channel before being able to make an accurate prediction. The observation window plays a role in how quickly we can predict load changes. Moreover, detection time also determines the length of the slot used in Peek-n-Sneak protocol.

Figure 11 shows overall accuracy of predictions for both high and low throughput classes for different observation windows. When the observation window is less than 3 seconds the number of samples available for power ratio parameter and pilot power are few, leading to low accuracy (65%). The accuracy steadily improves to 75% with an increase in the size of the observation window mainly owing to increased number of observations available for LoadSense. However, accuracy does not improve significantly beyond 3 seconds, which suggests that a 3-second observation of channel condition is sufficient to capture most of the load characteristics in a cell and predict the throughput class for the next few seconds effectively. Also, it is preferable to have a short detection time in order to keep the random backoff overhead of Peek-n-Sneak low. We observed similar behavior on LTE networks. For the rest of our experiments we choose a detection time of 3 seconds for both 3G and LTE.

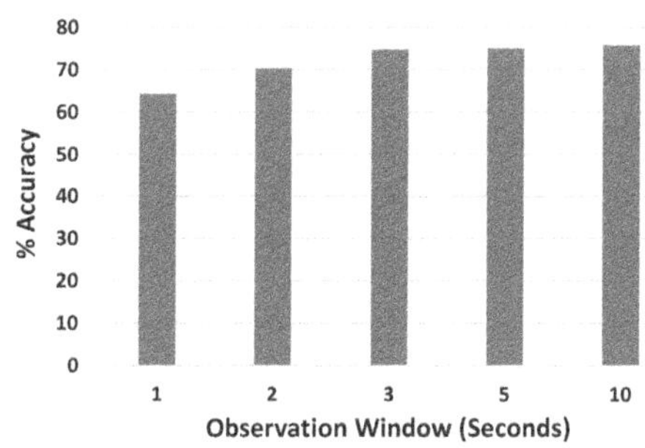


Figure 11: Detection time vs Accuracy for 3G

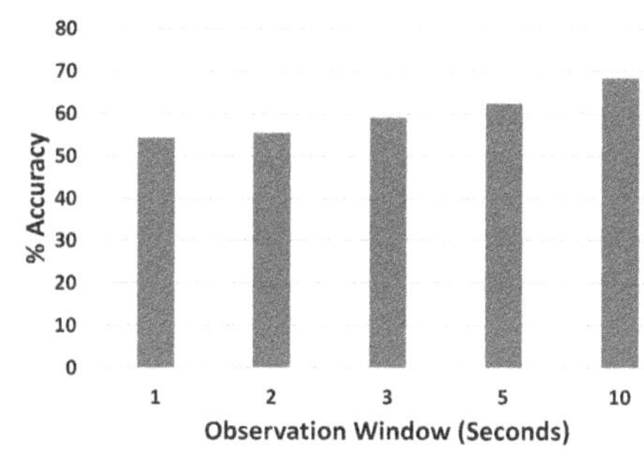


Figure 12: Detection time vs Accuracy for 3G using RIL APIs

We also evaluated the detection time needed when using the RIL APIs to poll the modem directly from the phone. Figure 12 shows the prediction accuracy for different observation windows. The main issue with the current implementation of RIL is that it provides very coarse grained samples. We find that even at 10 second interval, the accuracy achieved is still below 70% due to very few samples of channel measurements. In addition, a large detection time elongates the slots used in the Peek-n-Sneak protocol and reduces efficiency. Thus, we employ the desktop-assisted setup to obtain fine-grained channel measurements for the rest of the experiments. Note that this issue is not an inherent bottleneck since the modem is able to provide fine-grained measurements through the tool. This just shows that the current set of RIL APIs is not well suited for our needs.

### 6.1.2 *Throughput Threshold*

Next, we evaluate the sensitivity of detection accuracy with respect to the throughput threshold parameter that is chosen for classifying the low and high throughput classes. Figure 13 shows the accuracy for different threshold values. For 3G networks, we ob-

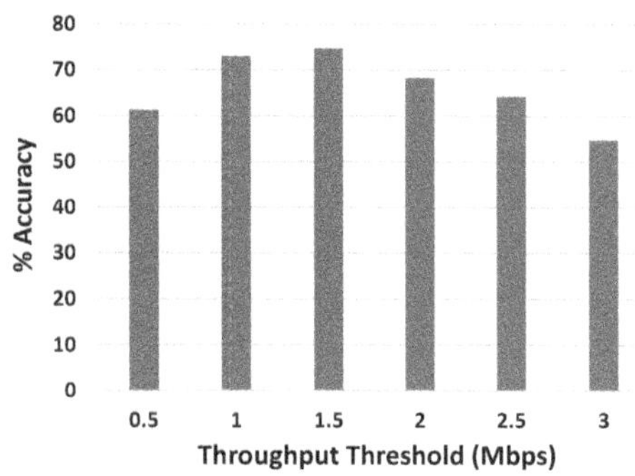


Figure 13: Throughput threshold vs Accuracy for 3G

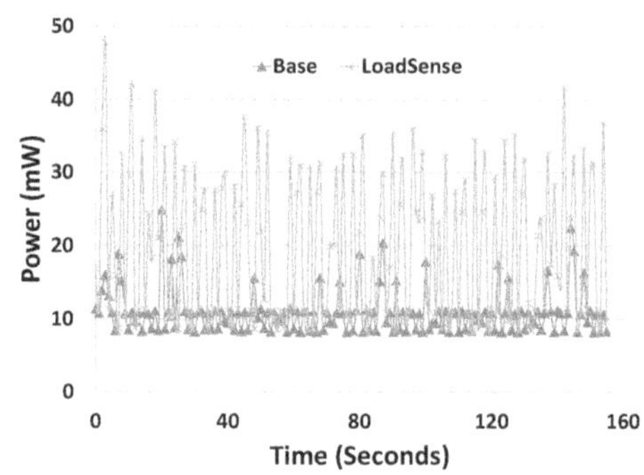


Figure 14: Power draw with and without LoadSense

served that accuracy peaks at around 1.5 Mbps throughput. For values both above and below this threshold the accuracy is lower. A deeper look at the dataset revealed that 1.5 Mbps is close to the median value for the throughputs we observed in the 3G network. The SVM based technique in LoadSense is able to learn a good classifier when the threshold value splits the dataset into equal sized classes. In LTE experiments we observed the throughput threshold value which achieves best accuracy is 7 Mbps. While we can improve the accuracy for different throughput thresholds by tuning the classifier or using a different classifier, we believe using the median throughput to separate the high/low classes is a reasonable operating point for a primitive such as LoadSense.

For the rest of the experiments, we choose 1.5 Mbps for 3G and 7 Mbps for LTE as the thresholds respectively for classifying busy and idle periods. We consider the channel to be Busy (Idle) when predicted throughput is Low (High).

#### *6.1.3 Energy Consumption*

Energy consumption has two components – (1) Sensing energy spent running LoadSense continuously in the background and (2) Transfer energy spent for the actual data transfer as well as overheads (wakeup and tail). Due to the engineering constraints of our system implementation, we used a combination of two setups to estimate total energy. To compute sensing energy, we used the mobile only implementation of our system which invokes RIL call periodically (once per second) to capture the computational overhead. Since the desktop assisted implementation achieves the best accuracy, we use this to monitor the radio on time and RRC state changes and use these values to estimate the transfer energy spent (including the CPU energy of the background transfer with the display switched off) during the course of an experiment. We then compute the sum of these two components to estimate the total energy spent. Note that, if the cellular modem implemented the LoadSense primitive, the cost of the first component can be eliminated.

Figures 14 shows a snapshot of power drawn by the device over time without LoadSense and with LoadSense, respectively. The average power draw increases only by 12mW from 10mW to 22mW corresponding to sensing overhead of running LoadSense continuously. In the experiments to follow, for computing total energy cost of Peek-n-Sneak we add both the transfer energy as well as the above sensing energy cost (12mJ).

#### *6.1.4 Location Sensitivity*

In addition to just measuring load in a cell with background traffic that already exists, we also looked at settings when we used our own clients to generate traffic in a controlled setting. The objective is to determine how well LoadSense can be used to detect the presence or absence of synthetic background traffic at different locations inside a cell. In addition, this analysis forms the basis for the Peek-n-Sneak protocol which uses LoadSense to implicitly inform the outcome of a contention round to other clients running LoadSense. We used one mobile client referred to as interferer to periodically download data for 60 sec and remain idle for 60 sec. Another mobile client referred to as observer runs LoadSense continuously to detect whether the channel is busy or idle. Note that in this experiment, we know for sure that the channel is loaded when interferer is active. However, since we do not have control over other users in a cell, there can be times when interferer is idle, but the channel could still be busy.

We vary the locations of the observer while keeping the interferer in one location inside an office building. The distance between the clients are as far apart as 800 meters at some locations, where the observer is outdoors. During each experiment we ensured that both clients were attached to the same cell tower. At each location we run LoadSense every 3 seconds for a duration of 10 mins, which accounts for a total of 200 predictions per location. Figure 15 and 16 depict the accuracy of predictions using LoadSense at four different locations using 3G and LTE, respectively. At each location, accuracy is shown for two periods – times when the interferer is on and times when the interferer is off. Overall, LoadSense detects presence of background interferer accurately more than 80% of the time irrespective of the location of the observer in both 3G and LTE networks. The accuracy drops by 10-20% in the case of idle period prediction but this could be due to lack of accurate ground truth information for classifying idle periods (there could be other active users attached to the cell that we are unaware of). This experiment shows that the detection accuracy of LoadSense is high enough to be useful for coordinating background data transfers. Each client running Peek-n-Sneak can use LoadSense to coordinate their contention, since they can effectively detect each others downloads.

### 6.2 Macro-benchmarks

We evaluate Peek-n-Sneak using multiple phones using a variety of synthetic and real workloads.

To evaluate Peek-n-Sneak in a typical multi-phone setting, we setup 6 stationary phones connected to the same cell and performed a combination of experiments with foreground and background traffic. The objectives of the experiment are twofold – (1) to evaluate the impact of the Peek-n-Sneak protocol on energy consumption and latency, and (2) to see how well Peek-n-Sneak performs in a network where other clients do not employ Peek-n-Sneak. A client may not employ Peek-n-Sneak if it is either performing foreground

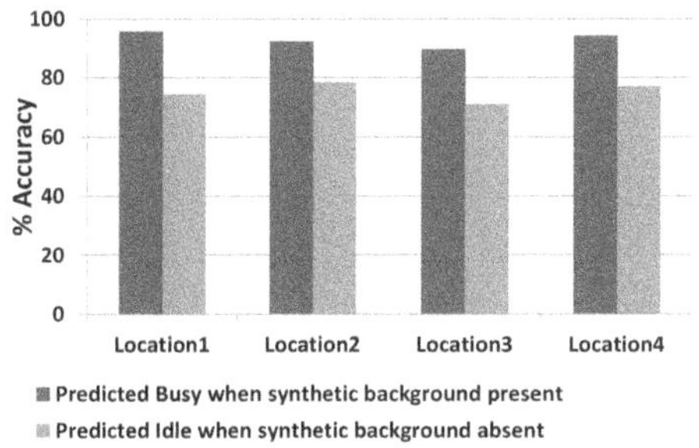


Figure 15: Detecting synthetic background traffic from different locations in a 3G cell

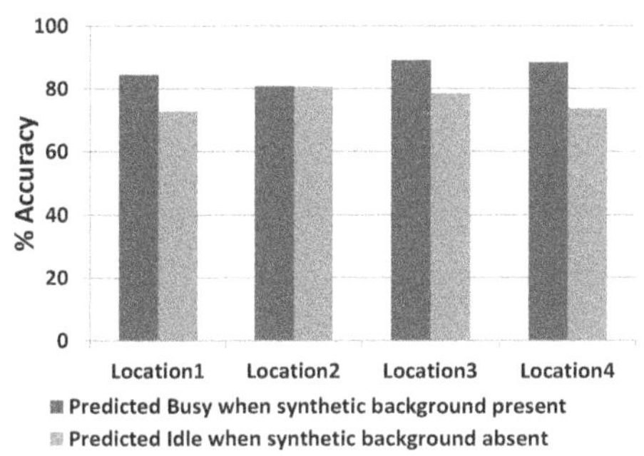


Figure 16: Detecting synthetic background traffic from different locations in a LTE cell

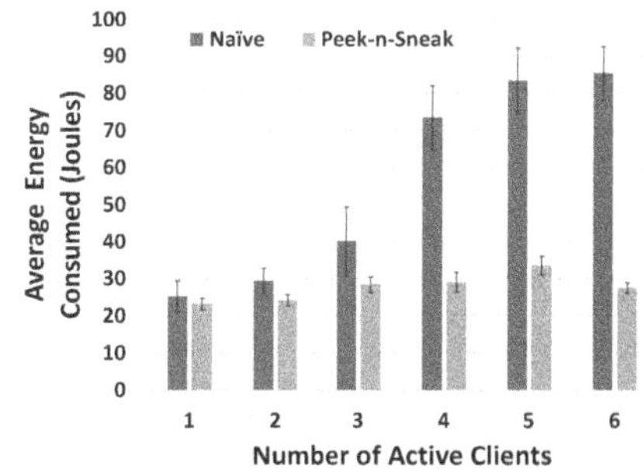


Figure 17: Average total energy consumption for Naive and Peek-n-Sneak with increasing load

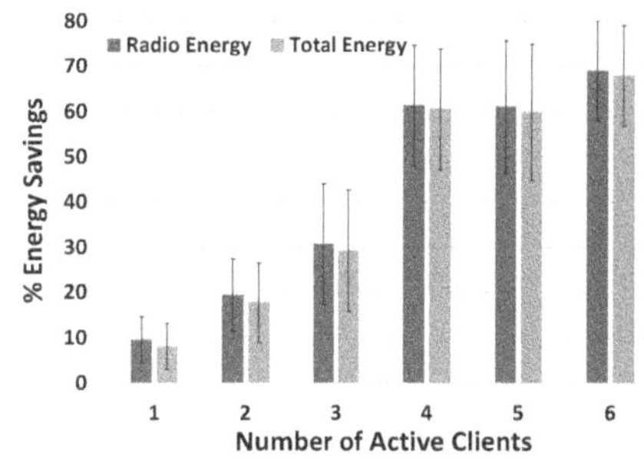


Figure 18: % savings for Peek-n-Sneak with increasing load consisting of only background downloads

transfers which cannot be time-shifted or if it does not implement Peek-n-Sneak. The latter setting captures the benefits of Peek-n-Sneak during an incremental deployment of the protocol.

### *6.2.1 Multiple Phone Experiments*

For these experiments, we emulate a periodic syncing background workload where each phone downloads 5 MB of data from an Internet server every 15 mins. We ensure that downloads across the clients are not synchronized since in realistic settings the syncing schedules of individual phones are independent of each other. In the beginning of the experiment, every client sleeps for a random duration of time (up to 4 mins), before initiating a sync request for download. In the first set of experiments we look at a *homogeneous* setup where all clients are using Naive or all are using the Peek-n-Sneak protocol. Naive clients basically download data as soon as the request is generated (as is the common practice today), while in Peek-n-Sneak, the clients download data according to the protocol with a deadline set to 15 mins (if a low load opportunity does not arise, the download is triggered anyway to ensure completion within 15 mins). The numbers in the plots are an average of 5 runs. Due to complexity of settings up multiple clients, experiments were conducted over several days at different times of the day.

We vary the number of active clients in each experiment from 1 to 6 and run either Naive or Peek-n-Sneak on each client. In each configuration, we performed 5 runs and computed the average metrics over these runs. Figure 17 shows the average total energy in Joules consumed by Naive and Peek-n-Sneak for different number of active clients. As mentioned earlier, we include the compute overhead of running LoadSense while the client is waiting for the right opportunity to download. First, we see that as the number of active clients increase, energy consumption for each client increases significantly for the Naive approach. This is due to increased contention between different downloading clients. Peek-n-Sneak implicitly serializes downloads and each client gets to access the channel without contention from other active clients. Thus, energy consumption only increases by 23% when going from 1 to 6 active clients using Peek-n-Sneak, while with the Naive approach, the corresponding energy increase is as high as 340%. Energy savings come at the cost of increased latency. The average latency (Figure 19) to download is higher with Peek-n-Sneak, but remains within 3 mins of when the sync request is generated. Moreover, for background workloads, which are not initiated by the user, a small increase in latency may not impact user experience.

Figure 18 shows the percentage savings for Peek-n-Sneak over Naive for radio energy and total energy. The compute overhead of running LoadSense and Peek-n-Sneak is very low and does not impact total energy savings. Average energy savings go up to 62% in the 6 client experiment, mainly owing to reduced contention and also since LoadSense ensures that the expected throughput is high, before initiating a download, thereby resulting in shorter download time. In the experiments, we find that download throughput in Peek-n-Sneak is 150% higher compared to Naive with 6 clients. However, the improved throughput gains do not translate to equivalent energy savings mainly due to the cost of aborted transfers (and the associated overheads such as radio tails). Since there can be background data transfers that are not under our control, Peek-n-Sneak clients stop the data transfer as soon as the throughput drops below the low threshold and then again looks for periods when it can download. Every interruption causes additional energy due to radio wakeup and tail overheads.

Next, we perform experiments with a combination of Naive and Peek-n-Sneak clients. The Naive clients can be seen either as foreground clients that want the data downloaded right away or as background clients that do not implement Peek-n-Sneak (corresponding to an incremental deployment scenario).

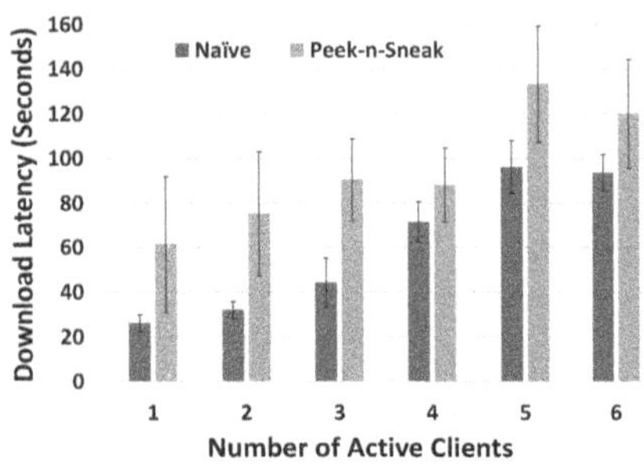


Figure 19: Average download latency for Naive and Peek-n-Sneak with increasing load consisting of only background downloads

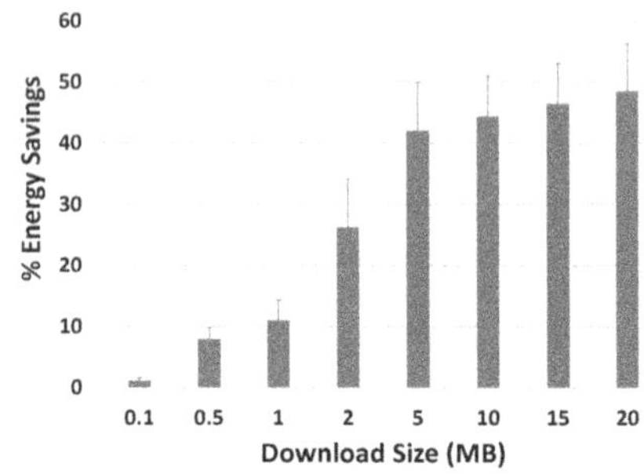


Figure 21: % savings for Peek-n-Sneak for different download sizes

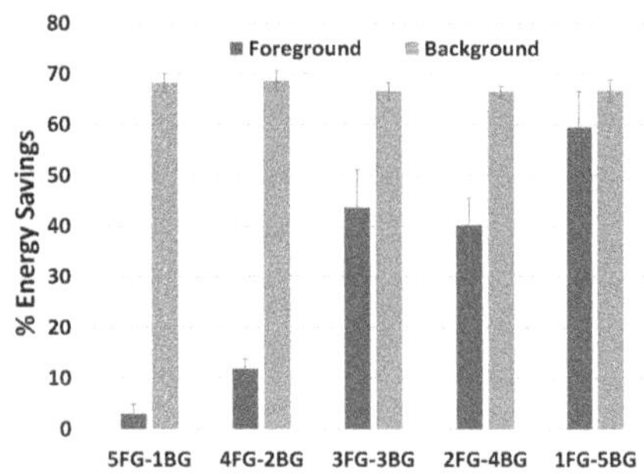


Figure 20: % savings for Foreground and Peek-n-Sneak clients for different Foreground-Background client combinations

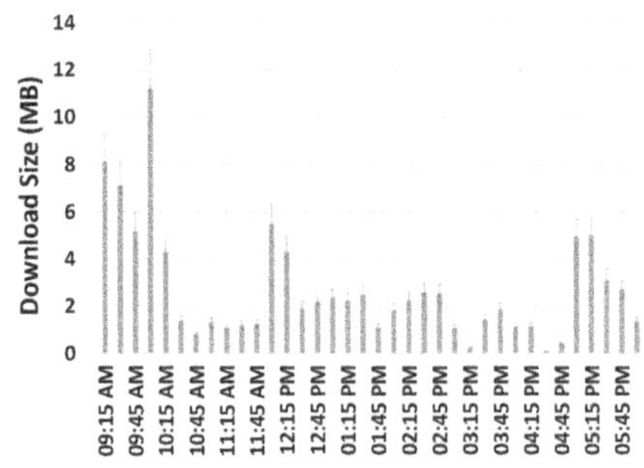


Figure 22: Average download size in MB per 15 min sync interval during work hours for Email and RSS feed reader applications

Similar to the previous setup we have 6 clients, and we choose different combinations of clients doing foreground traffic (Naive) and clients doing background traffic (Peek-n-Sneak). Figure 20 shows energy savings for foreground clients and background clients separately compared to the case where all 6 clients follow Naive irrespective of whether they are doing foreground or background traffic. The first thing to note here is that even in a scenario where there is only 1 client following Peek-n-Sneak and 5 naive clients performing foreground traffic, we achieve savings as high as 68% for the Peek-n-Sneak background client. The energy savings remain stable above 65% even as the number of background clients increase. This is due to implicit coordination achieved by Peek-n-Sneak which serializes the data transfers. A beneficial side-effect of Peek-n-Sneak is that even clients with foreground traffic achieve energy savings as a result of reduced contention from the Peek-n-Sneak clients. As the proportion of background clients running Peek-n-Sneak increases, energy savings for foreground clients steadily improves, reaching as high as 60%. This experiment shows that Peek-n-Sneak clients can coexist and achieve savings even in networks where other clients may not be following the protocol, as is typically the case during incremental deployment of new protocols.

### 6.2.2 *Workload Size*

So far we only looked at fixed size background workloads. We now evaluate the impact of varying background workload size on the savings achieved by Peek-n-Sneak. In this scenario, we had 1 phone downloading the specified workload using Peek-n-Sneak while we had 5 other phones performing foreground traffic in the same cell (similar to the heterogeneous setup in the previous experiment with 6 clients).

In this experiment, we vary the download size over a wide range of values that correspond to different real-world background workloads (email sync, app updates and music downloads). We repeat each experiment 10 times using both Naive and Peek-n-Sneak approaches to perform the download using the 3G network and measure the average savings of Peak-n-Sneak over Naive. Figure 21 shows download size varying from 100 KB to 20 MB and the corresponding average total energy savings achieved by Peek-n-Sneak. For small download sizes (<1 MB) we find that radio overheads (wakeup and tail) dominate the energy cost of the actual data transfers, resulting in negligible energy savings. We find that savings steadily increase with download sizes up to a certain point (5 MB) and then saturates (46%). The reason for the saturation is that large background downloads are often interrupted by presence of foreground traffic. While the Peek-n-Sneak protocol avoids downloading during these periods, it still ends up paying the cost of putting the radio to sleep (tail overhead) and waking it up, thereby limiting the energy savings.

### 6.2.3 *Real Workloads*

In this experiment, we collected real world traces for two background applications – email and RSS feed reader – that are configured to sync every 15 mins. The RSS reader is setup to download feeds from popular news sites and blogs. Figure 22 shows the average download sizes during each 15 min interval averaged over two separate days from 9am to 6pm. We replayed the traces with Peek-n-Sneak and computed energy savings. Again, as before, we had five other phones generating foreground traffic.

Figure 23 shows the savings achieved during each sync interval for Peak-n-Sneak as compared to Naive. We find that Peak-n-Sneak achieves an overall energy savings of 29% for the background workload averaged over two days.

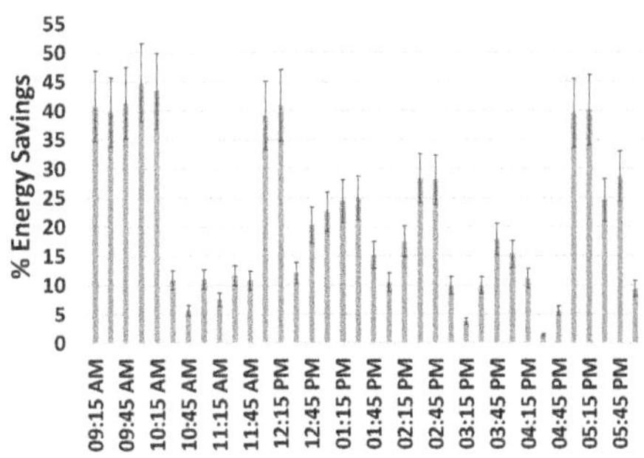


Figure 23: % savings for Peek-n-Sneak per sync in 3G

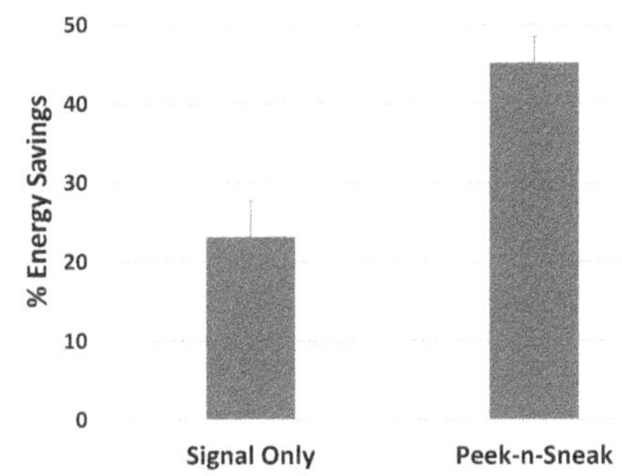


Figure 24: % energy savings for Peek-n-Sneak and Signal-only in mobile settings

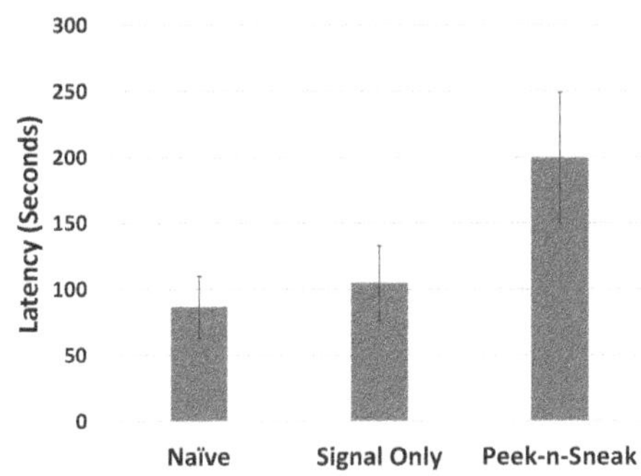


Figure 25: Average download latency for Naive, Signal-only and Peek-n-Sneak

### *6.2.4 Mobile Experiments*

In these experiments, we apply LoadSense in mobile settings as well where throughput variation is due to a combination of both signal and load effects. Since the mobile client remains in a cell for a short period of time and channel conditions differ from cell to cell, we disabled the random backoff in the Peek-n-Sneak protocol. We simply employ LoadSense to identify periods when the throughput is expected to be high to initiate a data transfer. We abort the transfer when throughput falls below the default threshold. We compare this scheme with the Naive scheme that simply downloads when the request is generated. In addition, we also compare this with a scheme that uses only signal to predict high throughput periods. Prior work [15] has shown that signal correlates well with expected throughput. We performed 25 mobile experiments while driving around in different parts of Bangalore at various times of the day on BSNL 3G network. An experiment consisted of running Naive, Signal-only and Peek-n-Sneak schemes separately on a particular route while downloading 10MB of data in 30 mins(two back-to-back 5 MB sync workloads).

Energy savings for Signal-only scheme and Peek-n-Sneak over Naive averaged over 25 runs is shown in Figure 24. Peek-n-Sneak achieves an average total savings of 45% across these runs while Signal-only achieved 23% savings. Thus, load awareness leads to a doubling of the energy savings compared to the Signal-only scheme. This is because often there are times when the signal is quite good, but the cell is congested. Peek-n-Sneak is able to avoid downloading data until both load and signal conditions are good, thereby increasing energy savings.

Figure 25 shows the average time (in seconds) when the download finished for the three schemes. Clearly latency increases for both schemes compared to Naive as a result of waiting for the right time to download. Latency for Peek-n-Sneak is the highest (2.3x of Naive) as it is more conservative in downloading data. However, in absolute terms, the additional delay is only about a couple of minutes, which may be acceptable for background data transfers.

# 7. DISCUSSION

**Other applications.** Besides optimizing energy for background applications, LoadSense can be applied in other settings. For example, the typical signal bars shown on a phone indicate merely the signal strength but does not take into account interference or congestion in the cell; LoadSense can be used to provide an indication of the expected throughput for a foreground application, which might be a more meaningful indicator for the user. Also, LoadSense can be used to estimate the number of people in a region. For example, one can estimate road traffic conditions by correlating it with number of active users in a cell.

**Multi-user MIMO.** LTE standard allows multi-user MIMO where multiple antennas at the base-station can transmit different streams to different clients at the same time. A mobile client may observe total power in the channel increasing while available throughput does not decrease until all streams at the base-station is exhausted. LoadSense for such networks will require dynamic calibration to learn the relation between interference levels and expected throughput in such cells. However, in our experiments, we did not observe such behavior. Perhaps this is because most LTE deployments today use Frequency Division Duplex (FDD) which separates uplink and downlink transmissions on different frequency bands and implementing MU-MIMO on FDD systems is challenging.

**Changing cellular standard to broadcast load information.** Clearly, the base station has the best knowledge of load levels in a cell and if cellular standards allow the base station to broadcast this information, LoadSense at the mobile clients would not be necessary (though Peek-n-Sneak would still be necessary for coordination among different nodes). However, even if the standards supported such a feature, LoadSense may still be needed as operators may not be willing to continuously broadcast cell load information for competitive reasons.

# 8. RELATED WORK

**Cellular measurement studies.** Several papers have examined the performance and other characteristics of cellular networks using measurements [12, 13, 17]. Study of spatio-temporal characteristics of base station load in [13] show low correlation between neighboring base stations and significant temporal changes in base station load. These characteristics corroborate our measurement study and imply that time- and space-shifting techniques, as employed in this paper for the static and mobile scenarios, will likely be effective in "water-filling" unused cellular capacity using background traffic.

**Throughput estimation** Throughput estimation is typically performed using active measurements, albeit using as few packets as possible. For example. for estimating throughput on wired networks, there is a long list of research papers and tools available [3, 4, 7, 8, 16]. Other work have extended these techniques and developed new tools to estimate throughput over 802.11 standard-based wireless LANs [10, 11].

However, to our knowledge, there does not exist any tool to date that can accurately estimate throughput in cellular networks. In fact, authors in [9] show that conventional bandwidth estimation tools are ineffective in estimating throughput in cellular networks. Furthermore, in order to save energy, we require *passive* estimation of throughput when the cellular radio is in the RRC disconnected state. Even sending a few packets to estimate cellular load can result in significant drain in energy, thereby wiping out the gains of such a load sensing approach. Therefore, instead of estimating throughput, we use signal and interference power measurements of the cellular radio to simply determine if the cell is loaded or not. This is analogous to carrier sensing used in WiFi and exploited by systems such as Idle Sense [6] to optimize throughput.

**Cellular energy optimization** Bartendr [15] is a system that uses predicted mobility and future signal strength values to preferentially schedule communication when the signal strength is high, thereby reducing energy consumption due to mobile communication. However, Bartendr does not account for the current load in a given cell. Therefore, preferentially scheduling communication at a high signal strength alone may not be enough for reducing energy consumption if the current cell is highly loaded. In this paper, we show that incorporating load sensing in mobile settings (which also encompasses signal-based scheduling since load estimation takes mobile's signal strength into account) can result in significant energy savings. There are also techniques that optimize radio tail energy [14] by ensuring that transmissions from applications are coordinated but these energy optimization are complementary and additive to the energy savings obtained by scheduling transmissions when the cellular network is lightly loaded.

# 9. CONCLUSION

Obtaining good throughput is key to reducing the energy consumption of background communication over cellular networks. We have shown experimentally that throughput depends not only on the link quality but also on the cellular load. Given this, we have developed the *LoadSense* technique, to obtain a measure of cellular load and predict the expected throughput class, while incurring little overhead. In turn, LoadSense enables the *Peek-n-Sneak* protocol, which allows a set of devices to implicitly coordinate their (background) communications, with a view to benefitting them all in terms of higher throughput and lower energy drain.

On a broader note, cellular networks are reputed to be closed, operator-controlled entities. Even so, our work shows that it is possible for end devices to glean information indirectly and be smart about how they communicate, for the benefit of both the devices and the network. Such a win-win proposition could nudge operators towards greater openness.

# 10. ACKNOWLEDGEMENTS

We thank our shepherd, Thyaga Nandagopal, and the anonymous reviewers for their constructive comments. We thank Ajay Manchepalli for helping us collect measurements in US.

# 11. REFERENCES


[1] iPhone 4s Review. http://bit.ly/uLXlUm.

[2] Samsung Galaxy S2 Review. http://bit.ly/qjMdYv.

[3] C. Dovrolis, P. Ramanathan, and D. Moore. Packet-dispersion techniques and a capacity-estimation methodology. *IEEE/ACM ToN*, 12(6):963–977, 2004.

[4] A. Downey. Using pathchar to estimate internet link characteristics. In *In Proceedings of ACM SIGCOMM*, 1999.

[5] H. Falaki, D. Lymberopoulos, R. Mahajan, S. Kandula, and D. Estrin. A first look at traffic on smartphones. In *Proceedings of the 10th annual conference on Internet measurement*, pages 281–287. ACM, 2010.

[6] M. Heusse, F. Rousseau, R. Guillier, and A. Duda. Idle sense: An optimal access method for high throughput and fairness in rate diverse wireless lans. In *ACM SIGCOMM*, 2005.

[7] N. Hu and P. Steenkiste. Evaluation and characterization of available bandwidth probing techniques. 21(6), 2003.

[8] M. Jain and C. Dovrolis. End-to-end available bandwidth: measurement methodology, dynamics, and relation with tcp throughput. In *In Proceedings of ACM SIGCOMM*, 2002.

[9] D. Koutsonikolas and Y. C. Hu. On the feasibility of bandwidth estimation in 1x evdo networks. In *In Proceedings of the ACM Mobicom International Workshop on Mobile Internet Through Cellular Networks (MICNET 2009)*, September 2009.

[10] K. Lakshminarayanan, V. N. Padmanabhan, and J. Padhye. Bandwidth estimation in broadband access networks. In *ACM/USENIX Internet Measurement Conference*, October 2004.

[11] M. Li, M. Claypool, and R. Kinicki. Wbest: a bandwidth estimation tool for ieee 802.11 wireless networks. In *In Proceedings of IEEE LCN*, 2008.

[12] X. Liu, A. Sridharan, S. Machiraju, M. Seshadri, and H. Zang. Experiences in a 3g network: interplay between the wireless channel and applications. In *MobiCom*, 2008.

[13] U. Paul, A. Subramanian, M. Buddhikot, and S. R. Das. Understanding traffic dynamic in cellular data networks. In *In Proceedings of IEEE INFOCOM*, 2011.

[14] F. Qian, Z. Wang, A. Gerber, Z. Mao, S. Sen, and O. Spatscheck. TOP: Tail Optimization Protocol for Cellular Radio Resource Alocation. In *Proceedings of the eighteenth IEEE International Conference on Network Protocols*, Kyoti, Japan, October 2010.

[15] A. Schulman, V. Navda, R. Ramjee, N. Spring, P. Deshpande, C. Grunewald, K. Jain, and V. N. Padmanabhan. Bartendr: A practical approach to energy-aware cellular data scheduling. In *Proceedings of the 16th Annual International Conference on Mobile Computing and Networking (Mobicom)*, Chicago, Illinois, September 2010.

[16] J. Strauss, D. Katabi, and F. Kaashoek. A measurement study of available bandwidth estimation tools. In *In Proceedings of ACM Internet Measurement Conference (IMC)*, 2003.

[17] W. L. Tan, F. Lam, and W. C. Lau. An empirical study on 3G network capacity and performance. In *INFOCOM*, May 2007.

# ParkSense: A Smartphone Based Sensing System For On-Street Parking

Sarfraz Nawaz, Christos Efstratiou, Cecilia Mascolo
Computer Laboratory, University of Cambridge, UK
{firstname.lastname}@cl.cam.ac.uk

## ABSTRACT

Studies of automotive traffic have shown that on average 30% of traffic in congested urban areas is due to cruising drivers looking for parking. While we have witnessed a push towards sensing technologies to monitor real-time parking availability, instrumenting on-street parking throughout a city is a considerable investment.

In this paper, we present ParkSense, a smartphone based sensing system that detects if a driver has vacated a parking spot. ParkSense leverages the ubiquitous Wi-Fi beacons in urban areas for sensing unparking events. It utilizes a robust Wi-Fi signature matching approach to detect driver's return to the parked vehicle. Moreover, it uses a novel approach based on the rate of change of Wi-Fi beacons to sense if the user has started driving. We show that the rate of change of the observed beacons is highly correlated with actual user speed and is a good indicator of whether a user is in a vehicle. Through empirical evaluation, we demonstrate that our approach has a significantly smaller energy footprint than traditional location sensors like GPS and Wi-Fi based positioning while still maintaining sufficient accuracy.

## Categories and Subject Descriptors

C.3 [**Special-Purpose And Application-Based Systems**]

## General Terms

Design; Experimentation; Measurement

## Keywords

Smartphone Sensing; On-street Parking; Wi-Fi Fingerprinting

## 1. INTRODUCTION

In metropolitan city centers and dense urban areas around the world, parking space is an expensive and often scarce resource. This scarcity leads to high demand for parking space and during busy periods of the day, it is common for drivers to spend a significant amount of time searching for available spots. While off-street parking garages are usually equipped with necessary infrastructure to estimate the number of unoccupied spaces, the situation with on-street parking is less favorable. This lack of information on the availability of on-street spaces is usually frustrating for users and leads to cruising drivers looking for vacant spots.

A study [21] of major downtown areas has shown that 30% of the traffic in these congested areas is in fact due to cruising vehicles. This situation can be alleviated by providing real-time occupancy information to cruising drivers. In [19] the authors show, through a simulated model of an urban city center, that when real-time occupancy of on-street parking is disseminated to drivers, it results in a reduction of 15% in total travel time. In a survey reported in [18], it is shown that 30% of the 483 surveyed drivers changed their intended parking destination in response to road-side guidance signs indicating space availability at car parks. It is reasonable to expect similar behaviour change when users are presented with on-street parking availability information. If this information is accessed before the start of the journey, it can also potentially result in a change of transport mode, for example, a user might decide not to drive if there are no spaces available in the vicinity of his/her intended destination.

A number of on-going research efforts are aiming at systems that can offer real-time parking availability estimations. These efforts rely on specialized infrastructure, either embedded in roads [4] or on vehicles [17] to capture real-time space occupancy. However, there are significant costs involved in instrumenting large cities. On the other hand, smartphone applications such as ParkMobile[1] and PaybyPhone[2] that allow users to view where parking spaces are located and also pay for these, have seen a wider adoption. Considering the ease of deployment and maintenance costs, it is reasonable to assume that soon the majority of urban parking will be managed and paid for through smartphones.

Motivated by this trend, we develop ParkSense, a smartphone based sensing system that can detect if a driver has vacated a previously occupied parking space. The primary design goal of ParkSense is to minimize its impact on the battery life of the user's device while still maintaining an accuracy level that could allow estimations on parking availability. The requirement for low energy prevents us from using traditional location sensors available on smartphones which typically impose a significant energy cost. ParkSense,


*MobiCom'13,* September 30–October 4, Miami, FL, USA.
Copyright 2013 ACM 978-1-4503-1999-7/13/09 ...$15.00.
http://dx.doi.org/10.1145/2500423.2500438.

[1] `http://www.parkmobile.co.uk/`
[2] `http://paybyphone.co.uk/`

therefore, uses the wireless interface to sense user mobility. It takes advantage of the widely deployed Wi-Fi access points in urban environments that periodically transmit their SSIDs as beacons. ParkSense uses robust Wi-Fi signature matching based on the beacon reception ratio to detect a user's return to the parked vehicle. We show that, in our outdoor scenario, this beacon reception ratio based signature matching performs significantly better than signal strength based functions used by previous location tracking approaches [14, 15]. ParkSense also utilizes a novel approach to detect if the user has started driving by observing the rate of change of visible access points. The primary contributions of this work are as follows:

- We develop a smartphone based sensing system for on-street parking space occupancy that can be readily integrated into systems in use today.
- We show through micro-benchmark energy measurements and experiments from actual devices that our approach is much more energy efficient as compared to traditional location sensors. Our approach consumes less than 30% of the energy of possible alternatives based on traditional location sensors on smartphones.
- We empirically demonstrate through a four month user trial, the feasibility of using smartphone based sensing to detect unparking events in order to estimate parking availability.

The rest of this paper is organized as follows. In the following section, we discuss the motivation and the design guidelines that led us to ParkSense in more detail followed by the analysis of energy consumption of traditional location sensors available on current smartphones. We then present our approach and the results from our four month long user study. We conclude with a discussion of some of the limitations of our approach and how these can be mitigated.

## 2. MOTIVATION

The majority of on-street parking spaces are managed through legacy parking meters where the driver has to pay a fixed amount for a predefined duration, or pre-pay for the expected time that they intend to leave their vehicle. The side-effect of this model is that the majority of the drivers tend to over-pay for their parking time to avoid being penalized with large fines for overstaying. This makes information collected through such systems unreliable for estimating parking availability. Furthermore, as the majority of the legacy parking meters are offline, there are no mechanisms to capture accurate real-time availability of parking spaces which can be very precious to route drivers to appropriate parking areas. While the situation is rapidly changing with electronic and smartphone based payments for parking, the legacy model of pre-payment is still prevalent.

The proliferation of mobile phone based parking payment applications offers a unique opportunity to capture parking availability information through the users' mobile devices. In the central London borough of Westminster, over 9,000 on-street parking spaces managed by the local city council, accept only electronic payments for parking, with a smartphone application as the predominant means of payment. This smartphone based system is being gradually rolled out to other parts of London and also in other UK cities. In this work, we explore the feasibility of augmenting such parking payment mobile applications with sensing capabilities that would allow the accurate detection of available parking space for on-street parking. Through a series of consultations with domain experts and parking management companies, we identified that the primary objective is to design a mobile phone sensing service capable of detecting when a driver vacates a parking spot, with minimal impact on the driver's mobile device. Indeed, considering that phone-based parking payment applications can accurately capture the time when a driver occupies a space, the main challenge is to discover when that space is vacated — in most cases long before the payment has expired.

We established a close collaboration with a major company offering phone-based parking payment systems in the UK in order to explore the requirements for a parking availability estimation system. During this process we discussed the possiblity of relying on user feedback about parking duration, expecting users to report through their mobile phone when they unpark their car. However, such solution was considered unreliable. Previous attempts to rely on user feedback about parking availability, such as Google OpenSpot [1] have failed to gain traction, with users often forgetting to report when they depart from a parking spot, thus not allowing a reliable estimation of city-wide parking availability. The possiblity of using financial rewards to incentivise unparking reporting was dismissed as well. In most on-street parking areas in the UK, there are a number of stakeholders involved in managing them. Parking prices are planned and managed by local city authorities, often based on a pricing strategy that is intented to incentivize drivers to avoid certain locations at different times of the day. Payment technologies, such as smartphone based payments, are typically outsourced to specialised companies. For such companies to accept the incorporation of a parking availability detection system on their mobile applications, it was important to avoid any interference with the pricing scheme managed by the local authorities. Offering financial rewards to drivers related to their parking behaviour was considered such interference. Furthermore, domain experts raised concerns that linking the use of such application with financial rewards would carry the risk of motivating users to try to deceive the system in order to maximise their fiancial gains. Based on these observations we, therefore, aimed for a system that can detect unparking without user intervention.

Unparking detection through mobile phone sensing can have a significant impact on the battery life of users' mobile device. Therefore, for any such system to be accepted, the primary concern is to minimize the battery consumption required for detecting an unparking event. On the other hand, using such information to estimate parking availability means that the accuracy requirements can be relatively low. The SFpark [4] system, an infrastructure based parking detection system deployed in the city of San Francisco, considers 70% detection accuracy as acceptable [3] for estimating parking occupancy. This assessment is justified by the fact that a parking availability information system estimates availability based on aggregated data from multiple users in a given area. Inaccuracies in the sensing data are therefore less important as long as the number of participating users is high. Based on these observations, we attempt to design a detection mechanism with minimal energy requirements for the user's device (in order to facilitate wider adoption), while relaxing the need for high accuracy that perhaps could be achieved through more expensive sensing.

The key requirements for the design of such system are: (i)

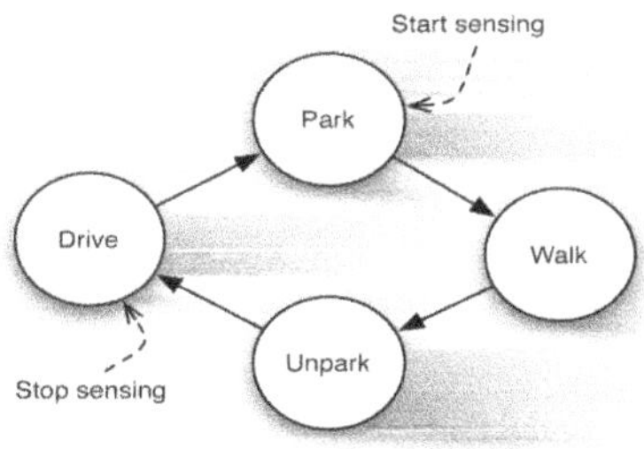


Figure 1: In a *pay-by-phone* parking application, sensing is initiated when the driver has parked and paid. Detection of unparking requires tracking the driver until they return to their vehicle and drive away.

considering that parking is initiated by payment, the system should be able to detect the time at which the driver returns to the vehicle and unparks, (ii) the system should be able to detect unpacking incidents without user intervention with minimal energy overhead, (iii) the system should not collect user location information beyond the parking location.

# 3. ALTERNATIVE SENSORS

Using mobile phone sensing to detect when a driver vacates a parking space can be considered a special case of an activity detection problem. It can be defined as a sequence of specific actions that are expected by the driver: (i) initiate a parking incident through mobile phone payment, (ii) walk away from the vehicle, (iii) return to the vehicle, (iv) drive away (Figure 1). This sequence of actions is primarily related to the relative location of the driver and the vehicle. A typical approach for detecting these actions could be to rely on localization technologies readily available on current smartphones. In this section, we explore the feasibility of detecting these actions using location sensors.

## 3.1 GPS Based Location

GPS based location tracking could be considered a natural choice for our application. Continuous tracking of users, after they have parked their vehicles, could allow us to determine when they return to their vehicles. Furthermore, estimation of the user's speed from the GPS sensor can be used to discover if the user is driving again after returning to the parked vehicle. However, there are several issues with this approach as we further discuss.

It is well known that GPS receivers require a significant amount of time to acquire an initial fix and to produce a location estimate after being switched on. The time required to acquire an initial fix is also unpredictable because it depends on several factors such as the time since last fix and surrounding environment affecting the signal multipath [13]. While Assisted GPS aims to shorten this delay by acquiring ephemeris data through cellular networks, the time required to search and acquire satellite signals is unavoidable. This delay is typically translated to additional energy consumption by the GPS chip.

While new GPS chips have significantly improved energy consumption, GPS sensors are still very power hungry. Figure (2a) shows the instantaneous current drawn by a Samsung Galaxy S2 running a location-based application that requests a GPS reading every 10s. The measurement was collected outdoors where the phone had a clear view of the sky. The "baseline" current drain of the device, when the GPS is switched off is 36.3 mA. The mean current consumption jumps to 115mA when the API requests location from the GPS sensor. In this particular case, it takes about 45s for the GPS to acquire an initial fix and subsequent requests take on average 7s. The energy consumed for the initial fix is 23,447mJ and the mean energy consumption for subsequent requests is 2,831mJ.

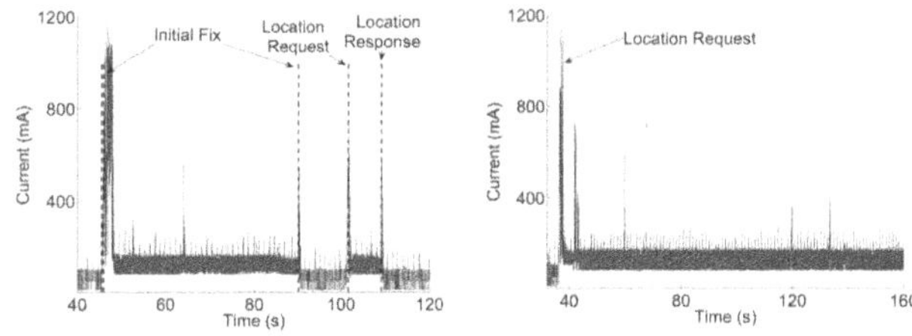


(a) Outdoors (b) Indoors

Figure 2: Energy consumption of GPS sensor

This measurement represents a best case scenario as the phone is outdoors with a clear view of the sky. In our parking application, it is highly likely that the user will move indoors after parking his or her vehicle. While it is well known that GPS receivers struggle to estimate location without a clear line of sight to satellites [9, 14], the energy consumption is also significantly higher in these scenarios. Figure (2b) shows the current consumption on the same smartphone as our previous experiment when it is moved indoors. In this case, not only is the sensor unable to estimate location, the device current consumption also stays constantly high at 120mA.

## 3.2 Network Based Location

An alternative location API available on current smartphones is network based location. This requires the mobile device to perform a scan for surrounding Wi-Fi access points. The captured access point SSIDs are transmitted over the cellular network to a remote server which translates this SSID set into a location coordinate using a wardriving database. Although this enables the mobile device to quickly acquire location coordinates, this approach is more suited for one off queries rather than periodic location updates due to the high energy consumption of the cellular radio interface. Figure (3) shows the current consumption for a single location query using the network based location API on both Samsung Galaxy S2 and Samsung Galaxy S1 devices. It shows that the device continues to draw high current even after the location response is received due to the 3G tail. The total energy cost of performing a single network based location request is 8,229mJ and 3,920mJ for Samsung Galaxy S2 and S1 respectively.

In addition to its energy characteristics there are other issues with this approach. As network based localization relies on wardriving data, it offers relatively coarse grained location. Due to the high energy costs of network based location queries, smartphone operating systems also aggressively cache the location responses thus making this approach less suitable for continuous tracking.

We now briefly analyse the energy consumption of Wi-Fi scanning which will form the basis of our approach for detecting unparking events. Figure (4) shows the current

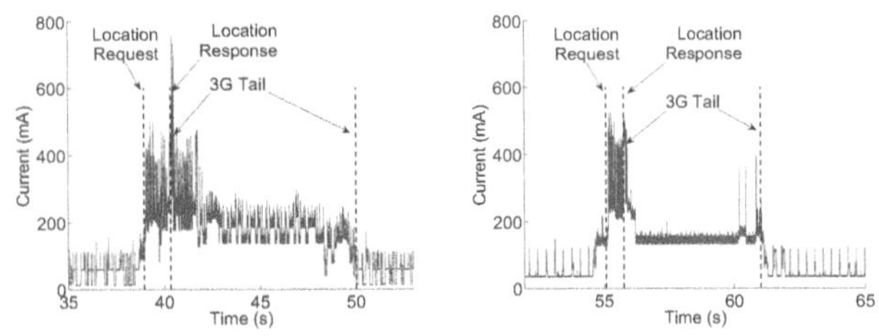


(a) Samsung S2 (b) Samsung S1

Figure 3: Energy consumption of network location

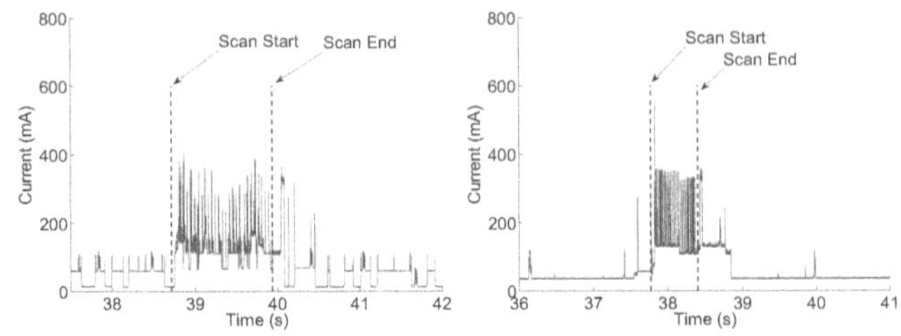


(a) Samsung S2 (b) Samsung S1

Figure 4: Energy consumption of Wi-Fi scanning

consumption of both of our test devices while performing a passive scan for Wi-Fi access points. The mean current consumption for Samsung Galaxy S2 and S1 is 114mA and 140mA, respectively. A passive scan usually takes a fixed amount of time. It takes 1.2s and 0.65s to complete the scan resulting in an energy cost of 512mJ and 335mJ on Galaxy S2 and S1, respectively.

### 3.3 Accelerometer

Although an accelerometer is not an alternative sensor for tracking the location of a user, in our specific scenario it can be used to detect the actual activity of the driver. The accelerometer is an attractive option because of its low energy consumption. It has been exploited in a number of activity detection systems [8] to detect physical activities, such as "walking", "cycling", "driving", etc. However, achieving high accuracy through accelerometer data alone can be quite challenging. Challenges include the variability of the readings depending on the phone placement — traces from a phone attached to the vehicle's dash board will be very different to those from a phone in the driver's pocket — and whether the classifier is trained over a dataset collected from the actual user.

In the parking scenario, the accelerometer can assist in detecting the transition between a driver walking back to their vehicle and driving. However, if used without any additional information regarding the relative location between the driver and the vehicle, it can lead to erroneous results. For example, simply detecting the change between walking and riding a car could lead to wrong inferences for users who park their car in order to use public transportation, such as busses or trains — a common scenario in metropolitan centers. A more practical use of the accelerometer in this scenario could be to act as a low power sensor that can trigger more accurate detection through location based sensing [23].

This shows that while current smartphones are equipped with a range of sensors and location technologies, these are not suitable for our application scenario either due to high energy consumption or dependence on user specific factors. Following the analysis of possible sensing modalities, we now embark on the design of a novel approach motivated by the specific requirements of our application.

## 4. WIRELESS BASED SENSING

The primary motivation for the design of ParkSense is to build a mobile phone application that can detect the evacuation of parking spaces, while minimizing the impact on the user's mobile device. We saw in the previous section that performing passive wireless scans is the lowest energy operation as compared to other location sensors. This motivates us to explore the wireless interface as a sensor to sense driver mobility.

Current smartphone based parking payment systems require the user to make a payment for the amount of time that they intend to stay in on-street parking before they leave the vehicle. These users generally use a smartphone application provided by the parking management company where they enter a unique location code and their payment details to pay for parking while they are still at the parking location. Each set of parking slots has a unique location code that is clearly marked on a sign on the pavement beside the parking space. When the payment transaction completes, the user can leave the vehicle. Leaving the vehicle without making the payment leaves them open to parking infringement fines and tickets. ParkSense captures a wireless signature during this payment phase by running multiple Wi-Fi scans when the user is at the parking location waiting for the transaction to complete. This wireless signature consists of the SSIDs of the Wi-Fi access points and the number of times a beacon frame was received from each access point. Let us represent this Wi-Fi signature with sets

$$\mathbf{S_p} = \{s_p(1), s_p(2), \ldots s_p(n)\} \quad \text{and}$$
$$\mathbf{W_p} = \{w_p(1), w_p(2), \ldots w_p(n)\}$$

where $s_p(i)$ is the SSID and $w_p(i)$ is the beacon reception ratio for access point $i$ and $n$ is the total number of access points observed in all the scans. The beacon reception ratio $w_p(i)$ is the fraction of scans for which the access point $i$ was visible i.e. $w_p(i) = v_p(i)/m$ where $v_p(i)$ is the number of scans in which a beacon frame was received from access point $i$ and $m$ is the total number of scans. ParkSense saves this signature and then periodically performs new wireless scans as the user moves away from the vehicle. From each successive window of size $m$, it creates a new signature with $\mathbf{S}_t$ and $\mathbf{W}_t$ in the same manner as described above. It uses these periodically generated signatures to decide if the user has returned to the parked vehicle.

This is similar to Wi-Fi fingerprint based localization [6]. However, as opposed to traditional localization where each fingerprint is assigned a coordinate in the geographic space, we do not perform any translation from the fingerprint to the real coordinates. This allows us to do away with any other external input (either from the user or any other sensor like GPS) and thus the sensing relies only on performing passive Wi-Fi scans. This makes this approach significantly more energy efficient. Detecting that the user has vacated a parking spot can be decomposed into two sub-problems,

1) sensing that the user has returned to the parked vehicle location 2) detecting that the user is in a moving vehicle after returning to the parking location. In the following subsections, we describe how ParkSense functions to sense these scenarios.

## 4.1 User Returning to Vehicle

ParkSense detects the return of the user to the parked vehicle by comparing the periodically generated signature sets $\mathbf{S}_t$ and $\mathbf{W}_t$ with the saved signature $\mathbf{S}_p$ and $\mathbf{W}_p$. However, this is a challenging problem because wireless signals are affected by multi-path fading, device placement close to the body and the changing environment in urban areas. The access points are usually located within the buildings and other infrastructure that attenuate the radio signals significantly. Therefore, the signal strength of radio signals received by the mobile device is usually just above the radio transceiver sensitivity making it difficult for the radio to receive the beacon frames. This manifests in a continuously changing wireless environment even if the user or the mobile device is stationary. To overcome these issues, we define the Wi-Fi signatures over a set of scans rather than a single scan. We also use the beacon reception ratio as opposed to the signal strength in our Wi-Fi signatures. It has been shown that the beacon reception ration can be more robust and a better indicator of distance in outdoor urban environments [7] as compared to received signal strength. From $\mathbf{W}_p$, we define a set of normalized reception ratios $\hat{\mathbf{W}}_p$ as,

$$\hat{\mathbf{W}}_p = \{\hat{w}_p(1), \hat{w}_p(2), \ldots, \hat{w}_p(n)\} \quad (1)$$

where $\hat{w}_p(i) = w_p(i)/\sum_i^n w_p(i)$. These normalized beacon reception ratios can be thought of as weights assigned to access points. An access point that was visible in all the scans gets a higher weight whereas the ones that appear in only a few scans get lower weights assigned to them. We then define the matching between saved signature and the current signature as,

$$M = \sum_{i=1}^{l} \hat{w}_p(i) \quad for \quad s_p(i) \in \mathbf{S}_p \cap \mathbf{S}_t \quad (2)$$

where $0 \leq M \leq 1$ and $l = |\mathbf{S}_p \cap \mathbf{S}_t|$. Therefore, the matching function is just the sum of normalized weights of access points that are common to both signatures. When no beacons are received from access points that were seen at the parking location, the matching $M = 0$ and it increases as more and more of those access points re-appear. Access points that were seen more frequently at the parking location result in a larger increase in $M$ as opposed to those that were observed infrequently. This matching function takes into account all of the access points initially observed at the parking location and does not discard the ones with low reception ratios. It merely trusts them less than those that were frequently seen.

Here we must point out that Eq. (2) relies on the normalized weights from $\hat{\mathbf{W}}_p$ only and does not use $\mathbf{W}_t$. To observe if this has any effect on the signature matching performance, we define two more matching functions. Eq. (3) defines a matching function that penalizes the access points according to the difference between the saved reception ratios and currently observed values. Eq. (4), on the other hand, defines a function that removes the reception ratio completely and uses the percentage of saved access points as the matching function. We will refer to Eq. (2) as Weighted, Eq. (3) as Weighted Difference and Eq. (4) as Percentage. In Section 6 we will compare the performance of these to signal strength based signature matching functions.

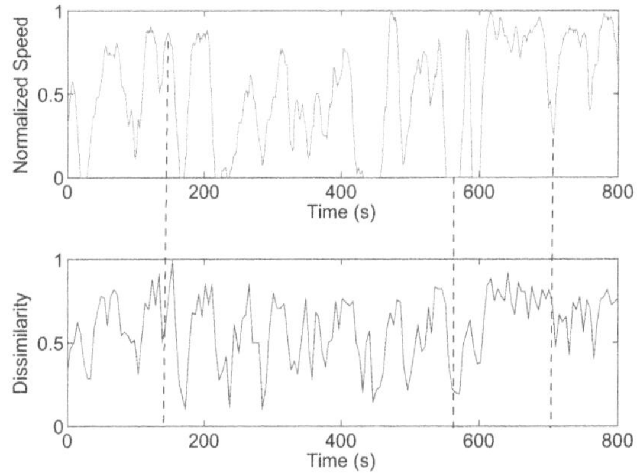


Figure 5: Comparison of normalized GPS speed and Jaccard dissimilarity between successive Wi-Fi signatures.

$$M = \sum_{i=1}^{l} \hat{w}_p(i)(1 - |w_p(i) - w_t(i)|) \quad (3)$$

$$M = \frac{|\mathbf{S}_t \cap \mathbf{S}_p|}{|\mathbf{S}_p|} \quad (4)$$

## 4.2 User Driving Away

When the user is in a vehicle that is moving at a typical urban road speed, the successive wireless signatures observed by the mobile device bear very little similarity as the vehicle comes within range of access points that may be located in buildings beside the road and then moves away from them quickly. A vehicle traveling in urban traffic tends to follow a certain pattern. It accelerates quickly, travels at a certain speed, decelerates and then comes to a stop due to queues, traffic lights or road junctions. In fact, the entire journey of a vehicle in an urban area is composed of these start stops known as driving cycle in transportation research [11]. In order to demonstrate this, we collect a GPS trace from a mobile device in a vehicle traveling in urban traffic. Figure (5) shows the speed of the vehicle for this particular trip in the top plot. It shows that in urban traffic, a vehicle continuously speeds up and then stops either due to other vehicles or traffic lights.

But what effect do these drive cycles have on the wireless beacons observed by the mobile device inside the vehicle? In order to answer this question, we take a trace of Wi-Fi scans collected by the same mobile device. These scans were divided into windows of size m=4 (We will show in Section 6 that other window sizes are possible and that the window size has little impact) and for each window, we create the signature sets $\mathbf{S}_t$ and $\mathbf{W}_t$. Then we compute the Jaccard similarity [12] between each pair of successive windows as,

$$J = \frac{|\mathbf{S}_t \cap \mathbf{S}_{t-1}|}{|\mathbf{S}_t \cup \mathbf{S}_{t-1}|} \quad (5)$$

Jaccard similarity is merely the ratio of the number of access points observed in both windows to the total number

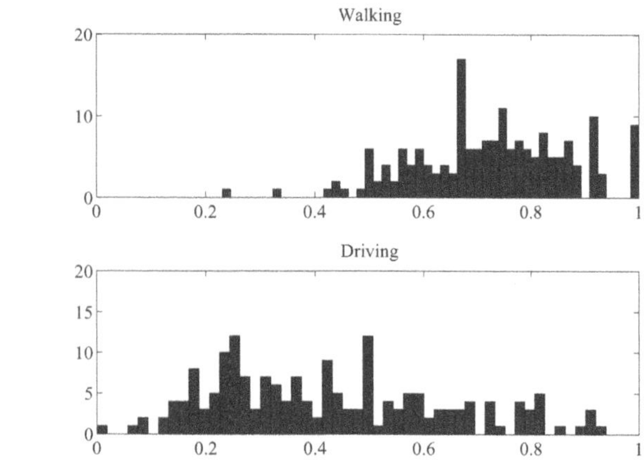


Figure 6: Comparison of the distribution of Jaccard Index for walking and driving in an city center.

of access points in the two windows. As the vehicle speeds up, we expect the successive windows to be different (low similarity) and as the vehicle slows down, these successive windows to be more and more similar. In order to make the visual comparison easy, we plot the dissimilarity $1 - J$ (also known as the Jaccard distance) between each pair of successive windows and the normalized GPS speed in Figure (5). This shows that there is a strong correspondence between the wireless beacons observed by the smartphone and the speed at which the user carrying the phone is traveling. Therefore, the wireless signature can be used as a proxy to estimate user mobility.

However, one might ask, what does the wireless signature look like when the user is not in the vehicle but continuously moving. Could this be mistaken for vehicular movement? In order to answer this, we collected another trace where a user carrying the same mobile device walked in the same urban area where the vehicle was traveling. Figure (6) shows the distribution of Jaccard Index for a user walking in the same urban area. It also compares it with the one obtained from the vehicle trace and shows that the Jaccard Index for the vehicular trace varies much more than pedestrian type mobility. In order to detect that a user is moving away in a vehicle, we need a mechanism that can detect a change from ordinary pedestrian mobility to vehicular mobility by inspecting the distribution of the Jaccard Index. In the following paragraphs, we briefly describe an algorithm for this.

### *Page-Hinckley Test*

The Page-Hinckley Test (PHT) also known as Cumulative Sum (CUSUM) test is a widely used statistical algorithm for detecting a changes in processes [10]. It uses sequential observations of the process and detects if the process mean has shifted by more than the specified amount. The sequential nature of the algorithm is particularly attractive for our application where the results of Wi-Fi scans arrive periodically. As the name suggests, the algorithm sequentially computes cumulative sums using the following two equations,

$$S_{hi}(i) = \max(0, S_{hi}(i-1) + x_i - T - k) \quad (6)$$

$$S_{lo}(i) = \max(0, S_{lo}(i-1) + T - k - x_i) \quad (7)$$

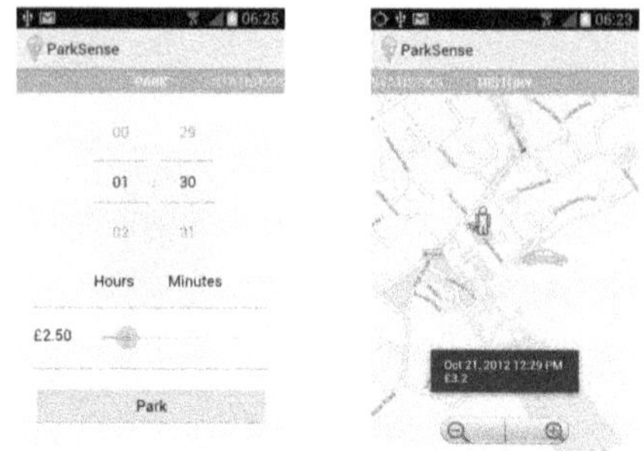


Figure 7: Android App used for collecting realistic data during user study.

where $S_{hi}(0) = S_{lo}(0) = 0$, $x_i$ is the process mean usually calculated from a sample of $q$ observations, $T$ is the target value of mean for which the process is considered to be under control and $h$ and $k$ are design values. When the value of $S_{hi}(i)$ or $S_{lo}(i)$ exceeds $h$, the process is considered to have undergone a change. The value of $k$ is calculated as,

$$\bar{\sigma} = \sigma/\sqrt{q} \quad (8)$$

$$k = \delta\bar{\sigma}/2 \quad (9)$$

where $\sigma$ is the process standard deviation and $\delta$ is the amount of shift in the process mean that we want to detect expressed as a multiple of standard deviation of sample means. We use this approach to detect when the mean of the Jaccard Index J computed over successive windows drops below a threshold which indicates that the user is moving in a vehicle in urban traffic.

## 5. EXPERIMENTAL STUDY

We developed a smartphone application for Android OS that was released through Google Play (Figure 7). The application was launched as a parking logger allowing users to record where they parked their vehicle and collect statistics about parking payments. Essentially the application emulates the behaviour of a pay-by-phone parking application where users enter the amount of time that they intend to park and the amount of money that they had paid when they parked their vehicles. When a parking event is triggered by the user, the application records the wireless signature of the parking location and then continues to perform Wi-Fi scans and saves this data in a log file. Users can then mark the unparking event by pressing a button. This triggers the GPS sensor which is used to collect the data during driving. The smartphone application communicates with a back-end service hosted on Google App Engine to upload the logged data using a RESTful API. The application displays all the previous parking locations, durations and payments on a map. The same information is also available from a webpage where the users can login to view these details on a larger map in a browser window.

The data collection period lasted four months. During this period, 59 traces in 4 different cities were collected. Out of these 59 traces, the GPS data was available for 45 parking sessions. On inspection, we observed 41 of these sessions are complete sessions where the users eventually unpark and drive away. However, the remaining 4 traces were incomplete where the users appear to have triggered unparking but did not return and drive away. Nevertheless,

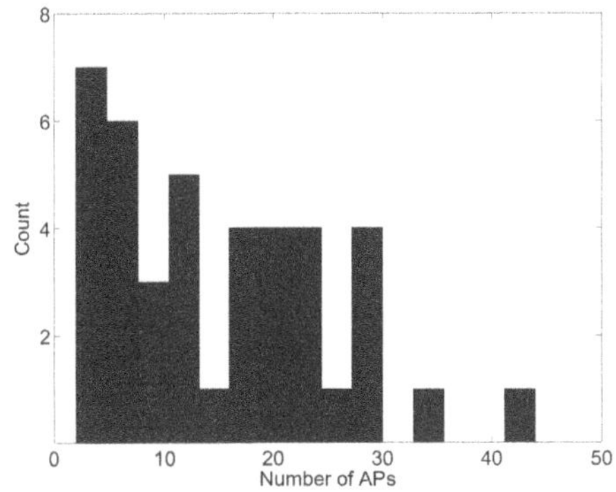


Figure 8: Distribution of APs at parking locations

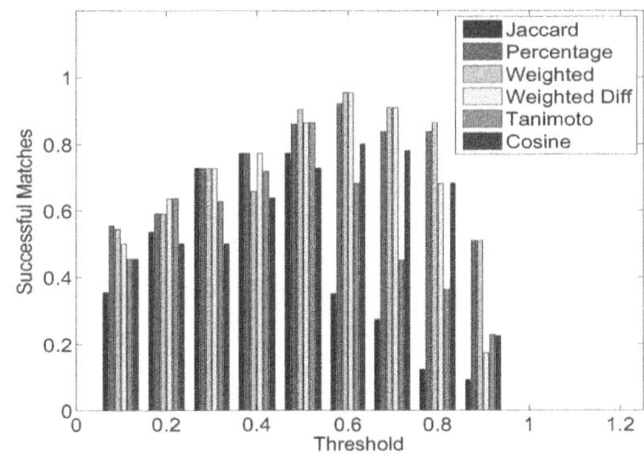


Figure 9: Comparison of different signature matching techniques.

we include these traces in our evaluation to test for false positives for driving detection. In our traces, the minimum parking duration is 15 minutes, longest one is 3.5 hours and the mean difference between the paid and actual parking time is 30 minutes. Figure (8) shows the distribution of access points observed at these parking locations. All the traces were collected from actual on-street parking at various locations.

# 6. EVALUATION

In this section, we evaluate the performance of our Wi-Fi based sensing approach to detect unparking events. First we evaluate the accuracy of the signature matching functions proposed in Section 4.1, then we look at the ability of the Wi-Fi signals to predict the mobility of the user, as described in Section 4.2, and finally we investigate the overall accuracy of the system in detecting unparking events.

## 6.1 Signature Matching

Previous research on Place Learning [14] and Proximity estimation [15] use a signal strength based similarity metric known as Tanimoto Coefficient to calculate similarity between Wi-Fi signatures. These applications are focused on indoor environments where the received signal strength from different access points located in the environment is usually quite high. Our outdoor application scenario, on the other hand, requires us to work with Wi-Fi signals that are usually severely attenuated. Under these conditions, the beacon reception ratio has previously been shown [7] to be a more robust choice. There are also several other general similarity metrics, including Jaccard Index and Cosine Similarity. We compare the three signature matching functions, Weighted, Weighted Difference and Percentage Intersection, proposed in Section 4.1 with the signal strength based Tanimoto Coefficient, signal strength based Cosine similarity and the Jaccard Index for comparing periodically captured signatures to the one saved during parking.

All of these matching functions produce a match value $0 \leq M \leq 1$ with zero for no match and one for a perfect match. We also have to choose a threshold $\tau$ such that $M \geq \tau$ is considered a match. If $\tau$ is set too high, it will result in a lower ratio of successful detections of the user returning to the parked location. This can be caused by irregular changes of the wireless signature due to multi-path fading, changing environment, missing or low reception ratio access points and thus rarely matching completely with the saved signature. If $\tau$ is set too low, it can result in false positives. For example, if the user parks the vehicle and walks to a nearby location, some of the access points will keep appearing in periodic scans and can cause a false match, indicating that the user has returned to the parking location when in reality he/she has not done so. Figure (9) shows the percentage of correctly identified user returns in 41 of our driving away traces as we vary the matching threshold $\tau$. It shows that our reception ratio based matching functions are able to correctly identify more than 90% of user returns with a threshold $\tau = 0.6$. The cosine similarity captures 80% of returns with Tanimoto just above 60%. As expected, the performance of all matching functions drops as the value of the threshold $\tau$ is reduced (resulting in false positives) or increased (resulting in missing user return).

In our traces, the scanning interval is 2s i.e. after every 2s the application performed and logged a scan. However, while the user is away, the scanning rate can be reduced significantly to save energy. We adopt an approach for adaptive scanning where the scanning frequency is throttled down when it is estimated that the user is far from the parked vehicle. Specifically, the approach that we adopt is to perform a single scan infrequently. If none of the access points $s_p(i)$ that were captured during the parking event appear in this scan, we can continue to perform infrequent scans. If, however, any of the captured access points appear again, it triggers frequent (2s) scanning and thus signature matching. This frequent scanning times out if the match value $M$ does not appear to increase or exceed the threshold $\tau$ indicating that the user is staying in the vicinity of parking location but not approaching it. If this happens, the next trigger to fast scanning is done on access points $s_p(i)$ that have not been observed so far to avoid continuous triggering. We explored the potential duration of infrequent scanning interval, by subsampling the collected traces captured by our mobile application. We found that in our traces an interval of up to 60s can be maintained with this approach, without affecting the accuracy of detection.

## 6.2 User Driving

In Figure (5), we showed that there is a strong correspondence between the Jaccard Index calculated over successive windows and user speed. Now we quantify this correspondence. We split the traces where the drivers unparked and

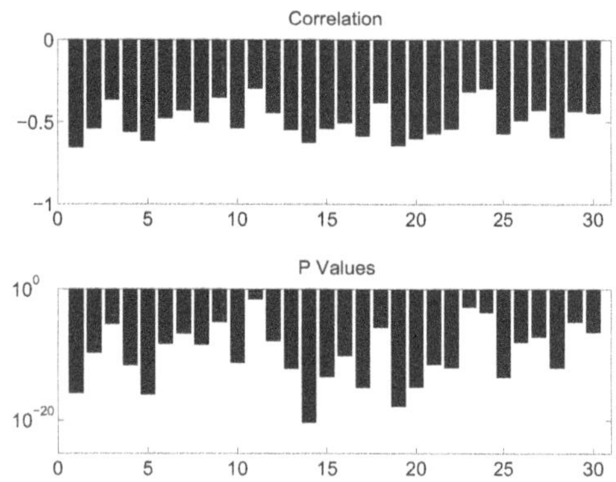


Figure 10: Correlation between normalized GPS speed and Jaccard Index computed over successive scan windows.

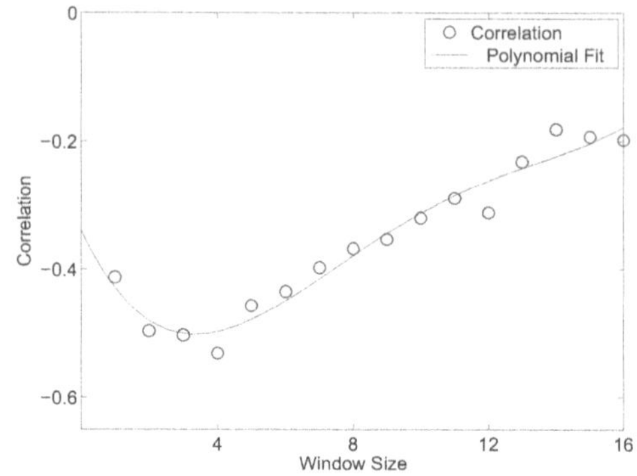


Figure 11: Optimal window size.

drove away from parked locations into parking and driving periods using the GPS ground truth. Then we calculate the Jaccard Index over successive windows of Wi-Fi scans (with window size m=4) during the driving portion of the trace. And finally, we calculate the correlation between the user speed obtained from GPS and the Jaccard similarity over adjacent scan windows. Figure (10) shows the correlation coefficients for a random sample of 30 traces: a strong correlation between vehicle speed and the Jaccard similarity calculated from the Wi-Fi scans as the user moves in an urban space is evident. The coefficients are negative because, as the user speed increases, the similarity between scan windows becomes small and vice versa. Figure (10) also plots the P-values for these coefficients. These values are extremely small (on the order of $10^{-15}$ to $10^{-20}$), which suggests that the associated correlation values are indeed significant. To determine the best window size for sensing, we vary it and observe its effect on the correlation coefficients. Figure (11) shows that as the window size increases, the median correlation between user speed and the Jaccard similarity goes down. It shows that the maximum (negative) correlation is achieved with window size of 4.

## 6.3 Sensing Accuracy

We now look at the sensing accuracy of the complete system i.e. the ability of the system to detect unparking events. An unparking event consists of a user return (indicated by the wireless signature match) followed by the system sensing (using the PHT test) that the user is moving at high speed. We first look into how the parameters of the PHT are set. In Figure (6), we showed that the distribution of the Jaccard Index calculated over successive scan windows is quite different for a user that is walking along a road in an urban space as opposed to the one traveling in a vehicle in typical urban traffic. We take a random sample of 10 traces from our 41 driving traces and use these as a training set for our detection algorithm. The sample is split into portions of when the user is away from the vehicle and when the user is traveling in the vehicle. Figure (12) shows the distribution of the standard deviation of Jaccard similarity for the two portions of these traces. It shows that the standard deviation of Jaccard Index is about 0.16 before driving and rises above 0.22 when the users drive away. We, therefore, choose $\sigma = 0.22$, $\delta = 1$ (to detect a change as small as one standard deviation) and sample size $q = 5$ to calculate $k$. Figure (6) shows that the mean of Jaccard Index is around 0.5 when the user is traveling in the vehicle. Thus, we choose a target mean value of $T = 0.55$ and use PHT (Equations (6) and (7)) to detect when the mean value of Jaccard Index calculated over successive windows falls below $T$ indicating that the user is driving. Furthermore, for the driving away detection we used a time threshold for the maximum duration of the detection run. This was set to 15min after the user has returned to the vehicle, so as to keep the duration of any background sensing within reasonable bounds.

From the 41 traces where the users actually unparked and drove away, ParkSense was able to detect user returns in 38 instances. The misses are due to the fact that the urban radio environment is dynamic and at times can lead to beacons with high reception ratio to disappear during the scan window. Out of these 38 instances, ParkSense was able to sense that the user is driving in 34 cases within the 15min time window. On average, PHT took 5.3min to detect driving. The remaining instances where ParkSense was not able to detect driving was due to users driving slowly or stopping for extended periods of time. It is clear that as the drivers eventually speed up and the mean Jaccard Index falls, driving will eventually be detected. This, however, requires the sensing process to run longer in order to capture such special cases. For the 4 non driving cases where users accidentally marked return to vehicle but did not drive, it was able to correctly detect non driving behaviour in all 4 instances.

The accuracy of the detection mechanism depends on the selected parameters for configuring PHT (values of $\sigma$, $\delta$, $T$ and maximum sensing duration). These parameters can be fine tuned in the deployed system by collecting data from probe vehicles. It is possible to use some of the users as probes by triggering the GPS sensor when a return to vehicle is detected and using the GPS trace as ground truth to fine-tune the specific parameters. These fine tuned parameters can then be passed to the mobile devices of new users during the payment transaction. Finally, as discussed in Section 2 since the purpose of the ParkSense app is to feed data into a parking availability information system, we anticipate that possible detection inaccuracies will be smoothed out when data from multiple users is aggregated for a given location.

## 6.4 Special cases

In all the traces we collected through the ParkSense application, the behavior of the users followed the pattern shown

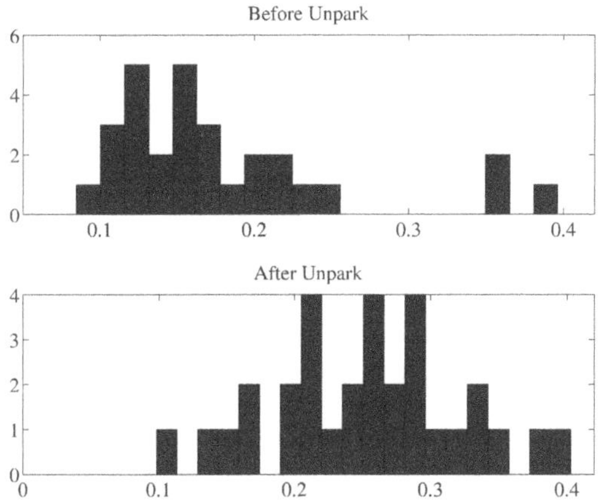


Figure 12: Standard deviation of the Jaccard Index calculated over successive windows before and during driving.

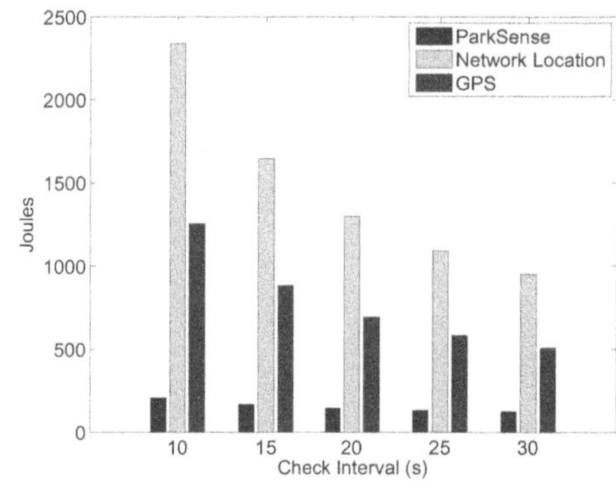


Figure 13: Energy cost of detecting an unparking event.

in Figure (1). However, there are situations where the user may not follow this particular pattern. Example cases are:

- After parking, the driver returns to the parking location and drives away in a friend's car. If the two cars are close to each other, the ParkSense application will falsely detect such an action as "unparking".
- A driver parks a vehicle and makes a payment that triggers sensing. However, the driver then gives the keys to someone else, who unparks the vehicle. ParkSense will not be able to detect this unparking event.
- The driver returns and unparks as expected. However, immediately after vacating the space, he/she gets stuck in the traffic. In this scenario, ParkSense may not accurately detect the release of the space, considering that the car has not yet driven away. In this particular case ParkSense will eventually detect the evacuation when the vehicle moves at a speed higher than the walking speed.

Although these are rare scenarios, and we have not witnessed any such cases during our deployment, nevertheless they can have an impact on the estimated parking availability. Such errors can be mitigated through a more conservative recommendation engine for parking availability, where users are directed to areas where more than one space might be available. Current infrastructure based systems already take this approach by reporting only coarse-grained availability of parking spaces. These systems label streets with high, moderate or low probability of finding a space as opposed to reporting the exact number of available spaces.

## 6.5 Energy Consumption

The energy consumption of sensing an unparking event depends on the number of wireless scans performed during each phase of our approach i.e. detecting a return to the parked vehicle and sensing that the user is driving. Thus the total energy consumption for a parking session can be given as,

$$E_{ParkSense} = E_{scan}\left(\frac{t_{away}}{t_{check}}\right) + E_{scan}\left(\frac{t_{drive}}{t_{scan}}\right)$$

where the two parts of above equation represent the energy consumed during the two phases of our approach. During the first phase it performs infrequent scans to check if a user is returning to the parked vehicle by observing if any of the access points captured during parking payment has reappeared. It then switches to frequent scans to perform signature matching and driving detection. In the above equation, $t_{check}$ is the interval with which infrequent scans are performed, $t_{away}$ is the time the user spends away from the vehicle, $t_{drive}$ is the time required to detect that the user has started driving, $t_{scan}$ is the wireless scanning interval during this second phase and $E_{scan}$ is the energy required to perform one wireless scan. The mean value of $E_{scan}$ for Samsung Galaxy S2 (from Section 3) is 512mJ, the mean value of $t_{away}$ in our traces is 42 minutes, the mean value of $t_{drive}$ (from Section 6.3) is 5.3 minutes and $t_{scan}$ is 2s. Based on these values, Figure (13) shows the energy consumption of our approach for different check intervals. The energy consumption of a possible alternative approach that relies on GPS can be given as,

$$E_{GPS} = 2\ E_{Fix} + E_{indoor}\left(\frac{t_{away}}{t_{check}}\right) + E_{outdoor}\left(\frac{t_{drive}}{t_{sample}}\right)$$

This assumes the typical scenario in which the user moves indoors during $t_{away}$. The GPS sensor looses its initially acquired fix and consumes $E_{indoor}$ amount of energy for each location request during this period. As the user moves out and starts driving, it acquires a fix again with the energy cost of $E_{Fix}$ and then starts consuming $E_{outdoor}$ energy for each location estimate generated every $t_{sample}$ seconds. We use $E_{Fix} = 23,447$mJ, $E_{outdoor} = 2,831$mJ and $E_{indoor} = 4,428$mJ (assuming that it is kept on for at least 10s) from Section 3 and $t_{sample} = 10$s for these calculations.

Another possible alternative approach would be to use the network based location. The energy consumption of this approach can be given as follows,

$$E_{Network} = E_{netloc}\left(\frac{t_{away}}{t_{check}}\right) + E_{netloc}\left(\frac{t_{drive}}{t_{sample}}\right)$$

where $E_{netloc}$ is the energy required to perform one network based location query. We use $E_{netloc} = 8,229$mJ calculated in Section 3 for these calculations. Figure 13 compares the energy consumption of both of these possible alternatives to our approach. It shows that the energy consumption of our approach is significantly smaller than both of these alternatives. The cost of our approach is only 11% of the energy

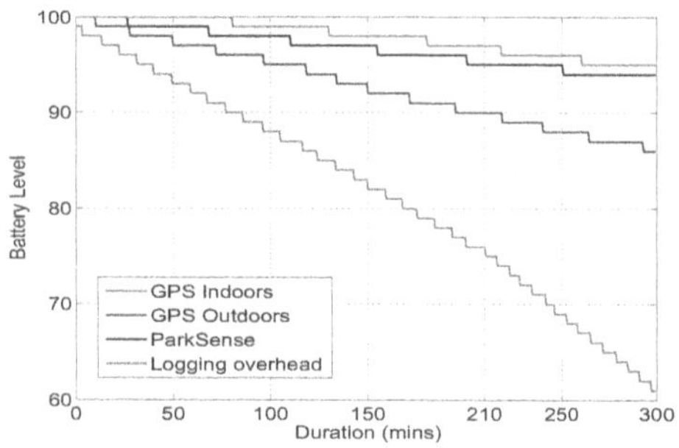


Figure 14: Battery level for various sensing approaches.

consumption of network based location and 21% of the energy consumption of GPS based approach.

In our traces, the longest parking session is 3.5 hours. With a typical 1650mAh phone battery and a 60s check interval that can trigger frequent scanning, the predicted energy consumption of our approach is around 1% of the battery life. In order to verify this, we run a series of experiments on a Samsung Galaxy S2 phone. For each experiment, the battery is fully charged and an application is run that samples the selected sensor at 60s intervals. It also logs the remaining battery level reported by the operating system. Figure (14) shows the results of these experiments. It shows that in the standby mode the phone consumes 3% of the battery due to the battery logging overhead. With our approach of Wi-Fi scanning at 60s intervals, it consumes only 5% of the battery, a small increase of 2% over the standby mode. On the other hand, battery usage for periodic sampling from the GPS sensor depends on where the phone is located during sensing. If the phone is outdoors with a clear view of the sky, GPS is able to acquire periodic location fix and consumes about 10% of the battery. However, it consumes 24% of the battery when it is indoors where it is difficult to acquire a fix. This presents the upper and lower bounds for the energy consumption of GPS sensor. In our parking application, we expect that most of the users will move indoors after parking. This not only increases the energy consumption but also makes it difficult to duty cycle the GPS sensor based on user distance from the parking location as the GPS sensor typically fails to produce a location estimate in this case. Another issue that makes it difficult to duty cycle GPS in an energy efficient manner is the unpredictable time required to acquire a fix [16]. On the other hand, our Wi-Fi based approach is free from these issues due to the fixed response time and energy consumption of the wireless transceiver.

Energy consumption for location sensing may be further reduced in some cases through the use of a low energy sensor such as acceleromter that can trigger more expensive sensing when needed (as described in Section 3.3). Such techniques are orthogonal to any of the aforementioned methods. Therefore, the difference in energy consumption will still follow the same relative trend.

# 7. RELATED WORK

## 7.1 Location Tracking Systems

There are previous pieces of work that use Wi-Fi signature matching for tracking user location. In [9] authors use Wi-Fi signature matching to learn places that can be of significance to a user. They use signature matching to sense user dwell time and mark places with large dwell times as significant. In [14], the authors present another approach that can detect more fine-grained places using signature matching. However, these approaches are focused on sensing in indoor environments and therefore use signal strength based matching functions to discriminate between nearby places in buildings, offices etc. These matching functions perform well in these environments where signal strength is high due to proximity to access points. But, as we have shown, these signal strength based functions do not perform well in our outdoor scenario where the RSSI is usually low. In [7], authors show that beacon reception ratio is a more robust indicator of distance in outdoor environments. They use it to estimate distances to access points. These distances are then used for performing localization. There is a large body of work on Wi-Fi fingerprint based localization [6]. These approaches use parameters of the signal strength distribution to form a fingerprint for a location. This makes them susceptible to changes in signal strength which is common in outdoor environments.

## 7.2 Parking Detection Systems

A number of smart street parking aids systems have been proposed. The SFPark project [4] is trialling the use of wireless sensor nodes embedded into asphalt at each parking location for real-time occupancy detection in down-town San Francisco. The occupancy information is collected in a central server and then provided to users looking for parking spots. A similar trial is under way in central London [2] and commercial ventures like StreetLine [5] are commercializing this technology. However, the main issue with this approach is the extremely high cost of the complete system that hinders large scale deployment. For example, the SF-Park project proposes to cover only 25% of the parking spots in San Francisco at the total cost of 19.8 million US dollars, and this does not account for the system maintenance once in place. Similarly, the trial installation in London covers only 137 parking spots. Such systems have not been widely adopted often because they require large investments and long term commitments from local governments.

Mathur et. al. [17] propose a mobile sensor network for collecting road side parking spot occupancy. They use a vehicle equipped with a GPS receiver and an ultrasound transceiver attached to the passenger side as a mobile sensor. As the vehicle drives forward, the ultrasound transceiver measures its distance to the road side objects and thus used to estimate if the space is occupied or vacant. The authors propose to equip all the vehicles that routinely travel across the urban space, such as taxis, buses, police vehicles etc. with this sensing technology.

Google OpenSpot [1] smartphone application is a crowdsourcing alternative and allows drivers to mark a parking spot as *open* if they were vacating the parking location. Other drivers looking for parking could view these empty spots on their smartphones. The main drawback of this approach is the lack of incentive for the drivers to submit a report. Yan et. al. [24] try to address this problem by designing an online auctioning system around the availability of a parking spot, offering financial incentives to participating users. The drawback of this approach is that it still requires manual user intervention for the system to be useful. This often leads to users either forgetting or not caring enough to send availability reports. An approach that automatically detects user departure from a parking location can overcome such problems.

### 7.3 Transport Modality Detection

Significant research efforts have concentrated on the detection of transportation modes using smartphone sensing. Typical approaches rely on accelerometer or a combination of accelerometer and location sensing (e.g. GPS). In [20] authors use a combination of accelerometer and GPS data and achieve a 93.6% accuracy in detecting user's mode of transportation. Although such mechanisms are valuable for a general purpose activity detection framework, they come at the expense of power hungry modalities, such as GPS. Other pieces of work have explored the use of accelerometer as a low power sensor that can trigger the use of expensive sensing such as GPS. In [22] authors perform a light-weight activity classification on continuous accelerometer data in order to trigger GPS tracking when the user is within a public mode of transportation such as bus or underground. We consider this approach complementary to the Wi-Fi sensing presented in the paper. Although not the focus of this paper, suspending sensing when the user is not moving can certainly allow further reductions in energy consumption.

## 8. CONCLUSIONS

We have presented an approach to on-street parking real-time information management through mobile phone wireless sensing. Our approach takes advantage of the low power consumption of the Wi-Fi radio to effectively report when drivers leave parking spots. In contrast to other approaches that either use fixed sensing infrastructure or user originated information, our aim was to devise an automatic framework to capture real time parking occupancy. Our evaluation reports on accuracy and power efficiency of the approach with respect to both a GPS and network location based solution. We present robust signature matching based on beacon reception ratio and a novel approach to driving detection.

In terms of future work, our plan is to negotiate with the developers of one of the exiting parking payment applications to incorporate this technique in their framework.

## 9. ACKNOWLEDGMENTS

This research has been funded by the EPSRC Innovation and Knowledge Centre for Smart Infrastructure and Construction project (EP/K000314).

## 10. REFERENCES

[1] Google open spot: A useful application that no one uses. `http://www.androidauthority.com/google-labs-open-spot-a-useful-application-that-no-one-uses-15186/`. [Online; accessed 4-December-2012].

[2] London parking technology trial. `http://www.westminster.gov.uk/services/transportandstreets/parking/bay-sensor-technology/`. [Online; accessed 4-December-2012].

[3] Parking sensor performance standards and measurement. `http://sfpark.org/wp-content/uploads/2011/09/SFpark_SensorPerformance_v01.pdf`. [Online; accessed 10-March-2013].

[4] SFPark. `http://sfpark.org`. [Online; accessed 4-December-2012].

[5] Street Line. `http://www.streetline.com`. [Online; accessed 4-December-2012].

[6] Paramvir Bahl and Venkata N. Padmanabhan. Radar: An in-building rf-based user location and tracking system. In *INFOCOM*, pages 775–784, 2000.

[7] Yu-Chung Cheng, Yatin Chawathe, Anthony LaMarca, and John Krumm. Accuracy characterization for metropolitan-scale wi-fi localization. In *Proceedings of the 3rd international conference on Mobile systems, applications, and services*, MobiSys '05, pages 233–245, New York, NY, USA, 2005. ACM.

[8] Sunny Consolvo, David W. McDonald, Tammy Toscos, Mike Y. Chen, Jon Froehlich, Beverly Harrison, Predrag Klasnja, Anthony LaMarca, Louis LeGrand, Ryan Libby, Ian Smith, and James A. Landay. Activity sensing in the wild: a field trial of ubifit garden. In *Proceedings of the SIGCHI Conference on Human Factors in Computing Systems*, CHI '08, pages 1797–1806, New York, NY, USA, 2008. ACM.

[9] Jeffrey Hightower, Sunny Consolvo, Anthony LaMarca, Ian Smith, and Jeff Hughes. Learning and recognizing the places we go. In *Proceedings of the 7th international conference on Ubiquitous Computing*, UbiComp'05, pages 159–176, Berlin, Heidelberg, 2005. Springer-Verlag.

[10] D. V. Hinkley. Inference about the change-point from cumulative sum tests. *Biometrika*, 58(3):509–523, 1971.

[11] WT Hung, HY Tong, CP Lee, K. Ha, and LY Pao. Development of a practical driving cycle construction methodology: A case study in hong kong. *Transportation Research Part D: Transport and Environment*, 12(2):115–128, 2007.

[12] P. Jaccard. Distribution de la flore alpine dans le bassin des drouces et dans quelques regions voisines. *Bulletin de la Société Vaudoise des Sciences Naturelles*, 37(140):241–272, 1901.

[13] Elliott D. Kaplan and Christopher Hegarty. *Understanding GPS: Principles and Applications.* Artech House Publishers, 2 edition, November 2005.

[14] Donnie H. Kim, Younghun Kim, Deborah Estrin, and Mani B. Srivastava. Sensloc: sensing everyday places and paths using less energy. In Jan Beutel, Deepak Ganesan, and Jack A. Stankovic, editors, *SenSys*, pages 43–56. ACM, 2010.

[15] M.B. Kjærgaard, M. Wirz, D. Roggen, and G. Troster. Mobile sensing of pedestrian flocks in indoor environments using wifi signals. In *Pervasive Computing and Communications (PerCom), 2012 IEEE International Conference on*, pages 95–102. IEEE, 2012.

[16] Mikkel Baun Kjærgaard, Jakob Langdal, Torben Godsk, and Thomas Toftkjær. Entracked: energy-efficient robust position tracking for mobile devices. In *Proceedings of the 7th International Conference on Mobile Systems, Applications, and Services (MobiSys 2009)*, pages 221–234. ACM, 2009.

[17] Suhas Mathur, Tong Jin, Nikhil Kasturirangan,

Janani Chandrasekaran, Wenzhi Xue, Marco Gruteser, and Wade Trappe. Parknet: drive-by sensing of road-side parking statistics. In *Proceedings of the 8th international conference on Mobile systems, applications, and services*, MobiSys '10, pages 123–136, New York, NY, USA, 2010. ACM.

[18] Mike McDonald and Kiron Chatterjee. VMS in urban areas - Results of cross-project collaborative study. Technical Report TR1101 D3.3.1-a, Transport Sector of the Telematics Applications Programme (T-TAP), March 2000.

[19] Nadereh Moini, David Hill, and Rooholamin Shabihkhani. Impact assessments of on-street parking guidance system on mobility and environment. In *Transportation Research Board 92nd Annual Meeting*. Transportation Research Board, 2013.

[20] Sasank Reddy, Min Mun, Jeff Burke, Deborah Estrin, Mark Hansen, and Mani Srivastava. Using mobile phones to determine transportation modes. *ACM Trans. Sen. Netw.*, 6(2):13:1–13:27, March 2010.

[21] Donald C. Shoup. Cruising for parking. *Transport Policy*, 13(6):479 – 486, 2006.

[22] Arvind Thiagarajan, James Biagioni, Tomas Gerlich, and Jakob Eriksson. Cooperative transit tracking using smart-phones. In *Proceedings of the 8th ACM Conference on Embedded Networked Sensor Systems*, SenSys '10, pages 85–98, New York, NY, USA, 2010. ACM.

[23] Yi Wang, Jialiu Lin, Murali Annavaram, Quinn A. Jacobson, Jason Hong, Bhaskar Krishnamachari, and Norman Sadeh. A framework of energy efficient mobile sensing for automatic user state recognition. In *Proceedings of the 7th international conference on Mobile systems, applications, and services (MobiSys 2009)*, pages 179–192, New York, NY, USA, 2009. ACM.

[24] Tingxin Yan, Baik Hoh, Deepak Ganesan, Ken Tracton, Toch Iwuchukwu, and Juong-Sik Lee. A crowdsourcing-based parking reservation system for mobile phones. Technical Report UM-CS-2011-001, Department of Computer Science, University of Massachusetts, Amherst MA, 2011.

# How Voice Calls Affect Data in Operational LTE Networks

Guan-Hua Tu, Chunyi Peng, Hongyi Wang, Chi-Yu Li, Songwu Lu
University of California, Los Angeles, CA 90095, USA
{ghtu, chunyip, hywang, lichiyu, slu}@cs.ucla.edu

## ABSTRACT

Both voice and data are indispensable services in current cellular networks. In this work, we study the inter-play of voice and data in operational LTE networks. We assess how the popular CSFB-based voice service affects the IP-based data sessions in 4G LTE networks, and visa versa. Our findings reveal that the interference between them is mutual. On one hand, voice calls may incur throughput drop, lost 4G connectivity, and application aborts for data sessions. One the other hand, users may miss incoming voice calls when turning on data access. The fundamental problem is that, signaling and control for circuit-switched voice and packet-switched data have dependency and coupling effect via the LTE phone client. We further propose fixes to the identified issues.

## Categories and Subject Descriptors

C.2.1 [**Computer-Communication Networks**]: Network Architecture and Design—*Wireless Communication*; C.4 [**Performance of Systems**]: *Design Studies*

## Keywords

Cellular Networks; Mobile Data Services; Voice Call

## 1. INTRODUCTION

Voice and data are both services indispensable to cellular networks. The IP-based, mobile data access is vital to the surge of smartphones and tablets. In parallel, cellular voice has been the killer application to carriers and users for years. In a legacy 3G network, voice calls are supported via the circuit-switched (CS) path, and data are offered via its packet-switched (PS) route. However, the 4G LTE[1] technology decides to use PS delivery only. This is good news for IP-based mobile data, but poses challenges for voice support. In the absence of CS delivery, LTE carriers have been using a popular solution to voice service, called circuit-switched fallback (CSFB) [1]. CSFB leverages the deployed 3G/2G infrastructure and its CS delivery. It relays LTE voice calls to the legacy 3G/2G networks and enables CS-based voice service. Due to its simplicity and no extra deployment cost, most carriers, including four of the top-five worldwide operators [2, 3, 7, 8] and two major US carriers, have deployed or are planning to deploy CSFB.

[1]In this paper, we will use 4G and LTE interchangeably.


*MobiCom'13,* September 30–October 4, Miami, FL, USA.

http://dx.doi.org/10.1145/2500423.2500429.

In this work, we study the inter-play between voice calls and data services in operational LTE networks. Our objective is to understand how well the CSFB voice works with the PS data over LTE. We are interested in identifying scenarios where they may interfere with each other in both expected and unanticipated manners. We quantify their mutual impact, identify root causes, and design solution fixes.

At a first glance, the above problem seems to be either ill-posed or pretty trivial. In fact, the 4G LTE networks used by data service and the 3G/2G networks used by CSFB voice are indeed independent in operations. Voice and data thus have little mutual dependency. The only merging point is that, the 4G LTE phone has to switch its radio back to 3G/2G networks during a voice call. While it is anticipated that ongoing data may suffer from reduced throughput during the call, there is little beyond this expected performance degradation. However, our study shows this is not true.

Our experiments over two US operational LTE carriers (called as OP-I and OP-II) have yielded four findings, one expected and three unanticipated. First, we indeed observe throughput slump for data sessions up to 83.4% when the 4G LTE user falls back to 3G for voice calls. This drop is caused by the speed gap between LTE and 3G, but also incurred by data suspension and losses during CSFB-triggered handoffs between 4G and 3G. The good news is that this degradation occurs mainly during the voice call for OP-I ; However, for OP-II, the degradation may last even after the call ends (see Finding 2). Second, we discover that 4G LTE users may lose 4G connectivity due to voice calls. They will not return to 4G afterwards. The lost connectivity lasted more than 10 hours and showed no sign of limit. The issue occurs when certain background data traffic is running in some voice call scenarios. In particular, it happens when the voice call fails to be established (for OP-I), or no matter if the call is established (for OP-II). We identify that it is caused by the state machine "loophole" that 3G is unable to switch back to 4G under certain scenario. Third, data applications may abort (about 2-5% on average and 15% in the worst case in our tests) when a voice call ends. The network may implicitly detach the user, despite ongoing data sessions, when migrating the user back to 4G after CSFB calls. Consequently, the state or signaling triggered by CS voice also affects PS data service. Last, we discover that PS data may also affect CS voice. CS calls may not be available when the mobile turns on its PS service. The network state can then be changed by PS, thus leading to transient unavailability of CS. Table 1 summarizes all these four findings.

The above findings confirm that, the interference between voice and data in CSFB-capable LTE is mutual. Although these experi-

| Finding | Operators | Detail | Root Cause | Section |
|---|---|---|---|---|
| Throughput slump | OP-I, OP-II | Data throughput decreases (up to 83.4% observed); OP-I: only during the call, OP-II: during and after the call | Handoffs triggered by CSFB and speed gap between 3G and 4G | Section 4 |
| Losing 4G connectivity | OP-I, OP-II | Never returns to 4G after the CSFB call under certain data traffic; OP-I: when the call fails to be established, OP-II: any CSFB call | State machine "loophole" in 3G→4G transition | Section 5 |
| Application aborts | OP-I, OP-II | Application aborts occasionally (3.4% for OP-I, 5.7% for OP-II) after the call; | Network state changed by CS-domain operation (here, network detach caused by CSFB voice calls) | Section 6 |
| Missing incoming call | OP-I, OP-II | Misses all incoming calls temporally (for several seconds) while enabling the PS service | Network state changed by PS-domain operations | Section 7 |

**Table 1: Finding summary.**

mental cases do not necessarily represent the common usage scenarios, they do showcase worst, yet possible settings. It indeed reveals complicated dependency and coupling effects between voice and data. These effects are induced by the fundamental design of CSFB, as well as its implementation loopholes. We further devise solutions that coordinate with the LTE phone to fix these issues.

The rest of the paper is organized as follows. Section 2 introduces the 4G/3G architecture and voice support via CSFB. Section 3 describes our study methodology and the addressed issues. Sections 4, 5, 6 and 7 present each individual finding and explore its root causes. Section 8 proposes our solution fix. Section 9 discusses alternatives to CSFB. Section 10 compares with the related work, and Section 11 concludes this paper.

# 2. BACKGROUND

We introduce the 4G LTE architecture and its legacy 3G network. We then describe how voice and data services are provided.

**Cellular network:** Figure 1 illustrates the LTE architecture, as well as its legacy 3G network, i.e., UMTS (Universal Mobile Telecommunication System). The LTE network offers PS data service. It consists of core network, radio access network (RAN) and user equipments (UEs, i.e., mobile devices). Its RAN uses eNodeB (LTE base station) to offer radio access to UEs. Its network core is IP-based, consisting of MME (Mobility Management Entity) to handle user mobility (e.g., location update or paging UEs), and 4G gateways that route packets between the Internet and the 4G RAN.

In contrast, 3G network supports both PS and CS to offer data and voice, respectively. Its RAN uses RNS (Radio Network System) to provide radio access. Its core network has several main elements: (1) GMSC/MSC (Gateway Mobile Switch Center), which pages and establishes CS services (e.g., voice calls) with mobile users; (2) HLR/VLR (Home/Visitor Location Register), which stores user information (e.g., location updates); (3) 3G gateways, which route PS packets between the internet and the RAN. There exist 3G technology variants, such as 3G HSPA (High Speed Packet Access) that offers data rate up to 14.4–42 Mbps. Note that 3G architecture is also applicable to 2G; We only describe 3G since 2G is seldom observed in our study.

**Voice calls (and data) for 4G LTE users:** Since the LTE network uses PS only, it is unable to use CS to support voice, which traditionally requires guaranteed service quality. Instead, LTE uses CSFB that supports voice calls in the legacy 3G CS network. LTE also claims VoLTE (voice-over-LTE) as its ultimate voice solution [9], to be discussed in Section 9.

In CSFB, when a 4G user is called, the incoming call is routed to the GMSC in 3G networks. GMSC then queries HLR/VLR to learn which MSC the 4G user is located at, and forwards this call to the serving MSC. The MSC subsequently pages the user device through MME. Once the UE is found, MME migrates it from 4G

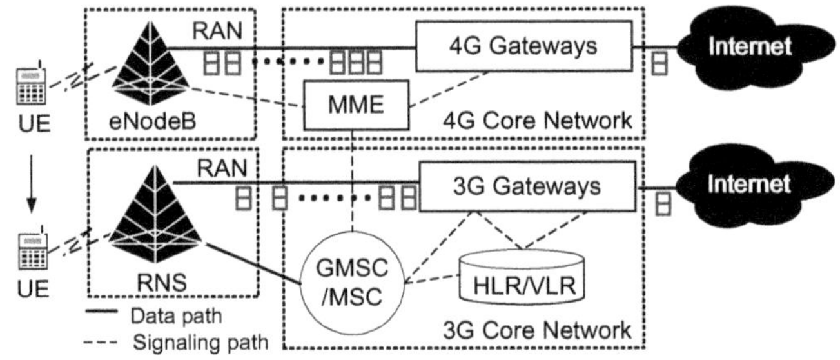


**Figure 1: 4G/3G network architecture and CSFB.**

LTE networks to 3G networks via triggering inter-system handoff (i.e., from 4G to 3G). After the UE successfully connects to 3G RANs, the MSC establishes the voice call with UE. In the meantime, ongoing data sessions are also transferred to 3G networks together with voice. The outgoing call performs similarly except it sends MME a request to switch to 3G networks.

# 3. STUDYING CSFB IN OPERATIONAL LTE NETWORKS

In this section, we describe our experimental methodology and identify the key problem aspects to be studied.

## 3.1 Experimental Methodology

We conduct experiments in two major US LTE operators, denoted as OP-I and OP-II, for privacy concerns. They together serve more than 138M mobile subscribers and cover almost 50% US market share [13]. We use six phone models of LG Optimus G, Samsung Galaxy S3, S4 and Stratosphere, HTC One, and Apple iPhone5, running two mobile operating systems: Android and iOS. For OP-II, we use Galaxy S4 and iPhone5 only. They run popular applications (e.g., YouTube) or conduct data sessions with our deployed servers, including Apache Web server, FTP and TCP/UDP servers. For further performance analysis, our deployed TCP/UDP server adds a sequence number in each data packet to/from the UE. We primarily collect and analyze traces from Android phones, and Apple iPhone5 is used for verification experiments.

In each experiment, we collect five traces if available: (1) *Wireshark:* We use the Wireshark for packet capture traces on mobile devices and our deployed servers. (2) *TcpParms:* We use *getsockopt*, a socket API to periodically log TCP parameters, such as retransmission timeout or congestion window, on both our TCP server and mobile devices (root is required) . (3) *UdpSeq:* To verify whether out-of-order delivery is observed by CSFB-induced inter-system handoffs, we log the sequence number carried in the received UDP datagram and timestamps on our deployed UDP servers and mobile devices. (4) *NetworkStatus:*

Mobile devices also record network status information given by Android PhoneStateListener class. The *NetworkTrace* periodically collects phone status information including *timestamp*, *operator*, *network type*, *cell identifier*, *RSSI* (Signal Strength) and *IP address*. The record interval is 100ms. (5) *CallEvents:* Mobile devices also log all incoming-call events on phones via PhoneStateListener and outgoing-call events, e.g., ringing, and current timestamp.

## 3.2 Issues to Study

In operational LTE networks, data service is offered via the IP-based, PS service, while the voice service is provided through mechanisms such as CSFB. Since CSFB is probably the most popular mechanism in practice to support voice in LTE networks, we focus on it in this study. We discuss other alternatives of VoLTE and SVLTE in Section 9.

Conventional wisdom states that such data and voice will not *interfere* each other, or at least not to the degree beyond expectation. Anyway, data is going through the 4G LTE infrastructure, while voice is going through the separate 3G/2G networks. However, our study shows that this is not the case. We carry out our research along both directions: (I) How does CSFB voice affect the ongoing data service in LTE networks? and (II) How does the data session in LTE networks affect the voice service? While the results for (II) are presented in Section 7, the details for (I) need more elaboration and are given in Sections 4 - 6. As data service becomes increasingly important for mobile devices, it deserves more attention. In particular, we cover three aspects, expected, and unexpected, even certain worst-case scenario, regarding how voice affects data in the context of LTE networks:

1. How much is the performance degradation when voice calls occur? This is the somewhat expected case for performance penalty. The data session falls back to 3G/2G networks during a CS voice call and then returns to 4G data networks while the call ends. We seek to understand how TCP and UDP transport protocols react to such scenarios, as well as worse-than-expected instances (Section 4).
2. Can the data session go wrong when call completes or is never established? If it indeed occurs, it will be unanticipated exceptions for CSFB. We seek to show certain extreme cases of losing LTE connectivity and getting stuck in 3G even when voice calls complete or never start and explore their root causes (Section 5).
3. Can voice calls incur other negative performance impact beyond throughput degradation? In particular, we will illustrate cases of application abort when voice calls are underway and identify their root causes (Section 6).
4. Can the PS data also affect the CS voice call under certain conditions? If it is indeed observed, it shows that both data and voice have mutual interference on each other's operations (Section 7). We also explore its root cause.

Table 1 summarizes our findings over two US carriers on the above four issues. We elaborate them in Sections 4 to 7.

# 4. THROUGHPUT SLUMP

In this section, we first examine how data performance is affected by voice calls using CSFB in the *normal* case. The user might experience throughput slump during voice calls due to the handoff from 4G to 3G. This observation matches our expectation and recent reports [10]. We elaborate on what happens to TCP/UDP based data sessions and study the impact of regular CSFB calls. We finally report *worse-than-expected* findings: performance degradation under multiple handoffs (OP-I) or even *after* the voice call (OP-II).

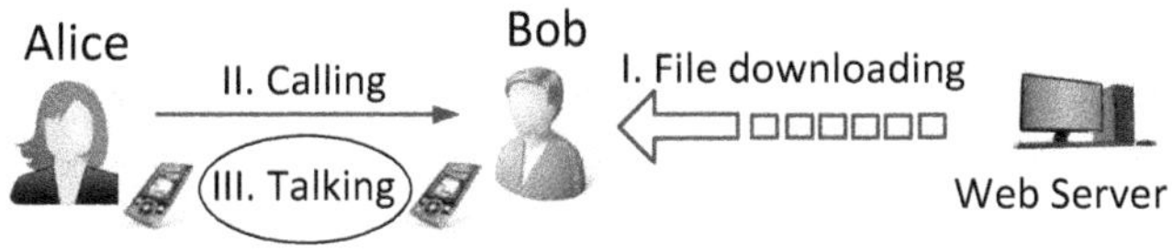


**Figure 2: Alice calls Bob while he is downloading a file.**

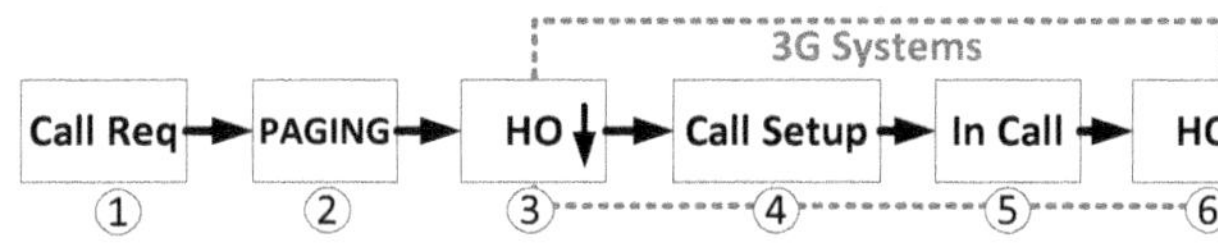


**Figure 3: CSFB event flow for an incoming call.**

## 4.1 An Illustrative Example

We use an example to illustrate the normal case performance. Bob is downloading a file to his Samsung Galaxy S3 via the high-speed 4G LTE network. Everything goes well until he receives a call from Alice. The call lasts about 22 seconds. The procedure is illustrated in Figure 2. Figure 4(a) records the data throughput, network type, and call events observed at Bob's phone using OP-I carrier. At the beginning (up to 29.8th second before the call), Bob enjoys high-speed data access up to 14 Mbps; During the voice call (during the interval [42s, 64s]), the throughput drops from 14 Mbps to 9 Mbps; When the call ends (about 64th second), the throughput increases to 14 Mbps in about 2 seconds. That is, the data throughput decreases by 35.7% (i.e., $(14-9)/14$) *during* the call.

**Cause:** The observed throughput slump is caused by CSFB. Figure 3 shows the CSFB event flow for an incoming call. We make four observations. First, when answering the incoming call, a handoff procedure from 4G to 3G is triggered. This inter-system handoff takes place (Step 3) even *before* the call is fully established (Step 4). Figure 4(a) shows that, Bob's phone call starts ringing around 33th second and is answered at 42th second. In contrast, the first handoff (LTE to 3G UMTS) completes at 31st second, earlier before the events of ringtone and call answering. Interestingly, at 35.4th second right after the first handoff, the network performs a second handoff (UMTS to 3G HSPA), which upgrades to higher-speed 3G HSPA networks (14.4 - 42Mbps theoretically). Second, the call proceeds during [42s, 64s] until the call hangs up. The phone stays in the 3G HSPA network during this period. Third, once the call completes, the phone switches back to 4G after two handoffs (HSPA to UMTS, followed by UMTS to 4G) at 65th and 66.4th seconds. Note that, the 4G CSFB standard [1] does not require that users be immediately switched back to 4G after the call ends, or how many handoffs be triggered to switch to 4G. The sixth step is OP-I's implementation choice. We will see OP-II's behaviors later. Last, we observe two data transmission suspensions (i.e., rate is 0 Mbps): 6.4 seconds during [29.8s, 36.2s] and 1.5 seconds during [64.3s, 65.8s]. Both periods are accompanied with handoffs. These handoffs lead to data transmission suspension [1]. Once the handoff is completed, the data transmission resumes.

We next address two issues: (1) How does TCP/UDP react to the above case? (2) Is there any worse-than-expected result, except the performance degradation caused by staying in 3G during the call? In particular, is there any difference between the handoff triggered by CSFB calls and the traditional, mobility-induced handoff?

## 4.2 TCP/UDP under Normal Voice Calls

**TCP:** In the above example, TCP data transmission is suspended during [29.8s, 36.2s] and [64.3s, 65.8s]. Figure 5 plots TCP logs

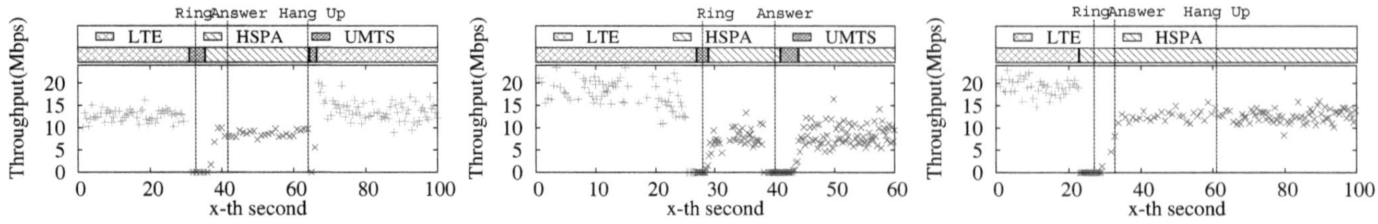


(a) OP-I (b) OP-I, more handoffs (c) OP-II

**Figure 4: Logs of data throughput (4G:+, 3G:×), network type (LTE, HSPA, UMTS) and call event (marked by black dashed lines) observed at Bob's phone in normal case of answering Alice's call. (a) OP-I: one 4G→3G handoff triggered; (b): OP-I: multiple handoffs triggered; (c): OP-II: no handoff back to 4G when the call ends.**

in [29s, 38s] at the TCP server in the example of Figure 4(a). Note that the server clock is slightly out of sync (about 0.2s to 0.3s) from the mobile's trace. We make three observations on the TCP trace. First, no packet delivery during handoffs results in multiple TCP timeouts. Around the 29.7th second, no ACKs are received for the packet with sequence number 44636389. Accordingly, the server retransmits it four times (at 29.7s, 30.6s, 32.3s, 35.8s, respectively). Second, large RTO may impede fast TCP recovery. The retransmission timeout (RTO) gradually doubles, here, 0.436s, 0.872s, 1.744s, 3.488s, 6.976s during [29.1s, 35.6s]. Large RTO values imply that TCP responds slowly once the network connection resumes. In this case, the fourth retransmission succeeds (another packet sent at 35.9s) and the suspension lasts around 6 seconds. Third, the TCP congestion window is about 244 MSS during [29s, 36s]. It does not reduce immediately upon retransmission timeout, thus different from the TCP specification (RFC 5681). The congestion window update is deferred when data transmission resumes. We believe this is a TCP implementation variant in Linux.

**UDP:** We observe behaviors similar to TCP, except that the suspension time for UDP is shorter. Since UDP does not have congestion and flow control mechanisms, its transmission resumes immediately after the PS service is available. In contrast, TCP RTO may not expire yet though the PS service resumes. We conduct experiments to test this hypothesis. Before a voice call comes, we start a 100 Kbps UDP downlink session and a TCP downlink flow on our 4G phone. As expected, average data suspension durations for UDP and TCP are 5.4 and 6.4 seconds, respectively. It takes longer for TCP to resume its transmission. We further observe out-of-order data delivery upon 4G→3G and 3G→4G handoffs.

## 4.3 Worse Than Expected

As expected, data performance degrades during the voice calls due to the speed gap[2] between 4G and 3G and data suspension during handoffs triggered by CSFB. Next, we are curious about whether any worse-than-expected results happen. We uncover two cases of further performance degradation: (1) due to more handoffs (OP-I), and (2) even after the call (OP-II).

**More handoffs (OP-I):** Handoffs are critical to data performance. Upon handoff, data transmission suspends, thus incurring TCP/UDP throughput decrease. Each CSFB call triggers two network switches: 4G → 3G upon call arrival and 3G → 4G after the call ends. In OP-I (Figure 4(a)), one 4G → 3G switch is enabled by two handoffs of LTE→ UMTS (before the phone rings) and UMTS→ HSPA (before the call is answered).

We next examine whether there is any difference between the handoff triggered by CSFB voice calls and the conventional handoff induced by mobility. Our study shows that the difference indeed

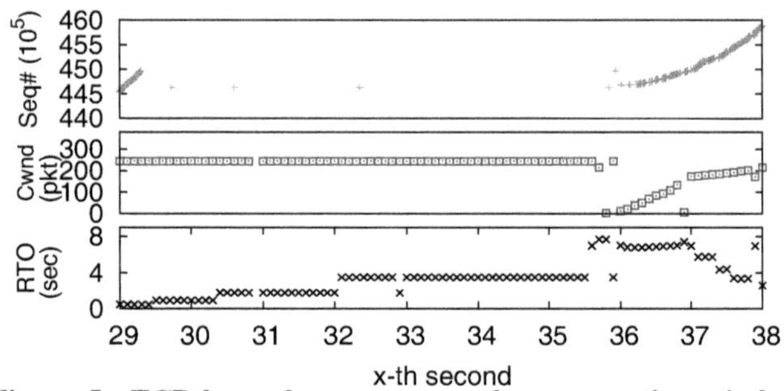


**Figure 5: TCP logs of sequence number, congestion window and retransmission timeout observed at Bob's TCP Server in the example of Figure 4(a).**

exists; More handoffs may be triggered by call-related events. We run a 100 Kbps UDP session while answering an incoming voice call. We repeat this experiment for 367 runs. In 218 runs, the handoff results are the same as the above example. However, in the remaining 149 runs, two additional handoffs ( HSPA→ UMTS and UMTS→HSPA) are triggered by the call-answering operation, as shown in Figure 4(b). Consider the speed of HSPA and UMTS (up to 14.4-42 Mbps and 2 Mbps for HSPA and UMTS, respectively). The mobile user suffers from another performance drop at around 40th second. Note that, the additional HSPA↔UMTS handoffs differ from the mobility-induced one. It is triggered by a call-answering event while the phone remains at the *same* location, performing data and voice services. In contrast, the traditional handoff to 3G UMTS typically occurs upon mobility (i.e., users move out of a HSPA cell).

**No handoff back to 4G (OP-II):** We observe similar performance drop during the call in both carriers. However, after the call ends, data throughput still remains low for OP-II, different from the throughput increase for OP-I. Figure 4(c) plots the mobile trace at Bob's phone using OP-II. In this example, Bob experiences a throughput slump from 19Mbps to 12.7Mbps during the call [31s, 61s]. However, the throughput still remains around 12.7Mbps after the call. We observe similar behaviors with different phone models (e.g., Galaxy S4 and iPhone5): the handoff occurs before the phone rings and the throughput remains similar after the call ends. Undoubtedly, it adversely imposes larger impact on data throughput. The mobile loses its 4G connectivity even after the voice call. This occurs because no handoff is invoked immediately after the call ends. We will explore its root cause in Section 5.

We further explore why these handoffs are invoked and whether they can be eliminated for performance improvement. Unfortunately, the inter-system handoff (4G→3G) is mandatory to support CSFB in order to access the 2G/3G circuit-switched service for voice calls. The additional handoff (HSPA ↔ UMTS) is the OP-

[2]More measurements can be found in Section 5.4.

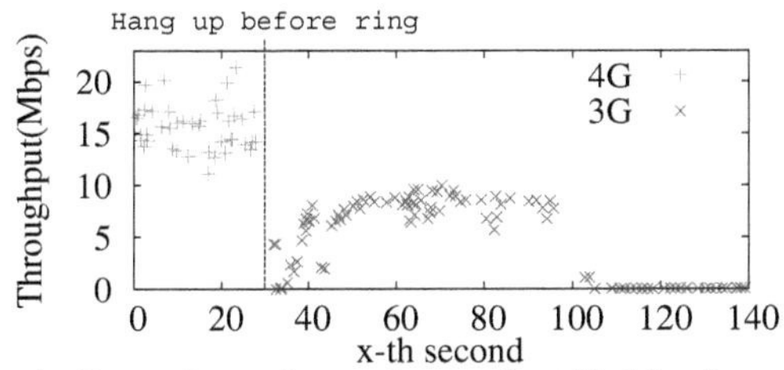


**Figure 6: Data throughput observed at Bob's phone if Alice immediately hangs (the outgoing call) up in OP-I carrier.**

I's implementation choice; it is not required in OP-II. The handoff back to 4G is also part of the operator's design choice. The CSFB standard never specifies when to switch back to 4G networks. In practice, OP-I decides to perform this handoff immediately, while OP-II does not.

# 5. LOSING 4G CONNECTIVITY

We observe that LTE users permanently lose 4G connectivity due to CS voice calls under certain conditions. In an extreme test scenario, the mobile phone is stuck in 3G networks longer than 10 hours and shows no sign of exiting. It remains in 3G networks even when the user drives on the route with stronger 4G signal. The condition of losing 4G connectivity varies among two operators. Compared with OP-II, OP-I has more complex settings.

## 5.1 OP-I: When the Call Fails to Establish

Our test scenario can be illustrated via the Alice-Bob example. However, after Alice calls Bob, she *immediately hangs up* because she realizes that it is too late to call Bob at 10PM. For Bob, his phone never rings and the call is never established. Assume that Bob has been downloading a file before the call. Contrary to our expectation, we discover that Bob gets stuck in the 3G network for a long time (or even unlimited duration). Figure 6 plots the data throughput measured at Bob's phone. It shows that Bob never returns to the 4G network even after the download halts at 100th seconds. The same is observed on all phone models using OP-I. Note that only some background data service keeps on running. Throughout this process, Bob is not even aware of what happens!

We now explore the root cause to lose 4G connectivity. It turns out that a loophole (in fact, a loop) in Radio Resource Control (RRC) state transition forces the 4G user to remain in 3G. RRC is the function that regulates the connection establishment and release between the UE and the core network.

Figure 7(a) plots the simplified RRC state transition in 3G/4G standards [1]. We do not consider 2G here since it is not observed in our experiments. We make two observations. First, the switch between 3G and 4G networks is enabled via the handover procedure (that occurs between 3G `FACH/DCH`[3] and 4G `CONNECTED` states) or the cell reselection procedure [1] (that is invoked between 3G `IDLE` and 4G `IDLE` states). Second, within 3G or 4G, the state transition (e.g., 3G `FACH/DCH` ↔`IDLE` or 4G `CONNECTED`↔`IDLE`) is determined by the connection establishment/release. For example, a RRC connection shall be established before the PS/CS service is used, or be released when the CS/PS service is in no use or remains idle for a long time.

The above RRC state machine brings an inherent risk of getting stuck in one network (e.g., 3G). In case the loop between 3G `FACH/DCH` and 3G `IDLE` is formed, the mobile user will be unable to escape from 3G. Unfortunately, our experiments confirm that such a loop indeed exists under certain conditions in OP-I. In particular, for an unestablished call, the RRC enters into the 3G loop with some ongoing data services.

[3]FACH and DCH are two RRC states that offer RRC connections for data delivery. FACH offers a RRC connection at lower speed with low power consumption, whereas DCH offers it at full speed with higher power consumption [1, 27].

**Unestablished Call State:** In the normal case, the mobile user moves back to the 4G network quickly (in about 2–4 seconds) after the call ends. However, the time prolongs if the call is not established. It occurs in two scenarios. One is that the 4G user is called but the caller hangs up immediately (usually within 4–6 seconds). The other is that the user makes an outgoing call and immediately hangs up after the handoff to the 3G network is done. In both cases, the mobile phone falls back to the 3G network though no call has been established.

The unestablished call state does make it longer move back to the 4G network. Figure 7(d) shows the call setup procedure (Step 4 of Figure 3) for the incoming call case. When the MSC sends a call-setup request to a 4G phone, it waits for the response from the phone in order to update its state as `Call_Received`. However, when the call is canceled before entering the `Call_Received` state (in the above two scenarios), the MSC will *not* update its call state. The user thus stays longer in the 3G network. This implies that the call state plays a critical role in the handoff operation. The unestablished call changes the trigger condition for handoffs, thus taking longer time to go back to 4G.

The duration to stay in 3G is largely independent of locations and phone models. We test with all phone models at four locations with different base stations. Each test repeats 20 runs. In the absence of data service, the duration to remain in 3G ranges from 7 to 8 seconds, varying slightly with locations. With background data traffic, we observe similar results independent of locations. We figure out that the duration is determined by other factors to be discussed in Section 5.3.

**Data Services in Parallel:** We discover that, the phone can stay in the 3G network for an extended period of time if some data service is ongoing in parallel. We run a large number of tests to study when and under what conditions the switch (back to 4G) takes place. We run the unestablished call experiments with a constant-rate UDP *uplink* session to our deployed server on Samsung Galaxy S3 and LG Optimus G. We vary the inter-packet spacing (i.e., packet interval) from 1 to 24 seconds, using 1B and 1KB UDP payload sizes. Each test repeats 20 runs. We observe similar results for both phone models, and only describe the results on Samsung Galaxy S3. Figure 8 plots the duration in 3G since the phone moves to 3G. The upper and lower lines mark the maximal and minimal durations in 3G. The 180-second duration implies that the phone never returns to 4G in 3 minutes. It clearly shows that the phone might get stuck in 3G under certain conditions. The condition specifics will be elaborated in Section 5.3.

In summary, we infer the RRC state transition machine for OP-I in Figure 7(b). The 4G→3G handoff is triggered when the call arrives (or is initiated), and the 3G→4G handoff occurs when the call ends after its establishment. However, if the call is not established (i.e., hanging up too early), the 3G→4G handoff will not be invoked. Note that, no handoff for the unestablished call is not designed without rationale. If the call is not successfully established, the caller would probably redial shortly. For a call terminated in the unestablished call state, immediate handoff from 3G to 4G could trigger more handoffs. Consequently, the UE still stays at the 3G `FACH/DCH` state. In this case, the cell reselection procedure turns out to be the only way back to 4G. Note that the cell reselection is only triggered in the 3G `IDLE` state. Our study demonstrates that

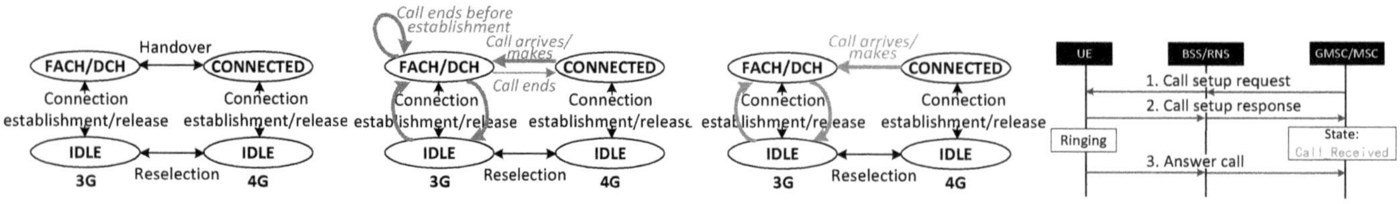

(a) 3G/4G standard [1] (b) CSFB for OP-I (c) CSFB for OP-II (d) Call setup procedure

**Figure 7: Simplified RRC state transition machine and call setup procedure.**

under certain data operations (the details are in Section 5.3), the UE may not enter the 3G IDLE state, or switch back to 3G FACH/DCH before triggering the cell reselection. Consequently, a RRC loop (marked by bold blue lines in Figure 7(b)) is created when the call is not established under certain background data traffic.

## 5.2 OP-II: Once the Call Attempt is Made

Losing 4G connectivity becomes easier in OP-II than in OP-I. The user is prone to losing 4G connectivity, no matter whether the call is established or not. Figure 4(c) shows an example of losing 4G connectivity after the call completes. We test various call operations (answering/rejecting an incoming call, unestablished incoming call, or making an outgoing call) to examine its dependency on the call event. We find out that, once the 4G→3G handoff is triggered under any call attempt, the UE gets stuck in 3G as long as some background data traffic is present.

Similar to the OP-I test, We run constant-rate UDP *uplink* session tests with different packet sizes and intervals. The only difference is that the call is established and completes in this experiment. Figure 9 plots the duration being stuck in 3G with packet intervals for 1B/1KB packets. We observe that, the rule in OP-II is much simpler. When the packet interval is smaller than 9s (1B packet) or 13s (1KB packet), the 4G user is unable to return to the LTE network.

Consequently, we deduce the RRC state transition for OP-II in Figure 7(c). Different from OP-I, no handoff path (back to 4G) exists when the call ends. The switch from 3G to 4G is thus invoked only through the cell reselection. Similarly, when the RRC loop in 3G FACH/DCH and 3G IDLE (marked by red bold lines) is formed, the UE loses its 4G connectivity. The conditions to form the 3G RRC loop will be discussed in Section 5.3.

## 5.3 RRC Loop Under Data Services

We now examine when or under what data services the 3G RRC loop is formed. We mainly address the OP-I case that is more complicated, and then describe the OP-II case.

### 5.3.1 *OP-I Case*

Figure 8 plots the 3G duration under various packet intervals for OP-I. We make four observations. First, when the packet interval is smaller than certain threshold (10 seconds for 1B packets and 15 seconds for 1KB packets), the phone never returns to 4G. Second, when the packet interval is larger than another threshold (15 seconds for 1B packets and 20 seconds for 1KB packets), the phone definitely returns to 4G. Third, for both packet sizes, there exist two interesting transition intervals. For 1B packets, these two intervals are 10 seconds and 15 seconds (with larger duration variance). The phone is likely to return to 4G with these packet intervals. For packet intervals in between (i.e., 11–14s), the phone never returns to 4G. For 1KB packets, the pattern is similar but the two transition intervals are 15s and 20s. Finally, compared with no data transmission, it stays longer (about 40 seconds) in 3G even when it can return to the 4G network.

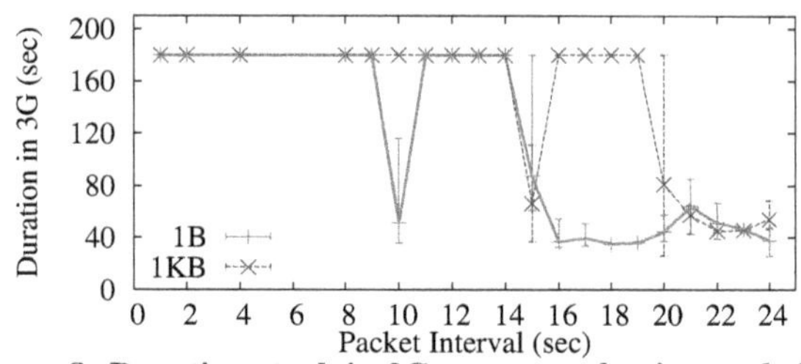

**Figure 8: Duration stuck in 3G versus packet intervals for two 1B/1KB packets in case of an unestablished call via OP-I.**

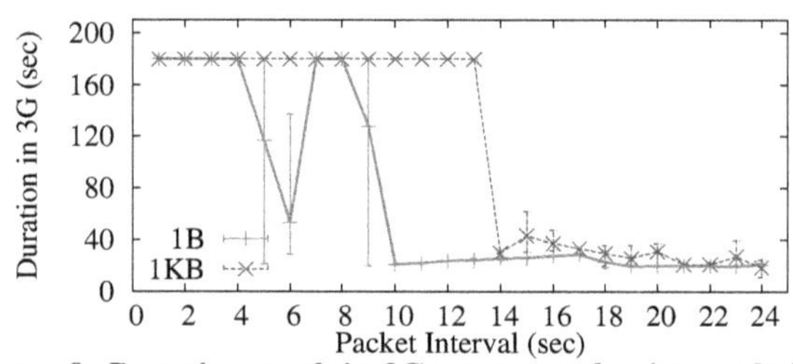

**Figure 9: Duration stuck in 3G versus packet intervals for two 1B/1KB packets in case of a complete call via OP-II.**

At the first glance, these findings are not anticipated, particularly the inconsistent performance with packet intervals in the transition zone. Three questions need to be answered: (1) Why does the switch remain *sensitive* to several packet intervals and yield the non-monotonic pattern for all packet intervals? (2) What occurs when the packet interval is set as 10s, 15s, and 20s? (3) How is it related to packet sizes? We examine event traces and finally derive the trigger conditions for the 3G RRC loop. We summarize these rules for $3G \rightarrow 4G$ switch in OP-I in Table 2, and then use our trace analysis to explain what happens and how each rule is applied. In summary, the above observations reveal how such mechanisms interact with each other.

These rules exhibit both standard specifications and carrier-specific operations. They also correspond to the state machine derived in Section 5.1. Note that the UE can be switched from 3G RRC IDLE to 4G RRC IDLE only via the cell re-selection procedure. Rule 1 states that this cell reselection is triggered by a timer $T_{3G\rightarrow 4G}$, which is set to 5s according to our measurements. Note that the timer $T_{3G\rightarrow 4G}$ is not specified by the standards, but chosen by the operator's implementation.

Rule 2 regulates the traditional 3G RRC transition between DCH/FACH and IDLE. The transition is controlled by another timer $T_{idle}$. When this timer expires, RRC jumps from DCH/FACH to IDLE; Upon packet delivery, it immediately switches to DCH/FACH and resets $T_{idle}$. In our experiments, we find that $T_{idle} = 10$ seconds and is operator specific, consistent with prior studies [27].

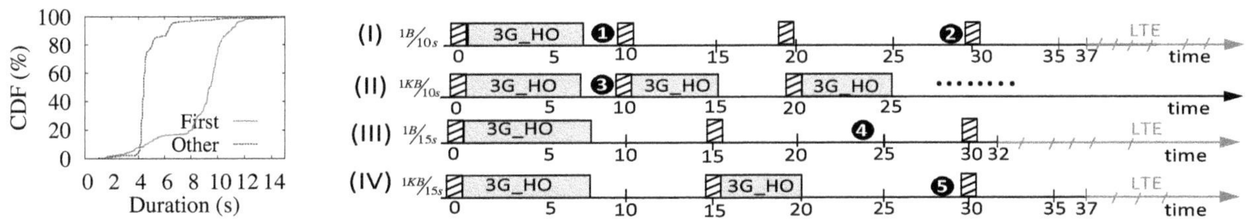


(a) Intra-3G handoff time (b) Example traces

**Figure 10: Illustration of event traces for data flows with various packet intervals and packet sizes.**

| | |
|---|---|
| **Rule 1** | The phone immediately performs the switch back to 4G when the timer $T_{3G\rightarrow 4G}$ times out; $T_{3G\rightarrow 4G}$ is only started when the UE enters into the 3G `IDLE` state; |
| **Rule 2** | The RRC state switches from `DCH/FACH` to `IDLE` when the timer $T_{idle}$ times out; It switches to `FACH/DCH` immediately upon any data delivery; |
| **Rule 3** | $T_{3G\rightarrow 4G}$ is reset once an intra-3G[a] handoff occurs. |
| **Rule 4** | The intra-3G handoff occurs when a data transmission request occurs in either condition: (1) the UE is in 3G `IDLE` state, (2) the packet size is larger than a threshold (210-220B in our measurement) or for the first packet. |

**Table 2: Rules for $3G \rightarrow 4G$ switch upon an unestablished call (i.e., the call state is not `Call_Received`) for OP-I.**

[a] In this work, we define the intra-3G handoff as handover events within different types of 3G networks, i.e., among UMTS/HSDPA/HSPA/HSPA+ [1].

Rule 3 implies that the users will not go back to 4G LTE when it is at the `FACH/DCH` state, which is specified in [1]. This is because the user triggers an intra-3G handoff to perform data transmission (Rule 4), its RRC state is hence changed from `IDLE` to `FACH/DCH`. The timer $T_{3G\rightarrow 4G}$ should be reset since the user leaves the `IDLE` state.

In Rule 4, we observe that intra-3G handoffs (i.e., HSPA$\leftrightarrow$UMTS) might happen. The operator usually switches the mobile device to proper radio access technologies (e.g., UMTS or HSPA) based on its transmission rate and data volume. The first condition in Rule 4 is obtained from our traces. It is not in the standard specifications; we believe it is also an operator-dependent choice.

Our measurements also indicate that, an intra-3G handoff typically takes about 5 seconds, but 8–10 seconds for the first time. Figure 10(a) plots the CDF for the intra-3G handover duration. To derive the packet size threshold used in Rule 4, we run experiments using variable-sized payloads at 8-second intervals (i.e., it remains in 3G). It turns out that the payload threshold is 210–220B. These parameter settings are also operator specific.

We briefly illustrate how these rules are applied so that the 3G duration varies with packet intervals as shown in Figure 8. In all our experiments, the first packet is immediately sent out once the phone switches to 3G, shown by those packet boxes at time 0 in Figure 10(b). We look at two easy-to-understand cases, while more cases can be found in Appendix A. In the first case, when the interval is smaller than $T_{idle}$, the phone never returns to 4G. It has no chance to enter the 3G `IDLE` state and trigger the timer $T_{3G\rightarrow 4G}$ back to 4G. In the second case, when the packet interval is larger than 20 seconds (i.e., $T_{idle}+T_{3G\rightarrow 4G}+T_{3G-HO} \approx 10+5+5 = 20$), the phone can always return to 4G. No matter whether an intra-3G handoff is triggered or not, the packet interval is large enough to enter the `IDLE` state and trigger the $3G \rightarrow 4G$ timeout. This also explains why the transition interval for 1B is 5 seconds smaller than that for 1KB. The decisive factor for the 1B/1KB discrepancy is whether an intra-3G handoff is triggered. By Rule 4, 1KB packet delivery always triggers such an intra-3G handoff as long as it is still in 3G, whereas 1B packet does so only when the RRC state is 3G `IDLE`. The intra-3G handoff takes about 5 seconds. In more cases (all four cases of Figure 10(b) and other combinations of packet intervals and sizes) in Appendix A, we confirm that the duration in 3G is mainly determined by how the RRC state and the two timers of $T_{3G\rightarrow 4G}$ and $T_{idle}$ evolve under these rules.

### 5.3.2 *OP-II Case*

We next derive the trigger conditions for the RRC loop for OP-II. Our trace analysis shows that OP-II follows the above four rules but Rule 4 and the parameters vary slightly. Figure 9 shows that the transition intervals for 1B and 1KB packets are around 9s and 13s, respectively. Our traces indicate that the difference between 1B and 1KB packets lies in whether intra-3G handoffs are incurred; Intra-3G handoffs (HSPA$\rightarrow$HSPA+) occur for 1KB packets, but not for 1B packets (except for the first packet, the same as OP-I). Moreover, we test with various packet sizes and find out that the occurrence of intra-3G handoffs only depends on the packet size (here, the threshold is about 940–950B). This slightly differs from Rule 4 for OP-I. In OP-II, Rule 4 works under the second condition (an intra-3G handoff occurs when the packet size is larger than 940-950B or for the first packet). Our measurements show that an intra-3G handoff takes about 4–5 seconds (but 8-12 seconds for the first time), similar to Figure 10(a). We infer that the 3G$\rightarrow$4G switch is also controlled by two timers, $T_{3G\rightarrow 4G}$ for the cell reselection and $T_{idle}$ for the state transition from 3G `FACH/DCH` to `IDLE`. Based on our measurements, we infer that $T_{3G\rightarrow 4G} \approx 6$s, $T_{idle} \approx 3$s. The derivation is similar to that for OP-I, and is omitted due to space limit. Note that, these parameters are operator-specific choices.

For both cases of OP-I and OP-II, some may argue that the loss of 4G connectivity is an operator-specific implementation issue. We admit that the operator's choice does matter. Indeed, the standards do not stipulate under what conditions the handoff/switch should be initiated, though they do specify such handoff/switch mechanisms for CSFB [1]. They leave the flexibility to the carriers. For example, the operator can decide whether a handoff back to 4G is triggered immediately after the call ends or not. However, our study shows that, the loss of 4G connectivity is caused by the flaw (i.e., the state loop) between CSFB and the RRC finite state machine. The interplay of functions and states used in both CS and PS domains results in unanticipated effect. The two timers create the 3G RRC loop so that the phone never returns to 4G.

## 5.4 Performance Impact

We examine the impact of being stuck in the 3G network from three aspects: duration in 3G, mobility, and throughput gap.

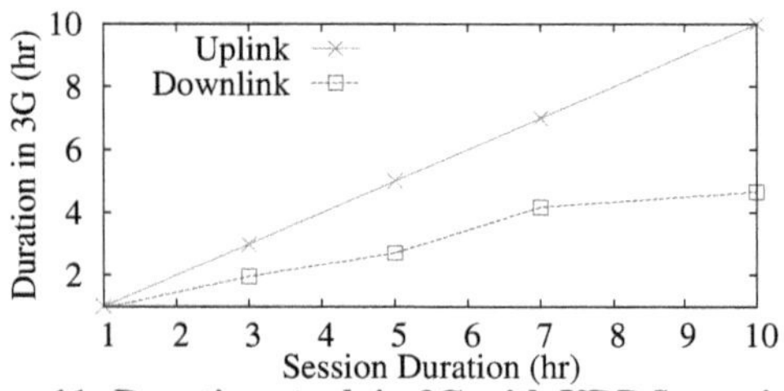


**Figure 11: Duration stuck in 3G with UDP flows vis OP-I.**

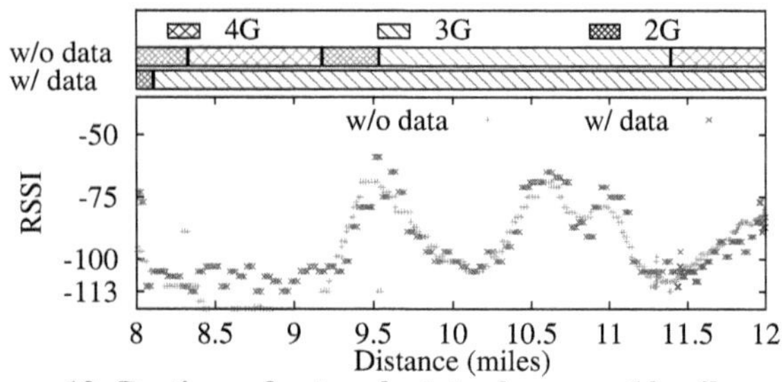


**Figure 12: Portions of network status logs on a 12-mile route.**

**Duration in 3G:** In the unestablished call case, we run an 8s-interval UDP data flow for various durations from 1 hour to 10 hours. Figure 11 plots the average duration in 3G with downlink and uplink data flows. Specifically, we measure the interval from the time when the call ends to the instant when the UDP session stops. It is not surprising to see that the phone gets stuck in 3G as long as the data flow is alive (10 hours are observed and there is no sign of limit). Interestingly, we find that the duration in 3G for the downlink case is usually shorter than the uplink case, e.g., we observed 2 hours in 3G networks during a 3-hour data session test. This is because not all UDP downlink packets can be sent successfully under packet loss. The longer the session lasts, the more likely a packet interval goes beyond the transition threshold (15/20 seconds). We also test with TCP flows; Both uplink and downlink flows perform similarly to the UDP uplink case (never expires), because TCP retransmits packets upon losses.

**Mobility:** We also examine whether a 4G user may go back to LTE networks under mobility where handoffs are triggered. We repeat the above experiment when driving on a 12-mile local route. It takes about 35~45 minutes. Note that the call ends before driving, i.e., the 4G user gets stuck in 3G before driving starts. In the meantime, we bring another 4G phone without any data session. It is used to collect network status events such as network type and RSSI. Figure 12 plots a portion of the network status logs at two phones over this route via OP-I. The results for OP-II are similar. It is easy to see that, the 4G phone freely switches among 2G, 3G and 4G networks in the absence of data; however, the 4G phone with data only switches among 2G and 3G networks. It never goes back to 4G LTE networks, even though the 4G LTE network signals are stronger than 2G/3G in certain areas, e.g., [11.5, 12].

**3G/4G Speed Gap:** To quantify the performance impact of being stuck in 3G networks, we measure the speed of 4G LTE and 3G HSPA networks at different hours of a day. We use the SpeedTest tool [6]. Figure 13 plots the average uplink and downlink speed of 3G/4G networks at different times. 4G outperforms 3G in most cases, especially at midnight (with lighter traffic) and for the uplink. For example, 4G users experience 83.4% uplink improvement and 53.8% downlink gain at 11PM. Over all test hours, the average improvement is 70.4% and 31.9% for uplink and downlink, respectively. However, the downlink gap between 3G and 4G shrinks at

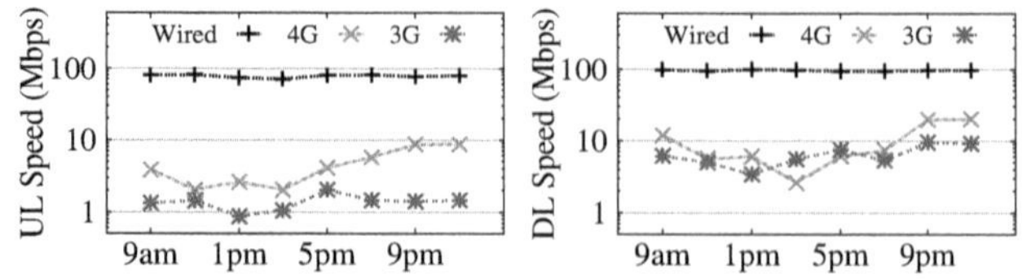


**Figure 13: 3G/4G speed at different hours of a day via OP-I (Left: uplink; Right: downlink).**

| Application | Type | TCP/UDP | Behavior |
|---|---|---|---|
| Webkit | Bursty | TCP | Respond slowly, seldom abort |
| Gmail | Bursty | TCP | Respond slowly, occasionally abort |
| Facebook | Interaction | TCP | Respond slowly, seldom abort |
| AndFtp | Transferring | TCP | Transmit slowly or abort later |
| Skype | Interaction | UDP | Suspend, abort later |
| Youtube | Streaming | TCP | Suspend (abort if call unestablished) |
| PPStream | Streaming | UDP | Suspend (abort if call unestablished) |
| Pandora | Streaming | TCP | Suspend |

**Table 3: Application behavior when voice call arrives**

other times. To our surprise, 4G performs worse than 3G at 3PM (1.8 Mbps vs. 4 Mbps). This shows that, the deployed LTE network might not achieve what it claims at all times. We also note that, the 3G/4G speed varies with locations (depending on the radio link quality and the traffic load). In general, throughput drop occurs when 4G users get stuck in 2G/3G networks.

# 6. DATA APPLICATION ABORT

We find that voice calls might even result in data application aborts in operational LTE networks. In this section, we first show real application behaviors under various call operations, such as dialing and answering a call. We then diagnose the root cause for application aborts.

## 6.1 Popular Applications

We test eight popular mobile applications while receiving a CS voice call. These applications include web browsing (via WebKit), FTP downloading, Gmail, Facebook, Skype voice calls, Youtube, PPStream (P2P video streaming), and Pandora (music playback over radio broadcast). We observe that these applications might behave abnormally when the voice conversation ends on all the phone models for both carriers. Upon voice call completion, five applications except Youtube, PPStream and Pandora might abort, and Pandora suspends for tens of seconds until the playback status turns from "stopped" to "playing." YouTube and PPStream might abort in other calling scenarios.

**FTP downloading:** In our experiment, a mobile client downloads a 121 MB file from our FTP server. Figures 14(a) and 14(b) show the error dialog at the mobile client and the TCP trace captured by Wireshark at our FTP server. When the voice call ends around the 47th second, the mobile client experiences a socket exception error, i.e., `sendto failed`, in Android OS. File downloading stops afterwards. On the FTP server side, it first attempts to retransmit packets (10 retries over 33 seconds are observed) to the client and finally tears down the TCP connection, since no response is heard from the client. Note that mobile phone aborts earlier at 48s before the server tears down the TCP connection at 82s.

**Skype voice calls:** When the CS call ends, Skype is designed to resume its original call session; However, it may still fail similarly to FTP, and the root cause will be discussed in Section 6.3. The difference is, during the CS voice call, Skype holds its ongoing call but FTP download keeps going. Skype is not allowed to simultane-

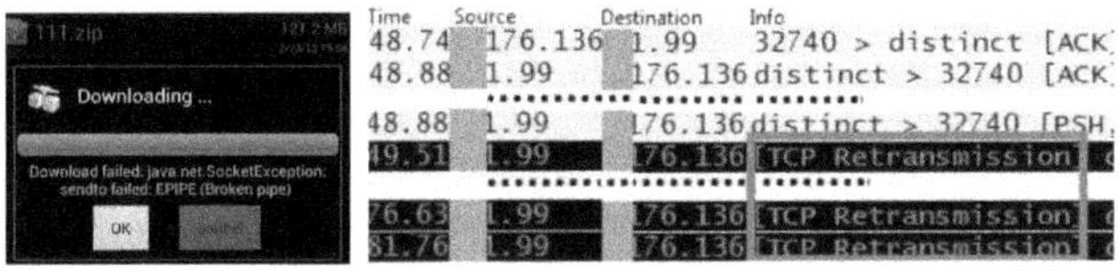


(a) Error at the client (b) Wireshark traces at the server

**Figure 14: An example of FTP application abort.**

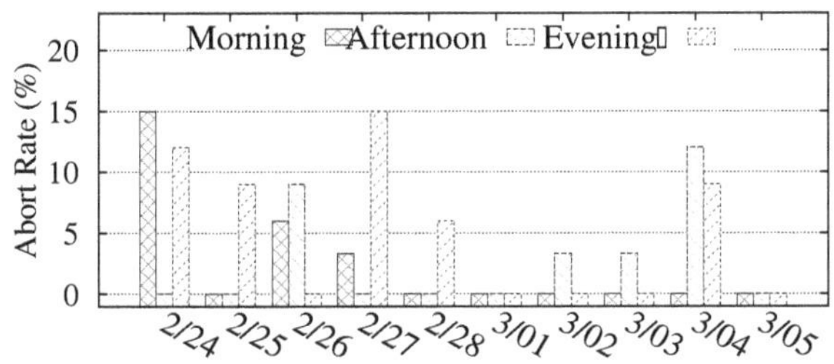


**Figure 15: 10-day FTP downloading abort ratio (OP-I).**

ously work with CS voice calls due to the conflicting usage of the speaker. So are YouTube, PPStream and Pandora.

**Web, Facebook and Gmail:** Similar to FTP, they are unable to fetch the attempted web content when they abort upon call completion. It is clearly observed when they fetch big-sized data, e.g., a high-resolution image or an email attachment. For short data sessions (e.g., fetching a html page), the abort takes places but with negligible effect.

**Youtube and PPStream:** Upon call arrival, both video streaming operations pause. They never automatically resume when the call ends (i.e., a manual replay is required). However, when an incoming call hangs up before reaching the client, Youtube and PPStream might still abort.

**Pandora:** Similar to Skype call, it is suspended upon the call arrival and resumed automatically after the call ends.Except that the suspension lasts tens of seconds, no other abnormal (i.e., being aborted) behaviors are observed.

Table 3 summarizes these application behaviors, including application aborts and "slow response" due to throughput slump described in Section 4. In fact, application aborts depend on how these applications handle the failure of data sessions, which is triggered by an completed call, in their own manners. The first five applications abort because they do nothing once the original data sessions terminate, whereas Pandora automatically starts a new session once the old one fails. Youtube and PPStream do not take action since they already stop their data sessions once a voice call starts. Note that applications do not abort every time a call completes. We next study when and how often these applications abort.

## 6.2 How Often Application Aborts

We conjecture that these application aborts are caused by voice calls. In our test scenario, a 4G user dials out and hangs up the outgoing call later. In the meantime, we run FTP downloading. The results for other applications are similar. For OP-I, we use Samsung Galaxy S3 and LG Optimus G at two locations (home and campus), during the morning (9am-12pm), the afternoon (1-5pm), and the evening (7-10pm), for 10 days, from February 24 to March 4, 2013. For OP-II, we test Samsung Galaxy S4 and iPhone 5 from June 17–21, 2013. Each test has at least 15 runs. We observe similar abort ratios, independent of the phone model.

Figure 15 plots the 10-day abort percentage for OP-I. The applications do abort but only with certain probability. It confirms that

| Seconds | OP | EVENT | TYPE | CID | RSSI | IP |
|---|---|---|---|---|---|---|
| 52.84 | OP-I | CALL | HANG UP | | | 10.xx.xx.51 |
| 53.41 | OP-I | NET | UMTS | 5****075 | -67 | 10.xx.xx.51 |
| 54.30 | OP-I | NET | UMTS | 5****075 | -67 | 10.xx.xx.51 |
| 55.26 | Unknown | NET | Unknown | n/a | -113 | n/a |
| 56.28 | Unknown | NET | Unknown | n/a | -113 | n/a |
| ... | ... | ... | ... | ... | ... | ... |
| 69.26 | OP-I | NET | LTE | 1*****223 | -70 | 10.yy.yy.11 |

**Table 4: Logs of network status at the mobile phone.**

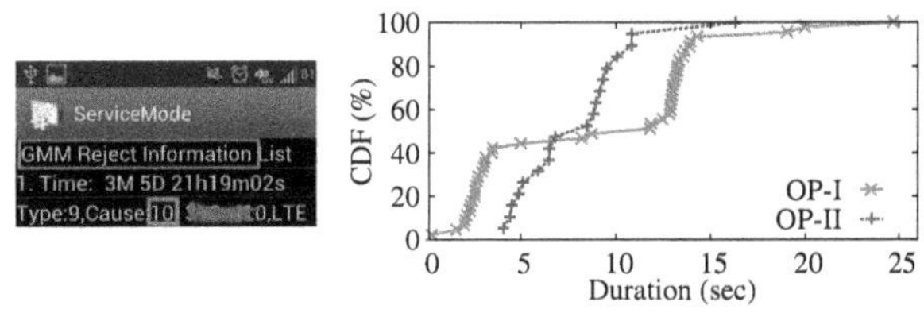


(a) Implicit detach (b) CDF of Reattach time

**Figure 16: Cause of being kicked out and reattach time.**

operational LTE networks are still largely successful. In two worst-case settings (a morning slot and an evening slot), about 15% of tests fail. However, over the 10-day period, the average failure percentages for the morning, afternoon and evening are merely 2.4%, 2.7%, and 5.1%. For OP-II, the average abort ratio is 5.7% in the 5-day test.

## 6.3 Root Cause: Being Detached

We now explore the root cause for application aborts. We find that it is because the mobile phone is detached from the cellular network when performing an 3G→4G handoff to return to the LTE network after a voice call. Table 4 logs the network status at the phone when an application aborts using OP-I. The call conversation ends at 52.84s. In 2.42 seconds, the user is kicked out of the carrier network (indicated by "unknown"). It also loses its original IP address. This disconnection lasts for about 14 seconds before the 4G phone reconnects to the network. However, upon reconnection, the phone is assigned a brand new IP address. Consequently, the original data session fails and those applications not supporting automatic application-level recovery finally abort.

Another plausible root cause is that power consumption at the UE exceeds the permissible budget when initiating and maintaining radio access bearers for simultaneous voice call and data service. If it were correct, we would observe it when users concurrently access voice and data services, and application abort rate may also depend on phone models. However, our experiments show that this never occurs. Application abort only happens after the call ends, i.e., the UE is being switched back to 4G. The application abort rate observed on different phones is also similar.

To find out why 4G users are kicked outside the cellular network, we enable the service mode of Samsung S3 where low-level cellular network traces can be observed. Figure 16(a) displays the screen snapshot when an application aborts. It states that, the GMM (GPRS Mobility Management) operation [1] is rejected due to an error (cause ID: 10). In this case, an inter-system handoff (from 3G to 4G) request is rejected because it has been implicitly detached [1]. The "Implicit Detached" indicates that the phone is detached by the network without any notification. It typically occurs when the network fails to communicate with the UE. Once this error occurs, the UE has to perform re-attach procedure to associate with carrier networks again [1]. A new IP address will be assigned for OP-I, whereas the same IP address is used for OP-II. However, the NAT (Network Address Translation) mapping for the UE is no longer available. The UE is thus unable to receive packets using the same data session no matter whether the IP address changes.

No packet delivery is allowed until this procedure completes. Figure 16(b) plots the CDF of reattach time. It shows that, 90% of re-attaches would finish within 15 seconds for OP-I, and 95% of re-attaches is shorter than 11s for OP-II.

We are not sure why the network detaches the user when a CSFB call ends, due to lack of status information inside the network. It might be caused by the failure of inter-system (3G to 4G) handoff, due to insufficient resources (resource occupied by CSFB) or unsynchronized user information between 3G and 4G [1].

# 7. REVERSE IMPACT: MISSED CALLS

We next show how the PS data service may adversely affect CS voice calls. We find that 4G LTE users may miss their voice calls while starting PS data access. When the caller makes a call but the callee starts PS data access almost simultaneously, the caller hears success signals (e.g., alerting tone) so that he/she believes that the call has been made but is not answered. In the meantime, the callee receives no incoming-call request (e.g., no ringing or vibrating). Everything else operates normally, but the callee is unaware of missing a call.

We test it with two experiments. First, we make a call while the callee starts to turn on its PS data network (i.e., network attach). In all test runs ($>20$), all calls have been missed. Second, we make a call when the data network is either off or already on, i.e., the callee does not turn on his/her PS data network while caller makes call; In this case, all calls have succeeded. The same results are observed on all phones for both carriers. We note that, in case of missing calls, the caller may have an option to leave a message if his/her voice-mailbox feature is enabled. The voice-mailbox feature is free in the US, so the adverse effect of missing calls can be greatly relieved. However, not all operators support free voice-mailbox features, so missed calls may incur inconvenience.

**Root cause:** We analyze the *NetworkStatus* trace logged on the callee's phone. With an incoming call request, the callee is implicitly detached by the network (same as Section 6). During the period (before network re-attach completes), the mobile loses connectivity with carrier networks. We next seek to understand why the caller hears an alerting tone, thus misinterpreting that the call has been established.

We examine the incoming CSFB call flow of Figure 3. In Step 2 (Paging), the MSC pages the UE through MME. Following the *mobile terminated call procedure* [1] in the CSFB standard, the UE will respond with `Service Request` [1] to the MSC, then the MSC sends an indication (i.e., an alerting tone) to the caller. In fact, it happens before the handoff to 3G networks occurs; The caller is acknowledged no matter whether the callee is kicked out of carrier networks or fails to handover to 2G/3G networks. This results in *asynchronous* call status at the caller and the callee. This scenario differs from the call establishment process in 3G networks, where the caller hears the alerting tone only after the callee is found by the network via paging. We believe that it is a fundamental issue in cellular networks, rather than a operator-specific implementation choice (despite observed in both operators). PS data and CS voice are performed independently on their data plane, but share common network states on the control plane. Imprudent control in one domain may impose unexpected impact on the other domain.

# 8. SOLUTION

We now describe our solution to mitigating the negative impact incurred by CSFB voice calls in 4G LTE networks. We use a combination of techniques to address all four issues: performance degradation of TCP-based data sessions in the presence of CSFB calls, unexpected application abort, lost 4G connectivity, and missed calls during PS service.

**Mitigating TCP performance degradation** We first note that the TCP issue is due to inter-system handoffs; it cannot be fixed from the CSFB protocol itself since the handoffs are a fundamental feature of CSFB. We follow the popular middlebox-based approach [30] in our solution. Our scheme differs from the related work [12,22,24] in that we focus on voice-triggered handoffs rather than mobility-induced handoffs. We split the TCP connection into two sessions: one between the middlebox and the application server, and the other between the middlebox and the UE. The UE detects handoffs induced by CSFB, and sends suspension request to the middlebox. Upon receiving a suspension request, the middlebox freezes its retransmission timer and caches data packets from the application server for about 15 seconds. The parameter is chosen because 90% of data suspension time is less than 15 seconds (Figure 16(b)) in both handoff and application-abort cases. Once receiving a resumption request from the UE after the handoff completes, the middlebox immediately retransmits its cached packets to the UE. Note that the timeout value in CSFB is decided by the UE, rather than the operator, thus different from the mobility-induced handoff case. Our prototype implementation on Android phones and the middlebox proxy shows that, our solution is 2-50% faster in packet reception recovery than the standard TCP, and the average improvement is 18%. The main merit of our solution is that it can be readily integrated with existing carrier middleboxes, but it also incurs more complexity and handles only the TCP flows.

**Handling lost 4G connectivity** In our solution, we let the carrier initiate the inter-system handoff (i.e., 3G $\rightarrow$ 4G) to switch the user back to 4G when both conditions are met: (1) no ongoing voice call exists; (2)the duration the user stays in the 3G network is longer than certain threshold (e.g., 60 seconds). Our scheme not only addresses the issue of lost 4G connectivity, but also avoids unnecessary handoffs. The downside is that, the carrier has to maintain a timer for each 4G user to record how long (s)he stays in 3G. In contrast, another possible solution is that the operator immediately switches the user back to the 4G LTE network once the call completes. However, it may lead to more CSFB-induced handoffs since the caller may redial for incomplete call conversation (e.g., the Operator-I's scenario). Moreover, it may lead to a potential security loophole that incurs significant inter-system handoffs on the 4G user via repetitively dialing and hanging calls up from the malicious user.

**Handling application abort** This issue can be addressed by either an in-network approach (e.g., following Operator-II's IP assignment policy that assigns the same IP address to the UE and keeps the NAT mappings after the UE reattaches to carrier networks), or an out-of-network approach (e.g., via the middlebox).

Our solution is still based on the middlebox. We borrow ideas from Cisco AnyConnect [4], which offers a mobile VPN scheme that allows for the UE to reconnect its VPN server via different IP addresses to proceed the session established earlier. We do not require secure connections that encrypt each transmitted packet, but enable the mobile device to connect to the proxy server with a different IP address. The UE is thus able to resume data sessions that are established earlier between the middlebox and the application server. Our scheme thus saves computing power and energy consumption at the mobile device. The downside is that the middlebox may pose as the bottleneck for the transmission rate to the UE.

**Handling missed call** Our solution slightly modifies the current CSFB specification. Upon receiving `Service Request` (introduced in Section 7), the MSC does not send an indication of user alert to the caller. This notification is deferred until `Call Setup Response` arrives at the MSC. Consequently, Alice will not hear the alert tone before Bob successfully hands over to the 3G network and enters `Call_Received` state. Our tests show that, in the current practice of 4G LTE CSFB, Alice hears the alert tone about one second before Bob's phone rings. Therefore, our solution may increase only one second based on our estimate to establish the voice call when the caller hears the alert tone. We thus address the issue with little cost (about 1-second extra waiting time). The downside is that our proposal requires modifications on the CSFB specification.

# 9. DISCUSSION

We now discuss two solution alternatives to CSFB to support voice calls over 4G LTE.

**CSFB: An interim solution to VoLTE or not?** Some people may argue that, CSFB is only an interim voice solution, and all its problems will disappear once the ultimate solution of VoLTE is deployed. However, the global deployment of VoLTE is not foreseen in the near future. VoLTE is only supported by three small operators so far, MetroPCS (US), SK Telecom and LG Uplus (both in South Korea) [5]. Most operators, including four of the top-five global operators, China Mobile, Vodafone, Bharti Airtel, and Telefonica, make plans to deploy or have deployed CSFB as their voice solution in 4G LTE networks [2,3,7,8].

In fact, VoLTE has several drawbacks that may impede its large-scale deployment. They include high technology complexity, challenges to ensure guaranteed service for voice, and more energy consumption of mobile clients. VoLTE is purely PS based, and offers voice service via its IMS (IP Multimedia Subsystem) [1]. The first version of IMS was released in 2002. During the past decade, operators have little incentive to deploy IMS, because of its high cost in deployment and maintenance, as well as its operation complexity [16]. Moreover, it poses challenges to deliver guaranteed service for voice calls on top of the IP-based best-effort service. Fundamentally, it is the old, challenging Internet QoS problem, and cellular networks need extra mechanisms to ensure carrier-grade quality when migrating CS voice calls into the PS domain. Last, the client may consume more power when using VoLTE. We run two experiments to estimate the power consumption via VoLTE. The tests do not intend to be very accurate but show us some hints on the energy aspect of VoLTE. One experiment is to make a CS voice call only, and the other is to deliver a 12.2 Kbps data flow that emulates the traffic of a voice call in VoLTE [18]. We measure the power consumption of the client device while its LCD screen is off. The CS call takes 0.96 W while the PS data service takes 1.42 W. Another measurement conducted in [17] shows that the energy consumption of a VoLTE call can be twice as much as that of a 2G call. Therefore, VoLTE may pose potential energy issues for the client device. Moreover, to retain the capability of being paged for an incoming call, the mobile device may have to power on its data network interface all the time but not on demand.

**SVLTE: Alternative to CSFB?** SVLTE (Simultaneous Voice and LTE) offers an alternative solution to voice call in 4G LTE. It allows for a phone to simultaneously use both networks, thus avoiding the issues raised by CSFB. However, this technique is only applied to CDMA 1xRTT [29]; it is not compatible with LTE plus 3G UMTS systems that are widely deployed. More importantly, it requires *two radios*, one for PS and one for CS. Therefore, power consumption may become a concern. We measure the power consumption of a SVLTE-capable phone (Samsung Stratosphere). Upon answering a voice call with/without background data service (50 Kbps), the phone consumes power at about 1.0 W and 2.39 W, respectively. When both radios are on to support both CS and PS, the phone consumes extra 0.97 W than VoLTE. This issue has been reported by [15] and our measurement results are similar.

# 10. RELATED WORK

Cellular networks have been an active research area in recent years. However, the interplay of voice calls and data services in 4G LTE networks has remained largely unaddressed in the research community.

How to better support voice calls in LTE networks has appeared in the literature [9, 14, 20, 21, 23]. All such studies seek to improve the voice service quality, but do not study the potential mutual impact of voice and data, which is the focus of this work. Various performance aspects of 2G/3G/4G networks have been studied, and new solutions have been proposed, e.g., [11,19,22,24–26,28]. These studies mainly focus on wireless data, whereas we examine interactions between voice and data.

Our proposed solution fix also bears similarity to existing designs. Our goal is to address the four identified new issues. We thus borrow several ideas freely from the literature and do not claim novelty. The general middlebox-based solution is a popular industry practice [30]. How to improve TCP under mobility-triggered handoffs has been well documented in early papers, e.g., [22,24], though our handoff events are induced by CSFB voice calls.

# 11. CONCLUSION

With the success of the Internet, the 4G LTE technology has also adopted packet-switched (PS) delivery while abandoning the circuit-switched (CS) model. The PS service facilitates mobile data but causes problems for voice calls, which required guaranteed (carrier-grade) service. Given the undisputed importance of both data and voice, LTE carriers have used CSFB as a popular interim solution to CS voice. In this work, we use experiments to study how the CSFB-enabled voice interacts with the PS-based data in operational LTE networks. To our surprise, voice and data indeed interfere with each other. Voice may cause data to reduce throughput, abort applications, and lose 4G connectivity. Data may also cause the voice service to miss incoming calls.

We believe that the identified issues lie in both the design of the CSFB technology and its engineering implementation. The key features, including the finite state machine, the inter-dependency between data and signaling, and the third-party triggered handoff, are all fundamental to CSFB. Therefore, the problems stem from the design of CSFB. They include (1) deadlocked state transitions in the finite state machine of RRC, (2) unexpected coupling between signaling and data; and (3) arbitrary triggering of handoffs by a third party without security protection. The fundamental problem is that, users demand both data and voice services on the LTE phone device. Voice and data thus interact with each other since both use the shared radio. While the support for PS-based data tends to be simple, the signaling and control operations to enable CS-based voice are complex. Throughout the life cycle of a voice call, any procedure may go wrong. Consequently, any failure or exception in the process may affect both voice and data through the phone. The goal of this work is to better understand such systems by exposing some of such cases and devising solution fix at the early stage of global LTE deployment.

Our somewhat biased results should not be interpreted as the common failures of operational LTE networks with CSFB. It remains largely successful in practice. Some may argue that the problem will be short lived, since CSFB is only an interim solution. Therefore, all identified problems would disappear once the ultimate VoLTE solution is deployed. However, current practice shows that VoLTE does not look promising within the 3–5 year horizon. Most operators, including four of the top-five worldwide operators have committed to CSFB. Moreover, another alternative SVLTE also has its own drawbacks. Given the growing interest on CSFB for LTE, we seek to locate the problem and find its solution.

## 12. ACKNOWLEDGMENTS

We greatly appreciate the insightful and constructive comments from our shepherd, Dr. Li Erran Li, and the anonymous reviewers. We also thank Zhe Wen and Xingyu Ma for their contributions at the early stage of this work and all participants in the experiments.

## 13. REFERENCES

[1] 3GPP Specification: TS23.060, TS23.401, TS23.228, TS23.272, TS24.008, TS36.331, TS36.304. http://www.3gpp.org.
[2] Bharti Airtel to offer voice services to LTE customers via GSM #MWC13. http://www.nokiasiemensnetworks.com.
[3] China Mobile selects Nokia Siemens Networks for large, multi-city, TD-LTE deployment. http://www.nokiasiemensnetworks.com.
[4] Cicso AnyConnect Secure Mobility Client. http://www.cisco.com.
[5] MetroPCS, SK Telecom, LG Uplus Claim VoLTE First. http://www.telecomengine.com.
[6] Speedtest.net - Ookla. http://www.SpeedTest.net.
[7] Telefonica Germany achieves to transfer a phone call from LTE to UMTS without interruptions. http://blogthinkbig.com.
[8] Vodafone Supports CSFB. http://www.webwire.com/ViewPressRel.asp?aId=170837.
[9] Voice over LTE. http://www.gsma.com/technicalprojects/volte.
[10] iphone 5 review, 2013. http://www.anandtech.com/show/6330/the-iphone-5-review/18.
[11] P. K. Athivarapu, R. Bhagwan, S. Guha, V. Navda, and et.al. Radiojockey: mining program execution to optimize cellular radio usage. In *ACM MobiCom*, Aug. 2012.
[12] H. Balakrishnan, V. N. Padmanabhan, S. Seshan, and R. H. Katz. A Comparison of Mechanisms for Improving TCP Performance over Wireless Link. In *ACM SIGCOMM*, 1996.
[13] CNET. Competitive wireless carriers take on at&t and verizon, 2012. http://news.cnet.com/8301-1035_3-57505803-94/competitive-wireless-carriers-take-on-at-t-and-verizon.
[14] A. Dhananjay, A. Sharma, M. Paik, J. Chen, and et.al. Hermes: Data Transmission over Unknown Voice Channels. In *MobiCom*, 2010.
[15] B. Ekelund. LTE, Telephony and Battery Life, 2012. `http://www.stericsson.com/technologies/VoLTE_power_consumption_white_paper_R6.pdf`.
[16] Ericsson. Current status of IMS deployment strategies & future developments, 2012. http://www.itu.int/.
[17] K. Fitchard. Voice calls over 4G LTE networks are battery killers, 2012. http://gigaom.com/2012/11/28/volte-calls-consumer-twice-the-power-of-2g-voice-calls/.
[18] GSMA. IR.92: IMS Profile for Voice and SMS, Mar. 2012.
[19] J. Huang, F. Qian, A. Gerber, Z. M. Mao, S. Sen, and O. Spatscheck. A Close Examination of Performance and Power Characteristics of 4G LTE Networks. In *ACM MobiSys*, June 2012.
[20] Y. Jouihri and Z. Guennoun. Best selection for operators starting lte deployment towards voice services. In *IEEE ICMCS*, May 2012.
[21] M. Keeley. Deployment Challenges Await In VoLTE QoS User Equipment, 2012. http://mobiledevdesign.com/tutorials/deployment-challenges-await-in-volte-qos-user-equipment-1210/.
[22] X. Liu, M. Seshadri, A. Sridharan, H. Zang, and S. Machiraju. Experiences in a 3G Network: Interplay between the Wireless Channel and Applications. In *ACM MobiCom*, Sep. 2008.
[23] J. Namakoye and R. Van Olst. Performance evaluation of a voice call handover scheme between LTE and UMTS. In *AFRICON*, 2011.
[24] C. Paasch, G. Detal, F. Duchene, C. Raiciu, and et.al. Exploring Mobile/WiFi Handover with Multipath TCP. In *CellNet*, Aug. 2012.
[25] C. Peng, G. hua Tu, C. yu Li, and S. Lu. Can We Pay for What We Get in 3G Data Access? In *ACM MobiCom*, Aug. 2012.
[26] C. Peng, C.-y. Li, G.-H. Tu, S. Lu, and L. Zhang. Mobile Data Charging: New Attacks and Countermeasures. In *CCS*, Oct. 2012.
[27] F. Qian, Z. Wang, A. Gerber, Z. M. Mao, and et.al. Characterizing Radio Resource Allocation for 3G Networks. In *IMC*, Nov. 2010.
[28] G.-H. Tu, C. Peng, C.-Y. Li, X. Ma, H. Wang, T. Wang, and S. Lu. Accounting for roaming users on mobile data access: Issues and root causes. In *ACM MobiSys*, June 2013.
[29] A. D. V. Vanghi and B. Vojcic. *The cdma2000 System for Mobile Communications: 3G Wireless Evolution*. Pearson Education, 2004.
[30] Z. Wang, Z. Qian, Q. Xu, Z. Mao, and M. Zhang. An Untold Story of Middleboxes in Cellular Networks. In *ACM SigComm*, Aug. 2011.

# APPENDIX

## A. CASE ANALYSIS OF 3G DURATION

We use case study to analyze 3G durations and validate how each handoff rule take effects in each case of Figure 10(b). In particular, we will see how two timers and intra-handoff events affect the time back to 4G.

**Case (I): 1B/10s** The first packet packet delivery triggers an intra-3G handoff (Rule 4) and then it enters into DCH/FACH (see ① in the plot). Since the first intra-3G handoff usually takes a longer time (about 8-10 seconds), the second packet (at 10th second) is delivered via 3G since it is still in DCH/FACH. In this case, the packet interval is very close to $T_{idle}$ (also 10s); Thus, the 3G duration is sensitive to whether the packet arrives before $T_{idle}$ times out. In this example, the third packet arrives slightly earlier before RRC becomes IDLE, whereas the fourth packet (at the 30th second) arrives after that (see ②). Therefore, at 30th second, the timer $T_{3G\rightarrow 4G}$ is set and the handoff to 4G is triggered 5 seconds later. Finally, it returns to 4G at 37th second (i.e., the handoff takes about 2 seconds).

In the best case, the handoff timer is triggered just before the 3rd packet, and the duration is about $(20+7)=27$ seconds. We observe that the duration varies dramatically due to its time sensitivity and goes up to 120 seconds. The detailed trace analysis shows the fourth packet does not trigger an intra-3G handoff. We find that it is because starting the timer $T_{3G\rightarrow 4G}$ happens almost at the same time as the request to trigger an intra-3G handoff. We gauge that, the handoff to 4G has higher priority than an intra-3G handoff and thus the intra-3G handoff is dismissed. We attribute this rule to the operator-specific implementation. It has been validated while we slightly increase the interval. The intra-3G handoff is triggered if the interval is larger than 10s, or in [11s, 14s]. Hence $T_{3G\rightarrow 4G}$ is reset and the phone never returns to 4G.

**Case (II) 1KB/10s** It never returns to 4G since the packet interval is smaller than 15 ($T_{idle} + T_{3G-HO} \approx 10+5$) seconds. It stays in FACH/DCH state and each packet transmission triggers an intra-3G handoff (see ③ in the plot). It also explains why the phone never returns to 4G when the 1KB-packet interval is smaller than 15 seconds.

**Case (III) 1B/15s** The difference from Case (I) is, before the third packet arrives, RRC turns into IDLE at about 25th second (10 seconds after the 2rd packet delivery) and thus the timer $T_{3G\rightarrow 4G}$ is set (Rule 1). It is also sensitive whether $T_{3G\rightarrow 4G}$ times out before the next packet arrival. If so, it triggers an handoff back to 4G, as shown in Figure 10(b). Otherwise, $T_{3G\rightarrow 4G}$ is reset and the duration in 3G is prolonged. This is why the duration also fluctuates around 15th second. When we slightly increase the interval (e.g., 15.5 seconds), the timer $T_{3G\rightarrow 4G}$ times out always before the next packet arrival. It returns to 4G similar to all the $> 15s$ case.

**Case (IV) 1KB/15s** Here, it is sensitive to how long the intra-3G handoff lasts. If the intra-3G handoff finishes within 5 seconds (e.g., 4.5 seconds), RRC turns IDLE and $T_{3G\rightarrow 4G}$ is set before next packet arrival. Otherwise, the triggered intra-3G handoff is to reset the $3G \rightarrow 4G$ handoff timer. Similarly, we induce that 20s is another transition interval for 1KB packets. For those intervals in [16s, 19s], the packet interval is larger than 15 seconds ($T_{3G-HO} + T_{idle}$), but is not large enough to wait for $T_{3G\rightarrow 4G}$ timeout. The subsequent intra-3G handoff resets this timer, so it will never return to 4G. It is also similar to the 1B-packet case with the interval in [11s, 14s].

In addition, it also explains the duration remaining in 3G without ongoing data. The timer 3G→4G handoff is set at the start, and the handoff is usually triggered 5 seconds later when it falls back to 3G. The handoff takes another 2–3 seconds to finish. This is why it is smaller than the one with data (at least first two packets are sent in 3G).

# FluidNet: A Flexible Cloud-based Radio Access Network for Small Cells


Karthikeyan Sundaresan
NEC Labs America, Inc.
karthiks@nec-labs.com

Mustafa Y. Arslan
NEC Labs America, Inc.
marslan@nec-labs.com

Shailendra Singh
UC Riverside
singhs@cs.ucr.edu

Sampath Rangarajan
NEC Labs America, Inc.
sampath@nec-labs.com

Srikanth V. Krishnamurthy
UC Riverside
krish@cs.ucr.edu



## ABSTRACT

Cloud-based radio access networks (C-RAN) have been proposed as a cost-efficient way of deploying small cells. Unlike conventional RANs, a C-RAN decouples the baseband processing unit (BBU) from the remote radio head (RRH), allowing for centralized operation of BBUs and scalable deployment of light-weight RRHs as small cells. In this work, we argue that the intelligent configuration of the front-haul network between the BBUs and RRHs, is essential in delivering the performance and energy benefits to the RAN and the BBU pool, respectively.

We then propose *FluidNet* - a scalable, light-weight framework for realizing the full potential of C-RAN. *FluidNet* deploys a logically re-configurable front-haul to apply appropriate transmission strategies in different parts of the network and hence cater effectively to both heterogeneous user profiles and dynamic traffic load patterns. *FluidNet* 's algorithms determine configurations that maximize the traffic demand satisfied on the RAN, while simultaneously optimizing the compute resource usage in the BBU pool. We prototype *FluidNet* on a 6 BBU, 6 RRH WiMAX C-RAN testbed. Prototype evaluations and large-scale simulations reveal that *FluidNet* 's ability to re-configure its front-haul and tailor transmission strategies provides a 50% improvement in satisfying traffic demands, while reducing the compute resource usage in the BBU pool by 50% compared to baseline transmission schemes.


## Categories and Subject Descriptors

C.2.1 [**Network Architecture and Design**]: Wireless communication


## Keywords

Cellular, Cloud RAN, DAS, FFR, Front-haul


## 1. INTRODUCTION

Mobile network operators are facing the pressure to increase the capacity and coverage of their radio access networks to meet the exponential growth in data traffic demand [8]. While leveraging the increased spatial reuse from smaller cells is a promising direction, every new cell adds to the capital and operational expenses borne by the operators. To address this problem, cloud-based radio access network (C-RAN) architectures have been considered by several operators [17] and service providers [15] as a cost-efficient way of realizing small cells. Unlike typical RANs where the baseband units (BBUs) and the radio units are situated together, the C-RAN concept (depicted in Fig. 1) migrates the BBUs to a datacenter (i.e., the BBU pool) hosting high performance general purpose and DSP processors, while providing high-bandwidth optical transport to the remote antennas called remote radio heads (RRHs). We define the high-bandwidth optical transport that carries the cellular signals between the BBUs and the RRHs to be the *front-haul* part of the network, whose bandwidth requirements could be significantly higher (tens of Gbps) than that of the backhaul depending on the nature of the signals (digital/analog, layer 1/2) carried [17]. The decoupling of the BBUs and radio units in a C-RAN allows for sophisticated centralized techniques for interference management, where the BBUs in the pool can seamlessly cooperate to improve the RAN capacity. In addition, the deployment of radio units is made light-weight and can be realized in a fast and scalable manner for small cells (other benefits of C-RAN are detailed in [17]).

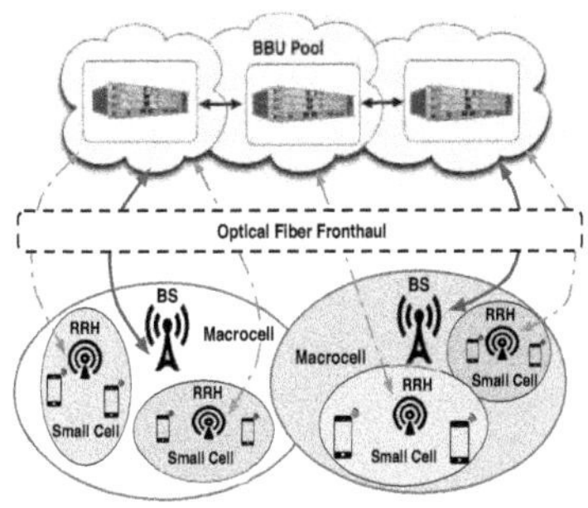


Figure 1: C-RAN Architecture.

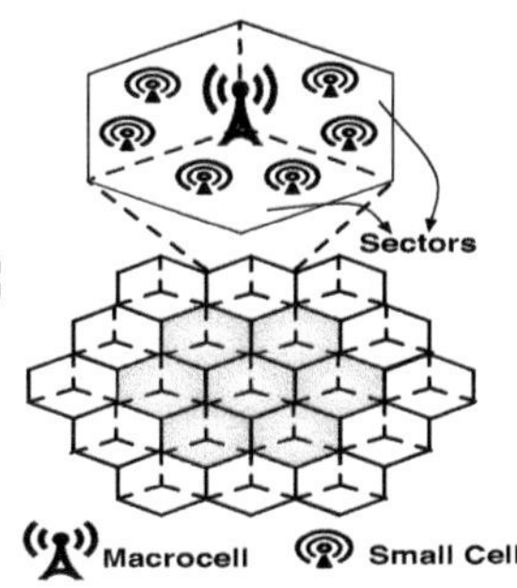


Figure 2: Network Deployment.

In this work, we argue that the front-haul that is unique to a C-RAN has a critical role in delivering its performance and cost benefits. We note that although the BBUs are decoupled from the RRHs in terms of physical placement, there exists a one-to-one logical mapping between BBUs and RRHs in that one BBU is assigned to generate (receive) a signal (e.g., LTE or WiMAX frame) to (from) an RRH (although the mapping can change over time). This one-to-one mapping allows for generating a distinct frame for each small cell (deployed in the form of a RRH), which is key for enhancing



*MobiCom'13*, September 30–October 4, 2013, Miami, FL, USA.



http://dx.doi.org/10.1145/2500423.2500435.

the network capacity via techniques such as dynamic fractional frequency reuse (dynamic FFR [4]) or coordinated multi-point transmissions (e.g., LTE CoMP [22]). We contend that this notion of a fixed, one-to-one mapping is not optimal in a practical cellular network deployment for two reasons.

**RAN Performance:** First, these techniques primarily apply to static users. The mobile users will have to bear frequent handoffs (exacerbated by smaller cells) and the associated performance penalties. In addition, tracking a mobile user's location and channel may be difficult for such techniques. In fact for mobile clients, a traditional distributed antenna system (DAS [11]) is arguably better suited. In a DAS setting, the same signal (carrying the user's data) is transmitted simultaneously by multiple small cells to provide coverage benefits (which in turn reduces handoffs) and diversity gain. DAS can be realized by changing the one-to-one to a one-to-many logical mapping in the C-RAN front-haul.

**BBU Energy Consumption:** Second, the one-to-one mapping requires several BBUs to be active and generating frames, which consumes energy in the BBU pool. However, the enhanced capacity of techniques such as [4, 22] may not be needed in all parts of the network or at all times (e.g., 50% of cells carry 5% of net traffic [5]). When the traffic load is low in a region (e.g., coverage area of multiple small cell RRHs), a single BBU may suffice to serve the offered load (via a DAS mapping). This in turn reduces the number of BBUs and hence the compute resources (e.g., CPU cores, DSPs), thereby allowing energy savings in the BBU pool.

Given the above observations, we envision a C-RAN architecture with a novel, flexible front-haul that supports one-to-one as well as one-to-many logical mappings between BBUs and RRHs. Our vision is to utilize this architecture *to address the traffic needs of users (static and mobile) while leveraging the energy savings made possible by the traffic load heterogeneity (i.e., temporal and spatial load variations in the network).*

Towards realizing this vision, we present *FluidNet* - a flexible C-RAN system for small cells that houses an intelligent controller in the BBU pool, which dynamically re-configures the front-haul (at coarse time scales) based on network feedback to cater effectively to both heterogeneous user and traffic profiles. This allows *FluidNet* to maximize the amount of traffic demand satisfied on the RAN for both static and mobile users, while at the same time optimizing the compute resource usage in the BBU pool. Briefly, *FluidNet* adopts a two-step, scalable approach: based on spatial traffic distribution and demand from users, *FluidNet* first determines the optimal combination of configurations (one-to-one and one-to-many, i.e., DAS and FFR strategies) needed to support the traffic demand from a set (termed *sector*) of small cells. Then, it employs a novel and efficient algorithm (with an approximation factor of $\frac{3}{2}$) to consolidate (cluster) the configurations of multiple sectors in the network to further reduce the compute resource usage without compromising on the traffic demand satisfied. *FluidNet* is both standards and technology agnostic. It allows for desirable features such as co-existence of multiple mobile operators and technologies (LTE, WiMAX, WiFi) in the same C-RAN, while employing different front-haul configurations tailored to each of their respective traffic.

We prototype *FluidNet* on a small-scale WiMAX C-RAN testbed with 6 BBUs and 6 RRHs, employing radio-over-fiber (RoF) as the front-haul. With *FluidNet* 's algorithms, the logical BBU-RRH configurations are determined and executed on the fly. Real-world experiments with COTS WiMAX clients show that featuring flexible front-haul configurations and hence strategies, allows *FluidNet* to provide a 50% improvement in traffic demand satisfaction, while also reducing the compute resource usage in the BBU pool by 50% compared to baseline DAS and FFR strategies. Complementary, standards-calibrated (3GPP) simulations for large networks show that the clustering component in *FluidNet* helps further reduce the compute resource usage by 50% during low traffic load periods. Our contributions are as follows:

- We propose *FluidNet* - a light-weight, scalable framework to determine the optimal use of strategies (DAS, FFR) to cater to dynamic user and traffic profiles, while realizing them through appropriate configurations that help minimize compute resource usage in the BBU pool.

- We design efficient algorithms with performance guarantees in determining the appropriate configurations.

- We build a small-scale C-RAN system with 6 BBUs-RRHs; prototype *FluidNet* on it; and conduct over-the-air experiments, complemented by standards-calibrated large-scale simulations to demonstrate its feasibility and benefits.

# 2. BACKGROUND

## 2.1 C-RAN Primer and Related Work

The C-RAN architecture, depicted in Fig. 1, includes three components: (i) remote radio heads (RRH), (ii) pool of baseband units (BBUs), and (iii) the front-haul (optical fiber based transport network).

**RRHs:** These are simple, light-weight radio units with antennas. Several proposals have focused on making RRHs power-efficient and scalable (e.g., [15, 9]) to support multiple bands and technologies (e.g., 3G, 4G).

**BBU Pool:** This helps migrate bulk of the base station (BS) processing of a large set of cells to a datacenter [17], allowing for easier realization of interference (e.g., CoMP [22, 3], HetNet [13]) and mobility management solutions.

On the energy front, [7, 21, 16] have looked at the benefits of switching off entire macrocell BSs based on prevailing traffic conditions. Moving the processing to a central entity in C-RAN allows for fine-grained use of resources in the pool and hence better energy savings (evaluated in Section 7). Further, these savings can be obtained without having to switch off an entire BS (allowing RRHs to be ON) and hence sacrificing performance or coverage.

For the BBU pool, there are several proposals for the use of heterogeneous platforms consisting of general-purpose processors as well as DSPs for compute-intensive baseband functions [10, 12]. Recently, [6] focused on assigning processor cores in a homogeneous platform to different BBUs in the pool, to meet latency requirements. Being complementary to [6], we focus on optimizing the use of BBUs themselves, which has an impact not only on compute resource usage in the BBU pool (especially in a heterogeneous platform) but also on RAN performance.

**Front-haul:** Optical fiber with wavelength multiplexing serves as the front-haul and distributes signals from the BBU pool to the RRHs either as (i) digitized radio signals over CPRI (common public radio interface) [1], or (ii) analog radio signals via radio-over-fiber (RoF) [19]. While CPRI is more robust than RoF over long distances, it requires more transport bandwidth.

Optical front-haul is already used in several DAS deployments [11]. Recently, [14] articulated the need for a re-configurable front-haul in a C-RAN, but did not offer a solution. Our focus is to design and build a dynamically re-configurable front-haul along with the intelligence to adaptively determine the appropriate configurations.

## 2.2 Overview of Strategies

**Fractional Frequency Reuse (FFR):** FFR is the mechanism for radio resource management (RRM) in cellular networks, whereby inter-cell interference is addressed. Unlike WiFi, the synchronous operation of downlink (BS-MS) and uplink (MS-BS) transmissions across cells requires transmissions to be intelligently scheduled to manage interference. In the popular 1-3 FFR scheme for macrocell networks, the spectrum is divided into four fixed-size bands. One band is used by all the cell-interior clients (in each cell), who do not see interference due to the close proximity to their BS, while the other three bands are used (by cell-exterior clients) in an orthogonal manner between the three sectors (Fig. 2) of a cell to mitigate interference with sectors of adjacent cells. Thus, while the band used by cell-interior clients is reused in each cell, the reuse of the other three bands are subject to the spatial reuse possible. Recently, dynamic FFR approaches [4] have been proposed specifically for small cells, and determine the number and size of bands to be used by each small cell only based on the aggregate traffic demand from its cell-interior and cell-exterior clients; they allow for better spectral utilization and do not rely on planned sectorization (unlike macrocells). Note that the FFR schemes only determine the set of spectral resources assigned to cells - scheduling of clients within those resources is done by each cell locally (based on per-client feedback) to leverage multi-user diversity.

We adopt [4] for FFR in *FluidNet*, although other FFR schemes can also be easily used. While point-to-point MIMO is automatically incorporated in FFR, other cooperative techniques such as multi-user MIMO and co-ordinated multi-point transmissions (CoMP) can also be applied under FFR.

**Distributed Antenna Systems (DAS):** In DAS, a common signal from a single source is delivered to multiple RRHs and transmitted simultaneously. This provides larger coverage and has been adopted by operators for both indoors and outdoors [11]. Unlike FFR that is focused on capacity, increasing the foot-print of the signal across multiple transmit points (small cells) under-utilizes the spectrum in DAS without scope for any spectral reuse.

**Relation between Strategies and Configurations:** Since interfering cells will be operating on potentially different spectral bands in FFR, different frames (with specific preamble, control, etc.) have to be generated for each cell, thereby requiring a one-to-one logical mapping (configuration) between a BBU and an RRH. This is the conventional mapping considered in C-RAN currently. However, in DAS, a single frame is transmitted by multiple RRHs, which in turn can be accomplished using a single BBU, thereby requiring a one-to-many mapping.

# 3. MOTIVATION AND MODEL

## 3.1 Motivation for a Reconfigurable Front-haul

With the help of a simple experiment conducted on a WiMAX C-RAN testbed (details in Section 6), we now motivate why a one-to-one signal mapping between BBUs and RRHs is highly sub-optimal. Consider a system with 3 BBUs and 3 RRHs, serving three clients as shown in Fig. 3, where each RRH interferes with its neighbor's client.

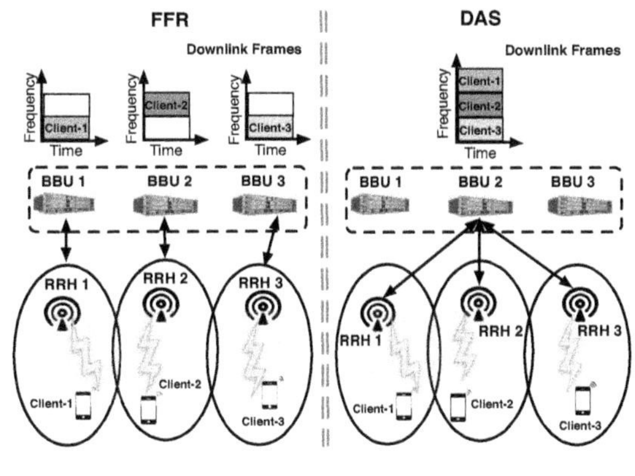


**Figure 3: 3 BBU-RRH setup for DAS vs FFR.**

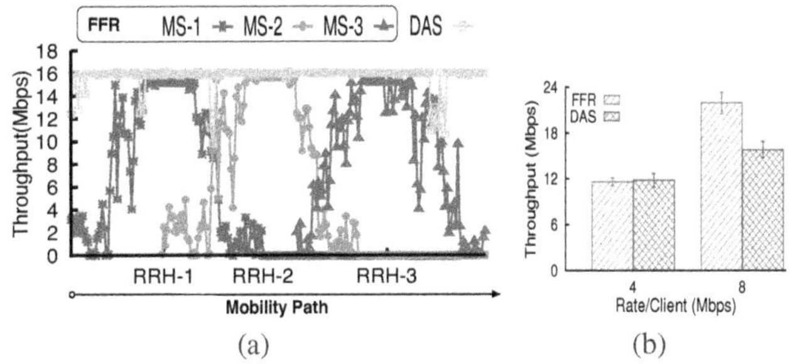


**Figure 4: (a) Effect of mobility. (b) Effect of traffic load.**

1. **Traffic Heterogeneity:** Consider a scenario, where the clients are static, but their data rate varies (see Fig. 4(b)). When the total rate (e.g., 8 Mbps per client = 24 Mbps) exceeds the max. data rate supported by all the sub-channels in one frame ($\approx$ 16 Mbps in our testbed), the increased capacity with FFR (by reusing orthogonal half of sub-channels as in Fig. 3) is essential to meet the traffic demand, while DAS is limited to one frame's capacity of 16 Mbps. On the other hand, at low load (e.g., 4 Mbps per client), DAS's capacity is sufficient to serve the clients with just one BBU, allowing the other two BBUs to be off. This is unlike in FFR, where all the BBUs have to be active to generate different frames to the RRHs; it lowers compute resource usage and thus enables significant energy savings in the BBU pool.

2. **User Heterogeneity:** Now, let all the three clients be mobile, moving between the 3 RRHs. Catering to the mobile clients through dynamic FFR from individual RRHs is very challenging for multiple reasons - (a) with small cells, there are frequent handoffs, whose associated latency has an adverse impact on throughput, (b) there is increased signaling load on the front-haul and the mobile core network due to frequent handoffs, (c) it may be hard to track the mobile user to specific small cells to efficiently apply dynamic FFR and leverage reuse. Even notwithstanding such drawbacks and assuming ideal handoffs for FFR, Fig. 4(a) clearly shows DAS' ability to deliver consistent coverage and performance for mobile users. Note that while relegating the mobile user to the macrocell is one option, DAS is ideal for such mobile users, since it achieves a coverage similar to a macrocell, while also increasing the link capacity (through shorter links and diversity gain, see Fig. 3).

Thus, while dynamic FFR is best suited for static users in high traffic load conditions, employing DAS also has benefits both from RAN performance (for mobile traffic) as well as BBU resource usage (for low traffic) perspectives. Given this, it is imperative for the front-haul to be re-configurable to realize flexible combinations of one-to-one and one-to-many BBU-RRH mappings.

## 3.2 Problem Definition

### 3.2.1 *Network Model*

Given that small cells have to co-exist with macrocells, we consider a large number of small cells to be deployed as an under-lay to an operator's macrocell network (Fig. 2). Since a macrocell will interfere with the small cells, thereby limiting their spatial reuse ability, two kinds of RRM solutions have been considered in literature: (i) macrocells and small cells operate on different carrier frequencies, and (ii) both use the same frequency but orthogonalize their radio resources at coarse time scales. We consider the former model and focus entirely on the downlink operation of small cells for ease of exposition. However, our solutions are equally applicable to the latter model and to uplink as well. Further, while small cells themselves could be deployed in an un-planned manner, we leverage the over-lay of macrocells and borrow the notion of logical sectors (from macrocells) to refer to the location of small cells.

### 3.2.2 *Objective*

Recall from Section 3.1 that while FFR (one-to-one configuration) supports the maximum amount of traffic through reuse, it does not save on computing resources in the BBU pool. On the other hand, while DAS (one-to-many configuration) minimizes the resource usage and caters to mobile traffic, it under-utilizes the spectrum. By appropriately employing FFR and DAS in combination in different parts of the network, *FluidNet* 's goal is to strike a fine balance between them. Specifically, subject to the primary requirement of supporting as much traffic ($D$) as the optimal configuration ($D_{OPT}$), *FluidNet* strives to minimize the corresponding amount of compute resources needed in the BBU pool (resource usage $RU$, defined in Sec. 4) for the purpose.

$$\min_{\Gamma} RU_{\Gamma}, \quad \text{subject to} \quad D \geq \lambda \cdot D_{OPT} \tag{1}$$

where $\Gamma$ represents a possible configuration, and $\lambda$ is the fraction of (optimum) traffic demand that must be satisfied (e.g., $\lambda = 0.99$). The optimal configuration would depend on the relative composition of mobile and static traffic and their priorities ($D_{OPT} = D_{FFR}$ when there is only static traffic demand). We assume mobile traffic to be prioritized over static traffic, albeit other models are also possible. Also note that minimization of compute resource consumption is only subject to satisfying as much of the traffic demand as possible and does not come at the expense of the latter.

*BBU Usage as a resource metric:* The main components of energy consumption in a traditional base station (BS) are those of air conditioning ($\approx$ 2 KW) and the BS equipment itself ($\approx$ 0.7 KW) [17]. A C-RAN system helps towards both these components by not only simplifying the cell site to a RRH (eliminating the need for air conditioning), but also consolidating the BS processing in the BBU pool. With respect to the latter component, reducing the number of BBU units and hence the frames that need to be processed, has a direct impact on energy consumption for two reasons. (1) BBU processing involves layer 1 (framing, FFT/IFFT, decoding, etc.), layer 2 (HARQ, resource/QoS scheduling, etc.) and layer 3 (connection management) functions. While layer 3 and part of layer 2 can be handled by generic processors, some of the time-sensitive layer 2 (resource scheduling) and layer 1 (framing, FFT/IFFT, decoding) functions are typically handled by dedicated DSPs for each BBU. (2) When DAS is employed, the traffic demand of multiple cells is handled without any spectral reuse. Hence, while the (traffic) load-dependent processing component is limited to that needed to handle the total number of slots (e.g., resource blocks in LTE) in a single frame, the basic processing component (FFT/IFFT) scales with the number of cells (frames) and soon dominates the former (see [6] for realistic values). Note that optimizing the BBU usage is complementary to assigning compute resources (e.g., GPPs) to the BBUs themselves, for which solutions such as [6] can be leveraged.

# 4. DESIGN ELEMENTS IN FLUIDNET

We motivate *FluidNet* 's design by addressing key aspects relevant to the operation of transmission strategies and its impact on the compute resource usage in the BBU pool.

## 4.1 Granularity and Choice of Configurations

A strategy (configuration) is applied to a set of small cells. In macrocells, each sector has its own cell ID and is the smallest granularity for RRM operations. Given this, *FluidNet* adopts *sector* (referring to set of small cells located within the logical sector) to be the minimum granularity for configurations.

Depending on the user and traffic profiles in a sector, one has to determine the appropriate transmission strategy: DAS or FFR. However, picking either DAS or FFR in *isolation* often results in in-sufficient or spare spectral resources respectively, in handling the offered traffic load. Hence, *FluidNet* employs a flexible *combination* of DAS and FFR (called *hybrid* configurations) in each sector. It devotes the right fraction of spectral resources between the two configurations, thereby supporting the offered traffic load with the least possible use of BBU resources.

## 4.2 Realization of Hybrid Configurations

Since two configurations cannot co-exist in the same time-frequency resource, hybrid configurations have to be multiplexed either in time or frequency. If multiplexed in time, a hybrid configuration can be realized at the granularity of an epoch spanning several super-frames (10 ms each in LTE), where a contiguous subset of the sub-frames (1 ms each) operate in a DAS configuration, while the rest operate in FFR. If multiplexed in frequency, the operator's spectrum can be divided into coarse spectral blocks (separate carriers in a multi-carrier scenario such as LTE-advanced; e.g., similar to orthogonal channels in WiFi), which are then split between the two configurations (see Fig.5). The fraction of carriers allocated to the configurations is such that the traffic load is satisfied with the least possible use of BBU resources. Since a DAS configuration minimizes the use of BBU resources but supports the least amount of traffic, this is equivalent to finding the largest allocation to the DAS configuration that is capable of sustaining the offered load.

Note that, frequency-multiplexing allows appropriate number of BBU resources to be assigned to each carrier (based on the configuration using it), which do not have to be changed unless the hybrid configuration itself is updated (which happens at coarse time scales; order of minutes). This is unlike time-multiplexing, where the assignment of BBU resources has to be re-mapped even within a hybrid configuration, i.e. switches between DAS and FFR (granularity of super-frames - tens of ms). Although feasible, the time scales of the latter may limit the potential for resource and energy savings in the BBU pool. Hence, *FluidNet* adopts multiplexing configurations in the frequency domain.

## 4.3 Clustering for Reduced Resource Usage

In regions of the network with low traffic load, it is possible to support the traffic demand from multiple sectors jointly with a single DAS configuration. While aggregating such sectors reduces the compute resource usage in the BBU pool, it must be done in a scalable manner. *FluidNet* proposes a novel clustering mechanism for this purpose.

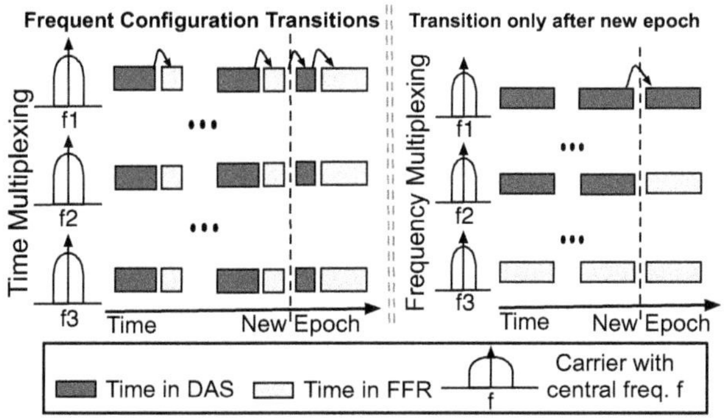


**Figure 5: Realizing Hybrid Configurations.**

To capture the BBU resource usage for a hybrid configuration in a sector, we define the resource usage metric, RU:

$$RU(b_i, n_i) = b_i \cdot 1 + (B - b_i) \cdot n_i \tag{2}$$

where, $n_i$ is the number of small cells in sector $i$ and $b_i$, the number of carriers (out of $B$ total) allocated to its DAS configuration. In every carrier, the number of BBU units needed for DAS is one, while it is equal to the number of small cells ($n$) for FFR. Thus, $RU$ captures the effective number of BBU units needed to support the offered load on the given spectral resources (OFDMA resources in $B$ carriers).

Using the RU metric, *FluidNet* employs a scalable algorithm (details in Section 5) that clusters two neighboring sectors ($i$ and $j$) at a time, until either their net offered load cannot be supported or the RU of the resulting cluster ($i \cup j$) cannot be improved, i.e.,

$$RU(b_{i\cup j}, n_i + n_j) > RU(b_i, n_i) + RU(b_j, n_j) \tag{3}$$

where $b_{i\cup j}$ captures the new split of carriers between DAS and FFR in the cluster). While applying DAS to serve user traffic on $b_{i\cup j}$ resources is straight-forward (shared between users without any reuse), dynamic FFR now has to be applied on $B - b_{i\cup j}$ carriers for a larger number of cells ($n_i + n_j$). The latter, being a non-trivial RRM process, could become computationally intensive as the size of the cluster increases. Hence, for large clusters, *FluidNet* can run its FFR solution seperately in each cluster's constituent sectors (for scalability), albeit on the same set of $B - b_{i\cup j}$ carriers.

## 4.4 Handling User Mobility

So far we had assumed that the offered traffic load in a sector or cluster can be scheduled on any of the carriers operating on either DAS or FFR. Recall that for mobile (mainly vehicular) users, a DAS configuration is essential not just for reducing compute resource usage but even for performance. Identifying such mobile users can be done in many ways (e.g., mobile operator maintains user's mobility state). Then the offered traffic load from vehicular users can be isolated from the rest of the traffic and scheduled on resources supporting the DAS configuration. Hence, the net traffic load from mobile users in a sector or cluster would place a constraint on the minimum number of carriers that need to be allocated to its DAS configuration. Subject to this constraint, the rest of the operations (resource allocation, multiplexing, clustering, etc.) are performed as mentioned above.

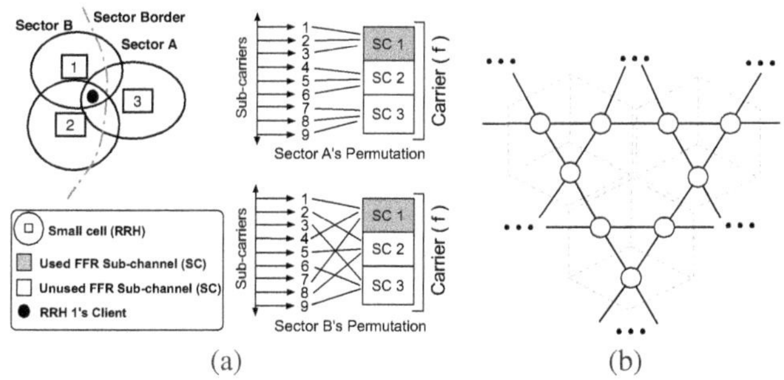


**Figure 6: (a) Handling Inter-sector Interference. (b) Sector graph.**

## 4.5 Handling Interference across Sectors

Since FFR is executed at the sector granularity for scalability, interference is managed only between cells within a sector. The conventional (simple) solution to handle interference across sectors (or clusters) is to consider all external interference as noise. A more sophisticated approach is to make implicit provisions in the transmission strategy of a sector for alleviating interference across sectors (and hence clusters) without any coordination. Recall that, in a carrier allocated to FFR, only a subset of the sub-channels (called resource blocks in LTE) are used by any of the cells in the sector to account for intra-sector interference (e.g., cells 1 and 2 in Fig. 6(a)). When coordination across sectors is allowed, these sub-channels would be further chosen so as to avoid interference between sectors. However, in the absence of any coordination (for scalability), the sub-carriers constituting the sub-channels in the carrier can be *permuted differently* across sectors. While this does not provide the same performance as performing FFR over the interfering sectors jointly, it does provide an interference averaging (alleviating) effect (cells 1 and 3 in Fig. 6(a)). Note that, this is not possible when operating in DAS, where all sub-channels in the carrier are used in every interfering sector.

*FluidNet* determines the sector-exterior traffic that is prone to interference from neighboring sectors and operates it in an FFR configuration to alleviate interference. Hence, similar to the minimum set of carriers needed for DAS (for mobile traffic), *FluidNet* reserves a minimum set of carriers for FFR to accommodate sector-exterior traffic.

# 5. ALGORITHMS IN FLUIDNET

## 5.1 Overview of Solution

The sequence of operations in *FluidNet* for every epoch (spanning several minutes) is as follows.

**Step 1:** For every sector, obtain the aggregate traffic demand (over the previous epoch) from each of its small cells. Determine the minimum set of carriers needed for the DAS and FFR configurations based on traffic demand from mobile and sector-exterior traffic respectively.

**Step 2:** Determine the optimal multiplexing (in frequency) of DAS and FFR configurations for each sector. This would automatically classify the appropriate traffic that needs to be scheduled on a particular configuration. Based on the resulting allocation of carriers to the configurations, determine the RU metric for the sector.

**Step 3:** Cluster sectors two at a time based on their RU metric until either their net offered load cannot be supported or the RU of the resulting cluster cannot be improved.

**Step 4:** For each cell in the cluster, apply the configurations on their allocated carriers as determined by the cluster's RU metric and assign respective traffic to carriers allocated to their appropriate configurations.

We now describe each of the steps in detail.

## 5.2 Estimation of Radio Resource Demand

Each small cell maintains an estimate of the aggregate traffic demand from its users in the current epoch (of length $T$ s). Given a traffic demand ($d_{c,u}$ in bits) from a user $u$ in cell $c$, this is translated to the corresponding radio resource demand per sub-frame (i.e. OFDMA resource slots/ms). For this, the average MCS (modulation and coding rate, $\ell_{c,u}$) used to serve the user in the epoch is kept track of and used to obtain the radio resource demand per sub-frame as $r_{c,u} = \frac{d_{c,u}}{T \cdot 1000 \cdot \ell_{c,u}}$ slots. Each cell ($c$) classifies its net user traffic demand $d_c$ as either mobile or non-mobile. The non-mobile category is further classified as cell-exterior or cell-interior traffic (for FFR purposes) based on presence or absence of interference respectively from neighboring small cells. At the end of the epoch, every cell ($c$) then provides 3 parameters as input to the central controller: aggregate radio resource demand from mobile ($d_{c,mob} = \sum_{i \in mob} r_{c,i}$), cell-interior ($d_{c,int} = \sum_{i \in int} r_{c,i}$) and cell-exterior ($d_{c,ext} = \sum_{i \in ext} r_{c,i}$) traffic. Note that with centralized processing in C-RAN, there is no associated feedback overhead in providing this information.

Each sector ($j$) then further aggregates the radio resource demands from mobile traffic in each of its small cells ($D_{j,mob} = \sum_{c \in j} d_{c,mob}$). The minimum radio resource demand needed for its DAS configuration is then the smallest number of carriers needed to satisfy the net mobile traffic demand, i.e, $b_{DAS} = \min_{b \cdot M \geq D_{j,mob}} b$, where $M$ is the number of OFDMA resource slots on each carrier. Similarly, to determine the minimum radio resource demand for FFR, it aggregates the cell-exterior traffic from all its small cells that are on the edge of the sector ($D_{j,ext} = \sum_{c \in edge(j)} d_{c,ext}$), scales them by $\alpha = 0.25$, and obtains $b_{FFR} = \min_{b \cdot M \geq \alpha D_{j,ext}} b$. Note that approximately only half of the cell-exterior traffic of the sector-edge cells will be vulnerable to other small cells from neighboring sectors. Further, every alternate sector-edge cell would be able to reuse the radio resources in the sector. Accounting for both these aspects, reduces the radio resource demand approximately by a quarter that is captured by $\alpha$.

**Remarks:** (1) Since *aggregate* traffic demand from a sector of small cells changes slowly at coarse time scales, determining configurations for every epoch (order of minutes) based on the aggregate demand is both appropriate and robust. For the same reason, it also suffices to estimate the *approximate* radio resource demand from sector exterior traffic. (2) *FluidNet* requires only one parameter (mobile traffic demand) from each small cell in addition to those already required by FFR schemes (i.e. cell-interior and cell-exterior traffic demands). However, one can eliminate the former and simplify *FluidNet* 's design by not catering to mobile and sector-exterior traffic separately (i.e. $b_{DAS} = b_{FFR} = 0$).

## 5.3 Optimal Sector Configuration

With the estimates of aggregate radio resource demands, *FluidNet* determines the optimal split of carriers between DAS and FFR configurations in a sector ($j$) as follows. With $b_{DAS}$ and $b_{FFR}$ serving as the minimum number of carriers needed for the DAS and FFR configurations, *FluidNet* uses an iterative approach (Algorithm 1) to determine the optimal split ($b_j, B - b_j$) by starting with $b_{FFR}$ as the minimum set of carriers needed for FFR and allowing it to expand till the radio resource demand can be satisfied or if the limit of $B - b_{DAS}$ carriers is reached. Since mobile and sector-exterior traffic demands are already accounted for, to check if net radio resource demand can be met, *FluidNet* essentially needs to check only if the remaining resource demand ($\sum_{c \notin edge(j)} d_{c,ext} + \sum_{c \in j} d_{c,int}$) can be accommodated by the current split (say $b, B - b$) in the iteration, with $b - b_{DAS}$ and $B - b - b_{FFR}$ carriers in DAS and FFR configurations respectively. Note that this would involve running an FFR scheme on $B - b - b_{FFR}$ carriers first (step 3), wherein to maximize the amount of traffic demand satisfied through FFR, the cell-interior traffic ($\sum_{c \in j} d_{c,int}$) that provides maximum spatial reuse is assigned to FFR prior to the cell-exterior traffic ($\sum_{c \notin edge(j)} d_{c,ext}$). The remaining traffic demand ($D - D_{FFR}$) is then scheduled through DAS on the $b - b_{DAS}$ carriers (step 4).

If the total number of carriers $B$ is small, then a simple, sequential iteration (with increments of one carrier) would suffice. However, if $B$ is large, then the FFR operation in each iteration could be computationally expensive. In this case, *FluidNet* employs binary search, where the split is moved to the left if the traffic demand cannot be met (steps 8-9), and moved to the right if spare resource slots ($f_{DAS}$, normalized to total # resource slots in a carrier $M$) remain in DAS configuration after demand satisfaction (steps 5-6). It converges at the split (say $b_j$), where the number of carriers allocated to FFR cannot be further reduced, while still satisfying the demand. Binary search reduces the number of iterations and hence FFR operations from linear ($O(B)$) to logarithmic ($O(\log_2(B))$). After convergence, the RU of the sector is computed using Eqn. 2 as $RU(b_j, n_j)$.

**Algorithm 1** Optimal Configuration for Sector $j$

1: Initialize $b_{low} = b_{DAS}$, $b_{high} = B - b_{FFR}$, $b = b_{high}$, $D = \sum_{c \notin edge(j)} d_{c,ext} + \sum_{c \in j} d_{c,int}$
2: **while** $b_{high} \neq b_{low}$ **do**
3: $(f_{FFR}, D_{FFR})$ = Schedule_FFR$(B - b_{FFR} - b, D)$
4: $(f_{DAS}, D_{DAS})$ = Schedule_DAS$(b - b_{DAS}, D - D_{FFR})$
5: **if** $f_{DAS} > 0$ **then**
6: $b_{low} \leftarrow b$; $b \leftarrow \frac{b + b_{high}}{2}$; $b_{cur} \leftarrow b$
7: **else**
8: **if** $D - D_{FFR} - D_{DAS} > 0$ **then**
9: $b_{high} \leftarrow b$; $b \leftarrow \frac{b + b_{low}}{2}$
10: **end if**
11: **end if**
12: **end while**
13: $b_j \leftarrow b_{cur}$

In addition to RU, every sector keeps track of two metrics: spare radio resources ($\beta_j$) and reuse factor ($r_j$) in the sector (for use in clustering). Note that since minimum set of carriers are determined for FFR configuration, spare resource slots, if any, will appear only in the DAS configuration. This is normalized to the total number of slots ($M$) in each carrier to yield $\beta_j$. Similarly, reuse factor determines the number of actual resource slots needed to support the traffic demand in the sector (and captures the average reuse resulting from FFR): $r_j = \frac{\sum_{c \in j} d_{c,mob} + d_{c,ext} + d_{c,int}}{(B - \beta_j)M}$.

THEOREM 5.1. FluidNet *'s iterative scheme converges to the optimal split of carriers between FFR and DAS configurations in each sector w.r.t. the objective in Eqn. 1.*

The proof is deferred to [20] in the interest of space.

## 5.4 Properties of RU Metric

We present properties of the RU metric that are relevant for clustering (proofs are deferred to [20]). For ease of exposition, we do not consider mobile traffic in the discussions.

PROPERTY 5.1. *When two sectors $i, j$ are clustered, the split of carriers in the resulting cluster has to be the minimum of those in the constituent sectors ($b_{i \cup j} = \min\{b_i, b_j\}$) to maximize RU.*

PROPERTY 5.2. *RU metric does not satisfy the "local" property, i.e. if clustering sectors $i, j, k$ improves the RU, then this does not mean that clustering a subset of its constituent sectors also improves RU.*

$$RU(b_{i\cup j\cup k}, n_i + n_j + n_k) \leq \sum_{\ell=\{i,j,k\}} RU(b_\ell, n_\ell)$$
$$! \Rightarrow RU(b_{i\cup j}, n_i + n_j) \leq RU(b_i, n_i) + RU(b_j, n_j)$$

PROPERTY 5.3. *To cluster sectors $i$ and $j$ (with say $b_i \leq b_j$), we need all of the following to be satisfied.*

1. *Both sectors must have spare radio resources in the DAS configuration, i.e. $\beta_i < b_i$ and $\beta_j < b_j$.*
2. *The aggregate traffic from the DAS and FFR configurations of the two sectors must be satisfied by the new split of carriers in the cluster. Equivalently, $b_j - r_j(b_j - b_i) \leq \beta_i + \beta_j$.*
3. *The RU of the resulting cluster must be improved. Equivalently, $b_j \leq \frac{n_j}{n_j - 1} b_i$.*

## 5.5 Clustering of Sectors

Based on the above established properties, *FluidNet* designs a light-weight clustering algorithm (Algorithm 2) to improve the RU of configurations applied in the network. Representing as a graph $G = (V, E)$, each sector forms a vertex in the graph, while an edge $e = (u, v)$ exists between two vertices ($u$ and $v$) if the corresponding sectors are adjacent (Step 1). Each edge $e$ carries a weight ($w_e$), which evaluates property 5.3 in identifying if the corresponding sectors $u$ and $v$ can be clustered, and if so assigns the resulting RU of the cluster as its weight ($w_e = RU(\min\{b_u, b_v\}, n_u + n_v)$). If however, clustering is not feasible, then this is denoted by $w_e = \infty$ (Step 2).

**Algorithm 2** Clustering of Sectors

```
1: Construct Sector Graph: G = (V, E), V = {sectors}, E =
   {e = (u, v)} : v = N(u)
2: w_e = RU(min{b_u, b_v}, n_u + n_v) if Property 5.3 is satisfied;
   and w_e = ∞ otherwise
3: Let G' = (V', E'); initialize V' = V, E' = E
4: while (1) do
5:    Pick u = Rand(V')
6:    Select v* = arg min_{v:e=(u,v)∈E'} w_e
7:    if v* ≠ ∅ then
8:       Contract (u, v*) in V', i.e. (u, v*) → u'
9:       Add edges in E', (u', v) : (u, v) ∈ E or (v*, v) ∈ E
10:      Update edge weights in E' w_e', ∀e' = (u', v) : v ∈
         N(u') &v ∈ V'
11:   else
12:      Exit
13:   end if
14: end while
15: Output clustered graph G' = (V', E')
```

With the above weighted graph, *FluidNet* clusters sectors through a graph coarsening approach. At each step, it picks a random vertex $u$ (Step 5), then selects the neighboring vertex $v$ (Step 6) that when clustered together minimizes the resulting RU ($v = \arg\min_{e \in E'} w_e$, where $e = (u, v)$). It then contracts $u$ and $v$, along with edges between them to a new clustered node $u'$ (Steps 7-9). Weights of edges incident on $u$ and $v$ are updated after the contraction (Step 10). The process is repeated until no more clustering is possible. Each vertex in the final graph ($v \in V'$) represents the clustering of sectors in the network for improved RU (Step 15). Further, the RU of each clustered node, represents the common split of carriers between the DAS and FFR configurations for all sectors in that cluster.

Recall that RU does not satisfy the local property (property 5.2). Hence, while local clustering schemes are light-weight and scalable, they might miss out on potential clusters that improve the RU. To reduce the impact of such sub-optimality, *FluidNet* leverages the structure of the sector graph as follows. The logical 3-sector operation of macrocell networks results in a graph that has only cliques of size 3 and cycles of size 6 (see Fig.6(b)). This special form of $G$ is called a "sector graph". Hence, *FluidNet* includes the following optimization, where in addition to computing the weight of each edge, it also computes the weight of each clique ($w_{(u,v,w)} = RU(\min\{b_u, b_v, b_w\}, n_u + n_v + n_w)$). Hence, it first starts contracting (clustering) all possible cliques ($\frac{|V|}{3}$ in number) before moving to the contraction of edges. This would help improve RU from potential 3-sector (clique) clusters, which would not otherwise result from their constituent 2-sector (edge) clusters.

As with most clustering problems, it can be shown that the problem of finding the network-wide configuration with the smallest RU is NP-hard. We have the following performance guarantee (proof deferred to [20]) for *FluidNet* .

THEOREM 5.2. FluidNet *'s algorithms yield network-wide transmission configurations with a RU that is within a factor of $\frac{3}{2}$ and 2 from the optimal for sector and general graphs respectively.*

## 5.6 Scalable Realization

While carriers assigned to DAS and FFR (say $(b', B - b')$) in a cluster are fixed for an epoch and determined by the cluster's resulting RU (computed based on aggregate radio resource demands from previous epoch), DAS and FFR strategies are applied to appropriate incoming traffic demand at finer time scales (order of seconds) during the epoch. Further, the DAS traffic of all the constituent sectors simply share the radio resources through a common DAS configuration on $b'$ carriers. However, the FFR for the constituent sectors is executed individually within each sector (and not jointly), albeit on the same set of $B - b'$ carriers. This keeps the complexity of running FFR schemes low (restricted to cells in a sector). Not running FFR jointly across all sectors in the cluster will result in inter-sector interference. However, this does not hurt the estimated RU of the cluster since it is implicitly incorporated in the RU of the constituent sectors prior to clustering. Further, adopting a two-step approach - first determining the RU-optimal DAS-FFR configuration in each sector, then improving RU of the network by clustering sectors through a light-weight process, forms the key in ensuring scalability of operations in *FluidNet* .

# 6. PROTOTYPE OF FLUIDNET

## 6.1 Architecture

The core intelligence of *FluidNet* resides in the central processing entity managing the BBU pool, which consists of two key components.

1. **Resource Manager:** The resource manager is responsible for two key functionalities: (i) determining the appropriate

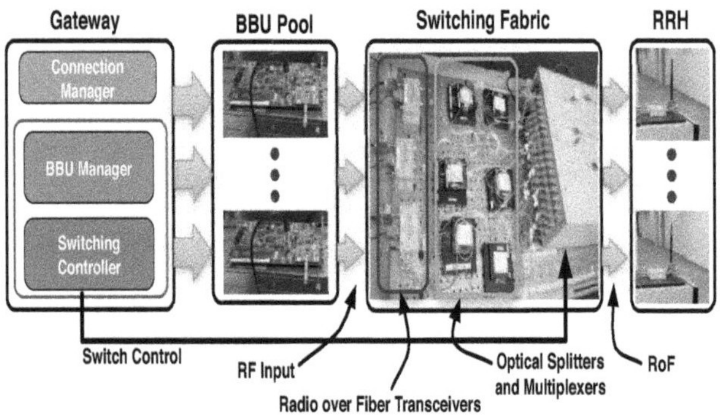


**Figure 7: Testbed components of *FluidNet*.**

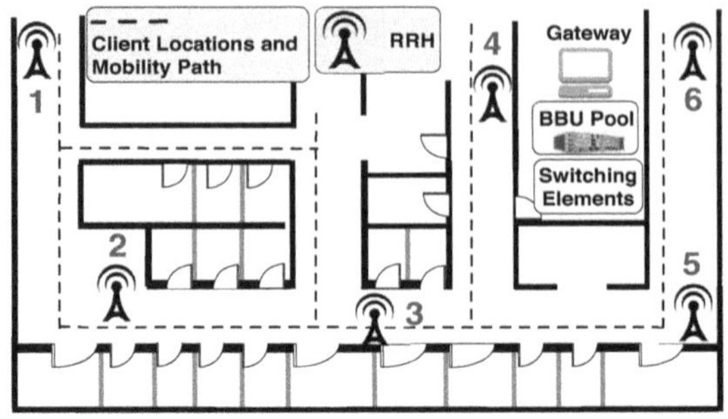


**Figure 8: Testbed deployment**

number of BBU units (using *FluidNet* 's algorithms) needed to generate distinct frames and how these frames from BBUs are mapped to specific RRHs, and (ii) assigning compute resources (DSPs, cores, etc.) to each BBU unit. *FluidNet* focuses on the former functionality and is complementary to the processor scheduling problem addressed by studies with the latter functionality [6].

2. **Switching Element:** While the resource manager determines the logical mapping of BBU signals to RRHs, the switching element is responsible for realizing these mappings. Since some BBU frames are sent to multiple RRHs (as in DAS), while other frames are sent individually to specific cells (as in dynamic FFR), the switching element allows for both unicast and multicast switching. Based on the configuration determined by the resource manager on a given carrier, the switch module activates the appropriate set of output ports for an incoming BBU signal depending on the intended set of recipient RRHs. Since a BBU pool may potentially serve tens to hundreds of small cell RRHs, to ensure scalability, the switching fabric may be composed of multiple smaller-size switches (as opposed to one big switch). The size of the switches may be chosen to tradeoff the level of multicasting capability (e.g., for DAS) with cost.

## 6.2 Implementation

We have built a full-fledged, small-scale C-RAN testbed, capable of over-the-air transmissions. Given that LTE requires licensed spectrum, our set-up is currently based on WiMAX (with an experimental license). However, both LTE and WiMAX being OFDMA-based, our testbed suffices to demonstrate the proposed concepts in *FluidNet* that are equally applicable to LTE as well. Our testbed is depicted in Fig. 7.

**BBU Pool, clients and gateway:** Since our focus is on the fronthaul configuration, we consider six WiMAX BSs (from PicoChip [18]) directly as our BBUs. We use netbooks with USB WiMAX dongles as the clients. *FluidNet* 's algorithms to determine configurations, are implemented in the WiMAX gateway, whose primary role is to manage the traffic flows from/to the clients. In our set-up, a single gateway is instrumented to manage all the 6 BBUs and their clients. The gateway also hosts the controller to instruct the switch for mapping of BBU signals to RRHs. We implement the controller using LabVIEW and communicate the desired configurations to the switch via serial port (RS232).

**Radio-over-Fiber:** Ideally, baseband signals should be transported in the digital domain between BBU pool and RRHs to allow for scalable, low-latency switching between configurations. However, the lack of commercially available products to manipulate the baseband signals between BBU pool and RRHs in the digital domain (over CPRI), has prompted us to pick an alternate design, wherein we employ analog RF signal transmission based on radio over fiber (RoF) techniques. With latencies of about 5 $\mu$s/Km over the fiber, we have verified that RoF can retain the signal synchronization between RRHs as well as the timing constraint between downlink and uplink signals for reasonable distances of around 10 Km between the BBU pool and RRHs. With RoF, the modulated RF analog signal from a BBU is converted into an optical carrier using a COTS optical transceiver, and delivered to RRHs on a single mode optical fiber.

**RRHs:** Since all the signal processing (even modulation and RF up/down-conversion) is done at the BBU pool, our RRH design is simple and consists of an optical transceiver attached to an antenna. The optical wavelengths (carrying multiple RF signals) are photo-detected and converted back to the RF domain (for over-the-air transmission) by the optical transceiver. On the uplink (from RRHs to BBUs), the operations are similar but in reverse order.

**Switching Element:** Since BBU signals are carried as analog RoF, to realize various configurations, we enable switching in the optical domain, which is controlled from the gateway. Since our optical switch supports only one-to-one switching, we enable flexible switching (one-to-one and one-to-many) indirectly by using optical splitters and multiplexers with CWDM. While the latency in switching between configurations is negligible if implemented in the digital domain, it could be appreciable in the optical domain depending on the sophistication of the switch. With our inexpensive optical switch that reconfigures individual port switches, this could amount to 1 s. This is still acceptable if hybrid (DAS, FFR) configurations are realized in the frequency domain (across spectral carriers), where they need to be changed only with appreciable load changes at the granularity of several seconds or minutes.

The gateway controls the optical switch to turn on or off each independent path from each BBU to any RRH to create various configurations. Since each switch in our testbed is limited to supporting all configurations in a set-up with at most 4 BBUs and 4 RRHs, we employ two such switches jointly to serve our 6 BBU-RRH system.

# 7. PERFORMANCE EVALUATION

## 7.1 Prototype Evaluation

### 7.1.1 Set-up

**Testbed:** Our testbed consists of six small cell RRHs deployed in an indoor office setting, driven by six physical BBUs co-located in a single room through optical fiber (see Fig. 8). There are six

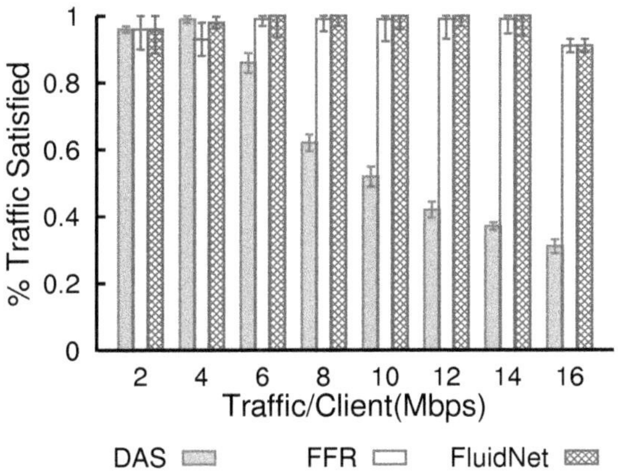


**Figure 9: Traffic satisfaction with variable traffic demand.**

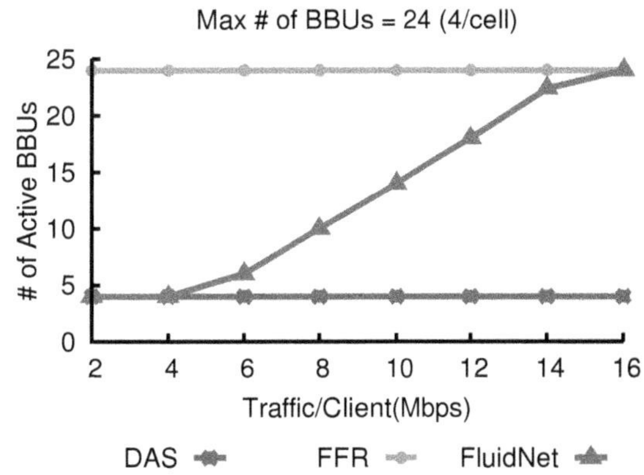


**Figure 10: Energy efficiency with variable traffic demand.**

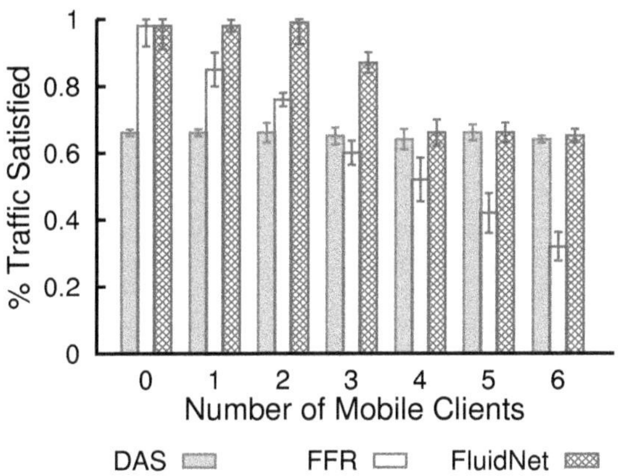


**Figure 11: Mobile: Traffic satisfaction.**

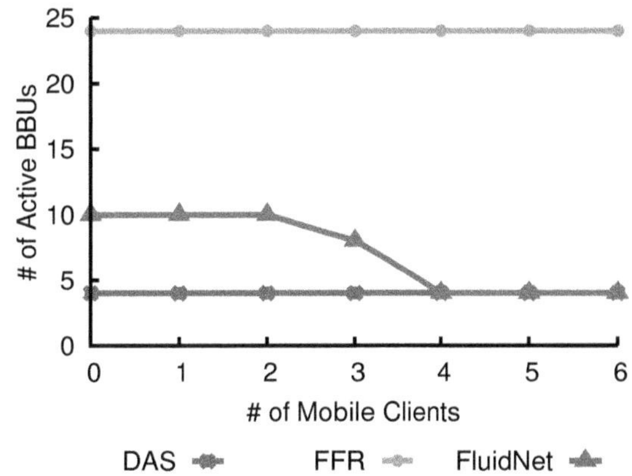


**Figure 12: Mobile: Energy efficiency.**

clients, each associated to one of the six cells. All the small cells are assumed to be in a single sector of a macrocell. The BBUs can generate WiMAX RF signals over two 10 MHz bands: at 2.59 GHz and 2.61 GHz, for which an experimental FCC license has been acquired to conduct over-the-air transmissions. Hence, we consider four spectral blocks (i.e., carriers), each with 5 MHz bandwidth to realize hybrid configurations. Since our BBUs are BSs themselves, we can operate a BS and hence an RRH on only one carrier at any given time. Due to this technical difficulty, we run DAS and FFR configurations sequentially on the appropriate blocks to realize the hybrid configuration for the sector. This would equivalently amount to 4 logical BBUs (one per carrier) per small cell and hence a maximum of 24 logical BBUs in the system.

**Strategies and Metrics:** We evaluate *FluidNet* against both the DAS scheme (labeled "DAS") and an FFR scheme (labeled "FFR") for baseline comparison (we consider other baselines in simulations). For FFR, our topology allows each small cell to operate on half the set of sub-channels, while being orthogonal to those of its neighbors. In DAS, a single BBU frame serves all the RRHs and clients. Traffic loads (2 - 16 Mbps) and profile (static, mobile) of clients are the parameters studied. The maximum net throughput that can be delivered in a WiMAX frame (at 64 QAM) in our set-up is around 16 Mbps for 10 MHz bandwidth. Each experiment takes 180 seconds and is repeated multiple times with varying client locations. Impact of rate adaptation is isolated by picking the MCS that delivers maximum throughput for a client (we try all MCSs). The fraction of the offered load supported and the effective number of BBU units consumed in the process are the metrics of evaluation.

### 7.1.2 *Impact of Traffic Heterogeneity*

With six static clients, we study the percentage of average traffic satisfied and the number of BBUs required by each scheme with varying per-client traffic demand in Figs. 9 and 10, respectively. With high load, FFR is essential to support the traffic demand, while DAS can support only a third of the demand (Fig. 9). When the load is low, DAS is sufficient and activates only a sixth of the BBUs required by FFR (Fig. 10). While *FluidNet* blends the best of DAS and FFR under extreme load conditions, its benefits are more pronounced in the intermediate regime (e.g., 10 Mbps demand per-client), where it outperforms both DAS and FFR. By employing hybrid configurations and adapting them to traffic profiles, *FluidNet* sustains twice as much traffic as DAS and requires only half the BBUs activated by FFR.

### 7.1.3 *Impact of User Heterogeneity*

We vary the number of mobile clients in a six client scenario, with each client's traffic fixed at 8 Mbps. To eliminate the adverse impact of handoffs in FFR (triggers, delays, etc.), we move a mobile client at pedestrian speed only in the vicinity of its RRH (sample path in Fig. 8). In contrast, seamless coverage and lack of handovers, allow a client to be moved in all deployment areas with DAS and *FluidNet* . Hence, the results in Figs. 11 and 12 are optimistic for FFR. We see that with increasing fraction of mo-

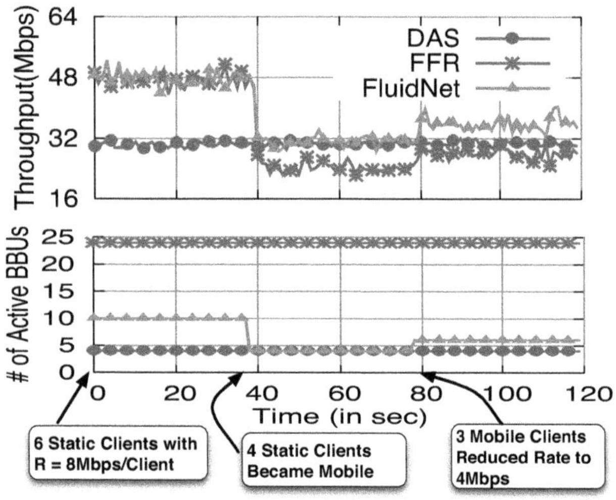


**Figure 13: Network Dynamics.**

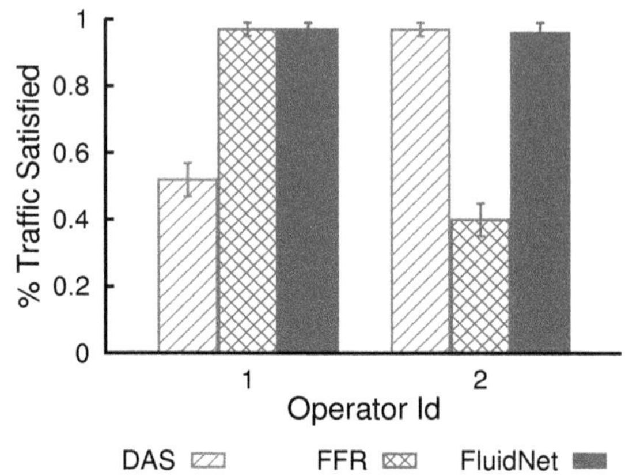


**Figure 14: Two Operators: Traffic satisfaction.**

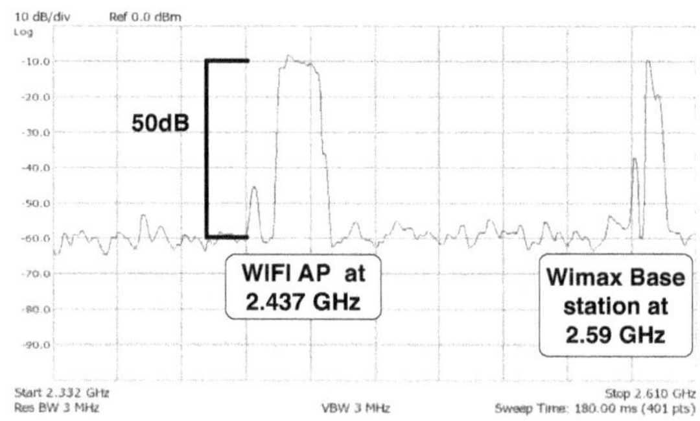


**Figure 15: Signal Spectrum: WiFi + WiMAX.**

bile traffic, FFR's performance degrades and ends up being much worse than that of DAS (Fig. 11). We observed that, even without handovers, when a client moves away from its RRH, its link deteriorates and faces high interference from the control region of frames of neighboring RRHs in FFR (only data part of the frame is protected in FFR). While DAS's coverage provides consistent link quality, it under-utilizes the spectrum when mobile traffic is low. *FluidNet* strikes a fine balance between the two configurations to support as much as 50% more traffic, while incurring a BBU energy consumption that is only slightly more than that of DAS.

### *7.1.4 Adaptation to Network Dynamics*

We now evaluate *FluidNet* 's adaptability to network dynamics. We start with six static clients, each with a 8 Mbps traffic load. Two events are triggered, one at 40 seconds into the experiment and another at 80 seconds. In the first event, four of the clients become mobile. Then at the 80 second mark, one of the mobile clients becomes static again and the remaining mobile clients reduce their rate to 4 Mbps. From Fig. 13, we see that *FluidNet* tracks FFR performance initially (albeit at less number of BBUs activated), when there are more static clients inducing a high traffic load. When a majority of the traffic demand becomes mobile at the first event, unlike FFR that suffers in performance, *FluidNet* immediately (but for a short transition delay) adapts its configuration to track DAS performance that is optimal for the updated network conditions. Similarly, when the traffic load of static clients starts to dominate, while still involving mobile clients at the second event, *FluidNet* employs a hybrid configuration to sustain a higher traffic load compared to both DAS and FFR, while incurring a BBU usage comparable to DAS. This clearly indicates *FluidNet* 's ability to effectively adapt its configurations to varying network conditions.

### *7.1.5 Multi Operator/Technology Customization*

One of *FluidNet*'s key features is its ability to allow for multiple operators to customize the configurations needed to serve their respective clients simultaneously. To illustrate this, we design an experiment with three BBUs and three RRHs. There are two operators, one operating at 2.59 GHz and the other at 2.61 GHz, each with 10 MHz bandwidth. Both operators share the same set of three RRHs to cater to three clients each simultaneously. While all clients for operator 1 are static and impose a net rate requirement of 21 Mbps, those for operator 2 are all mobile with a net rate requirement of 12 Mbps. To check transmission feasibility on our front-haul over longer distances, the fiber between BBUs and RRHs is made to be a 10 Km fiber spindle. Fig. ?? presents the spectral graph from one of the RRHs captured using a spectrum analyzer. It is clearly seen that both the operators are able to co-exist simultaneously on the same front-haul without any interference to each other's RF signal. Furthermore, this is achieved over a large distance of 10 Km, which demonstrates feasibility for an outdoor cellular deployment. Also, Fig. 14 shows that *FluidNet* tailors the right configuration for each operator to provide maximum satisfaction of traffic demand.

This is also evident from Figs. 15 and 16, where a single operator uses two different access technologies (WiFi and WiMAX) to serve five clients (each with 10 Mbps traffic rate) through 3 RRHs. Two of the clients on WiFi (2.43 GHz) are static and associated to two of the RRHs, while the other three are on WiMAX (2.59 GHz) and mobile. It is interesting to see that *FluidNet* is capable of simultaneously supporting an asynchronous (WiFi; one-to-one for CSMA) and synchronous (WiMAX; one-to-many for DAS) access technology for the same operator. *FluidNet*'s support for multiple operators and technologies are very useful features in a C-RAN, given the growing popularity of RAN-sharing and dual carrier small cells (for WiFi offload).

## 7.2 Simulation

**Set-up:** We use a 3GPP-calibrated system simulator to create a outdoor heterogeneous cellular network, with 19 macrocell sites (each has three sectors) and ten small cells per sector. Thus, the network has a total of 627 cells (57 macro + 570 small) based on the scenarios defined in 3GPP 36.814 [2]. We distribute 3600 small cell

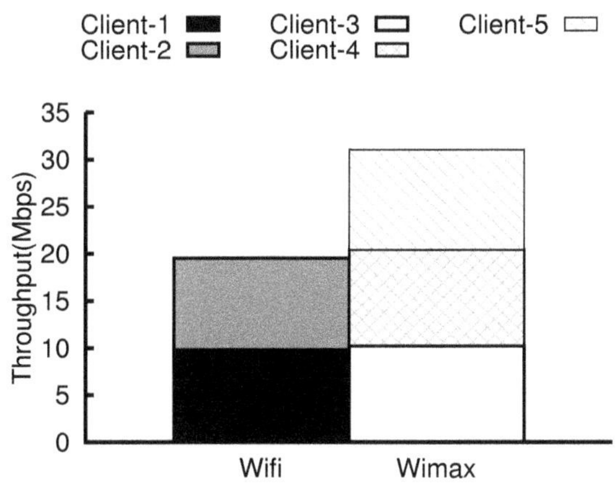


**Figure 16: Traffic Satisfaction: WiFi + WiMAX.**

clients according to the '4b' distribution [2]. We assume that the macrocells and their clients use pre-determined spectral resources orthogonal to the ones used by the small cells and their clients, and thus ignore the interference from/to the macrocell network.

To generate traffic demands, we resort to emulating a typical operational day in outdoor cellular networks. Since we do not have access to such operator data (and public data does not exist to the best of our knowledge), we use the reported peak hour distribution from [7] as follows. We mark each sector (and the small cells in it) as either "business" or "residential". As seen in Fig. 2, we geographically determine that the central, shaded sectors are business sectors (there are a total of 21 such sectors with 210 small cells in them) and peripheral sectors are residential sectors (36 of them exist). The small cells in a business sector hit their peak loads between 10 a.m. and 4 p.m. and residential cells have peak hours between 4 p.m. and 8 p.m. The traffic outside the peak hours is chosen such that there is a gradual increase until the peak interval and a decrease after that.

We compare *FluidNet* against three other schemes. The first (labeled "FFR") is a pure FFR solution running with a fixed cluster size corresponding to a macrocell (3 sectors = 30 small cells). The second (labeled "DAS") is a pure DAS solution with opportunistic clustering. When the total load of neighboring sectors is less than a frame's worth of resources (i.e., the max. capacity of DAS), they are merged in a DAS cluster and thus served by one BBU. The third (labeled "GRID") is reported in [7] and addresses energy consumption by turning small cells off during non-peak periods.

**Traffic Heterogeneity:** We first simulate a network where no clients are mobile. Each result is the average of five different runs with randomly selected traffic demands from clients, subject to the spatio-temporal traffic distribution.

Figs. 17(a) and 17(b) plot the traffic satisfaction ratio and the energy consumption (*RU*), respectively. We first see that *FluidNet* has a competitive traffic satisfaction ratio with FFR (is only 3% worse on average). The slight reduction is because FFR explicitly accounts for inter-sector interference by considering a cluster size of three sectors. In contrast, *FluidNet* applies FFR at a granularity of one sector and resorts to resource permutations to address inter-sector interference in a scalable manner. We also see that while having a competitive traffic ratio, *FluidNet* is much more (*3x* on average) energy efficient than FFR. DAS, albeit the most energy efficient strategy, suffers from lack of spatial reuse and hence satisfies only 65% of the traffic on average.

When compared with GRID, while the fraction of traffic satisfied does not differ considerably, *FluidNet* activates *2.2x* less BBUs than GRID. This is due to the fact that while energy savings from BS-switching approaches such as GRID are inherently limited based on physical proximity of cells, *FluidNet* can cluster arbitrarily large numbers of cells to yield more energy savings. This is exemplified in Fig. 17(e) where we plot the temporal progression of clusters in *FluidNet*; clusters (color-coded) are seen to shift spatially from residential areas in the morning to business areas in the evening. White (uncolored) sectors are clusters of size one (i.e., cannot be merged with other sectors due to high traffic load). To closely look at clustering in *FluidNet* during non-peak hours, we compare *FluidNet* with and without the clustering component (the latter called "*FluidNet-NC*"). As seen in Fig. 17(c), even without its clustering component *FluidNet* outperforms GRID. Further, while *FluidNet* - NC requires 80 BBUs on average, *FluidNet* requires only 43 BBUs, resulting in much lower energy consumption. This shows that clustering is critical in realizing high energy savings.

In summary, *FluidNet* effectively exploits the spatial and temporal load asymmetry in the network and yields more energy savings than state-of-the-art solutions while satisfying a high fraction of the traffic demand.

**User Heterogeneity:** We now evaluate *FluidNet* with vehicular mobility. Here, we take the peak traffic hour of the day (4 p.m.) and investigate the traffic satisfaction ratio (averaged over 5 runs) with varying percentage of mobile clients. Each client moves at 60 miles per hour, only within its sector. From Fig. 17(d) we see that DAS performance is not affected by mobility since it results in a uniform signal quality for mobile clients; the network capacity is unchanged. With FFR, performance degrades as we increase the percentage of mobile clients (due to handovers and degraded SNR). With *FluidNet* , increasing number of mobile clients results in more carriers being allocated for DAS. While associating mobile traffic with DAS is beneficial in most of the cases, it can lead to lower performance (compared to FFR) when *all* the traffic is mobile. Ideally, one would need to identify the tradeoff between DAS (uniform per-client SNR but no spatial reuse) and FFR (degraded client SNR but high spatial reuse) for mobile traffic, and make careful decisions.

## 8. DISCUSSIONS AND REMARKS

We presented *FluidNet* - a framework for dynamically re-configuring the front-haul of a C-RAN to meet the dual objective of improved RAN performance with reduced resource usage in the BBU pool. Our evaluations show promising benefits towards these goals. Going forward, we would like to consider the following.

**Applicability to other C-RAN Models:** Since *FluidNet* focuses on *logical* front-haul configurations, it can work with any front-haul (e.g., microwave wireless) as long as the latter can support the data rates needed for transport of BBU signals. Similarly, it also applies in a partially-centralized C-RAN model [17], where more processing is entrusted to the RRHs to reduce the load on the front-haul. However, the energy savings in this model needs to be investigated.

**Co-existence with Carrier Aggregation:** LTE-advanced systems will support multiple component carriers and carrier aggregation. Carrier split for configurations in *FluidNet* can be realized much more easily with multiple component carriers. However, the interaction of FFR and DAS with joint scheduling on multiple carriers needs further study.

**Migrating to Digital Front-Haul Transmissions:** Instead of using RF over Fiber, we would like to migrate our BBUs to those that provide access to digital I-Q streams that can be transported

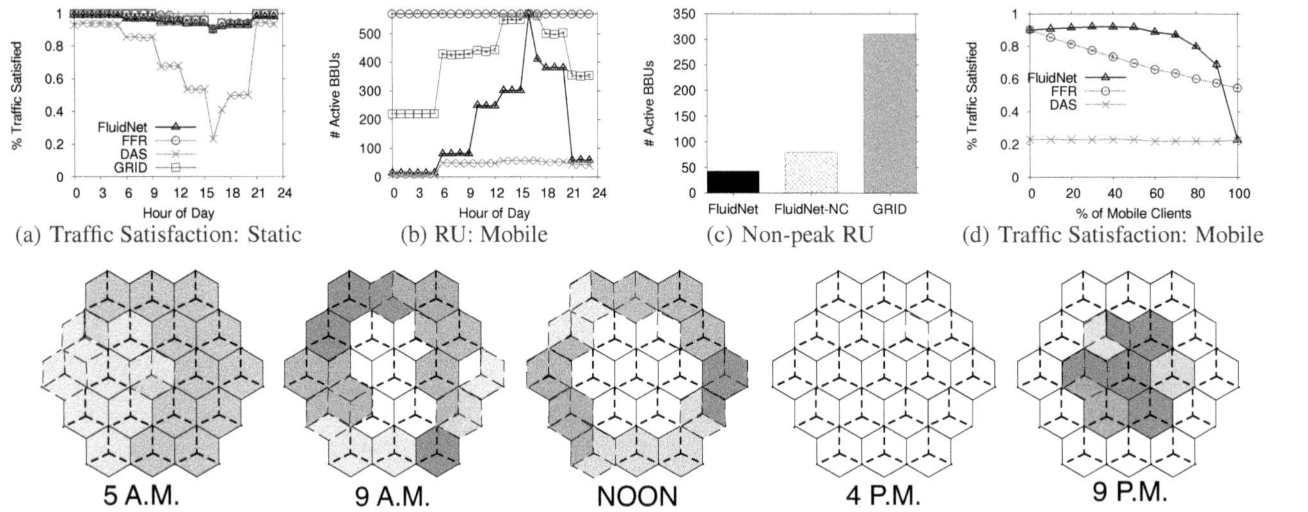


(a) Traffic Satisfaction: Static (b) RU: Mobile (c) Non-peak RU (d) Traffic Satisfaction: Mobile

(e) Temporal Progression of Clusters

**Figure 17: *FluidNet* has comparable traffic satisfaction ratio to FFR (a), and is *3x* and *2.2x* more energy efficient than FFR and GRID respectively.**

over CPRI. This would allow for scalable realization of our configurations in the digital domain.

# 9. REFERENCES


[1] Common radio public interface. www.cpri.info.

[2] G. T. 36.814. Evolved Universal Terrestrial Radio Access (E-UTRA): Further advancements for E-UTRA physical layer aspects. http://bit.ly/Ysh6Cq.

[3] J. Andrews, W. Choi, and R. Heath. Overcoming Interference in Spatial Multiplexing MIMO Cellular Networks. In *IEEE Wireless Communications*, volume 14, Dec 2007.

[4] M. Y. Arslan, J. Yoon, K. Sundaresan, S. V. Krishnamurthy, and S. Banerjee. FERMI: A Femtocell Resource Management System for Interference Mitigation in OFDMA Networks. In *ACM MobiCom*, Sept 2011.

[5] U. Barth. How to reduce green house emissions from ICT equipment: Wireless Networks, EARTH research project. In *ETSI Green Agenda*, Nov 2009.

[6] S. Bhaumik, S. P. Chandrabose, M. K. Jataprolu, G. Kumar, A. Muralidhar, P. Polakos, V. Srinivasan, and T. Woo. CloudIQ: A Framework for Processing Base Stations in a Data Center. In *ACM MobiCom*, Aug 2012.

[7] P. Chunyi, L. Suk-Bok, L. Songwu, L. Haiyun, and L. Hewu. Traffic-Driven Power Saving in Operational 3G Cellular Networks. In *ACM MobiCom*, Sept 2011.

[8] Cisco. Cisco Visual Networking Index: Global Mobile Data Traffic Forecast Update, 2012-2017, Feb 2013.

[9] Ericsson. AIR: Antenna Integrated Radio. http://bit.ly/dLOIAu.

[10] T. Flanagan. Creating cloud base stations with TI's KeyStone multicore architecture. http://bit.ly/ztLLcz.

[11] T. D. Forum. www.thedasforum.org/news/.

[12] Intel. Heterogeneous Network Solution Brief. http://intel.ly/ZIMRcI.

[13] H. Li, J. Hajipour, A. Attar, and V. Leung. Efficient HetNet Implementation Using Broadband Wireless Access With Fiber-Connected Massively Distributed Antennas Architecture. In *IEEE Wireless Communications Magazine*, Jun 2011.

[14] C. Liu, K. Sundaresan, M. Jiang, S. Rangarajan, and G. Chang. The Case for Re-configurable Backhaul in Cloud-RAN based Small Cell Networks. In *IEEE Infocom*, 2013.

[15] A. Lucent. lightRadio Network: A New Wireless Experience. http://bit.ly/VpR4Cb.

[16] M. Marsan, L. Chiaraviglio, D. Ciullo, and M. Meo. Optimal energy savings in cellular access networks. In *IEEE GreenCom*, Jun 2009.

[17] C. Mobile. C-RAN: The Road Towards Green RAN. http://bit.ly/YalzuW.

[18] Picochip. http://www.picochip.com.

[19] M. Sauer, A. Kobyakov, and A. Ng'oma. Radio Over Fiber for Picocellular Network Architectures. In *IEEE Journal on Lightwave Technology*, volume 25, 2007.

[20] K. Sundaresan, M. Arslan, S. Singh, S. Rangarajan, and S. Krishnamurthy. Fluidnet: A flexible cloud-based radio access network for small cells. In *NEC Laboratories Technical Report*, Mar 2013.

[21] D. Tipper, A. Rezgui, P. Krishnamurthy, and P. Pacharintanakul. Dimming Cellular Networks. In *IEEE Globecom*, Nov 2010.

[22] Q. Wang, D. Jiang, J. Jin, G. Liu, Z. Yan, and D. Yang. Application of BBU+RRU Based Comp System to LTE-Advanced. In *IEEE ICC Workshops*, Jun 2009.

# Last Call for the Buffet: Economics of Cellular Networks

Jeremy Blackburn‡♭, Rade Stanojevic‡, Vijay Erramilli‡, Adriana Iamnitchi♭
Konstantina Papagiannaki‡
Telefonica Research, Barcelona (Spain)‡
University of South Florida♭

## ABSTRACT

Voice and data traffic growth over the last several years has become a major challenge for cellular operators with a direct impact on revenues, infrastructure investments, and end-user performance. The economics of these operators depend on various incentives used to attract users in the form of unlimited, buffet-like voice/sms/data packages. However, our understanding of the effects of user behavior under these offerings on operator revenues/costs remains poor. Using two years of detailed usage information of $\sim 1$ million users across three services, voice, sms and data, combined with payment and cost information, we study how user behavior affects the economics of cellular operators. We discover that around 20% of the users consume more resources than what they pay for and hence are non-profitable. In addition to the individual user behavior, we study how the user interactions in the call graph affect the operator's revenues and cost, drawing on tools from social network analysis. We develop a framework that incorporates both the individual and social user behavior for studying how volume caps influence the revenues and the traffic costs. Using this framework we empirically show that volume caps can increase the difference between the revenues and the traffic costs of the studied operator by a factor of 2, while affecting only 16% of the existing user base.

## Categories and Subject Descriptors

K.6.2 [**Management of computing and information systems**]: Pricing and resource allocation

## General Terms

Economics

## Keywords

User behavior, Network effects, Cross-subsidization


*MobiCom'13,* September 30-October 4, Miami, FL, USA.


## 1. INTRODUCTION

The network services industry (wired and wireless) has experienced high growth in every corner of the world in the previous decades. This growth has been fueled by technology advancements, increase in demand for connectivity among end-users as well as pricing mechanisms that can lead to profits and are conducive to attract and engage users. The growth of the subscriber base is seen as one of the most important metrics to reflect success. Towards this end, pricing schemes tend to be simple; a flat rate and contain an abundant amount of communication units (all-you-can-eat buffet plans) to attract a large user base.

The wide-scale adoption and profitability of such pricing schemes is predicated on several premises. First, it has been reported that users prefer flat rate pricing schemes due to their inherent predictability [17]. Second, it is assumed that most users will consume only a small amount of the purchased packages, thus not generating a large aggregate traffic cost [26]. And third, the cost of delivery for many network services on a per service unit basis has been a small fraction of the retail price; common examples include sms service or residential (cable/DSL) broadband where the marginal cost of delivery of a 160-character sms or 1GB of wired data is significantly lower than the retail price the providers charge for the service [16, 24].

However, in recent years many network operators, specially those in mature markets, have seen their revenues and profits saturating or even decaying [30, 28]. Consider mobile broadband that has contributed a relatively small fraction of the total revenues but is projected to be the main cash cow for providers in near future [28]. Fig. 1 depicts an estimation of current and future costs for delivering a gigabyte of mobile data among north American carriers with current retail prices of $10-20, leaving very little margins for profits [1]. There are several reasons for this loss of revenue – intense competition, regulation and user behavior [28].

In this paper, we focus on understanding the effect of user behavior on revenues and traffic costs in cellular networks. In particular, we rely on a large (anonymized) dataset of $\sim 1M$ customers of a cellular operator that consists of their entire usage behavior across voice calls, sms and data usage, as well as their billing details and costs incurred *by* the operator, to answer the following questions: (i) how do users respond to flat/unlimited tariff structures, (ii) how such user behavior affects the revenues and costs of operators and (iii) how operators can optimize their profit under the presence of costly user behavior. Our dataset (Sec. 2) has unique properties to aid us in answering the above questions more accurately.

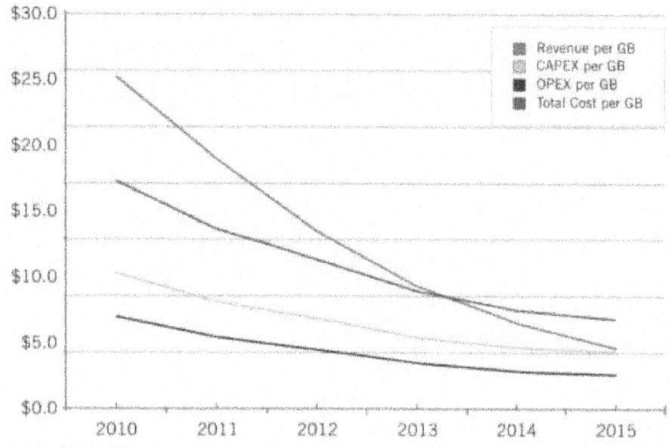


**Figure 1: North American mobile data carriers: estimate of costs and revenues per GB of mobile data, 2010-2015, [1].**

First, the pricing plans offer unlimited volume units, hence the usage of subscribers is the real communication needs of users and second, the cost information we have per service unit is an accurate proxy for the true cost of delivery.

For the first question, we extract the amount of revenues and traffic costs per customer of the operator from our dataset and we find that 20% of the users lead to more cost to the network than revenue (Sec. 3). This result points to two conclusions – first, unlimited, buffet-type plans attract such unprofitable user behavior and second, this unprofitable user behavior is *cross-subsidized* by other users[1].

Digging deeper into user-behavior, we find that defining the value of a user in the network only in terms of her individual revenue and cost is myopic. We find that by understanding network effects – how users interact with other users in the network and how users attract other users to join the network can give a more accurate value of a user in the network. In order to study network effects, we rely on tools from social network analysis (Sec. 4). Finally, in order to answer the third question, we develop a case for using volume caps as a means to remove unprofitable user behavior and increase profits (Sec. 5).

Our main results can be summarized thus:

- Using the fine-grained usage and billing data from the customers of a mobile virtual network operator with $\sim 1M$ customers, and the traffic cost information, we demonstrate that around 20% of customers generate higher traffic cost than what they pay to the operator and hence are subsidized by other customers.

- We show that the usage of the non-metered services (3G data, sms and on-net calls) is highly (negatively) correlated with the profitability of the customer, and that customer profitability is assortative: connected customers are likely to have similar profitability.

- As with many other services that involve social interaction, the social graph (observed via voice calls and sms) has non-trivial impact on the revenues and the costs of the operator. We quantify the relationship between the social network structure and the operator's revenues and costs.

- Finally, by integrating the individual user behavior and user interaction behavior we develop a framework for studying the impact of volume caps on the operator's revenue and costs. We show that simple capping strategies can increase the difference between the revenues and the traffic costs by almost a factor of 2 while affecting only 16% of the customers.

[1]Unlimited volume in the wired access network have lead to cases where few heavy users were being cross-subsidized by other users and led to practices like throttling/blocking peer-to-peer traffic [5, 11], bringing into focus the notion of net-neutrality [4].

## 2. BACKGROUND AND DATA

In this section, we first provide background for concepts we use throughout the paper. We then discuss the dataset we study.

### 2.1 Background

In this paper, we deal with cellular networks. Cellular networks around the world have a very diverse set of pricing plans. In general, pricing plans can be thought of as being on a spectrum, where on one end lies a single flat rate for 'unlimited' usage and on the other end lies pure usage based pricing (UBP) where every unit of service (voice minutes, sms, data) consumed is 'metered' and charged. Most operators, however offer plans that lie somewhere in the middle of the spectrum. The typical offerings are monthly plans – payments are done on a monthly basis and a specific flat rate is charged for a bundle of services – specific volumes of voice/sms/data. 'Unlimited' plans are those bundles where the volumes of different services have no cap on usage every month. If a maximum usage limit is specified, then the plan is referred to as 'flat up to a cap' or just capped. Any volume used more than the volume cap is either metered and the extra volume is charged proportional to the usage, or the service is degraded for the extra volume (eg. 3G to 2G). 'Tiered' plans with different flat-rate prices for different volume caps are used to offer choice to the user. We note here that tiered plans are also a type of usage based pricing (UBP).

We focus on cellular network operators setting the retail prices for the sole purpose of maximizing profits. Pricing can also be dictated by other factors like regulation, but we do not deal with that here. In the process of user acquisition and retention many of the operators choose to offer 'incentives' of various forms including: (1) *handset incentives*, where the operator offers a handset for a discounted price, usually requesting the commitment from the customer to remain within the network for an extended period of time (12-24 months); (2) *traffic incentives*, where the operator offers a number of free service units (eg. voice minutes or sms messages) or an unlimited service quota for a particular service like data. Many operators also offer *social* incentives to attract new customers. These incentives normally come in the form of unlimited volume of voice minutes or sms between users of the same network and are incorporated in the pricing plans/tariffs. Hence, if a user has many of her contacts in a certain network, then it would be rational for her to join this network. Combined with word-of-mouth marketing where customers of an operator explicitly or implicitly advertise the operator, it is clear that a user's activity with other users in the network also plays a role in the revenue/cost structure of an operator.

| Tariff | On-net voice | On-net sms | Off-net Voice | SMS | 3G data | Price |
|---|---|---|---|---|---|---|
| PAYG | Free | Free | 1★/min | 0.6★/txt | $\frac{2★}{20MB}$ per day | 0 |
| Bundle 1 | Free | Free | 60min | unlmtd | $\frac{2★}{20MB}$ per day | 50★ |
| Bundle 2 | Free | Free | 250min | unlmtd | unlmtd | 100★ |
| Bundle 3 | Free | Free | 400min | unlmtd | unlmtd | 150★ |
| Bundle 4 | Free | Free | 800min | unlmtd | unlmtd | 200★ |
| Bundle 5 | Free | Free | 1500min | unlmtd | unlmtd | 250★ |

**Table 1: Tariffs. Note that SMS is unlimited across all bundles, while 3G data is unlimited across most**

## 2.2 Data

The data used in this paper belongs to a national Mobile Virtual Network Operator(MVNO), with around one million customers. In contrast to conventional Mobile Network Operators (MNO) that own the radio spectrum and cellular network infrastructure, MVNOs utilize the infrastructure of one (or more) MNOs by effectively purchasing the access to network services (voice/sms/data) at wholesale rates. In general, MVNOs provide their own customer and billing service. Similar to most other MVNOs, the one we study targets price-conscious segment of the market.

There are several types of data we use:

- *Usage data.* An anonymized record is stored for *every* call, sms and data session generated (initiated or received) by every customer of the network over a period of 27 months, from late 2009 to early 2012. The usage records contain the calling number, the receiving number (for voice calls and sms), the time-stamp, the duration of the call/data session as well as the volume of the data transmitted in the data session. This enables us to understand usage of different services on a per-user basis.

- *Payment information.* An anonymized record is stored for every service payment by every customer, over the same period of 27 months. We can thus correlate the usage with payment.

- *Traffic cost information.* We have the cost the MVNO has to pay to its cellular provider per minute of a voice call, per sms and per $MB$ of data sent. The real figures are proprietary but one minute of voice calls, one sms and one $MB$ of 3G data wholesale prices are within the same order of magnitude. The cost information helps us figure out the traffic cost on a per customer basis. The cost the MVNO pays to its provider is a linear function of the usage, in that if the MVNO users aggregately generated $M$ minutes of voice calls, $S$ txt messages and $D$ *Mbytes* of mobile broadband traffic over a billing period, the MVNO must pay

  $$C(M, S, D) = p_M \cdot M + p_S \cdot S + p_D \cdot D,$$

  where $p_M, p_S$ and $p_D$ are the wholesale prices of one minute of voice calls, one sms and one *Mbyte* of mobile broadband, respectively.

The tariffs offered by the operator are listed in Table 1. The customer can choose between the pay-as-you-go (PAYG) tariff in which each service unit (off-net calls[2], sms and 3G data) are charged separately, or she can purchase one of the bundles that has a fixed number of free off-net voice minutes and unlimited/non-metered[3] data and sms services. Once a bundle is purchased, it expires in one month, and then the user can choose whether to purchase another bundle or continue using the service in a pay-as-you-go manner. At any time, the voice calls and sms between the customers of the network are non-metered.

**Why data from a MVNO?**

We use data from a MVNO for the following reasons: (i) The data we have has unlimited tariffs. This enables us to study user behavior in the *absence* of caps; the demand put on the network is natural demand and not self-regulated and constrained by the caps/metering [3]. (ii) As mentioned earlier MVNOs purchase the access for network services from a cellular operator that owns the network infrastructure at *wholesale* rates. The wholesale rates closely match the real production cost of the network services and are a good proxy for the *real cost* of the generated traffic, and do not include other overheads like marketing etc. In addition, the MVNO we consider does not offer handset incentives and offers only traffic based incentives – hence any users who joined this MVNO have done so for reasons other than handset incentives. (iii) MVNOs typically have very limited budgets for personnel and customer acquisition/retention. Thus, the overall costs of the MVNOs (including the one we study here) are dominated by the traffic cost [30]. Finally, most of the analysis we perform can easily be extended to data from a cellular operator that owns its infrastructure and radio network. We discuss these issues in more detail in Sec. 7.

# 3. USER BEHAVIOR: INDIVIDUAL LEVEL

In this section, we analyze user behavior under the different tariffs presented in Sec. 2, in terms of consumption – that gives us cost to the operator and in terms of revenues – what users pay. We focus on individual user behavior and how that relates to revenues/cost.

## 3.1 How much does each user contribute?

The first question we ask: what is the contribution of each user to the overall revenues and costs of the operator? For this, we look at the payments made by the user and the cost imposed by the user when she uses non-metered services.

We define the balance $B(u)$, for each user $u$, as the difference between the total revenue she paid for the network services to the operator ($R(u)$) and the total traffic cost she generated for the operator ($C(u)$):

$$B(u) = R(u) - C(u).$$

For each user, we possess the billing records over the 27 month period, from which we derive the revenue the user raised. We use the voice/sms/3G-data usage records to calculate the traffic cost to the provider each user imposes by adding the cost of voice calls, sms and 3G data generated by

[2]We refer to interactions, voice or sms, between two customers of the operator as on-net, and to interactions in which only one end is the customer of the operator as off-net.

[3]The exception is the Bundle 1 that has metered data service.

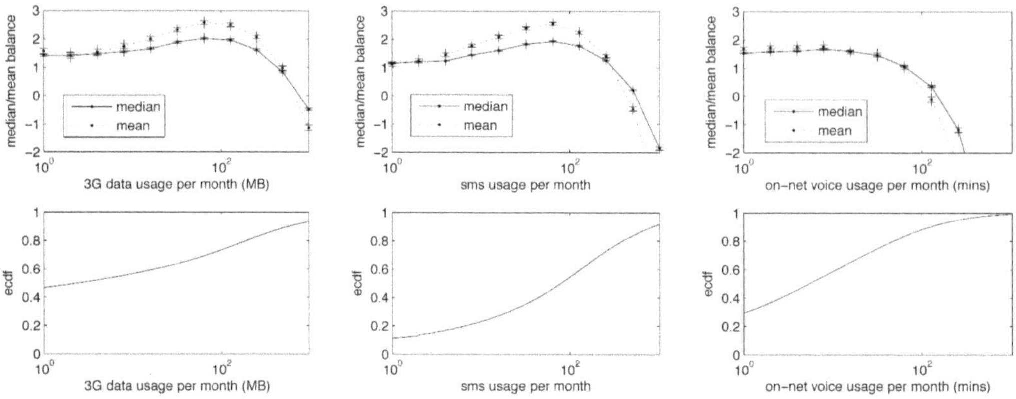


**Figure 3: The median/mean per-user balance (normalized) vs. amount of non-metered service (top). Empirical CDF of the amount of non-metered services (bottom) consumed. $x$-axis is in log-scale.**

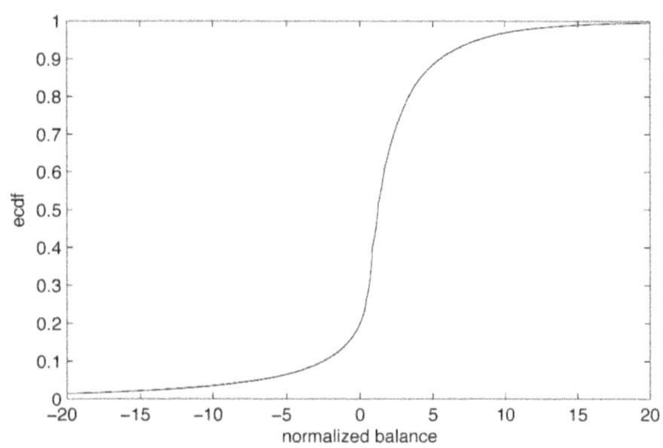


**Figure 2: Empirical CDF of per-user balance (normalized to have mean equal to 1). Around 20% of users have negative balance!**

the user, charged at the wholesale rates of $p_M$/min, $p_S$/sms and $p_D/MB$, as described in Sec. 2. The balance measures how profitable the user is for the operator. Users with large balance are very profitable for the operator, while users with negative balance generate uncovered costs that must be subsidized by those with positive balance. In Fig. 2 we plot the empirical CDF of the balance normalized[4] to have mean equal to 1, and in the rest of the paper we use use this scalar value $b(\cdot)$ to refer to balance instead of $B(\cdot)$:

$$b(\cdot) = \frac{B(\cdot)}{average(B(\cdot))}.$$

We observe that around 20% of users have **negative** balance, and hence must be subsidized by other users. In addition, while the empirical distribution of $b(\cdot)$ is bell-shaped, the tails are long with the minimum (= -443) and maximum (= 157) values far away from the mean compared to the standard deviation ($\sigma$ = 6.75). Overall, the total balance of users who are subsidized $|\sum_{u:b(u)<0} b(u)|$ is greater than the whole total balance of all users $\sum_u b(u)$, see Eqn .(1) in Sec. 5.

Balance, as defined above, clearly depends on consumption of non-metered services (3G data, sms and on-net voice calls). One would guess that users who consume more of the

[4]We perform normalization in order to protect the proprietary information related to revenues and costs.

| | $r$ | $p$ | 95% conf. |
|---|---|---|---|
| $V_{off}$ v. Data | 0.080 | $< 0.01$ | 0.077, 0.082 |
| $V_{off}$ v. SMS | 0.228 | $< 0.01$ | 0.225, 0.230 |
| $V_{off}$ v. $V_{on}$ | 0.145 | $< 0.01$ | 0.142, 0.147 |

**Table 2: Correlation coefficients of unmetered service usage.**

non-metered services are less likely to be profitable. In Fig. 3 we quantify this dependence between balance and usage, by evaluating the mean and median balance among users consuming $x$ units of non-metered service (MB of 3G data, sms, mins of on-net calls), for $x \geq 0$. We do not show the instances of very small ($x < 1$) and very large ($x > 1000$) usage, in order to depict the behavior of the majority of the users. The median balance is positive for users that use low amounts of the non-metered services. However, once the usage of the non-metered services crosses a threshold the balance decays below zero. Such thresholds, beyond which the median balance turns negative are: 796MB (for 3G data), 552 sms messages (for texting) and 150 mins (for on-net calls).

**Main takeaways:** We find that 20% of the users have negative balance; imposing a higher cost on the operator than the revenues they generate. We also find, somewhat intuitively, that costs are correlated to usage of non-metered services. We later show in Sec. 5 that significant improvements in the overall profit of the operator are possible by treating these 'subsidized' customers with caps.

## 3.2 Is off-net voice a good proxy for costs?

Table 1 shows that the charge the customer $u$ pays for the service in most bundles is related to the amount of off-net voice minutes she uses ($V_{off}(u)$), while the cost she generates for the operator also depends on the amount of the non-metered services she uses: on-net calls ($V_{on}(u)$), sms ($S(u)$) and 3G data ($D(u)$). If these service usages were strongly correlated, in other words if one of them could be a good proxy for estimating the other, then metering that one service could align the revenues with the costs users generate. However looking at the consumption of these 4 services we see low levels of correlations between the usage per-service (see Fig. 4 and Table 2), indicating that the total traffic cost per-user (aggregated cost for all services availed) is weakly correlated with the revenues that depend only on the usage of one service ($V_{off}(u)$).

**Main takeaways:** We observe no correlation between the usage levels per service across the customers of the operator.

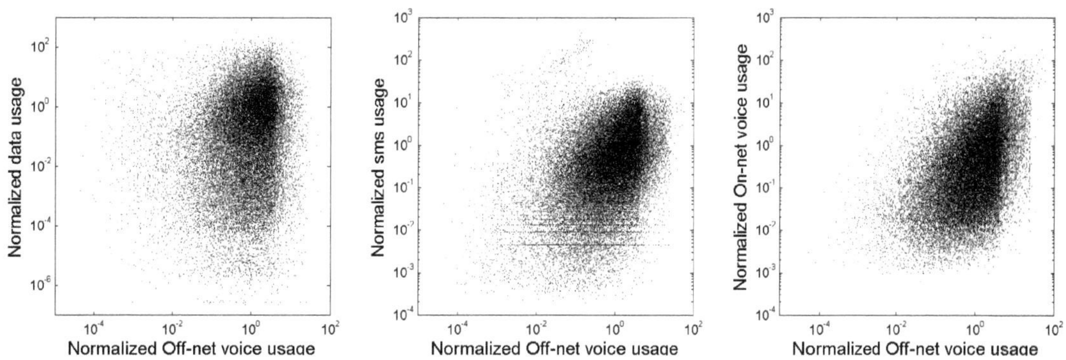


**Figure 4: Correlation between the metered Off-net voice usage and non-metered: 3G data, sms and on-net voice usage. Each dot represents a single user.**

By metering one service, while the costs depend also on the other three services whose usage is not correlated with the metered one, the revenues can be highly disconnected with the costs, as demonstrated in Fig. 2.

# 4. USER BEHAVIOR: CALL GRAPH

In the previous section, we looked at user-behavior in isolation and how the behavior in terms of usage impacts revenues and costs of an operator. In this section, we look at user-behavior in the social network defined by the call graph. This is important for two reasons. First, there are social incentives in place – from Table 1 we see that calls and sms made to other users in the network are non-metered and are free – and user behavior with these incentives in place can affect costs and revenues. Second, again because of the social incentives the users in the network can play an active role in the growth (or contraction) of the network, and this facet should be accounted for in a user's balance.

## 4.1 User balance in the call graph

In Sec. 3, we saw that the balance of a user is negatively correlated with the amount of non-metered services she uses. We expand the analysis to the social network (as represented by all other users contacted via calls/sms) of a user. Intuitively, since the balance is negatively correlated with the amount of on-net minutes (as we see in Fig. 3) we expect to see similar correlation between the balance and the number of on-net contacts (contacts within the same operator) of the user, which we confirm in Fig. 5. We observe that for users with 1 or more on-net contacts, the mean balance is significantly smaller than the median and that for users with 5 or more on-net contacts the mean balance is negative.

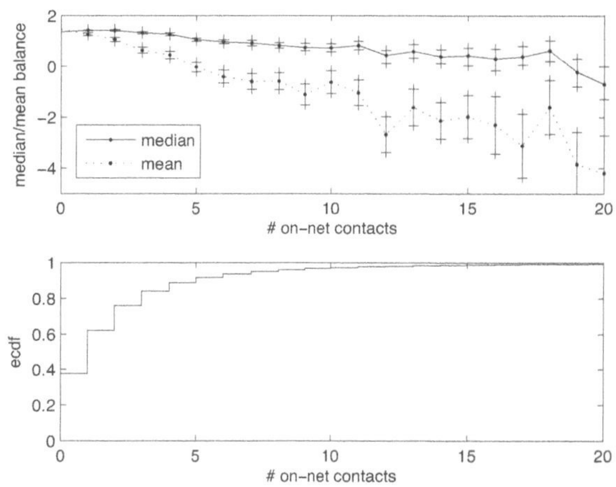


**Figure 5: The median/mean balance vs number of contacts. Users with many contacts have low expected balance. Cutoff in the figure at #on-net contacts $\leq$ 20 is made to increase the readability of the figure. In addition < 1% of users have #on-net contacts> 20.** max**#on-net contacts>** 100.

The notion of similarity in behavior between users can be captured by the *assortativity coefficient*; which is a measure of correlation between nodes in a graph. Intuitively, it is a measure of users to engage with 'similar' users. In our case, we are interested in assortativity with respect to user balance. Specifically, the assortativity coefficient, defined as the Pearson correlation coefficient of the balance vector between all pairs of connected users, is 0.27, indicating a high assortativeness[5]. In Fig. 6 we plot the dependence between the mean and median balance across contacts of users with balance (approximately) equal to $b$, where we vary $b$. The monotonic increasing nature of the mean/median contact balance, is another indicator of the high assortativity of the balance in the studied social network.

**Main takeaway:** We find that heavy users interact more with other heavy users and vice-versa. Hence in our data we see that social incentives sometimes hurt the operator more than help it.

## 4.2 Number of on-net contacts

In this section we show evidence that social contacts can play a role of attractors in the organic growth of the operator's user base, and quantify such effect using a simple metric. While we note here that establishing pure causality – users joined for social contacts only – is beyond the scope of this work, previous work has looked into the (major) role of network effects on the choice of an operator [2].

The operator we study has nation-wide coverage and serves relatively small fraction (< 5%) of the population in the country. Given our voice calls and sms data we can detect

[5]For example the node-degree in Facebook social network has assortative coefficient of 0.23 that is interpreted as high [8].

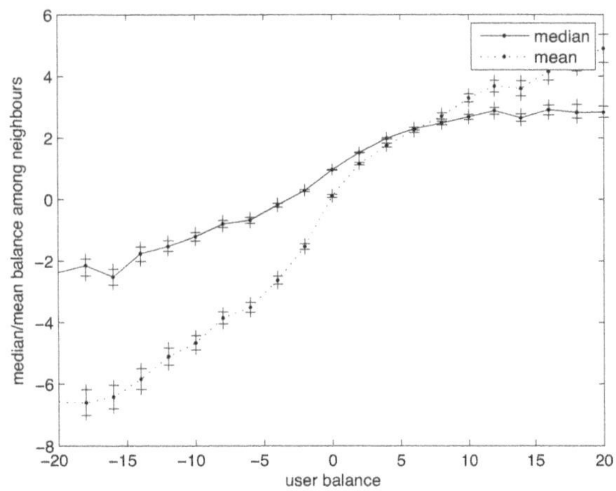


**Figure 6: The median/mean balance among the contacts of users with balance $\approx b$, for $b \in [-20, 20]$. User balance is assortative: contacts are likely to have similar balance.**

whether a user (on-net or off-net) is a contact with an existing customer of the operator. We define a mobile user $v$ to be the *contact* of a customer $u$ if there is at least one interaction (voice or sms) between $u$ and $v$ in *both* directions[6].

For $k = 0, 1, 2, \ldots$ we use $N_k$ to denote the number of customers of the operator with exactly $k$ contacts in the operator and we use $F_k$ to denote the number of national mobile users (both on-net and off-net), with exactly $k$ contacts in the operator. Hence $N_0$ denotes the number of existing customers of the operator who have 0 contacts within the operator. Likewise, $F_0$ denotes the number of all mobile users in the country who have 0 contacts in the operator.

We can compute $N_k$ for any $k \geq 0$ and $F_k$ for $k \geq 1$, from our data since it archives any voice or sms interaction in which one (sending or receiving) party is a customer of the operator. However, computing $F_0$ is not as straightforward, since we possess no information regarding the communications that happen outside the operator. To estimate $F_0$ we use the estimate of the total number, $T_0$ of mobile phone users in the country [32] and use:

$$F_0 = T_0 - \sum_{k \geq 1} F_k.$$

To understand the relationship between the number of contacts of $u$ that are customers of the operator and the likelihood that $u$ is customer of the operator we define the following metric

$$p_k = \frac{N_k}{F_k}, \quad k = 0, 1, 2, \ldots$$

Thus, $p_k$ is the fraction of users from the entire mobile user base with $k$ contacts in the operator. In Fig. 7 we report the values of $p_k$. We can observe that the likelihood of a user with no contacts in the operator ($k = 0$) to be a customer of the operator is small, while such likelihood increases with $k$, and flattens out around $k = 5$; having more that 5 contacts in the operator does not affect the chances of being the customer of the operator.

[6]Thus the contact relationship is symmetric: if $u$ is contact with $v$, then $v$ is contact with $u$.

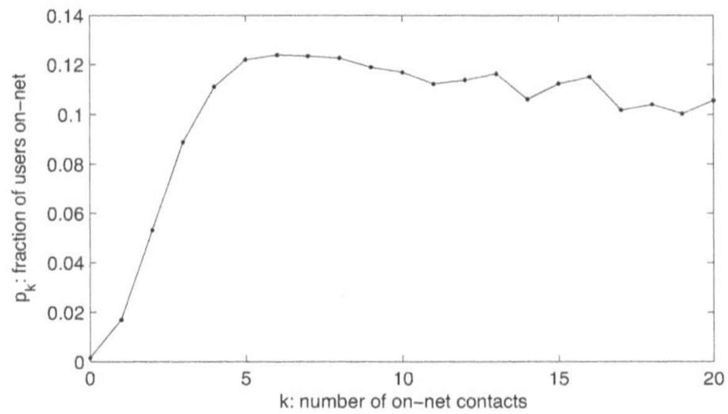


**Figure 7: Number of contacts in the operator vs. likelihood of being the customer of operator. Having more contacts in the operator increases chances of being a customer of the operator up to $k = 5$.**

**Main takeaways:** The parameters $p_k$ determine the impact of social ties in the growth of the network from a macroscopic point of view. In Sec. 5 we will use the parameters $p_k$ to evaluate the effects of node removal on its contacts and the impact of such cascade removal process on the revenues and costs of the operator.

## 4.3 Revisiting user balance: Incorporating social effects

The previous result shows that users within the operator can play a role in attracting other users. In Sec. 3, the *value* of each user is the user's balance. However, it can be the case that a heavy user, with a negative balance can attract other users to the operator who contribute positively. Hence the effective value of the user to the operator should reflect this facet. To examine this, we use the call graph between customers of the operator to model their interactions. The undirected edges of this graph are weighted with the total duration of calls between contacts, a known proxy for social strength [19].

The balance for each node is then distributed between each of its contacts, proportional to the duration of calls (acting as a proxy for social strength). In this way, the aggregate balance across nodes remains the same but each node's balance is now derived entirely from the balance of its contacts and their behavior patterns.

We compare differences between user balance calculated in Sec. 3 and user balance using social relations in Fig. 8, that plots the density distribution of balances in the range [-10, 10]. The network calculation "squeezes" the distribution, resulting in more borderline profitable customers. This points to the fact that there is a fraction of users who are themselves costly users but nonetheless bring in profitable users, underscoring the importance of considering network effects in assigning values to customers.

**Main takeaways:** Users join the service to take advantage of social incentives, and there are users who at face value are subsidized, but who are profitable with respect to the other service users they interact with.

# 5. VOLUME CAPS: WHY AND HOW?

In this section we study how volume caps affect the revenues and costs for the operator. We incorporate our findings

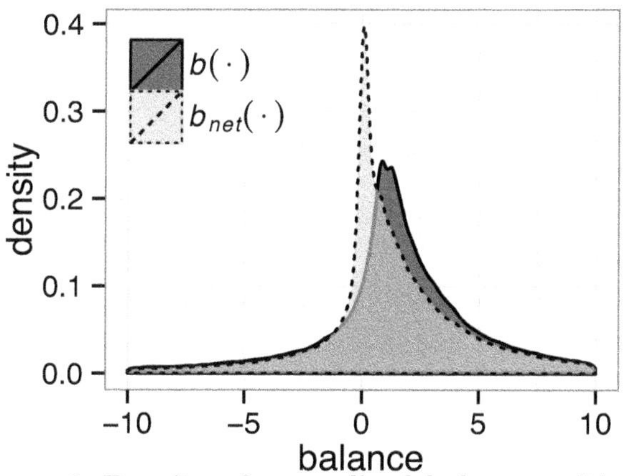


**Figure 8: Density of normalized balances with two calculation types: 1) local ($b(\cdot)$), and 2) network ($b_{net}(\cdot)$).**

from previous sections in the design of cap-based solutions. To understand the impact of the caps on user behavior, and hence the revenues and costs, we study two models. In the first model the users affected by the cap are only those that cross the cap. The second, more general model also takes into account the social ties between the users to capture the social network effects that can arise due to the introduction of caps.

We calculate optimal volume caps under the two models, with the goal of optimizing profits. We demonstrate that significant improvements with regards to the aggregate balance are possible; by using optimal caps one can expect the relative increase in the total balance of 107% (for the net-oblivious model) and 90% (in the net-aware model) that is close to the maximum of 124% that one can obtain by removing non-profitable users (and them only) from the network (as we show next). We also show that setting caps on only one of the three non-metered services (3G data, sms and on-net calls) can increase the total balance, although the gains in these cases are not as large as they are in the case of capping all three services. Before we describe our solutions, we first discuss why we need caps.

## 5.1 Why volume caps?

From our findings in Sec. 3, we saw that certain users cost more to the operator than what they contribute to the revenues. A natural question to ask in this context is: what can be the possible increase in the profit of the operator by eliminating these users; users with a negative balance, how much would the total (aggregated over all users) balance change? The following coefficient gives the answer:

$$\gamma = \frac{\sum_{u:b(u)>0} b(u)}{\sum_u b(u)} = 2.24 \qquad (1)$$

The amount spent on subsidizing the users with the negative balance is (1.24×) larger than the total balance, hence eliminating the users has a great potential to increase the aggregate balance without charging more for the service. However, eliminating as a policy is not desirable. First there are contractual obligations. Second, there have been instances of negative press when heavy users have been pushed out of the network [33]. Another solution can be to remove social incentives – however as we saw in Sec. 4, social incentives do help in driving growth and any solution that disrupts the social mechanics could backfire, resulting in the loss of both subsidized users and their subsidizing friends.

Volume caps have been suggested as a *simple* mechanism to alleviate cross-subsidization and increase profits [18]. In addition, it is also posited that volume caps in cellular networks are used for sustainability reasons; curbing runaway growth that can lead to operators being "crushed by capital spending" [18]. Our contribution is to design and study simple caps using real data, while incorporating user behavior.

We stress that more complex solutions with more pricing tiers on segmented user base and price differentiation [12] or has different form of social incentives, may offer even higher gains than those we compute with caps. However we demonstrate that simple cap-based solutions have potential to eliminate the bulk of the cross-subsidizations and hence there is limited room for extracting higher profit without increasing the prices on existing customers. The problem of profit maximization beyond cap-based solutions remains open and is out of scope of the present paper.

## 5.2 Optimizing caps

To quantify the effects of caps on the users and the operators we use two models, the *net-oblivious* and the *net-aware*, that we describe below.

### 5.2.1 Net-oblivious model

In the net-oblivious model, we assume that if a user consumes more service units than what the cap offers, she either quits the network or the overage charges compensate for the extra traffic she consumes, thus bringing her balance to zero. More formally, if the user $u$ consumes $s_u$ smses, $d_u$ $MB$ of mobile broadband and $f_u$ minutes of on-net calls, on average and the operator packages have caps of $x$ sms, $y$ $MB$ of mobile broadband and $z$ minutes of free on-net calls, we say that $u$ is *affected* by the caps if she consumes more service than the cap quota in at least one of the three services. In the net-oblivious model: if a user $u$ is affected by the cap we assume that she is not customer of the operator and hence has balance zero, otherwise neither her usage nor charge is affected by the caps and thus her balance remains the same:

$$b_u^{(x,y,z)} = \begin{cases} 0 & \text{if } (s_u > x) \vee (d_u > y) \vee (f_u > z) \\ b(u) & \text{otherwise} \end{cases}$$

The users with large consumption of non-metered services are the ones that are cross-subsidized and putting a cap on how much of the free services they obtain in the package they purchase should reduce the instances of cross-subsidization and increase the total balance $B(x, y, z)$ defined as:

$$B(x, y, z) = \sum_u b_u^{(x,y,z)}. \qquad (2)$$

To find the optimal caps we consider the solution of the optimization problem:

$$(x_{opt}, y_{opt}, z_{opt}) = \underset{x\geq 0, y\geq 0, z\geq 0}{\arg\max}\ B(x, y, z). \qquad (3)$$

One can observe that in this model the user affected by caps either does not change her behavior in terms of their usage and payments in case she remains under the cap, or has zero balance if she crosses the cap.

**Data**: $G = (V, E)$: Social graph
$(x, y, z)$: caps
$s_u, d_u, f_u$: average per service usage of customer $u \in V$
$p_k$: probability that a user with $k$ contacts is customer of the network
**Result**: Compute set $A$ of affected nodes

```
begin
    A = ∅;
    Ē = E;
    for u ∈ V do
        if s_u > x or d_u > y or f_u > z then
            affected (u);
        end
    end
end
affected (u)
begin
    A = A ∪ u;
    for v : (u, v) ∈ Ē do
        k = #{w : (w, v) ∈ Ē};
        with probability 1 − p_{k−1}/p_k : affected (v) Ē = Ē \ (u, v);
    end
end
```

**Algorithm 1:** Finding the set $A$ of affected nodes.

Clearly, the relative total balance $RTB$, relative to the baseline total balance $\sum_u b(u)$, is upper-bounded by

$$\frac{B(x, y, z)}{\sum_u b(u)} \leq \gamma = 2.24$$

from Eq. 1

### 5.2.2 Net-aware model

In Sec. 4.2 we uncovered evidence that social connections impact the growth of the operator's user base. Hence, eliminating the instances of losing customers[7] (those with $balance < 0$), may affect whether their social contacts join the network or not. The net-aware model, is a generalization of the net-oblivious model described above, in which each user affected by the cap can affect her contacts, by pulling them out from the network. The process of pulling out the contacts is recursive, and is driven by the parameters derived in Sec. 4.2 that map the likelihood of user $u$ being the customer of the operator to the number of the contacts $u$ has in the operator's network.

In the net-aware model, we consider the social graph $G = (V, E)$ with the nodes being the customers of the operator and the edges between the nodes if the customers have interacted using the network infrastructure (via voice calls or sms). In this graph, we define two sets of nodes: $A$ contains the set of nodes affected by the cap and $A^c$ those not affected by the cap. The balance of user $u$ is either 0, if she is an affected node, or her original balance, $b(u)$, if she is not affected:

$$\bar{b}_u^{(x,y,z)} = \begin{cases} 0 & \text{if } u \in A \\ b(u) & \text{if } u \in A^c \end{cases}$$

To decide which nodes are affected we perform the following recursive procedure. Every node that uses more than $x$ sms or more than $y$ $MB$ of mobile broadband or more than $z$ minutes of free on-net calls is added to the set $A$ of affected nodes. Each time a node $u$ is added to set $A$, every contact $v$ of $u$ is added to $A$ with the probability $1 - \frac{p_{k-1}}{p_k}$, where $k$ is the number of contacts of $v$ among yet non-affected nodes (including $u$) and $p_k$ is the probability that a user (from a pool of *all* mobile users in the country) is the customer of the operator conditioned on the fact that she has $k$ contacts that are customers of the operator. The parameters $p_k$ are estimated in Sec. 4 and provide the basis for the macroscopic behavior model that captures the relationship between the social network of a user and the social pressure that makes her a customer of the operator. Note that the conditional probability that node $v$ with $k > 0$ contacts on-net remains the customer of the operator after one of the contacts leaves the operator is indeed $\frac{p_{k-1}}{p_k}$. Hence the probability that she gets affected is $1 - \frac{p_{k-1}}{p_k}$. The pseudocode of the described procedure is shown in Algorithm 1.

[7]By either discouraging them to join the network in the first place, or decreasing their satisfaction level by increasing their bill via caps to compensate for the cost they generate for the operator

Once the set of affected nodes is computed the total balance is:

$$\bar{B}(x, y, z) = \sum_u \bar{b}_u^{(x,y,z)}. \quad (4)$$

And the optimal caps are those that maximize the total balance:

$$(\bar{x}_{opt}, \bar{y}_{opt}, \bar{z}_{opt}) = \underset{x \geq 0, y \geq 0, z \geq 0}{\arg\max}\ \bar{B}(x, y, z). \quad (5)$$

Empirically, the probabilistic nature of the procedure that determines the set of affected nodes has very small influence on the total balance: in our data, the sample standard deviation of $\bar{B}(x, y, z)$ is 2 orders of magnitude smaller than the sample mean, and hence for the analysis of how caps affect the total balance, we use single instance of the procedure to calculate the total balance $\bar{B}(x, y, z)$.

*Remark.* Note that in both of the described models, the notion of cap we use refers to capping the average usage, rather than usage at any given month. The inherent variability of per-customer usage volumes, on month-to-month basis, can be resolved simply by allowing customers to migrate non-used parts of the package (mins, sms, MB) towards the next month's cycle.

## 5.3 Data-driven evaluation

In the previous section, we described two models of implementing caps. Both of our models are rather conservative in that they rely on the assumption that the 'heavy' customers are not likely to generate any profit for the operator, while the non-heavy users remain unaffected by the caps in both the service payment and the service usage. In this section, we will empirically evaluate the impact of the caps in both models.

For that purpose we use the following metric which we refer to as the RELATIVE TOTAL BALANCE, as the ratio between the total balance of the system with caps and the total balance of the system with no caps.

$$\text{RELATIVE TOTAL BALANCE}(x, y, z) = \frac{B(x, y, z)}{\sum_u b(u)}$$

We report on the RELATIVE TOTAL BALANCE for both models while varying the cap values (same number of free sms, $MB$ of 3G data and on-net minutes) in Fig. 9. We also plot the absolute maxima of RELATIVE TOTAL BALANCE obtained by solving the optimization problems using a brute-force greedy approach.

We can infer the following from our results. First, carefully designed caps can significantly increase the total balance:

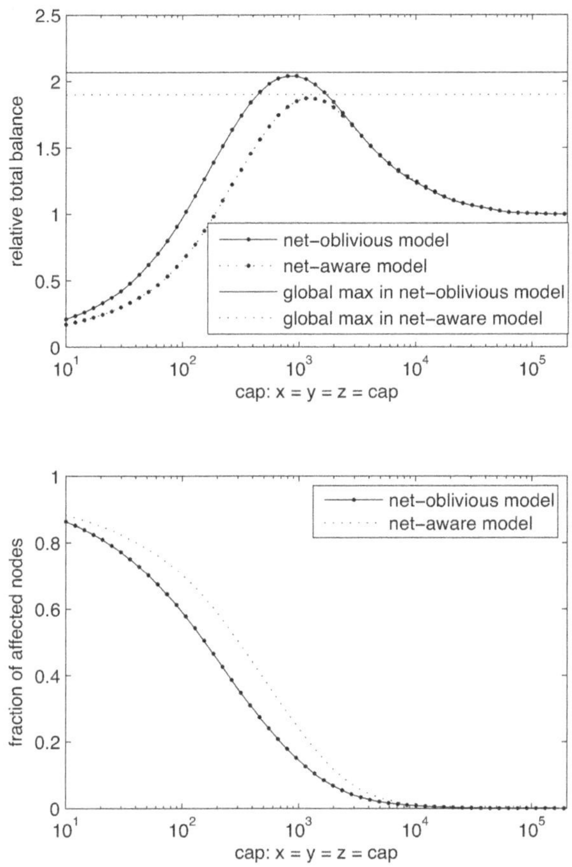


**Figure 9: Top: The relative total balance$(x, x, x)$, when the cap contains the same number of $x$ free sms, $x$ $MB$ of 3G data and $x$ on-net minutes. The straight lines represent the absolute maxima of relative total balance$(x, y, z)$, which is equal to 2.07 in the net-oblivious, and 1.90 in the net-aware model. Bottom: The fraction of affected customers.**

a factor of two increase can be expected in both models. Second, in the net-aware model one can expect lower total balance, though the impact of cap-initiated social pruning – users leaving due to network effects appears to be relatively small, and results in relatively small difference between the total balance in the two models of under 10%. This small difference can be in part attributed to the high-assortativity of the balance, shown in Fig. 6, where nodes with low balance are likely connected with the nodes with low balance too. Third, the cap in the simple form of $x$ smses, $x$ $MB$ of 3G data and $x$ free minutes of on-net calls, can recover most of the gains. Additionally, the optimal $x$ that maximizes the total balance is around $\bar{x}_0 = 1150$ in the net-aware model and around $x_0 = 800$ in the net-oblivious model. Having slightly higher cap means that less nodes are directly affected by the cap and hence less nodes are affected indirectly by the social pruning. Overall around 16% of nodes are affected by caps at the optimal point in both models.

The absolute maxima of RELATIVE TOTAL BALANCE is achieved for:

$$(x_{opt}, y_{opt}, z_{opt}) = (931sms, 1240MB, 354min)$$

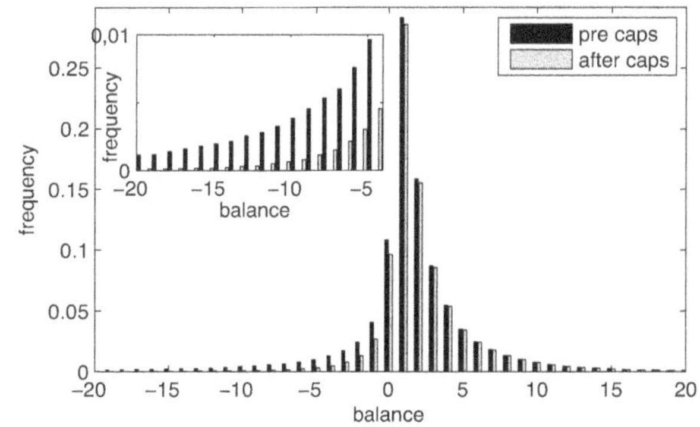


**Figure 10: Histogram of per-user balance with and without caps. The net-aware model for computing the affected nodes used, with optimal cap $(1361sms, 1650MB, 471min)$. Most users with positive balance remain non-affected, while a large fraction of those with negative balance get removed due to caps.**

in the net-oblivious model and

$$(\bar{x}_{opt}, \bar{y}_{opt}, \bar{z}_{opt}) = (1361sms, 1650MB, 471min)$$

in the net-aware model.

In Fig. 10 we depict the distribution of the balance per customer without caps and with caps in the optimal case of net-aware model. We observe that almost no users with balance $>1$ (= the mean) are affected by the cap, some customers are affected when the balance is close to zero, and almost all customers with large negative balance are affected by caps.

We finish this section by quantifying how capping individual services may affect the total balance. In Fig. 11 we plot the RELATIVE TOTAL BALANCE when one of the three originally-non-metered services is capped, while the other two are not, thus we look at the caps of form: $(x, \infty, \infty)$, $(\infty, y, \infty)$ and $(\infty, \infty, z)$. From this figure, we can observe that capping one of the services can indeed provide certain improvement in the total balance, although the relative increment is much smaller than in the case of capping all three services. One can expect increase of up to around 40% when the 3G data or sms services are capped and around 25% increase when the on-net voice calls are capped. Hence to fully exploit the potential of the caps the operator should consider capping all three services.

# 6. RELATED WORK

If we consider the history of telecommunication services there is a distinctive trend of charging 'flat' fees for services: telegraph, post, fixed and mobile telephony, residential broadband, etc. This practice is justified by the customers' preference for convenient and simple tariffs as well as very low cost for the provider for accounting and delivering the service [17, 25]. In addition, users are willing to pay extra money for the convenience of not worrying about high bills that can result due to usage based pricing (UBP) [17, 25]. The focus of this work is *not* to study the historical precedents of flat-rate pricing nor is it to study the reasons why users may prefer flat-rate schemes. The focus is to understand, at large, the user behavior in terms of consumption

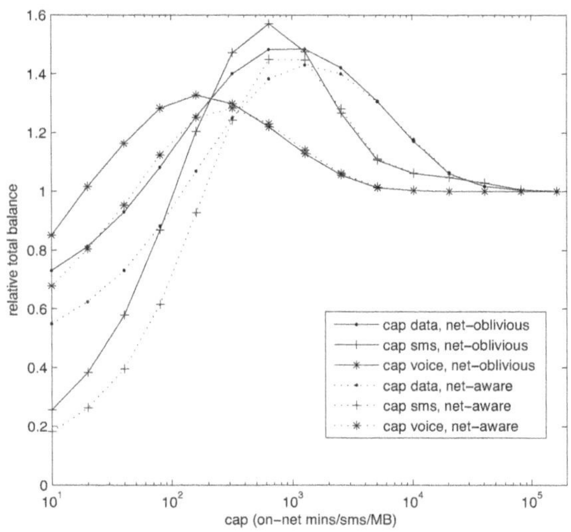


**Figure 11: The relative total balance when only one service is capped. In the net-aware model the maxima are 1.43 for capping only sms, 1.42 for capping only 3G data, and 1.25 for capping only on-net voice.**

under such schemes and how the behavior affects economics of a cellular provider, using real data.

There has been a lot of work on pricing issues in the Internet, including discussing relative merits and demerits of usage based pricing (UBP) in access and cellular networks [18, 16, 13]. The general consensus is UBP is used in access networks to raise revenues [18] while it is used in cellular networks to cope with congestion and runaway growth [18, 13]. It has also been suggested that UBP can be used to put an end to cross-subsidization [18, 13]. Our focus in this paper is not to study the underlying reasons to enforce UBP, but to quantitatively assess the effects of flat rate/UBP-tiered schemes using a large scale longitudinal dataset as well as investigate network effects in enforcing UBP schemes to end cross subsidization.

Most recently, the research community is starting to recognize the importance of pricing mobile broadband. Authors of TUBE [9] demonstrate that time-dependent pricing of mobile-broadband is powerful tool for reducing the peak-hour traffic in congested cells. While we do not investigate effects of temporal variability of demand here, we note that it plays important role in defining the traffic cost. Our time-independent approach in deriving the optimal caps, is driven by an implicit goal of simple tariffs. The design of more sophisticated, time-dependent and dynamic tariffs can benefit the efficiency of the provider, albeit it is not clear how large such benefits can be. On a more practical side, authors of [20, 21] investigate how accurate is the mobile broadband metering systems, isolate several sources of inaccuracy in such systems and describe various method for exploiting them. We note that the large variability of per-user demand has been documented in various domains in wired [6] and wireless [7] networks.

## 7. DISCUSSION

In this section we briefly discuss various factors that may affect the applicability of the observed results in other networks/operators. We also examine the implications of our findings on the end users, the operators and the mobile communications ecosystem in large.

Mobile network operators (MNO) that own radio spectrum and network infrastructure have a cost model that is not as simple and elastic as the one employed by MVNOs. In contrast to MVNOs that use and purchase the service on-demand, the MNO costs and revenues are not directly connected with the volumes of the usage of their customers. However, if the network has been planned optimally, the MNO capacity should closely match the demand generated by its customers. We believe that our results can offer insights on how the user behavior affects the revenues and usage of the cellular services and be instrumental in the process of network planning with the goal of maximizing the profits for the operator. We recall here that our dataset, that has tariffs with unlimited volume, lets us extract close to the 'actual' usage demands – usage demands that otherwise would be biased by self-regulation if volume caps had been in place.

The studied cost model is rather simple in that it treats each service unit equally in terms of cost, independent of the time or place of the request. The cost of delivering a service indeed depends whether the request was made in the peak-hour, the middle of the night, in an urban cell or a rural cell. The cost model we study averages all these conditions in order to simplify the billing of a service with millions requests (voice, sms, 3G data) per day. Other types of cost function, that take into account the spatial and/or temporal, variability of the traffic cost can easily be integrated in the studied model [27, 15, 9], though such considerations are out of scope of the present paper. Our analysis in this paper takes a rather static view on the user behavior, determined by their average usage and payment information. Understanding the dynamics of the studied phenomena would be an interesting direction for future research.

Additionally, we would like to stress that independently of whether the mobile provider is MNO or MVNO, targets low-income or high-income segments of the market, understanding the user behavior is a critical factor that drives not only the quarterly balance sheet, but also long-term strategy and network development. Therefore, the relationship between the users' usage patterns on revenues and cost, studied holistically, is pivotal in determining how future networks will evolve.

**Dealing with caps: user's perspective**

While the cost of delivery of mobile broadband is expected to decay due to the technological advancements, the decay is unlikely to be as quick as one may have wished; see Fig. 1. With the nontrivial cost of delivery of mobile broadband, some form of usage based pricing (UBP) with caps for network services appears inevitable as we have shown using our data. Given that majority of Internet users are accustomed to the non-metered Internet access, it will be interesting to observe their response to such UBP as well as the reaction from mobile app developers that would need to take a price-aware approach when designing apps that use mobile broadband and other network services.

Some early approaches to dealing with UBP, are reflected in several interesting projects regarding cap sharing that include Airmob [14] and Shair [10]. These projects are aimed at sharing available capacity across devices. Our results seem from Sec. 3 where we show that there is little correlation between usage of different services seems to indicate that it is indeed possible to share across different services. We have provided economic motivations for capacity sharing based solutions. From an app developer point of view, in addition to designing apps that judiciously consume data, they can themselves pay for part of the traffic the users generate [23]. Authors of [22] demonstrate that mobile broadband traffic has around 20% of redundant traffic that could be cached on the phone. Another method is to use existing network primitives when needed; a user who has exceeded the data caps and wants to use an over-the-top (OTP) app like Whatsapp can have some of her messages delivered via the sms channel – provided the user has sms capacity. Many existing operators have open APIs where this is feasible [31, 29].

# 8. CONCLUSIONS

This paper studies user behavior in terms of usage of different network services (voice calls, sms, data) and how the behavior affects revenues and costs of a cellular operator. In order to conduct this study, we use a large anonymized trace of over a million users spread over two years that consists of all usage information per user, the associated costs in delivering each service as well as their billing information for each user. Using the data, we characterize the individual user profitability and show that 20% of the users cost more to the operator than what they contribute as revenues. These heavy users are therefore being cross-subsidized by other users. We find that assigning value to a user without looking into her activity in the call graph, or without incorporating the role she can play in growing the network due to social network effects is myopic. We therefore quantify the social network effects and this enables us to more accurately assess the value of each user to the network. Armed with our knowledge, we study how volume caps affect the revenues and the costs of the operator and find that the difference between the revenues and the traffic costs can almost double by affecting just 16% of the user base.

To the best of our knowledge, this is the first work to provide insights on how user behavior impacts the economics of cellular operators, along with the viability of certain offerings (all-you-can buffet plans), quantitatively. We hope the findings of this work can help to plan new pricing mechanisms, do efficient network planning and provide motivation to develop new technologies to curb the increasing cellular traffic costs.

# 9. ACKNOWLEDGEMENTS

The authors would like to thank the reviewers of the paper for constructive comments, as well as our shepherd Vishnu Navda for his help.

# 10. REFERENCES


[1] Tellabs report, 2011. http://www.tellabs.com/news/2011/index.cfm/nr/142.cfm.

[2] Daniel Birke and G M Peter Swann. Network effects and the choice of mobile phone operator. *Journal of Evolutionary Economics*, 16(1-2):65–84, 2006.

[3] M. Chetty et al. You're capped: understanding the effects of bandwidth caps on broadband use in the home. In *Proceedings of ACM CHI*, 2012.

[4] Jon Crowcroft. Net neutrality: the technical side of the debate: a white paper. *ACM SIGCOMM CCR*, 37(1), 2007.

[5] Marcel D. et al. Glasnost: Enabling end users to detect traffic differentiation. In *NSDI*, pages 405–418, 2010.

[6] C. Estan and G. Varghese. New directions in traffic measurement and accounting. In *Proc. of ACM SIGCOMM*, 2002.

[7] H. Falaki et al. Diversity in smartphone usage. In *Proc. of ACM Mobisys*, 2010.

[8] M. Gjoka et al. Walking in facebook: A case study of unbiased sampling of osns. In *Proceedings IEEE INFOCOM*, 2010.

[9] S Ha et al. Tube: time-dependent pricing for mobile data. In *Proceedings of ACM SIGCOMM*, 2012.

[10] Pan Hui et al. Sharing airtime with shair avoids wasting time and money. In *Proceedings of ACM HotMobile 2009*.

[11] C. Kreibich et al. Netalyzr: illuminating the edge network. In *Proceedings of ACM IMC*, 2010.

[12] A. Lambrecht et al. Price discrimination in service industries. *Marketing Letters*, pages 1–16, 2012.

[13] Daniel A. Lyons. The impact of data caps and other forms of usage-based pricing for broadband access. In *Working Paper no 12-27, Mercatus Center, at George Washington Univ.*, 2012.

[14] MIT Media Labs. Airmobs Project, 2012. https://www.media.mit.edu/research/groups/viral-spaces.

[15] M. Motiwala et al. Towards a cost model for network traffic. *ACM SIGCOMM CCR*, 42(1):54–60, 2012.

[16] P. Nabipay, A. Odlyzko, and Z.L. Zhang. Flat versus metered rates, bundling, and "bandwidth hogs". In *NetEcon*, 2011.

[17] A. Odlyzko. Internet pricing and the history of communications. *Computer Networks*, 36:493–517, 2001.

[18] A. Odlyzko et al. Know your limits: Considering the role of data caps and usage based billing in internet access service. In *Public Knowledge*, 2012.

[19] J.-P. Onnela et al. Structure and tie strengths in mobile communication networks. *PNAS*, 104(18):7332–7336, 2007.

[20] C. Peng et al. Can we pay for what we get in 3g data access? In *Proceedings of ACM MOBICOM*, 2012.

[21] C. Peng et al. Mobile data charging: new attacks and countermeasures. In *Proceedings of ACM CCS*, 2012.

[22] F. Qian et al. Web caching on smartphones: Ideal vs. reality. In *Proceedings of the Mobisys*, 2012.

[23] H. Raj et al. Splitting the bill for mobile data with simlets. In *Proceedings of ACM HotMobile*, 2013.

[24] S. Keshav. Estimating the cost of SMS, 2008.

[25] S Soumya et al. Pricing data: A look at past proposals, current plans, and future trends. *CoRR*, abs/1201.4197, 2012.

[26] R. Stanojevic, V. Erramilli, and K. Papagiannaki. Cognitive bias in network services. In *Proc. of ACM HotNets*, 2012.

[27] R. Stanojevic, N. Laoutaris, and P. Rodriguez. On economic heavy hitters: shapley value analysis of 95th-percentile pricing. In *Proceedings of the ACM IMC*, 2010.

[28] Telco 2.0 Initiative. European Mobile: The Future's not Bright, it's Brutal, 2012. http://www.telco2research.com/articles/EB_European-mobile-future-brutal-telco_Summary.

[29] Telefonica. Bluevia Network API, 2013. http://bluevia.com/en/home/B.

[30] Upnext Mobile. White paper. How Iliad is shaping the future of mobile telecoms, 2012. http://upnextmobile.com/post/17945556081/freemobilefuturetelecoms.

[31] Verizon. Verizon Network API, 2013. http://developer.verizon.com/content/vdc/en/verizon-tools-apis/verizon_apis/network-api.html.

[32] Wikipedia. List of countries by mobile phones, 2012. http://en.wikipedia.org/wiki/List_of_countries_by_number_of_mobile_phones_in_use.

[33] Wired. Comcast bans Seattle man from Internet for his Cloudy Ways, 2011. http://www.wired.com/business/2011/07/seattle-comcast/.

# Network Coding for Content-Based Intermittently Connected Emergency Networks

Joshua Joy, Yu-Ting Yu, Mario Gerla
UCLA
{jjoy,yutingyu,gerla}@cs.ucla.edu

Samuel Wood, James Mathewson
Suns-Tech
{sam,james}@suns-tech.com

Mark-Oliver Stehr
SRI International
{stehr}@csl.sri.com

## ABSTRACT

First responders at the edge of the network rely on situation awareness updates to arrive in a timely matter, even when the fixed infrastructure is unavailable. The technical advancements of the commercial mobile phones make them capable of supporting such requirements under very disruptive network conditions. In this demo, we present a network architecture that exploits partial caches by utilizing network coding to deliver large files (e.g. images) to first responders. The architecture is based on a content centric network platform called ICEMAN(Information CEntric Mobile Ad-hoc Networking) and runs on Android phones. We demonstrate our system in a file dissemination scenario in a CORE/EMANE network emulation. We measure file delivery ratio, latency, and network overhead and report significant improvements that network coding achieves over fragmentation.

## Categories and Subject Descriptors

C.2.1 [**Network Architecture and Design**]: Distributed networks

## General Terms

Design, Performance, Reliability

## Keywords

Network Coding, Ad-Hoc, MANET, ICN

## 1. INTRODUCTION

Tactical and emergency response scenarios require efficient, robust, and secure network communications to quickly deliver data for situational awareness applications. The dynamic and resource limited constraints in these networks require that nodes opportunistically communicate with limited global knowledge, and make efficient use of the scarce available bandwidth. However, despite the remarkable increase in sensing, storage, processing, and communication capabilities in mobile devices, efficient dissemination and storage of content on the volatile network edge remains a challenge. In this study we fragment a file into segments, called fragments. Then, before transmission we explore two options. In the fragmentation option, we transmit fragments as independent entities. The destination is responsible for reassembly. In the Network Coding option, blocks are linearly combined and coded as later discussed. The destination decodes and reassembles. We show that Network Coding helps to improve the number of files delivered compared to fragmentation in scenarios with intermittent connectivity and severe disruptions.

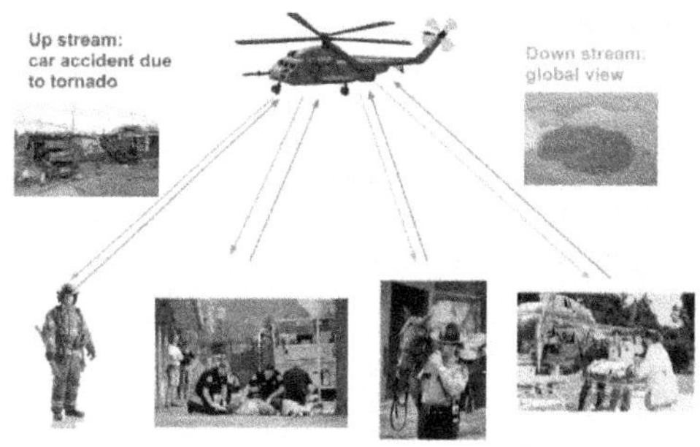


Figure 1: First responders in an emergency situation share location and images with each other. Overhead, a helicopter circles transmitting the global view down to the first responders. Simultaneously, the first responders upload to the helicopter their local view of the situation. Due to the intermittent connectivity, only partial images are often received, cached and shared. The image file completion may require repeated contacts between ground teams with each other (exchanging the partial caches) and with the helicopter [1, 2]

More specifically, due to intermittent connectivity, we face the following challenges during file transfer and dissemination:

- *Last coupon problem*: Network disconnections or partitioning may frequently occur, thus, requiring a file to be transmitted in a piecemeal fashion, possibly with pieces arriving out of order. Missing pieces make it difficult for a receiver to reliably reconstruct a file.
- *End-to-end connectivity not guaranteed*: Nodes must store and cache partial files; then wait for the next contact opportunity to resume transmission.
- *Partial caches*: Various caches may contain different pieces of a file. A receiver does not know which caches contain which pieces of the file in advance.


*MobiCom'13,* September 30–October 4, 2013, Miami, FL, USA.
ACM 978-1-4503-1999-7/13/09.
http://dx.doi.org/10.1145/2500423.2505291 .

- *Busy caches*: If a requestor does not receive a response from a cache that contains the missing segments, it may turn out that the cache is busy serving other requestors. Thus, the requestor must wait for this or another cache to respond.

Network coding can help overcome these challenges and improves file delivery in scenarios with severe disruptions. We show that network coding with a carefully designed content-based network can address each of the above challenges. In particular:

- *Eliminate Last Coupon Problem*: By using network coding, the last coupon problem (also known as the "coupon collector's problem", i.e. waiting for the last missing piece) is mitigated since each coded block received is innovative (i.e., helpful) with a high probability and helps filling in the gaps. Thus, even if network partitions occur, more files will be delivered with coding compared to not coding.
- *Overcoming Intermittent Connectivity*: Since end to end connectivity is not guaranteed and transmissions are connectionless, we cache blocks at intermediate nodes. A requestor can then exploit nearby caches for network-coded blocks. The neighbors push coded blocks from their cache.
- *Exploit Partial Caches*: Nodes cache partial files with innovative blocks. Since each coded block is as helpful as any another, nodes can make efficient use of intermittent contacts by transmitting arbitrary innovative blocks at the next contact and transmission opportunity.
- *Take Advantage of Peer Caches*: When a requestor does not receive a response from a nearby cache because it is too busy to answer requests, it can exploit other nearby caches to collect blocks, since each network-coded block is as good as any other.

## 2. ICEMAN ARCHITECTURE

ICEMAN (Information CEntric Mobile Ad-hoc Networking) [11, 12] enables flooding of interests and epidemic dissemination of interests and content. ICEMAN is implemented in the Haggle framework [5, 6, 9, 10]. Haggle is an open-source content-centric networking architecture originally aiming at pocket-switched networks, a particular form of delay-tolerant networks (DTN) that use a store and forward paradigm. Several extensions and significant changes where made to the Haggle framework to better support MANETs and DTNs with richer connectivity as well as message ferrying. An extensive overview of ICEMAN with implementation details and performance reports can be found in [11, 12].

## 3. NETWORK CODING REVIEW

We first begin with a quick overview of network coding [7, 4]. We start with a *source node* that wishes to disseminate a file F. The source node first subdivides F into a set of fragments. The fragments are then coded into a set of $m$ vectors $\mathbf{v_1}, ..., \mathbf{v_m}$ in an n-dimensional vector space over a finite field $\mathbb{GF}_p$ where p is a prime number. These vectors are then linearly combined by drawing from the finite field $\mathbb{GF}_p$ an encoding coefficient $\mathbf{e_i}$ to create $m$ coded blocks $\mathbf{b_1}, ..., \mathbf{b_m}$. The set of coefficients used to create the vector is called the encoding vector $\mathbf{e}$ which is $[\mathbf{e_1}, ...\mathbf{e_n}]$.

To reconstruct the file, a node must recover enough linearly independent coded blocks to be able to perform matrix inversion. Formally, we take the transpose of the received vectors such that $\mathbf{E^T} = [\mathbf{e^T}_1, ..., \mathbf{e^T}_n]$, $\mathbf{B^T} = [\mathbf{b^T}_1, ..., \mathbf{b^T}_n]$ and $\mathbf{V^T} = [\mathbf{v^T}_1, ..., \mathbf{v^T}_n]$. Then we compute $\mathbf{E^{-1}B}$ which is the reconstruction of all the original blocks in the file. In practice, Gaussian Elimination is used to speed up the decoding process [7, 4].

## 4. NETWORK CODING IMPLEMENTATION

To improve the delivery of content, ICEMAN supports fragmentation and network coding. We segment a large file into fragments (in case of fragmentation) or blocks (in the case of network coding). This overcomes the problem arising when file transmissions are atomic and intermittent connectivity causes repeated unsuccessful attempts to retransmit the entire file. Inspired by CodeTorrent [8], we exploit that peer nodes can become seeds. This is the case after the peer has accumulated enough innovative network-coded blocks and has reconstructed the original file. These seeds then serve as a source of new innovative blocks. Network coding and fragmentation differ in a key aspect: With network coding the source and seed nodes generate innovative blocks with high probability, while fragmentation can select only from a finite set of fragments (the same set for sources and caches). This capability allows network coding to efficiently solve the "coupon collector's problem", while the fragmentation approach has to wait precisely for the missing fragments.

In order to study the effects of partial caches, we apply a simple LRU caching policy for collecting blocks (or fragments) and for aging and timing out these blocks (or fragments). Additionally, after a seed successfully reconstructs a file using blocks or fragments, the blocks used for reconstruction are aged after inactivity. Blocks which are generated by the source or a seed are kept in the LRU cache for a defined period of time and are then expired.

## 5. DEMO DESCRIPTION

With reference to the scenario in Figure 1, we will demonstrate that with intermittent connectivity, fragmentation typically requires multiple helicopter passes while network coding can reconstruct the published original file within a single pass. The helicopter is an example of a highly mobile node, which could also be a UAV or a ground vehicle. The system used in the demo, ICEMAN, is a fully functional peer-to-peer information-centric architecture running on Android phones and utilizing UDP broadcast for the dissemination of interest and content. Figure 1 describes the demo scenario. Because of intermittent connectivity only partial images (i.e. fragments or blocks) can be directly shared in both directions between helicopter and first responders arriving at the aftermath of the emergency (say, a tornado).

The demo will consist of an emulated scenario utilizing the CORE emulator [3] in which network coding and fragmentation run side by side to download the files. Attendees will be able to visually appreciate that network coding is the first to complete the downloads all the files first, while fragmentation experiences significant download delay due to the "coupon collector's problem". One phone in each group acts as the helicopter, while the remaining three phones act as the first responders with actual ICEMAN code running in emulation mode. The network connectivity is emulated by CORE.

The demo will be using ad-hoc WiFi mode on the Android phones, so no additional wireless access is required. Space is required for a laptop and eight Android phones.

# 6. EVALUATION

In this section we report typical measurements collected in previous experiments. To isolate the effects of coding from fragmentation, we evaluate each strategy individually. We implement network coding above the transport layer; e.g. network coding occurs at the application layer for both TCP and UDP broadcast. Naturally, TCP handles congestion control while UDP does not. Moreover, when utilizing UDP broadcast, RTS and CTS is disabled at the MAC layer.

In Figure 3, we evaluate a thirty node scenario using CORE emulation with EMANE 802.11 network simulation. There are three groups of ten member first responder teams each roaming in an open field. Connectivity is sparse. The rescue teams exchange various types of files with each other (stream, data and commands) taking advantage of the times when they are in contact. During a disaster, these images will direct resources and first responders to where they are needed the most. Time can be a critical factor during these rescue situations. The node movement follows the Nomadic Community Mobility model which will represent search and rescue movement. In this model, members of a team perform a random walk around their reference point which in turn follows a Random Waypoint Model. Occasionally teams pass one another and benefit from brief periods of high connectivity.

Figure 3 reports the number of files downloaded for each strategy, within a given delay tolerance. Asymptotic performance is reached as delay grows to infinity. We can observe that network coding outperforms fragmentation (for a given latency) regardless of the underlying transport technology, UDP broadcast or TCP. This is mainly tied to network coding's ability to overcome the "coupon collector's problem". Comparing different transport techniques, we must recall that this is a file distribution scenario where a file must be broadcast to all neighbors. While TCP provides reliable block transfer on a single link, it cannot compete with the broadcast advantage of UDP. UDP with Network Coding fares particularly well as Network Coding provides the ability to recover from losses, thus matching the reliability of TCP.

# 7. ACKNOWLEDGMENTS

This work was supported by the Defense Advanced Research Projects Agency (DARPA) and SPAWAR Systems Center Pacific (SSC Pacific) under Contract N66001-12-C-4051. The views expressed are those of the author and do not reflect the official policy or position of the Department of Defense or the U.S. Government. We thank Victor Perez, and Shao-Cheng Lu for their input.

# 8. REFERENCES

[1] http://www.nesec.org/images/haz_tornado_car.jpg.

[2] http://www.fire.uni-freiburg.de/other_rep/research/rus/rus_re_1bor_16.jpg.

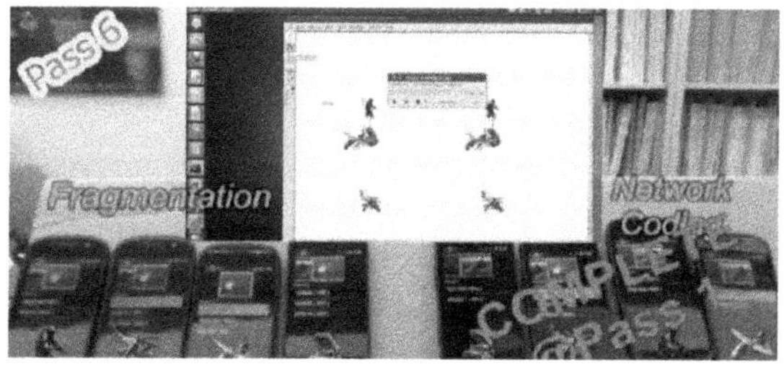


Figure 2: Screenshot capture of demo. Fragmentation (on the left) always requires multiple helicopter passes to reconstruct the file. Network coding (on the right) reassmbles the file in only a single pass.

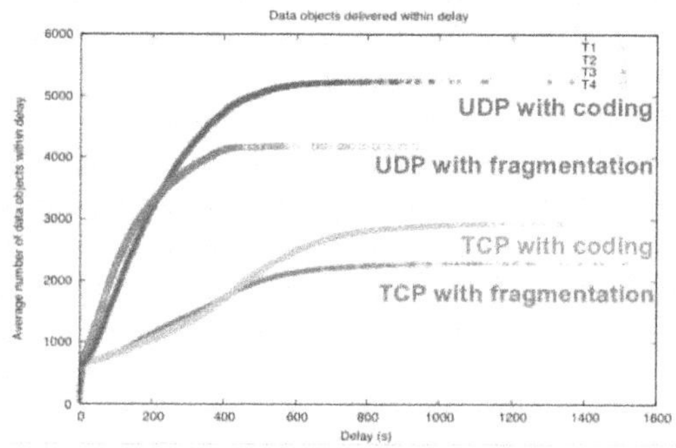


Figure 3: The size of the files range from 250 KB to 1MB. All nodes serve as publishers and subscribers of content.

[3] J. Ahrenholz, C. Danilov, T. Henderson, and J. Kim. Core: A real-time network emulator. In *Military Communications Conference, 2008. MILCOM 2008. IEEE*, pages 1–7, 2008.

[4] C. Fragouli, J.-Y. Le Boudec, and J. Widmer. Network coding: an instant primer. *ACM SIGCOMM Computer Communication Review*, 36(1):63–68, 2006.

[5] Haggle - A content-centric network architecture for opportunistic communication. https://code.google.com/p/haggle/.

[6] Haggle: An innovative Paradigm for Autonomic Opportunistic Communication Research project funded by the European Commission under the Information Society Technologies Programme of the 6th Framework between January 2006 and June 2010. http://www.haggleproject.org/.

[7] T. Ho, M. Médard, R. Koetter, D. R. Karger, M. Effros, J. Shi, and B. Leong. A random linear network coding approach to multicast. *Information Theory, IEEE Transactions on*, 52(10):4413–4430, 2006.

[8] U. Lee, J.-S. Park, J. Yeh, G. Pau, and M. Gerla. Code torrent: content distribution using network coding in vanet. In *Proceedings of the 1st international workshop on Decentralized resource sharing in mobile computing and networking*, pages 1–5. ACM, 2006.

[9] E. Nordstrom, P. Gunningberg, and C. Rohner. A search-based network architecture for mobile devices. Technical report, Uppsala University, 2009.

[10] E. Nördstrom, P. Gunningberg, and C. Rohner. A search-based network architecture for mobile devices. *TR, Department of Information Technology, Uppsala University*, 2009.

[11] S. Wood, J. Mathewson, J. Joy, M.-O. Stehr, M. Kim, A. Gehani, M. Gerla, H. Sadjadpour, and J. Garcia-Luna-Aceves. ICEMAN: A practical architecture for situational awareness at the network edge. http://www.csl.sri.com/users/stehr/CBMEN/iceman-arch-2013.pdf, 2013.

[12] S. Wood, J. Mathewson, J. Joy, M.-O. Stehr, M. Kim, A. Gehani, M. Gerla, H. Sadjadpour, and J. Garcia-Luna-Aceves. ICEMAN: A system for efficient, robust and secure situational awareness at the network edge. http://www.csl.sri.com/users/stehr/CBMEN/iceman-eval-2013.pdf, 2013.

# Demo: Adaptive Video Streaming for Device-to-Device Mobile Platforms

Joongheon Kim, Feiyu Meng, Peiyao Chen, Hilmi E. Egilmez, Dilip Bethanabhotla, Andreas F. Molisch, Michael J. Neely, Giuseppe Caire, and Antonio Ortega
University of Southern California, Los Angeles, CA 90089, USA
{joonghek, feiyumen, peiyaoch, hegilmez, bethanab, molisch, mjneely, caire}@usc.edu, antonio.ortega@sipi.usc.edu

## ABSTRACT

This demo abstract describes an initial design of a new adaptive video streaming protocol for device-to-device WiFi-based mobile platforms and its software implementation. For the demonstration, two mobile servers and two mobile users will be deployed verifying that our device-to-device adaptive video streaming implementation works with desirable user experience.

## Categories and Subject Descriptors

C.2.2 [**Computer-Communications Networks**]: Network Protocols; C.2.3 [**Computer-Communications Networks**]: Network Operations; C.2.4 [**Computer-Communications Networks**]: Distributed Systems

## General Terms

Algorithm, Design, Management

## Keywords

Adaptive Video Steaming, Android, Device-to-Device, Mobile Platforms

## 1. INTRODUCTION

Recently, the USC Communication Sciences Institute has been investigating device-to-device wireless protocols and architectures [1][2][3]. Among the research contributions, the algorithm proposed in [3] introduces joint transmission scheduling and admission control for adaptive video streaming in device-to-device wireless networks or small-cell networks. As presented in [3], there are two types of devices, i.e., *helpers* and *users* where helpers are mobile video clouds, i.e., they contain video files which can be requested by users, and users are mobile smartphones which request video service. In this given network configuration, helpers are responsible for transmission scheduling, i.e., each helper decides which user can download requested video from helpers in each time slot in terms of sum rate maximization where the video contents within helpers consist of a sequence of chunks. When users receive these chunks from helpers via wireless links, they can playback the independently decodable video chunks one-by-one. While the helpers schedule the transmission of chunks, users select the quality mode for the next video chunk to be received. Eventually, this protocol can achieve desired performance in terms of network utility maximization as shown in [3]. In this demo abstract, we describe the WiFi-based software design and implementation of our previous contribution in [3] on top of Android mobile platforms. However, there is one practical limitation which is described as follows. According to the proposed algorithm in [3], multiple helpers select their users which have the maximum value of $Q_u^h(t)C_u^h(t)$ where $Q_u^h(t)$ and $C_u^h(t)$ stand for the queue backlog size from helper $h$ to user $u$ at time $t$ and the channel capacity of the link from helper $h$ to user $u$ at time $t$, respectively. Now, for the system that has multiple helpers and a single user, the helpers will always select the single user on every time slot. However, it is not allowed in terms of WiFi-based wireless systems because multiple access points (APs) are not allowed in a single WiFi network (note that our software design defines helpers as APs and users as non-AP stations). We design and implement a new feature for WiFi-based mobile platforms named *greedy pull for minimum delay (GPMD) strategy* instead of the transmission scheduling. With this GPMD strategy, each user selects its helper which has the chunk that is required in terms of a *playback order* at each time slot. Then, the selected helper should stream the chunk to the user and the amount of transmitted chunk is determined by the maximum WiFi link date rate. Note that multiple chunks can be transmitted if the channel is good, otherwise, parts of a chunk can be transmitted if the channel suffers. In this demo , we design and implement the software architectures of the proposed GPMD-based adaptive streaming for device-to-device Android mobile platforms.


*MobiCom'13*, September 30–October 4, Miami, FL, USA.

ACM 978-1-4503-1999-7/13/09.
http://dx.doi.org/10.1145/2500423.2505292.

## 2. MODELS AND ALGORITHMS

### 2.1 A Reference Network Model

Suppose that the given network is defined by a bipartite graph $\mathcal{G} = \{\mathcal{U}, \mathcal{H}, \mathcal{E}\}$, where $\mathcal{U}$, $\mathcal{H}$, and $\mathcal{E}$ stand for the sets of users (mobile smartphone users), helpers (mobile video cloud servers), and edges for all pairs $(h, u)$ such that there exists a potential WiFi wireless link from $h \in \mathcal{H}$ and $u \in \mathcal{U}$, respectively. The helper is defined as a device which has a set of videos. When users (i.e., mobile phones) want to watch a specific video, they search neighbor helpers and download the sequence of the chunks of the desired videos. For each chunk, users can download it from different helpers. Therefore, helpers (i) contain video files and (ii) serve user requests via WiFi wireless links. On the other hand, users (i) request videos and (ii) downstream the sequence of the chunks of the requested video.

## 2.2 An Operational Framework

In terms of video data structure, a video consists of a sequence of chunks. In [3], the unit of service processes of transmission queue is in bits. However, bit-level transmission control is not allowed in current Android API (SDK Version 4.1). To cope with this problem, we define the concept of *sub-chunk* where a single chunk consists of a sequence of sub-chunks. With this concept, we can control the amount of transmitted bits in terms of the number of transmitted sub-chunks depending on the channel conditions. The dynamics of the transmission queue at each helper for each user is modeled as follows where $t \in \{0, 1, \cdots\}$:

$$Q_u^h(t+1) = \max\left\{Q_u^h(t) - \mu_u^h(m,t), 0\right\} + c_u^h(m,t) \quad (1)$$

where $\forall(h,u) \in \mathcal{E}$ and $Q_u^h(0) = 0, \forall h \in \mathcal{H}, \forall u \in \mathcal{U}$. In addition, $c_u^h(m,t)$ and $\mu_u^h(m,t)$ stand for the number of bits of incoming chunk with quality mode $m$ at time $t$ and the number of bits of processed one or more sub-chunk(s) with quality mode $m$ at time $t$, respectively. Note that if the channel is good, a helper can transmit more sub-chunks in a given time interval. The users can employ three different algorithms: (i) selecting helpers for each chunk placement (i.e., Sec. 2.2.1), (ii) selecting helper which should transmit one or more sub-chunk(s) to the user based on the GPMD strategy (i.e., Sec. 2.2.2), and (iii) selecting quality mode for each chunk (i.e., Sec. 2.2.3). Therefore, users can handle entire protocol behaviors and helpers just transmit chunks to requested users with desired quality mode.

### 2.2.1 Chunk Placement

For each time slot, each user determines which helper should place/stream the next chunk. When each time slot starts, each user sends packets requesting the next video chunk to all neighbor helpers, and each helper replies back the current queue backlog size to the user. Then, the user select the helper which has the smallest queue backlog size and the user sends one packet to the helper for letting it know that the helper should send the next chunk in its queue. If there are multiple helpers which has the smallest queue backlog sizes, the user performs a random selection.

### 2.2.2 Greedy Pull for Minimum Delay

For each time slot, each user selects its helper which has to transmit sub-chunks to the user. In our previous work [3], transmission scheduling is defined and implemented at helpers and the objective of the function is sum rate maximization. Then, one user can be selected by multiple helpers due to the fact that helpers are operating in a fully-distributed manner. Moreover, if only one user exists in the system, then all helpers select the single user on every time slot. Unfortunately, this kind of system cannot be supported by WiFi-based mobile platforms, because having multiple APs in a single WiFi network is not allowed. Thus, we design an alternative algorithm at user side, named *greedy pull for minimum delay (GPMD)*. Suppose that a user is receiving a sequence of chunks from helpers, and the sub-chunks of the desired video exist within the local storage of the user. Then, the user checks the playback order of its own list of sub-chunks. When the user figures out that a sub-chunk is not yet received from helpers and urgent in terms of playback order, then user requests that sub-chunk from the helper. If the channel condition is good enough, the user is able to download not only this sub-chunk but also the sub-chunks within the FIFO queue of the currently serving helper. The amount of sub-chunks to be transmitted from helpers to users is determined by the channel state of the WiFi link.

### 2.2.3 Quality Mode Selection

For each user, the quality mode $m_u(t)$ is computed by

$$m_u(t) = \arg \min_{m \in \{H,L\}} \left\{Q_u^h(t) \cdot kB_v(m,t) - VD_v(m,t)\right\} \quad (2)$$

as explained in [3] where H and L stand for high-quality and low-quality, respectively. In addition, $D_v(m,t)$ and $kB_v(m,t)$ stand for the video quality measurement index and the number of bits for video $v$ with quality mode $m$ at time $t$. Last, $V > 0$ means a control parameter which affects an utility-delay tradeoff [3].

# 3. IMPLEMENTATION

## 3.1 A Protocol Operation Overview

For the first time slot, the implemented protocol starts when a user broadcasts a request of desired video to neighbor helpers. Then, the neighbor helpers reply back packets to the requested user with the information of their queue backlog sizes. In this initial stage, there are no sub-chunks in the queues yet, i.e., all neighbor helpers will reply back to the user with zero. Then, the user selects one helper which has the shortest queue backlog size. According to the fact that the queue backlog sizes of all neighbor helpers are zero at this moment, the user performs a random selection where the selected helper is denoted as $h'$. Now, the user transmits one packet to inform $h'$ about: (i) $h'$ is selected as the serving helper, (ii) desired chunk of the requested video (note that the user needs the first chunk at this initial stage), (iii) maximum link rate between current user and $h'$, and (iv) desired quality mode for the requested chunk computed by (2). Then, $h'$ sends the sub-chunks of the first chunk into the queue with desired quality. Note that there is no video sub-chunk transmission from helper to user in this initial time slot, i.e., just the sub-chunks are pushed into the queue. For the next time slot, the user requests the next chunk (i.e., the second chunk)from neighbor helpers. Then, the neighbor helpers reply back packets to the user with their queue backlog sizes. After that, the user selects the helper which has the shortest queue backlog size and follows the same procedure discussed before (chunk placement procedure). In terms of video chunk transmission, if the user have not received any chunks , i.e., the user requests the first sub-chunk of the first chunk along with computed quality mode located at $h'$. On the helper side, $h'$ transmits the sub-chunks with desired quality mode (H or L)within the given time slot interval. If the channel condition is good, the $h'$ may transmit more sub-chunks, but in the worst case, it can transmit only one sub-chunk. If the *helper*, $h'$, cannot

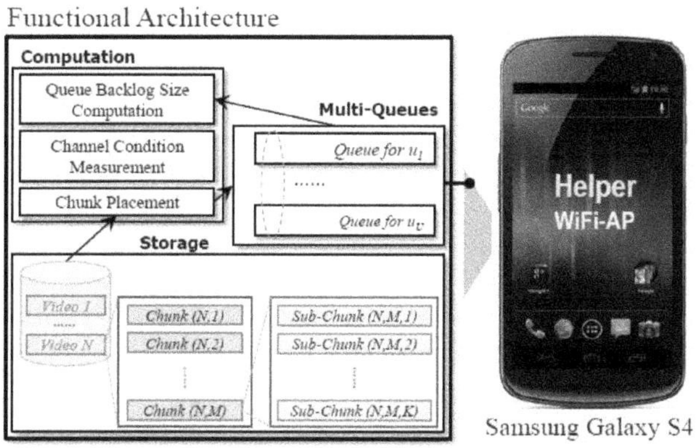


(a) Helper Software Architecture

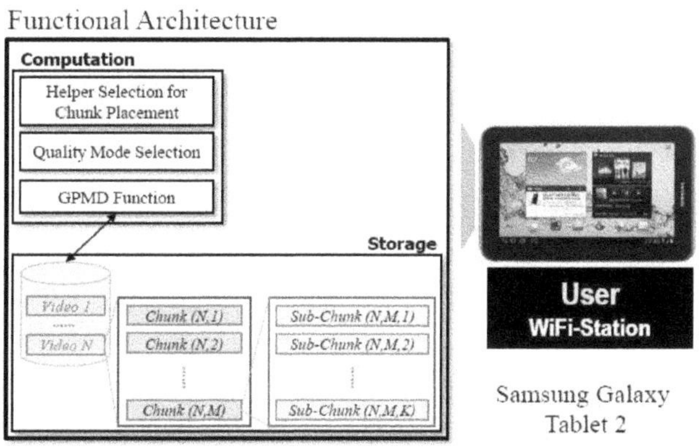


(b) User Software Architecture

**Figure 1: Device Software Architectures**

send the all sub-chunks of the first chunk, then it can be transmitted later when the helper is scheduled. In the following time slots, the previous operations are repeated until helpers transmit the last sub-chunk of the last chunk.

## 3.2 Helper Implementation

The software for helper side is implemented on top of Samsung Galaxy smartphones with Android platforms. The helpers in this system are set to WiFi-APs, i.e., they work as WiFi APs. Therefore, the users can also periodically measure achievable link rates or RSSI measures from the helpers, because the corresponding functions are allowed in WiFi AP-centric systems, such as `getRssi()` defined by the classes in the Android API's `android.net.wifi` package. For multi-user support, the helpers can create multiple TCP sockets for the multiple users which want to download sub-chunks from the helpers. The roles of helpers are as follows: (i) returning the queue backlog sizes when they receive chunk requests from users, (ii) placing sub-chunks when they are selected by users for specific chunk service, and (iii) transmitting a number of sub-chunks depending on the channel conditions. The corresponding software architecture is illustrated in Fig. 1(a).

## 3.3 User Implementation

The software for user side is implemented on top of Samsung Galaxy tablet with Android platforms. The roles of users are (i) determining which helpers should be selected for chunk placements, (ii) selecting helpers for the GPMD strategy in terms of sub-chunks downloading, and (iii) selecting quality modes for each chunk. The corresponding software architecture is illustrated in Fig. 1(b).

# 4. DEMONSTRATION

## 4.1 Settings

For the demonstration, two helpers and two users will be used (Samsung Galaxy S4, ID: GI9250). To do this setting, four AC-power sources are required (110V) and one table for deploying devices is also required. In addition, one easel for presenting the poster which describes our system and algorithm is also needed. Additional wireless resources such as AP are not required. In terms of space, one easel for a poster and one table for four phones are required.

## 4.2 Video

Throughout this demo, we use standard test sequences "Bridge" and "Highway" both of which have 2000 frames with CIF ($352 \times 288$) resolution. Each video sequence is divided into 10 chunks and then encoded using ffmpeg encoder [4] at 25 fps so that each chunk corresponds to 8 seconds. In order to generate two different quality levels per video, we encode each video at rates 250 kbps and 50 kbps corresponding to high quality and low quality streams, respectively. Our demonstration video clip is available in [5].

# 5. CONCLUDING REMARKS

This demo abstract presents a practical implementation of an adaptive video streaming protocol for device-to-device mobile software platforms. In the given network, users can dynamically select helpers and video quality modes (two quality levels) for adaptive video streaming. In addition, we proposed the GPMD strategy to deal with the implementation issues or limitations in our previous work [3].

## Acknowledgments

This work is supported in part by the Intel VAWN projects.

# 6. REFERENCES

[1] N. Golrezaei, A.F. Molisch, A.G. Dimakis, and G. Caire. Device-to-device collaboration: a new architecture for wireless video distribution. *IEEE Communications Magazine*, 2012.

[2] N. Golrezaei, K. Shanmugam, A.G. Dimakis, A.F. Molisch, and G. Caire. FemtoCaching: wireless video content delivery through distributed caching helpers, In *INFOCOM'12: Proceedings of IEEE International Conference on Computer Communications*, 2012.

[3] D. Bethanabhotla, G. Caire, and M.J. Neely. Joint transmission scheduling and congestion control for adaptive streaming in wireless device-to-device networks. In *Asilomar'12: Proceedings of Asilomar Conf. Signals, Systems, and Computers*, 2012.

[4] `http://ffmpeg.org/`

[5] `https://www.youtube.com/watch?v=uRqwnCWDCsw`

# A Lane-Level Cooperative Collision Avoidance System Based on Vehicular Sensor Networks

Lien-Wu Chen
Department of Information Engineering and Computer Science, Feng Chia University, Taichung, 407, Taiwan
lwuchen@fcu.edu.tw

Po-Chun Chou
Department of Information Engineering and Computer Science, Feng Chia University, Taichung, 407, Taiwan
lunenknight@gmail.com

## ABSTRACT

In this paper, we design and implement a lane-level cooperative collision avoidance (LCCA) system using vehicle-to-vehicle communications. The LCCA system applies vehicular sensor networks to preventing chain vehicle collisions, which allows vehicles with merely onboard sensors to prevent such collisions on the road because of sharp stops. To the best of our knowledge, this is the first CCA system that does not use inaccurate GPS locations and costly roadside infrastructures to avoid chain vehicle collisions. LCCA employs inter-vehicle communications and onboard sensing to form warning groups, where each warning group is a set of vehicles that drive along the same lane and every pair of adjacent cars is within a certain distance. Only single-hop transmissions are needed to join/leave a warning group, thus keeping the group maintenance overhead low. When a sudden braking is taken in a warning group, LCCA can quickly propagate warning messages among group members. This paper demonstrates our current prototype.

**Categories and Subject Descriptors:** C.2.1 [Network Architecture and Design]: Distributed networks

**General Terms:** Algorithms, Design, Management

**Keywords:** Collision Avoidance, IEEE 802.11p, Traffic Safety, V2V Communication, Vehicular Sensor Network

## 1. INTRODUCTION

Recent advances in vehicular communication technologies and embedding sensing MEMS make *vehicular sensor networks (VSNs)* possible. VSNs combine the advantages of both *vehicular ad hoc networks (VANETs)* and *wireless sensor networks (WSNs)*, which consists of many sensor nodes deployed on roads or vehicles to detect various phenomenons to facilitate vehicular applications. Many VSN applications have been developed, such as environment monitoring, traffic safety, mobile surveillance, and vehicle security.

In this work, we design a *Lane-level Cooperative Collision Avoidance (LCCA)* system to prevent chain collisions among vehicles even there is no global positioning system (GPS) onboard. GPS is a worldwide localization technology adopted by vehicles, which consists of a number of satellites transmitting periodical coded signals. GPS receivers with multiple radio channels can observe multiple GPS satellites at once and obtain a distance measurement from each satellite signal. A GPS receiver can compute its location in three dimensions from four distance measurements. However, the distance measurement contains global and local errors caused by atmospheric and multi-path effects, respectively, with a typical accuracy range of $10 - 50$ meters.

During satellite signals that originate in the atmosphere and travel to the surface of Earth, global errors consisting of satellite clock errors, ephemeris errors, ionospheric delays, and tropospheric delays are generated. In particular, the effect of global errors on receiver measurements varies from one geographical area to another. Local errors depend on the hardware accuracy and surrounding environment of the receiver that are caused by the receiver hardware itself and multipath effects without line of sight.

GPSs are generally assumed to be deployed on vehicles by most safety protocols and applications in VANETs [1, 2, 3, 4, 5]. However, the current geographical locations of vehicles can not be accurately estimated due to GPS errors. In addition, the availability of GPS is uncertain as the vehicles enter areas where GPS signals may not be detected such as inside tunnels, streets between high buildings, etc. On the other hand, in the traditional CCA system, the vehicle encountering an emergency situation will broadcast warning messages to all other vehicles behind it. But a large number of messages are generated and flooded in the VANET. In addition, redundant messages are produced for the same emergency event. Thus, message collisions are occurred very often with the increasing number of vehicles on the road, which lead to a substantially high delay in delivering the warning message.

To eliminate the above GPS error and message collision problems, we design the LCCA system consisting of dynamic grouping and message forwarding schemes with GPS-less protocols. To the best of our knowledge, this is the first CCA

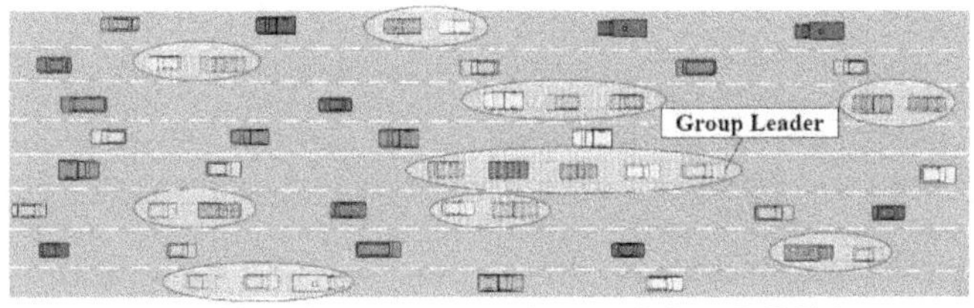


**Figure 1: Warning groups formed by LCCA on a highway.**


*MobiCom'13*, September 30–October 4, Miami, FL, USA.
ACM 978-1-4503-1999-7/13/09.
http://dx.doi.org/10.1145/2500423.2505293.

system that avoids chain vehicle crashing without using inaccurate GPS locations and merely rely on vehicle-to-vehicle communications to dynamically form warning groups. A warning group is a set of adjacent cars within a certain distance driving along the same lane. Only single-hop transmissions are needed to join/leave a warning group, thus keeping the group maintenance overhead low. When a sudden brake event is detected in a warning group, LCCA can quickly propagate warning messages among its group members. Fig. 1 shows an example of warning groups formed by LCCA on a highway.

## 2. SYSTEM DESIGN

In the LCCA system, each vehicle is equipped with an image sensor (e.g., video camera) and a distance sensor (e.g., magnetic sensor or laser range finder) in its front end. The image sensor is to recognize the license plate number (i.e., communication ID) of the vehicle in the front, whereas the distance sensor is directional and to detect the distance from one vehicle to another in its front. With this sensor, a vehicle can also estimate the relative velocity of the vehicle in its front. For the absolute velocity, it is obtained through the On Board Diagnostics (OBD [6]) interface. All vehicles have WAVE/DSRC [7] radio interfaces to freely communicate with each other.

A vehicle will join a warning group as its following distance with the vehicle in its front is less than the safety distance. On the contrary, a vehicle will leave a warning group as its following distance is more than or equal to the safety distance. When a group vehicle performs an emergency brake (i.e., the deceleration of brake is more than a predefined threshold), it will immediately send a warning message to all other group vehicles behind it. The warning message is assigned the highest priority than other control messages or data packets for its emergency. Group vehicles beyond the transmission range of the braking vehicle will be warned through a multi-hop manner. Thus, drivers can become aware of emergency brake before they actually see the braking light of the vehicle in the front.

Our goal is to design an efficient lane-level CCA system for vehicles to join/leave a warning group. In addition, when any vehicle in a warning group performs an emergency brake, the system needs to immediately broadcast a warning message to all behind group vehicles. The warned vehicles could slow down their speeds in advance to reduce the chances of chain vehicle collisions. In the lack of vehicles' self-locations, we consider the following issues:

1. Vehicle Grouping: How do we construct a warning group that can be joined/left by vehicles in the same lane so that the control overhead is minimized?

2. Member Updating: How do we update a warning group as some members change their lanes or following distances so that the group maintenance overhead is minimized?

3. Group Warning: How do we quickly propagate a warning message to all members behind the braking vehicle through multi-hop forwarding so that the warning message cost is minimized?

4. Forwarder Decision: How do we explicitly specify an optimal forwarding vehicle so that the number of rebroadcasted warning messages is minimized?

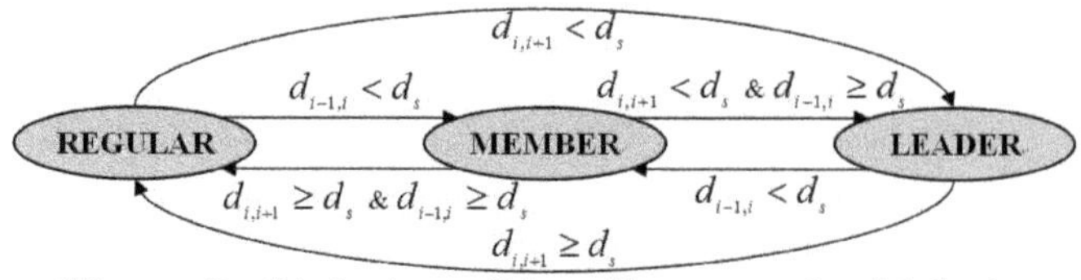


**Figure 2: State transition diagram of vehicle $i$.**

## 3. LANE-LEVEL COOPERATIVE COLLISION AVOIDANCE

Based on our previous work [5], we further design a new GPS-less framework consisting of a distributed grouping mechanism and a receiver-based forwarding scheme. The dynamic grouping of vehicles is employed to notify related vehicles with the emergency event, which keeps control and warning messages in local. To minimize the number of warning message transmissions for emergency brakes in a group, the receiver-based forwarding scheme specifies the optimal group vehicle to rebroadcast the warning message without infrastructure and GPS supports.

For dynamic grouping, after a vehicle $i$ gets on the road, the safety distance $d_s$ supposed to be maintained by $i$ is equal to $s_i \times \eta$ meters, where $s_i$ is the current speed of $i$ and $\eta$ is the statistical factor for the safety distance between vehicles. For example, $\eta = 0.55$ by using the two-second rule [8]. If $d_{i-1,i} \geq d_s$, it means the distance between $i$ and $i-1$ is enough for $i$ to deal with the emergency brake of $i-1$. There is nothing to do for both onboard units of $i$ and $i-1$. Conversely, if $d_{i-1,i} < d_s$, it means $i$ may not react in time to the emergency brake of $i-1$ such that a crashing is possible to happen.

When $d_{i-1,i} < d_s$, $i$ will send a message $M_{join}$ to $i-1$ for joining $i-1$'s warning group. Then, $i-1$ will reply a message $M_{reply}$ to $i$ for indicating the group leader ID (i.e., $\text{ID}_{GL}$) and $i-1$'s group number (i.e., $\text{GN}_{i-1}$) in the warning group, and add $i$ to its warning list $L_{i-1}$. If $i-1$ has kept $d_s$ from vehicle $i-2$ in its front, $i-1$ will serve as the GL. $\text{ID}_{GL}$ and $\text{GN}_{i-1}$ will be passed to $i$ by $i-1$ and $\text{GN}_i = \text{GN}_{i-1} + 1$, where $\text{GN}_{GL} = 1$. On the other hand, when $d_{i-1,i}$ is getting larger than $d_s$, $i$ will send a message $M_{leave}$ to $i-1$ for leaving $i-1$'s warning group. Then, $i-1$ will remove $i$ from its $L_{i-1}$ since $d_{i-1,i}$ is enough to deal with the emergency brake of $i-1$. Note that $M_{join}$, $M_{reply}$, and $M_{leave}$ messages are only transmitted in single hop so that the control overhead to join/leave a warning group is localized and thus minimized.

For example, there is a sequence of vehicles $A$, $B$, and $C$ in the same lane. If $B$ detects $d_{A,B} < d_s$, it sends $M_{join}$ to $A$. $A$ adds $B$ into its $L_A$ and replies $M_{reply}$ to $B$ that indicates $\text{ID}_{GL} = A$ and $\text{GN}_A = 1$. According to $M_{reply}$, $B$ can calculate its $\text{GN}_B = \text{GN}_A + 1 = 2$. Similarly, if $C$ detects $d_{B,C} < d_s$, it sends $M_{join}$ to $B$. $B$ adds $C$ into its $L_B$ and replies $M_{reply}$ to $C$ that indicates $\text{ID}_{GL} = A$ and $\text{GN}_B = 2$. According to $M_{reply}$, $C$ can calculate its $\text{GN}_C = \text{GN}_B + 1 = 3$.

The state transition diagram of vehicle $i$ is shown in Fig. 2, where vehicle $i$ is in front of vehicle $i+1$ and behind vehicle $i-1$ in the same lane. There are three possible states for vehicle $i$:

- *REGULAR*: $i$ keeps in $d_s$ from $i-1$ and so does $i+1$ from $i$.
- *MEMBER*: $i$ does not keep in $d_s$ from $i-1$.
- *LEADER*: $i$ keeps in $d_s$ from $i-1$, but $i+1$ does not keep in $d_s$ from $i$.

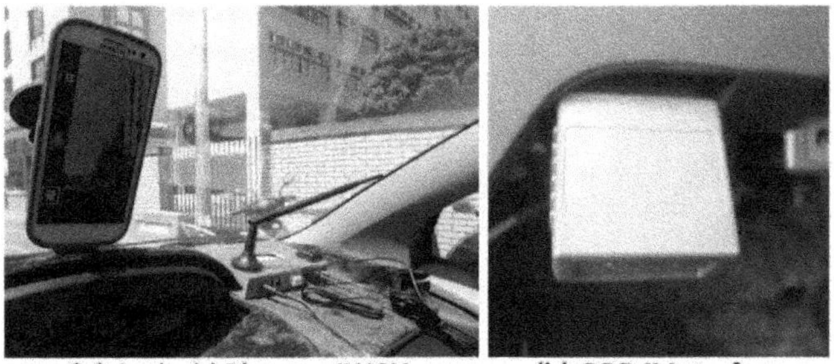

Figure 3: LCCA hardware components.

Whenever $i$ transits to the LEADER state, it broadcasts a $M_{update}$ message to all behind group member $j$ for updating $ID_{GL}$ to $ID_i$ and $GN_j$ to $GN_j - GN_i$. Whenever $i$ is in the LEADER/MEMBER state and performs an emergency brake, it immediately broadcasts a $M_{warn}$ message to all behind group members. A vehicle only accepts a $M_{update}/M_{warn}$ message from the vehicle in front of it in the same warning group. The forwarding of $M_{update}/M_{warn}$ is through a multi-hop manner as some behind group members are out of the transmission range of $i$. In our framework, the redundancy of $M_{update}/M_{warn}$ will be completely eliminated by the proposed receiver-based forwarding scheme (due to space limitation, the detailed mechanism is omitted). Note that we can also simply use general broadcast forwarding to relay $M_{update}/M_{warn}$ to all behind group members.

# 4. PROTOTYPE IMPLEMENTATION

We have developed a prototype of LCCA. In our prototype, the radio interface is implemented by ITRI WAVE Communication Unit (IWCU [9]), which has two IEEE 802.11p interfaces and one Ethernet connector. Vehicle grouping and warning operated in LCCA can send UDP packets via standard socket APIs, such as sendto() and recvfrom(), and IWCU can convert UDP packets to WAVE short messages (WSMs [10]).

The image sensor is implemented by the camera of an Android phone recognizing the license plate number of the vehicle in the front to obtain the communication ID. In addition, the camera also recognizes the license plate size to detect the distance from itself to the vehicle in its front. As shown in Fig. 3(a) and Fig. 3(b), the Android phone communicates with an IWCU and an OBD II interface through Wi-Fi and Bluetooth, respectively. The Ethernet connector of the IWCU is connected to a Wi-Fi access point for communications with the Android phone. The 802.11p interfaces are set to WAVE/DSRC mode for communications with neighboring vehicles. The graphical user interface (GUI) in the Android phone shows the messages received from neighboring vehicles and status of vehicles in the warning group.

Fig. 4 shows the indoor demonstration of LCCA. As shown in Fig. 4(a), we use three Android phones on the separate modeled cars to simulate traffic flows on a road segment with four lanes (two lanes per direction). As shown in Fig. 4(b), the GUI shows the license plate tag and warning group status. The Android Augmented Reality (AndAR [11]) Library is adopted to recognize the license plate number and tag size of the vehicle in the front. In our demonstration, the first vehicle (i.e. green car) is joined by the second one (i.e., red car) as the distance between them is smaller than a predefined safety distance, as shown in Fig. 4(c). Then, the third vehicle (i.e., blue car) joins the warning group formed by the first and second ones, as shown in Fig. 4(d). After the warning group is formed, the first one of these three vehicles takes an emergency brake by pushing a button on the GUI to broadcast a warning message. As shown Fig. 4(e), the group vehicles behind the braking car are notified, and the drivers are warned by the alarming sign and high frequency sound while other vehicles ahead or in different lanes discard the warning message.

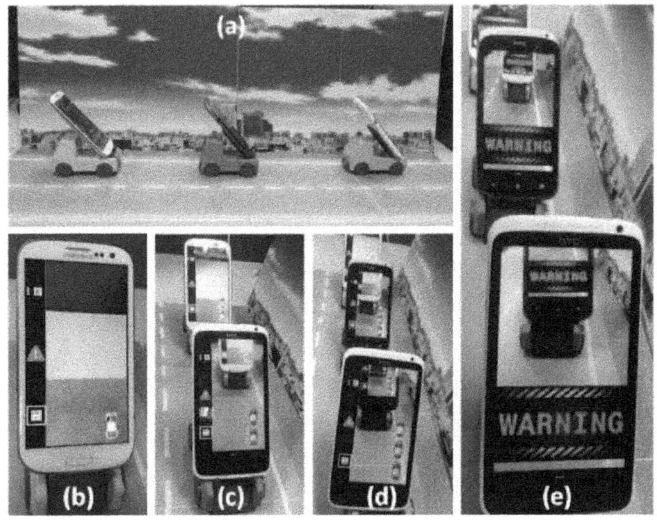

Figure 4: Indoor demonstration of LCCA.

# 5. ACKNOWLEDGMENTS

This research is supported in part by NSC under Grant No. NSC101-2221-E-035-090 and NSC102-2221-E-035-031-MY3.

# 6. REFERENCES

[1] T. Taleb, A. Benslimane, and K. B. Letaief. Towards an Effective Risk-Conscious and Collaborative Vehicular Collision Avoidance System. *IEEE Transactions on Vehicular Technology*, 59(3):1474-1486, Mar. 2010.

[2] Y. Zang, L. Stibor, H.-J. Reumerman, and H. Chen. Wireless Local Danger Warning Using Inter-Vehicle Communications in Highway Scenarios. In *14th European Wireless Conference (EW)*, pages 1-7, June 2008.

[3] D. Djenouri. Preventing Vehicle Crashes Through a Wireless Vehicular Sensor Network. In *24th Biennial Symposium on Communications*, pages 320-323, June 2008.

[4] F. Ye, M. Adams, and S. Roy. V2V Wireless Communication Protocol for Rear-End Collision Avoidance on Highways. In *IEEE International Conference on Communications (ICC)*, pages 375-379, May 2008.

[5] L.-W. Chen, Y.-H. Peng, and Y.-C. Tseng. An infrastructure-less framework for preventing rear-end collisions by vehicular sensor networks. *IEEE Communications Letters*, 15(3):358-360, Mar. 2011.

[6] On Board Diagnostics. http://www.obdii.com/background.html.

[7] D. Jiang and L. Delgrossi. IEEE 802.11p: Towards an International Standard for Wireless Access in Vehicular Environments. In *IEEE Vehicular Technology Conference (VTC-Spring)*, pages 2036-2040, May 2008.

[8] Luis. Two Second Rule [Online]. In *http://www.studydriving.com/safetyon-the-road/the-two-second-rule/*, May 2007.

[9] ITRI WAVE Communication Unit. http://www.itri.org.tw.

[10] IEEE P1609.3/D5.0. Draft Standard for Wireless Access in Vehicular Environments (WAVE) - Networking Services. Mar. 2010.

[11] Android Augmented Reality. http://code.google.com/p/andar/.

# Demo: Secure M2M Cloud Testbed

Heikki Mahkonen
heikki.mahkonen@ericsson.com

Teemu Rinta-aho
teemu.rinta-aho@ericsson.com

Tero Kauppinen
tero.kauppinen@ericsson.com

Mohit Sethi
mohit.m.sethi@ericsson.com

Jimmy Kjällman
jimmy.kjallman@ericsson.com

Patrik Salmela
patrik.salmela@ericsson.com

Tony Jokikyyny
tony.jokikyyny@ericsson.com

NomadicLab
Ericsson Research, Finland

## ABSTRACT

This demo presents a Machine-to-Machine (M2M) service platform running on an OpenStack cloud environment. Access to this platform is secured with authentication based on 3GPP standardized Generic Bootstrapping Architecture (GBA). The M2M network in this testbed consists of Raspberry Pi gateways and resource-constrained devices such as Arduinos. These devices have associated sensors, that report physical data such as temperature, and actuators such as LEDs, that respond to actuation commands. In this demo, the sensor data is authenticated and integrity protected end-to-end with public-key elliptic curve digital signature algorithm (ECDSA). Lastly, the demo testbed includes a web-based cloud management interface referred to as the "IoT Portal". This portal allows a system administrator to specify pre-configured Virtual Machine (VM) images with custom applications. As an example, a M2M Web service is installed into the VMs. This web service collects and displays authenticated and verified sensor data and can also be used to send actuator commands.[1]

## Categories and Subject Descriptors

C.2.4 [**Computer Systems Organization**]: Computer-Communication Networks—*Distributed Systems*

## Keywords

Cloud computing; Generic Bootstrapping Architecture; Internet of Things; Machine-to-Machine; OpenStack; Security

## 1. INTRODUCTION

Internet of Things (IoT) encompasses a wide variety of technologies, objects and protocols. Physical objects that are part of IoT, no longer act as unresponsive nodes but rather understand and react to the environment they reside in. Such objects, referred to as smart objects, form the building blocks of the Internet of Things. In order to ensure smooth and successful deployment of these smart objects, as an important first step, it is necessary to develop experimental prototypes that study the feasibility of different protocols and technologies. To this end, our testbed presents a prototype platform that provides resource-constrained smart objects with secure connectivity to a cloud environment over the Internet. Using a cloud service allows easy and dynamic deployment of services, as well as, facilitates network operators and enterprises with a platform where services can be managed centrally on a large scale.

The rest of this paper is structured as follows. In Section 2, we present relevant background information about the secure M2M and Cloud solution implemented in our testbed. Section 3 then gives a detailed overview of the demonstration. Lastly, Section 4 provides a conclusion.

## 2. BACKGROUND

### 2.1 Machine-to-Machine Network

In the testbed demo, we prototype smart object devices with Arduino[2] development boards. They have associated sensors, that report physical data such as temperature, and actuators such as LEDs, that respond to actuation commands. Since these devices are constrained in the amount of energy available to them, we rely on energy-efficient IEEE 802.15.4 short-range radio boards (Digi XBee[3]) for communication. To enable seamless interaction between users and devices across heterogeneous networks, it is important that these devices are accessible over the Internet. We therefore use a Java OSGi[4] based M2M Gateway (GW) device running on a Raspberry Pi[5] development board to provide Internet connectivity to the smart object network.

### 2.2 Cloud Environment

We use the OpenStack[6] platform (Grizzly 2013.1 distribution) running on Linux servers with Ubuntu 12.04 as the

[1]Demo URL: `http://users.piuha.net/nomadiclab/smct.mov`

[2]`http://www.arduino.cc/`
[3]`http://www.digi.com/xbee/`
[4]`http://www.osgi.org/Main/HomePage`
[5]`http://www.raspberrypi.org`
[6]`http://www.openstack.org/`


*MobiCom'13,* September 30–October 4, 2013, Miami, FL, USA.
ACM 978-1-4503-1999-7/13/09.
http://dx.doi.org/10.1145/2500423.2505294 .

cloud backend in our testbed. This backend operates on the KVM[7] hypervisor and utilizes Open vSwitch[8] networking. VM instances for the smart object devices that are part of the M2M network are managed and run by the OpenStack "compute" component. Assignment of IP addresses and connectivity management for the VMs is controlled by the "networking" component of OpenStack. Lastly, the "image service" component is responsible for storing pre-configured VM images which are used when spawning new VMs.

Our M2M service platform includes a web interface for management of the cloud backend. This management interface, referred to as the "IoT Portal", consists of components written in PHP, JavaScript and shell scripts (for issuing OpenStack commands), and runs on an Apache web server. It interfaces with an SQL database for storing data and configuration information. With the IoT Portal, a system administrator can obtain an overview of gateways, registered devices, their corresponding VM instances, IP addresses, the status of the VM instances, and other configuration data. Through its interface, the IoT Portal also allows specification of VM templates to ensure that devices of a certain class (for example, a specific vendor, type or subscriber) can be assigned VMs with different configuration data such as memory, disk space, operating system, and software packages. Moreover, the IoT Portal can also specify if a VM instance for a device class can be shared by several devices in that class, or if a new instance needs to be created for each device.

The M2M gateway communicates with cloud backend through a REST API. The IoT portal creates a new VM instance for new devices joining the M2M network if it does not already have an instance, or if the device class does not have a shared instance. It is possible for the IoT portal to acquire software and configuration options for a new VM instance from an external source, for example, a device vendor service. In our cloud backend, custom software and configurations can be installed into a VM instance using the Puppet[9] automation software.

## 2.3 Authentication and Security

Secure authentication and bootstrapping of devices can be non-trivial in smart object networks. Generic Bootstrapping Architecture (GBA) [1] is a 3GPP standard for secure and flexible authentication of a user to application services. GBA relies on the Authentication and Key Agreement (AKA) protocol and utilizes SIM credentials along with the operator infrastructure to setup a shared secret between a user equipment (e.g. mobile phone) and an application server. Since GBA can be used with little or no user interaction, and the fact that it provides strong authentication, we believe that it is a potential candidate protocol for secure authentication and bootstrapping of devices. In our demo testbed, we use GBA for secure authentication and provisioning of gateway devices.

A smart object network that contains resource-constrained sensor devices, may have several intermediaries between the sensor where the data is generated, and the cloud, where the sensor data is stored. These intermediaries may include gateways, firewalls and caching proxies. The sensor data stored in the cloud may also later be accessed by user applications running on different devices. In order to ensure data authenticity and integrity end-to-end in such a multi-hop environment, it is beneficial to have asymmetric public-key based digital signatures which can be used to sign data at its origin (sensors). This data can later be verified for its authenticity and integrity by caching proxies, end-user applications consuming the data or any other intermediary. As shown by Sethi et al. [2], it is possible to use Elliptic Curve Digital Signature Algorithm (ECDSA) to sign data even on 8-bit micro-controllers. In this demo, we use the same library (Relic[10]) and configuration to demonstrate end-to-end data authenticity and integrity from sensors to the cloud with digital signatures.

# 3. DEMO OVERVIEW

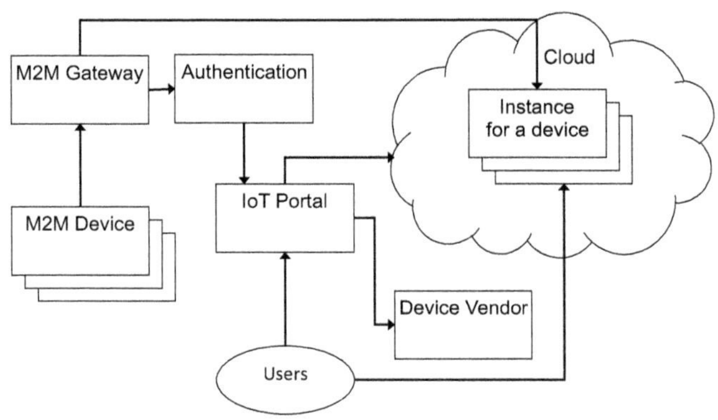


**Figure 1: Secure M2M Cloud Testbed**

Figure 1 shows the components of the testbed. The M2M network has resource-constrained smart object devices and GWs. These devices use IEEE 802.15.4 radios for communication in the M2M network and are connected to the Internet through GWs. Each GW in the M2M network first authenticates itself to the cloud backend using standard 3GPP Generic Bootstrapping Architecture [1]. The Network Application Function (NAF) service is part of the authentication infrastructure and is located at well-know address (domain name). It is responsible for providing the correct IoT Portal address to an authenticated GW based on the GBA credentials presented by the GW. Henceforth, when an authenticated GW receives an attach request from a resource-constrained device in the M2M network, it requests the IoT Portal to register the new device. The portal may use an existing VM instance or, if needed, may create a new VM instance for this device. Thereafter, the address of this VM instance is communicated to the GW. The IoT portal in this demo uses VM templates when instantiating new VMs. These templates have pre-configured operating system (Ubuntu 12.04 amd64) and Apache web server along with a custom M2M web service. If the device is a sensor, then this web service can be used for collecting as well as viewing sensor data. On the other hand, if the device is an actuator, this web interface can be used to send and view the status of actuation commands.

The demo message sequence shown in Figure 2 is as follows:

[7]`http://www.linux-kvm.org/`

[8]`http://openvswitch.org/`

[9]`http://puppetlabs.com/`

[10]`http://code.google.com/p/relic-toolkit/`

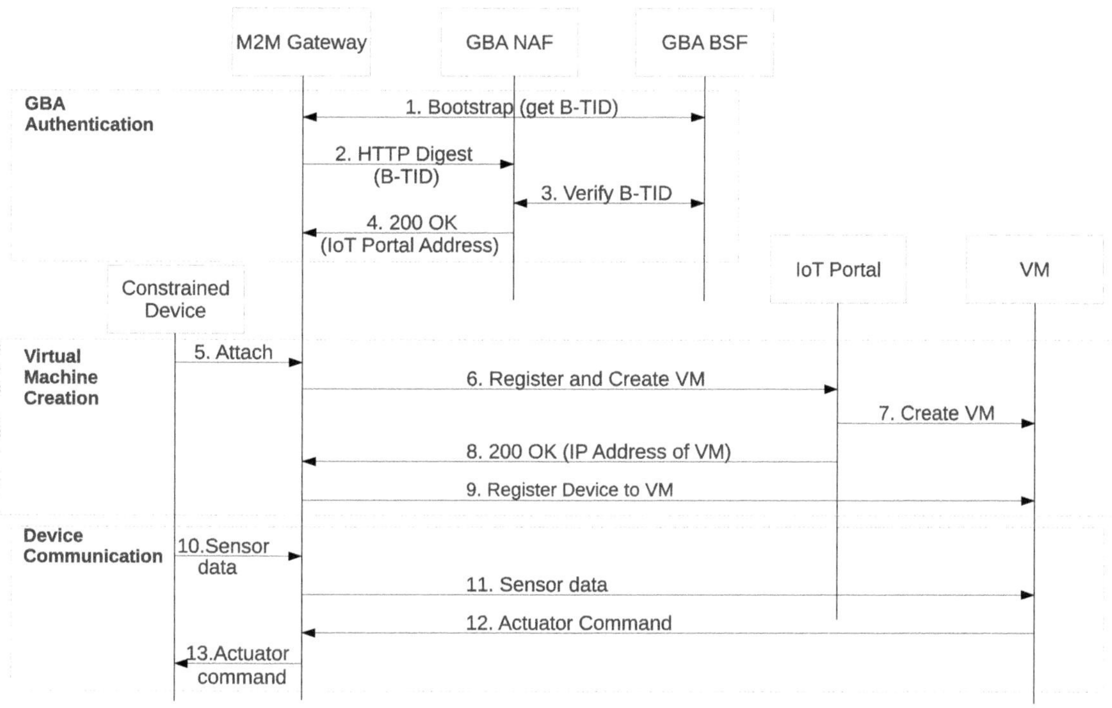


**Figure 2: Testbed demo sequence**

1. The GW performs GBA [1] bootstrapping with the Booststrapping Server Function (BSF) and both generate a key $K_s$. The GW also obtains the bootstrapping context identifier (B-TID).
2. Using the B-TID, the GW performs HTTP Digest authentication with the NAF.
3. The NAF requests the BSF for a key matching the received B-TID. Using the B-TID, the BSF generates a key $K_s$NAF, which is then communicated to the NAF.
4. The NAF, on verifying the digest, replies with an OK message that may contain configuration data, such as the IoT Portal address. Also, the NAF and the GW now share a secret key, $K_s$NAF which can be used to securely transfer the configuration data.
5. Device sends an attach request to the GW.
6. GW request a new VM for the newly joined device.

7–8. A new VM is created and its IP address is communicated to the GW.

9. The GW registers this new device to the M2M web service in the VM.

10–11. If the device is a sensor, it can start sending signed data to the GW which is forwarded and stored in the VM. A user can use the web service in the VM to view collected and verified data.

12–13. If however, the device is an actuator, the gateway would forward actuation commands to the device from the web service and return any status updates from the device to the web service.

## 3.1 Demo Requirements

Our demo requires a demo stand with a table to hold a laptop, a display, and a few M2M devices. The demo requires electricity and Internet access. The minimum required setup time is 1 hour.

# 4. CONCLUSIONS

We demonstrate a system where devices are automatically and securely provisioned and connected to a cloud backend. We note that there are many benefits of placing M2M services into the cloud. Firstly, potentially billions of objects can be managed centrally, removing the need to have local server deployments for services and management. Secondly, it enables dynamic configuration of service and networking resources, which can be instantiated and scaled as per need basis. Thirdly, data published by these smart object can be accessed from anywhere on the Internet and they can also be managed remotely. Fourthly, the solution is completely horizontal, that is, the same platform can be used by any application and user. Services can reside in separate secure domains within the cloud. Lastly, the solution provides lower OPEX and CAPEX by enabling faster deployment of M2M services with minimal configuration and maintenance.

# 5. ACKNOWLEDGMENTS

This work was partly done in the Internet of Things program[11] of Tivit (Finnish Strategic Centre for Science, Technology and Innovation in the field of ICT), funded by Tekes.

# 6. REFERENCES

[1] 3GPP. TS 33.220 - Generic Bootstrapping Architecture (GBA), 2007.

[2] M. Sethi, J. Arkko, and A. Keranen. End-to-end security for sleepy smart object networks. In *LCN Workshops 2012*, pages 964–972. IEEE, 2012.

[11] `http://www.internetofthings.fi/`

# PiCode: 2D Barcode with Embedded Picture and ViCode: 3D Barcode with Embedded Video*

## Innovative System for Transmitting Data from Display to Camera

Wenjian Huang
Hong Kong University of Science and Techonology
Clear Water Bay, Hong Kong
whuangad@ust.hk

Wai Ho Mow
Hong Kong University of Science and Techonology
Clear Water Bay, Hong Kong
eewhmow@ust.hk

## ABSTRACT

As 2D barcodes become more and more popular, their new applications, like mobile marketing, give a strong motivation for embedding visual information in them. Information stored on a 2D barcode, being printed on paper or shown on a display device, can be delivered to people via a camera phone with suitable decoding software. The barcoding system can be viewed as a communication system with key functional modules, including channel coding, modulation, channel estimation, demodulation and channel decoding. By applying advanced communications principles, a way to integrate a picture into a 2D barcode (called PiCode) is developed. By extending the idea, a way to integrate a video clip into a series of 2D barcodes (called ViCode) is also developed. To realize PiCode and ViCode, new modulation and demodulation schemes are designed. Based on our channel estimation technique, a new decoding scheme for low-density parity-check codes is devised to provide more robust error rate performance than traditional 2D barcodes. A US patent and a Chinese patent have already been filed based on the innovative methods developed for PiCode.

## Categories and Subject Descriptors

C.2.1 [**Network Architecture and Design**]: Wireless Communication

## General Terms

Algorithms, Human Factors, Performance, Reliability

## Keywords

2D Barcode, 3D Barcode, Embedded Picture and Video, Encoder, Decoder, Display-Camera Communication Channel

*This work was supported by the Hong Kong Research Grants Council (DAG05/06.EG16).


*MobiCom'13*, September 30–October 4, 2013, Miami, FL, USA.
ACM 978-1-4503-1999-7/13/09.
http://dx.doi.org/10.1145/2500423.2505295.

## 1. INTRODUCTION

Recently, QR codes appear everywhere not only for inventory, but also for mobile marketing. A typical scenario of the the latter application is that a company logo is embedded in the centre of a QR code in order to promote the company brand to potential customers. Unfortunately, the logo in the QR code is often too small to see and the brand image it represents may even be distorted in order to be fit it in the small area. Therefore, it is highly desirable to design a 2D barcode with perfect integration of the code and the picture. This motivates us to develop a new kind of picture-embedding 2D barcode, called PiCode. A US patent [1] and a Chinese patent [2] have already been filed based on the innovative methods developed for PiCode. Further extending the concepts behind PiCode and 2D barcode in general, we also investigate new ways to increase barcode storage capacity by developing 3D or video barcode, which roughly refers to a video series of 2D barcodes, and to embed in it a low-resolution video clip, called ViCode. Our design approach is based on the interpretation of a barcoding system as a 2D communication system with an image processing frontend so as to draw inspiration from advanced communications theory.

**Figure 1: QR code with embedded picture (Left) and PiCode (Right)**

### 1.1 PiCode

The PiCode system mainly includes two parts: i) modulation & demodulation; ii) channel coding. Some barcodes use color to store more information [3], but we use color in barcodes to deliver visual information to human. The first part is about how to add visual information in the barcode and how to recover the stored data from the barcode. Existing 2D barcodes, like QR code and Data Matrix code, usually use black and white square modules to modulate the data bits, which present no meaningful visual information to human. Our approach is to use color in 2D barcode represent the color of a modified version of the embedded image while the data bits are used to adjust the intensity of the embedded image. This process unavoidably induces additional distortion and therefore improving system robust is one of our design emphases. The second part describes the methods adopted for channel estimation, low-density parity-check (LDPC) code and the associated log likelihood ratio (LLR) assignment for iterative decoding. They aim to improve system performance and response time relative to existing barcodes. We have already set up a PiCode demo website at `http://www.picode.info`.

## 1.2 ViCode

The MIT Media Lab reported a very fast display-camera transmission system by ultilizing the idea of 3D barcode (also called video barcode) with a professional camera, an extra-high resolution display and high-performance computational devices [4], and this proved the huge potential of 3D barcode. For a practical mobile phone platform, another 3D barcode demo was built which can achieve a transmission rate of around 2Kbps [5]. As an extension of PiCode, our ViCode is the first ever attempt to embed a video clip in a 3D barcode which can transmit data at a very high rate using commonly available mobile phones. ViCode is ideal for mobile applications which require higher storage capacity than what 2D barcodes can ever provide, such as storing a brochure, a ringtone, a photo, an app file, and so on. The data storage capacity of ViCode is unbounded because of the extra time dimension and the data transmission rate of our existing implementation is already exceeding 100Kbps. Our demo video is available at `http://youtu.be/rqxHDH2EtVY`.

# 2. PICODE SYSTEM

## 2.1 Modulation & Demodulation

For modulation, the embedded image is first converted to a gray scaled one, and resized to have an aspect ratio of 1:1 (i.e., a square shape). In the embedding process, a module, which refers to one of the many small squares composing a PiCode, is used to represent a single bit of the encoded data. Each module is realized by choosing one of two pre-defined tilting patterns according to whether the data bit is 0 or 1.

The gray level of the modules may be heavily distorted in the barcode image captured by a camera. The thresholding detection method commonly used in existing barcode system may not be sufficient in our case. In general, it is difficult for the demodulator to determine the threshold for deciding whether data is 0 or 1 in the presence of severe distortion. The decoding performance is sensitive to the choice of the decision threshold and may be significantly degraded due to the choice of mismatched threshold.

Before the demodulation step, we first detect the finder pattern of the 2D barcode and synchronize each data block based on the timing pattern. By using tilting patterns composed of two concentric squares with different gray levels, the demodulator can decide whether the data bit is 0 or 1 from the differential gray level between the inner and outer parts of a tilting patten, without the need of estimating a threshold. In this way, reliability is improved with less complexity.

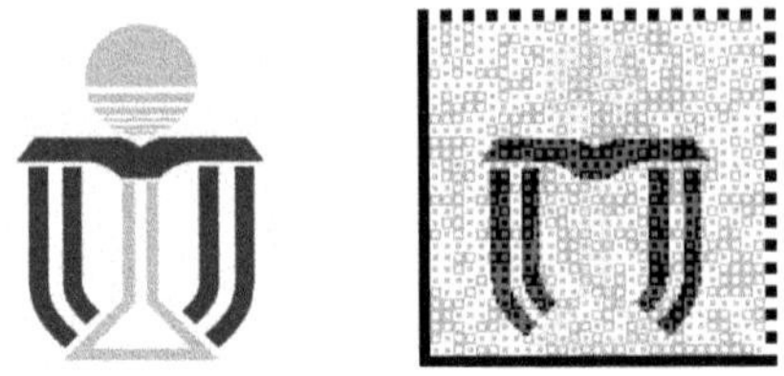

**Figure 2: Original picture (Left) and its associated PiCode (Right)**

## 2.2 Channel Coding

PiCode uses soft decoding, instead of the information lossy hard decoding widely applied in existing barcode systems. The demodulator estimates the histogram of intensity difference between the inner and outer parts of every module. Since there are only two tilting patterns, the histogram typically show two peaks. From the histogram, the channel parameters and hence the LLR can be estimated. For example, by assuming the additive white Gaussian noise channel model, the distributions of the aforementioned intensity difference conditioned on the data bit, whether it is 1 or 0, are symmetric. Hence the histogram can be divided into two symmetric parts. By calculating the mean and variance of each part, the LLR of each symbol can be estimated. To realize this soft decoding advantage, we adopt a regular LDPC code with iterative decoding. RS code is famous for its burst error correction capability. However, it is not ideal for random bit error correction because one bit error suffices to cause a multi-bit symbol error. Since the major distortion to the aforementioned intensity difference between the inner and outer parts of every module is induced by edges and sharp changes in the embedded picture, the errors occurred in PiCode are closer to random errors, instead of burst errors. Compared with the Reed Solomon (RS) code that is used in QR code and Data Matrix code, LDPC offers a distinctive performance advantage in terms of bit and block error rate. For barcode decoding, the image capturing and decoding processes are repeated until the first decoding success. Hence, a lower block error rate also translates to a shortened average response time in our PiCode system.

# 3. VICODE SYSTEM

## 3.1 System Structure

ViCode can be viewed as a 3D barcode extension of PiCode. As a 3D barcode, ViCode can store much more information than any single 2D barcode because of the added time dimension. In addition, ViCode can also show an embedded video clip or animation, which is ideal for attracting consumer's eyeballs in mobile marketing applications.

The ViCode system produces, instead of a single barcode image, a series of 2D barcodes, which can be shown as a video clip or even a video stream. The camera then captures each frame of ViCode and decode these frames in combination, which allows a much higher data capacity than decoding frame by frame. To achieve good performance, the inter-frame and intra-frame channel coding should be optimized. Advanced communication techniques including Orthogonal Frequency Division Multiplexing (OFDM), LDPC and maximum distance separable (MDS) code, are applied to make the system sufficiently robust and fast.

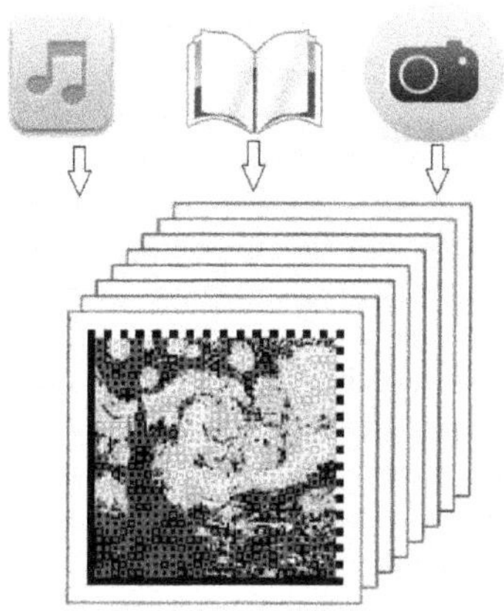

**Figure 3: A ringtong, a brochure, a photo, and so on can be stored in ViCode which can be later retrieved using a mobile phone conveniently.**

## 3.2 ViCode Encoder and Decoder

### *3.2.1 ViCode Encoder*

The function of the ViCode encoder is to convert a information bitstream and a video clip into a ViCode. Firstly, the bitstream is encoded using a LDPC code. Then OFDM is used to modulate it so as to facilitate accurate frequency offset estimation at the decoder. After scaling & quantization, a set of 2D barcodes are formed. Next, inter-frame MDS encoding, which can achieve the capacity of binary erasure channel, is performed. Finally, a video clip is embedded to form a ViCode, which is then showed on a display device.

### *3.2.2 ViCode Decoder*

The function of the ViCode decoder is to recover the information bitstream from a video stream (or an image series) representing a ViCode. Firstly, the camera continuously captures a series of images, to which a novel Moiré effect elimination algorithm based on the camera parameters, distance and angle is applied. Then a fast spatial synchronization algorithm is performed. After estimating and compensating the frequency offset, OFDM demodulation is carried out. Next the intra-frame LDPC decoding and inter-frame MDS decoding are employed to retrieve the information bitstream.

# 4. CONCLUSIONS

Both our PiCode and ViCode can offer excellent performance in the terms of decoding robustness and data capacity, compared with existing 2D and 3D barcodes available in mobile phone platforms. More importantly, they can also provide eye-appealing visual information, such as a picture or video clip, meaningful to people. They are therefore very promising tools for mobile marketing applications. By integrating PiCode or ViCode into a company logo, commodity packages, electronic billboards, digital signage, TV advertisement, and so on, it can effectively connect potential customers to commercial products. In the near future, when Google glasses become popular, PiCode and ViCode may appear everywhere because they can deliver various form of data to people at no (or very low) cost while they are simply looking at a PiCode or ViCode in the guise of an eye-appealing picture or video clip.

# 5. REFERENCES


[1] Wai Ho Mow, Chiu Yeung Au, Cheuk Yin Chiu, Ka Shun Li, and Wenjian Huang. *A Method for Embedding Visual Information in Two Dimensional Bar Codes.* US Patent, Application No. 13/866,028, Filing date: May 3, 2013.

[2] Wai Ho Mow, Chiu Yeung Au, Cheuk Yin Chiu, Ka Shun Li, and Wenjian Huang. *A Method for Embedding Visual Information in Two Dimensional Bar Codes.* Chinese Patent, Application No. 201310160620.7, Filing date: May 3, 2013.

[3] Devi Parikh and Gavin Jancke. Localization and Segmentation of a 2D High Capacity Color Barcode. In *Proceedings of 2008 IEEE Workshop on Applications of Computer Vision (WACV'08)*, pages 1–6, 2008.

[4] Samuel David Perli, Nabeel Ahmed, and Dina Katabi. Pixnet: Lcd-camera pairs as communication links. In *Demo of ACM SIGCOMM, 2010*, pages 451–452, 2010.

[5] Xu Liu, David Doermann, and Huiping Li. VCode – Pervasive Data Transfer Using Video Barcode. *IEEE Transactions on Multimedia*, 10(3):361–371, 2008.


# APPENDIX

# A. DEMO SETUP

## A.1 Equipment to be used for the demo

An exhibition stand, an iPad, an Android phone and two podia to keep them in upright positions.

## A.2 Space needed and setup time required

Space: 150cm Height × 40cm Width × 40cm Length
Setup Time: 15 minutes

## A.3 Additional facilities needed including power and Internet/wireless access

Access to power for charging an iPad and an Android phone. Wireless access is not necessary.

# Demo: Flexible Array of Inexpensive Radios

Jiansong Zhang Kun Tan
Microsoft Research Asia
Beijing, China
{jiazhang, kuntan}@microsoft.com

## ABSTRACT

In this demo, we propose to use multiple inexpensive off-the-shelf radios to build the FAIR system that can be flexibly configured to realize (1) non-contiguous spectrum access (2) MIMO and beamforming (3) constructing wider-band radio. While non-contiguous spectrum access and MIMO/beamforming are naturally supported by the FAIR system, we further develop radio bonding technique for constructing wider-band radio. Radio bonding provides a cost effective alternative to proprietary radio development that it can realize a non-existing wider-band radio using multiple commodity narrower-band radios. We demonstrate FAIR and radio bonding based on Sora 2.0.

## Categories and Subject Descriptors

C.2.1 [**COMPUTER-COMMUNICATION NETWORKS**]: Network Architecture and Design—*Wireless communication*

## Keywords

FAIR; Radio Bonding; Wider-band Radio; Sora2.0

## 1. INTRODUCTION

Non-contiguous spectrum access [4, 6] has been shown effective for handling spectrum fragments in unlicensed bands, *e.g.* the fragments due to narrow-band devices like zigbee in ISM bands or the fragments due to incumbents in white spaces. Recently, non-contiguous spectrum access has even been adopted into WiFi standards that a 80+80 MHz mode is introduced in 802.11ac [3]. However, from radio design point of view, non-contiguous spectrum access posts new challenges. First, the fragments could span a very wide range in spectrum. For example, in 802.11ac 80+80MHz mode, two 80MHz channels can span up to 645MHz. Second, there can be strong interference in between the fragments for which we need to either do analog filtering or reserve additional dynamic range to prevent radio saturation. To construct a radio for non-contiguous spectrum access, if we follow the traditional way of building a single radio chain, the radio will be very difficult (if not impossible) to realize. Particularly for the ADC component, the requirements will be 645MHz sampling rate to fulfill Nyquist sampling rate as well as over 100dB dynamic range to tolerate possible strong interference in between. Adding dynamically configurable band-reject filters could be a way to reduce the requirements, but these analog filters are non-trivial to design and implement.

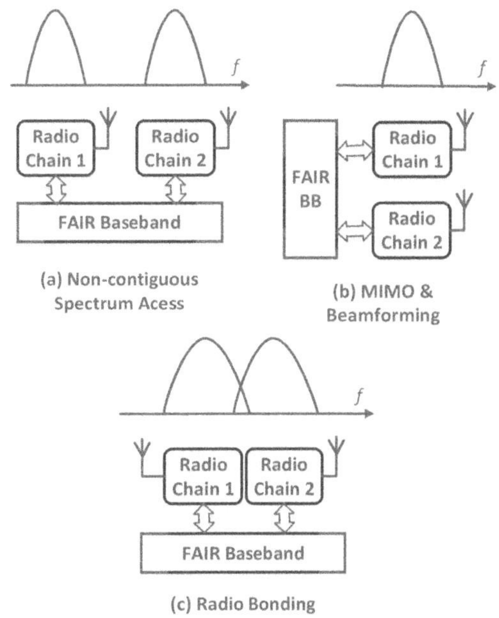


**Figure 1: (a) FAIR naturally realize non-contiguous spectrum access (b) As a multiple radio system, FAIR supports MIMO and beamforming (c) radio bonding in FAIR provides a cost effective alternative to proprietary radio development for constructing wider-band radio**

Using multiple radio chains is a more practical solution. Take 802.11ac as an example, if we use two radio chains to implement the 80+80 mode, each radio will only need 80MHz sampling rate and the interference in between will be naturally rejected by baseband filter of the radios. Recently, benefit from the adoption of MIMO (Multiple Input Multiple Output) technique, wireless devices equipped with multiple radio chains have already been ubiquitous in access points and laptops. Moreover, the chipset industry are keeping devoting effort for more compact and more energy efficient solution. Nowadays, chipset with multiple radio chains can be even equipped in mobile devices like Microsoft Surface and some other latest tablets [2].


*MobiCom'13,* September 30–October 4, 2013, Miami, FL, USA.
ACM 978-1-4503-1999-7/13/09.
http://dx.doi.org/10.1145/2500423.2505296.

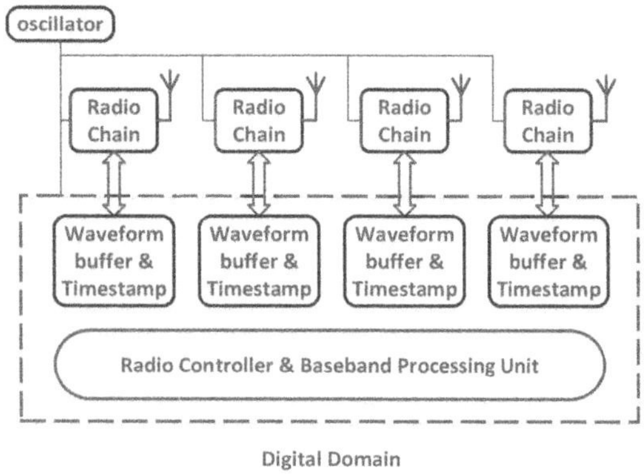


**Figure 2: FAIR Architecture**

In this demonstration, we propose the system FAIR (Flexible Array of Inexpensive Radios) in which multiple inexpensive off-the-shelf radios can be flexibly configured to realize many features that are in high demand, including (1) Non-contiguous spectrum access (2) MIMO and beamforming (3) constructing wider-band radio. While non-contiguous spectrum access and MIMO/beamforming are naturally supported in FAIR by setting multiple radio chains into different or the same central frequency, we further develop radio bonding technique which bonds multiple radio chains to construct a wider-band radio. Radio bonding provides a cost effective alternative to proprietary radio development if we need to construct a wider-band radio which is not available as commodity. Technically, radio bonding is also different from previous multi-radio architecture [5] because it can be viewed as a single radio from PHY/MAC layer and above. Figure 1 (c) illustrates the idea of radio bonding while Figure 1 (a)(b) shows FAIR can naturally support non-contiguous spectrum access and MIMO/beamforming.

We implemented FAIR using Sora 2.0 which equips four 20MHz 802.11a/g radios. The demonstration scenario focuses on radio bonding. We implemented a 40MHz 802.11n PHY using two 20MHz FAIR radios for radio bonding. Then we demonstrate a wireless link between this FAIR based implementation and a commodity 40MHz 802.11n access point.

## 2. FAIR ARCHITECTURE

The architecture of the FAIR system is shown in Figure 2. FAIR contains multiple radio chains that each can independently transmits and receives waveform in a limited bandwidth. These radio chains are off-the-shelf radios thus inexpensive and sophisticated, like 20MHz/40MHz 802.11n radios presently or 80MHz/160MHz 802.11ac radios in the near future. All the radio chains in FAIR share a common oscillator to drive ADC/DAC and generate carrier frequency. Clock sharing facilitates FAIR baseband by avoiding central frequency offset and sampling frequency offset among the radio chains.

All the radio chains are connected to a common digital domain logic via ADC output and DAC input. Inside this digital domain, each radio chain has a corresponding TX waveform buffer and RX waveform buffer. Then, all these buffers are connected to a common baseband processing unit for various FAIR baseband processing. In order to realize different features, different baseband algorithms are invoked from this baseband processing unit. Besides, there is a radio controller which controls parameters for all the radio chains, *e.g.* central frequency, bandwidth, gains, *etc.*. This centralized radio controller fulfills the basic frequency configuration requirement for enabling different features, *i.e.* MIMO/beamforming, non-contiguous spectrum access and radio bonding, in a single FAIR system. For example, we configure the radio chains to be different central frequencies for non-contiguous spectrum access, whereas we configure the radio chainss to be the same central frequency for MIMO and beamforming. Radio bonding could be viewed as a special case of non-contiguous spectrum access that the radio chains are configured on adjacent frequencies.

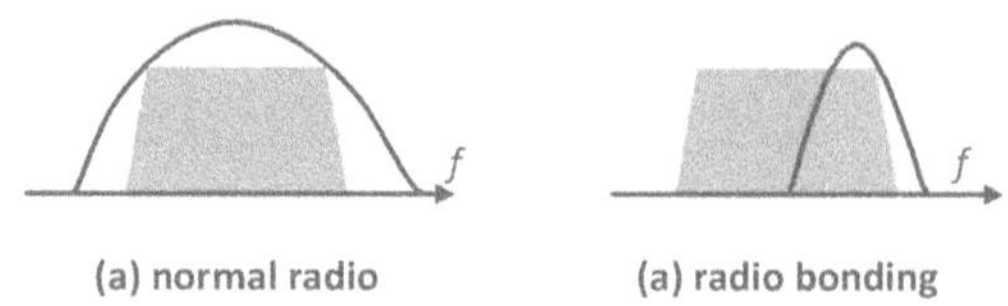


**Figure 3: In radio bonding, each narrower-band radio receives only a portion of the whole signal which is distorted by non-rectangular analog filters**

The whole digital domain logic could be implemented in different forms, *e.g.* ASIC, programable hardware like FPGA, graphic processor, general purpose processor, or a combination of several/all. In this demo, we use Sora software radio system that most of the digital domain logic is implemented in CPU while the other is implemented in FPGA.

### 2.1 Time Synchronization

Besides clock sharing mentioned above, time synchronization among multiple radio chains is also critical. For example, MIMO transmitter requires precise control that samples on different radio chains are sent out at exactly the same time, whereas at receiver side baseband processor needs to exactly know which samples are taken from the same time. Similarly, time synchronization is also critial to radio bonding and non-contiguous spectrum access.

In order to enable time synchronization, we added a hardware clock in FAIR which is shared for all the radio chains. At each ADC output, timestamps are inserted to digital samples based on this shared hardware clock. On the other hand, this hardware clock will be checked when digital waveform is going to DAC inputs. With the help of this shared hardware clock, FAIR transmitter can precisely synchronize waveform for all the radio chains and FAIR receiver can identify samples taken at the same time.

### 2.2 Radio Bonding

Radio bonding is to bond two or more radios to construct a wider-band radio. It provides a cost effective alternative to proprietory radio development while a wider-band radio is not yet available as commodity. For example, at the time of this demonstration that 160MHz 802.11ac device is not available, by applying radio bonding, we could build a 160MHz 802.11ac radio by bonding four 40MHz 802.11n radios or two 80MHz 802.11ac radios, thereby enabling 802.11ac 160MHz mode.

The biggest challenge which makes radio bonding non-trivial to accomplish is the distortion caused by band limited analog components and rate limited ADC of the narrower-band radios. As shown in Figure 3 (b), each narrower-band radio in radio bonding only receives a portion of the whole signal. Since the filters are not ideal rectangular filters, the received signal is distorted. In contrast, as shown in Figure 3 (a), in a normal radio the filters always have wider passband than signal width therefore the signal is never distorted. In addition to distortion, there is also a unique phase offset added by each radio chain. This phase offset is introduced in down-

Figure 4: Sora 2.0 Hardware

converter where the received signal is mixed with a phase-unknown carrier frequency LO (Local Oscillator).

In oder to address these challenges, we introduce modeling and compensating techniques. Specifically, to deal with signal distortion, we build a model for the filters and measure parameters for all the radio chains. To deal with phase offset, we estimate phase offset among the radio chains in advance. Then during signal receiving, we compensate both signal distortion and phase offset before adding the signal from multiple radio chains together. Finally, the whole signal is recovered and can be viewed as if it is received by a single wider-band radio.

# 3. SORA 2.0

We implemented FAIR using Sora 2.0 [1]. As shown in Figure 4, sora 2.0 hardware is a stand-alone box which connects to a PC via a up to 8-lane PCIe cable. Each sora 2.0 box equips four 20MHz 802.11a/g radios or 40MHz 802.11n radios. These four radios share a common reference clock for sampling and synthesizing carrier frequency so that it is capable to implement MIMO and beamforming. All the radios are mounted on a RAB (Radio Adapter Board) for radio configuration and further mounted to a RCB (Radio Control Board) to transmit digital waveforms into and from PC through the PCIe link.

Sora 2.0 comes with a SDK (Software Development Kit) which contains Windows drivers and a 802.11n baseband sample featuring 2x2 MIMO. The FAIR baseband implementation is based on sora UMX (User Mode eXtension) with which all the baseband codes are runing in user mode.

# 4. DEMONSTRATION

The demonstration scenario is shown in Figure 5. We focus the demonstration on radio bonding that we implemented the single stream 40MHz mode of 802.11n PHY using two 20MHz radios. To demonstrate, we set up a wireless link between this FAIR based 40MHz 802.11n and a commodity 40MHz 802.11n radio. We show that this FAIR based implementation can seamlessly communicate with the commodity 802.11n device by transmitting bidirectional bitstreams between them.

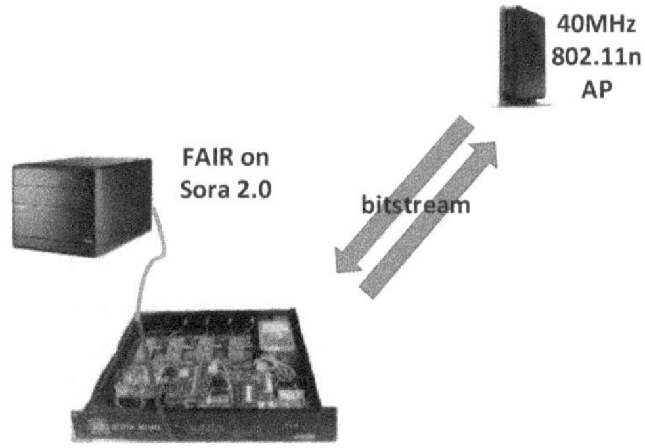


Figure 5: Demonstration scenario

## 4.1 Facility Requirements

Our facility requirements can be listed as follows.

- **Equipment Requirement:** A Sora 2.0 kit is needed which contains a Sora hardware box, a desktop PC running software radio algorithms and accessories. In addition, a 802.11n AP is needed as a wider-band radio and a laptop is needed to control the AP.

- **Space Requirement:** There is no special requirements for the exhibition space. A normal desk or table will work. On the desk or table, a Sora 2.0 box, a desktop PC, an AP and a laptop will be placed.

- **Power and Internet Requirement:** The power plug is needed for Sora 2.0 box, desktop PC, AP and laptop. In the demo, the Wi-Fi connection might be required.

# 5. REFERENCES


[1] Sora: Microsoft research software radio platform for academic use. *http://research.microsoft.com/en-us/projects/sora/academickit.aspx.*

[2] Mobile MIMO: Disruptive Technology For Tablets And Super Phones. *Marvell white paper*, 2011.

[3] *P802.11ac/D2.0, Jan 2012 - IEEE Draft Standard for IT - Telecommunications and Information Exchange Between Systems - LAN/MAN - Specific Requirements - Part 11: Wireless LAN Medium Access Control and Physical Layer Specifications - Amd: Enhancements for Very High Throughput for operation in bands below 6GHz.* IEEE Press, 2012.

[4] E. Chai, J. Lee, S.-J. Lee, R. Etkin, and K. G. Shin. Building efficient spectrum-agile devices for dummies. In *Proceedings of the 18th annual international conference on Mobile computing and networking*, Mobicom '12, pages 149–160, New York, NY, USA, 2012. ACM.

[5] R. Draves, J. Padhye, and B. Zill. Routing in multi-radio, multi-hop wireless mesh networks. In *Proceedings of the 10th annual international conference on Mobile computing and networking*, MobiCom '04, pages 114–128, New York, NY, USA, 2004. ACM.

[6] K. Tan, H. Shen, J. Zhang, and Y. Zhang. Enable flexible spectrum access with spectrum virtualization. In *Dynamic Spectrum Access Networks (DYSPAN), 2012 IEEE International Symposium on*, pages 47–58, 2012.

# Demo: OverDrive - an Overlay-based Geocast Service for Smart Traffic Applications

Martin Florian, Simeon Andreev, Ingmar Baumgart
Institute of Telematics
Karlsruhe Institute of Technology (KIT)
76131 Karlsruhe, Germany
florian@kit.edu, simeon.andreev@student.kit.edu, baumgart@kit.edu

## ABSTRACT

For smart traffic applications like dynamic route planning, communication between traffic participants is of high importance. Traditional approaches rely on centralized, server-based communication architectures, which raises scalability and privacy concerns. To address these problems, we proposed *OverDrive* [5], an overlay-based geocast service that is applicable in smart traffic scenarios and not prone to the shortcomings of centralized designs. Here, we present an interactive demonstrator of the OverDrive protocol that visualizes OverDrive's neighborhood structures and routing approach in a realistic and highly mobile traffic scenario. Our demonstrator is realized as an extension to the overlay simulation framework *OverSim* [2].

## Categories and Subject Descriptors

C.2.1 [**Network Architecture and Design**]: Distributed networks; C.2.2 [**Network Protocols**]: Routing protocols

## Keywords

Geocast, Overlay networks, Peer-to-peer

## 1. INTRODUCTION

The increasing availability of Internet access in vehicles offers a variety of new opportunities to assist road users. Examples for such *smart traffic* applications, which leverage communication capabilities, are *dynamic route planning* (e.g., *Waze*[1]) or the *localization and reservation of charging stations* for electric vehicles. Current solutions mainly follow a centralized, server-based approach for communication, which has several inherent drawbacks:

- Lack of privacy, as all communication and service provision is handled by the service provider. Even given approaches for increasing the privacy in centralized setups, providers might not be motivated to implement them.
- Questionable scalability: With over 50 million vehicles in Germany alone, centralized solutions might quickly lead to performance bottlenecks.
- Inhibited innovation potential and service quality, as successful services are unlikely to share their user base with competitors. In this way, service models that depend on a large user base are difficult to deploy and cannot develop their full potential.

Decentralized overlay networks providing *geocast* services [5, 4, 6] are a recent development with a lot of potential for resolving these drawbacks. Roughly, the idea is the creation of a logical *overlay network* on top of a cellular communication network based on the *Internet Protocol (IP)*. In this overlay network nodes propagate their location to other participating nodes and use this information for choosing overlay neighbors and forwarding messages. With *OverDrive* [5], this approach was specifically adapted to smart traffic scenarios, introducing mechanisms for dealing with high degrees of node mobility.

In the following, we present a demonstration of the applicability of OverDrive in realistic traffic scenarios with high degrees of mobility. Since a demonstration with real vehicles would be unfeasible, we simulate the mobility and communication behavior of participating nodes using the overlay simulation framework *OverSim* [2]. Two of the simulated nodes are tracked and controlled using tablet computers, giving a feel for a possible implementation in real life. Through user interaction, these nodes can initiate the sending of geographic queries to arbitrary points in geographic space. The messages are routed over the overlay and answered by the traffic participants currently residing closest to the target point, all without requiring any form of centralized coordinator. On a separate monitor, the internal functioning of the OverDrive protocol can be observed. Both the neighbor selection logic and the routing mechanism are visualized on top of real street maps.

## 2. THE OVERDRIVE PROTOCOL

As a geocast overlay, *OverDrive* [5] provides an interface for delivering messages to geographic regions, respectively to the nodes within these regions. In the scope of this demo,

[1] `http://www.waze.com/`


*MobiCom'13*, September 30–October 4, Miami, FL, USA.
ACM 978-1-4503-1999-7/13/09.
http://dx.doi.org/10.1145/2500423.2505297.

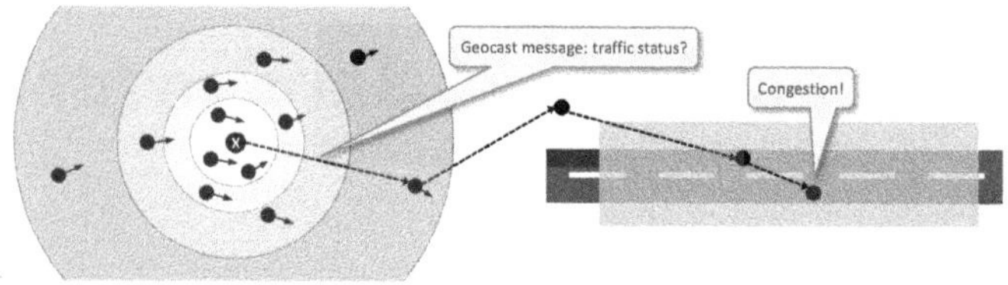


Figure 1: Geographic routing and neighborhood structure in OverDrive.

we will focus on *geographic unicast messages (GUMs)* addressed to points in geographic space and delivered to the one overlay node that is closest to the target point in terms of geographic distance. Technically, OverDrive is based around two concepts:

- An overlay neighborhood structure based on a partitioning of geographic space into concentric rings with exponentially increasing radii. Each node attempts to *satisfy* all of its rings, i.e., for each ring, to form connections with a certain number of nodes in the geographic area covered by that ring.
- A greedy routing mechanism for forwarding messages to nodes in a desired geographic area. Messages are forwarded using connections from the aforementioned overlay neighborhood structure.

The neighborhood structures of individual nodes are maintained using *find neighbor requests* and *location update* messages. Find neighbor requests are sent to random points within unsatisfied rings. The requests are routed like regular GUMs. The final recipient of the request answers with a list of nodes suitable as overlay neighbors to the requester. The speed and movement direction of nodes is also taken into account when considering their suitability as overlay neighbors, as similar movement patterns between overlay neighbors leads to a higher stability in overlay links. Location updates are used for the communication of a node's current location and speed to its overlay neighbors. This is done as rarely as possible, by keeping the information up to date only to the extent that a correct allocation to rings is possible.

An overview of the routing in OverDrive can be seen in Fig. 1. The figure depicts a possible application for the geocast service, namely the sending of a GUM to a road segment lying ahead of the requester. From all of its neighbors, the requester greedily choses the one neighbor that is closest to the destination region in terms of geographic distance. The request is sent via the cellular network and standard IP to this neighbor, who then forwards it according to the same rule, sending it to the one of its overlay neighbors that is closest to the destination. Once the message arrives at a node residing in the target area, that node might, depending on the application, decide to answer the query by directly sending a response (via IP) to the requester.

More details about the mechanisms involved in the overlay-based geocast service OverDrive can be found in our original publication [5].

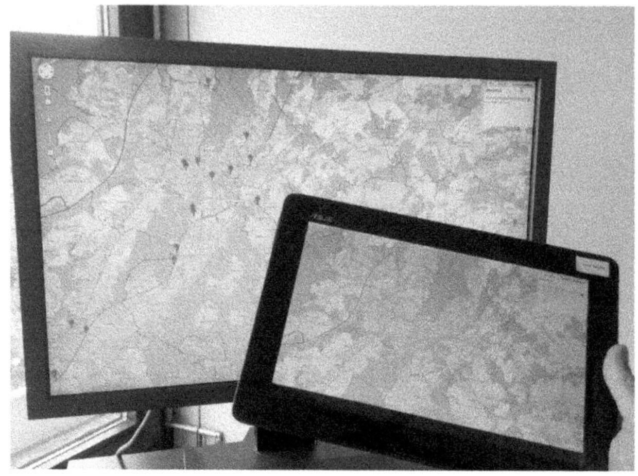

Figure 2: Visualization view and tablet computer showing application view.

## 2.1 Demo Setup and Functionality

Hardware-wise, our demo consists of a notebook computer, two tablet computers and an optional additional computer monitor. Since the demonstration of a geocast protocol using a large number of vehicles moving on real streets is unfeasible, the mobility and communication behavior of around 1000 vehicles is simulated instead on the notebook using and extended version of the overlay simulation framework *OverSim* [2].

The two tablets are used for tracking the movement of two of the simulated vehicles. They provide an *application view* similar to that of popular navigation applications, with a map centered on the current position of the tracked vehicle. The application view allows the initiation of GUMs to arbitrary points on the map. These messages get routed according to OverDrive's routing logic. Once a GUM reaches its final recipient, the location of this recipient is shown on the application view. Clearly, this functionality is only a placeholder for more sophisticated real-life applications like querying about the traffic situation at a given location.

On an additional *global view* on a separate monitor, the internals of the OverDrive protocol can be inspected. This includes the neighborhood structures of nodes, parts of the neighbor selection logic and the path that GUMs initiated from the application views take through the network.

## Internal Realization

In [5], OverSim was extended by a new geographic underlay abstraction that allows the modeling of nodes moving in geographic space that communicate using cellular communication technologies. Communication latencies are influenced by the location of a node. The node positioning information is available to overlay implementations and applications running on the simulated nodes, thus emulating the existence of positioning sensors like GPS receivers. Additionally, a *pathfinding* movement model was implemented for the simulated vehicles. Vehicles choose random start- and endpoints upon joining the simulation and follow a shortest-path route between these points. For the road network underlying the simulation, the highway network of the German state of

**Figure 3: Demonstrator setup and global view.**

Baden-Wuerttemberg, as extracted from *OpenStreetMap*[2] map data, is used.

For the purposes of this demo, and for allowing the better visualization of any type of protocol for which the geographic location of nodes is of importance, additional extensions were made to OverSim. A new *dynamic scheduler* was implemented that allows the explicit setting and on-the-fly changing of the simulation speed. In our demo, we use this functionality for aligning the simulation time with real time and speeding up the simulation when this is more convenient for explaining the inner workings of OverDrive. In addition to the new scheduler, we integrated a lightweight *webserver*[3] into OverSim that allows the visualization of OverDrive nodes and data structures as well as the tunneling back, via a web interface, of commands into the running simulation in OverSim. The actual web-based demo views are based on the *Google Maps JavaScript API*[4] and map material from the OpenStreetMap project. From the views, the running simulation can be influenced directly, e.g., by initiating the sending of GUMs or by changing the simulation speed. A schematic of the demo setup, together with a screenshot of the global view, can be seen in Figure 3.

As mentioned, the additions to OverSim made for this demo can easily be reused for visualizing other protocols and scenarios in which node movement and the geographic location of nodes is of importance. In addition to overlays for smart traffic scenarios, this includes, for example, works in the area of user-centric networking [1].

## 3. CONCLUSION

We present a live demonstration of the overlay-based geocast protocol *OverDrive* applied in a realistic traffic scenario with a high degree of mobility. Since a demonstration using real vehicles moving on real streets is unfeasible, node movement and communication behavior is simulated instead using the overlay simulation framework OverSim. Using application views running on tablet computers and a separate global view on the whole simulation, both a possible real-life application of OverDrive as well as the internal workings of the protocol can be demonstrated. Future work on OverDrive includes the assessment of the privacy characteristics of the approach [3] and the development of privacy-preserving mechanisms specifically tailored for geocast overlays. Additionally, the potential for leveraging existing cellular network infrastructure for minimizing the communication load in the wireless segment will be explored.

## 4. REFERENCES


[1] I. Baumgart and F. Hartmann. Towards secure user-centric networking: Service-oriented and decentralized social networks. In *Proceedings of the 5th IEEE Conference on Self-Adaptive and Self-Organizing Systems Workshops (SASOW)*, pages 3–8, Ann Arbor, Michigan, USA, Oct. 2011.

[2] I. Baumgart, B. Heep, and S. Krause. OverSim: A Flexible Overlay Network Simulation Framework. In *Proceedings of the* $10^{th}$ *IEEE Global Internet Symposium (GI '07) in conjunction with IEEE INFOCOM 2007*, pages 79–84, Anchorage, AK, USA, May 2007.

[3] M. Florian and I. Baumgart. Privacy in Overlay-based Smart Traffic Systems. In *Proceedings of the IEEE Workshop on Privacy and Anonymity for the Digital Economy (PADE 2013)*. IEEE, Oct. 2013.

[4] C. Gross, D. Stingl, B. Richerzhagen, A. Hemel, R. Steinmetz, and D. Hausheer. Geodemlia: A Robust Peer-to-Peer Overlay Supporting Location-Based Search. In *Proceedings of the* $12^{th}$ *IEEE International Conference on Peer-to-Peer Computing (IEEE P2P'12)*, pages 25–36, Tarragona, Spain, Sept. 2012.

[5] B. Heep, M. Florian, J. Volz, and I. Baumgart. OverDrive: An Overlay-based Geocast Service for Smart Traffic Applications. In *Proceedings of the 10th Annual Conference on Wireless On-Demand Network Systems and Services (WONS)*, Mar. 2013.

[6] M. Picone, M. Amoretti, and F. Zanichelli. GeoKad: A P2P Distributed Localization Protocol. In *Proceedings of the* $8^{th}$ *IEEE International Pervasive Computing and Communications Conference (PERCOM 2010) Workshops*, pages 800–803, Mannheim, Germany, Mar. 2010.


[2] `http://www.openstreetmap.org/`
[3] `http://code.google.com/p/mongoose/`
[4] `https://developers.google.com/maps/documentation/javascript/`

# Demo v(t) CSMA: A Link Scheduling Algorithm in Wireless Networks with Improved Delay Characteristics

Ahmed Elbagoury, Moustafa Youssef
Wireless Research Center, Alexandria University
and E-JUST, Egypt
{ahmed.elbagoury, moustafa.youssef}
@ejust.edu.eg

Dongyue Xue, Eylem Ekici
Department of Electrical and Computer
Engineering, the Ohio State University, USA
{xued, ekici}@ece.osu.edu

## ABSTRACT

Efficient scheduling of wireless resources has always been one of the most challenging tasks for wireless networks. To achieve throughput-optimality, traditional back-pressure algorithms calculate a maximal weight matching at each time slot. However, these algorithms need centralized scheduling with high complexity, and thus are not suitable for practical distributed implementations. A class of distributed queue-length-based CSMA algorithms have been proposed that achieve throughput optimality, which we refer to as regular throughput-optimal. These algorithms suffer from two problems: large delays, and temporal starvation. In this demo we demonstrate the operation of the v(t)-regulated CSMA algorithm that mitigates these two problems while provably retaining throughput optimality. The demo allows the participants to see the the performance advantage of v(t)-regulated CSMA over queue-length-based CSMA algorithms and change the different system parameters.

## Categories and Subject Descriptors

C.2.1 [**Computer-Communication Networks**]: Network Architecture and Design—*Distributed networks, Wireless communication*

## General Terms

Algorithms, Experimentation, Performance

## Keywords

Optimal wireless scheduling; CSMA-based scheduling; Delay-based scheduling

## 1. INTRODUCTION

Efficient scheduling of wireless resources has always been one of the most challenging tasks for wireless networks. To achieve throughput-optimality, traditional back-pressure algorithms calculate a maximal weight matching at each time slot. However, these algorithms need centralized scheduling with high complexity, and thus are not suitable for practical distributed implementations. A class of distributed queue-length-based CSMA algorithms have been proposed in literature [2] that achieve throughput optimality (CSMA algorithms). Although these CSMA algorithms have been proved to be throughput-optimal they suffer from the following problems: (1) Temporal starvation, where links usually undergo prolonged periods of inactivity followed by a prolonged period of activity, which leads to bursty service and undesirable jitter performance. (2) Undesirable delay performance. This behavior of regular throughput-optimal CSMA algorithms leads to the scheduling of links with short queues while there exist unscheduled links with longer queues in the network, resulting in long average packet delays.


*MobiCom'13*, September 30–October 4, Miami, FL, USA.
ACM 978-1-4503-1999-7/13/09.
http://dx.doi.org/10.1145/2500423.2505298.

## 2. GOALS

In this demo, we consider a time-slotted wireless network, where wireless nodes are implemented on TelosB motes. Each link is backlogged with a constant arrival rate $\lambda$. We demonstrate v(t)-regulated CSMA [1] which solves both the temporal starvation and undesirable delay performance problems ***while provably retaining throughput optimality***. In v(t)-regulated CSMA, only links with weights above a certain threshold qualify to be scheduled. Since link weights are chosen as increasing functions of packet queue lengths, only links with sufficiently large queue lengths are scheduled.

The demo will present two algorithms v(t)-regulated CSMA and QCSMA, which is a state-of-art scheduling algorithm [2]. The rich user interface will allow the attendees to compare the two algorithms and change the different system parameters.

### 2.1 Basic Idea of v(t)-regulated CSMA

The v(t)-regulated CSMA algorithm establishes a vector of thresholds $(\eta_l)_{l\in L}$, such that, if the packet queue of an active link $l$ has a link weight below threshold $\eta_l$, the active link $l$ relinquishes the wireless resource and becomes idle. Since link weights are chosen as increasing functions of packet queue lengths, only links with sufficiently large queue lengths are scheduled [1]. In comparison, under regular throughput-optimal CSMA algorithms, when a link occupies the channel, even if it has few packets (or even no packets) in its queue, it is highly likely that this link will remain scheduled for a considerably long period of time [2]. By always scheduling links with sufficiently large queue lengths, the v(t)-regulated CSMA algorithm potentially results in a reduction of packet delays in these scheduled queues, which outweighs the increase in delay of the packets in the other unscheduled queues (which have fewer packets). In addition, under the proposed algorithm, the switch between schedules becomes more frequent than under regular throughput-optimal CSMA algorithms, mitigating the temporal starvation problem.

The v(t)-regulated CSMA algorithm starts by choosing a set of non-conflicting links $x(t)$. For any link $l \in x(t)$, if its neighboring links in the interference set $N_l$ are not scheduled in the previous time slot, or do not have a link weight above the threshold $\eta$, then link $l$ is scheduled for service ($\mu_l(t) = 1$) with a link activation probability of

$$p_l \triangleq \frac{e^{w_l(t)}}{1+e^{w_l(t)}}$$

Where $w_l(t)$ is the link weight chosen as an increasing function of queue length $Q_l(t)$. Therefore, the v(t)-regulated CSMA algorithm ensures that only links with sufficiently large queues (such that the corresponding link weights $w_l(t)$ are larger than the thresholds ) can be scheduled.

## 2.2 Implementation

Figure 2 shows the the hardware testbed setup of the demo. Five TelosB motes are connected to one laptop through a USB hub. The demo implements a time-slotted wireless network, where all nodes are within the communication range of each other, leading to a 10-link topology shown in Figure 3. The interference model employed is the one-hop interference model.

The system works as follows: On each mote, each of the two algorithms (v(t)-regulated CSMA and Q-CSMA) alternately runs for a a time slot then the other algorithm runs. This makes the two algorithms experience almost the same channel conditions.

The application running on the laptop collects the information from all the motes at the end of each time slot. After each cycle, i.e. running one slot for each algorithm, the application calculates the different statistics for both algorithms and updates on the GUI. This is performed in parallel while performing the next cycles on the physical motes.

The application also shows all the control messages sent from both algorithms and their internal state (Figure 1(a)). Each node is represented by a circle that is colored according to the node state (sent RTS, sent CTS, scheduled or not scheduled) during each time slot. The program also allows the user to change different system parameters including the packets arrival rate and the of value of $\eta$ used by v(t)-regulated CSMA.

The demo has two modes of operation: (a) Automatic mode: where the cycles are advanced automatically with a speed controlled using a slider. The user can pause the demo at any time and (b) Manual mode: where the user can single step the demo to see specific events.

# 3. DEMO EQUIPMENT

The demo uses the following equipment:

- Five TelosB motes.
- USB cables used to connect the motes to the laptop.
- One laptop as an application server.
- Standard power supply for the equipment above.

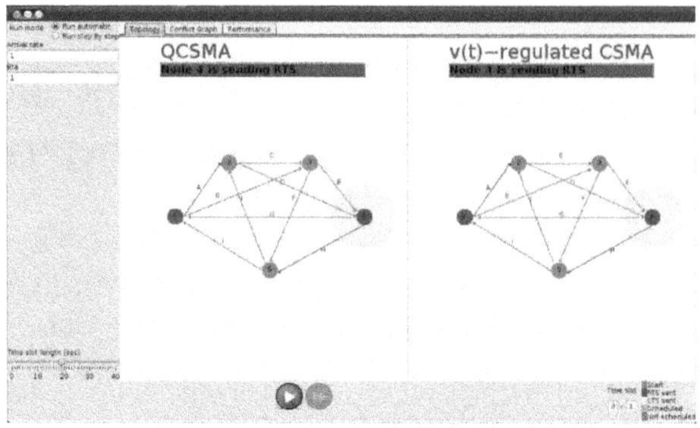


(a) Network topology.

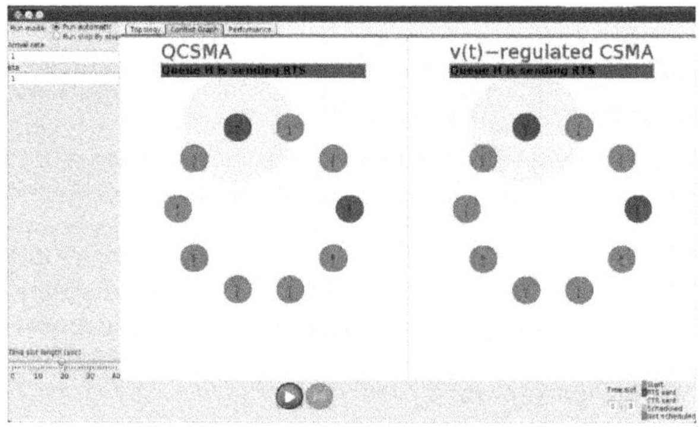


(b) Conflict graph.

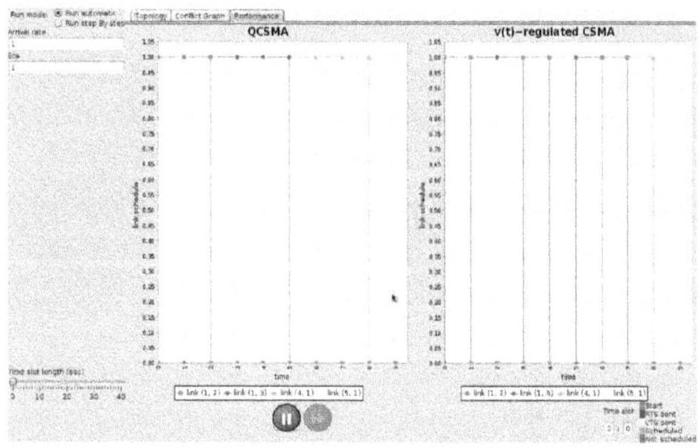


(c) Performance metrics.

**Figure 1: The applications GUI.**

# 4. SPACE NEEDED

The demo requires minimum space for spreading the trusted and un-trusted sensors. Typical required space is 6×6 feet.

# 5. SETUP TIME

The system setup requires less than 30 minutes to connect the components.

# 6. DEMO VIDEO

A video showing the system in action and its characteristics can be found at:
`http://youtu.be/fetuUs_pCpY`.

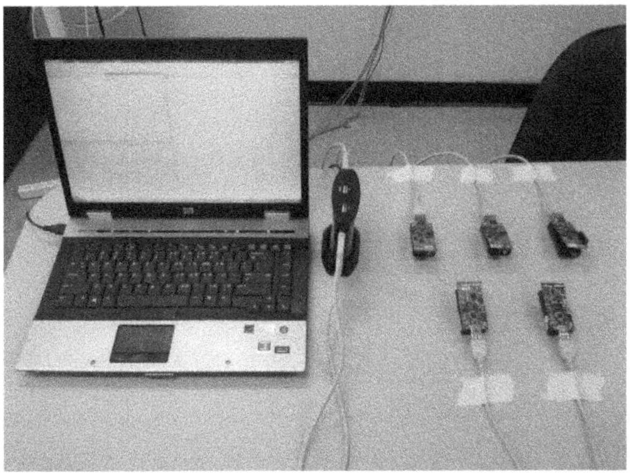

**Figure 2: Hardware testbed setup.**

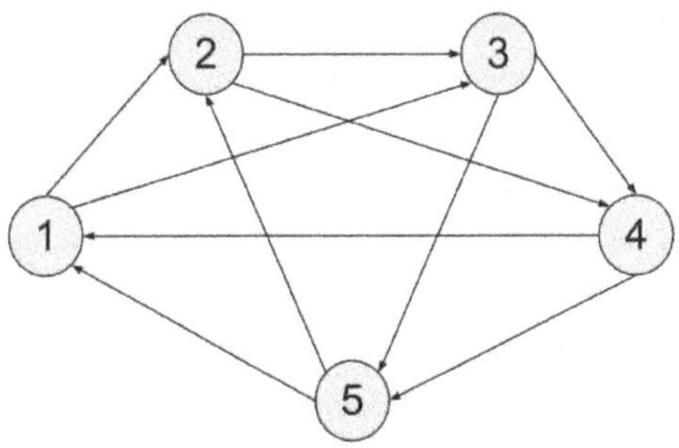


**Figure 3: Network topology for implementation.**

# 7. CONCLUSIONS

This demo allows the attendees to experience with wireless scheduling algorithms showing how to achieve better delay characteristics on actual motes. Attendees will have the opportunity to change the different system parameters and see their effect in real times.

# 8. REFERENCES


[1] Xue Dongyue and Ekici Eylem. On reducing delay and temporal starvation of queue-length-based CSMA algorithms. In *Communication, Control, and Computing (Allerton), 50th Annual Allerton Conference*, pages 754–761. IEEE, 2012.

[2] R. Srikant Jian Ni, Bo Tan. Q-CSMA: queue-length based CSMA/CA algorithms for achieving maximum throughput and low delay in wireless networks. In *INFOCOM'10 proceedings of the 29th conference on Information Communications*, pages 271–275. ACM, 2010.

# Demo: Mobile Network Performance Evaluation Using The Radio Frequency Network Channel Emulation Simulation Tool(RFnest™)

Justin Yackoski, Babak Azimi-Sadjadi, Ali Namazi,
Alexey Bogaevskiy, Jason H. Li, Yalin Sagduyu, and Renato Levy
jyackoski, babak, anamazi, abogaevskiy, jli, ysagduyu, rlevy@i-a-i.com
Intelligent Automation, Inc., Rockville, MD, USA

## ABSTRACT

In this demonstration, we present new capabilities of Intelligent Automation Inc. (IAI) Radio Frequency Network Emulation Simulation Tool (RFnest™) [1][1]. RFnest™is a Field Programmable Gate Array (FPGA) based network channel emulator that allows all of the channels of a full network of radio nodes to be emulated in real time, with all communication nodes experiencing a realistic channel impulse response. This allows RFnest™to be used for protocol testing, replaying field tests, and model validation. RFnest™has a modular design with three main capabilities: 1) FPGA based emulation hardware with RF front ends that allows nodes with real radios to send their RF signal over an emulated channel without any modification to the radio, 2) modeling of time-varying channel impulse responses within the emulation hardware, with channel properties based on mobility defined with a scripted or interactive Graphic User Interface (GUI) environment, and 3) integration with network emulators and monitoring functionality that allows the user to instantiate, manage, and monitor real and virtual network nodes within the scenario. In the new version of RFnest™we now support:

- Frequency programmability: The new RFnest™allows users to change the center frequency through software from 800 Mhz to 2.7GHz.
- Increased bandwidth: RFnest™supports a bandwidth of 60 MHz.
- Higher fidelity channel modeling: Through software and hardware updates RFnest™support wireless channels with up to 20 taps and a wide range of Doppler frequencies.
- MIMO: RFnest™now supports different combination of MIMO channel between transmitters and receivers.

We will demonstrate the capabilities of RFnest™with scenarios, including multi-hop bulk data transfer in mixed real virtual network, bulk data transmission at 900MHz and video transfer between two real nodes.

[1] *www.i − a − i.com/rfnest*


*MobiCom'13*, September 30–October 4, 2013, Miami, FL, USA.

http://dx.doi.org/10.1145/2500423.2505299 .

## Categories and Subject Descriptors

B. Hardware
B.4 INPUT/OUTPUT AND DATA COMMUNICATIONS
B.4.4 Performance Analysis and Design Aids**
Subjects: Simulation**

## Keywords

Network, Emulation Simulation, FPGA, Radio Frequency

## 1. INTRODUCTION

Wireless network evaluation is mainly done either through software simulation such as ns-2/3, Opnet and Qualnet or hardware testbeds such as ORBIT in WINLAB. Both of these approaches lack fidelity needed for accurate and realistic evaluation of a network. Software simulations usually use simplistic physical layer modeling that ignores effects such as nonlinearity, filtering, and inter modulation that are caused by hardware. On the other hand testbeds are not repeatable and controllable and cannot emulate a representative geometry of a specific scenario.

The goal of RFnest™is to provide a repeatable and controlable propagation environment for a network of wireless nodes (currently 12 nodes and in near future up to 96 nodes) so that radios with real MAC, Network, and Transport protocols communicate with each other in a dynamic RF propagation environment. In short RFnest™provides:

- network evaluation in a **controlled, repeatable, and realistic mobility model environment** with the **same radios used in the field.**
- a **hybrid** software/hardware network emulator to provide **scalability** as well as **high fidelity**.
- **replaying of field tests** with all their complexity in a lab environment.
- **model validation** by creating identical scenarios for real radios and radio models.

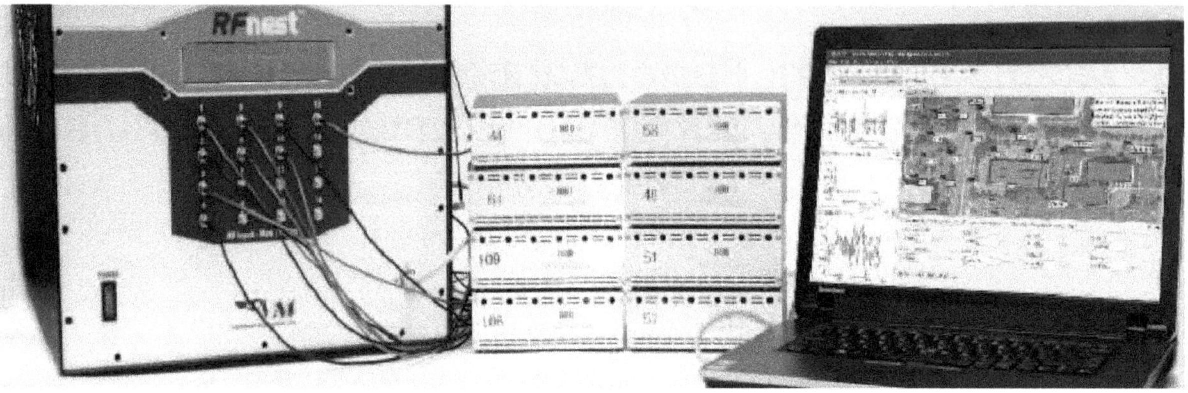

Figure 1: RFnest$^{TM}$setup.

## 2. HARDWARE

Several radios can be hooked up to RFnest$^{TM}$and the channel between all of them (full mesh) is emulated by RFnest$^{TM}$. Essentially, RFnest$^{TM}$is a bank of Software Defined Radios (SDRs) that are all connected to a central powerful processing unit (Virtex7 FPGA). The SDRs interface with the radios under test, and the central FPGA emulates the channel between them. Figure 1 shows the RFnest$^{TM}$hardware and software setup with connected radios.

The 12 node RFnest$^{TM}$currently consists of one main Xilinx Virtex7 FPGA for emulating the wireless channels and 12 RF interface nodes. Each RF interface node includes a Spartan6 FPGA, an analog-to-digital Converter (ADC), a digital-to-analog converter (DAC), and an RF front end. This hardware (HW) interfaces with software components, including the channel models, through a Gigabit Ethernet link.

The current HW has the following specifications:

- RF Band: 800MHz to 2.7GHz
- Instantaneous Bandwidth: 60 Mhz
- Sample Resolution: 16-bit DAC, 12-bit ADC
- Output Dynamic Range: 96 dB (digital)

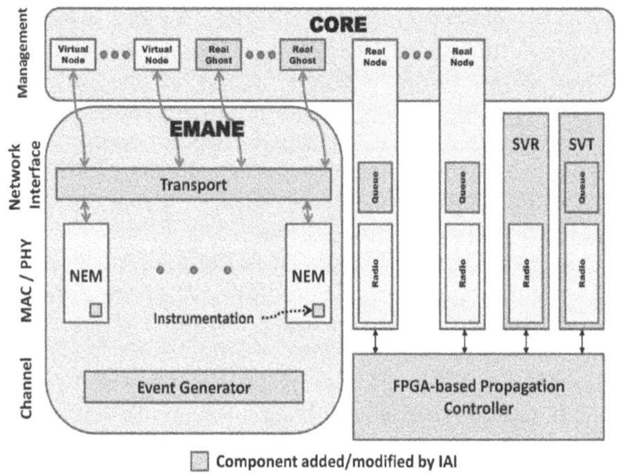


Figure 2: Our EMANE- and CORE-based architecture.

## 3. SOFTWARE

[2]The RFnest$^{TM}$software architecture is shown in Figure 2. In a wireless network, there are essentially two aspects of each node that must be considered. First, the operating system stack, meaning the network layer and above, must exist or be emulated. Second, each node must have either a real wireless radio or a virtual radio via MAC and PHY layer simulation model. Building upon existing methods of creating and connecting these aspects, we have created additional components which allow an integration between the real and virtual radios [1].

CORE (Common Open Research Emulator) [2] is used to manage the scenario being tested, including creating the emulated virtual nodes via Linux network namespaces, configuring EMANE (Extendable Mobile Ad-hoc Network Emulator), allowing the user to move nodes via the GUI, and configuring the routing and other network behaviors on both the real and virtual nodes. CORE uses EMANE's event notification API and PHY/MAC models.

EMANE [3] provides a simulation infrastructure for wireless communication that includes a library of various PHY and MAC models. These models can be either used directly or modified to simulate new protocols. EMANE provides several key features that are heavily used by our emulation architecture. EMANE has an event service API for use by other emulators (such as CORE), mobility generators, terrain data, as well as various PHY, MAC, and other models provided both by EMANE and by third parties. This allows us to easily integrate with existing radio models and other software written for EMANE with little to no changes. For example, we use the EMANE event service to receive node position updates from CORE.

EMANE provides virtual network devices which allow emulated nodes (i.e., those created by CORE) to communicate over what appears to be a normal network device. The virtual network device serves as an entry point for providing packets to and from the PHY and MAC models. We have made significant use of this extendable nature to develop new or modified EMANE components.

[2]Parts of the text in this section are taken from [1]

To allow interaction between real nodes using our emulation hardware and virtual nodes created by CORE and EMANE, we have created an EMANE transport which serves as a bridge between data sent between the EMANE radio simulation models and the Surrogate Virtual Receiver (SVR) / Surrogate Virtual Transmitter (SVT) (see [1] for more details). In EMANE, a transport is responsible for transferring packets between each node's OS stack and the corresponding simulated MAC and PHY layer. By monitoring the MAC addresses specified in packets, our EMANE transport decides whether to keep each packet sent by a virtual node within the "virtual world" (i.e., within EMANE's models) or to give the packet to the SVT. Similarly, packets received from the SVR which are addressed to a virtual node are injected into the EMANE simulation.

# 4. DEMONSTRATION

In this demonstration we will connect several radios with different frequency band and bandwidth in a dynamic propagation environment and we show the performance of the wireless network as a function of time. The overall demonstration scenario is shown in Figure 3.

**Figure 3: Emulated scenarios using RFnest$^{TM}$;multiple nodes and scenarios are demonstrated at the same time**

The details of the demonstration are described below:

- **Multi-hop Bulk Data Transfer in Mixed Real Virtual Network at 2.4 GHz:** In this scenario, two real radios are sending bulk data (e.g. a file transfer) and we want to observe the behavior of the network at a larger scale. To do this, we add a number of virtual nodes (created using CORE and EMANE) to the network. These virtual nodes communicate with the real nodes via surrogate radios controlled by RFnest$^{TM}$. The virtual nodes become part of the routing topology and actually carry the packets. As the real node moves throughout these virtual nodes, the routing protocol adjusts appropriately. In this scenario neither the real nor the virtual nodes are aware if they or their neighbors are real or virtual. This scenario allows us to see that the behavior of particular routing protocols which can be unstable when many routing options are present.
- **Bulk Data Transmission at 900MHz:** In this scenario, two radios are configured to operate at 900MHz frequency and the are sending bulk data. As one of the nodes moves back and forth, we can observe the changes in throughput shown on the graph labeled "900".
- **Video Transfer Between Two Real Nodes at 2.4 GHz:** In this scenario, live bi-directional video is being sent between the two blue nodes (Video1 and Video2). The real-time throughput is shown on the left side of the figure, the routing paths being attempted are shown by blue arrows, and the signal strength is indicated by the straight lines between nodes. We demonstrate how an aircraft flying over a mountainous terrain communicates a video capture of the environment to a ground station. The wireless multipath channel is estimated using IAI's ray-tracing based channel-modeling software that accounts for the effects of terrain and antenna patterns of aircraft and ground station. The multipath channel coefficients are then communicated to RFnest$^{TM}$that emulates the channel so that real radios operating within 2.4 GHz representing the aircraft transmitter and ground station receiver communicate over the estimated wireless multipath channel. The effects of the channel, such as blockage of line of sight, are captured in the quality of the video feed received by the ground station receiver.

# 5. REFERENCES


[1] J. Yackoski, B. Azimi-Sadjadi, A. Namazi, J. H. Li, Y. Sagduyu, and R. Levy, "RF-NEST: Radio Frequency Network Emulator Simulator Tool," MILCOM 2011.

[2] J. Ahrenholz, C. Danilov, T.R. Henderson, and J.H. Kim, "CORE: A real-time network emulator", Proc. of IEEE MILCOM, Nov. 2008, pp 1-7, San Diego, CA USA.

[3] , Naval Research Laboratory, "Extendable Mobile Ad-hoc Network Emulator (EMANE)", url = "http://cs.itd.nrl.navy.mil/work/emane/.

# Demo: Decoding IEEE 802.11a/g/p OFDM in Software using GNU Radio

Bastian Bloessl[*], Michele Segata[*†], Christoph Sommer[*] and Falko Dressler[*]

[*]Institute of Computer Science, University of Innsbruck, Austria
[†]Dept. of Information Engineering and Computer Science, University of Trento, Italy

{bloessl,segata,sommer,dressler}@ccs-labs.org

## ABSTRACT

We just released an Open Source receiver that is able to decode IEEE 802.11a/g/p Orthogonal Frequency Division Multiplexing (OFDM) frames in software. This is the first Software Defined Radio (SDR) based OFDM receiver supporting channel bandwidths up to 20 MHz that is not relying on additional FPGA code. Our receiver comprises all layers from the physical up to decoding the MAC packet and extracting the payload of IEEE 802.11a/g/p frames. In our demonstration, visitors can interact live with the receiver while it is decoding frames that are sent over the air. The impact of moving the antennas and changing the settings are displayed live in time and frequency domain. Furthermore, the decoded frames are fed to Wireshark where the WiFi traffic can be further investigated. It is possible to access and visualize the data in every decoding step from the raw samples, the autocorrelation used for frame detection, the subcarriers before and after equalization, up to the decoded MAC packets. The receiver is completely Open Source and represents one step towards experimental research with SDRs.

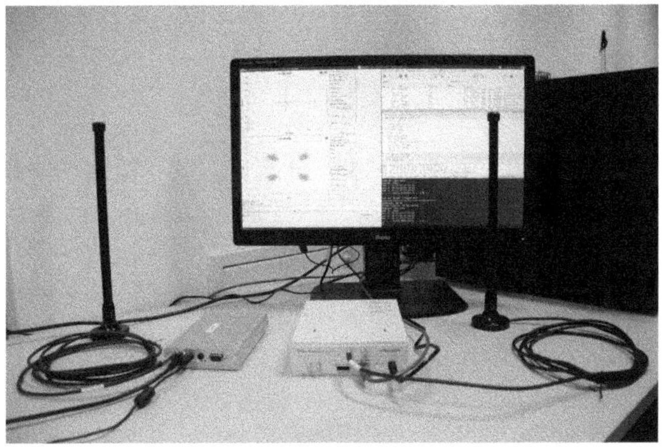

**Figure 1: Overview of the demonstration setup. While the GNU Radio receiver is decoding WiFi frames, visitors can interact with the setup by grabbing one of the dipole antennas, move them around, and watch the impact live on the graphical outputs.**

## Categories and Subject Descriptors

C.2.1 [**Computer-Communication Networks**]: Network Architecture and Design—*Wireless communication*; C.4.3 [**Performance of Systems**]: Measurement Techniques

## Keywords

IEEE 802.11a/g/p, OFDM, Receiver

## 1. INTRODUCTION

Given the wide range of applications from IEEE 802.11 a/g/p to WiMAX and to LTE Advanced, Orthogonal Frequency Division Multiplexing (OFDM) gained a lot of attention in the wireless networking community both in industry and in academia. There are many new algorithms that have been proposed for frame detection, frequency offset correction, and channel estimation [2, 4, 7]. Furthermore, OFDM and its applicability in different scenarios and channels has been studied analytically and by means of simulation [4, 5].

Yet, the possibility to conduct experimental research in this field is extremely limited. In particular, we'd like to mention the custom radio prototypes [9], which are usually based on Field-Programmable Gate Arrays (FPGAs), i.e., rather complex and inflexible.

Even though this approach offers high performance, investigations typically have to focus on small parts of the receive chain, as an implementation of the complete transceiver, together with the design of the hardware platform, incurs substantial effort. Furthermore, the code for custom devices can neither be reused nor verified, nor can results be reproduced by other researchers.

Matt Ettus, the developer of the *USRP* series of devices, supplies an initial GNU Radio OFDM receiver using maximum likelihood estimation [8] and pseudonoise (PN) sequence correlation [6] that did, however, not provide the required bandwidth for WiFi.

To overcome current limitations, we developed a complete OFDM receiver based on GNU Radio and fitted for operation on an *Ettus USRP N210*. This is, to the best of our knowledge, the first prototype of such a Software Defined Ra-


*MobiCom'13*, September 30–October 4, Miami, FL, USA.
ACM 978-1-4503-1999-7/13/09.
http://dx.doi.org/10.1145/2500423.2505300.

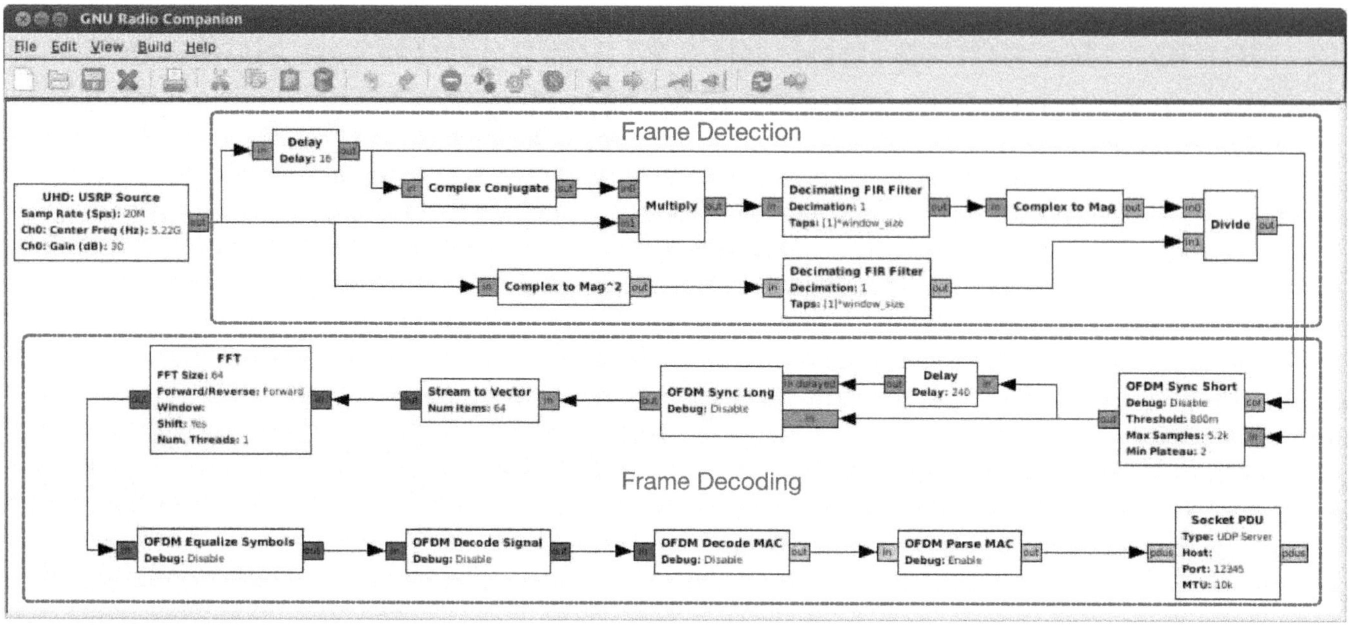


**Figure 2: Overview of the blocks comprising the OFDM receiver in GNU Radio Companion.**

dio (SDR) based OFDM receiver supporting all typical WiFi variants and channel bandwidths up to 20 MHz. Its counter part, the corresponding GNU Radio-based WiFi transmitter, is also already published by Fuxjäger et al. [3].

## 2. OUR GNU Radio OFDM RECEIVER

As illustrated in Figure 2 the structure of the OFDM receiver is completely exposed to GNU Radio Companion, a graphical tool to setup and configure signal processing flow graphs. The receiver is divided into two functional parts: The first part, depicted in the top half, is responsible for frame detection. The second part, shown in the bottom half, is responsible for decoding the frame. More technical details on the implementation can be found in [1].

We already performed several interoperability tests and verified that the receiver is compatible with off-the-shelf hardware. Table 1 summarizes the results from interoperability tests using different IEEE 802.11a/g/p transmitters conducted in our testbed.

The objective of this demo is to highlight the very straightforward use of the OFDM receiver. In our opinion, the usage is eased by the modularity of the receiver where each of the functional blocks depicted in Figure 2 is responsible for a very specific task. Furthermore, this modularity also offers the possibility to compare different receive algorithm by reimplementing one block with an alternate algorithm and compare the alternative implementations directly by means of simulations with captured input traces or with over the air measurements. Finally, given the possibility to reconfigure the receiver live while it is running, one can also get a feeling for how different parameters impact the performance of the receiver.

| NIC | Standard | Bandwidth | |
|---|---|---|---|
| MacBook Pro | 802.11a/g | 20 MHz | ✓ |
| Intel Ultimate-N 6300 | 802.11a/g | 20 MHz | ✓ |
| Air Live X.USB | 802.11a/g | 20 MHz | ✓ |
| Cohda MK2 | 802.11p | 10 MHz | ✓ |
| Unex DCMA-86P2 | 802.11a/p | 10/20 MHz | ✓ |

**Table 1: Selection of WiFi and IEEE 802.11p devices we verified to be interoperable with the receiver.**

## 3. DEMONSTRATION SETUP

The setup of the demo is depicted in Figure 1. We can see an *Ettus USRP N210* connected to a desktop PC. The second device, which acts as sender, uses an off-the-shelf IEEE 802.11a/g/p Unex DCMA-86P2 WiFi card.

In order to demonstrate the capabilities of the OFDM receiver, we extended it with various graphical outputs that visualize every step of the decoding process. More precisely, we plot the raw complex base band signal as acquired from the SDR in time domain on the top right position in Figure 3. This plot shows the raw input data the receiver is on which the receiver is operating on.

Furthermore, we can visualize the autocorrelation of the incoming sample stream. The autocorrelation of the input samples is relevant for the receiver since it is used to recognize the repeating pattern of the short preamble, which is used by the frame detection algorithm to trigger subsequent decoding operations. This visual output is particularly helpful to find a robust configuration that offers a good trade-off between missing frames and triggering the decoding process just by chance. Even though papers propose certain numeric thresholds for these algorithms we found this indeed helpful, since according to our experience with real hardware and its imperfections these thresholds do not always work too well.

Moving into the frequency domain, we show a constellation plot of the subcarrier symbols after compensation of channel induced phase rotations. A typical screenshot of such a constellation plot is depicted in Figure 3. The QPSK-modulated symbols and the deviation from the ideal positions can clearly be seen. This plot supports an intuitive estimation of receiver performance, channel quality, and bit error rates.

While the constellation plot shows that we manage to equalize the subcarriers reasonably well, we still did not show that we manage to decode the actual payload. For that reason, we output all frames in the PCAP format, which is the de-facto standard for packet capturing and is understood by all network monitoring software. Following Linux, we prepend each frame with a Radiotap header[1], which allows us to annotate frames with further metadata like encoding, bandwidth, channel, and so on. With the help of a Linux pipe, we connect Wireshark directly to the receiver and are able to monitor the traffic live.

In addition to that, we implemented the required blocks to connect the receiver with the Linux network stack. This is done by removing the WiFi MAC header and replacing it with an Ethernet header and feeding the decoded packet into a TUN/TAP interface.[2] Note that one could also capture packets from that virtual interface, but without a Radiotap header we would lose the possibility to annotate frames with metadata.

On the sending side we use a MiniPC built using standard PC components, which is additionally equipped with a Unex DCMA-86P2 WiFi card. This card is based on an Atheros chipset and with minor modifications of the Linux kernel (i.e., removing regulatory domain restrictions), we can use this card to send IEEE 802.11a/g/p frames. More precisely, we can set the channel bandwidth to 10 MHz and 20 MHz and also utilize frequencies at around 5.9 GHz that are dedicated to Intelligent Transportation System (ITS). By setting up static routing and ARP entries on the MiniPC, we can establish a unidirectional communication between the WiFi card and the SDR.

In order to make the demo more interactive for visitors, we connect two large dipole antennas with a pretty long cable to both devices. This way, visitors can grab the antennas and move them around, while watching the impact on the receiver. The constellation plot of the symbols on the different carriers shows very clearly the impact of different antenna placements.

# 4. REQUIREMENTS FOR THE DEMO

Our equipment consists of a MiniPC from which we send the WiFi frames and a desktop PC where the OFDM receiver is running on. In order to provide the visitors a clear presentation of the live graphs, we connect a screen or a small projector to the desktop PC. In total, we need 4 power plugs (2 PCs, SDR and screen). We do not require much space, a normal table is large enough for the setup. It would be nice if we could pin a poster beside the booth, as this aids to give more detailed explanations of the receiver structure.

Accompanying this demo paper, we made a video that shows the demonstration setup and in particular how visitors can interact. The video, a list of related publications, and all software can be found on our website.[3]

[1] `http://www.radiotap.org`
[2] `https://www.kernel.org/doc/Documentation/networking/tuntap.txt`
[3] `http://www.ccs-labs.org/software/gr-ieee802-11/`

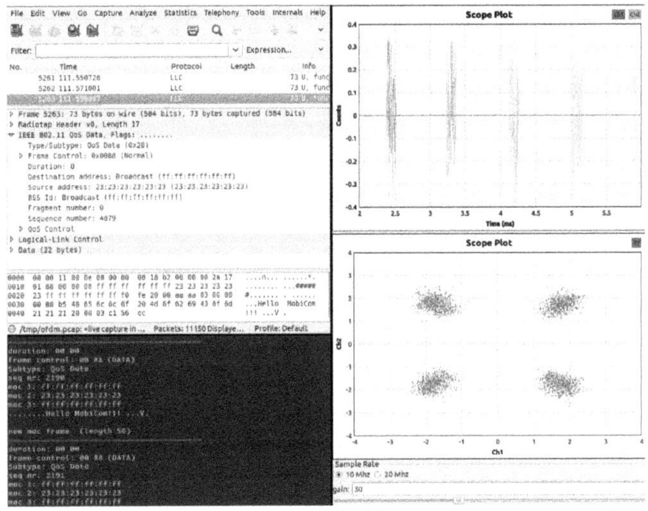


**Figure 3: Screenshot of the live visualizations while the receiver is running: Packets in Wireshark (left), time domain signal (right), and constellation plot of (here) QPSK-modulated symbols (bottom right).**

# 5. REFERENCES

[1] B. Bloessl, M. Segata, C. Sommer, and F. Dressler. An IEEE 802.11a/g/p OFDM Receiver for GNU Radio. In *ACM SIGCOMM 2013, 2nd ACM SIGCOMM Workshop of Software Radio Implementation Forum (SRIF 2013)*, Hong Kong, China, August 2013. ACM.

[2] L. Chia-Horng. On the design of OFDM signal detection algorithms for hardware implementation. In *IEEE GLOBECOM 2003*, pages 596–599, San Francisco, CA, December 2003. IEEE.

[3] P. Fuxjäger, A. Costantini, D. Valerio, P. Castiglione, G. Zacheo, T. Zemen, and F. Ricciato. IEEE 802.11p Transmission Using GNURadio. In *6th Karlsruhe Workshop on Software Radios (WSR)*, pages 1–4, Karlsruhe, Germany, March 2010.

[4] T. Hrycak, S. Das, G. Matz, and H. G. Feichtinger. Practical Estimation of Rapidly Varying Channels for OFDM Systems. *IEEE Transactions on Communications*, 59(11):3040–3048, November 2011.

[5] M. Morelli and U. Mengali. A Comparison of Pilot-Aided Channel Estimation Methods for OFDM Systems. *IEEE Transactions on Signal Processing*, 49(12):3065–3073, December 2001.

[6] T. Schmidl and D. Cox. Robust frequency and timing synchronization for OFDM. *IEEE Transactions on Communications*, 45(12):1613–1621, 1997.

[7] E. Sourour, H. El-Ghoroury, and D. McNeill. Frequency Offset Estimation and Correction in the IEEE 802.11a WLAN. In *IEEE VTC2004-Fall*, pages 4923–4927, Los Angeles, CA, September 2004. IEEE.

[8] J.-J. van de Beek, M. Sandell, and P. O. Borjesson. ML estimation of time and frequency offset in OFDM systems. *IEEE Transactions on Signal Processing*, 45(7):1800–1805, 1997.

[9] A. van Zelst and T. C. W. Schenk. Implementation of a MIMO OFDM-based wireless LAN system. *IEEE Transactions on Signal Processing*, 52(2):483–494, Feburary 2004.

# ArgosV2: A Flexible Many-Antenna Research Platform

Clayton Shepard, Hang Yu, and Lin Zhong
Department of Electrical and Computer Engineering
Rice University, Houston, TX
{cws, hang.yu, lzhong}@rice.edu

## ABSTRACT

Many-antenna base stations are a rapidly growing field in wireless research. A plethora of new theoretical techniques have been recently proposed for many-antenna base stations and networks. However, without experimental validation, it is difficult or impossible to predict the practicality and performance of these techniques in real hardware, under complex, rapidly varying, real-world conditions. Indeed, there is a significant demand for a flexible many-antenna research platform which supports rapid prototyping and validation of new massive-MIMO techniques.

Leveraging our experience building *Argos*, a 64-antenna base station prototype, we have designed and built *ArgosV2*, a compact, powerful, and scalable many-antenna research platform based on WARP. In addition to the physical hardware and mechanical design, we are developing a software framework, *ArgosLab*, which will provide synchronization and channel estimation, greatly reducing the development effort for a wide range of massive-MIMO techniques. ArgosV2 is intended to provide ultimate scalability and programmability for experimental massive-MIMO research. The modular architecture and real-time capability of ArgosV2 can support up to 100s of base station antennas and 10s of users with streaming applications. For our demonstration, we will unveil a 96-antenna base station which supports real-time streaming applications to 32 users simultaneously.

## Categories and Subject Descriptors

C.2.1 [**Computer-Communication Networks**]: Network Architecture and Design—*Wireless Communication*

**Keywords:** Many-Antenna, Massive-MIMO, Large-scale Antenna Systems (LSAS), MU-MIMO, Distributed-MIMO, Network-MIMO, Beamforming, Conjugate, Zero-forcing

## 1. INTRODUCTION

Due to the popularization of mobile devices such as smartphones, tablets and data-hungry applications, mobile data traffic is growing exponentially. One approach to satiate this increasing demand for wireless capacity is large-scale MU-MIMO, which is commonly referred to as *massive-MIMO*. Massive-MIMO theory predicts that with $M$ antennas on the base station, or in the network, up to $M$ users can be served simultaneously, leading to a linear increase in network capacity. Not surprisingly, many wireless researchers are envisioning the next generation base stations to have hundreds, or even thousands, of antennas which realize the benefits of massive-MIMO [1]. Over the past few years, there has been a plethora of new massive-MIMO techniques proposed, such as [2, 3, 4, 5], and many more.

However, to date, most research regarding massive-MIMO has been restricted to theory that is based on analytical or simulation results. The lack of an experimental platform has prohibited the validation of theoretical results and understanding of the impact of real-world factors on the performance of massive-MIMO. Our previous work [6] demonstrated that a properly designed architecture can realistically scale up to 100s of antennas serving 10s of users simultaneously; however, our initial prototype used antiquated hardware which was bulky, and not flexible and powerful enough to enable real-time wideband MU-MIMO applications. We believe it is critical for the area of massive-MIMO to have an experimental research platform that allows rapid prototyping of new massive-MIMO techniques for real-time streaming applications. Leveraging our experience from the initial Argos prototype, we have refined the Argos design to be more powerful, compact, robust, and scalable; this substantial revision we refer to as *ArgosV2*. Unlike Argos, ArgosV2 supports rapid prototyping of real-time many-antenna applications with extreme scalability, programmability, portability, and performance. We draw the parallel from ArgosV2 to similar platforms used for rapid implementation and testing of small-scale wireless techniques, such as WARP and Sora [7, 8], which have proven to be invaluable for novel research in PHY and MAC designs.

Building a many-antenna base station to function as a multi-purpose research platform is non-trivial. On one hand, ArgosV2 must have *real-time* capability, i.e., it must support streaming applications. Fast variation of real-world wireless channels, however, is a serious challenge for any MU-MIMO base station, and is the fundamental limiting factor for the performance of massive-MIMO. This is because the many-antenna base station must have accurate channel state information (CSI) to calculate the precoding vectors for each user. The presence of channel fading requires the base station to continuously collect the CSI to each user, within the channel coherence time, which can be as short as 100s of microseconds. As a result, the baseband processing for massive-MIMO must be done rapidly by ArgosV2, so that the base station and users can send downlink and uplink data transmission within the channel coherence time. On the other hand, as a research platform, ArgosV2 must support programmability of various massive-MIMO techniques such as conjugate beamforming, zero-forcing, MMSE, Tomlison-Harashima, etc. Depend-


*MobiCom'13*, September 30–October 4, Miami, FL, USA.
ACM 978-1-4503-1999-7/13/09.
http://cms.acm.org/forms/2013-40395/5168/66/5168_66_1.pdf.

ing on this massive-MIMO algorithm, often substantial portions of the baseband processing have to be done centrally, whereas other parts can be implemented in a distributed fashion for a performance and scalability gain [6]. Not surprisingly, realizing the real-time capability and programmability of ArgosV2 is quite challenging, requiring a careful and flexible design of the base station architecture which enables both centralized and distributed processing in order to accommodate the diverse plethora of emerging massive-MIMO techniques. In addition to the computational and hardware challenges facing a massive-MIMO research platform, we have found that the mechanical and form-factor design are critical components of a flexible, scalable, and usable system. Furthermore, most massive-MIMO techniques share a common requirement of time/frequency synchronization and channel estimation. However, these components are tedious and difficult to implement from scratch, thus we are developing a software framework, *ArgosLab*, to provide these key components out-of-the-box. Finally, to conduct experiments with real-world propagation environments and mobility, we have also developed a battery-powered compact mobile client, *ArgosMobile*.

## 2. ARGOSV2 DESIGN

The ArgosV2 platform design can be separated into three categories: 1) the mechanical design, 2) the hardware design, and 3) the software framework. Additionally, we have created ArgosMobile to facilitate real-world experimentation with massive-MIMO techniques.

### 2.1 Mechanical Design

From our previous experience in building a many-antenna base station, we have found the mechanical design and form-factor of ArgosV2 is critical for usability, reliability, scalability, resiliency, and performance. The basis of ArgosV2's mechanical design is a custom polycarbonate rack, shown in Figure 1. Each rack houses 12 WARPv3 boards on dado-style shelving, for a total of 48 radios. These radios are cabled to 48 panel-mount female SMA connectors spaced a half-wavelength apart at 2.4 GHz; this is the most compact 2D-array design which allows full performance with antennas mounted directly to the rack. The rack was carefully designed to present the SMA connectors on a 9.75 by 29.75 inch face, allowing racks to be stacked next to or on top of each other (using 1/4 inch clips), while maintaining half-wavelength spacing between connectors across racks, both vertically and horizontally. Should different antenna spacing be required, perhaps to test a distributed-MIMO setup or an even more compact array for the 5 GHz band, this configuration enables cables to be easily attached to the panel-mount SMA connectors, allowing antennas to be placed anywhere. For easy-access, troubleshooting, assembly, and field-replacement, the dado-shelves can slide either forward or backward in the rack; all the shelves are held firmly in place by four full-length stops, which can be quickly removed to gain access to all of the WARP modules. This also allows shelves to be easily removed to be placed in remote locations to function as standalone APs, or as part of a distributed antenna system, for maximum flexibility.

We also designed a polycarbonate ArgosHub [6], which uses similar dado-style shelving to house the clock, time-sync, power, and data distribution for up to 32 WARP modules (128 antennas). The hub was designed to be 19.75 inches wide with casters on the bottom, allowing two racks to attach flush to it, creating a single portable base station unit. Moreover, the modular design allows the base station to be easily scaled up with more racks, or split in to multiple small base stations, as well as quickly disassembled and re-assembled for additional portability (such as for placement on inaccessible rooftops). Hubs can be easily daisy-chained or placed in a tree topology to support more radios.

(a) Front side (b) Back side

**Figure 1: The ArgosV2 base station rack accommodates 12 WARP boards with 48 antennas; multiple racks can be easily connected using an ArgosHub to scale up the base station to support hundreds of antennas.**

Polycarbonate was chosen for its good impact resistance, as well as low cost and weight. While polycarbonate has relatively good anti-static properties, compared to acrylic, to ensure full protection against static discharge damage, we coated the racks and hub Lycron anti-static spray. Ventilation holes were strategically placed to promote airflow around the boards, and the racks were thermally tested to verify that the WARP boards do not overheat; we found that under continuous operation the temperatures of all boards stabilized below 50° C, which is well below the maximum operational temperature rating of 85° C.

This carefully planned mechanical design ensures that ArgosV2 is well-suited for diverse research environments, where usability, reliability, scalability, resiliency, and performance are critical.

### 2.2 Hardware Design

ArgosV2 is based on the fundamental Argos system design described in [6]. This hierarchal modular design facilitates both distributed and centralized processing, which are required for massive-MIMO techniques. We leverage the new WARPv3 as the radio module to provide powerful, distributed, real-time processing at the radios. Additionally, most massive-MIMO techniques require tight time and frequency synchronization; we use ArgosHub to provide this synchronization, along with power and data distribution.

For frequency synchronization, ArgosHub utilizes 2 daisy-chained AD9523 clock distribution reference boards, each with a very low noise, accurate CrysTek CVHD-950 VCXO. Time synchronization is implemented using FPGA GPIO

**Figure 2: The autonomous ArgosMobile client is comprised of a 4-antenna WARP board, a battery, and an 802.11n bridge, which enables massive-MIMO experiments in real-world conditions with high mobility.**

over twisted pair cabling. We chose a readily available 1300W server power supply to provide 12V DC power to the WARP modules. Finally, data distribution is achieved using a Netgear GS752TXS 48-port 1 GbE switch with 4 10GbE SFP+ ports, which provides 2 Gbps to each WARP module and up to 40 Gbps to the central controller, which may be comprised of a single server, an FPGA, or even a full compute cluster depending on performance requirements. While it would be advantageous to enable processing in the switch, as described in [6], it is not necessary for most research applications given the high-bandwidth of the switch, and would require an expensive custom design.

The ArgosV2 hardware design leverages off-the-shelf components to provide a powerful and flexible platform that is capable of accommodating the rigorous computational demands of emerging massive-MIMO techniques.

## 2.3 Software Framework

Massive-MIMO techniques share strict requirements for synchronization and CSI collection, and many use common precoders, which are time-consuming and difficult to implement efficiently. As part of our ongoing work to facilitate rapid prototyping and experimentation, we are designing ArgosLab, a software framework which works with ArgosV2 "out-of-the-box" to provide synchronization, reciprocity calibration, and channel estimation, as well as hardware accelerated linear precoding. Our goal is to enable researchers to develop and test massive-MIMO techniques in real-time, and in real-world environments, without having to spend months, or even years, developing the complex hardware and software required to enable such experimentation.

## 2.4 ArgosMobile

A critical component of ArgosV2 is the ArgosMobile, shown in Figure 2, as it enables experimentation in real-world propagation environments. ArgosMobile is an autonomous battery-powered mobile client that uses a WARP board to support up to 4 antennas, enabling client-side MIMO techniques. Additionally, ArgosMobile includes a standard 802.11 dual-band WiFi interface for out-of-band feedback and control; this feature is subtle, but crucial for accelerating development, as it allows testing of specific techniques without requiring a fully-functional network stack. The battery-life in the ArgosMobile shown is approximately 8 hours, though we are working on newer versions which use batteries that are half the size. These new ArgosMobiles will be much smaller, lighter, and weather-resistant, which make them easier to deploy for outdoor and mobile experimentation.

# 3. DEMONSTRATION

We demonstrate our 96-antenna prototype implementation of ArgosV2 transceiving to 4 ArgosMobiles, each with 4 antennas, for a total of 16 simultaneous streams. While the base station supports streaming to many more clients, due to space constraints, as well as hardware availability, it is not practical to demonstrate more simultaneous streams, nor would it be particularly beneficial. Even with 16 clients we require a fairly substantial amount of space (2 or 3 tables, or around 10'x20') as well as a dedicated 20A power outlet for our demonstration.

# 4. CONCLUDING REMARKS

With the plethora of emerging work on massive-MIMO, it is critical for the community to have a research platform which supports rapid prototyping and experimental validation of proposed techniques. In order to fulfill this need, ArgosV2 holistically considers the hardware, software, and mechanical requirements to create a scalable, powerful, portable, and programmable design.

## Acknowledgements

This work was funded in part by NSF grants CRI 0751173, MRI 0923479, NetSE 101283, MRI 1126478 and CNS 1218700. Clayton Shepard was supported by an NDSEG fellowship. We thank Ashutosh Sabharwal, Edward Knightly, Patrick Murphy, Chris Hunter, and Nathan Zuege for their input, support, and help.

# 5. REFERENCES

[1] E. G. Larsson, F. Tufvesson, O. Edfors, and T. L. Marzetta, "Massive MIMO for Next Generation Wireless Systems," *arXiv:1304.6690 [cs.IT]*, 2013.

[2] T. Marzetta, "Noncooperative cellular wireless with unlimited numbers of base station antennas," *IEEE Trans. on Wireless Communications*, 2010.

[3] A. Ashikhmin. and T. Marzetta, "Pilot Contamination Precoding in Multi-cell Large Scale Antenna Systems," in *IEEE Int. Symp. Information Theory (ISIT)*, 2012.

[4] S. Mohammed and E. Larsson, "Per-Antenna Constant Envelope Precoding for Large Multi-User MIMO Systems," *IEEE Trans. Communications*, 2013.

[5] C. Shepard, N. Anand, and L. Zhong, "Practical Performance of MU-MIMO Precoding in Many-antenna Base Stations," in *Proc. ACM CellNet Workshop*, 2013.

[6] C. Shepard, H. Yu, N. Anand, E. Li, T. Marzetta, R. Yang, and L. Zhong, "Argos: Practical many-antenna base stations," in *Proc. ACM MobiCom*, 2012.

[7] Rice University Wireless Open Access Research Platform. `warp.rice.edu`.

[8] K. Tan, J. Zhang, J. Fang, H. Liu, Y. Ye, S. Wang, Y. Zhang, H. Wu, W. Wang, and G. M. Voelker, "Sora: High Performance Software Radio Using General Purpose Multi-core Processors," in *Proc. USENIX NSDI*, 2009.

# Demo: Online Evaluation of Sensing Characteristics for Radio Platforms in the CREW Federated Testbed

Virgilios Passas[⊕], Kostas Chounos[⊕], Stratos Keranidis[⊕], Wei Liu[⋆], Lieven Hollevoet[†], Thanasis Korakis[⊕], Iordanis Koutsopoulos[⊕], Ingrid Moerman[⋆] and Leandros Tassiulas[⊕]
[+]Department of Computer and Communication Engineering, University of Thessaly, Greece
[○]Centre for Research and Technology Hellas, CERTH, Greece
[⋆]Ghent University - iMinds, Gent, Belgium
[†]IMEC Wireless Research, Leuven, Belgium
{vipassas, hounos, efkerani, korakis, jordan, leandros}@uth.gr
{wei.liu, ingrid.moerman}@intec.ugent.be
{lieven.hollevoet}@imec.be

## ABSTRACT

Cognitive radio systems have gathered a lot of research interest during the last decade. Accuracy of spectrum sensing and efficiency of free spectrum utilization are considered as the primary objectives in this emerging technology, which promises a boost in wireless network performance, through exploitation of underutilized licensed frequency bands. As the focus of researchers is usually on these two major challenges, other aspects have been in part underestimated. In this work, we consider two factors that are rather important for evaluation of cognitive platforms, namely sensing delay and energy efficiency. The first is related to the latency induced by the spectrum sensing process and its impact on sensing efficiency, which is tightly connected to both the QoS performance of secondary users and the protection of primary users. On the other hand, energy consumption is considered as a crucial issue in all types of wireless communications, due to restricted battery autonomy of mobile devices, as well as for moving towards "greener" solutions in telecommunications. Therefore, it is important to extend existing testbed experimentation tools and develop new ones, in order to equip cognitive testbeds with such advanced monitoring capabilities. In this work, we present a monitoring procedure that has been directly integrated in the experimentation tools of the CREW testbed federation and demonstrate how it aids in the online evaluation of four different cognitive platforms in terms of the aforementioned metrics.

## Categories and Subject Descriptors

C.2.1 [**Computer-Communication Networks**]: Network Architecture and Design - Wireless Communications


*MobiCom'13,* September 30–October 4, Miami, FL, USA.
ACM 978-1-4503-1999-7/13/09.
http://dx.doi.org/10.1145/2500423.2505303.

## Keywords

Spectrum Sensing, Energy Consumption, CREW project

## 1. INTRODUCTION

Cognitive Radio Networking is a rapidly evolving research thrust in wireless communications nowadays, aspiring to create a major paradigm shift in the wireless landscape through Dynamic Spectrum Access and Management. In order to enable realistic cognitive radio experimentation, several devices that feature spectrum sensing capabilities have been developed. In this work, we will investigate the sensing characteristics of 4 different sensing devices under common spectrum sensing scenarios. The scenarios include spectrum sensing of a specific channel band through FFT processing of the captured data to characterise the Power Spectral Density (PSD) over the specified bandwidth. Under these reference scenarios, we will evaluate the 4 different devices in terms of the achieved sensing delay and resulting energy consumption.

## 2. HARDWARE PLATFORMS

Devices under investigation are the well-established Universal Software Radio Peripheral (USRP) E110 Embedded Series [1], the USRP N210 Networked Series [2], the prototype IMEC Sensing Engine (SE) [3] and a commercial wireless network interface card (NIC) that features the Atheros AR9380 chipset [4]. The USRP devices are commercial SDR platforms, which mainly consist of two parts, a fixed mother board and a plug-in daughter board. The former contains ADC/DAC and an FPGA and the latter provides basic RF front-end functionality. We will equip both USRP devices with the XCVR2450 daughterboard, which operates in the 2.4 GHz and 5 GHz bands. The feature that differentiates the E110 from the N210 device is that it is equipped with an ARM Cortex-A8 cpu processor and thus does not require the use of a host pc for measurement processing. USRP N210 is capable of monitoring 25 MHz of bandwidth, limited by the maximum bandwidth of Gigabit Ethernet, while the USRP E110 device is limited to bandwidth sizes up to 8MHz, due to the reduced sampling rate and processing capabilities.

The IMEC SE consists of two core components: an analogue RF front-end SCALDIO (SCAlable raDIO) and a DIg-

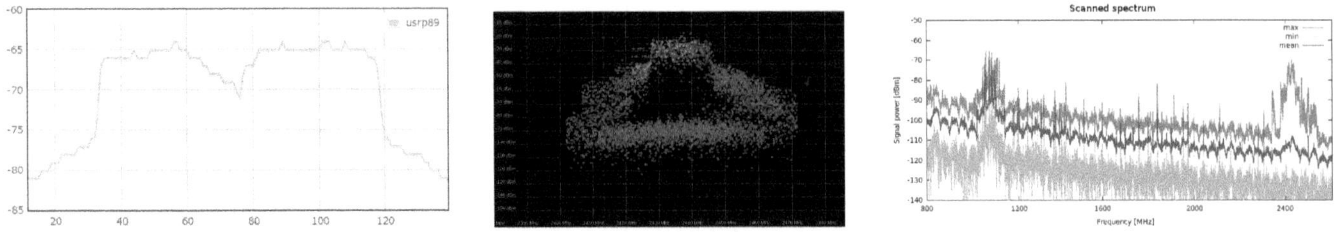


(a) USRP N210 - FFT 128 bin (b) Atheros AR9380 - FFT 56 bin (c) IMEC SE - FFT 128 bin

**Figure 1: Screenshots of PSD estimations for different devices and configurations**

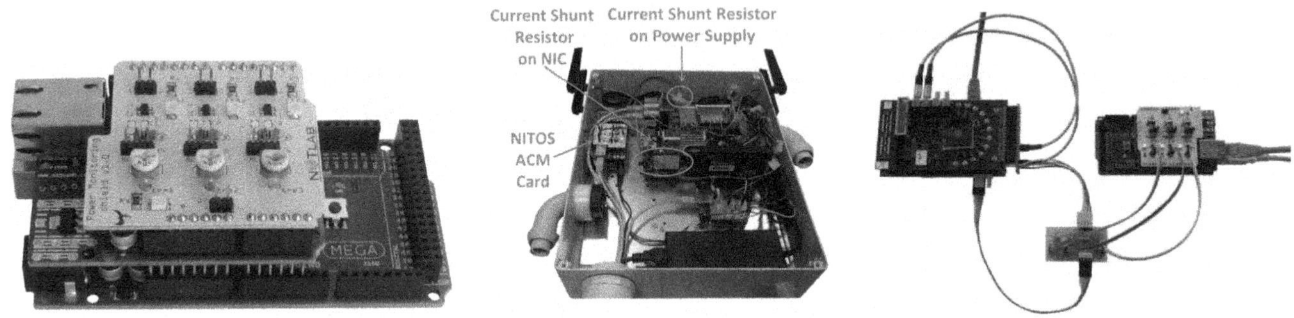


(a) NITOS ACM card (b) Testbed node attached with the developed hardware solutions (c) Energy Consumption Monitoring of the IMEC Sensing Engine

**Figure 2: Hardware components and modifications to sensing devices**

ital Front-end For Sensing (DIFFS). Both these ICs are low-power and flexible and targeted towards implementation of a cognitive radio as a mobile device. SCALDIO is a fully reconfigurable analog transceiver that features an FFT accelerator core, enabling the engine to perform spectral analysis with a default FFT size of 128 samples. The receiver RF operating frequency is programmable from 0.1 to 6 GHz and the channel bandwidth is programmable between 1 and 40 MHz.

The Atheros AR9380 chipset, which is also 3x3 MIMO compatible, is capable of performing spectrum sensing, by exploiting the open-source driver compat-wireless version 3.9 and above. AR9380 can generate $4\mu s$ long spectral snapshots for any 20MHz wide channel among the 38 available ones in the 2.4 GHz and 5 GHz bands. The default driver implementation supports FFT calculations of 56-bin size, where each bin is used to characterise the PSD of each one of the OFDM subcarriers that are being used by IEEE802.11n standard. This NIC is enabled for spectrum sensing, so that interference of different wireless technologies (e.g. Zigbee) that operate on the same channel can also be detected.

## 3. METRICS AND EXPERIMENTATION

Considering the fact that the aforementioned sensing devices feature varying sensing capabilities, we will test them under two reference scenarios, to comparatively evaluate their performance in terms of sensing delay and energy efficiency. The first scenario includes the sensing of 8 MHz bandwidth of the 2.4 GHz band and the characterisation of the observed PSD. We decided to set the limited bandwidth of 8 MHz, so that all devices are able to gather measurements without the need of switching their central frequency. Under this scenario, we will evaluate the sensing delay capabilities of the considered devices, which significantly varies due to the variance of both the measurement collection and measurement processing time across different platforms. Moreover, we will also consider a second scenario where the targeted band is 100 MHz wide, so that all devices will have to perform channel switching to provide for proper monitoring of the whole band. In this second scenario, we will also evaluate the sensing efficiency of all devices, which is related to the portion of time, during which spectrum is being continuously monitored. Indicative screenshots that correspond to PSD spectrum characterisation for different devices and FFT configurations are presented in Fig. 1. More specifically, Fig. 1(a) represents PSD estimation of the USRPN210 that monitors 25 MHz bandwidth of a single Wi-Fi channel with 128-bin FFT, while Fig. 1(b) represents data gathered through the Atheros AR9380 device and characterises the PSD of 11 consecutive Wi-Fi channels in the 2.4 GHz band. These results have been collected through 8 repetitive scans on the central frequency of each channel, where in each step 56-bin FFT calculations are performed. Finally, Fig. 1(c) illustrates the PSD estimation of the IMEC SE for the entire band between the 800 and 2600 MHz, as captured through 128-bin FFT calculations.

The considered devices include both embedded solutions (USRPE110 and IMEC SE) that do not require the use of a host machine for measurement processing and devices that are not capable of self-processing (USRP N210 and AR9380) and thus are attached to external PCs. As a result, the energy expenditure that each device results in significantly varies. We will assess this interesting sensing performance - energy consumption tradeoff, by using the NITOS ACM card [5] that is able of gathering power measurements with increased sampling rate and accuracy. The NITOS ACM card is presented in Fig. 2(a), while Figures 2(b) and 2(c) show how we attach the card to a host PC, its NIC and the IMEC SE accordingly.

The two aforementioned experimental scenarios will be demonstrated live and the obtained results will be presented in parallel with the experiment execution.

## 4. DEMO REQUIREMENTS

For the purposes of this demonstration, we will bring:

- our projector and laptops
- the 4 Sensing devices available at the CREW Testbed and also 4 NITOS ACM cards,

while we will also require:

- a desk of 2 meters length to place the equipment,
- power supply plugs for all the devices.
- 20 minutes for setup and testing.

## 5. CONCLUSIONS

In this demo paper, we demonstrate a framework that enables evaluation of cognitive devices, in terms of sensing delay and resulting energy consumption. In particular, we present a monitoring procedure that has been directly integrated in the experimentation tools of the CREW facilities and demonstrate how it aids in the online evaluation of 4 different cognitive platforms in terms of the aforementioned metrics.

## 6. ACKNOWLEDGEMENTS

The authors acknowledge the support of the European Commission through IP project CREW (FP7-258301).

## 7. REFERENCES

[1] *"USRP E110 Embedded Series"*, https://www.ettus.com/product/details/UE110-KIT.
[2] *"USRP N210 Networked Series"*, https://www.ettus.com/product/details/UN210-KIT.
[3] *"IMEC Sensing Engine"*, http://www2.imec.be.
[4] *"Atheros AR9380 Chipset"*, http://goo.gl/51Mg7.
[5] *"Energy Characteristics of NITOS NICs"*, http://nitlab.inf.uth.gr/NITlab/papers/EnergyTR.pdf.

# Demo: NTMobile: New End-to-End Communication Architecture in IPv4 and IPv6 Networks

Hidekazu Suzuki
Faculty of Science and Technology
Meijo University
Nagoya, Japan
hsuzuki@meijo-u.ac.jp

Katsuhiro Naito
Graduate School of Engineering
Mie University
Tsu, Japan
naito@elec.mie-u.ac.jp

Kazuma Kamienoo
Graduate School of Science and Technology
Meijo University
Nagoya, Japan
123430013@ccalumni.meijo-u.ac.jp

Tatsuya Hirose
Graduate School of Science and Technology
Meijo University
Nagoya, Japan
tatsuya.hirose@wata-lab.meijo-u.ac.jp

Akira Watanabe
Faculty of Science and Technology
Meijo University
Nagoya, Japan
wtnbakr@meijo-u.ac.jp

## ABSTRACT

With the spread of mobile devices, there is a growing demand for direct communication between users. However, under recent complex IP networks, it is extremely hard to establish a direct connection between devices. In order to solve the problem, authors have been proposing a new end-to-end communication architecture called "Network Traversal with Mobility" (NTMobile). In NTMobile, applications in the mobile device establish an end-to-end connection by using virtual IPv4/IPv6 addresses in the NTMobile network independent from real IP networks.

In this demo, we will show that Android smartphones can make free communication with each other without any constraint such as an NAT traversal problem in IPv4 networks and incompatibility between IPv4 and IPv6 architectures.

## Categories and Subject Descriptors

C.2.5 [**Computer-Communication Networks**]: Local and Wide-Area Networks—*Internet*; C.5.3 [**Computer System Implementation**]: Microcomputers—*Portable devices*

## General Terms

Design, Experimentation, Performance, Verification

## Keywords

Android, Handover, IPv4/IPv6, Mobility, NAT traversal


*MobiCom'13,* September 30–October 4, Miami, FL, USA.
ACM 978-1-4503-1999-7/13/09.
http://dx.doi.org/10.1145/2500423.2505304.

## 1. INTRODUCTION

In recent years, high performance mobile devices such as smartphones and tablet computers are rapidly spreading all over the world. Users can get access to the Internet at any time and from anywhere by using 3G/LTE and Wi-Fi technologies. Global mobile data traffic has been growing explosively, therefore, it is desired that the traffic will be offloaded onto the fixed network through Wi-Fi [1]. In the Internet, the network changes when the mobile device switches to a different communication interface or to another Wi-Fi access point.

Most of today's network services are built on the IPv4 network. However, IPv4 architecture has a serious problem caused by IPv4 global address exhaustion. Private address networks are generally constructed using Network Address Translation (NAT) routers. Recently, Career Grade NAT (CGN) technology [2] is being introduced in ISP networks, and transition to IPv6 has been gradually progressing. However, since IPv6 architecture does not have compatibility with IPv4, it is not possible to communicate between these networks directly. Thus, it is thought that a situation of IPv4 and IPv6 coexisting networks lasts for a fairly long period of time.

In such a complex network, it is necessary to securely establish reliable connection between mobile devices directly as much as possible wherever these devices are. In addition, it is also important to achieve IP mobility in order to maintain the established connection even if the mobile devices move to another network during communication.

We have been proposing a new End-to-End communication architecture, called "Network Traversal with Mobility" (NTMobile) that can achieve connectivity and mobility simultaneously in IPv4 and IPv6 networks [3, 4, 5]. This paper describes the overview of NTMobile architecture and how to establish an end-to-end connection in the today's complex network. In this demo, we will show that Android smartphones and tablets implemented with NTMobile functions can start communication (by using a network

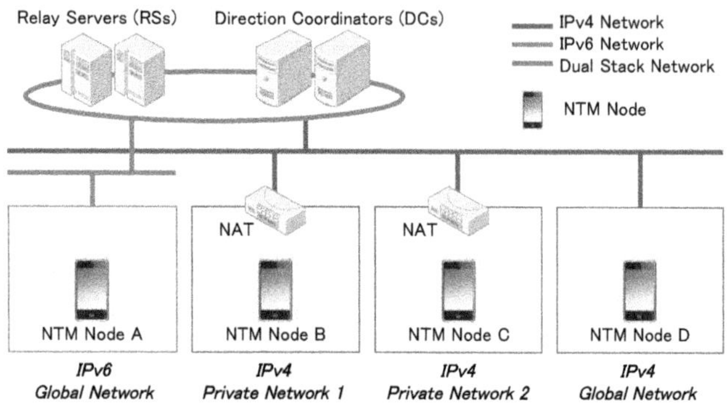


**Figure 1: System configuration.**

camera application) between various network environment, those are IPv4 global network, IPv4 private network, IPv6 global network and dual stack network. Moreover the video streaming is maintained even if these devices move to another network.

## 2. NTMOBILE

In the NTMobile architecture, mobile devices establish a connection by their virtual IP addresses which are not existed in real networks. By performing NTMobile operation, applications can make communication without being affected by switching of networks, existence of NAT on the communication route, and even by the difference between IPv4 and IPv6 networks. On the other hand, all packets based on virtual IP addresses are sent through a UDP tunnel between mobile devices. As the UDP tunnel is established in a direct route, except in certain specific situations, mobile devices always make tunnel communication through the optimal route.

### 2.1 System Configuration

The overview of NTMobile system configuration is shown in Figure 1. NTMobile consists of NTM nodes, Direction Coordinators (DCs), and Relay Servers (RSs).

An NTM node is a mobile device and has two kinds of addresses, those are, a real IP address assigned by the connected network and a virtual IP address assigned by DC. The virtual IP address is a permanent IP address in the NTMobile network and is not exited in the real network. Both of virtual IPv4 and IPv6 addresses are assigned in NTM nodes.

DC is a coordinator to manage the assignment of virtual IP addresses and direct NTM nodes to establish tunnels. DC stores information of NTM nodes such as Fully Qualified Domain Name (FQDN), real IPv4 and IPv6 addresses, virtual IPv4 and IPv6 addresses, and IPv4 global address of NAT router when the NTM node is behind the NAT router.

RS is a server to relay packets between NTM nodes under certain circumstances; e.g., when both of communicating NTM nodes are located behind different NAT routers, when an NTM node communicate with a general node which does not have NTMobile functions, and when NTM nodes are located in different address families, that is, IPv4 network and IPv6 network like the case of NTM node $A$ and NTM node $B$ as shown in Figure 1. In these cases, tunnels are established with RS which is set in the dual stack network, and communication between NTM nodes is made via RS.

DC and RS are placed in the dual stack network, and they can be multiplexed depending on the size of networks and the number of NTM nodes. Therefore, NTMobile system has scalability and can be applied to quite large scale networks.

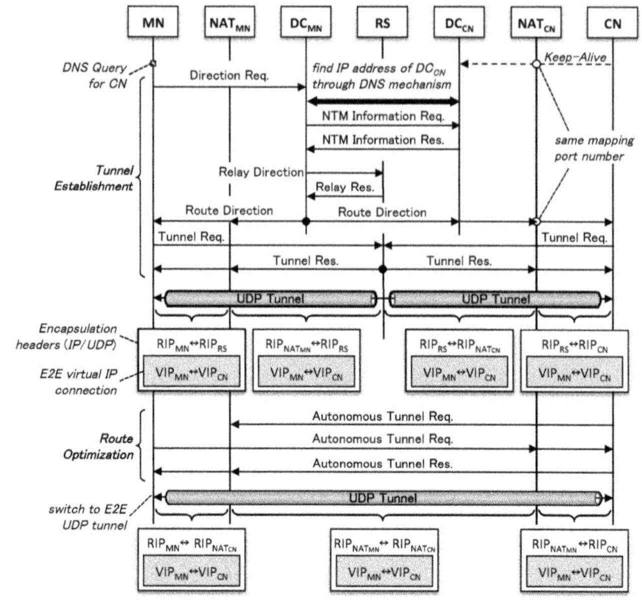


**Figure 2: Signaling for creating tunnel between different IPv4 private networks and switching to direct communication route by a route optimization procedure.**

### 2.2 Signaling for Creating Tunnel

Figure 2 shows the signaling for creating tunnel between NTM nodes, and the relationship between a virtual IP connection and a UDP tunnel of real IP addresses. It is assumed that an NTM node $N$ completed a registration process, and IP address information of NTM node $N$ is stored in $DC_N$. Unique virtual IPv4 and IPv6 addresses are assigned to each of NTM nodes. When an NTM node $N$ is located behind a NAT router, the NTM node periodically sends keep-alive messages to $DC_N$ in order to maintain a mapping in $NAT_N$ for receiving the signaling from $DC_N$.

NTM node "MN" initiates the following NTMobile signaling when a DNS query from a DNS resolver is detected. First, MN sends a Direction Request message to $DC_{MN}$ for requesting a tunnel creation between MN and CN. $DC_{MN}$ finds the IP address of $DC_{CN}$ with the DNS name resolution mechanism. Then, $DC_{MN}$ obtains the address information of CN from $DC_{CN}$ by exchanging of NTM Information Request and Response messages. After that, $DC_{MN}$ determines how to create a tunnel based on IP address information of MN and CN, and directs MN and CN by Route Direction messages (including both of IP address information) to create a tunnel between them.

In the case shown in Figure 2, the Route Direction message for CN located behind $NAT_{CN}$ can be transmitted via $DC_{CN}$ because the mapping for this signaling in $NAT_{CN}$ is maintained by the keep alive between $DC_{CN}$ and CN. MN

**Table 1: Communication patterns and their communication route in NTMobile system.**

| Location of an initiator's NTM node | Location of a correspondent NTM node | | | |
|---|---|---|---|---|
| | IPv4 Global | IPv4 Private 1 | IPv4 Private 2 | IPv6 Global |
| IPv4 Global | ◎ | ◎ | ◎ | ○ |
| IPv4 Private 1 | ◎ | ◎ | ◎ | ○ |
| IPv4 Private 2 | ◎ | ◎ | ◎ | ○ |
| IPv6 Global | ○ | ○ | ○ | ◎ |

◎: Optimal route
○: Communication route via RS

and CN exchange Tunnel Request and Response messages directly with each other to create a direct tunnel between them. In the particular cases, both of MN and CN create tunnels with RS.

After the above signaling, the DNS resolver in MN reports the virtual IPv4 and IPv6 addresses of CN to its application. In this way, an MN's application recognizes that the CN is located in the NTMobile network.

## 2.3 End-to-End Communication

When MN establishes an End-to-End connection with CN by using their virtual IP addresses, packets are encapsulated by UDP packets with real IP addresses and are transmitted to the destination using the created tunnel. Therefore, the virtual IP connection in the NTMobile network is established through the UDP tunnel in the real network.

In the case when an MN and a CN are located in different IPv4 private networks, it is possible to switch from the communication route via RS to the direct tunnel communication route by conducting a route optimization procedure [6]. In the NTMobile system, NTM nodes can freely communicate with each other without any constraint, as shown in Table 1.

## 2.4 Handover

When an NTM node moves to another network during the communication and its real IP address is consequently changed, a UDP tunnel is recreated in the same way as at the beginning of the communication. For example, if the MN moves from IPv4 private network to IPv6 global network, the UDP tunnel changes from the direct route to the route via RS. However, even the tunnel route is changed, mobility is realized because the connection between MN and CN established by their virtual IP addresses is surely maintained.

# 3. DEMONSTRATION

We will demonstrate the NTMobile system with Android smartphones and tablets. Figure 3 shows the configuration of demonstration. As NTM nodes, we will use Samsung Galaxy Nexus and SONY Xperia Tablet Z in which our NTMobile function is implemented. DC and RS will run as virtual machines on Apple MacBook Pro. We will construct an IPv4 global network, two IPv4 private networks, an IPv6 network, and a dual stack network with YAMAHA RTX1200 router and four Wi-Fi routers. These Wi-Fi routers provide network connections for Android smartphones and tablets.

In this demo, we will show the following:

(1) Android devices can start communication with each other in any case by using network camera application.

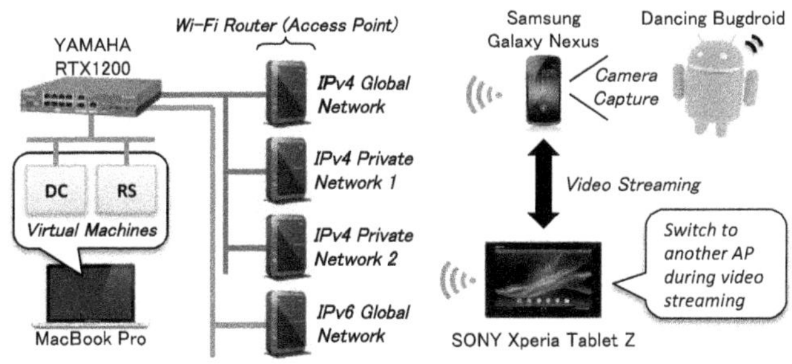


**Figure 3: Configuration of demonstration.**

(2) The video streaming is maintained even if the Android devices move to another network.

Our demonstration requirements are as follows:

(i) One table (W1500×D500) is needed.

(ii) We can complete the setup within an hour.

(iii) Total power consumption of 500W is needed.

(iv) No Internet access.

Finally, we provide a short video clip that gives an overview of NTMobile on YouTube[1], and also explain NTMobile in detail on our website [7].

# 4. REFERENCES


[1] Cisco. Cisco Visual Networking Index: Global Mobile Data Traffic Forecast Update, 2012–2017, February 2013. `http://www.cisco.com/en/US/solutions/collateral/ns341/ns525/ns537/ns705/ns827/white_paper_c11-520862.pdf`.

[2] S. Perreault, I. Yamagata, S. Miyagawa, A. Nakagawa, and H. Ashida. Common Requirements for Carrier-Grade NATs (CGNs). RFC 6888, IETF, April 2013.

[3] H. Suzuki, K. Kamienoo, T. Mizutani, T. Nishio, K. Naito, and A. Watanabe. Design and Implementation of Establishment Method of Connectivity on NTMobile. *IPSJ Journal*, 54(1):367–379, January 2013. (in Japanese).

[4] K. Naito, K. Kamienoo, T. Nishio, H. Suzuki, A. Watanabe, K. Mori, and H. Kobayashi. Proposal of Seamless IP Mobility Schemes: Network Traversal with Mobility (NTMobile). In *Proc. IEEE GLOBECOM 2012*, pages 2572–2577, December 2012.

[5] K. Kamienoo, H. Suzuki, K. Naito, and A. Watanabe. Implementation and Evaluation of NTMobile with Android Smartphones in IPv4/IPv6 Networks. In *Proc. IEEE GCCE 2012*, October 2012.

[6] H. Noudou, H. Suzuki, K. Naito, and A. Watanabe. A Proposal of Autonomous Route Optimization in NTMobile. *IPSJ Journal*, 54(1):394–403, January 2013. (in Japanese).

[7] project NTMobile. `http://www.ntmobile.net/`.


[1] `http://www.youtube.com/watch?v=MmVWnSOs85w`

# BEEINFO: Data Forwarding Based on Interest and Swarm Intelligence for Socially-aware Networking

Jie Li, Li Liu, Feng Xia
School of Software, Dalian University of Technology
Dalian 116620, China
f.xia@acm.org

## ABSTRACT

Socially-aware networking provides a promising paradigm for data forwarding by exploiting the involved nodes' social properties in mobile social networks. However, individuals' learning capability and awareness to the dynamic environment have not been well explored in the literature. In this paper, we give a brief introduction of an interest-based scheme called BEEINFO. Inspired by swarm intelligence, BEEINFO takes advantage of individuals' perceiving and learning capability to gather information of density and social tie during communication. Moreover, it classifies communities based on nodes' interests and distinguishes data forwarding into situations of inter-community and intra-community. Furthermore, BEEINFO performs efficient message scheduling and buffer management to improve performance. The simulation results show that BEEINFO outperforms PROPHET and Epidemic in message delivery ratio, overhead and hop count, except for average latency.

## Categories and Subject Descriptors

C.2.2 [**Computer-Communication Networks**]: Network Protocols; H.1.2 [**Information Systems**]: User/Machine Systems—*human factors*

## Keywords

Socially-aware networking; Forwarding; Interest; Swarm intelligence

## 1. INTRODUCTION

Socially-Aware Networking (SAN) is an emerging paradigm to solve problems of networks consisting of mobile nodes with social properties, e.g. social relationship, and mobility patterns. These characteristics can be utilized to design efficient data forwarding protocols in e.g. mobile social networks.

In particular, social relations of mobile nodes have generally long-term features and they are more stable than node mobility patterns. *Community, interest, social tie*, etc. are the commonly used social concepts in SAN. For instance, people are usually interested in some files or data in specified categories. Moreover, people with the same interest tend to meet frequently, bonding each other with social tie and forming a community. Additionally, individuals' regular mobility pattern is important to predict the future mobility. Many experiments [1, 7, 8] proved the high efficiency of socially-aware methods, involving the above properties. However, SAN is faced with some challenges, including how to conduct community construction and detection, predict future encounters, and calculate social relationship efficiently. These are correlated with some facts, such as the changing network topology, the constrained resources, the threat of potential congestion caused by information exchange.

These challenges are due to the lack of adaptability to dynamic environments. It is essential to find an appropriate solution. Fortunately, swarm intelligence has provided some clues to detect and adapt to the changes of environment context in a timely fashion. For example, Artificial Bee Colony (ABC) algorithm [2] imitates the bees' behaviors to search for nectar, as well as their ability to detect the changing density of nectar sources.

In our work, BEEINFO is designed as an artificial BEE colony inspired INterest-based FOrwarding scheme under the framework of SAN. BEEINFO takes advantage of mobile users' social properties, mobility regularities and learning capability to detect the dynamic environment, including density and social tie. Additionally, it classifies the community based on personal interests, eliminating the cost by community detection and construction. Furthermore, the interest information is small enough to predict density and social tie, saving resources, e.g. buffer and energy. All these features contribute to the novelty of BEEINFO.

## 2. INSPIRATION FROM ARTIFICIAL BEE COLONY

ABC algorithm imitates the natural bees' behavior of searching for nectar sources. In the process, the scout bees search in a random direction and gather information simultaneously. Once the best sites are spotted, some of the scout bees are assigned as follower bees to work on the sites. With the back and forth, the bees evaluate and maintain the density of left nectar source for the future detection.

The process reveals bees' awareness and learning capability, which is of crucial use to improve individuals' adaptability to dynamic environments. This further leads to the following inspirations when we design BEEINFO. 1) We de-


*MobiCom'13,* September 30–October 4, 2013, Miami, FL, USA.
ACM 978-1-4503-1999-7/13/09.
http://dx.doi.org/10.1145/2500423.2504569.

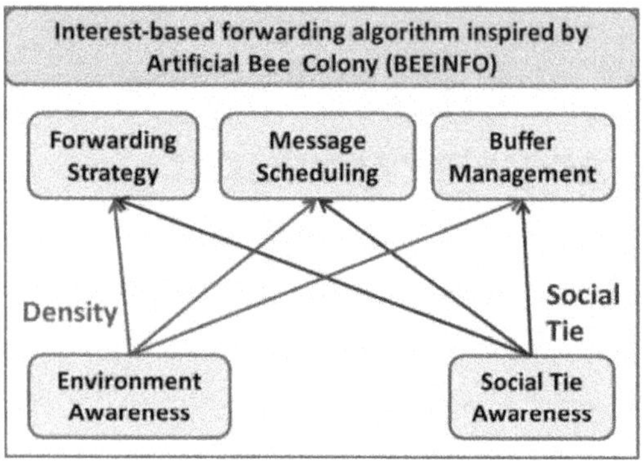


**Figure 1: Components of BEEINFO.**

fine *density* to identify the number of passing nodes with different interests. The bigger the density, the more nodes can be met. 2) *Social tie* should be maintained by nodes and it denotes the strength of social relationship between nodes with the same interest. 3) Nodes update the information of density and social tie when being in contact.

# 3. DESIGN OF BEEINFO

## 3.1 Overview

Fig. 1 depicts the five components of BEEINFO: *environment awareness*, *social tie awareness*, *forwarding strategy*, *message scheduling*, and *buffer management*. Environment awareness and social tie awareness provide density and social tie information separately, which are essential to make decisions in forwarding, scheduling message, and managing buffer. This structure stands on the following assumptions: 1) each node maintains its one and only interest, 2) nodes with the same interest belong to the same community, and 3) nodes follow their regular mobility patterns.

## 3.2 Environment and Social Tie Awareness

In BEEINFO, environment awareness and social tie awareness gather density and social tie information, respectively. To be specific, density is the number of nodes a mobile user encounters over a time window $T$. In addition, considering the influence of the past and present information, BEEINFO predicts density based on the exponentially weighted moving average, similar to [3]. After that, an evaporation process is performed to weaken the influence of previous density.

$$Density_i(t) = \sum_{t=0}^{T} n \tag{1}$$

$$\begin{aligned} Density_i(t+\Delta t) &= \alpha \times Density_i(t-\Delta t) \\ &\quad +(1-\alpha) \times Density_i(t) \end{aligned} \tag{2}$$

$$Density_{new} = Density_{old} \times \gamma^k \tag{3}$$

Eqs. (1), (2) and (3) describe the computational formulation of density, where $\alpha$ is community density prediction factor, $\gamma$ is evaporation factor and $k$ is the time interval towards last update.

We use similar method to measure, predict and evaporate social tie, as shown in (4), (5) and (6). In (4), $\lambda_{i,j}$ is the contact frequency and $d_{i,j}$ is the contact duration of $i$ and $j$ in time window $T$. $\beta$ in (5) is social tie prediction factor. $\gamma$ and $k$ keep the same.

$$SoTie_{i,j}(t) = (\lambda_{i,j} \times d_{i,j}(t))/T \tag{4}$$

$$\begin{aligned} SoTie_{i,j}(t+\Delta t) &= \beta \times SoTie_{i,j}(t-\Delta t) \\ &\quad +(1-\beta) \times SoTie_{i,j}(t) \end{aligned} \tag{5}$$

$$SoTie_{new} = SoTie_{old} \times \gamma^k \tag{6}$$

## 3.3 Forwarding Strategy

Forwarding strategy is the core of BEEINFO. The information of destination node (DN), including ID and interest, is contained in the message. When a source node (SN) meets with an intermediate node (IN), firstly, they compare their interests and see if they belong to the same community, and then compare density or social tie information to decide whether IN is a good forwarder. Specifically, density is for inter-community forwarding and social tie is for intra-community process. Note that when making a decision, BEEINFO follows the rule that intra-community forwarding is prior to inter-community process. After comparison, our scheme takes different actions to deal with distinct situations, as described below.

(1) If DN, SN and IN belong to the same community, it is intra-community forwarding. The node with the higher social tie will be selected as the forwarder among SN and IN.

(2) DN and SN are in the same community, but IN is an outside node. In this situation, IN is not a suitable forwarder and BEEINFO needs a node in the same community with DN for intra-community forwarding.

(3) When IN and DN belong to the same community but SN is an outside node, IN will be chosen as a forwarder and the message will be transmitted from SN to IN.

(4) SN and IN belong to the same community but not the destination community where DN belongs. It is inter-community forwarding. The node with the higher density to DN will be chosen as forwarder among SN and IN.

(5) If SN, IN and DN are in three communities, it satisfies the inter-community forwarding scenario. BEEINFO will perform the same action as in (4).

## 3.4 Message Scheduling and Management

Message scheduling and buffer management share the same rule with Forwarding Strategy. Besides, they both exclude or discard the expired or successfully delivered messages without influencing those messages under transmission. The difference between them lies in the priority of impact factors.

In message scheduling, intra-community messages are processed first. Then those with higher social tie (or density for inter-community) are transmitted, followed by the newer ones. Buffer replacement has the reverse order, meaning that the inter-community messages are replaced first, and then those with lower density (or social tie for intra-community) and finally it is the older messages being replaced .

# 4. EVALUATION AND DISCUSSION

We have conducted preliminary simulations on BEEINFO, PROPHET [5], and Epidemic [6]. The simulations were conducted with the Opportunistic Network Environment Simulator [4] in Points of Interest (POIs) movement

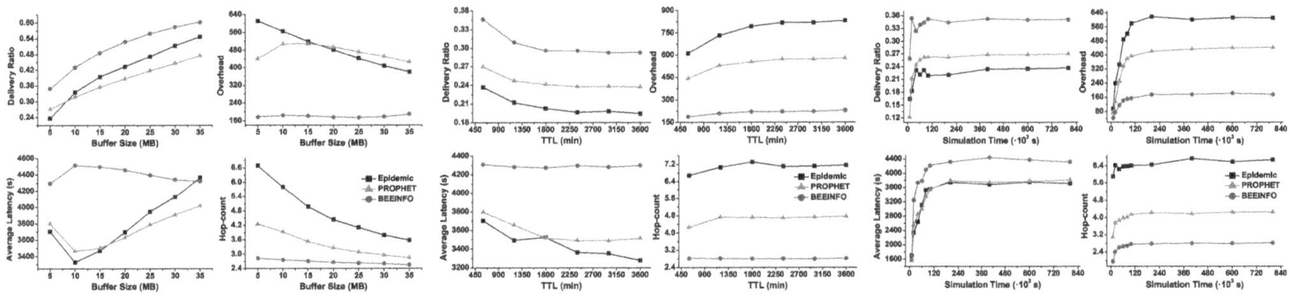

(a) Buffer size (b) TTL (c) Simulation time

**Figure 2: Performance with respect to buffer size, TTL and simulation time.**

model. Basically, there are four POI groups and each group consists of 40 nodes with same interest, indicating one community. In each POI scenario, there is a high probability for a node to meet others in the same community and a low possibility to move to other POIs. Additionally, we set a POI5 group to represent the place that all the nodes may reach with the same probability.

The protocols' performance is evaluated over various buffer sizes (5~35 MB), TTLs (600~3600 min) and simulation times (10000~800000 s). Nodes move with speeds from 0.5 m/s to 1.5 m/s in the area of 8000 × 7800 $m^2$. The message size varies in the range of 500~1024 kB. To calculate density and social tie, $\alpha$ and $\beta$ are both assigned 0.3, and $\gamma$ is 0.98. Other parameters are set with default values and not listed here given the limited space.

The metrics to evaluate the protocols are message delivery ratio, overhead, average latency and hop count. Overhead is the ratio of relayed messages (delivered messages excluded) and delivered messages.

We ran the simulation 10 times and calculated the average values. The results in Fig. 2 display that generally BEEINFO keeps the same trends with PROPHET and Epidemic, in terms of delivery ratio, overhead and hop count. Specifically, BEEINFO achieves the highest delivery ratio, with the changing parameters. The overhead of BEEINFO is far lower than those of PROPHET and Epidemic, and keeps less than 160. Besides, it takes less than 3 hops to successfully deliver messages for BEEINFO, which is also the best among the protocols. The data also show that BEEINFO is not as sensitive as PROPHET and Epidemic to buffer size, TTL, and simulation time concerning overhead and hop count. The results of BEEINFO are stable, but those of the other protocols fluctuate in some occasions, such as the overhead of PROPHET with buffer size and the hop count of Epidemic with TTL.

Nonetheless, BEEINFO experiences the highest average latency. This is caused by the fact that it does not transmit messages until it chooses a proper forwarder and it costs time. However, Fig. 2(a) shows an encouraging phenomenon, which is BEEINFO's latency declines after reaching the peak about 4496s, when buffer size increases. The reason is that BEEINFO controls message redundancy more effectively, with message scheduling and buffer management. Besides, the latency of BEEINFO is also more stable than PROPHET and Epidemic, especially when TTL and simulation time are considered.

The conclusions we reach from the experiments are: 1) BEEINFO outperforms PROPHET and Epidemic in delivery ratio, overhead and hop count, except for average latency; 2) TTL and simulation time have the least effect on BEEINFO.

Our research on BEEINFO provides a foundation for upper layer application design, such as automatic information sharing in an academic conference. However, we need to explore more on what causes the high latency and how to reduce it. Besides, there are more fields we need to concentrate on as well, including 1) how message copies affect the performance, 2) if interest and the relation of interests can make a difference or not, and 3) how the protocols perform under the circumstances of real traces/datasets.

## 5. REFERENCES


[1] K. Chen, H. Shen, and H. Zhang. Leveraging social networks for p2p content-based file sharing in disconnected manets. *IEEE Trans. Mob. Comput., PrePrint*, December 2012.

[2] S. K. Dhurandher, S. Misra, P. Pruthi, S. Singhal, S. Aggarwal, and I. Woungang. Using bee algorithm for peer-to-peer file searching in mobile ad hoc networks. *J. Netw. Comput. Appl.*, 34(5):1498–1508, September 2011.

[3] R. Jain, K. K. Ramakrishnan, and D. M. Chiu. Grant: Inferring best forwarders from complex networks' dynamics through a greedy ant colony optimization. Technical report, INRIA, RR-7694, 2011.

[4] A. Keränen, T. Kärkkäinen, and J. Ott. Simulating mobility and dtns with the one (invited paper). *J. of Commun.*, 5(2):92–105, February 2010.

[5] A. Lindgren, A. Doria, and O. Schelen. Probabilistic routing in intermittently connected networks. *SIGMOBILE Mobile Comput. Commun. Rev.*, 7(3), 2003.

[6] A. Vahdat and D. Becker. Epidemic routing for partially connected ad hoc networks. Technical report, Technical Report CS-200006, Duke University, 2000.

[7] J. Wu, M. Xiao, and L. Huang. Homing spread: community home-based multi-copy routing in mobile social networks. In *Proc. IEEE INFOCOM*, 2013.

[8] M. Xiao, J. Wu, and L. Huang. Community-aware opportunistic routing in mobile social networks. *IEEE Trans. Comput.*, to be published, 2013.

# CRESCENT: a Modular Cost-Efficient Open-Access Testbed for Cognitive Radio Networks Routing Protocols


Abdelrahman Asal
a.asal@alexu.edu.eg

Ahmad Mamdouh
a.mamdouh@alexu.edu.eg

Ahmed Salama
a.salama@alexu.edu.eg

Moamen Elgendy
m.elgendy@alexu.edu.eg

Moamen Mokhtar
m.mokhtar@alexu.edu.eg

Muhammed Elsayed
m.elsayed@alexu.edu.eg

Department of Computer and Systems Engineering
Alexandria University



## ABSTRACT

Cognitive Radio Networks (CRNs) provide a solution to increase the utilization of the scarce radio frequency spectrum. Building testbeds for CRNs is one of the main challenges that can affect the wide deployability of such networks. Many testbeds were proposed for testing CRN routing protocols, but most of them are either pure simulations or require high deployment cost for buying and maintaining the needed hardware devices on a large scale. We propose *CRESCENT*: a modular framework for testing CRNs routing protocols with cost-efficient and large-scale deployability. *CRESCENT* is based on general purpose computers without the need for any special devices leveraging their built-in Wi-Fi interfaces as the default interface. The framework is built on top of Click modular router to ensure the ease of the development of new routing protocols while providing new modules that are essential for cognitive radio protocols.



## Categories and Subject Descriptors

C.2.1 [**COMPUTER-COMMUNICATION NETWORKS**]: Network Architecture and Design—*Wireless communication*; C.2.2 [**COMPUTER-COMMUNICATION NETWORKS**]: Network Protocols—*Protocol verification*

## Keywords

Cognitive radio networks; Cognitive routing protocols; Emulation; Testbeds.


## 1. INTRODUCTION

The huge increase in wireless devices highlighted the problem of wireless spectrum scarcity in today's networks that are characterised by a static spectrum assignment policy. Spectrum utilization varies from 15% to 85% [1] distributed temporally and spatially. These variations and the current inefficient use of spectrum led to the emergence of cognitive radio networks (CRNs) as an important solution that allows dynamic spectrum allocation. This is achieved by giving secondary unlicensed users access to use the spectrum when the primary licence users are inactive.

CRN protocol designers are concerned with testing the behavior of their protocols with real environmental conditions [6]. Most of the current testbeds for CRNs protocols focus on the physical or MAC layers. Usually, they either use simulations, which may be limited in capturing the real channel conditions, or use high cost hardware per node, e.g. [4], which limits their scale. Even though these high cost testbeds may be needed to implement the details of the physical or MAC layers protocols, there are many cases in which this high complexity is not necessary. This is especially true for implementing routing protocols for CRNs, where the protocol designer may not be interested in implementing and managing the details of the physical or MAC layer protocols.

In this work we propose *CRESCENT*: a novel architecture with modular implementation for a large-scale and open-access testbed where the protocol designers can deploy and benchmark CRNs protocols using a powerful and easy-to-use GUI. CRESCENT is a modular low-cost testbed which uses commodity computers with off-the-shelf Wi-Fi cards with the ability to extend the RF-Frontend to use USRP and/or WARP boards.

The remainder of the paper is organized as follows: In Section 2, we present our system architecture and implementation. Finally, Section 3 presents a case study for a typical CRNs protocol on both our framework and ns-2.



*MobiCom'13*, September 30–October 4, 2013, Miami, FL, USA.
ACM 978-1-4503-1999-7/13/09.
http://dx.doi.org/10.1145/2500423.2504570.


## 2. SYSTEM ARCHITECTURE

*CRESCENT* represents our second generation CRN routing testbed architecture that extends our *CogFrame* architecture [5]. In particular, *CRESCENT* provides (a) more functionalities including emulation modules for PU behavior, mobility, and topology management; (b) remote testbed access for centralized control and management; (c) low-end hardware support, e.g. Raspberry Pi; (d) protocols library for easier deployment; and (e) enhanced GUI for configuration, management, animation, and analysis.

*CRESCENT* is built on top of the Click modular router [3]. This allows it to inherit Click modularity and extensibility and to facilitate the implementation of various routing pro-

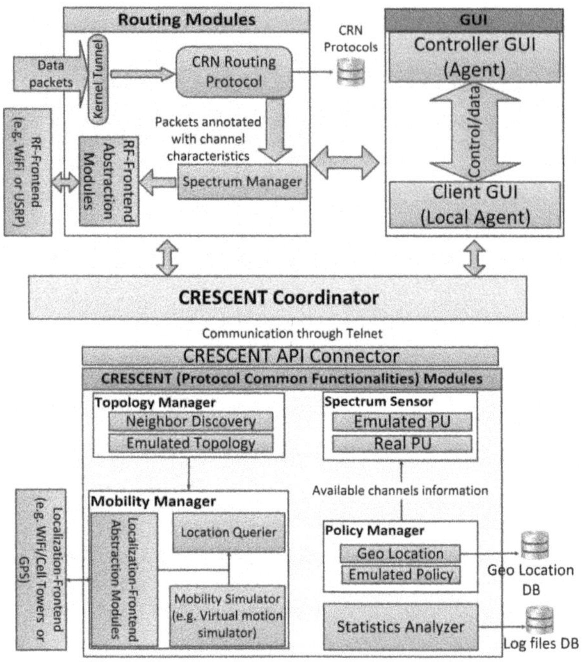


Figure 1: *CRESCENT* Architecture

tocols and nodes configurations while providing the common functionalities required by CRN protocols. *CRESCENT* is designed as a low-cost testbed that can be deployed on commodity computers with typical RF interfaces, without the need for attaching any other special hardware. In particular, *CRESCENT* makes use of the MAC and PHY protocols of conventional 802.11 cards, allowing the user to focus only on the implementation of the routing protocols, with integration with USRP and WARP boards if needed. *CRESCENT* also provides a set of common CRN functionalities, via an API, to separate the development of the protocol from the details of PHY and MAC layers.

Figure 1 depicts *CRESCENT* architecture. *CRESCENT* is composed of four main components: 1) Routing modules, 2) *CRESCENT* modules, 3) *CRESCENT* Coordinator and 4) *CRESCENT* Agent and GUI.

## 2.1 Routing Modules

The routing modules are built on top of Click modular router, they are responsible for routing the incoming packets and managing the spectrum. They consist of:

- Router elements: These are Click elements implemented by the protocol designer describing the behavior of the protocol. Developing a new protocol requires only the implementation of the protocol Click elements. This enables the user to test and compare different protocols together easily.

- Spectrum manager: This module is provided by *CRESCENT* to manage the spectrum by handling channel switching, transmission power and rate by interacting with the RF-Frontend abstraction module.

- RF-Frontend abstraction module: This module provides an abstraction layer for the users to handle different RF-frontend devices. No restrictions are made on the wireless interface hardware making it possible to use any RF interfaces ranging from conventional Wi-Fi cards to software defined radios, such as USRPs [4].

- Protocol database: *CRESCENT* provides a library of CRN protocols that can be used by CRN protocol designers. This significantly reduces the development time and overhead.

## 2.2 CRESCENT Modules

These modules are supported by *CRESCENT* to provide the common CRN functionalities hiding PHY and MAC layers details from the protocol designer. They can provide both emulated and real information through a unified API. *CRESCENT* provides emulated scenarios such as virtual primary users and virtual node motion. This allows it to model complex scenarios over limited hardware, if needed.

- Spectrum sensor: This module is responsible for providing spectrum information such as available channels, channels quality, and primary users existence. Spectrum sensing information can be sensed by Wi-Fi cards or USRP boards to provide real information about the spectrum, or it can provide emulated environment measurements by supporting virtual primary users allowing complex and extreme scenarios.

- Topology manager: This module is responsible for maintaining the topology of the participating nodes in the experiment. Two modes of operation are provided: (a) physical sensing of neighbors, where each node senses its surrounding and identifies its neighbors or (b) through enforcing a certain topology by emulating different channel qualities on the links between neighboring nodes.

- Policy manager: Policy manager provides the protocol designer with the available spectrum channels and transmission regulations which can be collected either from geo-location databases or by enforcing certain policy information.

- Mobility manager: *CRESCENT* provides different modes of mobility, either through mounting the nodes on robots moving in predefined paths, or by emulating mobility through virtual motion where motion parameters are defined at the beginning of the experiment (e.g. the velocity, acceleration and the direction of motion). Location determination can be done using different localization technologies (e.g. GPS, Wi-Fi, or cellular localization techniques) or through simulated localization. The mobility manager manages the mobility of certain nodes and provides the interface to query the location at any given instance of time.

- Statistics analyzer: It is responsible for the aggregation of the statistics files from each node with the collaboration of the *CRESCENT* agent and performs statistical analysis producing different CRN metrics used to evaluate the protocol. Big data can be analyzed through large-scale parallel computing paradigms and files can be stored in a distributed database.

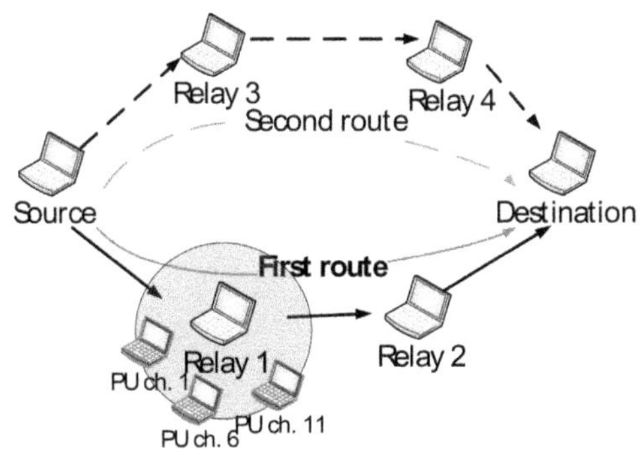


Figure 2: Experiment scenario with three primary users becoming active sequentially at Relay 1.

## 2.3 CRESCENT Agent and GUI

*CRESCENT* provides two graphical user interfaces to help the protocol designer configure and monitor the behavior of each node in the experiment.

1. Controller GUI: It provides a set of functionalities starting from the collection of nodes information (e.g. Ethernet IP and Hardware addresses), setting the network topology, visualizing the experiment statistical metrics, and animating the experiment dynamics.

   *CRESCENT* also provides an agent module that communicates with all the machines involved in the experiment to collect their information, distributes configuration files automatically, and aggregates their statistics files. The agent plays a crucial role to support large-scale deployment of *CRESCENT* as it enables the user to perform many complex tasks easily via the GUI.

2. Client GUI: This module is run on all the nodes involved in the experiment and provides real-time information regarding each node including loss ratio, number of channel switches, primary user status, wireless interfaces information, among other protocol-specific information.

## 2.4 CRESCENT Coordinator

The routing modules and the controller GUI interact with *CRESCENT* modules through the Coordinator. The coordinator provides a unified API that facilitates the separation and abstraction of the common CRN functionalities supported by *CRESCENT* and the router elements written by the protocol designer.

# 3. CASE STUDY

We implemented a location-aided routing protocol for CRNs [2] over both *CRESCENT* and ns2. We had to implement only two modules to fully have a running version of the protocol on *CRESCENT*. We used the scenario shown in Figure 2 where there are three available channels (1, 6 and 11) corresponding to the non-overlapping channels of 802.11b. Figure 3 shows the results collected from *CRESCENT* and ns2. At the beginning, none of the PUs is active and the source selected Relay 1 as the next hop based on the routing protocol. Virtual PUs were scheduled to appear at Relay 1 on channels 1, 6 and 11 sequentially at different times, leading to interruption in service during channel switching on

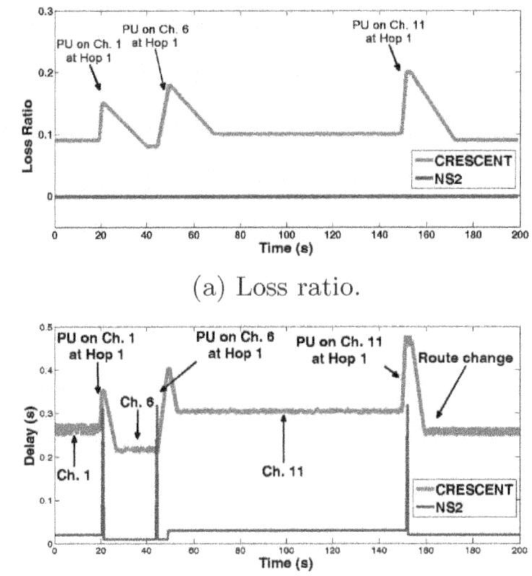


(a) Loss ratio.

(b) End-to-end delay.

Figure 3: Performance comparison between CRESCENT and ns2 for the scenario in Figure 2.

the same route. After all PUs are active concurrently, the source decided to change the route to go through Relay 3.

The figure shows that *CRESCENT* provides more realistic results than ns2 that has instantaneous switching time.

## Acknowledgments

This work is supported in part by a grant from the Egyptian National Telecommunication Regulatory Authority (NTRA).

# 4. ADDITIONAL AUTHORS

Moustafa Youssef (Wireless Research Center, Alexandria University and E-JUST, email: `moustafa.youssef@ejust.edu.eg`).

# 5. REFERENCES

[1] I. F. Akyildiz, W.-Y. Lee, M. C. Vuran, and S. Mohanty. Next generation/dynamic spectrum access/cognitive radio wireless networks: a survey. *Comput. Netw.*, 50(13):2127–2159, Sept. 2006.

[2] K. Habak, M. Abdelatif, H. Hagrass, K. Rizc, and M. Youssef. A location-aided routing protocol for cognitive radio networks. In *ICNC*. IEEE, 2013.

[3] E. Kohler, R. Morris, B. Chen, J. Jannotti, and M. F. Kaashoek. The click modular router. *ACM Trans. Comput. Syst.*, 18(3):263–297, Aug. 2000.

[4] E. R. LLC. http://www.ettus.com/.

[5] A. Saeed, M. Ibrahim, K. Harras, and M. Youssef. A low-cost large-scale framework for cognitive radio routing protocols testing. In *ICC'13*. IEEE, 2013.

[6] M. Youssef, M. Ibrahim, M. Abdelatif, L. Chen, and A. V. Vasilakos. Routing Metrics of Cognitive Radio Networks: A Survey. *IEEE Communications Surveys and Tutorials*, to appear.

# OpenRoutes: Augmenting Backhaul Network Survivability with Reduced Redundancy- A Topology based Analysis

Venmani Daniel Philip*†
*Orange Labs, France Telecom R&D
Lannion, France
danielphilip.venmani@orange.com

Yvon Gourhant
Orange Labs, France Telecom R&D
Lannion, France
yvon.gourhant@orange.com

Djamal Zeghlache
†TELECOM SudParis & CNRS
Evry, France
djamal.zeghlache@telecom-sudparis.eu

## ABSTRACT
In this article we illustrate that, management of network resources can yield notably different performances leading to different restoration behaviors – for different network topologies. In consideration towards this, we first briefly summarize our earlier work on a novel fault restoration mechanism. The proposed mechanism addresses the problem of finding the minimum bandwidth cooperative route in the backhaul of mobile network operators that is shared among multiple operators. We then present our recent results on the extended performance evaluations of the same, for four different synthetic network topologies carried out using extensive simulations. Through these evaluations, we conclude on the best topology that mobile network operators should construct in order for them to maximally benefit by the proposed cooperative routing scheme to yield optimum performance for their capital expenditure.

## Categories and Subject Descriptors
C.2.1 **[Computer-Communication Networks]**: Network Architecture and Design-*Network topology*; C.2.3 **[Computer-Communication Networks]**: Network Operations.

## General Terms
Algorithms, Network design, Network survivability.

## Keywords
Maximally disjoint paths, Multi-topology wireless backhaul networks, Path computation algorithms.

## 1. INTRODUCTION AND BACKGROUND
*Network survivability* enables communication networks to sustain maximum network connectivity and quality of service (QoS) under failure conditions. Among others, one naive solution to guarantee the survivability is to over-provision the network links, often termed as *Redundancy*. Through a series of our earlier works including [1], we argued that it is not cost-efficient anymore to extend permanent backup paths (redundant paths) for every independent Mobile Network Operator (MNO) within the same geography– because the capacity which is allocated for the already existing backup paths is not *always* actively filled-in as much as the capacity allocated for the primary path. Consequently, we presented *OpenRoutes*, a failure restoration framework that minimizes network disruption - *cost-effectively*, wherein two or more MNOs cooperate with each other and share their already existing unused network resources (bandwidth capacities) on a mutually beneficial understanding, up to a certain extent without exceeding their limits on resource sharing; thereby diligently saving on the over-provisioning costs.

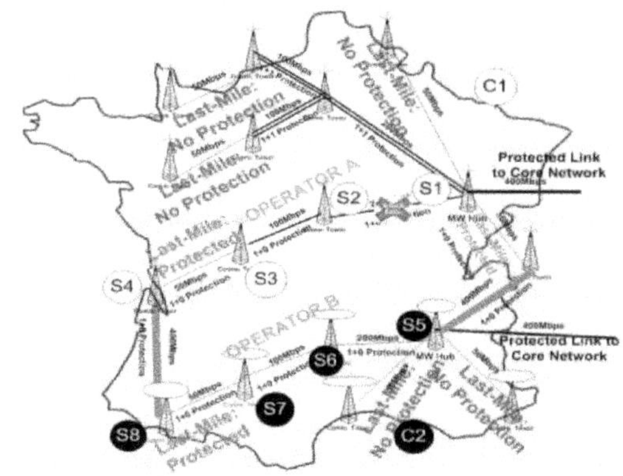


**Figure 1. An illustrative example network topology portraying resilience design flow using infrastructure sharing within the country France. Two MNOs: one at the top (north), another in south (with circles) are joined by just another additional link (green colour thick link), making a 'resilient' ring topology.**

Precisely, our approach re-routes failed connections according to their respective QoS requirements (according to different traffic classes) over maximally disjoint paths constructed across a backhaul network topology, that has emerged out of sharing between different MNOs, without affecting any of the other MNOs' already existing traffic flows. We formulated the problem as a multi-constrained non-linear optimization problem, providing the MNOs with a parameterized objective function which facilitates them to choose the desired paths based on the traffic patterns of their end-customers. This is defined as:

$$\textbf{Minimize:} \left( \left( \varepsilon \sum_{e \in E} \sum_{\lambda \in \Lambda} \tau_d \right) + \left( (\mathbf{1} - \varepsilon) \sum_{n=1}^{\mathcal{K}} \delta_n \right) \right) \quad (1)$$

The objective function illustrated above in (1) is designed to determine the shortest alternative path out of the $\mathcal{K}$ available paths from the combined backhaul topology while also ensuring that the selected shortest path has the optimal capacity to carry the disrupted connection satisfying its QoS requirements. This is finely tuned by the parameters $\tau_d$ and $\delta_n$ denoted in (1). $\tau_d$ indicates the end-to-end delays of each path. This is obtained by adding the


*MobiCom'13*, September 30–October 4, 2013, Miami, FL, USA.
ACM 978-1-4503-1999-7/13/09.

individual weights of each link associated with every path and $\delta_n$ in (1) represents the binary variable to determine whether the capacity of any link in the network is within the acceptable utilization range (i.e., above a fixed threshold limit that we defined as *Shareability Index*, $\theta_{ij}$) at a time instant t so that a disrupted connection has an optimal capacity path to traverse. Here, $\varepsilon \in [0, 1]$ is a small weighting coefficient that we have assigned arbitrarily such that it identifies between choosing a path with the least delay and the most optimal capacity. We solved the formulated ILP equation using three heuristics algorithms: (i) Least Length Shortest Paths (LLSP), (ii) Least Delay Shortest Path (LDSP) (*both based on the well-known Dijkstra's algorithm* [2]) for delay-sensitive real time traffic and (iii) Ant Colony Optimization (ACO) (*based on Ant-colony meta-heuristics* [3]) for bandwidth consuming traffic types. We evaluated our framework for the Sprint L3 topology (node: 44; edge: 106; average node degree: 4.82). This concludes the overview of our earlier work (Please refer [1] for extensive details on *OpenRoutes*).

## 2. EXTENDED ANALYSIS

Motivated by our earlier results from [1], in this work, we go forward to present the efficiency of our framework on four different topologies and determine the best topology that can maximally benefit MNOs if they conclude on backhaul resource sharing. This will allow us to quantify the network resource utilization that can be achieved for a particular topology, not just for a particular flow. Now we recall that the centre of our earlier work was heavily quantified, based on a new key metric that we defined as *Shareability Index* $(\theta_{ij})$. This metric characterizes the extent to which available capacity on a link is shareable among MNOs. In a way, it is representative of a specific topology's survivability with respect to the utilization range of the available capacity. We now tune the accuracy of this metric using four different topologies under a range of failure probabilities and present our results. The end result, therefore, accurately predicts the survivability of a given network topology, with reduced redundancy. To do this, we vary the value of $\theta_{ij}$ between 0 (0% allowed range- implying no network resource sharing between MNOs) and 0.50 (50% allowed range- implying sharing half of the available network resources in each link), in the topologies where we have carried out the experiments. Table I summarizes the different topologies that were used for the simulation, each exhibiting its own characteristics, such as - mesh, ring, grid and star. To measure the impact of our algorithms on them, we compare our results against the Shortest Path Routing (SPR) [2] and Beam Search Algorithm (BS) [4] as reference schemes.

**Table 1. Network Topologies Characteristics**

| Network Type | # of Nodes | # of Links | Average Node Degree |
|---|---|---|---|
| | Network Characteristics | | |
| Full-Mesh | 20 | 190 | 19.00 |
| Manhattan Grid | 25 | 40 | 3.20 |
| Ring | 25 | 25 | 2.00 |
| Star | 25 | 24 | 1.92 |

## 3. INFLUENCE OF TOPOLOGIES

In this section, we present numerical illustrations towards the realization of our scheme. Here the metric that was considered for the evaluation is *Blocking Probability (BP). BP* is defined as a measure of the number of connection requests rejected against the total number of connection requests. Our methodology for evaluations is described as follows: As a first step, we focus on determining the topology that yields the best performance for the proposed *OpenRoutes* restoration scheme. To do so, we evaluate and compare the performance of all the four topologies by combining the three heuristics *(LLSP+LDSP+ACO)* for the two cases: (i) when the MNOs do not share $(\theta_{ij} = 0)$and (ii) when the MNOs share$(\theta_{ij} = 0.5)$, in figure 2(a) and figure 2(b).

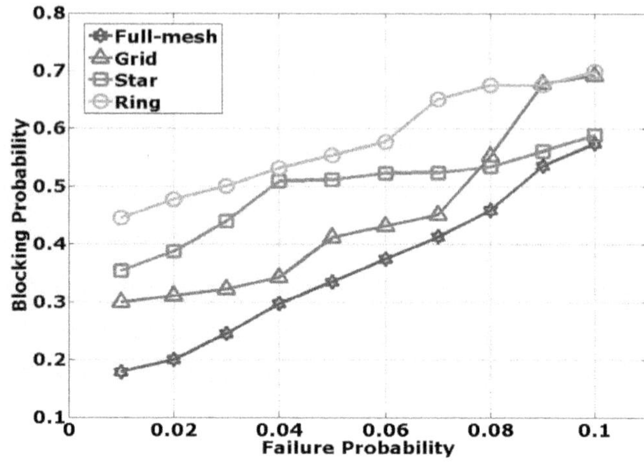


(a)

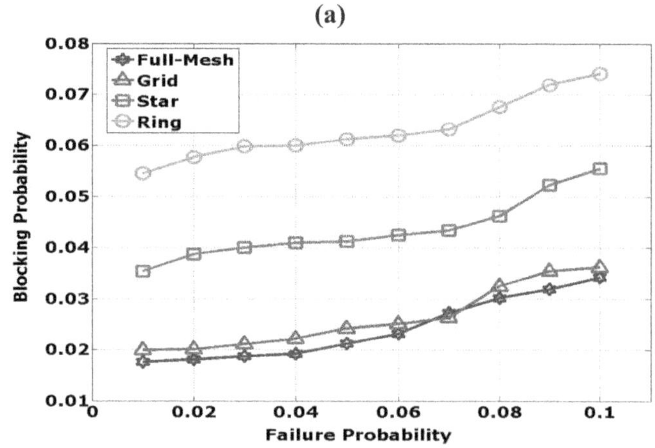


(b)

**Figure 2. Illustration of blocking probability for various topologies when all the three heuristics (LLSP+LDSP+ACO) are combined for (a) $\theta_{ij} = 0$ (no resource sharing) (b)$\theta_{ij} = 0.5$ (50% resource sharing).**

The performances of all three heuristics when combined yield the best results on the *full-mesh topology* than any other topologies in consideration. To give them a ranking, full-mesh performs the best, followed by grid, then star, then ring. Our justification to this is that it is due to the density of this 'mesh-like' topology which is larger than star or ring network topology. As the density decreases, it may no longer be possible for some pairs of intermediate nodes to communicate over short paths. Hence a decrease in density is typically accompanied by an increase in network diameter, which results in larger length, resulting in poor performance. Furthermore, unlike each of the other topologies in consideration such as grid, star and ring, messages sent on a full-mesh network, where every node in the topology is connected to every other node, can take any of several possible paths from source to destination, thus maximally benefitting from our restoration heuristics. On the other hand, considering the case of ring, this shows the least performance because a failure in any link disconnects the entire loop and thus the entire path is not available for the failed connections to traverse-through. Nevertheless, it has to be noted that the performance of all the topologies is better for $\theta_{ij} = 0.5$ than $\theta_{ij} = 0$. (Detailed analysis on the same is in the section below). Nonetheless, through our results, we are able to demonstrate that the survivability of disrupted connections due to resource sharing will have much higher availability in the presence of any number of failures (single or double link failures), if the contribution of the reconfiguration time from primary path to backup path towards unavailability is disregarded [since it is relatively small (on the order of tens of milliseconds) with respect to the manual failure repair time (on the order of hours) and the connection's holding time (on the order of weeks or months).

# 4. INFLUENCE OF SHARING

Having determined the best topology, we now illustrate the performance of our three heuristics *(LLSP, LDSP, ACO)* individually against the reference approaches and then combine all three heuristics into one *(LLSP+LDSP+ACO)* and compare against the reference approaches for the two cases- (i) when the MNOs do not share $(\theta_{ij} = 0)$ and (ii) when the MNOs share $(\theta_{ij} = 0.5)$. Figure 3 illustrates the performances for the *Full-mesh* topology alone which performs the best as ascertained by our earlier results. Observing from Figure 3, we can conclude that the total number of connections rejected when the MNOs share (Figure 3(b)) is lesser compared to when they do not share (Figure 3(a)). Taking a closer look at the obtained results precisely indicate the following observations. The reference shortest path routing (SPR) algorithm almost always performs well, be it in the case when the MNOs do not share or when they share. However, there is a slight difference in performance observed looking closely. Our algorithms *LLSP* and *LDSP* perform inferior to the *SPR* routing algorithm, when MNOs do not share but the performance gets augmented atleast by 50% when the MNOs share and gets in-par with the performance of the SPR algorithm. This is mainly due to the fact that *SPR* routing algorithm best fits in the case when the network links are not very congested (congested in the sense that there is no failure and hence no congestion encountered) and that there is always sufficient capacity available. As stated earlier, since *LLSP* and *LDSP* address the traffic classes which does not demand paths with more capacity, they find it very feasible to choose abundant paths with less capacity compared to the classic *SPR* - meaning that *LLSP* and *LDSP* succeeds as much as *SPR* routing algorithm in re-routing delay sensitive traffic. Moving forward, the performance of *ACO* shows a huge variation unlike the other two heuristics (LLSP, LDSP), when the MNOs share and when they do not share. Especially, the *BP* is the highest when the MNOs do not allow the others to share. This is because, *ACO* heuristics looks for optimal paths especially with more capacity to re-route bandwidth consuming traffic. Having said that, *ACO* performance is the best when there is resource sharing, implying that more paths with enough capacity to re-route bandwidth consuming traffic can be easily found in the case when the MNOs share. Adding to this, the performance when all three heuristics are combined is notably remarkable, seemingly much better than the reference schemes, when the MNOs share and it is notably not affected by the size of the network or the failure probability. This is because our approaches fundamentally makes sure that the overall congestion due to link failures is reduced as much as possible by "intelligently" using the unused resources of the network. Our simulation results show that, for sharing constraints those are not strict, our proposed heuristics approaches return solutions close to the optimum making their application for multi-constrained routing problems very promising.

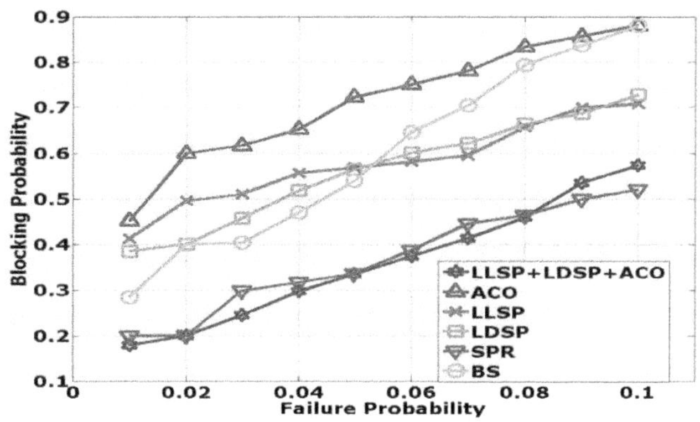


(a)

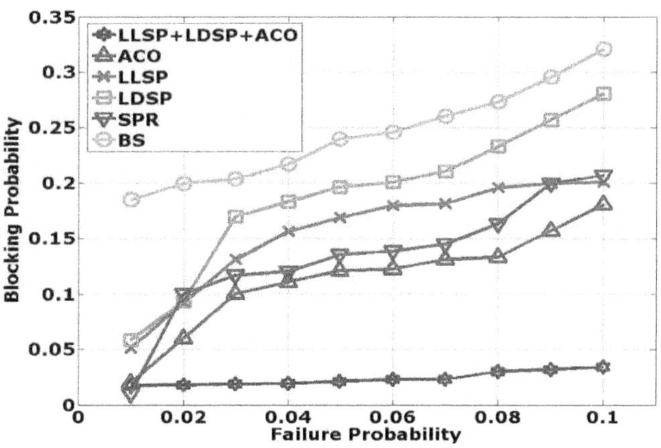


(b)

**Figure 3. Illustration of blocking probability (a) for $\theta_{ij} = 0$ (no resource sharing) (b) for $\theta_{ij} = 0.5$ (50% resource sharing) on a Full-mesh topology.**

# 5. CONCLUDING DISCUSSIONS

Topologies remain an important part of network design theory. In this article we extended our earlier analysis on backhaul resource sharing between several MNOs intended for its survivability, for four different synthetic topologies, each exhibiting different characteristics. Based on our results, we could conclude that it is most beneficial when two (or more) MNOs with already existing *mesh* topologies decide to cooperate and share their backhaul resources, in order to maximize their network resource utilization or in other words to minimize the disrupted connections resulting due to failure situations. Regardless, through our results, we have demonstrated that the management of resources can yield notably different performances leading to different restoration behaviors for different network topologies.

# 6. REFERENCES


[1] D.P.Venmani, Y.Gourhant and D.Zeghlache. OpenRoutes: Multi-operator Cooperative Routing over Maximally Disjoint Paths for the Survivability of Wireless Backhaul. In Proc. of IEEE/IFIP DRCN'13, Budapest, Hungary, Feb. 2013.

[2] E. W. Dijkstra. A note on two problems in connection with graphs. Numerische Mathematik, vol. 1, pp. 269–271, 1959.

[3] M.Dorigo and D.C.Gianni. Ant colony optimization: a new meta-heuristic. In Proc. of IEEE CEC, vol. 2, 1999.

[4] K.H.Kim and K.Y.Kim, Routing straddle carriers for the loading operation of containers using a beam search algorithm. Computers & Industrial Engineering, 36(1), 109-136, 1999.

# SilentSense: Silent User Identification Via Touch and Movement Behavioral Biometrics


Cheng Bo
Illinois Institute of Technology
Chicago, IL 60616, USA
cbo@hawk.iit.edu

Lan Zhang
Tsinghua University
Beijing, China
zhanglan03@gmail.com

Xiang-Yang Li
Illinois Institute of Technology
Chicago, IL 60616, USA
xli@cs.iit.edu

Qiuyuan Huang
University of Florida
Gainesville, FL 32605, USA
idfree@ufl.edu

Yu Wang
University of North Carolina at Charlotte
Charlotte, NC 28223, USA
yu.wang@uncc.edu



## ABSTRACT

In this work, we present *SilentSense*, a framework to authenticate users silently and transparently by exploiting the user touch behavior biometrics and leveraging the integrated sensors to capture the micro-movement of the device caused by user's screen-touch actions. By tracking the fine-detailed touch actions of the user, we build a "touch-based biometrics" model of the owner by extracting some principle features, and then verify whether the current user is the owner or guest/attacker. When using the smartphone, the unique operating pattern of the user is detected and learnt by collecting the sensor data and touch events silently. When users are mobile, the micro-movement of mobile devices caused by touch is suppressed by that due to the large scale user-movement which will render the touch-based biometrics ineffective. To address this, we integrate a movement-based biometrics for each user with previous touch-based biometrics. We conduct extensive evaluations of our approaches on the Android smartphone, we show that the user identification accuracy is over 99%.



## Categories and Subject Descriptors

H.4 [**Information Systems Applications**]: Miscellaneous

## Keywords

*SilentSense*, Mobile Device, Identification


## 1. INTRODUCTION

The blooming digital service for mobile devices has attracted more privacy concern, especially when people are sharing their personalized device to guest users. Since device owners are not willing to take distrust action to reduce permission deliberately before sharing [4], it would be good for devices to silently know exactly who is using it, so as to provide necessary privacy protection and access control.

The most popular mechanism for authentication is using enhanced password patterns [2] with an additional security layer, and establishing guest profiles for access control. Such methods are overelaborated, inconvenient and time consuming. Facial recognition [1] by front camera is another optional strategy to identify user. But it is still annoying to require users to accept frequent shooting. Besides, the accuracy is unstable with changing environment and frequent shooting is power-consuming.

The latest solution exploits the capacitive touch communication as a mechanism to distinguish different users [6], which has potential risk of being imitated. TapPrints [5] indicates that taps on the touch screen could be observed through sensitive motion sensors. Touchalytics [3] only exploits scrolling as biometric for continuous authentication while [8] only considers tap behaviors on certain digit patterns.

In this work, investigating the feasibility of utilizing the behavioral biometrics extracted from smartphone sensors for user identification, we propose *SilentSense*, a non-intrusive user identification mechanism to silently substantiate whether the current user is the device owner or a guest or even an attacker. Exploiting the combination of several interacting features from both touching behavior (pressure, area, duration, position) and reaction of devices (acceleration and rotation), *SilentSense* achieves highly accurate identification with low delay. A great challenge comes from the circumstance when the user is in motion, such as walking. The perturbation generated by the interacting will be suppressed by larger-scale user movement. While most of existing works neglect this circumstance, *SilentSense* is capable of identifying user in motion by extracting the motion behavior biometrics. As long as the current user is identified, necessary access control is triggered automatically.

Continuous monitoring sensors will provide minimum guest identification delay, but could cause unwanted energy consumption. Facing this challenge, we propose a novel model to estimate the current user leveraging the observation of owner's sociable habit. An online decision mechanism is designed for the timing to turn on or turn off sensors, which provides a balance between energy cost, delay and accuracy. Our online decision mechanism results in an adaptive observing frequency according to owner's social habit.



*MobiCom'13*, September 30–October 4, 2013, Miami, FL, USA.
ACM 978-1-4503-1999-7/13/09.
http://dx.doi.org/10.1145/2500423.2504572.


## 2. SYSTEM MODEL

*SilentSense* is designed as a pure software-based framework, running in the background of smartphone, which non-intrusively explores the behavior of users interacting with the device without any additional assistant hardware.

### 2.1 Main Framework

The framework model consists of two basic phases: *Training* and *Identification*, as shown in Figure 1. The training phase is conduct-

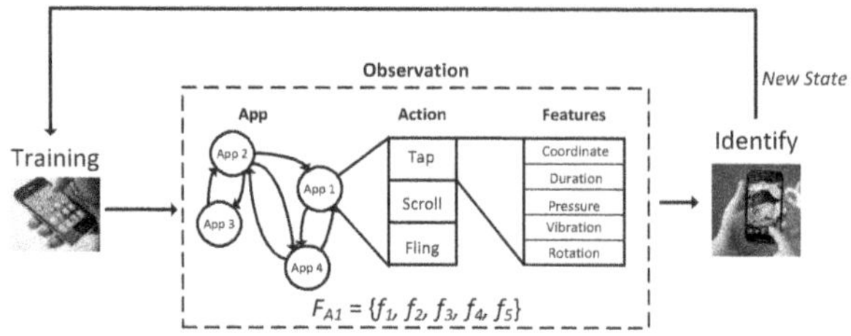


**Figure 1: Framework Overview.**

ed to build a behavior model when the user is interacting with the device, and the identification phase is implemented to distinguish the identity of the current user based on the observations of each individual's interacting behaviors.

Initially, the framework trains the owner's behavior model by retrieving two types of correlated information, the information of each touch-screen action and the corresponding reaction of the device. With the owner's behavior model, the current user will be identified through SVM classification. As personalized devices, the initial identification accuracy is usually not high enough because of lacking of non-owner's pattern. The model will upgrade the SVM model by adding newly observed features gradually through self-learning, which provides more accurate judgement.

## 2.2 Interacting Model

The operation of touchscreen based mobile device mainly consists of four gestures: Tap, Scroll, Fling, and Multi-touch. Different gestures usually have different touch features and lead to different device reactions. Interacting with certain app often involves a certain set of gestures. For a touch action $T_i$, we combine the app with its touch gesture and the features captured by this framework as one *observation*, denoted as $O_i = \{A_i, G_i, f_{i1}, \cdots, f_{in}\}$. here $A_i$ is the app being used, $G_i$ represents the gesture (*e.g.* tapp), and $f_{i,j}$ ($j \geq 1$) are features of the observed action.

Two types of features are used in this system: the touch features and reaction features. The touch features include touch coordinate on the screen, touch pressure and duration, which can be obtained from system API. To capture the reaction features, we notice that diverse gestures and positions for holding the device by individual users infer different amplitudes of vibration caused by each touch, which has already been proved by previous works ( [5, 7]). Such tiny reaction of the devices produces an identifiable patterns which could be observed via accelerometer and gyroscope.

## 2.3 Identification Process

The purpose of the framework is to identify the current user of the device, and prevent sensitive information leakage if the user is not the legal owner. Generally, the three important issues that users concern about are *delay*, *accuracy*, and *energy consumption*.

We employ SVM to judge the identity of the current user according to each interacting behavior observation. Since it is difficult to validate the correctness of the results because of lacking of ground truth, we denote $\varepsilon_i$ as the probability of the result, which is available for the SVM. Obviously, the accuracy of the identification process depends on the amount of observations, thus we denote $\theta_i(X_1, X_2, \cdots, X_i)$ as the probability of the identity based on the sequence of accumulated observation until $X_i$. With the number of observation increases, the framework will be more credible to provide the correct result, and the overall probability is generated according to historical creditability:

$$\theta_i(X_1, X_2, \cdots, X_i) = 1 - (\prod_{j=1}^{n}(1 - \varepsilon_j(X_j)))$$

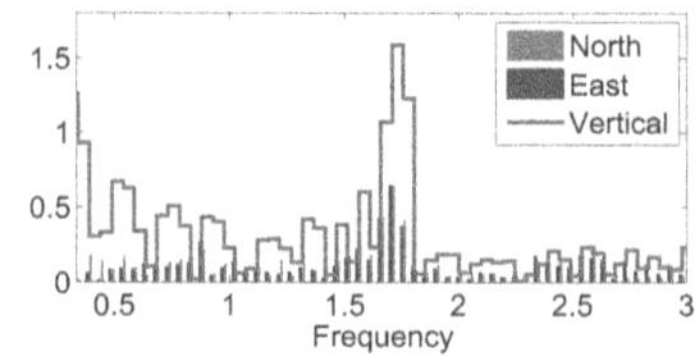


(a) The FFT result of 4 step acceleration in the earth coordinate system.

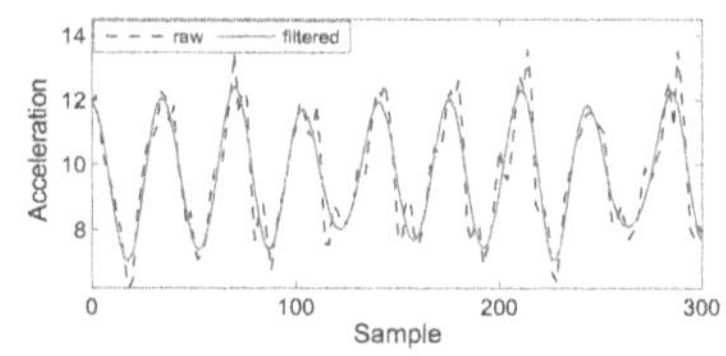


(b) The raw vertical acceleration and filtered acceleration.

**Figure 2: The frequency feature of acceleration in the earth coordinate system while walking.**

On the other hand, framework in mobile device cannot neglect the energy consumption, coming from feature extraction and running the identification. We assume the function of $U(E_t, \theta_t)$ as the utility that could be achieved under the energy budget $E_t$ and maintaining the reliable overall probability for the identification. The framework will make dynamic decision to balance the two factors so that the expected utility could be maximized. We can also set the threshold on the overall probability while minimizing the energy cost.

## 2.4 Motion Analysis

The amplitude of the sensory data extracted from the motion will be much larger than that of small perturbation caused by touch action, and the latter may be swamped by the former so that it fails to be extracted as a feature. In our work, we analyze the motion features, and use the walking features as part of the behavioral biometrics for identification.

To accurately capture the walking features of different users, three steps are conducted in our method. Firstly, considering a user could hold the phone in any attitude, we convert the raw acceleration vector in phone coordinate system into the earth coordinate system in real time. There are a lot of walking independent noise in the acceleration, which will greatly confuse the walking feature detection. We analyze the acceleration while walking in the frequency domain, Figure 2(a) shows that, the energy mainly locates around 2Hz, which is the user's walking frequency. The energy in other frequency comes from noise. To extract the pure walking acceleration, secondly, we filter linear acceleration with a band pass filter. Then we get the vertical acceleration in the gravity orientation and horizontal acceleration. Figure 2(b) shows the filtered vertical acceleration. A simple step detection algorithm can be performed on the filtered vertical acceleration in real time. Thirdly, we extract the walking feature from the processed acceleration data. The vertical displacement of a walker is directly correlated to his/her stride length and height, hence it is an important feature. Besides, the step frequency and horizontal acceleration pattern also vary with different users. To sum up, we extract four features of walking from $EA_v$ and $EA_h$: (1) Vertical displacement of each step by double integration of $EA_v$; (2) Current step frequency, calculated by the duration of each step; (3) Mean horizontal acceleration for each step; (4) Standard deviation of $EA_v$ for each step.

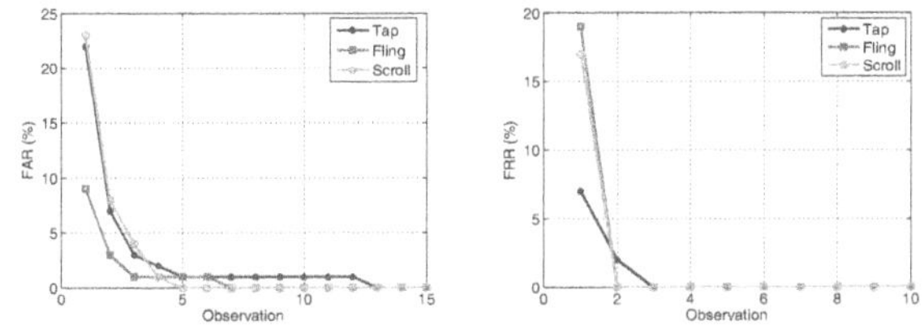


(a) FAR (b) FRR

**Figure 3: FAR, and FRR by different actions and different number of actions observed.**

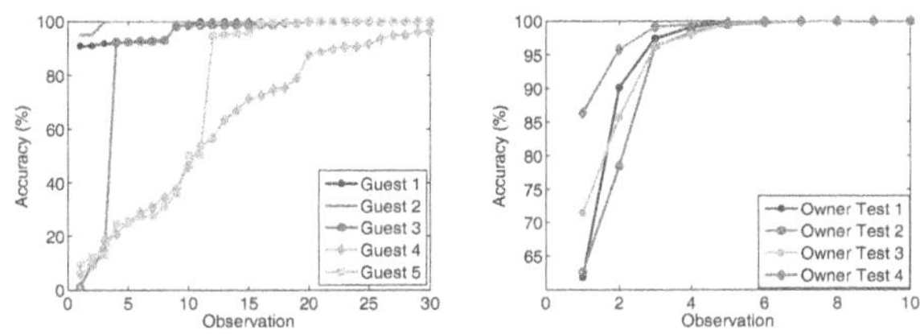


(a) Guest Accuracy (b) Owner Accuracy

**Figure 4: Identification based on combined operation.**

# 3. PRELIMINARY RESULTS

We implemented *SilentSense* on Android phone as a service running background. This service obtains the current app and touch events from system API, and captures sensory data from accelerometer and gyroscope.

## 3.1 Identification in Static Scenario

First, we explore the uniqueness of the behavior biometric in the static scenario. With more than 100 actions for each user, we analyze the key features of users extracted from both the touching behavior and reaction of smartphone. The analysis shows that there exists big diversity of each interacting feature among different users.

We evaluate the performance of operating in three different gestures through three different apps, including *Message*, *Album*, and *Twitter*. In Figure 3, we plot the false acceptance ratio (FAR), and false rejection ratio (FRR) of identifying user by different actions with different number of total observed actions. From Figure 3(a), the mean FAR of identification by one observation of tap is 22%, by one fling action is 9%, by one scroll action is 23%. The FAR is reduced to below 1% after observing about 3 fling actions and with about 13 observations the FAR achieves 0 for all three gestures. Surprisingly, Figure 3(b) shows that FRR almost achieves 0 with only 2 observations for each gesture. The experiments result show great discrimination of three gestures based on multiple features extracted by *SilentSense*.

Now, we evaluate the performance of *SilentSense* in a more general scenario, with 100 users interacting with smartphones freely as their daily usages, *i.e.*, the action sequences are random combinations of three types of gestures. Since the amount of training behavior data for the guest user is much smaller than that of the owner's data set (we assume user usually not lend phone to others very often), our experiments show that it is much faster to achieve a high accuracy for identifying the owner than identifying the guest. Even so, the framework could reach over a 80% accuracy within 10 observations for identifying a guest. Figure 4(a) takes the results from five random selected guests and plots how soon the framework could identify the guest. Similarly, as shown in Figure 4(b), the owner will be identified with in 6 observations. Overall, in a general scenario, with only one observation, the FAR and FRR are about 20%. But, with about 12 observations of various actions, the FAR and FRR are both reduced to nearly 0, meaning that there is no incorrect identification.

## 3.2 Identification in Dynamic Scenario

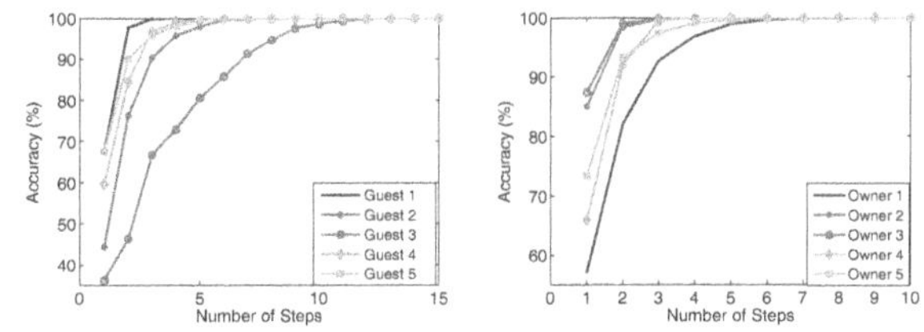


(a) Guest Accuracy (b) Owner Accuracy

**Figure 5: Identification based on walking feature.**

In the dynamic scenario, we extract 4 walking features, including vertical displacement, step duration, mean and standard deviation of horizontal acceleration and establish a SVM model for dynamic walking features. The same users are required to use the smartphone while they are walking freely. We collect their processed vertical and horizontal accelerations in the earth coordinate system. After collecting necessary information, we combine the walking features with touch event features to establish the SVM model. And such touch event features only contains the duration, pressure, and the operation mode. Figure 5 presents the achieved identification accuracy increases with observed steps. As shown in Figure 5(a), after 12 steps, the accuracy to identify a guest can achieve 100%. Similarly, Figure 5(b) shows that after 7 steps, the accuracy to identify the owner can achieve 100%.

# 4. ACKNOWLEDGMENTS

The research of authors is partially supported by NSF CNS-0832120, NSF CNS-1035894, NSF ECCS-1247944, NSF CNS-1050398, National Natural Science Foundation of China under Grant No. 61170216, No. 61228202, No. 61272426, China Postdoctoral Science Foundation funded project under grant 2012M510029 and 2013T60119.

# 5. REFERENCES

[1] Visidon applock. http://www.visidon.fi/en/Home.

[2] A. De Luca, A. Hang, F. Brudy, C. Lindner, and H. Hussmann. Touch me once and I know it's you!: implicit authentication based on touch screen patterns. In *CHI*, pages 987–996. ACM, 2012.

[3] M. Frank, R. Biedert, E. Ma, I. Martinovic, and D. Song. Touchalytics: On the applicability of touchscreen input as a behavioral biometric for continuous authentication. *IEEE TIFS*, 2013.

[4] A. Karlson, A. Brush, and S. Schechter. Can I borrow your phone?: understanding concerns when sharing mobile phones. In *ACM CHI*, pages 1647–1650, 2009.

[5] E. Miluzzo, A. Varshavsky, S. Balakrishnan, and R. R. Choudhury. Tapprints: your finger taps have fingerprints. In *ACM MobiSys*, pages 323–336, 2012.

[6] T. Vu, A. Baid, S. Gao, M. Gruteser, R. Howard, J. Lindqvist, P. Spasojevic, and J. Walling. Distinguishing users with capacitive touch communication. In *ACM MobiCom*, pages 197–208, 2012.

[7] Z. Xu, K. Bai, and S. Zhu. Taplogger: Inferring user inputs on smartphone touchscreens using on-board motion sensors. In *the 5th ACM Conference on Security and Privacy in Wireless and Mobile Networks*, pages 113–124, 2012.

[8] N. Zheng, K. Bai, H. Huang, and H. Wang. You are how you touch: User verification on smartphones via tapping behaviors. WM-CS-2012-06, http://www.wm.edu/as/computerscience/documents/cstechreports/WM-CS-2012-06.pdf

# Participant Recruitment and Data Collection Framework for Opportunistic Sensing: A Comparative Analysis

Güliz Seray Tuncay, Giacomo Benincasa and Ahmed Helmy
Department of Computer and Information Science and Engineering
University of Florida, Gainesville, FL 32611
{gstuncay, giacomo, helmy}@cise.ufl.edu

## ABSTRACT

Opportunistic sensing is a novel approach that exploits the sensing capabilities offered by smartphones and users' mobility to sense large scale areas without requiring the deployment of sensors in-situ. In this work, we propose a novel framework for fully distributed, opportunistic sensing which coherently integrates two main components that operate in DTN mode: i. participant recruitment and ii. data collection. We evaluate our approach by considering alternative implementations of the framework, and by measuring their performance via extensive trace-based simulations. Our results show how the performances of the considered protocols vary, depending on the particular scenario, and suggest guidelines for future development of distributed opportunistic sensing systems.

## Categories and Subject Descriptors

C.2.4 [**Computer-Communication Networks**]: Distributed Systems—*distributed applications*; C.2.2 [**Network Protocols**]: Routing Protocols

## Keywords

Crowdsensing, Opportunistic Sensing, DTN

## 1. INTRODUCTION

Recent advances in sensing capabilities, storage capacity, and computation power of smartphones–along with the increasing pervasiveness of their adoption–led to the development of people-centric applications that exploit the capabilities of these devices to crowdsource data collection about the users' surroundings. People-centric sensing has therefore become a viable approach for large-scale urban sensing activities that do not require the deployment of sensors in-situ. In opportunistic people-centric sensing, minimal or no interaction with the participants is required; in fact, opportunistic sensing applications may run in the background and opportunistically collect data with no need to interact with the participant. For example, an application as the one described in [1], that passively monitors 2G/3G data to assess the quality of mobile Internet from end-terminals, may benefit from the adoption of a distributed data collection model. The users would not need to upload their measurements using the cellular network, therefore saving bandwidth. High participation is crucial for the success of people-centric activities. Because of the low degree of interaction that the user is required to provide, opportunistic sensing may be a suitable and inexpensive way to achieve high participation; however, current approaches for people-centric sensing rely on centralized registries to recruit possible participants [2]. Moreover, the collected data is uploaded from the participants to remote servers by using cellular networks. These approaches may lead to privacy and economical concerns that may work as a disincentive for participation. It is therefore critical to devise alternative approaches to opportunistic sensing that are autonomous and fully distributed, and therefore potentially more privacy-preserving. We propose a generic mechanism to perform the *recruitment* and *data collection* activities in a completely distributed fashion. By doing so, we recognize that many different implementations may be applied, and therefore we also recognize the need for a framework to systematically evaluate these implementations. Our major contributions are summarized as follows:

- We introduce a unified distributed recruitment and data collection framework for opportunistic sensing.
- To assess the quality of the compared methods and identify their strengths and shortcomings, a systematic comparative analysis is conducted using a rich set of test suites and scenarios based on real wireless traces.
- The findings indicate guidelines for the use of DTN routing for opportunistic sensing based on sensing mission requirements and the sink model.

## 2. THE OVERALL FRAMEWORK

Opportunistic sensing activities consist of two phases: *recruitment* and *data collection*. The aim of the *recruitment* phase is to notify an upcoming sensing activity to the nodes that are likely to be able to take part in it. We call this set of nodes *candidate sensing nodes*. Since our focus is opportunistic sensing, where the users are not expected to change their behavior to take part in the sensing activity, some candidate sensing nodes may choose not to participate in the activity. We call the set of nodes that participate in the sensing activity, *sensing nodes*. The aim of the *data collection* phase is to return the sensory data that was collected by the sensing nodes to the organizer of the sensing activity.


*MobiCom'13*, September 30–October 4, 2013, Miami, Florida, USA
Copyright 2013 ACM 978-1-4503-1999-7/13/09.
http://dx.doi.org/10.1145/2500423.2504573 .

In order to perform distributed recruitment, we propose the use of *recruiter nodes* that advertise the sensing activity, while sensor data will be delivered to a set of *sink nodes*.

## 2.1 Implementation Details

We used **profile-cast** [3] and **opportunistic geocast** [4] (location-based) for recruitment, and **epidemic routing** [5] (context-oblivious), **prophet** [6] (encounter-based), **spray and wait** [7] (context oblivious) and modified versions of profile-cast and opportunistic geocast for data collection. In this section, we describe the modifications that we applied to these protocols.

### 2.1.1 Recruitment

Profile-cast can be used to perform the dissemination, and a profile which includes the locations in the sensing area can be used as the target profile. However, unlike the original version of profile-cast, where the aim is to reach nodes matching a certain target profile, for recruitment it is necessary to also reach the nodes that match only a *part* of the target profile. It is therefore necessary to change the similarity metric to evaluate the similarity between a subset of the locations and the behavioral profile of the nodes. Upon an encounter with a message holder, the encountered node's profile will be compared to the sets in the power set of the actual target profile and the message will be forwarded if for any of these sets the similarity is above the similarity threshold.

In opportunistic geocast, the expected visiting rate (EVR) is calculated for hexagonal cells that make up the entire routing space for a given geographical region. We modified this metric in such a way that EVR will be calculated for the buildings in the traces, not for the hexagonal cells. However, the two location representations are equivalent, since it is always possible to associate a building with its geographical location. We also devised a geographical dissemination protocol, **geo-dissemination**, which works in a similar way to opportunistic geocast, but nodes may keep a copy of the message and forward it several times.

### 2.1.2 Data Collection

When the locations visited by the sink are known a-priori, profile-cast may be used for the purpose of data collection; This location information can be used to describe the behavior of the sinks, and therefore included in the recruitment message, and used by the sensing nodes as a target profile for the data messages. Analogously to the recruitment case, data collection aims to reach *any* of the nodes that match the target profile. Because the sensing nodes are expected to greatly outnumber the number of data sinks and that they may produce a large number of messages, it is critical to limit the data replication by having the nodes run solely in gradient ascend mode. While this may significantly increase the delivery time, in many sensing applications it is not the case.

Opportunistic geocast can also be applied when the locations visited by the sink(s) are known. However, since broadcasting of collected data will result in a high communication overhead, this phase can be omitted and only the ascending gradient phase in the protocol can be applied to reach the sink(s).

When the sink locations are unknown, regular DTN routing protocols such as epidemic routing, prophet or spray and wait may be used without modification, if the sink IDs are known.

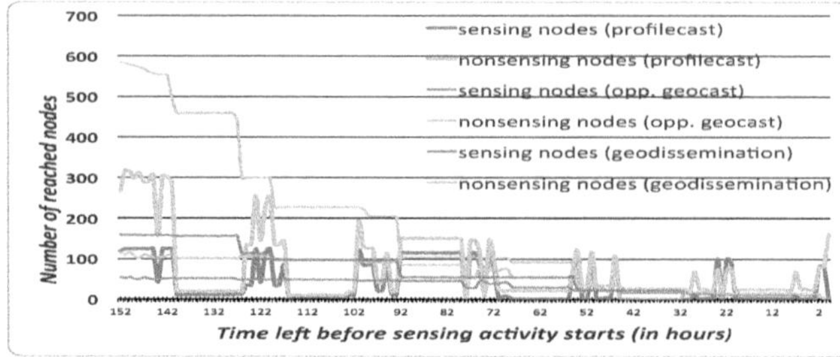


**Figure 1: Number of nodes that received the recruitment message (recruited and not recruited) versus time.**

## 3. EVALUATION AND RESULTS

In order to evaluate our approach, we developed a trace-driven simulation in a way analogous to what is described in [3]: we use the extensive WLAN traces that were collected on the USC campus in 2006 [8] and we assume users to be in communication range when they are associated with the same access point at the same time.

For the opportunistic sensing activity, we designed a test scenario in which the sensing activity is scheduled in the seven most visited locations of the USC campus. A single node, designated both as recruiter and data sink, is deployed one week before the start of the sensing activity, and is either static or continuously moves along a seven waypoint predefined path. The path of the sink is assumed to be included in the recruitment message and this behavior is continuously repeated along the duration of the sensing (from 8am to 8pm).

## 3.1 Recruitment

The recruiter node is configured to send a recruitment message every hour until the start of the sensing activity. We analyzed the traces and learned that the number of nodes that appear in the sensing area during the activity, and hence should be recruited, is 163.

### 3.1.1 Mobile sink for recruitment

The recruiter is mobile and travels between the top seven most visited locations. We compare the performances of profile-cast, opportunistic geocast and geo-dissemination for this scenario. While the size of the recruitment message may be negligible, we are still interested in limiting the number of unsolicited messages received by users that will not be able to participate in the sensing activity. Figure 1 shows the number of nodes that received at least one recruitment message for each of these protocols, and the portion of these nodes that will be able to take part in the sensing activity. Geocast recruits the smallest number of nodes (78) with the smallest overhead, and geo-dissemination recruits the highest number of nodes (159) with the highest overhead. Profilecast, on the other hand, achieves a trade-off between these protocols, by recruiting 126 nodes with a moderate overhead.

### 3.1.2 Static sink for recruitment

The sink is fixed at one the target locations or one of the two non-sensing locations for the duration of the re-

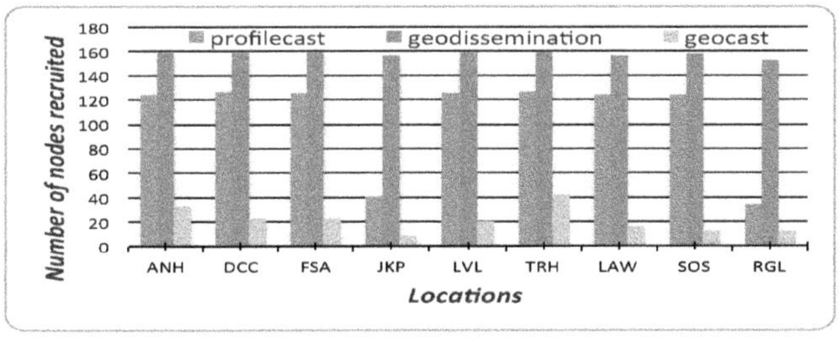


**Figure 2: Number of recruited nodes by the protocols for each fixed sink location. All locations except SOS and RGL are target locations from which users are recruited.**

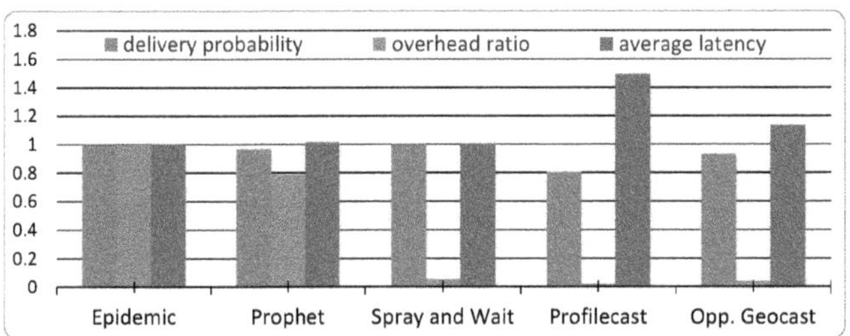


**Figure 3: Data collection performance comparison for mobile sink (normalized w.r.t epidemic routing)**

cruitment, and stays there until the end of data collection. Figure 2 shows the number of reached nodes by profile-cast, opportunistic geocast and geo-dissemination when the sink is static at a given location.

In case of a static sink, the number of nodes reached by opportunistic geocast decreases significantly. This shows that mobility has a considerable effect on the performance of this protocol. The overhead ratios of the protocols are similar to those in the mobile sink case. Profile-cast offers the best trade-off between the number of reached sensing nodes and reached non-sensing nodes, when the sink is mobile, and it still is a valid option when the sink is static.

## 3.2 Data Collection

We use the ONE simulator [9] to compare the performances of profile-cast, prophet, epidemic routing, spray and wait and opportunistic geocast DTN routing protocols. We focus on three major performance measures: 1) delivery ratio, 2) average delivery time and 3) overhead ratio.

### *3.2.1 Mobile sink for data collection*

The sink is mobile and travels between the top seven most visited locations. Figure 3 depicts the normalized performance metrics with respect to those of epidemic routing. The highlight of our results is that spray and wait leads to a delivery ratio as high as that of epidemic routing, an overhead ratio that is significantly lower than all protocols except profile-cast and opportunistic geocast, but it beats these two protocols in terms of latency.

### *3.2.2 Static sink for data collection*

The sink is fixed in one of considered locations, and collects data from all the eligible sensing nodes that are present in any of the target locations. Figure 4 shows the normalized average performances (with respect to epidemic routing) of all the nine locations. The performances of all protocols

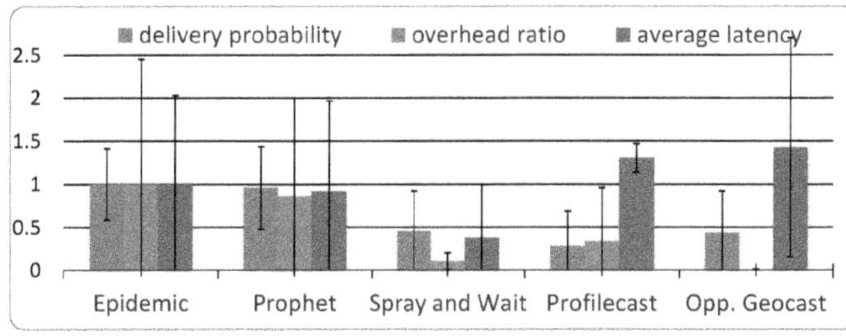


**Figure 4: Data collection performance comparison for static sink(normalized w.r.t epidemic routing)**

drop significantly for this scenario. The reason for this inefficiency is that the probability of encountering the sink drops drastically, and the messages need to follow a longer route, when it exists. In particular spray and wait's performance drops more significantly than that of other protocols since it blindly replicates messages to a limited number of nodes, without trying to select better forwarders. Figure 4 shows that prophet has the most consistent results with the mobile sink case; it is interesting to observe that although prophet starts collecting encounter information only after the start of the sensing activity, it still achieves a high delivery ratio.

# 4. CONCLUSION

In this work, we proposed a framework for autonomous and distributed recruitment and data collection in opportunistic sensing. We verified the feasibility of several applicable state-of-the-art DTN routing protocols for both the recruitment and data collection components, and provided a comprehensive analysis of their performances. Our results show that profile-cast is a reliable protocol for participant recruitment due to its comparably lower overhead and higher delivery rate. For the case of data collection, spray and wait outperforms the other protocols for the mobile sink case, although we showed that its performance degrades significantly when the sink only visits a subset of the sensed area, or does not visit the sensed area at all, and therefore there are only few, or no, direct encounters between the sensing nodes and the sink.

## References


[1] G. Hourton, G. Del Canto, J. Bustos, and F. Lalanne. Crowd-measuring: Assessing the quality of mobile internet from end-terminals. In *NetGCooP*, 2012.

[2] S. Reddy, D. Estrin, and M. Srivastava. Recruitment Framework for Participatory Sensing Data Collections. In *International Conference on Pervasive Computing*, 2010.

[3] CSI: A paradigm for behavior-oriented profile-cast services in mobile networks. *Ad Hoc Networks*, 2011.

[4] Y. Ma and A. Jamalipour. Opportunistic geocast in disruption-tolerant networks. In *IEEE GLOBECOM*, 2011.

[5] A. Vahdat and D. Becker. Epidemic routing for partially-connected ad hoc networks. Technical report, Duke University, 2000.

[6] A. Lindgren, A. Doria, and O. Schelén. Probabilistic routing in intermittently connected networks. *SIGMOBILE Mob. Comput. Commun. Rev.*, 2003.

[7] T. Spyropoulos, K. Psounis, and C. S. Raghavendra. Spray and wait: an efficient routing scheme for intermittently connected mobile networks. In *Proc. WDTN*, 2005.

[8] Mobilib: Community-wide library of mobility and wireless networks measurements. http://nile.cise.ufl.edu/mobilib.

[9] A. Keränen, J. Ott, and T. Kärkkäinen. The ONE Simulator for DTN Protocol Evaluation. In *Proc. SIMUTools*, 2009.

# SmartLoc: Push the Limit of the Inertial Sensor Based Metropolitan Localization Using Smartphone

Cheng Bo
Illinois Institute of Technology
Chicago, IL 60616, USA
cbo@hawk.iit.edu

Xiang-Yang Li
Illinois Institute of Technology
Chicago, IL 60616, USA
xli@cs.iit.edu

Taeho Jung
Illinois Institute of Technology
Chicago, IL 60616, USA
tjung@hawk.iit.edu

Xufei Mao
Tsinghua University
Beijing, China
xufei.mao@gmail.com

Yue Tao
Illinois Institute of Technology
Chicago, IL 60616, USA
ytao6@hawk.iit.edu

Lan Yao
Northeastern University
Shenyang, China
yaolan@mail.neu.edu.cn

## ABSTRACT

We present *SmartLoc*, a localization system to estimate the location and the traveling distance by leveraging the lower-power inertial sensors embedded in smartphones as a supplementary to GPS. To minimize the negative impact of sensor noises, *SmartLoc* exploits the intermittent strong GPS signals and uses the linear regression to build a prediction model which is based on the trace estimated from inertial sensors and the one computed from the GPS. Furthermore, we utilize landmarks (*e.g.*, bridge, traffic lights) detected automatically and special driving patterns (*e.g.*, turning, uphill, and downhill) from inertial sensory data to improve the localization accuracy when the GPS signal is weak. Our evaluations of *SmartLoc* in the city demonstrates its technique viability and significant localization accuracy improvement compared with GPS and other approaches: the error is approximately 20m for 90% of time while the known mean error of GPS is 42.22m.

## Categories and Subject Descriptors

H.4 [**Information Systems Applications**]: Miscellaneous

## Keywords

*SmartLoc*, Inertial Sensor, Localization

## 1. INTRODUCTION

Localization have attracted significant attentions in the past few decades, and numerous techniques [2, 11, 13] have been proposed to achieve high accuracy localization. In outdoor scenarios, GPS (Global Positioning System) or its variants are the most common technologies to provide accurate position [4] for various applications, such as trace and tracking [9, 12] in the wild, and environmental monitoring [7]. However, problems regarding low accuracy of GPS in critical regions such as metropolises have proposed the idea of war-driving and created the state of art large scale WiFi/GSM fingerprint database for positioning, like Skyhook [1]. These methods often sample and establish fingerprint databases, which are computationally intensive.

To study the severity of the GPS localization [6] errors in metropolises, we conducted comprehensive experiments in downtown Chicago to evaluate the performance of GPS positioning. Based on the experiment results, we observe that the GPS signals are very weak and unstable in some roads due to highrises, or even blocked completely in some complicated road structures, such as tunnels and underground. In addition, the largest location error we collected is over 100m on the ground, and nearly 400m in the underground segments. Thus, improving the location accuracy is imperative when the GPS signal is weak in metropolises.

In this work, we propose *SmartLoc*, a localization method which improves the localization accuracy in metropolises by leveraging embedded inertial sensors in smartphones to help improve the driving patterns according to various of road conditions. Although exploiting the data collected from inertial sensors has been used to measure the walking speed and distance of pedestrian in outdoor environment [3, 5, 8, 10], realtime localization of driving cars in metropolises is still far more challenging as such activity does not have a cyclic pattern in sensor data.

To address these challenges, during the dead reckoning process for calculating the current position of a car, we propose a dynamic trajectory model to estimate the driving speed and velocity based on current road condition, so that the impact of inherent noise and accumulated error could be reduced to a large extent. We also design a calibration strategy based on road infrastructures (*e.g.*, bridge, traffic lights, uphill, and downhill) and driving status (*e.g.*, turns, stops), which are inferred from the sensory data.

*SmartLoc* also exploits the current coarse-grained estimation of location to confine the search space, so that a much more accurate localization could be achieved through matching the road infrastructures and driving status.

## 2. APPROACH

The purpose of **SmartLoc** is to use inertial sensors in the smartphone to estimate the movement of the vehicle, and lively provide locations based on the traveling distance and orientation with high accuracy but low energy consumption. Remarkably, we not only address the inaccuracy caused by the complex infrastructures in downtown area, but also exploit them as landmarks in the map to improve the localization accuracy of localization.

### 2.1 Self-learning Predictive Model

According to the Newton's Law, we can obtain the distance after applying a double integration on the acceleration. However, the noises from the accelerometer will be accumulated also so that


*MobiCom'13,* September 30–October 4, 2013, Miami, FL, USA.
ACM 978-1-4503-1999-7/13/09.
http://dx.doi.org/10.1145/2500423.2504574.

the estimation error gets enormously huge in just several minutes. However, we observe from our preliminary experiments that the majority of the road segments with bad GPS signals (error $\geq$ 30m) are usually shorter than 400m, which takes only 20-30 seconds to drive through in a normal condition. On the one hand, such distance is long enough to navigate drivers to wrong places, on the other hand it is short enough to endure the errors to some extent. Therefore, we propose the following predictive dynamic trajectory estimating model which adaptively calibrates itself using GPS signals and dead reckoning.

**Velocity Estimator:** Because of the inherent noises and measurement errors, the traditional velocity estimation model is no longer reliable. In this case, we denote the velocity $V_i$ at the end of a timeslot $i$ as

$$V_i = V_{i-1} + \beta \cdot a_i \cdot \Delta t + \mu$$

where $\beta$ is the parameter to be learned and adjusted in real time, $a_i$ is the average measured acceleration during the timeslot $i$, and $\mu$ is the noise. When GPS signals are strong, both $V_i$ and $V_{i-1}$ could be achieved from the GPS directly, and the mean linear acceleration $a_i$ is extracted from the accelerometer. Then we regress the model to find the best $\beta$, and calculate the noise $\mu$ hiding behind. When the localization through GPS is unreliable, we use the trained model proposed to predict the velocity $V_i$.

**Distance Estimator:** For general cases, the trajectory distance gathered from GPS indicates the distance with some error. Therefore, letting $G(\Delta t_i)$ be the distance during a timeslot $i$ read from GPS, which could be presented as:

$$G(\Delta t_i) = \lambda_1 \cdot V_{i-1} \cdot \Delta t + \frac{1}{2} \cdot \widehat{a_i} \cdot \Delta t^2 + \eta$$

where $\widehat{a_i}$ is the actual acceleration in the time slot $i$. Here $\lambda_1$ is multiplied to reflect the error in the estimated speed $V_{i-1}$ for the time slot $i-1$. Since the known measured acceleration $a_i$ contains both inherent noise and measurement errors, by assuming that these error follows normal distribution, we define the measured acceleration as: $a_i = (1+\varepsilon)\widehat{a_i} + \delta$, where $\widehat{a_i}$ is considered as the true acceleration which cannot be obtained. Then, we use the following formula to estimate the distance $G(\Delta t_i)$:

$$G(\Delta t_i) = \lambda_1 \cdot V_{i-1} \cdot \Delta t + \lambda_2 \frac{1}{2} \cdot a_i \cdot \Delta t^2 + \lambda_3 \cdot \Delta t^2 + \lambda_4 \cdot \Delta t + \eta \quad (1)$$

where $\lambda_1, \cdots, \lambda_4$ are parameters to be learned by our regression model. When GPS signals are strong (GPS error is $\leq$ 20m), based on the $V_{i-1}$, $a_i$ is computed using the sensory data and the distance from GPS, we train our model using Eq. (1), which is in turn used to predict the distance $G(\Delta t_i)$ in the time slot $i$ when GPS signals are bad. From the predicted trajectory distance $G(\Delta t_i)$, the location at the timeslot $i$ could be estimated based on the obtained location, distance and orientation.

## 2.2 Calibration By Landmarks

The road infrastructures, including tunnels, bridges, crossroads and traffic lights, cause large noises in the GPS data, which results in large drift in the distance estimation if it is not treated rigorously. In this work, we exploit the precise location of these infrastructures that are available in Google Map to calibrate the localization without any extra cost.

**Traffic Light:** When the vehicle stops due to the traffic lights and drives through crossroads, unique patterns appear in the readings of sensors (Figure 1(a)). Actually, when vehicles encounters traffic lights, the whole process can be divided into two phases, braking and speeding up respectively. However, in rush hours with terrible traffic, the location where cars stop may not be near the crossroad, but with a certain distance from the crossroad. In this case, *SmartLoc* adjusts the moving distance based on the estimated stopping location from the empirical data, *i.e.*, subtracting the distance from the car to the crossroad. However, the distance between the car and the crossroad is determined by the traffic condition, it is difficult to measure the exact distance from the car to the crossroad. The main approach adopted by *SmartLoc* is to subtract the $\frac{n \cdot L}{2}$, where $L$ indicates the average length of a vehicle, and $n$ represents the current possible number of vehicles waiting for the green light. We calculate the number of vehicle based on the observed data, and $n$ is also related to different time periods.

**Turning:** Sometimes, vehicles may turn at intersections, which could be detected by sensors. Figure 1(b) indicates the centripetal force sensed by the accelerometer, and the scale of the acceleration depends on the speed at which the vehicle is turning. Simultaneously, the angular velocity sensed by the gyroscope also reaches up to 0.5 rad/s in our test case (Figure 1(c)), and the data from the magnetometer changes as well with a large fluctuation. Finally, the orientation of the smartphone also changes approximately 90 degrees when turning left or right. Although the angle may not be accurate enough due to the large noise in the magnetometer (the maximum error we experienced was approximately $30^o$), we are still able to correctly determine the road segment to which the car is turning by calibration. Figure 2(a) shows a case when vehicle turns from the north, the angle is from about $350^o$ to $100^o$, which is east. We also compare the measured angle difference for turning and lane changing (Figure 2(b)) since lane changing can be wrongly detected as a turning. The angle difference when a car changes its lane is much smaller than the one when a car make a turn.

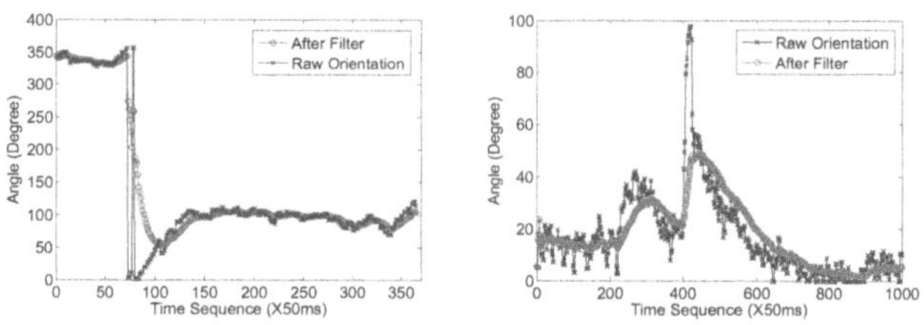


(a) Turning (b) Changing Lane

**Figure 2: Turning or changing lanes, and Driving Trace**

In fact, certain driving patterns, such as turing left or right and stopping for traffic lights or stop signs, can be more accurately detected and thus classified. To classify other road infrastructures, we collect the sensor readings of those patterns to store as the fingerprints, and then match the real-time sensor readings with the trained fingerprints. To improve the classification and the matching accuracy, we rely on the coarse-grained estimation of the location from dead-reckoning first, and then we further use our predictive regression model to confine the search space: only the road infrastructures (stored fingerprints) $I$ within a certain distance $\delta$ from the estimated location $x$ will considered as the matching candidate for the real-time pattern $P$ achieved from the sensor data. We select the infrastructure that maximizes the *weighted matching score*:

$$\alpha M(I,P) + (1-\alpha)e^{-D(x,L(I))}$$

where $M(I,P)$ is the matching score between the fingerprint of an infrastructure $I$ and the observed pattern $P$, $\alpha \in (0,1)$ is a constant, and $D(x, L(I))$ is the geodesic distance between the location $x$ and the location $L(I)$ of infrastructure $I$. Then, the estimated location $x$ is updated as the location $L(I^*)$ of the infrastructure $I^*$ which maximizes the weighted matching score.

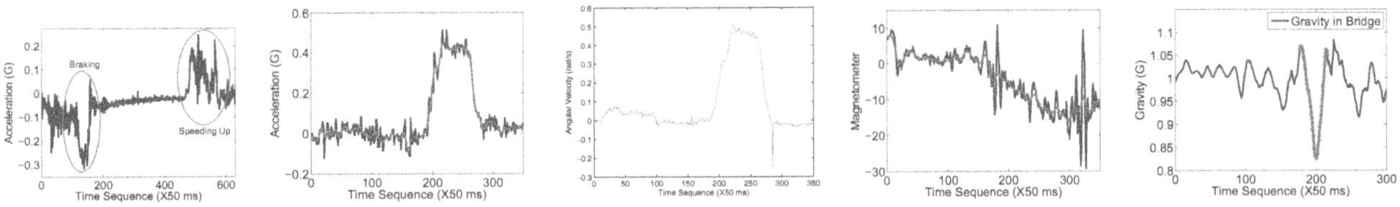


(a) Traffic lights (b) Centripetal force (c) Angular velocity (d) Magnetometer (e) Bridge

**Figure 1: Pattern of the sensor data collected in different road infrastructures when driving: (a) car stopping and crossing a traffic light; (b), (c), and (d) car turning $90^o$; and (e) car crossing a bridge.**

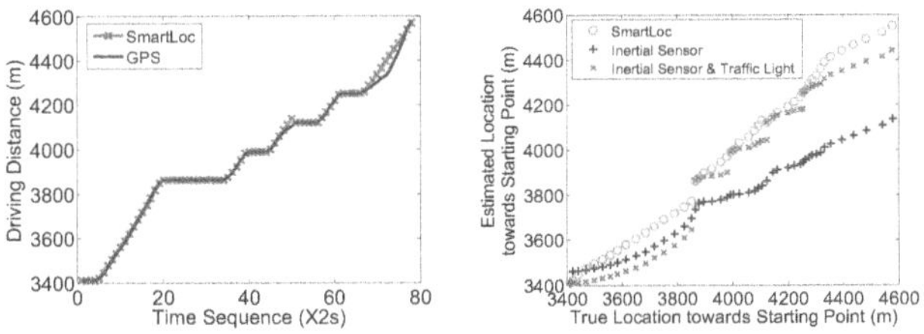


(a) SmartLoc (b) Overall Comparison

**Figure 3: Distance prediction comparison among three methods and ground truth.**

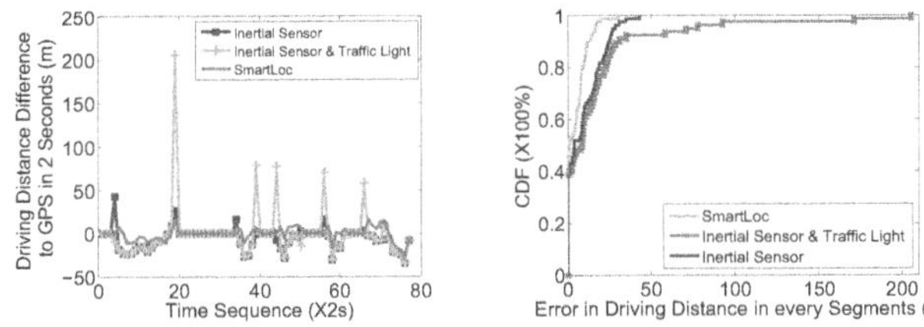


(a) Error of driving distance in each time slot (b) Error of driving distance in each segment.

**Figure 4: Comparison of three methods.**

# 3. PRELIMINARY RESULTS

We conduct a preliminary evaluations of SmartLoc in downtown Chicago for over 100 different road segments ranging from 1km to 10km. Since the inertial sensors provide the driving orientation, combined with driving distance from the location in last timeslot, the real-time location could be obtained. Thus, the key problem becomes estimating the trajectory distance.

SmartLoc calibrates the location as soon as it detects specific patterns, especially traffic lights and turnings. We compare the performance of three different methods in detail: using inertial sensors only, using sensors and landmark calibration, and using *SmartLoc* with all learning model and calibration.

In this experiment, we assume the first 3400m is with reliable G-PS signals, and the precise locations are accessible. The estimation starts from 3400m, and the first three figures in Figure 3 indicate the driving distance from the starting point versus the elapsed time. Surprisingly, after combining our predictive regression model and the noise canceling technique, *SmartLoc*'s result almost coincides with the ground truth, as shown in Figure 3(a). For the first 900m, the curve of *SmartLoc* nearly overlaps with the curve of the ground truth. For the first 450m, the vehicle passes three crossroads with all green lights, and the error is less than 20m in most of the time. After the final traffic lights, the vehicle has to drive at a relatively low speed because of the road construction. The predicted distance consequently deviates from the ground truth a little, but at the end of the road, the errors remain small. We plot all the estimated distances by three methods in Figure 3(b), with the X axis being the ground truth distance and Y axis being the predicted distance, *i.e.*, the perfect prediction will have a diagonal line. *SmartLoc* results are distributed almost along the diagonal line, and pure sensor approach deviates greatly.

The deviation of the results from the ground truth comes from the accumulated errors from all time slots. Based on the previous experiments, we plot the error in every time slot in Figure 4(a). *SmartLoc* with landmarks calibration has the smallest mean error of the estimated locations for all time slots: 90% of them are lower than 20m from the CDF in Figure 4(b). The other two approaches have larger errors, and the last figure describes the CDF of the total driving distance error.

# 4. ACKNOWLEDGMENTS

The research of authors is partially supported by NSF CNS-0832120, NSF CNS-1035894, NSF ECCS-1247944, National Natural Science Foundation of China under Grant No. 61170216, No. 61228202, No. 61272426, No. 61100182 China Postdoctoral Science Foundation funded project under grant 2012M510029 and 2013T60119.

# 5. REFERENCES

[1] Skyhook. http://www.skyhookwireless.com/.

[2] C. Bo, S. Tang, D. Ren, X.-Y. Li, X. Mao, Q. Huang, L. Mo, Z. Jiang, Y. Sun, and Y. Liu Locating Sensors in the Forest: A Case Study in GreenOrbs, *IEEE INFOCOM*, 2012.

[3] W. Chen, Z. Fu, R. Chen, Y. Chen, O. Andrei, T. Kroger, and J. Wang. An integrated GPS and multi-sensor pedestrian positioning system for 3d urban navigation. In *IEEE Joint Urban Remote Sensing Event*, pages 1–6, 2009.

[4] Y. Cheng, Y. Chawathe, A. LaMarca, and J. Krumm. Accuracy characterization for metropolitan-scale Wi-Fi localization. In *ACM MobiSys*, pages 233–245, 2005.

[5] I. Constandache, R. Choudhury, and I. Rhee. Towards mobile phone localization without war-driving. In *IEEE INFOCOM*, pages 1–9, 2010.

[6] W. Hedgecock, M. Maroti, J. Sallai, P. Volgyesi, and A. Ledeczi. High-accuracy differential tracking of low-cost GPS receivers. 2013.

[7] L. Mo, Y. He, Y. Liu, J. Zhao, S. Tang, X. Li, and G. Dai. Canopy closure estimates with greenorbs: sustainable sensing in the forest. In *ACM SenSys*, pages 99–112, 2009.

[8] G. Retscher. An intelligent multi-sensor system for pedestrian navigation. *Journal of GPS*, 5(1-2):110–118, 2006.

[9] B. Thorstensen, T. Syversen, T. Bjørnvold, and T. Walseth. Electronic shepherd-a low-cost, low-bandwidth, wireless network system. In *ACM MobiSys*, pages 245–255, 2004.

[10] H. Wang, S. Sen, A. Elgohary, M. Farid, M. Youssef, and R. Choudhury. No need to war-drive: Unsupervised indoor localization. In *ACM MobiSys*, pages 197–210, 2012.

[11] Z. Yang, Y. Liu, X.-Y. Li, Beyond Trilateration: On the Localizability of Wireless Ad-hoc Networks in *IEEE/ACM Trans on Netw.*, 2010 Vol. 18, pp 1806 - 1814.

[12] P. Zhang, C. Sadler, S. Lyon, and M. Martonosi. Hardware design experiences in zebranet. In *ACM SenSys*, pages 227–238, 2004.

[13] J. Zhao, W. Xi, Y. He, Y. Liu, X.-Y. Li, L. Mo, and Z. Yang, Localization of Wireless Sensor Networks in the Wild: Pursuit of Ranging Quality, in *IEEE/ACM Trans. on Netw.*, 21(1): 311-323 (2013)

# You're Driving and Texting: Detecting Drivers Using Personal Smart Phones by Leveraging Inertial Sensors

Cheng Bo
Illinois Institute of Technology
Chicago, IL 60616, USA
cbo@hawk.iit.edu

Xuesi Jian
Illinois Institute of Technology
Chicago, IL 60616, USA
xjian@hawk.iit.edu

Xiang-Yang Li
Illinois Institute of Technology
Chicago, IL 60616, USA
xli@cs.iit.edu

Xufei Mao
School of Software and TNLIST
Tsinghua University, China
xufei.mao@gmail.com

Yu Wang
University of North Carolina at Charlotte
Charlotte, NC 28223, USA
yu.wang@uncc.edu

Fan Li
Department of Computer Science
Beijing Institute of Technology
fli@bit.edu.cn

## ABSTRACT

In this work, we address a critical task of detecting the user behavior of driving and texting simultaneously using smartphones. We propose, design, and implement **TEXIVE** which achieves the goal of distinguishing drivers and passengers, and detecting texting operations during driving utilizing irregularities and rich micro-movements of users. Without relying on any external infrastructures and additional devices, and no need to bring any modification to vehicles, **TEXIVE** is able to successfully detect dangerous operations with good *sensitivity*, *specificity* and *accuracy*. We conduct experimental study of **TEXIVE** with the help of a number of volunteers using various vehicles and smartphones. Our results indicate that **TEXIVE** has a classification accuracy of 87.18%, and precision of 96.67%.

## Categories and Subject Descriptors

H.4 [**Information Systems Applications**]: Miscellaneous

## Keywords

**TEXIVE**, Smartphone, Classification

## 1. INTRODUCTION

One recent study indicates that there are at least 23% of all vehicles crashed and 1.3 million crashes in the US involve using cell phones (especially texting) during driving [2] although over 30 states and District of Columbia has forbidden texting message while driving [1]. Such severe security issue has stirred numerous researches and innovations on detecting and preventing driving and texting operations so that a number of distracted driving behavior detection approaches have been proposed, e.g., mounting a camera to monitor the driver [8], relying on acoustic ranging through car speakers [7], use adapter that provides vehicle speed reference readings to the phone [6], and cloud computing to recognize drivers' operations [3].


*MobiCom'13,* September 30–October 4, 2013, Miami, FL, USA.
ACM 978-1-4503-1999-7/13/09.
http://dx.doi.org/10.1145/2500423.2504575.

In this work, we address this critical task of detecting driving and texting activities. We propose **TEXIVE**, a system leveraging inertial sensors integrated in regular smartphones to distinguish drivers from passengers through recognizing rich micro-movement dynamics of smartphone users, and further detect driving and texting activities of drivers. Our main idea is to let **TEXIVE** recognize micro-movements by fusing multiple evidences collected from inertial sensors in smartphones, e.g., detecting whether a user is entering a vehicle or not, inferring which side of the vehicle he/she is entering, determining whether a user is siting in front or rear seats, or even detecting which side if multiple users in the car collaborate.

We collected the data from motion sensors when users are performing various activities and observed some unique patterns by converting the signal to the frequency domain using DCT and wavelet. To infer whether a user enters the vehicle from left side or right side of the vehicle, or sits in front or rear seats, we exploit the unique patterns mined from the rich dynamics in the accelerometer and magnetometer data observed during respective actions, and make cognitive decision based on machine learning techniques.

Unlike most related solutions, **TEXIVE** is designed based on regular smartphones without supporting from any external infrastructures and additional devices. In addition, **TEXIVE** does not bring any modification to vehicles. We conduct extensive experiments involving in a number of volunteers on various vehicles and smartphones and the results show that **TEXIVE** has a classification accuracy of 87.18%, and precision of 96.67%.

## 2. SYSTEM DESIGN

To address the challenge of distinguishing between driver and passenger, we will leverage the existing inertial sensors integrated in smartphones and exploit some unique and distinguishable patterns mined from a sequence of sensory data.

### 2.1 System Architecture Overview

We adopt a three-phase solution to accomplish the task: initial walking detecting, in-vehicle recognition, and evidence fusion respectively. Figure 1 illustrates the basic working flow of the system according to the three phases, and the functionality of detailed components is as follows.

**Activity Identification:** Generally, most of users get used to carry their smartphones all day long, which facilitate observing multiple activities. One of tasks is to identify related activities from a rich set of potential daily activities, including walking, sitting, standing or even ascending stairs. One thing deserves mention is that **TEXIVE** does **not** require *any* interaction from the user. We

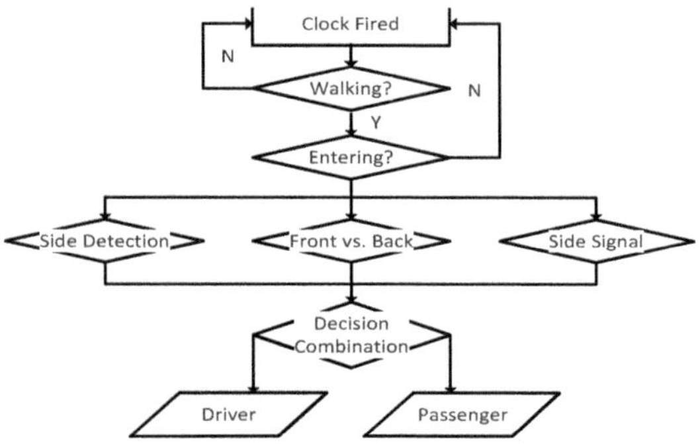


**Figure 1: The system overview**

study the temporal and spatial distribution of different activities as well, through constructing a Hidden Markov Model (HMM) [5] to personalize the model, and further optimize the energy consumption by carefully adjusting the duty-cycle.

**Detecting Boarding Side:** Although whether a user entering a vehicle from either side of the vehicle is a driver could be inferred most of time directly, we cannot guarantee the identity of the user precisely. Hence, it is still necessary to judge the boarding side for users. **TEXIVE** recognizes the entering activity based on direction of turning and sequence of lifting leg to judge the boarding side of a user. Turning and lifting actions on different sides of the vehicle could be reflected through inertial sensors, which will act divergent under different side and place of the body.

**Detecting Front vs. Back:** Our approach relies on the unique and distinguishable patterns reflected on the acceleration between front and back seats when vehicle is crossing a bump or pothole. According to our preliminary tests, the bump signal, although not guaranteed to happen, can always accurately determine whether the phone (user) is in front seats or rear seats.

## 2.2 Entering Vehicles?

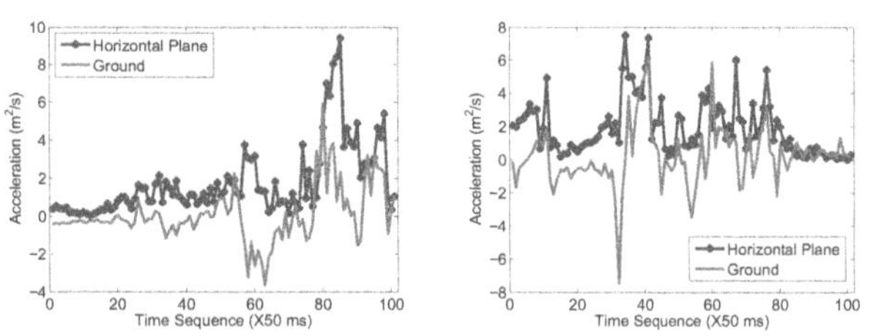


(a) Driver Side, Left Pocket (b) Driver Side, Right Pocket

**Figure 2: Data extracted from accelerometer in Horizon plane and ground when people enter vehicles.**

A key challenge of this system is to identify specific activities in real-time, especially determining whether a user will enter a vehicle or is just performing other activities, which have similar observable patterns. Empirically, the activity of getting into vehicle consists of five basic actions, including walking towards the vehicle, opening the door, turning the body, entering, and sitting down.

A study [4] indicates that most of the users carry their phone in trousers. We first collected 200 samples of entering vehicle from both driver and passenger sides in the parking lot by a group of volunteers with the smartphones in trouser pockets. We extract the linear acceleration and transform it to the Earth Frame Coordinate, to reduce the impact of irregular and unpredictable positions of smartphones in the pocket. The activity of entering the vehicle in both horizontal plane and ground direction is shown in Figure 2, in which the difference is obvious. With Naive Bayesian classifier, the accuracy and precision of distinguishing 40 cases of entering from nearly 296 other activities are 84.46% and 45.24%. Unfortunately, several other activities (sitting down mostly) could be misjudged as car-entering activity, which negatively impacts the performance. To overcome this, we propose a more comprehensive ambient-aware filter to improve the accuracy. The filter is based on the observation the sensed ambient magnetic field fluctuates more dramatically when approaching the vehicle than other activities.

## 2.3 Which Boarding Side?

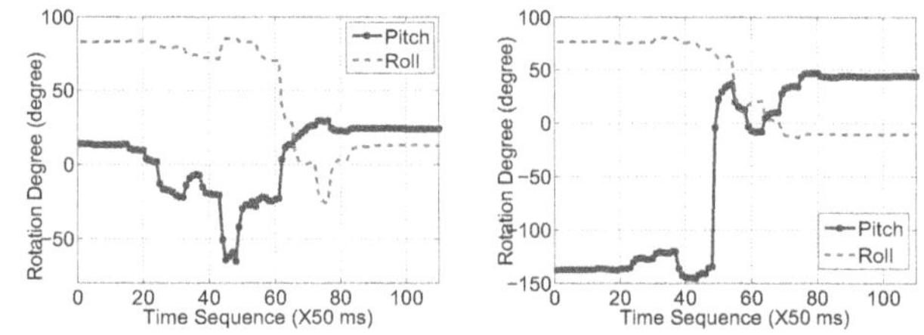


(a) Left Pocket, Driver Side (b) Right Pocket, Driver Side

**Figure 3: Side detection by observing rotation along BFC.**

The system conducts side-detection operations simultaneously with the entering-detection so that the detection delay is minimized. The pure acceleration-based determination may fail in judging the boarding side of a user because of the possibility that a user with his/her phone in left pocket boarding from the right side has similar observing pattern as that of a user with his/her phone in his right pocket boarding from the left side.

We found another key factor determining the direction of body rotation when entering from both sides. Usually, in order to face front, the driver has to turn left while the passenger will turn right before he/she enters into the car, and such small duration of action could be captured by the gyroscope sensor in both *Pitch* and *Roll*, shown in Figure 3. Although the orientation of vehicle is unknown and unpredictable, the turning-based determination is demonstrated to be robust during our evaluation. We also adopt Extend Kalman Filter to eliminate the internal mechanism noise of sensors.

## 2.4 Front or Back Seats?

Solving the front-or-back problem is inspired by the experience that when we drive through a bump or a pothole, people sitting in the back row feel more bumpy than those sitting in the front. The thought is verified in analyzing our data collected by driving through either bumps or potholes (Fig. 4).

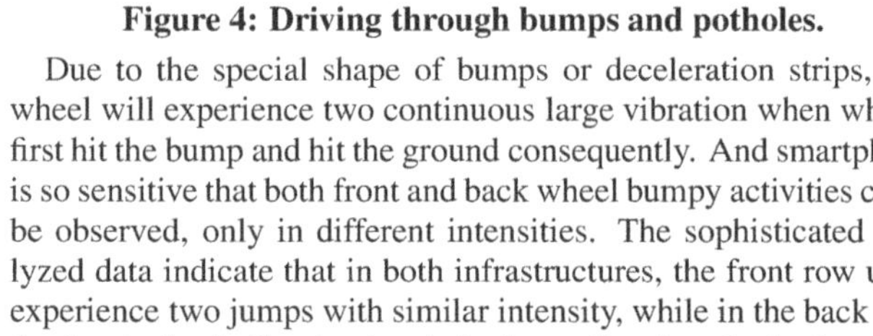


(a) Driving through bump (b) Driving through pothole

**Figure 4: Driving through bumps and potholes.**

Due to the special shape of bumps or deceleration strips, one wheel will experience two continuous large vibration when wheels first hit the bump and hit the ground consequently. And smartphone is so sensitive that both front and back wheel bumpy activities could be observed, only in different intensities. The sophisticated analyzed data indicate that in both infrastructures, the front row users experience two jumps with similar intensity, while in the back row, the front-wheel vibration is relatively smaller than the back-wheel, as shown in Figure 4(a) and 4(b) respectively.

## 2.5 Texting?

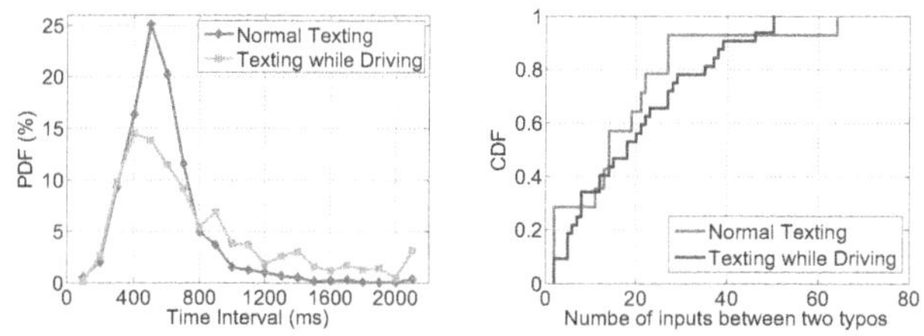


(a) The probability of different time interval between two inputs

(b) The typo frequency

**Figure 5: The information extracted from typing.**

**TEXIVE** triggers necessary warning when endangered texting activity is detected, and the key to satisfy the demand is detecting distracted behavior within a small amount of input or before touching the screen. Generally, typing is not a difficult task when user are fully concentrated, with fewer typo and higher typing speed. We conduct a set of experiments by a group of volunteers to compose multiple sentence in smartphone in both normal and driving scenarios, focusing on both the time interval between two inputs, and the frequency of typo.

We plot typing time interval between two inputs in Figure 5(a). We notice that the large difference in average typing speeds and standard deviation in two cases are generated from the fact that driver has to pause and watch the road after one word or phrase to keep alert. Therefore, the typo are more likely to happen in this case, as shown in Figure 5(b).

# 3. PRELIMINARY RESULTS

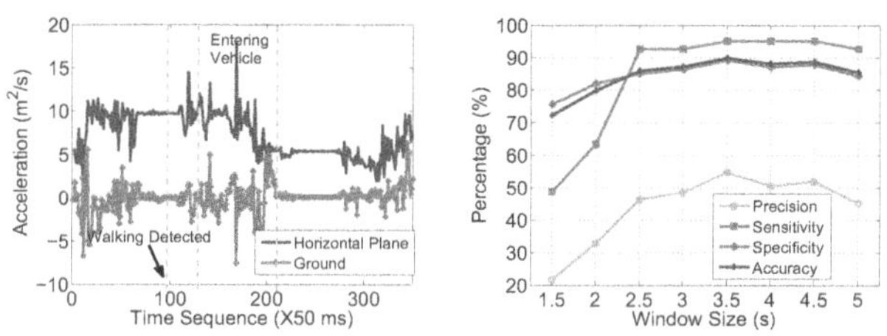


(a) Detecting the first arriving signal

(b) Recognition of entering vehicles

**Figure 6: Detecting entering vehicles.**

Initially, we evaluate the performance of entering activity detection, more specifically, the capability of both extracting entering pattern in a series of sensory data and distinguish from others.

Figure 6(a) illustrates the successful detection of first signal according to the protocol reflected in acceleration from the perspective of both horizontal and ground direction. The smartphone is put in the pocket, and **TEXIVE** perceives a walking activity from $112^{th}$ time slot, and the entering signal arrives 2 seconds later($133^{th}$ time slot). In addition, we evaluate the precision, sensitivity, specificity and accuracy with respect to different window sizes of the action. We set the window size ranging from $1.5s$ to $5s$ and plot the results in Figure 6(b), which indicates that generally the performance improves with the increment of window size. The system reaches a better performance when the window side is around $4s$ to $4.5s$, with both sensitivity are over $90\%$. After the behavior is determined, the detection of boarding side is followed. For both side, the accuracy reaches $85\%$ and the precision is as high as $95\%$ in the same window size.

We also take a number of comprehensive experiments in both parking lot and local roads to evaluate the efficiency of front-back distinguish using bumps and potholes. We drive through both one deceleration strip and one bump in the parking lot ten times each with different driving speeds. The test results in Table 1 indicates absolute correctness, 20 bumps are all successfully detected in both locations.

**Table 1: Bump in the parking lot**

| | Bump in Front | Bump in Back |
|---|---|---|
| Test in Front | 20 | 0 |
| Test in Back | 0 | 20 |

In local road test, the smartphone of driver detects 334 samples of readings and 23 of bumps and potholes, while the back seat passenger only detects 286 samples but 58 bumps and potholes. Although the number of bumps and potholes being detected by both smartphones are different, because of the starting time of passenger is behind the driver, both smartphones report they are in the right location with accuracy of $100\%$.

To detect driving and texting, we sample 20 different typing cases with 8 texting in normal condition and 12 in driving condition in the parking lot. The evaluation in texting detecting is reliable and feasible, the accuracy is $90\%$.

Based on our experiment, we notice that the performance of **TEXIVE** mainly depends on the first two phases. We test the performance of driver detection based on the fusion of all the phases, the precision is $96.67\%$ and accuracy $87.18\%$. Meanwhile, according to the real evaluation in Android smartphone, the recognition delay is only $0.2184$ second.

# 4. ACKNOWLEDGMENTS


The research of authors is partially supported by NSF CNS-0832120, NSF CNS-1035894, NSF ECCS-1247944, NSF CNS-1050398, National Natural Science Foundation of China under Grant No. 61170216, No. 61228202, No. 61272426, China Postdoctoral Science Foundation funded project under grant 2012M510029 and 2013T60119. The work of Fan Li is partially supported by the National Natural Science Foundation of China under Grant 60903151, 61370244 and Beijing Natural Science Foundation under Grant 4122070.


# 5. REFERENCES


[1] Insurance institute for highway safety. http://www.iihs.gov/.

[2] National highway traffic safety administration (nhtsa). http://www.nhtsa.gov/.

[3] H. Chu, V. Raman, J. Shen, R. Choudhury, A. Kansal, and V. Bahl. In-vehicle driver detection using mobile phone sensors. In *ACM MobiSys*, 2011.

[4] Y. Cui, J. Chipchase, and F. Ichikawa. A cross culture study on phone carrying and physical personalization. In *UI-HCII*, pages 483–492. Springer, 2007.

[5] L. Rabiner and B. Juang. An introduction to hidden markov models. *IEEE ASSP Magazine*, 3(1):4–16, 1986.

[6] Y. Wang, J. Yang, H. Liu, Y. Chen, M. Gruteser, and R. P. Martin. Sensing vehicle dynamics for determining driver phone use. In *ACM MobiSys*, 2013.

[7] J. Yang, S. Sidhom, G. Chandrasekaran, T. Vu, H. Liu, N. Cecan, Y. Chen, M. Gruteser, and R. Martin. Detecting driver phone use leveraging car speakers. In *ACM MobiCom*, pages 97–108, 2011.

[8] C.-W. You, N. D. Lane, F. Chen, R. Wang, Z. Chen, T. J. Bao, M. Montes-de Oca, Y. Cheng, M. Lin, L. Torresani, et al. Carsafe App: Alerting drowsy and distracted drivers using dual cameras on smartphones. *ACM Mobisys*, 2013.

# Making the Case For Computational Offloading in Mobile Device Clouds


Afnan Fahim
School of Computer Science
Carnegie Mellon University
Doha, Qatar
afnan@cmu.edu

Abderrahmen Mtibaa
ECE Department
Texas A&M University
Doha, Qatar
amtibaa@tamu.edu

Khaled A. Harras
School of Computer Science
Carnegie Mellon University
Doha, Qatar
kharras@cs.cmu.edu



## ABSTRACT

In this paper, we consider an environment in which computational offloading is adopted amongst mobile devices. We call such an environment a *mobile device cloud* (MDC). In this work, we highlight via emulation, experimenation and real measurements, the potential gain in computation time and energy consumption that can be achieved by offloading tasks within an MDC. We also propose and develop an experimental platform to enable researchers create and experiment with novel offloading algorithms in MDCs.


## Categories and Subject Descriptors

C.2.4 [**Computer Systems Organization**]: Computer Communication Networks—*Distributed Systems*


## Keywords

Computation Offloading, Measurements, Mobile Device Clouds


## 1. INTRODUCTION

Computational offloading, also known as cyber foraging, had greatly evolved over the past few years [4]. Recent examples of this work includes offloading tasks from mobile devices to remote cloud resources [2], automatically transforming mobile applications by partitioning its execution into offloadable tasks [1], and arguing the need for bringing computational resources closer to offloaders in order to save energy [5].

In this work, we consider environments in which computational offloading is performed *among a set of mobile devices* forming what we call a *Mobile Device Cloud (MDC)*. Such offloading context was also considered in Serendipity [6]. We build on their work by adopting an experimental approach highlighting the potential gain in energy and time which can be achieved by offloading computation among devices in an MDC. We investigate the possibility of saving energy and time by offloading sub-tasks to neighboring mobile devices.




*MobiCom'13*, September 30–October 4, Miami, FL, USA.
ACM 978-1-4503-1999-7/13/09.
http://dx.doi.org/10.1145/2500423.2504576 .


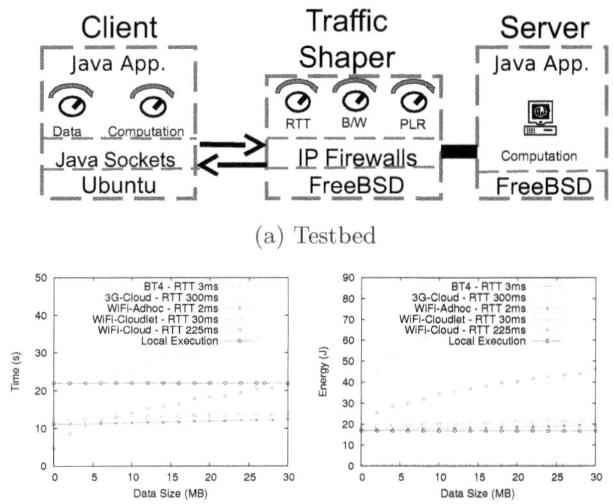


(a) Testbed

(b) Resp. time

(c) Energy cons

**Figure 1: Emulation testbed and preliminary results for moderate intensive tasks (30MFLOP)**

We implement an emulation testbed as a first step towards evaluating the potential gain of computational offloading in mobile environments. The testbed, shown in Fig. 1-(a), includes an offloading application running on a client, an offloadee server receiving tasks varying in data and computational needs from the offloader, and a traffic shaper situated between the client and server emulating various communication technologies. We identify five communication technologies that can be used to offload tasks, namely, Bluetooth 3.0, Bluetooth 4.0, WiFi Direct, WiFi and 3G. The testbed evaluates the gain achieved using any of the available communication technologies for different combinations of data and computation. Figs. 1-(b),(c) are a representative subset of the results that quantify the gain of offloading moderately intensive computational tasks to MDCs. Results for low and high computationally intensive tasks can be found in [3]. Overall, offloading to an MDC registers up to 80% savings in time as opposed to offloading to the cloud. We also observe up to 20% savings in time by offloading to an MDC as opposed to a cloudlets [5]. These results show the potential gain of computational offloading in MDCs.

The second step in our work is proposing an experimental platform, needed by the research community [6], to enable future evaluation and assessment of MDC-based solutions. In this platform, we provide an android-based API allowing future MDC experimental applications to be built. We also create a testbed that measures the energy consumed by a device while performing various tasks using different communication technologies. In addition, we build an offloading mobile application using our API while measuring the time taken to offload tasks to other devices and receive the result.

The last step in our work is utilizing the platform we built to carry out different MDC offloading experiments. These experiments conducted over several mobile devices guide us to the types of tasks that should be offloaded, and in what scenarios is it better to offload tasks to an MDC versus executing them locally on the offloader device. Our experimental results show that it is possible to gain time and energy savings, up to 50% and 26% respectively, by offloading within MDC, as opposed to locally executing tasks.

## 2. EXPERIMENTAL APPROACH

We believe there is a need for a generic flexible platform that can be utilized by researchers to freely test mobile cloud computing resource sharing and offloading solutions. This tool should decouple two main components that characterize any mobile application: the amount of data as well as the computational load that any task or job requires. These two components should also be easily broken down into distributable sub-tasks that researchers can control in real-time. Similar to simulation, this flexibility in the platform allows researchers to test their solutions over a fine-grained range of parameters that can represent a wider spectrum of current and future applications.

We introduce our mobile device cloud (MDC) experimental platform for mobile cloud computing research, shown in Fig. 2. We implement the MDC platform as an android application, called MDCloud, based on a set of APIs for mobile-to-mobile task offloading. This platform allows users to generate tasks with different computational loads (measured in total floating point operations and denoted in MFLOP) and relevant data input (measured and denoted in MB). It also provides APIs that enable building more specialized applications that can offload sub-tasks, set by the user, using various wireless technologies, such as WiFi, Bluetooth, or WiFi Direct. The user can select the number of connected devices from a pool of devices within its proximity, as well as the amount of data and computational load to be offloaded to each connected device. When the user executes a task generation and offloading scenario by pressing the send button, the original task is, therefore, fragmented and the selected percentages will be forwarded to remote devices while the remaining sub-tasks will run locally. The MDC platform enables the application to log the total response time for each task (*i.e.,* the time when the task was initiated to the time when the results are sent back to the initiating user). It also logs the task computational completion time for every device as well as the data transfer time separately.

In order for the MDC experimental platform to be complete, real-time power measurements are needed for various states of an application. We therefore set-up an energy measurement circuit, shown in Fig. 2, in order to measure the computational and communication energy consumption. We remove the battery from the phone, solder a DC power supply to phone's power input as shown in the figure, and supply a constant voltage that matches that of the battery. We measure the electric current drawn as a result of each event, such as sending or receiving data (using Bluetooth, WiFi, or WiFi direct) as well as a given computational load, and calculate the power consumed for each event. We run these events independently for the duration of one minute to smooth out any fluctuations that occur as a result of other OS-related tasks. Once we have the power for each event computed, we finally measure the duration taken for any event in our real experiments and calculate the resulting total energy consumed in Joules. We generate power usage profiles for various computational and data transmission demands, which are in turn used as input to the evaluation described in the next section.

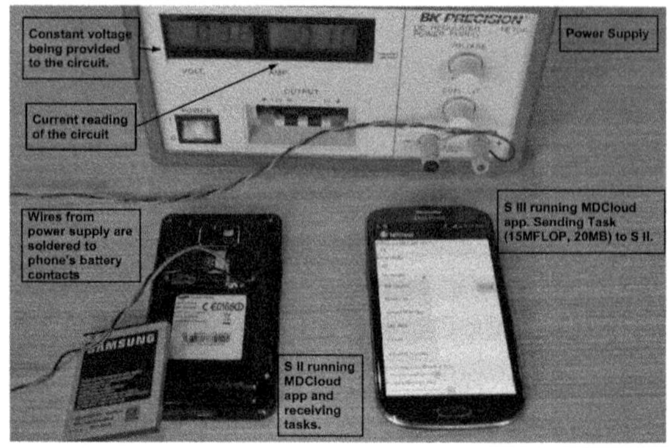


**Figure 2: MDC Experimentation Platform: measuring energy consumption on an S2 upon receiving a task (15MFLOP, 20MB) from S3 device**

| | SII | SIII |
|---|---|---|
| WiFi-Scanning | 455 mW | 520 mW |
| WiFi-Idle | 210 mW | 280 mW |
| Bluetooth-Idle | 36 mW | 40 mW |
| Bluetooth-Scanning | 540 mW | 400 mW |
| Bluetooth-Sending (10MB) | 370 mW | 280 mW |
| Bluetooth-Receiving (10MB) | 296 mW | 240 mW |
| WiFiDirect-Idle | none | 320 mW |
| WiFiDirect-Sending (10MB) | none | 920 mW |
| WiFiDirect-Receiving (10MB) | none | 640 mW |
| Execute Task (200MFLOP) | 648 mW | 320 mW |

**Table 1: Experimental energy readings on Samsung S2 and S3**

Table 1 compares different energy measurements while performing wireless transfers using Bluetooth (BT) and WiFi Direct (WiFi D.) between two Samsung SII devices and two Samsung SIII devices. We send the same data sizes using both Bluetooth and WiFi Direct, and show that Bluetooth is 80% to 120% more efficient than WiFi Direct. Moreover, we notice that sending data costs 10% to 25% more energy than receiving data independent of the wireless communication used. This confirms that WiFi Direct is an energy expensive technology; in fact, SIII with WiFi Direct radio on and connected to another SIII, consumes almost the same energy like the SIII sending via Bluetooth to another SIII device. We also measure the computational energy consumption by running a high load task on SII and SIII devices. We show that the local execution in an SII device costs almost double the energy required to send data via Bluetooth. Inspired by these results, one may expect that offloading data to more powerful mobile devices using a low energy wireless technology may be advantageous. This previous statement is highlighted by almost a 50% energy gain when using SIII to run the same task.

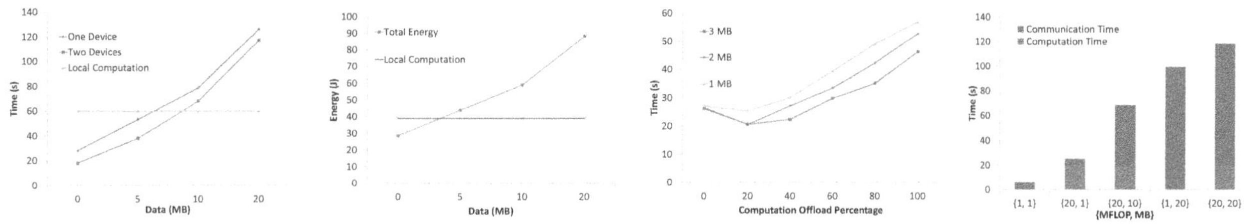


(a) Resp. Time (b) Energy Consumed (c) Offload Perc. (d) Comp. vs. Comm.

**Figure 3: Results from MDC Testbed Experiments**

# 3. EXPERIMENTAL ANALYSIS

We create an experimental testbed consisting of two Samsung Galaxy SII and two Samsung Galaxy SIII phones, all running our MDCloud application. We aim to obtain practical insights into making offloading decisions in mobile device clouds in order to make conclusions about appropriate strategies to be adopted for developing offloading algorithms. In all of these scenarios, we chose Bluetooth as the standard communication technology, because of its widespread availability in almost all modern smart devices.

Fig. 3 summarizes a subset of our experimental results. Additional results can be found in [3]. Ror a higher MFLOP value, we show larger gains in both energy and time conservation while offloading the task to another device using MDCs (Figs. 3-(a),(b)). We register up to 50% gain in time and 26% gain in energy by offloading half the task to one other device. This gain is further amplified when considering higher MFLOP values [3]. We note that this result corroborates the emulation experiments' results. Moreover, we show that offloading to more than one device further improves the gain with respect to time (Fig. 3-(a)). For example, we divide the offloaded task equally among the offloader and two offloadee devices such that each device carries out 33% of the task. We achieve up to 40% gain in time by offloading to two devices as compared to one. We can also observe that for higher data values, this gain is reduced because the overhead introduced by exchanging larger data sizes mitigates the gain achieved by distributing the computation among multiple devices.

We then vary the percentage of computation offloaded to the offloadee device, between 0% and 100%, in order to determine the optimal percentage to offload so as to maximize gains in time and energy. Determining such optimal distribution during runtime will be investigated in future work. Fig. 3-(c) shows the optimal time registered when 20% of the task is offloaded to the offloadee device and the rest is executed locally achieving up to 51% gain in time. In terms of energy, the best gain is registered while offloading 100% of the task to another device, yielding up to 16% conservation in energy [3].

We pose the following question: which factor (data or computation) consumes more energy during the offload operation? Fig. 3-(d) shows that communication can take up to 100 times more time than computation does. This is also shown when 25% increase in data costs 4x more time than a 25% increase of task complexity. This analysis shows that having more computation provides avenues for more gain to be achieved in terms of time and energy conservation, while having more data means a reduction in the energy and time that can be achieved by offloading tasks into an MDC.

# 4. CONCLUSION AND FUTURE WORK

In this work, we have motivated the use of mobile devices in creating mobile device clouds that can be used to save time and energy when it comes to executing computationally heavy tasks. We have shown the potential gain in both time and energy, up to 50% and 23% respectively, achieved by offloading to other devices in an MDC. These results were also corroborated by carrying out experimentation on our MDC testbed. We have presented different insights into the factors that affect the offloading decision by carrying out further experiments on our MDC testbed.

We have provided an MDC platform with an API that allows offloading algorithms to be tested on actual mobile device clouds consisting of multiple devices. We have used this platform to carry out experiments that have provided insights into how to decide whether to offload a particular task or not, and what potential strategies can be adopted for making such decisions. We have shown up to 50% gain in time and 26% gain in energy via offloading, corroborating our observations from the emulation testbed results.

While we have looked into making offloading decisions based on the contents of the task at hand, in the future, we plan to explore which device a task should be offloaded to, given information regarding devices within an MDC. Given typical user mobility and expected inter-device intermittent connections, we plan to leverage social context and contact history between devices to determine those that are more likely to respond the fastest, and thus, result in the most efficient offloading choice. For each of the strategies used to determine which device a task should be offloaded to, we would then run simulations against actual contact history data sets to discover which strategies are most energy and time efficient in real world scenarios.

# 5. REFERENCES

[1] B.-G. Chun, S. Ihm, P. Maniatis, M. Naik, and A. Patti. Clonecloud: elastic execution between mobile device and cloud. In *Proceedings of the sixth conference on Computer systems*, EuroSys '11, pages 301–314, New York, NY, USA, 2011. ACM.

[2] E. Cuervo, A. Balasubramanian, D. ki Cho, A. Wolman, S. Saroiu, R. Chandra, and P. Bahl. Maui: making smartphones last longer with code offload. In *MobiSys'10*, pages 49–62, 2010.

[3] A. Fahim, A. Mtibaa, and K. Harras. Making the case for computational offoading in mobile device clouds. Technical Report CMU-CS-13-119, Carnegie Mellon University, June 2013.

[4] J. Flinn. Cyber foraging: Bridging mobile and cloud computing. *Synthesis Lectures on Mobile and Pervasive Computing*, 7(2):1–103, 2012.

[5] M. Satyanarayanan, P. Bahl, R. Caceres, and N. Davies. The case for vm-based cloudlets in mobile computing. *Pervasive Computing, IEEE*, 8(4):14–23, 2009.

[6] C. Shi, V. Lakafosis, M. H. Ammar, and E. W. Zegura. Serendipity: enabling remote computing among intermittently connected mobile devices. In *MobiHoc*, pages 145–154, 2012.

# Toward Preserving Privacy and Functionality in Geosocial Networks

Mahmudur Rahman
Florida International University
Miami, FL

Jaime Ballesteros
Florida International University
Miami, FL

Bogdan Carbunar
Florida International University
Miami, FL

Naphtali Rishe
Florida International University
Miami, FL

Athanasios V. Vasilakos
National Technical University
of Athens, Greece

## Categories and Subject Descriptors

D.4.6 [**Security and Protection**]: Cryptographic controls; C.2.4 [**Distributed Systems**]: Distributed applications

## General Terms

Security, Verification

## Keywords

Privacy, Location verification, Social networks

## 1. INTRODUCTION

Storing user friend lists, preferences and messages, online social networks have become a significant source of sensitive personal information. A recent addition to this space, geosocial networks (GSNs) such as Yelp [1] or Foursquare [2], collect even user locations, through *check-ins* performed by users at visited venues. Overtly, personal information allows GSN providers to offer a variety of applications, including personalized recommendations and targeted advertising, and venue owners to promote their businesses through spatio-temporal incentives (e.g., rewarding frequent customers through accumulated badges). Providing personal information exposes however users to significant risks, as social networks have been shown to leak [3] and even sell [4] user data to third parties. There exists therefore a conflict. Without privacy people may be reluctant to use geosocial networks; without user information the provider and venues cannot support applications and have no incentive to participate.

In this work we take first steps toward breaking this deadlock, by introducing the concept of *location centric profiles* (LCPs), aggregate statistics built from the profiles of users that have visited a certain location. As we know, location privacy has been extensively studied before [5]. This work significantly extends the state of the art by (i) providing constructs that preserve the privacy of users when reporting private profile information (e.g., age, gender, location), and (ii) ensuring that the solutions enable providers to collect information needed to develop existing services. We introduce PROFIL$_R$ , a framework that allows the construction of LCPs based on the profiles of present users, while ensuring the privacy and correctness of participants. To relieve the GSN provider from costly involvement in venue specific activities, PROFIL$_R$ stores and builds LCPs at venues.


*MobiCom'13,* September 30–October 4, Miami, FL, USA.
ACM 978-1-4503-1999-7/13/09.
http://dx.doi.org/10.1145/2500423.2504577.

## 2. SYSTEM MODEL

We model the geosocial network (GSN) after Yelp [1]. It consists of a provider, $S$, hosting the system along with information about registered venues, and serving a number of subscribers. To use the provider's services, a client application needs to be downloaded and installed. Users register and receive initial service credentials, including a unique user id. We use the terms *subscriber* and *user* interchangeably to refer to users of the service and the term *client* to denote the software provided by the service and installed by users on their devices.

Participating venue owners need to install inexpensive equipment, present on most recent smartphones. This equipment can be installed and used for other purposes as well, including detecting fake user check-ins [6] preventing fake badges and incorrect rewards, and validating social network (e.g., Yelp [1]) reviews. We note that location verification solutions that do not rely on venue deployed equipment suffer from lack of ground truth problems (see [6] for a complete discussion of this topic). Besides ensuring the portability of our approach (e.g., can be installed anywhere inside the venue) this also implies solely a one-time cost for the venue owner (no monthly fees).

### 2.1 Location Centric Profiles

Each user has a profile $P_U = \{u_1, u_2, .., u_d\}$, consisting of values on $d$ dimensions (e.g., age, gender, home city, etc). Each dimension has a range, or a set of possible values. Given a set of users $\mathcal{U}$ at location $L$, the *location centric profile* at $L$, denoted by $LCP(L)$ is the set $\{S_1, S_2, .., S_d\}$, where $S_i$ denotes the aggregate statistics over the $i$-th dimension of profiles of users from $\mathcal{U}$.

In the following, we focus on a single profile dimension, $D$. We assume $D$ takes values over a range $R$ that can be discretized into a finite set of sub-intervals (e.g., set of continuous disjoint intervals or discrete values). Then, given an integer $b$, chosen to be dimension specific, we divide $R$

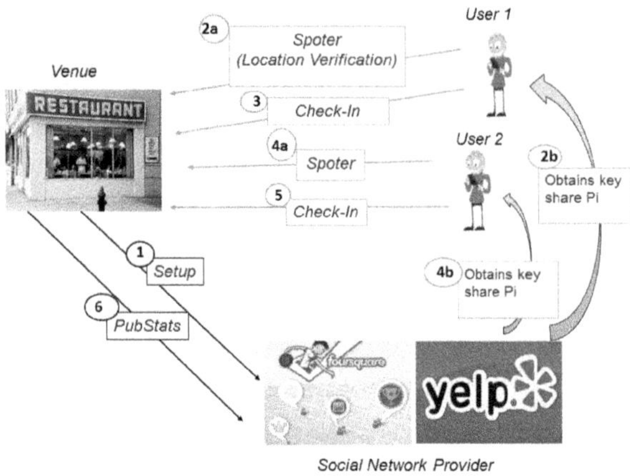


**Figure 1: Solution architecture ($k$=2).**

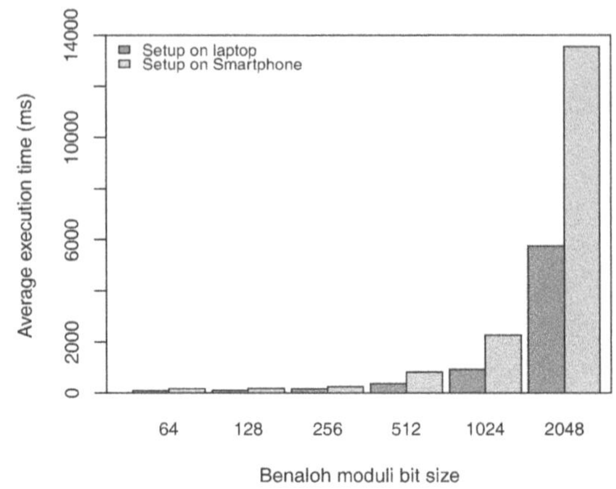


**Figure 2: *Setup* dependence on Benaloh mod size.**

into $b$ intervals/sets, $R_1, .., R_b$. For instance, gender maps naturally to discrete values ($b = 2$), while age can be divided into disjoint sub-intervals, with a higher $b$ value. We define the aggregate statistics $S$ for dimension $D$ of $LCP(L)$ to consist of $b$ counters $c_1, .., c_b$; $c_i$ records the number of users from $\mathcal{U}$ whose profile value on dimension $D$ falls within range $R_i$, $i = 1..b$.

## 3. PROFIL$_R$

Let SPOTR$_V$ denote the device installed at venue $V$. For each user profile dimension $D$, SPOTR$_V$ stores a set of *encrypted counters* – one for each sub-range of $R$. Initially, and following each cycle of $k$ check-ins executed at venue $V$, SPOTR$_V$ initiates *Setup*, to request the provider $S$ to generate a new Benaloh key pair [7].

When a user $U$ checks-in at venue $V$, it first engages in the *Spoter* protocol with SPOTR$_V$ . This allows the venue to verify $U$'s physical presence through a challenge/response protocol between SPOTR$_V$ and the user device. Furthermore, a successful run of *Spoter* provides $U$ with a share of the secret key employed in the Benaloh cryptosystem of the current cycle. For each venue and user profile dimension, $S$ stores a set $Sh$ of shares of the secret key that have been revealed so far.

Subsequently, $U$ runs *CheckIn* with SPOTR$_V$ , to first send its share of the secret key and to receive the encrypted counter sets. During *CheckIn*, for each dimension $D$, $U$ increments the counter corresponding to her range, re-encrypts all counters and sends the resulting set to SPOTR$_V$ . $U$ and SPOTR$_V$ engage in a zero knowledge protocol that allows SPOTR$_V$ to verify $U$'s correct behavior: exactly one counter has been incremented. SPOTR$_V$ stores the latest, proved to be correct encrypted counter set, and inserts the secret key share into the set $Sh$. Once $k$ users successfully complete the *CheckIn* procedure, marking the end of a cycle, SPOTR$_V$ runs *PubStats* to reconstruct the private key, decrypt all encrypted counters and publish the tally.

### 3.1 The Solution

Let $C_i$ denote the set of encrypted counters at $V$, following the $i$-th user run of *CheckIn*. $C_i = \{C_i[1], .., C_i[b]\}$, where $C_i[j]$ denotes the encrypted counter corresponding to $R_j$, the $j$-th sub-range of $R$. We write $C_i[j] = E(u_j, u'_j, c_j, j) = [E(u_j, c_j), E(u'_j, j)]$, where $u_j$ and $u'_j$ are random obfuscating factors and $E(u, m)$ denotes the Benaloh encryption of message $m$ using random factor $u$. That is, an encrypted counter is stored for each sub-range of domain $R$ of dimension $D$. The encrypted counter consists of two records, encoding the number of users whose values on dimension $D$ fall within a particular sub-range of $R$.

Let $RE(v_j, v'_j, E(u_j, u'_j, c_j, j)$ denote the re-encryption of the $j$-th record with two random values $v_j$ and $v'_j$: $RE(v_j, v'_j, E(u_j, u'_j, c_j, j)) = [RE(v_j, E(u_j, c_j)), RE(v'_j, E(u'_j, j))] = [E(u_j v_j, c_j), E(u'_j v'_j, j)]$. Let $C_i[j]++ = E(u_j, u'_j, c_j + 1, j)$ denote the encryption of the incremented $j$-th counter. Note that incrementing the counter can be done without decrypting $C_i[j]$ or knowing the current counter's value: $C_i[j]++ = [E(u_j, c_j)y, E(u'_j, j)] = [y^{c_j+1}u_j^r, E(u'_j, j)] = [E(u_j, c_j + 1), E(u'_j, j)]$.

In the following we use the above definitions to introduce PROFIL$_R$ . PROFIL$_R$ instantiates $PP(k)$, where $k$ is the privacy parameter. The notation $P(A(params_A), B(params_B))$ denotes the fact that protocol $P$ involves participants $A$ and $B$, each with its own parameters.

**Setup(V(),S($k$)):** The provider $S$ runs the key generation function $K(k)$ of the Benaloh cryptosystem [7]. Let $p$ and $q$ be the private key and $n$ and $y$ the public key. $S$ sends the public key to SPOTR$_V$ . SPOTR$_V$ generates a signature key pair and registers the public key with $S$. For each user profile dimension $D$ of range $R$, SPOTR$_V$ performs the following steps. First, initialize counters $c_1, .., c_b$ to 0. $b$ is the number of $R$'s sub-ranges. Then, generate $C_0 = \{E(x_1, x'_1, c_1, 1), .., E(x_b, x'_b, c_b, b)\}$, where $x_i, x'_i$, $i = 1..b$ are randomly chosen values. Store $C_0$ indexed on dimension $D$. Finally, initialize the share set $S_{key} = \emptyset$.

**Spoter(U(K),V(),S($k$)):** To ensure anonymity, $U$ needs to generate fresh random MAC and IP addresses for each run of Spoter (and CheckIn) with SPOTR$_V$ . No advantage can be gained by spoofing MAC and IP addresses. SPOTR$_V$ uses one of the location verification procedures proposed in [6] to verify $U$'s presence. Let $U$ be the $i$-th user checking-in at $V$. If the verification succeeds and $i \leq k$, $S$ uses the $(k, n)$ TSS to compute a share of $p$ (Benaloh secret key, factor of the modulus $n$). Let $p_i$ be the share of $p$. $S$ sends the (signed) share $p_i$ to $U$. If $i > k$, $S$ calls *Setup* to generate new parameters for $V$.

**CheckIn(U($p_i$, n, V), V(n, y, $C_{i-1}$, $S_{key}$)):** Executes only if the previous run of *Spoter* is successful. Let $U$ be the $i$-th user checking-in at $V$. Then, $C_{i-1}$ is the current

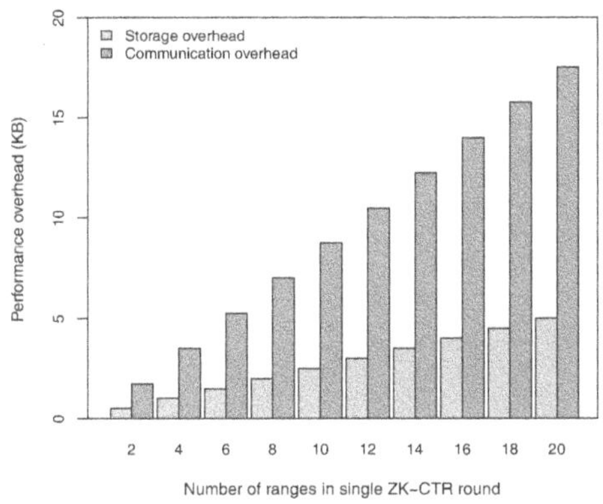


**Figure 3: Storage and communication overhead (in KB) as a function of range count.**

set of encrypted counters. SPOTR$_V$ sends $C_{i-1}$ to $U$. Let $v$, $U$'s value on dimension $D$, be within $R$'s $j$-th sub-range, i.e., $v \in R_j$. $U$ runs the following steps. First, generate $b$ pairs of random values $\{(v_1, v_1'), .., (v_b, v_b')\}$. Compute the new encrypted counter set $C_i$, where the order of the counters in $C_i$ is identical to $C_{i-1}$: $C_i = \{RE(v_l, v_l', C_{i-1}[l])|l = 1..b, l \neq j\} \cup RE(v_j, v_j', C_{i-1}[j]{+}{+})$. Then, send $C_i$ along with the signed (by $S$) share $p_i$ of the private key $p$ to $V$.

If SPOTR$_V$ successfully verifies the signature of $S$ on the share $p_i$, $U$ and SPOTR$_V$ engage in a zero knowledge protocol that allows $U$ to prove that $C_i$ is a correct re-encryption of $C_{i-1}$: only one counter of $C_{i-1}$ has been incremented. If the proof verifies, SPOTR$_V$ replaces $C_{i-1}$ with $C_i$ and ads the share $p_i$ to the set $S_{key}$.

**PubStats(V($C_k$,Sh,V),S(p,q))**: If $|Sh| < k$, SPOTR$_V$ aborts. Otherwise, if $|Sh| = k$, SPOTR$_V$ uses the $k$ shares to reconstruct $p$, the private Benaloh key. Then, use $p$ and $q = n/p$ to decrypt each record in $C_k$, the final set of counters at $V$, and publish the results.

## 4. EVALUATION

We have implemented PROFIL$_R$ using Android. For secret sharing, we used Shamir's scheme [8] and for digital signatures we used RSA. We have used Android Samsung Admire smartphones (800MHz CPU) and a Dell laptop (2.4GHz Intel Core i3, 4GB of RAM) for the server. For local connectivity the devices used their 802.11b/g Wi-Fi interfaces. We plot averages taken over 10 independent protocol runs.

We have first measured the overhead of the *Setup* operation. We set the number of ranges of the domain $D$ to be 10, Shamir's TSS group size to 1024 bits and RSA's modulus size to 1024 bits. Figure 2 shows the *Setup* overhead on the smartphone and laptop platforms, when the Benaloh modulus size ranges from 64 to 2048 bits. Note that even a resource constrained smartphone takes only 2.2s for 1024 bit sizes (0.9s on a laptop). Second, Figure 3 shows the SPOTR$_V$ storage overhead, only a fraction of the (single round client-to-SPOTR$_V$ ) communication overhead. For one dimension, with 20 sub-ranges, the overhead is 5KB.

## 5. RELATED WORK

Location and temporal cloaking techniques [9, 10] are a popular anonymization technique. PROFIL$_R$ provides an orthogonal notion of $k$-anonymity: instead of reporting intervals containing $k$ other users, we allow the construction of location centric profiles only when $k$ users have reported their location.

Golle et al. [11] proposed techniques allowing pollsters to collect user data while ensuring the privacy of the users. The privacy is proved at "runtime": if the pollster leaks private data, it will be exposed probabilistically. PROFIL$_R$ allows providers to collect private user data, however, they are never allowed direct access to private user data. Toubiana et. al [12] proposed Adnostic, a privacy preserving ad targeting architecture. Users have a profile that allows the private matching of relevant ads. While PROFIL$_R$ can be used to privately provide location centric targeted ads, its main goal is different - to compute location (venue) centric profiles that preserve the privacy of contributing users.

## 6. ACKNOWLEDGMENTS

This material is based in part upon work supported by the National Science Foundation under Grant Nos. CNS-0821345, CNS-1126619, HRD-0833093, IIP-0829576, CNS-1057661, IIS-1052625, CNS-0959985, OISE-1157372, IIP-1237818, IIP-1330943, IIP-1230661, IIP-1026265, IIP-1058606, IIS-1213026.

## 7. REFERENCES


[1] Yelp. http://www.yelp.com.

[2] Foursquare. https://foursquare.com/.

[3] Balachander Krishnamurthy and Craig E. Wills. On the leakage of personally identifiable information via online social networks. *Computer Communication Review*, 40(1):112–117, 2010.

[4] Emily Steel and Geoffrey Fowler. Facebook in privacy breach. http://online.wsj.com/article/SB10001424052702304772804575558484075236968.html.

[5] M. Humbert, T. Studer, M. Grossglauser, and J-P Hubaux. Nowhere to Hide: Navigating around Privacy in Online Social Networks. In *The Proceedings of 18th ESORICS*, 2013.

[6] B. Carbunar and R. Potharaju. You unlocked the Mt. Everest Badge on Foursquare! Countering Location Fraud in GeoSocial Networks. In *Proceedings of the 9th IEEE MASS'12*, 2012.

[7] Josh Benaloh. Dense probabilistic encryption. In *Proceedings of the Workshop on Selected Areas of Cryptography*, pages 120–128, 1994.

[8] Adi Shamir. How to share a secret. *Communications of the ACM*, 22(11):612–613, 1979.

[9] Marco Gruteser and Dirk Grunwald. Anonymous usage of location-based services through spatial and temporal cloaking. In *Proceedings of MobiSys*, 2003.

[10] Femi G. Olumofin, Piotr K. Tysowski, Ian Goldberg, and Urs Hengartner. Achieving Efficient Query Privacy for Location Based Services. In *Privacy Enhancing Technologies*, pages 93–110, 2010.

[11] P. Golle, F. McSherry, and I. Mironov. Data collection with self-enforcing privacy. In *ACM CCS 2006*, pages 69–78. ACM.

[12] V. Toubiana, A. Narayanan, D. Boneh, H. Nissenbaum, and S. Barocas. Adnostic: Privacy preserving targeted advertising. In *NDSS*, 2010.

# Spaceify - a Client-Edge-Server Ecosystem for Mobile Computing in Smart Spaces

Petri Savolainen†, Sumi Helal‡, Jukka Reitmaa†, Kai Kuikkaniemi†, Giulio Jacucci†,
Mikko Rinne ¬, Marko Turpeinen†, Sasu Tarkoma†
†HIIT/University of Helsinki/Aalto University, firstname.lastname@hiit.fi
‡Aalto University and University of Florida, firstname.lastname@gmail.com
¬ Aalto University, firstname.lastname@aalto.fi

## ABSTRACT

Spaceify is a novel edge architecture and an ecosystem for smart spaces — a technology that extends the mobile user view of today's common space services (e.g., WiFi) to a richer portfolio of space-centric, localized services and space-interactive applications.

## Categories and Subject Descriptors

D.4.7 [**Operating Systems**]: Organization and Design

## Keywords

client-edge-server, architecture, smart space, ecosystem

## 1. INTRODUCTION

Resource-poor mobile devices can benefit from utilizing external resources that are available both in the cloud and in the proximity of the device. For example, offloading computation to the cloud can both make the mobile applications faster and make the battery of the mobile device last longer [5]. Additionally, using a server found in the environment for the offloading can help to keep latencies at bay [6]. Besides the computational, storage and networking resources utilized in mobile offloading, Internet of Things (IoT) proposals add sensors and actuators in the list of utilizable resources in the environment of the mobile device.

The web programming model is becoming increasingly popular on the mobile devices with HTML 5 and mobile operating systems such as Firefox OS [1] and Tizen [3] adding support for installable web applications. However, the traditional client-server model of the web, combined with the sandboxed JavaScript execution environments on the devices offers little support for utilizing the resources available in the cloud and in the proximity of the devices.

In this poster we present the Spaceify ecosystem that is based on client-edge-server architecture. In the client-edge-server model, a web application is executed not only on a client and a server, but also on an *edge node* which is typically a smart access point — a resource-rich device through which the mobile devices are connected to the internet. In addition to offering its own computing and storage resources to be used, the edge node also acts as a central hub through which the resources in the space become available to the three-tier web applications.

Spaceify supports running both transient (i.e. JavaScript programs embedded in HTTP responses) and persistent code (installed native and JavaScript applications) on the edge nodes. From here on we will refer to the embedded JavaScript code executed on the Spaceify edge nodes as *Spacelets* and the installed code as *native applications* and *JavaScript applications*. This naming convention is analogous to the well-known convention of calling on-page pieces of Java code "Java applets" and installed Java code "Java applications".

The main two goals of the Spaceify ecosystem can be summarized as follows:

(1) To contribute to the digital transformation of physical spaces such as malls, schools, university campuses, downtown districts, etc. Currently, the web is accessible from many spaces via WiFi or cellular, but then the specificity of the space is washed out in the vast morasses of the web content and apps. What Spaceify aims at is to transform the space into a web of its own — a specialized, local web of things strictly inside the space, including services, people, and sensors.

(2) To provide significantly enhanced user experience by enabling intuitive and effective interactions of mobile users with the space. Spaceify aims to achieve this goal over an evolving mobile / ubiquitous device technology.

To achieve these goals we designed an architecture based on a friction-free ecosystem, in which we do not require new standards or any restrictive software layering other than existing web technology.

## 2. RELATED WORK

Satya et al. [6] highlighted the impact of latency on the user experience of mobile offloading. In order to achieve low latency, they proposed deploying *cloudlets*, the counterpart of Spaceify edge nodes, resource-rich computers one hop away from the mobile devices. Their solution is, however, concentrated only on making the computational and storage resources of the edge server available to mobile applications, and they do not address utilizing other resources that may be available in the environment. In contrast to lightweight web technologies used in Spaceify, their solution is virtual-machine-based, which can impose high overheads. Indeed, according to measurements of Satya et al. [6], launching a virtual machine to serve the mobile clients can take tens of


*MobiCom'13*, September 30–October 4, Miami, FL, USA.
ACM 978-1-4503-1999-7/13/09.
http://dx.doi.org/10.1145/2500423.2504578.

seconds even on a dedicated cloudlet. Finally, a major difference to cloudlets is that unlike cloudlets, Spaceify is based on an ecosystem with several well-defined roles that encourage, support and monetize adoption of its architecture. For instance, it gives return-on-investment incentives to space owners for installing an edge node in their premises.

Another work that relates to Spaceify is the Open Pluggable Edge Services (OPES) architectural framework [4]. Like Spaceify, OPES essentially utilizes a client-edge-server architecture for performing content adaptation to provide enhanced user experience. This is done by modifying the network traffic between the providers and the consumer of data through a protocol suite for invocation and tracking of OPES services. Unlike OPES, Spaceify addresses the problem of content adaptation by allowing external service providers to run software on-demand on the edge node in a restricted execution environment. This way external service providers can under pre-defined security policies access space-specific information such as user presence information or indoor map data on the edge node.

# 3. SPACEIFY ARCHITECTURE

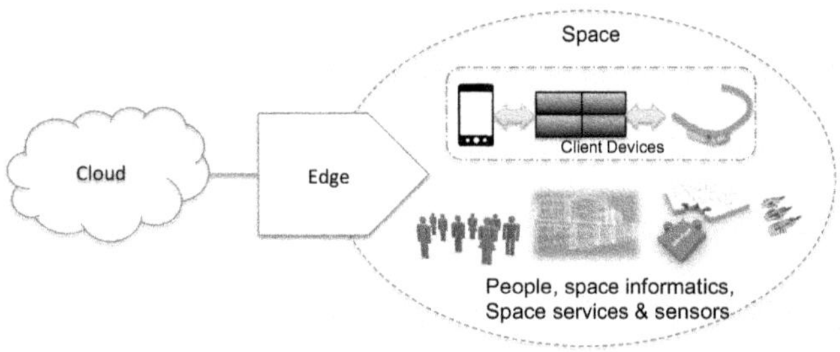


**Figure 1: A Spaceify System Instance**

A Spaceify system instance in Figure 1 consists of:

(a) A physical space containing mobile users, space specific services (e.g., shops and restaurants), space informatics (maps, models), sensors (such as WiFi and Bluetooth as location sensors, crowd sensors, capacity counters, noise sensors, and virtual sensors such as heat maps of hot activities and people). Mobile, wearable and other shared devices and interfaces are part of the space and represent client devices through which the mobile user may interact with the space services.

(b) An edge node that represents a specialized local computing and integration platform. It acts primarily as an efficient gateway to accessing and localizing the execution of web applications as will be shown later. It also acts as a point of integration of web applications, local space-specific applications, space sensors and mobile and other client devices. Such integration is designed to turn the smart space into a web of its own accessible seamlessly through multiple client devices (e.g., smart phone, public multi-touch displays, etc.) The seamless client device integration (maintaining sessions while switching among devices) is implemented in Spaceify but is not the focus on this poster.

(c) The web at large and its applications and services that may take part in localizing services in the space.

## 3.1 Edge Node Architecture

The edge node architecture shown in Figure 2 consists of three layers composed of open source components. The

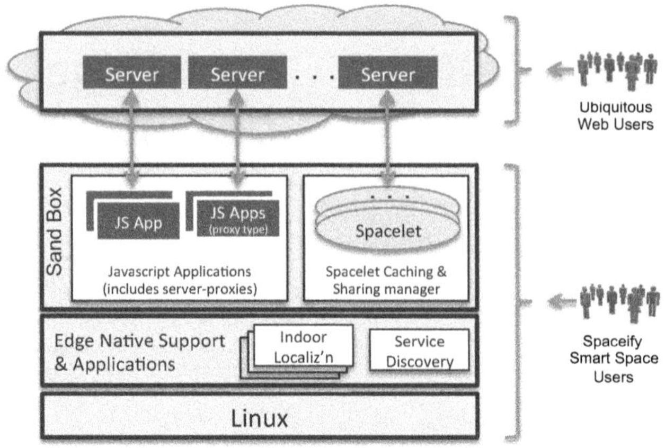


**Figure 2: A Spaceify Edge Node Architecture**

lowest layer is the GNU/Linux operating system on top of which the native Spaceify applications are installed using the default package management system of the underlying Linux variant. Spaceify system services such as Service discovery are also implemented as native Spaceify applications which makes the system highly modular. On the highest layer is the JavaScript sandbox in which JavaScript applications and Spacelets — dynamically downloaded applications provided by "Spaceified" web services — are run.

Native applications are intended for implementing services that require access to kernel services or specialized device drivers. Native applications are packaged in the package format of the underlying Linux variant (such as *.deb*) and sold in the Spaceify app store.

JavaScript applications are bought from the app store and permanently installed on the edge node by the Space owner. They are used for providing higher-level services such as storage or navigation that do not need direct access to the underlying operating system. They are distributed as *.zip* archives containing the JavaScript and other resource files along with the application manifest file. The packaging, installation and usage of Spaceify JavaScript applications is very similar to that of JavaScript applications on the Tizen mobile operating system [3].

The third Spaceify application type are Spacelets, which in contrast to JavaScript apps are not explicitly installed, but are transferred along HTTP responses from web services. The structure of the Spacelets is similar to that of JavaScript applications, consisting of JavaScript and resource files along with the manifest file.

On the edge node, Native applications, JavaScript applications and Spacelets (from here on referred collectively to as applications) can all provide services to each other and to the connected mobile devices. The services that are provided by native applications are often interfaces to hardware, such as indoor location devices, sensors and actuators. Building on low-level services provided by native applications, the JavaScript applications and Spacelets can then provide higher-level services such as indoor localization or persistent storage to each other and to code running on the connected mobile devices. Spaceify applications can be installed at will from the app store and web service providers can add Spacelets to their web content, which makes the Spaceify software stack extensible and ever-evolving.

This extensibility is achieved by allowing each application to run one local HTTP and one local WebSocket server.

One of the core components of the Spaceify stack is the Service discovery agent. It is a special native application that keeps track of which application is running on which port and what service it offers. Service discovery also implements access control by allowing and disallowing access to specific ports from specific applications using the Linux *iptables* mechanism.

Whenever a Spaceify application starts, it announces its presence and the name of the service it provides to the Service discovery agent. Whenever another application, running on the edge node or on a mobile device, needs some service from the edge node, it requests the service by its name from the Service discovery agent running on a well-known port in the address *edge.local*. The Service discovery agent goes through its list of registered services, checks whether the requester has rights to access this service, and in the positive case, returns the port number at which the requested service is running. While doing all this, the service discovery agent also creates an *iptables* rule that allows the requestor to access the server port of the requested service.

Resources and specific services available in a given Spaceify system may not be known beforehand to applications and application developers. They are typically chosen and deployed at the discretion of the space owner dynamically during the system operation.

# 4. SPACEIFY ECOSYSTEM

The spaceify ecosystem is based on well-defined roles that partly resemble those of well-established mobile ecosystems such as iOS or Android.

- **Spaceify inc.** develops and distributes the Spaceify software stack and runs an app store in which native and JavaScript applications are sold. Spaceify inc. also grants licenses to partner developers for developing native applications.
- **Partner developer** is a licensed developer of native Spaceify applications.
- **Application developer** develops JavaScript applications to be sold on the app store and installed on the edge nodes. JavaScript application development does not require a license.
- **Web service provider** hosts a web service that utilizes Spacelets. Hosting a "Spaceified" web service does not require a license.
- **Space owner** owns the physical space, the edge node and decides on the installation of software to the node. Space owner often employs a space system administrator to do the actual system administration work.

# 5. EXAMPLE: INDOOR NAVIGATION

This example demonstrates what we articulated in the first goal of Spaceify. It shows how map applications embedded in web pages that would normally return a google map utilizing GPS to the mobile user changes behavior inside a shopping mall, and returns an indoor map utilizing indoor localization technology instead. For example, a map returned when searching for *Pizza Hut* from home is therefore very different from the map returned for the same in a shopping mall, all be it using the same search. Let us now present our use case to explain the edge node architecture.

A shopping mall decides to acquire an accurate indoor navigation system for its customers. Quuppa [2] is chosen as the positioning hardware provider, and the hardware is installed in the mall and connected to the Spaceify edge node of the mall. As a partner developer, Quuppa has published the driver for their hardware as a Spaceify native application in the Spaceify app store. The system admin (works for the Space Owner) installs the Quuppa application on the edge node and configures the edge node so that all Spacelets from `maps.google.com` have the right to use the Quuppa application. This is done because Google has recently added support for accurate indoor navigation into Google maps, and routinely adds the *edge-manifest* HTTP header into all HTTP replies for the URL `maps.google.com`.

Next time a customer connected to the Internet through the edge node of the mall browses to `maps.google.com`, the edge node intercepts the *edge-manifest* HTTP header from the HTTP reply, and downloads the manifest file the header points to from Google. The edge node inspects the manifest file, checks the permissions required, downloads the required JavaScript files and maps generic service references in the manifest to actual available service interfaces found through the Service discovery agent running on the edge. For instance, "*bluetooth_indoor_positioning*" could be mapped to the Quuppa native application. Finally, the edge node starts the Spacelet according to the lifecycle policy stated in the manifest. After Google's indoor positioning Spacelet starts running it advertises its own presence using the Spaceify service discovery mechanism. Spacelet caching and sharing is not covered in this poster even though they are utilized by the edge node architecture.

As the customer's device receives the web page from `maps.google.com`, the JavaScript contained in the page checks for the existence of an indoor positioning Spacelet by querying for the service "*google_indoor_positioning*" at the well-known port of Spaceify service discovery agent running on the edge node. The on-page JavaScript then opens a WebSocket connection to the Spacelet at the port that was returned by the Spacelet service discovery, and starts receiving real-time data from the Google indoor positioning Spacelet based on which it displays a detailed indoor map to the user ready for inspection or navigation.

# 6. REFERENCES


[1] Firefox OS – Mozilla | MDN. `https://developer.mozilla.org/en-US/docs/Mozilla/Firefox_OS`. Retrieved July 4, 2013.

[2] Solution | Quuppa. `http://quuppa.com/solution/`. Retrieved July 4, 2013.

[3] Tizen | An open source, standards-based software platform for multiple device categories. `http://www.tizen.org`. Retrieved July 4, 2013.

[4] R. Chen A. Barbir, R. Penno, M. Hofmann, and H. Orman. An Architecture for Open Pluggable Edge Services (OPES). RFC 3835 (Informational), August 2004.

[5] A. Saarinen, M. Siekkinen, Y. Xiao, J. Nurminen, M. Kemppainen, and P. Hui. Can offloading save energy for popular apps? In *MobiArch'12*, pages 3–10.

[6] M. Satyanarayanan, P. Bahl, R. Caceres, and N. Davies. The case for vm-based cloudlets in mobile computing. *Pervasive Computing, IEEE*, 8(4):14–23, 2009.

# Reducing Power Consumption of IEEE802.11 Stations in Flexible Multicast Services

Yuta Morisawa
Graduate School of Information Science and Technology
The University of Tokyo
Tokyo, JAPAN
morisawa@akg.t.u-tokyo.ac.jp

Yoshihiro Kawahara
Graduate School of Information Science and Technology
The University of Tokyo
MIT Media Lab
Tokyo, JAPAN
kawahara@akg.t.u-tokyo.ac.jp

Tohru Asami
Graduate School of Information Science and Technology
The University of Tokyo
Tokyo, JAPAN
asami@akg.t.u-tokyo.ac.jp

## ABSTRACT

Wireless LAN multicast can provide high quality location-aware content service. However, our research revealed that multicast might cause a significant increase in the power consumption. Flexible Multicast Service (FMS) which is defined in the IEEE 802.11v enables power efficient multicast service. In this paper, we prove that the FMS strategy is not optimal and a little extension on FMS will achieve great improvement in power efficiency without throughput or delay penalties.

## Categories and Subject Descriptors

C.2.1 [Computer-Communication Networks]: Network Architecture and Design—Wireless communication

## Keywords

Wireless LAN, Power Saving, Multimedia Streaming

## 1. INTRODUCTION

Wireless LAN multicast is an efficient tool to provide location-aware content broadcast services. For instance, exhibition organizers provide video, map and music at the exhibition venue. However, in most cases, these contents are provided through unicast, meaning that quality of contents is sacrificed because of a bandwidth limitation as the number of user increases. In such a case, multicast has a large advantage in distributing high quality content streams simultaneously. However, Wireless LAN multicast has two big well known problems. First, the IEEE 802.11 standard does not define a retransmission mechanism in multicast[2]. Second, the standard limits the available data rate in multicast. Many excellent solutions have been proposed for these problems. However, to be best of our knowledge, there are few works which focus on the impact of background traffic on power efficiency of Wireless LAN stations. Our preliminary experiment shows that the power consumption of a mobile device increases by about 30% because of background multicast traffic. This power increase occurs whether stations join the multicast stream or not because multicast frames are treated as broadcast frames in IEEE 802.11 networks. FMS is a new power efficient mechanism defined in the IEEE 802.11v[2]. The overview of FMS is shown in Fig.1 (Original FMS). FMS defines a special unit named stream featured by a set of parameters such as MAC and IP addresses. APs transmit multicast that select a unique time interval for each stream. This time interval is larger than the original Delivery Traffic Indication Message (DTIM). A station may wake up at the interval specific to the multicast stream that the station wishes to join. FMS mechanism enables stations to avoid receiving unnecessary frames. However, FMS is not the optimal strategy because in FMS standard APs should transmit multicast streams which have the same delivery interval at the same time. Optimal choice and delivery pattern are out of scope of the standard and thus as shown in Fig.1 (Extended FMS), the power efficiency could be improved significantly by selecting the right interval and pattern for each stream. However, to decide the optimal delivery pattern, APs should consider many parameters, i.e. which stations to receive which streams, the number of multicast streams, the delivery interval, throughput, etc. We have modeled the delivery pattern and found that its computational complexity is $O(\alpha^N)$($\alpha$ is a natural number) when brute-force search is employed. Thus, an excellent algorithm for the problem is needed.

In summary, our contribution is as follows: (1) Background multicast streaming traffic causes the increase of power consumption of mobile devices by about 28%. (2) Computational cost to decide the optimal delivery is $O(\alpha^N)$. (3) The optimal delivery strategy of FMS can result in power savings of stations' by at most 45%.


*MobiCom'13*, September 30–October 4, Miami, FL, USA.
ACM 978-1-4503-1999-7/13/09.
http://dx.doi.org/10.1145/2500423.2504579 .

## 2. BACKGROUND

We investigate the impact of multicast traffic on stations' power consumption. We set up the experiment environment based on Thiagarajan' s work[5]. We used a Galaxy nexus SC-04D as a station and Buffalo WZR-AGL300NH as an AP. We used IEEE 802.11a for the wireless network. To mea-

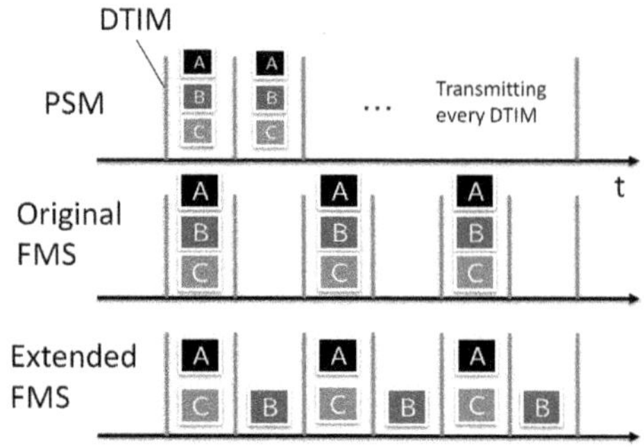


Figure 1: The timeline shows the frame transmission in three power saving mechanism.

sure the station's power consumption, we attached a small resistor serial to the power supply line. Measuring its voltage drops, we can calculate current using the Ohm' law. We also measured the battery voltage to calculate power consumption. The station is associated with the AP and the AP is connected to a PC via Ethernet. The PC transmits 960kbps multicast traffic destined for an unused group address to simulate the situation that station receives the stream in MAC layer but discard them after the station snoops into packets. We have conducted the experiment with or without the multicast stream. Each measurement lasted for 30 seconds and the result is an average of 10 measurements. The result shows that the power consumption was increased by about 28% when the AP transmits multicast frames. A Wireless LAN chip have Power Saving Mode (PSM) which enables the module to turn off its transceiver when there are no frames to transmit or receive (sleep). Though multicast streams prevented stations from sleeping and caused increased power consumption, multicast is by its nature a power efficient strategy to deliver the same content to multiple stations.

The most significant difference between FMS and PSM is the flexibility of delivery intervals of multicast streams. Again, Fig. 1 illustrates the timeline of both mechanisms. Although PSM regulates that APs should transmit every multicast stream in every DTIM, FMS still permits APs to modify the delivery intervals of multicast streams. In the Fig. 1(Original FMS), we assume that the transmission of the stream $A$ has 2-slot intervals. Destination stations should wake up at the first slot to receive a DTIM beacon and the stream $A$, and they switch to sleep again in the second slot. The interval is decided by the negotiation between the AP and stations. So, several streams may share the same interval. In original FMS, APs must transmit required streams together with other streams that share the same interval and the stations will receive all frames transmitted in the same DTIM period. That results in unnecessary power consumption. On the other hand, Fig. 1 (extended FMS) describes the extended FMS mechanism. We permit APs to shift the transmission timing between interval slots even though the streams share the same interval. Therefore, APs are able to optimize the transmission pattern for better power efficiency. Since APs only shift the transmission timing, the optimization does not cause any overhead.

We have modeled FMS transmission to analyze stations' power consumption. We assume a simple network which contains one AP, $M$ stations and $N$ multicast streams. Stations and streams are numbered from 1 to $M$ and $N$, respectively. In this paper, we only consider multicast frames. We left unicast frames, packet loss and AP's buffer overflow for future study. Our modeling is motivated by the Anastasi's work[3]. According to thier modeling formulation, stations' power consumption is the trade off between the number of stations' receiving frames and how often stations wake up. However, considering actual parameters, we can prove that the power consumption strongly depends on the number of frames received by the station. The intuitive reason is that multicast streams used for content streaming require a huge number of frames thus the impact of receiving frames is more significant. Moreover, the overhead of stations' waking up is insignificant. The overhead consists of receiving beacon frames and state transition of wireless LAN modules. Obviously, the number of receiving beacons is smaller than that of multicast frames. The overhead of state transition is also small because stations do not have to wake up to receive every DTIM beacon. Therefore, we can ignore these overheads and define the number of frames received by stations as a cost function $C$.

Let $S_i$ denote the delivery interval of stream $i$ and $T$ denote the least common multiple of $S_i (i = 1 \text{ to } N)$. The delivery pattern has $T_d T$ periodicity, where $T_d$ is a period of DTIM beacons. Then, it is relevant that we limit the target period to $[t_1 \ , \ t_1 + T_d T]$ where $t_1$ is the initial time when the first DTIM beacon is transmitted. We assume that the AP buffers all the frames and transmits them on and after the next opportunity. This assumption can ease our analysis and it obeys the IEEE 802.11 standard. We also assume that the streams are of fixed sized frames and constant flows (the arrival rates are denoted by $\lambda_i$). Under the assumption, we can derive the mean of stream $i$ frames' number which arrive in one DTIM period: $u_i$. $u_i$ is denoted by $\lambda_i S_i T_d$.

Let $t_k$ denote the time when $k$th DTIM beacon is transmitted and we define following binary variables. $l_{ik}$ means whether AP transmits stream $i$ in the period $[t_k, t_{k+1}]$. $l_{ik}$ becomes 0 when stream $i$ is not transmitted and becomes 1 when it is transmitted. $Z_{ij}$ means whether station $j$ receives stream $i$. $Z_{ij}$ becomes 0 if station $j$ does not receive stream $i$ and becomes 1 if station $j$ receive stream $i$.

Since we assume that the unicast flow does not exist, the stations keep active only when the AP indicates there are streams in the buffer which the stations want to receive. Then, let $s_{jk}$ denote whether station $j$ keeps active in the period $[t_k, t_{k+1}]$. $s_{jk}$ is given by

$$s_{jk} = P_N(i, l_{ik} Z_{ij}) \tag{1}$$

where

$$P_N(i, x_i) = x_1 \vee x_2 \vee x_3 \vee ... \vee x_N \tag{2}$$

Now we obtain the whole number of received frames as follows

$$C = \sum_{k=1}^{T} \sum_{j=1}^{M} \sum_{i=1}^{N} s_{jk} l_{ik} u_i \tag{3}$$

$C$ is the cost function to minimize the consumed power in the system. The variable in the equation is $l_{ik}$. Let $o_i$ denote the first $k$ which $l_{ik}$ becomes 1. Considering the periodicity of streams in the interval $S_i$, the maximum of $o_i$ should be $S_i - 1$. If $o_i = S_i$ were correct, the $l_{ik}$ would

| Streams | n1 | n2~4 | n5,6 | n7,8 |
|---|---|---|---|---|
| Throughput (λi)[bps] | 2.4K | 128K | 256K | 1M |
| Interval(Si) | 4 | 5 | 3 | 2 |

| STAs | m1 ~ m16 |
|---|---|
| Receiving Stream | n1 and RANDOM from n2~n8 |

Figure 2: The simulation parameters. There are 8 streams and 16 stations.

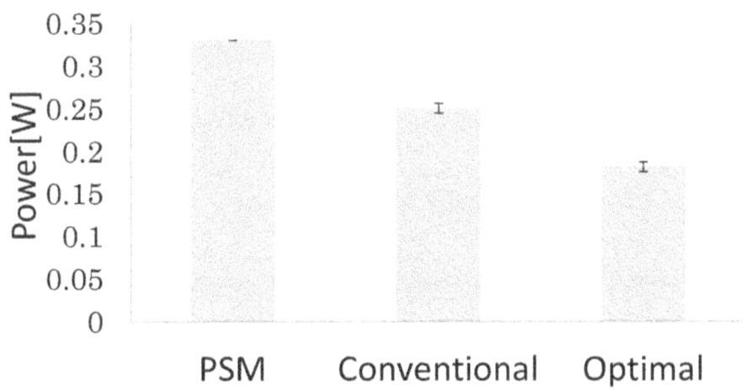


Figure 3: The NS2 simulation result. Power consumption of stations in three different conditions.

become 1 at $t_1 + T_d S_i, t_1 + 2T_d S_i, t_1 + 3T_d S_i$.... But the calculation period is $[t_1, t_1 + T_d T]$, then $l_{ik}$ should be 1 at $t_1$ for the interval constraint. This contradicts the definition of $o_i$. Thus, each $l_{ik}$ has $S_i$ patterns for transmission and the whole combination pattern is denoted by $\prod_{i=1}^{N} S_i$. If we use brute-force search to solve the problem, the computational complexity becomes quite large:$\mathcal{O}(\alpha^N)$($\alpha$ is a natural number). In addition, the calculation cost of $C$ is also substantial because of the triple summations:$\mathcal{O}(MTN^2)$. The brute-force search is infeasible because the AP has a small computational resource. Since $C$ includes the OR operation, Linear Programming (LP) cannot be adopted. Also, we have tried to utilize Dynamic Programming (DP) which is a well known algorithm to obtain the optimal solution. However, since the problem cannot be divided into correct subproblems, DP cannot be adopted. To our knowledge, the proper solution to the problem has not been proposed.

# 3. CASE STUDY

We investigate how the optimal delivery strategy can increase the power efficiency by simulation. We have implemented original and extended FMS on the network simulator NS-2. To analyze power saving mechanism, we adopt the Wireless LAN Power Management Extension patch[1]. It provides the basic power saving mechanism on both APs and stations. To our knowledge, there is no patch providing FMS mechanism, so we customized the patch for evaluating FMS. But we have implemented only transmission mechanisms rather than all FMS components because we cannot find documents which specify FMS implementation details. Even though our implementation is partial, the simulator is reliable because our focus is on the capacity of power consumption reduction.

We analyze a simple model: one AP and 16 stations in the network. The content server which provides certain contents and the content list in multicast streams is in the same network of the AP. Fig. 2 shows the list of streams and their throughputs. Evaluating all combinations of intervals and throughputs is a considerably tough work. Instead we evaluate a simple scenario which is, we believe, a more general case. All streams are at fixed speed traffic and of a fixed packet size (600Byte). We conduct the simulations for three delivery patterns: optimal FMS, conventional FMS and PSM. We have obtained the optimal pattern by using brute-force but we note that the calculation is quite heavy. The conventional pattern observes original FMS regulations. The stations consume power of 1.4W while transmitting frames, 0.9W while receiving frames, 0.8W in idle state, and 0.016W in sleep state[4]. Each simulation lasts 20 seconds and we show the result as an average of 100 simulation runs. The simulation results are shown in Fig. 3. As shown in the graph, the optimal delivery pattern reduces the consumed power of each station by about 28% compared to the Conventional FMS and about 45% compared to PSM. The result proves the power efficiency will be improved when the optimal delivery is achieved.

# 4. CONCLUSION AND FUTURE WORKS

We have the following findings: (1) the background multicast stream increases stations' power consumption by about 28%, (2) the computational complexity to solve the problem is $\mathcal{O}(\alpha^N)$ where $\alpha$ is a natural number, (3) Power can be reduced dramatically by adopting the optimal pattern of FMS. These findings motivated us to reduce the computational complexity. However, it is still challenging to decide the optimal pattern. APs should consider the number of streams and throughputs as well as the combination of stations and received streams. As a result, the calculation complexity would be too large for APs to conduct real time calculation. This will be the first priority in our future research.

# 5. ACKNOWLEDGMENTS


This work is funded by National Institute of Information and Communications Technology, Japan.


# 6. REFERENCES


[1] Wireless lan power management extension for ns-2. http://nspme.sourceforge.net/.

[2] IEEE Standard for Information technology–Telecommunications and information exchange between systems Local and metropolitan area networks–Specific requirements Part 11: Wireless LAN Medium Access Control (MAC) and Physical Layer (PHY) Specifications. IEEE STANDARDS ASSOCIATION, 2012.

[3] G. Anastasi, M. Conti, E. Gregori, and A. Passarella. Saving energy in wi-fi hotspots through 802.11 psm: an analytical model. In ESSLLI-2000, pages 24–26, 2004.

[4] M. Hashimoto, G. Hasegawa, and M. Murata. Energy efficiency analysis of tcp with burst transmission over a wireless lan. In ISCIT 2011, pages 292–297, 2011.

[5] N. Thiagarajan, G. Aggarwal, A. Nicoara, D. Boneh, and J. P. Singh. Who killed my battery?: analyzing mobile browser energy consumption. In WWW '12, pages 41–50, 2012.

# Demand-based Location Dependent Data Dissemination in VANETs


Susumu Ishihara
Graduate School of Engineering, Shizuoka University
3-5-1 Johoku, Naka-ku
Hamamatsu, Japan
ishihara@ishilab.net

Nobuhiro Nakamura
Graduate School of Engineering, Shizuoka University
3-5-1 Johoku, Naka-ku
Hamamatsu, Japan
nobu@ishilab.net

Yuya Niimi
Graduate School of Engineering, Shizuoka University
3-5-1 Johoku, Naka-ku
Hamamatsu, Japan
niimi@ishilab.net



## ABSTRACT

We propose a framework for efficiently disseminating large data items associated to locations where they are produced by vehicles and desired by drivers of different vehicles in a VANET. The framework consists of a scheme for aggregating drivers' demand for location dependent data using soft-state sketches, a scheme for understanding the condition of data dissemination, and a strategy for selecting data to be transmitted according to the aggregated demands and the condition of the existence of neighboring vehicles which have the same data.



## Categories and Subject Descriptors

C.2.2 [**Computer-Communication Networks**]: Network Protocols—*Routing protocols*

## General Terms

Algorithms

## Keywords

ad hoc networks, data dissemination


## 1. INTRODUCTION

If a driver can obtain a picture a place where he/she wants to go, he/she can easily know the current condition of the place and make a new driving plan to avoid traffic jams. Especially, if a service providing such an experience can be used in everywhere without relying on road and/or communication infrastructure, it will give much benefits to drivers. Using vehicular ad hoc networks (VANETs) will be a solution for the purpose since it does not rely on existing communication infrastructure.

Disseminating large image and video data to drivers using VANETs, however, is not easy. Of course, simply disseminating large picture data to all vehicles that are going to move to the position where the picture has been taken will incur large traffic. In addition, if multiple vehicles which have taken pictures send the different picture data to all vehicles which might need the pictures, the bandwidth of the VANET will be easily exhausted even if an effective data dissemination protocol is used. Thus efficient schemes to reduce traffic for disseminating images/videos which are produced by multiple vehicles is required.

In this paper, we propose a framework for efficiently disseminating large data items which are associated to locations where they are produced by vehicles and desired by drivers of different vehicles in a VANET (Figure. 1). We call such data *location dependent data*. In short, the proposed framework provides a way for demand-based many to many data dissemination. The framework consists of a scheme for aggregating drivers' demand for location dependent data, a scheme for understanding the condition of data dissemination, and a strategy for selecting data to be transmitted according to the aggregated demands and the condition of the existence of neighboring vehicles which have the same data.

Since the proposed framework disseminates only selected data according to aggregated demands from multiple vehicles and avoids duplicate transmissions of the same data from multiple vehicles, it can effectively use the communication resources in VANETs. Though effective schemes for many to many data dissemination in wide-area VANETs have been proposed, they are designed for smaller data such as traffic status and free parking lot information[1][2] compared with pictures and videos.

## 2. DEMAND-BASED LOCATION DEPENDENT DATA DISSEMINATION

The strategy used in the proposed framework is leveraging an efficient scheme for disseminating small data from multiple vehicles such as soft-state sketches[2] so that vehicles can understand the geographical distribution of demands to point of interest (POI) and who have the data related to the POI, and then disseminating location dependent data according to the collected information. The framework of the demand-based location dependent data dissemination consists of three components, *Demand Map*, *Supply Map*, and *Data dissemination engine*.



*MobiCom'13,* September 30–October 4, 2013, Miami, FL, USA.
ACM 978-1-4503-1999-7/13/09.
http://dx.doi.org/10.1145/2500423.2504580.

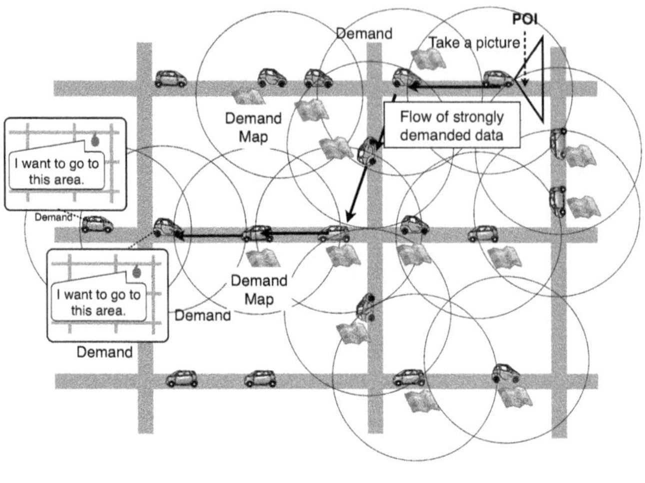


**Figure 1: Demand-based location data dissemination in a VANET.**

## 2.1 Demand Map (Dmap)

A demand map (Dmap) is a matrix that stores the strength of demands from a region to a POI. Figure 2 illustrates an example of a Dmap. Dmap is maintained at each vehicle. If a vehicle issues a new request to a POI, it updates its own Dmap so that the map reflects the new request, and the vehicle broadcast a portion of Dmap including the updated information by piggybacking it on a beacon. If a vehicle receives a portion of a Dmap from its neighboring vehicles, it updates its own Dmap according to the received information.

Each of requests issued by vehicles will lose its effect with time because the vehicle that has issued the request will leave the original position. Thus Dmaps have to support the temporal variation of demands. One of naive approaches for this purpose is to store the list of pairs of the ID of a vehicle that issued a request and its timestamp as an entry of the Dmap for each pair of a demand source region and a POI. However, it makes the size of the Dmap very large.

To effectively handle demand which lose its effect with time, we popose to use soft-state sketches proposed in [2] as a data structure for Dmap entries. The soft-state sketch is a data structure which has an ability to approximate aggregated values from different data sources instead of carrying specific values. In addition, it can handle the time to live of each data item.

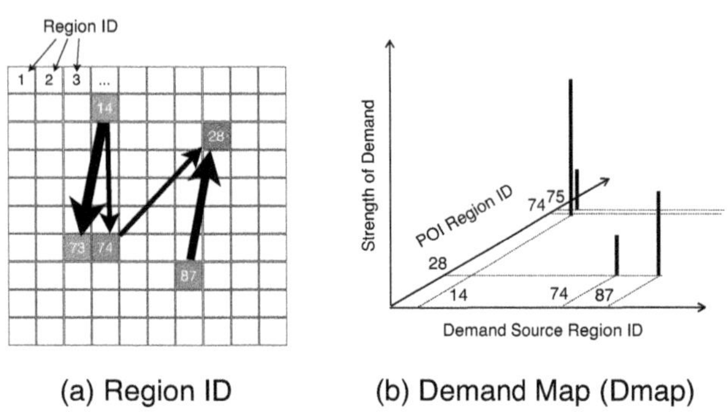


(a) Region ID (b) Demand Map (Dmap)

**Figure 2: Demand map.**

Note that the size of regions for demand sources regions and POIs do not have to be the same. If the size of a region for a POI is large, a data item which related to the region might be different from what the driver has requested to the POI. Thus, the size of regions for POIs should not be large. On the other hand, if the size of a demand source region is small, it will be difficult to aggregate multiple demands from different vehicles at different positions in the region. In addition, if the size is sufficiently large, a vehicle will be able to receive the requested data even if the vehicle has moved from the position where it has issued the request since the data should be disseminated within the region. Thus the size of regions for POIs should be small and one of demand source regions can be large.

## 2.2 Supply Map (Smap)

A supply map (Smap) is a table holding approximate numbers of vehicles that have copies of location dependent data items related to each POI. This information is used by each vehicle to determine whether it should send copies of location dependent data related to a POI if there is a strong demand to the POI. To share information for making supply maps, each vehicle periodically broadcasts a list of data items that it holds. Receiving the broadcasted list, each vehicle updates its Smap so that each entry of a POI hold the number of vehicles that have data items related to the POI.

## 2.3 Data Dissemination Engine (DDE)

Each vehicle has a data dissemination engine (DDE), which periodically selects and broadcasts a suitable data item from its local database of location dependent data items that it has received. According to the Dmap, the DDE on a vehicle assigns a high priority to a data item if the current position of the vehicle is on a suitable route between the position related to the data item and regions with strong demands in terms of multi-hop data transmission including store-carry-forward strategy. The DDE, however, lowers the priority if it knows there are many neighbors that have the same data item according to the Smap. As for concrete algorithms for data transmission, various effective schemes such as network coding based ones[3] and ones leveraging the road structure[4] can be used.

# 3. PRELIMINARY SIMULATION RESULTS

We conducted simulation of a simplified model of the proposed framework using a wireless network simulator, Sce-

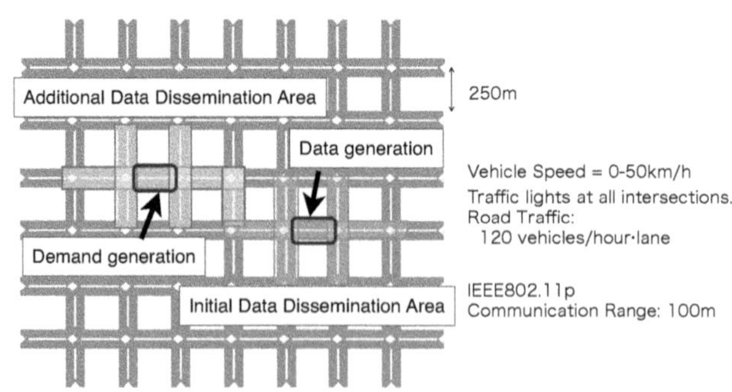


**Figure 3: Road map used for simulations.**

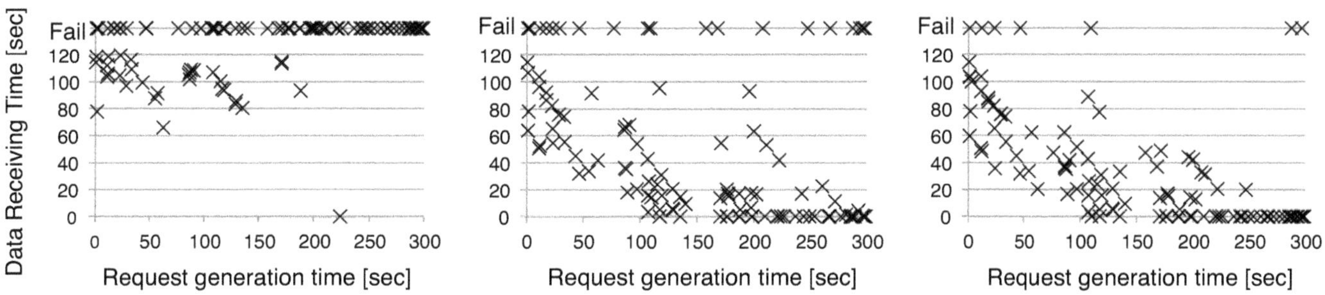


(a) No adaption of data dissemination area

(b) Data dissemination area is adapted to demands

(c) Data dissemination area is whole map area

**Figure 4: Simulation results of a simple model of demand-based data dissemination**

**Table 1: Request success ratio and data traffic.**

| | Success Ratio | Traffic |
|---|---|---|
| (a) No additional data dissemination area | 0.26 | 76 |
| (b) Adaptipve data dissemination area (Proposed) | 0.81 | 129 |
| (c) Data item is disseminated to all the area | 0.92 | 592 |

nargie by Space-Time Engineering[5] and a road traffic simulator, SUMO to illustrate the effectiveness of adaptively forming flows of delivering location dependent data according to the geographical distribution of demands. In the simulation model, we assumed that only vehicles passing through a road segment generate demands for data related to one location and only one data item related to the location is generated only once. The copies of data item are disseminated to the road segment where the data item has been generated and its neighboring segments using RD method[4], in which a copy of a data item is broadcasted at each intersection and at most one vehicle is delegated to broadcast the data item at the next intersection which the vehicle encounters within the term of validity of the data item. If a vehicle receives a demand piggybacked on a beacon, it enlarges the data dissemination area so that it can cover the road segment where the demand has been generated and the road segments between the original data dissemination area as shown in Figure 3. Vehicles broadcast the data item following the RD method. The size of the data item is 1kB. The beacon interval is 0.1 seconds.

Figure 4 (a)-(c) show the relationship between the time when a request generated by a vehicle and the time between the issue of a request and the reception of the requested data item. (a), (b), and (c) present the results of a case where additional data dissemination area is not used, a case where the additional data dissemination area is used (Proposed), and a case where the data item is disseminated to all the area even if no vehicle receives demands respectively. Table 1 shows the success ratio of requests and the number of transmissions of the copies of the data item. These results present the strategy (b) corresponding to the proposed framework effectively improves the success ratio compared with a case where no additional dissemination area is used and achieves sufficiently high success ratio with less data traffic compared with a case where the copies of the data item are disseminated to all the area (c).

# 4. CONCLUSION

The framework of demand-based location data dissemination in VANETs is proposed, and the simulation results of the simplified case of the framework present that the proposed framework suggest the potential to achieve high accessibility to location dependent data with small amount of data traffic. We are now working on developing detailed design of the framework and simulation models.

# 5. ACKNOWLEDGMENTS

This work was supported by KAKENHI 23300024.

# 6. REFERENCES

[1] T. Nadeem, S. Dashtinezhad, C. Liao, and L. Iftode, TrafficView: traffic data dissemination using car-to-car communication, ACM SIGMOBILE Mobile Computing and Communications Review, Vol.8, No.3, pp.6–19, 2004.

[2] C. Lochert, B. Scheuermann, and M. Mauve, Probabilistic aggregation for data dissemination in VANETs, in proc. of the fourth ACM international workshop on Vehicular ad hoc networks (VANET 2007), pp.1–8, 2007.

[3] U. Lee, J-S. Park, J. Yeh, G. Pau, and M. Gerla, CodeTorrent: Content Distribution using Network Coding in VANET, ACM MobiShare'06, pp.1–5, 2006.

[4] M. Yamanaka, G. Tsuchida, and S. Ishihara, A replica distribution scheme for location-dependent information on vehicular ad hoc networks, ACM VANET 2006, pp.98–99, 2006.

[5] Space-Time Engineering, http://www.spacetime-eng.com/

# SpyLoc: A Light Weight Localization System for Smartphones

Mostafa Uddin
Old Dominion University, USA
muddin@cs.odu.edu

Tamer Nadeem
Old Dominion University, USA
nadeem@cs.odu.edu

## ABSTRACT

In this paper, we propose and addresses the challenge of designing a light-weight high-accuracy indoor/outdoor localization system (*SpyLoc*) for off-the-shelf smartphones. In SpyLoc, we want to leverages both the acoustic interface (microphone/speaker) and the Wi-Fi interface at the kernel-level of the smartphones as well as the inertial sensors in the smartphones to achieve high localization accuracy. In the ranging-based approach, we utilizes the RF-Beep ranging scheme [?], and in dead reckoning-based approach, we fuses the inertial sensors of the smartphone to estimate the direction and the distance of user's movements.

In RF-Beep [?], we develope a ranging scheme that utilizes the Time-Difference-of-Arrival (TDoA) between the acoustic and the radio-frequency (RF) signal. The RF-Beep basically leverages the slow propagation speed of the acoustic signal with respect to the RF signal to estimate the relative range. The well known acoustic range based localization scheme, Cricket [?] also utilizes the same concept of using the difference in arrival times of concurrent transmissions of radio and ultrasound signals at the target device to infer the distance. Unlike the Cricket, which was designed with special hardware, our localization scheme is applicable to the smartphones. In RF-Beep, we address the different challenges of implementing such ranging scheme in smartphones by leveraging the existing functionalities of the audio driver and the WiFi driver. Further details on RF-Beep scheme could be found in [?]. The ranging based localization scheme typically requires at least three reference points (e.g., anchor points), in order to calculate the location. However all these three reference points must be in Line of Sight(LoS) to the target device. In *SpyLoc* localization system, we use the combination of both ranging-based and dead reckoning approaches to reduce the constraint of having three LoS anchor/reference points all the time.

The basic idea of the SpyLoc is to leverage the benefits of both the dead-reckoning and the ranging scheme to build a practical localization system. Given the high errors of the inertial sensors, SpyLoc uses a novel ranging scheme based on both the acoustic and WiFi interfaces to mitigate this error in order to improve the localization accuracy. Unlike the ranging-based or RF-based localization schemes that require multiple reference points (e.g., achor points), using the dead reckoning in SpyLoc reduces the required number of reference points to only one reference to locate and track users accurately. This low dependency on ranging scheme make SpyLoc practically applicable to high mobility environment. Finally, In the SpyLoc system, user's device (i.e. smartphone) works autonomously to determine its location. This system does not require any coordination from the nearby smartphones or from a central controller. Furthermore, this localization system does not require user's device to transmit any acoustic signal or RF messages to nearby smartphones. Therefore increasing the number of user's devices have no impact on the complexity of the SpyLoc system, which make SpyLoc a light-weight localization system. In addition, such characteristics make the localization system privacy preserving and energy efficient for the user's smartphone.


*MobiCom'13*, September 30–October 4, Miami, FL, USA.

ACM 978-1-4503-1999-7/13/09.
http://dx.doi.org/10.1145/2500423.2504581.

## Categories and Subject Descriptors

H.4 [**INFORMATION SYSTEMS APPLICATIONS**]: Miscellaneous

## Keywords

Localization, Mobility, Smartphones, Range

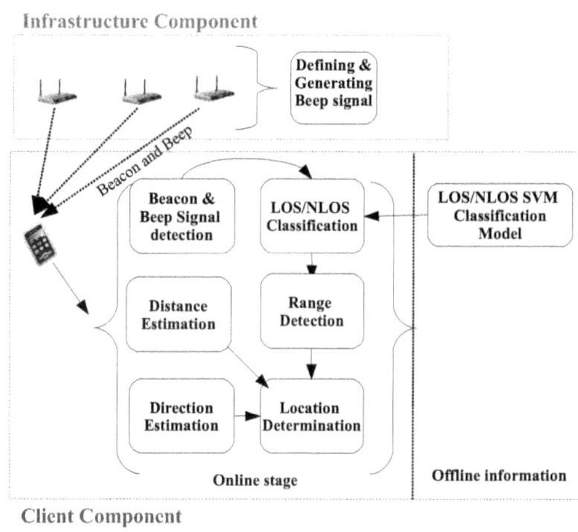


Figure 1: Architecture overview of the different components of SpyLoc localization system

## 1. SPYLOC LOCALIZATION SYSTEM

In this sections, we introduce the SpyLoc system architecture and the challenges. Figure 1 shows the different modules of SpyLoc system. Similar to many localization systems, SpyLoc consists of two main components: infrastructure component that runs on infrastructure hardware, and client component that runs on the user's device (i.e. smartphone). In this paper, we refer to an infrastructure device running the SpyLoc infrastructure component by a *beacon device*. The beacon device periodically broadcasts a RF message (i.e. Wi-Fi beacon frame), which we refer to as a *beacon*. In addition, the beacon device also generates an acoustic signal, *beep* following each broadcasted beacon message. In a practical scenario, a beacon device could be an Access Point (AP) with additional acoustic interface (i.e. speaker, mic and sound driver). A user's smartphone running SpyLoc client component (e.g., SpyLoc application) will capture the beacon messages and the corresponding beep signals from the surrounding beacon devices. Using the captured beacon messages and the corresponding beep signals in addition to the inertial sensors in smartphone, SpyLoc application will infer the user's location.

In a typical usage scenario, while the user runs the SpyLoc application in the smartphone, it will initially collect the beep signals from the surrounding beacon devices along their corresponding beacon messages. After collecting the *beep* signal and the *beacon* message, the application determines the relative ranges between the user's smartphone and the corresponding beacon device. Then, the application combines three estimated ranges from three different beacon devices to estimate the user's initial location. After fixing the user's initial location, later on SpyLoc uses the inertial sensors to track the distance and the direction of the user's locations. However, In indoor environments, using the inertial sensor of the smartphone to detect the distance and the direction of the user's movement is extremely challenging due to surrounding noises from the ferromagnetic devices. Therefore, In SpyLoc we utilize the range estimation to calibrate and calculate the accurate location of the user. However, In SpyLoc, our objective is to just limit the range calculation from one beacon device.

In summary, SpyLoc localization system possess the following interesting features:

- SpyLoc exploits the multiple interfaces in the smartphones by utilizing both the RF interface and acoustic interface to design high-accurate localization scheme.
- SpyLoc does not require any central controller or backend server to coordinate between neighboring devices. In this system, user's smartphone calculate the location locally and no collaboration with neighboring devices is required. In addition, The user's application does not require to share any acoustic or WiFi information with any nearby device or access point. This enables to preserve and protect the user security and privacy.
- The SpyLoc application running by the users does not require any customized hardware. This enables any off-the-shelf smartphone to adopt and use the developed application.
- SpyLoc only needs one ranging estimation from the beacon device after knowing the user's initial position. In addition, such ranging requirement is only required to calibrate the estimated location by the dead reckoning approach. This enables SpyLoc to be light-weight and practically applicable during user's mobility.
- SpyLoc only requires one way transmission; the transmission of the beacon messages and the beep signals by the beacon devices. Furthermore, estimating one range from one beacon device eliminates the need to switch the Wi-Fi channel to receive multiple beacon messages from the multiple beacon devices. Therefor, the development of the SpyLoc is energy efficient application for user's smartphones.

In the following subsection, we provide a brief overview of the infrastructure component and the client component.

## 1.1 Infrastructure Component

The beacon device (e.g. Wi-Fi AP), which runs the infrastructure component of the SpyLoc system, periodically generates a RF beacon message followed by a beep signal. A single frequency sinusoidal acoustic signal defines the basic sound that we refer to as *tone* in the paper. A mixture of such tones (i.e., set of frequencies) defines the beep signal. Typical human hearing perception diminishes after 18kHz. Therefore, we utilize the 18kHz-21kHz audio frequency range, which is perceptible to the most of the off-the-shelf smartphones [?]. From experiments, we found that if the frequency space between two adjacent tone is 250Hz, then it is sufficient to avoid the interference and detect the tones on the client side. Therefore, we select 10 tones(i.e frequencies) $(f_1, f_2, ..., f_{10})$ from 18kHz-21kHz audio range, we can have up to $2^{10}$ unique beep signals. One of the major challenge in the infrastructure component is, *How to uniquely and autonomously define the tones of the beep signal for each beacon device?*

In selecting the tones we utilize the last ten bits of the MAC address from the Wi-Fi Interface card of the beacon device. In this last ten bit sequence, each bit position correspond to one tone among the 10 tones, $\{f_1, f_2, ..., f_{10}\}$ (i.e. the $0th$ bit map to $f_1$, $1th$ bit map to $f_2$, and so on). A value of 1 in one bit position indicates that corresponding tone will exists in the beep signal and vice versa for the value of '0'. For example, if the MAC address of a beacon device is $c4 : 2c : 03 : 3a : 2c : a1$, that has last ten bits as 0010100001, then the selected tones of the beep signal for that beacon device would be $\{f_1, f_6, f_8\}$. Selecting a tone is such way has almost $1\%$ ( $= (10*100)/2^{10}$) chance of having same tones for two different beacon device, if we consider 10 beacon devices in one place within each other proximity. Note that, at different public places we didn't found any cases where two Wi-Fi AP have same last 10 bit MAC address in one place.

In addition with the above designing of the *beep* signal, designing the RF message for each beacon device is challenging. In designing the infrastructure component, we leverage the existing WLAN setup, so that we can reduces the barrier of deploying our localization system. Therefore, we use the existing WLAN to generate the RF beacon message without imposing any overhead on the WLAN traffic. For example, we use the Wi-Fi beacon frame as our beacon message. In addition, we add the location information of the AP in the payload of the the Wi-Fi beacon frame, so that the client application can calculate the location locally. Furthermore, In the scenario of multiple APs, we also need to address the challenge of mapping each *beep* signal with the corresponding RF *beacon message* from a AP. As defining the beep signal in a unique way for each beacon device, help us to reduce the ambiguity of mapping the beep signal to the correct beacon message. In the implementation, we use a timeout of 100ms of detecting the beep signal after receiving the corresponding beacon message, which is also the normal periodicity of the beacon message (i.e. beacon period).

## 1.2 Client Component

In SpyLoc, client component consists of following modules:

**Distance Estimation module:** This module has two submodules i) *Step Detector*, and ii) *Personalized Step Model*. The step detector uses the commonly used accelerometer and the gyroscope sensors of the smartphone to detect and track the user steps. Typically, these sensor reading shows a noticeable periodic pattern for human steps, unless the smartphone is not carried by the user. However, the duration of each periodic pattern varies dynamically with the change of human walking speed. Numerous, paper address this challenge by building a standard model to consider unique fixed length step duration for each user [?]. The dynamic nature of human walking speed is quite natural in indoor environment. Therefore, using a fixed step duration for each user might create error in each step, which will accumulate over the time. Therefore, In SpyLoc we leverages our own customized Dynamic Time Wrapping (DTW) algorithm propose a robust and online step duration detection technique that address the dynamic nature of human walking speed. In the implementation, we use a fixed step length and our own DTW algorithm to calculate the final distance traveled by the user.

**Direction Estimation:**This module utilizes the geomagnetic and gyroscope sensors to detect the direction of the user. In indoor environments, using the inertial sensor of the smartphone to detect the direction of the user's movement is extremely critical due to surrounding noises from the ferromagnetic devices. Therefore in current implementation, we use the function *getRotationMatri* provided by the android API to collect more cleaner ration sensor reading.

**Location Determination module:** The location determination module is responsible to estimate the user's final location based on both the range estimation and the dead reckoning approach using inertial sensors. If the user is in the LoS of at least three beacon devices, location determination module applies the triangulation technique to estimate the user's actual location. However, in scenarios where the users is moving, (e.g. walking or running) such triangulation technique is not always practically applicable due to time limitation of computations. In addition, existence of three beacon device (e.g WiFi AP) in LoS is not always a practical scenario. Therefore, our location determination module utilizes the inertial sensors to predict the user's location.

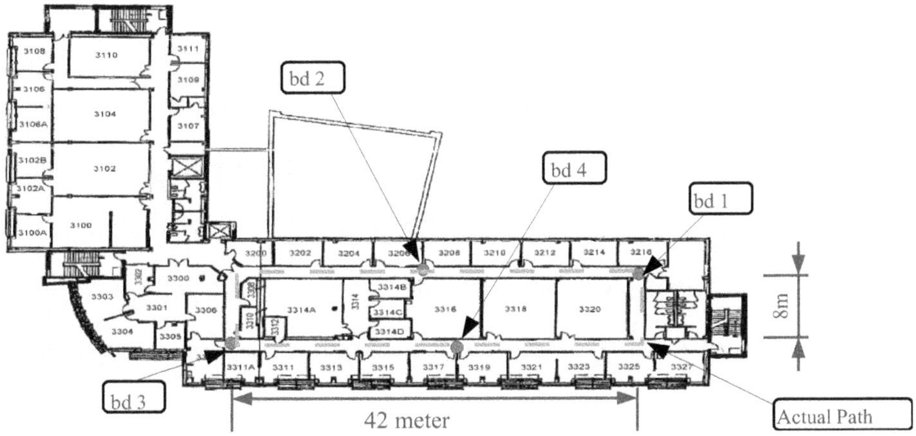


9(a)

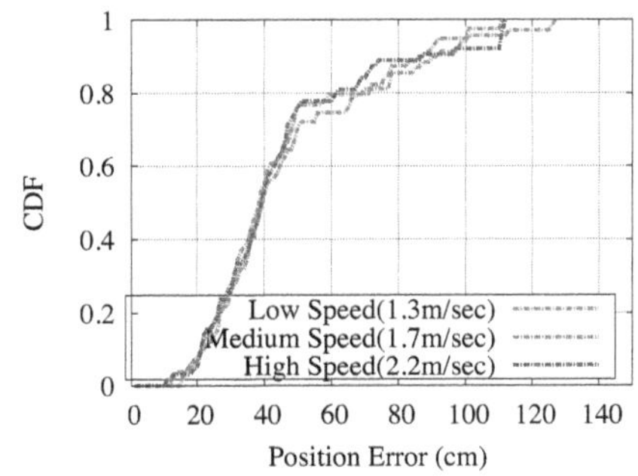


9(b)

Figure 2: (a) Indoor experiment setup at department building, following the green line as a route. (b) CDF of the estimation error for following the route in 2(a) at different speed.

However, such technique is not highly reliable in predicting the location. Since localization error in dead reckoning scheme get cumulated over time. Thus, instead of using three ranges from three beacon devices, our location determination module uses one range estimation to calibrate the estimated location from the inertial sensors. In situation where no LoS beacon device exists, location determination module relies on the inertial sensors to predicts the location.

The variation in direction estimation due to the noise, we assume the following gaussian model for the rotation sensor reading $\theta$,

$$\theta = \mathcal{N}(\theta_\mu, \theta_\sigma), \tag{1}$$

where $\theta_\mu$ is the mean and $\theta_\sigma$ is the variation. Therefore, lets assume the direction/distance estimation module provides possible set of locations,

$$L = \{l_1, l_2, ..., l_i, ..., l_N\}$$
$$l_i \equiv (x_i, y_i) \; i = 1, 2, .., N \tag{2}$$

Now In SpyLoc, with a single LoS, we use the following calculations to infer the user's final location by selecting the location point that is closest to the range $r$ from the only beacon device.

$$d_{min} = \min_{l_i} |r - \sqrt{(a - x_i)^2 + (b - y_i)^2}| \tag{3}$$

where $a, b$ are the center coordinate of the only LoS beacon device.

## 2. EVALUATION

Figure 2(a) shows the location of the beacon devices and the actual followed route(green line). Note that, during this experiment we use one range estimation and the inertial sensors to calibrate user's final location.The plot 2(b) shows the CDF of the estimation while we follow the route in 2(a) at different speed. In this experiment, we found estimation error less then 90cm for 90% of the times for different speed. These results proofs the feasibility and the efficiency of our SpyLoc system under different mobility condition of the user.

## 3. CHALLENGES AND FUTURE WORK

In future work we like to address the following challenges in details:

- The commonly used human step length model [?]infer the user's step length from the time duration of a steps.

$$s = \frac{a}{f} + b, \tag{4}$$

where $s$ is the step length in meter, $f$ is the time duration of a step in second, and $a, b$ are person-dependent constants. In SpyLoc client application, we want to leverage the ranging scheme and the step detection algorithm to build the above model for each person with no or minimal efforts.

- We like to utilize the sensor fusion technique to collect more cleaner rotation/direction sensor reading. However, despite the surrounding noise, these sensor also possess some biased noise. We like to address this challenge by following some pre-defined steps to calibrate the rotation sensor reading.
- We observe that the range detection from the NLoS *beacon device* shows less accuracy compare to the LoS *beacon device*. Therefore, we want to address the challenge of differentiating the LoS *beacon device* from the NLoS *beacon device* before estimating the range.
- In range estimation, knowing the temperature of the environment is important to calculate the speed of the sound. In our best knowledge, smartphones usually don't have the temperature sensor to provide the temperature of the surrounding environment. However, we want to utilizes the audio interface of the smartphone and the propagation speed of the acoustic signal to estimate the environment temperature.

# Concurrent-MAC: Increasing Concurrent Transmissions in Multi-AP Wireless LANs

Ghazale Hosseinabadi and Nitin Vaidya
Dept. of Electrical and Computer Engineering, University of Illinois
Urbana, IL, USA
ghossei2@illinois.edu, nhv@illinois.edu

## ABSTRACT

This paper presents the design and performance evaluation of Concurrent-MAC, a MAC protocol for increasing concurrent transmissions in multi-AP wireless LANs. Based on SINR values between stations and APs, sets of concurrent transmitters are identified by the backhaul of APs. A station gaining access to the channel, schedules a set of its neighbors for concurrent transmissions. Neighbors chosen for concurrent transmission can start transmitting on the channel, immediately after they overhear the privilege given to them for concurrent transmission. Our simulation results show that, in dense wireless LANs, Concurrent-MAC can improve aggregate throughput significantly compared to 802.11 DCF.

## Categories and Subject Descriptors

C.2.2 [**Computer-Communication Networks**]: Network Protocols

## Keywords

Concurrent Transmissions, MAC-Layer, Wireless LANs

## 1. INTRODUCTION

Deployment of Wireless Local Area Networks has grown rapidly in the past few years. IEEE 802.11 DCF is the MAC protocol commonly used in wireless LANs. 802.11 DCF employs *Carrier Sense Multiple Access with Collision Avoidance (CSMA/CA)* scheme. In 802.11 DCF protocol, a station willing to transmit, senses the wireless channel to determine if the channel is busy or idle. If the channel is sensed busy, the station has to defer its transmission until the medium becomes idle. The main drawback of carrier sensing mechanism is that, by simply comparing received power level with a carrier sense threshold, the information regarding which station is transmitting on the channel, is lost. Some stations might be eligible for concurrent transmissions while some might not, which is directly related to the SINR values at the receiver. Concurrent transmissions are transmissions that overlap in time. The ideal MAC protocol must prevent concurrent transmissions by interfering links and allow concurrent transmissions by non-interfering links.

IEEE 802.11 protocol is designed based on a "single AP-multiple stations" architecture, in which each AP serves multiple stations and each station is associated with only one access point at a time. But in current deployments of WLANs, it is observed that, in many cases, multiple APs are present in the vicinity of each station [1]. In this paper, we refer to WLANs in which stations are covered by multiple APs as *multi-AP WLANs*. In multi-AP WLANs, due to the broadcast property of the wireless channel, packets sent by a station can be received by any of the APs present in the station's transmission range.

We believe that a new MAC protocol that efficiently utilizes the presence of multiple APs to increase network throughput should be designed for multi-AP WLANs. In this paper, we design a MAC protocol, called *Concurrent-MAC*, which exploits the presence of multiple APs and increases concurrent transmissions to improve the uplink throughput in multi-AP wireless LANs. As we have found in this work, in multi-AP WLANs, there are many instances in which nearby stations can transmit concurrently. Although the concurrent packets might collide in some of the APs, they can be captured by some other APs. Our protocol, Concurrent-MAC, exploits the presence of the infrastructure to measure the path loss between stations and APs. Based on path loss information, central controller calculates the Signal to Interference and Noise Ratio (SINR) for different sets of transmitters to exactly find out which stations can transmit concurrently. Each station is then given an accurate list of its exposed neighboring stations. Whenever a station gains access to the channel, it gives a privilege to a set of its neighboring exposed stations to transmit concurrently. In a multi-AP WLAN, two nearby stations might not be eligible for concurrent transmission if they are restricted to transmit to their associated APs. On the other hand, two nearby stations might be eligible for concurrent transmissions if their packets can be received by any AP. Our protocol, Concurrent-MAC, enables stations to transmit concurrently, if their concurrent transmissions can be captured successfully by the backhaul of APs.


*MobiCom'13*, September 30–October 4, Miami, FL, USA.
http://dx.doi.org/10.1145/2500423.2504582
ACM 978-1-4503-1999-7/13/09.

## 2. RELATED WORK

Related work falls into two main areas:

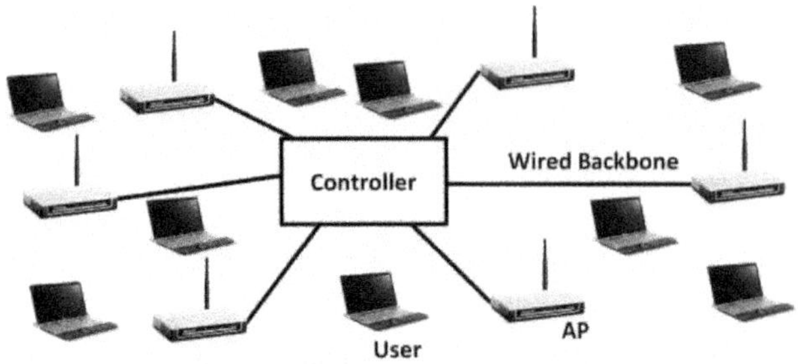


Figure 1: System architecture

**Coordinating multiple APs in WLANs:** Miu et al. [2] has designed the Multi-Radio Diversity (MRD) wireless network, which uses path diversity to improve throughput of WLANs. MRD has proposed a frame combining method which attempts to find the correct version of the transmitted frame even if it is received erroneously at all APs. Zhu et al. [3] has proposed an AP association algorithm for deciding which APs to associate with. Their proposed heuristic selects an AP to be included in the set of associated APs of a station, if the addition of that AP will increase the throughput of the station by more than a threshold.

**Solving the exposed terminal problem of 802.11 DCF:** [4] proposes *CMAP (Conflict Maps)*, a MAC protocol which allows concurrent transmissions by exposed terminals in wireless networks. CMAP tries to find out which stations can transmit concurrently and which can not. In CMAP, initially, all stations transmit concurrently, even if their transmissions collide. Stations then measure the loss probability to figure out which nearby stations are interfering stations and which are exposed stations, based on which, the stations build conflicting transmissions map. A station willing to transmit on the channel, considers the current transmitters and consults the conflict maps, to decide whether to transmit or defer.

# 3. CONCURRENT-MAC DESIGN

Figure 1 shows the multi-AP WLAN architecture we consider in this paper. Similar architecture has been proposed for multi-AP WLANs in the literate [2], [3]. APs are connected to a central component called *controller* via a wired backbone. In our protocol, Concurrent-MAC, a station is not explicitly associated with an AP and a station's packets might be received by any of the nearby APs. The APs are configured such that they receive or overhear packets transmitted by close by stations. Concurrent-MAC runs an opportunistic token passing protocol, where a token (or a privilege) is given by a transmitting station to a set of its neighbors. In this paper, we use the terms privilege and token interchangeably. Concurrent-MAC has two major components:

1. A probe phase to determine the sets of concurrent transmitters.
2. An opportunistic token passing protocol to enable concurrent transmissions.

## 3.1 Probe Phase

In this phase, stations transmit a number of packets in a round robin manner. APs located in the reception range of each station receive the probe packets based on which the channel gain between stations and APs can be measured. APs forward the channel gain information to the controller. From this information, the controller finds the set of the stations that can transmit concurrently. Stations can transmit concurrently, if their packets can be captured by different APs. Each station is then given a list of concurrent neighbors sets, where concurrent neighbors of a station can reliably transmit concurrently with the station. Stations use concurrent stations information to schedule their neighbors for concurrent transmissions.

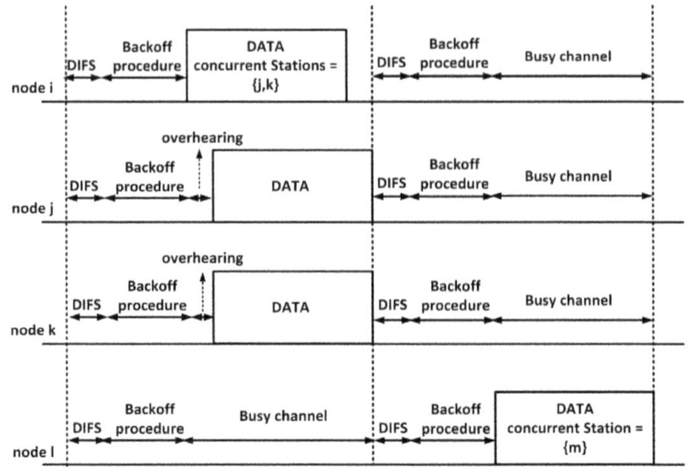


Figure 2: Access method of Concurrent-MAC protocol

## 3.2 Enabling Concurrent Transmissions

Channel access mechanism of Concurrent-MAC is shown in Figure 2. In Concurrent-MAC, when station $i$ transmits on the channel, it gives privilege to a set of neighboring stations, e.g. stations $j$ and $k$. If privileged stations $j$ and/or $k$ were sensing the channel as idle before transmission of $i$ starts, and if they overhear the privilege given to them by station $i$, they will start transmitting on the channel immediately. Non-privileged stations (e.g. station $l$ in Figure 2) have to defer their transmission till when the channel becomes idle. This process of giving a privilege to a set of neighbors repeats in each successful channel access. Whenever a station transmits on the channel, a set of concurrent transmissions might start. Compared to 802.11 DCF protocol in which nodes determine the channel as idle or busy just based on some heuristics, Concurrent-MAC provides an accurate method for enabling concurrent transmissions which can be received successfully by the backhaul of APs.

# 4. EVALUATION

We simulate Concurrent-MAC and 802.11a in ns-2 to measure and compare performance of these two MAC protocols. The network is a wireless LAN in which stations and APs are placed uniformly at random in a square area. We use a log-distance path loss model with path loss exponent of four to simulate the indoor office environment. Traffic is full buffer CBR. IEEE 802.11 RTS/CTS mechanism is turned off. Packet payload size is 1500 bytes. Each simulation lasts for 30 seconds and the presented results are averaged over 5 runs. We run the simulations for two network sizes, i.e.,

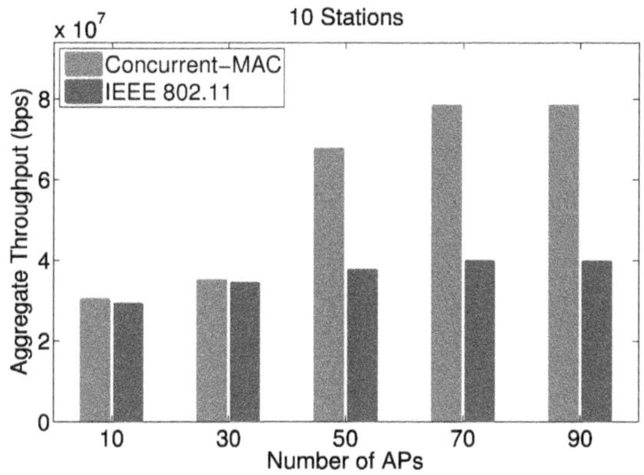


Figure 3: Single hop network (area = 15mx15m)

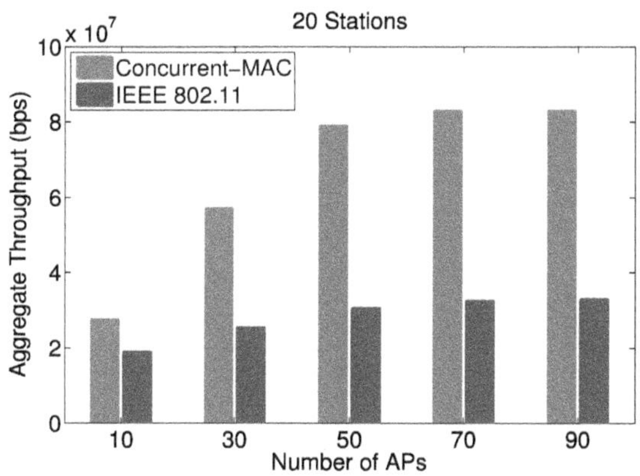


Figure 4: Single hop network (area = 15mx15m)

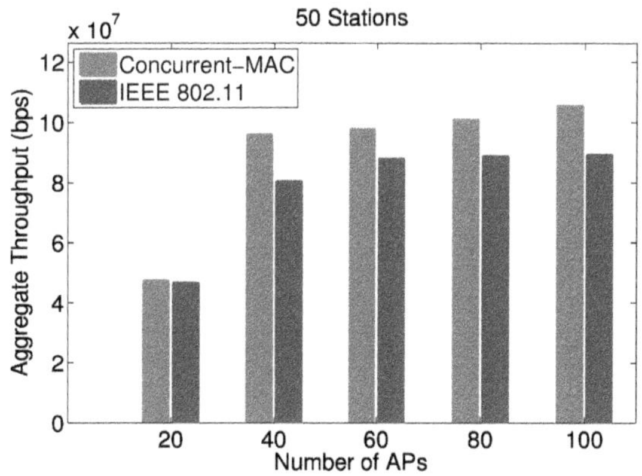


Figure 5: Multi-hop network (area = 50mx50m)

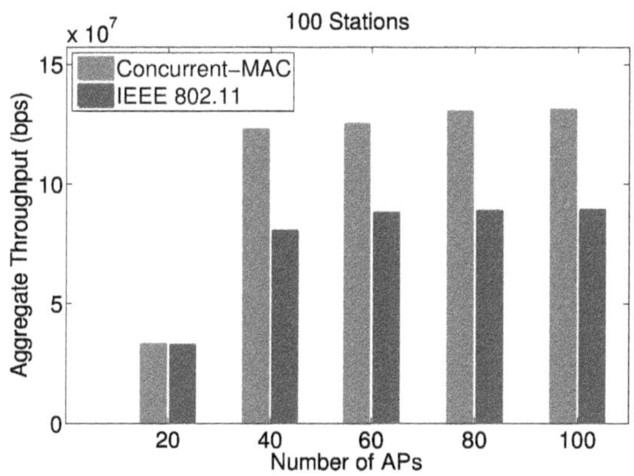


Figure 6: Multi-hop network (area = 50mx50m)

$15m$x$15m$ and $50m$x$50m$. We vary the number of stations and APs in the area to investigate the effect of stations and APs density on the concurrent transmissions and network throughput.

Figures 3 and 4 plot the throughput in a single hop network of size $15m$x $15m$. With our simulation parameters, carrier sense range is $25m$. As can be seen in these figures, throughput gain obtained by Concurrent-MAC compared to IEEE 802.11 can be up to a factor of 2.5 as we increase the number of stations and APs in the area. The reason is that increasing number of stations and APs increases the number of concurrent transmissions in the network. The aggregate throughput of 802.11 DCF and Concurrent-MAC, for a multi-hop network of size $50m$x$50m$ is presented in Figures 5 and 6. As we observe in these figures, aggregate throughput is increased by up to 52% by exploiting the presence of many APs in the area.

# 5. CONCLUSION AND FUTURE WORK

In this paper, we presented the design and performance evaluation of Concurrent-MAC. Concurrent-MAC is a MAC protocol that uses an opportunistic overhearing mechanism to schedule network stations for concurrent transmissions in multi-AP WLANs. The main design goal of Concurrent-MAC is to increase aggregate throughput by allowing concurrent transmissions that can be received successfully by the backhaul of APs. Our simulation results show that Concurrent-MAC can achieve significant improvement in system throughput compared to 802.11 DCF. In future, we want to explore the effect of rate adaptation on increasing the number of concurrent transmissions in Concurrent-MAC. As we have observed in our simulations, by decreasing the rate, we might be able to increase the number of concurrent transmissions.

# 6. ACKNOWLEDGEMENTS

This research is supported in part by National Science Foundation award CNS 11-17539.

# 7. REFERENCES

[1] A. Akella, G. Judd, S. Seshan, and P. Steenkiste, Self-management in chaotic wireless deployments, In *MobiCom '05*, August 2005.

[2] A. Miu, H. Balakrishnan, and C. E. Koksal, Improving loss resilience with multi-radio diversity in wireless networks, In *Proc. of ACM MobiCom*, pp. 16-30, August 2005.

[3] Y. Zhu, Z. Niu, Q. Zhang, B. Tan, Z. Zhou, and J. Zhu, A multi-AP architecture for high-density WLANs: protocol design and experimental evaluation, In *Proc. of IEEE SECON*, pp. 28-36, June 2008.

[4] M. Vutukuru, K. Jamieson, and H. Balakrishnan, Harnessing exposed terminals in wireless networks, In *USENIX NSDI*, June 2008.

# How Long Are You Staying? Predicting Residence Time from Human Mobility Traces

Paul Baumann
Wireless Sensor Networks Lab
TU Darmstadt, Germany
paul.baumann@wsn.tu-darmstadt.de

Wilhelm Kleiminger
Institute for Pervasive Computing
ETH Zurich, Switzerland
kleiminger@inf.ethz.ch

Silvia Santini
Wireless Sensor Networks Lab
TU Darmstadt, Germany
santinis@wsn.tu-darmstadt.de

## ABSTRACT

Predicting the arrival and residence time of individuals at their relevant places enables a plethora of novel applications. In this work we first analyze the theoretical predictability of arrival and residence times and then evaluate the performance of eight different residence time predictors. We show that these predictors tend to underestimate the time a user will spend at her relevant places.

## Categories and Subject Descriptors

I.5.m [**PATTERN RECOGNITION**]: Miscellaneous

## Keywords

Predictability of human mobility; Arrival time; Residence time

## 1. INTRODUCTION

Places where a person "*spends a substantial amount of time and/or visits frequently*" [2] are typically referred to as *relevant places*. On a typical day, an individual might move from one relevant place to the other and spend different amounts of time in each place. The time spent at each place is referred to as *residence time* [6, 10, 11]. The times of the day at which a person arrives at or leaves from a place are called *arrival time* and *departure time*, respectively [6, 10, 11]. The ability to predict when a person will arrive and how long she will stay at a specific place is fundamental to enable a number of applications like, e.g., smart heating control or urban navigation [5]. A number of algorithms that can perform these predictions have been presented in the literature [6, 11, 9]. This poster abstract presents our preliminary results on investigating both the theoretical and practical limits of the prediction performance achievable by arrival and residence time prediction algorithms.

To investigate the predictability of arrival and residence times we build upon recent work by Song *et al.* [1]. In their work Song *et al.* focus on the problem of predicting the next place that will be visited by a person, provided that the sequence of places she visited so far are known. In this context, they define the *predictability* $\Pi$ as the "*upper bound that fundamentally limits any mobility prediction algorithm in predicting the next location based on historical records*" [7]. They also show how the value of $\Pi$ can be computed from the entropy $S_i$ of the sequence of places visited by a person – or *user* – $i$. Building upon this approach, we investigate the predictability of arrival and residence times. Our analysis allows to evaluate how close the performance of existing algorithms are to the theoretical limits. In particular, we investigate the actual performance achieved by eight algorithms in predicting residence times and show that these values are underestimated by most algorithms.


*MobiCom'13,* September 30–October 4, 2013, Miami, FL, USA.
ACM 978-1-4503-1999-7/13/09.
http://dx.doi.org/10.1145/2500423.2504583.

## 2. PREDICTABILITY OF ARRIVAL AND RESIDENCE TIMES

In this section we present the results of our analysis of the predictability of arrival and residence times. To this end, we first introduce the mathematical notation and describe the setup of our study. We would like to point out that we focus on the average predictability of a user over a given period of time – as in Song *et al.* 's work [1] – and not on the *momentary predictability* as done in [8, 4].

### 2.1 Terminology and notation

We indicate with $L_j$, $j = 1 : N_L$, the j-th relevant place of a user $i$ and define the set $\mathcal{L} = \{L_1, L_2, \ldots, L_{N_L}\}$ as the set of $N_L$ places relevant to user $i$.[1] The places are ordered according to the total amount of time spent at each place, e.g., $L_1$ is the place at which the user spends most of her time ($L_1$ is typically the home). Locations visited by the user that cannot be associated to any relevant place are assumed to be "irrelevant" to the user and are marked using the symbol $L_x$. We further define the *mobility trace* $MT$ of a user $i$ as the sequence of places visited by the user during the observation period $T_{obs}$. The observation period is thereby virtually divided in *slots* of length $\Delta_s$. For instance, if the observation period is one day and the length of a slot is 15 minutes then the mobility trace will be a vector of 96 elements, whereby the elements of the vector take values in $\{\mathcal{L}, L_x\}$.

We further define the *arrival time trace* $AT(L_j)$ as the vector containing the ordered sequence of arrival times at place $L_j$. The length of the vector is not fixed a priori since the number of arrival events occurring in the mobility trace might vary from user to user and from place to place. The values of the elements of $AT(L_j)$ are the indexes of the time slots at which arrival events takes place. Using again the example above, in which $T_{obs} = 1$ day and $\Delta_s = 15$ minutes, the mobility trace has 96 elements. The first element (index 1) corresponds to the time slot spanning the period from 00:00 to 00:15 and the last elements (index 96) to the slot from 11:45 p.m to 12:00 p.m.. Consider for instance a user for whom $L_1$ is the home and that during the observation

[1]To simplify the notation, we omit the use of the subscript $i$. The quantities defined here however always refer to a specific user $i$.

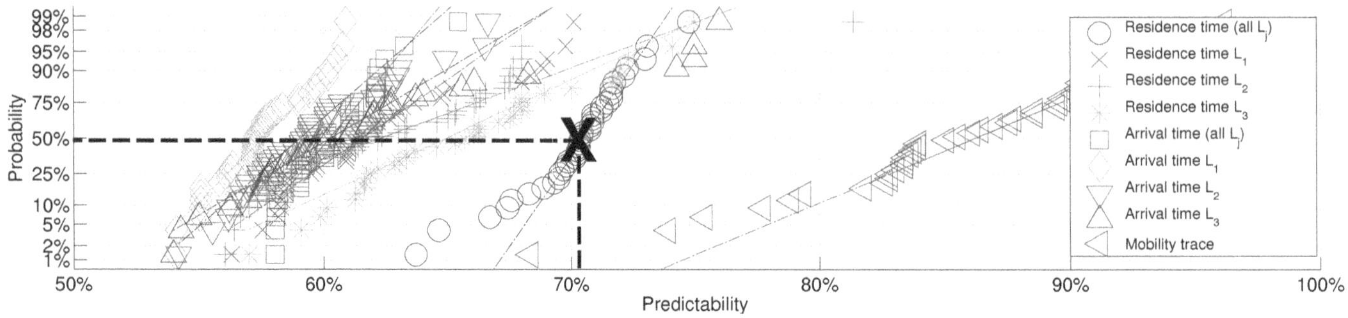


Figure 1: Normal probability plot of arrival time and residence time predictability vectors.

period had come back home at 17:00, then went out again and returned at 22:00. The corresponding arrival time trace for $L_1$ will be: $AT(L_1) = [68, 88]$. Arrival time traces of two different places can be combined: $AT(L_j, L_k)$ will for instance indicate the ordered union of the two vectors $AT(L_j$ and $AT(L_k)$. $AT(\mathcal{L})$ indicates the union of the arrival time trace of all $L_j, j = 1 : N_L$.

Finally, we define the *residence time trace* $RT(L_j)$ as the vector containing the sequence of residence times at place $L_j$. The length of a residence time is thereby indicated as the number of slots the user stays at place $L_j$ before moving to another place. Using again the example mentioned above and assuming the user stayed at home between 17:00 and 18:30 and then again from 22:00 to the end of the observation period (midnight), then: $RT(L_1) = [6, 8]$.

## 2.2 Evaluation setup

We run our analysis on data collected using smart phones in the context of the Lausanne Data Collection Campaign (LDCC) [3]. The subset of LDCC data available for this study consists of records collected from 38 users over about 1.5 years including a large amount of location data. We use the Wi-Fi scans available in the data set as input to the PlaceSense algorithm by Kim *et al.* [2]. This way, we derive the set $\mathcal{L}$ of relevant places for each user. We use the same parameter settings as in [2] apart from the value of the *sensitivity* parameter which is set to 30% as in [9]. We then derive the mobility trace of each user using a $\Delta_s$ of 15 minutes. The observation period varies depending on the amount of data available for each user. Minimum, maximum, average, and median of the observation periods is 86, 407, 203, and 189 days, respectively.

From these mobility traces we derive the vectors $RT(\mathcal{L})$, $RT(L_1)$, $RT(L_2)$, $RT(L_3)$, $AT(\mathcal{L})$, $AT(L_1)$, $AT(L_2)$, and $AT(L_3)$. We compute the predictability of these traces obtaining one data point per vector and per user. For instance, we compute the predictability associated with the sequence of values in $RT(\mathcal{L})$ for each of the 38 users and combine these values in the *predictability vector* $\Pi_{RT(\mathcal{L})}$. Similarly, we compute the predictability vectors $\Pi_{RT(L_1)}$, $\Pi_{RT(L_2)}$, $\Pi_{RT(L_3)}$, $\Pi_{AT(\mathcal{L})}$, $\Pi_{AT(L_1)}$, $\Pi_{AT(L_2)}$, $\Pi_{AT(L_3)}$. The predictability of the arrival time traces and residence time traces is computed using the same method used by Song *et al.* to compute the predictability of mobility traces [1][2].

## 2.3 Evaluation results

Figure 1 shows the normal probability plot of the predictability vectors $\Pi_{RT(\mathcal{L})}$, $\Pi_{RT(L_1)}$, $\Pi_{RT(L_2)}$, $\Pi_{RT(L_3)}$, $\Pi_{AT(\mathcal{L})}$, $\Pi_{AT(L_1)}$, $\Pi_{AT(L_2)}$, $\Pi_{AT(L_3)}$ and of the predictability of the mobility traces. On a normal probability plot[3], data showing a normal distribution fits on a line. The x-axis indicates the predictability, computed as described above. The y-axis indicates the probability that the arrival time, residence time, or mobility trace of a user shows a predictability equal or lower than the corresponding value on the x-axis. For instance, the large 'X' marker in Figure 1 shows that the residence time of 50% of the users has a predictability of 71% or less (when all locations in $\mathcal{L}$ are considered). This implies that the prediction accuracy achievable by an algorithm that predicts the residence time does not exceed 71% for about 50% of the users.

Figure 1 also shows that the overall predictability of the mobility traces is higher than that of the arrival times and residence times. This means that it is in general easier to predict the next location of a user rather than the arrival or residence time at specific locations. The curves in Figure 1 further show that the predictability of the arrival times at location $L_1$ is low (about 60%) and lower than the predictability of the arrival times at locations $L_2$ and $L_3$. Furthermore, the predictability of the arrival times is in general lower than the predictability of the residence times.

Figure 2 shows the Cumulative Distribution Function (CDF) of the residence time at places $L_1$, $L_2$, $L_3$, and $L_x$ averaged over all users in the data set. The curve corresponding to $L_1$ is significantly "smoother" than the $L_2$, $L_3$, and $L_x$. This indicates that the amount of time users spend at $L_1$ varies more than the time spent at other locations. This offers an explanation of the predictability values observed above: the high dispersion of residence times at $L_1$ increases the number of potentially predictable value, leading to an overall lower predictability.

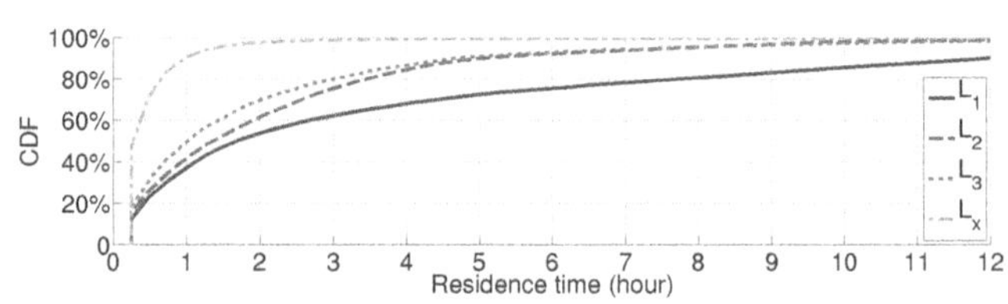


Figure 2: Cumulative distribution function of residence time for $L_1$, $L_2$, $L_3$, and $L_x$.

# 3. PREDICTION OF RESIDENCE TIME

After exploring the theoretical bounds for the predictability of users' arrival and residence times, in this section we focus on the accuracy achieved by existing, practical residence time prediction algorithms.

[2]The results by Song *et al.* are obtained under the assumption that the sequence of locations is the realization of a stationary ergodic process. This assumption is not likely to be fulfilled if long sequences (e.g., over several years) are considered. In our work, however, we consider shorter sequences (e.g., several months).

[3]http://www.mathworks.de/de/help/stats/normplot.html

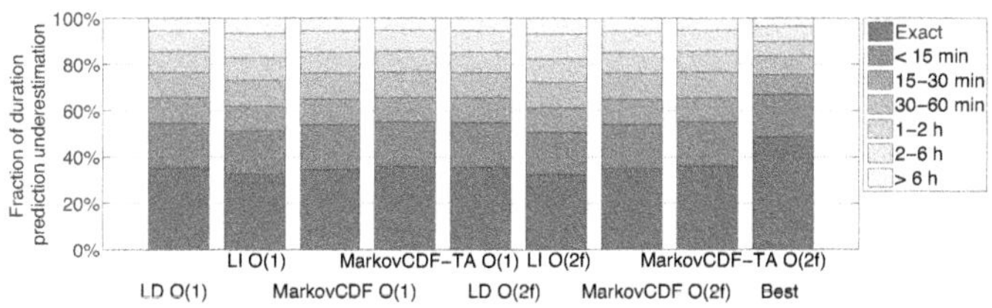


(a) Correct and underestimated residence time predictions.

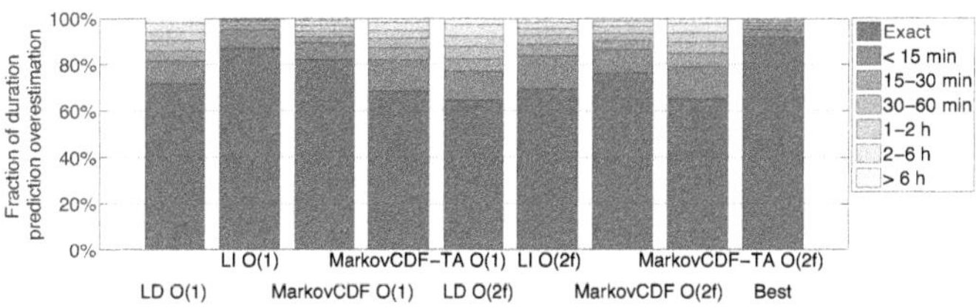


(b) Correct and overestimated residence time predictions

Figure 3: Fractions of residence time under- and overestimated predictions.

## 3.1 Prediction algorithms

We consider eight different residence time predictors selected from the literature [6, 11]. We use the location-dependent (LD), location-independent (LI), MarkovCDF, and MarkovCDF time-aided (MarkovCDF-TA) predictors. The Markov 1st O(1) and 2nd O(2) order location-dependent (LD) predictor with the fallback option O(2f) are described in [6, 11] and are used without further modifications. As a LI predictor we use the LD predictor by removing the explicit location dependency. For the predictors MarkovCDF and MarkovCDF time-aided (i.e., the residence time depends on the arrival time), we use the implementations proposed in [11]. We further consider a fictive algorithm – dubbed *Best* – which always takes, among the predictions computed by the other algorithms, the one known to result in the smallest prediction error. We use the same notation and data as described in Section 2 as well as the residence time traces $RT(L_j)$ ($RT(\mathcal{L})$ for the LI predictor).

## 3.2 Results

We use the algorithms described above to predict the residence time of each user at the locations $L_j, j = 1, \dots, N_L$. We compute the average prediction error of each algorithm and split the results into correct predictions, overestimation, and underestimations, i.e., zero, positive, or negative error values. Figure 3(a) shows the percentage of both correct and underestimated predictions (the percentage is meant over the total of correct and underestimated predictions) for each of the nine considered algorithms. Figure 3(b) shows the same data when along with correct also overestimated predictions are considered.

Apart from the *Best* algorithm – which, as expected, always shows the best performance – all the predictors exhibit similar percentages of prediction error ranges when the error is underestimated. The LI O(1) predictor however generates the highest number of underestimated predictions. Overall, the number of overestimations with respect to the correct predicitons is much smaller than the number of underestimations. In particular, location-independent Markov 1st order predictor together with the fictive *Best* approach produce the smallest amount of overestimated predictions.

This allows us to conclude that the considered residence time predictors tend to underestimate the time a user will spend at the location $L_j$. Further investigations on whether this consideration can be generalized and on what are the reasons for this behavior are part of our future work.

# 4. CONCLUSIONS

This poster abstract describes preliminary results on the analysis of predictability of arrival time and residence time and on the evaluation of the actual performance of residence time predictors. We observe that arrival time traces have an overall lower predictability than residence time traces and that the higher the amount of time a user spends at a specific place, the lower is the corresponding arrival and residence time predictability. Our analysis of the performance of residence time predictors shows that most predictors tend to underestimate the time a user will spend at her relevant places.

# 5. ACKNOWLEDGEMENTS

This work has been partially supported by the Collaborative Research Center 1053 (www.maki.tu-darmstadt.de) funded by the German Research Foundation and by the Priority Program Cocoon (www.cocoon.tu-darmstadt.de) funded by the LOEWE research initiative of the state of Hesse, Germany.

# 6. REFERENCES


[1] C. Song *et al.* Limits of Predictability in Human Mobility. *Science*, 327(5968):1018–1021, 2010.

[2] D.H. Kim *et al.* Discovering Semantically Meaningful Places from Pervasive RF-Beacons. In *11th Intl. Conf. on Ubiquitous Computing (UbiComp'09)*, 2009.

[3] J. Laurila *et al.* The Mobile Data Challenge: Big Data for Mobile Computing Research. In *10th Intl. Conf. on Pervasive Computing (Pervasive'12)*, 2012.

[4] J. McInerney *et al.* Exploring Periods of Low Predictability in Daily Life Mobility. In *10th Intl. Conf. on Pervasive Computing (Pervasive'12)*, June 2012.

[5] J. Scott *et al.* PreHeat: Controlling Home Heating Using Occupancy Prediction. In *13th Intl. Conf. on Ubiquitous Computing (UbiComp'11)*, Sept. 2011.

[6] L. Song *et al.* Predictability of WLAN Mobility and its Effects on Bandwidth Provisioning. In *25th Intl. Conf. on Computer Communications (INFOCOM'06)*, 2006.

[7] M. Lin *et al.* Predictability of Individuals' Mobility with High-resolution Positioning Data. In *14th Intl. Conf. on Ubiquitous Computing (UbiComp'12)*, 2012.

[8] P. Baumann and S. Santini. On the Use of Instantaneous Entropy to Measure the Momentary Predictability of Human Mobility. In *14th IEEE Workshop on Signal Processing Advances in Wireless Communications (SPAWC'13)*, 2013.

[9] P. Baumann *et al.* The Influence of Temporal and Spatial Features on the Performance of Next-place Prediction Algorithms. In *2013 ACM Intl. Joint Conf. on Pervasive and Ubiquitous Computing (UbiComp'13)*, 2013.

[10] S. Scellato *et al.* NextPlace: A Spatio-temporal Prediction Framework for Pervasive Systems. In *9th Intl. Conf. on Pervasive Computing (Pervasive'11)*, 2011.

[11] Y. Chon *et al.* Evaluating Mobility Models for Temporal Prediction with High-granularity Mobility Data. In *10th Intl. Conf. on Pervasive Computing and Communications (PerCom'12)*, 2012.

# Measuring Human Queues Using WiFi Signals


Yan Wang
Stevens Institute of Technology
Hoboken, NJ 07030, USA
ywang48@stevens.edu

Jie Yang
Oakland University
Rochester, MI 48309, USA
yang@oakland.edu

Hongbo Liu
Stevens Institute of Technology
Hoboken, NJ 07030, USA
hliu3@stevens.edu

Yingying Chen
Stevens Institute of Technology
Hoboken, NJ 07030, USA
yingying.chen@stevens.edu

Marco Gruteser
Rutgers University
North Brunswick, NJ 08902, USA
gruteser@rutgers.edu

Richard P. Martin
Rutgers University
North Brunswick, NJ 08902, USA
rmartin@rutgers.edu



## ABSTRACT

We investigate using smartphone WiFi signals to track human queues, which are common in many business areas such as retail stores, airports, and theme parks. Real-time monitoring of such queues would enable a wealth of new applications, such as bottleneck analysis, shift assignments, and dynamic workflow scheduling. We take a minimum infrastructure approach and thus utilize a single monitor placed close to the service area along with transmitting phones. Our strategy extracts unique features embedded in the signal traces to infer the critical time points when a person reaches the head of the queue and finishes service, and from these inferences we derive a person's waiting and service times. We develop a feature driven approach in our system. Extensive experiments conducted both in the laboratory demonstrate that our system is robust to queues with different waiting time. We show that in spite of noisy signal readings, our methods can measure important time periods in queue (e.g., service and waiting times) to within a 10 second resolution.



## Categories and Subject Descriptors

H.4.m [**Information Systems Applications**]: [miscellaneous]

## General Terms

Measurement, Experimentation

## Keywords

Human Queue, WiFi, Smartphone


## 1. INTRODUCTION

The popular usage of smartphones and their data-intensive apps has created novel opportunities to exploit such network traffic for monitoring and optimizing real-world processes. Research has shown, for example, how cellular call data records can be used to infer large scale transportation patterns (e.g., [1]) or how cellular signal traces allow inferring the level of congestion on roadways [2]. In this work, we ask whether signal power readings from phone traffic are also sufficient, to monitor a much finer-scale, yet common, process: human queues.



*MobiCom'13*, September 30–October 4, 2013, Miami, FL, USA.
ACM 978-1-4503-1999-7/13/09.
http://dx.doi.org/10.1145/2500423.2504584.


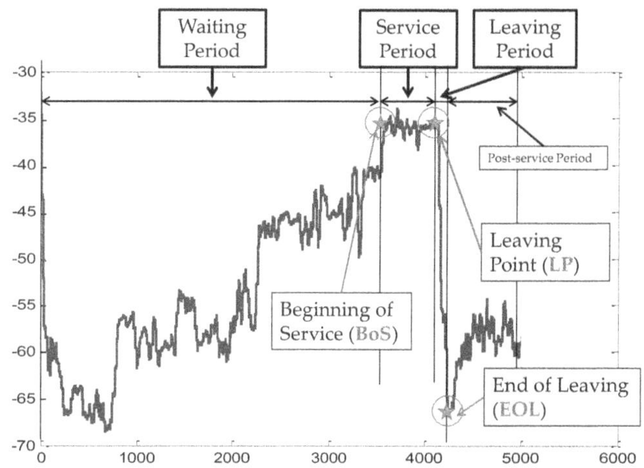


**Figure 1: Illustration of special queue-related patterns embedded in the RSS trace collected from a smartphone in a human queue.**

Such queues are a familiar and often frustrating occurrence, for example in retail stores, banks, theme parks, hospitals and transportation stations. Note that we interpret the concept of a queue loosely, people do not need to stand in line but could sit in a waiting room and do not always need to be served in a strict first in, first out order. Real-time quantification of the waiting times and service times in such queues, allows optimizing service processes across ranging from retail, to heath care, to transportation and entertainment. For example, many hospital emergency departments surveys have average waiting times of several hours [3]. More complete wait and service time statistics allows customers, travelers, managers and service providers make changes to their behavior and processes. For example, an airport checkpoint might be experiencing abnormal delays and require intervention by diverting screeners from queues with shorter waiting times. Customers also can benefit, for example, knowing at what times retail store checkout lines can be expected to be shorter.

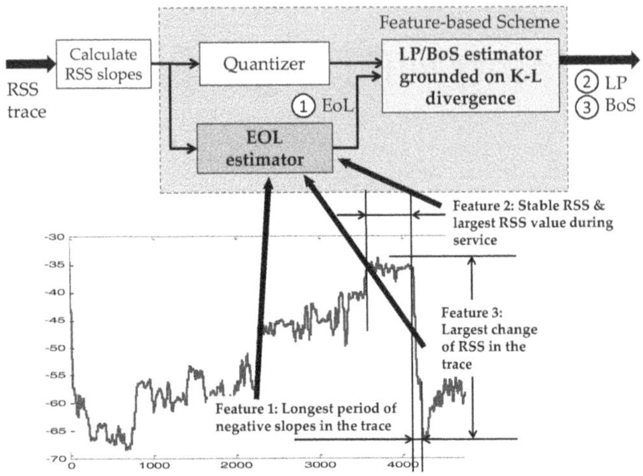


**Figure 2: Flow of feature-driven scheme to find EoL, LP, and BoS in a time-reversed way.**

Existing solutions to the queue monitoring problem often rely on cameras [4] or special sensors (e.g., infrared [5] or floor mats [6]) at multiple locations. Bluetooth signals emanating from phones have also been used to measure travel times between two sensing points, both at airports [7] and for vehicle traffic [8]. All these solutions require multiple sensors to fully monitor a single queue, which increases installation and system cost. In addition, prior techniques using wireless networks were too coarse-grained to differentiate between the waiting time and service time and vision techniques face increased privacy issues.

Our approach uses only a single sensor, a WiFi monitor near the head of the queue that measures the received signal strength of packets emitted from phones. Intuitively, the received signal power should follow a known pattern. As the person moves towards the service point, the phone moves closer to the monitor and the received signal power should increase. When the person is receiving service, the signal power should be very strong and relatively constant. Finally, when the person exits the service point, there should be a rapid decline in signal strength. For example, Figure 1 presents the RSS trace of a smartphone in a queue collected from a single WiFi monitor at the service desk in a coffee shop. We observe that the captured RSS trace reflects the patten of the distance between the person carrying the phone to the service desk. In particular, the RSS exhibits the following unique patterns: (1) the RSS has a slowly increasing trend during the *waiting period*; (2) it then becomes stable at high RSS values when the person carrying the phone is in the *service period*; and (3) it finally drops quickly when the person is leaving the service desk after got service in his *leaving period*.

Accurately discerning the points where the person begins and ends service is challenging, however, in this single-point monitoring system, because the multi-path, shadowing, and fading components of a signal are quite dynamic due to the movement of many people. We therefore investigate a direct feature-driven approaches for extracting the waiting and service times from a signal trace. We experimentally evaluate our approach in a laboratory with 90 traces. We find our approach is robust and able to measure the waiting time to with average errors less than $10s$.

## 2. FEATURE-DRIVEN QUEUE PARAMETER DETERMINATION

We find that the important periods of a human queue are separated by three critical time points, namely Beginning of Service (BoS), Leaving Point (LP), and End of Leaving (EoL). By deducing these three time points, our system is able to track the important queue time periods including waiting, service, and leaving periods.

Toward this end, we develop a *feature-driven* scheme in our system to identify the critical time points in a human queue. The feature-driven approach utilizes the unique features extracted from RSS traces to identify these time points. We next describe the details of this approach.

When designing the feature-driven scheme, we consider directly applying the features associated with the leaving period in the RSS trace to determine the EoL, LP, and BoS in a time-reversed manner. Because the RSS value changes dramatically when people leave the queue after service, the features associated with the leaving period are the most obvious and easy to be extracted. In particular, we identify three features extracted from the RSS trace associated with the leaving period:

1. The leaving period has the *longest* consecutive negative-slope segments of the selected RSS trace.
2. The RSS values before the leaving period are stable with the *highest* amplitude of the selected RSS trace.
3. The leaving period experiences the *largest* decreasing of RSS in the selected RSS trace.

The feature-driven scheme consists of three components: *EoL Estimator*, *Quantizer*, and *LP/BoS Estimator*. We illustrate the flow of the feature-driven scheme in Figure 2.

**EoL Estimator.** Assume there is a group of $M$ segments with consecutive negative slopes in the RSS trace $\mathbb{G} = \{G_1, \ldots, G_M\}$, and each segment $G_i$ lasts for a period of $T_i = t_1^i - t_0^i$, where $t_1^i$ and $t_0^i$ denote the starting time and the ending time of that segment, respectively. The EoL estimator determines the time $t_0^i$ to be EoL when a segment $G_i$ is most likely to be a leaving period. To determine the likelihood of being a leaving period, we first define the significance of the three features described above as: 1) $\frac{T_i}{\max(\mathbb{T})}$, where $\mathbb{T}$ denotes time length of all the segments in $\mathbb{G}$; 2) $\frac{S_i}{\max(\mathbb{S})}$, where $S_i$ is the average RSS over a time window $L$ before $t_1^i$, and $\mathbb{S}$ denotes all such average RSS; 3) $\frac{R_i}{\max(\mathbb{R})}$, where $R_i$ is the ratio of the RSS at $t_0^i$ and $t_1^i$, and $\mathbb{R}$ denotes all such RSS ratio, respectively. We further define an utility function which is a weighted sum of the significance of the three features:

$$u_i = \alpha \cdot \frac{T_i}{\max(\mathbb{T})} + \beta \cdot \frac{S_i}{\max(\mathbb{S})} + \gamma \cdot \frac{R_i}{\max(\mathbb{R})}, \qquad (1)$$

where $\alpha$, $\beta$, and $\gamma$ are the weights. The leaving period thus can be determined as the segment $G_i$ that maximizes the utility function $u_i$. And the time $t_0^i$ of such a segment $G_i$ is then declared as the EoL. To determine the weights in Equation (1), we use a heuristic approach by counting the occurrence of each feature in a small portion of the collected traces (e.g., 20 traces) and respectively using the ratio of each feature's occurrence to the number of traces as their weights. For example, if feature 1 has been found true for 10 times in 20 traces, the weight for feature 1 is then 0.5. Based on our experiments, we empirically find that when $\alpha = 0.4$, $\beta = 0.8$ and $\gamma = 0.8$, the unique features can be extracted from the RSS trace accurately.

Meanwhile, we compute the slopes of each RSS sample in the selected RSS trace. A *Quantizer* performs normalization and quantization on the computed RSS slopes.

**LP/BoS Estimator.** Our feature-driven scheme then takes the input from the EoL Estimator together with the quantized RSS slopes to identify the leaving point (LP) and beginning of service point

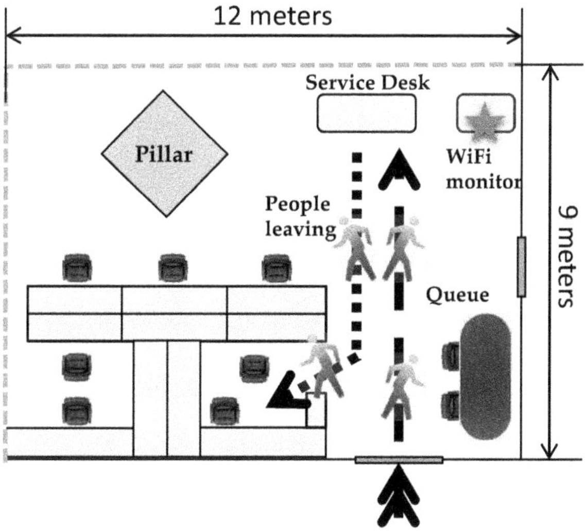


**Figure 3: Illustration of experimental setup for queue measurement in the laboratory.**

(BoS) in the queue following the temporal-reversed order. The LP/BoS Estimator takes the view point that the leaving point separates the service period and the leaving period, and thus the WiFi signals before LP is relatively stable whereas they drop dramatically after the leaving point. This useful observation indicates that the distributions of WiFi signal changes (i.e., slopes of RSS) before and after the leaving point are significantly different. This inspires us to identify LP by using the KL-divergence technique to examine the distribution difference of WiFi signal changes. And LP is determined as the time point (prior to EoL) separating the RSS slopes into two parts that present the most different distributions from each other.

In particular, we calculate the distributions of quantized RSS slopes before and after each time point $t_j$ occurring before EoL, respectively denoted as $P(K_{j-1})$ and $Q(K_j), j = [1, \dots, J]$, where $J$ is number of time points occurring before EoL. The K-L divergence between these two distributions are derived as:

$$D_{KL}(P(K_{j-1}) \| Q(K_j)) = \sum_{q \in Q} P(K_{j-1} = q) \ln \frac{P(K_{j-1} = q)}{Q(K_j = q)}, \tag{2}$$

where $Q$ is the set of all possible values for quantized RSS slopes. LP is then determined as the time point $t_j$, which maximizes the K-L divergence value:

$$t_j = \arg\max_{t_j}(D_{KL}(P(K_{j-1}) \| Q(K_j))). \tag{3}$$

Similarly, our scheme can also employ the KL-divergence technique to identify BoS, since WiFi signals is relatively stable during the service period while they exhibit an obvious increasing trend in the waiting period.

# 3. PERFORMANCE EVALUATION

We next show our system implementation with the input RSS from single antenna as well as the maximum RSS from two antennas at the WiFi monitor, and evaluate their impacts.

**Experimental Setup.** We conduct experiments with human queues in a laboratory setup as shown in Figure 3. We place a WiFi monitor equipped with two antennas at the service desk to capture WiFi signals. We develop an Android app to send beacon packets at the rate

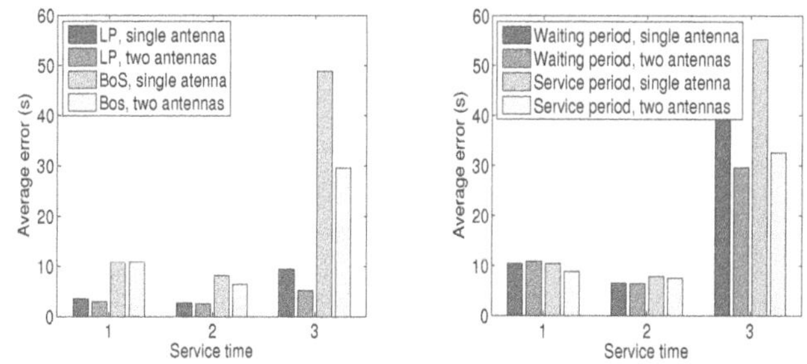


(a) LP & BoS

(b) Waiting & service times

**Figure 4: Performance comparison of the single-antenna and two-antenna approach under different service times in laboratory.**

of $10pkt/sec$. We experiment with three different service times, $30s$, $60s$, and $180s$, representing *short*, *normal* and *long* service times, respectively. In total we collect 90 traces in the laboratory environment and we use two-fold cross-validation for evaluation. We calculate the estimation error of the relevant time points and important time periods with regard to the manually logged ground-truth.

**Experimental Results.** We first study the performance of the feature-driven scheme based on the signals received from a single and two antennas at the WiFi monitor. Figure 4 (a) compares the average error of estimating the LP and BoS under different length of the service time. We observe that the feature-driven scheme performs well with both single and two antennas under short (30s) and normal (60s) service times with the average error less than 10s. We find that with two antennas the system has better performance, especially under the long service time (180s). Moreover, Figure 10(b) depicts the average error of tracking the waiting and service times derived from the estimated BoS and LP. We observe the average error of both waiting and service times is less than 10s under short and normal service times. Under the long service time, using two antennas outperforms using single antenna for over 30%, although both schemes experience performance degradation.

# 4. REFERENCES


[1] S. Isaacman and et.al., "Human mobility modeling at metropolitan scales," in *ACM MobiSys*, 2012.

[2] G. Chandrasekaran and et.al., "Vehicular speed estimation using received signal strength from mobile phones," in *ACM Ubicomp*, 2010.

[3] I. of Medicine (US), *Hospital-Based Emergency Care: At the Breaking Point*. National Academy Press, 2007.

[4] "Expo 2010 Shanghai China." http://en.expo2010.cn/, 2010.

[5] U. Stilla, E. Michaelsen, U. Soergel, S. Hinz, and H. Ender, "Airborne monitoring of vehicle activity in urban areas," *ISPRS*, 2004.

[6] D. Bauer, M. Ray, and S. Seer, "Simple sensors used for measuring service times and counting pedestrians," *Transportation Research Record*, 2011.

[7] D. M. Bullock and et.al., "Automated measurement of wait times at airport security," *Transportation Research Record*, 2010.

[8] I. Siemens Industry, "Measure travel time and speed between multiple controller locations." http://www.mobility.siemens.com, 2011.

# T-Mobile QoE Lab – How We Are Making Your Mobile Browsing Faster and Research Problems That We Are Facing


Jie Hui
QoE Lab, T-Mobile U.S.A
12920 SE 38th Street
Bellevue, WA 98006
Jie.hui@t-mobile.com

Kevin Lau
QoE Lab, T-Mobile U.S.A
12920 SE 38th Street
Bellevue, WA 98006
Kevin.lau@t-mobile.com



## ABSTRACT

T-Mobile is looking at all possible ways to optimize quality of user experience (QoE) for our customers in balance with our network resources and device energy consumptions.

In the mobile smart phone world, the misperception that people often held about use experience is the faster the network speed is, the faster the phone CPU speed is, the better the quality of experience (QoE) is. On the contrary, we intend to use three practical examples to unveil the mystery behind the mobile network black box and illustrate it is the end-to-tend (E2E) latency impacts the QoE of one of the most commonly used data services – mobile browsing.

A lengthy E2E latency due to rarely-understood and hard-to-uncovered phone or network issues may render a very poor browsing page loading speed even if you have a super hero dual core smart phone with the fastest 4G network speed. In order to understand the E2E latency better in the transient wireless channel conditions and optimize data QoE in a much faster way, we advocate the use of the Cross-device/network evaluation methodology.

Finally, we presented a few research questions that we are facing and solicit research community's input.



## Categories and Subject Descriptors

C 2.1 [**Computer-Communication Networks**]: Network Architecture and Design – *Wireless communication.* C 4 [**PERFORMANCE OF SYSTEMS**]: Measurement techniques, Performance attributes

## General Terms

Performance, Experimentation, Measurement

## Keywords

Quality of User Experience (QoE), mobile browsing, smart phone, end-to-end latency, 4G wireless network, transient state




*MobiCom'13*, September 30–October 4, 2013, Miami, FL, USA.
ACM 978-1-4503-1999-7/13/09.


## 1. THE IMPACT OF E2E LATENCY ON MOBILE QOE

Looking into most commonly used service - mobile browsing, this section uses three examples to illustrate some rarely understood conditionings by mobile device and network, and therefore demonstrates the importance of E2E latency on mobile QoE.

Through the examples, we also advocate looking into anomalies in long tails, and the methodology of driving optimizations with thread of identifying issues of "device QoE" to understanding "traffic pattern" to root-cause analysis of the "mobile conditioning", because practice proves with this methodology we are able to uncover a network design issue which has existed for eleven years since beginning of the product but unnoticed till now.

### 1.1 Mystery 1: Long DNS Lookup Time

#### *1.1.1 Device QoE*

The first network round trip time (RTT) in mobile browsing is DNS lookup time if the IP address for the site is not yet resolved and cached in the mobile device.

However, we found discrepancy between network viewed average DNS lookup time (around 200ms) and individual device test results:

- Network side: aggregated average DNS lookup = 222 ms;
- Device side: 'Curious George' engineers looked into distribution of DNS lookup time from device testing and found outliers (10s+), such as shown in Figure 1.

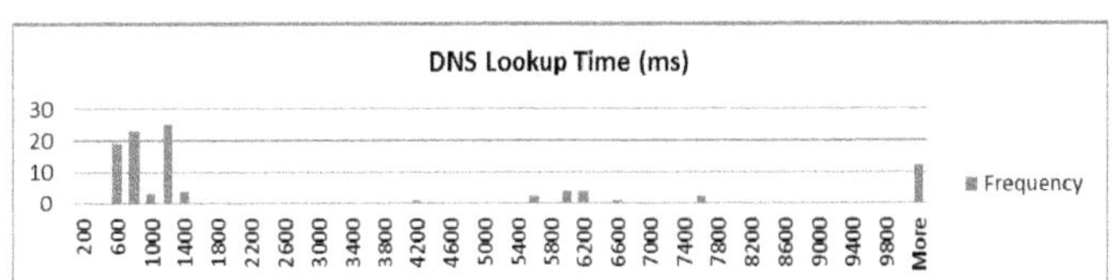


**Figure 1. DNS lookup time distribution of device testing.**

#### *1.1.2 Traffic Pattern*

When we analyze the traffic pattern (Figure 2) from packet trace, we can see the DNS response is lost therefore device will retransmit DNS Query after a timeout (in the case, it is 5s in

The views presented in this publication are as individuals from the authors and do not necessarily reflect any position of T-Mobile USA, Inc.

Android system). Here UE stands for User Equipment, and RAN stands for Radio Access Network. UE and device or mobile device will be used interchangeable in this publication.

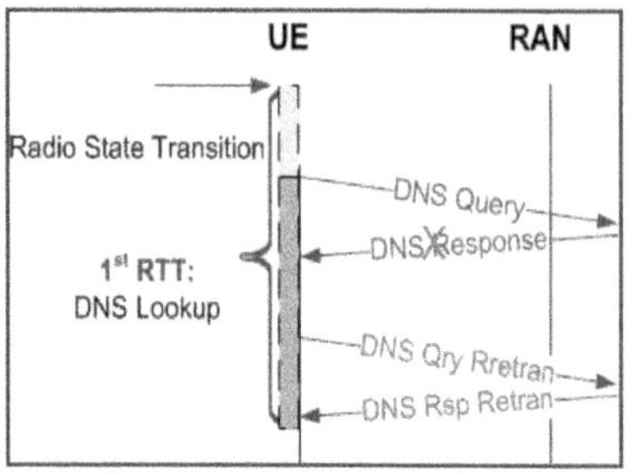


**Figure 2. Traffic pattern of Mystery 1.**

### *1.1.3 Mobile Conditioning*

Cross layer analysis in Figure 3 shows the root cause of Data Stall #1 associated with Mystery 1 is that Radio network controller corrupts downlink packets due to cipher key out-of-synch after radio state transition (Cell PCH → Cell FACH).

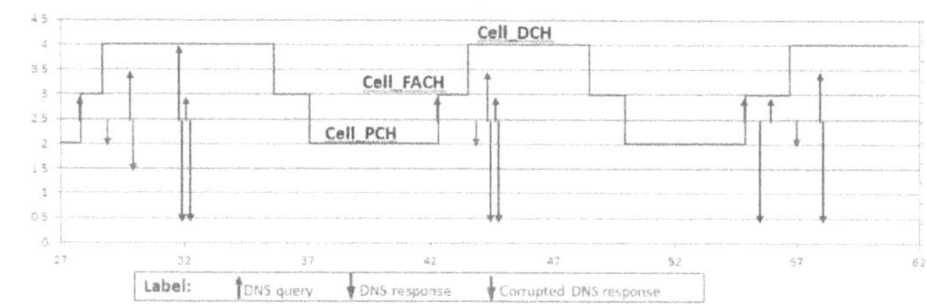


**Figure 3. Cross-layer analysis of Mystery 1.**

After the problem is fixed, the benefits show DNS lookup time during this erroneous scenario (DNS lookup sent during Cell_PCH state) is reduced on average from 3.7s to 0.7s as shown in Figure 4.

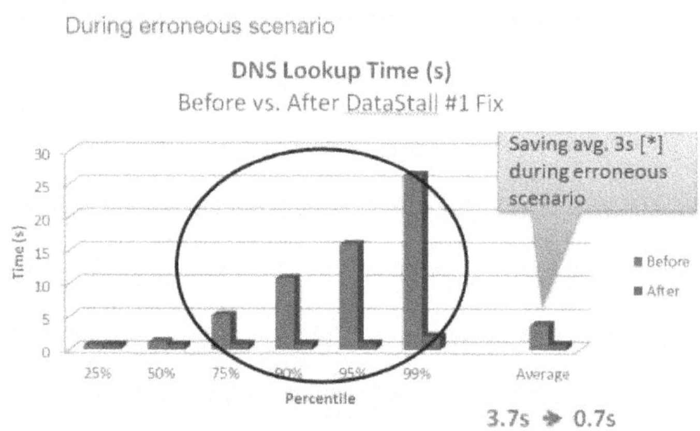


**Figure 4. Before and after comparison of Data stall #1 fix.**

## 1.2 Mystery 2: Long TCP Connect Time

### *1.2.1 Device QoE*

When we look into the next RTT of browsing, the TCP connection time based on TCP three-way handshaking from SYN to SYN/ACK also is still not ideal with 95% percentile close to 4s.

### *1.2.2 Traffic Pattern*

Analysis of packet trace shows traffic pattern as in Figure 5. TCP SYN/ACK from network side in response to the TCP SYN was delayed extensively in the RAN and causes the device to retransmit the TCP SYN again.

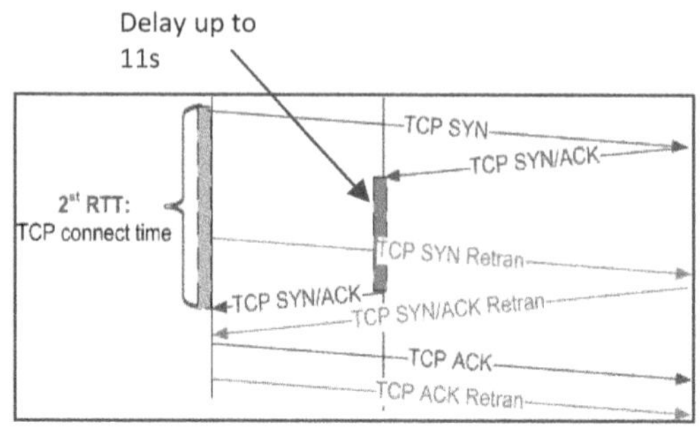


**Figure 5. Traffic pattern of Mystery 2.**

### *1.2.3 Mobile Conditioning*

Cross layer analysis shows the root cause of Data Stall #2 associated with Mystery 2 is that Radio network controller scheduler unnecessarily buffer DL packets up to 11s due to a bug in credit based scheduling algorithm between NodeB and RNC → causes UL RLC retransmissions and RESETs.

After the problem is fixed, the benefits show TCP connect time is reduced on average from 0.95s to 0.8s.

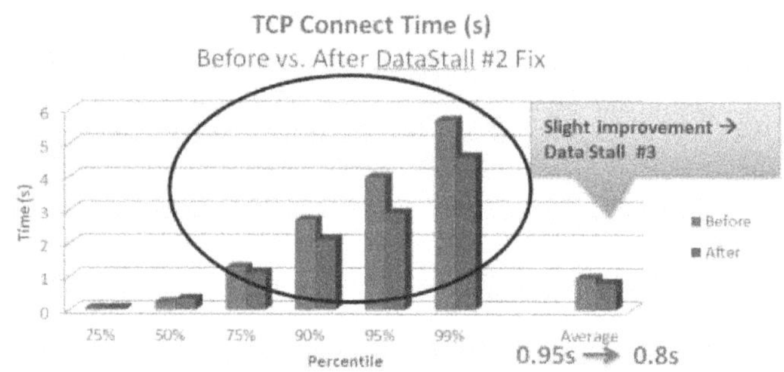


**Figure 6. Before and after comparison of Data stall #2 fix.**

## 1.3 Mystery 3: TCP Connect Time Still Long

### *1.3.1 Device QoE*

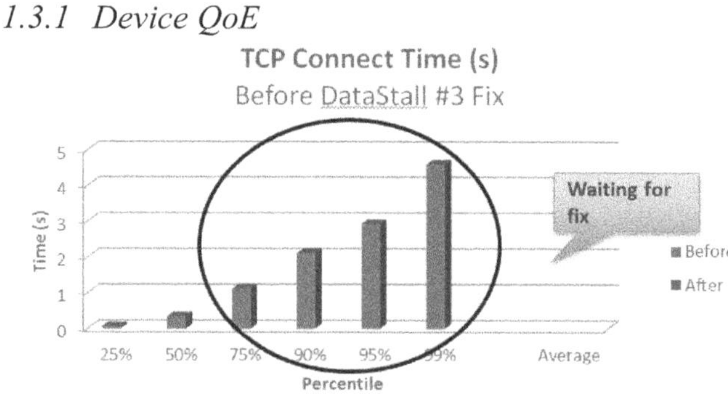


**Figure 7. Distribution of TCP connect time in Mystery 3.**

The TCP RTT after data stall 2 is fixed still shows 95% percentile close to 3s as shown in Figure 7 based on device testing, though improved over before.

### *1.3.2 Traffic Pattern*

Analysis of packet trace shows traffic pattern as in Figure 8. TCP SYN from the device in the uplink is dropped by the RAN therefore causes the device to retransmit the TCP SYN again.

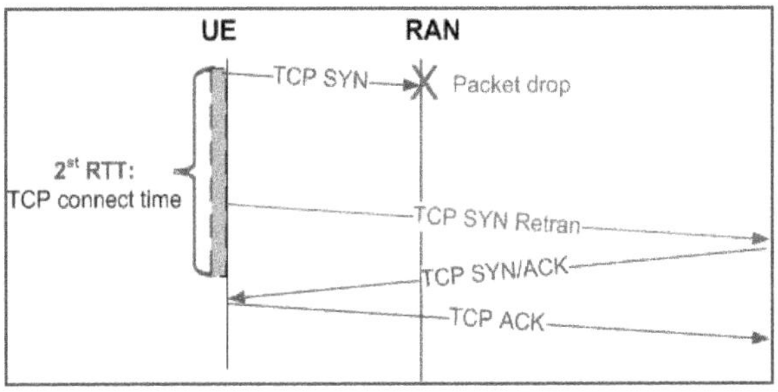


**Figure 8. Traffic pattern of Mystery 3.**

### *1.3.3 Mobile Conditioning*

Cross layer analysis shows the root cause of Data Stall #3 is that Radio network controller UL scheduler drops UL packets during channel switching from DCH to FACH, same problem happens during other radio state or transport channel switchings such as HS←→R99, DCH←→FACH.

## 2. QOE LAB

The three case studies presented above were done in QoE lab of T-Mobile. Unique approach is taken in the lab:

- Measure end user experiences from the device perspective
- Seek success by improving not only averages but also the spread and long tail
- Leverage key industry and academic partners for joint R&D and Real User Measurement (RUM)
- Analyze cross functionally to achieve cross layer intelligence and automation

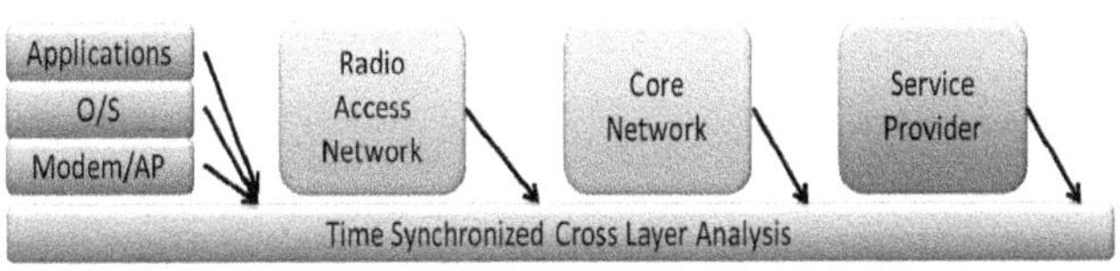


**Figure 9. Cross-Layer/Network Approach Taken in QoE Lab.**

We are looking for top minds from research community to help answer the questions that we are facing.

### 2.1 Transient State Performance and Resilience

Research Problem:

- Automatically characterize and instrument transient state mobile application performance. Here transient state means the transition among the radio states of cellular network as shown in Figure 10 of either 3G/4G network or LTE network, including transitions in-between Cell_DCH and Cell_FACH or Cell/URA_PCH in UMTS/HSPA network, or connected mode and IDLE mode in LTE network, also includes the handover, cell-reselection or link failure recovery transient states.
- Packet loss and retransmissions observed during transient states
- Cross-layer analysis and optimizations are still not fully explored!

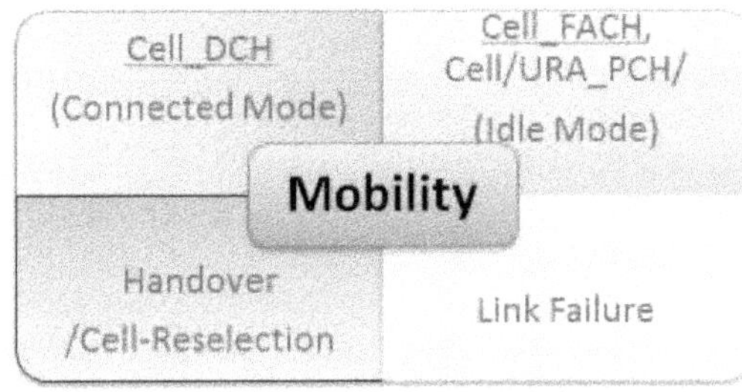


**Figure 10. Radio states of cellular network.**

### 2.2 Interactive Traffic Modeling and Scheduling

Research Problem:

- 3GPP radio scheduling designed mostly with Full Buffer Traffic model
- Higher layer scheduling (RNC, SGW) is not considered

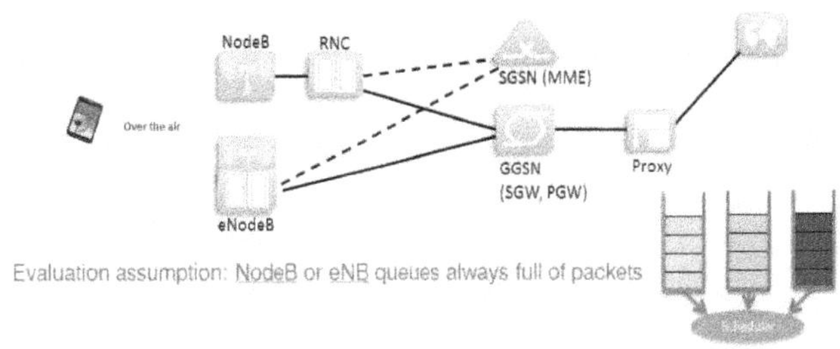


**Figure 11. Cellular network architecture and current evaluation methodology of full traffic model.**


## 3. ACKNOWLEDGMENTS

Our thanks go to our colleagues in T-Mobile for their contributions and support: Jason Chang, Aaron Drake, Himesh Bagley, Jeff Smith, Pablo Tapia, Antoine Tran, Kranthi Sontineni, Helen Oh, Eric Johnson, Pablo Lopez, Warren McNeel, Randy Myerson, and John Murphy.

# Comparing Wireless Network Usage: Laptop vs Smart-Phones

Udayan Kumar  Jeeyoung Kim  Ahmed Helmy

{ukumar, jk2, helmy}@cise.ufl.edu

University of Florida, Gainesville, USA

## 1. INTRODUCTION

The proliferation of smart-phones has been simply unprecedented. Unlike laptops, smart-phones have a much smaller form factor, are ultra mobile, include a rich set of sensors (e.g., location, motion), and are tightly coupled with the users. These factors pose a fundamental question regarding the characteristics in mobile users' on-line behavior for these devices, and how their differences (vs laptops) impact networking protocols and services.

Several existing research studies (mobility models [1], behavior models [2]) have been parametrized/designed using real WLAN traces, assuming that movement detected in the traces is indicative of real user movement. The vast majority of the devices in these traces have been laptops. For recent traces, with the presence of always-on mobile devices (smart-phones), we are able to study mobility more accurately, and at a finer granularity. Several fundamental questions are raised: Will the usage be any different? Do we need to revisit the mobility models? The goal of this work is to study difference in the usage characteristics of smart-phones and laptops to shed light on the preceding questions. The main challenges in our study include the collection of extensive recent traces, the classification of mobile devices, and the analysis of various behavioral metrics on a large-scale. To the best of our knowledge, this is the first work that compares laptops and smart-phone on the basis of wireless network usage and behavior.

The result of our analysis shows significant differences between usage of smart-phones and laptops. The differences include shorter session durations for smart-phones (by 67% as compared to laptops), higher number of sessions per day (2 times that of laptops) and visiting new location (3 times that of laptops). We find that these differences are significant and will allow researchers to create better models and future services.

## Categories and Subject Descriptors

C.2.m [**Computer Communication Networks**]: Miscellaneous


*MobiCom'13,* September 30–October 4, Miami, FL, USA.
ACM 978-1-4503-1999-7/13/09.
http://dx.doi.org/10.1145/2500423.2504586.

| MAC | Start Time | Duration | AP/Location |
|---|---|---|---|
| 00:11:22:33:44:55 | 01 Jun 2011 21:00:51 | 3000secs | CS_buildingAP1 |
| 11:22:33:44:55:66 | 01 Sept 2011 21:01:30 | 10secs | ECE_buildingAP2 |
| 01:02:03:04:05:06 | 01 Sept 2011 22:11:00 | 200secs | MSL_buildingAP1 |
| 10:20:30:40:50:60 | 01 Sept 2011 22:15:30 | 600secs | MACA_buildingAP1 |

*Table 1:* Wireless Association Trace sample after Processing (MAC address are faux to protect privacy)

## Keywords

Network usage, laptop, smart-phone, mobile device

## General Terms

Measurement

## 2. RELATED WORKS

The majority of work on data-driven analysis of mobile networks uses traces from Crawdad [3] and MobiLib [4] that do not include smart-phones. Recently, a handful of works studied smart-phone usage. Authors in [5] compared browsing behavior differences between laptops and smart-phones. Their results indicate that smart-phones abort a large portion of video streaming which the authors feel is due to inadequate browser caching in smart-phones. Another work [6] focuses on discovering why smart-phones are more pervasive in terms of usage. Authors in [7] study the use of smart-phone and laptop/pc in business environment and find that smart-phones can make employees work overtime due to ubiquitous access to office emails. Smart-phone use by non-mobile business user is studied here [8]. Researchers studied the confidence a user has in sending/accessing private information over smart-phones [9]. The above studies show some usage difference between smart-phones and laptops. However, to the best of our knowledge, this study is the first to compare the usage differences based on network access and mobility patterns.

## 3. DATA SET

In this work we analyze wireless association traces collected at University of Florida (UF) from Sept. 2011 to Dec. 2011. For each wireless association, there is : 1. MAC address of the device associating, 2. Time of the association, 3. Duration of the association and 4. Name of Wireless Access Point (AP), as shown in Tab. 1. The MAC address is used as a unique identifier of a device throughout the trace (here we assume that very few users change the MAC address of their devices). In this trace period almost 120K unique devices make more than 46 Million associations. There are 1700 unique Access Points throughout the campus.

**Identification of Smart-phones and Laptops:** In the WLAN association trace we collected (Tab. 1), there is no explicit 'device type' information to allow classification of devices into laptops or smart-phones, and the MAC addresses are partially anonymized. However, the manufacturer of

| Make | Smart-phone | Laptop |
|---|---|---|
| Apple | 12485 | 4121 |
| Rim | 1495 | |
| Samsung | 2292 | |
| HTC | 2096 | |
| Murata | 469 | |
| Motorola | 405 | |
| Huawei | 49 | |
| Sony Ericcson | 9 | |
| Asus | | 392 |
| Intel | | 14781 |
| HP | | 82 |
| LiTE-ON | | 4530 |
| Atheros | | 23 |
| Total | 19300 | 23929 |

*Table 2:* Number of devices detected as Smart-phone and Laptops along with the manufacturers

the wireless network card can be inferred (i.e., identified uniquely) from the first 3 octets of a MAC address (a.k.a. the Organizationally Unique Identifier - OUI), which were kept intact in our trace even after anonymization.

There are several manufacturers that either make only smart-phones (e.g., HTC, RIM, Nokia) or only laptops (e.g., Asus, Dell, HP, Lenovo) but not both (and if they do, the market share in the other segment was less than 1% until the end of the trace period in 2011). However, there are manufacturers such as Apple and Samsung that manufacture both. To distinguish between smart-phones and laptops coming from the same manufacturer, we conduct a user survey where users of different smart-phones were asked to give the first 3 octets of their WiFi MAC address.

The assumption here is that a manufacturer will not use the same MAC address range for both smart-phones and laptops. This assumption is reasonable, since WiFi cards used in laptops are different from those used in smart-phones, thus they are manufactured separately. Hence assigning MAC addresses from the same range may call for unnecessary collaboration and is not commonly practiced. In our survey we did not find any overlapping MAC address ranges between laptops and smart-phones. In our survey, we provide detailed instructions for finding and sharing the MAC address for iOS, Android, and Windows phone OS.

A total of 95 responses were received for our survey that provided us with 30 unique MAC address ranges. These surveys were conducted from Dec 2011 to Jan 2012. Tab. 2 gives the details of our classification.

# 4. ANALYSIS

In this section, we present our results and analysis based on the processing of the traces. The analysis is divided into three main parts based on the temporal, spatial and load characteristics (details [10]). First, we discuss the temporal characteristics, including the overall average duration of sessions for both devices and the session start (i.e., initiation) times in terms of time-of-day. Second, we investigate the spatial aspects with analysis of the number of unique APs visited, the location predictability of users, and the radius of gyration (RG) to estimate the centroid of the user's movements. Finally, we analyze the load characteristics with the number of session made per day by each device kind.

The metrics are evaluated mainly for three sets (i.e., categories) of traces; the first includes 19,300 smart-phones, the second includes 23,929 laptops, and the third includes 120K devices overall. Note that we are interested in analyzing and comparing the mobility during on-line activity (i.e., not physical mobility), which is faithfully captured by WLAN traces.

## 4.1 Average Session Duration

Average session duration can be used to distinguish between the amounts of time spend on-line by different devices. It may also be indicative of user activities. To compute this

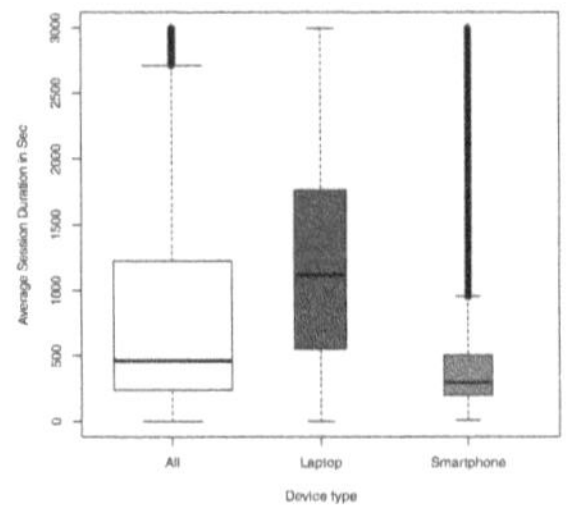

*(a)* Average Session Duration per user. For clarity the plot only shows average session duration less than 3000 sec

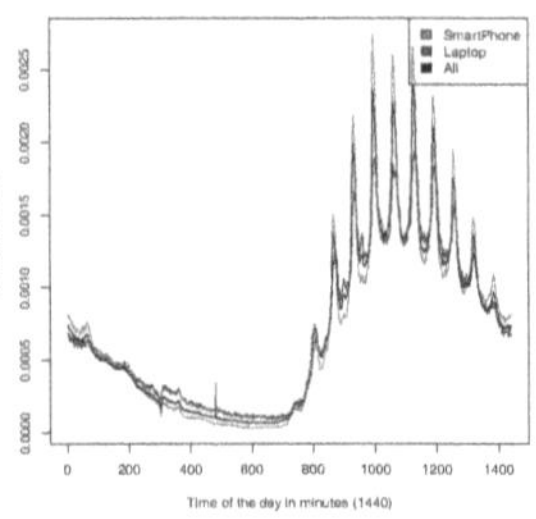

*(b)* PDF for session starts in minutes

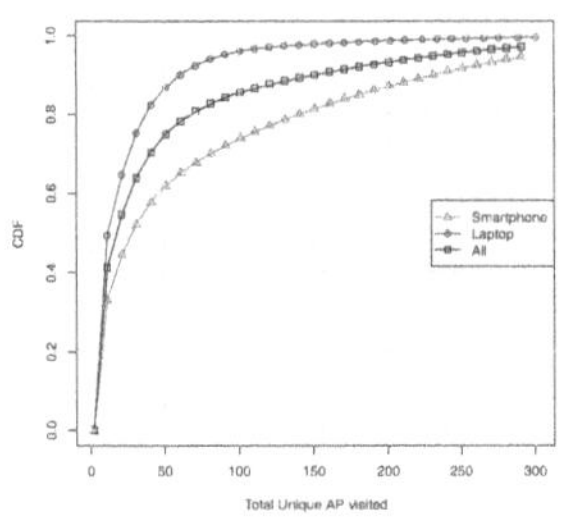

*(c)* CDF for unique APs visited for entire trace period. Graph is clipped at 300 APs for clarity

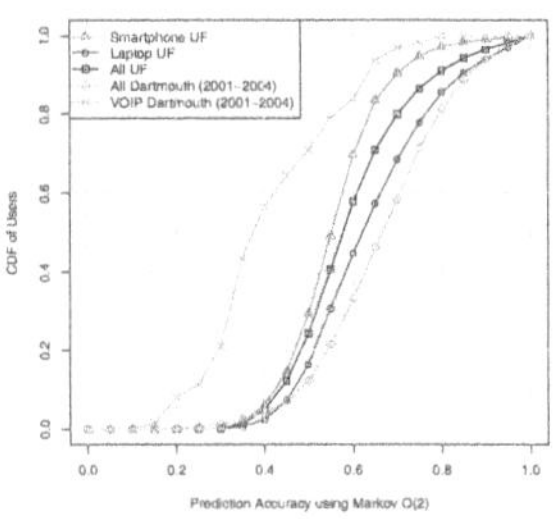

*(d)* CDF of Predictability using Markov O(2) predictor

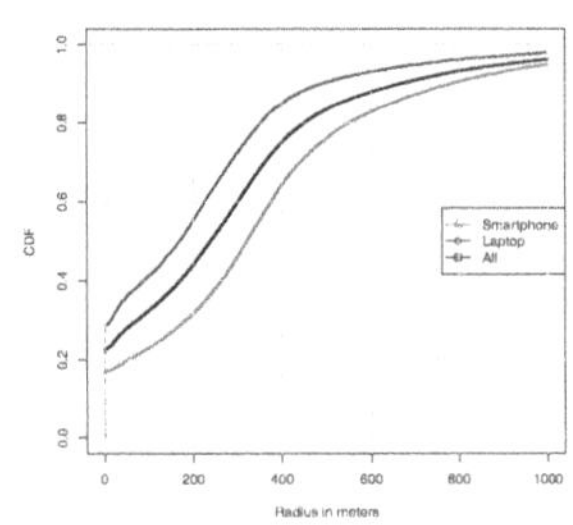

*(e)* CDF of Radius of Gyration

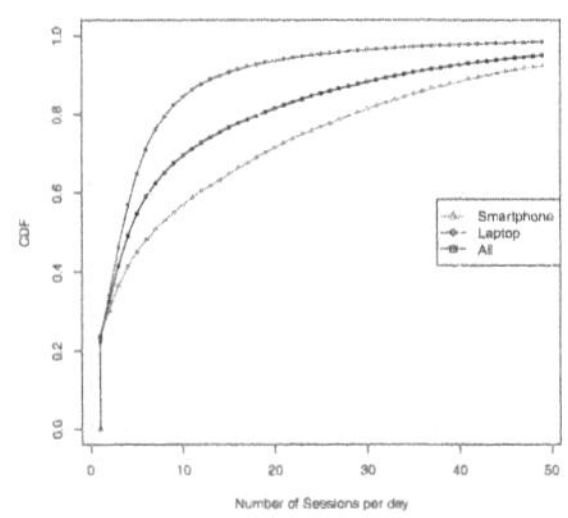

*(f)* CDF for number of sessions per day. Clipped at 50 session for clarity

*Figure 1:* Analysis Metrics

metric we calculate the average session duration for each of the devices in different categories. The results are plotted in Fig. 1a. We find that an average session for a laptop user is 1900 sec long (~31 min) and that of a smart-phone user is 630 sec (~10 min). This indicates that laptop users on average have 3 times longer sessions than a smart-phone user. The session duration for all devices is 1222 sec (~20 min).

## 4.2 Session start time

For each category of devices, we look at the PDF of starting a session with respect to time (in minutes). To measure this empirical metric we create 1440 bins denoting the total number of minutes in a day. Each bin contains the normalized number of sessions that start during that respective minute. Fig. 1b shows the PDFs for each device category. It is interesting to note that the PDF of session is low from 0 to 800 mins (12am to 1pm) and then it starts to rise. Another interesting feature on this graph is the presence of 10 spikes between 800 and 1400 minutes. These 10 spikes correlate with 10 hours and occur whenever the class period changes. The spikes are more prominent for smart-phone users than laptop users during class breaks. We note that between two adjacent spikes (i.e., during classes) the probability of laptops starting a session is greater than smart-phones. In-between classes there is a gap of 15 mins which makes smart-phones the easily accessible device for quick browsing and work needs, thus the spikes in smart-phone usage. However, during class, laptops provide most of the browsing, class material access and other work needs so there is a higher probability of sessions created by laptops in the periods between the spikes. This metric, yet again shows us the temporal usage differences between smart-phones and laptops.

## 4.3 Unique APs Visited

The number of unique APs visited through the trace period can tell us about the mobility experienced by these devices. Questions such as what kind of device is more mobile can be partially answered by this metric (APs remain at fixed location, accessing more unique AP implies visiting more unique locations). Fig. 1c displays the CDF of number of unique AP visited. We note that approximately 50% of the laptop users visit less than 12 unique APs, however, for smart-phone users this number is 28. The average number of unique APs accessed by laptops is 26 where that of smart-phones is 75 (almost 3 times the number visited by laptops). We also note that barely 1% of laptop users visit more than 200 unique APs, whereas there are at least 13% smart-phone users visit more than 200 unique APs (max is 600 which is approximately 1/3 of the total number of APs).

## 4.4 Predictability

Many applications utilize prediction to achieve functionality (or improve performance), including caching, paging, resource allocation, and capacity planning. Here we look at the user location predictability of these devices. The predictor attempts to predict the next AP that the device will access next, given the history of AP accesses. We use a Markov O(2) predictor (considers past two locations). Earlier studies [10] find this as the best predictor. Predictability results are shown in Fig. 1d. We observe 7% difference in the average prediction accuracy between the laptops and smart-phones, with smart-phones being harder to predict. To show a more fundamental trend that is evolving over the years [1], we add two more curves on this particular graph (Fig. 1d) that include prediction accuracy of the always-on voice-over-IP (VoIP) devices and regular WLAN devices collected from Dartmouth college during from 2001 to 2004 ([11]). As we can see the gap between the prediction accuracy difference between always-on devices (e.g., VoIP devices and smart-phones) and laptops has closed significantly (down from 30% to 7%). On plausible trend could be that users are migrating more predictable activities (traditionally done on laptops) to the more capable smart-phones. We have yet to do a thorough investigation on this cause but intend to work on this in the future.

## 4.5 Radius of Gyration

Radius of Gyration (RG) measures the standard deviation between a user's movements and the user's center of mass which is the centroid of all the user's movements. A higher RG indicates the user going farther away from the center of mass. Comparing average RG of smart-phone users with laptop users can point out the mobility differences based on the area that they have traveled. Since actual coordinates of AP were not available, we used the Geo-coordinates of the buildings (centroid) to represent the location of the APs. Hence we would not be able to distinguish distance traveled inside buildings. Fig. 1e shows the CDF of RG for smart-phones and laptops. On average, a laptop user travel 255 meters from the center of mass, whereas a smart-phone user travels 449 meters which is almost twice the distance covered by laptop user.

[1]A complete evolution study is out of scope of this paper, and is addressed in more details in [11] over a period of 10 years.

## 4.6 Number of Sessions per Day

The number of sessions per day is indicative of the load a wireless device puts on the network systems including dhcp, authentication, dynamic configuration change of APs, etc. This metric is also related to temporal characteristic of the wireless device. Fig. 1f shows the empirical CDF comparing laptops and smart-phones. We find that only 15% of the laptop user make 10 or more session per day, however, more than 40% of smart-phones make more than 10 sessions a day. Also the average number of sessions per day for laptops is 7 where as it is 16 for smart-phones (almost twice that of laptops).

# 5. CONCLUSION

In this paper we study the changing patterns of network usage between laptops and smart-phones. We analyze four month long traces that consist of 120K unique devices and among those devices we selected two subsets of data each consisting of approximately 20K unique devices of laptops and smart-phones respectively. The method we introduced for device classification is systematic, robust and repeatable. We investigated three main sets of metrics with respect to temporal, spatial and load characteristics.

This is the first study we are aware of to investigate the spatio-temporal differences between smart-phones and laptops based on large-scale WLAN trace analysis. It is evident from our study that these differences are dramatic, both in time and space, and warrant further research. More importantly, the behavioral shift from laptops to smart-phones (and other devices, e.g., tablets) is likely to grow at a faster pace in the future. This calls for the re-evaluation of existing mobility and network behavioral models and the protocols affected by those models (e.g., prediction, routing, caching). More so, perhaps the re-design of such models and protocols is needed based on new data-driven approaches. In our future work, we plan to conduct further analysis of net-flow traces to provide another perspective on the difference between smart-phones and laptops from a traffic and flow points of view.

# 6. REFERENCES


[1] F. Bai and A. Helmy, Chapter 1 A SURVEY OF MOBILITY MODELS in Wireless Adhoc Networks. Springer, 2006.

[2] U. Kumar, G. Thakur, and A. Helmy, "Protect: proximity-based trust-advisor using encounters for mobile societies." in IWCMC'10.

[3] "CRAWDAD," August 2013. [Online]. Available: http://crawdad.cs.dartmouth.edu/data.php

[4] W. jen Hsu, D. Dutta, and A. Helmy, "Trace: Structural analysis of user association patterns in university campus wireless lans," IEEE Transactions on Mobile Computing, Nov 2012.

[5] I. Papapanagiotou, E. M. Nahum, and V. Pappas, "Smartphones vs. laptops: comparing web browsing behavior and the implications for caching," SIGMETRICS Perform. Eval. Rev., June 2012.

[6] A. Oulasvirta, T. Rattenbury, L. Ma, and E. Raita, "Habits make smartphone use more pervasive," Personal and Ubiquitous Computing, vol. 16, pp. 105–114, 2012.

[7] A. K. Karlson, B. R. Meyers, A. Jacobs, P. Johns, and S. K. Kane, "Working overtime: Patterns of smartphone and pc usage in the day of an information worker," in Pervasive '09.

[8] P. Bao, J. Pierce, S. Whittaker, and S. Zhai, "Smart phone use by non-mobile business users," in MobileHCI '11.

[9] E. Chin, A. P. Felt, V. Sekar, and D. Wagner, "Measuring user confidence in smartphone security and privacy," in SOUPS '12.

[10] U. Kumar, J. Kim, and A. Helmy, "Changing patterns of mobile network (wlan) usage: Smart-phones vs. laptops," in IWCMC'13.

[11] J. Kim and A. Helmy, "The evolution of wlan user mobility and its effect on prediction," in ACM IWCMC 2011.

# Radio Environment Mapping with Mobile Devices in the TV White Space

Ayon Chakraborty and Samir R. Das
Stony Brook University
Stony Brook, NY 11794, USA
{aychakrabort,samir}@cs.stonybrook.edu

Milind Buddhikot
Alcatel-Lucent Bell Labs
Murray Hill, NJ 07974-0636,USA
milind.buddhikot@alcatel-lucent.com

## ABSTRACT

In this paper, we envision a scenario where mobile devices perform at least part-time spectrum sensing in a collaborative fashion under the control of a central server. The goal is to create an adequate 'radio environment map' for the 'white spaces' that will be useful for spectrum management decisions. We lay out the research challenges, describe a prototype implementation using a DTV receiver dongle interfaced with an Android-based mobile device, and present preliminary performance measurements.

## Categories and Subject Descriptors

C.2.1 [**Network Architecture and Design**]: Wireless Communications.

## Keywords

TV Whitespace, Spectrum Sensing, Radio Environment Map.

## 1. INTRODUCTION

As regulators worldwide are deregulating the TV white spaces (TVWS) for unlicensed use, there is a significant interest in understanding the nature of such white spaces and the real spectrum opportunities in time and space so that they can be gainfully exploited. So far the understanding in the TVWS has been mostly driven by models that use terrain data and TV transmitter (primary) characteristics/schedule to estimate the signal strengths observed at different frequencies at a given location. There are several existing services such as Spectrum Bridge, Google Spectrum Database, MSR WhiteFi etc. that essentially use such model-based methods.

However, such model-based approaches have limited applicability in several scenarios. First, they can only model large-scale propagation characteristics and are unable to accurately describe spectrum occupancy in the urban canyons and in indoor spaces. Even in outdoor spaces, occasionally significant errors are possible. Second, such models are geared towards modeling the primary behavior that have powerful transmitters and antennas at a significant height. It is unclear whether such modeling will provide enough accuracy to estimate coverage of secondary transmitters that are of lower power and are at lower heights. Overall at best, modeling-based approaches can provide fairly conservative estimates leading to loss of spectrum use. This is more relevant in heavily populated urban regions, where the 'spectrum holes' are already limited due to relatively heavy primary occupancy [6]. This is also where the need for spectrum is the greatest.

### 1.1 Mobile Spectrum Sensing

We propose an alternative where model-based methods to evaluate spectrum occupancy is replaced or supplemented by actual spectrum measurements via coordinated spectrum sensors that are either add-on or integrated into mobile client devices [5, 8]. These include smartphones, tablets, e-readers, wearables such as glass or watch, or similar future platforms. While the general concept of distributed, coordinated spectrum sensing is hardly new, much of the existing work has considered lab-grade spectrum analyzers or powerful SDR-based spectrum sensing [4]. These devices are large, expensive, power-hungry and often require external computers. It is not conceivable that such systems will be widely deployed in practice to perform the task of large-scale spectrum sensing.

Modern mobile platforms provide an attractive alternative. They have multicore processors and GPUs to provide enough compute power and also provide backend network connectivity. They are also everywhere as a significant and growing fraction of humanity possesses one or more of these devices. Further, they are often idle. While they may lack appropriate radio interfaces for white spaces at this time, early prototypes have already been demonstrated [5, 8].

There are several challenges, however. Fundamentally, the challenges boil down to architectural design and accuracy versus resource use tradeoffs:

**Architecture.** An end-to-end framework must be developed such that spectrum data will be collected from numerous sensors and collated at the backend (a central server or cloud-based platform) to create the radio environment map (REM). The REM is essentially the power-spectral density (PSD) as a function of location. Preferably, the central server also acts as a form of 'spectrum manager' and is responsible for the actual use of the REM in making spectrum allocation decision for the secondaries.

**Accuracy.** It is unclear whether inexpensive radios integrated onto a phone and with small, built-in antennas can perform sensing with the needed accuracy. Also, due to re-


*MobiCom'13,* September 30–October 4, Miami, FL, USA.
ACM 978-1-4503-1999-7/13/09
http://dx.doi.org/10.1145/2500423.2504587 .

source limitations, the sensing could be sparse in frequency, time and space, and also the data may be compressed. See below.

**Resource.** While mobile devices are often idle and may have ample processing power, they are energy poor. The radio front end can also have limitations in the sense of tunability and sampling rate. Thus, spectrum sensing must be controlled by the central server for optimally exploiting the radio capability for a given power budget. The cost of network connectivity is also an issue. The spectrum data may need to be compressed before transmission or may have to be analyzed partially (e.g., the FFT on the I/Q samples can run on the mobile).

In this poster paper, we limit ourselves to only one part of these challenges. We develop a prototype platform using commodity devices – DTV receiver dongle interfaced with an Android-based mobile device. Then, we perform preliminary experiments demonstrating that such a low-power platform can still perform adequate radio environment mapping even with measurements at a low spatial resolution.

# 2. MOBILE TVWS SENSOR

While current generation smartphones have several radio interfaces they do not operate in the TV band. Also, in general an interface to tune to arbitrary frequencies in the operating band and obtain I/Q samples is absent. Past work has considered developing custom, small form-factor boards with RF front ends, ADC and FPGA that can be interfaced with the phone [5]. Chip-level design of the wideband frontend of an SDR receiver has also been demonstrated [8]. However, these are research prototypes and are not widely available. Instead for our work, we rely on commodity devices to understand the potential of our techniques. We use a commodity Digital TV receiver dongle (DTV receiver with an USB interface with the form factor of a thumb drive) that has a chipset (Realtek RTL2832U demodulator) with the ability to export I/Q samples. Such dongles can be used as inexpensive software radio receivers as the demodulator (RTL2832U) supports a debugging mode where it passes the IQ samples directly from the tuner's ADC to the device. The dongle is provided with an aerial TV plug and is interfaced to a mobile device via the USB port. This forms a miniature spectrum sensor. We have connected a low gain antenna to the dongle. However, in principle such antennas can be built inside the phone.

## 2.1 Hardware Prototype

We have used the EzCap Digital ATSC TV dongle. The dongle uses a Rafael R820t tuner supporting the ATSC standard. The tuner works with DVB-T, ISDB-T and DTMB standards as well. Figure 1 shows our prototype spectrum sensor. The dongle has a USB 2.0 interface and can be interfaced to any mobile device that supports USB OTG (on-the-go) so that it can host a USB accessory. We have used a PiPo Smart S1 tablet, equipped with Rockchip RK3066 dual-core processor, running Android Jelly Bean (v4.1.1) operating system for the initial prototyping. Our system can easily be ported to any Android tablet or phone that has USB OTG support.

## 2.2 Software Implementation

The Open Source Mobile Communications (Osmocom) [1] has a community-supported project developing software support for using DTV dongles as above as functioning SDR receivers. We have ported the existing Linux libraries and drivers for these dongles to the Android platform. The overall system consists of two units: first, the mobile client (local unit) and second, a central server (remote unit) meant for logging sensing data.

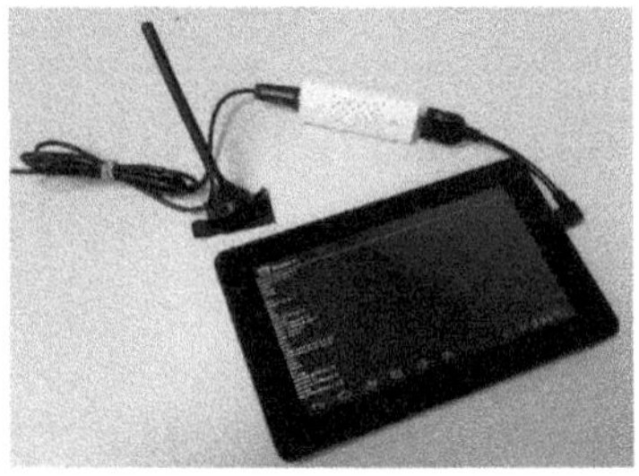

**Figure 1: The DTV dongle with external antenna interfaced with the Android tablet.**

**Mobile Client:** This unit comprises of the mobile device with GPS support interfaced with the dongle. The mobile client thus acts as a mobile spectrum sensing agent. The application running in the mobile can set the center frequency and the sampling rate. Additionally, the mobile device runs a TCP server that streams I/Q data (geo-location tagged) to the central server. The latter can also send requests to the mobile client to start, stop change the center frequency or sampling rate of the scan.

**Central Server:** The server receives I/Q data from the mobile client and computes the power spectral density (PSD) by employing standard FFT techniques on the stream of incoming I/Q samples. This unit forms the central repository of the sensing data and is responsible for computing the Radio Environment Map (REM) from the data. The server can also start, stop and/or schedule scans on specific clients depending on the needs. The central server also responds to queries regarding spectrum availability from secondary devices given its location and makes or helps in spectrum allocation decisions. A set of APIs are being developed for interfacing the client with the server for smooth interfacing and for promoting independent software developments.

Our initial work in creating and evaluating REM is presented in Section 3. Energy optimization issues, scheduling of spectrum scans and spectrum allocation issues are part of our ongoing work and are not directly addressed in this poster.

# 3. CREATING RADIO ENVIRONMENT MAP

The goal in this section is to demonstrate that even with low resolution spatial sampling commodity platforms as our prototype can map the radio environment with a fairly good accuracy. To demonstrate this we use an industry-standard portable RF signal and spectrum analysis platform, ThinkRF WSA4000 [2], that provides the baseline spectrum measurements. For the purpose of our work, ThinkRF measurements form the ground truth dataset. ThinkRF provides a sampling rate of 125 Ms/s. A 16K bin FFT is used at the backend to create the power spectral density with each FFT bin corresponding to roughly a 7.6 KHz bandwidth. The dongle runs at a substantially slower rate of 1 Ms/s. Here, a 1K bin FFT is used providing a bin size of 1 KHz.

Concurrent but independent measurements are done in a continuous fashion in both the dongle-based prototype as

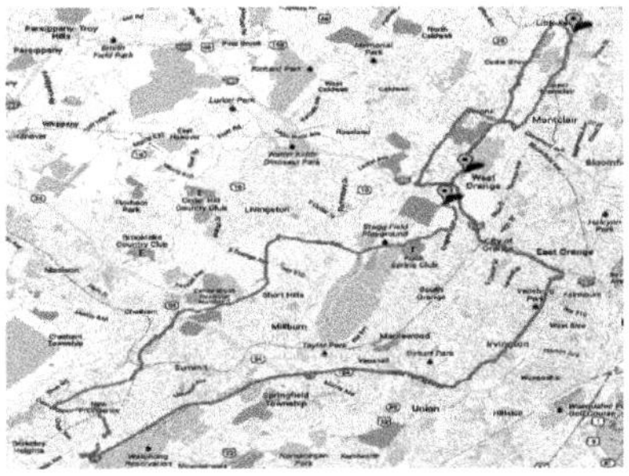

**Figure 2: Measurement route (roughly 60 miles) and locations of 3 TV towers. Two of the towers transmit on 1 channel each and the other transmits on 2 channels. These 4 channels are studied.**

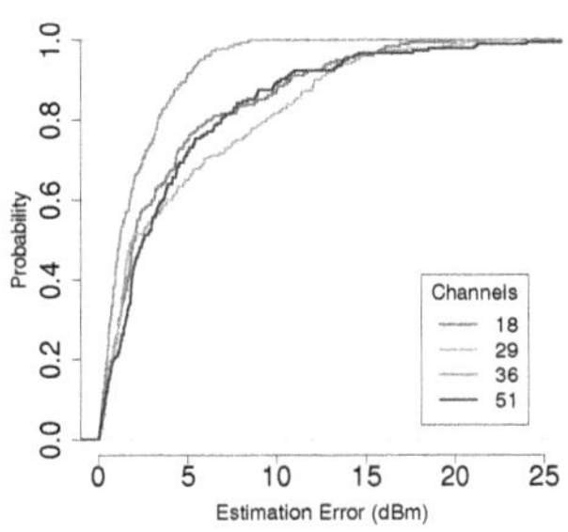


(a) 6 miles

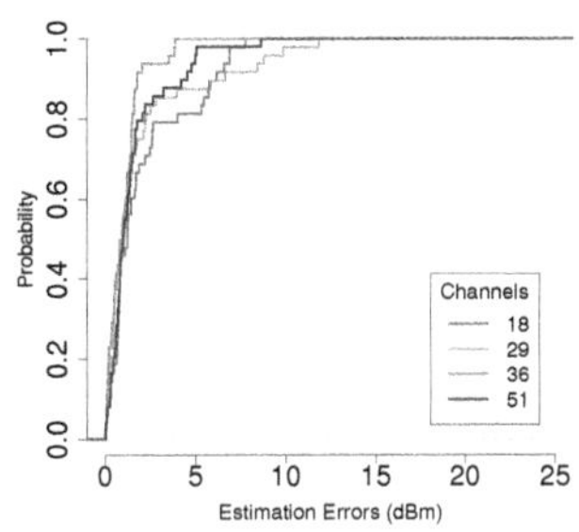


(b) 1.5 miles

**Figure 3: CDF of absolute estimation error by using subsets of the dongle data set for the 4 TV channels studied. Two cases are evaluated where the chosen subset of measurement samples has average measurement distance of 6 miles and 1.5 miles.**

well as the ThinkRF platform from a mobile van driven along a 60 mile loop in and around Essex county in New Jersey (see Figure 2). The measurements are done in a continuous fashion. They are geo-tagged using a separate external GPS receiver and stored in a database. Since the dongle is substantially slower than the ThinkRF (by more than an order of magnitude), the dongle is used to scan only 4 specific TV channels that are reasonably prominent in the area (see Figure 2). This way reasonably frequent measurements can be collected. At the end of the experimental runs, our database has collected roughly 1100 ThinkRF measurements and roughly 200 dongle measurements for each of the 4 channels. Before the map creation, the dongle has been calibrated against the ThinkRF platform using a signal generator. The signal generator generates a tone at the frequency of interest at specific transmit power levels. Both devices are placed at a specific location (one at a time) near the signal generator and the average received power is computed for each frequency bin after the FFT. The differences are recorded and are used as bin-specific corrections for the dongle measurements for the analysis we present here.

## 3.1 Interpolation

Recently, there has been several works in employing standard methods of spatial statistics in mapping the radio environment (see, e.g., [9]). Empirical measurement-based work has also been done [7]. We take the same basic approach by assuming the radio signal strength at each frequency to be a random field in 2D that is sampled at some random (spatial) intervals. The samples are presented by our data set. We use different randomly chosen subsets of dongle measurements we have collected (roughly with average measurement distance of 1.5 miles and 6 miles for two cases studied) and use these to interpolate the 2D field of signal strength separately for each 7.6 KHz frequency bin. We use Ordinary Kriging [3, 7] as the interpolation method as also used in prior work.

To validate the results, we compare the interpolated values at each frequency bin from the actual measured ground truth (ThinkRF measurements) for each location where ground truth measurement is available (roughly 1100 locations). The absolute error (in dBm) is plotted in the form of a CDF separately for each of the 4 channels. See Figure 3. Note the error statistics is excellent. The median error is $1-3$ dBm for the 6 mile case and less than 1 dBm for the 1.5 mile case. This shows that very sparse measurement density can be tolerated. Mobile phone density in urban areas will be certainly one to two orders of magnitude relative to these values, though scheduling issues may lessen the actual measurement density. We also anticipate error performance to improve further by using more sophisticated interpolation.

# 4. CONCLUSION AND FUTURE WORK

Mobile spectrum sensing present several research challenges, but when addressed right, such systems enable adequate radio environment maps for the white spaces with very little infrastructure cost. In this work, we have laid out the vision of such systems, presented a prototype implementation and performed preliminary validation experiments. The entire gamut of challenges mentioned in the paper forms parts of our ongoing and future works.

# 5. REFERENCES

[1] The open source mobile communications (Osmocom), SDR project. `http://sdr.osmocom.org/`.

[2] thinkRF WSA4000 Spectrum Analyzer. `thinkrf.com/product/wsa4000/`.

[3] A. Alaya-Feki, S. Ben Jemaa, B. Sayrac, P. Houze, and E. Moulines. Informed spectrum usage in cognitive radio networks: Interference cartography. In *Proc. IEEE PIMRC*, pages 1–5, 2008.

[4] A. Iyer, K. Chintalapudi, V. Navda, R. Ramjee, V. N. Padmanabhan, and C. R. Murthy. Specnet: Spectrum sensing sans frontieres. In *8th USENIX Symposium on Networked Systems Design and Implementation (NSDI)*, 2011.

[5] S. Kallioinen, M. Vaarakangas, P. Hui, J. Ollikainen, I. Teikari, A. Parssinen, V. Turunen, M. Kosunen, and J. Ryynanen. Multi-mode, multi-band spectrum sensor for cognitive radios embedded to a mobile phone. In *Proc. ICST CROWNCOM Conf.*, 2011.

[6] S. Mishra and A. Sahai. How much white space has the FCC opened up? *IEEE Communication Letters*, 2010.

[7] C. Phillips, M. Ton, D. Sicker, and D. Grunwald. Practical radio environment mapping with geostatistics. In *Proc. IEEE DySpan Symp.*, 2012.

[8] S. Pollin, L. Hollevoet, F. Naessens, P. Van Wesemael, A. Dejonghe, and L. Van der Perre. Versatile sensing for mobile devices: cost, performance and hardware prototypes. In *Proc. 3rd ACM workshop on Cognitive radio networks*, 2011.

[9] M. Wellens, J. Riihijarvi, M. Gordziel, and P. Mahonen. Spatial statistics of spectrum usage: From measurements to spectrum models. In *Proc. IEEE ICC*, 2009.

# V-Scope: An Opportunistic Wardriving Approach to Augmenting TV Whitespace Databases

Tan Zhang and Suman Banerjee
Department of Computer Sciences
University of Wisconsin-Madison, USA
{tzhang, suman}@cs.wisc.edu

## ABSTRACT

The recently released TV whitespaces offer a promising land for wireless communications. The secondary users of TV whitespaces today rely on spectrum occupancy databases to determine vacant TV channels for unlicensed communications. However, the accuracy of these databases (that depend solely on propagation models as per guidelines of the FCC) may be low. In this paper, we propose V-Scope - a vehicular sensing framework aimed to collect wide-area spectrum measurements for evaluating the accuracy of these databases. A key design feature of *V-Scope* is to leverage spectrum sensors mounted on public vehicles for collecting and reporting measurements from the road (opportunistic wardriving). We have currently deployed a version of our system on a single public transit bus traveling across a mid-sized city in the US. Based on measurements collected at over 1 million locations across a 100 square-km area, we find that databases tend to over-predict the coverage of certain TV broadcasts, unnecessarily blocking the usage of whitespace spectrum in a large area (up to 42% measured locations). We further propose ways of leveraging these measurements to enhance existing propagation models in databases.

## Categories and Subject Descriptors

C.2.1 [**Computer-Communication Networks**]: Network Architecture and Design—*Wireless communication*

## Keywords

TV Whitespaces; Spectrum Sensing; Opportunistic Wardriving

## 1. INTRODUCTION

Wireless providers are facing spectrum crisis when trying to meet the growing demand of mobile users. The recently released TV whitespaces (512MHz-698MHz) have become an effective solution to the spectrum crunch. However, there exists a fundamental challenge to correctly identify vacant and good channels for unlicensed usage. The state-of-art approach is to rely on a spectrum occupancy database that solely uses propagation models to predict the strength of primary signals. However, such approach can sometimes have low accuracy in urban environment. In this work, we propose *V-Scope* - a vehicle sensing (wardriving) framework aimed to collect wide-area measurements for evaluating and augmenting commercial databases. An unique feature of *V-Scope* is to leverage whitespace spectrum sensors mounted on public buses for this purpose, thus avoiding costly and laborious measurement campaigns while collecting measurements at an unprecedented scale.

In a whitespace network, a spectrum occupancy database plays a central role in assigning operating channels to secondary devices (TVBDs). On one hand, it distributes unused TV channels to TVBDs based on their locations, thereby fulfilling the FCC's requirement of protecting licensed signals. As per FCC's ruling [2], there exist three types of primary incumbents to be protected, i.e., digital TV, analog TV and wireless microphones. To detect TV signals, the database leverages well-known propagation models (e.g., R6602 [2]) to estimate the signal strength at the locations of TVBDs. It concludes a channel as being occupied if the estimated power is above a reception threshold (-84dBm). To protect microphones, the database reserves two dedicated channels for their exclusive usage, and allows more to be reserved upon request. On the other hand, the database (e.g., SpectrumBridge [4]) might inform TVBDs with channel quality in whitespaces predicted by the model. Hence, the accuracy of a spectrum database largely affects the protection of primary incumbents and channel selection by TVBDs.

Unfortunately, the database has inevitable inaccuracy in achieving above functions. First, it is inaccurate in predicting the coverage of a TV broadcast, which leads to either waste of whitespace spectrum or harmful interference to primary incumbents. The underlying reason is that its propagation model is tuned to average propagation conditions, and unable to capture the environment-induced variation, e.g., shadowing and multipath fading of specific objects and topologies. Our measurement shows this variation can be as high as 25dBm for two locations separated by merely 10 meters. Second, a database is incapable of estimating the power of unlicensed mobile transmitters operating in whitespace channels, some of which can cause high-power interference to other unlicensed communications. The incapability of predicting the coverage of a mobile transmitter is because the propagation model usually requires accurate information about the mobile transmitter, e.g., location and transmission power, which is rarely available to the database and might change frequently. Both these factors motivate the need of spectrum sensing, which provides spectrum measurements for better tracking local propagation characteristics.

In this paper, we propose an opportunistic whitespace sensing infrastructure-*V-Scope*, which uses spectrum sensors mounted on public vehicles to collect large-scale measurements. Since the public vehicles usually travel at a low speed, across wide area and for long time, *V-Scope* can leverage a few spectrum sensors to collect


*MobiCom'13,* September 30–October 4, Miami, FL, USA.
ACM 978-1-4503-1999-7/13/09.

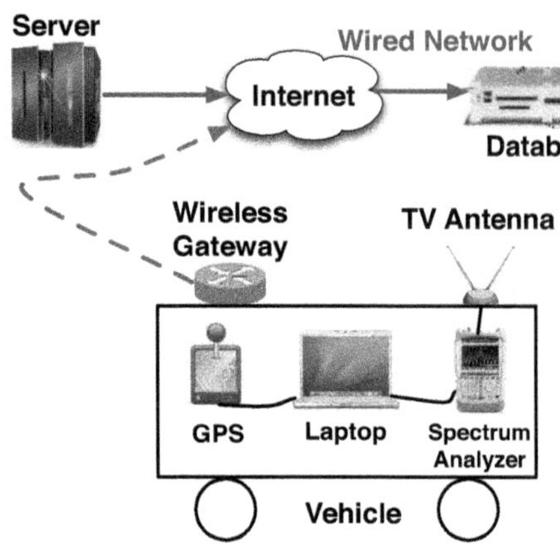


Figure 1: System architecture of *V-Scope*.

wide-area measurements for augmenting databases. Further, it obviates the need for expensive spectrum sensing hardware and their overheads in the end TVBD devices, while organically bringing some of the advantages of spectrum sensing. As a key component in *V-Scope*, we propose a zoom-in pilot detection algorithm that can reliably detect TV signals at -120dBm and operate in real-time.

We have deployed *V-Scope* on a single public transit bus in Madison, WI. Since our bus operator tends to rotate their buses through multiple routes in the course of each day, we have been able to collect spectrum measurements at more than one million locations over a 100 sq. km. area for a two week period. Our measurements show that commercial databases that are based solely on propagation models have significant inaccuracies (up to 42% of measurement locations). Furthermore, we find the quality difference among whitespace channels tends to be high due to interference from mobile transmitters, which can hardly be predicted by the existing propagation models. Finally, we propose how to use measurements collected by *V-Scope* to refine existing propagation models.

## 2. V-SCOPE DESIGN

In this section, we first describe the architecture of *V-Scope* and then present our primary detection algorithms.

**System architecture:** *V-Scope* consists of a central server and multiple clients. Each client is envisioned to run on a different vehicle. Figure 1 shows the overall architecture of *V-Scope*. We use a laptop at the client to control all the measurement procedures running in parallel. Specifically, the laptop instructs the spectrum analyzer to sweep across all the TV channels in the UHF band. The spectrum analyzer transfers spectrum samples (FFTs) to the laptop over Ethernet. Upon receiving all the samples for each channel, the laptop performs a set of real-time analysis, e.g., primary detection and power calculation. In the meanwhile, the laptop obtains the vehicle's location from a GPS module. It includes this GPS reading into the analysis results, and upload them to the central server using some wide-area networks, e.g., cellular networks.

The server is equipped with an Ethernet connection to receive measurement results. It uses the GPS reading to query the database for vacant channels. It stores the database's response with the measurements for later comparison. One design caveat is to use the central controller instead of each client to query the database. This is due to the intention of reducing burden on the wireless link. Moreover, the client is robust to connection outage by storing the measurements in the local disk and uploading them asynchronously. Since the TV signal remains stable for long period of time (order of days), the extra round-trip delay over Ethernet and the brief outage period (usually <2s) introduce negligible inaccuracy to the measurements.

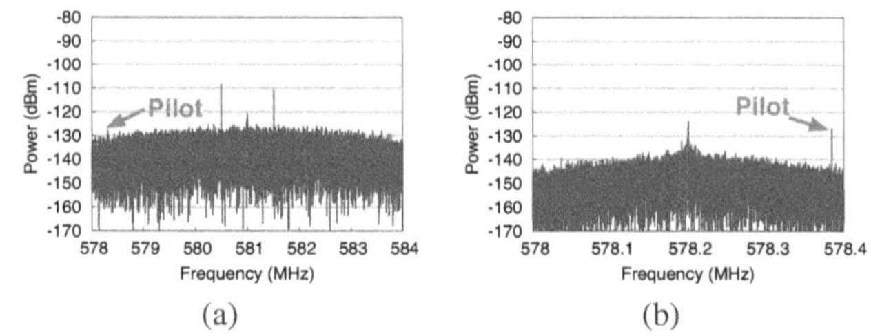


Figure 2: Spectrum of a digital TV signal at -114dBm. (a) Full-channel capture; (b) Zoom-in capture at first 488KHz band.

**Zoom-in pilot detection:** Central to our measurement is a set of algorithms to detect primary incumbents. We adopt the same detection criteria as the sensing-based TVBDs [2], i.e., to detect primary signals as low as -114dBm. The reason for being able to detect such weak signal is to *account for the transmission range of TVBDs*.

Detecting a weak TV signal is very challenging because most of spectrum analyzers generate thermal noise at a much higher power. For example, our high-end device (WSA4000 [5]) produces -91dBm noise over a 6MHz TV channel. This requires a detection algorithm to identify primary signals at very harsh SNR (-23dB). We note alternative approaches of using amplification hardware (e.g., directional antennas or low noise amplifiers). However, it causes significant distortion that reduces detection accuracy.

Our algorithm leverages two interrelated techniques, i.e., zoom–in and pilot tracking. For pilot tracking, both analog and digital TV signals have pilots to assist decoding. These pilots are at a specified frequency and more robust to noise than other spectral components. Moreover, TV standards [1] specify a fixed difference in power between a TV signal and its pilot. For example, the pilot in digital TV should be 11.3dB below the total power. Thus, we simplify the detection task by tracking pilots at an equivalent strength.

Unfortunately, even the pilot of a weak TV signal can be overwhelmed by noise. Figure 2(a) shows such a weak TV signal. We leverage a zoom-in technique to reduce noise. It configures the spectrum analyzer (through decimation) to capture at very narrow bands (488KHz). This reduces the amount of noise passing through the radio front-end, thus effectively improving SNR by 12dB. Figure 2(b) shows the beginning fraction of the TV channel where the same pilot signal is present. We observe a clear peak at 578.38KHz in front of reduced noise. Now, we can reliably detect a weak TV signal by tracking its pilot.

Combining the two ideas, our final algorithm takes two narrowband captures at fixed frequencies of a TV channel. We extract the pilots by searching for the maximum FFT bin $(f_{max}, p_{max})$ within a predetermined frequency range $(f_{start}, f_{end})$. Upon detecting this maximum bin, we include all the continuous FFT bins around it as part of the pilot, if they have a power $p_i$ higher than a threshold $(p_{max} - \delta)$. Formally, $Pilot = \{(f_i, p_i) : (f_i, p_i) \in FFT, p_i \geq p_{max} - \delta \wedge f_i \geq f_{start} \wedge f_i \leq f_{end}\}$. We extract several features (e.g., power, center frequency and bandwidth) from the pilot bins, and feed them into a decision tree based classifier for TV detection.

## 3. EVALUATION

In this section, we present our results about the performance of a commercial database. We highlight our findings that the database tends to over-predict the coverage of TV broadcasts, causing up to 42% lost in whitespaces. We start by benchmarking the accuracy of our primary detection algorithms.

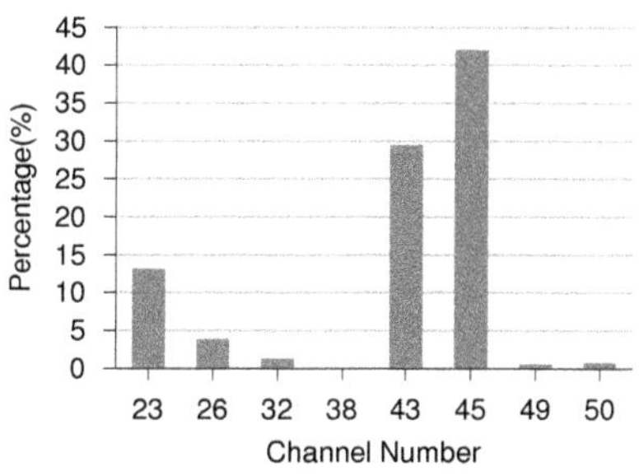


Figure 3: Fraction of whitespace loss in a model-driven database.

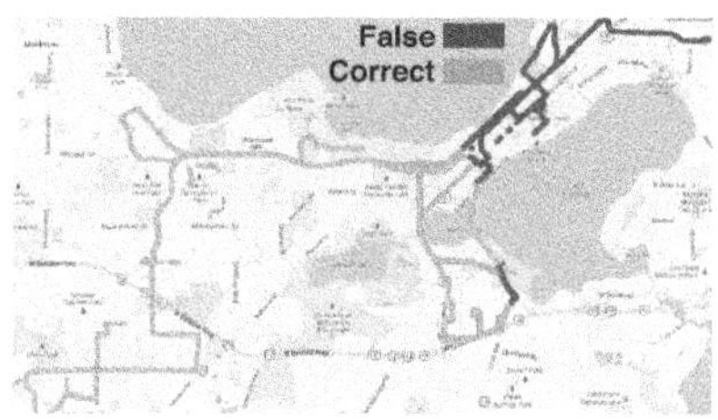


Figure 4: Prediction errors of a model-driven database in channel 45.

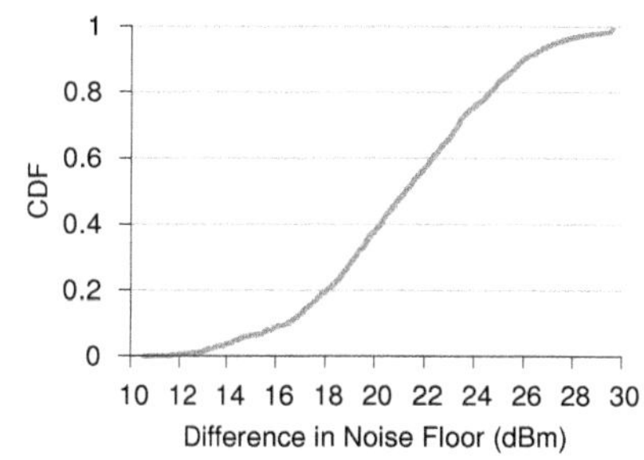


Figure 5: Quality difference in whitespace channels at same locations.

**Accuracy of detection algorithms:** We collect spectrum traces from 31 TV channels in the UHF band at different indoor locations. Using a high-end TV tuner, we identify that five channels have digital TV broadcasts, one has analog broadcast, and the rest has noise or microphone signals. We further attenuate the TV signals to obtain traces at a wide range of power (-40dB to -114dB at 10dB step). We apply a standard cross-validation procedure by randomly choosing 90% of the traces as the training data to detect the remaining 10%. Table 1 shows our algorithm has very low error rates (<5%). We also measure the detection latency and find it to be less than 1s. This short delay enables *V-Scope* to conduct very dense measurements, e.g., 10m separation in our deployment.

**Accuracy of spectrum databases:** We now evaluate the accuracy of a commercial database from SpectrumBridge [4] in predicting whitespace spectrum. The dataset is collected on a metro bus during a two-week period, containing measurements at more than 1 million distinct locations over a 100 sq. km. area around Madison, WI. All 31 channels in the UHF band were measured, among which 8 channels had active TV broadcasts in part of the measured area. We define two types of prediction errors, i.e., false positive and false negative. A false positive is the case where the database mis-predicts an occupied channel as whitespaces. The opposite is a false negative. We find very low (<0.4%) false positive rates in all these TV channels, which is similar to the prior report [3]. This demonstrates that current databases can faithfully protect TV broadcasts. However, Figure 3 shows high false negative rates in channels that have TV broadcasts. The worse channel (45) has 42% area unnecessarily blocked for unlicensed usage.

To reveal the underlying reason, Figure 4 shows the locations of false negatives in channel 45 from traces collected in one day. We note most prediction errors are densely located at the east side of the city. This is because at the east side stands several tall buildings blocking TV signals. The database failed to capture this shadowing effect, thus over-predicting the coverage of a TV broadcast.

**Difference in channel quality:** We compare the noise floor of different whitespace channels at each measured location. Figure 5 shows the CDF of maximum difference between the best channel and the worst channel. We note that the median quality difference can be 21dBm at same locations. This indicates that randomly selecting a whitespace channel can lead to poor communication performance. After examining spectrum waveforms, we identify large variation is mainly due to microphone transmissions and small variation is caused by both microphones and adjacent channel leakage from TV broadcasts. Since the database can hardly predict the signal strength from these mobile transmitters, spectrum measurements are necessary in facilitating channel selection by whitespace devices, and can be opportunistically performed by *V-Scope*.

| Detected / Groundtruth | Digital | Analog | MIC |
|---|---|---|---|
| **Digital** | 94.9 | 0.7 | 4.4 |
| **Analog** | 0.5 | 97.4 | 2.1 |
| **MIC** | 1.2 | 0.7 | 98.1 |

Table 1: Accuracy of primary detection algorithms.

# 4. FUTURE WORK AND CONCLUSION

**Developing measurement-driven models:** The measurements collected in *V-Scope* can be used to construct local propagation models that can better capture a propagation environment. A set of geostatistical interpolation methods (e.g., regression, Kriging) can be used to construct these local models, which we intend to explore.

**Augmenting spectrum occupancy databases:** *V-Scope* can be leveraged to build a hybrid database, which uses measurements or predictions from local models when available. There are a variety of open challenges for building this database, e.g., the scalability issue in storing local measurements, when to switch between local and global models, and how frequent should measurements be repeated.

In conclusion, we present the design and deployment of a vehicular sensing infrastructure called *V-Scope*. *V-Scope* is able to collect large-scale measurements in TV whitespaces by using spectrum sensors mounted on public vehicles. We are currently developing approaches to augmenting the database with these measurements.

## Acknowledgments

Tan Zhang and Suman Banerjee are supported by the US National Science Foundation through awards CNS–1040648, CNS–0916955, CNS–0855201, CNS–0747177, CNS–1064944, and CNS–1059306.

# 5. REFERENCES


[1] A. T. S. Committee. Atsc digital television standard - part 2: Rf transmission system characteristics, December 2011.

[2] FCC. Unlicensed operation in the tv broadcast bands, second memorandum opinion and order, 2010.

[3] R. Murty, R. Chandra, T. Moscibroda, and P. V. Bahl. Senseless: A database-driven white spaces network. *IEEE Transactions on Mobile Computing*, 2012.

[4] Spectrum Bridge Inc. Spectrum bridge database. http://www.spectrumbridge.com/Home.aspx.

[5] ThinkRf. The thinkrf wireless signals intelligence platform. http://www.thinkrf.com/.

# Exploring Indoor White Spaces in Metropolises


Xuhang Ying
Dept. of Information Engineering
The Chinese University of Hong Kong

Jincheng Zhang
Dept. of Information Engineering
The Chinese University of Hong Kong

Lichao Yan
Dept. of Information Engineering
The Chinese University of Hong Kong

Guanglin Zhang
Institute of Network Coding
The Chinese University of Hong Kong

Minghua Chen
Dept. of Information Engineering
The Chinese University of Hong Kong

Ranveer Chandra
Microsoft Research
One Microsoft Way
Redmond, WA 98052



## ABSTRACT

It is a promising vision to utilize white spaces, *i.e.*, vacant VHF and UHF TV channels, to satisfy skyrocketing wireless data demand in both outdoor and indoor scenarios. While most prior works have focused on exploring outdoor white spaces, the indoor story is largely open for investigation. Motivated by this observation and that 70% of the spectrum demand comes from indoor environments, we carry out a comprehensive study of exploring *indoor* white spaces. We first present a large-scale measurement of outdoor and indoor TV spectrum occupancy in 30+ diverse locations in a typical metropolis Hong Kong. Our measurement results confirm abundant white spaces available for exploration in a wide range of areas in metropolises. In particular, more than 50% and 70% of the TV spectrum are white spaces in outdoor and indoor scenarios, respectively. While there are substantially more white spaces in indoor scenarios than in outdoor scenarios, there is no effective solution for identifying indoor white spaces. To fill in this gap, we propose the first system WISER (for White-space Indoor Spectrum EnhanceR), to identify and track indoor white spaces in a building, without requiring user devices to sense the spectrum. We discuss the design space of such system and justify our design choices using intensive real-world measurements. We design the architecture and algorithms to address the inherent challenges. We build a WISER prototype and carry out real-world experiments to evaluate its performance. Our results show that WISER can identify 30%-50% more indoor white spaces with negligible false alarms, as compared to alternative baseline approaches.



## Categories and Subject Descriptors

C.2.1 [**Computer-communication networks**]: Network Architecture and Design-Network topology; C.4 [**Performance of systems**]: Design studies, Measurement techniques





## Keywords

TV white spaces, clustering algorithms, sensor placement


## 1. INTRODUCTION

The skyrocketing growth of mobile devices and applications has triggered a need for additional radio frequency (RF) spectrum to satisfy this demand. Since most of the frequency spectrum has been licensed for different purposes (satellite, TV, radio, RADARs, cellular, *etc.*), a recent concept of dynamic spectrum access (DSA) is being explored to provide additional spectrum with little disruption to existing licensed users and their devices.

A recent manifestation of DSA is in the TV spectrum. In 2008, the FCC passed a historic ruling that allowed unlicensed devices (similar to Wi-Fi) to operate in the locally unoccupied TV spectrum (also called the TV white spaces or simply white spaces). Devices, similar to the Wi-Fi devices of today, are required to detect the available spectrum before using it for communication. Per a 2010 FCC Second Order and Report [6], the white space devices can detect available spectrum using either spectrum sensing or by querying a geo-location web service over the Internet.

Most white space devices and standards are being designed around querying the web service for spectrum availability. This is primarily because spectrum sensing is expensive – in cost, energy consumption and complexity of the circuitry. Furthermore, it is more difficult to accurately detect TV signals using spectrum sensing at low thresholds with commercial, off-the-shelf hardware. In contrast, the geo-location approach does not require any hardware and is easier to implement. Devices report their locations to a web service, which in turn returns a list of TV channels that can be used at that location[1]. See [8] for a survey on this line of approach. However, this approach suffers from inherent inefficiency. The geo-location service uses propagation modeling to determine the available spectrum, and hence, is very conservative in the channels it returns for a given location. For example, the propagation models used by the FCC do not account for buildings, and man-made obstructions that exist in urban areas. In a measurement study in [36],

[1]To avoid interference to white space users from wireless microphone usage, wireless microphone users are suggested to register the location and frequency usage to the geo-location database. In this way, the database can exclude the frequency occupied by wireless microphone at the location and within its estimated interfering neighbors from the returned list.

an in-operation geo-location database service reports only half of vacant channels across a major city.

In this paper we carry out measurement-driven analysis and design to white space networking in indoor environments. We first carry out a large-scale measurement across 30+ diverse locations in a typical metropolis, and reveal that more than 50% and 70% of the TV spectrum are white spaces in outdoor and indoor scenarios, respectively. While there are significantly more white spaces in indoor scenarios than in outdoor scenarios, there is no effective solution for identifying indoor white spaces. Given that most people are indoors 80% of the time [24] and 70% of spectrum demand comes from indoor environments [12], it will be extremely useful if it were possible to use the vacant TV channels in indoor scenarios.

We therefore take the next step, and propose a system, called WISER (for White-space Indoor Spectrum EnhanceR), that increases the number of TV channels available for indoor white space networking, while (i) not requiring client devices to sense the spectrum, (ii) building more accurate white space database locally by integrating outdoor and indoor sensing, and (iii) not interfering with TV transmissions.

WISER enables buildings to become "white space enabled" using an innovative approach of profiling, sensor placement, and integration with geo-location databases. It provides a technique for building owners or managers to get their building profiled for white space use, based on which WISER strategically determines a few locations to place RF sensors. These sensors capture the additionally available white space spectrum in the building. Ideally we would require a very dense placement of RF sensors to obtain every additionally available channel. However, such approach can be very expensive due to the large number of RF sensors[2]. Hence, we propose an innovative clustering scheme to reduce the number of sensors needed to (i) capture the white space variation in indoor environments, yet (ii) provide most of the additional channels for indoor use.

Throughout this paper we make the following contributions:

- In Section 2, using comprehensive measurements in Hong Kong, we show that more than 50% and 70% of the TV spectrum are white spaces in outdoor and indoor scenarios, respectively. Further, in Section 3, we reveal that indoor white spaces expresses interesting location correlation and channel correlation. These characteristics provide insights in identifying and utilizing indoor white spaces.

- In Section 4, we propose an indoor white space identification system, called WISER, that allows additional white space spectrum to be used indoors. To the best of our knowledge, this is the first system that can use the additional white spaces without requiring client devices to sense the spectrum. Our approach is rather general, and can be additionally used in other spectrum monitoring applications. In Section 5, we present channel and location clustering algorithms to reduce the number of sensors used by WISER to monitor white space spectrum.

- In Section 6, we build a proof-of-concept WISER prototype, deploy it in a building floor, and evaluate its performance by real-world experiments across a four-month duration. In particular, we demonstrate that WISER can identify 30%-50% more indoor white spaces with negligible false alarms, as compared to alternative baseline approaches.

[2]For the purpose of identifying white spaces, an RF sensor consisting of USRP1, a TVRX receive-only daughter board and an antenna still costs around 1K US dollars. Hence, reducing the total sensor cost is an important system design consideration.

Given that indoor environments are crowded, and have the most spectrum demand, our system provides a new principled approach to make additional spectrum available in these environments. Last but not the least, we remark that WISER is not limited to the TV white space spectrum. It can be similarly applied to any other portion of the spectrum where dynamic spectrum access techniques will be adopted.

# 2. INDOOR/OUTDOOR WHITE SPACE AVAILABILITY MEASUREMENT

## 2.1 Objective

We carry out a large-scale indoor/outdoor white space measurement in a typical metropolitan city Hong Kong. The purpose of our measurement is two-fold. First, we aim to understand the difference between the indoor and outdoor white space availability patterns. Such understanding motivates our investigation on exploring indoor white spaces. Second, while various measurement studies have been reported in the literature, we find a large-scale indoor/outdoor measurement is missing. Such large-scale measurement is critical for properly evaluating the potential of white space networking in metropolises, where different districts observe diverse spectrum occupancy patterns.

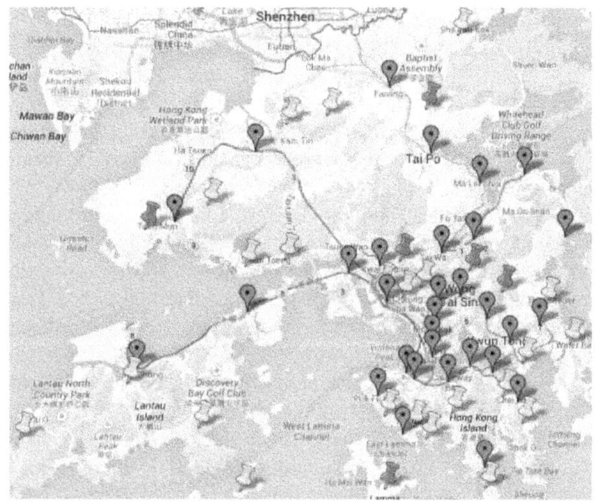


Figure 1: A map showing the six principal TV transmitting stations, 23 fill-in TV transmitting stations [5], and 31 diverse measurement locations that cover all 18 districts in Hong Kong. Principle and fill-in TV stations are labeled using red and yellow pin-shape markers, respectively. Measurement locations correspond to blue droplet-shape markers. Each measurement location is covered by 1-5 TV stations (2.2 on average) [4], and the distance to its nearest TV station ranges from 0.97 km to 9.35 km (3.25 km on average).

## 2.2 Methodology

### 2.2.1 *Equipment and Setup*

The measurement equipment consists of a USRP [9], a Log Periodic PCB Antenna, a laptop computer, and a battery bank. We use the USRP board coupled with a TVRX receiver-only daughter board and a GNU Radio platform [3] to construct a spectrum analyzer, for measuring and detecting TV signals in the 470-806 MHz TV spectrum band. We calibrate the measurement device using a RF signal generator to obtain accurate power reading in dBm. We

| | Outdoor | | | | Indoor | | | | Indoor Bonus |
|---|---|---|---|---|---|---|---|---|---|
| | Urban | Sub-urban | Rural | Overall | Urban | Sub-urban | Rural | Overall | Overall |
| White Space Ratio (%) | 44.1 | 55.9 | 60.9 | 53.6 | 67.9 | 74.7 | 73.3 | 72 | 18.4 |
| Number of Vacant Channels | 18.5 | 23.5 | 25.6 | 22.5 | 28.5 | 31.4 | 30.8 | 30.2 | 7.7 |
| Total Vacant Spectrum (MHz) | 148 | 188 | 204 | 180 | 228 | 251 | 246 | 242 | 62 |

Table 1: Summary of the indoor and outdoor white space measurement results.

use energy detection to detect analog signals by comparing the receiving power spanning 100 KHz centered at their visual carriers against -104.2 dBm. For digital TV signals, we use a feature-based detection scheme similar to that in [22] for accurate detection; the scheme is able to detect digital TV signal strength as low as 96 dBm/8 MHz. More details can be found in our measurement report [36].

### 2.2.2 *Measurement Locations and Design*

We measure the indoor/outdoor white space availability at 31 diverse locations in Hong Kong, including Hong Kong Island, Kowloon Peninsula, and New Territories. These locations cover all the 18 districts of Hong Kong, which have very different terrain and population characteristics [1]. For example, the urban area such as MongKok has the world-highest population density and the skyscrapers in the area have deep influence on the signal propagation. While in remote areas such as Yuen Lang, the population and tall-building densities are much lower. Fig. 1 shows the six principal TV stations, 23 fill-in TV stations[3] and 31 measurement locations. More details (*e.g.*, effective radiated power, polarization, *etc.*) about the TV broadcasting network of Hong Kong are available in [7]. All measurement locations are in well populated commercial/residential areas; thus our measurement results capture the representative spectrum occupancy patterns in Hong Kong.

At each location we measure the indoor/outdoor spectrum occupancy pattern of the TV bands at three time instants, one in the morning, one at noon, and one in the evening. The indoor measurements are taken inside various commercial buildings at the selected locations. The time interval between two adjacent measurements is 4 hours. In each measurement, we scan all 42 analog and digital TV channels multiple times. These channels are in the frequency range of 470-806 MHz with 8 MHz channel spacing [32]. For ease of discussions, they are labeled as CH 1 to CH 42. Using feature-based TV signal detection schemes, we analyze the measurement results and identify locally unoccupied channels. These unoccupied channels are labeled as white spaces available at the corresponding locations.

## 2.3 Observations

We summarize the indoor and outdoor white space measurement results in Table 1. In particular, we first group the 31 measurement locations into three areas, namely urban, sub-urban, and rural, according to the population density [1]. Then we summarize the indoor and outdoor white space results for each area.

Several observations can be made from the results. First, similar to the US and Europe, there are a large number of vacant TV channels in Hong Kong – more than 50% of the TV channels are white spaces. Together with existing white space measurement studies [13, 20, 26], our measurements confirm abundant white-space networking potential in metropolises, different areas in Hong Kong observe very different white space availability patterns. For example, in outdoor scenarios, there are on average 5 more vacant channels in the sub-urban area than in the urban area, corresponding to 54 MHz additional spectrum. Third, there are more indoor white spaces than the outdoor white space, which is mainly due to the signal attenuation because of the blocking effects of walls. In particular, in indoor scenarios, there are on average 72% of the 42 TV channels are white spaces, 18.4% higher than that in outdoors. This corresponds to 7.7 additional vacant channels and a total amount of 62 MHz spectrum. The amount of overall indoor white spaces is 242 MHz, enough to support one additional Wi-Fi service in operation.

Furthermore, the indoor white spaces are less fragmented than the outdoor ones. The average length of contiguous vacant channels is 3.84-channel in indoor scenarios as compared to 1.87-channel in outdoor scenarios. This indicates the indoor white spaces is of better "quality" than the outdoor ones, since it is easier to design wireless devices to communicate over contiguous channels than over fragmented ones.

# 3. INDOOR WHITE SPACE CHARACTERISTICS MEASUREMENT

Complementary to our large-scale indoor/outdoor availability measurements, we also conduct intensive indoor measurements to gain necessary understanding of indoor white space characteristics.

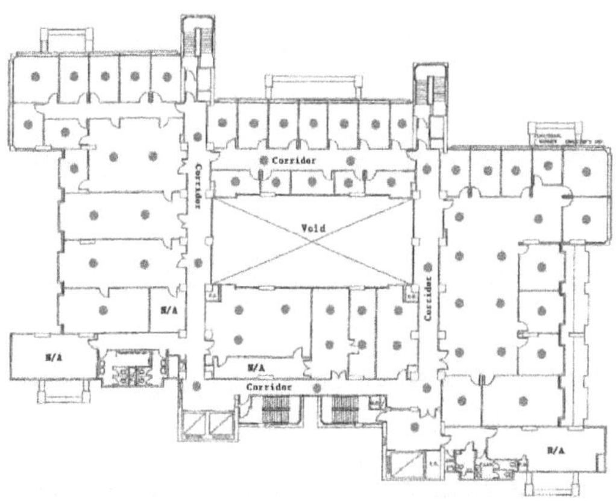


Figure 2: A map showing the 65 measurement locations on the 7th floor of a building. Each measurement location corresponds to a dot in red color on the map.

## 3.1 Methodology

### 3.1.1 *Equipment and Setup*

The same equipment described in Section 2.2.1 is used for indoor white space characteristics measurement, except an omnidirectional antenna with a gain of 0 dBi.

### 3.1.2 *White Space Threshold*

In our measurements, we label a TV channel as locally unoccupied if the corresponding channel receiving power is less than

[3]There are several tens of additional fill-in TV stations, but their precise location information is not available online, and we are unable to estimate their broadcasting coverage accordingly.

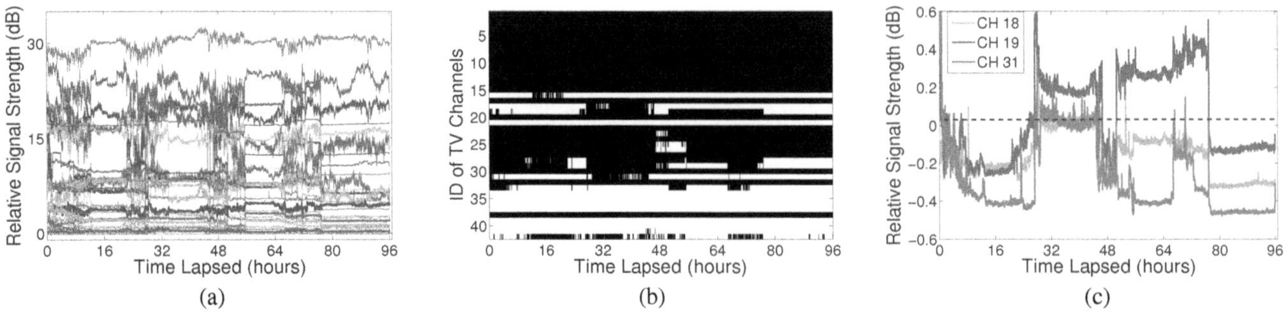


Figure 3: (a) Relative signal strength (in dB) for all 42 TV channels in a 96-hour window. (b) Channel occupancy statuses for all 42 channels in the same 96-hour window. White spaces are denoted in white, and occupied channels in black. (c) Three TV channels (CH 18, 19 and 30) that move up and down around the white space thresholds (*e.g.,* the dotted line). They become white spaces from time to time.

or equal to a pre-set white space threshold, and as occupied otherwise. This energy-detection based identification method is faster but less sensitive as compared to those used in our indoor/outdoor large-scale measurements. We adopt the method to do fast profiling of the white space availability at a large number of dense locations in an operational building. We set the white space thresholds to be -84.5 dBm/8 MHz for the digital TV signals and -104.2 dBm/100 KHz for analog TV signals (centered at their visual carriers). These values are the maximum readings out of detected power spanning the corresponding bands in all empty channels based on long-time sensing results. While these white space thresholds used for determining channel vacancy may seem aggressive due to hardware limitations, we believe that the observations drawn from the measurement results are general and our system is not tied with these thresholds. We note that if improved hardware is in use to allow a highly-conservative sensing threshold of -114 dBm as suggested by FCC, then the identified unoccupied channels are safe to use, in the sense that secondary users using these channels will not cause interfere with primary TV users within a considerably large neighborhood. See [6] for detailed discussions on setting interference-safe sensing threshold for TV white space networking.

#### *3.1.3 Measurement Locations and Design*

As shown in Fig. 2, a total of 65 indoor locations on one floor of a building are selected for measurement. At each indoor location, every channel is scanned five times. We observe <1% difference in recorded signal strengths beyond five-time measurements. During each scanning, each channel is measured for 0.2 seconds. The recorded signal is then processed by a GNURadio FFT program with a bin size of 2048 and a resolution of 3.9 KHz. We then record the maximum values observed at each bin for the channel during each scanning and compute the average value for that bin. For a digital channel, we compare the total channel power over 8 MHz centered at the middle of a TV channel against the white space threshold of -84.5 dBm. For a analog channel, we compare the power spanning 100 KHz centered at the frequency of its visual carrier against -104.2 dBm.

We conduct two types of indoor measurements, namely *indoor long-time sensing* and *indoor one-time profiling*. Indoor long-time sensing is for understanding temporal features of indoor white spaces. We measure the received signal strengths for all 42 TV channels at a typical indoor location consecutively for 96 hours. Indoor one-time profiling is to probe spatial features of indoor white spaces for a typical indoor environment. We mount the measurement equipment onto a movable cart and run a Python script to scan all TV channels automatically. We then profile the 65 indoor locations one by one. The duration for profiling one location is about 1.5 minutes, and the whole process lasts roughly three hours. We can obtain a 65x42 matrix containing absolute signal strengths (in dBm) for 42 channels at the 65 indoor locations. To facilitate comparison, we convert the absolute signal strengths to the relative signal strengths by comparing them against the corresponding white space thresholds. We collect a total of 13 one-time profiling data in two periods in four months.

### 3.2 Long-Time Indoor Sensing Results

There are several observations from the long-time indoor sensing. First, from Fig. 3a, there are *strong* channels whose relative signal strength exceed a large threshold most of the time. For instance, we observe 14.29% channels with >10 dB relative signal strength 95% of the time across the 96-hour interval, which means they are *long-term occupied* at the typical indoor location. Second, for *weak-to-normal* channels, their signal strengths express a *short-term stable yet long-term unstable* pattern. Third, we observe intermittent white spaces availability from Fig. 3b. This results from the temporal signal strength variation in weak-to-normal channels. These observations suggest that to extract the maximum indoor white space potential, it suffices to identify strong channels via long-time sensing and then focus resources to track the slow-varying white space availability of weak-to-normal channels.

### 3.3 One-Time Spectrum Profiling Results

We have the following observations from one-time spectrum profiling results. First, as shown in Fig. 4, a channel may express *spatial variation* in its relative signal strength and white space availability across different indoor locations. Such *spatial variation* is caused by complex outdoor and indoor signal propagation and attenuation patterns due to various factors, for example the blocking effects of indoor walls. This implies potential white space loss if indoor white space availability is directly inferred from outdoor availability results.

Second, seen from Fig. 5a, for a given channel, there is also strong correlation in signal strengths and white space availability across different locations. This suggests that we can infer the channel vacancies of multiple correlated locations from those of one or a few representative locations. We refer this observation as indoor white space *location correlation.*

In addition, seen from Fig. 5b, we observe that for multiple channels, there are strong correlation in their signal strengths and white space availability patterns across all locations. The similarities among these channels can be due to that they share the same trans-

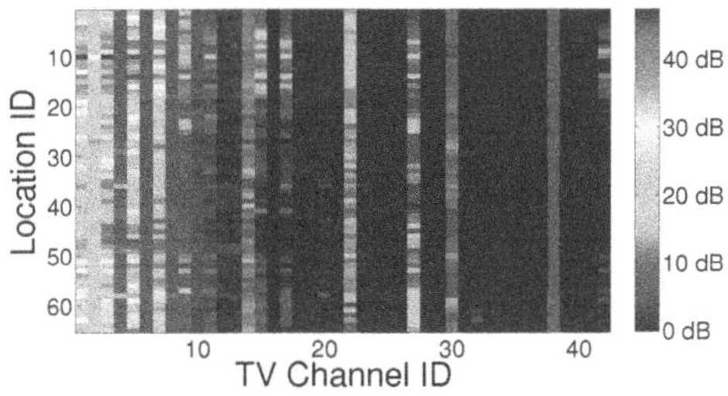


(a)

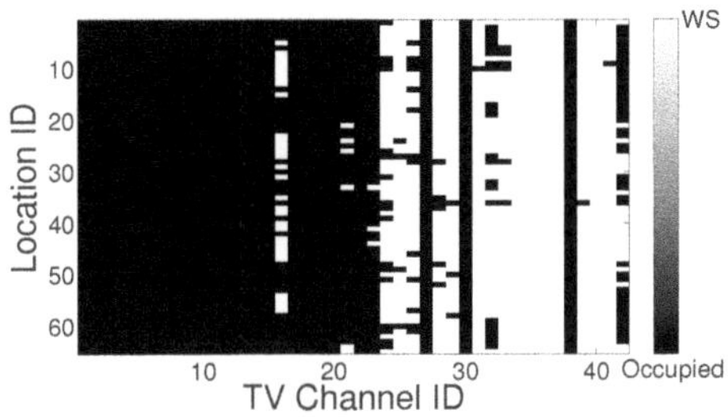


(b)

Figure 4: (a) Typical spatial map of channel relative signal strengths extracted from one-time spectrum profiling data. We observe signal attenuation patterns across different locations. (b) Typical spatial map of indoor white spaces (denoted in white, occupied channels in black) extracted from one-time spectrum profiling data. We observe different channel vacancy patterns across different locations.

mission tower, similar loss and attenuation patterns in their propagation. This suggests that we can group these "similar" channels together into a group, and infer the vacancies of this group of channels from those of a representative channel in this group. We refer this observation as indoor white space *channel correlation.*

The above observations on location correlation and channel correlation are drawn based on one-time profiling results. They have the potential to form useful guidelines in designing indoor white space identification systems. One important question stands on the way, however, is *whether the correlation among channels and locations are stable across different time epochs.*

## 3.4 Stability of Indoor Channel Correlation and Location Correlation

To study the stability of the channel correlation and location correlation, we cluster channels and locations according to their similarity using one-time profiling data collected across seven days in the first two-week period. We then compare one of the clustering results (*e.g.,* the first day) with other clustering results. If the channel correlation and location correlation are stable over time, then we should see consistent clustering results in these seven days. We should otherwise observe discrepancy in clustering results.

To filter out the noise in profiling data while maintain necessary information about signal strengths, we first quantize the relative signal strengths as described in Section 4.5.3. We then apply the clustering algorithms described in Section 5, and compute the Rand Index [33] of the clustering results to exam their consistency. The Rand Index is commonly accepted as an objective criterion for comparing two clustering results. A Rand Index of 1 indicates two identical clustering results, and 0 indicates total disagreement.

To facilitate the illustration for Fig. 6, we define *a channel group* as a group of channels that exhibit similar signal strengths across

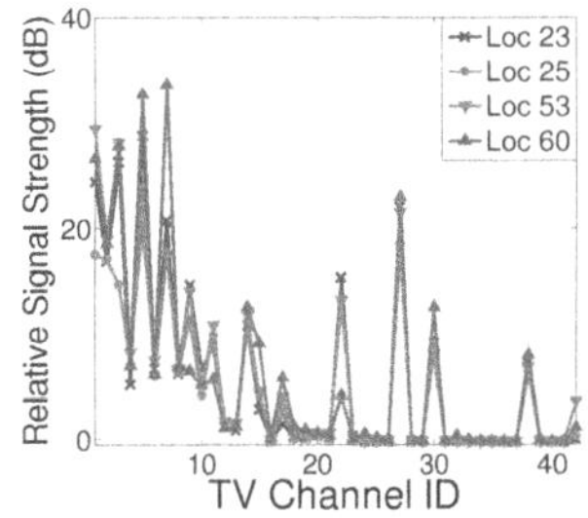


(a)

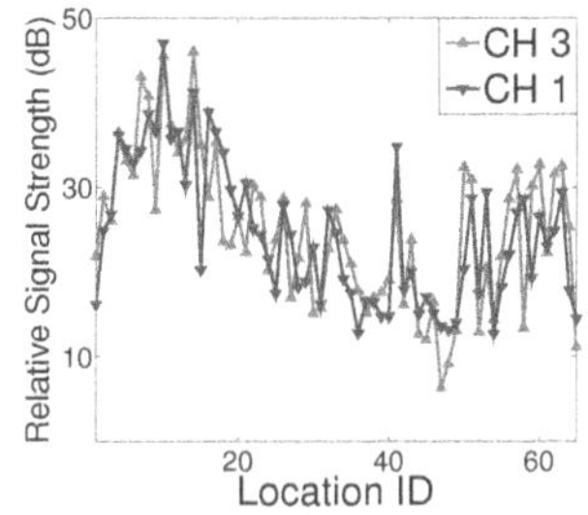


(b)

Figure 5: (a) Location 23, 25, 53 and 60 receive close signal strengths from many TV channels. Each line represents the relative signal strengths received at an indoor location for 42 channels. We observe strong location correlation. (b) CH 1 and 3 exhibit very close signal strengths at different indoor locations. Each line represents the relative signal strengths for a channel at 65 indoor locations. We observe strong channel correlation.

different indoor locations, and *a location group* as a group of locations that receive similar signal strengths for a particular set of channels. As shown in Fig. 6a, when we have three or more channel groups, the average Rand Index reaches 0.79 and keeps rising. It means that we would obtain very similar channel clustering results, and the channel correlation is very consistent across different days. Fig. 6b shows that the average Rand Index has exceeded 0.80 when there are 10 or more location groups for a group of channels (*i.e.,* CH 1, 3, 5 and 7), which indicates that location correlation also exhibits consistency in time. These observations imply that *the correlations among channels and locations are very likely to be stable in time*, which is critical in gauging our designs of the indoor white space identification system, to be discussed in the next section.

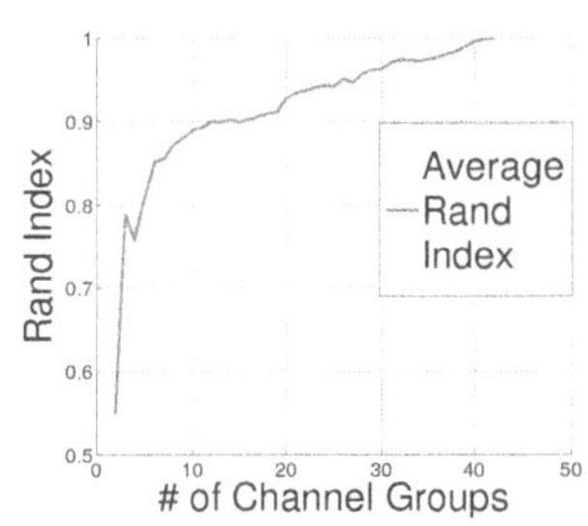


(a)

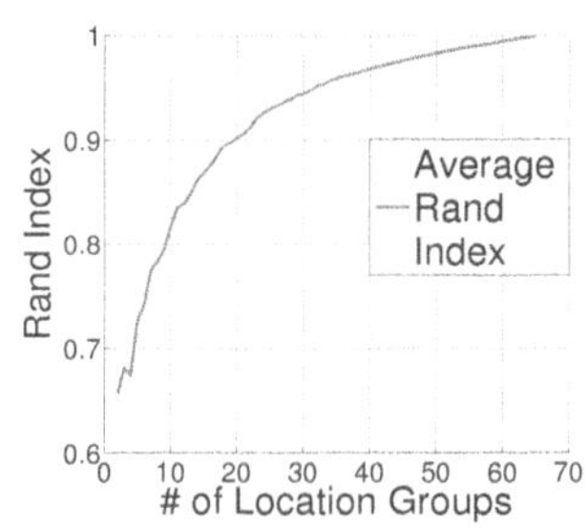


(b)

Figure 6: (a) Channel correlation is consistent across different days. The input is a matrix of quantized relative signal strengths for 42 channels at 65 locations. We would obtain highly similar channel clustering results with more then three channel groups. (b) Location correlation consistency across different days. The input is a matrix of quantized relative signal strengths at 65 locations for 4 channels (*i.e.,* Ch 1, 3, 5 and 7). We would obtain highly similar location clustering results with more than five location clusters. In both figures, clustering result of data in the first day serves as a main reference. Both curves start with two groups. The Rand Index is 1 when there is only one group.

## 3.5 Summary

In summary, our results from long-term sensing, one-time profiling, and correlation stability verification reveal the following important observations:

- Strong channels are long-term stable; weak-to-normal channels are short-term stable but long-term unstable.
- *Location correlation*: given a channel, there are strong correlations in its signal strength and white space availability across multiple indoor locations; these correlations are stable in time.
- *Channel correlation*: there are strong correlations in multiple channels in their signal strengths and white space availability patterns across all locations; these correlations are stable in time.

The first observation suggests that to extract the maximum indoor white space potential, it suffices to identify strong channels via long-time spectrum sensing and then track the slow-varying white space availability of weak-to-normal channels. The rest two observations suggest that we can focus on monitoring representative channels at representative indoor locations, and inferring the availability of other channels at other locations by exploiting the location and channel correlations. These observations will be utilized in designing indoor white space identification systems in the next section.

# 4. WISER - WHITE SPACE INDOOR SPECTRUM ENHANCER

In this section, we first explore the design space of an indoor white space identification system. We then present WISER's architecture, which consists of real-time sensing module, white space database, and indoor positioning module.

## 4.1 Design Objective and Design Space

A well-performed indoor white space identification system needs to (i) minimize false alarms (*safety*), and (ii) identify as many white spaces correctly as possible (*efficiency*). In addition, the sensor cost is also a major consideration, as RF sensors can be expensive. We define the following three metrics to evaluate a system:

- *False Alarm Rate (FA Rate):* the ratio between the number of channels that a system mis-identifies as vacant and the total number of vacant channels that the system identifies. A system with lower *FA Rate* is safer.
- *White Space Loss Rate (WS Loss Rate):* the ratio between the number of channels that a system mis-identifies as occupied and the total number of actually-vacant channels. A system with lower *WS Loss Rate* is more efficient.
- *Sensor Cost:* the total cost of all RF sensors in use.

Generally, there are several approaches to identify indoor white spaces. The *outdoor-sensing-only (OS-Only)* approach performs spectrum sensing locally on the rooftop using one outdoor sensor, and only reports channels that are available outdoors for indoor use. Despite of the low sensor cost, this approach is too conservative to be efficient, as it fails to take into account of the significant attenuation on TV signals due to the blocking effects of indoor obstacles (*e.g.*, walls).

Under the second approach called *one-time-profiling-only (OTP-Only)*, we only profile indoor locations once, then label every channel at each location as either 1 (vacant) or 0 (occupied), and store such information in the white space database for later retrieval. However, this approach assumes the indoor white space availability to be time-invariant, which does not hold according to our indoor white space measurements in Section 3. As a result, this approach fails in both safety and efficiency; in particular, violating safety would cause severe harm to primary users.

The third approach is *sensor-all-over-the-place.* This approach deploys dense indoor sensors to monitor indoor white spaces. Although this scheme can achieve the ideal safety and efficiency, it comes with a forbidden sensor cost.

In summary, none of the above approaches could achieve a satisfactory performance at low cost. To tackle this problem, we propose an indoor white space identification system called WISER with excellent safety and efficiency at lower sensor cost as compared to the above baseline solutions.

## 4.2 WISER Overview

As shown in Fig. 7, WISER consists of three components, namely real-time sensing module, white space database, and indoor positioning module. WISER takes users' locations as the inputs and outputs the indoor white space availability at the given locations.

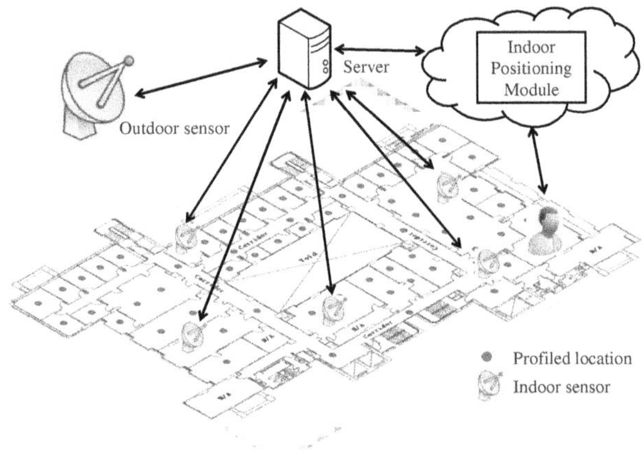


Figure 7: Architecture schema of WISER.

## 4.3 Indoor Positioning Module

In WISER, a user determines its indoor location by using the indoor positioning module. Indoor positioning has been widely explored in recent years. Many wireless technologies can be integrated into indoor positioning, including IR, ultra-sound, RFID, WLAN, and Bluetooth. See [17] for a recent survey. Since indoor positioning is developing into a mature technology, WISER simply uses one existing system as the indoor positioning module. It is conceivable that the indoor positioning accuracy will affect WISER's performance. We will study the relationship between indoor positioning accuracy and the performance of WISER in Section 6.

## 4.4 White Space Database

The white space database receives real-time channel signal strength reported from the sensors in the real-time sensing module, as well as the corresponding up-to-date indoor white space availability. After obtaining its indoor position, user queries the white space database to retrieve a list of vacant channels for communication with a separate white space networking infrastructure. To handle dynamics of wireless microphones, wireless microphone users are suggested to register the location and frequency usage to the white space database, so that WISER can exclude the frequency occupied by wireless microphone at the location and within its estimated interfering neighbors from the returned list.

## 4.5 Real-time Sensing Module

Given an indoor environment, the real-time sensing module performs real-time outdoor and indoor spectrum sensing, and reports the results to the white space database. To realize this functionality, we first conduct one-time spectrum profiling at a sufficient number of indoor locations. To exploit the observation in long-time measurement (Section 3.2), we then group the channels into strong and weak-to-normal channels. We also identify some permanently available channels based on the long-time outdoor sensing, and focus on the remaining weak-to-normal channels. Then, we perform channel-location clustering to leverage channel and location correlations (Section 3). Last, we place indoor sensors based on the results of channel-location clustering to optimize the use of a limited number of sensors and then send real-time data to server periodically.

### *4.5.1 One-Time Spectrum Profiling*

One-time spectrum profiling aims to learn the indoor white space characteristics, including channel and location correlations. These locations should be as dense as possible. For example, in our study, 65 measurement locations are profiled including almost every room and corridor on an indoor floor, as shown in Section 3.4. For a non-profiled location, its indoor white space availability is assumed to be the same with the nearest profiled one. The profiling data will serve as the main reference to determine indoor sensor locations. Ideally, we should profile all measurement locations simultaneously. However, since we observed that indoor white spaces tend to be stable with moderate variation in the short term (*e.g.,* hours), we base WISER deployment on the asynchronous one-time profiling within three hours.

### *4.5.2 Channel Grouping*

We first group TV channels into two basic classes: strong channels and weak-to-normal channels (including permanently vacant channels) based on one-time and long-time measurements. Weak-to-normal channels have a higher chance to be white spaces due to signal variation and attenuation.

We motivate the simple grouping scheme with the following reasons. First of all, such classification is general. In fact, for a particular area, TV services are broadcast via one or more major TV towers in several channels. These channels usually carry strong signals and are distinguishable from others. In addition, due to stable TV broadcasting arrangement in the long run (*e.g.,* years), the obtained grouping result will also be stable accordingly unless dramatic changes occur (*e.g.,* shutdown of a TV tower). Moreover, it is efficient to group channels into such two basic classes. Because by exploiting "always on" nature of some TV channels, indoor sensors can focus on other time-varying channels rather than these stably strong ones.

### *4.5.3 Channel-Location Clustering*

The channel-location clustering aims to obtain *channel-location (CL) groups*, each of which contains locations with similar signal strengths for channels with similar propagation patterns. In our current solution, we obtain CL groups by first clustering the channels according to their received signal strengths across the locations. Then, for each channel cluster, we group the locations according to the received signal strength distribution among those channels. More details will be described in Section 5. Nonetheless, conducting joint channel-location clustering is an alternative method, and is left for future work.

To reduce the undesirable impact of noise, we introduce a *uniform quantizer* for received signal strengths before conducting channel-location clustering, which is defined as below:

$$S_q = \begin{cases} -1, & S_r \le 0 \\ \left\lfloor \frac{S_r}{Q} \right\rfloor, & S_r > 0 \end{cases}$$

where $S_r$ is the received relative signal strength compared to the pre-set white space thresholds, $Q$ is the quantization step (*e.g.,* 5 dB), and $S_q$ is the quantized relative signal strength.

### *4.5.4 Indoor Sensor Placement*

Given a set of CL groups, we aim to deploy indoor sensors to fulfill (i) *coverage* requirement: every CL group is covered by at least one sensor, and (ii) *performance* requirement: safety is guaranteed and efficiency is maximized, given a number of indoor sensors. The brute-force way is to enumerate all possible combinations to find the best one. Instead of adopting this inefficient approach, we propose a greedy algorithm that could achieve local optimum with guaranteed system performance, as described in Section 5.

To avoid interference with primary users, indoor white space availability shared within each CL group is derived from real-time sensing results in a conservative way. First of all, if a particular CL group is covered by multiple indoor sensors, indoor white spaces are determined by comparing the maximum received signal strength for a channel with the white space thresholds as follows:

$$WS(C_x) = \begin{cases} 1, & S_{max}(C_x, L_{sensors}) < WSThr_x \\ 0, & otherwise \end{cases}$$

where $WS(C_x)$ means the white space availability for channel $x$ at all locations in the CL group, $S_{max}(C_x, L_{sensors})$ means the maximum received signal strength among multiple sensor locations for channel $x$ in the CL group and $WSThr_x$ is the white space threshold for channel $x$.

Second, if a CL group is covered by only one indoor sensor, a *protection range* (in dBm) needs to be added to minimize false alarm rate as follows:

$$WS(C_x) = \begin{cases} 1, & S(C_x, L_{sensors}) < WSThr^*_x \\ 0, & otherwise \end{cases}$$

where $WSThr^*_x = WSThr_x - PR_x$, and the $PR_x$ is the protection range for channel $x$ for this CL group. To exploit the statistics of received channel signal strength deviation in a CL group in training data sets, we obtain $PR_x$ by multiplying a constant (3 by default) with the standard deviation of all received signal strengths in channel $x$ at locations in the CL group. This constant measures how conservative we are and can be used to control the FA rate.

## 5. ALGORITHM

In this section, we first discuss the intuition of algorithms we use in deploying real-time sensing module. We then present the channel-location clustering and indoor sensor placement algorithms.

## 5.1 Algorithm Intuition

As revealed in Section 3.4, there exists consistent correlation among channel signal strength at different locations. An intuitive way to extract such correlation is clustering. Given one-time profiling data, we treat signal strengths across different indoor locations for a channel as a feature vector, and cluster similar channels together to obtain channel clusters. Then for each channel group, we treat signal strengths in different channels of the channel group at a location as a feature vector, and perform location clustering accordingly. In this way, we obtain CL groups (recall that CL group stands for channel-location group). Within each CL group, the channels share similar signal strength at the locations; hence, intuitively we can use one sensor per CL group to monitor signal strengths of the channels (in the group) at the locations (in the group). Following the above intuition, we design Algorithm 1 and Algorithm 2. As the next step of the above intuition, we need to deploy one sensor (or more) per CL group (*i.e.,* coverage requirement), and enable WISER to correctly identify as many indoor white spaces as possible (*i.e.,* performance requirement). These two requirements are very important in designing our indoor sensor placement algorithm (Algorithm 3) and its ranking mechanism (Algorithm 4). More details will be discussed later in this section.

## 5.2 Proposed Algorithm

The proposed algorithm takes quantized relative signal strength and the number of indoor sensors as inputs, and outputs a list of sensor locations. In the case of multiple feasible sensor placement options, the one with least FA rate (with first priority) and least WS Loss rate is chosen, namely "least-false-alarm-first" criterion.

### *5.2.1 Channel-Location Clustering*

As stated in Section 4.5.3, the channel-location clustering aims to cluster locations that receive similar channel signal strength for certain channels into the same group. We do so by first grouping the channels according to their receiving signal strengths at all indoor locations, and then within each channel group clustering the locations according to their receiving signal strengths of this group of channels. In our algorithm designs, we adopt Ward's minimum variance method [23] as the linkage criterion, and Euclidean distance as the similarity metric owing to their widespread popularity.

**Algorithm 1** Channel Clustering

1: **Input:** $S$: the $M \times N$ training data set
   {$M$ is the total number of locations, $N$ is total number of channels to be clustered}
   $k$: the number of channel clusters
2: **Output:** $k$ channel clusters with sizes of $M \times n_1$, $M \times n_2$, ..., $M \times n_k$, where $\sum_{i=1}^{k} n_i = N$
3: **if** $k == N$ **then**
4:   **return** $N$ channel clusters with a size of $M \times 1$
5: **end if**
6: let each channel object ($M \times 1$) be a cluster
7: compute the proximity matrix
8: **repeat**
9:   merge two "closest" clusters based on the linkage criterion
10:   update the proximity matrix
11: **until** $k$ clusters remain
12: **return** $k$ channel clusters with sizes of $M \times n_1$, $M \times n_2$, ..., $M \times n_k$, where $\sum_{i=1}^{k} n_i = N$

As mentioned in Section 5.1, we need deploy a given number of sensors for CL groups. One straightforward way to determine the number of CL groups is to let it be equal to the number of sensors. With a larger number of CL groups, we may not guarantee the coverage requirement; with fewer CL groups, it tends to be a waste of sensor resources, which is undesirable. Provided a number of CL groups, the next question is how to decide the desirable number of channel clusters, and also the desirable number of location clusters for each channel group. There are various ways to probe the true number of clusters, including a model-based approach [16]. In this study, we are more interested in the relationship between the number of indoor sensors and system performance instead of seeking for the true number of channel or location clusters. In our current solution, we permutate all possible numbers of channel clusters, and assign numbers of location clusters to channel clusters that are proportional to sizes of channel clusters. For instance, given 20 CL groups, we may try out 3 (or other possible numbers from 1 to 20) channel clusters, and obtain clusters with sizes of 8, 16 and 16 via channel clustering. Then, we will assign 4, 8 and 8 location clusters to 3 channel clusters accordingly before location clustering. Note that when multiple combinations are possible, WISER will choose the one according to the "least-false-alarm-first" criterion.

**Algorithm 2** Location Clustering

1: **Input:** $S_i$: the $M \times N_i$ channel cluster
   {$M$ is the total number of locations to be clustered, $N_i$ is total number of channels}
   $k_i$: the number of location clusters
2: **Output:** $k_i$ location clusters with sizes of $m_1 \times N_i$, $m_2 \times N_i$, ..., $m_{k_i} \times N_i$, where $\sum_{j=1}^{k_i} m_j = M$
3: **if** $k_i == M$ **then**
4:   **return** $M$ location clusters with the size of $1 \times N_i$
5: **end if**
6: let each location object ($1 \times N_i$) be a cluster
7: compute the proximity matrix
8: **repeat**
9:   merge two "closest" clusters based on the linkage criterion
10:   update the proximity matrix
11: **until** $k_i$ clusters remain
12: **return** $k_i$ location clusters with sizes of $m_1 \times N_i$, $m_2 \times N_i$, ..., $m_{k_i} \times N_i$, where $\sum_{j=1}^{k_i} m_j = M$

The channel clustering algorithm is illustrated in Algorithm 1. As shown in Line 6-7, we let each channel object be its own cluster at the initial stage and compute pair-wise proximity matrix (*i.e.,* Euclidean distance). Then we apply Ward's minimum variance method to merge two "closest" clusters and update the proximity matrix accordingly (Line 9-10). We repeat the process until a required number of clusters is obtained. In case of multiple training data sets as the input, we can extend the dimension of channel objects by treating signal strengths across different locations across different days for a channel as a 2-dimension vector, and perform channel clustering in the same way. One potential advantage of training with multiple data sets is that we can improve clustering accuracy and be robust to noise in individual data sets. The location clustering algorithm (Algorithm 2) is conducted in a similar way, except that we let the vector containing signal strengths in different channels at a location be a location object during the whole process. We find our cluster algorithms achieving decent performance in experiments to be discussed in Section 6. However, they do not necessarily achieve the best possible performance for the problems considered in this study. It would be an interesting direction to consider alternative linkage criteria and similarity metrics in the clustering algorithm design to further improve the performance.

### *5.2.2 Indoor Sensor Placement*

As mentioned in Section 4.5.4, we need to meet coverage and performance requirements in determining sensor location based on the result of channel-location clustering. To avoid brute-force enumeration of indoor sensor locations (*e.g.,* $C_{65}^{N}$ given 65 indoor locations and $N$ indoor sensors), we introduce a greedy sensor placement algorithm as shown in Algorithm 3. Initially, all CL groups are not covered, and all indoor locations are candidates for sensor placement. We rank candidates according to their ranks (Line 5). More details about the ranking algorithm (Algorithm 4) will be illustrated later. In Line 6-12, we check for each candidate one by one, starting from the highest ranking one, whether any not-covered CL groups can be covered if we place one sensor at that location. If yes, we remove the covered CL groups from the not-covered list, add this location to the sensor location pool and repeat the process for the remaining candidate locations; otherwise, we exam the next candidate until a suitable one is found. Our algorithm terminates the while loop (Line 4-13) when all initially not-covered CL groups are covered by at least one sensor. Since one indoor location may belong to different CL groups with respect to different channel groups, it is possible that we are able to cover multiple CL groups by deploying one sensor, and cover all CL groups with fewer sensors. Hence, upon the termination of the while loop, our algorithm guarantees that all CL groups will be covered. If there are still additional quota for sensor locations, we rank remaining candidates again and choose higher-ranking locations consecutively until the expected number of sensor locations is reached (Line 14-17).

**Algorithm 3** Indoor Sensor Placement

1: **Input:** $N$: given sensor quota
2: **Output:** $L$: a set of sensor locations
3: **Initialize:** $L \leftarrow NULL$
4: **while** there are not-covered Channel-Location groups **do**
5: $C \leftarrow$ remaining ranked candidate locations
6: **for** $i = 1$ to length($C$) **do**
7: **if** $C[i]$ can cover any not-covered Channel-Location group **then**
8: $L \leftarrow L + C[i]$
9: $N \leftarrow N - 1$
10: **break**
11: **end if**
12: **end for**
13: **end while**
14: **if** $length(L) < N$ **then**
15: $C \leftarrow$ ranked remaining candidate locations
16: $L \leftarrow$ first $(N - length(L))$ candidates in $C$
17: **end if**
18: **return** $L$

The ranking algorithm is crucial in fulfilling the performance requirement, as illustrated in Algorithm 4. At each stage, we rank candidate locations by comparing their "contribution" to the overall performance, which is quantized in items of evaluated FA rate and WS Loss rate after their individual participation in the current sensor pool. In Line 5-8, we first add a candidate location to existing sensor location pool, and then compute corresponding FA rate and WS Loss rate $f'$ and $w'$. We repeat the process for all candidate locations, and then compare their FA rates and WS Loss rates. By applying the "least-false-alarm-first" criterion, we will finally obtain the desirable ranking for given candidate locations (Line 10).

# 6. PROOF-OF-CONCEPT WISER PROTOTYPE AND EXPERIMENTS

In this section, we deploy a proof-of-concept WISER prototype and conduct actual experiments across four months to evaluate its performance. The WISER prototype takes user indoor positions as inputs, and outputs a list of vacant channels at the positions. Our objectives are: (i) to evaluate the performance of the deployed WISER prototype, and compare it with alternative solutions in a typical indoor scenario; (ii) to demonstrate its ability of providing accurate indoor white space information across a long period of time (in this case four months) and that there is no need to re-configure WISER frequently; (iii) to demonstrate how to choose a suitable number of indoor sensors for the target indoor scenario; (iv) to illustrate the impact of indoor positioning errors on WISER's performance.

**Algorithm 4** Candidate Location Ranking

1: **Input:** $S$:already selected sensor locations, $M$:candidate locations
2: **Output:** $M'$: ranked candidate locations
3: **Initialize:** $F \leftarrow NULL$ {FA rate}, $W \leftarrow NULL$ {WS Loss rate}
4: **for** $i = 1$ to $length(M)$ **do**
5: $S' \leftarrow S + M(i)$
6: $[f', w'] \leftarrow$ evaluated performance for $S'$
7: $F[i] \leftarrow f'$
8: $W[i] \leftarrow w'$
9: **end for**
10: $M' \leftarrow$ ranked $M$ according to $(F, W)$ {Candidate locations with less FA rate (first priority) and less WS Loss rate get higher ranking}
11: **return** $M'$

## 6.1 Scenario and Settings

### *6.1.1 Scenario*

We build a proof-of-concept WISER prototype for one floor of a typical office building to evaluate its performance using actual experiments. As shown in Fig. 2, this scenario contains individual office rooms with various sizes, common rooms of larger sizes, and corridors, all of which are separated by walls or glass. A total of 13 one-time spectrum measurements were taken during the months of October 2012 to March 2013 with the same equipment and procedures as described in Section 2.2.1.

### *6.1.2 Settings*

We set the white space threshold to be -84.5 dBm/8 MHz for digital TV channels and -104.2 dBm/100 KHz for analog channels. To capture real-world outdoor sensing, we perform outdoor long-time sensing for 30 hours by placing the equipment on the rooftop. We observe 5 channels who signal strengths are always far below the white space threshold, and hence treat them as outdoor-sensor-reported white spaces. We also remove 11 long-term strong channels (whose received signal strengths are 10 dB higher than the white space threshold) that have little chance to be white spaces indoors even in the presence of signal attenuation, and focus on tracking the availability of the remaining channels to maximally extract the indoor white space potential.

To ensure the quality of channel-location clustering , we use two sets of one-time profiling data as inputs into the clustering algorithm. We are aware of the potential over-fitting problem in clustering, and with only one one-time profiling data set, the deployed WISER tends to cause severe false alarms in the future prediction. It turns out that WISER can effectively alleviate the potential over-fitting problem by using two data sets. We use the remaining 11 data sets for actual experiments.

## 6.2 Performance Evaluation

For any indoor WS identification system, we are interested in the FA Rate and WS Loss Rate as defined in Section 4.1. The objectives of this experiment are (i) to quantify the performance of our WISER prototype using the above two metrics, (ii) to compare it with the performance of WISER with those of two alter-

| Exp. ID | 1 | 2 | 3 | 4 | 5 | 6 | 7 | 8 | 9 | 10 | 11 | Avg. |
|---|---|---|---|---|---|---|---|---|---|---|---|---|
| **Extra White Space (%)** | 30.14 | 44.99 | 37.79 | 34.20 | 31.76 | 50.37 | 39.62 | 35.51 | 35.20 | 40.00 | 43.40 | 38.47 |
| **WISER False Alarm Rate (%)** | 0.16 | 0.23 | 0.14 | 0.15 | 0 | 1.08 | 1.09 | 0 | 0.15 | 0.41 | 0.50 | 0.36 |

Table 2: Extra white spaces and FA rate achieved by our WISER prototype as compared to the OS-Only approach in eleven experiments across four months.

natives OS-Only and OTP-Only discussed in Section 4.1, and (iii) to demonstrate WISER's ability to providing accurate white space information in a long period of time.

In this experiment, the WISER prototype consists of a total of 20 indoor sensors and one outdoor sensor. OTP-Only labels channels at each location as 0 (occupied) or 1 (available) based on one of the training data sets for the WISER prototype, and use this information to report white spaces in the future. We assume perfect indoor positioning accuracy at this stage and will study the impact of indoor positioning errors in Section 6.4.

We have several observations. First, as shown in Table 2, our WISER prototype is able to identify 30-50% more white spaces with negligible average FA rate (*i.e.,* 0.36%) as compared to OS-Only. Fig. 8a shows that OTP-Only is not suitable for identifying indoor white spaces in long term due to its unacceptable false alarm rate, and WISER outperforms OS-Only as shown in Fig. 8b. Second, WISER is able to provide accurate indoor white space information with negligible false alarms across a long period of time – four months in our experiments. Note that as WISER is built on channel-location correlations that are determined by surrounding environments, such as building structures, nearby buildings, *etc.*, it needs to be re-calibrated when environment changes substantially (*e.g.,* a skyscraper is built nearby). Although WISER may give a FA rate of 1% occasionally, one can systematically lower WISER's FA rate by using more training data sets as inputs and using more conservative signal strength threshold in determining white spaces. We believe that our principled design behind WISER is general and does not depend on particular choices of system design parameters and inputs.

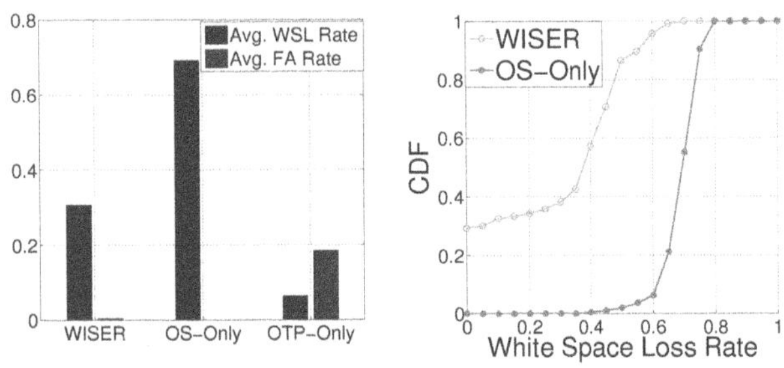


(a) (b)

Figure 8: (a) Averaged FA rate and WS Loss rate for WISER, OS-Only and OTP-Only. The FA rate is 18.53% for OTP-Only, which may cause severe interference to primary users. As compared to OS-Only, WISER is able to report 38% more white spaces on average with negligible false alarm rate. (b) Averaged CDF curves of WS Loss rate for WISER and OS-Only. With OS-Only, 90% locations would suffer a WS Loss rate of 60%. This number is <5% if using WISER. Note that we excluded OTP-Only from this comparison, as OTP-Only will result in high FA rate despite of its seeming high WS Loss rate, which makes itself undesired in the first place. Also, we did not plot the CDF curves for the FA rate for WISER and OS-Only, as both of them result in negligible FA rate and their CDF curves for the FA rate are not very informative.

## 6.3 Number of Indoor Sensors to Use in WISER

For a specific indoor scenario, it is important to balance between WISER performance and the sensor cost. To understand their relationship, we vary the number of indoor sensors during WISER deployment and evaluate WISER performance in actual experiments under the same setting.

As shown in Fig. 9, the WS Loss rate and FA rate decrease accordingly with more sensors. Note that the average FA rate drops to 0.4% when there are over 18 indoor sensors and remain rather low afterwards. To meet certain safety requirement (*e.g.,* less than 0.4% average FA rate in this example), the optimal number of indoor sensors would be 18; if the worst-case FA rate needs to be lower than 1.0%, WISER requires a minimum of 20 indoor sensors. In practice, we would jointly consider safety, efficiency and sensor cost to determine the optimal number of indoor sensors required. It also implies that for a typical indoor scenario, we could conduct multiple sets of one-time profiling, using some of them for WISER deployment and others for probing the suitable sensor number.

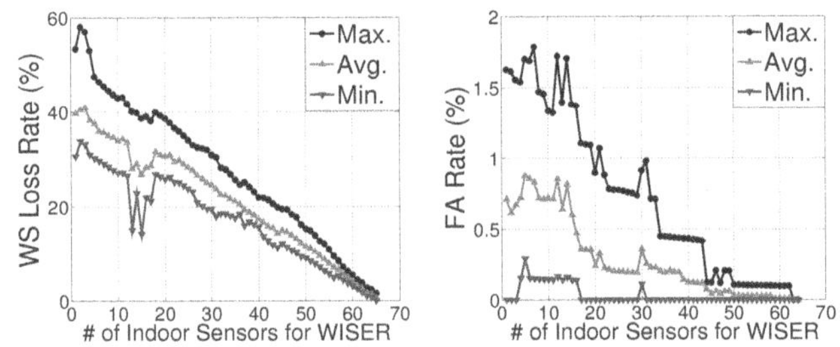


(a) (b)

Figure 9: (a) The average, minimum (best-case), and maximum (worse-case) WS Loss rate v.s. the number of indoor sensors. The more indoor sensors are used, the lower WS Loss rate WISER is able to achieve. (b) The average, minimum (best-case), and maximum (worst-case) FA rate v.s. the number of indoor sensors. The FA rate tends to be high with fewer indoor sensors used, and gets lower when the number of indoor sensors increases. The average rate becomes stable when there are more than 18 indoor sensors.

## 6.4 Impact of Indoor Positioning Errors

Previous experiments show that WISER has good performance if the indoor positioning is accurate. In practice, indoor positioning may incur errors. Therefore, it is important to evaluate the performance of our WISER prototype in the presence of indoor positioning errors.

Ideally, WISER returns the accurate indoor WS information at the user's position that is determined by the indoor positioning system without any false alarms. However, due to positioning errors, the user could appear in anywhere within the circle that is centered at the reported position with a radius of a certain positioning error (in meter). Positioning errors are problematic as they can manifest themselves in terms of both white space loss and (even worse) false alarms. To avoid false alarms, WISER returns the commonly

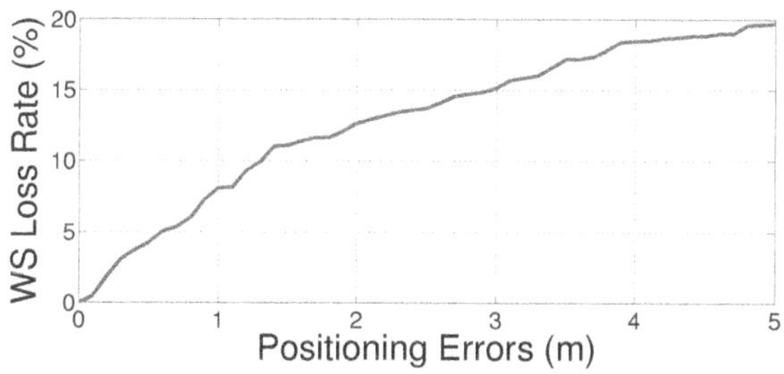


Figure 10: Additional WS Loss rate (averaged) introduced by indoor positioning errors. The WISER prototype consists of 20 indoor sensors and one outdoor sensor.

available channels within the circle, which would result in an additional loss of white spaces. In this way, indoor positioning errors will not result in additional false alarms. To quantify this impact of positioning errors, we compute WS Loss rates of WISERs with and without positioning errors respectively, and measure this additional loss against the positioning error. We show the average case for the 65 locations in Fig. 10. Note that with a positioning error of 5 meters, we would incur an average of 20% additional WS loss. To ensure the efficiency of WISER, the indoor positioning system should incur positioning error less than a couple of meters.

# 7. RELATED WORK

Existing works on TV White Space mostly focus on outdoor scenarios. These works include setting up a single Wi-Fi like AP system [10], implementing a network system for dynamic spectrum access [14, 37], and designing a prototype system for spectrum sensing [11]. In this paper, we develop a white space identification system for indoor scenarios where outdoor solutions do not perform well. We first carry out a large-scale measurement of outdoor and indoor white spaces, and then design WISER based on our observations. In fact, several measurement studies have investigated the opportunity for using white spaces in outdoor environments. Some of them focus on metropolitan cities including Chicago [26, 34], Singapore [20] and Guangzhou [13]. However, those measurements are limited in scope, whereas our outdoor measurement is a large-scale one that better capture the spectrum occupancy patterns across the entire city. Meanwhile, there are existing works focus on quantitative analysis on the availability of white spaces. In [29], the authors provide a theoretical analysis on the spectrum opportunity of TV white spaces in United Kingdom. [21] investigates the UHF white spaces in 11 Europe countries via an estimated methodology. Both the measurements and quantitative results show that there exists abundant white space spectrum in those cities. Different from their quantitative analysis based on propagation models or coverage maps, we base our analysis on more accurate local spectrum measurements.

As spectrum sensing is no longer compulsory due to sensing efficacy, the FCC mandated the use of a geo-location service at a given location [2]. The geo-location approach has been widely studied [15, 18, 25, 28]. These works use databases to store dynamic white space information for clients querying. However, in metropolitan cities, such as Hong Kong, wireless environment tends to be more complicated due to blocking effects of high density buildings and uneven distribution of TV towers in Hong Kong [36]. Actually, by comparing calculated results using different models and ground-truth measurements, the model-based approach fails to identify many vacant TV channels, and local spectrum measurements may obtain more accurate white space availability results. In [19], the authors investigate the white space availability in a different perspective. They quantify the white space availability in terms of pollution from existing television stations and self-interference, as well as the expected transmission rage of white space devices.

Although 70% of spectrum demand comes from indoors [12], there is little prior work on indoor white space availability. In [30], the authors assess the feasibility of white space devices in short-range indoor environment with focus on interference mechanisms. In [31], the authors perform a series of measurements in both laboratory and real environments to verify an indoor TV white space opportunity prediction model. They both focus on how to utilize indoor white spaces instead of how to identify them. An evaluation of spectrum availability in both indoor and outdoor environments is presented in [35]. The authors perform local spectrum sensing in the band from 20 MHz to 3 GHz on the rooftop and in a room of an office building, and confirm that considerably less occupancy was measured. In [27], an experimental spectrum sensor test-bed is built to investigate indoor radio environmental map, and it is recognized to be extremely challenging unless sophisticated conditions are considered. In this paper we analyze the temporal and spatial characteristics of indoor white spaces, and propose an innovative system to identify additional indoor white spaces.

# 8. CONCLUSIONS AND FUTURE WORK

White spaces promise to provide additional spectrum for wireless applications. However, the current rulings in the US and Canada (and being considered elsewhere), use a geo-location database to determine spectrum availability, which although works reasonably well, has severe limitations in both outdoor and indoor settings.

In this paper, we carry out a measurement-driven approach to explore white space networking potential in Hong Kong, with the focus on indoor environments. We show that the indoor white spaces have different characteristics from the outdoor ones. For example, there are more contiguous unutilized TV channels indoors, which are able to support high bandwidth communication. We then propose a system, called WISER, that is able to utilize the additional white space channels without requiring the clients to actually sense the wireless medium. Our system is incrementally deployable. Any interested building can adopt our techniques to make the building "white space enhanced" and utilize the additionally available vacant TV channels.

There are several interesting and important future directions that could be explored. First, it would be very interesting to extend our 2-dimensional system design, deployment and experiments to 3-dimensional (*i.e.*, from one floor to multiple floors in the building) by jointly exploring channel, location and space correlations. Second, it is also important to evaluate WISER's performance on different test-beds (*e.g.*, halls, residential buildings, *etc.*) other than office buildings. Third, it is also interesting to improve the indoor sensor placement by taking into account of "hotpot" locations with human activities.

## Acknowledgements

We would like to thank Wei Zhang, for his help with clustering analysis, and our shepherd, Moustafa Youssef, for helpful comments in improving the presentation of the paper. In addition, we are grateful to the anonymous reviewers for their insightful comments. The work described in this paper was partially supported by National Basic Research Program of China (Project No. 2012CB315904 and 2013CB336700) and several grants from the University Grants Committee of the Hong Kong Special Administrative Region, China (Area of Excellence Grant Project No. AoE/E-02/08 and General Research Fund Project No. 411010 and 411011).

## 9. REFERENCES


[1] Districts of hong kong. http://en.wikipedia.org/wiki/Districts_of_Hong_Kong.

[2] Fcc frees up vacant tv airwaves for "super wi-fi" technologies and other technologies. http://www.fcc.gov/sptf/reports.html.

[3] Gnu radio. http://gnuradio.org/redmine/projects/gnuradio/wiki.

[4] Hong kong digital terrestrial tv coverage & reception database. http://app1.ofca.gov.hk/apps/ubs/map.asp.

[5] Location of the digital terrestial television (dtt) stations and the estimated coverage in hong kong. http://www.digitaltv.gov.hk/general/pdf/coverage.pdf.

[6] Second memorandum opinion and order. http://hraunfoss.fcc.gov/edocs_public/attachmatch/FCC-10-174A1.pdf.

[7] Television broadcasting network of hong kong. http://www.ofca.gov.hk/filemanager/ofca/common/industry/broadcasting/television/free_tv/tvbnet.pdf.

[8] Tv white space geolocation database. http://ieee802.org/19/pub/Workshop/5_Gibson-ComSearch.pdf.

[9] Universal software radio peripheral. http://www.ettus.com.

[10] P. Bahl, R. Chandra, T. Moscibroda, R. Murty, and M.Welsh. White space networking with wi-fi like connectivity. In *Proc. of ACM SIGCOMM*, 2009.

[11] R. Balamurthi, H. Joshi, C. Nguyen, A. Sadek, S. Shellhammer, and C. Shen. A tv white space spectrum sensing prototype. In *Proc. of IEEE DySPAN*, 2011.

[12] V. Chandrasekhar, J. Andrews, and A. Gatherer. Femtocell networks: a survey. *Communications Magazine, IEEE*, 46(9):59 –67, september 2008.

[13] D. Chen, S. Yin, Q. Zhang, M. Liu, and S. Li. Mining spectrum usage data: a large-scale spectrum measurement study. In *Proc. of ACM MOBICOM*, 2009.

[14] S. Deb, V. Srinivasan, and R. Maheshwar. Dynamic spectrum access in dtv whitespaces: Design rules, architecture and algorithms. In *Proc. of ACM MOBICOM*, 2009.

[15] X. Feng, J. Zhang, and Q. Zhang. Database-assisted multi-ap network on tv white spaces: Architecture, spectrum allocation and ap discovery. In *Proc. of IEEE DySPAN*, 2011.

[16] C. Fraley and A. E. Raftery. How many clusters? which clustering method? answers via model-based cluster analysis. *The Computer Journal*, 41(8):578–588, 1998.

[17] Y. Gu, A. Lo, and I. Niemegeers. A survey of indoor positioning systems for wireless personal networks. *Communications Surveys Tutorials, IEEE*, 11(1):13 –32, quarter 2009.

[18] D. Gurney, G. Buchwald, L. Ecklund, S.Kuffner, and J.Grosspietsch. Geo-location database techniques for incumbent protection in the tv. In *Proc. of IEEE DySPAN*, 2008.

[19] K. Harrison, S.M. Mishra, and A.Sahai. How much white-space capacity is there. In *Proc. of IEEE DySPAN*, 2010.

[20] M. Islam, C. Koh, S. Oh, X. Qing, Y. Lai, C. Wang, Y. Liang, B. Toh, F. Chin, G. Tan, and W. Toh. Spectrum survey in singapore: Occupancy measurements and analyses. In *Cognitive Radio Oriented Wireless Networks and Communications, CrownCom 2008.*, 2008.

[21] V.D. Jaap, R. Janne, A. Andreas, and M.Petri. Uhf white space in europe: a quantitative study into the potential of the 470-790 mhz band. In *Proc. IEEE DySPAN*. IEEE, 2011.

[22] P. Jallon. An algorithm for detection of dvb-t signals based on their second-order statistics. *EURASIP Journal on Wireless Communications and Networking*, 2008:28, 2008.

[23] J. Jr. Hierarchical grouping to optimize an objective function. *Journal of the American statistical association*, 58(301):236–244, 1963.

[24] N. Klepeis, W.Nelson, and W.Ott. The national human activity pattern survey (nhaps): A resource for assessing exposure to environmental pollutants. *Journal of Exposure Analysis and Environmental Epidemiology*, 11:231–252, 2001.

[25] D. Makris, G. Gardikis, and A. Kourtis. Quantifying tv white space capacity: A geolocation-based approach. In *IEEE Communications Magazine: Topics in Radio Communications*. IEEE, 2012.

[26] M. McHenry, P. Tenhula, D. McCloskey, D. Roberson, and C. Hood. Chicago spectrum occupancy measurements & analysis and a long-term studies proposal. In *Proc. of the first international workshop on Technology and policy for accessing spectrum*. ACM, 2006.

[27] E. Meshkova, J. Ansari, D. Denkovski, J. Riihijarvi, J.Nasreddine, M.Pavloski, L.Gavrilovska, and P.Mahonen. Experimental spectrum sensor testbed for constructing indoor radio environmental maps. In *Proc. of IEEE DySPAN*, 2011.

[28] R. Murty, R. Chandra, T. Moscibroda, and P. Bahl. Senseless: A database-driven white spaces network. In *Proc. of IEEE DySPAN*, 2011.

[29] M. Nekovee. Quantifying the availability of tv white spaces for cognitive radio operation in the uk. In *Proc. IEEE ICC Workshop: Cognitive Wireless Networks and Systems*. IEEE, 2009.

[30] E. Obregon and J. Zander. Short range white space utilization in broadcast systems for indoor environment. In *Proc. of IEEE DySPAN*, 2010.

[31] R. Obregon, L. Shi, J. Ferrer, and J. Zander. Experimental verification of indoor tv white space opportunity prediction model. In *IEEE CROWNCOM*. IEEE, 2010.

[32] Office of the Communications Authority. Hong kong table of freqency allocaitons. Technical report, Office of the Communications Authority, 2012.

[33] W.M. Rand. Objective criteria for the evaluation of clustering methods. *Journal of the American Statistical Association*, 66(336):846–850, 1971.

[34] T. Taher, R. Bacchus, K. Zdunek, and D. Roberson. Long-term spectral occupancy findings in chicago. In *Proc. IEEE DySPAN*, pages 100–107. IEEE, 2011.

[35] M. Wellens, J. Wu, and P. Mahonen. Evaluation of spectrum occupancy in indoor and outdoor scenario in the context of cognitive radio. In *Cognitive Radio Oriented Wireless Networks and Communications*, 2007.

[36] L. Yan and M. Chen. Exploring white spaces in metropolises: A measurement study in hong kong. Technical report, The Chinese University of Hong Kong, 2011.

[37] L. Yang, W. Hou, L. Cao, B. Zhao, and H. Zheng. Supporting demanding wireless applications with frequency-agile radios. In *Proc. of ACM NSDI*, 2010.

# CSpy: Finding the Best Quality Channel without Probing

Souvik Sen
HP Labs

Božidar Radunović
Microsoft Research

Jeongkeun Lee
HP Labs

Kyu-Han Kim
HP Labs

## ABSTRACT

Wireless performance depends directly on the quality of the channel. A wireless transmitter can improve its performance by estimating and transmitting on only the strongest channel, which can be of significantly higher quality than a weak channel (yielding up to 100% rate improvement). It is considered impossible to predict the quality of the unseen channels. Thus, the only way to identify the strongest channel is by probing each channel individually, incurring large overheads. The key contribution of this paper is a discovery of previously unobserved properties of the wireless channel that makes it possible to predict the the strongest of a set of channels from the measurements collected *only on a single channel*. We confirm the properties through measurements and present a theoretical analysis that explains their nature. Our proposed system, *CSpy*, utilizes these observations to predict the strongest channel. CSpy is the first to reliably estimate the strongest channel by utilizing channel responses extracted from off-the-shelf wireless chipsets, without probing any additional channels. By tracking the strongest channel, CSpy improves performance by up to 100% in comparison to channel agnostic schemes.

## Categories and Subject Descriptors

C.2.1 [**Network Architecture and Design**]: Wireless communication

## General Terms

Algorithm, Design, Experimentation, Performance

## Keywords

Wireless, Cross-Layer, Channel Estimation

## 1. INTRODUCTION

There has been extensive research towards improving wireless performance using both link layer (scheduling, coordination, rate-control) and physical layer (MIMO, coding, beamforming) innovations. Most of these techniques try to achieve the highest performance that can be obtained under a given channel condition. However, wireless performance is ultimately limited by the quality of the channel that the link is operating on. The channel qualities vary significantly across the frequency band [1–3]. E.g., a few of the 21 available channels in the 5GHz band may be strong, and the others weak. TV whitespaces can provide more opportunities, with up to 40 available channels [4]. Due to environmental changes and user mobility, the qualities of these channels vary over time and *across channels*. We find that the quality of the strongest channel can be significantly better than the weakest, or even an average channel. Thus, it is possible to improve the wireless performance if we can successfully track and communicate on the strongest channel at all times.

Wireless signals traverse multiple paths before arriving at the receiver. The signals traversing different paths undergo different attenuations, delays and phase shifts. The phase shifts are further affected by the carrier frequency. The channel qualities at different frequencies thus depend on how different complex multipath signal components combine at the receiver. Due to the phase shift induced by the carrier frequency, signals from some paths that add constructively at one frequency may combine destructively at another frequency. Because of a large number of paths in a multi-path channel and a limited resolution of the receivers, it is considered impossible to predict the quality of any channels other than the ones being observed. This is why all of the existing channel estimation algorithms (e.g. [1, 5, 6]) use channel probing to identify the *Strongest Channel Index (SCI)*[1]. But probing is expensive. Moreover, identifying the strongest channel is not a one time operation and tracking the strongest channel will require frequent channel probes, incurring a very high overhead.

In this paper we present a novel technique that allows us to *determine the strongest channel from a set of channels while probing only a single channel from the set*. We first present extensive channel measurements showing that links at different locations with the same strongest channel index exhibit similarities in their multi-path structures. This is surprising, given that channels at different locations are typically assumed independent [7, 8]. We then analyse the observed correlation under a well-known Saleh-Valenzuela (SV) channel model [9]

[1]We define strongest channel index as the channel which yields the highest expected throughput across all available channels.


*MobiCom'13*, September 30–October 4, Miami, FL, USA.

and show how to construct a simple estimator that can provably determine on average the strongest of the two adjacent channels. This analysis also helps us identify the intrinsic characteristics of the channel that make the prediction possible. However, even constructing such a simple estimator of SCI was not obvious. We thus turn to machine learning techniques to help us automatically learn the best estimator using a training set of observed channel. We find that the the performance of the machine learning estimator improves as it is trained with diverse set of environments, e.g., indoors vs. outdoors. However, it is possible to infer the strongest channel with up to 80% accuracy using our approach, without probing any additional channel. Further, by using the strongest channel, wireless performance can be improved by up to 100%.

Translating the above key ideas to a real system entails a host of technical challenges. First, how are various channel profiles in practice, in different real-world environments, amenable for prediction? Second, is it possible to determine the strongest channel even if it is far away from the current operating channel? Third, how do we deal with mobile scenarios where the channel can change frequently? In such mobile scenarios, even if it is possible to find the SCI on a per-packet basis, tracking the strongest channel may incur prohibitive channel switching costs.

To address the above questions, we present a system called *CSpy*. To the best of our knowledge, CSpy is the first system that is able to predict the best channel without probing. We show that CSpy performs well under realistic channel conditions, providing significant performance gains over channel agnostic approaches and no channel probing overhead. Moreover, we leverage physical layer information to estimate the coherence time of the channel, and trigger channel switching only if estimated SCI can be used for reasonable duration. Also, note that inferring the strongest channel index is orthogonal to detecting the least used channel [10–12]. Ideally, both should be combined (as in e.g. [13]), but this is out of scope of our current work. The main contributions of this paper are as follows:

- **A measurement study to understand the channel quality across the 5GHz frequency band in a typical office environment.** We find that the achievable throughput gain by tracking the strongest channel, compared to fixed channel strategies, can be substantial (up to 100%). The channels with the same SCI resemble to each other while they differ from channels with different SCIs.
- **A theoretical analysis on the effect of multi-path on channel inferring capability.** We prove that even with limited multipath information from a single 20MHz channel, it is possible to determine the strongest amongst the adjacent channels in a typical indoor environment.
- **A learning based approach to determine the strongest channel by utilizing the channel responses extracted from off-the-shelf WiFi chipsets.** We extract the multipath information from commodity chipsets, and utilize it to determine the strongest channel index.
- **A demonstration of performance gains.** We implement CSpy algorithms in our test-bed, and quantify our gains for various scenarios. We show that we can predict the SCI among 5 adjacent channels on each side achieving 85% throughput of the optimal "oracle" algorithm, and yielding around 50% gain in rates over an average channel, and up to 2.5x gain over the worst channel.

The subsequent sections expand on each of these contributions, including controlled measurements, followed by analysis, design, and evaluation.

## 2. MULTIPATH CHANNEL RESPONSE

We start with a quick primer on channel response, how it affects the link quality and why it is difficult to predict it.

**Channel impulse response (CIR):** The wireless signal from the transmitter to the receiver traverses through multiple paths, undergoing reflections, diffractions, and scattering. Essentially, the received signal contains multiple time-delayed, attenuated, and phase-shifted copies of the original signal. If $x(t)$ is the transmitted signal at time $t$, and $h(t,\tau)$ captures the *Channel Impulse Response (CIR)* at time $t$ to an impulse transmitted at time $t-\tau$, the received signal is [7]:

$$y(t) = \int_{-\infty}^{\infty} h(\tau)x(t-\tau)d\tau + w(t), \tag{1}$$

where $w(t)$ is additive white noise. The channel impulse response $h$ can be considered time-invariant during the packet duration (thus we drop the dependency on $t$), and is defined as:

$$h(\tau) = \sum_{p=0}^{P-1} A(p)\delta(\tau - \tau(p)), \tag{2}$$

where $A(p) = a(p)e^{i\phi(p)}$ is a complex response of path $p$, $P$ is the (very large) number of paths between the transmitter and the receiver and $a(p), \phi(p), \tau(p)$ are the attenuation, phase and delay of the signal traversing on path $p$. The Fourier transform $H(f) = \mathscr{F}(h(t))$ of CIR is often called the *Channel Frequency Response (CFR)*. An equivalent of (1) in frequency domain is

$$Y(f) = X(f)H(f), \tag{3}$$

where $Y(f) = \mathscr{F}(y(t))$ and $X(f) = \mathscr{F}(x(t))$ are Fourier transform of the received and transmitted signal, respectively.

**Extracting channel information from commodity chipsets:** Most modern digital radios use OFDM communication, and transmit signals across orthogonal subcarriers at different frequencies. An OFDM receiver implementation includes a channel estimation logic in the hardware as a part of basic operations. Some WiFi chipsets, such as Atheros 9390, can export the estimated discrete CFR to the driver. Let $f_c$ be the carrier frequency of channel $c$, $W$ be the bandwidth of the radio and $n$ be the number of subcarriers. In most 802.11 a/g/n receivers, we have $W = 20$ MHz and $n = 64$. The reported discrete CFR $\hat{\mathbf{H}}^c = [H(f_c - W/2), H(f_c - W/2+1), \cdots, H(f_c - W/2+n-1)]$ is a complex vector that describes the quality of channel $c$ at each subcarrier. Figure 1 shows examples of a few discrete CFR vectors.

The channel impulse response $\hat{\mathbf{h}}^c = \mathscr{D}^{-1}\hat{\mathbf{H}}^c$ can be obtained by applying an inverse (fast) discrete Fourier transform on the CFR. By applying the aforementioned transforms we get

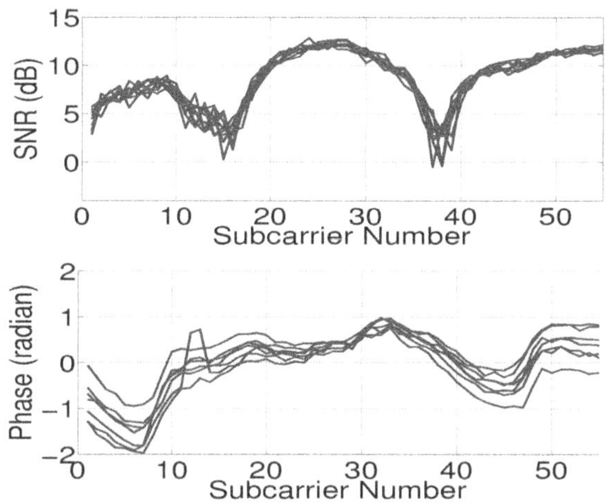


**Figure 1: Magnitude (top) and phase (below) of CFR reported for $10$ consecutive packets.**

a discrete CIR $\hat{\mathbf{h}}^c$ with $n$ number of taps:

$$\hat{\mathbf{h}}^c = [\hat{h}^c[0], \ldots, \hat{h}^c[n]] \; where$$

$$\hat{h}^c[l] = \frac{1}{P} \sum_{p=0}^{P-1} A(p) e^{-2\pi(f_c - W/2)\tau(p))} \frac{1-e^{-i2\pi W \tau(p)}}{1-e^{i2\pi(l/n - W\tau(p)/n)}}. \quad (4)$$

Intuitively, $\hat{h}^c[l]$ approximately aggregates the effects of paths $p$ with $\tau(p) \in [l/W, (l+1)/W]$. Figure 2 shows an example of a discrete CIR vector. Note from (4) that $\hat{\mathbf{h}}^c$ changes with the carrier frequency $f_c$, since it is a sum of complex vectors whose phase shift depends on the carrier frequency.

**Difficulty of predicting the quality of unseen channels:** Our goal is to predict a performance of an unseen channel $c'$ using an observed discrete CIR $\hat{\mathbf{h}}^c$ from a different channel $c \neq c'$. We will now argue that it is impossible to do so without assuming some structure on the amplitude $a(p)$ and phase $\phi(p)$ of each individual path. To see that, consider the system of equations (4) jointly for channels $c$ and $c'$. This system has $2n$ equations and $P$ unknown complex variables $A(p)$. Because the number of paths $P$ is very large (c.f. [9]), much larger than the number of subcarriers $n$, this system is underdetermined and has infinitely many solutions. Thus, there exists a set of values for $\{a(p), \phi(p)\}_{p=0,\cdots,P-1}$ that would achieve any discrete CIRs $\hat{\mathbf{h}}^c$ and $\hat{\mathbf{h}}^{c'}$ in channels $c$ and $c'$. Without some assumption on the channel *we are not able to infer anything about channel $c'$ only by observing channel $c$.* In reality, the channel $\{a(p), \phi(p)\}_{p=0,\cdots,P-1}$ has some structure which we will exploit. In the subsequent section we will first show that we can indeed make some prediction about unseen channels and in Section 4 we will explain why it works.

**Metric for determining channel quality:** Channel quality can be measured by the per-packet SNR metric that 802.11 drivers usually provide in the form of Received (or Relative) Signal Strength Indicator (RSSI). However RSSI is known to be an unreliable indicator of channel quality [14–16]. In search of a better metric, we find that the effective SNR (eSNR) value, as described in [14] can correctly capture the quality of the channel from the CFR. eSNR first uses the CFR to compute the SNR and bit-error rate (BER) of each subcarrier. From the subcarrier-specific BER, a channel-wide BER is computed and translated into eSNR. eSNR can further be used to determine the highest bit-rate that the channel can support. As shown in [14], eSNR can estimate the correct bit-rate of the channel with great accuracy, and performs significantly better than the per-packet SNR metric. Out of all the available channels in the 5GHz frequency band, we define the strongest channel index (SCI) as the channel that supports the highest bit-rate. We also adjust for link layer overheads (using [17]) to calculate the *Expected Throughput* of a channel from the bit-rate prescribed by the eSNR metric. In the rest of our paper we use the eSNR-based expected throughput metric to compare the throughput of the different channels from their CFR vectors.

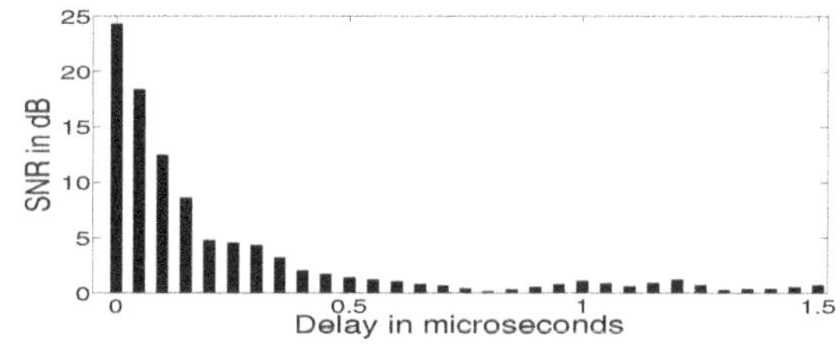


**Figure 2: Amplitude of a part of a CIR vector obtained from a CFR after applying IFFT.**

# 3. MEASUREMENT AND HYPOTHESES

This section aims to show that PHY layer CIR information can be an indicator of the strongest channel. We also demonstrate that tracking the strongest channel can indeed improve the network performance. We present three main hypotheses if CIRs from a single channel can be used to infer the strongest channel:

1. *The quality of the channel varies across frequency.* Wireless performance can be significantly improved by identifying and tracking the strongest channel, in comparison to a random fixed channel.
2. *Links with the same strongest channel shares some statistical similarity in their multipath structure.* It is possible to identify some features from the CIR information that can indicate the SCI.
3. *Links with different strongest channel index exhibits different multipath characteristics.*

To verify our hypotheses, we first describe our experimental methodology, followed by the key findings.

## 3.1 Measurement Setup

Our initial experiments were conducted at $10$ locations in an office building. We use laptops equipped with Atheros 9390 WiFi card operating on the 5GHz frequency spectrum as transmitters and receivers. We instrument the Atheros 9390 driver to extract the CFR information on a per-packet basis. The Atheros firmware exports a subset of the CFR (56 out of 64 subcarriers), and we only use these to compute the CIR. Although there are 21 available channels in the 5GHz frequency band, the Atheros 9390 driver is not Dynamic Frequency Selection (DFS) enabled [18] and hence can operate on only $9$ of the 21 available channels. Hence, we perform experiments on channel indices $36 - 48$ and $149 - 165$ only.

We design experiments to measure the quality of all the $9$ available channels at 5GHz. We make necessary driver modifications at both the transmitter and the receiver to cycle

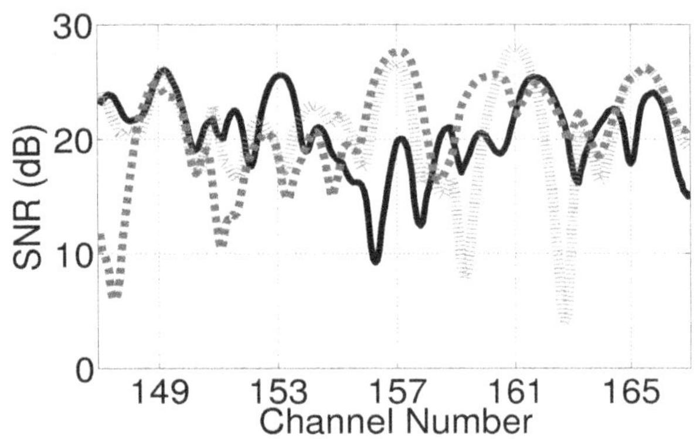


**Figure 3: Magnitude of CFR vectors collected from channels $149-165$.**

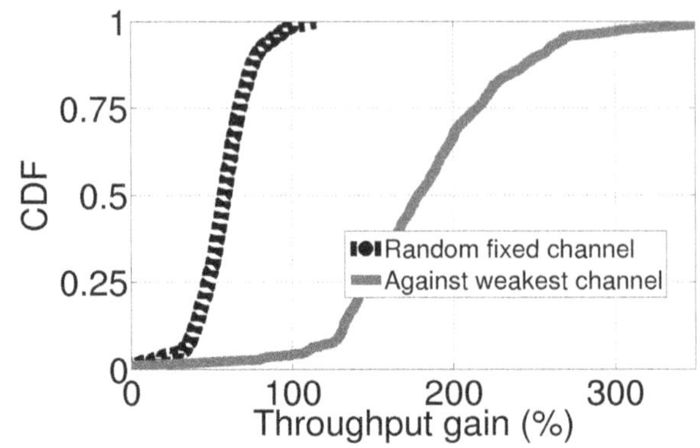


**Figure 4: Distribution of expected throughput gain by using the strongest channel.**

through the channels. The transmitter starts from channel 36 at 5GHz and transmits 10 short packets, before switching onto the next channel. To maintain synchronization, the receiver also follows the same predefined sequence. Due to software restrictions, a single round takes considerable amount of time – approximately 70ms. To ascertain no arbitrary multipath changes within a single round, we consider only those measurements where the channel characteristics were highly correlated across two consecutive rounds. We use the measurements to verify our key hypotheses in the following subsection.

## 3.2 Measurement and Verification

**Hypothesis 1:** *The quality of the channel varies across frequency.*

The CFR vectors, collected from a single round of transmissions, provide a snapshot of the characteristics of the channels across all the available frequencies in the 5GHz band. Figure 3 shows 3 such snapshots of 5 different channels. We observe that the CFRs across different frequencies are quite dissimilar. To understand how the wireless performance may vary across different channels, we compute the expected throughput from the CFRs. Figure 4 plots the difference between the expected throughput of the strongest channel over the weakest and a random fixed channel. Evidently, the performance gap is considerably large. On average, the expected throughput of the strongest channel is almost $2-3$ times than that of the weakest channel. Thus, we conclude that *the channel quality varies significantly across frequency. If we can identify the strongest channel, wireless performance will improve significantly.*

**Impact of temporal variations:** Channel quality can change over time due to environmental changes. Figure 5(a) illustrates the performance of a single link across 5 different channels over a duration of 50 seconds. A single channel demonstrates gradual but significant throughput variations due to the slow fading caused by environmental variations. We find that the performance also varies widely across channels. The quality of a channel depends on how the different multipath components combine at its operating frequency. As the environment changes, the multipath structure of the signal also changes. The multipath components may combine constructively at one frequency and destructively on another, while over time, the multipath structure can change in such a way that the previously stronger channel becomes weaker and vice versa. Thus, we find that the strongest channel index also changes over time (figure 5(b)). *It is not enough to identify the strongest channel only once, we need to track it to maximize performance.*

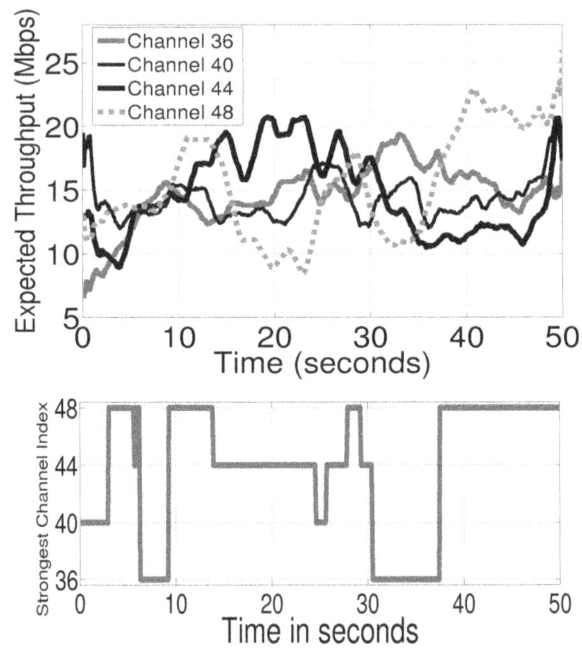


**Figure 5: (a) The expected throughput of a particular link for different channels. (b) SCI changes over time.**

**Hypotheses 2:** *Links with the same strongest channel shares some statistical similarity in their multipath structure.*

The channel quality depends on the multipath characteristics observed at a location. If at some instance, two links have similar multipath characteristics, they will also probably have the same strongest channel. To verify this hypotheses, let group $G_{i,j}$ contain all the CIRs collected from channel number $i$ when the SCI was $j$. In other words, each group contains CIRs from the same channel, but collected at different times and locations, such that the SCI was the same at those instances. According to our hypotheses the CIRs belonging to the same group should be similar to each other. We find the similarity between two CIRs, $a$ and $b$, by using the the cross correlation metric:

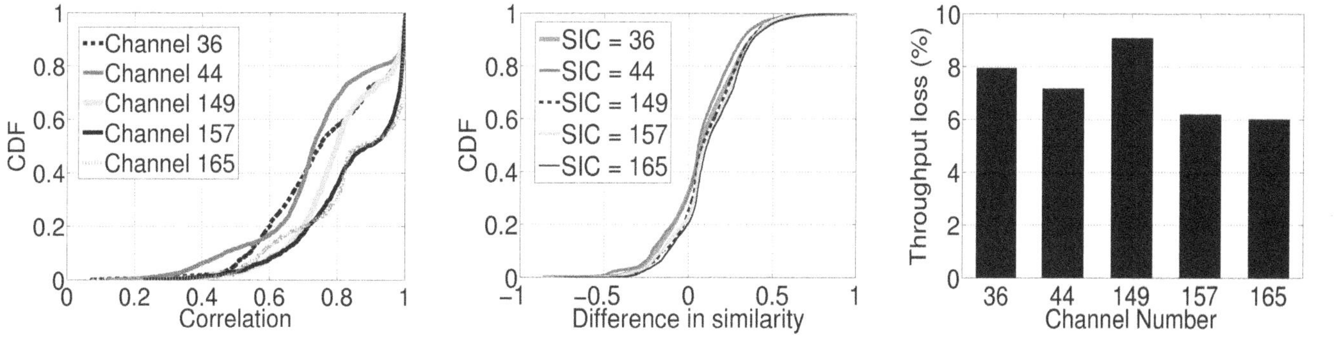


**Figure 6: (a) Similarity between the CIRs gathered from channel 36 at different locations when the SCI was the same. (b) CDF of difference in similarities $C_{own} - C_{others}$, observed at different locations, for different SCI values. (c) Throughput loss due to mispredicting the SCI.**

$$c(\mathbf{a}, \mathbf{b}) = \frac{\sum_s a_s b_s}{\sqrt{\sum_s a_s^2}\sqrt{\sum_s b_s^2}}. \tag{5}$$

Figure 6(a) shows that CIRs from the same group have high correlation, suggesting that the same SCI may imply similar multipath structure. If we can apriori learn some unique features about the multipath, we may be able to infer the SCI by observing the CIR from a single channel. Our observation in figure 6(a) may appear coincidental. However we will explain in section 4 why it may be possible to identify such differentiating features about the multipah at all.

**Hypotheses 3:** *Links with different strongest channel index exhibits different multipath characteristics.*

We evaluate the (dis)similarity between two groups of CIRs that were collected from the same channel but had a different SCI. Whenever a CIR from a group $G_{i,j}$, is more similar to the CIRs of a different group, $G_{i,k}|_{k \neq j}$, than those from its own group, we will mispredict the strongest channel. To evaluate the probability of such mispredictions, we arbitrarily choose a test CIR from a group $G_{i,j}$, and use correlation to find the similarity between the test CIR with a randomly chosen CIR from the same group. The correlation value, denoted as $C_{own}$, indicates *similarity* of a sample test CIR with responses which have the same SCI. Now, for the CIRs from all other groups, $G_{i,k}|_{k \neq j}$, we find the *similarity* of a randomly chosen CIR with the test CIR – we denote this similarity as $C_{others}$. If a test CIR is more similar to a different group than its own group, we will naturally misclassify its SCI.

Figure 6(b) plots the CDF of the difference in similarities, $C_{own} - C_{others}$, for 5 different strongest channels. If the difference is negative, then the SCI is likely to be misclassified. We find that the CIRs are often sufficient to correctly classify the SCI. However, in some cases more than 25% of the responses are misclassified. To understand these mispredictions, figure 6(c) plots the difference in expected throughput between the mispredicted strongest channel and the correct strongest channel. We find the performance gap is small, implying that there can be multiple strong channels with similar quality. As long as we can infer one of the stronger channels, we will be able to improve the wireless performance.

**Impact of resolution on SCI detection:** Ideally we want to find out all the multipath signal components that traverse between the transmitter and the receiver. However, due to limited (20MHz) bandwidth of WiFi, we can only determine a discrete channel impulse response (CIR). From equation (4) in section 2, it is clear that the discrete CIR depends on the operating frequency of the WiFi chipset. Thus, we expect that the structure of the CIR will vary across channels. Adjacent channels may have a relatively similar CIR structure and CIRs from widely separated channels can be quite dissimilar (figure 7). Thus, it is not possible to use the CIRs collected from a single channel in the 5GHz frequency band, to infer the strongest channel in the 2.4GHz band. However, we will show in our evaluation that it is possible to predict the strongest channel, amongst atleast a few adjacent channels with reasonably high accuracy.

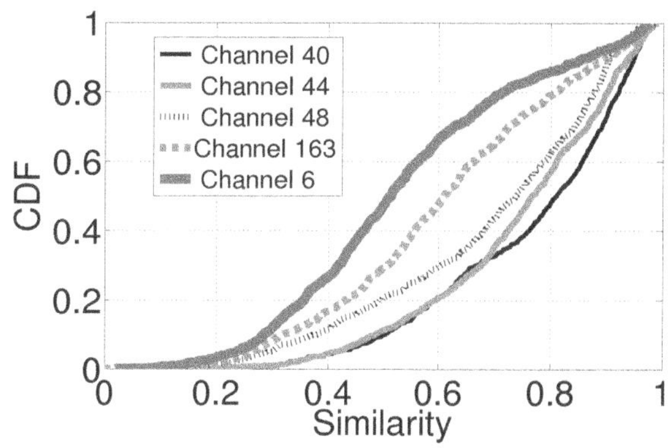


**Figure 7: Similarity of aggregate CIRs collected from channel 36 with other channels. The similarity is high for nearby channels (40, 44, 48), but low for channel 163 and even lower for channel 6 which is in 2.4GHz.**

# 4. WHY DOES PREDICTION WORK?

Measurement results from the previous section clearly show that we can predict the best among the adjacent channels based on the observations from the current channel. However, as discussed in Section 2, this is surprising, and has to follow from a certain structure of the channel response. The goal of this section is to explain the intuition of why are we able to make any prediction at all. To this end, we construct a simplified channel model and a simple predictor based on the observations in the current channel and prove that it is able to predict the best among the two adjacent channels. Note that the actual prediction algorithm we use in our implementation is different, and described in the following section. The actual algorithm is more general but is not amenable to a simple theoretical analysis. In this section we are deliberately focusing on a simple but analytically tractable scheme, to illustrate the intuition of why the prediction is possible at all.

Firstly, we define a predictor. Let

$$\Delta^c = \tan(\measuredangle \hat{h}^c[1]) - \tan(\measuredangle \hat{h}^c[0]))$$

be the phase difference between the first and the second tap of the CIR of channel $c$ (where $\measuredangle x$ denotes the phase of a complex number $x$). Note that this is purely based on the observations we make in channel $c$. We claim that when $\Delta^c < 0$ in channel $c$ we expect that channel $c+1$ is better than channel $c-1$. Secondly, we defined a simplified channel model. We start with a well known Saleh-Valenzuela (SV) channel model [9]. The key observation from [9] we use is that the path phases $\phi(p)$ are random (i.e. $\phi(p)$ and $\phi(q)$ are independent when $p \neq q$) and uniformly distributed on $[0, 2\pi]$. Also, let $T_d$ be the delay spread of the channel such that $a(p) = 0$ for $\tau(p) > T_d$ (and $a(p)$ can be an arbitrary value for $p$ such that $\tau(p) \leq T_d$). This is also in accordance with the SV model. We then have the following proposition

PROPOSITION 1. *Let us consider a $W = 20$MHz bandwidth radio and a channel with the delay spread $T_d = 20$ns. Under the assumptions on the channel model above, we have*

$$\mathbb{E}\left[\Delta^c\left(\left|\hat{h}^{c+1}(0)\right|^2 - \left|\hat{h}^{c-1}(0)\right|^2\right)\right] < 0 \qquad (6)$$

PROOF. Due to a lack of space we only give a sketch of the proof and ignore little-$o$ terms. First, let $\hat{A}(p) = a(p)e^{i\hat{\phi}(p)} = A(p)e^{-2\pi(f_c - W/2)\tau(p))}$. It is easy to see that the phase $\hat{\phi}(p)$ is also random, uniformly distributed in $[0, 2\pi]$ and independent across paths. Using Taylor expansions (and omitting little-$o$ terms) we then obtain the following approximation

$$\Delta^c = \tan(\measuredangle \hat{h}^c[1]) - \tan(\measuredangle \hat{h}^c[0])) \approx \left.\frac{\partial \tan(\measuredangle \hat{h}^c[l])}{\partial l}\right|_{l=0}$$

$$\approx \sum_{p,q} a(p)a(q)\sin\hat{\phi}(p)\cos\hat{\phi}(q)\left(\frac{n}{W\tau(p)} - \frac{n}{W\tau(q)}\right).$$

Also, we have

$$\left|\hat{h}^{c+1}(0)\right|^2 =$$

$$= \frac{1}{n^2}\sum_{p,q} a(p)a(q)\cos\left(\hat{\phi}(p) - \hat{\phi}(q) - 2\pi W(\tau(p) - \tau(q))\right).$$

We are interested in $\mathbb{E}[\Delta^c\left|\hat{h}^{c+1}(0)\right|^2]$. Note that $\mathbb{E}[\sin(\hat{\phi}(p))] = \mathbb{E}[\cos(\hat{\phi}(p))] = 0$. Since different paths have independent phases, the expectation of all cross-products containing different phases will be zero (e.g. $\mathbb{E}[\sin(\hat{\phi}(p))\cos(\hat{\phi}(q))] = 0$ for $p \neq q$). Taking this into account when expanding the terms in $\mathbb{E}[\Delta^c\left|\hat{h}^{c+1}(0)\right|^2]$, and with some elementary manipulations, we get

$$\mathbb{E}[\Delta^c\left|\hat{h}^{c+1}(0)\right|^2] \approx \frac{1}{n^2}\sum_{p=0}^{P-1}\sum_{q=0}^{p-1} 2a(p)a(q)$$

$$\times \sin\left(2\pi W(\tau(p) - \tau(q))\right)\left(\frac{n}{W\tau(p)} - \frac{n}{W\tau(q)}\right).$$

Let us order the paths such that $\tau(p) > \tau(q)$ for $p > q$. We then have in every term that $\tau(p) - \tau(q) > 0$ and $W(\tau(p) - \tau(q)) \leq WT_d < \frac{1}{2}$, thus each sine term is positive and each term in the sum is negative. Consequently, we have $\mathbb{E}[\Delta^c\left|\hat{h}^{c+1}(0)\right|^2] < 0$. Similarly we get $\mathbb{E}[\Delta^c\left|\hat{h}^{c-1}(0)\right|^2] > 0$ for channel $c-1$. $\square$

The interpretation of the proposition is as follows. Measurements show that most of the channel energy is concentrated in the first tap $\hat{h}^c(0)$. Term $\left|\hat{h}^{c+1}(0)\right|^2 - \left|\hat{h}^{c-1}(0)\right|^2$ is thus proportional to the difference in qualities between channels $c+1$ and $c-1$. If this term and $\Delta^c$ were uncorrelated, then the expectation of the product would be zero. Since the expectation is negative, this implies that negative $\Delta^c$ yields positive difference between channel qualities of $c+1$ and $c-1$, on average. Thus if one observes negative $\Delta^c$, it can conclude that channel $c+1$ is better (on average) than channel $c-1$ and conversely for positive $\Delta^c$ channel $c-1$ is most likely better than channel $c+1$.

We further verify the finding of Proposition 1 on the measured data. In Figure 8(a) we plot the empirical PDF functions of the simple estimator (6) over all measured channel responses. We verify that the observation from Proposition 1 holds, and that the mean is negative. Moreover, we see that the simple estimator has 70% accuracy(figure 8(b)) in practice when predicting the strongest of the adjacent channels.

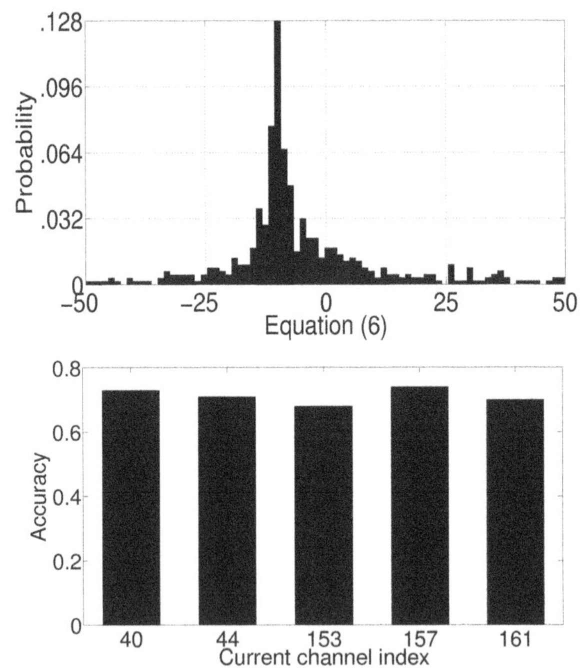


**Figure 8: (a) The empirical PDF of the estimator (6) calculated over the entire set of measured CIR samples. (b) Accuracy of strongest adjacent channel prediction for different current channels.**

The main high-level intuition behind the result is that the prediction works because the phases of different paths are uniformly random and independent from each other. Thus if we carefully construct an estimator based on relative phases, as it was shown in this example, we can recover a bias that is correlated with the channel quality. But constructing such an estimator is a difficult task. In the subsequent section we will use machine learning techniques to systematically explore the space of estimators and construct the best one for our problem, which improves the accuracy and expands the prediction range.

# 5. DESIGN AND IMPLEMENTATION

In this section we present the design and implementation details of CSpy. We have seen in Section 4 a simple predictor that is able to predict the strongest of two adjacent channels. However, this simple predictor captures only one specifics of the underlying channel structure. There might be others that can further improve the accuracy and expand the prediction power to more distant channels, but as we have seen, they are not easy to discover. Instead, we use machine learning techniques to train a predictor on a large training set and automatically discover various hidden correlations. We first describe the feature representation and selection process, and then define the classifier. We further describe another important building block that estimates the coherence time of the channel, and finally we present an overview of the entire system design.

## 5.1 Feature representation and selection

The analysis from Section 4 tells us that the relative phase differences between the first two taps can provide some information on SCI. Thus we decided to generalize this observation and use a feature vector that encodes relative phases of all taps. To obtain such a vector we take a complex discrete CIR vector observed by the NIC and we normalize its amplitudes and phases: we divide the discrete CIR vector by its amplitude and we subtract the phase of the first tap from the phases of all taps. Such a normalized feature vector then effectively encodes the descriptions of phases of different taps relative to the phase of the first one.

We obtain the discrete CIR vector by applying the inverse FFT on a discrete CFR vector obtained from a NIC, as described in Section 2. We extract the discrete CFR estimated for each received packets from Atheros 9390 chipsets with minor driver modifications. We note that the 802.11n standard allows higher resolution CFR reports, than the Atheros 9390 chipsets, that can further improve the performance of our system [19]. The extracted CFR measurements contains arbitrary phase offsets due to the lack of synchronization between the transmitter and the receiver.[2] We use the techniques described in [8, 20] to compute the phase offset and adjust the phase of each CFR before utilizing them for further calculations.

Finally, we note that the $l$-th tap of the discrete CIR vector $\bar{\mathbf{h}}$ predominantly contains the aggregate of paths with delays $\tau(p) \in [l/W, (l+1)/W]$, as discussed in Section 2. We observe that most of the significant multipath components appear in the first few taps of $\bar{\mathbf{h}}$. This is because the major multipah signals from the transmitter arrive at the receiver within a short time period called the *delay spread* [21], which is around 50ns in indoor environments. In our evaluation, we will show that the first 10 taps, which carries most of the energy, of the CIR vector $\bar{\mathbf{h}}$ can be a reliable indicator of the SCI. Using more taps will only increase the classification complexity, without any noticeable improvement in performance.

## 5.2 Training and Classification

Another takeaway from Section 4 is that the predictor (6) works well under a fairly general channel model assumption. This suggests that a simple classifier should be effective on a large class of channel profiles. Therefore, we decided to use a multi-class support-vector machine (SVM) as a simple linear classifier. In the training phase we collect CIR samples from multiple channels at various locations. For each channel we train our classifier on the training set comprising $\{\hat{\mathbf{h}}^c(x), \text{SCI}(x)\}_x$ over all locations $x$. Once a new CIR is obtained in the wild, we apply the classifier on it, derive the SCI and switch to the best channel. Since SVM is a linear classifier, it is simple and fast to calculate.

It is important to note that our classifier does not need to be trained on samples from each individual location. It is not built to learn all possible channel responses. It is designed to learn correlations that exist under very general assumptions, like the one illustrated in Section 4. In practical terms this means that we can train the classifier in one building and may be able to use it in another, as we demonstrate in our evaluation in Section 6. We also emphasize that the performance of the classifier does not reflect directly in the classification accuracy. Often, even if the classifier misestimates the SCI of the current location, the estimated channel can still have good performance. We evaluate this aspect in detail our evaluation.

## 5.3 Tracking the Strongest Channel

Even if it is possible to identify the strongest channel, channel switching may not always be beneficial due to the switching cost. To understand how quickly the SCI changes due to changes in the environment, we collected a few CFR measurements by tuning both the transmitter and the receiver at channel 36 using a 40MHz bandwidth. We disabled channel switching as it introduces an unacceptable overhead ( 3ms in our implementation) in our measurement. We postprocess each CFR vector over 40MHz to create CFRs of 4 consecutive 10MHz channels, and compute the strongest amongst only these 4 channels. Figure 9 shows that for a static link, we may need switch the channel only every $1-2$s and thus the switching cost can be amortized. We observe that although environmental variations affect the channel characteristics, the strongest channel may not always be more affected than other weak channels. However, if the link is mobile, the strongest channel remains consistent only for less than $50ms$. Thus, to track the SCI of a mobile link, we may need to switch channels frequently, which may incur some overhead.

Although it is difficult to estimate the exact duration for which the SCI can be used, the same duration is proportional to the coherence time of the channel ($T_c$). We compute the channel coherence time as the time-lag beyond which the correlation of the CFR vectors is less than 0.6. To amortize the cost of the channel switching time, CSpy ascertains that the strongest channel can be used for a duration significantly more than the channel switching duration($T_s$). It prescribes a channel change only when $T_c > kT_s$ where $k$ is a constant. We use $k = 10$ in our implementation to prevent CSpy from hurting

[2]This is not a problem for a conventional OFDM receiver that only needs to remove, but not learn the channel response.

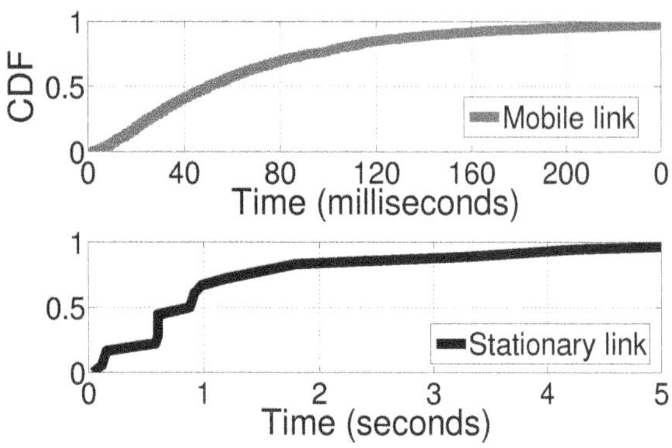


**Figure 9: Time duration between two consecutive channel changes while tracking the strongest channel.**

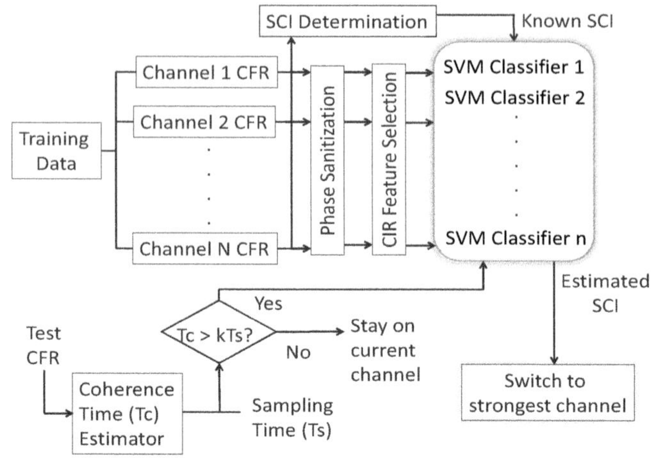


**Figure 10: CSpy design.**

performance by triggering frequent channel switching. Observe that the SCI coherence time (50ms under mobility) is almost 5x longer than the channel coherence time (typically 10ms for walking speeds). Moderately fast switching time in recent chipsets (3ms in our implementation) and a reasonable SCI coherence time allows us to tightly track the SCI in most scenarios.

### 5.4 Overall System Design

Figure 10 presents the overall design of CSpy. CSpy trains a SVM classifier with the CIR feature vectors, obtained from the CFR readings, after appropriate phase and amplitude sanitization. It groups the CIR feature vectors according to the empirically determined SCI. Once the classifier is trained with sufficiently diverse set of CIR readings, it can be used to infer the strongest channel. During run-time, CSpy estimates the CIR feature vector as well as the channel coherence time from the CFR readings obtained from a single channel. It classifies the CIR vector using the previously trained classifier, to obtain the SCI. Finally, CSpy switches to the strongest channel only if the coherence time of the channel is significantly more than the channel switching time.

## 6. EVALUATION

We evaluate CSpy across 70 different links in two different office buildings, and a parking lot. We conduct experiments to answer 2 key performance questions. (1) What is CSpy's strongest channel estimation accuracy? (2) How much performance gain can CSpy achieve by tracking the strongest channel? We begin by explaining our evaluation methodology.

### 6.1 Experiment Design

We employ a trace-driven simulation approach to evaluate CSpy. We use the same measurement setup as described in section 3.1 and collect traces during daytime. At 70 fixed locations, we cycle through 9 different channels and gather the CFRs. For each round, we compute the strongest amongst the all the channels by using the expected throughput metric. We also collect 8 walking traces from a single 40MHz channel (channels 36 bonded with channel 40), and thereafter divide the CFR into 4 contiguous 10MHz channels. We use only these 4 channels to evaluate CSpy's performance under mobility. [3] To evaluate CSpy's performance for a particular link $l_i$, we train the SVM classifier using the CIR features collected from all other links $l_j|_{i \neq j}$. Unless specified, we use the 10 taps specified in Section 5.1 as our feature vector.

**Metrics and comparison:** We use the following three metrics to evaluate CSpy's performance: (1) Accuracy – the fraction of cases when the expected throughput of the estimated SCI is within 90% of the actual strongest channel. (2) False positives (FP) – the fraction of cases in which the classifier estimates a weak channel, whose expected throughput is less than the average throughput across all available channels. In other words, false positives account for scenarios when CSpy hurts performance by switching to a weak channel. (3) Throughput – We compute CSpy's throughput as the expected throughput of the estimated SCI, aggregated over time. We also compute the optimal throughput from the known SCI determined empirically. Apart from the optimal scheme, we compare CSpy with a scheme which always uses a fixed channel and a probing scheme which periodically scans all possible channels to determine the SCI.

### 6.2 SCI Estimation Performance

Accurate estimation of the SCI will help in improving the wireless throughput by switching to a stronger channel. Otherwise, CSpy may hurt performance by switching to a weak channel. Figure 11(a) shows CSpy's SCI estimation performance across 50 locations in a single building. Evidently, CSpy's classification technique can determine the SCI from the observed CIR with a median accuracy of 83%. In rare occasions (mean 2.5%) CSpy underperforms and estimates a weak channel as the SCI. However, we observe poor accuracy (less than 50%) at a few locations. Careful investigation showed that these locations received packets at weak signal strengths, that results into low fidelity of the estimated CIRs [8].

CSpy collects the CIR from the current operating channel and utilizes it to estimate the strongest channel. Figure 11(b) further analyzes CSpy's performance and shows the accuracy/ false-positives on a per operating channel basis. The accuracy varies across different channels because the richness of the CIRs may vary across channels. We find that the channels at the edge of the frequency band, indices 36, 161, 165,

[3] It is not possible to evaluate all possible channels because the multipath structure changes frequently under mobility.

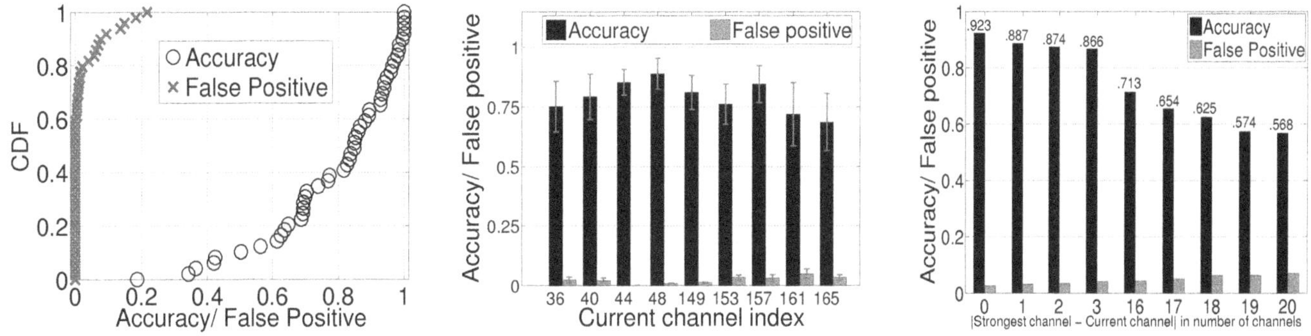


**Figure 11: Mean accuracy/false-positive of SCI determination (a) at 50 different locations, (b) for CIRs collected from different operating channels, (c) with increasing frequency gap between the operating channel and the actual SCI.**

performs poorly in comparison to other channels. Due to the dependency of the CIR on the operating frequency (section 3.2), CSpy's SCI determination accuracy is low if the SCI is far away (in terms of frequency) from the current operating channel (figurel 11(c)). Nonetheless, it is still possible to use the CIRs from a single channel to reliably estimate the strongest channel within a few $(4-5)$ adjacent channels.

**Effect of training data:** CSpy trains an SVM classifier with CIRs collected from different locations. The diversity of the training data affects CSpy's SCI estimation accuracy. The accuracy increases with the amount of training data (figure 12(a)). By using the training data from 30 locations, it is possible to estimate the SCI with 79% accuracy.

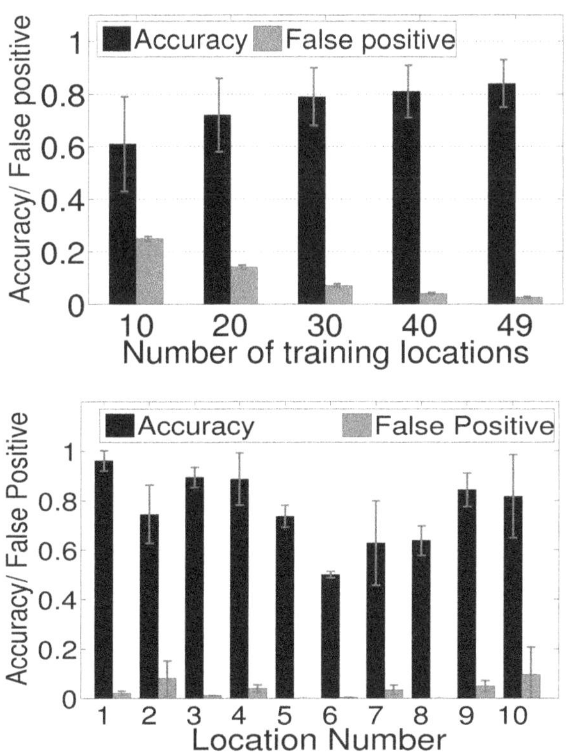


**Figure 12: SCI estimation performance (a) at 50 locations with different number training locations in the same building, (b) in the second building by using the training data collected from only the first building.**

The CIR features used in CSpy depend solely on the properties of the multipath components, and does not specifically depend on the location they are collected from. Thus, we find that we can train the classifier in the first building and use it to correctly classify the CIRs observed at 10 different locations in a second building (figure 12(b)). Figure 13 presents the accuracy and false-positive graphs for the parking lot experiment. In this scenario, we placed the transmitter right outside the first building, and collected traces at 10 random locations in the adjacent parking lot. We achieved only a modest accuracy in estimating the SCI at the outdoor locations by using the training data collected *only* from the indoor measurements, implying that outdoor and indoor channel characteristics in our measurements are quite different (figure 13(a)). Of course, the accuracy improves if the classifier is also trained with outdoor measurements (figure 13(b)). We further observe that although training separate classifiers for indoor and outdoor measurements may be possible, it improves CSpy's performance only marginally. We conclude that if a single classifier is sufficiently trained with a variety of CIRs, it may be able to determine the strongest channel at any location with reasonable accuracy.

**Effect of feature length:** The SCI estimation performance depends on the length of the chosen CIR feature vector. If the length is small, the estimation accuracy may not be satisfactory, whereas, if we use all the 56 complex taps of the CIR vector as the distinguishing feature, it may complicate the classification operation. Figure 13(c) plots the performance of SCI estimation for different feature lengths. Accuracy plateaus after a feature length of 10 because most of the multipath signals arrive at the receiver within a short duration. Figure 13(c) also specifies the average runtime of the classification operation for different feature lengths using a 2.8GHz CPU. As expected, the runtime as well as accuracy increases with the feature length. CSpy uses a feature length of 10 for training and classification to strike a balance between runtime and performance.

## 6.3 Performance Gain from SCI Detection

In this subsection we demonstrate how CSpy improves the wireless performance by tracking the strongest channel. In a typical WLAN scenario, a wireless link operates on a single fixed channel and does not exploit diversity across channels. CSpy tracks channel quality variations, and switches to the strongest channel whenever necessary. Figure 14(a) demonstrates that CSpy provides similar throughput gain over any

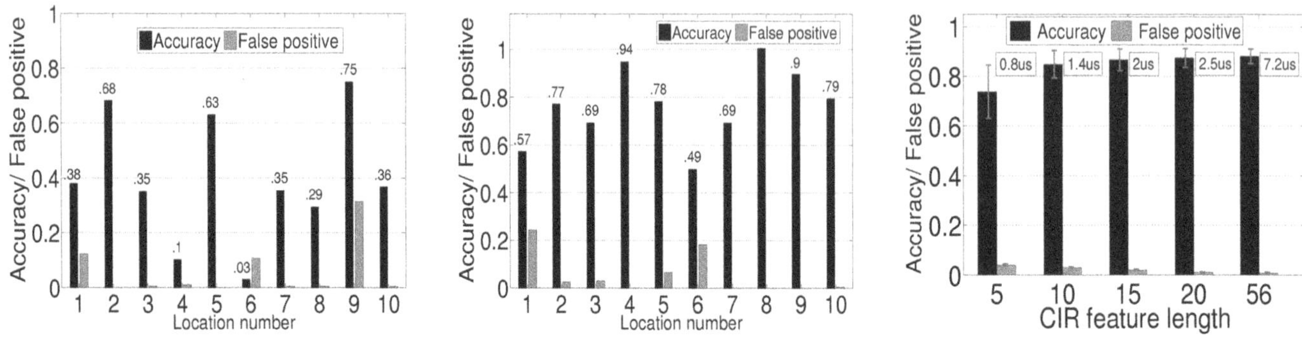


**Figure 13: SCI estimation performance at 10 locations in the parking lot by using the training data collected from (a) the first, and the second building only, (b) the parking lot as well as from the two buildings. (c) SCI estimation performance for different CIR feature lengths.**

fixed channel scheme. Because channel conditions change quite randomly at different locations, we also find that CSpy's throughput gain varies across different locations, with gain of upto 100% (figure 14(b)) over an average channel. When the current operating channel is the weakest of all the possibilities, CSpy can provide upto 250% improvement in throughput. On average, CSpy also achieves 85% of the throughput achieved by an optimal algorithm which always picks the correct SCI (figure 14(b)).

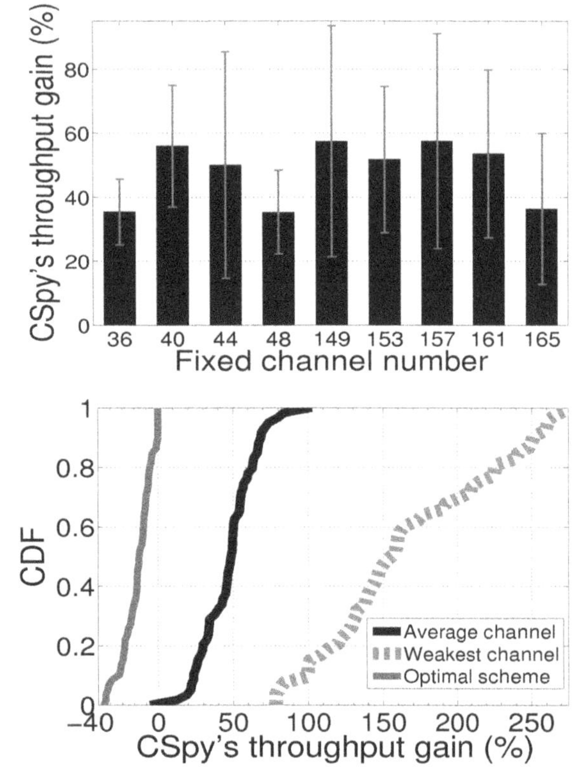


**Figure 14: CSpy's throughput gain (a) against fixed channel scheme, (b) against the weakest, an average channel, and the optimal scheme, across 60 indoor locations.**

**Comparison with probing schemes:** Probing all the available channels incurs an overhead (approximately $40ms$ in our implementation) because it requires scanning across all the available channels, along with packet exchanges to evaluate the channel qualities. Probing-based schemes are inapplicable in mobile scenarios because the overhead is often more than the channel coherence time of a mobile link. Even for static links, it is difficult to avoid the trade-off between probing frequency and SCI estimation accuracy. Frequent probing can track the SCI but incurs large overhead, whereas, the estimated SCI becomes stale if the channels are probed only occasionally. CSpy outperforms probing-based mechanisms by eliminating the need of periodic channel scanning (figure 15).

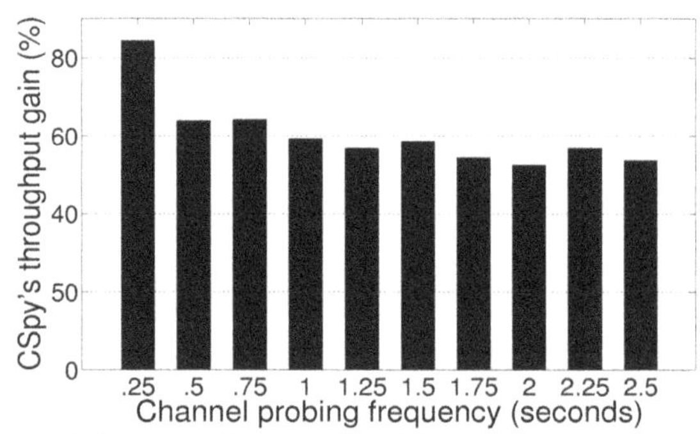


**Figure 15: Throughput gain of CSpy over a probing-based scheme.**

**Effect of mobility:** The SCI may change frequently for mobile links, and thus it may not be always beneficial to switch channels due to the costs involved. CSpy switches to the strongest channel if the estimated coherence time is significantly more the channel switching overhead. To evaluate CSpy's performance under mobility, we include the channel switching time (3ms in our implementation) as an overhead in our simulation. Figure 16 shows reduced throughput gain when the link is mobile because CSpy pays a higher overall switching cost. However, thanks to the light-weight estimation scheme, CSpy can still achieve a moderate performance improvement (median 24%) in mobile scenarios, when the channel is changing frequently.

# 7. RELATED WORK

Opportunistic channel selection is a well studied area in the context of cognitive radio systems [10–12, 22–26]. The goal of most of these studies is to reduce the effect of interference by communicating on channels that are either free or sparsely occupied. WiFi based multi-channel solutions also aim at avoiding channels which are heavily occupied by other

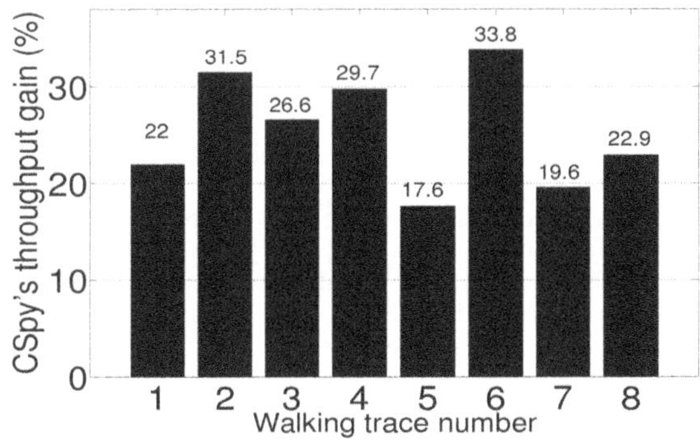

**Figure 16: Throughput gain of CSpy for 8 different walking traces**

devices. Early proposals required multiple radios to monitor all the available channels [27], which was later resolved using temporal synchronization [28], and channel hopping [29]. Interference-aware channel assignment was also studied in the context of mesh networks [30] and WLANs [31]. Authors in [32, 33] demonstrate that wireless throughput can be improved by allocating spectrum based on bandwidth demand. Recently PHY layer information has been exploited to select channels based on occupancy. Authors in [34] use a subset of OFDM subcarriers to detect narrowband interference, while Jello [35] identifies idle spectrum fragments using power spectrum density maps. While channel selection solutions optimize for a free or lightly-used channel, CSpy's aim is to determine the strongest channel that can deliver the highest PHY bit-rate. CSI-SF [36] combines CFRs from two adjacent channels to reconstruct the CFR of one bonded channel and use it for channel quality prediction; this still requires probing individual sub-channels.

Cellular networks [7] uses opportunistic scheduling by assessing the channel quality of all the registered users and serving clients which have a better channel quality. The concept of opportunistic scheduling has also been applied in multi-channel systems mostly by using probes [1, 5, 6, 37]. The main idea is to evaluate the quality of all the channels to a client by using short probe packets, and thereafter estimate and utilize the strongest channel. The issue is that probing techniques require frequent channel switching which incurs a large overhead. Author in [1] attempts to reduce the probing overhead in the context of whitespaces by utilizing opportunistic sampling, but still incurs a prohibitive overhead in finding the strongest channel. CSpy can be used in the cellular systems to remove or reduce the probing overhead. Cellular systems also employ coherence time based training to predict throughput and bitrate based on SNR [38]. While CSpy can benefit from this framework, it relies on features of multipath to estimate the strongest channel.

## 8. DISCUSSION AND FUTURE WORK

**Dependency on training:** As we discuss in Section 5.2, our training algorithm learns the generic properties of CIR. As our evaluation demonstrates, we need to retrain the classifier only for different types of environment: an indoor-trained classifier works in various indoor environments but not outdoors, and vice verse. This is expected, given that the proof of Proposition 1 depends on the channel's delay spread. We leave the full classification of different classes of environments and how to deal with them for future work.

**CSpy in WLAN scenarios:** This paper demonstrates the feasibility of improving the performance of a single link by estimating and communicating on the strongest channel. Our findings are directly applicable to scenarios where the transmitter has only one receiver to cater to, e.g., wifi-direct, wireless tethering, wireless displays, etc. If the transmitter (AP) has to serve multiple receivers (clients), it can either choose a fixed channel that is the strongest for majority of the clients, or periodically switch between the strongest channel of each client. Of course, CSpy can perform significantly better if the AP can switch to the strongest channel on a per-packet basis, for each individual client, without incurring large switching costs. This may be possible by using sophisticated physical layer techniques such as RODIN [39] and WiFi-NC [40]. IEEE 802.11ac also defines an enhanced RTS/CTS mechanism that enables the AP and a client to find and use the best subchannel within a given 40 or 80 MHz bonded channel on a per-packet basis, but it incurs a large RTS/CTS probing overhead. CSpy can also be incrementally deployed across multiple APs, although APs employing CSpy may experience a higher performance than those without CSpy.

**Combining CSpy with interference-aware channel selection:** Wireless throughput depends on both channel quality and the degree of interference. In some cases, a highly loaded channel may offer better performance over a less loaded channel, if the quality of the highly loaded channel is better. Balancing the channel quality and medium access in an optimal and distributed way is still an open research problem. CSpy optimizes for the former, without considering the effect of interference. Since channels at different locations are independent [7, 8, 41], it is reasonable to assume that SCI will be random and independent at different locations. Thus we speculate that using the channel quality as the channel selection metric across the entire network will yield a balanced distribution of links across channels. Alternatively, one can combine the existing works on interference-aware dynamic channel selection schemes [13, 42, 43] with CSpy. We leave both these directions for future work.

**SCI estimation and MIMO:** It is straightforward to extend CSpy to a MIMO system. However, MIMO already exploits channel diversity through spatial diversity, hence the expected gains of CSpy over MIMO will be smaller. Indeed, we measure a smaller but still substantial gain of 29% over an average channel and 62% over the weakest channel in the same experimental setting with 2x2 MIMO. This will further decrease with a larger number of antennas. But CSpy could potentially be beneficial in a different MIMO setting, similar to WLAN scenario discussed above, where an AP with a large number of antennas serves multiple clients concurrently. Since in this case the AP effectively assigns one antenna to each client, CSpy can guide the client and channel selection to improve the overall performance.

**CSpy for bandwidth selection**: In this paper, we assumed channels having homogeneous bandwidth. Recent wireless technologies allow various bandwidth options (20, 40, or 80 MHz in IEEE 802.11ac). In order to maximize the performance gain, not only the center frequency (channel index) but also the width of channel should be optimally decided. Thus, training and classifying heterogeneous bandwidth options, along with the channel index, is a natural next step.

# 9. CONCLUSION

Finding a quality channel has been a long-sought but still critical problem in wireless communications, particularly with the systems using unlicensed bands. While existing solutions rely on either active or passive measurements (probings), we propose a mechanism that can find the best quality channel among the candidate channels, purely based on the measurement done in one single channel. We leverage the multipath structure embedded in channel frequency response (CFR), which is a byproduct of OFDM/MIMO processing, to infer the best quality channel. Although the limited granularity of CFR doesn't allow us to reconstruct the CFRs of unseen channels, the aggregate multipath structure extracted from CFR has enough information for us to employ a machine learning classifier to find the best channel. To our best knowledge, this work is the first to present a viable solution to find the best quality channel without probing, and with reasonable accuracy (80%). Our evaluations show reasonable classifier training overhead and realtime classification overhead, hinting an immediate deployment in production networks.

# 10. ACKNOWLEDGMENT

We sincerely thank Prof. Kyle Jamieon for shepherding our paper, as well as the anonymous reviewers for their valuable comments and feedback. We would also like to extend our gratitude to Sungro Yoon.

# 11. REFERENCES

[1] B. Radunovic et al. Dynamic channel, rate selection and scheduling for white spaces. In *ACM CONEXT*, 2011.
[2] Jeongkeun Lee et al. Understanding the effectiveness of a co-located wireless channel monitoring system. In *IEEE ICC*, 2010.
[3] Anand Subramanian et al. Understanding channel and interface heterogeneity in multi-channel multi-radio wireless mesh networks. *PAM*, 2009.
[4] M. Mishra et al. How much white space is there? *University of California, Berkeley, Tech. Rep. UCB/EECS-2009-3*, 2009.
[5] P. Chaporkar et al. Scheduling with limited information in wireless systems. In *ACM MobiHoc*, 2009.
[6] A. Sabharwal et al. Opportunistic spectral usage: Bounds and a multi-band csma/ca protocol. *IEEE ToN*, 2007.
[7] D. Tse and P. Viswanath. *Fundamentals of Wireless Communication*. Cambridge University Press, 2005.
[8] S. Sen et al. Spot localization using phy layer information. In *MobiSys*, 2012.
[9] A. Saleh et al. A statistical model for indoor multipath propagation. *IEEE Journal on Selected Areas in Communications*, 1987.
[10] R. Murty et al. Senseless: A database-driven white spaces network. *IEEE Transactions on Mobile Computing*, 2012.
[11] H. Zheng et al. Device-centric spectrum management. In *IEEE DySPAN*, 2005.
[12] Q. Zhao et al. Decentralized cognitive mac for opportunistic spectrum access in ad hoc networks: A pomdp framework. *IEEE Journal on Selected Areas in Communications*, 2007.
[13] N. Ahmed and S. Keshav. SMARTA: a self-managing architecture for thin access points. In *CoNext*, 2006.
[14] D. Halperin et al. Predictable 802.11 packet delivery from wireless channel measurements. In *ACM SIGCOMM*, 2010.
[15] M. Vutukuru et al. Cross-layer wireless bit rate adaptation. In *ACM SIGCOMM*, 2009.
[16] S. Sen et al. Accurate: Constellation based rate estimation in wireless networks. In *USENIX NSDI*, 2010.
[17] R. Chandra. A case for adapting channel width in wireless networks. In *ACM SIGCOMM*, 2008.
[18] WIFI Aliance. Spectrum sharing in the 5 ghz band-dfs best practices. *Spectrum and Regulatory Committee*, 2007.
[19] E.H. Ong et al. Ieee 802.11 ac: Enhancements for very high throughput wlans. In *IEEE PIMRC 2011*.
[20] D. Halperin et al. Tool release: gathering 802.11 n traces with channel state information. *ACM SIGCOMM CCR*, 2011.
[21] S. Ghassemzadeh et al. Measurement and modeling of an ultra-wide bandwidth indoor channel. *IEEE Transactions on Communications*, 2004.
[22] I. Akyildiz et al. Next generation/dynamic spectrum access/cognitive radio wireless networks: a survey. *Computer Networks*, 2006.
[23] S. Huang et al. Optimal sensing-transmission structure for dynamic spectrum access. In *IEEE INFOCOM 2009*.
[24] H. Kim et al. In-band spectrum sensing in cognitive radio networks: energy detection or feature detection? In *ACM MobiCom*, 2008.
[25] N. Chang et al. Optimal channel probing and transmission scheduling for opportunistic access. In *MobiCom'07*.
[26] S. Yoon et al. Quicksense: Fast and energy-efficient channel sensing for dynamic spectrum access networks.
[27] N. Jain et al. A multichannel csma mac protocol with receiver-based channel selection for multihop wireless networks. In *IEEE ICCN*, 2001.
[28] Jungmin So et al. Multi-channel mac for ad hoc networks: handling multi-channel hidden terminals using a single transceiver. In *ACM MobiHoc*, 2004.
[29] P. Bahl et al. Ssch: slotted seeded channel hopping for capacity improvement in ieee 802.11 ad-hoc wireless networks. In *ACM MobiCom*, 2004.
[30] K. Ramachandran et al. Interference-aware channel assignment in multi-radio wireless mesh networks. In *IEEE INFOCOM*, 2006.
[31] E. Rozner et al. Traffic-aware channel assignment in enterprise wireless lans. In *IEEE ICNP*, 2007.
[32] T. Moscibroda et al. Load-aware spectrum distribution in wireless lans. In *IEEE ICNP*, 2008.
[33] S. Rayanchu et al. Fluid: Improving throughputs in enterprise wireless lans through flexible channelization. *ACM MobiCom*, 2011.
[34] H. Rahul et al. Learning to share: narrowband-friendly wideband networks. *ACM SIGCOMM*, 2008.
[35] Lei Yang et al. Supporting demanding wireless applications with frequency-agile radios. In *USENIX NSDI*, 2010.
[36] Riccardo Crepaldi et al. CSI-SF: Estimating wireless channel state using csi sampling & fusion. In *Infocom*, 2012.
[37] P. Chaporkar et al. Optimal joint probing and transmission strategy for maximizing throughput in wireless systems. *IEEE Journal on Selected Areas in Communications*, 2008.
[38] A. Schulman et al. Bartendr: a practical approach to energy-aware cellular data scheduling. In *ACM Mobicom*, 2010.
[39] E. Chai et al. Building efficient spectrum-agile devices for dummies. In *ACM MobiCom*, 2012.
[40] K. Chintalapudi et al. Wifi-nc: Wifi over narrow channels. In *USENIX NSDI*, 2012.
[41] Junxing Zhang et al. Advancing wireless link signatures for location distinction. In *MobiCom*. ACM, 2008.
[42] A. Anandkumar et al. Opportunistic spectrum access with multiple users: learning under competition. In *IEEE INFOCOM*, 2010.
[43] G. Kasbekar et al. Opportunistic medium access in multi-channel wireless systems: A learning approach. In *Allerton*. IEEE, 2010.

# Interference Alignment by Motion

Fadel Adib[†1] Swarun Kumar[†1] Omid Aryan[1] Shyamnath Gollakota[2] Dina Katabi[1]

[1]Massachusetts Institute of Technology
{fadel, swarun, omida, dk}@mit.edu

[2]University of Washington
gshyam@cs.washington.edu

[†]Co-primary authors

## ABSTRACT

Recent years have witnessed increasing interest in interference alignment which has been demonstrated to deliver gains for wireless networks both analytically and empirically. Typically, interference alignment is achieved by having a MIMO sender precode its transmission to align it at the receiver. In this paper, we show, for the first time, that interference alignment can be achieved via motion, and works even for single-antenna transmitters. Specifically, this alignment can be achieved purely by sliding the receiver's antenna. Interestingly, the amount of antenna displacement is of the order of one inch which makes it practical to incorporate into recent sliding antennas available on the market. We implemented our design on USRPs and demonstrated that it can deliver 1.98× throughput gains over 802.11n in networks with both single-antenna and multi-antenna nodes.

**Categories and Subject Descriptors** C.2.2 [**Computer Systems Organization**]: Computer-Communications Networks

**Keywords** Interference Alignment, Interference Nulling, Sliding Antennas, Motion-based Interference Management, MIMO, Wireless

## 1. INTRODUCTION

Recent advances in MIMO technology have demonstrated the practicality of interference alignment and its throughput gains [7, 26, 15, 13]. These systems leverage the MIMO capability of the transmitter to precode the signal and align it along a particular spatial direction at the receiver. In contrast, this paper investigates a simple question: Can we perform interference alignment with single-antenna transmitters? Furthermore, can interference alignment be performed purely by the receiver without cooperation from the senders? A positive answer to these questions could extend the gains of interference alignment to scenarios with single antenna systems, such as sensors, hence improving the overall throughput of these networks. Furthermore, the ability to do alignment purely at the receiver eliminates the need to send feedback from the receiver to the senders to inform them about the direction along which they should align their signals.

Motivated by the above questions, we investigate whether a receiver can perform interference alignment by simply adjusting the position of one of its antennas. Our intuition is that this may be possible due to two reasons. First, indoor settings are rich in multipath. Hence, at any point in space, the perceived channel is a combination of many channels that correspond to the various paths that the signal traverses. Even a small shift in the antenna location would cause some of these paths to become shorter and others longer, leading to a significant change in the resulting channel. Second, channels are continuous functions over space.[1] This means that the receiver can gradually slide its antenna, measure the channels, and keep moving the antenna in the direction that increases the alignment between the senders.

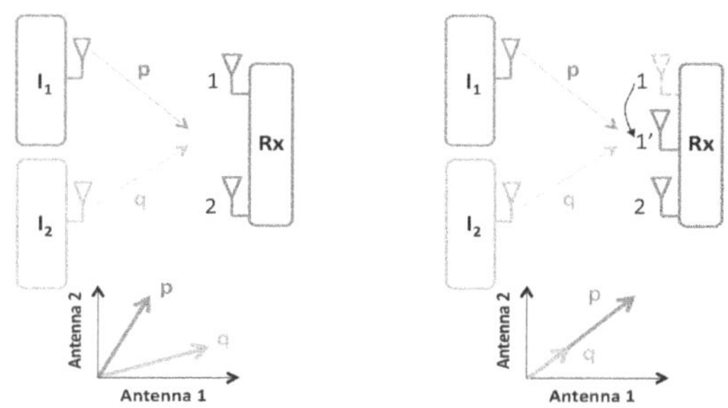


(a) **Before Sliding** (b) **After Sliding**

**Figure 1: Interference Alignment by motion.** Consider two single-antenna interferers $I_1$ and $I_2$ and a two-antenna receiver $Rx$. Initially, the two interferers are not aligned in the antenna space of $Rx$. Then, $Rx$ slides one of its receive antennas so that $I_1$ and $I_2$ are aligned in the antenna space.

To test this intuition, we used USRP radios to experiment with the scenario in Fig. 1. In this setup, we have two single-antenna interferers and a two-antenna receiver. We mount one of the receive antennas on an iRobot Create robot to emulate a sliding antenna. We measure the channels and gradually adjust the position of one of the receive antennas, moving it in the spatial direction that increases the alignment between the interferers, as in Fig. 1(b). The experiments have confirmed our intuition: alignment can indeed be performed by sliding the receiver's antenna. What is perhaps even more surprising is that the required antenna displacement was typically an inch or less. Multiple experiments in two campus buildings in both line-of-sight (LOS) and non-line-of-sight (NLOS) scenarios showed that in 84% of the settings, the required antenna displacement was less than one inch. The implications of our results are two-fold: First, they show for the first time that interference alignment can be achieved via motion. Second, the fact that the required displacement is of the order of one inch, means that motion-based interference alignment can be incorporated into recent sliding antennas available on the market.[2]

To gain insight into these empirical results, we have extended past signal propagation models to incorporate the effects of multi-

[1]The channel is a linear combination of multiple continuous waveforms [27], and, hence, is continuous over space and time.

[2]Recent USB Wi-Fi adapters have sliding antennas whose positions can be manually adjusted to improve the SNR [28].


*MobiCom'13,* September 30–October 4, Miami, FL, USA.

ACM 978-1-4503-1999-7/13/09
http://dx.doi.org/10.1145/2500423.2500449 ...$15.00.

path on interference alignment. Our results reveal that the presence of a reflector near the receiver creates significant spatial diversity, causing the channel to change dramatically (from combining constructively to combining destructively) within an inch or two. Since the receiver is typically situated on some platform which serves as a reflecting surface (e.g., a table, the floor, etc.), it is likely that it experiences reflections from at least one nearby reflector, enabling motion based interference alignment.

We introduce MoMIMO, a technique that enables MIMO interference management through mobility. Besides motion-based interference alignment, our study of MoMIMO reveals several other interesting capabilities:

- First, MoMIMO also provides interference nulling. Specifically, a single-antenna receiver can slide its antenna position to cancel an unwanted interference signal from a single-antenna transmitter, hence enabling single-antenna nodes to exploit MIMO nulling.
- Second, the process of sliding antennas to seek positions of interference alignment or nulling can be automated using a Stochastic Hill Climbing algorithm, as described in §6.
- Third, both uplink and downlink traffic benefit from motion-based MIMO techniques. This stems from the reciprocity of wireless channels, which ensures that motion-based alignment or nulling on the downlink, causes interference alignment or nulling on the uplink (see §7).

We implemented MoMIMO on an indoor network of USRP N210 software radios. To emulate a sliding antenna, we mounted the antennas on an iRobot Create robot. We conducted our experiments at a bandwidth of 20 MHz in the 2.4 GHz Wi-Fi band, both in line-of-sight and non-line-of-sight scenarios. Our results show the following:

- MoMIMO reduces the interference-to-noise ratio (INR) of undesired signal by an average of 22 dB for interference alignment and 15 dB for interference nulling.
- In a network of multiple transmitter-receiver pairs that use a combination of alignment and nulling, MoMIMO achieves an average throughput gain of 1.98$\times$ over 802.11n in networks with both single-antenna and multi-antenna nodes.
- MoMIMO's Stochastic Hill Climbing algorithm requires a mean displacement of the receive antenna of 0.44 inches for interference alignment and 1.17 inches for nulling.[3]
- Due to reciprocity, MoMIMO's interference alignment and nulling on the downlink also reduces the INR on the uplink to below the noise floor (i.e., the mean INR on the uplink is below 0 dB).
- MoMIMO is robust to sudden channel changes in otherwise static environments. It adopts a fail safe mechanism that falls back to 802.11n if the channel changes significantly, and recovers its gains once the channel is stable.

**Contributions:** This paper has three main contributions: (1) It is the first to demonstrate the feasibility of interference alignment and nulling purely via motion. Furthermore, it reveals that the required displacement is about one inch, and hence can potentially be supported by sliding antennas similar to those used in recent products [28]. (2) It presents a stochastic hill climbing algorithm that automatically repositions the antenna to achieve interference alignment or nulling. (3) The paper implements its design and demonstrates large throughput gains over real wireless channels.

[3]Alignment is easier to satisfy because many options exist for the direction along which two senders may be aligned, which provides extra flexibility for the choice of channels.

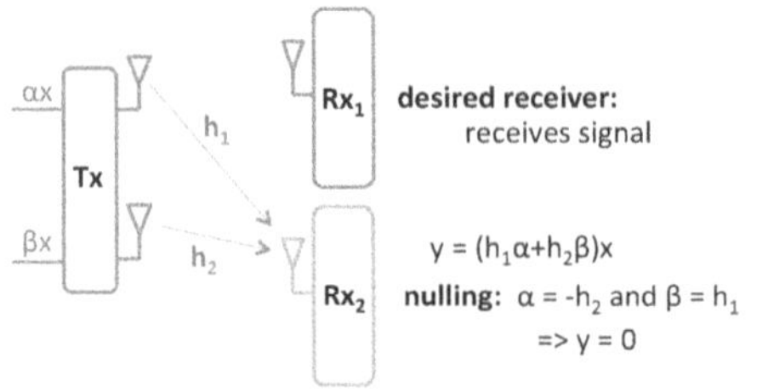


**Figure 2: Interference Nulling.** The transmitter cancels its signal at $Rx_2$ by precoding it, while $Rx_1$ can still receive its signal $x$.

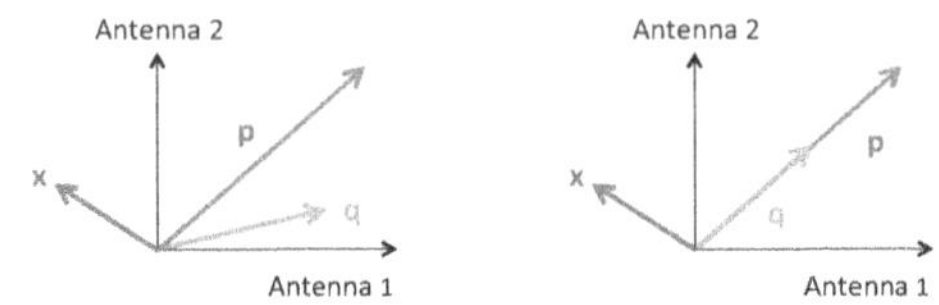


(a) **Before Alignment** (b) **After Alignment**

**Figure 3: Interference Alignment.** $q$'s transmitter performs precoding in order to align $q$ along the same direction as $p$ in the antenna space of the receiver.

## 2. BACKGROUND

We briefly introduce interference nulling and alignment.

**(a) Interference Nulling:** Interference nulling enables a MIMO node to transmit signals, and at the same time cancel them out at particular receiver (other than its own). Consider the example in Fig. 2; it consists of a two-antenna transmitter Tx and two single-antenna receivers $Rx_1$ and $Rx_2$. Let $h_1$ and $h_2$ denote the wireless channels from the two transmit antennas of Tx to the single antenna of $Rx_2$. Suppose the transmitter wants to send a signal $x$ to $Rx_1$ without interfering at $Rx_2$. The transmitter can then send $\alpha x$ on its first antenna and $\beta x$ on its second antenna. Then, $Rx_2$ would receive: $y = (\alpha h_1 + \beta h_2)x$. Hence, the transmitter can null its signal to this receiver, simply by picking $\alpha = -h_2$ and $\beta = h_1$. This process of encoding the transmitted signal across multiple antennas (i.e. multiplying by $\alpha$ and $\beta$) is referred to as *precoding*, and is used in both nulling and alignment.

**(b) Interference Alignment:** Recall the following basic properties of MIMO systems [27, 15]:

- An $N$-antenna receiver receives signals on each of its $N$ antennas. These signals can be represented as one vector in an $N$ dimensional space.
- An $N$-antenna receiver can decode up to N independent signals.

Suppose a 2-antenna receiver receives two signals – a desired signal $x$ and an interfering signal $p$. As mentioned above, these signals can be represented as vectors in a 2-D space, and the MIMO receiver can decode them. However, let's say another interferer joins the network, so that the 2-D space has a third vector $q$, as in Fig. 3(a). Unfortunately, the receiver can now no longer decode. So, how can the transmitter of $q$ avoid interfering at the receiver?

The transmitter of $q$ can precode its transmission to rotate the vector $q$ and align it along the same direction as $p$; this technique is called *interference alignment.*[4] In effect, the receiver now obtains only two vectors, one vector is the desired signal $x$, and the other is the sum of interferences $p$ and $q$, as shown in Fig. 3(b). Now, the receiver can eliminate all interference by projecting the received

[4]Specifically, to align the vector $q$ along the vector $p$, the transmitter uses a precoding matrix $M$, such that, $p^{\perp}qM = 0$, where $p^{\perp}$ denotes the vector space orthogonal to $p$ [15, 7].

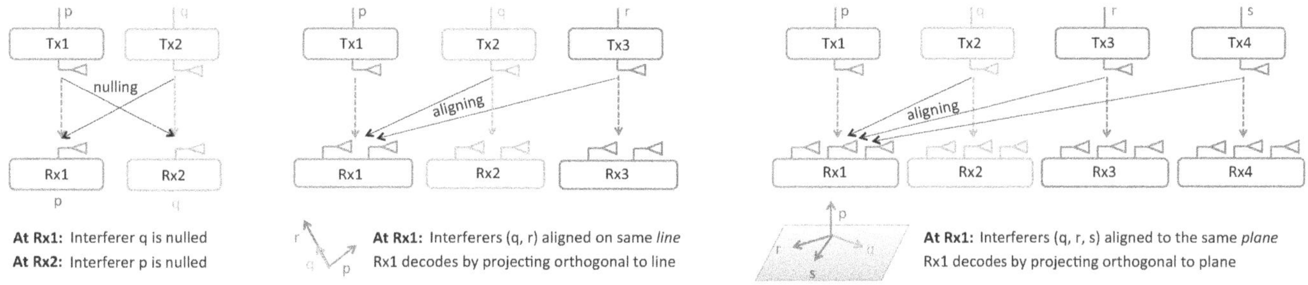


(a) **Nulling by motion** (b) **Alignment by motion** (c) **Scaling Motion-based Alignment**

**Figure 4: MoMIMO enables concurrent transmissions.** The figure shows three examples: **(a) Nulling:** Rx1 slides its antenna to null interference from Tx2, and Rx2 slides its antenna to null interference from Tx1. Hence, the network supports 2 concurrent transmissions. **(b) Alignment:** Rx1 slides its antenna to align interference from Tx2 and Tx3. Similarly, Rx2 and Rx3 slide their antennas to align their interferers. Thus, the network can support 3 concurrent streams. **(c) Scaling Alignment:** Rx1 slides one of its antennas to align interference from Tx2, Tx3 and Tx4. Similarly, Rx2, Rx3, and Rx4 each slide one of their antennas to align their interferers. Thus, the network supports 4 concurrent streams.

signal on a direction orthogonal to the direction of the aligned interference.

## 3. SCOPE OF MOMIMO

MoMIMO enables wireless nodes to perform techniques such as interference alignment and nulling by sliding one of their antennas by an inch or two. MoMIMO applies to both single antenna and multi-antenna nodes, i.e., MoMIMO enables both single and multi-antenna nodes to manage interference in a manner that increases the number of concurrent streams beyond what is available purely by the number of antennas on these nodes.

MoMIMO is not meant for mobile or hand-held devices, but is instead targeted for relatively static environments, with stable interference patterns. Examples of such scenarios include: (1) A home Wi-Fi access point that suffers interference from the neighboring apartment. (2) A sensor network collection point suffering from interference. (3) Wireless as a replacement for wires at homes and offices, e.g., a Wi-Fi link used to connect a TV to a DVD player [24], wireless surveillance cameras [3], etc. (4) Flyways in Data centers [11].

## 4. MOMIMO IN A NETWORK

We begin by presenting examples that illustrate how MoMIMO can provide significant throughput gains for wireless networks. We explain when nodes may use motion-based alignment and when they use motion-based nulling. For this section, we assume that it is possible to find locations that satisfy the desired interference alignment or interference nulling, by using small position adjustments of an inch or two. We will validate this assumption both empirically in §9 and analytically in §5.

### 4.1 Motion-Based Interference Nulling

Consider two co-located single-antenna transmitter-receiver pairs: Tx1-Rx1 and Tx2-Rx2 (Fig. 4(a)). Say these nodes are initially at positions where they interfere strongly (i.e. the interference to noise ratio (INR) from Tx1 to Rx2 and Tx2 to Rx1 is high). In such a scenario, 802.11 permits only one of Tx1 and Tx2 to transmit at any given time, i.e., the maximum number of concurrent streams is one.

Recall that because Tx1 and Tx2 are single-antenna transmitters, they cannot perform standard interference nulling to each other's receivers. This is because standard interference nulling requires a node to precode its signal across *multiple transmit antennas* as discussed in §2.

In contrast, MoMIMO can leverage motion-based nulling to send two concurrent streams that do not interfere with each other. Specifically, each receiver makes small adjustments to its antenna position by one or two inches until the signal from the interfering transmitter is nulled (i.e. below the noise floor). In this example, Rx1 adjusts its antenna until it nulls Tx2's interference. Similarly, Rx2 adjusts its antenna until it nulls Tx1. Now that there is no interference between the two streams, Tx1 and Tx2 can transmit concurrently to their respective receivers.

**Reciprocity:** We now have the receive antennas at positions where Tx1 and Tx2 can transmit concurrently, without interference. But what happens when Rx1 and Rx2 need to transmit their acknowledgments concurrently to Tx1 and Tx2? Interestingly, we notice that there is no need for any new adjustments in antenna positions, i.e. the ACKs do not interfere at Tx1 and Tx2. This is because reciprocity in wireless channels also leads to reciprocity in motion-based nulling (details in §7). Thus, once receivers perform motion-based nulling, they not only receive their desired signals concurrently, but also deliver ACKs to their transmitters, interference-free.

**Multiplexing Gains:** MoMIMO's motion-based interference nulling, can enable two concurrent streams in this setting, i.e., a $2\times$ multiplexing gain over 802.11.

### 4.2 Motion-Based Interference Alignment

Consider three co-located transmitter-receiver pairs: Tx1-Rx1, Tx2-Rx2 and Tx3-Rx3, as shown in Fig. 4(b). The transmitters have only one antenna each, while the receivers are two-antenna nodes. Once again, these nodes are in positions where they interfere strongly with each other. Therefore, 802.11 permits only one of Tx1, Tx2, and Tx3 to transmit packets at a given point in time; hence, the maximum number of concurrent streams is one.

Recall that since Tx1, Tx2, and Tx3 have only one antenna each, they cannot align their interfering signals along a common spatial direction at each receiver. This is because such alignment requires the transmitter to precode its signal across *multiple transmit antennas* as explained in §2.

In contrast, MoMIMO leverages motion-based alignment to send three concurrent streams that do not interfere with each other. Let's consider the two-antenna receiver Rx1, which receives its desired signal from Tx1 and unwanted interference from both Tx2 and Tx3. To mitigate this interference, Rx1 performs motion-based alignment by adjusting one of its antennas so that the signals from its two interfering transmitters, Tx2 and Tx3, are aligned in its 2-D space (see Fig. 4(b)). Now Rx1 obtains only two signal vectors in this 2-D space: the signal from its desired transmitter (Tx1) and the sum of the interference from the unwanted transmitters Tx2 and Tx3. Thus, as in standard interference alignment (see §2), the receiver can eliminate all interference by projecting its received sig-

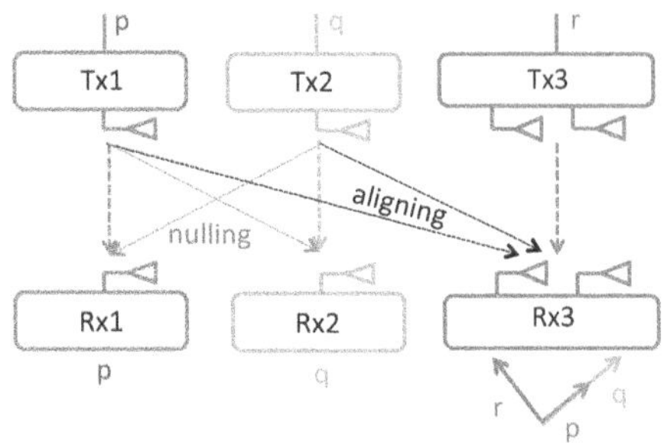


**Figure 5: MoMIMO in heterogeneous networks.** The two single antenna pairs perform nulling as in Fig. 4(a). Rx3 slides one of its antennas to align Tx1 and Tx2; similarly, Tx3 slides one of its antennas to align ACKs from Rx1 and Rx2. Tx3 also precodes its signal to null at Rx1. The network can support 3 concurrent streams.

nal along a direction orthogonal to that of the aligned interference. Similarly, Rx2 can decode its desired signal concurrently by adjusting one of its antennas to align interference from Tx1 and Tx3; while, Rx3 adjusts one of its antennas to align interference from Tx1 and Tx2.

**Reciprocity:** We now have the receive antennas at positions where Tx1, Tx2 and Tx3 can transmit concurrently without interference. Suppose the receivers want to send ACKs back to their respective transmitters, concurrently. These ACKs may still interfere with each other at the transmitters. For example, Rx1's ACK would cause interference at Tx2 and at Tx3. To address this issue, Rx1 can precode its transmission using standard interference nulling, such that it is nulled at Tx2. Fortunately, nulling the ACK at Tx2 also automatically nulls the ACK at Tx3 as well. This desirable phenomenon is due to channel reciprocity and will be further explained in §7. Hence, Rx2 and Rx3 can perform a similar procedure so that the receivers concurrently deliver ACKs to their transmitters, interference-free.

**Multiplexing Gains:** MoMIMO's motion-based interference alignment can enable three concurrent streams in this setting, i.e., a 3× gain over 802.11. We note that even if the receivers employed uplink multi-user MIMO (as in [26]) instead of standard 802.11, the maximum number of concurrent streams would be two, still 1.5× less than that of MoMIMO.

**Scaling:** MoMIMO's interference alignment scales beyond the setting in Fig. 4(b). For e.g., in a setup with four single-antenna transmitters and four 3-antenna receivers (shown in Fig. 4(c)), it can enable four concurrent streams, i.e., a 4× gain over 802.11.

### 4.3 Combining Alignment and Nulling

MoMIMO's throughput gains can be generalized to heterogeneous networks that require combining both motion-based alignment and motion-based nulling. Consider the scenario in Fig. 5, with two pairs of single-antenna nodes, and one pair of two-antenna MIMO nodes. Note that in 802.11n, only one of Tx1, Tx2, and Tx3 can transmit packets at any given time.

In contrast, MoMIMO can exploit both motion-based alignment and nulling to deliver three concurrent streams. To begin with, recall that Tx1, Tx2, Rx1 and Rx2 form a topology similar to the one in Fig. 4(a). Thus, to enable concurrent transmissions, Rx1 can simply slide its antenna to null Tx2, and Rx2 can similarly slide its antenna to null Tx1, as in §4.1.

We still need to make sure that Tx3 can transmit concurrently without interfering with the ongoing transmissions. To this end, we exploit interference alignment, as in §4.2. Specifically, Rx3 slides one of its antennas to *align* Tx1 and Tx2's signals. In addition, Rx3 precodes its transmission using standard interference nulling, such that it is nulled at Tx1; by reciprocity, Rx3's transmission is automatically nulled at Tx2 as explained in §7. Similarly, Tx3 slides one of its antennas to *align* the ACKs from Rx1 and Rx2; it also precodes its transmission such that it is nulled at Rx1 (and, hence, Rx2).

**Multiplexing Gains:** In this setting, 802.11n can send 1.33 concurrent streams on average assuming fair time-sharing between streams.[5] In contrast, MoMIMO's motion-based alignment and nulling enables three concurrent streams, i.e. a 2.25× gain over 802.11n. Note that using interference alignment and nulling without motion in this setup will only enable two concurrent streams at any time. Hence, MoMIMO can still achieve a 1.5× gain over advanced techniques that leverage standard nulling and alignment, e.g. n+ [15].

Finally, we note that in this section, we have assumed that it is feasible to find nearby locations that achieve the desired alignment and nulling. In §9, we revisit these topologies and provide extensive measurements that span line-of-sight and non-line of sight scenarios in multiple buildings, all of which confirm the gains of MoMIMO.

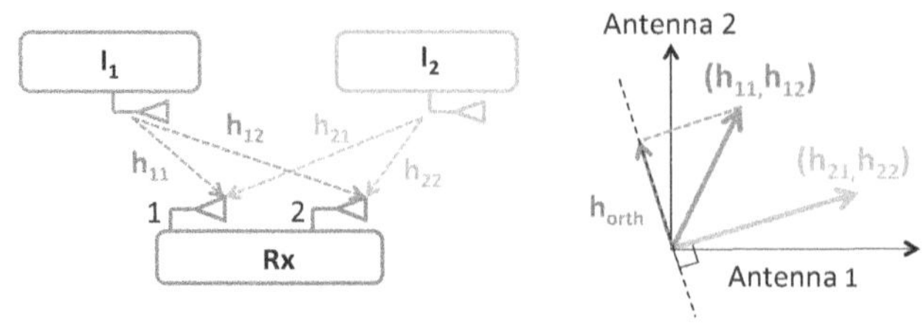


**Figure 6: Interference Alignment.** We wish to align the signals received from the two interferers $I_1$ and $I_2$ along the same direction. The goodness of alignment is determined by the *residual interference*; it is the projection of an interferer along a direction orthogonal to the desired alignment, and denoted as $h_{orth}$.

## 5. MoMIMO Analysis

In this section, we extend signal propagation models to capture how multipath effects enable motion-based alignment. We also give insights for why the required displacement is relatively small and is about one or two inches.

In order to quantify alignment, we need to pick a metric that reflects the goodness of alignment. So, how do we choose this metric? Suppose, a receiver *Rx* wants to align a given interferer *I* along a particular direction $\vec{v}$ in its antenna space. If the interferer is perfectly aligned with $\vec{v}$, then its projection along $\vec{v}^{\perp}$ (i.e. the direction orthogonal to $\vec{v}$) is zero. In contrast, if the interferer is poorly aligned with $\vec{v}$, its projection on $\vec{v}^{\perp}$ is large. In fact, the larger this projection is, the worse the alignment is. In the rest of this section, we analytically quantify the goodness of alignment in terms of *residual interference* after alignment [8, 20]. This quantity, which we denote $h_{orth}$ is defined as the projection of the interference along the direction orthogonal to that of the desired alignment.

Consider the setup in Fig. 6, where we wish to slide antenna 1 of the receiver Rx to align the signal $\vec{h}_1$ from $I_1$ along the same direction as the signal $\vec{h}_2$ from $I_2$. Let $h_{tr}$ denote the channel from interferer $I_t$ to receive antenna *r*. We then write the residual inter-

[5] In any time slot, Tx1, Tx2 or Tx3 sends 1, 1, or 2 streams respectively. Thus, on average, 802.11n sends $\frac{1+1+2}{3} = 1.33$ streams.

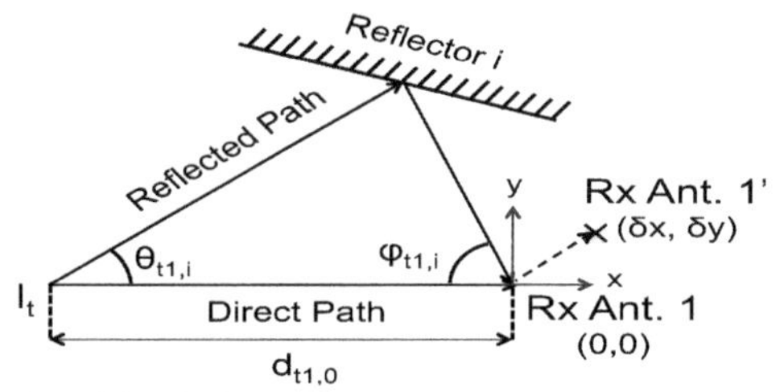


**Figure 7: Specifying Reflectors.** We specify the location of reflector $i$ with respect to interferer $I_t$ by: $\theta_{t1,i}$, the angle of departure of the signal from interferer $I_t$ and $\phi_{t1,i}$, the angle of arrival of the reflected signal at receive antenna 1.

ference after alignment $h_{orth}$ as:

$$\begin{aligned} h_{orth} &= \vec{h}_1.\vec{h}_2^{\perp} && (1)\\ &= (h_{11}, h_{12}).(-h_{22}, h_{21}) && (2)\\ &= -h_{11}h_{22} + h_{12}h_{21} && (3)\end{aligned}$$

where $\vec{h}_2^{\perp}$ denotes the vector orthogonal to $\vec{h}_2$.[6]

Let's study how the value of these channels $h_{tr}$ and the resulting $h_{orth}$ change as a function of reflectors in the environment. Say that we have $n$ reflectors in the environment. Then the channel between any interferer $I_t$ and receive antenna $r$ is the sum of the channel along the direct path between the two, $h_{tr,0}$, plus the channels along all the reflected paths, $h_{tr,i}$, for all reflectors $i = 1, \ldots, n$. We can use standard propagation models [27] to express these channels as a function of path length. Specifically, the channel on the direct path $h_{tr,0}$ is:

$$h_{tr,0} = \frac{1}{d_{tr,0}} e^{-2\pi j \frac{d_{tr,0} f}{c}} \quad (4)$$

where $d_{tr,0}$ is the length of the direct path between interferer $I_t$ and receive antenna $r$, $c$ is the speed of light, and $f$ is the frequency of the transmitted signal.

Similarly, the channel along the $i^{\text{th}}$ reflected path as:

$$h_{tr,i} = \frac{\gamma_i}{d_{tr,i}} e^{-2\pi j \frac{d_{tr,i} f}{c} + j\pi} \quad (5)$$

where $\gamma_i$ is the reflection coefficient of the reflector, and $d_{tr,i}$ is the total distance traversed by the reflected signal – i.e., $d_{tr,i}$ is the sum of the two segments of a reflected path, the segment from the interferer $I_t$ to the reflector and the segment from the reflector to the receive antenna $r$.

Thus, the channel from interferer $I_t$ to receive antenna $r$ is:

$$\begin{aligned} h_{tr} &= h_{tr,0} + \sum_{i=1}^{n} h_{tr,i} = \frac{1}{d_{tr,0}} e^{-2\pi j \frac{d_{tr,0} f}{c}} + \sum_{i=1}^{n} \frac{\gamma_i}{d_{tr,i}} e^{-2\pi j \frac{d_{tr,i} f}{c} + j\pi}\\ &= \sum_{i=0}^{n} \frac{\gamma_i}{d_{tr,i}} e^{-2\pi j \frac{d_{tr,i} f}{c} + \alpha_i}\end{aligned}$$

Where $\gamma_0 = 1$, $\alpha_0 = 0$, and $\alpha_i = j\pi$ for $i = 1, \ldots, n$.

We can substitute these channels in Eqn. 3 that defined $h_{orth}$ to understand how reflectors impact the residual interference after alignment. As we substitute, remember that we are only sliding antenna 1 on the receiver, while antenna 2 is fixed. Therefore, we consider channels $h_{12}$ and $h_{22}$ to antenna 2 to be constants, for the rest of our analysis.

$$\begin{aligned} h_{orth} &= -h_{22}h_{11} + h_{12}h_{21}\\ &= -h_{22} \sum_{i=0}^{n} \frac{\gamma_i}{d_{11,i}} e^{-2\pi j \frac{d_{11,i} f}{c} + \alpha_i} + h_{12} \sum_{i=0}^{n} \frac{\gamma_i}{d_{21,i}} e^{-2\pi j \frac{d_{21,i} f}{c} + \alpha_i}\\ &= \sum_{t=\{1,2\}} \sum_{i=0}^{n} \frac{\gamma_{t1,i}}{d_{t1,i}} e^{-2\pi j \frac{d_{t1,i} f}{c} + \alpha_i}\end{aligned}$$

Where $\gamma_{11,i} = -h_{22}\gamma_i$ and $\gamma_{21,i} = h_{12}\gamma_i$, are constants.

The above equation computes the residual interference after alignment for a particular position of the receive antenna. We are interested in how $h_{orth}$ changes as the receive antenna slides by $(\delta x, \delta y)$, which we denote by $h_{orth}(\delta x, \delta y)$. To derive $h_{orth}(\delta x, \delta y)$, we express the location of reflector $i$ based on two angles for any interferer $I_t$ and receive antenna $r$: the angle of departure ($\theta_{tr,i}$) and angle of arrival ($\phi_{tr,i}$), as shown in Fig. 7. Given these values, we can show that $h_{orth}(\delta x, \delta y)$ is:

$$h_{orth}(\delta x, \delta y) = \sum_{t=\{1,2\}} \sum_{i=0}^{n} \frac{\gamma_{t1,i}}{\tilde{d}_{t1,i}} e^{-2\pi j \frac{\tilde{d}_{t1,i} f}{c} + \alpha_i} \quad (6)$$

Where $\tilde{d}_{t1,i}$ is given by:

$$\begin{aligned} \tilde{d}_{t1,i} &= \sqrt{(2c_{t1,i}\sin^2\beta_{t1,i} - d_{t1,0} - \delta x)^2 + (c_{t1,i}\sin(2\beta_{t1,i}) - \delta y)^2}\\ c_{t1,i} &= \frac{d_{t1,0}\sin\phi_{t1,i}}{\sin\phi_{t1,i} - \sin\theta_{t1,i}}\\ \beta_{t1,i} &= (\phi_{t1,i} - \theta_{t1,i})/2\end{aligned}$$

The proof for the above equations follows from the geometry of the reflectors in Fig. 7. It is provided in Appendix A.

Eqn. 6 shows how sliding a receive antenna impacts alignment, or more precisely, the residual interference orthogonal to the desired alignment. As Eqn. 6 is fairly complex, in the following sections, we extract insights from it considering specific scenarios.

### 5.1 Impact of a Reflector on Motion-Based Alignment

We first consider the case of single randomly positioned non-absorbent reflector (i.e., $\gamma_i = 1$). Of course in reality, an indoor scenario would have many absorbent reflectors. However, studying this simplified case allows us to understand the trends that control how a reflector impacts alignment. Later in §5.2, we use these insights to understand the impact of many absorbent reflectors.

Recall that our objective is to understand, given that the receive antenna is at an arbitrary initial position, how much displacement is needed to move it to a location that achieves alignment (i.e., minimizes $|h_{orth}|^2$, the residual interference after alignment). To compute this displacement, we numerically compute $|h_{orth}|^2$ using Eqn. 6. Recall that the impact of the reflector on the signal from each interferer $I_t$ is defined by the angle of arrival ($\phi_{t1}$) and the angle of departure ($\theta_{t1}$) of the signal, as shown in Fig. 7. Since we have two interferers and one reflector, in this example, we have four parameters: $\theta_{11}$, $\theta_{21}$, $\phi_{11}$ and $\phi_{21}$, which determine this displacement.

Fig. 8(a) plots the mean displacement from an arbitrary initial position of the receive antenna to a position that achieves alignment by minimizing $|h_{orth}|^2$ locally.[7] The figure shows that the displacement is small when either $\phi_{11}$ or $\phi_{21}$ is large. Specifically, when either $\phi_{11}$ or $\phi_{21}$ is between 90° and 180°, the required mean displacement varies between about 0.6 inches and 1.2 inches. We note

[6]Note that, in practice, $\vec{h}_2^{\perp}$ is a unit vector. We ignore normalization of $\vec{h}_2^{\perp}$ for simplicity.

[7]Our analysis of $h_{orth}$ also reveals that these points of local minima, on average, decrease $|h_{orth}|^2$ below the noise floor, provided the environment has reflectors close to the receiver, that are behind it with respect to either sender.

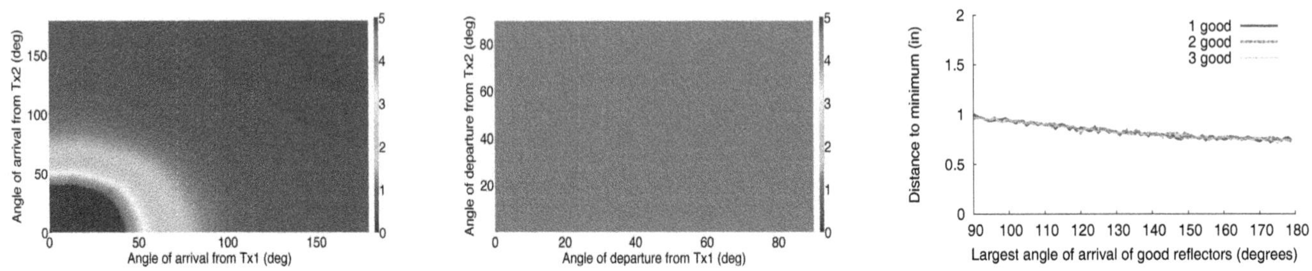


(a) **Displacement across $\phi_{11}$ and $\phi_{21}$** (b) **Displacement across $\theta_{11}$ and $\theta_{21}$** (c) **Displacement with many reflectors over $\phi_{max}$**

**Figure 8: Displacement (in inches) to position of alignment** (a): Across $\phi_{11}$ and $\phi_{21}$, with fixed arbitrary $\theta_{11}$ and $\theta_{21}$. We cap the maximum at 5 inches for ease of viewing. (b) Across $\theta_{11}$ and $\theta_{21}$, with $\phi_{11}, \phi_{21} = 90°$. Geometry restricts $\theta_{11}, \theta_{21} \leq 90°$. (c) With 10 reflectors placed at random locations across $\phi_{max}$, the largest angle of arrival among the good reflectors with respect to any interferer.

that this displacement and the results in Fig. 8(a) are based on Eqn. 6 for $f = 2.5$ GHz, which is the typical carrier frequency of 802.11. Hence the displacements of 0.6 and 1.2 inches correspond to distances of $\lambda/8$ and $\lambda/4$ respectively. The required displacements are even smaller at higher frequencies, where the wavelength is shorter, for e.g., in the 5 GHz Wi-Fi band.

So what does $\phi_{11}$ or $\phi_{21} > 90°$, mean in terms of the physical location of the reflector? Recall from Fig. 7 that $\phi_{t1}$ denotes the angle along which reflected signal arrives at at the receiver from interferer $I_t$. Thus, if $\phi_{t1} > 90°$, then this reflector is behind the receiver with respect to interferer $I_t$. Hence, we arrive at the following insight:

**Insight 1:** Reflectors which are behind the receiver with respect to the interferer (i.e. $\phi_{11}$ or $\phi_{21} > 90°$) enable a displacement on the order of 1 or 2 inches to a position that enables alignment. We call such reflectors *good reflectors*.

Note that it is common for most receivers in wireless networks to be placed on some platform (e.g. a table, the floor, etc.), which is usually behind the receiver with respect to at least one interferer, and hence serves as a good reflector.

One may wonder if the displacement to a position of alignment depends on either $\theta_{11}$ or $\theta_{21}$, given that $\phi_{11}$ or $\phi_{21}$ are fixed at values $\geq 90°$. In fact, we observe that the angles of departure have no impact on the displacement, once we fix the angles of arrival. In particular, Fig. 8(b), demonstrates that the required mean displacement is constant versus $\theta_{11}$, $\theta_{21}$, for the case when $\phi_{11}$ and $\phi_{21}$ are both fixed at 90°.

## 5.2 Motion-Based Alignment with Multiple Reflectors

While our discussion so far focused on a single reflector, the natural question to ask is how does the displacement to a position of alignment change, given a large number of reflectors in the environment. To this end, we extend our analysis to multiple absorbent reflectors. In particular, we pick multiple reflectors with random angles of departure and arrival and an absorption coefficient chosen randomly between $[0.2, 0.6]$ [14]. We use our model in Eqn. 6 to evaluate how these reflectors affect the mean displacement required from an arbitrary location to reach a position that achieves alignment by locally minimizing $|h_{orth}|^2$.

We consider a scenario with 10 randomly positioned reflectors with different angles of arrival and departure. We consider the following three cases: (1) Only one of these reflectors is a "good reflector" with respect to either interferer $I_1$ or interferer $I_2$. (2) Two reflectors are "good reflectors" with respect to either interferer. (3) Three reflectors are "good reflectors" with respect to either interferer.

Fig. 8(c) plots the mean displacement needed to reach a position of alignment, i.e. minimize $|h_{orth}|^2$. We plot this quantity across the largest angle of arrival, $\phi_{max} = \max_{t \in \{1,2\},i} \phi_{t1,i}$, among all the good reflectors with respect to either interferer. The figure reveals the following insight:

**Insight 2:** As long as at least one good reflector exists in the environment, i.e. one reflector is behind the receiver with respect to either interferer, the mean displacement needed to reach a position of alignment, is in the vicinity of $\lambda/8$ to $\lambda/4$, i.e. around 1 or 2 inches, for 2.4-2.5GHz transmissions.

While our analysis so far has focused on interference alignment, it can readily be extended to interference nulling. In particular, we can consider nulling as a special case of alignment where $h_{orth}$ is the projection along the direction of the receive antenna where the signal needs to be nulled (i.e., one of the axes in the antenna space). Hence, the analysis of $h_{orth}$ is similar.

# 6. STOCHASTIC HILL CLIMBING

In this section, we present a Stochastic Hill Climbing algorithm that automatically adjusts the receive antenna to seek positions of interference alignment or nulling. To find these positions, the algorithm minimizes the *Interference to Noise Ratio* (INR) from the interfering transmitter(s). For interference nulling, INR is the ratio of the power of the interfering transmitter to the power of noise. For interference alignment, we define the INR as follows. Let $(\alpha, \beta)$ denote the direction along which the projected power from the interfering signals is minimum. Recall that the received signal must be projected along this direction, to decode the desired signal. Thus, we define the INR for alignment as the ratio of the power of the interfering signals projected along this direction, to the noise power $\sigma^2$. For a system with two single-antenna transmitters and a two-antenna receiver, the INR can be computed based on the wireless channels as:

$$INR = \frac{1}{\sigma^2} \min_{\alpha,\beta} |h_{11}\alpha + h_{12}\beta|^2 + |h_{21}\alpha + h_{22}\beta|^2$$

where $h_{ij}$ is the channel from transmitter $i$ to receive antenna $j$ in Fig. 6. The solution of this minimization problem has a closed form (Proof in Appendix B):

$$INR = \frac{1}{2\sigma^2}\left(|h_{11}|^2 + |h_{21}|^2 + |h_{12}|^2 + |h_{22}|^2\right) - \frac{1}{\sigma^2}\sqrt{\left|\frac{|h_{11}|^2 + |h_{21}|^2 - |h_{12}|^2 - |h_{22}|^2}{2}\right|^2 + |h_{11}h_{12}^* + h_{21}h_{22}^*|^2} \quad (7)$$

Because channels are continuous functions over space, the INR profile is continuous and smooth. In other words, an incremental movement in any given direction would lead to a gradual increase or decrease in INR. Hence, to minimize the INR, a receiver can slide its antenna gradually until it reaches a local minimum.

We leverage this intuition in designing our stochastic hill climbing algorithm to reduce the INR (pseudo-code in Alg. 1). At a high level, our algorithm proceeds as follows: the receiver continuously monitors the INR from its interferer(s) (using Eqn. 7). Initially, it picks an arbitrary direction, and slides one of its antennas in that direction. Specifically, it slides the antenna either forward or backward, depending on which of those decreases the INR. It continues to move the antenna along that direction until the INR reaches a local minimum (in that direction). Then, it rotates the antenna either clock-wise or counter clock-wise about a small arc (of radius a few mm), whichever decreases the INR. Again, the receiver keeps rotating that antenna until the INR reaches a local minimum. The receiver repeats the above process, switching between translations and rotations, until it reaches a local minimum (in both translation and rotation). If the INR at the local minimum is below the noise floor, the algorithm terminates. Otherwise, the receiver moves the antenna to a random location and repeats the process again.

In practice, across all experiments in §9, the stochastic hill climbing algorithm converges to an INR below the noise floor in an average of 3 tries.

**Algorithm 1** Pseudo-code for Stochastic Hill Climbing

```
mode = +1                                   ▷ 1: Translate, -1: Rotate
direction = +1                              ▷ 1: Forward, -1: Reverse
attempts = 0
▷ Loop while INR is above 0 dB
while INR > 0 dB do
    switch mode
        case +1:  TRANSLATE(direction);     ▷ In Translate Mode
        case −1:  ROTATE(direction);        ▷ In Rotate Mode
    end switch
    prev_INR = INR                          ▷ Previous INR of sender
    INR = GETINR()                          ▷ Update INR based on channels
    if INR > prev_INR then                  ▷ If INR increased
        direction = −direction              ▷ Switch direction
        attempts = attempts + 1
    end if
    if attempts == 2 then                   ▷ Hit a minimum
        mode = −mode                        ▷ Switch modes
        attempts = 0
    end if
    if At local minimum with INR > 0 dB then
        ▷ Move to Random Location
    end if
end while
```

## 7. RECIPROCITY

In this section, we show how MoMIMO leverages channel reciprocity to allow concurrent uplink transmissions (such as ACKs). Consider two wireless nodes $i$ and $j$. Let $h_{ij}$ and $h_{ij}^{rev}$ denote the forward channel from $i$ to $j$ and reverse channel from $j$ to $i$, respectively. Then reciprocity [7] states that:

$$h_{ij}^{rev} = t_i h_{ij} r_j \quad (8)$$

Where $t_i$ and $r_j$ are fixed constants that depend purely on nodes $i$ and $j$ respectively.

Eqn. 8 has an interesting consequence for interference nulling. Specifically, when MoMIMO adjusts $j$'s receive antenna so that $h_{ij} \approx 0$, this also results in $h_{ij}^{rev} \approx 0$. Hence, nulling the downlink channel from interferer $i$ to receiver $j$ by motion, also nulls the uplink channel from $j$ to $i$.

Reciprocity can also be exploited for interference alignment. Consider two single-antenna nodes $I_1$ and $I_2$ causing interference at a two-antenna receiver Rx, as shown in Fig. 6. MoMIMO moves one of Rx's receive antennas to a position of interference alignment, so that (Eqn. 3):

$$h_{11}h_{22} - h_{21}h_{12} \approx 0 \quad (9)$$

Now, suppose the two-antenna receiver Rx needs to send a single stream on the uplink without interfering with $I_1$ or $I_2$. It precodes its signal by $(-h_{12}^{rev}, h_{11}^{rev})$ so that the effective uplink channel at interferer $I_1$: $-h_{12}^{rev}h_{11}^{rev} + h_{11}^{rev}h_{12}^{rev} = 0$, is nulled. Interestingly, because the receive antenna is in a position of alignment at the downlink, this precoding also nulls the effective uplink channel at $I_2$. Specifically, from Eqn. 8 and 9, the effective uplink channel at $I_2$ is:

$$\begin{aligned} -h_{12}^{rev}h_{21}^{rev} + h_{11}^{rev}h_{22}^{rev} &= -t_1h_{12}r_2t_2h_{21}r_1 + t_1h_{11}r_1t_2h_{22}r_2 \\ &= t_1t_2r_1r_2(h_{11}h_{22} - h_{21}h_{12}) \approx 0 \end{aligned}$$

Thus, MoMIMO's interference alignment and nulling by motion provides not only concurrent downlink transmissions, but by leveraging precoding and reciprocity, also enables concurrent uplink transmissions.

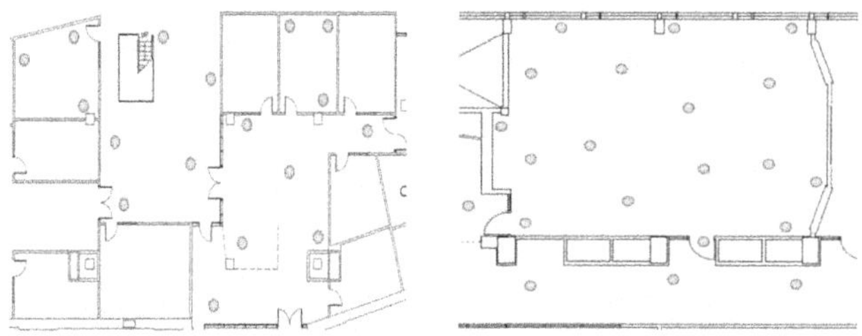

**(a) Testbed in Bldg. 1** **(b) Testbed in Bldg. 2**

**Figure 9: Testbed topology.** The figure depicts the cropped floor plans of two buildings where the experiments were conducted. The red marks on the floor plans depict locations for wireless nodes. Different random subsets of these locations for the transmitters and receivers are picked for different experiments.

## 8. EXPERIMENTAL SETTING

We describe our experimental environment, which is used to illustrate the gains of MoMIMO.

**Implementation:** Nodes in our experiments are equipped with USRP-N210 software radios [5] and RFX 2400 daughter-boards. They communicate in the 2.4 GHz Wi-Fi band using 20 MHz signals. We implement OFDM directly in the USRP Hardware Driver (UHD). We use various 802.11 modulations (BPSK, 4QAM, 16QAM, and 64QAM), coding rates, and choose between them using the effective-SNR bitrate selection algorithm [10]. Our implementation periodically measures the channels by listening to packets from the desired and interfering transmitters. It tracks the INR of the interfering signals for interference alignment or nulling.

To emulate sliding antennas, the antenna of each USRP is mounted on an iRobot Create robot, controlled by an ASUS EEPC 1015PX netbook. We implement stochastic hill climbing in a fully distributed manner using iRobot Create's Open Interface. Each receiver measures INR for interference alignment or nulling in real-time from the software radio(s), and automatically maneuvers the robot to minimize INR from any interferer(s). It also queries the robot sensors to ensure that the robot does not move beyond 2 inches from its initial position as it seeks to minimize its INR.

**Tested Environments:** We evaluate MoMIMO in indoor settings, in line-of-sight (LOS) and non-line-of-sight (NLOS) scenarios, and in two different buildings.

Our main experiments were conducted in Building 1 depicted in Fig. 9(a), which hosts a computer science department. The building is built mostly of flat reinforced concrete slabs and columns.

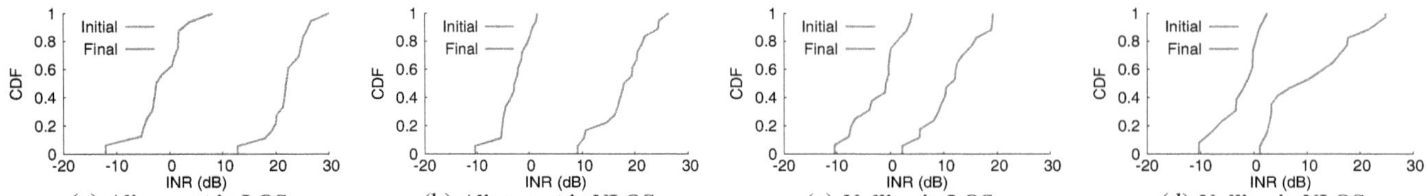

(a) **Alignment in LOS** (b) **Alignment in NLOS** (c) **Nulling in LOS** (d) **Nulling in NLOS**

**Figure 10: INR before and after applying MoMIMO's alignment or nulling.** The figure depicts the CDF of motion-based alignment in (a), (b) and nulling in (c), (d). Our experiments are performed in line-of-sight scenarios in (a), (c) and non-line-of-sight scenarios in (b), (d).

The enclosure of the exterior walls is of metal and brick. The interior walls are gypsum with steel sheet metal studs. The rooms are standard offices with several desks, chairs, cabinets, and computer workstations.

We also ran experiments in Building 2, which is constructed in 1963, and has thick concrete interior walls. We performed our experiments in a large classroom connected to a long corridor with the layout as shown in Fig. 9(b). The classroom consists of several desks and chairs.

**Metrics:** To evaluate MoMIMO's effectiveness at achieving interference alignment and nulling, we measure the *interference to noise ratio (INR)*. In the case of nulling, the INR is computed as the total received interference power after running the stochastic hill climbing algorithm. In the case of alignment, the INR is measured after running the stochastic hill climbing algorithm by projecting the interference signals orthogonal to the desired alignment direction, and computing the interference power after projection. In both cases, an INR less than 0 dB means that MoMIMO has reduced the interference below the noise level.[8]

Other metrics of interest include the throughput, which we measure using the effective-SNR metric as described in [10], and the required antenna displacement for nulling or alignment, which we measure as the distance from the initial location of the antenna to its location after running the stochastic hill climbing algorithm.

## 9. EMPIRICAL RESULTS

We evaluate the performance of MoMIMO in the testbed environment described in §8.

### 9.1 Microbenchmarks

We first investigate whether local antenna adjustments, using our stochastic hill climbing algorithm, can indeed deliver interference alignment and nulling. To do so, we quantify the INR after MoMIMO's alignment and nulling, and check whether it can be reduced below the noise level, i.e., 0 dB.

**Interference Alignment:** We experiment with the setup in Fig. 6, which consists of two single-antenna interferers and a 2-antenna receiver. We place these nodes randomly in our testbeds in both line-of-sight (LOS) and non-line of-sight (NLOS) scenarios. The two interferers concurrently transmit packets back-to-back. The receiver estimates the total power received on both of its antennas; this power constitutes the initial INR. The receiver then runs stochastic hill climbing until the two received signals are aligned. Subsequently, it computes the final INR as the projection of the received signals along the direction orthogonal to the desired alignment as described in §6. We repeat this experiment 20 times, each time placing the interferers and receiver at different locations in our topology.

Figs. 10(a) and 10(b) show the cumulative distribution functions (CDFs) of both the initial and final INRs in these experiments for LOS and NLOS scenarios. The figures show an average INR reduction of about 22 dB in both LOS and NLOS scenarios. Note that the median residual INR is $-0.5$ dB and $-2.5$ dB, in LOS and NLOS respectively, which is below the noise floor, thereby enabling significant throughput gains.

The CDFs also show that in a few percent of the runs, the INR after alignment may be above the noise level by a few dBs. These runs correspond to cases of very strong interference, over 25 dB, and hence the few dB of residual INR. Even in these scenarios, the reduction in INR is large and exceeds 20 dB. Overall, the figure shows that motion-based alignment produces similar accuracy to multi-antenna alignment [15], but requires only single antenna transmitters.

**Interference Nulling:** We place a single-antenna interferer and a single-antenna receiver randomly in our testbed, in both LOS and NLOS scenarios. The interferer transmits a stream of packets back-to-back. The receiver slides its antennas following the stochastic hill climbing algorithm in order to null the signal from the interferer. Upon convergence, it computes the final INR. We repeat this experiment 20 times, each time placing the nodes in different locations in our testbed.

Figs. 10(c) and 10(d) show the CDFs of the initial and final INRs in these experiments for both line-of-sight (LOS) and non-line-of-sight (NLOS) scenarios. The figure shows that after MoMIMO nulling, the median residual INR is $-0.3$ dB in LOS and NLOS, and median reduction in INR is about 15 dB. Our results show that motion-based nulling effectively cancels interference and brings it to the noise level.

In comparison with the alignment experiments, we note that the initial INR for nulling is much lower. This is because in alignment, the initial INR is due to two interferers, whereas here it is due to only one interferer.

### 9.2 Throughput Comparison

We assess the throughput benefits of MoMIMO against two baselines: standard 802.11n and n+ [15]. We compare against n+ to show that MoMIMO delivers gains even when compared with a system that employs advanced MIMO techniques.

For this experiment, we use the heterogeneous network topology in Fig. 5. We note that other topologies like those in Fig.4(b) and 4(c) show a bigger gain for MoMIMO, as explained in §4. However, we chose to present empirical results for the heterogeneous network topology because it is more complex than the others and requires combining both motion-based nulling and alignment.

Recall from §4 that the heterogeneous network in Fig. 5 has two single-antenna transmitter-receiver pairs and one 2-antenna

[8] To be able to evaluate the INR accurately, packets sent by the interferer contain a header with twenty known OFDM symbols. This allows us to measure INR up to an accuracy of -13 dB by averaging the wireless channel across these repeated symbols. While this allows us to accurately measure the residual interference, in practice, pushing the INR below -3 dB is unnecessary. Thus 2-3 known OFDM symbols are sufficient for this accuracy.

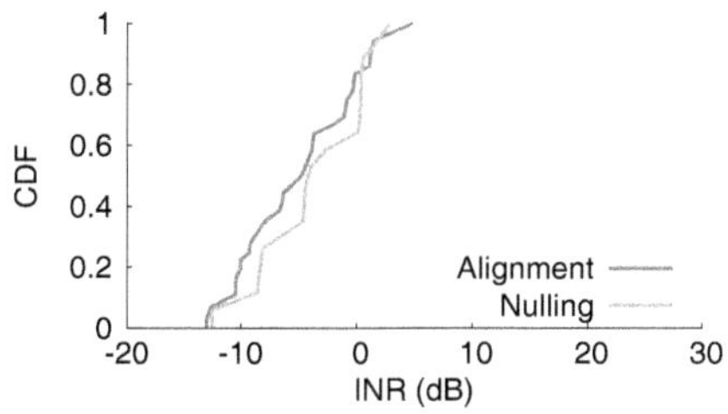

**Figure 12: Leveraging Reciprocity.** CDF of INR and Reciprocal INR for interference alignment and nulling.

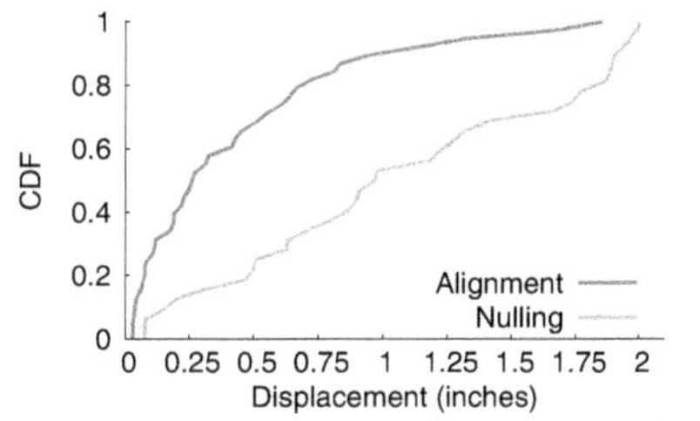

**Figure 13: Displacement for INR reduction.** CDF of the total displacement of the receiver from its initial position, across multiple experiments, for interference alignment or nulling.

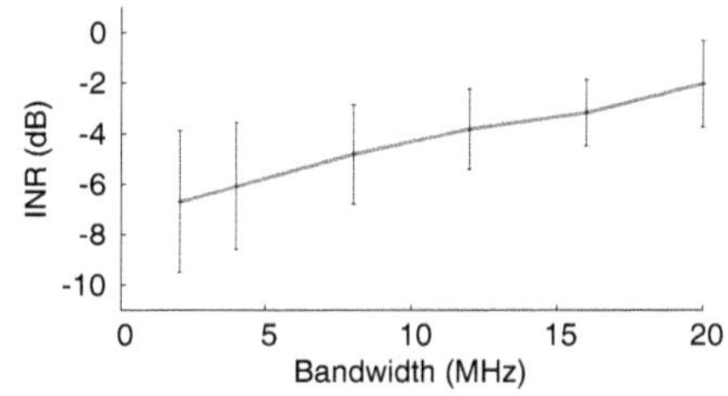

**Figure 14: INR across Bandwidth.** Plot of the mean and standard deviation of the INR at the converged position for interference alignment across bandwidth.

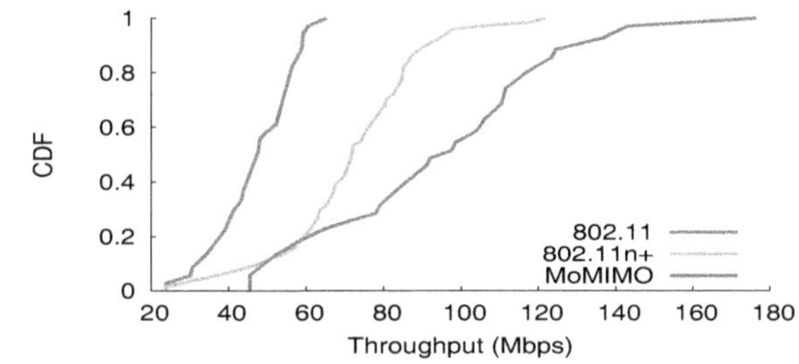

**Figure 11: Total Network Throughput.** Total network throughput of all three schemes: 802.11n, n+, and MoMIMO.

transmitter-receiver pair. For this network, MoMIMO uses sliding antennas to null the signal of Tx1 at Rx2 and that of Tx2 at Rx1. It also needs to align the signals of Tx1 and Tx2 at Rx3. In this case, MoMIMO can deliver 3 concurrent streams. In contrast, 802.11n has to budget the wireless medium between the three Tx-Rx pairs which yields an average of 1.33 concurrent streams, while n+[15] can enable 2 concurrent streams.

For each run of our experiments we pick a random subset of the nodes in the testbed to represent the nodes in the heterogeneous network in Fig. 5. We consider a single long-lasting flow from each sender to its receiver. We repeat the experiment at 20 randomly chosen locations. At each location, we record throughputs for MoMIMO, 802.11n and n+.

For each of the MoMIMO runs, the network initially uses 802.11n with each pair transmitting in a different time slot. During this phase, the nodes do not transmit concurrently; instead they measure the channel and run stochastic hill climbing. Once stochastic hill climbing reaches the desired nulling and alignment, we allow the nodes to transmit concurrently.

Fig. 11 shows CDFs of the obtained throughput in MoMIMO as well as those of 802.11n and n+. On average, MoMIMO achieves a throughput gain of 1.98× over 802.11 and 1.31× gain over n+. In comparison, the expected throughput gains for this heterogeneous network as reported in §4.3 are 2.25× over 802.11n and 1.5× over n+. Thus, our experimental gains are close to the expected ones. Note that both MoMIMO and n+ suffer from a slight performance dip in comparison to their theoretical gains; this is due to small residual interference power after alignment and nulling.

## 9.3 Reciprocity

Reciprocity enables MoMIMO to perform motion-based alignment/nulling on the forward path and still enjoy alignment and nulling on the reverse path, thereby enabling ACKs to be transmitted concurrently without interference. In this section, we evaluate how eliminating interference by applying MoMIMO on the forward path translates into eliminating interference on the reverse path.

Here, we use the same experiments described in §9.1 for both alignment and nulling. The difference however is that after we align/null along the forward path, we reverse the direction of the transmission, i.e., make the receiver transmit and the previous transmitter receive. For the case of alignment and as described in §7, the receiver also precodes the ACK to null it at one of the aligned senders. Our objective is to show empirically that this naturally leads to nulling the signal at the other sender. Hence we measure the corresponding reciprocal INR. For nulling we simply want to show that nulling in the forward direction leads to nulling in the reverse direction. Hence we measure the reverse INR.

Fig. 12 plots the CDFs of the reverse INRs for both alignment and nulling. Each CDF is taken over 20 different runs with different node locations. The figure shows that indeed applying stochastic hill climbing in the forward direction virtually eliminated the INR in the reverse direction as well, reducing it below the noise level (i.e., below 0 dB).

## 9.4 Displacement

Next, we would like to quantify the amount of displacement by which MoMIMO needs to slide the antennas to achieve alignment or nulling. To do so, we measure the displacement between the initial and final positions of the receive antennas in the throughput experiments in §9.2.

Fig. 13 plots the CDFs of this displacement for both alignment and nulling. As expected, since we restricted the motion of the antennas to within a 2 inch radius, the maximum displacement across all experiments is 2 inches. Further, the figure shows that MoMIMO's stochastic hill climbing algorithm needs a mean displacement of 0.44 inches for interference alignment and 1.17 inches for interference nulling. Alignment is easier to satisfy as many options exist for the direction along which two senders may be aligned, which provides extra flexibility for the choice of channels.

## 9.5 Impact of Channel's Bandwidth

Our previous experiments use a bandwidth of 20 MHz, the common setting for 802.11. In this experiment, we evaluate how channel bandwidth impacts MoMIMO's performance.

As in §9.1, we consider two single-antenna interferers and a two-antenna receiver. The receiver performs stochastic hill climbing by moving one of its antennas to align the signals from the two single-antenna interferers. Upon convergence, we fix the initial position of the receiver and repeat the experiment for different channel bandwidths: 2MHz, 4MHz, 8MHz, 16MHz, and 20MHz. For each channel width, we repeat this experiment in 10 randomly chosen locations in our testbed.

Fig. 14 plots the mean and standard deviation of the INR at the receiver as a function of the bandwidth, averaged over all our experiments. The plot reveals that the INR rises by an average of

5 dB as the bandwidth is increased from 2MHz to 20MHz. This is expected because a receiver perceives greater frequency diversity across OFDM subcarriers with increased bandwidth. Nevertheless, even at 20MHz, the mean INR across these experiments was around -2 dB, which is well below the noise floor. Thus, even though the performance of MoMIMO is impacted by an increase in bandwidth due to frequency diversity, MoMIMO continues to provide a significant reduction in INR.

### 9.6 Performance in Dynamic Environments

In this experiment, we study how MoMIMO responds to changes in the wireless channel. MoMIMO nodes incorporate a fail-safe mode that responds to channel changes by defaulting to 802.11n and re-running the stochastic hill climbing algorithm. Specifically, during the periods in which the receive antenna is still moving and has not reached a nulling/alignment position, as well as in which the nulling/alignment position has changed, the nodes fall back to 802.11n and do not transmit extra concurrent streams beyond what is allowed by 802.11n. Note that this behavior is natural in MoMIMO since, once the nulling does not hold, the receiver immediately starts hearing the interference. Similarly, if the alignment does not hold, the receiver sees the interference signal in the whole 2-D space as opposed to along a single direction. Thus, if the channel changes enough to disturb alignment or nulling, the receiver can detect this effect in real-time and fall back to standard 802.11n.

To assess MoMIMO's fail safe mechanism, we repeat the experiment in §9.2, which uses the heterogeneous network. We focus on the two-antenna receiver (Rx3 from Fig. 5), which slides its antenna to align the signals from the two single-antenna interferers Tx1 and Tx2. We consider a scenario where the interferers (Tx1 and Tx2) are inside an office with an open door and the receiver is outside the office. Before starting the experiment, the receiver runs the stochastic hill climbing algorithm to align the two single-antenna transmitters. Our experiment spans 30 seconds. At $t = 15.4$ seconds, we close the door so that the interferers (Tx1 and Tx2), and the receiver are no longer in line-of-sight of each other. We track the INR of alignment at the receiver for the full duration of 30 seconds. We also measure the receiver's throughput obtained based on the effective SNR [10] metric.

Fig. 15(a) plots a trace of the measured INR over time. The trace depicts a distinct spike of about 8 dB in INR at $t = 15.4$ seconds, when the door is closed. However the stochastic hill climbing algorithm responds quickly, reducing the INR to around 0 dB by $t = 16.6$ seconds. Note that the delay of 1.2 seconds was partly due to the limitations of the iRobot Create which is programmed to move at an average speed of 20 mm/s for accurate maneuverability.

Fig. 15(b) plots the throughput of the MIMO receiver over time, under identical settings for 802.11 and MoMIMO. At $t = 15.4$ seconds, the spike in INR caused by the change in channel triggers MoMIMO's fail-safe mechanism. Hence, MoMIMO ceases concurrent transmissions, and falls back to 802.11n's throughput levels (around 17 Mb/s on average). During this period, stochastic hill climbing moves the antenna but without activating concurrent transmissions. Once stochastic hill climbing causes the INR to fall close to the noise level MoMIMO switches on concurrent transmissions. By $t = 16.6$ seconds, the average throughput is around 24 Mb/s, restoring MoMIMO's original gains over 802.11n for the new channel.

## 10. RELATED WORK

Related work falls in the following two categories:

**(a) MIMO Interference Management:** Recent years have witnessed advances in MIMO interference management from both the theoretical [17, 2] and the empirical research communities [26, 7, 15, 22, 6, 21, 23]. Past systems implementing interference alignment [15, 7, 13] typically require multi-antenna senders that are aware of channel state information. Blind interference alignment [18], does not require channel state information at the transmitter, but needs symbol-level time synchronization between transmitters and receivers. Some theoretical work proposes interference alignment for single-antenna nodes either in frequency [25], or in time [19]. In contrast, MoMIMO is the first system to demonstrate that interference alignment and nulling can be performed purely by moving the receive antennas by just about one or two inches.

**(b) Exploiting Motion to Improve Wireless Performance:** Prior work demonstrated that mobility improves the performance of wireless network. For instance, Grossglauser and Tse [9] show that a wireless network of freely moving nodes has a higher capacity than a network with stationary nodes. Also, research from the robotics community [1, 12, 16] has leveraged mobility to improve the quality of wireless channels. For example, in [1, 12], robots improve their connectivity by maintaining a line-of-sight path to their access points. Other work observes that a robot can improve its throughput by sampling different locations in the environment, and choosing the one that maximizes its throughput (due to a higher SNR) [16]. Furthermore, recent work has leveraged node movement to improve beamforming [4] and energy consumption [29]. Additionally, some recent products allow the user to manually slide the antenna to avoid dead spots and improve the SNR [28].

MoMIMO builds on this past work but differs from it by being the first to show that motion enables MIMO-type interference alignment and nulling. Said differently, past work uses motion to improve the SNR but does not show that motion enables MIMO multiplexing gains.

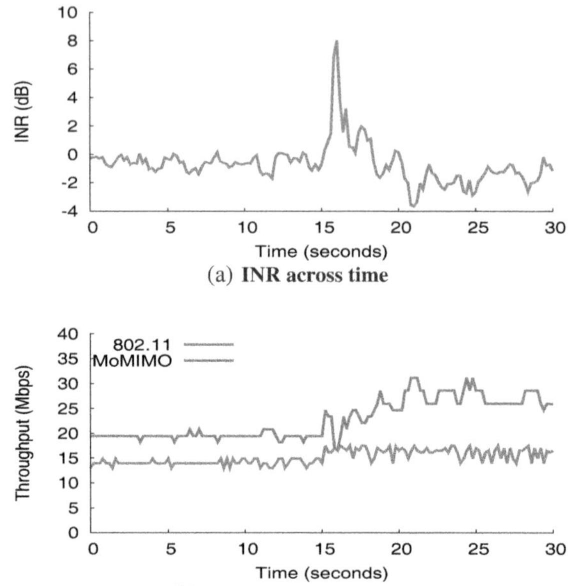

(a) **INR across time**


(b) **Throughput across time**

**Figure 15: Performance of Interference alignment in Dynamic Environments.** The plot shows a trace of the INR and throughput for 30 seconds, where at $t = 15.4s$, the channels change from line-of-sight to non-line-of-sight.

## 11. CONCLUSION

In this paper, we introduced MoMIMO, a technique that demonstrated, for the first time, that interference alignment and nulling can be achieved, even with single-antenna transmitters, by simply moving the receive antenna. We also showed that the amount of antenna displacement needed is fairly small ($\sim$ one inch); hence, MoMIMO can be achieved by sliding antennas.

This paper focused on demonstrating the feasibility and potential gains of MoMIMO. Important topics for future work include: 1) designing a medium access protocol that leverages the synergy between motion and interference alignment as demonstrated by MoMIMO; and 2) studying MoMIMO's gains in different classes of dynamic environments, e.g. static vs. mobile clients.

We believe MoMIMO presents a new paradigm for interference management, especially in settings of long-lived interference patterns such as home networks and data-center flyways. Further, we envision that future systems may exploit motion-based interference alignment and nulling to enable new applications at the intersection of networking and robotics, where mobility is already innate.

## 12. ACKNOWLEDGEMENTS

We thank Omid Abari, Haitham Hassanieh, Ezz Hamad, Jue Wang, Arthur Berger, Diego Cifuentes, Peter Iannucci, Zack Kabelac, Nate Kushman, Jonathan Perry, Hariharan Rahul, Lixin Shi, the reviewers, and our shepherd, Li Erran Li, for their insightful comments. This research is supported by NSF. We thank members of the MIT Center for Wireless Networks and Mobile Computing: Amazon, Cisco, Google, Intel, Mediatek, Microsoft, ST Microelectronics, and Telefonica for their support.

## 13. REFERENCES

[1] R. Arkin and T. Balch. Line-of-sight constrained exploration for reactive multiagent robotic team. *AMC*, July 2002.

[2] V. Cadambe and S. Jafar. Interference alignment and spatial degrees of freedom for the k user interference channel. In *IEEE ICC*, 2008.

[3] Samsung wireless smartcam. `http://www.samsungsv.com/Model/Detail/26/SNH-1011N`.

[4] N. Chatzipanagiotis, Y. Liu, A. Petropulu, and M. M. Zavlanos. Controlling groups of mobile beamformers. In *IEEE CDC*, 2012.

[5] USRP N210. `http://www.ettus.com`. Ettus Inc.

[6] S. Gollakota, F. Adib, D. Katabi, and S. Seshan. Clearing the RF smog: making 802.11n robust to cross-technology interference. In *ACM SIGCOMM*, 2011.

[7] S. Gollakota, S. Perli, and D. Katabi. Interference Alignment and Cancelation. In *ACM SIGCOMM*, 2009.

[8] K. Gomadam, V. R. Cadambe, and S. A. Jafar. Approaching the capacity of wireless networks through distributed interference alignment. In *IEEE GLOBECOM*, 2008.

[9] M. Grossglauser and D. N. C. Tse. Mobility increase the capacity of ad hoc wireless networks. *IEEE/ACM Transactions on Networking*, 2002.

[10] D. Halperin, W. Hu, A. Sheth, and D. Wetherall. Predictable 802.11 packet delivery from wireless channel measurements. In *ACM SIGCOMM*, 2010.

[11] D. Halperin, S. Kandula, J. Padhye, P. Bahl, and D. Wetherall. Augmenting data center networks with multi-gigabit wireless links. In *ACM SIGCOMM*, 2011.

[12] M. A. Hsieh, A. Cowley, V. Kumar, and C. J. Taylor. Towards the deployment of a mobile robot network with end-to-end performance guarantees. 2006.

[13] S. Kumar, D. Cifuentes, S. Gollakota, and D. Katabi. Bringing cross-layer MIMO to today's wireless LANs. In *ACM SIGCOMM*, 2013.

[14] O. Landron, M. Feuerstein, and T. Rappaport. A comparison of theoretical and empirical reflection coefficients for typical exterior wall surfaces in a mobile radio environment. *IEEE Transactions on Antennas and Propagation*, 1996.

[15] K. C.-J. Lin, S. Gollakota, and D. Katabi. Random access heterogeneous MIMO networks. In *ACM SIGCOMM*, 2011.

[16] M. Lindhe, K. H. Johansson, and A. Bicchi. An experimental study of exploiting multipath fading for robot communications. In *Robotics: Science and Systems*, 2007.

[17] M. Maddah-Ali, A. Motahari, and A. Khandani. Communication over MIMO X channels: Interference alignment, decomposition, and performance analysis. *Information Theory, IEEE Transactions on*, 2008.

[18] K. Miller, A. Sanne, K. Srinivasan, and S. Vishwanath. Enabling real-time interference alignment: promises and challenges. MobiHoc, 2012.

[19] A. S. Motahari, S. O. Gharan, M. A. Maddah-Ali, and A. K. Khandani. Forming pseudo-MIMO by embedding infinite rational dimensions along a single real line: Removing barriers in achieving the dofs of single antenna systems. *CoRR*, 2009.

[20] S. W. Peters and R. W. Heath. Cooperative algorithms for MIMO interference channels. *IEEE Transactions on Vehicular Technology*, 2011.

[21] H. Rahul, S. S. Kumar, and D. Katabi. Jmb: Scaling wireless capacity with user demand. In *ACM SIGCOMM*, 2012.

[22] W.-L. Shen, Y.-C. Tung, K.-C. Lee, K. C.-J. Lin, S. Gollakota, D. Katabi, and M.-S. Chen. Rate adaptation for 802.11 multiuser MIMO networks. In *ACM MobiCom*, 2012.

[23] C. Shepard, H. Yu, N. Anand, E. Li, T. Marzetta, R. Yang, and L. Zhong. Argos: Practical many-antenna base stations. In *ACM MobiCom*, 2012.

[24] Sony bravia wireless link module. `http://www.lg.com/us/tv-accessories/lg-AN-WL100W-wireless-media-kit`.

[25] C. Suh and D. Tse. Interference alignment for cellular networks. In *Allerton*, 2008.

[26] K. Tan, H. Liu, J. Fang, W. Wang, J. Zhang, M. Chen, and G. M. Voelker. SAM: enabling practical spatial multiple access in wireless LAN. In *ACM MobiCom*, 2009.

[27] D. Tse and P. Vishwanath. *Fundamentals of Wireless Communications*. Cambridge University Press, 2005.

[28] Netgear a6200 usb wi-fi adapter with sliding antennas. `www.netgear.com/home/products/wireless-adapters/ultimate-wireless-adapters/a6200.aspx`.

[29] Y. Yan and Y. Mostofi. Co-optimization of communication and motion planning of a robotic operation in fading environments. In *IEEE ASILOMAR*, 2011.

# APPENDIX

## A. LENGTH OF REFLECTED PATHS

In this section, we derive the length of reflected paths given the position of an arbitrary reflector. Recall from §5 that any reflector $i$ can be specified in terms of two angles $\theta_{t1,i}$ and $\phi_{t1,i}$. Consider a transmitter $I_t$ and receive antenna $R_1$ separated by a distance $d_{t1,0}$. We can write the position of the reflector in terms of $c_{t1,i}$, its distance from the transmitter, and $\beta_{t1,i}$ its angle to the axis $I_tR_1$ (Figure 16). First, it is easy to see that $\beta_{t1,i} = \frac{\phi_{t1,i} - \theta_{t1,i}}{2}$. Now, by using sine-rule on $\Delta PI_tR_1$, we have:

$$PI_t = d_{t1,0} \frac{sin(\phi_{t1,i})}{sin(\phi_{t1,i} + \theta_{t1,i})} \quad (10)$$

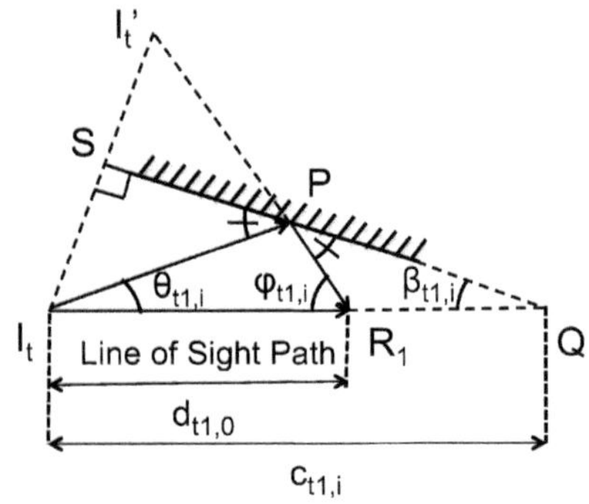


**Figure 16: Reflected Path.** We consider a transmitter $I_t$ and receive antenna $R_1$. Signals arrive at $R_1$ from the direct line-of-sight path and a path due to reflector specified by the tuple $(\theta_{t1,i}, \phi_{t1,i})$, where $\theta_{t1,i}$ denotes the angle of departure of the signal from interferer $I_t$ and $\phi_{t1,i}$ denotes the angle of arrival of the signal at receive antenna $R_1$

Using sine rule on triangle $PI_tQ$:

$$c_{t1,i} = PI_t \frac{sin\left(\frac{\phi_{t1,i}+\theta_{t1,i}}{2}\right)}{sin\left(\frac{\phi_{t1,i}-\theta_{t1,i}}{2}\right)} = \frac{d_{t1,0}sin(\phi_{t1,i})sin\left(\frac{\phi_{t1,i}+\theta_{t1,i}}{2}\right)}{sin(\phi_{t1,i}+\theta_{t1,i})sin\left(\frac{\phi_{t1,i}-\theta_{t1,i}}{2}\right)}$$
$$= \frac{d_{t1,0}sin(\phi_{t1,i})}{2cos\left(\frac{\phi_{t1,i}+\theta_{t1,i}}{2}\right)sin\left(\frac{\phi_{t1,i}-\theta_{t1,i}}{2}\right)} = \frac{d_{t1,0}sin(\phi_{t1,i})}{sin(\phi_{t1,i})-sin(\theta_{t1,i})}$$

Now suppose the receive antenna $R_1$ is initially at the origin (0,0). Then the transmitter is at a coordinate ($-d_{t1,0}$, 0). Let us denote $I_t'$ as the symmetric point of the transmitter about the reflector. Note that since $PI_t = PI_t'$, $PI_t + PR_1 = PI_t' + PR_1 = I_t'R_1$. Hence the length of the reflected path to any receive antenna coordinate $R_1$ is $I_t'R_1$.

Clearly $\angle I_t'I_tR_1 = \pi/2 - (\frac{\phi_{t1,i}-\theta_{t1,i}}{2}) = \pi/2 - \beta_{t1,i}$. From $\Delta QI_tS$ we have $SI_t = SI_t' = csin\beta_{t1,i}$. Hence $I_t'I_t = 2c_{t1,i}sin\beta_{t1,i}$. Hence the coordinate of $I_t'$ is $(2c_{t1,i}sin^2\beta_{t1,i} - d_{t1,0}, 2c_{t1,i}sin\beta_{t1,i}cos\beta_{t1,i}) = (2c_{t1,i}sin^2(\beta_{t1,i}) - d_{t1,0}, csin(2\beta_{t1,i}))$.

Thus the length of the reflected path when the receive antenna is moved to any position $(\delta x, \delta y)$ is:

$$d'_{t1,i} = \sqrt{(2c_{t1,i}\sin^2(\beta_{t1,i}) - d_{t1,0} - \delta x)^2 + (c_{t1,i}\sin(2\beta_{t1,i}) - \delta y)^2}$$

where, $c_{t1,i} = d_{t1,0}\sin\phi_{t1,i}/(\sin\phi_{t1,i} - \sin\theta_{t1,i})$ and $\beta_{t1,i} = (\phi_{t1,i} - \theta_{t1,i})/2$.

## B. MINIMIZING INTERFERENCE TO NOISE

Consider two transmitters and a single two-antenna receiver. Let $h_{ij}$ denote the channel from transmitter $i$ to receive antenna $j$. Our goal is to minimize the interference to noise ratio (INR) for alignment, given by:

$$INR = \frac{1}{\sigma^2}\min_{\alpha,\beta}|h_{11}\alpha + h_{12}\beta|^2 + |h_{21}\alpha + h_{22}\beta|^2$$

where $|\alpha|^2 + |\beta|^2 = 1$ and $\sigma^2$ is the noise power.

Without loss of generality, we can choose $\alpha$ to be a positive real, and $\beta = \sqrt{1-\alpha^2}e^{j\theta}$, where $\theta \in [-\pi, \pi]$. Hence, our goal is to minimize:

$$\begin{aligned}
&|h_{11}\alpha + h_{12}\beta|^2 + |h_{21}\alpha + h_{22}\beta|^2\\
=&(|h_{11}|^2 + |h_{21}|^2)\alpha^2 + (|h_{12}|^2 + |h_{22}|^2)|\beta|^2\\
&+ 2\mathrm{Re}\{\alpha\beta^*(h_{11}h_{12}^* + h_{21}h_{22}^*)\}\\
=&(|h_{12}|^2 + |h_{22}|^2) + \alpha^2(|h_{11}|^2 - |h_{12}|^2 + |h_{21}| - |h_{22}|^2)\\
&+ 2\alpha\sqrt{1-\alpha^2}\mathrm{Re}\{(h_{11}h_{12}^* + h_{21}h_{22}^*)e^{-j\theta}\}
\end{aligned}$$

We choose $\theta = \pi + \angle(h_{11}h_{12}^* + h_{21}h_{22}^*)$, so as to minimize the third term. Hence, we need to minimize:

$$\begin{aligned}
&(|h_{12}|^2 + |h_{22}|^2) + \alpha^2(|h_{11}|^2 - |h_{12}|^2 + |h_{21}| - |h_{22}|^2)\\
&-2\alpha\sqrt{1-\alpha^2}|h_{11}h_{12}^* + h_{21}h_{22}^*|
\end{aligned}$$

Let $A = (|h_{11}|^2 - |h_{12}|^2 + |h_{21}|^2 - |h_{22}|^2)$, $B = |h_{11}h_{12}^* + h_{21}h_{22}^*|$ and $C = (|h_{12}|^2 + |h_{22}|^2)$. Hence, we wish to minimize:

$$INR = \frac{1}{\sigma^2}(A\alpha^2 - 2B\alpha\sqrt{1-\alpha^2} + C) \quad (11)$$

To do so, we set its derivative with respect to $\alpha$ to zero, i.e.

$$\begin{aligned}
2A\alpha - 2B\sqrt{1-\alpha^2} + 2B\alpha^2/\sqrt{1-\alpha^2} &= 0\\
2A\alpha\sqrt{1-\alpha^2} - 2B(1-2\alpha^2) &= 0\\
A^2\alpha^2(1-\alpha^2) &= B^2(1-2\alpha^2)^2\\
\alpha^4(A^2+4B^2) - \alpha^2(A^2+4B^2) + B^2 &= 0
\end{aligned}$$

The above equation is quadratic in $\alpha^2$. Solving, we have:

$$\alpha = \sqrt{\frac{1}{2} - \frac{A}{2\sqrt{A^2+4B^2}}}$$

Substituting $\alpha$ in Eqn. 11:

$$INR = \frac{1}{\sigma^2}\left(A\left(\frac{1}{2} - \frac{A}{2\sqrt{A^2+4B^2}}\right) - 2B\sqrt{\frac{1}{4} - \frac{A^2}{4(A^2+4B^2)}} + C\right)$$

$$INR = \frac{1}{\sigma^2}\left((A/2 + C) - \frac{A^2}{2\sqrt{A^2+4B^2}}) - 2B^2\sqrt{\frac{1}{A^2+4B^2}}\right)$$

$$INR = \frac{1}{\sigma^2}\left((A/2 + C) - \frac{1}{2}\sqrt{A^2+4B^2}\right)$$

Substituting for $A$, $B$ and $C$ in the above equation, we have:

$$INR = \frac{1}{2\sigma^2}\left(|h_{11}|^2 + |h_{21}|^2 + |h_{12}|^2 + |h_{22}|^2\right) -$$
$$\frac{1}{\sigma^2}\sqrt{\left|\frac{|h_{11}|^2 + |h_{21}|^2 - |h_{12}|^2 - |h_{22}|^2}{2}\right|^2 + |h_{11}h_{12}^* + h_{21}h_{22}^*|^2}$$

Which precisely corresponds to Eqn. 7.

# Understanding RFID Counting Protocols

Binbin Chen
Advanced Digital Sciences Center
Illinois at Singapore Pte. Ltd.
Republic of Singapore
binbin.chen@adsc.com.sg

Ziling Zhou *
School of Computing
National University of Singapore
Republic of Singapore
zhouzl@comp.nus.edu.sg

Haifeng Yu
School of Computing
National University of Singapore
Republic of Singapore
haifeng@comp.nus.edu.sg

## ABSTRACT

*Counting the number of RFID tags, or* RFID counting, *is needed by a wide array of important wireless applications. Motivated by its paramount practical importance, researchers have developed an impressive arsenal of techniques to improve the performance of RFID counting (i.e., to reduce the time needed to do the counting). This paper aims to gain deeper and fundamental insights in this subject to facilitate future research on this topic.*

*As our central thesis, we find out that the overlooked key design aspect for RFID counting protocols to achieve near-optimal performance is a conceptual separation of a protocol into two phases. The first phase uses small overhead to obtain a rough estimate, and the second phase uses the rough estimate to further achieve an accuracy target. Our thesis also indicates that other performance-enhancing techniques or ideas proposed in the literature are only of secondary importance. Guided by our central thesis, we manage to design near-optimal protocols that are more efficient than existing ones and simultaneously simpler than most of them.*

## Categories and Subject Descriptors

C.2.1 [**Network Architecture and Design**]: Wireless Communication; C.2.8 [**Mobile Computing**]: Algorithm/Protocol Design and Analysis; C.3 [**Special-Purpose and Application-Based Systems**]: Real-time and embedded systems

## General Terms

Algorithms, Design, Experimentation, Performance, Theory

## Keywords

RFID; Counting; RFID counting protocols; Lower bounds; Two-phase

*This work was partly done when Ziling Zhou was a research intern at Advanced Digital Sciences Center.


*MobiCom'13,* September 30–October 4, Miami, FL, USA.

ACM 978-1-4503-1999-7/13/09 ...$15.00.
http://dx.doi.org/10.1145/2500423.2500431.

## 1. INTRODUCTION

Radio-frequency identification (RFID) technology uses RFID tags and RFID readers (or simply called *tags* and *readers*) to monitor objects in physical world. A tag is a low-cost microchip that can be attached to an object. It can store some information (including a unique ID) and can communicate with a reader through wireless channel. Over the past decade, RFID technology has enjoyed significant growth. With more than 3 billion tags sold in 2012, RFID technology has by now impacted applications ranging from inventory control, supply chain management, to people tracking. A common basic functionality needed by many of these applications is *RFID counting* — to count the number of tags and thus the number of tagged objects in certain physical area [17]. For example:

- Wal-Mart [2] puts tags on individual clothes. Here RFID counting provides information about sales trend and speeds up the restocking process.
- Purdue Pharma [4] has tagged millions of its tablet bottles. Here RFID counting ensures the right amount of its products are passing through its manufacturing, packaging, and shipping process.
- Many events (e.g., TechEd [1] and Bonnaroo festival [3]) distribute RFID wristbands to their visitors. Here RFID counting helps reveal the number of people around.

Often in such scenarios, it is desirable to simply count or just estimate the number of tags without explicitly identifying individual tags. This helps to significantly reduce the processing time, preserve people's privacy, and avoid the cost incurred for handling a large amount of unnecessary information. In addition to its direct utility, RFID counting can also serve as a preprocessing step and help other tasks. For example, even if one were still to identify individual tags, knowing the rough number of tags can make the identification process much more efficient [12, 20]. As another example, one can use RFID counting to help find popular categories in a large collection of tags [19].

In this paper, we will consider two common versions of RFID counting problem. The first *single-set RFID counting* problem is simply to count the number of tags in a given physical area, using a single stationary reader whose radio range covers that entire area. In the second *multiple-set RFID counting* problem, the reader's radio range cannot cover the whole area. Instead, the (single) reader becomes mobile and sequentially visits a number of locations, so that the union of the coverages at these locations can cover the whole physical area. Note that the coverage at different locations may overlap and hence double counting needs to be avoided.

In both versions of the problem, a key performance metric is the amount of time needed to count or estimate the total number of tags, which will be the focus of this work. Since exact results are often not necessary for many applications (e.g., for the earlier example application scenarios) and since the overhead of exact counting is fundamentally high,[1] as in most prior efforts [9, 12, 13, 16, 18, 24, 25], we will focus on approximate counting.

**Previous efforts.** Given the paramount practical importance of RFID counting, there have been a steady stream of recent research efforts on efficient RFID counting. To reduce the overhead (time) needed to count (i.e., to improve the *performance*), these efforts have developed an impressive arsenal of novel techniques, such as probabilistic framed ALOHA [12], multi-resolution probing [13], lottery frame protocol [16], first non-empty slot based estimation [9], probabilistic estimating tree [24], average run based estimation [18], and zero-one estimator [25].

While these efforts all aim at reducing the overhead of RFID counting, they often approach the problem from rather different perspectives without being guided by a central principle. This has led to ad hoc research outcomes where different researchers view different aspects of RFID counting protocols as key. For example, some researchers focus on using novel statistical quantities to estimate the count [9, 16, 18], some researchers put more emphasis on obtaining optimal trade-offs among different protocol parameters [13, 18], while others resort to gradually refining the parameters via an adaptive iterative process [9, 12].

The fundamentals of the RFID counting problem get easily buried among all these research outcomes — At this point, it is far from clear whether all these techniques are equally important or whether one technique plays the dominant role. Such a lack of deep understanding hinders future research on RFID counting — if we would like to advance the state of the art, should we combine all these techniques despite the resulting complexity? Or should we focus on improving one of them and ignore others?

**Our goal.** Given such a lack of fundamental understanding into the RFID counting problem, this paper aims to gain deeper insights to facilitate future research. Specifically, we aim to answer the following three key questions, none of which have been posed or answered in prior efforts:

- *Question 1:* Given the long list of protocols in the literature, how much room is there for further improvement?
- *Question 2:* What are the key aspects that determine a RFID counting protocol's performance? What are the techniques that are only of secondary importance?
- *Question 3:* Guided by the answers to the earlier two questions, can we easily design simple protocols that outperform existing ones?

**Our results.** Our main contributions are precisely the answers to these three questions:

- *Answer 1: Lower bounds.* To determine how much improvement is still possible, we obtain strong lower bounds on the overhead of RFID counting, by leveraging a recent breakthrough result on communication complexity [5]. Our lower bounds show that it is *impossible* for a single-set RFID counting protocol to use only $o(\frac{1}{\epsilon^2 \log \frac{1}{\epsilon}} + \log\log n)$ time slots for all inputs. Here $n$ is the number of tags to count, and $\epsilon$ is the relative error on the final output of the protocol (since we are considering approximate counting). In each *time slot*, the reader may broadcast $O(1)$ bits to the tags, and all the tags combined can send back $O(1)$ bits to the reader. A similar lower bound is obtained for multiple-set RFID counting.

  We then compare these lower bounds with the asymptotic overhead of existing protocols. Such comparison readily reveals that:

  - For single-set RFID counting, some existing protocols' performance is already asymptotically close to optimal. Improvements are still possible though one should not expect huge improvements.
  - For multiple-set RFID counting, existing protocols' performance is further away from optimal. Larger improvements hence seem still possible.

- *Answer 2: The overlooked key design aspect for approaching optimal performance.* We identify that a key design aspect for single-set RFID counting protocols to approach optimal performance is to have two conceptual phases: The first phase uses roughly $\Theta(\log\log n)$ slots to obtain a rough estimate with constant (e.g., $0.5$) relative error, and the second phase uses roughly $\Theta(\frac{1}{\epsilon^2 \log \frac{1}{\epsilon}})$ slots to eventually obtain a final estimate with the desired relative error of $\epsilon$. Our thesis further indicates that many other performance-enhancing techniques or ideas proposed in the literature are only of secondary importance. We also generalize this answer to multiple-set RFID counting protocols.

  It is worth noting that our answer to this question is quite surprising because prior efforts [9, 12, 13, 16, 18, 24, 25] often view various other aspects of RFID counting protocols as key, and have overlooked this two-phase aspect. Those efforts also attribute their performance improvements to various clever techniques on those aspects (e.g., the use of novel statistical quantities to do the estimation, the use of complex optimization techniques to tune various parameters, and the use of iterative process to refine the estimation). Our answer implies that all those design aspects are perhaps less important than originally thought.

  As direct evidence to support our claim, this paper carefully examines the source of performance gains in some existing RFID counting protocols. For example, some recent protocols [9, 18] attribute their performance improvements over prior protocols to the use of the novel statistical quantities to do the estimation. Quite surprisingly, in our experiments, we find that these novel quantity does not necessarily improve the performance of these protocols: Replacing these novel quantities with some old quantity from some earlier protocol [13] either improves the protocols' performance or provides comparable performance in our experiments. We further show that the source of performance gains in these protocols is their two-phase design, despite that such a two-phase design was not considered as the key.

- *Answer 3: Simple & more efficient RFID counting protocols.* Guided by our answers to the earlier two questions, we set out to search for more efficient RFID counting protocols while keeping our design as simple as possible. We manage to design such protocols by simply putting together a few basic building blocks (with some rather minor adaptations) from the literature. We do *not* claim novelty on these building blocks – instead, we aim to show that simply putting them together in a *proper manner* as guided by our earlier answers is already sufficient to outperform existing protocols. This serves as an ultimate validation of the utility of our earlier findings.

  Specifically, our RFID counting protocols are significantly simpler than most existing protocols — for example, we do not need iterative refinement or to solve optimization problems to tune parameters. Despite the simplicity, our experiments show that our single-set (multiple-set) RFID counting protocol is around $100\%$ ($500\%$) faster than the best existing single-set (multiple-set) RFID counting protocol. Furthermore, our protocols are *near-optimal* and are within a small $O(\log \frac{1}{\epsilon})$ factor from the lower bounds, for both single-set and multiple-set RFID counting.

[1] As implied by our formal lower bound results in Section 3.

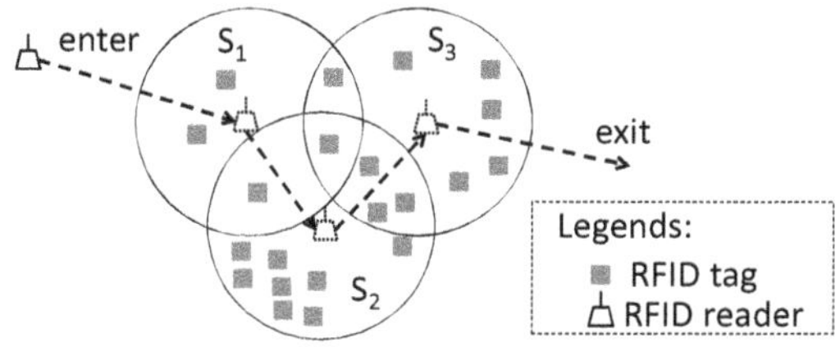


**Figure 1: A multiple-set RFID counting example: A mobile reader sequentially visits three locations.**

**Roadmap.** The next section formalizes the RFID counting problem. Section 3 proves lower bounds on the overhead of single-set and multiple-set RFID counting. Section 4 reviews major existing RFID counting protocols. Section 5 presents our thesis on the overlooked key design aspect of RFID counting. Section 6 provides direct and immediate evidence to support our thesis by examining the source of performance gain of some recent protocols. Section 7 demonstrates the utility of our insights by applying them to construct new protocols that are both simple and more efficient. Section 8 and Section 9 discuss variant models and related work. We conclude in Section 10.

# 2. PROBLEM FORMULATION

This section formalizes the RFID counting problem. We define the overhead of RFID counting protocols mainly for later studying the asymptotic lower bound on the problem and the asymptotic upper bound achieved by the protocols. Hence our formulation here will only be concerned with asymptotic overhead.

**Single-set and multiple-set RFID counting.** In the *single-set RFID counting* problem, the reader covers a certain physical area. Let $S$ denote the set of tags in that area, and let $n = |S|$. The goal of the counting protocol is to produce an estimate $\hat{n}$ for $n$, so that $Pr(|\hat{n} - n| \leq \epsilon n) \geq 1 - \delta$, with the probability taken over the random coin flips done by the randomized protocol. Here $\epsilon$ and $\delta$ captures the target estimation quality, and should be specified by the end user. We also refer to $\epsilon$ as the *relative error* of $\hat{n}$. We call $\hat{n}$ as having $(\epsilon, \delta)$ *estimation quality* and call $\hat{n}$ itself as an $(\epsilon, \delta)$ estimate.

In the *multiple-set RFID counting* problem (Figure 1), a mobile reader sequentially visits $k$ locations exactly once.[2] At location $i$, the reader's radio range covers a set $S_i$ of tags. Let $n_i = |S_i|$. The goal of the counting protocol is to produce an $(\epsilon, \delta)$-approximation $\hat{n}$ for $n$, where $n = |S_1 \cup S_2 \cup ... \cup S_k|$. Usually $n \neq n_1 + n_2 + ... + n_k$ since the $S_i$'s may overlap. Note that such formulation of the multiple-set RFID counting problem implicitly but fully captures more general application scenarios. For example, it also captures the setting where a static reader takes a sequence of snapshots of mobile tags and then counts the total number of tags.

Since we aim for $(\epsilon, \delta)$ estimation quality, the RFID counting protocols are essentially Monte Carlo randomized algorithms [15]. In our reasoning on asymptotic overhead, we will adopt the following standard way of treating $\delta$ in Monte Carlo algorithms [15]: We will only require the protocol to achieve constant $\delta$ (e.g., 0.2). It is well-known that to achieve a smaller $\delta$, one can repeat the protocol $O(\log \frac{1}{\delta})$ times and then take the median of the $O(\log \frac{1}{\delta})$ outputs as the final output. A constant $\delta$ helps simplify our discussion.

**Abstracting RFID counting protocols.** In an RFID counting protocol, the reader communicates with tags in synchronized time slots. In Section 1, we explained that in each time slot the reader and the tags can exchange $O(1)$ bits. Without loss of generality, from now on, we will assume that in each time slot the reader may send $O(1)$ bits to the tags, while all the tags collectively can either send a single bit of "1" or send nothing.[3] Such treatment is without loss of generality because our formalization here is only for reasoning about asymptotic overhead — one can easily use $O(1)$ slots to send $O(1)$ bits. We say that a tag *responds* in a slot iff it sends back a "1" bit. If there exists at least one tag responding in a slot, the slot becomes *non-empty*. Otherwise the slot is *empty*.

Now consider a given slot. Since the tags are distributed, each tag will need to unilaterally determine whether it will respond, based on its id, random numbers generated locally, and its current state (since the protocol may be stateful), and the bits received from the reader. For our formal reasoning later, it will be convenient to imagine that in each slot the reader conceptually specifies a boolean *predicate function* $f$. A tag responds in the slot iff it satisfies the predicate $f$. Note that the RFID counting protocol may be stateful — this is captured by allowing the function $f$ to take the local state (i.e., local variables) of the tag as an input as well.

**Measure of goodness.** Our measure of goodness (or *performance*) of an RFID counting protocol is the amount of time it needs. When studying asymptotic behavior, this is the same as the total number of slots used by the protocol. Hence we define the *asymptotic overhead* of a protocol to be $O(x)$, if for all inputs, it needs $O(x)$ slots on expectation for achieving the accuracy target. Here the expectation is taken over the coin flips done by the randomized protocol.

# 3. LOWER BOUNDS ON THE OVERHEAD OF RFID COUNTING PROTOCOLS

We first consider single-set RFID counting, and then generalize to multiple-set RFID counting.

**Single-set Counting: Lower bound as a function of $\epsilon$.** We will use a standard *reduction* approach to obtain our novel lower bound on the overhead of a RFID protocol. For readers not familiar with reduction, following is a quick explanation. To prove that a problem $\mathcal{A}$ (in our case, the RFID counting problem) is hard and hence to obtain a lower bound for the complexity of any protocol that solves $\mathcal{A}$, a common approach (called *reduction*) in complexity research is to establish a connection with another hard problem $\mathcal{B}$. Namely, one first shows that any protocol for solving $\mathcal{A}$ can be used, as a black box sub-procedure, to solve $\mathcal{B}$. Next since $\mathcal{B}$ is hard, any protocol for solving $\mathcal{B}$ must incur large overhead. This in turn can be translated back to reason about the hardness of $\mathcal{A}$.

The key step/challenge in reduction is to choose a proper $\mathcal{B}$ and then to show how to construct a protocol for solving $\mathcal{B}$, given any protocol for solving $\mathcal{A}$. We choose the *Hamming Distance Estimation* (HDE) problem as the hard problem $\mathcal{B}$. HDE is a two-party communication complexity problem, where the two parties Alice and Bob are given $n$-bit strings $x$ and $y$ as input respectively. They would like to estimate the hamming distance between $x$ and $y$, with $(\epsilon, \delta)$ estimation quality, while minimizing the number of bits they need to exchange. A recent breakthrough result by Chakrabarti and Regev [5] implies that even for a constant $\delta$, solving the HDE problem requires $\Omega(1/\epsilon^2)$ bits of communication between Alice and Bob (for $\epsilon \geq 1/\sqrt{n}$).

With HDE as problem $\mathcal{B}$, our goal now is to design a protocol for solving HDE, using any given RFID counting protocol $\mathcal{P}$ as a building block. To do so, Alice and Bob will locally *simulate* an execution of $\mathcal{P}$. Specifically, they will simulate $n$ RFID tags, with IDs from 1 through $n$. We want tag $i$ to be *present* and be included

[2]Some researchers (e.g., [18]) consider a *simpler* variant of the problem by assuming *parallel* access to all sets through multiple readers. Section 8 discusses this simpler variant.

[3]Some protocols (e.g., [12]) assume that the reader can further distinguish whether a single tag or multiple tags send a bit. We will cover this extended model in Section 8.

in the RFID counting result iff $x[i] \neq y[i]$. All other tags $j$ where $x[j] = y[j]$ should be *absent* and will not be included in the count. This will make the RFID count to exactly equal the hamming distance between $x$ and $y$, hence solving the HDE problem once we know the count.

Now to properly simulate the execution of $\mathcal{P}$ with those present tags, Alice/Bob needs to determine which slots in the simulated execution of $\mathcal{P}$ are empty. Doing so enables Alice/Bob to simulate the responses received in all these slots and feed those into $\mathcal{P}$ to obtain the final count. For each slot, we will show that Alice and Bob can determine whether it is empty by only exchanging $O(\log \frac{1}{\epsilon})$ bits. Consider the first slot. $\mathcal{P}$ must have specified a predicate $f$ for the first slot. Alice/Bob can thus locally determine the set of tags (e.g., tag 2, 6, and 7) that satisfy $f$. Next Alice computes a short fingerprint of size $O(\log \frac{1}{\epsilon})$ for the (potentially long) string $x[2]x[6]x[7]$ and sends to Bob. Bob similarly computes the fingerprint over $y[2]y[6]y[7]$ and compares the two fingerprints. For now assume no fingerprint collisions (collisions will be properly addressed in our proof). Then the two fingerprints differ iff $x[2] \neq y[2]$ or $x[6] \neq y[6]$ or $x[7] \neq y[7]$, which in turn is equivalent to tag 2 or tag 6 or tag 7 being present, and also equivalent to the first slot being non-empty. Alice and Bob now have successfully determined whether the first slot is empty or not. Emptiness of later slots can be sequentially determined in a similar way.

Formalizing the above intuition will lead to the following theorem, whose proof is in our technical report [6]:

THEOREM 1. *No single-set RFID counting protocol can output an* $(\epsilon, 0.2)$ *estimate with* $o(\frac{1}{\epsilon^2 \log \frac{1}{\epsilon}})$ *overhead, for* $\epsilon \in [1/\sqrt{n}, 0.5]$.

**Single-set Counting: Lower bound as a function of $n$.** One naturally expects that the number of slots needed by an RFID counting protocol will increase with $n$ as well. For example, to approximate every possible tag count between 1 to $n$ within a relative error of 0.5, a deterministic RFID counting protocol needs to be ready to output $\Omega(\log n)$ different values, with *at least* one in each of ranges $[1, 2]$, $[4, 8]$, $[16, 32]$, ... These $\Omega(\log n)$ different values require at least $\Omega(\log \log n)$ bits (i.e., slots used by the RFID counting protocol) to encode. To extend this argument to randomized RFID counting protocols with $(\epsilon, \delta)$ guarantee, we leverage Yao's well-known minimax principle [22] on the complexity of randomized algorithms. Doing so will eventually yield a similar log log lower bound (see our technical report [6] for full proof):

THEOREM 2. *No single-set RFID counting protocol can output an* $(\epsilon, 0.2)$ *estimate with* $o(\log \log n)$ *overhead, for* $\epsilon \leq 0.5$.

**Single-set Counting: Putting everything together.**

COROLLARY 3. *No single-set RFID counting protocol can output an* $(\epsilon, 0.2)$ *estimate with* $o(\frac{1}{\epsilon^2 \log \frac{1}{\epsilon}} + \log \log n)$ *overhead, for* $\epsilon \in [1/\sqrt{n}, 0.5]$.

This corollary also implies the difficulty of exact counting: Exact counting is no easier that approximate counting with $\epsilon = \frac{1}{\sqrt{n}}$, where $o(\frac{n}{\log n})$ overhead is already impossible.

**Multiple-set Counting: Lower bounds.** Recall that in multiple-set RFID counting, the RFID reader sequentially sees a sequence of (potentially overlapping) sets $S_1, S_2, ..., S_k$. The goal is to estimate the size of the union of all these sets. We can show that in the worst case, to estimate the size of the union, it is actually *necessary* for the protocol to estimate with similar accuracy the size ($n_i$) of each individual set $S_i$. Formalize such intuition, together with our single-set RFID counting lower bound, would lead to the following theorem, whose proof is in our technical report [6]:

THEOREM 4. *No multiple-set RFID counting protocol can output an* $(\epsilon, 0.2)$ *estimate with* $o(\sum_{i=1}^{k}(\frac{1}{\epsilon^2 \log \frac{1}{\epsilon}} + \log \log n_i))$ *overhead, for* $\epsilon \in [1/\sqrt{\min(n_1, n_2, \ldots, n_k)}, 0.25]$.

**Key implications of our lower bounds — how much room is there for further improving RFID counting protocols?** As we will show in Section 5, in terms of asymptotic overhead, the best existing single-set RFID counting protocol incurs an overhead of $O(\frac{1}{\epsilon^2} + \log \log n)$. This is already close to our lower bound. Improvements may still be possible though one should not expect huge improvements. For multiple-set RFID counting, the best existing protocol incurs an overhead of $O(\frac{k}{\epsilon^2} \log \log(\sum_{i=1}^{k} n_i))$. It exhibits a larger gap from our lower bound — in particular, this overhead is multiplicative while our lower bound is additive. Hence significant asymptotic improvement seems still possible.

# 4. REVIEW OF THE MAIN IDEAS IN EXISTING PROTOCOLS

This section concisely reviews major RFID counting protocols in the literature (Table 1). This serves to set up the stage for our later discussion on which design aspects are key for RFID counting protocols. For each protocol, we will highlight which design aspects are believed by the original authors as the key aspects of that protocol. Throughout this section, we use $\tilde{n}$ to denote a rough estimate on $n$ (e.g., with constant relative error), and $\hat{n}$ to denote the final estimation on $n$ with $\epsilon$ relative error.

These protocols adopt some common concepts. Each of these protocols is comprised of a sequence of *trials*, where each trial is a sequence of slots. At the beginning of a trial, the reader sends a command to the tags. This causes the tags to initialize their local state machines and potentially load new random numbers. Next in each slot within that trial, a tag will respond or not respond based on the command, its local state, and its random number. For all existing protocols, a tag does not carry state across trial boundary. Due to the processing needed at the beginning of a trial, in certain physical implementations of RFID systems, a trial may incur an additional *per-trial overhead.* If there is indeed such overhead, this extra overhead will be in addition to the time needed for all the slots in that trial [7].

The number of slots in a trial is called the *length* of the trial. Recall that a slot is either empty or non-empty, depending on whether there is at least one tag responding in that slot. A non-empty slot is called a *collision* slot iff at least two tags respond in that slot.

One simple way of running a trial, as adopted by multiple protocols, is to start a trial of length $l$ and let each tag *participate* in that trial with a certain probability $p$, with total $np$ tags participating on expectation. Here we say a tag *participates* in such a trial iff it chooses a uniformly random slot within that trial and then responds in that slot, and we call such a trial a *balls-and-bins trial.* The value of $n$ can then be estimated from various statistical quantities on the status of the slots. A basic principle, which will help us understand these protocols, is that usually we want to use a $p$ value such that $np$ is on the same order as $l$. This ensures that we see a healthy mixture of empty and non-empty slots in the trials, maximizing the amount of information carried about $n$. Besides such balls-and-bins trials, existing protocols have also developed alternative ways to use the slots of a trial, as will be described later in the corresponding protocols.

**Unified probabilistic estimation (UPE) [12].** In UPE, all trials are balls-and-bins trials with the same length (e.g., 30). In the first trial, all tags participate. Depending on the number of empty slots observed in this trial, the protocol will branch into several different execution paths. We will focus on the most important execution path, which corresponds to large $n$ and where the protocol observes no empty slots in the first trial. In such a case, the protocol proceeds sequentially to the second trial, the third trial, and so on, with each tag participating with $p = 0.1^{i-1}$ probability in the $i$th trial. This process stops once the protocol sees an empty slot in a trial. The

| Protocol | Venue | Key source of performance gains, as believed by the authors |
|---|---|---|
| UPE [12] | MobiCom'06 | i) proper randomization; ii) use of empty and collision slots for estimation |
| EZB [13] | INFOCOM'07 | i) multi-resolution probing; ii) various parameter optimization techniques |
| LOF [16] | PerCom'08 / TPDS'11 | small length of the trials |
| (Enhanced) FNEB [9] | INFOCOM'10 | use of the indices of the first non-empty slots for estimation |
| PET [24] | ICDCS'11 / TMC'12 | use of the binary search to find the index of the last nonempty slot |
| ART [18] | MobiCom'12 | use of the average run length of non-empty slots for estimation |
| ZOE [25] | INFOCOM'13 | i) each trial has a single slot; ii) two-phase design |

**Table 1: Major Existing RFID Counting Protocols**

protocol then generates a rough estimate $\tilde{n}$ based on the current $p$ and the number of collision slots in the current trial (i.e., the trial with at least one empty slot), and the first phase ends. In each trial of the second phase, the protocol uses the rough estimate $\tilde{n}$ so far to calculate an optimal $p$, and has each tag participate with probability $p$. Next using the new information received in this trial, the protocol amends $\tilde{n}$. This iterative process continues until the protocol believes that the estimation accuracy of $\tilde{n}$ is high enough.

The authors [12] attribute UPE's performance to the proper use of randomization, i.e., carefully choosing the probability for tags to participate in trials (called *probabilistic framed ALOHA* scheme), and the unified use of empty slots and collision slots to do the estimation. The basic idea of randomization has been inherited by virtually all follow-up research on the problem. Despite that UPE does have a rough estimation phase followed by an accurate estimation phase, this two-phase design is not mentioned as a key aspect of UPE by the authors. Multiple later protocols, including the authors' own follow-up work [13], abandon this two-phase approach.

**Enhanced zero based estimator (EZB) [13].** EZB partitions the entire domain for the possible values of $n$ into logarithmic number of narrow ranges: $[1, r)$, $[r, r^2)$, $[r^2, r^3)$, .... Here $r$ is some parameter to be explained later. Each of these narrow ranges has the property that the max of the range is at most $r$ times larger than the min. EZB works on each range sequentially and independently. For each range, EZB uses a certain number of balls-and-bins trials with a certain length. In each such trial, tags participate with some probability $p$. Here the number of trials and trial length are the same for all ranges, while the value of $p$ depends on the range. Finally for each range, EZB uses the number of empty slots in the trials, together with the probability $p$, to estimate $n$. EZB then combines all estimates from all ranges to obtain the final output. EZB uses various involved optimization techniques to choose the optimal values for the various parameters such as $r$ and $p$. Intuitively, EZB works because the count $n$ must be in one of these ranges. Since each range is narrow, one can pick a single $p$ value such that for any value $x$ within that range, $xp$ is on the same order as the length of the trial. This enables $n$ to be properly estimated, as long as $n$ is in that range.

The authors [13] attribute EZB's performance gain to its unique narrow range design (called *multi-resolution probing*) and the various parameter optimization techniques.

**First non-empty slots based estimator (FNEB) and enhanced FNEB [9].** Enhanced FNEB has two phases, while FNEB is exactly the same as the second phase of enhanced FNEB, so we only review enhanced FNEB. A trial in enhanced FNEB is similar to a balls-and-bins trial as it lets each tag uniformly randomly choose an integer from the range of 1 to $l'$. Here $l'$ is some parameter to be explained later. Different from a balls-and-bins trial, a trial here does not use $l'$ slots to sequentially scan the whole range. Instead, it does so only for the first few slots. If any of them is non-empty (i.e., its index is chosen by some tag), the trial ends immediately and returns the index of that slot. Otherwise, the trial continues with a binary search to find the smallest integer $j$ that has been chosen by at least one tag. Imagine the protocol uses a balls-and-bins trial, the $j$th slot would be the first non-empty slot it sees. Therefore $j$ is still called the index of the first non-empty slot here.

To start, enhanced FNEB requires the user to input an upper bound on $n$. The protocol determines the $l'$ used in its first trial by solving an optimization problem parameterized with this upper bound. The protocol then uses the index of the first non-empty slot in its first trial to generate a rough estimate $\tilde{n}$. Intuitively, this index carries information about $n$ since for a given $l'$, the larger the value of $n$, the smaller this index will likely be. Next the protocol determines the $l'$ used in its second trial by solving the same optimization problem, this time parameterized with the rough estimate $\tilde{n}$. The second trial then proceeds in the same way as the first trial, and amends $\tilde{n}$. This iterative process continues until the protocol believes that the estimation quality of $\tilde{n}$ is good enough. Next the protocol moves on to the second phase where all trials use the same value of $l'$, which is obtained by solving the optimization problem again but parameterized using the $\tilde{n}$ from the first phase. The protocol then combines the first non-empty slot information from all of its second-phase trials to produce a final estimate.

The authors [9] consider their use of the first non-empty slots as the key improvement of (enhanced) FNEB over prior protocols. This design enables (enhanced) FNEB to end a trial as soon as it finds the index of the first non-empty slot. Despite that enhanced FNEB has two phases, these two phases are introduced by the authors only as an "enhancement" instead of a key design aspect.

**Lottery frame protocol (LOF) [16].** LOF consists of multiple independent trials. For each trial, a tag randomly chooses a slot according to a geometric distribution where the $i$th slot is chosen with $\frac{1}{2^i}$ probability. A tag then responds in its chosen slot. LOF finds the index $j$ of the first empty slot by sequentially going through the slots. A trial ends immediately and returns $j$ when the protocol sees the first empty slot. The value of $j$ carries useful information about $n$: On expectation, $\frac{n}{2^i}$ tags respond in the $i$th slot, and $j$ tends to take a value around $\log(n)$. Finally, LOF combines the information obtained from all of its trials to produce a final estimate.

The authors [16] attribute LOF's improvement over prior protocols to its small trial length.

**Probabilistic estimating tree (PET) [24].** Similar to LOF, PET does a sequence of independent *trials*, where in each trial each tag randomly chooses a positive integer $i$ according to the same geometric distribution as LOF. But instead of determining the $j$ in LOF, PET finds the maximum $j'$ such that there exists some tag choosing $j'$. The intuition why such $j'$ carries useful information about $n$ is similar to $j$ as in LOF. In addition, PET (implicitly) requires an upper bound $x$ on the maximum $j'$. These two changes enable PET to perform a more efficient binary search on the slot index range of $[1, x]$ to find the maximum $j'$, instead of sequentially going through the slots. In the first slot of this binary search, PET asks all tags whose chosen integer falls within $[x/2, x]$ to respond. If the slot is empty (non-empty respectively), PET can then focus on the range of $[1, x/2]$ ($[x/2, x]$ respectively) in the next slot.

The authors [24] attribute PET's improvement over prior protocols to the efficient way of using binary search to determine the maximum $j'$.

**Average run based tag estimation (ART) [18].** The first trial in ART is roughly the same as a trial in LOF. ART uses this trial to obtain a rough estimate $\tilde{n}$ on $n$. The quality of this rough estimate is low since different from LOF which uses many trials to estimate, ART only uses a single trial. All the following trials are balls-and-bins trials, where each tag participates independently with certain probability $p$. The length of these trials and the $p$ used in these trials are all the same. ART then observes which slots in each trial are non-empty. Next it calculates the average *run length* of non-empty slots (i.e., the average length of sequences of consecutive non-empty slots), and uses such information to generate a final estimate. Such average run length carries information about $n$ since the larger the value of $n$, the more non-empty slots, and the larger the average run length. The total number of trials, the length of the trials, and the probability $p$ used in ART are determined by solving an involved optimization problem with the rough estimate $\tilde{n}$ being an input parameter.

The authors [18] attribute ART's improvement over prior protocols to its novel use of run length to do the estimation. While ART does have two phases (with the first phase having a single trial), the authors neither emphasize this aspect nor attribute ART's performance gain to this aspect.

**Zero-One Estimator (ZOE) [25].** ZOE is independent of and concurrent with our work. ZOE has two explicit phases, where the first phase gets a rough estimate $\tilde{n}$ and the second one obtains the final estimate. As a key design decision, each trial in ZOE has a single slot, so we directly describe slots here. In its first phase, ZOE aims to find a $j$ such that if all tags participate in a slot with a probability of $1/2^j$, the probability of the slot being empty is around $1/e$. To find such a $j$ efficiently, ZOE (implicitly) requires an upper bound $x$ on the number of tags so that it can does a binary search over $[0, \log x]$. Each step of the binary search uses a constant number of slots. In each such slot, the tags respond with probability of $1/2^i$ where $i$ is the current value tested in the binary search. The protocol then observes the fraction of empty slots, and determines how to continue the binary search. With a suitable $j$ found by the first phase, ZOE's second phase uses a certain number of slots where the tags participate in each slot with probability of $1/2^j$. The number of slots needed in the second phase is determined by the required estimation quality. ZOE eventually estimates $n$ from the fraction of empty slots observed in the second phase.

The authors [25] attribute ZOE's improvement over prior protocols to the following two design aspects: i) each trial having only a single slot so that this slot can potentially collect information from all tags, and ii) having two explicit phases. While this concurrent work of ZOE does emphasize the importance of its two-phase design, the thesis identified in this paper is still not discovered in ZOE: ZOE believes that its unique design of each trial having a single slot is also key to ZOE's performance. Our thesis, on the other hand, suggests that the two-phase design is the key while other aspects are only secondary. Guided by our thesis, a protocol designer would not be overly concerned with sticking to ZOE's idea of having a single slot in each trial. Section 7.3 will show that *not* having a single slot in each trial, as in our protocol, enables us to get better performance in our experiments.

# 5. WHICH DESIGN ASPECTS ARE KEY?

So far we have reviewed major RFID counting protocols in the literature, each with its own unique techniques. Given such a myriad of interesting techniques, which techniques are the actual dominant factors for good performance? Which techniques are less important? If one would like to outperform the state-of-the-art, which existing technique should one builds upon? To answer these questions, we aim to identify the key aspects of efficient RFID counting protocols.

| | |
|---|---|
| UPE [12] | – |
| EZB [13] | $O(\frac{1}{\epsilon^2}\log n)$ |
| LOF [16] | $O(\frac{1}{\epsilon^2}\log n)$ |
| FNEB [9] | $O(\frac{1}{\epsilon^2}\log n)$ |
| Enhanced FNEB [9] | $O(\frac{1}{\epsilon^2}+\log n)$ |
| PET [24] | $O(\frac{1}{\epsilon^2}\log\log n)$ |
| ART [18] | $O(\frac{1}{\epsilon^2}+\log n)$ |
| ZOE [25] | $O(\frac{1}{\epsilon^2}+\log\log n)$ |

**Table 2: Asymptotic Overhead of Single-Set Protocols**

While experimental study can help reveal about which aspects in these protocols are more important than others, we notice that what we are looking for could very well be buried deep under the vast amount of experimental data. Thus we start by first systematically investigating and comparing the asymptotic overhead of these protocols, with respect to the $n$ and $\epsilon$. Interestingly, as we will soon see, such a simple investigation already sheds much light onto the question.

It is worth noting that such a systematic comparison of the asymptotic behavior has never been done before: The end-to-end performance of some protocols [12, 18] has not been formally analyzed, while the performance of other protocols [9, 13, 16, 24] has been analyzed and presented in a rather detailed form. These more precise but complex forms unfortunately prevent a direct comparison across the protocols and bury the key insights we are searching for.

**Asymptotic overhead of single-set RFID counting protocols.** UPE [12] and ART [18] do not come with end-to-end overhead analysis. We find that the estimator used by UPE is biased, hence UPE cannot be used when $\epsilon$ is small. This is consistent with the findings by the original authors of UPE in their follow-up work [13] and will be validated by our experiments in Section 7.3. We have analyzed ART by ourselves, which shows that it uses $O(\log n)$ slots in the first phase and $O(\frac{1}{\epsilon^2})$ slots in the second phase. This implies a total overhead of $O(\frac{1}{\epsilon^2}+\log n)$. For space limitation, we leave the full analysis, which is straightforward and uses rather standard approaches, to our technical report [6].

The other existing protocols, i.e., EZB [13], (enhanced) FNEB [9], LOF [16], PET [24], and ZOE [25], all come with detailed analysis on the number of slots needed. Here all we do is to simplify their more precise results to asymptotic forms (with adaption to our formulation when necessary), for later comparison. More details about these protocols can be found in our technical report [6].

Table 2 summarizes the asymptotic overhead of these single-set RFID counting protocols. At this point, it is clear that the protocols have either additive overhead or multiplicative overhead. Additive overhead is obviously lower, and it comes from a conceptual separation of two phases in these protocols, with the first phase taking $O(\log n)$ or $O(\log\log n)$ slots and the second phase taking $O(\frac{1}{\epsilon^2})$ slots. The $\log n$ and $\log\log n$ term are about 16 and 4 respectively, for $n = 100,000$. (When $n$ is small, almost all known protocols can complete fast, so further improvement is less interesting.) Unless the hidden constant in a multiplicative overhead protocol is comparably smaller, additive overhead protocol will be more efficient. Our experiments in Section 7 will show that this is indeed the case.

Bring our lower bound from Section 3 into the picture makes this key observation even clearer. There we proved that it is impossible to reduce the overhead of a single-set RFID counting protocol to $o(\frac{1}{\epsilon^2\log\frac{1}{\epsilon}}+\log\log n)$. Now it is clear that $\Theta(\log\log n)$ slots are for the first phase, while the remaining $\Theta(\frac{1}{\epsilon^2\log\frac{1}{\epsilon}})$ slots are for the second phase.

**Our thesis.** Our observations above lead us to conjecture the following thesis, which will be validated in the remainder of this paper:

> *The key design aspect for single-set RFID counting protocols to achieve near-optimal performance is to have two phases, where the first phase uses roughly $\Theta(\log\log n)$ slots to obtain a rough estimate with constant (e.g., 0.5) relative error, and the second phase uses roughly $\Theta(\frac{1}{\epsilon^2 \log \frac{1}{\epsilon}})$ slots to eventually obtain a final estimate with the desired relative error of $\epsilon$. Furthermore, other techniques/ideas proposed in the literature are only of secondary importance.*

While this thesis is almost obvious from our discussion so far, somewhat surprisingly, it has never been identified by any of the previous efforts (including the concurrent work on ZOE [25]). Instead, existing protocols often overlook the two-phase design and often attribute their improvements to a diverse set of design aspects other that the two-phase design. Our thesis implies that all the following design aspects, emphasized by previous efforts, are far less important than originally thought:

- using various novel statistical quantities to do the estimation (such as using the average run length in ART [18] and using the index of the first non-empty slot in FNEB [9]);
- using an iterative process to refine the estimation over many iterations (such as in UPE [12] and enhanced FNEB [9]);
- using complex optimization techniques to tune various parameters (e.g., to trade off the trial length with the number of trials as in EZB [13], FNEB [9], and ART [18]);
- using a single slot in each trial as in ZOE [25].

**Generalizing to multiple-set RFID counting protocols.** We naturally generalize our thesis to the multiple-set setting: There the protocol should have two phases at each location $i$ for $1 \le i \le k$, where the first phase uses roughly $\Theta(\log\log n_i)$ slots to obtain a rough estimate, and the second phase uses roughly $\Theta(\frac{1}{\epsilon^2 \log \frac{1}{\epsilon}})$ slots.

Existing multiple-set RFID counting protocols[4] (EZB, FNEB[5], LOF[6], and PET) all focus on other aspects of the protocol instead of having the above two phases, and incur multiplicative overhead. Specifically, EZB, LOF, and FNEB all incur $O(\frac{k}{\epsilon^2}\log(\sum_{i=1}^{k} n_i))$ overhead, while PET incurs $O(\frac{k}{\epsilon^2}\log\log(\sum_{i=1}^{k} n_i))$ overhead. Such multiplicative overhead contrasts sharply with the additive overhead of our new SRC$_M$ protocol (Section 7.2), which has applied our thesis on the two-phase design. Hence in the multiple-set setting, these previous efforts have not even implicitly applied our thesis.

# 6. SOURCE OF PERFORMANCE GAIN — TWO CASE STUDIES

An ultimate way of validating our thesis is to see whether applying such a design principle enables new protocols that are significantly better than existing ones. We will do so later in Section 7. This section instead aims to provide direct and immediate evidence to support our thesis, by carefully examining the source of performance gains in existing protocols. We will focus on two recent protocols, ART [18] and enhanced FNEB [9], as two prominent examples. As reviewed in Section 4, ART uses the average run length of non-empty slots as a *gauge* for estimation and attributes its performance gain over prior protocols to this unique gauge. Similarly, the authors of enhanced FNEB [9] consider the novel use of the first non-empty slots as a *gauge* being the key source of performance gain.

We will show that quite surprisingly, in our experiments, these two novel gauges do not necessarily improve the performance of ART and enhanced FNEB: Replacing these two novel gauges with a simple gauge (i.e., the number of empty slots in balls-and-bins trials) from the earlier EZB protocol [13] either improves the performance or provides comparable performance in our experiments. We further show that the actual source of performance gains in these two protocols is their (implicit) two-phase design, despite that such a two-phase design was not considered as the key.

## 6.1 Source of Performance Gain in ART

For all experimental results presented in this section, we use $n = 100,000$ and a constant $\delta = 0.2$ unless otherwise mentioned — we have performed extensive experiments under other settings (e.g., with smaller $n$) and observe similar trends (see our technical report [6]). Our evaluation in this subsection adopts the same setting as the original ART paper [18]. Specifically, we assume that each slot takes 0.3ms, and each trial incurs an additional overhead of 1ms.

**ART outperforms EZB.** To identify the source of performance gain in ART [18], for clarity, we focus on ART's performance gain when compared with a specific prior protocol EZB [13]. As a sanity check, we first perform experiments to see whether ART indeed outperforms EZB, as claimed in [18]. Figure 2 summarizes our experimental results, showing the amount of time needed for ART and EZB to achieve a certain target relative error $\epsilon$. Consistent with [18], we observe that ART significantly outperforms EZB — more than 200% faster.

**ART's novel gauge and ART's performance.** Next we proceed to test whether this performance gain comes from ART's novel run length based gauge. To do so, we keep everything else unmodified in ART except that we replace ART's novel run length based gauge with the old gauge in EZB. This old gauge in EZB is based on the number of empty slots. We call this protocol as the revised ART. If the run length based gauge were indeed the source of ART's performance gain, the revised ART should perform significantly worse than ART. Quite surprisingly, as shown in Figure 2, the revised ART actually outperforms the original ART.

**Resolving the contradiction.** To resolve such contradiction with the claims from [18] that ART's novel gauge is the source of performance gain, we trace back and examine the reasoning in that work. There the authors [18] compare the variance of ART's average run length based gauge with the variance of other old gauges, including the gauge in EZB (and hence the gauge in revised ART). They show that the variance of ART's gauge is smaller, leading to the conclusion that ART's gauge is the source of performance gain. Again as a sanity check, we examine the variance of ART's gauge and EZB's gauge as observed in our experiments. Consistent with [18], we also observe that ART's gauge has smaller variance (Table 3). On the other hand, however, we find that smaller variance of a gauge does not necessarily translate to better accuracy of the final estimate. Table 3 also presents the variance of the final estimate as generated by ART and revised ART (which uses EZB's gauge). Despite ART's gauge has smaller variance than EZB's, the variance of ART's final estimate is actually larger than that of revised ART's final estimate. Note that this is consistent with the better performance of revised ART as we observed in Figure 2.

[4]Other protocols are not for the multiple-set RFID counting problem. Among those, ART only works for a simpler variant of the multiple-set problem (see Section 8).

[5]Enhanced FNEB no longer works in the multiple-set problem.

[6]Here LOF requires an upper bound $x$ on the number of tags, and can no longer end a trial when it sees the first empty slot.

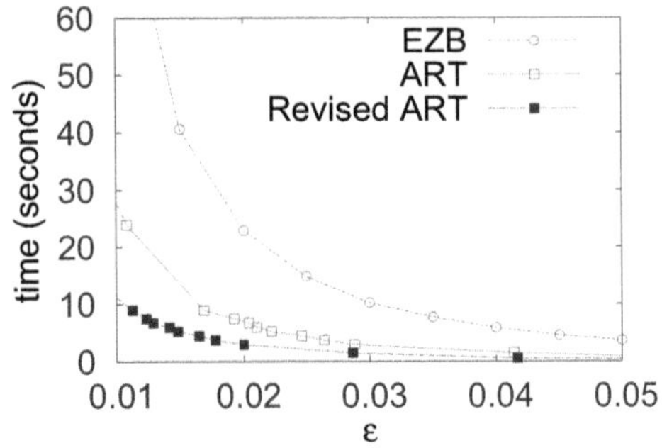


**Figure 2: Time needed to achieve relative error $\epsilon$ under $\delta = 0.2$.**

| | ART | Revised ART |
|---|---|---|
| With 2000 time slots: | | |
| Var($gauge$) | 0.080 | 4.8 |
| Var($\hat{n}$) | 12 $\times 10^6$ | 8.0 $\times 10^6$ |
| With 4000 time slots: | | |
| Var($gauge$) | 0.045 | 2.4 |
| Var($\hat{n}$) | 7.0 $\times 10^6$ | 3.9 $\times 10^6$ |

**Table 3: Variances of gauges and estimates under ART and revised ART.**

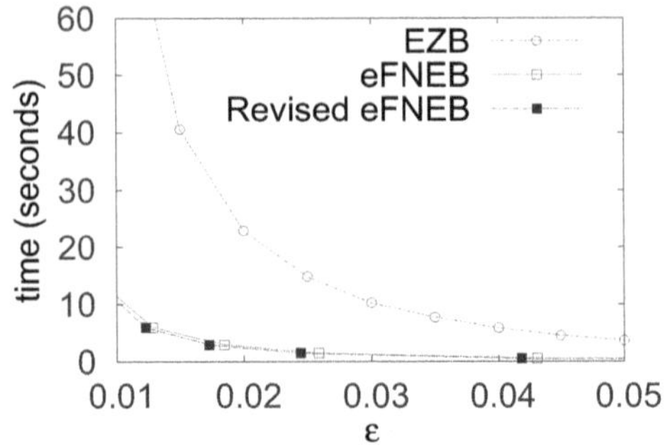


**Figure 3: Time needed to achieve relative error $\epsilon$ under $\delta = 0.2$.**

The fundamental reason behind these results is that in order for the final estimate to have better accuracy, the gauge needs to not only have small variance but also be *sensitive* to the count. In other words, under different number ($n$) of tags, the value of the gauge should ideally be very different. This ensures that we can easily differentiate different $n$ even if the value of the gauge is a bit off from its expectation. In fact, if we were not concerned with such sensitivity, it would be trivial to design a gauge with zero variance: We simply let the value of the gauge always be a constant regardless of what $n$ is. Clearly such gauge cannot be used to accurately estimate $n$. Hence the reason that the variance of ART's final estimate is larger is exactly that ART's gauge is less sensitive than EZB's. Intuitively, such insensitivity can even be partly observed from the fact that under practical parameters, the value of ART's gauge has a smaller domain that EZB's.

**The actual source of performance gain.** It will shed much light onto the problem if we view the revised ART protocol from a different perspective. Namely, one can alternatively view the revised ART protocol as a variant of the EZB protocol — the only main difference between these two is that EZB does not have a rough estimate from a first phase. Thus EZB has to divide the possible domain for $n$ into $O(\log n)$ narrow ranges and process them sequentially. In comparison, revised ART has a rough estimate from its first phase to identify the correct range to process.

Hence one can view revised ART as adding a first phase to EZB. This implies that the performance gain of revised ART over EZB comes from having two phases as suggested by our thesis. In turn, this is also the source of the performance gain in ART.

## 6.2 Source of Performance Gain in Enhanced FNEB

Using the same approach as above, we continue to examine the source of the performance gain of enhanced FNEB [9] over EZB. Here our evaluation adopts the same setting as [9], where each slot still takes 0.3ms (as in [18]) but there is no per-trial overhead. As shown in Figure 3, our experiments first confirm that enhanced FNEB significantly outperforms EZB. To test whether this performance gain comes from FNEB's unique first non-empty slot gauge, we revise the enhanced FNEB by using EZB's gauge in its second phase while keeping all other design in enhanced FNEB unchanged. Our revised version of enhanced FNEB provides comparable performance as the enhanced FNEB (specifically, our revised protocol outperforms enhanced FNEB slightly by around 6%), showing that FNEB's novel gauge does not necessarily improve its performance.

The original authors of (enhanced) FNEB [9] attribute the performance gain to their novel gauge, because they believe that such gauge enables (enhanced) FNEB to end a trial as soon as it sees the first non-empty slot and thus reduces the number of slots per trial. While this is obviously true, the total overhead of a protocol also depends on the number of trials needed. For example, when $\delta = 0.2$, to achieve $\epsilon = 0.01$, enhanced FNEB uses on average around 2 slots per trial but it needs to invoke around $16,000$ trials. To achieve the same estimation quality with EZB's gauge, each trial uses 242 slots and only around 120 trials are needed. Hence the total number of slots needed by EZB's gauge is comparable to that needed by FNEB's gauge.

Exactly as in the case of revised ART, here one can alternatively view the revised version of enhanced FNEB as adding a first phase to EZB. This directly leads to our conclusion that the actual source of the performance gain in enhanced FNEB is having two phases as suggested in our thesis.

# 7. DESIGNING BETTER RFID COUNTING PROTOCOLS

Guided by our thesis in Section 5, this section aims to design new RFID counting protocols that are more efficient than existing ones and also simultaneously simpler than most of them. We will design our protocols by simply putting together various basic building blocks in the literature. We do *not* claim novelty on these building blocks – instead, we aim to show that simply putting them together in a *proper manner* as guided by our thesis is already sufficient to outperform existing protocols. This serves as an ultimate validation of the utility of our thesis.

## 7.1 SRC$_S$: Our Simple RFID Counting Protocol for Single-Set

For single-set RFID counting, our thesis suggests that the protocol should have two conceptual phases, the first one does a rough estimation, while the second one generates the final estimate. When designing these two phases, we will use as simple building blocks as possible. This is because: i) more complex designs tend to have larger hidden constants, and ii) our thesis indicates that other performance tricks only have minor effects in further improving performance.

**Our SRC$_S$ protocol.** Algorithm 1 summarizes the main steps of our SRC$_S$ protocol. The first phase of our SRC$_S$ protocol is exactly the same as the simple LOF protocol [16] as reviewed in Section 4. Recall that LOF does a sequence of independent trials with each trial using $O(\log n)$ slots. For $\delta = 0.2$, our protocol invokes LOF to do 10 trials, using total $O(\log n)$ slots. It then uses LOF's output as the rough estimate $\tilde{n}$. By LOF's analysis [16], $\tilde{n}$'s relative error is below 0.5 with at least $\frac{9}{10}$ probability. Given such a $\tilde{n}$, the second phase of SRC$_S$ (as we will soon describe) guarantees to output an estimate $\hat{n}$ of relative error below $\epsilon$ with probability of $\frac{8}{9}$. Combining the guarantees from these two phases ensures that $\hat{n}$'s relative error is below $\epsilon$ with probability of $\frac{9}{10} \times \frac{8}{9}$, which corresponds to

**Algorithm 1 Our SRC$_S$ protocol** (for $\delta = 0.2$)

1: Invoke LOF with 10 trials to get $\tilde{n}$;
2: Start a balls-and-bins trial of length $l$, and let each tag *participate in the trial* with probability $p = max(1, 1.6l/\tilde{n})$;
3: Count the number of empty slots $z$ in the trial;
4: Output $\ln(z/l)/\ln(1 - p/l)$.

$\delta = 0.2$. To achieve a $\delta$ smaller than 0.2, one can sequentially invoke $m$ ($m$ being some odd integer) independent instances of Algorithm 1 and then take the median of their outputs as the final output. Asymptotically, it is well-known that $m = O(\log \frac{1}{\delta})$ suffices [15]. Obtaining a concrete value of $m$ for a certain target $\delta$ is not hard: Each instance of Algorithm 1 has $1 - 0.2 = 0.8$ probability to generate a "good" result with at most $\epsilon$ relative error. For the median to have at most $\epsilon$ relative error, it suffices to have at least $(m + 1)/2$ good results among the $m$ results. With all instances being independent, we simply pick the smallest $m$ such that $\sum_{i=(m+1)/2}^{m} \binom{m}{i} \times 0.8^i \times 0.2^{m-i} \geq 1 - \delta$. Since $m$ is usually small (e.g., $m$ only needs to be 41 even for $\delta = 10^{-5}$), the value of $m$ can be trivially determined via brute-force calculation.

The second phase of SRC$_S$ simply consists of a single trial with $l$ slots, and each tag participates in this trial (i.e., responds in a uniformly random slot in the trial) independently with probability $p$. We will explain the two parameters $l$ and $p$ later. The expected fraction of empty slots in this trial will thus be $(1-p/l)^n$. Our protocol determines the observed number of empty slots in this trial, denoted by $z$. Obviously, $z$ directly carries information about $n$. The protocol finally generates the final estimate $\hat{n}$ by solving the equation $(1 - p/l)^{\hat{n}} = z/l$, which leads to $\hat{n} = \ln(z/l)/\ln(1 - p/l)$. The second phase of our protocol is rather similar to subprocedures used in UPE [12] and EZB [13]. The only (minor) difference is that we further simplify the design and use a single trial instead of doing multiple trials. This simplification actually also slightly improves our performance: By putting all slots into the same trial, whether a slot is empty becomes negatively correlated with each other. Such negative correlation makes the total number of empty slots concentrate better near its expected value.

The parameter $l$ is uniquely determined by the target relative error of $\epsilon$, and there are two ways to do so. The first approach is to set $l = \frac{65}{(1-0.04^{\epsilon})^2}$, which is $O(\frac{1}{\epsilon^2})$ (see the proof of Theorem 5 in our technical report [6], where we have proved that such $l$ is sufficiently large). The second approach is to directly construct a numerical lookup table. This lookup table is constructed by running the algorithm under a wide range of $n$ values, and then observing the $l$ needed to achieve a certain $\epsilon$. See our technical report [6] for a sample table. Between the two approaches, since mathematical analysis is often a loose approximation, in practice, using a lookup table usually offers superior performance. The parameter $p$ is set to be $\max(1, 1.6l/\tilde{n})$, so that the expected number of tags responding is on the same order as $l$. The constant 1.6 here provides the best estimation performance (see analysis in [12, 13]).

The following theorem summarizes the end-to-end guarantee of our SRC$_S$ protocol, whose proof is in our technical report [6]:

THEOREM 5. *Our SRC$_S$ protocol outputs an $(\epsilon, 0.2)$ estimate with $O(\frac{1}{\epsilon^2} + \log n)$ overhead.*

**Incurring $O(\log\log n)$ slots in the first phase.** The first phase of the design above incurs $O(\log n)$ slots. It is possible to use only $O(\log\log n)$ slots by using a revised version of PET protocol [24] instead. As reviewed in Section 4, PET does a sequence of independent trials. In each trial, each tag randomly chooses a positive integer according to a geometric distribution. Given a proper upper bound $x$ (from the end user) on $n$, PET uses a binary search over $[1, \log x]$ to find the maximum $j'$ such that there exists some tag choosing $j'$. Hence the number of slots incurred in PET for each trial is $O(\log\log x)$. It is possible for $x$ to be much larger than $n$, in which case this will still not give us $O(\log\log n)$ complexity. To always have $O(\log\log n)$ complexity, we slightly modify PET so that the user does not input $x$: In each trial before the binary search, the protocol uses some extra slots. In the $i$th extra slot, tags that have chosen an integer larger than or equal to $2^{i-1}$ will respond. This process stops once the protocol observes an empty slot. Let the corresponding $i$ in this empty slot be $y$. Next the protocol does a binary search as before, except that now the binary search is done over $[1, 2^{y-1}]$ instead of $[1, \log x]$. This binary search will take another $y$ slots at most. It can be easily shown that $y = O(\log\log n)$ on expectation. Hence the total overhead will be $O(\log\log n)$ slots. See our technical report [6] for more details and the pseudo-code.

Under practical settings, however, the overhead for the second phase usually dominates and such improvement will be negligible. But we will need this revised PET later in our multi-set protocol.

## 7.2 SRC$_M$: Our Simple RFID Counting Protocol for Multiple-Set

For multiple-set counting, our thesis suggests that the protocol should have two conceptual phases at each location $i$ for $1 \leq i \leq k$. We will focus on achieving the two phases in a simple way.

**Protocol intuition.** Recall that SRC$_S$ conceptually works by throwing $np$ (on expectation) balls uniformly randomly into $l$ bins. The value of $n$ can then be inferred from the fraction of empty bins. We would like to design SRC$_M$ in a similarly simple way, i.e., by throwing $np$ balls (on expectation) into $l$ bins, where $n$ is the total number of tags in all sets (if there is no overlapping between sets, $n = n_1+n_2+\ldots+n_k$). The value of $l$ can still be determined by $\epsilon$ and our Theorem 6 later shows that $l = O(1/\epsilon^2)$. Imagine for now that magically, we can also properly set $p$ to be $\max(1, 1.6l/\tilde{n})$, where $\tilde{n}$ is a rough estimate for $n$ with constant relative error. With such value for $p$, the problem becomes trivial: At each location, the protocol simply does a balls-and-bins trial with participation probability of $p$, so that on expectation there are $np$ balls in total. The protocol records the outcome at each location and merges these results for producing a final estimate. The merging is done by considering a bin occupied as long as it is occupied in any of the $k$ locations. Note that this already takes care of potential overlaps between the $k$ sets – as long as we use the same random seed when doing these experiments, the same tag will always be hashed into the same bin, even if it appears in multiple sets.

So far we have assumed that the protocol can properly set $p$. However in the multiple-set setting, the protocol sees $S_1$, $S_2$, ..., $S_k$ sequentially and it is not possible to obtain $\tilde{n}$ until the last location. Observe however that at location $i$, the protocol can easily get a rough estimate $\tilde{n}'_i$ for the size of $S_1 \cup S_2 \ldots \cup S_i$ (by merging all the first phase results up to location $i$). Define $p_i = \max(1, 1.6l/\tilde{n}'_i)$ and we obviously have $p_i \geq p$ (note that $p_k = p$). Next note that these values of $p$ and $p_i$ do not need to be accurate, since the rough estimate is rough in the first place. Hence let us assume, without loss of generality, that they are both in the form of $1/2^x$ for some integer $x$. If not, we simply round them to the nearest value with such a form. When the reader finishes the first phase for the $i$th set, it knows $p_i$ but not $p$. Conceptually for set $S_i$, the protocol will do the balls-and-bins trial with participation probabilities $p_i$, $\frac{p_i}{2}$, $\frac{p_i}{4}$, $\frac{p_i}{8}$, ..., and so on. This ensures that one of the participation probability will equal $p$, regardless of what $p$ is. After processing all sets, we can then decide the proper value of $p$ and use the combined result for the corresponding trial to obtain the final estimate.

Naively doing the above trials with the infinite sequence of participation probabilities will result in infinite overhead. One can easily make things correlated to avoid this: For each participation

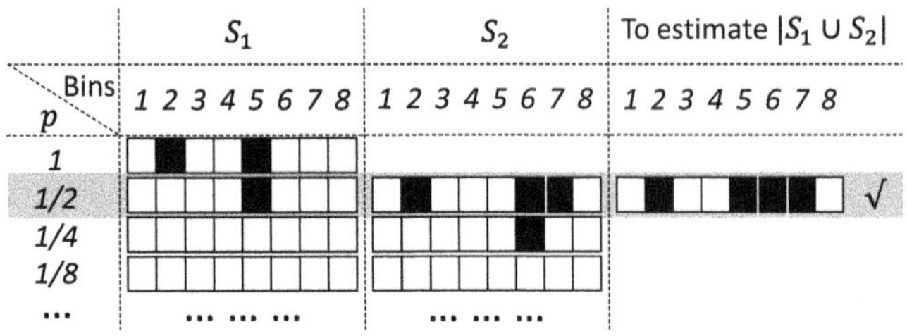


**Figure 4: An example run of SRS$_M$ with two reader locations: Each column corresponds to a bin (note that the same bins appear at both locations), and each row corresponds to a participation probability. A filled (non-filled) rectangle means an occupied (non-occupied) bin. At a given location, once a bin becomes non-occupied at a certain participation probability, there is no need to further examine smaller probabilities for this bin. In this example, the second phase of SRS$_M$ starts at the participation probability of 1 and $\frac{1}{2}$ respectively at the first and the second location. SRC$_M$ eventually merges the outcomes at the participation probability of $\frac{1}{2}$ from the two locations to estimate $|S_1 \cup S_2|$.**

probability except the first one, a tag flips a fair coin and participate iff the coin flip result is head and the tag participated in the previous participation probability. This would mean that in this sequence, a tag will keep participation, and then stop participating after a certain probability. In turn, this means that for a given bin in this sequence of experiments, it will initially be occupied and then will never be occupied again after a certain participation probability (Figure 4). This enables the protocol to do the following: Instead of checking all bins for a given probability, the protocol iterates through the bins. For each bin, the protocol checks whether it is occupied, for all the probabilities in the sequence. Note that the protocol can stop once the bin becomes empty. The rough estimate from SRC$_M$'s first phase ensures that its second phase sees a constant number of balls in each bin on expectation. From the mean of geometric distributions, one can easily see that on average, it only needs to move down the sequence of participation probabilities $O(1)$ steps for a given bin to become empty. Hence the total number of slots needed is just $O(1) \cdot l = O(\frac{1}{\epsilon^2})$.[7]

**Our SRC$_M$ protocol.** Our SRC$_M$ protocol implements the above intuitions. Algorithm 2 summarizes the main steps of our SRC$_M$ protocol (for $\delta = 0.2$). To achieve a $\delta$ smaller than 0.2, exactly as for SRC$_S$, one only needs to sequentially invoke multiple independent instances of Algorithm 2 and then take the median result. See Section 7.1 for how to determine the number of instances needed. For the parameter $l$, the only difference between SRC$_M$ and SRC$_S$ is that the participation probability used in SRC$_M$ needs to be rounded to the form of $1/2^x$. Taking this into account, we can either mathematically set $l = \frac{205}{(1-0.013^{\epsilon})^2}$, which is $O(\frac{1}{\epsilon^2})$ (see the proof of our Theorem 6 in our technical report [6]), or find its value from a numerical lookup table. The lookup table is constructed by running the algorithm under a wide range of $n$ values and then observing the $l$ needed to achieve a certain $\epsilon$. Note that $l$ does not depend on the number of sets and how the sets overlap (see more detailed reasoning in our technical report [6]), one only need to run the algorithm against a single set.

Given $l$, each tag determines which bin it will choose, and also the smallest participation probability for which it will still participate. At location $i$, our SRC$_M$ protocol has two phases. For a constant $\delta = 0.2$, the first phase invokes the revised PET protocol (with 30 trials), which was described at the end of Section 7.1. This incurs total $O(\log\log n_i)$ slots. SRC$_M$ then merges all the first phase results it sees so far to get a rough estimate $\tilde{n}'_i$ for the size of $S_1 \cup S_2 \ldots \cup S_i$. Such merging is possible since PET, and therefore the revised PET, is able to do multiple-set RFID counting. By PET's analysis [24], the relative error of $\tilde{n}'_i$ is below 0.5 with at least $\frac{9}{10}$ probability. The second phase now determines $p_i$ based on $\tilde{n}'_i$ in exactly the same way as in our SRC$_S$ protocol. We then round $p_i$ to the nearest $1/2^x$ for some integer $x$. The protocol then iterates through the $l$ bins. For each bin, the protocol uses a sequence of slots, which corresponds to participation probabilities $p_i$, $\frac{p_i}{2}$, $\frac{p_i}{4}$, ... For each slot, those tags who select this bin and still participate at the current participation probability will respond. The protocol records all such information and stops once an empty slot is observed. It then proceeds to the next bin.

At the last ($k$th) location, SRC$_M$ can merge the first phase results from all the $k$ sets to obtain a rough estimate for the size of the union of all $k$ sets, and it can compute a proper participation probability $p$ based on this rough estimate. By our design, SRC$_M$ must have collected the information regarding whether each bin is empty under $p$ for every location. SRC$_M$ then combines such information by setting a bin to be empty iff it is empty in all sets (see Figure 4). Let $z$ denote the number of empty bins in the combined $l$ bins, SRC$_M$ generates the final estimate $\hat{n}$ by solving the equation $(1-p/l)^{\hat{n}} = z/l$. See our technical report [6] for the proof for the following theorem about the end-to-end guarantee of our SRC$_M$ protocol:

**Algorithm 2** **Our SRC$_M$ protocol** (for $\delta = 0.2$)

```
Each tag uniformly randomly chooses a bin out of l bins, and
  chooses a positive integer y according to a geometric distribu-
  tion with parameter of 1/2;
Initialize A to an array of l elements with values of −1. A[j]
  will record the largest y chosen by a tag in the jth bin;
for each set S_i do
  Invoke revised PET with 30 trials, and merge its outcome
    with previous revised PET outcomes to get a rough estimate
    ñ'_i for the size of S_1 ∪ S_2 ... ∪ S_i;
  Find an integer x that minimizes |1/2^x − max(1, 1.6l/ñ'_i)|;
  for j = 1 to l do
    h = x;
    while true do
      Let all tags in the jth bin with y ≥ h respond;
      if (See a non-empty slot) then
        A[j] = max(A[j], h);
        h = h + 1;
      else
        Break;
      end if
    end while
  end for
end for
Consider the x used for the last set and let z be the number of
  elements in A with value no less than x;
Output ln(z/l)/ln(1 − 2^(−x)/l).
```

THEOREM 6. *Our SRC$_M$ protocol outputs an* $(\epsilon, 0.2)$ *estimate with* $O(\sum_{i=1}^{k}(\frac{1}{\epsilon^2} + \log\log n_i))$ *overhead.*

## 7.3 Evaluation Results

We conduct extensive simulations to compare the overhead of our protocols against all major existing protocols in the literature,

[7]A less efficient design would be to iterate through the sequence of participation probabilities. For each probability, one checks all bins. The process stops if all bins are empty. Such a design would need on expectation $O(\frac{\log(1/\epsilon)}{\epsilon^2})$ slots.

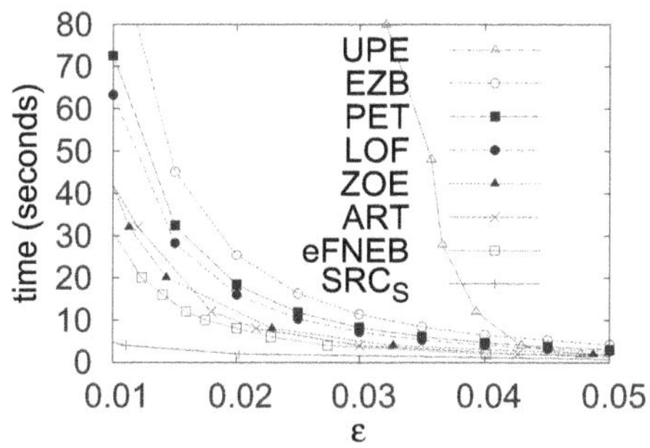


**Figure 5: Overhead of single-set protocols ($n = 10,000$).**

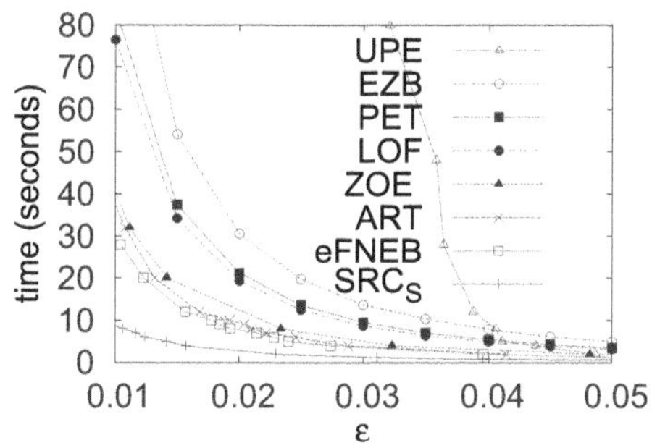


**Figure 6: Overhead of single-set protocols ($n = 100,000$).**

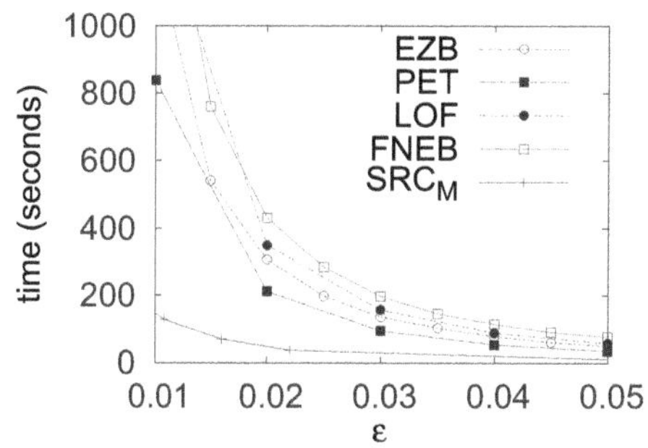


**Figure 7: Overhead of multiple-set protocols ($n = 100,000$ and $k = 10$).**

including UPE, EZB, (enhanced) FNEB, LOF, PET, ART, and ZOE. As in Section 6, we consider a constant $\delta = 0.2$ to simplify our discussion — we observe similar trends under all other values of $\delta$. When comparing the performance of these protocols, for each experiment, we first choose a time budget, then we simulate the protocols and observe their achieved relative error $\epsilon$ given such budget (i.e., overhead). This evaluation methodology is also taken by recent prior work [25]. An alternative evaluation methodology would be to compare the overhead of different protocols when achieving the same target $\epsilon$. We do not take this method since for several two-phase protocols (e.g., [18, 25]), when they mathematically decide the number of slots needed in their second phase, they assume a perfect estimate from their first phase. Since the estimate from the first phase is only a rough estimate, following their calculation will actually achieve a relative error that is somewhat larger than the target $\epsilon$. This will make the comparison inconsistent across the protocols. Unless otherwise mentioned, all our experiments use the following parameters derived from EPCglobal C1G2 standard [7]: a slot in UPE takes 0.8ms[8], a slot in all other protocols takes 0.4ms, and for all protocols each trial incurs an extra overhead of 1ms.

**Comparing SRC$_S$ with existing single-set protocols.** Figure 5 and Figure 6 present the overhead of our SRC$_S$ protocol against the overhead of existing single-set RFID counting protocols, for tag count of 10,000 and 100,000 respectively. As shown in the figures, SRC$_S$ is significantly (more than 1000%) faster than EZB, PET, and LOF. This is because asymptotically SRC$_S$ incurs additive overhead while EZB, PET, and LOF all incur multiplicative overhead (see Section 5). SRC$_S$ is at least 100% faster than ART, ZOE, and enhanced FNEB (eFNEB for short in the figures) in all of our settings. The difference between SRC$_S$ and these three protocols is relatively moderate, since all of them incur additive overhead. For each of them: SRC$_S$ is faster than ART, partly because the novel gauge used by ART does not perform as well as the simpler gauge used by SRC$_S$ (see Section 6), and partly because the quality of the rough estimate in ART is overly low. SRC$_S$ is faster than ZOE for the following two reasons. First, recall that ZOE uses a single slot for each trial, while SRC$_S$ puts all its slots in the second phase into a single trial. Therefore for the second phase of SRC$_S$, whether a slot is empty becomes negatively correlated with each other. Such negative correlation makes the total number of empty slots concentrate better near its expected value and thus provides higher estimation equality, as compared to a design using independent slots like ZOE. Second, each slot in ZOE needs to incur per-trial overhead since each of them corresponds to an individual trial, while the per-trial overhead is incurred much less often in SRC$_S$. For enhanced FNEB, recall that each of its trials also only uses a small number of slots. Therefore, the same two reasons that explain why SRC$_S$ is faster than ZOE also apply here.

[8]UPE requires a tag to send more bits in a slot to detect collision.

In addition, the quality of the rough estimate in enhanced FNEB is also lower than desirable. Finally, our results show that UPE cannot support relative error $\epsilon < 0.03$ due to its biased estimator. This is consistent with the findings by the original authors [13].

As we see, the overhead difference between SRC$_S$ and some existing protocols is partly due to the existence of per-trial overhead. To understand how significant this factor is, we have further compared the protocols when there is no per-trial overhead. We find SRC$_S$ continues to have the lowest overhead among all protocols. For example, when $\epsilon = 0.01$, SRC$_S$ is 20% to 100% faster than the most efficient existing protocol, i.e., ZOE. See detailed results in our technical report [6].

**Comparing SRC$_M$ with existing multiple-set protocols.** Figure 7 presents the overhead of our SRC$_M$ protocol against existing multiple-set RFID counting protocols. We perform extensive experiments under different values of $n$ and $k$, as well as different ways that the sets overlap with each other. Since they all show similar trends, Figure 7 presents a concrete setting, where a total of $n = 100,000$ tags (with index from 1 to 100,000) are distributed over $k = 10$ overlapping sets. For $i = 1, \ldots, 9$, the $i$th set is comprised of 11,000 tags with index from $(i-1) \times 10000 + 1$ to $i \times 10000 + 1000$. The last set is comprised of 10,000 tags with index from 90001 to 100000. In this setting, our SRC$_M$ protocol is around 500% faster than the most efficient existing multiple-set protocol, i.e., PET. In particular, while all existing protocols require more than 10 minutes to provide an estimate with relative error $\epsilon$ of 0.01, our SRC$_M$ protocol can achieve the same estimation quality in 2 minutes. The significant difference between SRC$_M$ and existing multiple-set protocols is mainly because asymptotically all existing multiple-set protocols incur multiplicative overhead, while SRC$_M$ incurs additive overhead (see Section 5).

Same to the single-set experiments, the overhead of multiple-set protocols partly comes from the per-trial overhead. To understand the significance of this factor here, we again evaluate a setting without per-trial overhead. We find that SRC$_M$ continues to be 300% faster than the most efficient existing protocol (see our technical report [6] for details).

## 8. VARIANT MODELS

This section discusses some variants of RFID counting problem.

**A simpler variant of multiple-set problem.** Some researchers (e.g., [18]) consider a simpler variant of the multiple-set RFID counting problem, where multiple readers jointly cover an area. These readers together count the total number of tags under their coverage. One can actually solve this simpler variant of our multiple-set problem using *any* single-set RFID counting protocol. Recall that a single-set protocol specifies a predicate for each slot. Roughly speaking, all readers send the same predicate to their sets. Together the readers return an empty slot to the single-set protocol iff every reader sees an empty slot. Note that this takes care of potential overlaps between sets, as long as a tag behaves identically for the same predicate from different readers.

**Capability to detect collision.** Some protocols (e.g., [12]) assume a reader can further detect collision, i.e., whether there are multiple tags responding in a non-empty slot. Though the reader becomes more capable in this variant model, we can still obtain a similarly strong lower bound result (with a small $\log \frac{1}{\epsilon}$ difference) as our original model. See our technical report [6] for the proof.

**Programmable tags vs. non-programmable tags.** Same as many recent research efforts on RFID systems (e.g., [9, 16, 20, 24, 25]), our $\text{SRC}_S$ and $\text{SRC}_M$ protocol target programmable RFID tags that can run customized code. There have also been research work (e.g., [18]) that focuses on non-programmable RFID tags. These non-programmable tags can participate in a protocol only via a pre-determined way (e.g., only via framed slotted Aloha as specified in C1G2 [7]). We are currently working on adapting $\text{SRC}_S$ and $\text{SRC}_M$ to non-programmable tags. We already have initial designs for adapted $\text{SRC}_S$ and $\text{SRC}_M$, as well as promising preliminary results, though a full discussion into the subject is beyond the scope of this paper.

## 9. RELATED WORK

Section 4 already reviewed major related RFID counting protocols [9, 12, 13, 16, 18, 24]. Same as this paper, these efforts all focus on improving the performance of RFID counting. There have also been efforts that optimize other metrics such as energy consumption [14]. In early days, researchers (e.g., [10, 23, 26]) focus on efficient identification of RFID tags. Obviously once all tags are identified, we will obtain an exact count of the tags. But the inherent $\Omega(n)$ complexity makes it impossible for large-scale RFID systems.

There are deep connections between RFID counting protocols and algorithms for counting the number of distinct elements in a data stream [11]. One can conceptually map a slot in RFID counting protocols to a memory bit in distinct element counting algorithms. Existing RFID counting protocols (including ours) have borrowed multiple ideas from distinct element counting algorithms (e.g., [8, 21]). These ideas include for example, the use of duplicate-insensitive statistical quantities to deal with the possible overlapping between sets in multiple-set RFID counting [9]. Furthermore, reduction from the Hamming Distance Estimation problem has also led to lower bounds on the memory space needed by distinct element counting algorithm [5]. Despite these deep connections, RFID counting and distinct element counting also have some fundamental differences. First, a memory bit in distinct element counting can be overwritten multiple times. A slot in RFID counting, however, can only be used once. Hence a distinct element counting technique that overwrites the same memory multiple times cannot be carried over directly to RFID counting. Second, RFID counting can have multiple passes/phases, while distinct element counting for data streams cannot.

## 10. CONCLUSION

In summary, we present three fundamental results about RFID counting protocols: We establish strong lower bounds for both the single-set and multiple-set problem. We show that the overlooked key aspect for RFID counting protocols is a conceptual separation of a protocol into two phases. Furthermore, other techniques/ideas proposed in the literature are only of secondary importance. Finally, we apply the obtained insights to design new protocols that are more efficient than existing ones and also simultaneously simpler than most of them. We hope that our results will help facilitate future research in this subject.

## Acknowledgments

This work is partly supported by the research grant for the Human Sixth Sense Programme at the Advanced Digital Sciences Center from Singapore's Agency for Science, Technology and Research (A*STAR), and partly supported by the Singapore National Research Foundation under its International Research Centre @ Singapore Funding Initiative and administered by the IDM Programme Office.

## 11. REFERENCES

[1] http://newzealand.msteched.com/.
[2] http://spectrum.ieee.org/riskfactor/computing/it/walmart-to-track-clothing-with-rfid-tags.
[3] http://www.exhibitionnews.co.uk/featuredetails/172/a-flick-of-the-wrist-rfid-wristbands-for-exhibitions.
[4] http://www.packaging-gateway.com/projects/purdue/.
[5] A. Chakrabarti and O. Regev. An optimal lower bound on the communication complexity of GAP-HAMMING-DISTANCE. In *STOC*, 2011.
[6] B. Chen, Z. Zhou, and H. Yu. Understanding RFID counting protocols. Technical report. Available at `http://www.comp.nus.edu.sg/~yuhf/rfid-tr.pdf`.
[7] EPCglobal. EPC Radio-Frequency Identity Protocols Class-1 Generation-2 UHF RFID Protocol for Communications at 860 MHz - 960 MHz Version 1.2.0. 2008.
[8] P. Flajolet and G. Martin. Probabilistic counting algorithms for data base applications. *Journal of Computer and System Science*, 31(2):182–209, 1985.
[9] H. Han, B. Sheng, C. C. Tan, Q. Li, W. Mao, and S. Lu. Counting RFID tags efficiently and anonymously. In *INFOCOM*, 2010.
[10] D. Hush and C. Wood. Analysis of tree algorithms for RFID arbitration. In *IEEE Symposium on Information Theory*, 1998.
[11] D. Kane, J. Nelson, and D. Woodruff. An optimal algorithm for the distinct elements problem. In *PODS*, 2010.
[12] M. Kodialam and T. Nandagopal. Fast and reliable estimation schemes in RFID systems. In *ACM MobiCom*, 2006.
[13] M. Kodialam, T. Nandagopal, and W. C. Lau. Anonymous tracking using RFID tags. In *INFOCOM*, 2007.
[14] T. Li, S. Wu, S. Chen, and M. Yang. Energy efficient algorithms for the RFID estimation problem. In *INFOCOM*, 2010.
[15] R. Motwani and P. Raghavan. *Randomized Algorithms*. Cambridge University Press, 1995.
[16] C. Qian, H. Ngan, Y. Liu, and L. Ni. Cardinality estimation for large-scale RFID systems. *IEEE Transactions on Parallel and Distributed Systems*, 22(9):1441–1454, September 2011.
[17] Y. Qiao, S. Chen, and T. Li. *RFID as an Infrastructure*. Springer, 2013.
[18] M. Shahzad and A. X. Liu. Every bit counts - fast and scalable RFID estimation. In *ACM MobiCom*, 2012.
[19] B. Sheng, C. Tan, Q. Li, and W. Mao. Finding popular categories for RFID tags. In *MobiHoc*, 2008.
[20] J. Wang, H. Hassanieh, D. Katabi, and P. Indyk. Efficient and reliable low-power backscatter networks. In *ACM SIGCOMM*, 2012.
[21] K. Whang, B. Vander-Zanden, and H. Taylor. A linear-time probabilistic counting algorithm for database applications. *ACM Transactions on Database Systems*, 15:208–229, June 1990.
[22] A. Yao. Probabilistic computations: Toward a unified measure of complexity. In *FOCS*, 1977.
[23] B. Zhen, M. Kobayashi, and M. Shimizu. Framed ALOHA for multiple RFID objects identification. *IEICE Transactions on Communications*, E88-B(3), March 2005.
[24] Y. Zheng and M. Li. PET: Probabilistic estimating tree for large-scale RFID estimation. *IEEE Transactions on Mobile Computing*, 11(11):1763–1774, November 2012.
[25] Y. Zheng and M. Li. ZOE: Fast cardinality estimation for large-scale rfid systems. In *INFOCOM*, 2013.
[26] F. Zhou, C. Chen, D. Jin, C. Huang, and H. Min. Evaluating and optimizing power consumption of anti-collision protocols for applications in RFID systems. In *ACM ISLPED*, 2004.

# Optimal Throughput and Delay in Delay-tolerant Networks with Ballistic Mobility


Federica Bogo
Dip. Ingegneria dell'Informazione
Università degli Studi di Padova (Italy)
bogofede@dei.unipd.it

Enoch Peserico
Dip. Ingegneria dell'Informazione
Università degli Studi di Padova (Italy)
enoch@dei.unipd.it



## ABSTRACT

This work studies delay and throughput achievable in delay-tolerant networks with ballistic mobility – informally, when the average distance a node travels before changing direction does not become vanishingly small as the number of nodes in the deployment area grows. Ballistic mobility is a simple condition satisfied by a large number of well-studied mobility models, including the i.i.d. model, the random waypoint model, the uniform mobility model and Levy walks with exponent less than 1. Our contribution is twofold.

First, we show that, under some very mild and natural hypotheses satisfied by all models in the literature, ballistic mobility is strictly necessary to achieve simultaneously, as the number of nodes grows, a) per-node throughput that does not become vanishingly small and b) communication delay that does not become infinitely large. Any network whose nodes exhibit a more "local" mobility pattern (e.g. Levy walks with exponent greater than 1, or Brownian motion) must sacrifice either a) or b), regardless of the communication scheme adopted – even with network coding.

Second, we present a novel packet routing scheme. Our scheme is relatively simple and does not rely on centralized control, replication, or static base stations. At the same time it achieves both non-vanishing throughput and bounded delay as the number of nodes grows, on any network with ballistic mobility (i.e. whenever they can be simultaneously achieved), asymptotically outperforming any existing communication scheme that exploits node mobility to boost throughput.



**Categories and Subject Descriptors:** C.2.1 [Computer-Communication Networks]: Network Architecture and Design - Wireless Communication

**General Terms:** Algorithms, Performance, Theory

**Keywords:** Mobile networks; Delay-tolerant networks; Opportunistic networks; Throughput; Interference; Omnidirectional antennas; Routing; Network coding; In-flight communication; Mobility models




*MobiCom'13,* September 30–October 4, 2013, Miami, FL, USA.



ACM 978-1-4503-1999-7/13/09 ...$15.00.
http://dx.doi.org/10.1145/2500423.2500432.


## 1. INTRODUCTION

This work identifies in *ballistic mobility* the key to obtaining simultaneously high per-node throughput and low delay in delay-tolerant mobile wireless networks. After a very brief recap of the intuition why mobility can boost throughput in delay-tolerant networks (Subsection 1.1), and of the large number of models developed for the problem (Subsection 1.2), this introduction provides a succinct review of the state of the art (Subsection 1.3) and a summary of our results and of the organization of the following sections (Subsection 1.4).

### 1.1 Interference and Mobility

In wireless networks, interference can seriously reduce the throughput available to each node. Consider a network of $n$ randomly deployed, *static* nodes equipped with omnidirectional antennas, each transmitting to a random destination either directly or through any number of relays. Then the maximum average throughput achievable by each node is only a fraction $O(1/\sqrt{n})$ of the peak throughput achievable by two nodes communicating in isolation [9].

[8] observed that throughput can be considerably improved (to a constant fraction of the peak throughput) if a constant fraction of the nodes is mobile, by accepting potentially large communication delays (this would be a reasonable tradeoff e.g. in many sensor network scenarios). Informally, when a source node $u_s$ generates a packet for a destination node $u_d$, it transmits the packet to the first mobile node $u_r$ passing "sufficiently close" that the Signal-to-Noise ratio between the two allows nearly peak throughput; when $u_r$ eventually wanders "sufficiently close" to the destination $u_d$, it can in turn relay the information nearly at peak throughput. A vast literature has since appeared analysing the delay-throughput tradeoffs in networks exploiting node mobility [7, 13, 14, 17, 11, 12, 19, 8, 2, 15, 5, 20, 22].

### 1.2 Too Many Models?

It turns out that the performance achievable strongly depends on the mobility pattern of the nodes, and on the communication model adopted. Unfortunately, different models are appropriate for different scenarios: for example the mobility of wild animals is different from that of microsensors in a fluid, and both are different from that of humans. Furthermore, one can often model the same situation with different degrees of accuracy vs. tractability, and this has further multiplied the number of models in the literature.

All models in the literature share, however, some common characteristics. All assume nodes moving in straight lines at constant speed between waypoints in a deployment area that is either a circle, a square, or a spherical or toroidal surface. Once a waypoint is reached, possibly after a waiting time drawn from some distribution, a new direction, distance and speed are selected and determine the next waypoint. Almost all mobility patterns observed tend to match this very general framework: inanimate objects tend to move in straight lines at constant speed between physical events that change their velocity vector, and animals and humans tend to take the shortest path between "points of interest" [18, 16].

The difference between mobility models lies in how direction, distance and speed between waypoints are selected [3]. All models choose the next waypoint randomly, possibly with some bounds on the maximum distance travelled, or choose a direction uniformly at random (bouncing off or "wrapping around" the edges of the deployment area) and a distance within an interval according to some probability distribution (typically either uniform or a power law privileging shorter distances). Speed is chosen randomly according to a distribution that may depend on distance travelled, but is otherwise independent of the direction of travel. In virtually all models a node's choices at each waypoint are independent from those at previous waypoints, and from those of other nodes (again, this seems a fair approximation of observed mobility patterns [18, 16]).

In terms of communication, the most widely used model is the Signal-to-Noise ratio (SNR) model [2, 8, 9, 15, 21, 24], where the critical parameter when a source $u_s$ attempts to transmit to a destination $u_d$ is the Signal-to-Noise ratio $\frac{S_{u_s}}{N_0+\sum_{u\neq u_s} S_u}$ between the source's signal power $S_{u_s}$ at $u_d$, and the sum of the signal power $S_u$ of every other transmitting node $u$ plus a constant background noise $N_0$. If the ratio exceeds some threshold, the source can communicate at peak throughput with the destination. Signal power is known to decay with distance from the source as a *piecewise* polynomial [10, 24], i.e. the ratio between the signal power received at distance $d_1$ and $d_2$ lies between $(d_1/d_2)^{-\gamma_{min}}$ and $(d_1/d_2)^{-\gamma_{max}}$. In practice, most of the literature assumes for simplicity strictly polynomial decay, i.e. $\gamma_{min} = \gamma_{max}$. Both $\gamma_{min}$ and $\gamma_{max}$ are generally assumed larger than 2, so that, if nodes are uniformly distributed and all transmit with identical power, the bulk of the noise afflicting a communication will come from the nodes closest to the receiver. This justifies the even simpler Relaxed Protocol (RP) model [7] where a source can transmit at peak throughput with a destination at distance $d$ if and only if every other node is at distance greater than $(1+\Delta)d$ from the destination.

The majority of the literature assumes that nodes can communicate only at waypoints ("end of flight"), and not while in transit between them ("in flight"). The only justification for this choice is that it makes the analysis far simpler; in almost every scenario assuming in-flight communication is more realistic. Note that if the distance between consecutive waypoints is of the same order as the average distance between a node and its closest neighbour (i.e. $\Theta(1/\sqrt{n})$ for $n$ nodes distributed in a unit square), there is little difference between in flight and end of flight – informally because the distance between any two nodes is unlikely to change drastically between two waypoints. However, ignoring in-flight communication can lead to strongly suboptimal performance for nodes moving on longer trajectories [11].

## 1.3 A Performance Comparison

Table 1 compares the various delay/throughput bounds in the literature, and those provided in this work. To allow a meaningful comparison we have rescaled all results to a common time and space scale (so results in the table may at first sight appear different from those in the respective articles, which use different units of measure). In particular, we assume that the diameter of the deployment area is 1; that the speed of the fastest node is 1 (meaning that spanning the diameter of the deployment area at maximum speed takes time 1); and that peak throughput achievable between nodes in the absence of interference is 1.

The random waypoint (RWP) model [15, 19, 20] and the i.i.d. model [14, 15, 22, 17, 11] both assume that the next waypoint is chosen uniformly at random; the former assumes speed is independent of distance travelled (and thus travel time is proportional to it), while the latter assumes speed is proportional to distance travelled (and thus travel time is independent of it). Similarly, truncated Levy walks (LW) and Levy flights (LF) [11, 12] assume, respectively, independent speed and independent travel time, but choose a random direction and a travel distance $d$ in the interval $\approx [1/\sqrt{n}, 1]$ with probability proportional to $d^{-(1+\alpha)}$. The uniform mobility (UM) model of [2, 5] is similar to a Levy walk in that direction is chosen uniformly and speed is independent of distance travelled, but the distance $d$ is chosen with probability $\Theta(e^{-d/\mu})$, with $\mu = \Theta(1)$. The Brownian motion (BM) model [8, 7, 19, 20, 13] can be seen as a truncated Levy walk/flight with $\alpha \to \infty$: nodes travel distance $\approx 1/\sqrt{n}$ between consecutive waypoints, all at the same speed.

Roughly speaking, *without in-flight communication, all schemes in the literature achieving $\Theta(1)$ throughput per node incur delay equal to the time required by a node to change direction $\Omega(n)$ times – i.e. delay $\Omega(\sqrt{n})$ to $\Omega(n)$ depending on the mobility model used.* Reducing throughput to $\lambda < 1$ allows a reduction in delay by a factor between $\lambda$ to $\lambda^3$ depending on the model and the scheme used (including the possibility of diversity routing over multiple paths and/or of a centralized scheduler coordinating transmissions [6]).

In-flight communication increases performance, but *no previous work achieves $\Theta(1)$ throughput with less than $\Theta(\sqrt{n})$ delay.* $\Theta(1)$ throughput is achieved with $O(\sqrt{n})$ delay in the i.i.d. model, in the BM model, in the RWP model and in the LF model with $\alpha \leq 0$. In the LW model with $\alpha > 1$ and in the LF model with $\alpha > 0$ throughput $\Theta(1)$ is only achieved with larger delays, respectively $\Theta(n^{\frac{\alpha}{2}})$ and $\Theta(n^{\frac{1+\alpha}{2}})$. Again, reducing throughput to $\lambda < 1$ allows a reduction of delay by a factor between $\lambda^{\frac{1}{2}}$ and $\lambda^{\frac{3}{2}}$. The only work presenting a considerably better tradeoff is [2]: in a network where mobile nodes represent a fraction $\eta$ of the node population and move according to the UM model, $\Theta\left(\eta\frac{1}{\log^2 n(\log n+1/\mu)}\right)$ throughput is achieved with $\Theta(1)$ delay. However [2] assumes that *all destinations are static, with all their positions known to every mobile node*, and states that achieving a better tradeoff than [8] with mobile destinations seems impossible.

## 1.4 Our Results

*This work presents the first scheme that achieves $\Theta(1)$ throughput with only $\Theta(1)$ delay.* This is a $\Theta(\sqrt{n})$ improvement in delay over the best results with mobile destinations in the literature. Our scheme works in both the SNR and the RP communication models (with in-flight communica-

Table 1: **Throughput and delay in different models. Coloured entries use in-flight communication.**

| Work | Mobility | Throughput $\lambda$ | Delay $D$ | Notes |
|---|---|---|---|---|
| [8] | BM | $\lambda = \Theta(1)$ | $D = O(\inf)$ | 2-hop routing |
| [2] | UM | $\lambda = \Omega\left(\frac{\min(m,n)}{n \log^3 n}\right)$ | $D = \Theta(1)$ | $m$ static nodes |
| [7] | BM | $\frac{1}{n} \leq \lambda \leq 1$ | $D(\lambda) = O(\sqrt{n}\lambda)$ | Multi-hop routing |
| [14], [15] | i.i.d. | $\frac{1}{n} \leq \lambda \leq 1$ | $D(\lambda) = O\left(\frac{n\lambda^3}{log^{9/2} n}\right)$ | Centralized scheduler.<br>Delay $\leq D$ for *each* packet w.h.p. |
| [15] | RWP | $\frac{1}{n} \leq \lambda \leq 1$ | $D(\lambda) = \Theta\left(\frac{\sqrt{n}\lambda^2}{log^{3/2} n}\right)$ | Partially obtained by simulation |
| [5] | UM | $\lambda = \Theta(1)$ | $D(\lambda) = O(n)$ | Replication |
| [19], [20] | BM | $\lambda = \Theta(1)$ | $D = O(\sqrt{n} log^2 n)$ | 2-hop routing |
| [19], [20] | RWP | $\lambda = \Theta(1)$ | $D = \Theta(\sqrt{n})$ | Only simulation results |
| [22] | i.i.d. | $\lambda_{0<d<1} = \Theta\left(\frac{1}{n^{\frac{1-d}{2}} \log^{\frac{5}{2}} n}\right)$ | $D(\lambda) = O\left(n^d\right)$ | Delay $\leq D$ for *each* packet w.h.p. |
| [17] | i.i.d. | $\frac{1}{\sqrt{n}} \leq \lambda \leq 1$ | $D(\lambda) = O(n\lambda)$ | Replication |
| [13] | BM | $\lambda = \Theta\left(\frac{1}{\sqrt{n}}\right)$ | $D = \Theta(1)$ | Centralized scheduler |
| [12] | LW | $\lambda = \omega\left(\frac{1}{\sqrt{n}}\right)$ | $D = \Omega\left(n^{\frac{\max(1,\alpha)}{2}}\right)$ | Only critical delay analysis |
| [12] | LF | $\lambda = \omega\left(\frac{1}{\sqrt{n}}\right)$ | $D = \Omega\left(n^{\frac{\alpha}{2}}\right)$ | Only critical delay analysis |
| [11] | i.i.d | $\frac{1}{\sqrt{n}} \leq \lambda \leq 1$ | $D(\lambda) = O(\sqrt{\max(1, n\lambda^3)})$ | 2-hop, multiple path routing |
| [11] | LF | $\frac{1}{\sqrt{n}} \leq \lambda \leq 1$ | $D(\lambda) = O(\sqrt{\min(n^{1+\alpha}\lambda, n^2)})$ | 2-hop, multiple path routing |
| This work | Non-ballistic (includes BM, $LW_{\alpha>1}$,$LF_{\alpha>0}$) | $\lambda = \Theta(1)$ | $D = \omega(1)$ | Regardless of replication, network coding or centralized scheduling |
| This work | Ballistic (includes i.i.d., RWP, UM, $LW_{\alpha<1}$, $LF_{\alpha<0}$) | $\lambda = \Theta(1)$ | $D = \Theta(1)$ | Multi-hop routing, no replication, no network coding, no centralized scheduler |

tion) for all *ballistic* mobility models: roughly speaking, all mobility models in which the positions of a node between time $t$ and time $t+1$ have $\Omega(1)$ probability of being $\Omega(1)$ distance apart. Ballistic mobility thus encompasses the random waypoint, i.i.d. and uniform mobility models, Levy walks with $\alpha < 1$, and Levy flights with $\alpha < 0$. The key to our scheme's performance is exploiting information about node positions for packet forwarding. Our scheme does not require centralized control, network coding or packet replication, and each node needs only have access to an accurate clock and gauge the position and velocity vectors *relative to itself* of nodes it successfully communicates with (a GPS is sufficient to guarantee this, but is not necessary).

Furthermore, we prove our result is strict in the sense that without ballistic mobility it is impossible to simultaneously achieve $\Theta(1)$ throughput and $\Theta(1)$ delay whether or not one uses in-flight communication, centralized omniscient control, multiple message copies, or network coding (as long as transmissions are omnidirectional).

The rest of this work is organized as follows. Section 2 introduces our mobility and communication models, formalizing the crucial notion of ballistic mobility. Section 3 proves that ballistic mobility is necessary to achieve simultaneously $\Theta(1)$ throughput and $\Theta(1)$ delay. Section 4 presents and analyses our routing scheme. Finally, Section 5 discusses the significance of our results as well as possible directions of future work.

# 2. A GENERAL NETWORK MODEL

This section describes our mobile network model. Our purpose is to make it as general as possible, so as to encompass the widest variety of "natural" models, including all models already in the literature. Subsections 2.1 and 2.2, below, describe respectively the mobility and communication models of the nodes. Subsection 2.3 introduces the crucial notion of ballistic mobility.

## 2.1 Mobility Model

$n$ mobile nodes $u_1, u_2, \ldots, u_n$ move within a deployment area $A$ that is either a square, a circle, a toroidal surface or a spherical surface, with diameter 1. We denote the position of node $u_i$ at any time $t$ by the vector $\mathbf{x}_i(t) = \langle x_i^1(t), x_i^2(t)\rangle$; given a pair of nodes $u_i$ and $u_j$, we denote their distance at time $t$ by $d_{i,j}(t)$. Every node travels in a straight line between intermediate waypoints; we refer to each such segment as a *trajectory*. Once at a waypoint, a new waypoint for that node is selected by choosing at random (independently from other waypoint choices for the same node or other nodes):

1. a direction uniformly in $[0, 2\pi[$
2. independently, a distance $d$ according to some distribution $D_d$ within the interval $[0, 1]$.
3. independently of the direction but not necessarily of the distance, a travel time (or wait time if $d = 0$). This induces a speed $s(d)$ according to some distribution $D_{s(d)}$ with support in $[0, 1]$ (i.e. maximum speed is 1).

We also require the speed distribution to satisfy a mild technical condition to avoid some pathological mobility patterns: if $s$ has a probability bounded away from 0 of exceeding a certain threshold $\bar{s}$, then it has probability density at least $\Omega(1/\bar{s})$ over an open interval of speeds of size $\Omega(\bar{s})$

containing $\bar{s}$ (this condition essentially prohibits node speeds from having infinitely small modes).

If the choices above would yield a waypoint beyond the boundaries of the deployment area (which is never the case for a toroidal or spherical surface, but may be the case with a square or circle), we allow the node to take an arbitrary path of length bounded by 1 at an arbitrary speed bounded away from 0 (including a path that leaves the deployment area at one point and re-enters at some other point); we call these arbitrary paths *out of boundary*, in order to distinguish them from *normal* trajectories. In this case we only place two mild technical conditions to avoid pathological situations: that at any given time the fraction of nodes on out-of-boundary paths be bounded away from 1, and that the steady state probability density of finding a node at any given point be roughly uniform across the deployment region, save possibly near the borders (where it can approach 0). This can be formalized using the definition of *ρ-uniform* distribution:

DEFINITION 1. *Consider a probability density function* $p(x)$ *with support* $X$ *and average* $\bar{p} = \frac{1}{|X|}\int_X p(x)$. *Given* $\rho > 0$, $p(x)$ *is* $\rho$*-uniform if* $\rho\bar{p} \le p(x) \le \frac{1}{\rho}\bar{p}$ *for every* $x \in X$.

We then require the existence of some arbitrarily small $\rho$ bounded away from 0, such that the node probability density is *ρ-uniform* at distance at least $\rho$ from the boundaries of the deployment area. Note that the absence of out-of-boundary paths automatically guarantees $\rho$-uniformity.

It is easy to verify that this very general model encompasses all mobility models we described in the previous section, including the i.i.d., RWP, UM, LW, LF, and BM models. But it can also encompass additional/more general mobility models. For example, experimental studies [18] suggest that the "correct" mobility model for long-range human mobility is a hybrid between the Levy walk and the Levy flight, that we call the *Levy run* (LR). In a Levy run, the probability of selecting the next waypoint at distance $d$ is still proportional to $d^{-(1+\alpha)}$, but speed grows with the distance as $d^{\alpha^*}$ for some non-negative $\alpha^* \le 1$ (Levy walks and flights are then the two extreme cases of $\alpha^* = 0$ and $\alpha^* = 1$).

## 2.2 Communication Model

We assume all nodes are identical and can freely and continuously adjust their transmission power between 0 and a given maximum (we remark that in our routing scheme in Section 4 nodes do not take advantage of this flexibility, and always transmit at maximum power or not at all). We denote by $T_i(t)$ the ratio between the transmission power of node $u_i$ at time $t$ and its maximum transmission power (so $0 \le T_i(t) \le 1$), and by $S_{i,j}(t)$ the power of the signal from node $u_i$ received at time $t$ by node $u_j$. We assume that $S_{i,j}(t)$ is proportional to the transmission power of $u_i$, and decreases with distance $d_{i,j}(t)$ between $u_i$ and $u_j$ according to a piecewise power law. More formally, we assume the existence of two constants $\gamma_{min}$ and $\gamma_{max}$ with $2 < \gamma_{min} \le \gamma_{max}$ such that, for any pair of nodes $u_h$ and $u_i$ with $T_h(t), T_i(t) > 0$, and any other node $u_j$ with $d_{h,j}(t) \le d_{i,j}(t)$, we have:

$$\frac{T_h(t)}{T_i(t)}\left(\frac{d_{h,j}(t)}{d_{i,j}(t)}\right)^{-\gamma_{min}} \le \frac{S_{h,j}(t)}{S_{i,j}(t)} \le \frac{T_h(t)}{T_i(t)}\left(\frac{d_{h,j}(t)}{d_{i,j}(t)}\right)^{-\gamma_{max}} \tag{1}$$

In the SNR model, denoting by $N_0$ the background noise and by $\beta$ the minimum Signal-to-Noise ratio for successful transmissions, the transmission from $u_i$ is received by $u_j$ if:

$$\frac{S_{i,j}(t)}{N_0 + \sum_{h \ne i} S_{h,j}(t)} \ge \beta \tag{2}$$

In the simplified RP model [7], at any given time any node is either silent or transmitting at full power (i.e. $T_i(t) \in \{0,1\}$ $\forall i, t$); the transmission from $u_i$ is received by $u_j$ if for every other node $u_h$ transmitting at $t$:

$$d_{h,j}(t) \ge (1+\Delta)d_{i,j}(t) \tag{3}$$

where $\Delta > 0$ is a system parameter. In either model, the peak throughput between two nodes in the absence of interference is 1, i.e. up to 1 unit of information can be exchanged in 1 unit of time – subdivided into packets we assume of identical size $P$ for simplicity. We also make the realistic assumption that 1 unit of information amounts to at least $k_{com}\sqrt{n}$ packets (so $P \ll 1$) each of at least $k_{id} \log n$ bits for two appropriate constants $k_{com}, k_{id} = \Theta(1)$: informally, each packet must hold sufficient information to identify its sender and be short enough to be exchanged by two nodes during the time ($\approx 1/\sqrt{n}$) they remain closest neighbours. Note that $\Omega(n)$ simultaneous packet exchanges, and thus $\Omega(1)$ per-node throughput (regardless of delay), require most transmissions to originate from one of the $O(1)$ closest nodes to the receiver – so this "short packets" assumption is shared, implicitly or explicitly, by most previous work.

Each node *generates* packets at a rate of at most $\lambda$ units of information per unit of time; each packet must be delivered (possibly through a number of intermediate relays) to a destination chosen uniformly and independently at random. We are interested in the maximum $\lambda$ sustainable while guaranteeing a given delivery delay for at least a constant fraction of the packets [2]. More precisely, we say that a communication scheme *achieves throughput* $\lambda(n)$ *and delay* $D(n)$ if there exists a probability $p > 0$ independent of $n$ such that, if every node generates $\lambda < \lambda(n)/p$ information per unit of time, each packet has probability at least $p$ of being delivered within time $D(n)$ of its generation.

## 2.3 Ballistic Mobility

Despite the generality of our mobility model, we prove in the following sections that a very simple condition is both necessary and sufficient to guarantee simultaneously $\Omega(1)$ throughput and $O(1)$ delay: *ballistic mobility.* Informally, mobility is ballistic if, as the number of nodes $n$ grows, at any given time a non-vanishing fraction of them is headed with non-vanishing speed towards a waypoint at non-vanishing distance. More formally:

DEFINITION 2. *A mobility model is ballistic if there exists some* $\epsilon > 0$ *independent of* $n$ *such that at any given time, choosing a node uniformly at random, with probability at least* $\epsilon$ *that node is headed with speed at least* $\epsilon$ *towards a waypoint at distance at least* $\epsilon$.

It is immediate to verify that the i.i.d., random waypoint, and uniform mobility models, as well as Levy flights with $\alpha < 0$, are ballistic. Similarly, it is immediate to verify that Brownian motion is *not* ballistic, since the distance between consecutive waypoints is $\Theta(1/\sqrt{n})$.

It is less obvious that Levy walks with $\alpha < 1$ are ballistic, since for any given $\epsilon > 0$ the probability that a node's next waypoint is selected at distance $\epsilon$ or greater is $\Theta(n^{-\alpha})$, which becomes vanishingly small with $n$. However, nodes selecting a distant waypoint spend a longer time to reach it, and thus the fraction of nodes on such "long" trajectories at any given time remains bounded away from 0 as long as $\alpha < 1$.

Similarly, it is easy to verify that Levy runs with $\alpha + \alpha^* < 1$ are ballistic, and that Levy runs with $\alpha + \alpha^* \geq 1$ (and thus Levy walks with $\alpha \geq 1$ and Levy flights with $\alpha \geq 0$) are not ballistic. Table 2 summarizes our classification between ballistic and non-ballistic models.

**Table 2: Ballistic vs. non-ballistic models.**

| Ballistic | Non-ballistic |
|---|---|
| i.i.d., UM, RWP, $LW_{\alpha<1}$, $LF_{\alpha<0}$, $LR_{\alpha+\alpha^*<1}$ | BM, $LW_{\alpha\geq 1}$, $LF_{\alpha\geq 0}$ $LR_{\alpha+\alpha^*\geq 1}$ |

# 3. BALLISTIC MOBILITY IS NECESSARY FOR $\Theta(1)$ THROUGHPUT AND DELAY

This section is devoted to the proof of the following:

THEOREM 1. *Without ballistic mobility, no communication scheme can simultaneously achieve $\Theta(1)$ delay and $\Theta(1)$ average per-node throughput – even assuming centralized control, perfect knowledge of all future node movements and packet destinations, and arbitrary network coding.*

PROOF. The cornerstone of our proof is the fact that, in the absence of ballistic mobility, as $n$ grows nodes tend to remain within a progressively smaller area during any given time interval. More formally:

LEMMA 1. *In the absence of ballistic mobility, for any arbitrarily small $\epsilon > 0$ there exists a sufficiently large $\bar{n}$ such that, with $n > \bar{n}$ nodes, choosing a node $u_i$ uniformly at random the expected maximum distance between any two positions of $u_i$ in the interval $[t, t+1]$ is strictly less than $\epsilon$.*

PROOF. Consider any arbitrarily small $\delta > 0$. One difficulty in the proof of the lemma is dealing with "out-of-boundary" paths (in deployment areas with boundaries). Denote by $\mathcal{E}_{out}$ the event that $u_i$ is within distance $\delta$ of the boundaries (a region of area $\Theta(\delta)$) at time $t$. By our mobility model, $\Pr(\mathcal{E}_{out}) < k_{out}\delta$ for some constant $k_{out}$ independent of $n$.

Suppose $\mathcal{E}_{out}$ does not take place, so that $u_i$ starts at distance greater than $\delta$ from the boundaries (this is automatically satisfied in deployment areas without boundaries such as spherical surfaces). Since mobility is not ballistic, for any arbitrarily small $\gamma > 0$ the event $\mathcal{E}_{long}$ that during an interval of duration 1 $u_i$ finds itself on a trajectory of length greater than $\gamma$ can be given a probability smaller than $\delta$ by choosing a sufficiently large $n$. We want to prove that, if neither $\mathcal{E}_{out}$ nor $\mathcal{E}_{long}$ take place, the probability of the event $\mathcal{E}_{max}$ that $u_i$ achieves a maximum distance $\delta$ or greater from its starting point is less than $\delta$ (which avoids "out-of-boundary" paths, and proves the lemma). We do so by proving that with probability greater than $1 - \delta$ the maximum distance during the (possibly shorter) interval $[t', t'']$ from the first to the last waypoint reached during $[t, t+1]$ is less than $\delta - 2\gamma$ (since on the way to its first waypoint, and while moving away from the last waypoint, the node covers less than $2\gamma$ total distance).

Simple geometric considerations show that the furthest point in a segment AB from a given point C (that may or may not belong to AB) is either A or B. Denote by $\Delta x_i^1, \Delta x_i^2$ the difference between the coordinates of the $i^{th}$ and $(i+1)^{th}$ waypoint during $[t', t'']$. To prove the bound on the maximum distance moved during $[t', t'']$, we can then just prove that:

$$\max_i \sum_{j=1}^{i} \Delta x_i^1 \leq \frac{\delta - 2\gamma}{2} \tag{4}$$

and an identical bound on $\max_i \sum_{j=1}^{i} \Delta x_i^2$. Since we are considering at least $\frac{1-2\gamma}{\gamma}$ independent variables, with mean 0 and variance bounded by $\gamma$, by the law of iterated logarithm the left-hand term of Equation 4 is in expectation $\Theta(\sqrt{\gamma \log\log(1/\gamma)})$. Since the probability that a non-negative variable exceeds $m$ times its expectation is less than $1/m$, by choosing a sufficiently small $\gamma$ the probability that Equation 4 is not satisfied can be made smaller than $\delta$.

Then, for any arbitrarily small $\delta > 0$, for all sufficiently large $n$ the probability that $u_i$ moves further than $\delta$ from its starting point during an interval of duration 1 is at most $\Pr(\mathcal{E}_{out}) + \Pr(\mathcal{E}_{long}) + \Pr(\mathcal{E}_{max}) < (k_{out} + 2)\delta$, proving the lemma. □

A simple consequence of Lemma 1 is the following:

COROLLARY 1. *In a deployment area of diameter 1, with an expected node density at most $\rho n = O(n)$ at any given point, in the absence of ballistic mobility in expectation $o(n)$ nodes enter or leave any given convex cell of the deployment area during any interval $[t, t+\Delta t]$ with $\Delta t = O(1)$.*

PROOF. Simple geometric considerations show that for any $\eta$, within a deployment region of diameter 1, the area within distance $\eta$ of the frontier of a generic convex cell is less than $3.1416 \cdot 2\eta$. By Lemma 1, for any arbitrarily small $\eta > 0$ and all sufficiently large $n$, the expected number of nodes further than $\eta$ from the frontier at $t$ that cross the frontier before $t + \Delta t$ is less than $\eta n$; and obviously the number of nodes closer to the frontier than $\eta$ at $t$ is less than $\rho \cdot 3.1416 \cdot 2\eta \cdot n$. □

We now prove the main theorem by contradiction. Assume without loss of generality that the memory capacity $M$ of each node is some integer multiple of $P$, and call *early* all throughput/packets with delay at most $1/\epsilon$, for some constant $\epsilon > 0$. Suppose that one can achieve in the absence of ballistic mobility for all $n$ at least $\epsilon$ average per-node early throughput during an interval $[t, t + \frac{2}{\epsilon}]$ (note that all early packets generated during the first half of the interval must arrive before the interval's end).

Considering only early packets generated and delivered during $[t, t + \frac{2}{\epsilon}]$, partition the deployment area into convex cells of diameter $r = \Theta(\sqrt{\epsilon})$ and area $\Theta(r^2) = \Theta(\epsilon)$ sufficiently small that, for any given cell, the probability of a packet's destination being within that cell's *$r-$neighbourhood* (i.e. in that cell or within distance $r$ of it) *at any time* during $[t, t + \frac{2}{\epsilon}]$ is less than $\frac{1}{4}\epsilon$ – this is possible by Corollary 1. For any such cell $A$, denote by $\mathcal{S}_A$ the set of nodes always within $A$ and by $\mathcal{D}_A$ the set of nodes never inside the

$r-$neighbourhood of $A$ during $[t, t+\frac{2}{\epsilon}]$. Then, with probability converging to 1 as $n$ grows, one such cell $A$ exists such that $|\mathcal{S}_A| \geq k_r \epsilon n$ for some $k_r = \Theta(1)$ (again, due to Corollary 1), the average per-node early throughput from $\mathcal{S}_A$ is at least $\frac{3}{4}\epsilon$, and the average per-node throughput to destinations outside $\mathcal{D}_A$ is at most $\frac{2}{4}\epsilon$; so the average per-node early throughput from $\mathcal{S}_A$ to $\mathcal{D}_A$ must be at least $\frac{1}{4}\epsilon$.

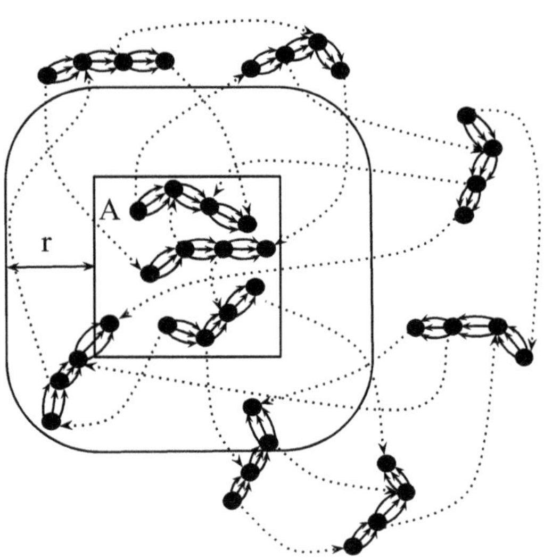


**Figure 1: A convex cell $A$ and its $r$-neighbourhood ($|\mathcal{S}_A| = 3$, $|\mathcal{D}_A| = 5$). Dotted and straight arcs model in-the-air and piggybacking information transfer, respectively.**

Note that all information is transferred either "in the air" or by "piggybacking" on mobile nodes. We can model this with a communication multigraph having a vertex at each point in the deployment area where a mobile node transmits or receives a packet, an arc from any transmission vertex to the corresponding reception vertex (modelling in-the-air information transfer), and $M/P$ arcs from any vertex to the vertex corresponding to the next transmission/reception from/to that same mobile node (modelling piggybacking information) – see Figure 1. As an arc marks a transfer of $P$ information units, the number of arcs in the minimum cut separating the $\mathcal{S}_A$-vertices from the $\mathcal{D}_A$-vertices equals:

$$mincut(\mathcal{S}_A, \mathcal{D}_A) \geq k_r \epsilon n \cdot \frac{1}{4}\epsilon \cdot \frac{1}{P} = \frac{k_r}{4} \cdot \frac{\epsilon^2 n}{P} \qquad (5)$$

A crucial observation is that Equation 5 holds even if network coding is used [1]. Thus there must be a set $\Pi$ of $\frac{k_r}{4} \cdot \frac{\epsilon^2 n}{P}$ arc-disjoint paths from the set of $\mathcal{S}_A$-vertices to the set of $\mathcal{D}_A$-vertices. Any such path $\pi$ alternates isolated in-the-air arcs with sequences of one or more piggybacking arcs (we only consider *maximal* sequences, i.e. sequences that are not proper subsequences of other sequences of piggybacking arcs in the path). Let the *range* of an in-the-air arc simply be its length, and let the range of a piggybacking sequence be the distance between its first and last vertex (rather than the sum of the lengths of individual arcs, which could be much larger by Lemma 1). Denote by $\delta_a(\pi)$ the sum of the in-the-air arc ranges of $\pi$, and by $\delta_b(\pi)$ the sum of the piggybacking sequence ranges. Then, remembering that each vertex in $\mathcal{S}_A$ has distance at least $r$ from every vertex in $\mathcal{D}_A$:

$$\delta_a(\pi) + \delta_b(\pi) \geq r \qquad (6)$$

The total number of in-the-air arcs over any set of arc-disjoint paths cannot exceed $\frac{n}{P} \cdot \frac{2}{\epsilon}$ (since the entire network cannot transmit more than $\frac{n}{P}$ packets per unit of time), so the total number of piggybacking sequences cannot exceed $2 \cdot \frac{2n}{\epsilon P}$. For any arbitrarily small $\eta > 0$, by Lemma 1 for all sufficiently large $n$ the maximum distance between two positions of a node during the interval $[t, t+\frac{2}{\epsilon}]$ is in expectation less than $\eta$. Then, in expectation for a sufficiently small $\eta = O(\epsilon^{\frac{7}{2}})$:

$$\sum_{\pi \in \Pi} \delta_a(\pi) \geq r|\Pi| - \sum_{\pi \in \Pi} \delta_b(\pi)$$
$$\geq r\left(\frac{k_r}{4} \cdot \frac{\epsilon^2 n}{P}\right) - \eta \cdot \frac{4n}{\epsilon P} \geq \frac{r|\Pi|}{2} = \Omega\left(\frac{\epsilon^{\frac{5}{2}} n}{P}\right) \qquad (7)$$

We easily prove that Equation 7 implies the existence of some $\eta > 0$ such that, for all $n$, at least $\eta n$ nodes can simultaneously transmit (successfully) at distance at least $\eta$. Suppose this were not the case: remembering that the diameter of the deployment area is 1 and that during the interval $[t, t+\frac{2}{\epsilon}]$ each node in the network transmits at most $\frac{2}{\epsilon P}$ packets, the sum of the distances of "long-range" transmissions would be less than $1 \cdot \frac{2}{\epsilon P} \cdot \eta n$, while the sum of the distances of all other transmissions would be less than $\eta \cdot \frac{2}{\epsilon P} \cdot n$ – yielding $\sum_{\pi \in \Pi} \delta_a(\pi) < \eta \cdot \frac{4n}{\epsilon P}$, which would violate Equation 7 for all sufficiently small $\eta$.

But we can prove, both in the SNR model and in the RP model, that no given $\eta > 0$ allows $\eta n$ nodes to successfully transmit to distance at least $\eta$ for all $n$ – leading to a contradiction and proving the theorem. In the RP model, each node successfully receiving from distance $\eta$ precludes any other successful transmission within distance $(1+\Delta)\eta$, so there are at most $O(\eta^2) = o(\eta n)$ such nodes at any given time in a deployment area of diameter 1. In the SNR model, if nodes $u_1, \ldots, u_{\eta n}$ are all transmitting simultaneously at time $t$ to a range between $\eta$ and 1, assuming without loss of generality that the transmission power of $u_{\eta n}$ is no higher than that of $u_1, \ldots, u_{\eta n - 1}$ and that its destination is some node $u_d$, we have:

$$\frac{N_0 + \sum_{h=1}^{\eta n - 1} S_{h,d}(t)}{S_{\eta n, d}(t)} \geq \sum_{h=1}^{\eta n - 1} \left(\frac{1}{\eta}\right)^{-\gamma_{max}} \qquad (8)$$

and the last term is greater than $\frac{1}{\beta}$ for all sufficiently large $n$, violating Equation 2. □

## 4. Θ(1) DELAY WITH Θ(1) THROUGHPUT

This section presents a simple routing scheme that achieves $\Theta(1)$ delay and $\Theta(1)$ throughput/node under any *ballistic* mobility model (and requires each node to store at most $O(1)$ units of information at any given time). The key to our scheme's performance is exploiting information about node positions for packet forwarding. The only previous work to do so is [2], which in fact achieves $\Theta(1)$ delay with only polylog $n$ throughput degradation (due in part to an overaggressive transmission policy). But [2] assumes (and relies heavily on) *static* destinations; without this assumption our task is far more challenging since node mobility makes positional information become quickly obsolete.

Subsection 4.1 describes the scheme and Subsection 4.2 analyses its performance, assuming (as most previous work) that packet destinations are chosen uniformly and independently at random, and that packets are the largest possible size (i.e. only $\Theta(1)$ packets, rather than $\Omega(1)$, can be exchanged between a node and its nearest neighbour in the $\Theta(1/\sqrt{n})$ time units before they move apart). Subsection 4.3 shows how these two assumptions can be easily removed.

## 4.1 Colouring, Sighting, Routing

We assume each node has access to an accurate clock and can assess the position and velocity vector *relative to itself* of any node it successfully communicates with. Note that nodes need not know their "global" position, the boundaries of the deployment area, the specific mobility pattern (as long as it is ballistic), the position of their next waypoint, or any other information about other nodes.

We assume direct communication between nodes takes place through a particular version of the Reservation Aloha protocol [4], where time is partitioned into slots of duration $k_{slot}/\sqrt{n}$ with $k_{slot} = \Theta(1)$, and each slot is in turn partitioned into 10 subslots. On the first subslot each node transmits a packet of the subslot's duration with independent probability $p_{tr} = \Theta(1)$; if the transmission is successful, the recipient transmits a reply on the second subslot, and then initiator and recipient alternate for the remaining subslots. If all 10 packets are successfully transmitted (note that due to mobility the "reservation" protocol may fail on any subslot), we say that the two nodes *sight* each other during that slot. Successful communication is obviously strongly dependent on distance: if two nodes are within distance $k_{enc}/\sqrt{n}$ (for some $k_{enc} = \Theta(1)$) at some instant $t$, we say they *encounter* each other at $t$.

For simplicity of exposition we associate to each integer from 1 to $n$ (and thus, implicitly, to each node) a unique *colour* from a set $C$. Packets exchanged in our scheme are of two types, *messages* and *sightings*. Messages are simply the data packets that our scheme must route from source to destination; each message is coloured with the same colour as its destination. Sightings carry information about node positions in the network: whenever a node $u_s$ sights a node $u_i$, $u_s$ generates a sighting of $u_i$ – i.e. a packet carrying the time of the encounter as well as the position and velocity vector of $u_i$ at that time. The latter are initially relative to $u_s$, but each subsequent node that receives $u_i$'s sighting recalculates them relative to itself, and adjusts the sighting accordingly, from the position and velocity relative to itself of the node transmitting the sighting. Each sighting is coloured with the same colour as the "sighted" node.

In addition to its permanent colour, each node "flies a banner" of $k_b\sqrt{n}$ colours changing over time, for some $k_b = \Theta(1)$ – a new colour is added to the banner at each time slot, replacing the oldest colour, according to a hash function $\mathcal{H} : C \times \mathbb{N} \to C$ shared by all nodes in the network that associates to each $\langle node, slot\rangle$ pair the colour entering the node's banner in that slot. While a node $u_i$ carries a colour in its banner we say $u_i$ is a *banneret* for that colour and for the corresponding node. The use of a hash function allows a banneret to efficiently communicate its banner colours to the nodes it meets, since those nodes can reconstruct all the $\Theta(\sqrt{n})$ colours in the banner from the colour of the banneret.

**Algorithm 1** Routing with ballistic mobility

*each node generates new messages for random destinations at an information rate* $\Theta(1)$
*at any time slot* $\mathcal{S}$*, any node* $u_i$ *keeps a set* $M_i(\mathcal{S})$ *of coloured messages and a set* $\Sigma_i(\mathcal{S})$ *of coloured sightings stored, and is associated to a banner* $B_i(\mathcal{S})$
**for** each time slot $\mathcal{S}$ **do**
  **if** $u_i$ and $u_j$ successfully communicate during $\mathcal{S}$ **then**
    *spotter/destination interaction:*
    $u_i$ stores in $\Sigma_i(\mathcal{S})$ a sighting of $u_j$
    $u_j$ stores in $\Sigma_j(\mathcal{S})$ a sighting of $u_i$
    *spotter/banneret interaction:*
    $u_i$ transmits to $u_j$ a (random) sighting in $\Sigma_i(\mathcal{S})$ whose colour is in $B_j(\mathcal{S})$, if any
    $u_j$ transmits to $u_i$ a (random) sighting in $\Sigma_j(\mathcal{S})$ whose colour is in $B_i(\mathcal{S})$, if any
    *source/banneret interaction:*
    $u_i$ transmits to $u_j$ a (random) message in $M_i(\mathcal{S})$ whose colour is in $B_j(\mathcal{S})$, if any
    $u_j$ transmits to $u_i$ a (random) message in $M_j(\mathcal{S})$ whose colour is in $B_i(\mathcal{S})$, if any
    *match message/sighting pairs:*
    $u_i$ matches messages in $M_i(\mathcal{S})$ with sightings in $\Sigma_i(\mathcal{S})$ of the same colour
    $u_j$ matches messages in $M_j(\mathcal{S})$ with sightings in $\Sigma_j(\mathcal{S})$ of the same colour
    *banneret/relay interaction:*
    $u_i$ transmits to $u_j$ a (random) message in $M_i(\mathcal{S})$ whose destination $u_j$ is projected to encounter, if any
    $u_j$ transmits to $u_i$ a (random) message in $M_j(\mathcal{S})$ whose destination $u_i$ is projected to encounter, if any
    *relay/destination interaction:*
    $u_i$ transmits to $u_j$ a (random) message in $M_i(\mathcal{S})$ with destination $u_j$, if any
    $u_j$ transmits to $u_i$ a (random) message in $M_j(\mathcal{S})$ with destination $u_i$, if any
  **end if**
**end for**

This is the linchpin of our construction. Informally, a node's banner states the colours of sightings and messages that node is "interested" in and will collect from those nodes it meets. Bannerets for a colour then act as rendezvous points for the sightings and messages of that colour, allowing each message to be routed in the "right" direction.

More precisely, after a node $u_s$ generates a sighting of $u_i$, it retains the sighting for some time $k_{ret}$ (with $k_{ret} = \Theta(1)$) and shares it with any banneret for $u_i$ sighted during that time; we say $u_s$ is acting as a *spotter* for $u_i$. If $u_s$ could share multiple sightings it has collected, it chooses a random one. Similarly, any source node that generates a message for a destination $u_d$ retains the message for time $k_{ret}$, and shares it with any banneret for $u_d$ sighted during that time, choosing a random message if multiple ones could be shared.

Once a banneret $u_b$ obtains both a message and a sighting of the same colour as a destination $u_d$, it can assess for each node $u_r$ it sights whether that node will encounter $u_d$ on its current trajectory (assuming $u_d$ maintains the same velocity vector it had when sighted); if so, $u_b$ transfers the message to $u_r$. In this case we say that $u_r$ is acting as a *relay* for the message to $u_d$. Again, if a banneret could transfer multiple messages (for which it has obtained the corresponding sightings) to a potential relay, it chooses a random one; and similarly, when a relay $u_r$ sights a destination for one or more messages it is relaying, it delivers to that destination one of those messages at random. Like spotters, bannerets retain sightings for time $k_{ret}$ before discarding them; and similarly, bannerets and relays retain messages for time $k_{ret}$ before discarding them.

Then, in addition to a source of a message and its destination, three more nodes are involved in the delivery of a message: the banneret, the spotter (which must encounter the destination before it encounters the banneret), and the relay (which must encounter the banneret after the source and spotter do, and before it encounters the destination). Note that each node, at any given time, is simultaneously acting in all five roles for many (in fact, $\Theta(\sqrt{n})$) messages.

Algorithm 1 shows the pseudocode of our routing scheme, while Figure 2 provides a visual intuition; finally, Table 3 summarizes the scheme's constants introduced in this subsection and used throughout the rest of the analysis.

**Table 3: Scheme constants.**

| Constant | Description |
|---|---|
| $k_{slot}$ | Slot duration is $k_{slot}/\sqrt{n}$ |
| $k_b$ | Each banner holds $k_b\sqrt{n}$ colours |
| $k_{enc}$ | Encounter distance is $k_{enc}/\sqrt{n}$ |
| $p_{tr}$ | Each node has probability $p_{tr}$ of transmitting in any given time slot |
| $k_{ret}$ | Sightings and messages are each retained for time $k_{ret}$ by any given node before being discarded by that node |

## 4.2 Analysis

This subsection is devoted to proving that, if each node generates messages for random destinations at an information rate $\Theta(1)$, then each message has probability $\Theta(1)$ of being delivered to its destination within time $\Theta(1)$.

Our proof proceeds in three steps. First, we show that with probability $\Theta(1)$ within time $\Theta(1)$ the source and a spotter from the destination both encounter a banneret, which in turn then encounters a relay to the destination. Then, we show that the probability that any of these encounters does not result in a sighting (i.e. that nodes involved fail to exchange information because of interference from other nodes) is bounded away from 1. Finally, we prove that the probability that during any such sighting the nodes involved fail to transmit the necessary data (because of conflicts with other data that should be transmitted in the same sighting) is also bounded away from 1.

To prove the first step we rely on two lemmas, informally stating that, given two nodes on "long" trajectories, any other node has probability $\Omega(1/\sqrt{n})$ of encountering either (Lemma 2, a result analogous to that in [11], but under a more general mobility model), and probability $\Omega(1/n)$ of encountering *both* (Lemma 3).

LEMMA 2. *Consider an arbitrary node $u_i$. Let $\mathcal{E}_i(t)$ be the event that at time $t$ $u_i$ is at distance $\Delta s = \Theta(1)$ from the deployment area's border (if any) on a normal trajectory it will maintain at least until time $t + \Delta t$ for some sufficiently small $\Delta t = \Theta(1)$. Choose another arbitrary node $u_j$. Conditioned on $\mathcal{E}_i(t)$, the probability that $u_j$ encounters $u_i$ during the interval $[t, t + \Delta t]$ is $\Omega(1/\sqrt{n})$.*

PROOF. Consider the trajectories of $u_i$ and $u_j$ during the interval $[t, t+\Delta t]$. With probability $\Omega(1)$ that of $u_j$ is normal and without waypoints. Conditioned on this event, simple geometric considerations show that with probability $\Omega(1)$ the trajectories of $u_i$ and $u_j$ meet at some point in space $\mathbf{x}_{enc}$, which $u_j$ has probability $\Omega(1)$ of reaching before the time $t_{enc}$ when $u_i$ does. By the mode condition in Subsection 2.1, with probability $\Omega(1/\sqrt{n})$ $u_j$ travels at some speed $s \in \left[\frac{|\mathbf{x}_i(t_{enc})-\mathbf{x}_j(t)|}{t_{enc}-t} - \frac{k_{enc}}{\sqrt{n}}, \frac{|\mathbf{x}_i(t_{enc})-\mathbf{x}_j(t)|}{t_{enc}-t} + \frac{k_{enc}}{\sqrt{n}}\right]$ – in which case it is within distance $\frac{k_{enc}}{\sqrt{n}}$ of $u_i$ at $t_{enc}$. □

LEMMA 3. *Consider a distance $\Delta s = \Theta(1)$ and a duration $\Delta t = \Theta(1)$ sufficiently small that, choosing a node uniformly at random, with probability $\epsilon = \Theta(1)$ it is travelling with speed greater than $\frac{\Delta s}{\Delta t}$ to a waypoint at distance greater than $\Delta s$ (note that $\Delta s$ and $\Delta t$ must exist if mobility is ballistic).*

*Choose two arbitrary nodes $u_h$ and $u_i$. Let $\mathcal{E}_{h,i}(t)$ be the event that they remain for (at least) an interval $[t, t + \Delta t]$ on two normal trajectories such that $\mathbf{x}_h\left(t + \frac{\Delta t}{3}\right)$ and $\mathbf{x}_i\left(t + 2\frac{\Delta t}{3}\right)$ are on a line at an angle $\theta = \Theta(1)$ with both trajectories, and are at distance $\frac{\Delta s}{3}$ from each other and at least $\frac{\Delta s}{3}$ from the border of the deployment area (if any). Choose another arbitrary node $u_j$. Conditioned on $\mathcal{E}_{h,i}(t)$, the probability that $u_j$ encounters $u_h$ during the interval $[t, t + 2\frac{\Delta t}{3}]$ and $u_i$ during the interval $[t + \frac{\Delta t}{3}, t + \Delta t]$ is $\Omega(1/n)$.*

PROOF. With probability $\Omega(1)$ the trajectory of $u_j$ is normal and without waypoints during $[t, t + \Delta t]$. Simple geometric considerations show that, for any arbitrarily small $\delta = \Theta(1)$, there is a probability $\Omega(1)$ that the line of the trajectory of $u_j$ will intersect the lines of the trajectories of $u_h$ and $u_i$ within distance $\delta$ respectively of $\mathbf{x}_h\left(t + \frac{\Delta t}{3}\right)$ and of $\mathbf{x}_i\left(t + 2\frac{\Delta t}{3}\right)$. Furthermore, for any arbitrarily small $\delta = \Theta(1)$ there is some sufficiently small $\eta = \Theta(1)$ such that, choosing any point $\mathbf{x}^1$ on the trajectory of $u_h$ within distance $\eta$ of $\mathbf{x}_h\left(t + \frac{\Delta t}{3}\right)$ and any point $\mathbf{x}^2$ on the trajectory of $u_i$ within distance $\eta$ of $\mathbf{x}_i\left(t + 2\frac{\Delta t}{3}\right)$, we have that $(1 - \delta)\frac{\Delta s}{3} < |\mathbf{x}^2 - \mathbf{x}^1| < (1 + \delta)\frac{\Delta s}{3}$. Note that $u_h$ and $u_i$ reach $\mathbf{x}^1$ and $\mathbf{x}^2$ within time $\eta$ of $t+\frac{\Delta t}{3}$ and of $t+2\frac{\Delta t}{3}$ (respectively). Then, by the mode condition in Subsection 2.1, for any such pair of points $\mathbf{x}^1$ and $\mathbf{x}^2$ the probability density of the speed of $u_j$ within the interval $\left[\frac{|\mathbf{x}^2-\mathbf{x}^1|-2\eta}{\Delta t/3+2\eta}, \frac{|\mathbf{x}^2-\mathbf{x}^1|+2\eta}{\Delta t/3-2\eta}\right]$ is $\Theta(1)$.

Assume then that the line of $u_j$'s trajectory does indeed intersect the trajectories of $u_h$ and $u_i$ within distance $\eta$ of $\mathbf{x}_h\left(t + \frac{\Delta t}{3}\right)$ and of $\mathbf{x}_i\left(t + 2\frac{\Delta t}{3}\right)$ – which, as we said, happens with probability $\Theta(1)$ – at two points $\mathbf{x}^1_{enc}$ and $\mathbf{x}^2_{enc}$ that $u_h$ and $u_i$ reach, respectively, at time $t^1_{enc}$ and $t^2_{enc}$. The interval of speeds that guarantee $u_j$ covers the distance $|\mathbf{x}^2_{enc} - \mathbf{x}^1_{enc}|$ in time $(t^2_{enc} - t^1_{enc}) \pm \frac{k_{enc}}{2\sqrt{n}}$ has size $\Omega(1/\sqrt{n})$, and thus the probability that $u_j$ chooses such a speed $\mathrm{v}$ is $\Omega(1/\sqrt{n})$. Conditioned on such a choice, the probability that the position of $u_j$ (on the line of its trajectory) at time $t$ is within distance $\mathrm{v} \cdot (t^1_{enc} - t) \pm \frac{k_{enc}}{2\sqrt{n}}$ of $\mathbf{x}^1_{enc}$ is also $\Omega(1/\sqrt{n})$ – meaning that the probability that $u_j$ will pass within distance $\frac{k_{enc}}{2\sqrt{n}}$ of $u_h$ and within distance $\frac{k_{enc}}{2\sqrt{n}} + \frac{k_{enc}}{2\sqrt{n}} = \frac{k_{enc}}{\sqrt{n}}$ of $u_i$ is $\Omega(1/n)$. □

Given a message generated at time $t_{gen}$ by a source $u_{src}$ with destination $u_d$, arbitrarily partition the set of all other

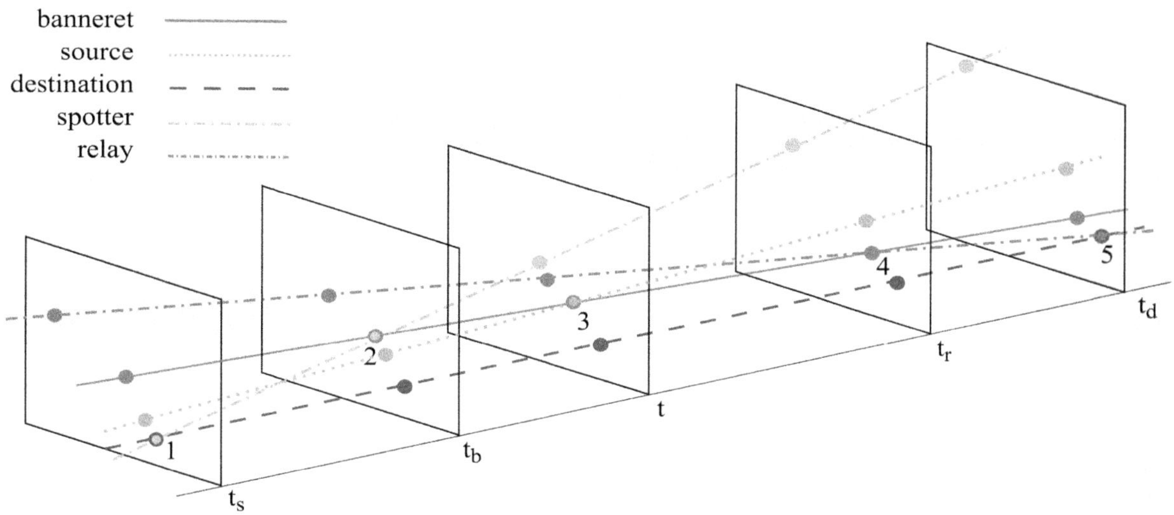


**Figure 2: Delivery of a message: 1. the spotter generates a sighting of the destination 2. the spotter transmits the sighting to the banneret 3. the source transmits the message to the banneret 4. the banneret transmits the message to the relay 5. the relay transmits the message to the destination.**

nodes into three subsets $U_1, U_2, U_3$ each of size at least $\lfloor \frac{n-2}{3} \rfloor$. Then, for some $k_1 \in \Theta(1)$, in $U_1$ there are with probability $1 - o(1)$ at least $(k_1 - o(1))\sqrt{n}$ bannerets for $u_d$ that will remain bannerets for $u_d$ for the next interval of time of duration $k_1$. With ballistic mobility $u_{src}$ has probability $\Theta(1)$ of having the properties that make Lemma 2 applicable. Then Lemma 2 ensures that, with probability $\Theta(1)$, one banneret $u_b$ encounters $u_{src}$ at some time $t < t_{gen} + k_{s-b}$ for $k_{s-b} = \Theta(1)$.

Similarly, $u_d$ has probability $\Theta(1)$ of having a trajectory, relative to $u_b$, that makes Lemma 3 applicable. Then with probability $\Theta(1)$, by Lemma 3, in $U_2$ one node $u_s$ (a spotter) will encounter $u_d$ at time $t_s$ and then $u_b$ at time $t_b > t_s$, and in $U_3$ one node $u_r$ (a relay) will encounter $u_b$ at some time $t_r > t_b$ and then $u_d$ at some later time $t_d > t_r$.

Given the trajectories of the source, destination, banneret, spotter and relay, we now prove that with strictly positive probability the destination sights the spotter and the relay, and the banneret sights the spotter, the source, and the relay – all in the "right" order. Note that these five nodes have some positional constraints, which *do* alter the probability distribution of the remaining nodes. The following lemma allows us to prove that such a perturbation is not too large:

LEMMA 4. *Assume that $n$ balls are $\rho$-uniformly distributed in a set of $m$ bins. Let $\mathcal{E}^i_a$ be the event that bin $i$ holds at least $a$ balls. Then, for any $u \geq n/m$ and any $d \geq 0$,* $\Pr(\mathcal{E}^i_{u+d} | \mathcal{E}^i_d) \leq \Pr(\mathcal{E}^i_u)$.

PROOF. Since the distribution is $\rho$-uniform, we can denote by $k_i/m$ the probability that a ball chooses bin $i$, for some $k_i = \Theta(1)$. The probability $p_i(x)$ that bin $i$ has exactly $x$ balls is

$$p_i(x) = \binom{n}{x} \left(\frac{k_i}{m}\right)^x \left(1 - \frac{k_i}{m}\right)^{n-x}, 0 \leq x \leq n \quad (9)$$

We must prove that

$$\frac{\sum_{x=u+d}^{n} p_i(x)}{\sum_{x=d}^{n} p_i(x)} \leq \sum_{x=u}^{n} p_i(x) \quad (10)$$

Equation 10 is immediately satisfied if $d = 0$. We then prove that for $d > 0$

$$\frac{\sum_{x=u+d}^{n} p_i(x)}{\sum_{x=d}^{n} p_i(x)} \leq \frac{\sum_{x=u+d-1}^{n} p_i(x)}{\sum_{x=d-1}^{n} p_i(x)} \quad (11)$$

Note that the right side of Equation 11 is a linear convex combination of the term on the left side and $\frac{p_i(u+d-1)}{p_i(d-1)}$. Also, the left side is a linear convex combination of $n-d+1$ terms, where the $j^{th}$ term is $\frac{p_i(u+d+j)}{p_i(d+j)}$ if $j \in [0, n-u-d]$, and 0 if $j \in [n-u-d+1, n-d]$. Therefore, it is enough to show that $\frac{p_i(u+d)}{p_i(d)} \leq \frac{p_i(u+d-1)}{p_i(d-1)}$ – the proof that $\frac{p_i(u+d+j)}{p_i(d+j)} \leq \frac{p_i(u+d+j-1)}{p_i(d+j-1)}$ for $j \geq 0$ is virtually identical. By Equation 9, this is true if:

$$\frac{\binom{n}{u+d-1}}{\binom{n}{d-1}} \geq \frac{\binom{n}{u+d}}{\binom{n}{d}} \quad (12)$$

and since Equation 12 can be simplified into $u(n+1) \geq 0$, which always holds given that $u, n \geq 0$, our claim follows. □

By Lemma 4 then, at any given time and in any region of space where the expected number of nodes would be $m$ and the probability that such a number exceeded $m' \geq m$ would be $p(m')$ in the absence of any constraints placed by the selection of source, destination, banneret, spotter and relay, the probability of witnessing more than $m' + 5$ nodes does not exceed $p(m')$. By allowing nodes to communicate, at any time slot, with a sufficiently low transmission probability $p_{tr}$, we can lower to an arbitrarily small $\epsilon$ the probability that, in any given time slot where a node *does* transmit, the transmission is unsuccessful because of interference from other nodes – while still guaranteeing a probability bounded away from 0 of a transmission. More formally:

LEMMA 5. *For any arbitrarily small $\epsilon > 0$ and arbitrarily large $\rho$, there exists a sufficiently small $p_{tr} = \Theta(1)$ such that, for all sufficiently large $n$, the following is true. Assume $n$ nodes are placed independently at random according to some* *distribution with an expected density no greater than $\rho n$ at any point of the deployment area, subject to arbitrary position and velocity constraints on 5 nodes $u_1, \ldots, u_5$. Then if $u_1$ encounters some node $u_i$ at some time $t_{enc}$ during a slot $[t, t+\frac{k_{slot}}{\sqrt{n}}]$ and chooses to transmit to $u_i$ during the slot, the probability of an unsuccessful transmission is less than $\epsilon$, both in the SNR and in the RP model.*

PROOF. First of all, note that if two nodes are at distance $d$ of each other at some time during a slot, they are never at distance greater than $d+\frac{2k_{slot}}{\sqrt{n}}$ or smaller than $d-\frac{2k_{slot}}{\sqrt{n}}$ during the same slot.

Let us consider the RP protocol. If $u_1$ encounters $u_i$, their distance is never greater than $\frac{k_{enc}+2k_{slot}}{\sqrt{n}}$ at any time during the slot. Thus, only nodes that, at time $t$, are within distance $r_0(n)=(1+\Delta)\frac{k_{enc}+2k_{slot}}{\sqrt{n}}+2\frac{k_{slot}}{\sqrt{n}}$ of $u_i$ can interfere. The expected number of such nodes, including $u_i$ and the arbitrarily positioned $u_2, u_3, u_4, u_5$, *transmitting* during the slot is by Lemma 4 at most $p_{tr}\left(5+\rho n\cdot 3.1416\,(r_0(n))^2\right)$ – which can be made *arbitrarily* smaller than $\epsilon$ by a suitable choice of $p_{tr}$ and is obviously an upper bound on the probability of at least one such node being present.

Let us leverage this result to prove the lemma in the SNR model, remembering that the choice of $\Delta>0$ in the RP model is arbitrary, and that for all sufficiently large $n$ and any $\tau$ in the slot $\frac{S_{1,i}(\tau)}{N_0}>\frac{\beta}{2}$ – so we need only prove that $\frac{S_{1,i}(\tau)}{\sum_{j\neq 1}S_{j,i}(\tau)}\geq\frac{\beta}{2}$ with probability greater than $(1-\epsilon)$. Consider a set of circles $C_0, C_1, \ldots$, all centred on the position of $u_i$ at time $t$, with the radius of $C_j$ being $r_j(n)=2^j\cdot(1+\Delta)\frac{k_{enc}+2k_{slot}}{\sqrt{n}}+2\frac{k_{slot}}{\sqrt{n}}$ (note that this matches the previous definition of $r_0(n)$). By the same arguments used for the RP model, any node outside $C_j$ at time $t$ will have a distance at least $2^j(1+\Delta)$ times that of $u_1$ from $u_i$ throughout the slot.

Denote by $M_j$ the set of nodes that at time $t$ are inside $C_j$ but not inside $C_{j-1}$ and will transmit during the slot. Noting that $r_{i+1}<2r_i$, in the worst case scenario where $u_2, \ldots, u_5$ are inside $C_0$, we have that $E[|M_j|]\leq 4E[|M_{j-1}|]$. For any $\tau$ in the slot we then have:

$$E\left[\max_\tau\frac{\sum_{j=1}^{\infty}\sum_{u_h\in M_j}S_{h,i}(\tau)}{S_{1,i}(\tau)}\right]\leq\sum_{j=1}^{\infty}E\left[\max_\tau\frac{\sum_{u_h\in M_j}S_{h,i}(\tau)}{S_{1,i}(\tau)}\right]$$
$$\leq\sum_{j=1}^{\infty}E\left[\frac{|M_j|}{(2^j(1+\Delta))^{\gamma_{min}}}\right]\leq\frac{E[|M_0|]}{(1+\Delta)^{\gamma_{min}}}\sum_{j=1}^{\infty}\left(\frac{4}{2^{\gamma_{min}}}\right)^j$$
$$\leq\frac{E[|M_0|]}{(1+\Delta)^{\gamma_{min}}}\cdot\frac{2^{2-\gamma_{min}}}{1-2^{2-\gamma_{min}}} \qquad (13)$$

and for a sufficiently small $E[|M_0|]$ the last term is less than $\frac{\epsilon}{2}\cdot\frac{2}{\beta}$, and thus $\Pr\left[\max_\tau\frac{\sum_{j=1}^{\infty}\sum_{u_h\in M_j}S_{h,i}(\tau)}{S_{1,i}(\tau)}\geq\frac{2}{\beta}\right]$ by Markov's inequality is less than $\frac{\epsilon}{2}$. Remembering (from the RP analysis) that all sufficiently small $p_{tr}=\Theta(1)$ can make $E[|M_0|]$ arbitrarily small for all $n$, and that the probability of *any* transmission (and thus noise) from nodes in $M_0$ is less than $E[|M_0|]$, all sufficiently small $p_{tr}=\Theta(1)$ yield:

$$\Pr\left[\max_\tau\frac{\sum_{j=0}^{\infty}\sum_{u_h\in M_j}S_{h,i}(\tau)}{S_{1,i}(\tau)}\geq\frac{2}{\beta}\right]<\frac{\epsilon}{2}+\frac{\epsilon}{2} \qquad (14)$$

making less than $\epsilon$ even in the SNR model the probability of excessive interference. □

By Lemma 5 then, the probability of having excessive interference during at least *one* of the 5 encounter slots is at most $5\epsilon$; and since in each encounter the probability that the appropriate node transmits is $p_{tr}=\Theta(1)$, the probability that *all* five encounters entail successful communication is at least $(1-5\epsilon)p_{tr}^5$ which is bounded away from 0 for all $n$.

The third and final step in our proof is showing that the three sightings of the banneret and the sighting of the relay and destination each have an independent probability bounded away from 0 of transmitting the necessary data (note that if the encounter between the spotter and the destination results in a sighting, the spotter automatically obtains the needed data, i.e. the sighting of the destination).

The union $B$ of all the colours in the banners flown by the banneret $u_b$ during the interval from the encounter with the spotter to that with the relay has cardinality $O(\sqrt{n})$. Similarly, the cardinality of the union $A$ of all the colours of the spotter's sightings, of the source's messages, and of the nodes encountered by the relay is $O(\sqrt{n})$ with probability $1-o(1)$. Remembering that, other than the colour of $u_d$, every remaining colour in $B$ is chosen uniformly and independently at random, the probability that $|B\bigcap A|=1$ is $\Theta(1)$. Since the probability that the source carries a second message of the same colour as $u_d$ is $O(1/\sqrt{n})$, the probability of the event $\mathcal{E}_b$ that at most one message needs to be exchanged at each of the $u_b$'s sightings with the spotter, source and relay in their respective roles is $\Theta(1)$.

Finally, let $t_d$ be the time the relay $u_r$ encounters the destination $u_d$, and consider the set $U$ of nodes other than $u_b$ encountered by $u_r$ during the time interval $[t_d-k_{ret}, t_d]$. $U$ has cardinality $O(\sqrt{n})$ with probability $1-o(1)$, and obviously includes all bannerets that may transmit to $u_r$ a message for $u_d$ still retained by $u_r$ at $t_d$ since messages are discarded after time $k_{ret}$. For the same reason, denoting by $B'$ the union of all colours in the banners of $U$ during the interval $[t_d-2k_{ret}, t_d]$, only messages whose colour is in $B'$ can be transmitted to $u_r$ in $[t_d-k_{ret}, t_d]$. And since banner colours are chosen uniformly and independently at random, the event $\mathcal{E}_r$ that the colour of $u_d$ is not in $B'$ is independent of $\mathcal{E}_b$ and has probability $\Theta(1)$.

Then, each message has probability $\Theta(1)$ of being successfully delivered to its destination; and if this happens, it must happen within time $3k_{ret}=O(1)$ since the source, banneret and relay can each hold messages for at most time $k_{ret}$ before discarding them.

## 4.3 Small Packets, Non-uniform Destinations

We have so far assumed that the size (in information units) of each packet is $\Theta(1/\sqrt{n})$ – the maximum that still guarantees $\Omega(1)$ packet exchanges between a node and its nearest neighbour before they move apart. It is extremely easy to see that the routing scheme of the previous section can be extended to deal with packets that are smaller by an arbitrary factor $m$ (as long as packets contain at least $k_{id}\log n$ bits, see Subsection 2.2) by simply having every node simulate $m$ virtual nodes, each of which receives an identical fraction $1/m$ of the host's bandwidth and storage. A virtual node uses the same unit of space (the diameter of the deployment area) and the same unit of time (the time required to span 1 unit of space at maximum speed) as the host, but its unit of information (that transmissible at full bandwidth in 1 unit of time) is $(1/m)^{th}$ of that of the host; so its storage requirements are also $(1/m)^{th}$ of the host's and it can transmit up to $\Theta(1)$ packets per encounter.

We have also assumed so far (as in virtually every other work on the subject) that the destination of each message is chosen uniformly and independently at random. This may not always be realistic. For example, a node sending a large file to another node may well be addressing 100% of its outgoing traffic to that destination until the file has been sent. Note that if a node generates $m$ messages for a given destination during an interval of duration 1, each has only a (non-independent) $\Theta(1/m)$ probability of being transmitted to a banneret and then delivered to the destination.

This issue can be easily addressed with a minor modification to our scheme: every message from a source to a destination is routed through an intermediate random node, in a fashion similar to that proposed in [23] for hypercubic networks. More precisely, we can assume that each node splits in two its communication bandwidth, reserving half for source-intermediary routing, and the other half for intermediary-destination routing. A message is routed from its source to a randomly chosen intermediary with the basic scheme. After being delivered to the intermediary at time $t$, it is stored and is scheduled to be "regenerated" at a time chosen uniformly and independently at random in $[t + \Delta^{min}, t + \Delta^{max}]$, with $\Delta^{min}, \Delta^{max} = \Theta(1)$. If multiple messages are scheduled to be regenerated simultaneously, all but (a randomly chosen) one are discarded. A message that is not discarded is finally routed to the destination with the basic scheme (see Algorithm 2). One can then easily prove the following:

THEOREM 2. *Let $\Delta t = \Delta^{max} + 6k_{ret} = \Theta(1)$, and consider a generic interval of time $[t, t']$ with $t' - t = \Theta(1)$. If there exists some $m \geq 1$ such that during the interval $[t - \Delta t, t' + \Delta t]$ (of duration $\Theta(1)$) messages for a total of at most $m$ units of information are generated in the network for a destination $u_i$, then choosing a banner hash function uniformly at random guarantees that each such message is delivered by Algorithm 2 within time $\Delta t$ of its generation with probability $\Omega(1/m)$.*

PROOF. Each message that successfully reaches its destination may spend at most time $3k_{ret}$ before reaching its intermediary, then at most time $\Delta^{max}$ before being regenerated, and then at most time $3k_{ret}$ before reaching its destination – for a total of at most $\Delta t$ time units before generation and delivery. Therefore, the only messages that may coexist at any point in time with those generated during $[t, t']$ are those generated during $[t - \Delta t, t' + \Delta t]$.

Note that since intermediate nodes are chosen uniformly and independently at random, the analysis of the source-to-intermediary phase proceeds exactly as in the basic case regardless of $m$. Then each message generated during $[t, t']$ has probability $\Theta(1)$ of reaching an intermediary that receives at most $O(m/n)$ units of information, i.e. $O(m/(nP))$ messages, for $u_i$ generated during $[t - \Delta t, t' + \Delta t]$. Each such message has then at least probability $\Omega(1/m)$ of being successfully transmitted to an appropriate banneret before being discarded. Conditioned on such an event, by exactly the same arguments used for the basic case, the message has probability $\Omega(1)$ of reaching its destination – proving the theorem. □

**Algorithm 2** Routing to non-uniform destinations

```
for each slot S do
  act as source
  M_gen ← {messages generated as source in S}
  if M_gen ≠ ∅ then
    select uniformly at random msg ∈ M_gen
    select uniformly at random an intermediary node u_j
    route msg to u_j with Algorithm 1
  end if
  act as intermediary
  for each message msg received at t ∈ S do
    select uniformly at random t_reg ∈ [t+Δ^min, t+Δ^max]
    schedule msg for regeneration at t_reg
  end for
  M_reg ← {messages scheduled for regeneration in S}
  if M_reg ≠ ∅ then
    select uniformly at random msg ∈ M_reg
    route msg to its original destination with Algorithm 1
  end if
end for
```

By Theorem 2 then, if the information rate at which the network generates messages for a given destination is $O(1)$, each will be delivered with probability $\Theta(1)$; if it is $m$ times higher, only a fraction $\Theta(1/m)$ of the messages will be delivered. This is clearly the best that can be achieved, since a single node cannot receive $\omega(1)$ information per unit of time. Note that the bounds on the rate need only hold over a window of duration $\Theta(1)$; shorter peaks are absorbed by the routing delay. Furthermore, note our scheme is "fair" in the sense that *each* message has a probability within a constant factor of every other for that destination of being delivered, regardless of where they are generated (as long as they are generated within the same timeframe).

## 5. CONCLUSIONS

This work does not add one more specimen to the already overpopulated "zoo" of mobility models for delay-tolerant networks. Instead, it considers the entire universe of all models satisfying some extremely mild and "natural" conditions (including all models that are present in the literature, and some that are not, like Levy runs) and draws a simple line: that of ballistic vs. non-ballistic mobility. Networks without ballistic mobility, as the number of nodes grows, witness either per-node throughput become vanishingly small, or communication delays grow infinitely large – regardless of centralized control or complex network coding schemes. Networks with ballistic mobility can instead adopt the routing scheme we propose and achieve simultaneously non-vanishing throughput and bounded delay.

Our scheme uses only simple routing, without any central coordination, network coding, or packet replication, and does not require nodes to adjust their transmission power. Each node needs only store $O(1)$ units of information at any given time, have access to an accurate clock, and gauge the position and velocity vectors *relative to itself* of those nodes it successfully communicates with. Also, our scheme works equally well for all ballistic mobility patterns, without requiring any knowledge of the distance and speed distribution – but still asymptotically outperforms all existing schemes, none of which achieves simultaneously non-vanishing throughput and bounded delay.

We remark that this work, for space limitations, only focuses on throughput and delay *asymptotics*. In particular, our goal is to highlight the role of ballistic mobility and to make our routing scheme and analysis as simple as possible. Thus, we omit considering a number of optimizations entailing only constant factors, even though such factors might be large and could easily spell the difference between a practical scheme and one of purely theoretical interest. Exploring a more practical version of our scheme (including not only performance optimizations, but also robustness to failing and/or malicious nodes) on real mobility traces, from people to sensors drifting in fluid media, is certainly one of the most obvious directions for future research.

From a theoretical point of view, one important assumption of our analysis (and of virtually all pre-existing literature) is that message destinations are chosen uniformly at random. Our scheme can be easily modified to deal with non-uniform destinations without asymptotic loss of performance by routing messages through random intermediate nodes. However, the lower bound of Section 3 does not hold if message sources choose very close destinations. In other words, if the majority of traffic is local, ballistic mobility is still sufficient to guarantee non-vanishing throughput and bounded delay, but may not be *necessary*. Is it possible to generalize our results, by relating the distance distribution of the "next waypoint" to the distance distribution of message destinations, and proving that if the two coincide one can simultaneously achieve $\Theta(1)$ per-node throughput and $\Theta(1)$ delay even in the absence of ballistic mobility?

## 6. ACKNOWLEDGEMENTS

This work was supported in part by Univ. Padova under Proj. AACSE. The first author was supported in part by fellowships from Univ. Padova and from Fondazione A. Gini. The authors would thank the anonymous referees for their constructive criticism and insightful comments.

## 7. REFERENCES

[1] R. Ahlswede, N. Cai, S. Li and R. Yeung. Network information flow. *IEEE Trans. on Inf. Theory*, 46:1204–1216, 2000.

[2] N. Bansal and Z. Liu. Capacity, delay and mobility in wireless ad-hoc networks. In *Proc. INFOCOM*, 2003.

[3] T. Camp, J. Boleng and V. Davies. A survey of mobility models for ad hoc network research. *Wireless communications and mobile computing*, 2:483–502, 2002.

[4] W. Crowther, W. Rettberg, D. Walden, S. Crustein and F. Heart. A system for broadcast communication: Reservation Aloha. In *Proc. HICSS*, 1973.

[5] R. de Moraes, H. Sadjadpour, and J. Garcia-Luna-Aceves. Throughput-delay analysis of mobile ad-hoc networks with a multi-copy relaying strategy. In *Proc. SECON*, 2004.

[6] R. D'Souza and J. Jose. Routing approaches in delay tolerant networks: a survey. *Int. J. of Computer Applications*, 2010.

[7] A. E. Gamal, J. Mammen, B. Prabhakar, and D. Shah. Throughput-delay trade-off in wireless networks. In *Proc. INFOCOM*, 2004.

[8] M. Grossglauser and D. Tse. Mobility increases the capacity of ad-hoc wireless networks. *IEEE/ACM Trans. on Netw.*, 10:477–486, 2002.

[9] P. Gupta and P. R. Kumar. The capacity of wireless networks. *IEEE Trans. on Inf. Theory*, 46(2):388–404, 2000.

[10] H. Hashemi. The indoor radio propagation channel. *Proceedings of the IEEE*, 81(7):943–968, 1993.

[11] Y. Kim, K. Lee, N. Shroff, and I. Rhee. Revisiting delay-capacity tradeoffs for mobile networks: the delay is overestimated. In *Proc. INFOCOM*, 2012.

[12] K. Lee, Y. Kim, S. Chong, I. Rhee, and Y. Yi. Delay-capacity tradeoffs for mobile networks with Levy walks and Levy flights. In *Proc. INFOCOM*, 2011.

[13] X. Lin, G. Sharma, R. Mazumdar, and N. Shroff. Degenerate delay-capacity tradeoffs in ad-hoc networks with Brownian mobility. *IEEE/ACM Trans. on Netw.*, 14:2777–2784, 2006.

[14] X. Lin and N. Shroff. The fundamental capacity-delay tradeoff in large mobile ad hoc networks. In *Proc. Med-Hoc-Networking*, 2004.

[15] X. Lin and N. Shroff. Towards achieving the maximum capacity in large mobile wireless networks under delay constraints. *J. of Communications and Networks*, 6(4):352–361, 2004.

[16] R. Metzler and J. Klafter. The restaurant at the end of the random walk: recent developments in the description of anomalous transport by fractional dynamics. *J. of Physics*, 37, 2004.

[17] M. J. Neely and E. Modiano. Capacity and delay tradeoffs for ad-hoc mobile networks. *IEEE Trans. on Inf. Theory*, 51:1917–1937, 2005.

[18] I. Rhee, M. Shin, S. Hong, K. Lee, and S. Chong. On the levy-walk nature of human mobility. In *Proc. INFOCOM*, 2008.

[19] G. Sharma and R. Mazumdar. On achievable delay/capacity trade-offs in mobile ad hoc networks. In *Proc. WiOpt*, 2004.

[20] G. Sharma and R. Mazumdar. Scaling laws for capacity and delay in wireless ad hoc networks with random mobility. In *Proc. ICC*, 2004.

[21] G. Sharma, R. Mazumdar, and N. Shroff. Delay and capacity trade-offs in mobile ad hoc networks: a global perspective. *IEEE/ACM Trans. on Netw.*, 15:981–992, 2007.

[22] S. Toumpis and A. Goldsmith. Large wireless networks under fading, mobility, and delay constraints. In *Proc. INFOCOM*, 2004.

[23] L. Valiant and G. Brebner. Universal schemes for parallel communication. In *Proc. STOC*, 1981.

[24] X. Zhou, Z. Zhang, G. Wang, X. Yu, B. Zhao, and H. Zheng. Practical conflict graphs for dynamic spectrum distribution. In *Proc. SIGMETRICS*, 2013.

# Exploring the Potential in Practice for Opportunistic Networks amongst Smart Mobile Devices

Shu Liu, Aaron D. Striegel
Department of Computer Science and Engineering, University of Notre Dame
Notre Dame, IN, USA
sliu6@nd.edu, striegel@nd.edu

## ABSTRACT

Wireless network providers are under tremendous pressure to deliver unprecedented amounts of data to a variety of mobile devices. A powerful concept that has only gained limited traction in practice has been the concept of opportunistic networks whereby nodes opportunistically communicate with each other when in range to augment or overcome existing wireless systems. One of the key impediments towards the adoption of opportunistic communications has been the inability to demonstrate viability at scale, namely showing that sufficient opportunities exist and more importantly exist when needed to offer significant network performance gains. We demonstrate through a large-scale, longitudinal study of smartphone users that significant opportunities are indeed prevalent, are indeed stable, and end up being reasonably reciprocal both on short and long-term timescales. In this paper, we propose a framework dubbed PSR (Prevalence, Stability, Reciprocity) to capture key aspects that characterize the net potential for opportunistic networks which we feel merit significantly increased attention.

## Categories and Subject Descriptors

C.4 [**PERFORMANCE OF SYSTEMS**]: Reliability, availability, and serviceability; C.5.3 [**COMPUTER SYSTEM IMPLEMENTATION** ]: Microcomputers—*Portable devices*

## Keywords

Relay; Opportunistic Networks; Proximity; Bluetooth; WiFi

## 1. INTRODUCTION

Over the past few years, a vast array of wireless devices and services have emerged that are fundamentally transforming how we as a society gather and react to information. Furthermore, the new wireless ecosystem has increased wireless data consumption at phenomenal rates with the most popular cited estimates slating traffic to double every year for the next five years [1]. Dubbed the *wireless data tsunami*, the dominant question for wireless service providers (carriers) is how to meet what appears to be an insatiable need for wireless data. Unlike wired networks, the spectrum available for wireless data is finite and typically entails massive costs for acquisition and infrastructure deployment. A wide variety of solutions have emerged ranging from simpler solutions such as better WiFi offloading to much more complex solutions such as small heterogeneous cellular networks.

One rich category of work that is complementary to existing techniques is the concept of *opportunistic communication*. Opportunistic communication refers to the concept which allows nodes to leverage sporadic, intermittent contacts when two nodes come into direct radio communication range [2]. When cellular or WiFi links are not available or not strong enough, opportunistic relaying introduces an alternative option for mobile device to get connected by working in tandem with one or more devices. From a conceptual standpoint for opportunistic networking, the design of the relaying protocol is critical, namely how does one select and manage appropriate relaying nodes as relays [3–7]?

Although opportunistic networking has received more attention as of late with the rise of various point-to-point technologies (WiFiDirect, LTEDirect) embedded in user devices, traction in terms of significant adoption remains elusive as the mere existence of point-to-point wireless technology is insufficient. Rather, infrastructure support (albeit at a software or protocol level) is still required that is impeded by the lack of shared, longitudinal data taking a serious look at the potential for opportunistic relaying amongst actual mobile device users to justify said investment in infrastructure. The actual gathering of said data though is in and of itself quite difficult, requiring one to overcome numerous issues with respect to privacy, cost, scale, and quite simply the amenability of the device to acquire said data. Thus, in the absence of real data and the difficulty in acquiring such data, opportunistic networking research has largely espoused synthetic or theoretical explorations of user mobility [8, 9].

A key aim of our work is to demystify the opportunities that exist for opportunistic relaying by bridging the gap with a large scale dataset across both a significant duration (15 months) and user pool (nearly 200 users). Critically, we demonstrate that not only is the opportunity for relaying more prevalent than expected, said opportunities are stable enough to be worthwhile to establish even with auxiliary security constraints and the opportunities are reciprocal across both short-term and long-term time scales even when con-


*MobiCom'13*, September 30–October 4, Miami, FL, USA.
Copyright 2013 ACM 978-1-4503-1999-7/13/09 ...$15.00.
http://dx.doi.org/10.1145/2500423.2500430.

sidering energy levels of the involved devices. Specifically, the key contributions of our paper are as follows:

- *Demonstrate the opportunity (prevalence) for relaying is indeed significant:* Through the analysis of a 15 month dataset of detailed smartphone data gleaned from nearly 200 smart phone users, we demonstrate that a typical user in our study could find devices amenable to relaying averaging nearly 60% of the time. To the best of our knowledge, we believe our study is the first to conduct a longitudinal study of relaying prevalence with demonstrating ample opportunities with respect to both raw relaying prevalence and useful relaying prevalence .

- *Demonstrate that said opportunities for relaying are not only prevalent but stable:* We show with our study data that relaying opportunities exist on average for durations of 6 or more minutes. Moreover, we show that the opportunities for relaying tend to be highly focused on a select subset of devices enabling enhanced levels of trust versus random, intermittent opportunities as espoused in the literature.

- *Demonstrate that said opportunities would largely be reciprocal:* In addition to opportunities being prevalent and stable (useful), we show that interactions for relaying would be overwhelmingly reciprocal in both short-term and long-term time windows, even when accounting for the energy levels of both parties involved in the relaying. We demonstrate this through the inclusion of actual traffic demands on fine temporal granularities, a unique feature of our dataset.

- *Propose a framework to evaluate the relaying potential for network traces:* While we believe our work is one of the first of its kind to fuse fine-grained proximity and traffic data over such a long period, we hope that others will embark on similar efforts to broaden the effective data pool available to the community. To that end, we view all of our data through the lens of what we dub the PSR (Prevalence, Stability, Reciprocity) framework, a framework for systematically evaluating the potential and quality of the proximity of mobile network trace data. Particularly, PSR can serve as a broad foundation for others to explore larger coverage areas, alternative populations, and different environments.

The rest of this paper is organized as follows. Section 2 provides an overview of the related work and Section 3 introduces the NetSense dataset. Based on the NetSense dataset, the framework to evaluate the potential for relaying is proposed in Section 4. Finally, Section 5 concludes the paper commenting in particular on shortcomings of the work and future areas for research.

## 2. RELATED WORK

The notion of what constitutes an *opportunistic communication* encompasses a wide variety of research and standardization efforts within the networking community. From the more traditional perspective, opportunistic relaying represents wireless nodes taking advantage of emergent opportunities to relay data towards its eventual destination originally espoused by [3] and expanded up by numerous others [4–7]. A key foundation for the evaluation of opportunistic networks arises from the characterization of inter-contact times [8, 9]. The work in [8] was one of the first works to highlight the importance of inter-contact time for studying opportunistic networks and analyzed the features of aggregate inter-contact times. In the work of [9], the mobility models proposed for opportunistic networks aim at reproducing the aggregate power-law distributions. The mobility models in turn provide powerful abstractions for the evaluation of various theoretical properties of opportunistic networks that is critical for understanding general limits of the overarching relay protocols. In contrast from these studies on statistical patterns of human mobility, we focus on the analysis to take in not only the proximity into consideration but also other elements such as traffic needs and battery influences which have to the best of our knowledge, not explored in a unified manner in the literature.

Complementary to the characterization of inter-contact time is the ability to unobtrusively measure the proximity of mobile nodes to one another. For the purposes of this paper, we are interested in techniques that are based on commonly available technologies in smartphones, i.e. GPS, Cell, WiFi and Bluetooth. Various techniques have emerged ranging from both academia through the concept of Location-based Service (LBS) functions [10–12] to automatically detect when a pair of mobile targets approach each other closer than a predefined proximity distance (as in Location Alerts of Google Latitude). Drawing in part on the prevalence of WiFi deployments in indoor environments, WiFi triangulation can be employed in tandem with cellular signals to reasonably detect locations at a much lower cost than GPS. Without calculating absolute location, NearMe [13] explores the algorithm for detecting proximity using Wi-Fi signatures (WiFi APs and signal strengths), allowing it to work with no a priori setup. Similarly, [14] uses GSM readings to explore the proximity of mobile targets. Conversely, the problem of inter-contact (proximity) detection can also be reduced to its most basic form simply asking whether two nodes are close rather than determining node proximity as a derivation from location. The MIT Reality Mining group was one of the pioneers in employing Bluetooth as a tool to infer the potential for social interactions among users capitalizing on the 10 m effective range of Bluetooth with agents on each mobile device [15, 16]. More recent works including the Nokia Data Challenge [17] also employed Bluetooth discoverable devices for proximity detection.

A key defining characteristic of the works adopting Bluetooth as a mechanism [15–18], for detecting proximity is the inclusion of a device-side agent for both detection and the enabling of devices as permanently discoverable with respect to Bluetooth. The inclusion of a device-side agent on a live user device introduces notable complexity with respect to user privacy and IRB (Institutional Review Board) concerns. Moreover, such studies tend to be frequently expensive to conduct due to the cost of subsidizing access costs at a sufficient level to yield effective participatory compliance. Although there are several notable wireless datasets including university campuses (MIT Reality [15], UCSD [19] and Dartmouth [20]), conference sites (Infocom [8]) and cities (Nokia [17]), most datasets are limited in size and scope in terms of capturing dyadic relationships, namely both sides of a potential proximity relationship for the purposes of truly

Table 1: Dataset Comparison

| Traces | Our Dataset | MIT Reality | UCSD | Dartmouth | Infocom | Nokia |
|---|---|---|---|---|---|---|
| Device | Smartphone | Cell Phone | PDA | Laptop PDA | iMote | Smartphone |
| # of Devices | 189 | 97 | 275 | 6,648 | 41 | 185 |
| Network Type | Bluetooth/WiFi | Bluetooth | WiFi | WiFi | Bluetooth | Bluetooth/WiFi |
| Contact Type | Direct/AP-based | Direct | AP-based | AP-based | Direct | Direct/AP-based |
| Duration (days) | 458 | 246 | 77 | 114 | 4 | 210 |
| Granularity (seconds) | 60/300 | 300 | 120 | 300 | 120 | N/A |
| # of internal contacts | 3,616,184 | 54,667 | 195,364 | 4,058,284 | 22,459 | N/A |
| Internal pairwise contact/day | 0.221 | 0.022 | 0.034 | 0.008 | 3.4 | N/A |
| Other proximity related data | Cell, Traffic, etc. | Cell | N/A | N/A | N/A | Cell, etc. |

evaluating opportunistic networking. For instance, both the MIT Reality and Infocom traces record when contact is detected by virtue of Bluetooth discovery, ample for characterizing the inter-contact times but not necessarily capturing energy levels nor traffic needs of the respective nodes. Alternatively, the UCSD and Dartmouth traces rely on WiFi for localization gathering either data via AP fingerprinting (UCSD) or SNMP logs directly from the AP (Dartmouth). The richest of the datasets is the data from the Nokia Data Challenge which includes both WiFi and Bluetooth data but the dataset is no longer public after the completion of the workshop. In contrast to prior works, our dataset includes nominal proximity (Bluetooth) / location data (WiFi, Google Location service) in addition to a complete view of the smartphone environment including WiFi signal strengths, energy levels, traffic demands, and the social context for the participants in the study (Facebook, SMS, etc.). Table 1 summarizes the most relevant studies and compares the works to our own reference study for this paper.

## 3. LARGE-SCALE PHONE DATASET

In August of 2011, two hundred participants were selected from the incoming freshmen class of Notre Dame and received a free Android smartphone and plan in exchange for agreement to participate in the two-year data collection project. Each Android device was rooted and a custom ROM installed (Cyanogenmod) to enable the device being permanently Bluetooth discoverable. A user-level agent was installed on each of the smartphones that extracted a wide variety of environmental and usage data from the phone at periodic intervals. The monitoring agent was installed to start automatically when the smart phone power was turned on and ran passively in the background. Tuning was conducted on the agent to ensure that even with WiFi enabled and Bluetooth always discoverable for a battery life potential at distribution of roughly one and a half days.

The agent itself is a multi-threaded block of modular code installed via an APK with updates to the agent delivered via customized text messages to the user prompting installation from our website. Data is locally spooled on the phone before being securely transmitted to one of two remote check-in servers. Data from the check-in server is then spooled locally before being conveyed to a database server not directly connected to the Internet with all accesses strictly logged and validated to protect sensitive user data. Critically, while the agent gathers various environmental data (application usage, wireless adapter tonnage, battery level, detected wireless and signal strengths, Bluetooth proximity) and communication patterns (SMS, e-mail, phone, and Facebook), the content of said communications are not recorded, only where, when, and with whom the communication occurred. All data recording is fully disclosed to the user upon entrance to the study with full approval of the university IRB for the procedure.

For the relevant portions of the paper, the critical aspects of the dataset are the respective wireless environmental readings, Bluetooth proximity, location (gleaned via Google Location services), device state (battery level, screen on / off), and data consumption. For example, the Bluetooth data includes the detailed values of timestamp, RSSI (Received signal strength indication), MAC address, and Bluetooth identifier (BTID) with a default sensing granularity of once per minutes. The wireless environmental data (primarily WiFi) has similar fields except the access point (AP) name is recorded and the granularity of sensing is three minutes. Traffic data includes breakdowns by application and wireless adapter (cell, WiFi) with respect to both downlink (Rx) and uplink (Tx) usage at intervals down to as low as once per minute.

The dataset used in the paper covers 15 months data (Oct 2011 - Dec 2012) and there are around 41 million Bluetooth records, 50 million WiFi scans and 1 million SMS messages. Data from the first two months of the study is excluded to allow for the new freshmen to have settled into a new routine and social arrangements. A reasonable degree of co-location exists amongst students in the study with students selected clustered amongst six primary dormitories equally divided amongst male and female students. Once entered into the study, students were free to re-locate at either the beginning of the spring semester (2012) or the start of their sophomore year. Moreover, the respective distribution levels within individual dormitories made it reasonably close to random chance amongst incoming freshmen for that dormitory if two participants in the study were selected as roommates. At the onset of the monitored period for the paper, approximately 11 students had dropped from the study reducing the data pool to 189 students.

Table 2 summarizes the details of the data across different months. For each of the respective metrics presented in the table, we reduce the sampling rate to five minutes slots scattered throughout the day where each day has the potential for 288 measurement points. The powered on percentage represents the number of slots when the phone monitor was active with a noticeable drop during later hours (12am - 8 am) but a notable uptick during the evening hours (4pm-12am). The screen on percentage is the duration when the phone screen is on and implies the average usage of the phone for either consuming data or conducting other communica-

Table 2: Monthly Data Summary

| Avg. Monthly Values per Phone | Nov 2011 | Apr 2012 | Jul 2012 | Nov 2012 |
|---|---|---|---|---|
| Powered On (%) | 73.7 | 70.6 | 51.3 | 61.2 |
| Powered On (%) (12am-8am) | 66.7 | 60.7 | 42.3 | 58.0 |
| Powered On (%) (8am-4pm) | 74.6 | 69.3 | 51.3 | 62.7 |
| Powered On (%) (4pm-12am) | 79.6 | 72.7 | 60.1 | 62.9 |
| Screen On (%) | 5.74 | 5.05 | 4.99 | 4.30 |
| Total Rx Traffic (MB) | 609.2 | 727.2 | 864.5 | 685.8 |
| Total Tx Traffic (MB) | 133.11 | 123.8 | 130.4 | 200.8 |
| # of Detected Distinct Bluetooth Devices | 961 | 746 | 310 | 681 |
| # of Detected Distinct Bluetooth Devices Within Project (RSSI >= -80 dBm) | 131 | 106 | <1 | 75 |
| # of Detected Distinct WiFi APs | 1218 | 1004 | 1777 | 1663 |
| # of Detected Distinct WiFi APs in Campus | 424 | 446 | <1 | 433 |

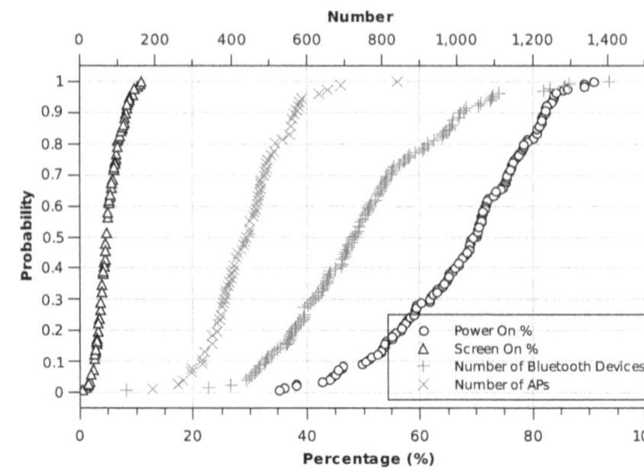


Figure 1: ECDF of Data in April 2012

tions (SMS, phone call, etc.). The monthly Bluetooth and WiFi records shows the average number of distinguished Bluetooth devices/WiFi APs detected per device across the month. University virtual APs are reduced to a single AP as each university router offers between two to four WiFi AP names.

Figure 1 exhibits the empirical distribution functions (ECDF) of different types of data in April 2012 to offer additional context for the data beyond the average values denoted in Table 2. Two percentage value ECDFs are plotted (power on, screen on) together with two detected environmental values (unique Bluetooth devices in the month, unique APs in the month). Scales for each of the two values are the lower axis for percentage and upper axis for raw numeric counts. Most notably, the average number of unique Bluetooth devices detected in April 2012 was 746 with some devices seeing as high as over 1000 devices and others seeing as low as slightly less than 200 unique devices. Table 2 also contains distinctions with respect to intra-study proximity and inter-study breakdowns of the various Bluetooth devices. As would be expected, intra-study detection dramatically trails off during summer break in tandem with detected university APs as the students leave campus.

## 4. EVALUATING PRACTICAL RELAYING

The dataset outlined in the prior section provides a fascinating opportunity to evaluate the actual prevalence with respect to opportunistic relaying in the 'wild' evaluating not only the prevalence itself but when intra-study proximity is involved, significant explorations with respect to the mutual benefits of relaying or collaborative efforts. For the purposes of evaluation, we are concerned with two types of opportunistic networking, namely relaying and collaboration. In the first case of relaying, a mobile node ($MN_i$) might relay the traffic from mobile node ($MN_j$) when $MN_j$ has a weak / non-existent wireless signal or $MN_i$ has a good signal to a preferred wireless medium (ex. WiFi) while $MN_j$ does not. In the second case of collaboration, $MN_i$ and $MN_j$ work together to overcome a lossy channel either by the use of striping across both nodes (ex. auxiliary relaying of TCP ACKs [21]) or striping across different wireless mediums (WiFi + cellular). Opportunistic communications would be provided through mobile-to-mobile communications (Bluetooth, WiFiDirect, LTEDirect). Both approaches to opportunistic relaying would require modifications to the wireless infrastructure as well as security concerns to establish any mobile-to-mobile communication which are beyond the scope of this paper. Rather, we focus on the more fundamental question of *does enough opportunity exist* and if so, *is it of reasonable quality to make it worthwhile*?

To that end, we seek to answer the following questions in this section of the paper summarized in terms of metrics in Table 3:

- *Environment*: How is proximity defined and what criterion should exist to enable opportunistic communication with respect to inter-node communications? What can be considered a 'good' opportunistic link in terms of the underlying physical link quality and at what granularity is such data recorded?

- *Prevalence*: What is the frequency that a mobile device detect other devices in proximity? To what extent is the detection symmetric for intra-study participants? How does the inter-contact times of nodes compare to prior work? Do opportunities exist when needed (traffic demand) making them useful versus simply available?

- *Stability*: To what extent are discovered opportunities stable enough that an overarching security mechanism could complete or relevant data exchanges could take place? Are there consistent patterns with regards to nodes appearing more common than others allowing expedited trust?

- *Reciprocity*: Even if opportunities are shown to be prevalent and stable, to what extent are the relationships likely to be reciprocal, namely both $MN_i$ and $MN_j$ will benefit on average equally in terms of both receiving assistance and giving assistance? When energy is factored in as a consideration for nodes not being willing participants, does any sort of prevalence or reciprocality disappear? Finally, reciprocality if it exists, does it exist exclusively in only longer-time scales or does it exist on reasonably short-time scales as well?

For the wireless network, we first being by defining several key attributes of the data. Each mobile node ($MN_i$) is

Table 3: Framework for Evaluating Prevalence, Stability, Reciprocity

| Criteria | | Term | Description |
|---|---|---|---|
| Prevalence | Sufficient Signal | $SS$ | Time with a 'good signal' vs. time powered on |
| | Symmetry | $Sym$ | Time when proximity is symmetric, has $SS$ vs. time powered on |
| | Diversity | $Div_n$ | Time with at least $n$ nodes with $SS$ detected vs. time nodes detected |
| | Effective Utility | $EU$ | Time with proximity of other nodes with $SS$, $Sym$, traffic to send vs. time with traffic to send |
| Stability | Duration | $D$ | Number of consecutive contact durations vs. instances of contact at $MN_i$ |
| | Total Appearances | $TA$ | Number of appearances of a device vs. total device appearances at $MN_i$ |
| | Continuous Appearances | $CA$ | Number of consecutive appearances of a device vs. appearances of multiple days at $MN_i$ |
| | Node Strength | $NS$ | Number of total appearances by $n$ most common peers |
| Reciprocity | Need Service | $Serv$ | Time when no auxiliary WiFi is present and traffic demand exists vs. time powered on |
| | Offer Assistance | $Assist$ | Time ween detected with $SS$ vs. time powered on |
| | Ratio Need vs. Assist | $R_{NA}$ | Time of $Serv$ vs. Time of $Assist$ |

considered to have a discrete set of samples at periodic intervals capturing the proximity of nearby nodes (Bluetooth), the signal strength from each detected Bluetooth node as received at $MN_i$, (ex. $MN_j \rightarrow MN_i$), each detected AP and also the signal strength for each AP as detected by $MN_i$ by virtue of the beacon signal strength. Each time slot is assumed to be five minutes long (for the purposes of assessing if the phone was on or off) though durations of contact are calculated using per-minute measurements. The term *Good RSSI* refers to thresholds for RSSI values that indicate the potential for excellent performance although in practice such performance may vary. Performance with respect to each node is normalized unless explicitly noted to the actual time that the phone was on (powered on, agent running) for that particular day or period. We do not give priority to any of the above metrics since they exhibit different attributes in various scenarios while the missing of any of them might lead to the failure of relaying protocol in general environment.

We use Bluetooth as the proximity mechanism for multiple reasons. First, the effective range of Bluetooth typically is on the order of 10 m or less. In contrast with other point-to-point technologies such as WiFiDirect and LTEDirect which have the potential for significantly longer ranges, Bluetooth in effect represents a minimum or floor to the potential for opportunistic communications as the various *Direct technologies would easily be able to cover the 10 m effective range of Bluetooth. Second, although Bluetooth is reasonably common amongst smart phones, the configuration of a device as being discoverable is fairly uncommon, largely for reasons of security. Despite the somewhat uncommon nature of discoverable Bluetooth (most devices require specific action to make themselves discoverable), a robust finding even with the limits of Bluetooth discoverability represents again a floor or minimum potential available. Critically, the act of gathering Bluetooth discoverable devices is reasonably power efficient allowing one to gather available devices at a reasonable pace (with associated signal strength for Bluetooth) without pairing and while still having a reasonable device battery life for the study. For reference, we do explore the potential when proximity is relaxed to consider proximity as derived by sharing common detected WiFi APs similar to [19].

## 4.1 Prevalence

The first question to pose is to what extent that opportunistic communication opportunities exist in practice. We

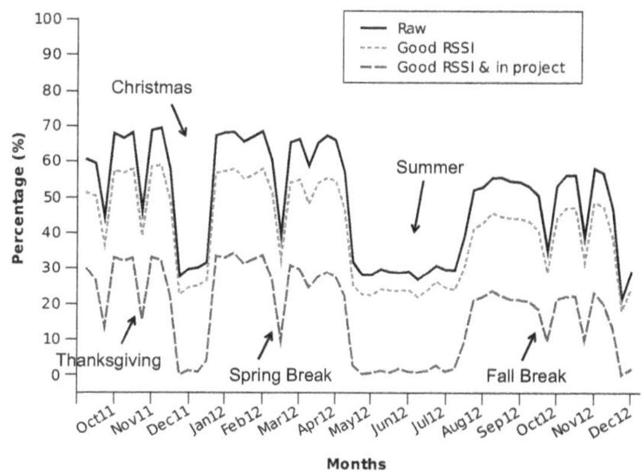


Figure 2: Bluetooth Proximity with Different Restrictions

begin with the most basic question with regards to the prevalence of discoverable Bluetooth devices and further refine our queries to explore various aspects of prevalence through the Prevalence criterion of the PSR framework. We posit several questions that include: (1) the extent to which discoverable Bluetooth devices exist, (2) the extent to which diurnal (daily) patterns play a role in discoverable devices, (3) and the extent to which Bluetooth views are symmetric. We further continue the explorations examining the prevalence of proximity to determine if the prevalence of such opportunities are still useful, namely (1) are such opportunities only available when there is no traffic and (2) how frequent do opportunities exist to augment access to 'better' wireless channels (ex. WiFi).

### *Bluetooth Proximity*

Figure 2 illustrates the average weekly Bluetooth proximity percentage with different restrictions across the study period. Various periods of interest representing various break periods are labeled in the graph. The percentage of time represents the percentage of time where an opportunity might exist for collaboration or relaying with a discoverable Bluetooth device. Further restrictions are placed on the data to filter for 'good RSSI' and candidates for opportunistic communications to exist only within the project (study). Notably, when completely unrestricted opportunities exist

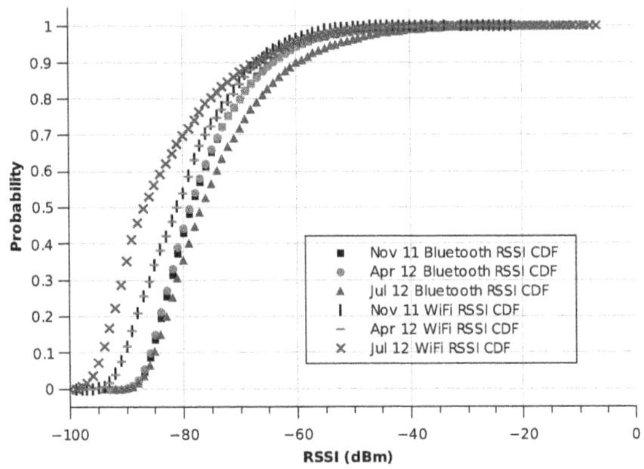


Figure 3: Bluetooth and WiFi RSSI Values ECDF

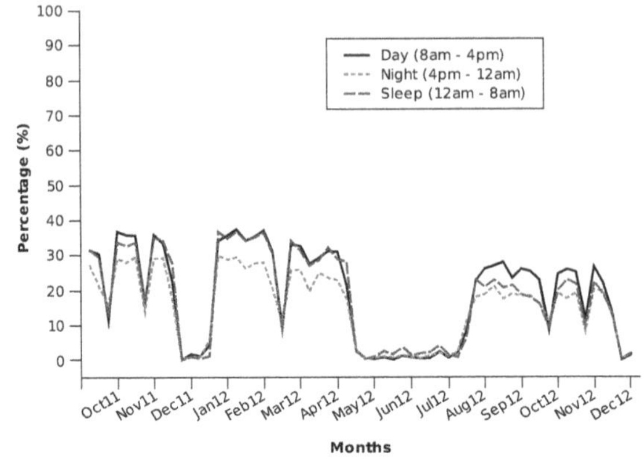


Figure 4: Diurnal Distribution of Bluetooth Proximity

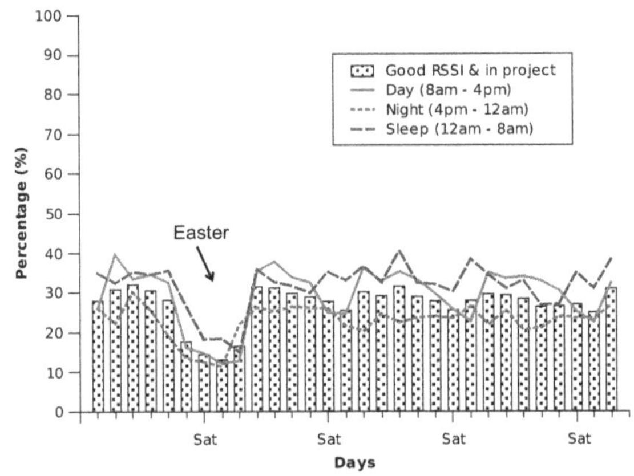


Figure 5: Diurnal Distribution of Bluetooth Proximity in April 2012

on the average of nearly 60% of the time when on campus, falling only slightly when good signal strength is added as a restriction. Even intra-study opportunities are quite prolific despite the fact that the 200 study participants represent less than one tenth of the freshmen class and less than 2.5% of the overall university student population. The slight drop from the fall of 2011 to the fall of 2012 can largely be attributed to students moving dorms and joining their respective majors and having less shared coursework versus their freshmen year.

Notably, the mere existence of the device being discoverable does not necessarily imply that the point-to-point link will be suitable for opportunistic communications. Figure 3 shows the ECDF of the Bluetooth and WiFi RSSI values in different months and more than 60% of the values are larger than -80 dBm. In particular, the data of July 2012 consider all the records including the Bluetooth devices outside the project and APs not under university control. Based on the work in [22], the RSSI value *-80 dBm* is used as a threshold to indicate good RSSI for direct mobile-to-mobile communication. As shown in Figure 2, even with the threshold of -80 dBm for the 'Good RSSI', there still exists more than 50% of the time slots, a fairly insubstantial drop from the raw detected Bluetooth devices.

Given that the students were selected from a core group of six dormitories, a natural skepticism should emerge from the data with regards to the diurnal effects of proximity, namely proximity does little good if it only occurs at night when the phone is not otherwise being used (ex. sleeping in the dorm room). Hence, we analyze the diurnal distribution of Bluetooth proximity by dividing one day into three parts: day time (8am to 4pm), night time (4pm to 12am) and sleep (12am to 8am). In this way, we are able to investigate the impacts of time durations on such proximity. Figure 4 shows the diurnal distribution with the twin restrictions of good RSSI and intra-study detected proximity only. The daytime proximity percentage from 8am to 4pm is larger than the value during nighttime and almost equal to the value of sleep time. The separation from in the fall of 2012 largely follows the classroom / major separation as noted in the raw and restricted graphs.

Beyond coarse diurnal metrics, significant day of week effects can also exist. Course patterns can vary dramatically between the Monday / Wednesday / Friday courses and Tuesday / Thursday courses. Similarly, weekends are much more likely to be quite diverse from normal weekday patterns. Figure 5 shows the daily Bluetooth proximity and diurnal distribution in April 2012 for a more detailed comparisons among the weekdays with each respective Saturday noted on the x axis. The peak values always appear at the beginning of the week and decrease slowly during the week. During the Easter holiday (April 6th - April 9th), the opportunities for proximity shrink dramatically as the students travel home for Easter break. The percentage does not drop to zero since there are some international students in the project and not all students travel home for Easter. Meanwhile, more Bluetooth proximity appeared in the later hours (broadly defined as sleep time) than daytime hours during weekend which indicates the participants spent more time in closer proximity to others during those time periods largely as a byproduct of social relationships.

## *WiFi Proximity*

While Bluetooth is used in the first part of the section to assess proximity, the next question to ask is to what extent could we infer proximity if we expanded our search to consider WiFi range via shared access points. For instance, in [19], WiFi signal strength is used to indicate proximity

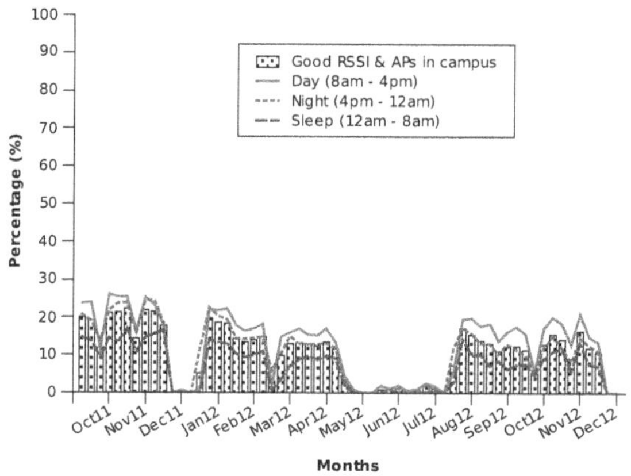


Figure 6: WiFi Proximity

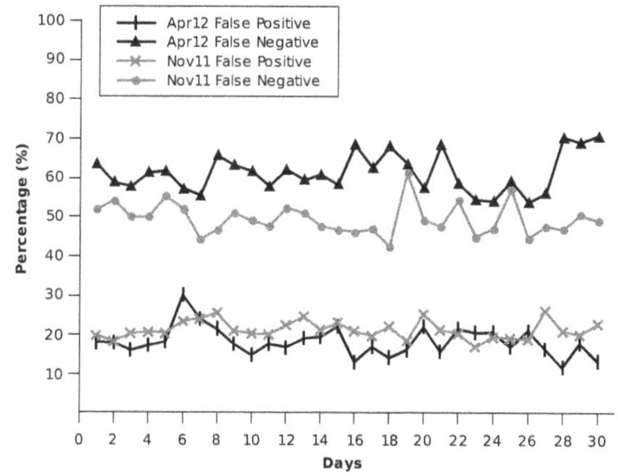


Figure 7: Comparison of Bluetooth Proximity and WiFi Proximity

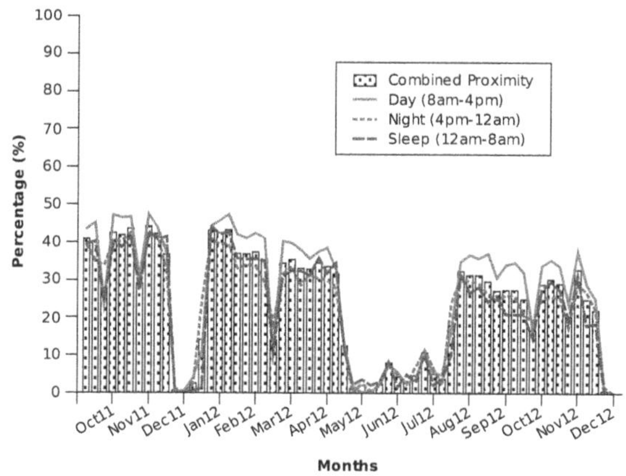


Figure 8: Combined Proximity (Fused Bluetooth / WiFi Detection)

when two devices are associated with the same AP. In our work, we further restrict the characterization to infer proximity if two mobile nodes detect two or more same access points. Barring the two APs being situated nearly on top of one another (note that university APs are filtered down to disambiguate virtual APs), one can reasonably infer that two nodes sharing the same two or more APs could be in WiFiDirect and / or LTEDirect range.

For appropriate range values within our study, we conducted experiments to evaluate the cutoff points for reasonable WiFi performance on the particular Android handset employed (Nexus S 4G). Channels were selected to be orthogonal to campus WiFi deployments (via a specially marked research channel space for our building) with distance, orientation, and other factors varied to get a wide variety of channel characteristics. Downloads were conducted over one hundred instances for each particular configuration and the results explored for throughput. Based on the experiment results of AP RSSI values and the corresponding throughputs, we note that -80 dBm can be the threshold to indicate good link quality with throughputs dramatically ramping up shortly after -80 dBm. At the same time, according to the RSSI distribution in Figure 3, there are more than 40% of records showing that APs in campus having RSSI values larger than -80 dBm. Therefore, we use -80 dBm as the good RSSI threshold for WiFi proximity.

For each device, we analyze the number of time slots when the device shares at least two of the same access points with another device (in-study devices only) and we calculate the percentage of such time slots. Figure 6 demonstrates the WiFi proximity and its diurnal distribution across the study period. During the holidays and summer, the percentage is almost zero as only university APs are considered for WiFi performance. Compared to other periods, WiFi proximity during daytime from 8am to 4pm represents a slight uptick though not statistically significant variation over other periods.

Interestingly, the WiFi result conveys less proximity than the noted Bluetooth proximity. Notably when compared to reference laptops or tablets, our prior work in [23] notes a roughly 10 dBm signal penalty for the smartphone used in our study.[1] In the work of [6] the RSSI discrepancy of different WiFi adapters is discussed as well. The net result is in addition to the detection of WiFi APs being hampered, reasonable placement of APs and auto-tuning of AP strength would result in significantly reduced probabilities of multiple mobile devices being able to detect one or more APs. In Figure 7, we compare the results of WiFi proximity and Bluetooth proximity in April 2012 and November of 2011. The false positive means the device detects other(s) in WiFi proximity which are not detected by Bluetooth proximity. On the other hand, the false negative means that the device does not detect some device in WiFi proximity but does detect the device in Bluetooth proximity. Notably, the false positive in the context of WiFi may not be a false positive but the false negative most certainly represents an incorrect result due to the aforementioned signal holes noted in [23].

Taking a bit more of an optimistic stance, we combine both WiFi proximity detection and Bluetooth proximity detection to create a combined proximity. Note that earlier proximity measurements used either exclusively Bluetooth

[1]Subsequent measurements indicated a 3-5dBm signal penalty in general for smartphone versus laptops.

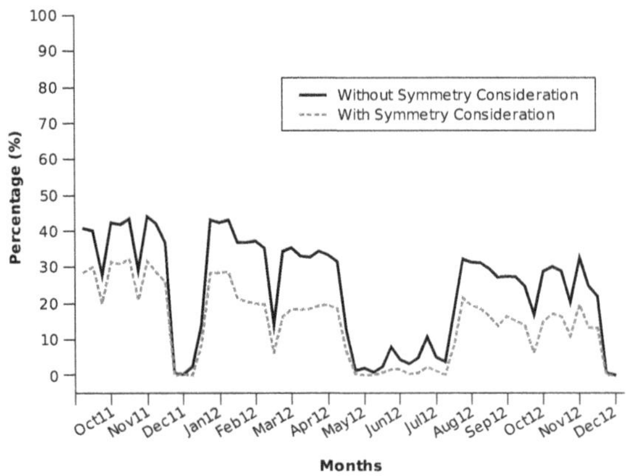


Figure 9: Combined Proximity with/without Symmetry

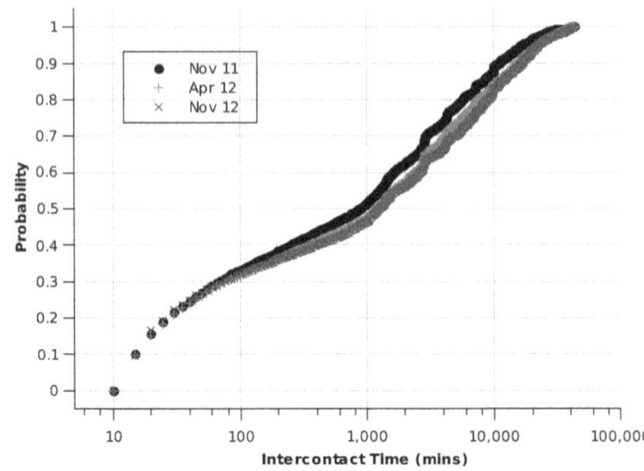


Figure 10: Inter-contact Time ECDF

or WiFi. Broadly defined, in one specific time slot, if the device can either detect other devices within the project with good Bluetooth RSSI or share at least two same APs in the campus with good WiFi RSSI, this time slot is counted as one of the slots when the device is in proximity with another device (intra-study only). Figure 8 illustrates such proximity across months. Compared to Bluetooth proximity only or WiFi proximity only, the percentage is increased to more than 40% trailing to roughly 30% by the end of the study, a nearly 10% increase over Bluetooth only considerations. The diurnal distribution keeps the same trend and the proximity percentage during the daytime being is the highest among the respective time periods. In the following sections, the measurements combine the Bluetooth and WiFi together to indicate proximity.

## *Symmetry*

For any two study participants that detect each other, there exists the opportunity to determine if symmetric detection exists, namely do both nodes detect each other and even if both nodes detect each other, do both nodes have a 'Good RSSI' to one another ($MN_i \rightarrow MN_j$ and vice versa)? Figure 9 compares the combined proximity with and without consideration of symmetry where symmetry is defined as both nodes seeing each other and having a 'Good RSSI.' Notably, roughly one third of the opportunities disappear in the study. Although the lack of symmetry does temper the earlier findings of prevalence, we note that Bluetooth is most appropriately viewed as a floor for potential interactions. The potential for asymmetry though between nodes does represent a consideration that merits further attention.

## *Inter-contact Time and Beyond*

Inter-contact time is defined as the time elapsed between two successive contact periods for a given pair of devices [8] which is another important characteristic of prevalence. For each pair of devices, we compute the inter-contact time as the time taken before the pair meet again. Figure 10 exhibits the empirical distribution of the inter-contact times obtained among different months. On average, the inter-contact time is around 1000 minutes which is more than 16 hours. The distribution varies only slightly with the earlier time periods (Nov 2011) exhibiting a shorter inter-contact time, in large part due to more shared coursework, reinforcing the findings from earlier graphs.

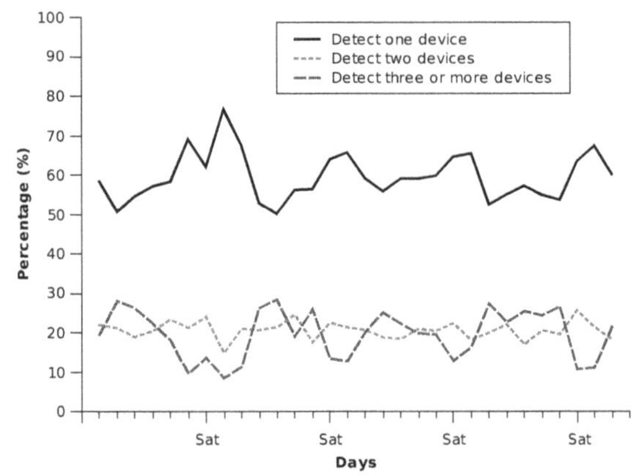


Figure 11: Distribution of Proximity Diversity (In-Study) in April 2012

While inter-contact time represents just one part of the puzzle, an related factor for the opportunity to be useful is with regards to the diversity of opportunities available. Relaying selection plays little role when there exists only a single device to choose from for relaying. Figure 11 shows the breakdown of detected devices in proximity through both Bluetooth and WiFi in April 2012 representing only cases where proximity occurred. In the figure, nearly 60% of time has only one peer is detected among all the possible opportunistic time slots. Meanwhile, there is nearly 20% of the time when two opportunities are detected and finally 20% when three or more opportunities are detected. In Figure 12, more details about the number of detected devices in April 2012 is illustrated with a diurnal distribution across the same month breaking down only cases where proximity was detected, i.e. 50% of daytime detections involved only a single device in the study. During the daytime, the chance to detect two or more devices in proximity is higher than other durations. Again, day time offers an increased potential for diversity in large part due to the increased mobility around the campus.

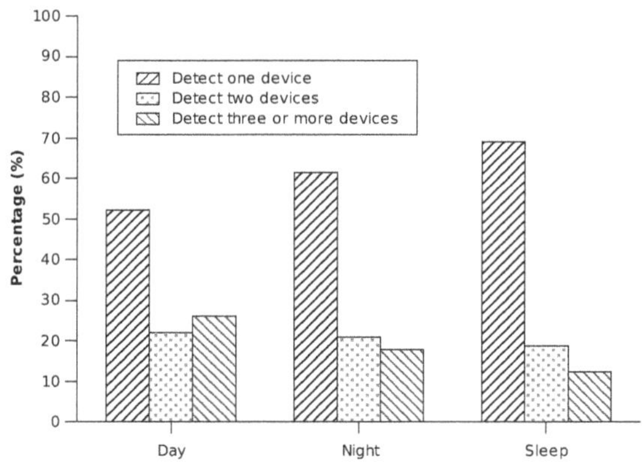


Figure 12: Diurnal Distribution of Proximity Diversity in April 2012

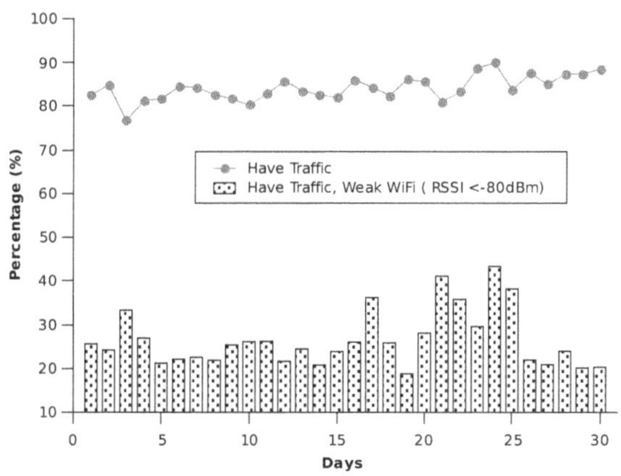


Figure 13: Weak WiFi Signal & Traffic

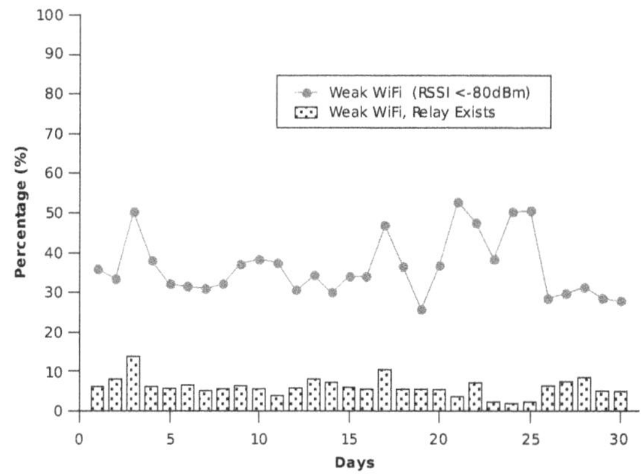


Figure 14: Relaying & Weak WiFi Signal

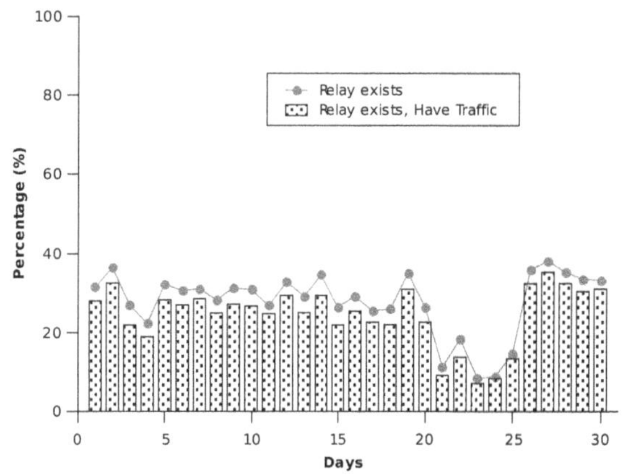


Figure 15: Traffic & Relaying

### *Measuring Effective Utility*

The final aspect for prevalence is the notion of effective utility, namely that the opportunity must occur when it is actually needed. From a general perspective, that need can happen when the following two conditions are satisfied: a) the node $MN_i$ has some traffic to receive or send but no direct / poor connection is available b) there is some other node $MN_j$ in proximity which can work together with the node. We analyze how often the devices really need relaying in the following three types of context.

The first context is when the device has traffic but does not have good WiFi connection. Figure 13 includes two sets of results in Nov 2012: one is the percentage of having traffic and the other is the percentage of having traffic but the device does not have good WiFi connection (all the detected access points have signal strength less than -80 dBm). Based on the results, there are more than 80% of time slots have traffic while 30% of time slots do not have good WiFi connection to do the transmission. Without WiFi, the traffic goes through the mobile link which further imposes pressure on mobile networks. However, relaying can work as an alternative to do the traffic offloading.

The second context is from the aspect of WiFi RSSI. With the prevalence of WiFi, it is interesting to investigate how often devices are not be fully covered by WiFi, i.e., detect no WiFi access points with RSSI larger than -80 dBm. In such case, relay is an option. In Figure 14, nearly 40% of the time the devices do not in good WiFi environment on average. There are around 10% of time slots do have relaying node(s) around while WiFi signal is not available or too weak.

In the third context, we consider the further benefits which relaying may produce. Besides WiFi and mobile network, relaying provides the third option to transmit traffic. When there is traffic need, the device may use relaying even it has established WiFi connection. Such cases happen when the relaying nodes have the content the device requests or the relaying communication has better link quality. Based on the results shown in Figure 15, the percentage is fairly high when relaying exists and there is traffic at the same time. Therefore, we posit that relaying can provide interesting opportunities for devices to send and receive traffic, not only in a passive way, but also in a proactive way.

## 4.2 Stability

Prevalence becomes of little use if the set of devices available for opportunistic communications are constantly in flux. While traditional opportunistic networking approaches as-

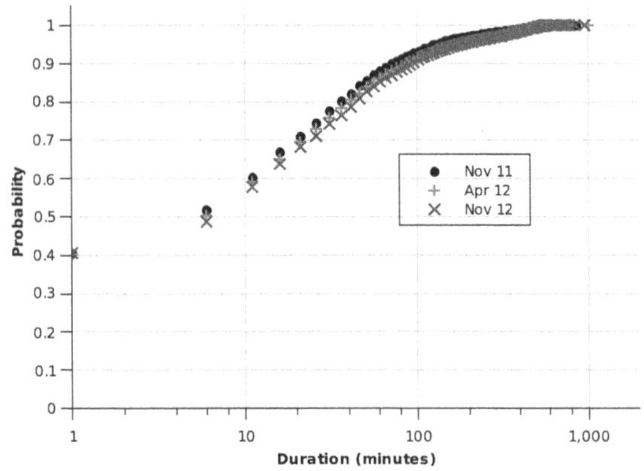


Figure 16: Proximity Duration ECDF

sume a degree of shared trust, there exists a non-zero cost for the establishment of secure point-to-point channels or at a minimum, the assurance that the device being considered for point-to-point communications is indeed legitimate. To that end, we evaluate the data through the lens of *stabilty*, namely to what extent are the devices available detected for communication likely to be available for a reasonable duration of time. Hence, the primary measure of stability lies in the distribution of contact durations with considerations for sufficient signal strength and symmetric connectivity detection. Put simply, candidates for opportunistic communications must exist for a reasonable duration of time (on the order of minutes, not simply seconds) to amortize the cost of point-to-point channel negotiation over the lifetime of the opportunity.

In a complementary sense, trust between various devices can be realized not only through duration but also through the repeated appearances in local proximity. Although an individual node may have long inter-contact times individually, the fact that a node appears consistently at multiple times per day or multiple times per week for a reasonably stable period of time implies a likely social construct or external relationship between the devices. Hence, a secondary metric for stability is the degree to which the most frequent nodes churn, i.e. the extent to which nodes appear for opportunities uniformly distributed and infrequent or are there nodes that appear dramatically more often than other nodes, potentially allowing for extended trust to be constructed by virtue of repeat appearances (or at a minimum, the trust exchange accelerated due to prior exchanges).

Hence, Figure 16 explores the most basic aspect of stability, namely the average duration of devices as present with regards to the locally detected nodes. Figure 16 exhibits the distribution of proximity durations of different months. Further filtering is applied where a node must have been seen at least once per day by that node for consideration for opportunistic communication. Nearly half of proximity lasts more than one time slot and the duration between 10 minutes and 45 minutes takes around 25%. Critically, the average stability of a connection falls at roughly 6 minutes, a considerable time period for conducting the security negotiations at the front of the communication.

In addition, we analyze the relationship between the number of relays and node strength in Figure 17. We define node

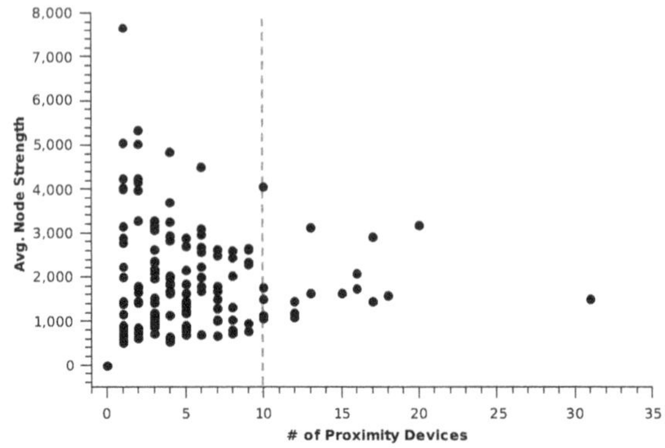


Figure 17: Number of Proximity Nodes vs. Node Strength

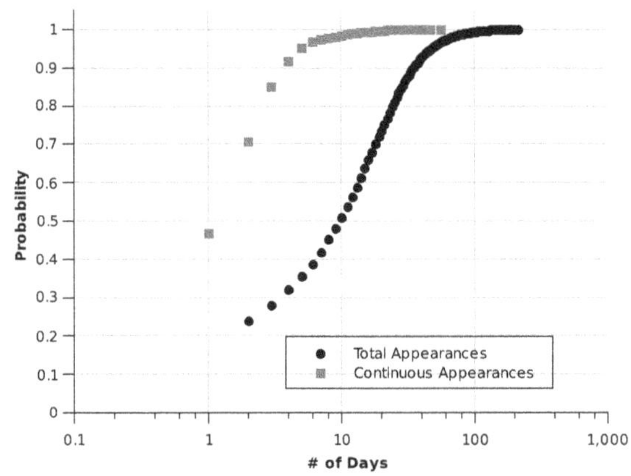


Figure 18: Total Appearances and Continuous Appearances in Day Counts ECDF

strength as follows: In one time slot, if the device detects a proximity device then the total appearance times of this peer is increased by one. Node strength is the total number of appearances of a proximity device in the period. Based on the data across 15 months, we compute the node strength of proximity nodes for devices. Using the threshold of 500 for node strength (have been seen almost at least once per day), we remove those infrequent proximity nodes and calculate the average node strength for each device. It is interesting that most of the nodes have less than 10 frequent proximity nodes (loosely correlating with their social circles) and the corresponding average node strength is relatively higher than those with more than 10 frequent relays.

While node strength captures the raw magnitude of total time spent together and indirectly infers longitudinal behavior, Figure 18 takes the concept further by examining the 'streakiness' over multiple days by which a potential peer is likely to appear across the entire duration of the study. The total appearances represents the distribution of how frequently a node is likely to appear whereby if the prospective peer is seen at least once in the day, it counts as being successfully seen for the purposes of consistency. Note that for the purposes of the graph, all nodes are considered rather than only the nodes with a reasonable degree of consistency to capture the full longitudinal nature of the study.

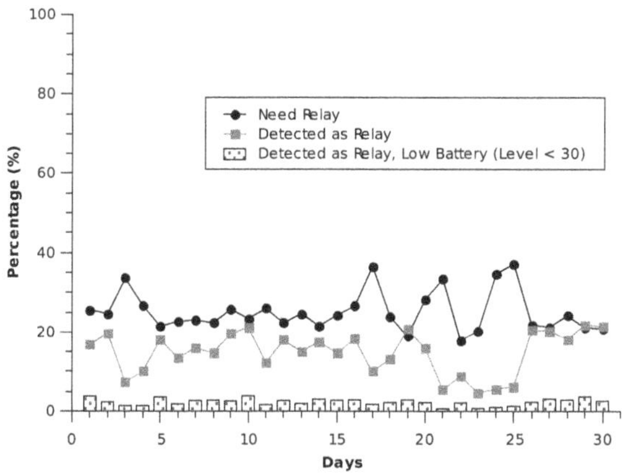


Figure 19: Distribution of Potential Interactions - Need vs. Serve (November 2012)

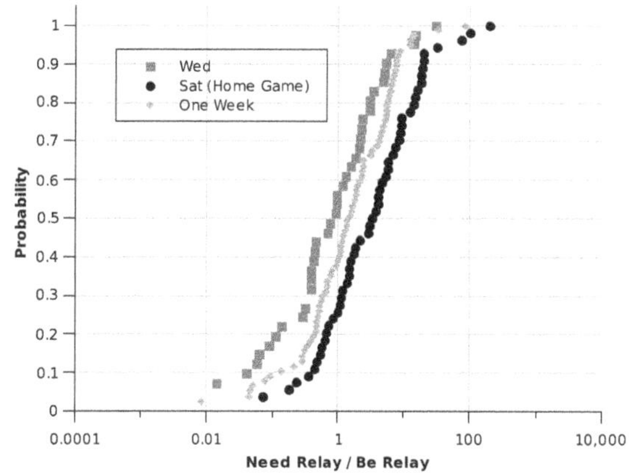


Figure 20: Ratio of Needing vs. Serving - One Week - November 2012

No filtering is done either for sufficiency of signal strength. Interestingly, several nodes eclipse nearly two-thirds of the time in the study in terms of consistency of meeting. It is those nodes that appear consistently that represent the stable foundation from which the prevalence can be effectively leveraged. The other plot in the graph captures the distribution of continuous days, namely if a node appears more than one day in a row, how long is the streak likely to continue with subsequent appearances over the next few days? The average number of continuous days is one day which means over 50% of the proximities did not happen continuously everyday.

## 4.3 Reciprocity

Finally, a key metric for evaluating the potential opportunistic communication is the degree to which reciprocity exists, ideally converging to an equal ratio of service versus need. Although altruism amongst nodes typically leads to a healthier network performance as a whole, the potential for increased energy consumption is of little consolation if the device is always helping but never benefitting. To that end, we posit that reciprocity amongst nodes must be taken into account when considering the overall utility of an opportunistic solution. Whereas much of the prior work is limited to evaluating only some aspects of prevalence and stability, interactions among pairs (dyads) in the study afford us the ability to evaluate the extent to which reciprocity exists both in short and long-term time scales with actual traffic patterns and actual energy constraints.

To that end, Figure 19 shows the daily average percentages with respect to needing assistance (relaying to another node) versus offering assistance (relaying for another node). The data is drawn strictly from intra-study interactions across the month of November 2012. A mobile node is defined as needing assistance if it has traffic but detects no WiFi access points with a sufficient signal strength ($> -80dBm$). A mobile node is defined as serving (offering assistance) if it has a good WiFi connection and has been detected by other nodes within the study. Hence, a value of 25% with respect to being detected as a relay denotes that another node ($MN_j$) in the study detected the node ($MN_i$), $MN_j$ had a good signal strength to the node $MN_i$, and $MN_i$ had a good signal strength for WiFi for 25% of the time that $MN_i$ was on for that day. Critically, a node needing relaying but detecting no nodes is similar to a node being willing to serve but yet no nodes needing its service. A further sub-division is done to breakdown the nodes filtered if battery level were taken into consideration, i.e. what percentage could no longer offer assistance if the battery level fell below 30% which barely has an impact, typically only a reduction of 1-3% for the number of times a node could offer assistance but would not due to energy constraints.

For a reasonable portion of the time, most nodes on average have an increased need for assistance versus the ability to serve. The primary exceptions emerge on weekends which also happen to correspond with football games, campus events, and travel. Figure 20 captures this relationship on both short-term (single day) and longer-term (one week) timescales drawing from a single week from Figure 19. The figure plots the distribution of the node having the potential to serve versus needing assistance. A ratio of one implies that the node had an equal number of time slots where the node could serve as a relay (detected, good WiFi) versus the node needing a relay. Whereas the traffic from the weekend shows much stronger need (due in part to the lack of WiFi at the football stadium), the nodes on the long-term scale have ratios much closer to one representing a reasonable reciprocity. Moreover, the typical weekday (as opposed to the game day scenario with limited WiFi) gravitates more closely to a balanced distribution as well.

# 5. CONCLUSION

In summary, our work is one of the first longitudinal and fine-grained studies that explores the practical potential for opportunistic communications with respect to smart devices. Whereas the natural intuition would be cast skepticism towards the potential for opportunistic communications (relaying or collaborative), we demonstrate through our explorations that opportunities for enhancements are not only prevalent but also sufficient, symmetric, and utilizable in our studied environment. Moreover, we find that such opportunities are stable in terms of having sufficient duration, low churn in peers, and relative consistency of peers. Finally, and perhaps most intriguingly, we show that the opportunities exhibit a reasonable degree of reciprocity for the short-term across weekdays and over the long-term when viewed across the entire week.

While we believe our work shows promising capabilities for practical mobile-to-mobile optimizations, the work is merely a first step that deserves further attention from the research community. Notably, several key aspects need to be explored including: (1) to what extent could one instrument a community outside of a campus drawing on either the Nokia Data Challenge or new efforts to explore a variety of audiences; (2) to what impact might the scale of coverage play a role, for instance would doubling or tripling the population yield considerably better results; And would other techniques besides Bluetooth and WiFi introduce more proximity opportunities (3) are there opportunities to improve content selection and distribution be that through Content Centric Networks (CCN) or other techniques (redundancy elimination); and (4) to what extent is there a 'critical mass' where opportunistic networks would seem useful either by analyzing subsets of the data or through theoretical explorations.

## Acknowledgement

This work was funded in part by the National Science Foundation through grant IIS-0968529. We would also like to thank our collaborators, Dr. Christian Poellabauer, Dr. David Hachen, and Dr. Omar Lizardo. Special thanks to Sprint who provides us more than 200 phones and free data plan making the data gathering a reality.

## 6. REFERENCES

[1] Cisco, "Cisco VNI mobile data traffic forecast 2012-2017," Feburary 2013.

[2] L. Pelusi, A. Passarella, and M. Conti, "Opportunistic networking: data forwarding in disconnected mobile ad hoc networks," *Communications Magazine, IEEE*, vol. 44, no. 11, pp. 134–141, 2006.

[3] J. Laneman, D. Tse, and G. Wornell, "Cooperative diversity in wireless networks: Efficient protocols and outage behavior," *Information Theory, IEEE Transactions on*, vol. 50, no. 12, pp. 3062–3080, 2004.

[4] A. Sendonaris, E. Erkip, and B. Aazhang, "User cooperation diversity. part I. system description," *Communications, IEEE Transactions on*, vol. 51, no. 11, pp. 1927–1938, 2003.

[5] A. Bletsas, A. Khisti, D. Reed, and A. Lippman, "A simple cooperative diversity method based on network path selection," *Selected Areas in Communications, IEEE Journal on*, vol. 24, no. 3, pp. 659–672, 2006.

[6] M. Lu, P. Steenkiste, and T. Chen, "Design, implementation and evaluation of an efficient opportunistic retransmission protocol," in *Proc. of MobiCom*. ACM, 2009, pp. 73–84.

[7] P. Bahl, R. Chandra, P. Lee, V. Misra, J. Padhye, D. Rubenstein, and Y. Yu, "Opportunistic use of client repeaters to improve performance of WLANs," *IEEE/ACM Transactions on Networking (TON)*, vol. 17, no. 4, pp. 1160–1171, 2009.

[8] A. Chaintreau, P. Hui, J. Crowcroft, C. Diot, R. Gass, and J. Scott, "Impact of human mobility on opportunistic forwarding algorithms," *Mobile Computing, IEEE Transactions on*, vol. 6, no. 6, pp. 606–620, 2007.

[9] H. Cai and D. Eun, "Toward stochastic anatomy of inter-meeting time distribution under general mobility models," in *Proc. of MobiHoc*. ACM, 2008, pp. 273–282.

[10] G. Treu and A. Küpper, "Efficient proximity detection for location based services," in *Proc. of WPNC*, 2005.

[11] A. Küpper and G. Treu, "Efficient proximity and separation detection among mobile targets for supporting location-based community services," *ACM SIGMOBILE Mobile Computing and Communications Review*, vol. 10, no. 3, pp. 1–12, 2006.

[12] L. Šikšnys, J. Thomsen, S. Šaltenis, and M. Yiu, "Private and flexible proximity detection in mobile social networks," in *Proc. of IEEE Mobile Data Management (MDM)*, 2010, pp. 75–84.

[13] J. Krumm and K. Hinckley, "The NearMe wireless proximity server," in *Proc. of UbiComp*. Springer, 2004, pp. 283–300.

[14] K. Li, T. Sohn, S. Huang, and W. Griswold, "Peopletones: a system for the detection and notification of buddy proximity on mobile phones," in *Proc. of MobiSys*. ACM, 2008, pp. 160–173.

[15] N. Eagle, A. Pentland, and D. Lazer, "Inferring social network structure using mobile phone data," *Proc. of the National Academy of Sciences (PNAS)*, vol. 106, no. 36, pp. 15 274–15 278, September 2009.

[16] N. Eagle and A. Pentland, "Social serendipity: Mobilizing social software," *Pervasive Computing*, vol. 4, no. 2, pp. 28–34, 2005.

[17] J. K. Laurila, D. Gatica-Perez, I. Aad, J. Blom, O. Bornet, T.-M.-T. Do, O. Dousse, J. Eberle, and M. Miettinen, "The mobile data challenge: Big data for mobile computing research," in *Proc. of Nokia Mobile Data Challenge Workshop*, 2012.

[18] S. Liu and A. Striegel, "Face-to-face proximity estimation using Bluetooth on smartphones," *Mobile Computing, IEEE Transactions on*, 2013.

[19] M. McNett and G. M. Voelker, "Access and mobility of wireless pda users," *ACM SIGMOBILE Mobile Computing and Communications Review*, vol. 9, no. 2, pp. 40–55, 2005.

[20] T. Henderson, D. Kotz, and I. Abyzov, "The changing usage of a mature campus-wide wireless network," in *Proc. of MobiCom*. ACM, 2004, pp. 187–201.

[21] M.-H. Lu, P. Steenkiste, and T. Chen, "Time-aware opportunistic relay for video streaming over WLANs," in *Proc. of Multimedia and Expo*. IEEE, 2007, pp. 1782–1785.

[22] J. Polastre, R. Szewczyk, and D. Culler, "Telos: enabling ultra-low power wireless research," in *Proc. of IPSN*, 2005, pp. 364–369.

[23] S. Liu and A. Striegel, "Casting doubts on the viability of WiFi offloading," in *Proc. of CellNet*. ACM, 2012, pp. 25–30.

# Fine-grained Spectrum Adaptation in WiFi Networks

Sangki Yun, Daehyeok Kim, Lili Qiu
The University of Texas at Austin
{sangki,dkim,lili}@cs.utexas.edu

**Abstract –** Explosive growth of WiFi traffic calls for new technologies to dramatically improve spectrum efficiency. In this paper, we propose an approach to adapt the spectrum on a per-frame basis. It consists of three major components: (i) a fine-grained spectrum access design that allows a sender and receiver to change their transmission and reception spectrum on demand, (ii) fast and accurate spectrum detection that allows a receiver to determine which spectrum is used by its sender on a per-frame basis by exploiting the IEEE 802.11 preamble structure, and (iii) an efficient spectrum allocation algorithm that determines which spectrum to use for each transmission by taking into account frequency diversity and interference. It can further be adapted to perform a joint assignment of spectrum, schedule, and access point (AP) for each frame. Using a SORA implementation and trace-driven simulation, we demonstrate the feasibility of per-frame spectrum adaptation and its significant benefit over existing channel assignment approaches. To our knowledge, this is the first per-frame spectrum adaptation prototype for WiFi networks.

## Categories and Subject Descriptors

C.2.1 [**Computer-Communication Networks**]: Network Architecture and Design—*Wireless communication*

## General Terms

Experimentation, Performance

## Keywords

IEEE 802.11, Dynamic Spectrum Access, Spectrum Allocation, Physical Layer

## 1. INTRODUCTION

**Motivation:** As WiFi traffic has grown explosively, new technologies have to be developed to dramatically improve spectrum efficiency and keep up with the users' ever increasing traffic demands. In response to this need, a recent trend in wireless standards is to adopt wider spectrum to increase data rates. For example, IEEE 802.11n [20] supports up to 40 MHz channels and IEEE 802.11ac [24] further increases the channel width up to 160 MHz. However, simply using larger channel width is not always desirable. For instance, IEEE 802.11n has a known problem that a node using a 40MHz channel can be easily starved by nodes using 20MHz channels [5, 35]. Moreover, a wider channel reduces the communication range due to less concentrated energy [3] and also increases energy consumption due to a higher sampling rate. In contrast, WIFI-NC [5] advocates using narrowband channels to reduce MAC overhead as well as improve energy efficiency at the cost of more guard bands or reduced SNR.


*MobiCom'13,* September 30-October 4, Miami, FL, USA.


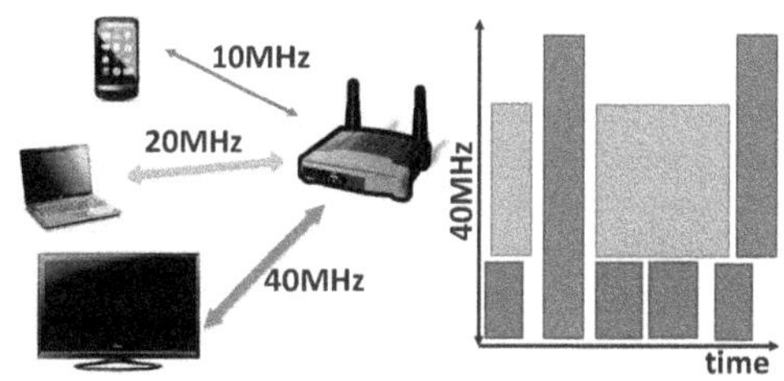


**Figure 1: Fine-grained spectrum adaptation (FSA) example scenario.**

Instead of fixing to a narrowband or a wideband, we believe the right approach is to determine spectrum based on the application need and current channel condition. By doing this, we can achieve the best of both worlds. This concept is illustrated in Figure 1, where an AP communicates with a mobile device on a 10MHz channel to conserve power and achieve a higher SNR over the same distance, communicates with a laptop on a standard 20MHz channel to balance power and bandwidth requirements, and communicates with HDTV on a wider channel to achieve high capacity. These transmissions need not be synchronized for maximum flexibility. The AP here may be either a sender or receiver of these transmissions. When it acts as a sender, it should be able to quickly switch the channel on a per-frame basis depending on which receiver the current frame is destined to; when it acts as a receiver, ity should be able to not only quickly switch the spectrum but also detect which spectrum the incoming transmission uses on a per-frame basis so that it can switch to the right spectrum to receive the incoming signals.

The need for dynamic spectrum adaptation further increases when the best channel changes quickly (*e.g.,* due to fast fading or dynamic traffic). If the receivers can promptly feed back the channel quality, which is made feasible with low overhead thanks to recent advances in feedback technologies, such as feedback compression [15], full duplex radios [6, 12], and embedding feedback in the data traffic [7], the transmitters can immediately adapt the spectrum to achieve high performance.

**Challenges:** In order to support the above functionalities, we need the following three fundamental capabilities:

- A sender or receiver should promptly switch to the desired spectrum. Tuning the spectrum parameter (*e.g.*, center frequency and channel width) in hardware incurs too long delay.
- A receiver should accurately detect the spectrum used by the transmission within a preamble time. There are many possible combinations of channel width and center frequency, which makes accurate and fast detection challenging.
- Given the capability of fine-grained spectrum access, it is important to determine which spectrum to use for each transmission to optimize performance and avoid interference.

**Our approach:** To address these challenges, we develop Fine-grained Spectrum Adaptation (FSA) that allows (i) a transmitter and a receiver to dynamically change the center frequency and channel width on a per-frame basis and (ii) a receiver to quickly identify the spectrum used by the sender based on the IEEE 802.11 preamble signature. In particular, a sender freely selects its channel width and center frequency without coordination with its receiver. It uses flexible baseband design to virtually change the spectrum, and optionally transmit multiple narrowband signals using one wideband radio. The receiver detects the transmission within the preamble detection phase using a novel spectrum detection method based on the special characteristics of the preamble in the frequency domain. Then it performs spectrum shaping, sampling clock and filter adjustment, and compensation for the center frequency difference of data symbols while fixing the hardware parameters. If multiple signals are transmitted, the receiver can decode all the signals from different subbands.

Built on the capability of per-frame spectrum adaptation, we then develop an algorithm to select the spectrum to use for each transmission according to the current channel condition. Different from OFDMA scheduling, which targets synchronous transmissions in cellular networks, our spectrum allocation works for unsynchronous transmissions (*i.e.*, transmissions from the same or different nodes are not synchronized) as common in WiFi networks. Our algorithm takes into account both frequency diversity and interference, and can support *joint* allocation of spectrum, schedule, and AP. Our algorithm is flexible: (i) an AP can use different spectrum to communicate with different clients or with the same client at different time depending on the current channel condition, and (ii) a frame can be allocated to non-contiguous spectrum or even to different APs if it improves performance.

Our main contributions can be summarized as follow:

- A baseband design that allows a sender and receiver to quickly change their frequency bands. It is fully compatible with 802.11a PHY: an FSA enabled device can communicate with a legacy 802.11a device that does not know FSA (Section 3.1).
- A simple yet effective algorithm that lets a receiver accurately determine which spectrum is used by the sender and how it is used by exploiting the IEEE 802.11 preamble structure (Section 3.2).
- An algorithm that selects the appropriate spectrum to use for each transmission by taking into account both frequency diversity and interference (Section 4).
- A SORA implementation that demonstrates the feasibility of spectrum adaptation on a per-frame basis and its performance benefit, and trace-driven simulations that show its effectiveness in more general scenarios. To our knowledge, this is the first WiFi compatible per-frame spectrum adaptation prototype (Section 5 and 6).

# 2. RELATED WORK

Our work is closely related to the following three broad areas: (i) spectrum virtualization, (ii) dynamic spectrum access, and (iii) spectrum allocation.

**Spectrum virtualization:** The signal bandwidth has long been considered to be determined by RF front-end, which takes non-negligible delay to change. In commercial hardware, changing the channel width takes over 1 ms; and even in advanced RF hardware, it takes more than 100 $\mu s$ [27]. Recently, spectrum virtualization techniques change the spectrum in baseband level while fixing the RF bandwidth [10, 32]. Using signal shaping techniques such as sampling rate conversion and frequency shifting, it changes spectrum with little overhead. This allows a sender to use different spectrum on a per-frame basis. However, [10, 32] do not consider how the sender and receiver agree which spectrum to use. Rodin [2] develops a new preamble for a receiver to identify the spectrum used by the sender. Different from Rodin, our approach is compatible with WiFi by leveraging the existing preamble in IEEE 802.11.

**Dynamic spectrum access:** Ranveer et. al. [3] show that dynamically changing channel width gives better throughput than using a static wide channel, and proposes SampleWidth to dynamically adjust the channel width. As it relies on RF for channel switching, the switching delay is significant. To reduce overhead, it adapts the channel width only infrequently. Moreover, an AP has to use the same channel width for all clients. Our FSA overcomes these issues by using faster and more flexible spectrum adaptation.

WiFi-NC [5] proposes using narrow channels to improve spectrum efficiency. This is based on the following insights: (i) the relative overhead of PHY/MAC is smaller in narrower channels, (ii) it is challenging to efficiently support heterogeneous channel widths, and (iii) the spectrum may be fragmented and only leave narrow channels available. However, narrow channels tend to incur a higher overhead due to more guard bands. While WiFi-NC uses sharp elliptic filters to achieve narrow guard bands, it incurs preamble dilation and requires a larger CP.

FICA [31] also advocates narrower sub-channels. Different from WiFi-NC, the subchannels in FICA are dependent and transmissions across different sub-channels should be synchronized within a few microseconds. Therefore, as pointed out in [5], FICA is essentially a wide single-channel system with multiple inter-dependent narrow sub-channels.

SWIFT [26] and JELLO [34] dynamically allocate spectrum depending on the narrowband interference or the traffic demand, but they require coordination for the spectrum agreement. ASN [35] allows adaptive subcarrier selection and detection using the preamble. But it assumes all nodes use the same OFDM structure and is only applicable when they use the same RF bandwidth. Also, its detection method is similar to STD, which significantly underperforms FSA as shown in Section 5.

The emerging IEEE 802.11ac standard supports up to 160MHz wide channel communication and provides dynamic bandwidth management mode that allows 20MHz subchannel communication [24]. It uses RTS and CTS exchange for spectrum agreement and incurs significant overhead.

**Spectrum allocation:** WhiteFi [1] provides WiFi like connectivity in TV spectrum. Its detection algorithm exploits different ACK time duration under different channel width. It requires storing the signal and defers decoding till the end of ACK reception, which increases decoding delay and complicates system design. In comparison, FSA detects the bandwidth using the preamble and the receiver can immediately start decoding as soon as it receives data signals. Moreover, the detection algorithm in WhiteFi works only when the center frequency of the sender and the receiver are aligned, which is not required by FSA.

FLUID [27] dynamically allocates spectrum. To address significant channel switching overhead, it uses two WiFi interfaces to hide the switching delay and also switches channel less frequently. Our work is inspired by FLUID and benefits from their proposed interference model, but differs from it in the following ways: (i) our spectrum adaptation is done on a per-frame basis (a few microseconds in FSA vs. above 4 ms in FLUID), (ii) our flexible baseband allows an AP to transmit multiple frames simultaneously on different spectrum, whereas FLUID allows an AP to transmit only one frame at a time, which limits spectrum efficiency, and (iii) we support allocating a frame to non-contiguous spectrum and perform joint AP assignment and spectrum adaptation.

# 3. FINE-GRAINED SPECTRUM ACCESS

We develop fine-grained spectrum access. It consists of a baseband design for a sender and receiver to quickly change the spectrum and spectrum detection scheme for a receiver to identify the spectrum used by the sender. Once the receiver detects the spectrum, the standard decoding is used to decode signals on the detected spectrum.

## 3.1 Baseband Design

We first introduce the baseband system design of FSA. As Analog to Digital Conversion (ADC), Digital to Analog Conversion (DAC), baseband to passband conversion, and passband to baseband conversion are performed in inflexible Radio Frequency (RF) front-end hardware, we describe how to implement FSA using flexible baseband signal processor. Our design goal is to support efficient spectrum change with negligible overhead. In this paper, since the maximum bandwidth of SORA is limited to 20MHz, we assume the physical bandwidth of the radio is 20MHz and confine possible channel widths to 5, 10, and 20MHz, but our system design is general enough to apply to wider band systems.

One easy way to communicate through narrow channel is to use a small number of subcarriers for data transmission in OFDM systems. Examples of such systems include FICA [31] and OFDMA. This approach is inflexible because it works only when transmitters in different spectrum are tightly synchronized with very small misalignment [5].

Another option is to use narrower subcarrier width. IEEE 802.11a standard uses this approach to support 5MHz and 10MHz channels in addition to the default 20MHz channels. Most commercial WiFi devices support it. This is also what we use in our system. By reducing the subcarrier width, most of the timing related values increase inversely proportional to the reduction ratio, while the basic PHY architecture remains the same. For example, an OFDM symbol duration is $4\mu s$ in 20MHz channel, and increases to $16\mu s$ in 5MHz. While the number of subcarriers remains constant (*i.e.*, 64), the bandwidth of each subcarrier is adjusted proportional to the channel width. For example, the subcarrier widths in 20MHz and 5MHz channels are 312.5KHz and 78.1KHz, respectively. The benefit of this approach is that nodes in different spectrum can independently communicate without the need to synchronize. However, most commercial devices incur non-negligible delay in changing the channel width, so it is too costly to change on a per-frame basis. Instead we use upsampling and downsampling to adjust subcarrier width without increasing delay.

**Transmitter:** Figure 2 (a) shows the baseband system design to send multiple narrowband signals using one wideband RF hardware. Based on the available channel and the application requirement, the sender decides which spectrum to use. If the channel

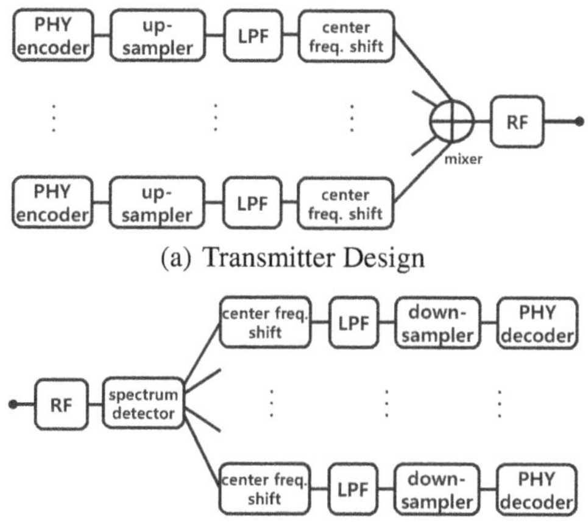

(a) Transmitter Design

(b) Receiver Design

**Figure 2: Baseband System Design.**

width is determined to be 5MHz or 10MHz, instead of changing the hardware sampling clock in RF-frontend, it performs upsampling in the baseband processor. Assuming that the signal rate is fixed, upsampling process adds interpolated samples for each signal. This increases the signal duration, which in turn decreases the spectrum width of the signal [23]. More specifically, upsampling by a factor of $N$ increases the sampling rate to N times by adding N - 1 interpolated samples for every signal and decreases the bandwidth to the ratio of $\frac{1}{N}$. Using the baseband signals generated by 802.11a PHY, we generate 10MHz and 5MHz bandwidth signals through upsampling by factors of 2 and 4, respectively. As upsampling process generates image of the signal outside the band, Low Pass Filtering (LPF) is required to avoid generating adjacent channel interference [23].

In addition to changing the channel width, if the transmitting spectrum and RF hardware have different center frequency, we need to shift the center frequency as follows. Suppose that the center frequency of the RF hardware is tuned to $f_c$, but the sender wants to use the center frequency $f_c + \Delta$ . This difference can be compensated in the baseband level as follow. Let $s[n]$ be the baseband signal that the sender transmits, and $\Delta$ be the difference between the desired and the hardware center frequency. We generate frequency shifted signal $s_{fs}[n]$ by multiplying $e^{j2\pi\Delta n}$ to each sample $s[n]$ (*i.e.*, $s_{fs}[n] = s[n]e^{j2\pi\Delta n}$). In RF hardware, this signal is converted into passband signal $x[n] = s_{fs}[n]e^{j2\pi f_c n} = s[n]e^{j2\pi(f_c+\Delta)n}$, which is the desired signal with center frequency $f_c + \Delta$.

If the sender transmits multiple signals through more than one subband, it unsamples all signals to 40MHz since the widest possible signal in our implementation is 20MHz and should be upsampled to 40MHz according to Nyquist Theorem while the narrower band signals is upsampled to the same level to ease processing. Then the sender adds the upsampled signals up at the mixer and delivers to the RF hardware, where it performs DAC and baseband to passband up-conversion to transmit the signals over the air. Since all signals have the same sampling rate regardless of their original data bandwidth, we can easily send them together. A similar technique has been used in SVL [32] and PICASSO [10].

**Receiver:** As shown in Figure 2, upon the arrival of a signal, the receiver performs passband to baseband down-conversion and ADC at the RF front-end and then uses the spectrum detector to determine which subband the sender uses for transmission. After the detector detects the start of the frame and estimates its channel width and center frequency, the receiver performs the following spectrum shaping. First, if the RF center frequency and the receiving spectrum are different, similar to the center frequency shifting at the sender side, the receiver compensates it by multiplying $e^{-j2\pi\Delta n}$ to the received baseband signals. Second, it filters the signal outside the channel width by LPF to avoid the adjacent channel interference. Third, it downsamples the signal to match the sampling rate to that of the transmitter (*e.g.*, downsampling by a factor of $\frac{1}{2}$ for 10MHz signal). After that, the signal is delivered to the 802.11a PHY decoder. While the decoder is decoding the signal that has already been detected, the detector keeps sensing the spectrum to detect new signal from the remaining idle spectrum. The detail of the spectrum detector is introduced in Section 3.2.3.

A natural question in the receiver design is whether spectrum can be changed quickly enough to match that of the sender before the receiver starts channel estimation using the preamble. When the receiver changes its filter bandwidth, it incurs some delay since it generates valid output only after filling a few samples in the sample memory registers. This delay is called filter group delay [23], and is negligible compared to the preamble duration. As we will show in Section 3.2, our spectrum detection algorithm requires 64 samples while the preamble for detection consists of 160 samples. As most digital filters provide enough cutoff bandwidth when the group delay is less than 20 samples, the remaining preamble samples after the spectrum detection are enough for the adjusted filter to take effect before the channel estimation takes place. Moreover, the frequency shifting and downsampling incur close to 0 delay since they are simple to compute.

Upon detecting one or more transmissions and their spectrum profile, a receiver tries to decode all the detected frames and discard the ones that do not have its address as the destination. To further reduce processing overhead, one may optionally use PN sequence to encode receiver address so that the receiver can use simple cross correlation to detect if the frame is destined to itself (*i.e.*, a spike in the correlation between the received signal and it address encoded in PN sequence indicates the frame has its address). The receiver then only decodes the ones destined to itself, instead of attempting to decode all the frames.

## 3.2 Detecting The Spectrum

To achieve the per-frame spectrum adaptation, the receiver should know which center frequency and channel width the sender uses for transmission. One way to enable this is to coordinate the spectrum usage before communication (*e.g.*, using RTS/CTS exchange or control channel). Such coordination incurs significant overhead. Moreover, RTS/CTS exchange may not be possible without a shared channel between the sender and receiver. Another option is to let the receiver detect spectrum based on the characteristics of incoming signals. This is challenging because the flexible spectrum access not only allows the sender to freely change the center frequency and bandwidth but also lets it potentially transmit multiple signals concurrently. This significantly increases the number of ways in which spectrum is used.

Without loss of generality, this section assumes the center frequency of the RF hardware is 0MHz (*e.g.*, a 20MHz signal spans from -10MHz to 10MHz). Also, we assume that the center frequency of an incoming signal is discrete and set to maximize the number of narrow channels in a 20MHz channel (*i.e.*, 10MHz channel uses -5MHz and 5MHz as center frequency, and 5MHz channel uses -7.5MHz, -2.5MHz, 2.5MHz, and 7.5MHz as center frequency). This reduces the number of possible channels with little impact on spectrum efficiency. Below we first introduce 802.11a frame detection in Section 3.2.1. Then we develop a simple baseline scheme that uses temporal and spectral analysis for spectrum detection in Section 3.2.2. In Section 3.2.3, we propose a novel spectrum detection method that exploits the 802.11a preamble signature in frequency domain.

### *3.2.1 802.11a frame detection*

To give better understanding on the spectrum detection method, let us briefly explain how a normal 802.11 receiver detects the frame. The 802.11a preamble consists of Short Training Field (STF) and Long Training Field (LTF), where STF is used for the frame detection and LTF is used for the channel estimation. STF has a special property in time domain. It has ten periods, each with 16 samples, altogether 160 samples. The 802.11a receiver takes advantage of this periodicity to detect the preamble. It first measures the energy of the received signal $r$ as $P = \sum_{k=1}^{L} r[k]r^*[k]$, where $L$ is the number of signals used for energy measurement and $^*$ represents the complex conjugate of the signal. If $P$ is higher than a given threshold, it performs auto-correlation check to see if the incoming signal is an 802.11a frame. The auto-correlation of the signal with $d$ delayed samples $C_d$ is:

$$C_d = \sum_{k=1}^{L} r[n+k]r^*[n+k-d].$$

The detection metric $m_d$ is calculated as $m_d = \frac{C_d}{P}$ [9]. As the preamble has a period of 16 samples, the receiver uses $m_{16}$ as the detection metric. If $m_{16}$ is higher than the threshold $\gamma$, it considers a valid 802.11a frame is detected and starts further processing.

### *3.2.2 Spectral and Temporal analysis based spectrum detection (STD)*

When the channel width of the transmitted signal is unknown to the receiver, it can be identified either by temporal analysis or spectral analysis of STF. Temporal analysis based detection detects the bandwidth of the signal using the characteristic of STF in the time domain. Specifically, the signal duration is inversely proportional to the bandwidth, so a narrowband signal lasts longer. For example, the duration of 20MHz and 10MHz signals are 50 $ns$ and 100 $ns$, respectively. When a receiver using a larger bandwidth gets STF from a transmitter using a narrower band, it sees more samples every period. For example, STF on a 10MHz channel takes 1600 $ns$ to transmit 16 repeated samples. A receiver using 20MHz will sample the signal every 50 $ns$ and get 32 samples every period. Similarly, an incoming 5MHz STF signal yields 64 samples every period to the receiver using 20MHz. The temporal detection estimates the channel width using this property by measuring the number of samples in each period of a received STF. xGiven the received signal, the receiver measures $m_{16}$, $m_{32}$, and $m_{64}$. If all $m_k$s are below $\gamma$, the signal is considered as non-802.11a signal and ignored. Otherwise, it selects the channel width that gives the best match.

Although the temporal detection is useful for estimating the channel width, it is still insufficient since it cannot identify the center frequency of the signal. Moreover, it does not work when the center frequencies of the sender and receiver are not aligned. Spectral analysis can be used to detect both the center frequency and the channel width by measuring the energy of the signal in the frequency domain. The receiver calculates Power Spectral Density (PSD) by performing Fast Fourier Transform (FFT) of the received signal to identify both the channel width and center frequency.

However, this approach cannot distinguish how many transmissions exist in the detected spectrum when multiple transmissions continuously occupy the spectrum. For example, suppose that 10MHz spectrum is occupied by two 5MHz channel signals. Only relying on the spectral analysis cannot tell whether it is one transmission on a 10MHz channel or two transmissions on two consecutive 5MHz channels. To address this issue, the temporal analysis and spectral analysis should be used jointly. When the spectral analysis detects spectrum is occupied from -5MHz to 5MHz, the temporal analysis is used to identify the exact channel width by comparing $m_{32}$ and $m_{64}$. If both $m_{64}$ and $m_{32}$ are below $\gamma$, the signal is ignored. Otherwise, if $m_{64}$ is higher than $m_{32}$, it considers the spectrum is occupied by two 5MHz signals; if not, it is considered as one 10MHz signal. This process is repeated for every possible spectrum combination in general and becomes computationally intensive when the sensed spectrum spans 20MHz due to many ways of occupying 20MHz spectrum.

### 3.2.3 *Our Detection: Fine-grained Spectrum Detection (FSD)*

In this section, we introduce a novel spectrum detection method that exploits the magnitude pattern of 802.11a STF in the frequency domain. The standard STF consists of 12 subcarriers with unit magnitude and 54 subcarriers with zero energy [19]. The interval between adjacent subcarriers with non-zero energy is 4 except some subcarriers near the guardband or the center, as shown in Figure 3 (a). We call such an interval as *subcarrier interval.* In Section 3.1, we mentioned that 5, 10, and 20MHz channel signals have different subcarrier widths. While the number of subcarriers is fixed to 64, the subcarrier width of 20MHz channel signal is four times and twice as that of 10MHz and 5MHz channel signals, respectively. We exploit this property to detect the channel width. Suppose a receiver whose channel width is tuned to 20MHz gets a signal from a sender using a 10MHz channel. Because the subcarrier width of the 20MHz receiver is twice as large as that of the 10 MHz sender, the signals of 2 subcarriers from 10MHz sender are merged into one subcarrier of 20MHz receiver, which reduces the subcarrier interval from 4 to 2 as shown in Figure 3 (b). Likewise, the subcarrier interval of 5MHz STF is 1 to the 20MHz receiver as shown Figure 3 (c).

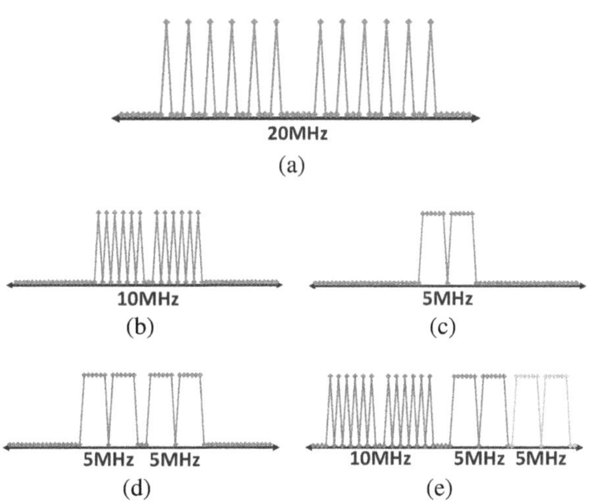


**Figure 3: Different patterns of received STF in the frequency domain when the receiver uses 20MHz channel and the transmitter uses spectrum as indicated in the graphs.**

These interval differences let us easily determine the channel width, center frequency, and number of channels. For example, comparing Figure 3(b) and (d), one can easily see the preamble pattern of one 10MHz channel transmission is visibly different from that of the two 5MHz transmissions in the same spectrum. Depending on the combination of the channels that the sender chooses, it generates 29 different preamble patterns on a 20MHz spectrum.

**ML detection algorithm:** The above observation on the preamble patterns in the frequency domain transforms the spectrum detection problem into a pattern matching problem. As different channel combinations yield different preamble patterns at the subcarrier level, the detector can identify the spectrum by determining the pattern of the transmitted preamble. We develop a Maximum Likelihood (ML) detection algorithm. It is optimal when the probabilities of all of the channel combinations are equal. Let $\mathbf{Y} \in R^{64}$ be the magnitude vector of the received preamble in the frequency domain generated by performing FFT-64 on the received STF signals, and $\mathbf{X}_i$ be one of the possible preamble magnitude patterns generated by the channel combination ($i \in \{1, ..., 29\}$). Let $P(\mathbf{X}_i \mid \mathbf{Y})$ be the likelihood function that the transmitted preamble magnitude pattern is $\mathbf{X}_i$ given the received preamble $\mathbf{Y}$. We use the ML detection to find $\mathbf{X}_i$ that maximizes the likelihood:

$$\begin{aligned}\hat{\mathbf{X}} &= \arg\max_i P(\mathbf{X}_i \mid \mathbf{Y}) \\ &= \arg\max_i \frac{P(\mathbf{Y} \mid \mathbf{X}_i)P(\mathbf{X}_i)}{P(\mathbf{Y})} \\ &= \arg\max_i P(\mathbf{Y} \mid \mathbf{X}_i).\end{aligned}$$

The second equality is according to Bayes Theorem, and the third equality is because $P(Y)$ is a constant and $P(X_i)$ is the same for all $X_i$ since we do not have a priori that a certain magnitude pattern is more likely.

Next we show the ML detection essentially finds $X_i$ that minimizes the Euclidean distance between the received signals and possible candidates across different subcarriers. Assuming Additive White Gaussian Noise (AWGN) channel and the probability distribution of all subcarriers are identical and independently distributed (i.i.d.),

$$P(\mathbf{Y} \mid \mathbf{X}_i) = \prod_{k=1}^{64} P(y^k \mid x_i^k) = \prod_{k=1}^{64} \frac{1}{\sqrt{2\pi\sigma^2}} e^{\frac{-(y^k - x_i^k)^2}{2\sigma^2}},$$

where $\sigma$ is noise variance of the channel and $x_i^k$ and $y^k$ represent the value of the $k$th element of $\mathbf{X}_i$ and $\mathbf{Y}$, respectively. As each transmitted subcarrier has either unit or zero magnitude, $x_i^k$ is either 1 or 0. The result of the above ML detection does not change over the log-likelihood function. So we have

$$\mathbf{ln}P(\mathbf{Y} \mid \mathbf{X}_i) = \mathbf{ln}\frac{64}{\sqrt{2\pi\sigma^2}} - \sum_{k=1}^{64} \frac{(y^k - x_i^k)^2}{2\sigma^2}.$$

As a result, ignoring the invariants over $i$, the ML detection finds $\mathbf{X}_i$ that minimizes $\sum_{k=1}^{64}(y^k - x_i^k)^2$, which is the Euclidean distance between $\mathbf{Y}$ and $\mathbf{X}_i$. The detection algorithm optimizes the following objective:

$$\hat{\mathbf{X}} = \arg\min_i \sum_{k=1}^{64} (y^k - x_i^k)^2.$$

**Binary detection to reduce the complexity:** Our above Euclidean distance based detection can yield high accuracy, but calculating the Euclidean distance between the received magnitude vector and every possible candidate can be computationally costly. To reduce the computational cost, we also propose a binary detection method. It first classifies $y^k$ to either 1 or 0 depending on its magnitude, and calculates $\sum_{k=1}^{64}(y^k - x_i^k)^2$. Because $x_i^k$ and $y^k$ are all binary numbers, $\mathbf{X}_i$ and $\mathbf{Y}$ can be represented as 64 bits sequences.

Then calculating $\sum_{k=1}^{64}(y^k - x_i^k)^2$ is simply counting the number of different bits between $\mathbf{X}_i$ and $\mathbf{Y}$ (*i.e.*, hamming distance). The resulting binary detection algorithm is represented as

$$\hat{\mathbf{X}} = \arg\min_i \mathbf{X}_i \oplus \mathbf{Y},$$

where $\oplus$ is bitwise XOR operation.

The complexity of the binary detection algorithm is $O(nk)$, where $n$ is the number of subcarriers and $k$ is the number of possible channel combinations. Specifically, in the proposed system design, $n$ is 64 and $k$ is 29. Due to simple XOR operation, this can be computed quickly. As shown in Section 5, the average processing time of the detection algorithm in SORA is $4\mu s$ with negligible variance. It will be much shorter if implemented in hardware chipset.

#### 3.2.4 Discussion

**Other WiFi standards:** The spectrum detection above exploits specific structure in IEEE 802.11a preamble. One might wonder if this detection is applicable to the other 802.11 wireless standards. Our detection method is applicable as long as the detection preamble has inherently similar structure to the 802.11a STF in the frequency domain. Fortunately, IEEE 802.11n and 802.11ac maintain the same design of STF, so FSD is directly applicable to them. For example, 802.11n 40MHz STF has 128 subcarriers; among them, there are 24 subcarriers with unit magnitude with 4 subcarrier intervals [20]. Similarly for 80MHz and 160MHz STF in 802.11ac [21].

Now the remaining issue is if the algorithm is scalable enough for detection on a wider spectrum. Increasing channel width increases the number of ways in which spectrum can be used, and makes detection more costly. To address the issue, we can combine coarse energy detection with fine-grained spectrum detection. In the carrier sensing process, an 802.11ac device is required to separately perform CCA for every 20MHz channel. If the signal is detected on a 20MHz channel, it further performs FSD to find the subband usage pattern. If the energy of the 20MHz channel is below CCA threshold, FSD is not performed. In the worst case, the signal spans a 160MHz channel and spectrum detection on a 160MHz channel is close to eight times as that on a 20MHz channel since the detection cost is dominated by identifying how each of the eight 20MHz channel is used. We believe the increased detection cost is acceptable considering that 802.11ac devices are inherently more powerful than 802.11a devices in order to handle up to eight times sample rate, up to 8 spatial streams, and more complex modulation and channel coding, such as 256-QAM and LDPC [21].

Once the spectrum is detected, the receiver decodes the signal on the detected spectrum using the decoding scheme as specified by the standard. Namely, FSA does not affect decoding. For example, if MIMO is used, MIMO processing is evoked during the decoding as usual.

**Detection accuracy:** Note that one may be concerned that STF is too short for us to reliably extract frequency domain signal and cause noisy results since we do not know when STF starts. Fortunately, this is not an issue since we only rely on the magnitude pattern in the preamble for detection. As long as the error in detecting starting time is within cyclic prefix (CP) (*i.e.*, a guard interval in OFDM), this error only affects phase but not magnitude and will be cancelled out during channel compensation. Therefore, we can get correct magnitude of the received STF as long as the FFT-64 window resides within 160 STF samples, and hence our detection is robust even for short STF.

**Antenna gain control (AGC):** As shown in the previous section, the transmitted STF signal varies according to the channel width. Since a receiver performs AGC using the received STF, one might wonder if it affects AGC. Since it is difficult to find the exact starting sample of STF when it is detected, the exact pattern of STF is not utilized in AGC [13, 8]. Instead existing AGC algorithms control the hardware gain parameter using the running average of the received STF magnitude. Since the average magnitude of transmitted STF remains the same across different channel widths, different STF patterns have little impact on AGC.

**Bidirectional traffic:** When there is bi-directional traffic, FSA can be applied independently in both directions. Namely, node $A$ can freely select the spectrum to transmit to node $B$ and node $B$ detects the spectrum in use based on the received preamble pattern and decodes the signals on the detected spectrum. Similarly, node $B$ freely selects the spectrum to transmit to node $A$ and node $A$ also detects the spectrum using the preamble pattern and decodes the detected signals. If one of the nodes, say node $A$ is an AP and communicates with multiple clients, the ACKs from the clients may overlap in time and the AP will detect the spectrum used by each ACK and decodes the ACKs in the order of their arrival time.

# 4. SPECTRUM ADAPTATION

## 4.1 Problem Specification

Given the capability of changing the spectrum on a per-frame basis, a natural question arises which spectrum should be assigned to a given transmission. In this paper, we consider the spectrum adaptation in an enterprise WLAN where all the APs are connected through an Ethernet and can be managed using a central controller. We focus on downlink traffic from APs to clients since downlink traffic often dominates the total traffic [16, 4].

While significant work has been done on channel assignment in WLAN, spectrum adaptation considered here differs from these existing works in the following important aspects. First, existing channel assignments assume an AP can transmit one frame at a time, whereas our flexible baseband design allows an AP to possibly transmit multiple frames simultaneously on different spectrum. Second, most channel assignment schemes (*e.g.*, [14, 17, 18, 28]) consider fixed channel width and center frequency. The flexible spectrum access enables us to dynamically change the channel width and center frequency and makes the channel assignment significantly different and have much larger search space. In particular, there can be an arbitrarily large numbers of channels in a given spectrum depending on the center frequency and channel width. Third, most existing channel assignments restrict an AP to use the same channel to communicate with all its clients for an extended duration of time. This is necessary due to significant overhead involved in changing the channels and also difficulties for the receivers to identify the spectrum used by the sender. [27] tries to alleviate the restrictions and consider flexible spectrum allocation. However, due to significant channel switching overhead (over 4ms) and the lack of per-frame spectrum detection at a receiver, its channel is adapted in a much longer time scale and it has to use multiple interfaces to hide the channel switching delay. Finally, our allocation problem differs from OFDMA scheduling (*e.g.*, [11]) in that OFDMA supports only synchronous transmissions while FSA can support asynchronous transmissions and allows a new mini-frame to start in the middle of other scheduled transmissions, which is common in asynchronous WiFi networks. Such an increased flexibility significantly increases the search space in the schedule and has the potential to yield better performance. It is feasible to use any part of the spectrum for a new transmission due to our fine-grained spectrum access and detection. Inspired by the existing works, we aim to completely remove all these restrictions and dynamically adapt the spectrum on a per-frame basis according to the instantaneous channel condition.

Our spectrum adaptation problem can be formulated as follows. Given a frame and SNR to the client across the entire spectrum, we decide which spectrum and start time should be assigned to the frame in order to optimize a given objective while ensuring interfering transmissions cannot overlap in time and spectrum. The objective we use in this paper is the finish time. In particular, we use the finish time of all transmissions as the primary objective; if this is equal, then we use the finish time of a new transmission to be scheduled as the secondary objective for tie-breaking when the primary objective is the same. Our algorithm can be easily extended to support other objectives.

## 4.2 Our Adaptation Algorithm

**Challenge:** The main challenge in the spectrum adaptation is the huge search space. Not only can a frame be placed in any part of the spectrum with different center frequency and channel width, but also a frame may not even occupy a continuous block of spectrum. This significantly increases the search space.

**Joint spectrum adaptation and scheduling:** In order to limit the search space, we use the following approach to discretize possible spectrum choices. We divide a frame into multiple mini-frames and divide the entire spectrum into multiple mini-channels. Our evaluation divides a frame with 1000-byte payload into 4 mini-frames, and uses 5MHz as the bandwidth of mini-channel. Then our goal is to determine where to place mini-frames (*i.e.*, which mini-channel and what is the starting time) to minimize finish time. A frame is allowed to occupy non-contiguous spectrum if needed.

We use the following greedy assignment with iterative improvement. For each incoming mini-frame, we first determine an initial assignment of the mini-channel and start time by going through all the mini-channels to find the one that optimizes our objective. Specifically, on each mini-channel we find the earliest start time such that the new mini-frame can transmit without interfering any existing scheduled transmissions while optimizing the finish time. We compute the finish time by measuring the SNR of the mini-channel and mapping the SNR to data rate according to the standard SNR to data rate mapping table (*e.g.*, the one in [25]). Next we go through each existing scheduled transmission to see if it is possible to swap the new transmission with one of them to further improve performance. If so, we swap with the existing transmission that gives the largest improvement. Otherwise, we stick to the initial assignment. Then we move on to the next mini-frame.

Figure 4(a) shows an example schedule, where $(i, j)$ denotes the mini-frame that is in the $i$-th frame's $j$-th chuck. This 2-D schedule exploits the fact that our baseband allows an AP to transmit multiple frames simultaneously if needed. In comparison, the existing channel assignments, including latest ones (*e.g.*, [1, 27]), assume an AP can only transmit one frame at a time, thereby limiting the spectrum efficiency. Moreover, as it shows, different mini-frames do not synchronize in time due to our flexible baseband design.

**Joint spectrum adaptation, scheduling, and AP assignment:** So far, we focus on the spectrum adaptation and scheduling, and implicitly assume that clients have already been associated with an AP. However, there is inter-dependency between the spectrum adaptation and AP association. Simply assigning to the closest AP or the AP with the highest SNR is not always the best choice (*e.g.*, such an AP may be overloaded). Therefore, we propose a simple extension to support joint AP assignment, scheduling, and spectrum adaptation, which considers a 3-D schedule: (AP, mini-channel, time) as shown in Figure 4(b). It uses the same search strategy as the above except that now it searches over the 3-D dimension: which AP, which mini-channel, and when to start in order to minimize finish time. As before, we first greedily find the earliest time to schedule the mini-frame and then use iterative improvement, which may swap the new mini-frame with one of the scheduled (but not yet transmitted) mini-frame if it improves performance.

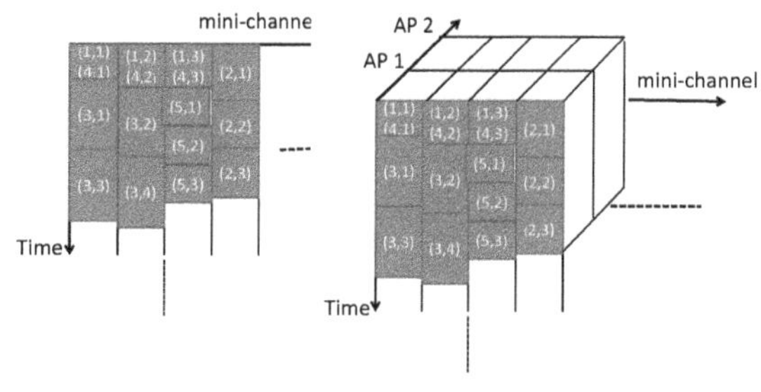


(a) 2-D schedule (b) 3-D schedule

**Figure 4: Example schedules, where $(i, j)$ denotes the mini-frame from $i$-th frame $j$-th segment.**

**Speed up:** To enhance efficiency, for each mini-frame, we consider only a few top APs and a few top mini-channels in terms of SNR under no interference as candidate APs and channels, and prune the remaining APs and mini-channels from the search. Our evaluation considers the top 25% APs and mini-channel combinations. Moreover, when considering candidates for swap, only the transmissions that interfere with the new transmission are considered since otherwise swapping with it does not affect the new transmission's schedule.

# 5. TESTBED EXPERIMENTS

We implement FSA in SORA [33] on top of its IEEE 802.11a OFDM implementation. Our implementation includes the entire baseband system design specified in Section 3 based on User-Mode Extension (UMX) and PHY API provided in SORA SDK 1.6. We use DELL XPS 850 with Intel i7 Quad-core processor and 8GB memory for testbed setup. Without FPGA-level modification, we enable sampling rate conversion, center frequency shifting, concurrent transmission of multiple frames in different subbands, fine-grained spectrum detection, and decoding a single frame from subband in real-time. However, due to the capacity limit of the general purpose processor, we cannot decode multiple frames concurrently transmitted through multiple subbands in real time on SORA, so decoding is done offline using the captured signal dump as follow. The narrowband signal generated by the SORA node is transmitted over the air, and the receiver captures it using the signal capturing tool provided by SORA SDK under various channel conditions. The captured signals are fed to the SORA receiver to evaluate the spectrum detection and frame decoding performance offline. In some experiments, we use USRP2 devices to generate narrowband interference to understand its impact.

## 5.1 Spectrum Detection

One of the key techniques in FSA is spectrum detection scheme that allows fine-grained spectrum access without coordination with the receiver. To evaluate the spectrum detection performance, we place the transmitter and the receiver in various locations and measure the detection performance in varying channel conditions from 0 to 20 dB SNR. To demonstrate the advantage of FSA detection algorithm, we compare its performance with the temporal and spectral analysis based detection method introduced in Section 3.2.2 in terms of the detection accuracy and delay.

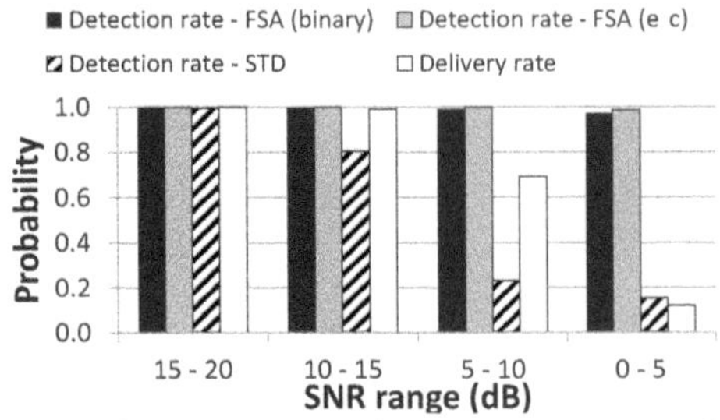


**Figure 5: Spectrum detection accuracy comparison.**

**Detection accuracy:** Figure 5 shows the detection accuracy under various SNR channels, where FSA and STD represent the proposed detection algorithm and spectral and temporal analysis based detection, respectively. We classify the measured results into 4 categories according to the SNR range, and plot the average detection probability in each range. Our testbed can run the proposed detection algorithm in real-time, but for fair comparison, we capture the received signal in the dump file and compare the detection performance using the same signal. To present the quality of the measured links, we plot the average frame delivery rate when the spectrum is known at the receiver and 6 Mbps rate Modulation and Coding Scheme (MCS) is used. Figure 5 shows that FSA achieves almost perfect detection performance. From 5 to 20 dB SNR range, FSA yields over 99% detection accuracy. In the severely degraded channel where the frame delivery rate is 10% (0 - 5 dB SNR in Figure 5), FSA still achieves 96% detection accuracy. The accuracy of FSA is comparable to that of the more computation intensive Euclidean Distance (ec) based detection, which is also our scheme and achieves accuracy of 98%. Therefore we focus on the binary detection due to its high accuracy and low computational cost in the remaining evaluation. In comparison, the detection accuracy of STD is unacceptable: when SNR is higher than 15 dB, it also shows close to 100% detection rate; but in 10 - 15 dB SNR range, its detection accuracy already drops to 80%, and when SNR is below 10 dB, its detection accuracy is only around 20%.

Why FSA and STD yield significantly different accuracy? FSA detects the spectrum using the magnitude patterns of the 64 subcarriers, which transforms the spectrum detection problem into pattern matching problem. With ML detection, it finds the pattern that gives the closest match. Assuming the binary magnitude, there are $2^{64}$ possible states of the subcarrier magnitude, but the number of possible preamble patterns is only 29, so the magnitude decision error of a few subcarriers is easily recovered in the ML detection process. The minimum hamming distance among the possible preamble patterns is 12. In coding theory, when the minimum hamming distance is $d$, the number of correctable errors is $\lfloor \frac{d-1}{2} \rfloor$ [30], which means FSA can tolerate mis-detection of 5 subcarriers magnitude. This implies that ideally our detection method is tolerable in a channel that gives 8% BER in BPSK modulation. On the other hand, the detection performance of STD relies on PSD analysis and temporal correlation check, which are sensitive to the channel noise. First of all, if PSD analysis mis-detects the allocated spectrum, there is no way to correct it. Moreover, when the estimated spectrum width is more than 10MHz, it performs temporal correlation comparison to identify the subband type, but this is unreliable in the low SNR channel.

Figure 6 evaluates the detection performance using various transmitted signal bandwidth in 0 - 20dB SNR channel. Increasing the spectrum width makes the detection more challenging because the power of STF is distributed over wider spectrum, which reduces the reliability, and a wider band also gives more possible subband

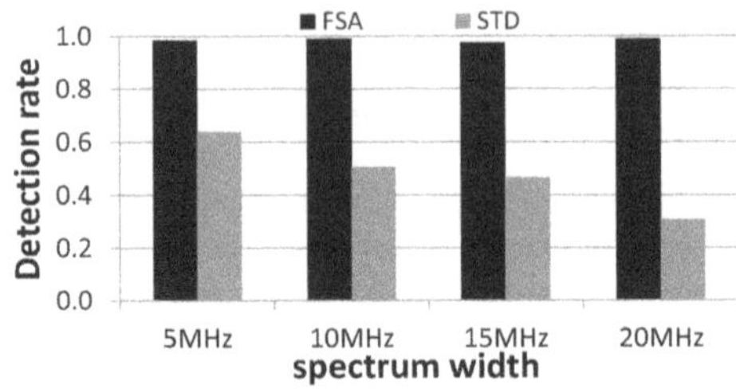


**Figure 6: Detection accuracy under different channel widths.**

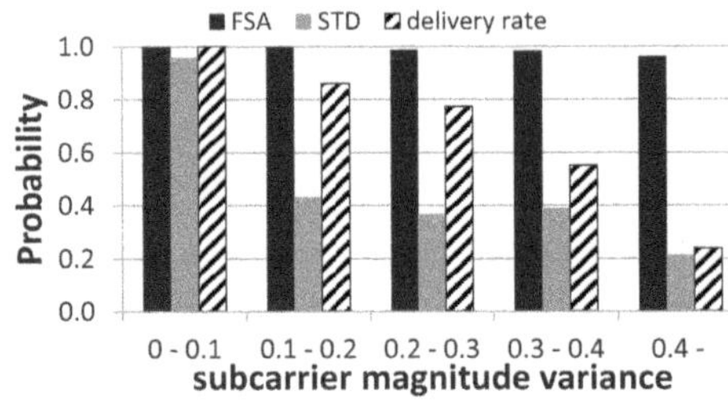


**Figure 7: Detection accuracy under different fading.**

combinations. The result in Figure 6 shows that FSA is not affected by the signal bandwidth while STD yields lower detection accuracy as the bandwidth gets larger.

Figure 7 compares the performance in different fading channel. We measure the intensity of the fading using the magnitude variance of the subcarriers in the received frame. We place the nodes at different locations so that each link experiences distinct fading intensity, and measures the detection accuracy using the received signal capture. If the channel is flat, every subcarrier has similar magnitude and the variance is small. If the channel is frequency selective (*i.e.*, severe fading), the variance becomes large. Based on our observation, a variance of less than 0.1 indicates a flat channel, and a variance of larger than 0.4 indicates severe fading. Figure 7 is measured in channel with SNR 0 to 20dB. It shows STD only works in flat fading channel and its performance significantly degrades in medium level fading channel. On the other hand, FSA achieves over 97% detection accuracy even under severe fading.

**Detection delay:** For the real-time spectrum adaptation, the detection algorithm needs to be processed within the preamble time. In 802.11a, it should be done in 8 $\mu s$ as the sampling rate and filtering parameters should be changed before LTF starts. Therefore, it is desirable that the detection algorithm is not only accurate but also computationally efficient. We compare the processing time of FSA and STD. This result is from our SORA testbed and it should be much shorter if it is implemented in the dedicated signal processing chipset, but this experiment demonstrates the relative complexity difference between FSA and STD. Figure 8 shows the cumulative distribution (CDF) of the detection delay when we measure the processing time of the detection algorithm 200 times for every

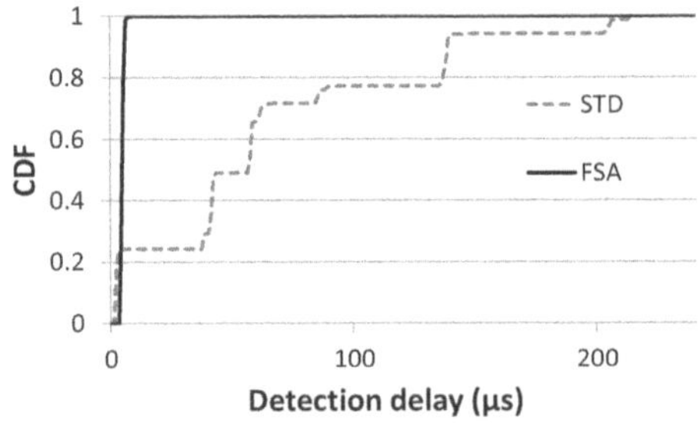


**Figure 8: CDF of spectrum detection delay.**

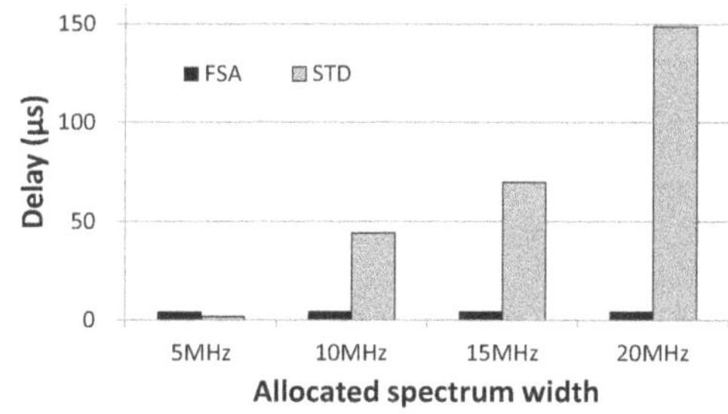


**Figure 9: Detection delay under different channel widths.**

possible subband allocation. It shows that FSA significantly outperforms STD. The median delay of FSA is 4.2 $\mu s$, which enables real-time detection even in SORA implementation. On the other hand, the median delay of STD is 56 $\mu s$. Their 95th percentile delays are 5.6 $\mu s$ and 204 $\mu s$, respectively. Moreover, the variance of FSA is only 0.44, whereas that of STD is 3218.

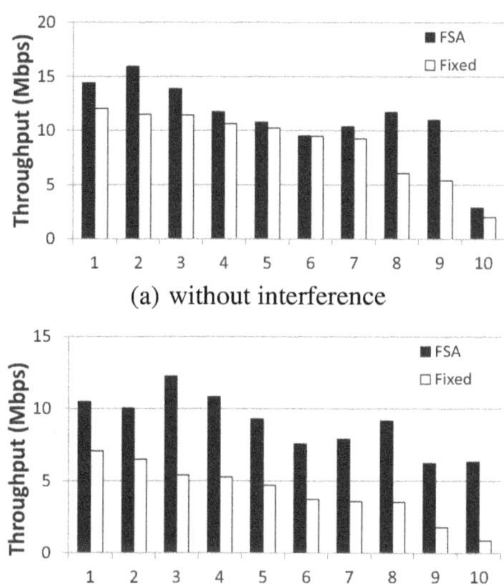


(a) without interference

(b) with interference

**Figure 10: Throughput comparison with and without narrowband interference.**

The reason for the huge detection delay variance of STD is that its processing time depends on the detected subband width as shown in Figure 9. When the detected bandwidth is 5MHz, the spectral analysis can determine the subband type without further processing and achieves detection delay of 1 $\mu s$. However, if the detected bandwidth is more than 5MHz, it performs low pass filtering, frequency shifting, and auto-correlation check to identify the subband type. When 20MHz channel width is detected, it iteratively performs filtering and frequency shifting several times to check many possibilities, which takes 149 $\mu s$ to process on average. On the other hand, FSA has almost constant computational cost regardless of the detected bandwidth, so its variance is small, which simplifies hardware implementation.

## 5.2 Spectrum Adaptation

Next we evaluate the performance gain of the fine-grained spectrum adaptation. We implement the spectrum allocation algorithm in Section 4 and compare its throughput with the fixed channel width approach. The channel bandwidth is 20MHz and the devices use flexible subband width from 5MHz to 20MHz as specified in Section 3. The AP selects the transmission rate from 6Mbps to 24Mbps based on the SNR feedback from the clients. We use 1 APs and 3 clients due to the limit of number of SORA nodes we have. When the AP allocates the spectrum and transmits the signal, the clients capture them. We evaluate the throughput by decoding them offline. We further evaluate larger scale networks using simulation in Section 6.

The testbed experiments evaluate the impact of the frequency diversity and how well FSA copes with the narrowband interference. For the latter case, we use a USRP2 device to generate 2MHz narrowband signal to interfere with some of the links in the testbed. We vary the location of the AP and clients, and report the average throughput from 10 runs with different channel conditions.

Figure 10 compares the throughput of FSA and the fixed channel width approach (fixed). The results are sorted by the throughput of the fixed channel width approach. In Figure 10(a), there is no interference and the throughput gain comes from the frequency diversity. In Figure 10(b), there is narrowband interference and the performance gain of FSA comes from both interference mitigation and frequency diversity. In the experiment without interference, FSA achieves the throughput gain of 27%. Since our allocation lets the AP use the subbands with higher SNR to communicate with each client, it improves link quality and increases the data rate. This gain increases with the number of clients or the width of spectrum [25]. But even with 3 clients and 20MHz spectrum, the gain is already significant.

When the clients are affected by the narrowband interference, the throughput gain of FSA increases to 110%. Though the interference is only 2MHz, it significantly degrades SNR for the fixed bandwidth approach. FSA avoids using the subbands with interference while taking full advantage of the subbands with high SNR.

# 6. SIMULATION

Next we use trace-driven simulation to evaluate the performance of spectrum adaptation.

## 6.1 Simulation Methodology

We compare the following spectrum assignment schemes: (i) random channel assignment with the fixed channel width (20MHz) and center frequency (RANDOM), (ii) greedy channel assignment that assigns the AP to the channel with least interference based on AP-to-AP interference again with the fixed channel width and center frequency (GREEDY), (iii) per-frame spectrum adaptation to change center frequency but fixing the channel width to 20MHz (FSA-fixed), (iv) per-frame spectrum adaptation with variable channel width where the minimum channel width is 5MHz (FSA-variable), and (v) FLUID-like scheme with a switching interval of 1 ms and 6 ms (FLUID - 1 ms/6 ms). Like FSA, FLUID also supports flexible channel widths, but an AP can transmit only one frame on any spectrum at a time, cannot split a frame across non-contiguous spectrum, and cannot change the spectrum within 6 ms to avoid the channel switching overhead. We also use 1 ms as the channel switching interval to reflect faster hardware in the future. We call the scheme FLUID-like since we did not implement the exact search heuristic described in [27] but use the same greedy search heuristic as FSA so that the performance difference between FSA and FLUID is due to the flexibility of the spectrum adaptation but not the quality of specific search algorithm, which can be applied to improve both protocols. For each spectrum assignment scheme, we run it with the following two different AP assignments: (i) assigning a client to the AP with the highest SNR (2D scheduling) and (ii) joint AP assignment (3D scheduling).

We collect the RSS traces using SORA nodes and varying the sender and receiver's locations. In this way, we measure RSS from 50 different links, each with 1000 frames. The traces report SNR

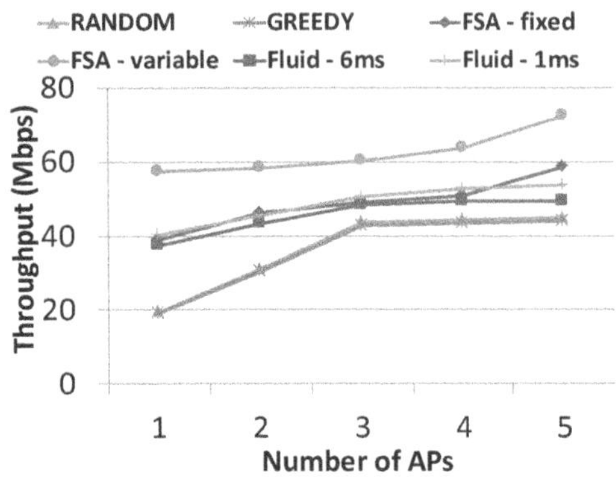


**Figure 11: Vary the number of APs using static AP assignment (30 clients and 20MHz)**

for every 5MHz channel across the entire 80MHz spectrum. We randomly map an AP-to-client link to one of the links in the traces. The SNR of the links ranges from 3dB to 20dB. We generate saturated traffic from the APs, record the finish time of different schemes, and calculate throughput as the total traffic transmitted divided by the time it takes. Transmission rate is selected as either 6Mbps, 12Mbps, or 24Mbps depending on the channel SNR.

In the simulator, each frame is divided into 4 mini-frames and a 20MHz channel is split into four 5MHz channels. In order to speed up FSA, we consider top 25% of mini-channels and APs in terms of SNR from the APs to the clients as candidate channels and APs.

## 6.2 Simulation Results

**Varying the number of APs:** Figure 11 compares different channel assignment schemes under the static AP assignment. We make several observations. First, as expected, FSA-variable > FSA-fixed ≈ FLUID > RANDOM and GREEDY. On average, FSA-variable out-performs static channel assignment (RANDOM and GREEDY) by 88% by adapting the spectrum per frame so that it can use the best spectrum for each transmission. FSA-variable out-performs FSA-fixed by 25% by leveraging fine-grained spectrum access instead of restricting to 20MHz channel. FSA-variable out-performs FLUID by 26% by supporting multiple transmissions, non-contiguous spectrum allocation, and more frequent spectrum adaptation. Second, as the number of APs increases, the throughput of all schemes improves quickly initially and then tapers off since the spectrum instead of the number of APs becomes the bottleneck when there are enough APs.

Figure 12(a) further compares different channel assignment schemes using joint AP assignment. FSA-variable > FSA-fixed > FLUID > RANDOM and GREEDY. On average, FSA-variable out-performs FSA-fixed by 47%, FLUID by 66%, and static channel assignment (RANDOM and GREEDY) by 155%. FSA-fixed out-performs FLUID since it can change center frequency more frequently whenever needed. Moreover, comparing Figure 11 and Figure 12(a), we observe that the benefit of joint AP and FSA-variable is 27% on average over its static AP assignment counterpart.

**Varying the spectrum:** Figure 12(b) compares various schemes as we vary the available spectrum from 20MHz to 80MHz. The relative ranking of various schemes stays the same. Moreover, as the spectrum becomes wider, the benefit of flexible channel adaptation increases due to more significant frequency diversity and narrowband interference in a wider spectrum. For example, FSA-variable out-performs the other schemes by 35% - 86% under one channel, and out-performs the others by 37% - 238% under four channels.

**Varying the number of clients:** Figure 12(c) compares various schemes as we vary the number of clients. As before, the flexible channel assignment with joint AP assignment performs the best. On average, FSA-variable out-performs FSA-fixed by 43%, FLUID - 6 ms by 85%, FLUID - 1 ms by 64%, and RANDOM and GREEDY by 126%. We can see that the number of clients does not significantly affect the performance in all the schemes. This is because that once the scheduling queue becomes saturated, the number of frames that can be processed within the same time is almost fixed for a given spectrum assignment scheme regardless of the number of clients.

## 6.3 Comparison with WiFi-NC

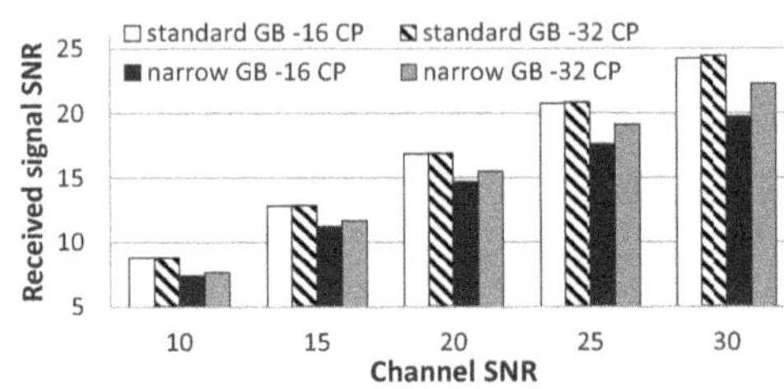


(a) RMS = $20ns$ (home environment)

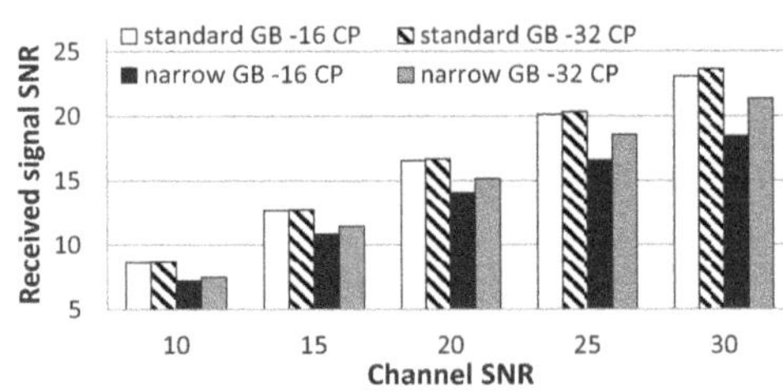


(b) RMS = $100ns$ (office environment)

**Figure 13: Received signal SNR in various channel SNR, CP size, guard band width and RMS.**

Next we use simulation to further compare FSA and WiFi-NC since the performance of WiFi-NC depends on the FFT configuration and Cyclic Prefix (CP). Similar to FSA, WiFi-NC also achieves the benefit of narrowband transmissions by dividing a channel into multiple subbands. The main difference is that WiFi-NC always uses a fixed narrow subband width while FSA uses variable widths. The downside of using variable channel width is that it requires an agreement between the sender and the receiver on the channel width. Section 5.1 shows we can accurately and efficiently detect the center frequency and channel width, so it is not a concern. A major limitation of the fixed narrow subband approach is that it needs more guard bands as the total channel width increases. To overcome it, WiFi-NC uses a very narrow guard band (*i.e.*, 100 KHz) and sharp cutoff filter. An inherent problem of the sharp cutoff filter is that it disperses symbols over time, which might increase inter symbol interference (ISI) [5, 23]. To enhance robustness against ISI, WiFi-NC uses a longer CP (*i.e.*, from 16 to 32) and increases FFT size from 64 to 128 to keep the ratio of data symbol to CP the same. However, this does not completely remove the overhead because (i) in some scenarios even CP with 32 samples is insufficient and can degrade SNR, and (ii) if we keep the CP size to 16 while increasing FFT size to 128, we can decrease the overhead ratio from $\frac{1}{4}$ to $\frac{1}{8}$.

In this section, we compare WiFi-NC and FSA using simulation. We first see the impact of the narrow guard band and sharp cutoff filtering in fading channel. Using MATLAB Signal Processing Toolbox, we design elliptic low pass filter with variable cutoff bandwidths. According to [5], we use 100KHz cutoff bandwidth filter generated by *ellipord* function in MATLAB. We model

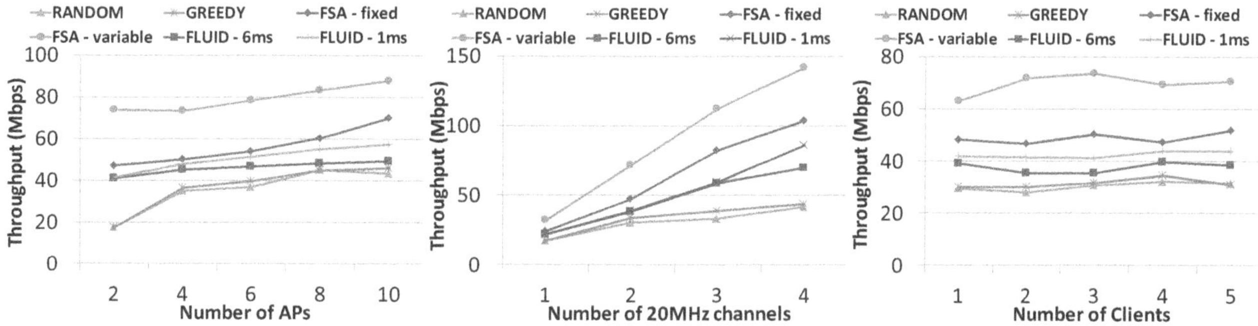

(a) Vary # APs (30 clients and 40MHz) (b) Vary spectrum (30 clients and 4 APs) (c) Vary # clients (4 APs and 40MHz)

**Figure 12: Comparison of channel assignment schemes with joint AP assignment**

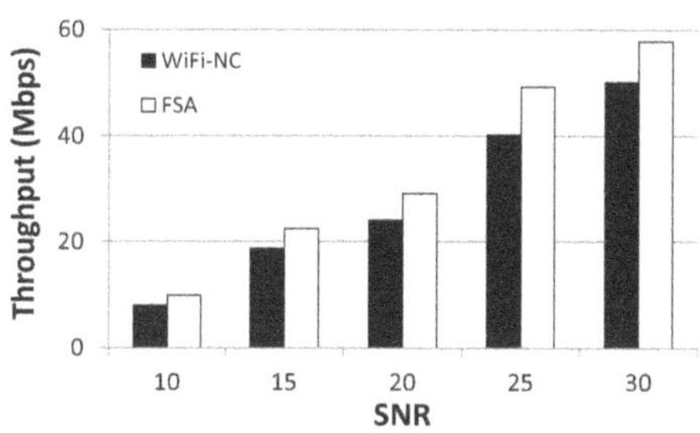

**Figure 14: Throughput comparison between WiFi-NC and FSA.**

the fading channel using Root Mean Square (RMS) of the delay spread. In home and office environment, RMSs are considered as 20 $ns$ and 100 $ns$, respectively [22]. Figure 13 compares the quality of the received signal in various guard band width, CP length, and delay spreads. We divide a 20MHz channel into four 5MHz subbands, where the guard band width of WiFi-NC is 100KHz and the guard band width of 802.11a standard 5MHz is 712KHz [19], respectively. The received signal in each subband is filtered by elliptic filter where the cutoff bandwidth is set to the guard band width. In Figure 13, the received signal SNR is measured according to the error vector magnitude (EVM) [29]. CP sizes are set to 16 and 32. The result shows that in both home environment (RMS of 20 $ns$ ) and office environment (RMS of 100 $ns$), the quality of the signal with standard guard band is not affected by the CP size. As the CP size of 16 is enough to compensate ISI even in 100 $ns$ RMS channel, increasing CP size does not improve the signal quality. On the other hand, the signal with narrow guard band experiences SNR reduction due to ISI from both multi-path fading and sharp filtering, and it is more serious when the CP size is 16. When the channel SNR is 30 dB and the RMS of the delay spread is 100 $ns$, SNR is 5dB lower than the signal with standard guard band in the same channel. A longer CP reduces the signal quality degradation, but even using a CP with 32 samples still yields 1-2 dB lower SNR than the signal with normal guard band, which suggests even a longer CP is required in this scenario.

Next we compare the throughput of WiFi-NC and FSA. We assume WiFi-NC and FSA use CP size of 32 and 16, respectively, while FFT size is fixed to 128. The channel bandwidth is assumed to be 40MHz, where FSA randomly divides it into 1 to 3 subbands. The guard band width of FSA is set to 600KHz, which is confirmed not to incur any SNR loss with CP size of 16 in 100 $ns$ RMS channel. We assume that the frame aggregation is used so that WiFi-NC and FSA have the same MAC overhead. RMS of the channel is set to 20 $ns$ to model the fading characteristic in home environment. Figure 14 shows the throughput in 5 different SNR channels. Here the transmission rate is selected as the one that gives the highest throughput in the given channel condition. The result shows FSA achieves 20% higher average throughput than WiFi-NC. The gains come from the following factors. First, as WiFi-NC uses longer CP than FSA, it has larger constant overhead (around 5% more). Second, even with a longer CP, the signal quality is still lower than FSA with a smaller CP due to sharp filtering. This yields more errors and reduces throughput.

# 7. CONCLUSION

In this paper, we develop the first per-frame spectrum adaptation approach and prototype for WiFi networks. It consists of a flexible baseband design, a fast and accurate spectrum detection method, and an effective spectrum adaptation algorithm. Through implementation and simulation, we show this fine-grained spectrum adaptation significantly out-performs the existing approaches. It can also be incrementally deployed by adding APs with this capability while supporting legacy clients and APs. As part of our future work, we plan to conduct field trials to further understand and improve its performance in different environments.

**Acknowledgements:** This work is supported in part by NSF Grants CNS-0916106 and CNS-1017549. We thank Sunghyun Choi and and anonymous reviewers for their valuable feedback.

# 8. REFERENCES

[1] P. Bahl, R. Chandra, T. Moscibroda, R. Murty, and M. Welsh. White space networking with WiFi like connectivity. In *Proc. of ACM SIGCOMM*, Aug. 2009.

[2] E. Chai, K. G. Shin, J. Lee, S.-J. Lee, and R. Etkin. Building efficient spectrum-agile devices for dummies. In *Proc. of ACM MobiCom*, 2012.

[3] R. Chandra, R. Mahajan, T. Moscibroda, R. Raghavendra, and P. Bahl. A case for adapting channel width in wireless networks. In *Proc. of ACM SIGCOMM*, Aug. 2008.

[4] Y. C. Cheng, J. Bellardo, P. Benk, A. C. Snoeren, and G. M. Voelker. Jigsaw: solving the puzzle of enterprise 802.11 analysis. In *Proc. of ACM SIGCOMM*, 2006.

[5] K. Chintalapudi, B. Radunovic, V. Balan, and M. Buettener. WiFi-NC: WiFi over narrow channels. In *Proc. of NSDI*, 2012.

[6] J. I. Choi, M. Jain, K. Srinivasan, P. Levis, and S. Katti. Achieving single channel, full duplex wireless communication. In *Proc. of ACM MOBICOM*, 2010.

[7] A. Cidon, K. Nagaraj, S. Katti, and P. Vishwanath. Flashback: Decoupled lightweight wireless control. In *Proc. of ACM SIGCOMM*, 2012.

[8] A. Fort and W. Eberle. Synchronization and AGC proposal for IEEE 802.11a burst OFDM systems. In *Proc. of IEEE GLOBECOM*, volume 3, pages 1335–1338. IEEE, 2003.

[9] J. Heiskala and J. Terry. *OFDM Wireless LANs: A Theoretical and Practical Guide*. SAMS, 2001.

[10] S. Hong, J. Mehlman, and S. Katti. Picasso: Flexible RF and spectrum slicing. In *Proc. of ACM SIGCOMM*, 2012.

[11] J. Huang, V. Subramanian, R. Berry, and R. Agrawal. In *Orthogonal Frequency Division Multiple Access Fundamentals and Applications*, chapter Scheduling and Resource Allocation in OFDMA Wireless Systems. Auerbach Publications, 2010.

[12] M. Jain, J. Choi, T. Kim, D. Bharadia, K. Srinivasan, P. Levis, S. Katti, P. Sinha, and S. Seth. Practical real-time full duplex wireless. In *Proc. of ACM MOBICOM*, 2011.

[13] V. P. G. Jimenez, M.-G. Garcia, F. G. Serrano, and A. G. Armada. Design and implementation of synchronization and AGC for OFDM-based WLAN receivers. *IEEE Transactions on Consumer Electronics*, 50(4):1016–1025, 2004.

[14] Y. Lee, K. Kim, and Y. Choi. Optimization of AP placement and channel assignment in wireless LANs. In *Proc. of IEEE LCN*, Nov. 2002.

[15] D. J. Love, R. W. H. Jr, , V. K. N. Lau, D. Gesbert, B. D. Rao, and M. Andrews. An overview of limited feedback in wireless communication systems. *IEEE JOURNAL ON SELECTED AREAS IN COMMUNICATIONS*, Oct. 2008.

[16] R. Mahajan, M. Rodrig, D. Wetherall, and J. Zahorjan. Analyzing the MAC-level behavior of wireless networks. In *Proc. of SIGCOMM*, 2006.

[17] A. Mishra, V. Brik, S. Banerjee, A. Srinivasan, and W. Arbaugh. A Client-driven Approach for Channel Management in Wireless LANs. In *Proc. of IEEE INFOCOM*, Apr. 2006.

[18] A. Mishra, V. SHrivastava, D. Agarwal, S. Banerjee, and S. Ganguly. Distributed Channel Management in Uncoordinated Wireless Environments. In *Proc. of ACM MOBICOM*, Sept. 2006.

[19] L. S. C. of the IEEE Computer Society. Wireless LAN medium access control (MAC) and physical layer (PHY) specifications. *IEEE Standard 802.11*, 2007.

[20] L. S. C. of the IEEE Computer Society. Wireless LAN medium access control (MAC) and physical layer (PHY) specifications, amendment 5: Enhancement for higher throughput. *IEEE Standard 802.11n-2009*, 2009.

[21] L. S. C. of the IEEE Computer Society. Part 11: Wireless LAN medium access control (mac) and physical layer (phy) specifications: Amendment 4: Enhancements for very high throughput for operation in bands below 6 ghz. *IEEE Standard 802.11ac-2013*, 2013.

[22] B. O'Hara and A. Petrick. *IEEE 802.11 Handbook: A Designer's Companion*. IEEE Press, 1999.

[23] A. V. Oppenheim and R. W. Schafer. *Discrete-Time Signal Processing*. Prentice Hall, 2009.

[24] Qualcomm. IEEE 802.11ac: The next evolution of Wi-Fi standards. *White paper*, May 2012.

[25] H. Rahul, F. Edalat, D. Katabi, and C. Sodini. FARA: Frequency-aware rate adaptation and MAC. In *Proc. of ACM MobiCom*, Sept. 2009.

[26] H. Rahul, N. Kushman, D. Katabi, C. Sodini, and F. Edalat. Learning to share: Narrowband-friendly wideband wireless networks. In *Proc. of ACM SIGCOMM*, Aug. 2008.

[27] S. Rayanchu, V. Shrivastava, S. Baneree, and R. Chandra. FLUID: improving throughputs in entreprise wireless LANs through flexible channelization. In *Proc. of ACM MobiCom*, Sept. 2011.

[28] E. Rozner, Y. Mehta, A. Akella, and L. Qiu. Traffic-aware channel assignment in enterprise wireless LANs. In *Proc. of ICNP*, Oct. 2007.

[29] R. A. Shafik, M. S. Rahman, and A. R. Islam. On the extended relationships among EVM, BER and SNR as performance metrics. In *Proc. of International Conference on Electrical and Computer Engineering (ICECE)*, Dec. 2006.

[30] B. Sklar. *Digital Communications: Fundamentals and Applications (2nd Edition)*. Prentice Hall, 2001.

[31] K. Tan, J. Fang, Y. Zhang, S. Chen, L. Shi, J. Zhang, and Y. Zhang. Fine grained channel access in wireless LANs. In *Proc. of ACM SIGCOMM*, Aug. 2010.

[32] K. Tan, H. Shen, J. Zhang, and Y. Zhang. Enable flexible spectrum access with spectrum virtualization. In *Proc. of Dyspan*, Sept. 2012.

[33] K. Tan, J. Zhang, J. Fang, H. Liu, Y. Ye, S. Wang, Y. Zhang, H. Wu, W. Wang, and G. M. Voelker. SORA: high performance software radio using general purpose multi-core processors. In *Proc. of NSDI*, April 2009.

[34] L. Yang, W. Hou, L. Cao, B. Zhao, and H. Zheng. Supporting demanding wireless applications with frequency-agile radios. In *Proc. of NSDI*, April 2010.

[35] X. Zhang and K. G. Shin. Adaptive subcarrier nulling: Enabling partial spectrum sharing in wireless LANs. In *Proc. of IEEE ICNP*, 2011.

# Observing Home Wireless Experience through WiFi APs

Ashish Patro, Srinivas Govindan, Suman Banerjee
Department of Computer Sciences, University of Wisconsin Madison
{patro, govindan, suman}@cs.wisc.edu

## ABSTRACT

We present a measurement study of wireless experience in a diverse set of home environments by deploying an infrastructure, we call WiSe. Our infrastructure consists of OpenWrt-based Access Points (APs) that have been given away to residents for free to be installed as their primary wireless access mechanism. These APs are configured with our specialized measurement and monitoring software that communicates with our measurement controller through an open API. We have collected wireless performance traces from 30 homes for a period in excess of 6 months. To analyze the characteristics of these home wireless environments, we have also developed a simple metric that estimates the likely TCP throughput different clients can expect based on current channel and environmental conditions. With this infrastructure, we provide multiple quantitative observations, some of which are anecdotally understood in our community. For example, while a majority of links performed well most of the time, we observed cases of poor client experience about 2.1% of the total time.

## Categories and Subject Descriptors

C.2.3 [**Network Operations**]: Network Monitoring; C.2.1 [**Network Architecture and Design**]: Wireless communication

## Keywords

Home WiFi networks; Deployment; Measurement; Interference; Characterization; WiSe

## 1. INTRODUCTION

Residential wireless networks have continued to become more complex and diverse over time. A typical home network today has different kinds of WiFi enabled devices such as laptops, handhelds (smartphones and tablets), printers, entertainment devices including game controllers (XBox, Wii), interactive television (e.g., Apple TV, Google TV), wireless HDTV transmitters [8], and wireless-based security cameras and other security systems. In addition, there is a plethora of other diverse wireless appliances in our homes — various cordless handsets, Bluetooth headsets, various types of sensors and actuators, and even microwave ovens that operate in the same unlicensed bands. Over the last decade or so, there has been a few individual studies that have tried to quantify the experience and performance of wireless networks. Most famous among them include Jigsaw for WiFi activities in a university campus [4], and a few in home environments [14, 5]. In such prior work, researchers have attempted to understand and evaluate specific wireless characteristics through passive observations by carefully deployed sniffers.


*MobiCom'13*, September 30-October 4, Miami, FL, USA.


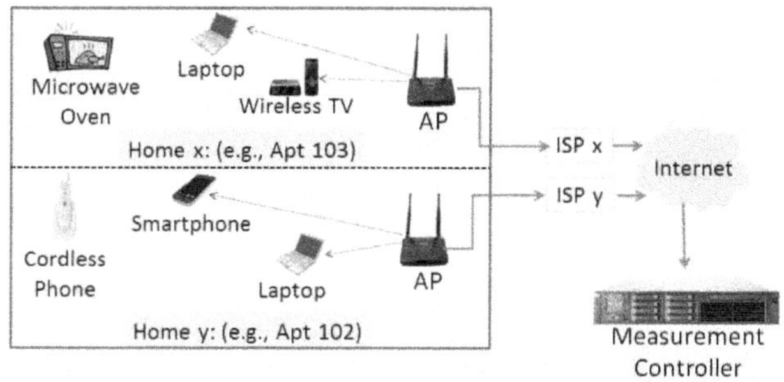


**Figure 1: WiSe measurement framework.**

Due to the above body of work and through various anecdotal experiences, our community has a broad understanding of WiFi performance in different settings. In general, we know that users are able to connect and get reasonably "good" performance most of the time, although there are instances where the networks appear to be frustratingly slow or unavailable. In this paper, we have attempted to perform a more systematic study of WiFi experiences in home environments and present a detailed characterization.

**A view through home WiFi APs:** Unlike prior wireless measurement studies that have deployed passive sniffers, in our work we have taken a significantly different approach — we have given away 30 of our own OpenWrt-based WiFi APs, enhanced with our network measurement and analysis software, to various home residents for free. We collect wireless-specific measurements *inline* using these WiFi APs as vantage points. Together, they form a unique type of wireless measurement infrastructure that we call WiSe (Wireless infrastructure for inline Sensing). Unlike out-of-band wireless sniffers that observe a subset of the traffic, *our WiFi APs can exactly observe all traffic to and from its clients,* correlate them with wireless performance, and can hence conduct types of measurements not possible otherwise (Figure 1).

The WiSe WiFi APs are equipped with dual WiFi NICs — one provides the AP functionality to clients, and the other serves some unique and additional measurement functions when necessary. Deployed over the last 6 months, the average WiFi AP observes more than 2 GB of data traffic per day.

In choosing residents to give these WiFi APs to, we attempted to maximize the mutual proximity of these APs in the bulk of our deployment. In fact, two-thirds of our APs are concentrated in two dense apartment buildings in the downtown area of an urban city.

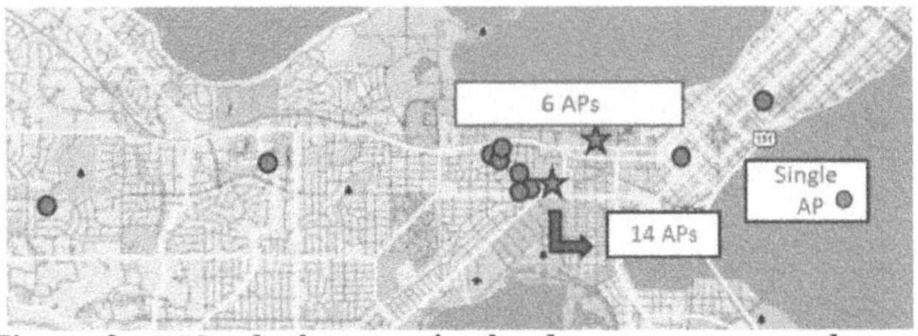


**Figure 2: WiSe deployment in the downtown area and some suburban locations in Madison, Wisconsin. The stars indicate the two apartment complexes and the other points indicate locations with deployment of single APs.**

Such a deployment allows multiple of our WiSe APs to often observe the same traffic from different vantage points enabling some specific types of wireless measurements. Some APs have been distributed to residents in homes further away from the city downtown that are much more suburban in nature. This allows for some comparisons between different types of wireless environments (Figure 2).

In a way, this measurement effort is related to the recent BISmark project [20] and the SamKnows effort [2] which focused on measurements of broadband ISP behavior across different communities. The key different between BISmark, SamKnows, and WiSe is that the first two projects primarily focus on characterization of the wired Internet path from the ISP's network into the home and not on the wireless network properties, while WiSe focuses solely on the wireless network properties and not on the rest of the ISP path. Our measurement infrastructure is quite stylized both in software and hardware to our specific wireless measurement goals.

**Objectives of measurement study and a wireless performance metric:** In this paper, our goal has been to evaluate our community's collective intuition of WiFi networks performance. In particular, we wanted to answer a number of questions such as: (i) how often do home WiFi networks provide us with good, mediocre, or bad performances? (ii) when the wireless performance is bad, what are likely causes of such experience and how persistent are these experiences? (iii) how much interference do we see in these environments from a) other WiFi sources and b) various non-WiFi sources?, and (iv) how do users configure their WiFi networks?

To evaluate and answer all of these questions, one of the first requirements is to define a wireless performance metric that can capture the overall "goodness" of the network. While a performance metric is necessary for our measurement study purposes, we believe that a good metric may have broader applicability.

In general, many different performance metrics are possible. In defining a metric, we posited four desirable properties for our purposes: (i) it should be easy to observe this metric from any passive vantage point and especially so for a WiFi AP; (ii) the computation of the metric should not require us to impose additional load on the wireless network; (iii) the metric should be relevant to only the wireless part of any user's end-to-end path and ignores potential latencies and bottlenecks that exist uplink from a WiFi AP at home; and (iv) it is application-agnostic.

As a result of this, we cannot use certain simplistic measures as our metric, e.g., end-to-end throughputs of all flows of different users — which is a function of upstream wired bottlenecks and also the individual applications that generate these flows. Instead, we propose a specific metric that can provide the following estimate — given the current wireless environmental conditions, what is the likely TCP throughput of a new flow between the AP and the different WiFi clients connected to the AP? Given that TCP elastically adjusts its throughputs to current conditions and bottlenecks, this metric would require to consider the busy time of the channel, signal quality to and from the client, consequent loss properties, and re-transmissions, and also overall airtime expended by the AP to and from its different clients. We call this metric, *WiFi-based TCP throughput* or Witt. Note that in computing our metric we do not conduct active TCP measurements, but instead estimate it *through a model based on various passive observations.* While it is possible to define many other metrics that capture the wireless experience, given the constraints of our measurement infrastructure and the goals of our study, we find this metric simple to compute, useful in understanding the wireless performance of WiFi environments, and fairly easy to explain to lay users of wireless networks. We provide a more precise definition of Witt in §3.

**Key contributions:** In this paper, we make the following main contributions.

- Present a unique measurement study of WiFi experience in home environments through the lens of WiSe APs across 30 homes (§2.3). Through our measurements we observed that while most of the WiFi clients experience moderate to good performance, poor performance plagues these environments about 2.1% of the time. The major cause of poor network performance (airtime, signal strengths) was dependent on the environment. Some APs experienced short periods of high impact interference (81% degradation) from external sources (e.g., microwaves). Also, majority of APs at homes tend to have static channel configurations over time, indicating that these APs do not adapt to interference or contention experienced by APs due to external sources.
- Describe the unique measurement and monitoring infrastructure deployed for this purpose that is being continually enhanced in scope and volume. The WiFi APs as part of this infrastructure support an open API through which wireless performance properties (WiFi and non-WiFi) are gathered and analyzed.
- Define a simple wireless performance metric, called Witt, that can be used to get a quick and easy measure of the wireless experience of a WiFi AP and its clients (§3).

## 2. WiSe INFRASTRUCTURE AND MEASUREMENT FRAMEWORK

Passive measurements of wireless systems, usually through carefully placed sniffers [4, 12] have been popular mechanisms to understand various properties of these systems. Our proposed approach in collecting measurements and understanding WiFi performance is passive as well. Unlike such prior wireless measurement efforts, our work (inspired in part by the BISMark project) places specialized measurement capabilities embedded into regular WiFi APs, and observes various wireless properties inline. This approach has various unique advantages as described next

**Inlined measurements from home WiFi APs:**. Measurement capability installed in WiFi APs provide a unique vantage point. This is a useful approach for collecting wireless measurements and understanding wireless properties for the following reasons. First, our infrastructure is able to observe all traffic to and from its clients without missing any data, unlike external passive sniffers. Second, APs can sometimes be re-configured by users to operate on different channels or with different transmit power levels. Since our measurement infrastructure sits inside these APs, we are both aware of these changes and can ensure that such changes do not affect our measurement process. Third, we can use different built-in functionalities in the APs to capture various types of information, e.g., CRC errors, CCA threshold settings, busy time of channel as reported by the AP's WiFi NICs, etc. The availability of this information directly from the AP itself proves to be particularly useful.

Perhaps, the most important benefit on inlined measurements is that we can provide better incentives to residents to deploy the

| Type | Description |
|---|---|
| AP statistics | Record aggregate statistics local to the AP such as airtime utilization, overheard beacons from external APs, total received packets, packet counts with CRC errors. |
| Client statistics | Record aggregate downlink statistics per associated client (e.g., Total packets sent, received, retried, client's signal strength at AP). |
| Non-WiFi devices | Report non-WiFi devices detected by the AP (type, start time, duration, RSSI), e.g., using Airshark [16]. |
| Per-packet summaries | Record packet summaries for all links overheard by the AP. Each packet summary contains: received timestamp, packet length, PHY rates, retry bit and RSSI (average overhead < 1%). |
| Flow statistics | Report aggregate flow level statistics (e.g., sent, recv, packet retries per domain). |

**Table 1: The data gathered by the WiSe framework through an open API about the wireless network by using each connected WiSe AP as a vantage point.**

measurement infrastructure. In our deployment so far, we have given away the APs for free to residents. The requirement to receive our AP is for the residents to deploy them *as their primary WiFi AP in their apartments and homes,* and a willingness to participate in our measurement framework. If for some reason, this AP has any problems, the users are incentivized to fix them (and inform us if necessary) almost immediately. In our prior experience, users are not always as meticulous in ensuring that passive sniffers stay online and functional for long running measurements.

**User privacy in our measurement study:** An infrastructure can potentially be highly intrusive to users. However, in this work, we have only needed to observe IEEE 802.11 frame header information for the most part, that do not carry any private information of users. As described to our Institutional Review Board, we have informed our participating users (and in some cases the relevant ISPs) that we do not capture user identifiable information in the study. In a few aspects when information such as flow types are analyzed (e.g., Netflix video), we have taken care to anonymize user and home identities (using an identity decoupling technique) in the measurements that this information cannot be mapped back to any individual user or home.

## 2.1 Infrastructure description

**WiSe Access Points:** For our study, we deployed OpenWrt [1] based APs using the ALIX 2d2 platform [6] (having a 500 MHz AMD Geocode CPU, 256 DDR RAM and slots for flash disk, Mini PCI and USB accessories). Each AP is equipped with two Atheros 9220 Mini-PCI WiFi NICs. The "primary" WiFi NIC is setup in the Access Point mode to allow users to connect their WiFi based devices to the AP. The "secondary" wireless NIC is used as back-up wireless NIC to perform various wireless measurements for the purpose of this study. The nodes were set to use a default transmit power of 17 dBm (50 mW). We also benchmarked our routers against commercial routers with similar configurations and achieved comparable performance under different workloads.

**Measurement controller:** A measurement controlling server collects periodic wireless measurements from the APs as well remotely configures the WiSe APs. Currently, our controller runs on a standard Linux server (3.00 GHz dual core CPU, 4 GB DRAM) with a public hostname. In our current setup, the controller is deployed in our lab's server cluster with public hostname/IP.

## 2.2 Measurements and Management API

In order for us to perform and collect measurements from WiSe APs, we have defined and implemented an open API that expose a set of simple capabilities. Our measurement controller uses this open API to specify all types of measurements necessary and also to remotely manage and configure the various APs. Table 1 provides a high level description of this open API. Over the last 6 months, we have incrementally added all of these capabilities into the WiSe APs to collect various statistics. We now briefly describe these different measurements performed over the course of this study.

**Basic Statistics.** Each WiSe AP periodically collects aggregate statistics (in 10 second intervals) such as overheard WiFi packets and beacons from neighboring APs present in the vicinity. These aggregate statistics include the total number of CRC errors for received packets and the per link packet transmission summaries for the overhead links. Local packet statistics collected the WiSe APs include aggregate statistics per local WiFi link (using kernel statistics), the nature of wired traffic by finding the TLDs (Top Level Domains) corresponding to the flows.

**Airtime utilization.** To measure the airtime utilization, we use the aggregate "busy time" statistics maintained by the Atheros NICs that we used with our APs. Whenever the energy level is detected to be higher than the CCA (Clear Channel Assessment) threshold (due to WiFi or non-WiFi sources), the channel is marked as busy, otherwise its marked as free. The driver records cumulative statistics about the total channel busy period observed over a period of time. In addition, the driver also records airtime utilization statistics due to local packet transmissions as well as utilization due to overheard WiFi packets only.

**Per-packet Summaries.** To perform WiFi interference analysis (§5.2), each WiSe AP records a short 10 byte per-packet summary for the WiFi data packet headers of its own links as well as the overheard data packets from other WiFi links on the same channel. Each packet's summary (grouped by link) contains the MAC timestamp (from driver) for the packet's transmission start time (32-bit timestamp with microsecond granularity), packet length, PHY rate, retry bit and RSSI. These statistics are periodically reported back to the controller to provide fine grained information about the WiFi activity on the channel. Across our deployment, the average WiFi packet size was between 900 bytes to 1000 bytes. So, it translates to only 1% average overhead per data packet.

**Non-WiFi device detection:** In our prior work, we designed a tool called Airshark [16] which demonstrates the feasibility of Atheros 9280-based WiFi NICs to detect non-WiFi devices (e.g., microwave oven, cordless phones) by using commodity WiFi NICs available in the market (e.g., Atheros 9280 chipsets). Airshark uses subcarrier-level energy samples received from the WiFi NIC as input to algorithms to detect the presence of different types of non-WiFi devices. For our work, we ported Airshark to run on our WiSe Access Points to detect the presence of non-WiFi devices in residential deployments. Since Airshark requires the WiFi NIC to be placed in monitor mode, we implement this functionality in the secondary WiFi NIC of the AP and have it scan all WiFi channels periodically. We also use the information to study the impact of non-WiFi interference in our deployments.

**Remote configuration of WiSe APs.** Our measurement controller can also allow automated management and remote configuration

| Location (AP IDs) | Count | Deployed Since |
|---|---|---|
| Bldg 1 (APs 1 - 14) | 14 | Sep 2012 |
| Bldg 2 (APs 25 - 30) | 6 | Dec 2012 |
| Others (APs 15 - 24) | 10 | Oct 2012 |

**Table 2: Summary of the deployment of WiSe Access Points**

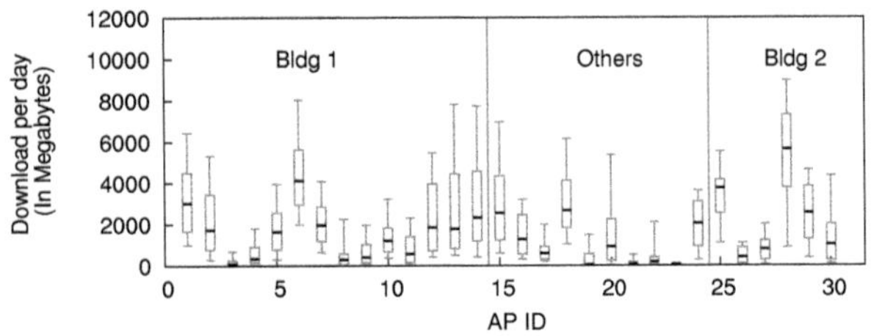


**Figure 3: Distribution of the daily data download over the WiFi network per WiSe AP (Sep 1, 2012 - Jan 31, 2013). 10th, 25th, 50th, 75th and 90th percentiles are shown in this figure.**

of the WiSe APs. The configuration capability includes picking channels of operation, choice of transmit power, and remote install of new software components if needed. Configurations are typically left to residents (using a local configuration utility), but this capability also allows us to remotely make any modifications when necessary (or requested by the residents). Configuration changes are installed only when the AP has no clients associated to it. This ensures that users are not affected by these choices.

## 2.3 Deployment

To understand the wireless characteristics in real home environments, we distributed our Access Points to volunteers who used them as the primary wireless APs inside their homes (Table 2) to connect all their WiFi devices. During this period, all APs were configured to use a randomly selected channel on different days to capture the impact of different channels on our APs. Channel changes were done sometime late at night when the APs had no associated clients. We now discuss the details of our deployment.

**Multiple APs within two residential apartments.** We collaborated with the property managers of two apartment buildings (Bldg 1 and Bldg 2) in the downtown area of our city to sign up volunteers, who wanted to be a part of our study in exchange for getting free wireless APs. Both these apartments were multi-storied with many 1-2 bedroom apartment units on each floor. In the case of Bldg 1, we focused our deployment on a specific portion of the building (5 floors) having 12 units per floor. We have currently given away 14 APs to Bldg 1 residents such that each of these floors have multiple APs (usually between 2 and 4). Bldg 2 is a 10-story building with dormitory style housing (1-2 bedrooms per apartment unit) in which the property manager provides its own wireless service to residents by deploying its own off-the-shelf APs. Hence, working with the property manager and the local ISP, in this building we deployed 6 APs on 2 consecutive floors (3 per floor) in the designated areas, that replaced their existing APs. We were told that these building APs were still the primary form of Internet access in this residential building. Thus, the two buildings had slightly different approaches to wireless AP deployment and provided us with some diversity in our measurements.

**Across different types of user homes.** We also distributed our APs to volunteers and colleagues staying at different low to high density residential units spread across different locations in our city (Others). This was done to capture the wireless network properties across different types of home environments.

| Causes | Indicator |
|---|---|
| Non-WiFi devices, Rate Anomaly, Heavy external traffic | Airtime utilization |
| WiFi and non-WiFi Interference, AP and Client Transmit Power + Signal Environmental/Location effects | Losses + Data Rates |
| Local WiFi clients sharing an AP | Local contention |

**Table 3: The list of potential factors can cause the degradation of a WiFi link's performance and potential indicators of these issues.**

**Volume of observed traffic.** Over the course of our deployment, we observed wide-ranging daily WiFi usage characteristics across our users (Figure 3). The median WiFi usage across users varied between a low 30 MB per day to over 5.6 GB per day. The 90th percentile usage for some users was as high as 8-9 GB per day. The usage of these wireless networks can be driven by a number of factors such as the kind of wireless devices used, wired access link capacity, the nature of the traffic/service used and user behavior.

# 3. QUANTIFYING WIRELESS EXPERIENCE THROUGH A METRIC

In order to analyze and understand the large volume of wireless performance data that we have observed, we wanted to categorize them through the use of a metric. In defining this metric, we set out some modest goals as outlined in Section 1 with our intent being two-fold: (a) to quickly identify the good and bad performances of our network, and (b) to be able to explain to residents or ISP personnel, how often there are performance problems of some type.

As discussed, there can be many different ways to approximate the "goodness" of a wireless network. In this paper, we wanted to pick something that is passively observable in real-time, captures the wireless experience alone, and is application-agnostic. We call our defined metric, Witt, and explain its construction next.

## 3.1 WiFi-based TCP Throughput metric

The idea of our proposed metric is fairly simple — it measures the *likely* TCP throughput between a client device and its AP (or a server located on the same uncongested LAN as the AP), given the current wireless conditions that exist. The metric is clearly, a property of the client and AP combined and the protocol used (802.11g vs. 802.11n). In this paper, we also consider the average value of the metric for the entire AP as a single aggregate. In such cases, we take the average of Witt for all its *active* clients. An active client (for this paper) is defined as one which has sent at least a minimum level of traffic in recent time window. We use a threshold of at least 500 packets in the last 10 second window — we want to bias the metric towards client devices that are imposing a higher load at the current time, than the ones that are less active.

Given that TCP-based flows are a dominant fraction of Internet traffic, this metric likely captures most of the user's experience when the wireless link is the bottleneck (short of analyzing performance on an application-by-application basis). We believe that such a metric would actually capture a lot of wireless properties on the network. Factors that imply poor wireless conditions, e.g., low signal strength, high degree of interference from various sources leading to losses, increased latency on the WiFi path due to reduced PHY rates or multiple re-transmission attempts, high airtime utilization leading to a reduced ability to send traffic, all will reduce the likely TCP throughput estimate, and vice versa. Thus, we focus on estimated TCP throughput as a direct measure of the link's performance.

| Feature | Correlation Coefficient |
|---|---|
| Airtime | 0.321 |
| CRC errors | 0.345 |
| Local contention | 0.463 |
| Signal strength | 0.536 |
| Effective rate | **0.882** |
| Effective rate + Airtime | 0.915 |
| Preferred "Link exp" model (Eqn. 2) | **0.958** |

**Table 4: Correlation of metrics with the observed TCP throughput (802.11g). The best individual and overall metrics are highlighted.**

| | Coefficients ($\beta_0, \beta_1$) | 95% Confidence interval for $\beta_1$ |
|---|---|---|
| 802.11g | (0.167, 0.422) | (0.403, 0.441) |
| 802.11n | (-0.493, 0.733) | (0.720, 0.746) |

**Table 5: Parameters of the linear model for predicting Witt.**

**Causes and indicators related to wireless performance.** Table 3 presents a short summary of such causes for poor performance experience by wireless links. The table also shows that the impact of multiple such causes can be captured by using a set of key indicators observed locally by the APs.

For example, the impact of non-WiFi activity as well as presence of WiFi traffic using low PHY rates (rate anomaly) can be observed by APs through an increase in *airtime utilization*, i.e., the fraction of airtime occupied by only external WiFi and non-WiFi transmissions . Similarly, an increase in packet losses for a link indicates the presence of factors such as WiFi or non-WiFi interference at the receiver, poor signal quality at the client, location dependent performance problems etc. High local contention at an AP caused by the presence of multiple clients with high traffic demand can reduce the available throughput capacity per client. In the next section, we use these indicators to build the Witt metric.

## 3.2 How to measure Witt?

A key objective of our metric is that it should be easy to obtain through passive observations at the AP and should not impose additional traffic. Hence, we built a simple model of Witt based on likely factors that will impact the metric. To do this, we first collected targeted ground truth data, built and tested our model of separate parts of the data, and then used it for analyzing wireless network performance. We first describe our ground truth measurements and then our model, leading to the metric.

**Ground truth measurements.** To collect ground-truth measurements of WiFi-based TCP throughput under different conditions, we placed 4 of our own clients (laptops) at 8 different deployment locations within the apartment buildings (excluding lab experiments). These laptops co-existed with the actual users of the WiSe APs and performed TCP downlink throughput runs (using iperf between APs and clients) that lasted 20 seconds each. This setup allowed to us create a scenario with the WiFi link being the bottleneck.

In the case of the actual home deployments, the clients ran throughput measurements in intervals of 5 to 10 minutes over the course of a week through which we collected hundreds of these measurements. Further, these clients connected to different APs within the apartment buildings to emulate different types of link conditions. These experiments were automatically conducted at different times of the day and hence, covered a diverse set of link characteristics, channel and operating conditions. Table 6 shows the distribution of different parameter values from our ground truth measurements.

**Creating the Witt metric.** To understand the impact of different factors on the observed throughput, we correlated the TCP throughputs from our clients with various wireless statistics recorded by the WiSe APs in 10 seconds intervals (Table 1). The following are some of the example statistical features that we tested to predict Witt: (i) airtime utilization, (ii) CRC error rate, (iii) client signal strength, (iv) local contention, and (v) effective rate — we define the last two precisely next.

| Parameter | Airtime | CRC errors | MAC retries | Signal (at AP) |
|---|---|---|---|---|
| Minimum | 17.6% | 1.2% | 6.2% | -71 dBm |
| 10th percentile | 20.5% | 6.4% | 13.3% | -70 dBm |
| 50th percentile | 38.3% | 17.2% | 24.9% | -61 dBm |
| 90th percentile | 47.5% | 41.6% | 56.7% | -52 dBm |
| Maximum | 72.5% | 98.8% | 86.4% | -49 dBm |

**Table 6: Parameter value ranges in our ground truth measurements.**

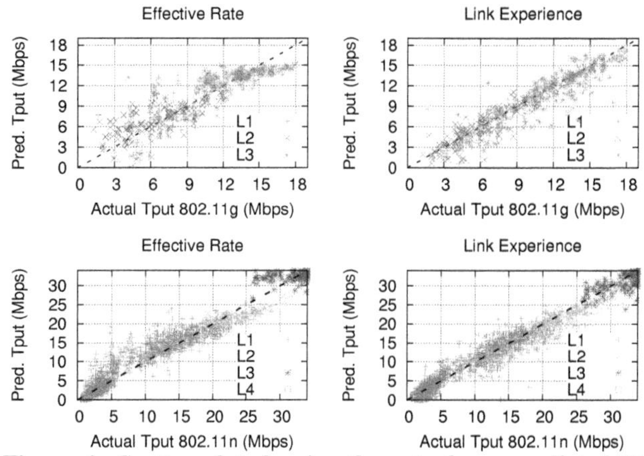


**Figure 4: Scatter plot showing the actual vs. predicted TCP throughput values for the 802.11g (top) and 802.11n (bottom) ground truth experiments by using "Effective Rate" and "Link Experience". Points near the "x=y" line indicate instances with accurate prediction of TCP throughput. Each set of points corresponds to a different WiFi link.**

- *Local contention (c):* the relative amount of other client traffic transiting through this AP as a fraction of total traffic passing through this AP. It captures the fraction of time the AP spends on transmitting (and receiving) traffic of its other clients, and hence, reduces the ability of this client to receive (and send) traffic.
- *Effective rate (r):* captures the net effect of packet losses and choice of PHY rate used on an AP-client link. It uses aggregate kernel statistics about the number of successful ($s_i$) and total packet ($p_i$) transmissions at each PHY rate ($r_1, ..., r_n$ ) used by an AP-client pair. It is defined as:

$$r = \frac{1}{\sum_i p_i} \sum_i s_i \cdot r_i, \ \ 1 \le i \le n \tag{1}$$

$$\text{link\_exp} = (1-a) * (1-c) * r, \ \ 0 \le a \le 1, \ \ 0 \le c \le 1 \tag{2}$$

Table 4 shows the correlation between these features available at the AP (individually and also in various combinations) and the observed TCP throughput from our ground truth measurements. Among all possible combinations tested (not all are shown in Table 4), the best combination of features that has the highest correlation is given by Equation 2. We call it the "link experience" model — which depends on a combination of airtime utilization from external sources ($a$), local contention ($c$), and effective rate ($r$). Together this model intuitively captures various aspects that govern the experience likely to be expected for a wireless link. Note that all these features

| Witt | >=16 Mbps | 8 - 16 Mbps | 4 - 8 Mbps | 1 - 4 Mbps | <1 Mbps |
|---|---|---|---|---|---|
| **Rating** | (V. Good) | (Good) | (Moderate) | (Poor) | (V. Poor) |

**Table 7: Using Witt to rate link quality.**

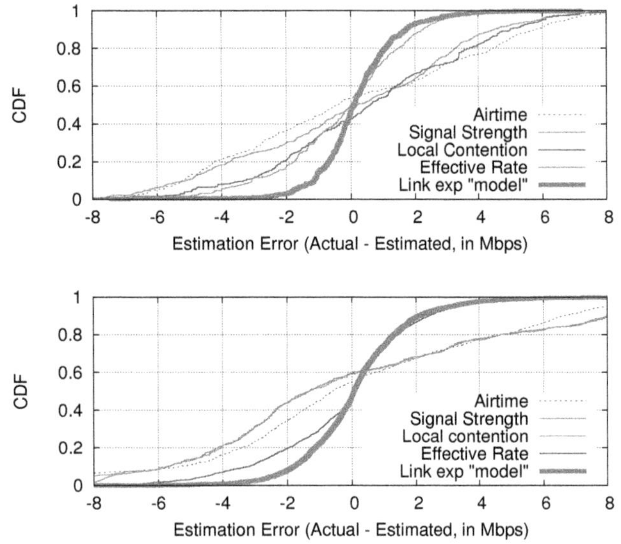


**Figure 5: CDF of errors between the actual and predicted TCP throughput values obtained by using different metrics for 802.11g (top) and 802.11n (bottom).**

are based on aggregate statistic per link (10 second intervals in our current system) and can be easily obtained using kernel statistics reported by wireless drivers.

Finally, to map "link experience" to Witt, we create a simple linear model between the two (Equation 3). We tested the fidelity of Witt by dividing our ground truth data into training and testing data sets, each corresponding to different days in our entire dataset. The parameters for our linear model as well as the error estimates for the slope, $\beta_1$ obtained using the training data, is indicated in Table 5. The small range of the the 95% confidence interval shows that the linear model is a reasonable estimate for predicting the throughput.

$$Witt = \beta_1 * \text{link\_exp} + \beta_0 \qquad (3)$$

**A subjective rating.** Based on the Witt value, we also use a subjective rating to classify links and APs into a range from *Very Good* to *Very Poor* based on the range of throughput observed (Table 7). Given that the highest Witt values estimated in our infrastructure approached 19 Mbps for 802.11g networks and 34 Mbps in 802.11n networks under best conditions, anything very low (1-4 Mbps) or lower was deemed poor or very poor. Further, our rating moved from across categories mostly with doubling of Witt value to indicate the ability of the APs to support higher TCP throughput.

## 3.3 Benchmarking the Witt metric

To evaluate the performance of the Witt metric, we present a couple of benchmarks in this section to compare the performance of the "link experience" model with other alternatives.

**Effective Rate vs. Link Experience.** As discussed earlier, effective rate exhibited the highest correlation amongst the individual features in estimating the TCP throughput. We used our ground truth TCP throughput measurements and compared them with the predicted TCP throughput values using the linear regression model (Equation 3) for effective rate and the link experience model. Figure 4

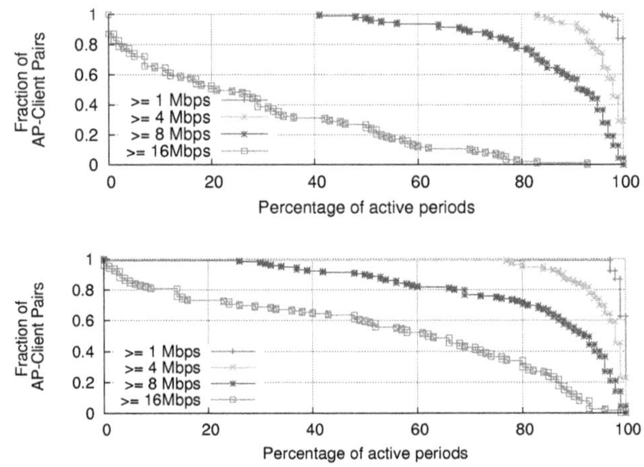


**Figure 6: Distribution of Witt across AP-client pairs using 802.11g (top) and 802.11n (bottom) in our deployment that were active for at least 20 days.**

compares the actual and predicted TCP throughputs for a few representative WiFi links from our ground truth experiments. It shows that the link experience model resulted in a better fit compared to effective rate. Only using effective rate as a feature can result in an overestimation of the link's TCP throughput (e.g., in the presence of high channel utilization) which leads to higher prediction errors. The link experience model also accounts for the potential reduction in TCP throughput due to factors such as high airtime and/or local contention which results in a better prediction.

**CDF of prediction errors using different features.** Figure 5 shows the CDF of the errors of our proposed link experience model to create the Witt metric in estimating the WiFi TCP throughput and compares that to the other alternatives. The figure shows that our proposed formulation performs effectively and better than the baseline metrics with an estimation error under 1.5 Mbps and 2 Mbps for more than 80% of 802.11g and 802.11n instances respectively. In summary, Witt provides a quick estimate of likely TCP throughput that an average WiFi link can achieve based on observed traffic characteristics at the AP and without requiring any active measurements.

# 4. USING Witt TO CLASSIFY WIRELESS EXPERIENCE IN THE WILD

The Witt metric allows us to classify links into different categories based on their performance from the large volume of data collected through our measurements (over 100 GB). In this section, we analyze on the impact of various factors (local and external) that affected the performance of WiSe APs. To study periods with WiFi activity at the APs, we focus on the periods when a WiSe AP has at least one *active* client (§3.3).

***How did the link performance vary across APs over time?***

During the course of our study, a diverse set of clients associated with the WiSe APs (e.g., laptops, handhelds, entertainment devices etc.). We measured their Witt values (§3) during active periods grouped their results based on their Witt values. Figure 6 shows the distribution of the performance experienced by AP-client pairs who were active for at least 20 days in our deployment. While a majority of our deployment consisted of 802.11g based WiSe APs, others used 802.11n based APs. For the different Witt threshold values used to characterize link performance in Table 7. For example, a line corresponding to >=16 Mbps shows the fraction of these links

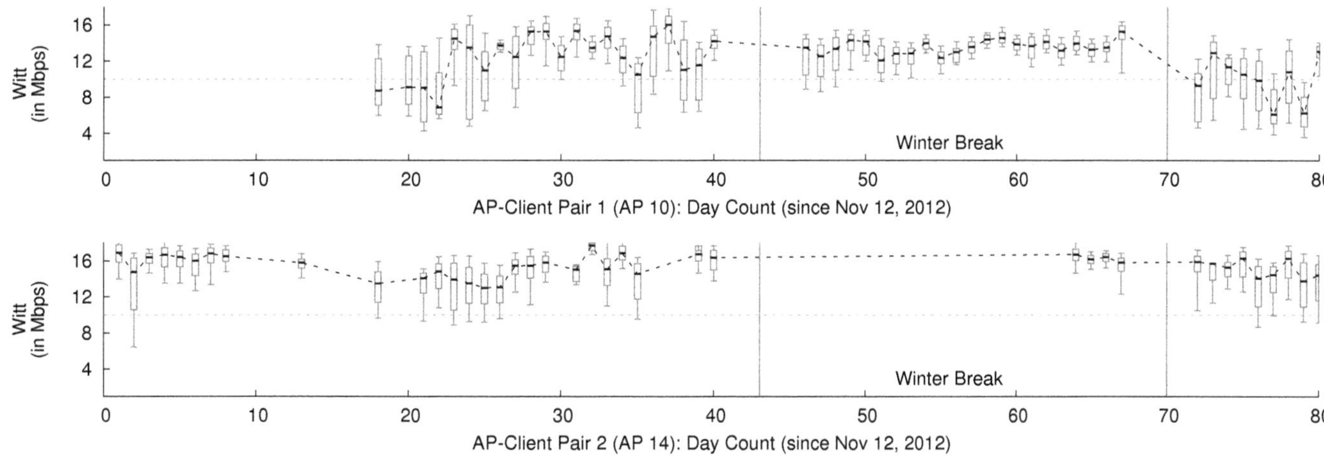


**Figure 8: Distribution of Witt for 2 different AP-client pairs in our deployment from 12 Nov 2012 to Jan 31, 2013 and shows their variation in performance over the span of this period. 10th, 25th, 50th, 75th and 90th percentiles are shown in this figure.**

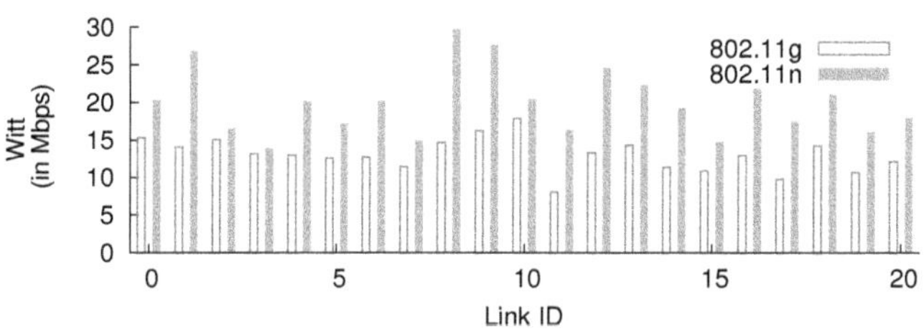


**Figure 7: Comparison of average Witt for AP - client pairs over 802.11g and 802.11n (3 days each).**

(an AP-client pair) whose Witt value was above 16 Mbps for a given percentage of their active periods.

The graph shows that a majority of links performed well for most of the time. For example, around 80% AP-client pairs experienced Witt >= 8 Mbps during more than 80% of their active periods. But, there were occasional periods for many AP-client pairs where the link performance was "Poor" (< 4 Mbps). About 8 % of these pairs experienced Poor performance (<4 Mbps) during more than 10% of their active periods, indicating some periods of poor performance which may be observed by users. In the later sections, we discuss the causes of poor performance across our different deployments.

**802.11g vs. 802.11n.** To study the performance gains of using 802.11n vs. 802.11g for a given link, we configured the 802.11n based APs to use 802.11g for a few days. Figure 7 compares the average Witt values on 802.11g vs. 802.11n for clients that support both protocols. The Witt values for most AP-client pairs increased between 12% to 100% due to usage of higher PHY rates (e.g., 65 Mbps) and use of 802.11n specific MAC layer optimizations such as frame aggregation. Interestingly, some clients experienced similar performance on both protocols (e.g., AP-Client pairs 2 and 3), indicating that using 802.11n did not ensure higher throughput for all clients. This can happen due to packet losses based on the link quality or the prevalence of interference from co-existing 802.11b/g WiFi transmitters on the same channel [19].

**Causes for "Poor" wireless experience.** During the course of 80 days from November 12, 2012 to January 31, 2013, we detected a *total of 186 and 2031 minutes* of the "Very Poor" and "Poor" instances respectively, across all 30 WiSe APs (average of 2.3 and 25 minutes,

| Indicators | | | | Bldg 1 | | Bldg 2 | |
|---|---|---|---|---|---|---|---|
| $A\uparrow$ | $S\downarrow$ | $L\uparrow$ | $R\downarrow$ | V. Poor | Poor | V. Poor | Poor |
| ✓ | × | × | × | 0% | 18.4% | 0% | 1% |
| × | × | ✓ | × | 24.2% | **49.5%** | 25.2% | **78.1%** |
| ✓ | × | ✓ | × | **61.8%** | 26.7% | 2.1% | 1.4% |
| × | ✓ | ✓ | × | 2.3% | 1.1% | 20% | 15.8% |
| × | ✓ | ✓ | ✓ | 9.4% | 0% | **51.6%** | 3.4% |
| Others | | | | 2.3% | 4.3% | 1.1% | 1.3% |

**Table 8: Distribution of causes responsible for "Poor" and "Very Poor" periods in Bldg 1 and Bldg 2. Each "cause" is composed of 1 or more of following indicators and corresponding threshold values: High Airtime ($A\uparrow, > 60\%$), High MAC Loss Rates ($L\uparrow, > 50\%$), Low signal strengths ($S\downarrow, < -70dBm$) and Low PHY rates ($R\downarrow, <= 12Mbps$). Others correspond to remaining combination of factors such as high contention, signal strengths etc.**

respectively per day across all APs). Thus, the "Very Poor" periods are rare but the "Poor" periods can occur intermittently depending on the link and the location. Overall, these cases accounted *for 2.1%* of the active periods during the 80 days.

In section 2.3, we had discussed that our deployments consisted of two apartments with multiple WiSe APs deployed within the same building. We aggregated the instances of poor wireless performance across WiSe APs in each of these apartments (Bldg 1 and Bldg 2). Table 8 breaks down the periods of poor wireless performance in our two apartment deployments to understand the causes of poor wireless performance at these APs. Each row in Table 8 is a combination of indicators of poor performance: high airtime (>60%) [9], high wireless MAC layer packet losses (>50%) indicating the fraction of wireless transmissions that were retried, low signal strengths (<-70dBm) and low PHY rates (<= 12Mbps). We use the signal strengths from clients observed at the APs as estimate of link quality at clients since we do not have access to the clients.

The table shows that the presence of both high airtime and wireless losses ($A\uparrow + L\uparrow$) were the main cause (61.8%) of "Very Poor" performance in Bldg 1. This can happen due to the network congestion at the WiSe APs and clients leading to high packet losses. In Bldg 2, the major cause of "Very Poor" performance (51.6%) was poor signal strengths (< -70dBm) which lead to high packet losses as well as usage of low PHY rates by the rate adaptation algorithm ($S\downarrow + L\uparrow + R\downarrow$). The impact of other factors ("Others"), such as period of high local contention (>0.5) from other clients associated to an AP was quite low at both locations ( <= 4.3%). The prevalence of low local contention at the wireless hop is due to the fact that it was not common for multiple clients associated to the same AP to generate high traffic demand during the same time interval (10 second intervals). In some cases where there were multiple *active clients* at the same AP, bottlenecks on the wired link or low traffic demand led to lower contention on wireless hop.

The most likely cause for the above observations about poor wireless performance is the *nature of the wireless deployments in the two buildings*. Bldg 1 has private APs per apartment unit resulting in a dense wireless deployment. Thus, some APs experience occasional high airtime utilization (> 60%) due to neighboring sources of traffic. Bldg 2 provides centralized wireless service to its residents and thus, some users can occasionally experience poor signal quality based on the client device and location. The impact of losses due to low signal strengths was much lower in Bldg 1 (<12%) due to good signal coverage within each apartment. But, performance issues can still arise due to the dense nature of these deployments. Finally, high WiFi loss rates ($L \uparrow$) was the major cause for "Poor" performance in both Bldg 1 and Bldg 2 (49.5% and 78.1% respectively). Some potential causes of these losses are packet reception issues at some clients or packet collisions at the receivers due to external WiFi/non-WiFi sources. Through our interference analysis from WiFi sources (§5.2) in Bldg 1, we were able to attribute at least 19% of these lossy cases during "Poor" periods to strong interference from external WiFi transmitters.

**Variability in wireless experience over time.** Figure 8 shows the Witt for 2 AP-client pairs (Bldg 1) across a period of 80 days since 12th November 2012. These were amongst the most actively used clients in our deployment and were chosen to show the diversity in link performance over time across different locations and clients. Amongst the 2 clients, the one at AP 14 experienced consistently good performance over this period due to low neighboring wireless activity (median Witt around 14 - 16 Mbps). On the other hand, the client at AP 10 experienced a higher fluctuation in performance as shown by the wide range of the observed median Witt across days. One of the reasons for this behavior was high airtime utilization caused by some neighboring WiFi transmitters at AP 10 (§5.1). The "Winter Break" corresponds to the period between Dec. 25, 2012 and Jan. 21, 2013 during which the wireless activity in Bldg 1 was lower compared to the other days[1]. During this period, the median Witt value for AP 10 was consistently high and stable (around 14 Mbps) compared to other periods of time due to less utilized wireless channel conditions. This observation indicates the high impact of neighboring wireless traffic at this AP.

**Summary.** The majority of the WiFi clients (>=80%) in our deployment of WiSe APs experienced "Good" wireless performance during most of their active periods while some clients (8%) experienced poor performance for greater than 10% of their active periods. Overall, the client's experience was poor during 2.1% of the total active periods across APs.The location and type of deployment (e.g., Bldg 1 vs. Bldg 2) influenced the causes of "Poor" instances. In a dense deployment of private APs (Bldg 1), high airtime utilization from neighboring APs was the major cause of performance degradation while low performance due to weak signal strengths were more prevalent in a centralized home deployment (Bldg 2). We also observed high variability in link performance over the day as well as during across a period of time (e.g., high Witt values during periods of low wireless traffic in the building).

[1]A large fraction of residents in the building are university students, and many of them were out of town during the break.

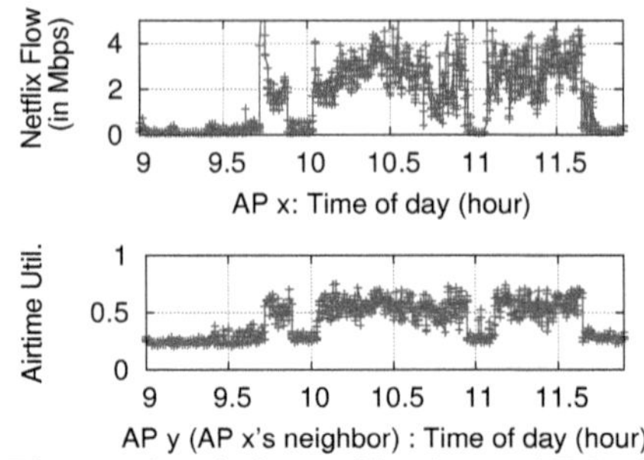


**Figure 9: Time-series airtime utilization at AP 9 with and without the presence of traffic from an external AP that used low PHY rates. AP 9 was inactive during this period.**

# 5. A MORE DETAILED VIEW

We now analyze the impact of external factors on the wireless clients in the wild: contention from transmitters using low PHY rates, hidden terminals and non-WiFi interference.

## 5.1 Contention from low data rate senders

The presence of transmitters using low PHY rates during the active periods of APs can cause their Witt to suffer. This is due to the rate-anomaly [21] problem caused by the loss in channel availability. Figure 9 shows an example of airtime utilization at WiSe AP 9 over a period of 2 hours in the presence and absence of traffic from an external AP (AP x). During AP x's activity, AP 9's airtime utilization (10 second average) increased from an average of 30% to around 65 - 70% due to the usage of low PHY rates by AP x. This was one of the major cause of "Poor" performance in Bldg 1 (§4).

**Prevalence and impact of contention from low rate senders.** We analyzed the presence of such transmitters and their impact on the WiSe APs from 12th Nov. to 21st Dec (40 days). Figure 10 (top and center) shows the duration of *active periods* per day (in minutes) and the number of days respectively, during the 40 day period, over which the WiSe APs experienced contention from external WiFi senders that transmitted at least 500 packets while using low average PHY rates (<= 15 Mbps). Thus, it only shows the impact on WiSe APs while they were sending actual traffic to their clients. Figure 10 (top) shows that some APs (e.g, APs 1, 6, 10, 28) experienced contention from such senders lasting over multiple minutes (median between 20 - 48 minutes). Figure 10 (center) shows that 4 WiSe APs faced at least 5 minutes of contention from such low PHY rate traffic during 10 or more days while they were transmitting data to their clients. This happened due to the presence of nearby external APs at these locations (both Bldg 1 and Bldg 2) that consistently used low PHY rates for some clients across multiple days. Figure 10 (bottom) compares the distribution of Witt at the impacted APs during active periods with and without (5 minutes before and after) such contention. Some APs experienced consistent reduction in Witt during the periods. For example the 75th percentile value for AP 10 reduced from 12.5 Mbps to 6 Mbps during such periods. These external APs was the main cause for the low values of Witt at AP 10 as observed in §4.

In addition to activity from external low PHY rate transmitters, the period of channel contention experienced (Figure 10, top) is also partially dependent on the activity at the AP itself. For example, AP 6 (Figure 3) was the most active AP in our deployment which resulted in the higher periods of contention (median of 40 minutes)

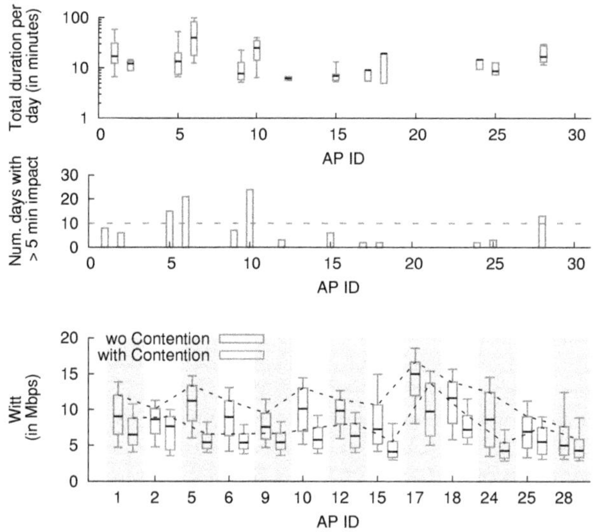


**Figure 10: (top) Candlestick graph showing the distribution of active periods per day (Y-axis in logscale) during which the WiSe APs experienced contention from external transmitters (using average PHY rate <= 15 Mbps), (center) Bar graph showing the total number of days during which WiSe APs experienced this contention for a minimum duration of 5 minutes (from 12th Nov. to 21st Dec, 40 days), (bottom) Witt during active periods for clients with and without contention from such transmitters.10th, 25th, 50th, 75th and 90th percentiles are shown here.**

experienced by it. While, it is not possible for us to determine the signal strength properties of these external links that used low PHY rates, we analyzed our traces and found that many of these transmitters sent large data packets while using conservative rate adaptation. These links switched to low bitrates after a single failure resulting in high usage of low data rates and thus, airtime usage.

## 5.2 Packet losses due to WiFi sources

High packet losses were a major cause for the "Poor" cases in our deployment. Amongst external factors, hidden terminal (HT) style interference at a wireless receiver from nearby links can reduce a link's Witt by increasing packet losses. We leveraged our deployment of 14 WiSe APs in Bldg 1, to collect timestamped (microsecond level) WiFi packet summaries (§2.2) for all observed WiFi traffic from multiple vantage points. These packet summaries from neighboring APs are time-synchronized and merged at the controller using prior techniques from [4, 18] using common data packet summaries present in both traces.

We use these synchronized and merged packets summaries from multiple APs in Bldg 1 to compute "hidden terminal events" in "epochs" of 15 seconds. We mark an epoch as a hidden terminal event for a WiSe AP when the loss rates for one of its links is 40% higher for packets *overlapped in time* by the interferer compared to packets *not overlapped by any other transmitter* [18]. When an epoch is marked as a hidden terminal event, the main cause is packet losses at the receiver caused by the overlapping packet transmissions from the interferer. To minimize false positives, we used a constraint requiring a minimum of 1000 WiFi packets for a link and a minimum of 100 packet overlaps from a potential interferer per epoch to check the presence of a conflict. Thus, our results are a conservative estimate of the interference experienced by the APs in Bldg 1.

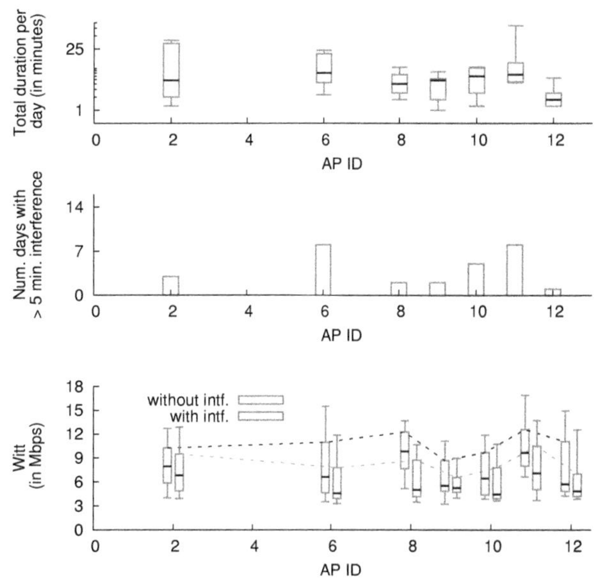


**Figure 11: (top) Distribution of time per day during which the WiSe APs in Bldg 1 experienced hidden terminal interference from external links. (center) Bar graph showing the total number of days during which WiSe APs experienced hidden terminal interference for a minimum duration of 5 minutes per day over a period of 2 weeks. (bottom) Distribution of Witt with and without the presence of HT interference (within 5 minutes of the interference event). Min, max, 25th, 50th and 75th percentiles are shown.**

***What was the impact of HT interference on APs in* Bldg 1*?***

We ran the interference detection measurements across APs in Bldg 1 for a period of two weeks (Figure 11). Across the 14 WiSe APs in Bldg 1, our analysis detected the occurrence of HT interference for 7 APs. Figure 11 (center) shows the number of days during which we detected at least 5 minutes of HT interference across different APs. During the two weeks, APs 6, 10 and 11 experienced HT interference between 5 - 8 days, indicating that some APs were repeatedly impacted by nearby WiFi interferers across multiple days. The median duration of interference per day (Figure 11, top) varied between 3 to 7 minutes but some APs (2, 6 and 11) experienced higher periods of interference (maximum of 23 - 87 minutes) during this two week period. Figure 11 compares the Witt of the impacted APs during periods with and without HT interference (within 5 minutes of HT event). The 75th percentile values dropped between 0.5 Mbps (AP 2) to 4.3 Mbps (AP 8) indicating high variation in impact of interference across some APs. AP 2 experienced minor reduction in throughput due to interference because, even though the loss rates for packets overlapped by the interferer increased by 40%, the proportion of these packets were low (< 20%) compared to the total transmitted packets.

Our analysis shows the HT interference can occur intermittently, mostly for short periods of time. The occurrence of such HT interference is a property of both the receivers' and interferers' traffic. We observed high burstiness of WiFi links in home environments. For example, in our deployment only about *10% of total periods of continuous activity at the* WiSe *APs lasted more than 3 minutes* at most APs (Figure 12). This is one of the reasons for the small periods of interference in homes. The length of these bursty periods are dictated by the nature of the underlying traffic and can be highly variable depending on the type of traffic. For example, we observed highest periods of continuous activity during video stream-

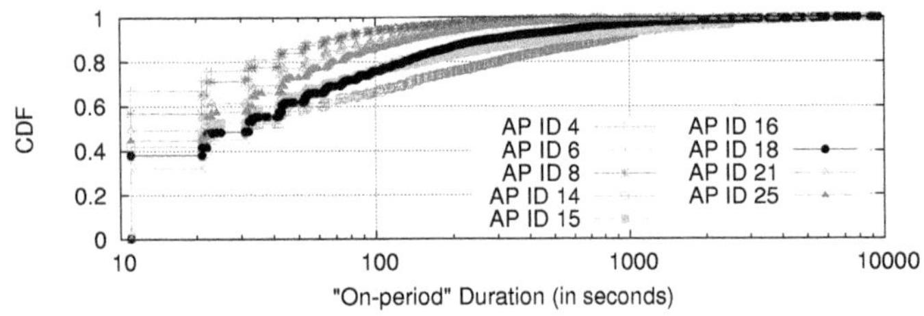


**Figure 12: Distribution of "on-periods" across different WiSe APs. We represent a consecutive period of 10 second intervals with more than 100 data packets each as the *on-period* of the APs.**

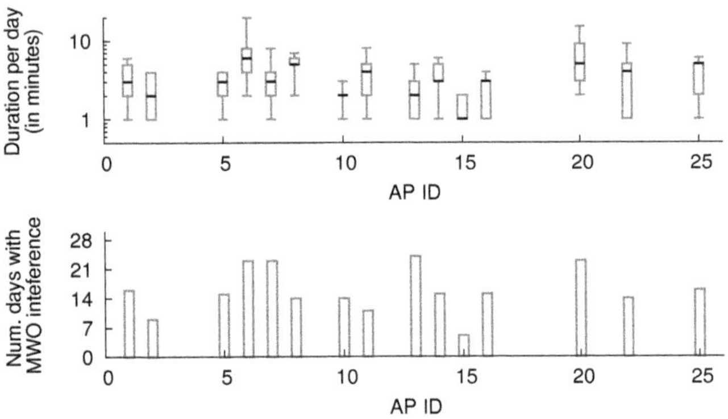


**Figure 13: (top) Distribution of duration per day during which microwave interference reduced Witt by 20%. (bottom) Number of days from a 30 day period, during which the APs experienced at least 1 minute of such interference.**

ing sessions (e.g., Netflix) which can download data in the order of 50 MB while buffering [15]. We found that, at APs 6 and 11, the periods of highest HT interference (39 and 87 minutes respectively) coincided with the usage of Netflix. The APs are more sensitive to such issues during these continuous periods of high activity, while short periods with bursty traffic are less likely to experience these performance issues from external sources due to the lower volume of the transmitted traffic.

## 5.3 Non WiFi interference activity

Another factor that can degrade the performance of WiFi links in homes is interference caused by commonly available non-WiFi devices, such as microwave ovens, Cordless Phones etc. Unlike WiFi transmissions, these devices do not sense the medium before transmitting energy into the spectrum. Different non-WiFi devices can impact WiFi links differently based on their transmit power, transmission protocol as well as their distance from the WiFi transmitters and receivers. By running Airshark [16], WiSe APs detect the presence of non-WiFi devices operating in their vicinity and report them to the controller (§2.2). In this section, we report the properties of non-WiFi interference in homes and quantify their impact on the Witt across the APs.

***How did non-WiFi interference impact nearby WiFi links?***
In this section, we focus on the impact of microwave oven devices on nearby links, since they were the most ubiquitous non-WiFi interferers in our deployment. Microwave ovens have a duty cycle of 50% with alternative periods of approximately 8ms of active and quiet periods (60Hz cycle). We compared the Witt for the active WiSe AP-client pairs with and without microwave oven activity

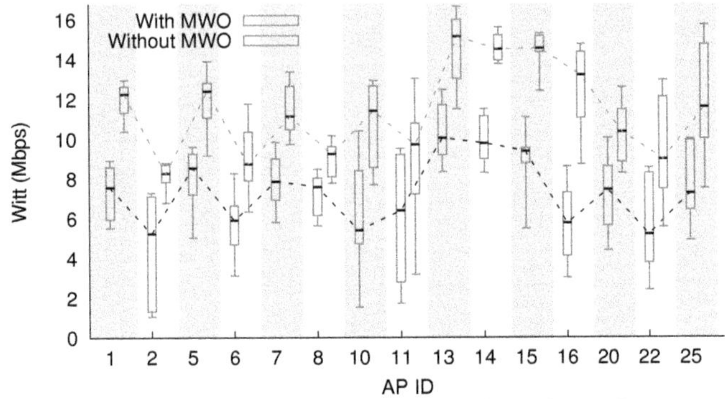


**Figure 14: Candlestick plot comparing the estimated average Witt for WiSe APs with active WiFi links during and after the completion of microwave oven activity. 10th, 25th, 50th, 75th and 90th percentiles are shown in this figure. The dotted line compares the 50th percentile values for both cases.**

(within 5 minutes of the activity). This allowed us to quantify their impact on these links by comparing their performance during these two periods. Since microwave ovens mainly impact channels 8 -11, we analyzed this data for a period of 30 days during which the APs were configured to use channel 11.

Figure 13 shows the duration per day and the number of days (from the 30 day period) during which different APs experienced at least 20% degradation of Witt in the presence of microwave oven activity. During this period, WiSe APs 6, 7, 13, 20 experienced microwave interference on more than 20 days. Most APs experienced short periods (median 1 - 5 minutes) of microwave oven interference during active periods. While these periods are short, they can cause significant reduction in Witt at some APs (e.g., AP 2, Figure 14).

Figure 14 compares the estimated average Witt for different WiSe APs during active periods with microwave oven activity and active periods without microwave oven activity (within 5 minutes). The dotted line compares the 50th percentile values of the Witt for both periods to focus on the performance during periods of high interference. Some APs (e.g., 2, 5 and 16) experienced high performance losses during periods of microwave activity. For example, the 25th percentile Witt dropped from 7.8 Mbps to 1.5 Mbps for AP 2 (in Bldg 1), indicating a performance drop of 81% due to microwave oven activity.

**Impact on airtime and effective rate.** To provide greater insight into the causes of the low Witt measured at some APs during periods of interference, Figure 15 shows the impact of microwave ovens on factors such as airtime and effective rate (§3). Figure 15 (left) shows the average airtime utilization (10 second average) across APs during the two periods. Some APs reported significant increase in airtime utilization in the presence of microwave ovens. For example, the 75th percentile value of airtime utilization for AP 16 increased from 0.33 to 0.70, indicating an absolute increase in airtime utilization of 37 percentage points due to the microwave oven. Other APs, such as AP 10, 11 and 22 also experienced high airtime utilization in the presence of microwave ovens (over 60%).

Figure 15 (right) shows the impact of microwave ovens interference on the effective rates. At some APs (e.g., APs 13 - 15), there was little reduction during most instances of interference. Thus, these APs were mostly impacted by higher airtime utilization at the sender. Other APs, such as APs 2 and 16 experienced high reduction for the effective rates due to microwave oven interference. For these APs, both high airtime utilization and packet losses contributed to a lower Witt. This analysis shows the diversity of impact of microwave

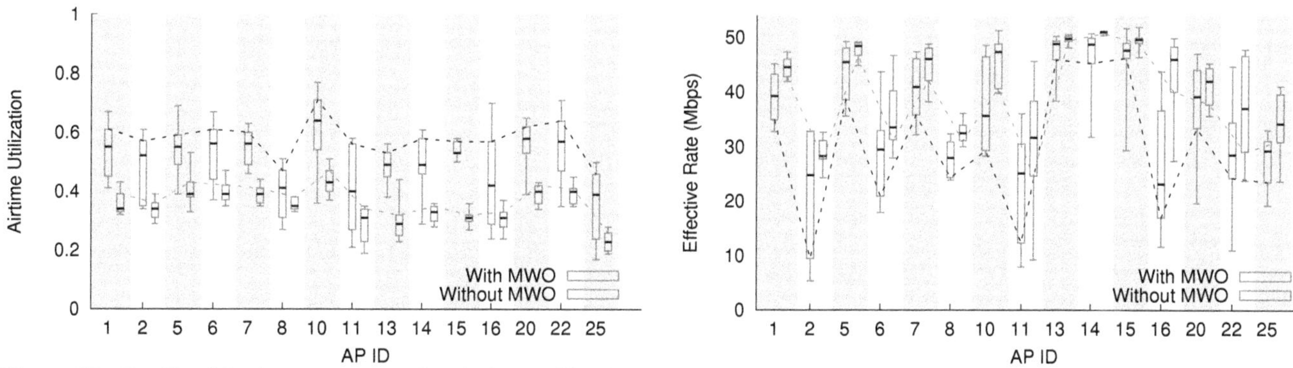


**Figure 15: Candlestick plot comparing the airtime utilization (left) and effective rates (right) for WiSe APs with active WiFi links with and without microwave oven interference. 10th, 25th, 50th, 75th and 90th percentiles are shown in this figure. The dotted line compares the 25th and 75th percentile values for airtime utilization and effective rate respectively.**

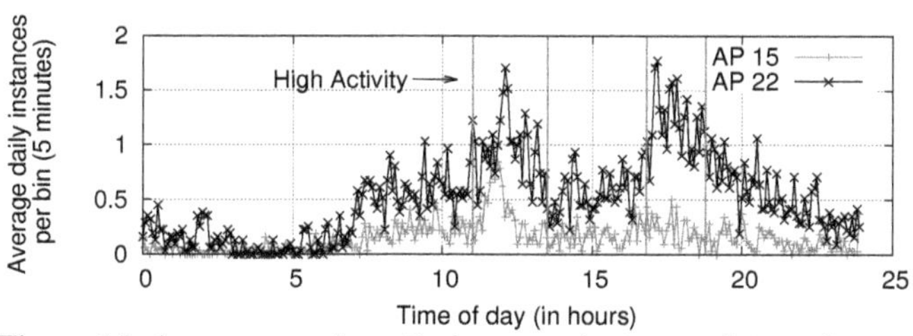


**Figure 16: Average number of microwave instances detected per 5 minute bin (on channel 11) at 2 WiSe APs experiencing low (AP 15) and high (AP 22) microwave oven activity (30 day period).**

ovens on WiFi links. Using different mitigation techniques based on the interferer type (e.g, channel hopping vs. fixed frequency) can be helpful for APs that experience high degradation in the link's performance. As discussed next, leveraging context information about non-WiFi device activity (e.g., time of day) can also be helpful in avoiding interference from these devices when they are more likely to be used.

***How does microwave oven activity vary across locations?***

Figure 16 provides an example of microwave oven activity at two different APs (channel 11). For this analysis, we computed the average number of microwave oven instances seen per 5-minute bin at each WiSe AP during the one month period. A value of 1 on the y-axis indicates that an average of 1 microwave oven instance was reported during the specific 5-minute bin of day over the one month period. AP 22 observed the highest activity during 11am - 1:30 pm and 5pm - 8pm. On the other hand, AP 15 observed low frequency of microwave oven activity on the same channel during most of the day except 10:30 am - noon. Learning about this *"time of day" context about non-WiFi device activity* can enable home APs to make better decisions in order to avoid the impact of such devices during periods of highest non-WiFi device activity. We plan to further explore this aspect in our future work in building mitigation mechanisms.

## 5.4 Channel Usage Patterns

Our deployment of WiSe APs across homes showed that WiFi links in dense deployments occasionally experience poor performance due to external sources. Changing channels can partially help in dealing with repeated performance issues on a channel (e.g., non-WiFi interference on a single channel).

To study the usage of channel selection algorithms by other home APs, we configured the WiSe APs to periodically scan all WiFi channels to overhear beacons from neighboring APs, especially to include external APs, on different channel. Table 9 shows the number of distinct WiFi channels used by these external neighboring APs observed by all WiSe APs as well for Bldg 1 only over a period of one month. It shows that around 56% of the overall 305 APs observed, used a single WiFi channel for the entire period, indicating the fact the majority of home APs used a static WiFi configuration, and are never re-assigned by residents after they are deployed. These channel configuration patterns were prevalent across different locations (as shown for Bldg 1), indicating that this property was not biased towards a particular location.

| Unique channels | Num. APs (Overall) | Percentage (Overall) | Num. APs (Bldg 1 only) | Percentage (Bldg 1 only) |
|---|---|---|---|---|
| 1 | 171 | 56.1% | 99 | 61.1% |
| 2 | 61 | 20% | 33 | 20.4% |
| >=3 | 73 | 23.9% | 30 | 18.3% |

**Table 9: Number of unique channels used by neighboring external APs as observed by the WiSe APs over a 1 month period. The table shows the overall values as well as the APs specifically observed in Bldg 1.**

Using a static channel assignment may not be an issue in low density deployments or if the link's experience is good for most of the time. But, as discussed in §4, some APs observed lower Witt values for various reasons. Such APs can benefit from channel re-assignments based on the performance experienced on the current channel.

## 5.5 Summary

1. The impact of interference (WiFi and non-WiFi) is dependent on both the link's and interferer's traffic. Majority of the interference durations were short (1 - 7 minutes) due to the bursty nature of traffic at homes. But, some links experienced extended periods of interference (tens of minutes) during periods of continuous activity due to either high airtime utilization (at sender) or packet losses (at receiver).
2. Even though most interference periods were short, some had a high impact on the APs. For example, microwave ovens caused high degradation of Witt at some APs (81%).
3. Learning context (e.g., time of day) about interference activity (e.g., periods of non-WiFi device usage at homes) can enable APs to avoid interference from such devices.
4. Majority of APs (56%) observed at homes used static channel configurations over time (30 days) indicating that they rarely or never get configured once they get deployed.

## 6. RELATED WORK

**Characterizing network performance.** The BISmark project [20] aims at understanding the performance of wired access networks in homes through the long-term deployment of gateways in homes serviced by a diverse set of ISPs. We use a similar approach but focus on building a framework to study the properties of dense residential wireless networks and deploy multiple APs within the apartment building. Previous studies [11, 4, 12, 3] have evaluated wireless network deployments in enterprises and homes by collecting passive traces or user traffic statistics. For example, Jigsaw [4] used a large number of passive sniffers in an enterprise WLAN to collect wireless packet traces for debugging wireless problems. Instead of using passive sniffers, we perform measurements directly through the wireless APs. This allows us to obtain more comprehensive information about the AP's view of the network in addition to packet level statistics (e.g., airtime utilization, non-WiFi devices etc.). By performing controlled experiments in three houses, authors in [14] observed high asymmetry in links and variability in link performance at different locations within homes. We measure the link performance in homes over time and identify the causes of occasional poor performance experienced by links. Prior work such as [5, 7] has focused on end-host techniques for measuring end to end performance in home networks. We use AP-centric techniques, since it allows us to monitor home WLANs by using a single instrumented vantage point.

**Wireless network debugging and diagnosis.** Prior work on model based techniques [10] require active network measurements to predict link capacity and build conflict graphs. Our focus is to passively estimate a wireless link's performance by only using coarse-grained local observations, since any additional traffic from the WiSe APs may impact the existing traffic. To avoid measurement overhead, passive techniques have been proposed [17, 18, 13] for detecting the presence of interference in WLANs. We build upon prior work from PIE [18] that uses microsecond level timing information to passively detect the presence of wireless interference for a link by comparing the link's loss rates in presence and absence of overlapping packets from a nearby WiFi sender. We ported Airshark [16] to the WiSe platform to detect the presence of non-WiFi devices near WiSe APs and measure their impact on user traffic.

## 7. CONCLUSION

We describe a unique measurement and management infrastructure, WiSe, to perform inline measurements of wireless properties in homes that uses APs as vantage points. We have been operating this infrastructure for more than 6 months in 30 homes. The deployed homes have diverse characteristics — some are in dense apartments while others are in sparser suburban neighborhoods, some residents directly own the APs while others use a shared infrastructure deployed in the apartment. We also present a simple metric to estimate the wireless TCP throughput in these deployments. Our infrastructure operates through a open API and so in the future other types of APs can be added to the infrastructure. We believe studies such as these can provide our community with valuable ground truth data. Hence, we also plan to release our anonymized wireless traces broadly to the community in the near future.

## 8. ACKNOWLEDGMENTS

We thank the participants in this study for their support. We also thank Nathan Moeller for his assistance in the initial stages of this deployment. We would like to acknowledge the anonymous reviewers and our shepherd, Alex Snoeren, whose comments helped bring the paper into its final form. Srinivas Govindan and Suman Banerjee are supported in part by the US National Science Foundation through awards CNS-1040648, CNS-0916955, CNS-0855201, CNS-0747177, CNS-1064944, and CNS-1059306.

## 9. REFERENCES

[1] "OpenWrt". https://openwrt.org/.

[2] "SamKnows". http://www.samknows.com/broadband/index.php.

[3] A. Akella, G. Judd, S. Seshan, and P. Steenkiste. Self-management in Chaotic Wireless Deployments. MobiCom '05.

[4] Y.-C. Cheng, J. Bellardo, P. Benkö, A. C. Snoeren, G. M. Voelker, and S. Savage. Jigsaw: Solving the Puzzle of Enterprise 802.11 Analysis. SIGCOMM '06.

[5] L. DiCioccio, R. Teixeira, and C. Rosenberg. Impact of home networks on end-to-end performance: controlled experiments. HomeNets '10.

[6] P. Engines. alix2d2. http://www.pcengines.ch/alix2d2.htm.

[7] C. Gkantsidis, T. Karagiannis, P. Key, B. Radunovic, E. Raftopoulos, and D. Manjunath. Traffic management and resource allocation in small wired/wireless networks. CoNEXT '09.

[8] H. Guru. "Do Wireless HDTV Systems Do The Job?". http://hdguru.com/do-wireless-hdtv-systems-do-the-job-lastest-models-reviewed/6178/.

[9] A. P. Jardosh, K. N. Ramachandran, K. C. Almeroth, and E. M. Belding-Royer. Understanding congestion in IEEE 802.11b wireless networks. IMC '05.

[10] A. Kashyap, S. Ganguly, and S. R. Das. A measurement-based approach to modeling link capacity in 802.11-based wireless networks. MobiCom '07.

[11] D. Kotz and K. Essien. Analysis of a Campus-wide Wireless Network. MobiCom '02.

[12] R. Mahajan, M. Rodrig, D. Wetherall, and J. Zahorjan. Analyzing the mac-level behavior of wireless networks in the wild. SIGCOMM '06.

[13] J. Manweiler, P. Franklin, and R. Choudhury. RxIP: Monitoring the health of home wireless networks. In INFOCOM, 2012.

[14] K. Papagiannaki, M. Yarvis, and W. S. Conner. Experimental Characterization of Home Wireless Networks and Design Implications. In INFOCOM 2006.

[15] A. Rao, A. Legout, Y.-s. Lim, D. Towsley, C. Barakat, and W. Dabbous. Network characteristics of video streaming traffic. CoNEXT '11.

[16] S. Rayanchu, A. Patro, and S. Banerjee. Airshark: Detecting non-WiFi RF devices using commodity WiFi hardware. IMC '11.

[17] C. Reis, R. Mahajan, M. Rodrig, D. Wetherall, and J. Zahorjan. Measurement-based models of delivery and interference in static wireless networks. SIGCOMM '06.

[18] V. Shrivastava, S. Rayanchu, S. Banerjee, and K. Papagiannaki. PIE in the sky: online passive interference estimation for enterprise WLANs. NSDI'11.

[19] V. Shrivastava, S. Rayanchu, J. Yoonj, and S. Banerjee. 802.11n under the microscope. IMC '08.

[20] S. Sundaresan, W. de Donato, N. Feamster, R. Teixeira, S. Crawford, and A. Pescapè. Broadband Internet Performance: A View From The Gateway. SIGCOMM '11.

[21] Tan, Godfrey and Guttag, John. Time-based fairness improves performance in multi-rate WLANs. In *Proceedings of the annual conference on USENIX ATC, 2004.*

# Symphony: Cooperative Packet Recovery over the Wired Backbone in Enterprise WLANs

Tarun Bansal†, Bo Chen†, Prasun Sinha and Kannan Srinivasan
Department of Computer Science and Engineering
The Ohio State University
Columbus, OH 43210
{bansal, chebo, prasun, kannan}@cse.ohio-state.edu
†Co-primary authors

## ABSTRACT

In this paper, we propose Symphony, a packet recovery architecture that encourages collisions among transmitters, and utilizes the unused capacity in the backbone to transmit recovered data packets and coordinate the efficient recovery of collided packets. Symphony improves the wireless throughput while incurring a low overhead on the typically under-utilized wired backbone. In Symphony, upon receiving the collided transmissions, the APs carefully suppress a subset of the transmissions. Realizing this idea in practice entails several challenges including identification of clients that have data to transmit and ensuring that the algorithm works despite imperfect time-synchronization and non-zero latency among APs. We present Symphony that addresses these challenges and show how it leverages Successive Interference Cancellation (SIC) to further increase the network throughput. Experiments performed on an USRP testbed shows that on an average, Symphony provides 43% and 187% higher throughput over Omniscient TDMA and IEEE 802.11, respectively. ns-3 based simulation results show that on an average, Symphony provides a throughput of up to 1.63x compared to omniscient TDMA and 5.6x compared to IEEE 802.11.

## Categories and Subject Descriptors

C.2.2 [**Computer-Communication Networks**]: Network Protocols

## Keywords

Wireless Networks; Cooperative Decoding

## 1. INTRODUCTION

APs in Enterprise Wireless Local Area Network (EWLAN) are typically connected using a wired backbone. *In this paper, we propose Symphony, a cooperative decoding approach that minimally uses the wired connection among APs to increase the throughput of wireless networks.* Symphony encourages collision of packets among transmitters at APs. On receiving multiple packets, APs suppress a subset of colliding transmitters. This reduces the number of transmitters in each slot. Eventually, the number of transmitters reduces to a small enough value such that the APs can cooperatively decode all the received packets.

Figure 1a shows a simple topology with two APs and four clients where the APs are connected to each other through a wired backbone. Assume that each of the clients needs to upload one packet to the backbone. For this topology, omniscient TDMA will take at least four slots to schedule the four transmissions (See Figure 1b). In Symphony, on the other hand, all the four clients transmit (See Figure 1c) in the first slot. At the end of the slot, Symphony suppresses Alice ($A$) and Bob($B$). In the next slot, only Carol($C$) and Don($D$) transmit. At the end of the second slot, $AP_1$ decodes the packet $D$ since $AP_1$ received it interference-free. After decoding, it sends the decoded bits of $D$ to $AP_2$ over the wired backbone. From the received bits, after correcting for different offsets, $AP_2$ recreates samples received from $D$ and subtracts them from the samples received in slot 2. After subtraction, it is left with only the samples corresponding to $C$ which $AP_2$ decodes. At the same time, $AP_1$ recreates the samples of $D$ as received in slot 1 and subtracts those samples from the samples received in slot 1. $AP_1$ then decodes the remaining samples to obtain $A$ and sends it to $AP_2$. Finally, $AP_2$ recreates the received samples of $A, C$ and $D$ for slot 1. After subtracting these samples from the samples received in slot 1, $AP_2$ decodes $B$. Using cooperation among APs and by using the backbone for exchanging decoded packets, Symphony enables the two APs to receive the four packets in two slots. Thus, by utilizing cooperation among APs to simultaneously decode multiple colliding transmissions, Symphony provides twice the throughput as compared to omniscient TDMA.

Cooperation among APs has been used before to increase wireless throughput. Authors in [17] focus on improving the client-AP association and AP channel assignment. Miu *et al.*[16], Woo *et al.* [22]and Gowda *et al.* [10] have respectively proposed techniques for bit-level, symbol-level and coarse symbol-level combining across different APs. In these solutions, a packet overheard by different APs is decoded cooperatively by multiple APs. However, in all these algorithms, all the APs cooperate to decode a single packet while in Symphony, APs cooperate to simultaneously de-


*MobiCom'13*, September 30–October 4, Miami, FL, USA.
Copyright 2013 ACM 978-1-4503-1999-7/13/09 ...$15.00.
http://dx.doi.org/10.1145/2500423.2500450.

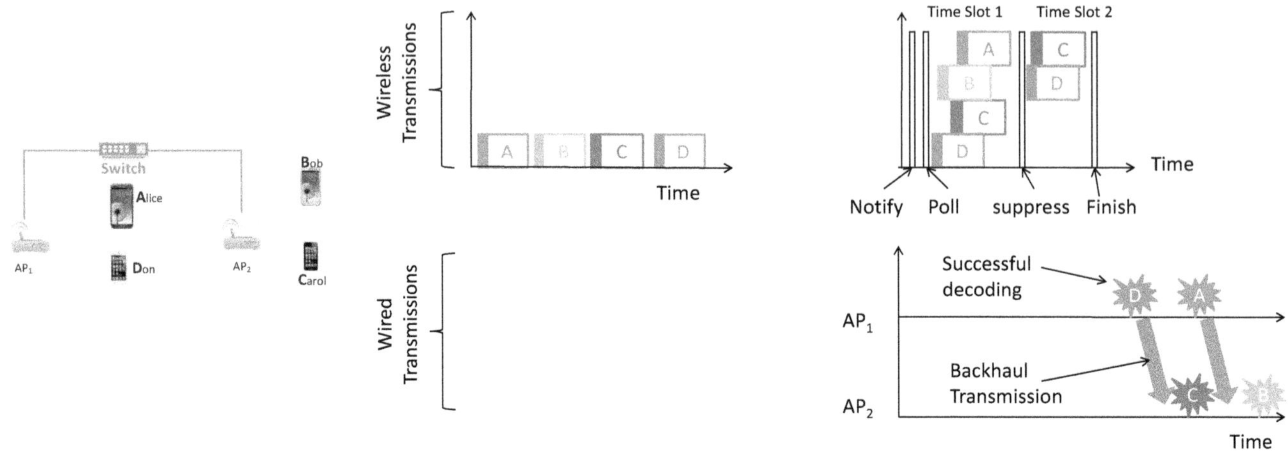


(a) Network Topology (b) Omniscient TDMA (c) Symphony

**Figure 1: Network topology and set of packets received by APs. (a) Network topology. $AP_1$ is assumed to be outside the interference range of Bob and Carol. (b) Omniscient TDMA takes a minimum of 4 slots. (c) Symphony can receive four packets in two slots. In Symphony, APs cooperatively decode packets in the reverse chronological order by first decoding the packets received in the last slot.**

code multiple packets. Further, symbol-level combining[16] across different APs is prohibitive due to significantly higher bandwidth requirements[22, 10] on the wired backbone. In Symphony, APs only exchange decoded packets which are typically much smaller in size compared to raw samples [22, 10]. The idea of exchanging packets on the backbone was also studied in [9]. However, unlike Symphony, [9] provides throughput improvement only when all the devices have at least two antennas.

Several prior works [21, 18, 14] have focused on increasing network throughput for downlink traffic in EWLANs while neglecting the uplink traffic. On the other hand, Symphony primarily improves the network throughput on uplink while allowing efficient schemes such as conflict-free TDMA scheduling[14] to be utilized over the downlink. We believe that upstream traffic is increasing rapidly due to rise in use of a wide-range of new storage paradigms, computing paradigms and applications, such as cloud computing, cloud storage, P2P file access, video conferencing, online gaming, VoIP, and traffic generated from the mobile devices (e.g., location information or sensor readings). Using cooperation to improve uplink wireless throughput is particularly challenging, since APs are not aware of which client has data to transmit making it difficult to schedule transmissions. Collecting this information from different clients is also cost-prohibitive.

Although the idea behind Symphony is simple, there are multiple challenges to realize it in practice.

1. **Set of nodes to suppress:** At the end of each slot, Symphony needs to determine the set of nodes to be suppressed. This set should be feasible (ensuring that the set of suppressed transmissions would be decoded in future) and large, so that all the collided transmissions can be decoded in a small number of slots.

2. **Synchronization and variable non-zero latency:** Cooperation among APs requires that APs be synchronized with each other and that their mutual-latency be low and predictable. However, our measurements described in Section 7.2 show that these requirements do not hold true in large networks.

3. **Absence of central controller:** In wireless networks, it may not be possible to set up a central controller that coordinates all the APs in the entire network due to the large size of the network. Thus, it is required that cooperative decoding should work in the absence of central controller.

4. **Knowledge of topology:** To cooperatively suppress a subset of transmitters, the APs need to know the network topology. This information (particularly the interference among non-AP nodes) is difficult to acquire for large scale networks [14, 9] and could lead to significant overhead.

5. **Difference in packet lengths:** It is possible that different transmitters may have different amount of pending data left. However, if the channel access time is fixed as shown in Figure 1c, then the users with less pending data may not fully use the access time leading to channel wastage.

The paper is organized as follows. Section 2 presents a brief overview of Mozart[2], a recently proposed collision recovery based MAC layer protocol. The next section describes a centralized algorithm that assumes the presence of a central server. In Section 4, we describe our distributed protocol, Symphony that handles all the above challenges. In Section 5, we explain how Symphony harnesses SIC to increase wireless throughput. The following section discusses some issues that makes our solution more practical. Section 7 and Section 8 outline the results from our USRP testbed experiments and ns-3 based simulations, respectively. Section 9 presents the state of the art and finally, Section 10 concludes our paper.

## 2. BACKGROUND

A recently proposed protocol, Mozart [2] uses packet subtraction and receiver controlled retransmissions to decode collided packets in the least possible number of slots. At the end of each slot, receivers in Mozart suppress one transmitter independently. In order to suppress some transmitter, receivers in Mozart need to identify which set of clients are transmitting. In [2], authors propose that transmitters should use Pseudo-random (PN) sequences to identify themselves. The PN sequences (implemented using Gold codes [7]) can be correlated by the receiver even under high interference [15]. Thus, by correlating received samples, the receivers in Mozart identify the IDs of as many colliding transmitters as possible. To harness SIC, Mozart's receivers need to estimate the individual RSS of each of the colliding transmitters. Mozart proposes three different approaches (PN sequence padding, cancellation, iterative estimation) which when combined significantly improve the accuracy of transmitter as well as the RSS estimation accuracy. In this paper, we use the methods proposed in Mozart [2] for sender identification and RSS estimation. Observe that *unlike Mozart, Symphony uses the wired backbone to cooperatively decode the collided packets.* This leads to a different set of challenges as described in Section 1.

# 3. COOPERATIVE PACKET SUBTRACTION

In this section, we present a simplified version of our algorithm, called Centralized Algorithm (CA) that works under a centralized framework. In Subsection 3.2, we explain the practical limitations of CA.

CA assumes the presence of a central server (CS) that coordinates different APs. CA also assumes that all the APs are synchronized with the CS and their mutual latency is zero. We relax these assumptions in Section 4 where we describe our distributed algorithm. CA works in multiple phases as described below (See Figure 1c):

1. **Polling:** First, using the wired backbone, the CS asks all the APs to simultaneously transmit poll packets on the air. The poll packets are encoded using PN sequences [15]. Use of PN sequences, allows the clients to correlate them even if multiple poll packets collide.
2. **Data Transmission:** Upon receiving the poll, the clients that have uplink data transmit their data packets. The clients also encode their IDs using their PN sequence and include it in the packet's header at the front. Due to simultaneous transmissions, multiple packets may collide at the APs. As explained in Section 2, each AP uses the PN sequence to determine the ID of as many colliding transmitters as possible, and then forwards this information to the CS using the wired backbone.
3. **Computing the set of suppressed clients:** On receiving the *best-effort* information about which AP received packets from which clients, the CS uses Algorithm 1 (explained in Section 3.1) to compute the subset of transmitters to be suppressed at the end of this slot. The algorithm described in Section 3.1 also determines which AP should suppress which client. All this information is conveyed by CS to the APs through the backbone.
4. **Transmitting the suppress packets:** Upon receiving the information about which nodes to suppress, the APs transmit the *suppress* packet that includes the PN sequence of the client that is suppressed. Similar to poll packets, here also use of PN sequences allows the clients to correlate them even if multiple suppress packets collide.
5. **Data retransmission:** Each client upon hearing the suppress determines if it is being suppressed: If so, it does not transmit (until it receives *finish*), otherwise, the client retransmits its data.
6. **Finish:** As the nodes are suppressed, the number of concurrent transmissions received by APs decreases with each slot. Eventually, it becomes possible for the APs to use cooperation and decode all the transmissions received in the last slot. As described in Section 1, this decoding is done in the *reverse chronological order* until all the received packets are decoded. At that point, the CS directs all APs to broadcast *finish*. The reception of a finish packet at the clients indicates that the data transmitted by the nodes has been successfully received at APs. This allows the nodes to transmit the next MAC-layer data frame.

Another way of scheduling transmissions may be that in the first slot, using the poll, APs gather the PN sequences of all the clients that have uplink data and then schedule different transmitters in a TDMA fashion. However, this approach does not work well since APs may not detect PN sequences from transmitters that have low SINR[2]. Thus, transmitters with low SINR will not be scheduled and get starved. On the other hand, the PN sequences of such transmitters will be detected in CA in later slots when the number of colliding packets become small. So, with the reverse chronological decoding of Symphony, the transmitters with low SINR will also be suppressed and eventually their packets would also be decoded.

To prevent overwhelming[10, 22] the wired backbone, one of the requirements for cooperative decoding is that APs should not exchange sample level information on the wired backbone[1]. The set of transmissions suppressed during a slot and the samples received at all the APs during that slot form a set of linear equations. Observe that, just because the set of equations is solvable, it does not imply that all the suppressed transmissions can be decoded without exchanging sample level information. Consider the example network shown in Figure 1a. If at the end of slot 1, the CS suppresses $A$ and $D$, then even though the set of linear equations has 2 variables ($A$ and $D$) and 2 equations (samples received at $AP_1$ and $AP_2$), still it is not possible to decode both $A$ and $D$ *without the exchange of samples.* Thus, we need another mechanism to compute the set of suppressed transmissions.

## 3.1 Computing the set of suppressed transmissions

At the end of each slot, the CS computes the set of suppressed transmissions. *This set should satisfy the following four requirements*: (*i*) **Feasibility:** It should be a feasible set such that the APs can successfully decode all the suppressed packets without exchanging sample-level information; (*ii*) **Optimality:** It should maximize the number of transmissions suppressed in this slot; (*iii*) **Optimality in future slots:** It should maximize the applicability of cooperative decoding in future slots; and, (*iv*) **Low backbone overhead:** It should minimize the number of decoded packets that need to be exchanged among APs, thereby reducing the overhead on the wired network.

[1]Although by exchanging coarse samples [10], it is possible to reduce the overhead in the backbone, it is not enough for our purpose since high fidelity representation of symbols is required to decode a packet in the presence of interference from other transmissions.

**Algorithm 1:** Computes the set of nodes to be suppressed in a given slot

1 **Input:** For every packet $P_i$ received in this slot by each AP $AP_j$, the transmitter of $P_i$ (identified using PN sequence).
2 **Output:** The acyclic subgraph showing: Set of packets (or corresponding transmitters) that should be sent suppress in this slot, which AP decodes which packet and how APs share decoded packets among themselves.
`// Phase 1: Computing dependence graph` $G_d = (V_d, E_d)$
3 $V_d \leftarrow \{v_{ij} : P_i$ received in this slot and $AP_j$ can decode $P_i$ in absence of external interference$\}$
4 $E_d \leftarrow \{(v_{ij}, v_{kl}) : v_{ij} \in V_d$ and $v_{kl} \in V_d$ and $P_i$ interferes at $AP_l$ and $v_{ij} \neq v_{kl}\}$
`// Phase 2: Computing largest IDAS`
5 $V_s \leftarrow \phi, E_s \leftarrow \phi, G_s \leftarrow (V_s, E_s)$
6 **while** *true* **do**
7   $v^* \leftarrow \phi, w^* \leftarrow \infty, E^* \leftarrow \phi$
8   **for** $v_{ij} \in V_d \backslash V_s$ **do**
9     $E_{ij} \leftarrow \{(v_{ij}, v_{kl}) : (v_{ij}, v_{kl}) \in E_d \wedge v_{kl} \in V_s\}$
10     $E_{ij} \leftarrow E_{ij} \cup \{(v_{kl}, v_{ij}) : (v_{kl}, v_{ij}) \in E_d \wedge v_{kl} \in V_s\}$
11     **if** $w_{ij} \leq w^*$ *and graph with* $V_s \cup \{v_{ij}\}$ *and* $E_s \cup E_{ij}$ *is acyclic* **then**
12       $w^* \leftarrow w_{ij}, v^* \leftarrow v_{ij}, E^* \leftarrow E_{ij}$
13   **if** $v^* \neq \phi$ **then**
14     $V_s \leftarrow V_s \cup \{v^*\}$`// Add` $v^*$ `to` $G_s$
15     $E_s \leftarrow E_s \cup E^*$
16   **else**
17     **break**
18 **return** $G_s$

Computing the largest set of feasible suppressed transmissions (while taking into account only the first two requirements) is a NP-Hard problem (shown in the technical report [1]). To that end, we propose a two-phased greedy algorithm that computes the set of suppressed transmissions by first constructing a *dependence graph* (Explained in Subsection 3.1.1) and then picking its maximum acyclic induced subgraph (Explained in Subsection 3.1.2). This acyclic graph corresponds to the set of transmissions that can be successfully suppressed in this slot. In this paper, we use $P_i$ to denote packet received from client $i$. We overload this term and also use $P_i$ to represent the client that transmitted the packet.

### 3.1.1 Phase 1: Constructing the dependence graph

When using cooperative decoding, decoding of one transmission may depend on successful decoding of another transmission. For the example network shown in Figure 1a, let's say that in the first slot, the CS suppresses $A$ and $B$. However, since $A$'s transmission interferes at $AP_2$, therefore, $B$'s transmission at $AP_2$ can be decoded only after the former transmission has been decoded at $AP_1$. In general, for two transmissions $\{P_i, AP_j\}$ and $\{P_k, AP_l\}$, if $P_k$ interferes at $AP_j$, then the transmission from $P_i$ can be decoded at $AP_j$ only after $P_k$'s transmission has been decoded. Thus, we say that the decoding of $P_i$'s transmission is *dependent* upon the decoding of $P_k$'s transmission. In this phase, the CS constructs a *dependence graph* for the current slot (Lines 3-4 of Algorithm 1)):

1. **Vertices:** Corresponding to each client-AP link in the topology, a vertex is created in the dependence graph. We use $v_{ij}$ to denote the vertex that corresponds to the link $\{P_i, AP_j\}$. $v_{ij}$ is created *iff* $P_i$ transmitted at least one packet in this slot and $AP_j$ is in the receiving range of $P_i$ (i.e., $AP_j$ can decode $P_i$ in the absence of interference).

2. **Edges:** Edges in the dependence graph capture the decoding dependence among different transmissions. A directed edge is added from vertex $v_{ij}$ to a vertex $v_{kl}$ *iff* (i) $P_i$ interferes at $AP_l$; and, (ii) $v_{ij}$ is not same as $v_{kl}$. The second condition forbids self-loops in the graph.

By creating vertices on the basis of transmission range and edges on the basis of the interference range, the algorithm is able to handle the differences between the transmission and interference range of practical radios. Figure 2a shows the dependence graph for the example network shown in Figure 1a at the end of slot 1. In the following discussion, we use $G_d$ to denote the dependence graph.

### 3.1.2 Phase 2: Computing the maximum vertex-induced directed acyclic subgraph (IDAS)

We prove (See technical report [1]) that a set of client-AP transmissions can be decoded if and only if the vertex induced subgraph of the corresponding set of vertices in $G_d$ is a DAG (Directed Acyclic Graph). For example, since transmissions $A \rightarrow AP_1$ and $B \rightarrow AP_2$ (See Figure 2a) are part of induced acyclic subgraph of the dependence graph, therefore both these transmissions can be suppressed at the end of slot 1. Thus, to compute the largest set of suppressed nodes in this slot, the CS computes the maximum Induced Directed Acyclic Subgraph (IDAS) of $G_d$. Algorithms for computing the maximum IDAS have been proposed before [6]. Although, those algorithms take into account the first and the second requirements discussed in Section 3.1, but they do not take into account the other two requirements. To that end, we now explain the greedy algorithm used by CS to compute the IDAS (denoted by $G_s = (V_s, E_s)$) of $G_d$.

CS works by greedily adding vertices while ensuring that $G_s$ stays acyclic. At any step, it may be possible to add any of the multiple vertices (each vertex corresponds to some client-AP pair in the dependence graph) available to $G_s$. However, different vertices may give different performance results. To that end, for each vertex that can be added to $V_s$, CS computes its *weight* and greedily adds that vertex that does not create a cycle in $G_s$ and has the lowest weight (Lines 8-15 of Algorithm 1). This process is repeated until no more vertices can be added to $G_s$ (Lines 6-17 of Algorithm 1).

**Computing the weight:** When adding a vertex (say $v_{ij}$) to $G_s$, the following equation is used to compute its weight:

$$\begin{aligned} w_{ij} &= w(P_i, AP_j) \\ &= |(v_{ij}, v_{kl}) : (v_{ij}, v_{kl}) \in E_d \wedge v_{kl} \in V_s| \\ &\quad \times |(v_{kl}, v_{ij}) : (v_{kl}, v_{ij}) \in E_d \wedge v_{kl} \in V_s| \end{aligned} \quad (1)$$

If on adding $v_{ij}$ to $V_s$, it has either fewer incoming edges or fewer outgoing edges, then this indicates that $v_{ij}$ has low probability of being part of some cycle in the future. This increases the possibility of extending $G_s$ to a larger acyclic induced subgraph in the following iterations. Further, fewer edges indicate that APs need to exchange fewer packets in the backbone. Thus, (1) assigns a lower weight to the vertices with either fewer incoming edges or fewer outgoing edges and thus, a higher priority. Therefore, by using (1), Algorithm 1 tries to take all the requirements into account that were discussed in Section 3.1.

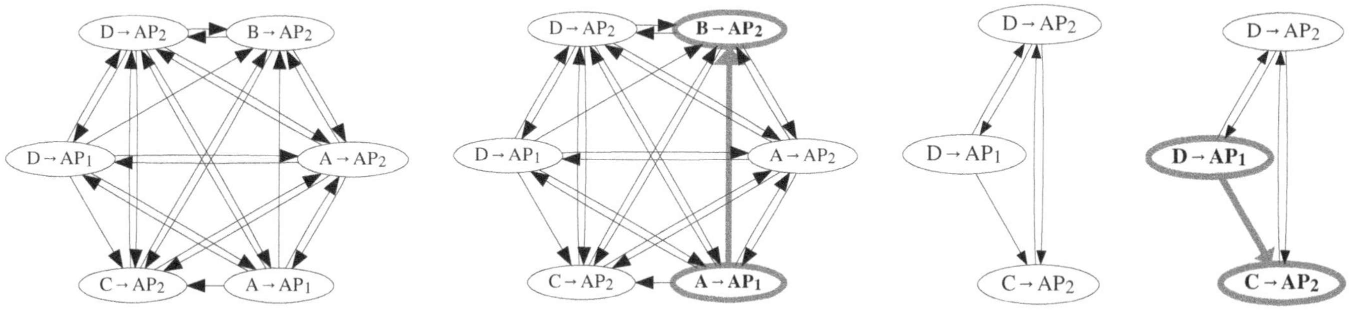


(a) $G_d$ at the end of slot 1

(b) Two vertices and one induced edge (shown in bold) form the Acyclic subgraph ($G_s$) at the end of slot 1.

(c) $G_d$ at the end of slot 2

(d) $G_s$ (shown in bold) at the end of slot 2.

**Figure 2: Dependence graph ($G_d$) and Induced Directed Acyclic Subgraph (IDAS denoted by $G_s$) at the end of the first and the second slot for the example network shown in Figure 1a.**

Figure 2b shows the computed IDAS for the dependence graph shown in Figure 2a. The subgraph shows that $AP_1$ suppresses $A$ while $AP_2$ suppresses $B$. After the APs send the suppress, only $C$ and $D$ transmit in the second slot. Figure 2c shows the dependence graph created by CA at the end of the second slot. Figure 2d shows the computed IDAS which shows that $C$ and $D$ are suppressed in this slot. Since, no other transmitters are left for transmitting, so, the CS would ask APs to send *finish*. Observe that the edges in the $G_s$ also reveal how the APs should exchange the decoded packets. For example, the directed edge from "$D \rightarrow AP_1$" to "$C \rightarrow AP_2$" indicates that decoding of $C$ at $AP_2$ is dependent upon decoding of $D$ at $AP_1$. Thus, $AP_1$ should send the decoded bits of $D$ to $AP_2$. The CS transmits this information to the APs so that they only exchange packets that are required, thereby reducing the overhead on the backbone.

## 3.2 Practical Challenges

Although the algorithm proposed before is good in theory, it is difficult to implement due to various challenges:

1. **Synchronization:** CA requires that all APs be time-synchronized to ensure correct correlation of PN sequences. As described in Section 2, receivers in CA use correlation of Gold codes to identify the set of transmitters. Gold codes guarantee that the circular cross-correlation of two instances of Gold code is bounded. For 127-symbol sequence Gold codes, the bound is 1/7[7]. So, the correlation works better when Gold codes collide only with other Gold codes, and not with arbitrary samples from data packets. This implies that CA needs to ensure that when an AP receives a set of collided transmissions, then the PN sequences in them only collide with other PN sequences. One way to satisfy this requirement is to ensure that all APs in the network poll and suppress in a synchronous fashion. Algorithms for synchronization in wired networks have been proposed before [11, 12], however, as the size of the network grows, ensuring synchronization across the entire network becomes difficult. Thus, a new method is needed to ensure that PN sequences collide only with other PN sequences so that they can be correlated with high accuracy.

2. **Unpredictable delays over the backbone:** In CA, the central server computes the set of suppressed transmitters and distributes that result to the APs. However, due to unpredictable delay, it is possible that this result may not arrive in time and thus, some of the APs may not be able to proceed.

3. **Non-uniform distribution of clients across APs:** The previous algorithm requires that all APs poll at the same time. In an enterprise network, it is possible that different APs have unequal number of neighboring clients with outstanding data. This may result in different APs finishing at different times, leading to lower throughput as all the finished APs in the network need to wait for the AP with the highest number of clients.

4. **Absence of central controller:** As discussed in Section 1, a central controller may not be present to control all the APs in the network.

# 4. SYMPHONY: DISTRIBUTED ALGORITHM

In this section, we explain the working of Symphony that takes into account the aforementioned challenges in Section 3.2.

## 4.1 System Structure

Using cooperative decoding requires multiple APs to collaborate, however, at the same time, it may not be possible for all the APs in the network to collaborate since the wired backbone delays from APs to the central controller may be unbounded. Further, if the central controller is overseeing a lot of APs, it may also become a bottleneck. Symphony handles these contradicting requirements by dynamically placing different APs in different *groups*. One AP in each group serves as the Group Head (GH) and executes Symphony independently from other groups. Putting APs in different groups allows Symphony to achieve multiple objectives: (i) When dynamically creating groups, it is ensured that the average round trip delay on the wired backbone from the AP to the GH is no more than a threshold ($\psi$ $\mu$s), thereby bounding the expected communication delay between the AP and the GH with high probability; (ii) If one AP has high number of clients, then only the APs in the same group are required to wait for this AP to finish; and, (iii) No central controller is required.

Implementing this dynamic group based structure leads to various **challenges**: (i) To avoid decoding failures due to conflicting *suppress* schedules, a client that is in the range of APs from different groups is not allowed to transmit (discussed below). Thus, it is important to dynamically change the composition of the groups so that all clients get an opportunity to transmit; and, (ii) The overhead of maintaining the groups should be minimized. The next subsection describes the group management algorithm used in Symphony.

## 4.2 Group Management

**Group creation and joining an existing group:** When a node (AP or client) turns *on* or whenever the node is not part of any group, it enters the *wait* stage where it waits to hear a *join* message on the wireless. This message includes the PN sequence of the GH that originated this message. In Symphony, the ID of a group is same as the ID of its GH. Therefore, the PN sequence included in *join* is also useful in determining which group a received message came from. If the node (say $n_i$) hears such a message, it joins the announced group if all of the following requirements are satisfied: (*i*) $n_i$ is not in *recovery*; (*ii*) $n_i$ has no wireless neighbor $n_j$ such that $n_j$ is a member of some other group and is under recovery; and, (*iii*) If $n_i$ is an AP, then the average round trip delay between $n_i$ and the GH on the wired backbone is no more than a threshold ($\psi\mu$s). If $n_i$ determines that it is eligible to join the group, then it immediately rebroadcasts the *join* message. Once $n_i$ rebroadcasts the message, we say that $n_i$ has joined the group and has entered recovery. On the other hand, if $n_i$ is an AP and it does not hear any *join* message within a certain time ($\theta$ $\mu$s) that satisfies all the requirements, then it exits the wait stage. Next, if $n_i$ checks if it has a wireless neighbor $n_j$ such that $n_j$ is a member of some other group and is under recovery. If $n_i$ has no such neighbor, then $n_i$ creates a new group and declares itself as the GH. Afterward, it broadcasts a *join* message.

**Data transmission:** A client broadcasts its data packet immediately after broadcasting the *join*. Once the APs receive the headers of the data packets transmitted by clients, the APs correlate the PN sequences in the headers to determine the IDs of clients that transmitted (See Section 2). This information is then sent by the APs to the GH that uses algorithm described in Section 3.1 to compute which AP will suppress which client. This result is then sent back by the GH to all the APs who use this result to suppress the clients at the end of the slot. However, due to unpredictable queuing delays on the backbone, it is possible that some APs do not receive the result back from the GH before the end of the slot. To handle such scenarios, the GH iteratively computes the set of nodes to suppress for the next $k$ slots and sends that to all the APs (We explain in Section 7.2 how $k$ is determined). Further, in the unlikely case when some AP does not hear back from GH for more than $k$ slots, then at the end of the slot that AP does not suppress any client.

**Finishing the recovery:** As the APs suppress transmitters, eventually the number of packets transmitted will be small enough such that they can be decoded. This marks the end of recovery. At the end of recovery, the APs need to take a few steps to ensure: (i) GH is dynamically changed to ensure that all APs have equal chance of being the GH; (ii) Members belonging to a small group have a non-zero probability of merging with a bigger group; (iii) Members belonging to a large group have a non-zero probability of splitting into multiple smaller groups; and, (iv) Next recovery starts as soon as possible. We now explain the steps taken by APs at the end of the recovery: (*i*) At the beginning of the last slot, the GH sends a message to the APs announcing that the recovery will finish at the end of this slot. This allows the APs to know when to enter the *wait* stage. (*ii*) Before the recovery is over, the GH randomly selects some other AP in the group to be the new GH. The current GH informs this new potential GH of this decision. This step ensures that all APs have equal chance of being the GH. (*iii*) Once the recovery is over, all APs enter the *wait* stage for a duration of $\theta$ $\mu$s as described in the beginning of Section 4. For all the APs, $\theta$ is inversely proportional to the number of APs in their group. This ensures that smaller groups wait for a longer time to receive a *join* message from other groups, and thus they have higher probability of merging into another group. Also, the value of $\theta$ is set to be low for the selected GH while it is higher for the other APs. This ensures that the selected GH has higher chances of becoming a GH. This also reduces the probability of multiple APs independently declaring themselves as GH. This allows Symphony to set $\theta$ to a low value, thereby reducing the overhead of group management.

## 4.3 Cyclic Padding

As discussed in Section 4.2, on receiving the *join* message, a client first rebroadcasts the message and then its uplink data. Consider the example network shown in Figure 3. Lets say Alice starts transmitting *join* message at t = T$\mu$s. join message is a 127-symbol PN sequence, so, at 20Mbps, it will take 6.35$\mu$s[15] to transmit. Further, due to hardware constraints, it may take Alice up to 2$\mu$s more before it can transmit the data packet. Thus, Alice will start transmitting data packet somewhere between $t = T+6.35\mu s$ and $t = T + 8.35\mu s$ (See Figure 3). $AP_1$ upon hearing the join message would immediately rebroadcast it. However, due to propagation delay (at most 1 $\mu$s [15]) and radio tx-rx turn around (at most 2 $\mu$s [15]), it may happen as late as $t = T + 9.35\mu s$. Continuing this computation, we can see that all neighboring clients of $AP_2$ will start transmitting before $t = T + 27.05\mu s$. Thus, for a given AP, the maximum difference between the start of the data transmission times of its neighboring clients is at most 20.70$\mu$s (See Figure 3 where Alice can possibly start transmitting data as early as $t = T + 6.35\mu s$ while Don may start as late as at $t = T + 27.05\mu s$). Thus, to ensure that the PN sequences in their data packet headers collide only with the PN sequences of other transmitters, the clients pad cyclic bits after their PN sequences. In Symphony, the length of the cyclic padding is set to 25$\mu$s.

By using circular padding and *join* messages broadcasted on wireless, Symphony ensures that it is possible to correlate the PN sequences without requiring global synchronization. By requiring GH to proactively compute the set of suppressed transmissions, Symphony is able to handle unpredictable and non-zero latency on the backbone.

# 5. HETEROGENEOUS DATA RATES AND PACKET SIZES

In Symphony, different transmitters may select different physical layer data rates due to differences in channel conditions. Since wireless channels are bidirectional in nature[9], the transmitters in Symphony use the received poll packet to estimate the channel to the receiver. This is similar to the Mozart's [2] approach of estimating the physical layer data

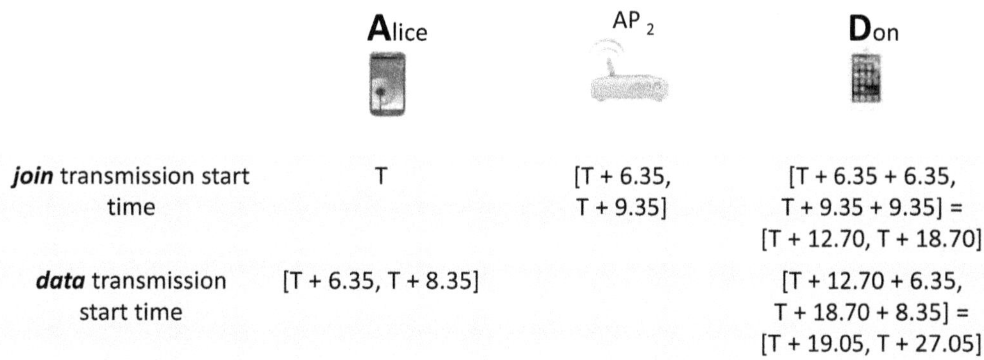


**Figure 3: Synchronization: The propagation delay is at most $1\mu s$, the length of 127 symbol PN sequence transmitted at 20Mbps is $6.35\mu s$ while the radio tx-rx turn around time is at most $2\mu s$ for a total duration of $9.35\mu s$[15]. For a given AP, the maximum difference between the start of the data transmission times of its neighboring clients is at most $20.70\mu s$**

rate. However, in Symphony, a client may receive poll from multiple APs. In that case, it estimates the channel with all the APs from whom it received the poll message and chooses the maximum possible data rate such that at least one AP can decode the transmitted packet. Estimating the channel requires the client to estimate the RSS of as many poll packets as possible. However, estimating the RSS of multiple colliding packets is not trivial due to high interference. As explained in Section 2, Symphony borrows the channel estimation technique proposed in Mozart for estimating the RSS of colliding packets.

In Symphony, the channel access time is fixed for all transmitters. A transmitter with better channel may transmit more bits than a transmitter with worse channel. However, it is possible that some transmitter may have good channel but not enough pending data to make complete use of the channel access time. This may lead to wastage of the channel. To minimize the channel wastage, such a transmitter in Symphony will reduce its data rate such that its transmission still fits in the slot size. This reduced data rate sometimes allows the receiver to simultaneously decode two transmissions using Successive Interference Cancellation (SIC) [20]. When using SIC, APs in Symphony decode two packets in the same slot and can suppress up to two transmissions in a single slot.

To implement SIC, the receivers in Symphony need to estimate the RSS of each of the colliding transmitters. For this, we borrow the idea proposed in Mozart[2] whereby PN sequences are used to estimate the RSS. Using SIC in Symphony requires making some changes to the way we construct the dependence graph:

1. In the dependence graph, instead of a vertex being a duplet, it can now be a triplet such that vertex $v_{ijk} = \{P_i, P_j, AP_k\}$ implies that $AP_k$ can decode packets from both $P_i$ and $P_j$ in a single slot using SIC where $P_i$ is the packet with higher RSS at $AP_k$. Such a vertex is added only if on the basis of estimated RSS and the physical layer data rates used, $AP_k$ determines that it can decode $P_i$ and $P_j$ simultaneously using SIC.

2. A directed edge is drawn from vertex $v_{ijk}$ to another vertex $v_{lmn} = \{P_l, P_m, AP_n\}$ *iff* either $P_i$ interferes at $AP_n$ or $P_j$ interferes at $AP_n$. Similarly, a directed edge is drawn from $v_{ijk}$ to vertex $v_{ln} = \{P_l, AP_n\}$ *iff* either $P_i$ interferes at $AP_n$ or $P_j$ interferes at $AP_n$. Finally, a directed edge is drawn from $v_{ln}$ to $v_{ijk}$ *iff* $P_l$ interferes at $AP_k$.

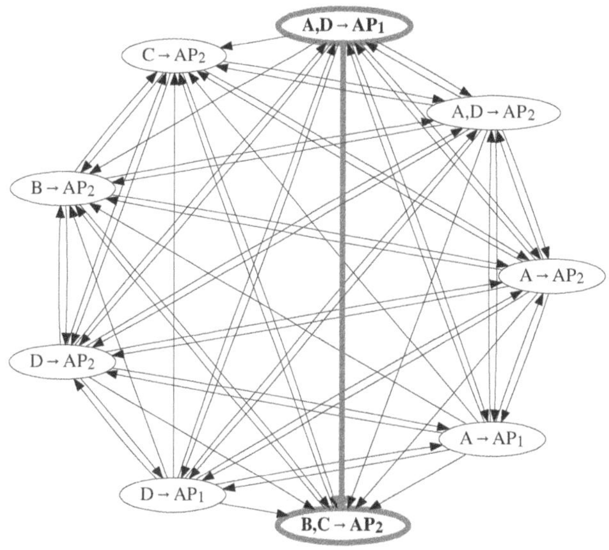


**Figure 4: Dependence graph for network topology shown in Figure 1a when using SIC. The chosen acyclic subgraph is also shown in bold.**

Figure 5 shows the dependence graph for the network topology shown in Figure 1a when using SIC. As before, to compute the set of suppressed transmissions, the GH picks an Induced Directed Acyclic Subgraph (IDAS) of the dependence graph. If the subgraph has vertices with three tuples, then the corresponding AP needs to suppress two transmitters. To maximize the probability of invoking SIC, Algorithm 1 is modified such that when greedily adding a vertex (Lines 8-15 of Algorithm 1), the GH first only considers the vertices with three tuples. If no such vertex is found, only then the GH adds the vertices with only two tuples.

## 6. DISCUSSION

In this section, we discuss some issues that need deeper investigation to make our solution more practical.

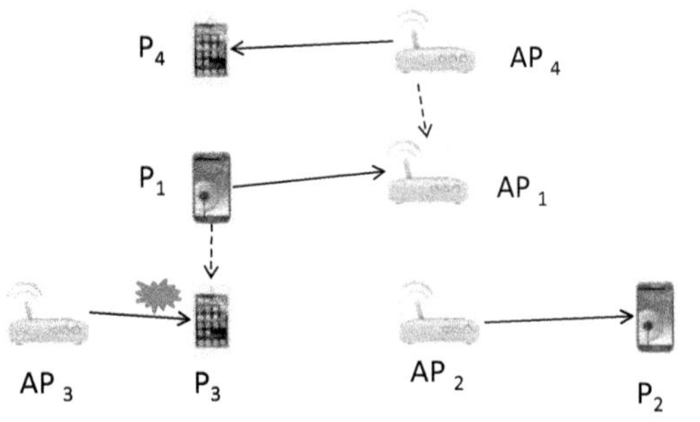


**Figure 5: Downlink-uplink coexistence.**

1. **Achieving gains on downstream traffic:** In EWLANs, it is generally easier to avoid collisions in downstream data as the APs are aware of which AP has data to send to which client. Multiple algorithms have been proposed in the literature that use this information to schedule downlink transmissions[21, 18, 14]. Symphony, on the other hand, improves performance for upstream data while allowing coexistence of downstream traffic.

In Symphony, due to differences in the distribution of clients, it is possible that for some AP, all its clients are suppressed sooner compared to clients of other APs. Symphony allows these *free* APs to transmit downlink traffic to their clients while other APs keep receiving uplink traffic. For the example network shown in Figure 5, once $AP_2$, $AP_3$ and $AP_4$ become free, they can start transmitting downlink traffic to their neighboring clients. The downlink transmission from $AP_2$ to $P_2$ will be successful while the transmission from $AP_3$ to $P_3$ will not be successful since it is interfered by $P_1$'s uplink traffic. The transmission from $AP_4$ to $P_4$ will also be successful. Although, this downlink transmission interferes with the uplink transmission at $AP_1$, it is still possible for $AP_1$ to decode $P_1$. For this, Symphony requires $AP_4$ to send its downlink packet to $AP_1$ on wired backbone. Using that, $AP_1$ recreates the samples of $AP_4$'s downlink packet and subtracts them from the received samples. Thus, in Symphony, the downlink traffic can coexist with the uplink traffic without causing interference to it.

Once all the APs in a group become free (i.e., they have transmitted *finish*), then the GH schedules interference-free downlink transmissions as discussed before in [14]. Apart from [14, 2], it is also possible to use other techniques proposed in the literature[21, 18] for achieving throughput gains on downlink traffic. Observe that, unlike other algorithms[14, 21], Symphony does not require any knowledge of the network topology. This reduces the overheads in Symphony compared to other algorithms.

2. **Packet subtraction:** In order to decode collided packets, APs in Symphony perform packet subtraction by recreating the samples. To increase the accuracy of subtraction, the APs need to correct for the phase, frequency and sampling offsets[8]. This problem of packet subtraction in presence of interference has been well studied [8, 2]. In our implementation, we use the scheme proposed in ZigZag[8] as it gave the best results.

3. **Sending ACK:** In Symphony, APs exchange the data packets among themselves on the backbone. However, this exchange may take some time due to the wired latency. In order to avoid wasting the channel during the decoding process, the APs immediately send *finish* to the clients without actually decoding the data packets. This allows clients to transmit new data packets when they receive a poll. While the next recovery is going on, the APs exchange the data packets on the wired backbone. Upon successful decoding, the APs send the *acks* to the different transmitters at the end of the next recovery period (during the *wait* period).

4. **Handling decoding errors:** After subtracting a packet, a small amount of *residual noise*[2] is left due to inaccuracies in correcting for the different offsets. If too many packets collide at the same AP, then as the AP cancels packets one-by-one, the residual noise builds up. This may result in an AP being unable to decode the packet of interest due to failed checksum. Further, this may also cause decoding error for the transmissions that are dependent on this transmission. In that case, the AP has two options: (*i*) Different APs may combine frames to correctly decode the received packet [16]. This is particularly useful in dense AP networks where multiple APs (including those who did not suppress any transmitter) may hear the transmission from the same client. (*ii*) If the previous option is not successful, then the APs send *ack* to only the transmitters that were decoded successfully.

5. **Mobility and fading:** It is possible that during recovery, a client may move and its set of neighboring APs may change. Symphony can handle such scenarios as clients in Symphony do not associate with any specific AP. However, if during the recovery, the client moves out of the range of *all* the APs in the group, then this may cause decoding error. In that case, the APs will use the mechanisms discussed above to handle the decoding error. It is also possible that during the recovery, due to fast-fading, some packet (say $P_i$) is temporarily not received by some of its neighboring APs. This does not cause any decoding error since in Symphony, the set of suppressed transmissions is computed only on the basis of transmissions received in that slot. So, in future when the APs receive the packet again, then it will be suppressed.

# 7. EXPERIMENTS

In this section, we describe the results from our experiments performed on the GNU radio platform and Universal Software Radio Peripheral (USRP) N210 version 4 radios with WBX daughterboards. In our experiments, we used BPSK with 1/2 convolutional code and the channel frequency was set to 1078 MHz. The phase offset, frequency offset and the sampling offset were cancelled as described in Section 6 while RSS estimation and transmitter identification were done as described in Section 2 and Section 5.

Besides Symphony, we also implemented a version of the IEEE 802.11 protocol. One of the challenges in implementing 802.11 was that USRP has different hardware parameters compared to the commercial 802.11 cards. So, similar to [2], we re-measured the optimum values of all 802.11 parameters (SIFS, DIFS, slot size, ACK timeout) for the N210 hardware. The transmission data rate was kept low (62.5 Kbps) to ensure that the delay between the host computer and the radio was *small* compared to the packet length so that the relative delay values would approximately match[2] the values from off-the-shelf wireless cards.

Apart from implementing our algorithm and IEEE 802.11, we also implemented two other algorithms: (i) **Mozart [2]**;

Table 1: Results from RTT measurements

| One-way distance (in hops) | Devices in between | Mean (in $\mu$s) | $\sigma$ (in $\mu$s) |
|---|---|---|---|
| 2 | One switch | 117 | 91.90 |
| 4 | 2 switches + 1 router | 829 | 182.96 |
| 5 | 2 switches + 2 routers | 2122 | 264.31 |

and, (ii) **Flex Omniscient TDMA**: Here, the clients do not associate with any particular AP but transmit data to and receive data from any of the neighboring APs. The schedule is greedily computed by a central omniscient scheduler. Two links are scheduled at different times *iff* transmitter of one of the link interferes at the receiver of the other link. The knowledge of which nodes have data to send to which other nodes, as well as the complete network topology is provided out-of-band (i.e., without any overhead) to the Flex-TDMA central scheduler and is 100% accurate.

## 7.1 Results

In our experiments, we placed two USRP APs in two different rooms (as shown in Figure 6a). Four USRP clients were placed at different locations in the three regions so as to create ten different topologies (hidden, non-hidden, mix etc.). In all the topologies, for 802.11 and Mozart, the clients associated to the AP with the strongest signal. Figure 6b shows the CDF of the throughput of clients for the four algorithms. Averaging over all topologies, Symphony (no SIC), Omniscient TDMA, Mozart (no SIC) and IEEE 802.11 provide a per node throughput (in Kbps) of 20.7, 14.4, 11.9 and 7.2, respectively. Thus, Symphony (no SIC) has an average throughput of 43%, 74% and 187% higher than Omniscient TDMA, Mozart (no SIC) and IEEE 802.11, respectively.

## 7.2 Measurements

Apart from implementing Symphony on the USRP testbed, we also made extensive measurements on the Ohio State University EWLAN. These measurements help us in better designing the algorithm and are also fed to the simulator (See Section 8). The measurements were conducted on a weekday between 10am-4pm (worst case analysis) with the routers and switches also serving the traffic from other desktops and APs on the EWLAN. All the switches and routers on the EWLAN had 1 Gbps interface speed. We measured the round trip time (RTT) between pairs of APs by transmitting and echoing back packets between multiple pairs of APs. The size of the packets was varied from 4-100 bytes to approximate the size of the control packets that would be transmitted from APs to the GH. Table 1 shows the result of the measurements. Using the three-sigma rule, we conclude that even with 5 hops of distance between a pair of APs, with 99.7% confidence, the RTT between the two APs will be less than 2914.93 $\mu$s (Mean + 3 times standard deviation).

So, the number of slots for which the GH proactively computes the set of suppressed transmissions ($k$ as discussed in Section 4.2) can be set such that $k \times T \geq 2914.93\mu s$ where $T$ is the channel access time (maximum duration of a data packet as discussed in Section 6). In our experiments and simulations, we computed $T$ as $\frac{1500\ bytes}{6\ Mbps} + \delta$ where $\delta$ is fixed time required for sending the data packet's header. Value of $k$ was set to 3.

# 8. SIMULATIONS AND EVALUATIONS

In this section, we explain the results from our ns-3 based trace driven simulations.

## 8.1 Setup

In our ns-3 based simulations, we randomly placed varying number of APs in a 750m $\times$ 750m field. The number of clients in the network were 5 times the number of APs. Each client associated with the AP from which it received the strongest signal. To generate traffic in the simulator, TCP connections were established between each client and its AP. For this, from the previously collected traffic traces during SIGCOMM[19], we computed the pdf distribution of packet sizes and also the pdf distribution of packet inter-arrival time over all connections. These two pdf distributions were then used to generate both uplink and downlink traffic in the simulation. To create network saturation condition, the number of connections between each client and its associated AP was set to 20.

Further, the results from the experiments were fed into the simulator as follows: (i) **PN-Sequence detection and RSS estimation accuracy**: The accuracy of correlating a PN sequence and estimating the transmitter's RSS depends on its SINR [2]. In the simulations, we used the values from [2] to model the PN sequence detection accuracy and the error in RSS estimation; (ii) **Residual noise level**: The level of the noise left after packet subtraction depends on the SINR of the canceled packet[2]. In simulations, we fed the power of the residual noise using the data shown in [2]; and, (iii) **Delays on backbone:** In our simulation, the APs were connected with each other through switched wired ethernet. To every switch, we connected three APs that were geographically close to each other. These switches were then connected to a router. The delay between two APs separated by $k$ hops, was randomly generated using the collected data as discussed in Section 7.2.

To compare the performance of Symphony with state of the art, we implemented various other algorithms: (i) **Mozart** [2]; (ii) **IEEE 802.11 without RTS-CTS**; and, (iii) **Flex Omniscient TDMA** as discussed in Section 7. The channel access time in both Mozart and Symphony was fixed to $\frac{1500\ bytes}{6\ Mbps} + \delta$ where $\delta$ is fixed time required for sending the data packet's header. In 802.11, the transmitters follow the data rate adaptation algorithm proposed in [13], while in Mozart and Symphony, the transmitters estimated the channel using the poll packet as described in Section 5.

## 8.2 Results

### 8.2.1 *Throughput*

Figure 7a compares the throughput of different algorithms. On an average, throughput of Symphony was observed to be 63% and 58% higher than TDMA and Mozart, respectively. Further, average throughput of Symphony was 5.6x compared to 802.11. Higher throughput of Symphony can be attributed to two factors: First, cooperative decoding as shown in Figure 1c allows APs in Symphony to simultaneously receive multiple packets. Secondly, when the transmitters have fewer data to send, then it results in throughput loss for TDMA that uses fixed slot length. Although, Symphony also uses fixed slot length, however, by using SIC to decode multiple packets, a single AP in Symphony is able to decode multiple packets simultaneously.

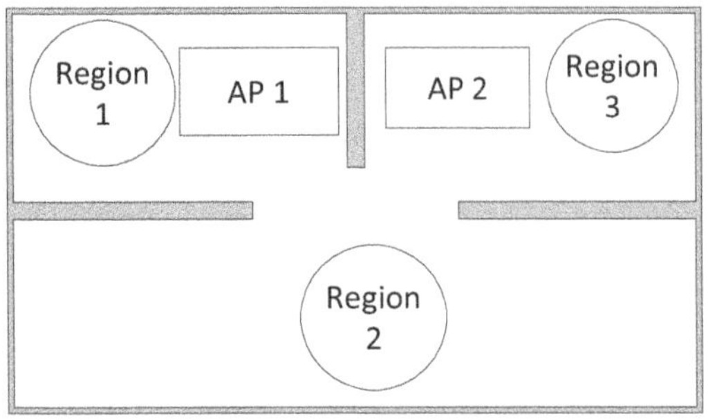


(a) USRP Testbed

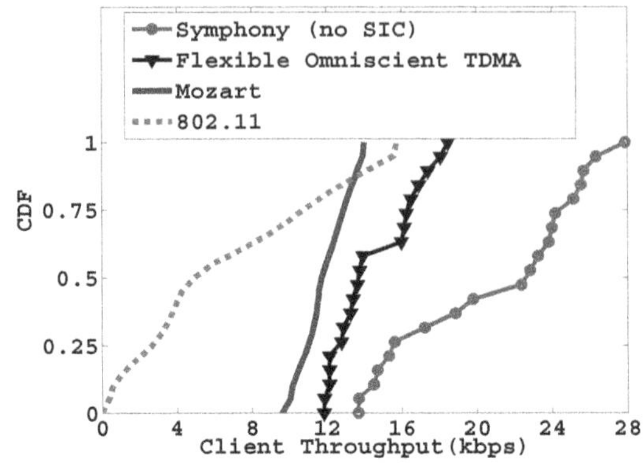


(b) CDF plot across different topologies

**Figure 6: Experiment testbed and results**

To further explore the throughput increase, we also plotted the percentage of data transmissions that were acknowledged by the receiver (See Figure 7b). This number is high for Symphony while for IEEE 802.11, the percentage of packets acknowledged is very low due to hidden terminal problem. Similar to Symphony, the percentage packets acknowledged for TDMA and Mozart were also close to 100%. Symphony had a slightly higher packet acknowledgment rate compared to Mozart since in the case of decoding failure in Symphony, multiple APs exchange frames to cooperatively decode a packet (See Section 6). In 802.11, the packet acknowledgment rate peaks as the number of APs and clients increase and then gradually decreases. This is because with increasing density of APs, it becomes possible for the clients to have stronger channel with the APs, thereby mitigating the effect of hidden terminal (due to data rate adaption and closeness to the AP). However, with increasing density, the probability of two clients picking the same backoff value and the probability of a hidden terminal also increases which decrease the packet acknowledgment rate. Due to these contradicting factors, the packet acknowledgment rate peaks when number of APs is 7.

Figure 7c shows the Jain's fairness index for different algorithms. Symphony has higher fairness since it allows all clients to participate. In other algorithms (including Flex Omniscient TDMA), if a client is in the range of multiple APs, then it may not get a chance to transmit to its AP since the channel in its neighborhood is very likely to be busy.

Figure 7d compares the percentage slots where SIC was used. Symphony uses SIC in more slots than Mozart since in Symphony, the AP can use SIC to suppress any pair of transmitters in its neighborhood. This increases the probability of finding a pair of transmitters that are eligible to be decoded simultaneously. Further, APs in Symphony also cooperate to use SIC to simultaneously transmit two packets to a single client resulting in higher applicability of SIC [20].

### 8.2.2 *Wired overhead*

In Symphony, APs exchange packets over the wired backbone. Theoretically, the number of unicast packets exchanged on wired backbone can be as many as $\frac{N\times(N-1)}{2}$-times the number of packets decoded on wireless (where $N$ is the number of APs in the network). However, Algorithm 1 minimizes this overhead by reducing the number of edges in the subgraph. Figure 8a shows the overhead as ratio of unicast data sent over wired over the wireless goodput. This ratio increases with increase in number of APs as expected but it plateaus as the number of APs go beyond a certain limit. This is because the broadcast nature of the wireless does not allow every AP in Symphony to suppress a packet. Thus, even with increase in APs, the number of APs that suppress at least one client do not increase, thereby also limiting the number of packets exchanged on the backbone. Further, at any time the ratio is less than 1 implying that for every packet decoded on wireless, at most 1 unicast transmission occurs on the wired backbone.

### 8.2.3 *Backoff Overhead*

APs in Symphony spend some time in backoff (or timeout) between every recovery. The amount of time spent is given by $\frac{100}{n}$ where $n$ is the number of APs in the group (See Section 4). Figure 8b shows the percent time spend by APs in backoff. APs in Symphony spend less than 1% time in backoff. In Symphony, the backoff overhead is amortized over the length of the recovery period. Further, unlike 802.11, the backoff in Symphony stays constant irrespective of the collision rate.

### 8.2.4 *Effect of wired ethernet latency*

Due to the unpredictable latency on the wired ethernet, the APs in Symphony proactively compute the schedule for the next 3 slots. To compute the effect of this latency on the optimality of the suppress schedule, we implemented a version of Symphony (called Symphony+) with latency on backbone set to zero. Figure 8c shows that throughput of Symphony+ is within 5% of Symphony indicating that the advance schedule computed by Symphony is close to optimal.

## 9. RELATED WORK

**Backbone usage:** The idea of using the wired backbone to increase wireless throughput is not new. In IAC[9], every node is assumed to have at least two antennas. The APs direct the transmitters in the network to align their transmissions such that the APs can cooperatively decode multiple packets. However, unlike [9], Symphony does not assume the

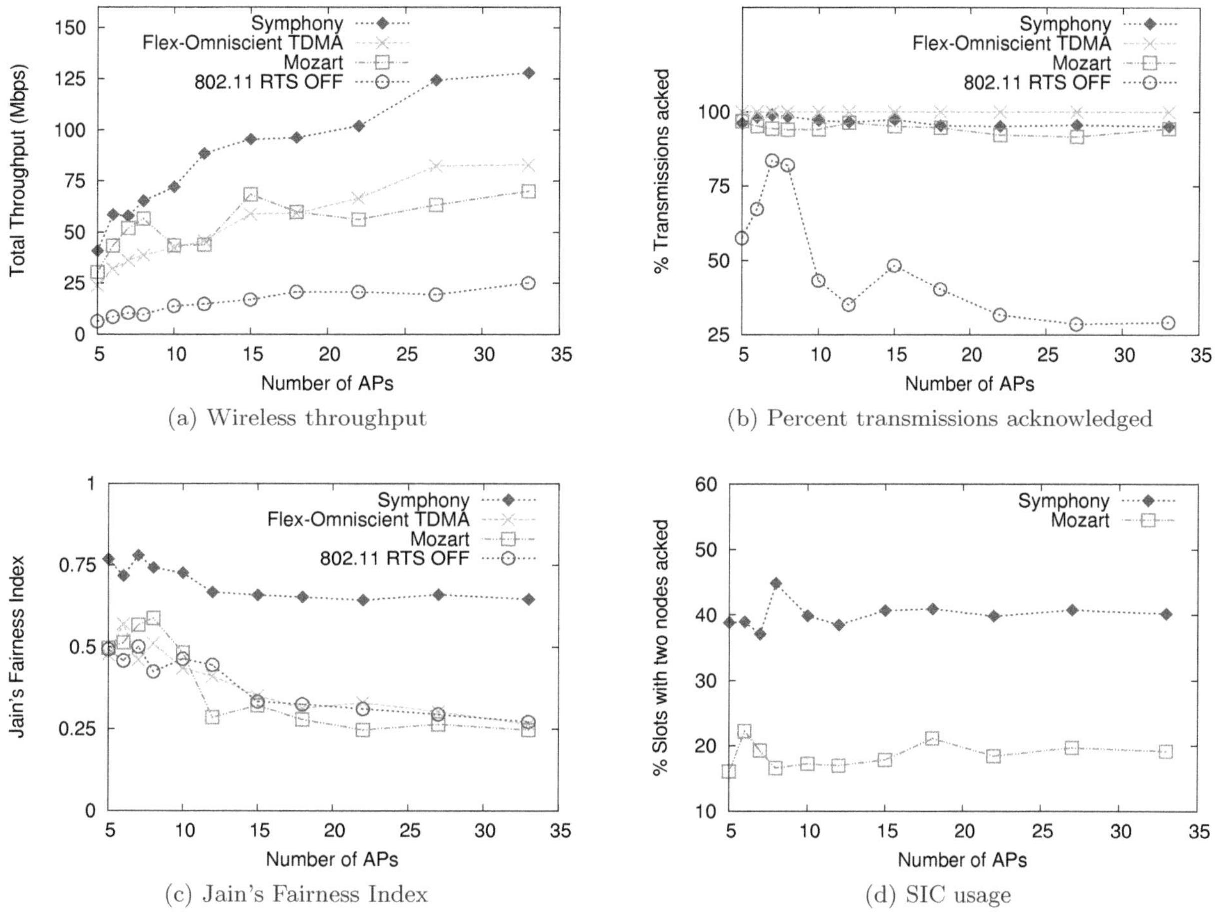


**Figure 7: Simulation results.**

presence of multiple antennas. In MegaMIMO[18], multiple APs cooperatively precode the transmissions such that each client receives only the packets intended for it while the other transmissions cancel-out. However, MegaMIMO requires that transmitters exchange decoded packets among themselves and thus, it works only for the downlink transmissions. On the other hand, Symphony improves the throughput for the uplink traffic.

In Epicenter[10], authors propose that APs should exchange coarse representation of symbols to decode corrupted bits. Similarly, authors in [16] also propose that APs exchange bits for decoding corrupted packets while Woo *et al.*[22] propose that APs should exchange raw samples. In all these algorithms, the APs cooperate to decode the same packet whereas in Symphony, APs encourage transmitters to collide and then cooperate to decode multiple packets simultaneously without exchanging the raw samples.

**Other MAC algorithms:** Algorithms proposed in [17, 4] focus mainly on client-AP association, channel assignment and power control. Authors in [14] propose implementing a backpressure based algorithm for downlink traffic. Similarly, CENTAUR[21] uses a central controller to reduce throughput loss due to hidden terminal and exposed terminal problems. However, their solution is also applicable only to downlink traffic. MiFi [3] also uses centralized coordination of APs and focuses on ensuring fairness. Contrary to the algorithms in [14, 21, 3, 5] that aim to decrease packet collisions, Symphony encourages transmitters to collide and then suppresses the packets so that all the colliding packets can be cooperatively decoded in minimum slots.

Mozart[2] is a recently proposed receiver oriented MAC layer protocol which was discussed in Section 2. In contrast to Mozart, Symphony focuses on leveraging communication in the wired backbone for cooperative decoding of collided packets. This leads to a different set of challenges as discussed in Section 1.

## 10. CONCLUSIONS

In this paper, we proposed Symphony, a novel backbone-based approach for cooperative packet decoding in Enterprise WLANs. We also designed an algorithm that computes the set of suppressed transmissions. To take into account the practical challenges of high latency, absence of synchronization and a central controller, we proposed a dynamic group based distributed algorithm. To reduce the throughput loss due to variations in packet lengths, we proposed that transmitters reduce their physical layer data rate while receivers use SIC to decode multiple packets simultaneously. Experiments conducted on the USRP testbed show that Symphony provides a throughput of 43% and 187% higher than Omni-

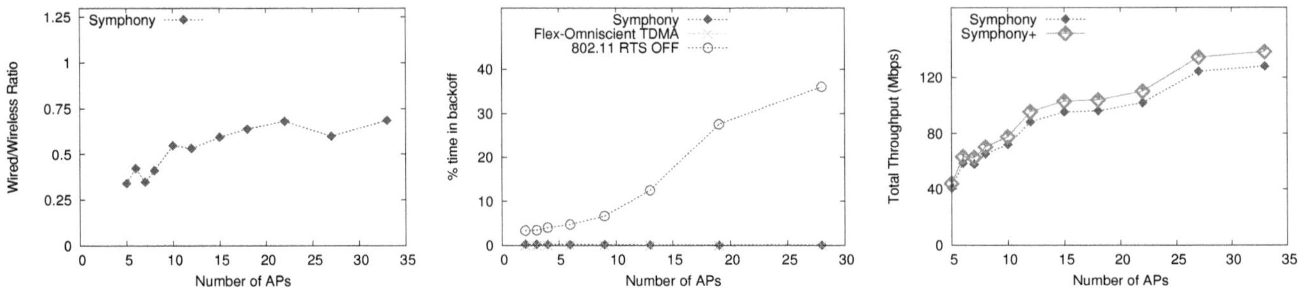


(a) Wired overhead for Symphony. (b) Time spent in backoff (c) Symphony+ has zero wired latency

**Figure 8: Simulation results: Overheads.**

scient TDMA and IEEE 802.11, respectively. Trace-driven simulations show that, throughput of Symphony is up to 1.63x compared to omniscient TDMA and 5.6x compared to IEEE 802.11.

## 11. ACKNOWLEDGMENTS

This material is based upon work partially supported by the National Science Foundation under Grant CNS-1161490.

## 12. REFERENCES


[1] Bansal, T., Chen, B., Sinha, P., and Srinivasan, K. Symphony. Tech. rep., 2013. `http://www.cse.ohio-state.edu/~bansal/symphonytechrep.pdf`.

[2] Bansal, T., Chen, B., Srinivasan, K., and Sinha, P. Mozart: Orchestrating Collisions in Wireless Networks. Tech. rep., 2013. `http://www.cse.ohio-state.edu/~bansal/mozart.pdf`.

[3] Bejerano, Y., and Bhatia, R. S. MiFi: A Framework for Fairness and QoS Assurance for Current IEEE 802.11 Networks with Multiple Access Points. *IEEE/ACM Transactions on Networking (TON) 14*, 4 (2006), 849–862.

[4] Bejerano, Y., Han, S.-J., and Li, L. E. Fairness and Load Balancing in Wireless LANs Using Association Control. In *Proc. ACM MOBICOM* (2004).

[5] Cidon, A., Nagaraj, K., Katti, S., and Viswanath, P. Flashback: Decoupled Lightweight Wireless Control. In *Proc. ACM SIGCOMM* (2012).

[6] Festa, P., Pardalos, P. M., and Resende, M. G. Feedback Set Problems. *Handbook of Combinatorial Optimization 4* (1999), 209–258.

[7] Gold, R. Optimal Binary Sequences for Spread Spectrum Multiplexing. *Information Theory, IEEE Transactions on 13*, 4 (1967), 619 –621.

[8] Gollakota, S., and Katabi, D. Zigzag Decoding: Combating Hidden Terminals in Wireless Networks. In *Proc. ACM SIGCOMM* (2008).

[9] Gollakota, S., Perli, S. D., and Katabi, D. Interference Alignment and Cancellation. In *Proc. ACM SIGCOMM* (2009).

[10] Gowda, M., Sen, S., Roy Choudhury, R., and Lee, S. Cooperative Packet Recovery in Enterprise WLANs. In *Proc. IEEE INFOCOM* (2013).

[11] Johannessen, S. Time Synchronization in a Local Area Network. *Control Systems, IEEE 24*, 2 (2004).

[12] Koutsonikolas, D., Salonidis, T., Lundgren, H., LeGuyadec, P., Hu, Y. C., and Sheriff, I. TDM MAC Protocol Design and Implementation for Wireless Mesh Networks. In *Proc. ACM CoNEXT* (2008).

[13] Lacage, M., Manshaei, M. H., and Turletti, T. IEEE 802.11 Rate Adaptation: A Practical Approach. In *Proc. ACM MSWIM* (2004).

[14] Laufer, R., Salonidis, T., Lundgren, H., and Le Guyadec, P. XPRESS: A Cross-Layer Backpressure Architecture for Wireless Multi-Hop Networks. In *Proc. ACM MOBICOM* (2011).

[15] Magistretti, E., Gurewitz, O., and Knightly, E. 802.11 ec: Collision Avoidance Without Control Messages. In *Proc. ACM MOBICOM* (2012).

[16] Miu, A., Balakrishnan, H., and Koksal, C. E. Improving Loss Resilience with Multi-Radio Diversity in Wireless Networks. In *Proc. ACM MOBICOM* (2005).

[17] Murty, R., Padhye, J., Chandra, R., Wolman, A., and Zill, B. Designing High Performance Enterprise Wi-Fi Networks. In *Proc. USENIX NSDI* (2008).

[18] Rahul, H., Kumar, S., and Katabi, D. MegaMIMO: Scaling Wireless Capacity with User Demand. In *Proc. ACM SIGCOMM* (2012).

[19] Schulman, A., Levin, D., and Spring, N. CRAWDAD data set umd/sigcomm2008. Downloaded from http://crawdad.cs.dartmouth.edu/umd/sigcomm2008.

[20] Sen, S., Santhapuri, N., Choudhury, R. R., and Nelakuditi, S. Successive Interference Cancellation: Carving Out MAC Layer Opportunities. *IEEE Trans. Mob. Comput. 12*, 2 (2013), 346–357.

[21] Shrivastava, V., Ahmed, N., Rayanchu, S., Banerjee, S., Keshav, S., Papagiannaki, K., and Mishra, A. CENTAUR: Realizing the Full Potential of Centralized WLANs Through a Hybrid Data Path. In *Proc. ACM MOBICOM* (2009).

[22] Woo, G. R., Kheradpour, P., Shen, D., and Katabi, D. Beyond the Bits: Cooperative Packet Recovery Using Physical Layer Information. In *Proc. ACM MOBICOM* (2007).

# Power and Thermal Challenges in Mobile Devices

Krishna Sekar
Broadcom Corporation
16340 W Bernardo Drive
San Diego, CA, 92127
1(858)385-8846
ksekar@broadcom.com

## ABSTRACT

In spite of significant advances in the development of low-power designs and power management techniques, power remains and will remain a first-class design constraint for mobile devices. The functionality integrated into mobile devices will only continue to grow with the increasing transition from PCs to super-phones. Power remains one of the critical hurdles to this transition, and without continued innovations in power management, the term "mobile" devices will be rendered moot. In addition to (and closely related to) power challenges in mobile devices are thermal challenges. Increasingly complex and rich functionality in mobile devices leads to higher power dissipation, and consequently, higher temperatures. However, thermal constraints are constant across successive device generations. Thermal limits, even more than power, will become the fundamental bottleneck to increasing the capabilities of such devices, making thermal management techniques crucial.

This paper discusses some of the major challenges in power management and thermal management for current and next-generation mobile devices from a semiconductor industry perspective. Specifically, this paper discusses challenges in three areas: process-variability-aware power management, thermally aware power management and thermal management for mobile devices. Broadcom mobile chipsets feature multiple such advanced power and thermal management techniques, with active on-going research and development in each of these areas.

## Categories and Subject Descriptors

C.5.3 [**Computer System Implementation**]: Microcomputers – *Portable devices*

## Keywords

Mobile devices; power management; thermal management; leakage power; process variability

## 1. INTRODUCTION

High-end mobile computation and communication devices have become ubiquitous today. The research firm IDC reports that for the first time, more smartphones were shipped in Q1 2013 than

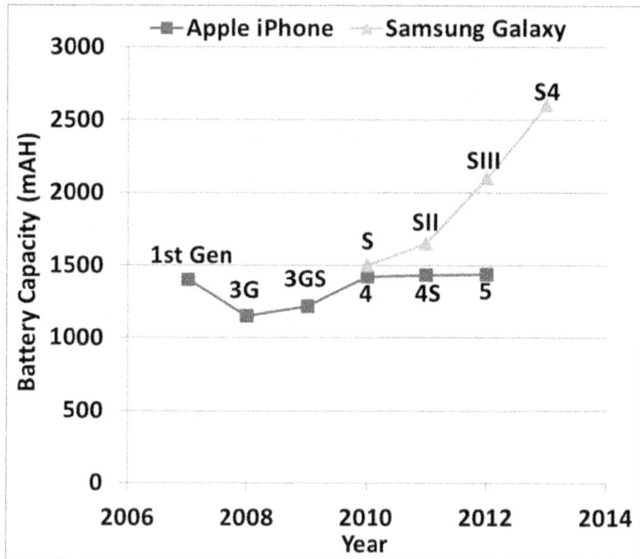


**Figure 1: Smartphone battery capacity evolution**

feature phones [1]. This trend will continue with the increasing availability of sub-$100 smartphones and tablet devices [2]. Significant advances in mobile technology have enabled this transition. Important among them has been the development of advanced low-power designs and power management techniques, allowing increasingly rich and complex feature-sets to be run on devices with only marginally increasing battery capacity. This is illustrated by Figure 1, which shows how the battery capacities of both Apple iPhones and Samsung Galaxy smartphone models have changed over successive generations of these devices [3][4]. Battery capacity has remained roughly flat between the 1st Generation iPhone and iPhone 5, while it has increased only 1.73 times between Samsung Galaxy S and S4. However, performance has increased by many times more. For example, the application processor performance has increased from up to 2000 DMIPS in Galaxy S with a single ARM8 processor at 1GHz [5][6], to up to 31500 DMIPS in Galaxy S4 with quad ARM A15 processors at 1.6GHz and quad ARM A7 processors at 1.2GHz[7][8], an increase of more than 15 times!

In spite of these advances, power remains and will remain a first-class design constraint to the continued advancement of mobile technology. Already users are implicitly expected to charge their mobile devices one or more times a day. Also, there is a limit to the battery size that can be accommodated in ever decreasing device form factors. However, the functionality integrated into such devices, and consequently their power consumption, will continue to grow as users increasingly transition to them from PCs as their primary means of information processing, consumption


*MobiCom'13*, September 30–October 4, 2013, Miami, FL, USA.

and communication. Without continued innovations in power management, this transition cannot fully come to fruition.

This paper discusses two such power management challenges in mobile devices:

- **Process-variability-aware Power Management:** With shrinking semiconductor process technology nodes, there is much greater variability between the device characteristics of individual dice. A power management policy which is optimized for a "nominal" die may be suboptimal for a "non-nominal" die. However, power management policies today are often process-variability agnostic. This is discussed in Section 2.

- **Thermally Aware Power Management:** Along with device variability, smaller process technology nodes also lead to much higher leakage power in semiconductor devices, making leakage power as important to manage as dynamic power. This is especially true at higher temperatures since leakage power increases exponentially with temperature. The power optimization techniques for leakage power may be very different from those for dynamic power. However, power management policies are usually temperature agnostic. Section 3 further discusses this challenge.

Closely related to, but distinct from, power challenges in mobile devices are thermal challenges. With multiple GHz+ application processors [9], advanced graphics capabilities [10], advanced LTE modems [11] and 5G WiFi [12] technologies, amongst others, modern mobile devices are capable of supporting very sophisticated functionality with high levels of performance. This leads to much higher power dissipation, and consequently, much higher temperatures. However, the thermal constraints of components inside a mobile device remain relatively constant. Furthermore, the thermal constraints on mobile device surface temperatures are also constant since the ability of human skin to tolerate temperature does not change. In fact, the problem is exacerbated with the decrease in the form factors of mobile devices which decreases their ability to dissipate the generated heat. This could lead to device overheating issues with very adverse consequences in terms of device usability, consumer safety, product liability, and negative publicity [13][14]. Thermal constraints, even more than power, will become the fundamental bottleneck to further integrating more functionality and performance in mobile devices.

Thermal challenges are being addressed today through the use of thermal management policies that typically throttle the performance of various components under high temperature conditions. However, without careful design, such policies could force devices to be throttled to a much lower level of performance for significant periods of time, invalidating the whole point of adding such advanced capabilities in the first place. This paper discusses the thermal management challenge in Section 4, advocating the need for optimized thermal management algorithms and policies that can intelligently manage the trade-off between application performance, power dissipation, thermal effects and user-perceived quality.

These challenges are being addressed through advanced power and thermal management techniques in various different Broadcom mobile chipsets today such as cellular baseband processors, mobile multimedia processors, power management ICs, cellular RF ICs, WiFi, Bluetooth, Global Positioning System (GPS), and Near-Field-Communications (NFC) systems, amongst others [15]. Broadcom is also pursuing active research and development in each of these areas.

# 2. PROCESS-VARIABILITY-AWARE POWER MANAGEMENT

## 2.1 Description

Continued advances in semiconductor device fabrication technology have enabled progressive reduction of transistor process geometries. Figure 2 shows how the process technology node (referring to the average half-pitch of a DRAM cell) has decreased over the years, from 130 nm in 2001, to 28 nm in 2013, and projected to reach 10 nm by 2022 [16]. This shrinking of transistor process geometries has been the main driving force behind Moore's law [17], which predicts that the number of transistors on integrated circuits doubles approximately every two years. It is the continued applicability of Moore's law that has enabled the revolution in mobile technology with faster, smaller and cheaper devices becoming available every successive generation.

However, with smaller process geometries, there is greater variability in device characteristics such as performance and power between individual dice. For example, in the 28 nm technology node, there could be up to 42% variability in performance and up to 51% variability in total power consumption [18]. This increasing die-to-die variability can be attributed to inherent limitations of the fabrication process especially for smaller process geometries. This trend has only become worse at smaller technology nodes, with increasing number of silicon dice whose characteristics vary from that of "nominal" or "typical" dice. Figure 3 shows the probability density function for the delay through a flip-flop (normalized to 1) fabricated in 65 nm and in 28 nm. At the 28 nm node, there are a larger number of dice whose delay is more than or less than that of nominal dice. Such devices are characterized as either slow or fast (i.e., non-nominal). The same trend applies to power consumption as well.

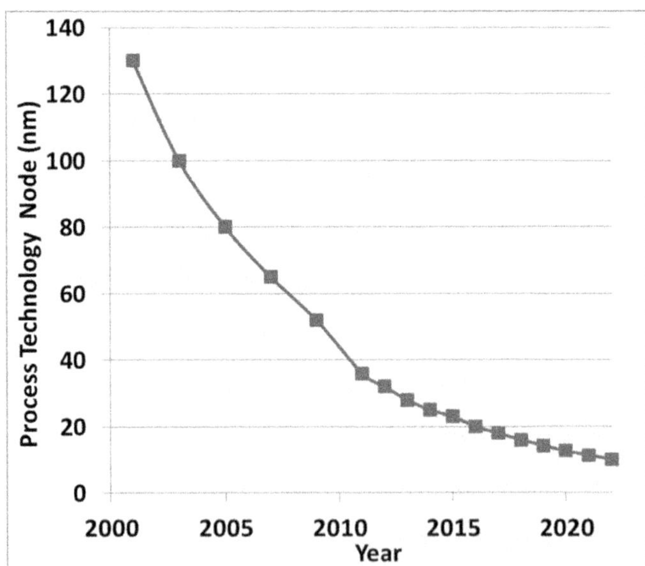


**Figure 2: Semiconductor process technology node evolution**

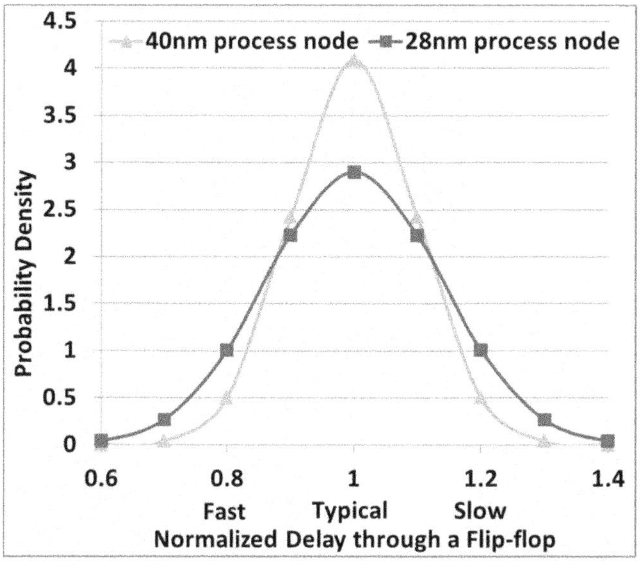


**Figure 3: Variability of delay through a flip-flop**

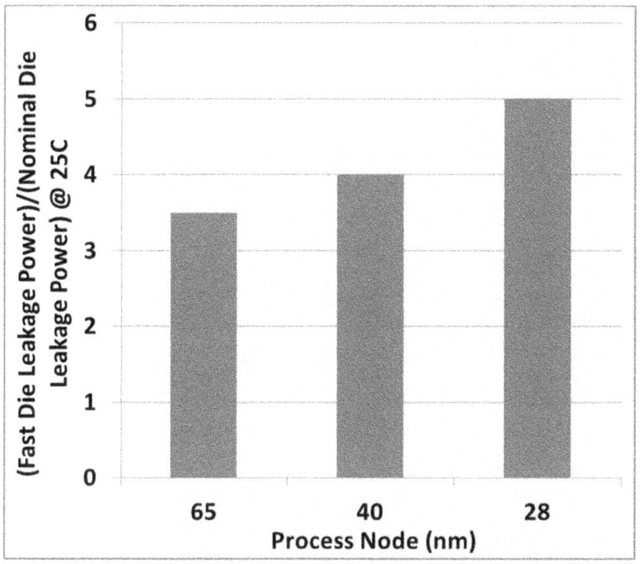


**Figure 4: Ratio of the leakage power of fast dice to leakage power of nominal dice for different process technology nodes**

To keep silicon yields high and the process node economical, non-nominal dice (within a certain standard deviation such as 2.5σ or 3σ) are still shipped and sold in end products. Therefore, in addition to an increasing number of non-nominal dice, the magnitude of difference between nominal and non-nominal dice has also been increasing with smaller process geometries. Figure 4 shows how the ratio between the leakage power of fast dice and nominal dice has been increasing with smaller technology nodes. The same trend holds true for dynamic power variability as well, albeit to a much smaller magnitude.

The consequence of device power variability is that **power is no longer a number, but a distribution**. However, power models and estimates typically used today are for nominal dice. Also, power management policies used today are usually customized for nominal dice and may not be optimal for the increasingly common non-nominal dice. This calls for *process-variability-aware power management policies*.

## 2.2 Motivational Example

One such commonly used power management technique is Adaptive Voltage Scaling (AVS). In AVS, slow dice are operated at a higher voltage compared to nominal dice, while fast dice are operated at a lower voltage, such that all dice can achieve a given target clock frequency. This exploits the fact that device speed is a function of the operating voltage. Fast dice, by virtue of being "fast", can still meet timing requirements at a lower voltage, while slow dice can be made to meet timing requirements by increasing their voltage. This, in turn, reduces the power consumption variability between different die types. Fast dice have higher leakage power consumption compared to nominal dice. Hence, reducing their voltage decreases their power consumption, bringing them closer to nominal dice. Similarly, increasing the voltage of slow dice, increases their power consumption, thereby, bringing them closer to nominal dice.

As another example, consider two power management policies for mobile devices: Dynamic Voltage and Frequency Scaling (DVFS) [19] and Run-Fast-and-Stop (RFS). In DVFS, the device is operated at the lowest possible voltage and frequency setting, such that it is just enough to meet its current computational requirements. DVFS operates under the principle that it is more power-efficient to run at the lowest voltage and frequency since, although it increases device active time, it reduces the overall power consumption due to the square dependence of dynamic power on voltage. DVFS is quite commonly used today in mobile devices. In contrast, in RFS, the device is operated at the highest possible voltage and frequency setting, such that the tasks are completed as soon as possible, and then the device is powered off. RFS operates under the principle that it is more power-efficient to keep the device powered off for as long as possible in order to minimize leakage power. These are two very different policies, and yet, each may be optimal for different die types. DVFS may be better suited for nominal and slow dice where dynamic power tends to dominate overall power consumption, whereas RFS may be better suited for fast dice where leakage power may dominate.

## 2.3 Challenge

A one-size-fits-all power management policy does not work very well any more, necessitating the need for process-variability-aware power management policies that are customized to the device characteristics they run on. Broadcom mobile chipsets feature such advanced power management policies, and Broadcom is actively engaged in further research and development in this area.

# 3. THERMALLY AWARE POWER MANAGEMENT

## 3.1 Description

As transistor process geometries have continued to shrink (Figure 2), the leakage power dissipated by semiconductor devices has increased exponentially. This is illustrated by Figure 5, which shows that the leakage power per gate increased by 2x going from 65 nm to 40 nm, and by 3x going from 40 nm to 28 nm. This trend is driven by multiple factors including thinner gate oxides, smaller channel lengths and smaller threshold voltages, and is expected to continue as process geometries shrink further. Additionally, the leakage power of fast dice increases much faster compared to that of nominal dice at smaller process technology nodes (Figure 4). In contrast, dynamic power per gate (for the same frequency) has decreased in every successive technology generation, due to reduction in the device operating voltage and load capacitances.

Therefore, leakage power is becoming a much more dominant factor in the total power dissipation of semiconductor devices.

This is especially true at higher temperatures since leakage power depends exponentially on temperature. Figure 6 shows how the leakage power of a nominal device in 28 nm scales with temperature, from 1x at 25°C to 30x at 125°C. At higher temperatures, leakage power could account for 40%-50% of the total power consumption of a device. Also, at smaller process geometries, dynamic power consumption also increases at higher temperatures although to a much lesser extent compared to leakage power. Furthermore, due to the increasingly rich and power-hungry computation and communication functionality integrated in small form-factor mobile devices today, device temperatures are expected to be significantly high for heavy-usage scenarios.

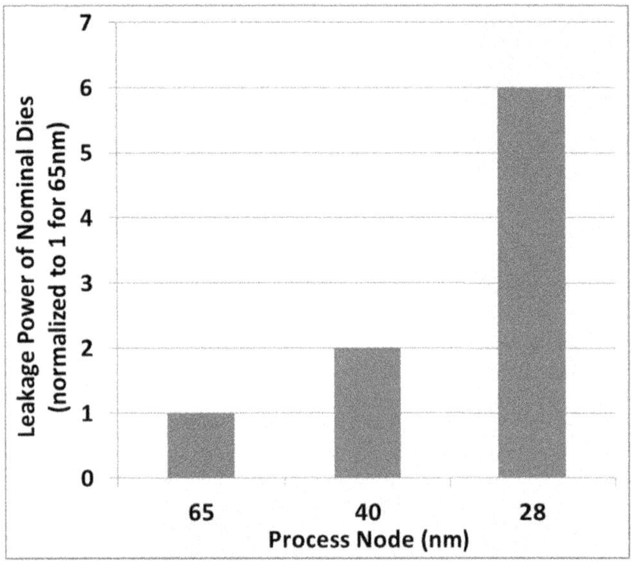


**Figure 5: Leakage power of nominal dice (normalized to 1 for 65 nm) for different process technology nodes**

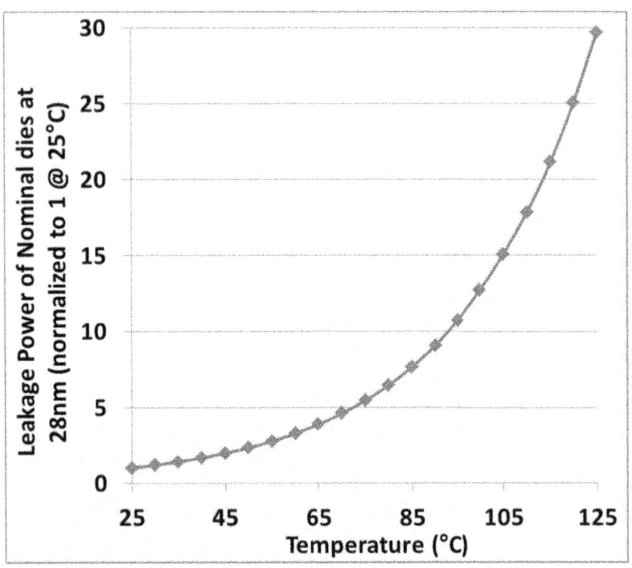


**Figure 6: Leakage power of nominal dice (normalized to 1 at 25°C) over temperature**

The consequence of the above is that **temperature has become a very important factor to consider in the context of power**. However, power models, simulations and estimates used today usually do not factor in temperature as a parameter. In fact, since temperature is itself a function of the power dissipation of a device, there is a positive feedback loop between power and temperature until the device reaches steady-state temperature (or in worst-case scenarios, there is thermal runaway). This calls for a "power-temperature cosimulation" methodology for accurate power estimation. Furthermore, power management policies typically used in mobile devices today are temperature agnostic.

## 3.2 Motivational Example

Consider, for example, two CPU power management policies used today in multi-CPU mobile devices: Dynamic Voltage and Frequency Scaling (DVFS) [19] and CPU Hotplug [20]. As described in Section 2.2, in DVFS, the CPU is operated at the lowest voltage and frequency setting which is just enough to meet the CPU load requirements. In contrast, in CPU Hotplug, one or more of the CPU cores are powered down or powered up depending on the CPU load requirements. DVFS is better optimized for dynamic power, while CPU Hotplug is better optimized for leakage power. Now, consider a dual-core mobile device. At low temperatures, due to the dominance of dynamic power, DVFS would be more power-efficient than CPU Hotplug; for processing the same CPU load, it may be better to operate two cores at a lower voltage and frequency than one core at a higher voltage and frequency. However, at high temperatures, due to the dominance of leakage power, the situation may completely reverse and CPU Hotplug may be more power-efficient.

## 3.3 Challenge

Temperature must be factored in as a critical parameter for all aspects of power on mobile devices, from power modeling, to estimation, to simulation and to thermally aware power management policies. This is the strategy adopted in Broadcom mobile chipsets, where temperature is incorporated as a first-class design parameter into all aspects of mobile device power modeling and management.

# 4. THERMAL MANAGEMENT

## 4.1 Description

Over the last several years, there has been an explosive growth in mobile technology, with ultra-high-end mobile devices becoming ubiquitous today. Such devices integrate a wide variety of sophisticated and high-performance computation and communication technologies, such as multiple GHz+ application processors, advanced LTE modems, advanced multimedia and graphics cores, 5G WiFi, GPS, Bluetooth and NFC chipsets, amongst others [15]. Now, for every successive technology node generation, the power dissipation per silicon gate has been decreasing. Therefore, the power consumption for the same use-case has been decreasing. However, due to the integration of more and more rich functionality (with a consequent increase in the number of gates), and increases in the operating frequencies to support such functionality, the overall power dissipated inside mobile devices has been increasing rapidly. Figure 7 illustrates how the power dissipation (normalized to 1W for Chip1) of some representative Broadcom mobile baseband processors has increased over the years for the heaviest usage scenario that they can respectively support and without any thermal management. From a 65 nm chip featuring a single ARM11 application processor, to a 28 nm chip featuring multiple advanced ARM application processors, the potential power dissipation has increased by almost 3 times. This trend is only expected to continue with further integration of even more advanced functionality in mobile devices.

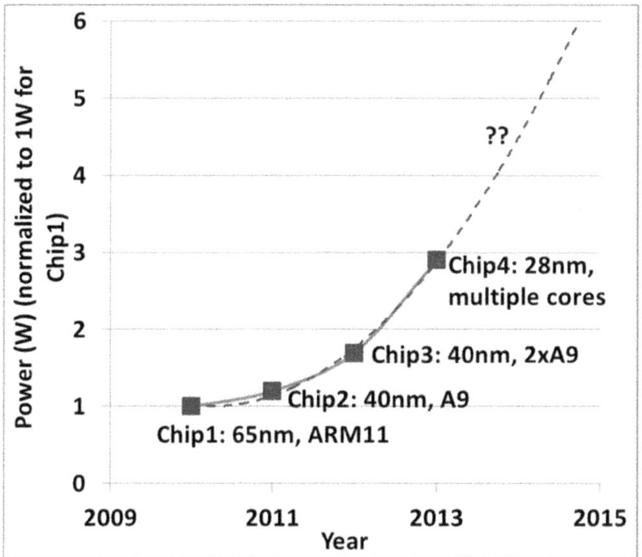


**Figure 7: Power dissipation of different representative cellular baseband processors under heaviest usage scenario (normalized to 1W for Chip1)**

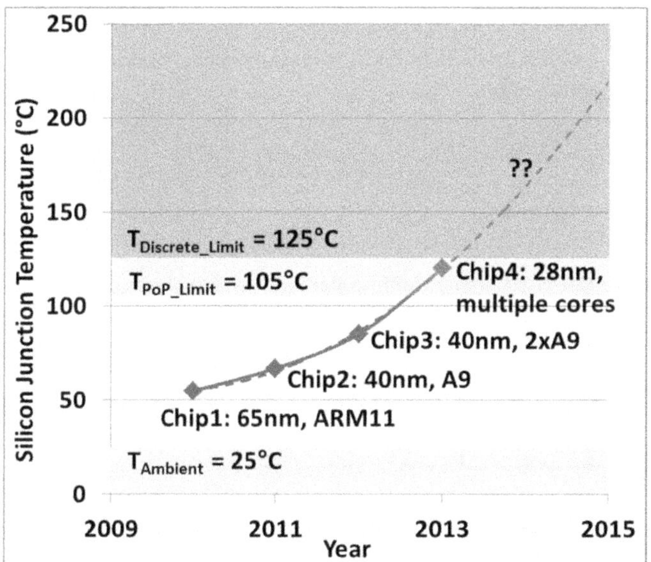


**Figure 8: Silicon junction temperature of different representative cellular baseband processors under heaviest usage scenario**

Due to increasing power dissipation, the temperatures inside mobile devices have been rapidly increasing. Figure 8 illustrates how the silicon die temperature has increased over the years corresponding to the same chips and power dissipations shown in Figure 7 (JEDEC thermal analysis assuming an ambient temperature of 25°C; without any thermal management). However, the fundamental thermal limits of components inside a mobile device have not changed. For example, in the elevated temperature range, low-power DRAM (LPDDR) devices have a thermal limit of 105°C [21], thereby limiting the maximum temperature of the underlying baseband processors in the case of Package-on-Package (PoP) systems. Similarly, the maximum baseband processor die junction temperatures are usually limited to 125°C to ensure correct device operation. Additionally, the thermal limits on mobile device surface temperatures have remained constant over the years since the ability of human skin to withstand temperature does not change. Furthermore, active cooling mechanisms such as fans, which are commonly used in laptops and PCs for thermal mitigation, are not feasible for use in phones and tablets. The thermal problem is further exacerbated by the fact that mobile device form-factors are becoming smaller and thinner, and therefore their ability to dissipate the generated heat has been decreasing.

One way to mitigate the thermal challenges in mobile devices is through better platform-level thermal design. This includes techniques such as thermally aware component placement and the use of materials such as heat spreaders and thermal interface material (TIM). However, such techniques provide limited improvements and are relatively expensive to use. Temperature, even more than power, is fast becoming the fundamental design bottleneck to the continued progress towards even more powerful mobile devices. Therefore, the design and development of better **thermal management** algorithms and policies has become imperative.

Thermal management policies typically rely on throttling the performance or functionality of various components in order to reduce their power dissipation, and consequently the temperature of mobile devices. However, by constraining the capabilities of the mobile device, thermal management will lead to some loss of performance. Therefore, without careful design of such thermal management policies, mobile devices could end up operating in much lower modes of performance than they are actually capable of for significant periods of time, thereby negating the usefulness of adding such high-performance features in the first place.

## 4.2 Motivational Example

Consider, for example, two thermal management policies and their effect on power and temperature as illustrated in Figure 9. Assume that the maximum temperature limit of the device is 100°C and the ambient temperature is 25°C. Under Policy1, the device is allowed to dissipate 3W of power until the temperature reaches the maximum limit of 100°C. At this point, the device is throttled to dissipate only 1W of power until the temperature cools down to 90°C, at which point throttling is disengaged. Figure 9 shows the power dissipation (Primary Y-axis, solid red line) and temperature (Secondary Y-axis, dotted red line) of the device over time under Policy1. The long-term average power dissipation of the device under Policy1 is 2.3W. In contrast, under Policy2, once the device reaches a temperature greater than 90°C, it is constantly throttled to dissipate only 2.3W of power. Figure 9 shows the power dissipation (solid blue line) and temperature (dotted blue line) of the device under Policy2. Both Policy1 and Policy2 dissipate the same amount of average power (2.3W), but under Policy2, the device temperature reaches only 95°C, and therefore has 5°C more thermal headroom. This thermal headroom can be translated to allowing the device to dissipate higher power than Policy1 (2.5W, 8.7% higher) while still keeping the temperature below the thermal limit of 100°C. Additionally, the effect of Policy1 and Policy2 on user-perceived application behavior could be very different. Policy1 could lead to visibly jerky application behavior due to the constant toggling between high and low performance modes, whereas Policy2 could lead to smoother, albeit lower, application performance.

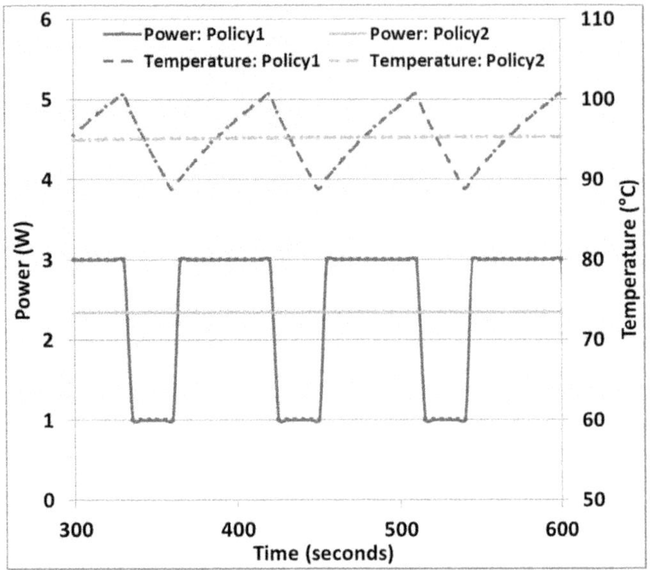


**Figure 9: Power and temperature under two different thermal management policies**

## 4.3 Challenge

It is of paramount importance to address the thermal challenge in mobile devices through the design of smart thermal management algorithms and policies that can effectively manage the trade-off between performance, power, temperature, and user experience. Such advanced thermal management features are available on Broadcom mobile chipsets today, with further research and development in this area being actively pursued.

# 5. CONCLUSIONS

Significant challenges remain today in the areas of power and thermal management for the continued advancement towards ever more sophisticated and feature-rich mobile computation and communication devices. This paper discussed three such challenges in the area of power management and thermal management. Broadcom is at the forefront of addressing many of these power and thermal challenges in various leading-edge mobile chipsets through innovate technologies, thereby enabling the continuation of the mobile revolution.

# 6. REFERENCES


[1] "More Smartphones Were Shipped in Q1 2013 Than Feature Phones, An Industry First According to IDC", IDC – Press Release, April 25th, 2013, http://www.idc.com/getdoc.jsp?containerId=prUS24085413

[2] "The global smartphone tipping point: '$100 or less'", CNET news article, February 29th, 2012, http://reviews.cnet.com/8301-13970_7-57387397-78/the-global-smartphone-tipping-point-$100-or-less/

[3] "List of iOS devices: iPhone", Wikipedia, http://en.wikipedia.org/wiki/List_of_iOS_devices#iPhone

[4] "Samsung Galaxy: Smartphones", Wikipedia, http://en.wikipedia.org/wiki/Samsung_Galaxy

[5] "Samsung Galaxy S", Wikipedia, http://en.wikipedia.org/wiki/Samsung_Galaxy_S

[6] "Cortex-A8 Processor: Specifications: Dhrystone Performance" http://www.arm.com/products/processors/cortex-a/cortex-a8.php

[7] "Samsung Galaxy S4", Wikipedia, http://en.wikipedia.org/wiki/Samsung_Galaxy_S4

[8] "List of ARM microprocessor cores: Cortex-A7 and Cortex-A15", Wikipedia, https://en.wikipedia.org/wiki/List_of_ARM_microprocessor_cores

[9] 'Broadcom 3G Baseband Processors", http://www.broadcom.com/products/Cellular/3G-Baseband-Processors

[10] "Broadcom Mobile Multimedia Processors", http://www.broadcom.com/products/Cellular/Mobile-Multimedia-Processors

[11] "Broadcom 4G Baseband Processors", http://www.broadcom.com/products/Cellular/4G-Baseband-Processors

[12] "Broadcom 5G WiFi", http://www.broadcom.com/products/features/5gwifi.php

[13] "Our test finds new iPad hits 116 degrees while running games", Consumer Reports, March 20th, 2012, http://news.consumerreports.org/electronics/2012/03/our-test-finds-new-ipad-hits-116-degrees-while-running-games.html

[14] "Does the new iPad have an overheating problem?", CNN, March 21st, 2012, http://www.cnn.com/2012/03/20/tech/gaming-gadgets/ipad-overheating

[15] "Broadcom Products", http://www.broadcom.com/products/

[16] "ITRS 2011 Edition: Lithography: 2011 tables: Table LITH2", International Technology Roadmap for Semiconductors, http://www.itrs.net/Links/2011ITRS/Home2011.htm

[17] Moore, Gordon E. (1965), "Cramming more components onto integrated circuits", in *Electronics*, Volume 38, Number 8, April 19th, 1965.

[18] "ITRS 2011 Edition: Design: 2011 tables: Table DESN10", International Technology Roadmap for Semiconductors, http://www.itrs.net/Links/2011ITRS/Home2011.htm

[19] A. R. Chandrakasan and R. W. Brodersen, *Low Power Digital CMOS Design*, Kluwer Academic Publishers, Norwell, MA, 1995.

[20] "CPU Hotplug", Linaro, https://wiki.linaro.org/WorkingGroups/PowerManagement/Doc/Hotplug

[21] "Low Power Double Data Rate 3 SDRAM (LPDDR3)", JEDEC LPDDR3 Standard, JESD209-3, May, 2012, http://www.jedec.org/standards-documents/docs/jesd209-3

# Towards a Virtual Cellular Network with Variable Grade Spectrum: Challenges and Opportunities*

[Invited Industry Track Paper]

Milind M. Buddhikot
Alcatel-Lucent Bell Labs
milind.buddhikot@alcatel-lucent.com

## ABSTRACT

In this paper, we make a case for future wireless networks that will seamlessly exploit many *variable grade* spectrum bands. The transformation we envision will be fueled by a fundamental change in the way networks use spectrum. The mix of spectrum options will include existing exclusively licensed and unlicensed bands and new *shared spectrum bands* where incumbent primary transmitters with interruptible, exclusive access share the band with cooperating (secondary) users. Such bands used in small cell deployments will be key to creating enormous wireless capacity needed to support future traffic demands. The nascent spectrum database technologies will morph into more dynamic spectrum databases and provide essential interference coordination, channel management and monetization. This trend when combined with infrastructure sharing enabled by cloud and SDN technologies will gradually lead to new deployment models. Such network transformation and democratization of spectrum access can fuel innovative business models and new regulatory regimes for wireless networks.

We illustrate the new architecture and component radio, database and security technologies using concrete example of incorporating shared spectrum in a small cell network.

## Categories and Subject Descriptors

C.2 [**COMPUTER-COMMUNICATION NETWORKS**]: Network Architecture and Design—*Wireless communication*

## Keywords

Shared spectrum, Spectrum databases, High capacity wireless, Future wireless networks

## 1. OVERVIEW OF THE WIRELESS LANDSCAPE AND KEY TRENDS

The 2010 National Broadband Commission [1] report published by FCC postulated that 1.2 to 1.7 GHz of new spectrum is required to sustain capacity expansion required to meet anticipated growth in wireless data traffic. Even if we discount this estimate, which some consider overzealous and inaccurate, by a factor of 3, still 600 MHz of new spectrum will be required. To that end, two US Government agencies – FCC and NTIA have been tasked to identify 500 MHz of new spectrum to be made available by 2015.

At the current point in the wireless network evolution, two types access networks exist: (1) licensed band cellular networks that are carefully engineered using expensive exclusively licensed spectrum to provide mobile access with national coverage. These are characterized by macro-cells with large coverage area realized using high power (e.g: 40-60 W) basestations. (2) Popular Wi-Fi networks operated in unlicensed spectrum (e.g.: 2.4 GHz, 5.8 GHz, 900 MHz) that provide indoor hot-spot coverage (e.g.: venues, hotels, homes, enterprise) and limited outdoor (e.g.: hot-zone) coverage realized using low power (40 mW-1W) access points. Despite their disparate characteristics, in early days these two access networks were often presented as competing ways to create wireless capacity. However, support of unlicensed and licensed bands on client devices and pressing need to relieve traffic overload in capacity starved cellular data networks caused by unforeseen growth in smart phone use and mobile video has pushed greater integration of these networks. This approach termed "Wi-Fi offloading" has provided some needed congestion relief to cellular networks. However, in many settings, Wi-Fi networks are experiencing congestion and despite continued improvements in Wi-Fi speeds (e.g: 802.11ac), many predict need for more unlicensed spectrum to support greater number of Wi-Fi channels.

As the traffic growth continues unabated, network operators continue to focus on ways improve capacity of their licensed band network. Techniques such as carrier aggregation, MIMO, enhanced inter-cell interference cancellation (eICIC), active antenna arrays (AAA) and increased sectorization are some of the techniques to increase capacity in macro-cells. However, these sophisticated techniques are expected to provide barely factor of 2 (in fact much less in many cases) capacity gains. This is also exacerbated by the fact that data traffic has different characteristics than voice traffic for which macro-cell coverage is suitable. Almost 60% of data traffic is generated indoor or in settings with minimal or no mobility – often termed portable access [4]. The corollary of this is that traffic is spatially clustered and exhibits temporal and spatial hot-spots. This characteristics can be matched perfectly if the coverage of the cell is matched to the spatial cluster size – leading to a concept of "small cells" – indoor femto/pico cells and outdoor metro/micro cells. This suggests a key design principle for future cellular networks:

*This work is supported in part by US National Science Foundation (NSF) grant CNS1117597.*


*MobiCom'13*, September 30–October 4, 2013, Miami, FL, USA.
Copyright 2013 ACM 978-1-4503-1999-7/13/09 ...$15.00.
http://dx.doi.org/10.1145/2500423.2505319.

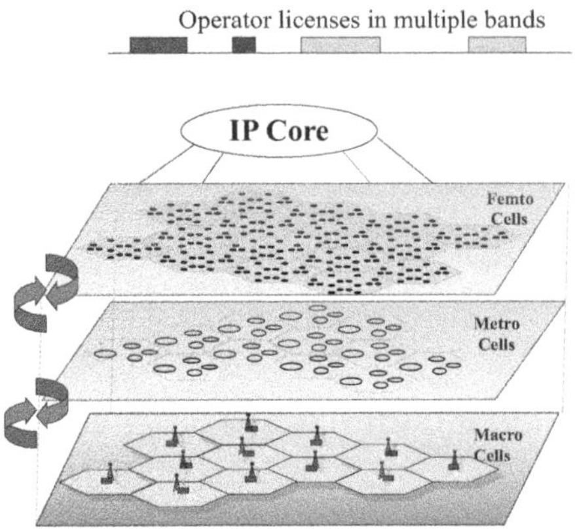


(a) Heterogeneous cellular network

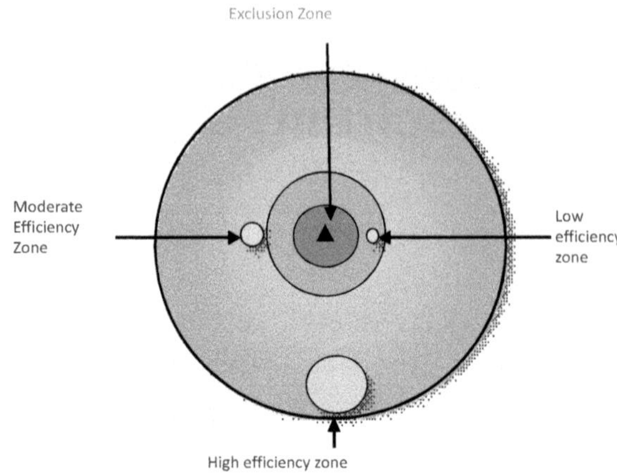


(b) Exclusion zones in shared carrier deployment

**Figure 1: Cellular hetnets**

> Wide geographical coverage is not as critical as high capacity in small spatial clusters, which suggests expansion of small cells instead of macro-cells as the key trend.

The natural question that arises is what spectrum band should these small cells operate in. If they use the same spectrum as that used in macro-cells they embed in, the client devices require no change in hardware. Such deployments – termed *shared carrier deployments* – require no new spectrum and in principle, no handset changes and are therefore quite attractive. The growth in small cell deployments transform the single tier network with macro-cells into a multi-tier heterogeneous networks – termed *hetnet* (Figure 1) (a) in short.

The hetnet approach in theory provides $O(N)$ growth in capacity for $N$ small cells. However, this has caveats in practice, especially for outdoor metro/micro cells due to co-channel interference across the hetnet tiers. The closer the metro cell is deployed to the macro-cell site, the greater the interference, resulting in coverage areas so small that it does not serve many users and fails to achieve traffic offload. In fact, realistic deployments introduce an exclusion zone around macro-cell site in which metro-cells should not be deployed. Such exclusion zone (Figure 1) (b) can be 30-40 % of the macro-cell coverage and often fall in the traffic hotspot regions.

Using different spectrum bands in each hetnet layer completely eliminates the interference interactions. However, such orthogonal carrier deployments require additional licensed spectrum bands suggesting need for more spectrum for true $O(N)$ capacity scaling and also, corresponding support of these bands in the client devices.

We note that licensed band small cells and unlicensed band access points are both inherently small cells and seamless hand-off from a macro-cell to a diverse licensed band small cell ("hard hand-off") or unlicensed access point ("Wi-Fi offloading or inter-technology hand-off") are fundamentally analogous. This represents a gradual blurring of boundaries between networks that were until recently competing approaches. However, the disparate business models for deploying these networks have made federated authentication and data path anchoring needed for seamless handoff rather challenging in practice. This suggests

> Sustained capacity expansion via integrated hetnet approaches will require support for greater number of spectrum bands in the network and client devices.

Let us visit the question of getting new spectrum. In almost all parts of the world, most of sub-6 GHz spectrum is already allocated for commercial or government (e.g: aviation, military) use. With exception of mobile broadband and ISM bands, many useful bands are spatio-temporally underused or unused. Naturally, it is tempting to think that users that use their spectrum less-profitably should be relocated to other bands and freed up spectrum should be re-purposed for mobile broadband. The *Incentive Auction NPRM* launched by FCC to shrink DTV band and release up to 120 MHz is an example of this approach. However, such "clearing" is impractical (e.g: JTRS links used by military in USA), expensive and slow (e.g.: $18 billion over 10-years to relocate 95 MHz of military bands) and fraught with uncertainties (e.g.: DTV band incentive auctions can fail to release any spectrum).

The only viable alternative left is that of "shared use" wherein two types or tiers of devices are allowed to use the band: the primary devices (users) that always have uninterrupted access to the band for their designated mission and the secondary devices (users) that can use the same spectrum bands in space and time when primary is not active. In the event primary needs access, the secondaries must immediately vacate the band. This requirement makes spatio-temporal availability of shared use spectrum statistical in nature.

The recent PCAST report [2] advocates that 1000 MHz of spectrum in 2700-3700MHz should be made available for such *shared use*. Following this recommendation, the recent FCC 3.5 GHz NPRM aims to release up to 150 MHz of spectrum in 3550-3700 MHz band used by multi-function radars and military and naval radars for use in small cells. These trends suggest a key design consideration for future:

> Future wireless networks must support new shared spectrum bands "encumbered" with high priority primary users. The network and client devices using these bands must be agile – i.e. capable of switching to new channels in the event of interruption of in-use channel.

A modern (e.g.: 4G LTE) cellular network consists of three main parts: (1) a radio access network (RAN) composed of basestations of various types (e.g: macro, micro, pico, femto) connected to a (2) packet core network consisting of IP-router based elements such as Service-GW (SGW) and Packet Data Network (PDN) gateway (P-GW) and a (3) control plane infrastructure consisting of authentication, signaling and billing infrastructures with servers such as Home Subscriber Serer (HSS), Mobility Management Entity (MME), AAA etc. The cloud based computing that has already transformed computing, storage and web services, can be applied to cellular networks to get benefits of demand responsive scalability, low CAPEX and OPEX by limiting the need for per-service, per-network or per-operator infrastructure and resulting improved reliability. Similarly, Software Defined Networking (SDN) or Network Function Virtualization (NFV) based on Open Flow paradigm can simplify and scale packet core functions. Another important trend is that of pooling of baseband processing functions in remote locations by exploiting availability of high speed fiber that can transport radio signals in digital I/Q format. Such centralized baseband processing can allow many wireless optimizations such as interference cancellation, joint scheduling across basestations, energy optimizations via sleep scheduling etc. This suggests:

> The cloud and SDN technologies may help reduce costs, improve performance and manageability by encouraging infrastructure sharing.

## 2. FUTURE WIRELESS NETWORK: A POSITION STATEMENT

This paper makes a case that over the next 10-years the confluence of the aforementioned trends will foster a slow, yet ultimately disruptive new transformation in wireless network architecture, deployment, value chain and business models. In the following, we record the salient changes we foresee.

**Operating in wide band, variable grade spectrum:** The artificial dichotomy of dedicated licensed band cellular networks and unlicensed band networks will disappear. The new wireless networks will employ mix of *variable grade* spectrum bands – (a) exclusively licensed, single owner, (b) unlicensed with no ownership and (c) shared use bands with one primary owner sharing with many coordinated or uncoordinated secondaries. The grade of the spectrum bands is characterized by *availability* and *quality* (e.g.: number of devices sharing the band, amount of co-channel and adjacent channel interference and propagation characteristics). For example, exclusively licensed bands that have guaranteed availability and have in-band interference protection (via exclusivity of transmission rights) and adjacent band/channel interference protection via stringent filtering requirements represent highest grade of spectrum. On the contrary, shared bands such as radar bands used by high powered fixed (e.g. Fixed Satellite Services (FSS) and mobile radars (e.g.: Naval Radars), public safety spectrum bands can have spatio-temporally variable spectrum availability. When these bands are available, the amount of in-band interference experienced by secondary users depends on the licensing model used. Similarly, dedicated unlicensed bands can have widely varying interference environment though they are guaranteed to be always available.

The main challenge is how to engineer the wireless network using mix of such spectrum bands to deliver performance that rivals performance of a network with equivalent amount of exclusively licensed spectrum.

**Moving control in the Cloud via dynamic databases for coordination:** The FCC rules in the context of DTV whitespace introduced a key architectural innovation in the form of a spectrum database (called TV Database (TVDB)). It was conceived as a compromise which sacrificed some spectrum usage efficiency to avoid complexity of distributed sensing based schemes for secondary use of DTV VHF and UHF band. This database (DB) approach, initially aimed at quickly bootstrapping secondary use ecosystem, will become a dominant architectural innovation for future. It can be further expanded to federal spectrum bands and in fact can be shown to be essential to guarantee security of primary occupancy information, scalable secondary use and reliable primary protection. However, DB functions in case of primary bands with more complex use patterns will become more dynamic and challenging to realize. Such a DB also resembles the centralized Self Organizing Network (SON) servers currently being developed for hetnets deployed in licensed cellular bands. In the long term, these various DB functions will converge into a single entity that manages various licensed and shared spectrum bands across multiple vendors, operators and primary users. The DB will also implement various spectrum access models – such as exclusive licensing, light licensing and unlicensed with a fine spatio-temporal granularity. By associating a market model (e.g: fixed priced transactions, real-time auctions) to first two methods of access, DB can create a real-time market for spectrum access or wireless capacity realized using such spectrum. In short, the spectrum DB will become heart of wireless network and its associated value chain.

**Infrastructure sharing** Though large scale small cell deployment is essential for capacity expansion, the economics of small cell deployment is challenging if every operator has to deploy its own small cells. The dominant components of cost will be the cell site and the backhaul required to connect small cell to the network. The cost of cell sites can be amortized across operators if small cells that support multiple frequency bands and multiple standards (e.g.: 3G / 4G) become feasible.

The wireline fiber based backhaul though ideal may not be available in exact location of small cell deployment and may be operated by different wireline operators. This may necessitate wireless backhaul solutions to ease deployments and reduce costs. However, since small cells are often deployed in clutter at 8-15 feet of height, such wireless backhaul must support near or non-line-of-sight (nLOS/NLOS) backhaul which needs sub-6 GHz spectrum that is in short supply. These constraints may encourage site and backhaul capacity to be shared. Specifically, SDN (Open Flow) technologies that offer centralized control of packet data paths can be key to realize such sharing in backhaul and wireless access.

**Regulatory transformation:** Here the analogy we can consider is that stock market trading. The human stock brokers shouting out stock sales on a exchange floor have given way to automated trading by algorithms that employ intelligence gathering tools that sniff all online information sources. Much the same way, FCC and its regulatory processes represent stock brokers of the old world. Increasingly spectrum management will be automated and fueled by "RF intelligence sources in the network" and centralized in the dynamic DBs. In such a future, role of FCC and NTIA will be redefined to DB-assisted enforcement of spectrum usage such as access fairness, collusion detection, market manipulation and RF compliance to spectrum lease.

**Business model transformation:** Current wireless network is a vertically integrated business where all aspects of wireless service offering – acquisition of licensed spectrum, deployment of network, marketing and management of customer facing service are integrated into a single entity. However, forces of sharing and virtualization can gradually transform this. Specifically, the business of spectrum DBs can be just "infrastructure service" instantiated on a cloud with real-time guarantees. Similarly, the entire control path of cellular networks – that deals with subscriber authentication, session tracking and billing can be virtualized into a Cloud business. Small cell RF-frontend deployment and management can be an independent business. Instantiation of customer services of variable QoS on such infrastructure can be another independent business. Much the same as Amazon Cloud services can be leveraged by vendors for web presence of their business without owning a server or a piece of software, wireless services can be commoditized.

The reduced emphasis on national coverage and emphasis on capacity instead of coverage realized using small cells and shared spectrum enables city and regional level operators to emerge. In fact, if the deployment of small cells, backhaul and DB based coordination are offered as commoditized services and subscriber authentication and billing become cloud services, small cells network can have microscopic scope – as small as a mall, airport or a building and such networks can go organically into a "stitched quilt" of a network.

The above does not suggest that the world as we know will overnight transform. Much the same way in real world we have public parks, house backyards and country clubs meeting needs of different people at different times and social status, mix of business models that provide various differentiators will emerge.

**Need for an exclusive license:** The question "do you need a exclusive license to operate a wireless network?" is rather provocative. The license is a tool to guarantee "certainty" – certainty in terms of interference environment, for business investment and guarantees in return of investment (ROI) and ultimately a level of service guarantee that can be quantified in simple monetizable plans a customer can understand. Interference certainty simplifies design of network and client devices, reduces cost of RF, baseband and network components and makes capacity calculations feasible. The certainty of investment return was key when expectation of deploying networks with national coverage was basis of wireless network business. These needs may not be necessarily valid going forward. A small cell network can be narrow in its spatial footprint –covering a city and such networks in disparate locations can be tied via roaming databases. Also, the licenses of future can be smaller in temporal and spatial scope and exclusivity of ownership limited to that small scope. In fact, advances in interference cancellation may allow multiple but limited number of operators to co-exist in a license scope – leading to non-exclusive, light licenses. Despite these advances, realizing performance similar to that of a exclusively licensed spectrum in a network with only *shared use* and unlicensed bands may have practical limitations. To compensate loss of a shared use channel or deterioration of an unlicensed band requires significant alternative bands and cost of channel switching may impair performance. As such we believe licenses – albeit with smaller spatio-temporal scope ("decimated licenses") and "controlled non-exclusivity" will be essential even in future to provide guarantees for high performance users and base level of service for all. By associating a monetary transaction and controlling the number of concurrent licenses via spectrum DB to such light licenses, the small cells can be provided arbitrary interference protection.

**Controlling market disruption:** Cellular networks today represent critical infrastructure with economic impact in excess of $1.6 trillion ($ 1trillion revenue, $550 B taxes, fees, 8.5 million jobs). The technology innovations have potential to create disruptive business models and strain cellular network operators whose revenues are already constrained due to slow growth in ARPU. It may be essential to craft regulation with two conflicting goals: (1) ensure incumbent interests are protected and enhanced and (2) new competition can be encouraged. For example, though in theory Dynamic DBs in its full potential can implement exclusive licenses, regulation need not bring existing licensed bands under such umbrella until technology and market mechanisms are designed and proven to be resilient. Similarly, for sharing to be feasible in many mission critical, sensitive spectrum bands, proof of primary protection and useful secondary capacity need to be demonstrated over sustained time period. This suggests conservative policy mechanisms that are relaxed over time leading to a slow evolution.

# 3. WHITECELLS: A CANDIDATE ARCHITECTURE FOR EVOLUTION

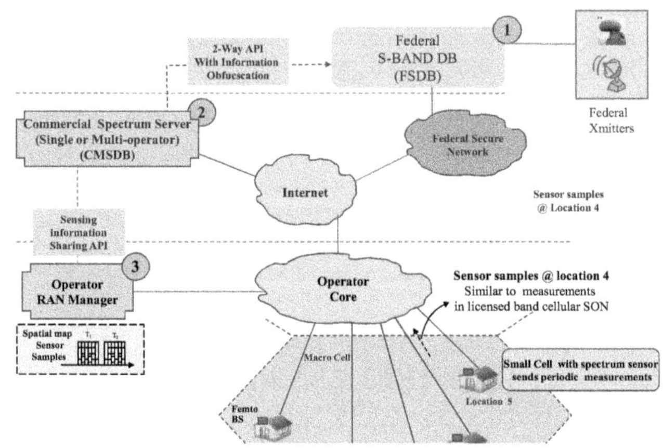


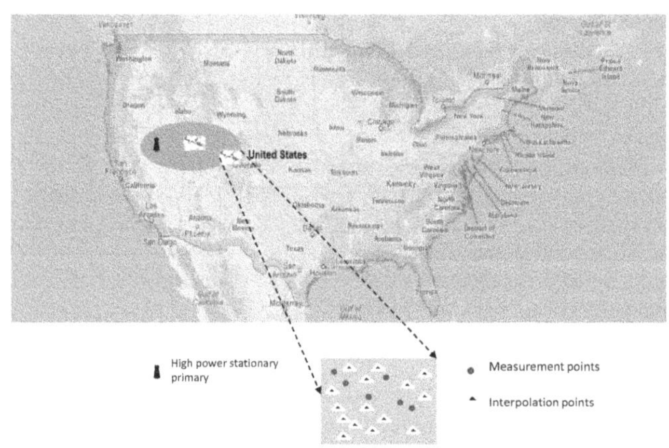


(b) Spatial interpolation technology

**Figure 2: Split dynamic database, whitecells and DREAM**

In the following, we propose a new architecture called *WhiteCells* (Figure 2) [3, 5] that helps realize some aspects of the evolution outlined above. In the cellular instantiation of this architecture, LTE RANs are augmented with new type of small cells called *whitecell* which support multi-band access operating in two types of bands: traditional licensed cellular and shared spectrum bands such as 2-4 GHz S-band radar bands and DTV whitespace bands in 470-700 MHz. Each whitecell also has a built-in wideband receive-only spectrum sensor that can rapidly scan all cellular and shared bands to characterize locally perceived spectrum activity. In the non-cellular version, whitecell only supports unlicensed and shared spectrum bands where interference protection can be obtained via obtaining shared spectrum band leases that are exclusive or near-exclusive. The salient aspects of our architecture are discussed in the following.

*Split Database:* Our architecture, instantiated for S-band, sists of a *Split Database* with two component DBs:

(1) Federal S-band DB (FSDB), likely managed by defer government establishment that securely handles all informatio primary and their spatio-temporal behavior. It is designed policies and security mechanisms to provide a obfuscated, tically impregnable access to primary channel availability. It only entity that can control which federal band channels (e.g band) channels are available for secondary use and also, can municate with Federal transmitters (e.g.: radars) to alter the rameters for enhanced co-existence.

(2) Commercial Multi-vendor S-band DB (CMSDB): is a da that controls the commercial LTE RANs of single or multipl vice providers, enabled with whitecells. Our model supports tiple CMSDBs similar to current TVDBs but does not need to communicate with each other as channel availability gran always common to all and each DB is free to decide how the allocated to secondary devices under its control. The split tecture also absolves FSDB to track secondary user populatio instead limits it to large spatial summaries and a few contact in the form of CMSDBs. This makes our approach very sca and also, maintains a strong wall of separation between con cial RANs and sensitive information about federal missions and transmitters. The CMSDB can be further broken into two layers: (1) the database layer that (a) receives spectrum demands and radio environment mapping (REM) data, (b) uses it to makes channel allocations, and (c) provides transaction or auction mechanism for awarding the leases, (2) a RAN manager (RANMAN) that coordinates the channel acquisition, configuration and release for the whitecells and uses the wideband spectrum sensors in them to collect REM measurements. In a cellular version of whitecells, RANMAN can be operator specific, where as in non-cellular scenarios, RANMAN can be implemented as a separate business.

*Tracking and Controlling secondary user population:* The mission critical nature of S-band federal transmitters, requires that all secondary use be expressly interruptible in the event mission parameters (e.g.: geographical scope of primary band use, tolerated interference etc.) are altered. This requires that unlike TVDB, the database in S-band should register and track secondary device characteristics (e.g.: location, TRX characteristics etc.) and activity (e.g: coverage region, secondary throughput) and also, maintain low latency logical channel of communication with it. This task is performed by the CMSDB+RANMAN layer, which is analogous to Small Cell Controller servers in current cellular deployments. This DB maintains a live secure TCP flow with each whitecell and commands channel allocation, de-allocations, sensing operations and collects sensing information. For example, in the event of a channel de-allocation, a message flows along the path: FSDB $\rightarrow$ CMSDB $\rightarrow$ whitecells $\rightarrow$ (broadcast message *Move to cellular channel*) to end-user devices (e.g: phones). Such message exchanges can be accomplished easily under 2-second duration.

*Dynamic Radio Environment Activity Mapping (DREAM)* aims at accurately tracking radio environment impact of primary and secondary device transmissions and ultimately assisting schemes (e.g.: channel allocation) for better co-existence. Based on knowledge of primary activity received from FSDB, the CMSDB schedules the whitecell sensors to collect dynamic secondary and primary user activity in S-band in 2 steps: *Step 1:* CMSDB dictates all secondary transmission to be shifted to cellular band to allow sensors only capture primary activity. *Step 2:* all sensors collect aggregate primary and secondary activity. These location tagged measurements are processed at each cell to create spatial and temporal summaries e.g. to estimate duty cycle of primary, max-min-median

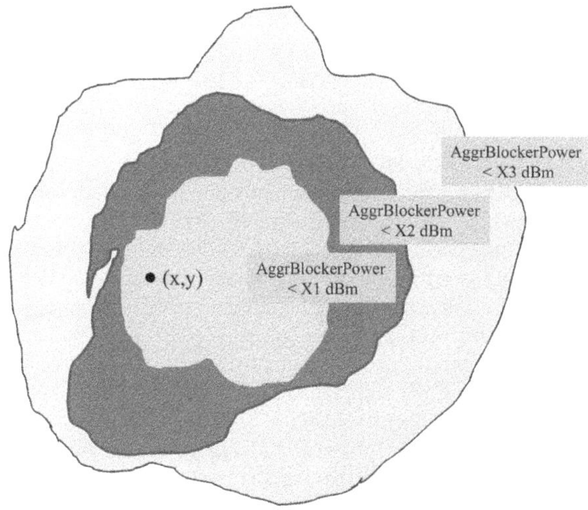


**Figure 3: Admissible Region Contours (ARC)**

energy, propagation loss range and uploaded to the CMSDB. These summaries can be used to better estimate the coverage of primary transmitters (e.g: service contours/coverage of radars) which are "exclusion zones" where secondary use can be precluded. They can be supplied to the FSDB to enable it to add enough spatio-temporal randomness to channel availability grants. Such randomness aims to increase statistical hardness of inferring primary behavior based on channel grant pattern observed at a single secondary user. These summaries will also be used (a) in CMSDB for allocation of available channels to secondary devices and (b) in whitecells to introduce randomness in packet-level scheduling of secondary packets transmitted in secondary use channel.

*Admissible Region Contours (ARC):* This innovation uses DREAM and is aimed at aiding optimum channel allocation and achieving better co-existence of secondary devices in S-band, by better tracking impact of primary devices on secondaries. The main objective of TVDBs is to provide primary protection and they are not mandated to provide any additional information to secondaries on impact of primaries on their channel use. In contrast, DREAM capability can easily track channel quality impact of primaries. If the CMSDB knows the receiver characteristics, it can estimate how much adjacent channel splatter from radar primaries and adjacent channel transmissions from secondaries increase interference in the desired channel. This aggregate interference varies from location to location and for a given receiver sensitivity and filter characteristics, it upper bounds the achievable maximum data rate. This idea can be captured in what we call Admissible Region Contours (ARC) (Figure 3) (similar to topographical contours in geographical maps and in fact, more dynamic version of protection contours in TVDBs) constructed such that each contour has an associated with it a maximum signal blocker power $P_{blk}$ (in dB scale). All points on or inside this contour experience at least $P_{blk}$ power. These contours when correlated with location of secondary device can help predict best case in-band interference and correspondingly, TDD receive performance and thus help better allocate channels. These contours change infrequently in the context DTV whitespace but require much more dynamically updates in S-band. For example, in case of naval radars mounted on cruisers, as the radar rotates, the primary energy received in the direction of targets and side lobes varies with rotation and the exclusion zone itself moves.

However, within the exclusion zones, the received energy can periodically change with a duty cycle and the ARCs change accordingly. The trade off of ARC update frequency, channel capacity variation and allocation performance dictates how fast ARCs should be computed.

*Spatial interpolation technology:* As the density of small cells increases, if the sensing is implemented naively where all cells perform sensing in all bands, inordinate amount of data may be generated towards the CMSDB. Since, the CMSDB knows the location, terrain, and transmit and receive characteristics of secondary devices, a spatial interpolation technique can use REM values at a limited subset of locations to predict values at other locations. If the set used for prediction is changed over time, it allows randomizing or scheduling the set of small cells which perform sensing, thus reducing the load on each cell.

*Integrated channel switching and aggregation:* The shared spectrum channels can be interrupted and unlicensed spectrum can deteriorate due to increased interference and therefore, capability to dynamically switch channels at RF level and transfer packet traffic over multiple channels in an aggregated fashion to achieve high capacity is critical. Such integration has been considered in current networks for mobility hand-offs across multi-technology networks and is extended to whitecells. However, channel bonding across disparate wireless interfaces is still not a mature technology and needs careful design. Layer-1 carrier aggregation mechanisms emerging in 802.11ac and LTE-Adv standards are baseband specific. An alternate approach could use inverse fair queueing based mechanisms that aggregate layer-2/layer-3 packet flows over multiple radio interfaces each using a different band. Though such an approach may be inferior in latency performance, it is baseband agnostic and can be far easier to implement in software in OS kernels used in access points and client devices.

*Whitecell hardware* and corresponding client devices need use of RF front ends and antennas that can operate in multiple bands – often wideband, such as 150 MHz wide in 3550 MHz band. The feasibility of building network and client devices that can operate in wider swaths of spectrum bands is the key enabler for whitecells. Even with today's technology, the A/D conversion and subsequent digital signal processing can be increasingly made wide-band tunable over 0 to 6 GHz and handle up to 40 MHz channels. However, building analog front ends that can tune over such wide-band under software control, meet adjacent channel splatter constraints across entire 6-GHz band for transmit and handle large blocker signals in nearby bands on the receive path appears elusive. In the near term, band specific filters leveraging promising switched filter banks can be used for cost effective design.

# 4. EPILOGUE

Our vision of future wireless networks presents new challenges and opportunities for equipment vendors, network operators and wireless industry on the whole.

To realize our vision, new generation of products – wide-band basestations, NLOS high capacity backhaul, virtualized control plane and packet core elements, spectrum databases, and network analytics will be necessary. As a leading supplier of 3G/4G networks world-wide and a recognized innovator, Alcatel-Lucent/ Bell Labs continues to be a pioneer in these technologies.

For incumbent operators, the network evolution we outlined can help reduce their "sunken costs" and help cost-effectively increase network capacity by reducing the capital expenditure. Over the course of evolution as vertically integrated operator business change to horizontal business, the operators can diversify into the new business.

The gradual flattening of network business also opens door for new competition to emerge. Such new organically growing networks though will not be a replacement for operator managed networks with clear pre- or post-paid monetization models and well defined service offerings. However, increased competition and "capacity where you need it most of the time" nature of these networks makes them very attractive for end-users.

Small cell networks in shared spectrum also will be relevant for rural broadband and fixed wireless to augment wireline infrastructure in many parts of the world.

In summary, we believe that innovation in wireless networking should now shift its focus from improving existing fixed band cellular or Wi-Fi networks to incorporating seamlessly multiple variable grade wide bands and in process unleash new wave of research and business opportunities.

# 5. REFERENCES


[1] Natioal broadband commission report. http://www.broadband.gov/plan/.

[2] PCAST report on federal government spectrum sharing. "http://www.whitehouse.gov/sites/default/files/microsites/ostp.

[3] M. M. Buddhikot, I. Kennedy, F. Mullany, and H. Viswanathan. Ultra-broadband femtocells via opportunistic reuse of multi-operator and multi-service spectrum. *Bell Labs Technical Journal*, 13(4):129–143, 2009.

[4] U. Paul, A. P. Subramanian, M. M. Buddhikot, and S. R. Das. Understanding traffic dynamics in cellular data networks. In *INFOCOM*, pages 882–890, 2011.

[5] S. Sen, T. Zhang, M. Buddhikot, S. Banerjee, D. Samardzija, and S. Walker. A dual technology femto cell architecture for robust communication using whitespaces (best paper). In *Proceedings of IEEE DySPAN 2012*, 2012.

# Panel: Indoor Localization - Ready for Primetime?

Marco Gruteser
Rutgers University
gruteser@winlab.rutgers.edu

## ABSTRACT

Indoor navigation and location tracking have been popular academic research topics in our community for more than a decade. This has lead to a vast amount of theoretical results, positioning techniques, and system prototypes that were developed in academia and industry research labs for efficient and accurate indoor localization and navigation. Marketplace adoption, however, has been slow—products have largely focused on outdoor positioning and navigation. Only recently has the industry buzz and investment in indoor positioning and navigation products picked up.

This panel will discuss whether indoor positioning solutions are finally ready for the marketplace. It will examine the limitations of the state of the art along dimensions such as precision, accuracy, energy consumption, complexity, and privacy and will debate in which areas, if any, further academic research is called for. The panelists will also discuss why adoption has been slow, whether any significant non-technical hurdles remain, and speculate which technical solutions are most likely to succeed.

## Categories and Subject Descriptors

C.2 [**Computer-Communicatino Networks**]: Miscellaneous

## Keywords

Indoor Positioning, Localization

## Panelists

To address this topic, this panel brings together experts in indoor location from industry research and academia. The panelists and their biographies follow.

### *Prof. Romit Roy Choudhury.*

Romit Roy Choudhury is an Associate Professor of ECE at the University of Illinois at Urbana Champaign (UIUC). He joined UIUC from Fall 2013, prior to which he was an Associate Professor at Duke University. Romit received his PhD in the CS department of UIUC in Fall 2006. His research interests are in wireless protocol design mainly at the PHY/MAC layer, and in mobile computing at the application layer. Along with his students, he received a few research awards, including the NSF CAREER Award, the Google Faculty Award, best paper at Personal Wireless Communications conference, Hoffmann Krippner Award for Engineering Innovations, etc. Visit Romit's Systems Networking Research Group (SyNRG), at http://synrg.ee.duke.edu

### *Prof. Moustafa Youssef.*

He is an Associate Professor at Egypt-Japan University of Science and Technology and Alexandria University. He has been working on location determination systems, including the Horus indoor localization system, PinPoint system, Nuzzer system, CellSense cellular localization system, systems for localization in sensor and ad hoc networks, among others. He has tens of papers in the world's most prestigious journals and conferences with thousands of citations on Google Scholar as well as ten issued and pending patents. Prof. Youssef is the recipient of the 2004 Invention of the Year award from the University of Maryland for his work in the Horus Location Determination System, the 2010 joint TWAS-AAS-Microsoft Award, the 2012 Egyptian State Award for Engineering Sciences, among others.

### *Dr. Ravi Palanki.*

He is with Qualcomm Research Silicon Valley, where he leads a team of engineers working on indoor positioning algorithms. He received his B.Tech. in EE from IIT Madras in 2000, and M.S. and Ph.D. in EE from Caltech in 2001 and 2004 respectively. During the course of his Ph.D., he was also a visiting researcher at NASA's Jet Propulsion Laboratory (JPL) and Mitsubishi Electric Research Labs (MERL), and has been with Qualcomm Corporate R&D subsequently. Dr. Palanki was a key member of the team that designed OFDMA-based wireless technologies and was responsible for the design and standardization of several key features for Long Term Evolution (LTE), the predominant 4G technology in the world. His research interests include wireless communications, information theory and probabilistic inference, and he has around 20 journal/conference papers and 200 approved/pending patents in these areas.

### *Dr. Jie Liu.*

He is a Principal Researcher and a Research Manager at Microsoft Research, leading the Sensing and Energy Re-


*MobiCom'13,* September 30–October 4, 2013, Miami, FL, USA.
Copyright 2013 ACM 978-1-4503-1999-7/13/09 ...$15.00.
http://dx.doi.org/10.1145/2500423.2500453.

search Group (SERG). His group conducts fundamental and systems research on sensing and energy-efficient computing. Before joining MSR in May 2004, he was a researcher at Palo Alto Research Center (formerly Xerox PARC). Since 2008, he also holds an adjunct professorship (Foreign PhD Advisor) at Harbin Institute of Technology, China. He received his Ph.D. degree from EECS, UC Berkeley in 2001 and his Master (1996) and Bachelor (1993) degrees from the Department of Automation, Tsinghua University, Beijing, China. He is a Distinguished Scientist of the ACM since 2011, has received the Exceptional Student Award from Tsinghua University (the highest student award) in 1996, the Leon O. Chua Award for outstanding research from UC Berkeley in 2001, the Technology Advance Award from PARC in 2003, and the Gold Star Award from Microsoft in 2008. He has also received, with co-authors, Best Paper Awards from RTAS 2010 and SenSys 2012.

# Using Crowd-Sourced Viewing Statistics to Save Energy in Wireless Video Streaming

Mohammad Ashraful Hoque, Matti Siekkinen, Jukka K. Nurminen
Aalto University School of Science, Finland
{mohammad.hoque, matti.siekkinen, jukka.k.nurminen}@aalto.fi

## ABSTRACT

Video streaming on smartphones is one of the most popular but also most energy hungry services today. Using mobile video services results in two contradictory sources of energy waste for smartphones: i) energy waste because of excessively aggressive prefetching of content that the user will not watch because of abandoning the session, and ii) excessive amount of tail energy, which is energy wasted by keeping the wireless interface powered on after receiving a chunk of content; this is caused by prefetching chunks that are too small. To remedy this, we propose a novel download scheduling algorithm based on crowd-sourced video viewing statistics. Our algorithm judiciously evaluates the probability of a user interrupting a video viewing in order to perform the right amount of prefetching. In this way, the algorithm balances the amount of the two above-mentioned kinds of energy waste. By simulations, we show that our scheduler cuts the energy waste to half compared to existing download strategies. We have also developed an Android prototype that implements the download scheduler together with a novel downloader that speeds up the download by exploiting the Fast Start technique. The prototype exhibits the desired properties of the scheduler, and its faster downloading mechanism yields further energy savings of up to 80% compared to the default Android YouTube app.

## Categories and Subject Descriptors

C.2.4 [**Computer-Communication Networks**]: Distributed Systems[Distributed Application, Client/Server]

## Keywords

Energy Saving; Mobile Multimedia; Tail Energy

## 1. INTRODUCTION

Energy consumption in modern smartphones has a significant impact on user satisfaction. Radio communication using the device's wireless network interfaces, such as Wi-Fi, 3G, and LTE, consumes a significantly large fraction of the total energy. This energy consumption is specifically of concern for services that are frequently used and that generate a lot of traffic. Mobile video streaming is a prime example of such services.

Today, mobile video services employ a range of techniques to deliver content to smartphones. The delivery mechanisms differ in the rate that the content is transmitted and in the amount of content prefetched and buffered by the player. The chosen technique depends on the behaviour of both the server and the client application [21, 16]. An aggressive prefetching technique improves user experience of watching a video but may lead to significant amount of unnecessarily downloaded content if the user abandons watching the video [11]. As a result, the associated downloading energy is also wasted. On the other hand, downloading the video content in small chunks reduces the probability of downloading unnecessary content but it is also energy inefficient because of the so-called *tail energy* present in mobile wireless communication. This energy is consumed as a result of keeping the radio powered on for a while after receiving or transmitting the last bit of content.

This paper presents a novel download scheduling algorithm which optimizes the energy consumption while streaming video to a mobile device via a wireless network interface (WNI). The novelty lies in the algorithm leveraging crowd-sourced video viewing statistics in order to quantify the probability of a user abandoning the watching of a video. The algorithm then calculates an energy optimal download schedule based on these probabilities. Extensive evaluations of our algorithm show that such statistics help to cut the energy waste to half compared to the best known alternative download strategies.

In summary, this paper makes the following contributions.

- We identify the sources of energy inefficiency in mobile video streaming and demonstrate that current download strategies suffer from these problems. Specifically, we formulate the problem of energy optimization of download scheduling in video streaming when users have a non-zero probability of abandoning the session.
- We design eSchedule, which is a download scheduling algorithm based on crowd-sourced video viewing statistics and power modeling. We show through simulations that this algorithm is able to cut the energy waste to half compared to currently existing other approaches.


*MobiCom'13*, September 30 - October 04 2013, Miami, FL, USA
Copyright 2013 ACM 978-1-4503-1999-7/13/09 ...$15.00.
http://dx.doi.org/10.1145/2500423.2500427.

- We present a YouTube-compliant Android prototype called StreamThrottler, which comprises two components: implementation of eSchedule and a novel downloader that downloads an individual chunk of content at the maximum bulk transfer capacity. We evaluate it on Samsung Galaxy SIII 4G and compare the performance of StreamThrottler to the default Android YouTube player.

The rest of the paper is structured as follows. The next section outlines the background to mobile video streaming, energy consumption and lists the factors that result in energy being wasted. Section 3 presents our novel download scheduler, called eSchedule, which we evaluate by applying simulations, in Section 4. Section 5 describes and evaluates the Android prototype called StreamThrottler. In Section 6, we discuss the practical issues associated with the player buffer, bandwidth fluctuation and audience retention information. Finally, we contrast our work with earlier research in section 7 before concluding the paper.

# 2. WIRELESS VIDEO STREAMING AND ENERGY CONSUMPTION

In this section, we discuss the different forms of energy waste that emerge during streaming video over wireless technologies. The focus is HTTP-based streaming over TCP because of its dominant status. We first briefly consider the different ways that streaming traffic is delivered from the server to the client and show the resulting energy consumption in each case. Then, we explicitly highlight the sources of energy waste that motivate us to propose the novel download scheduling scheme described in Section 3.

## 2.1 Video Streaming using HTTP over TCP

Today HTTP over TCP is by far the most commonly used protocol suite exploited by streaming services to deliver mobile videos [13]. The streaming services have to accommodate bandwidth fluctuation and jitter, which commonly occur due to the best-effort service of the Internet. To remedy these, content is prefetched from the streaming server and stored at the client player's playback buffer. This buffering is performed right at the beginning of the streaming session and, for this reason, it is commonly referred to as Fast Start.

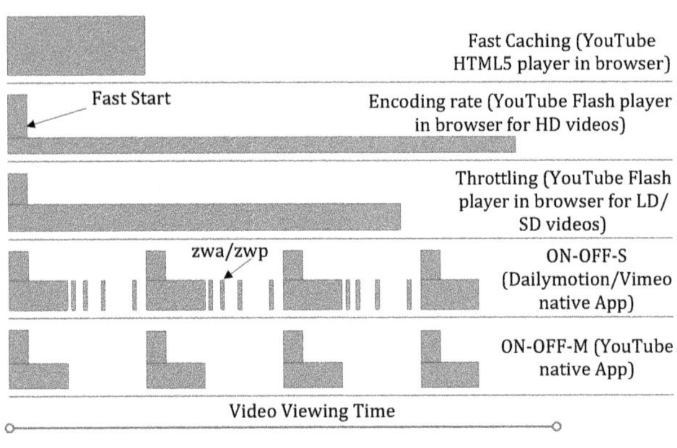


**Figure 1:** Typical mobile video streaming strategies with different mobile video services. HD refers to high definition videos (e.g., 720-1080p). LD and SD refer to low and standard definition videos respectively (e.g., 240-480p). The height of a rectangle represents the download rate and the width the download time.

Following the Fast Start buffering, the technique for delivering the remaining content varies and depends on the combination of the service, player implementation, and device characteristics. From the traffic pattern of YouTube, Dailymotion and Vimeo players in Samsung Galaxy SIII 4G (Android Jelly Bean 4.1.2) we identified a number of strategies employed by these video services for constant bit rate streaming (see Figure 1). YouTube exhibits all the streaming techniques in the Android platform with its combination of browser and the native players, except ON-OFF-S. The Dailymotion, and Vimeo applications apply ON-OFF-S.

Figure 1 shows large differences occur in the way the wireless interface is utilized, depending on the type of strategy. Fast Caching simply downloads the whole video in one go and the wireless interface is efficiently utilized. However, because users often do not watch the whole video, using this strategy may lead to a significant amount of content being unnecessarily downloaded [11].

Encoding rate streaming results from a situation where the server intends to send initially more data than the client player is able or willing to buffer. As a consequence, TCP flow control activates and allows the server to send the rest of the content at the rate at which the client player consumes it, i.e. encoding rate. This results in a light but continuous utilization of the wireless interface.

By throttling the sending rate, the server sends content to the client at a rate which is lower than the bulk transfer capacity but higher than the stream encoding rate. The YouTube Flash player in browser always specifies a throttling rate of 1.25 in the HTTP request and the server sends content at 1.25 times the encoding rate to the client.

The ON-OFF strategies are governed exclusively by the client players. There are two types: In the first, ON-OFF-M, the client player establishes a new TCP connection and makes a new HTTP request for each ON period and closes the connection after having received a chunk of content. In the second, ON-OFF-S, the client player uses a persistent TCP connection and simply stops reading from the TCP socket during an OFF period. Because the server has more data to send, TCP flow control messages, i.e. zero window probes (zwp) from the server and advertisements (zwa) from client, are exchanged during the OFF period. The YouTube player in Galaxy SIII buffers 100 s worth of content. When the buffer drains to 40 s, the player resumes downloading. Therefore, the duration of an OFF period is 60 s. The Dailymotion and Vimeo players buffer 20 MB of content. Figure 1 also shows that the players receive content at some throttled rate after the Fast Start phase using both ON-OFF mechanisms. In a manner similar to ON-OFF-M, GreenTube [16] also uses multiple TCP connections to download a video. It uses local viewing history of a user to determine the playback buffer size which in turn limits the amount of data to be downloaded during each connection.

The selection of the described streaming techniques does not depend on the wireless interface being used for streaming. The selection does not depend on the available bandwidth either. The ON-OFF mechanisms and throttling persist as long as the bandwidth is equivalent to the throttling rate. If the bandwidth is reduced further, the duration of an ON period increases using either of the ON-OFF mechanisms. However, Figure 1 illustrates that the selection depends on the service, player type, and the quality. A detailed study on how the video streaming services exhibit different streaming techniques can be found in [14].

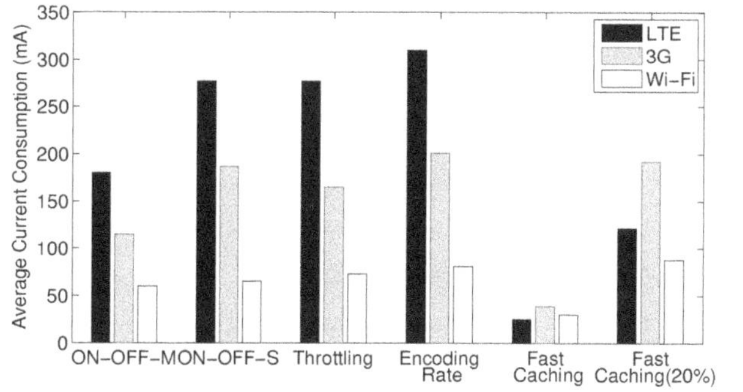


**Figure 2:** Avg. current consumed by Wi-Fi, 3G and LTE interfaces during streaming sessions of a 597 s video to Galaxy SIII 4G using different streaming techniques.

## 2.2 Energy Consumption

With regard to energy consumption, all the wireless network interfaces have a few characteristics in common. All of them have mechanisms to ensure that the radio is not kept fully powered on all the time. Consequently, they operate in different modes, which also map to different power states. For example, the states in Wi-Fi that employ a power saving mode (PSM) [3] are receive, transmit, idle, and sleep, of which the first three modes draw, by an order of magnitude of one, more power than the fourth mode. In 3G, the modes correspond to the different channel allocations (CELL_DCH, CELL_FACH, CELL_PCH and IDLE) [2]. An LTE device can be either connected or in idle mode and, if DRX is activated, the radio is switched on only for a short period, otherwise it remains in sleep mode during the connected mode [4].

Another common feature is that transitions from active to more passive states, i.e. decisions about switching the radio to sleep mode, are executed based on inactivity timers. The timer values of 3G and LTE may extend to ten seconds, whereas Wi-Fi switches the radio into sleep mode after only two hundred milliseconds. The timers in cellular networks are not specified in the standards but are set and controlled by the network operators. The energy consumed by keeping the radio on for the period specified by the inactivity timer is often called *tail energy* [10]. This tail energy is the price to pay for more efficient radio access network resource consumption and shorter application-level latency especially when using sporadically communicating applications. Modern smartphones try to avoid long tail energy by employing a different standard, namely Fast Dormancy (FD) [5]. The mobile devices use a shorter inactivity timer of 3-5 s [8]. FD enables a mobile device to switch directly from CELL_DCH to CELL_PCH or to IDLE state.

Using three video streaming services, YouTube, Dailymotion, and Vimeo, we executed several sessions on an Android phone, the Samsung Galaxy SIII 4G. For each streaming technique we conducted three sessions, each for a different WNI (Wi-Fi/3G/LTE). To understand what the different streaming strategies mean from an energy consumption point of view, we performed power measurements using the Monsoon Power Monitor [1]. We discovered that the smartphone used FD in the 3G network and the value of the inactivity timer was 5 seconds. However, the LTE network did not support DRX and the inactivity timer was of 10 seconds.

The total current measured during streaming comprises the idle current, the current draw required by playback and the current draw generated by the downloading, i.e. wireless interface usage. We calculated the playback plus idle current from the power traces by manually isolating a period following completion of the stream download and when only playback remains. We then computed the downloading current by subtracting the playback current from the total current. Figure 2 shows the computed downloading current. We observed that the playback plus idle current (not shown in the figure) varied 200-230 mA, which highlights the fact that the energy spent for downloading only is in most cases a very significant part of the total energy.

Among the different strategies we examined, it is clear that encoding rate streaming consumes the most energy because it keeps the radio active almost all the time. This is because the inactivity timers do not expire in between packet receptions. The phone consumes less current than the encoding rate when the server throttles the bit rate, because the device finishes downloading a little bit earlier. ON-OFF-S also leads to larger energy consumption when used over LTE and 3G because their long inactivity timer values combined with the TCP flow control traffic keeps the radio on most of the time. By contrast, ON-OFF-M is much more energy efficient. Compared to the discussed methods, Fast Caching draws very little current on average while the whole video is being watched. In Figure 2, we also present a case where the user abandons the session after watching 20% of the video, in which case the average current is clearly higher. The reason being that in the beginning the device does unnecessary work by downloading content that is never watched.

## 2.3 Sources of Energy Waste

Following on from the preceding section, we now identify the following four different factors that negatively impact the energy efficiency of a streaming service:

1. *Downloading content at a rate lower than the maximum possible rate*: The most energy efficient way to transmit data at a given moment is to use the full capacity of the wireless channel. This holds for all the types of wireless access (Wi-Fi, 3G, LTE). The reason is that the lower the rate, the greater is the time interval between the packets. Even though these intervals are small, the inactivity timers are active and the smartphone consumes energy.

2. *Auxiliary control traffic during periods when content is not being received*: As we observed with the ON-OFF strategy using a persistent TCP connection, this kind of traffic has a major impact on the energy efficiency because it keeps the client's radio powered on all the time in the worst case.

3. *Tail energy in non-continuous content reception*: The non-continuous download strategy, such as the ON-OFF-M, causes tail energy to be spent after the download of each chunk of content. This energy adds up to a significant amount especially when using 3G or LTE and if chunks are relatively small.

4. *Downloading unnecessary content*: In cases where users always watch the whole video, the most energy efficient streaming strategy would be Fast Caching because it

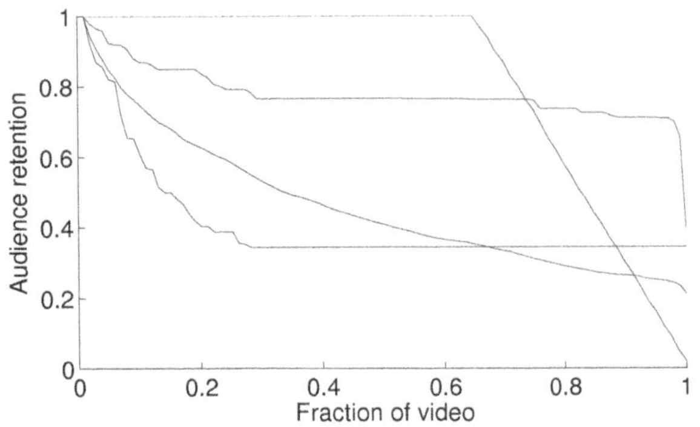


**Figure 3:** Audience retention graphs from YouTube videos.

minimizes the amount of time that the radio is kept powered on. However, since users often interrupt their viewing before the end of the video clip, such aggressive prefetching leads to unnecessary consumption of energy to download content that the user will never watch.

We note that while the first and second problems can be solved, for example, by alleviating server-side rate limits and by using non-persistent connections, the third and fourth problems are in fact contradictory: By downloading larger chunks to reduce the total amount of tail energy, the probability of downloading unnecessary content increases. We examine this tradeoff in the next section and propose an algorithm which optimally balances this tradeoff.

# 3. VIDEO STREAMING BASED ON CROWD-SOURCED VIEWING STATISTICS

## 3.1 Audience Retention

The fact that users do not always watch entire video clip transforms finding an energy optimal download schedule from using the trivial Fast Caching strategy into an optimization problem. The solution must strike a balance between two sources of energy waste: 1) prefetching content in large chunks in order to minimize the tail energy and 2) limiting that chunk size in order to reduce the amount of downloaded content that will never be viewed.

A key question in devising a solution is to estimate at what point a user will abandon watching the video. We propose to leverage crowd-sourced video viewing statistics. The underlying idea is that video clip specific statistics collected from all the previous viewing sessions give useful insights about how a new user will watch the video. It is natural that the viewing behaviour depends on how interesting and "capturing" or engaging the video clip is and the content type. We study the potential of using such statistics in download scheduling to save energy. We show that it helps to save significant amount of energy compared to strategies that do not leverage crowd-sourced statistics.

One source of such statistics is YouTube, which maintains *audience retention* data for each video clip [6]. These statistics are computed based on continuous feedback sent by the YouTube client applications during video streaming sessions [23]. Figure 3 shows examples of audience retention curves for some videos which we extracted from YouTube. Each curve always starts from one and shows, for a particular video clip, the fraction of the audience that is still watching at a given point of time. These examples highlight the fact that retention highly depends on the video clips: some retain clear majority of audience until the end while others lose most of the audience at the very beginning of the video.

## 3.2 eSchedule Algorithm

We designed a download scheduler that takes viewing statistics, such as the audience retention plotted in Figure 3, as input. We name it eSchedule. We assume that a mobile device is able to tell the scheduler at each moment the type of the network that it uses for data communication. In addition, it includes parameterized power models of communication using each different technology (i.e., Wi-Fi, 3G, and LTE including variants with and without DRX). Using the interrupt probabilities computed from the crowed-sourced viewing statistics, the scheduler computes the optimal download schedule, which is a sequence of variable size chunks that is estimated to minimize the energy consumption. Intuitively, if the amount of tail energy is large, e.g. when using 3G, and the viewing statistics suggest that many users watched a large fraction of the video, the scheduler will choose to download the large chunk of content. Conversely, if the amount of tail energy is small, e.g. when using Wi-Fi, and the statistics indicate that audience retention has been poor, the scheduler chooses small chunk sizes. Next, we model this approach as a stochastic optimization problem.

We divide the video viewing time into $n$ discrete time steps. Then, we consider the video viewing as a discrete time stochastic process $p_i(X)$, where $X$ takes value one or zero and describes whether the user watches the video segment corresponding to the $i$th time step. The audience retention $A_i$ (also defined in discrete time steps) describes the joint probability of watching all the segments from the beginning till the $i$th time step, i.e. $A_i = \prod_{k=1}^{i} p_k(X = 1)$.

The algorithm computes for each schedule an expected value of energy waste. We define the energy waste as the total tail energy and energy spent downloading data which is not watched. We obtain (1) for calculating the expected value of energy waste when downloading a video chunk corresponding to $T$ seconds of content starting from discrete time step $i$. In this case, $T$ represents an integer value. In the equation, $btc$ is TCP bulk transfer capacity, $P_{rx}$ is receive power, $E_i^{tail}(T)$ is the amount of tail energy for a chunk carrying $T$ seconds worth of content, and $\mathbb{E}[B_i^{waste}(T)]$ is the expected value of content that is downloaded and never watched because the user interrupts the session.

$$\mathbb{E}[E_i^{waste}(T)] = E_i^{tail}(T) + \frac{\mathbb{E}[B_i^{waste}(T)]}{btc} \times P_{rx} \quad (1)$$

Computing the tail energy is straightforward given that the algorithm knows the power states and inactivity timer values for each specific radio interface. This tail energy depends on the chunk size because the inactivity timer values corresponding to a specific radio interface can exceed $T$. The tail energy is added for a chunk even if the user interrupts viewing in the middle of downloading it. When downloading a chunk containing $T$ seconds worth of content, the expected value of the unnecessarily downloaded content is calculated using (2). This equation consists of two parts: the first one corresponds to the phase during which the chunk is being simultaneously downloaded and consumed, and the second one to the phase during which it is only being consumed.

$$\mathbb{E}[B_i^{waste}(T)] = \sum_{k=1}^{\frac{T\times r_s}{btc}} p_i^{int}(i+k)\left[btc\times k - k\times r_s\right] + \sum_{k=\frac{T\times r_s}{btc}+1}^{T} p_i^{int}(i+k)\left[T\times r_s - k\times r_s\right] \quad (2)$$

In the above equation, $r_s$ is the encoding rate of the streaming. We also need the probability of the user interrupting viewing ($p_i^{int}$). This probability needs to be re-evaluated each time the next chunk size is chosen by the scheduler during the streaming session. It is a conditional probability because it depends on the current viewing position and in addition on the audience retention. Therefore, it does not matter whether the viewing is continuous or not, since the probability to interrupt viewing is always computed from the current viewing position and it can be the new location in case of a forward or backward skip by the user. Thus, the probability for a user to interrupt during a discrete time step $j$ evaluated at time step $i$ (i.e., user is currently viewing at position $i, j > i$) is computed as follows:

$$\begin{aligned} p_i^{int}(j) &= p(\text{``abandon at j''}|\text{``curr. position i''}) = \frac{A_{j-1}p_j(X=0)}{A_i} \\ &= \frac{A_{j-1}(1-p_j(X=1))}{A_i} = \frac{A_{j-1}-A_j}{A_i} \end{aligned}$$

Each chunk can be of any size ranging from a defined minimum to the remaining video duration. Consequently, the number of all possible schedules grows exponentially as the video length grows. Even if we limit ourselves to considering only a certain granularity of chunk sizes, e.g. multiples of five second, it is infeasible to compute the number of all possible schedules, even for a video lasting only a few minutes (e.g., one minute video has more than two million possible schedules). The problem can be viewed as shortest path computation in which different sequential chunks represent different cost hops. The most efficient known algorithms for computing the shortest path scales according to $O(|E|+|N|log|N|)$, where $|E|$ is the number of edges and $|N|$ is the number of nodes. Our scheduling problem requires a path corresponding to each possible schedule which means that the number of edges grows exponentially as the video length extends, and it is infeasible to compute an optimal solution using exhaustive search. Hence, we use a heuristic, described in the next section.

## 3.3 Heuristic

Our approach is to limit the number of consecutive chunks when choosing the optimal size for the subsequent chunks. In this way, the algorithm finds a locally optimal schedule, i.e. it minimizes energy waste for the next chunks to be considered, but finding a globally optimal schedule is not guaranteed.

The heuristic we use is the expected value of energy waste per content download in Joules per second. The expected value is again calculated as shown in (1) and we obtain (3) as the heuristic.

$$Hr = \sum_{k=1}^{|S|}(\mathbb{E}[E_i^{waste}(T_k)]) / \sum_{k=1}^{|S|} T_k \quad (3)$$

eSchedule searches for a variable size chunk download schedule $S = (T_1, T_2, T_3, \ldots, T_n)$. Each time a new video chunk download needs to be scheduled, i.e. every time the amount of content in the playback buffer goes below a minimum threshold, the algorithm finds such an $S$ that minimizes $Hr$ and then selects $T_1$ as the next chunk size. The size of $S$ limits the number of consecutive chunks to consider in each scheduling decision. According to our tests, which used a video lasting ten minutes, having more than two consecutive chunks in the scheduling yields only minor improvements in overall energy efficiency.

# 4. PERFORMANCE EVALUATION

## 4.1 Simulation Setup

We implemented eSchedule in Matlab in order to compare it to the existing alternative approaches. Our colleagues helped us to collect audience retention information from 16 different YouTube videos[1]. Their durations range from one to eleven minutes and they had been viewed from a few hundred to five million times. Average stream encoding rates vary from 160 Kbps to 800 Kbps. The content includes recordings of illustrated discussions, music performances, advertisements, and martial arts exhibitions and lessons.

We divided the set of videos into short and long ones. The 10 short ones last less than five minutes and the 6 long ones more than five minutes. We simulated 1000 video streaming sessions for one user separately for both sets of videos. We simulate the behaviour of an average user: For each session, the video is randomly selected from the set and the abandoning time of viewing is randomly drawn from a probability distribution following the audience retention information of the selected video. For example, if the audience retention of a given video tells that not a single user abandoned the viewing during the first ten seconds, the simulations would also never draw an abandoning time shorter than ten seconds for that video. The video download schedule was computed with each considered algorithm, and the total energy consumed was calculated for each session.

We compare eSchedule to four other approaches: 1) to Oracle, which knows the viewing time for each session and downloads the content corresponding to that duration in one shot, 2) to downloading whole video at once, 3) to ON-OFF-M downloading 60-second chunks of content, which roughly corresponds to default YouTube Android app, and 4) to the algorithm used by GreenTube [16].

GreenTube resizes the download buffer size based on the user's viewing history stored locally in smartphones. It first computes an expected value of viewing time using this history. In turn, it finds a buffer size which will minimize the total energy consumed between the current and the end of the expected viewing time, also taking into account the power consumed during download and the tail energy. We implemented this algorithm, including maintaining local viewing history of the simulated user, on Matlab as well. In this way,

[1]These statistics are currently available only for the video owner in YouTube.

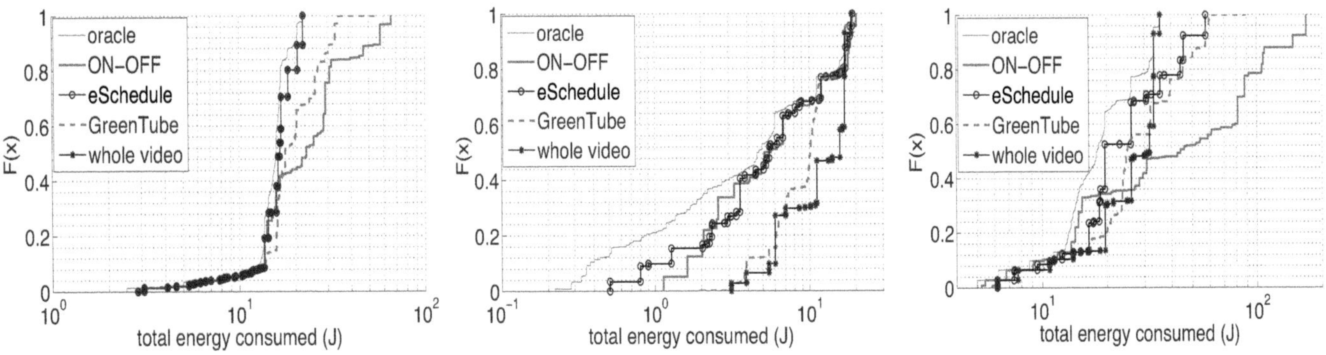


(a) short video over LTE (b) long video over Wi-Fi (c) long video over LTE

**Figure 4:** CDF plots of the downloading energy consumption when streaming videos.

| WNI | tail timers | power values | datarate |
|---|---|---|---|
| Wi-Fi | PSM: 0.2s | $P_{rx}$ = 0.78W, $P_{tail}$ = 0.435W | 10Mbit/s |
| 3G | FD: 5s | $P_{DCH}$ = 0.78W, $P_{tail}$ = 0.78W | 6Mbit/s |
| LTE | inactivity: 10s | $P_{rx}$ = 1.58W, $P_{tail}$ = 1.3W | 16Mbit/s |
| LTE+DRX | DRX: 0.75s | $P_{rx}$ = 1.58W, $P_{tail}$ = 1.3W | 16Mbit/s |

**Table 1:** WNI timer configurations and power consumption at different states of the interface.

we are able to compare our approach of using crowd-sourced per-video viewing statistics to GreenTube's approach of using local viewing statistics.

At the beginning of simulations, GreenTube's local viewing statistics were initialized to null as we considered that to be as realistic as initializing it with random statistics. They are updated according to the simulated viewing behaviour throughout the 1000 viewing sessions. In addition, the lower threshold of buffer size was reduced to 1 MB in order to allow GreenTube to use also small buffer sizes and to make the comparison fair.

Table 1 summarizes the network and power related parameters used in simulations. The data rates imply end-to-end bulk transfer capacity rather than the over-the-air data rate of wireless access network technologies. Most of the other parameters were identified during the measurements presented in Section 2.2. Only the DRX timer was assumed according to a vendor recommendation as the DRX was not enabled in the commercial network. The power models used are straightforward in that we assume a fixed power draw during each different state, namely reception of data, idle but radio on (tail power), and sleep. We used power values relative to each idle state of each WNI, namely 3G's CELL_PCH, LTE's idle, LTE's DRX sleep, and Wi-Fi's PSM sleep modes. Note that for 3G access we assumed Fast Dormancy as the Galaxy SIII supports. In the case of LTE, we considered both cases; with and without DRX.

## 4.2 Energy Consumption

In the first simulation round, we only included videos that are shorter than five minutes. The results show that downloading the entire video in one go is energy efficient in the case of short videos, especially when the amount of tail energy is high, such as with LTE (Figure 4(a)). Similarly, eSchedule responds to short videos by typically choosing in almost every case to download the whole video in one go. By contrast, for those videos longer than five minutes, we observe that downloading the whole video is less attractive. The performance of the ON-OFF strategy is fairly good when the tail energy is small, such as in the case of Wi-Fi (Figure 4(b)). However, when streaming over 3G and LTE, which exhibit large tail energy, the results are significantly worse (Figure 4(c)).

We computed the energy consumption overhead by subtracting the energy consumed by Oracle from the energy consumed by other strategies for each streaming session. We sum up this overhead for each test case and plot the results in Figure 5(a). In every configuration, eSchedule achieves overall the lowest energy consumption. On average, *eSchedule cuts the energy waste to approximately half when compared to the next best approach.*

The behaviours of the other competing download strategies are intuitive but GreenTube deserves more analysis. The reason why GreenTube in most cases consumes more energy than eSchedule is two fold. First, unlike eSchedule, which leverages "global" video viewing statistics, GreenTube uses "local" statistics and assumes that a given user will always watch each video in a similar fashion regardless of the content, thus, for example, the user will either always watch just a small fraction of each video or always watch the entire video. The vastly different shapes of audience retention graphs undermine this assumption.

The second reason is related to the way GreenTube optimizes its buffer size. To illustrate the problem, let us consider two situations: In the first one, the user has always watched roughly half of the video, and in the second, the viewing history is evenly distributed. Both cases suggest that the expected viewing time is half the video and thus GreenTube will choose the same download strategy. However, in the latter case, it is much less likely that the expected value will provide an accurate estimate. The consequence is large especially when the tail energy is significant, in which case an underestimated viewing time yields a large penalty (note the logarithmic scale in Figures). By way of comparison, eSchedule computes the download schedule based on the expected value of energy wasted and, thus, also considers the "shape" of the statistics when deciding the next chunk size.

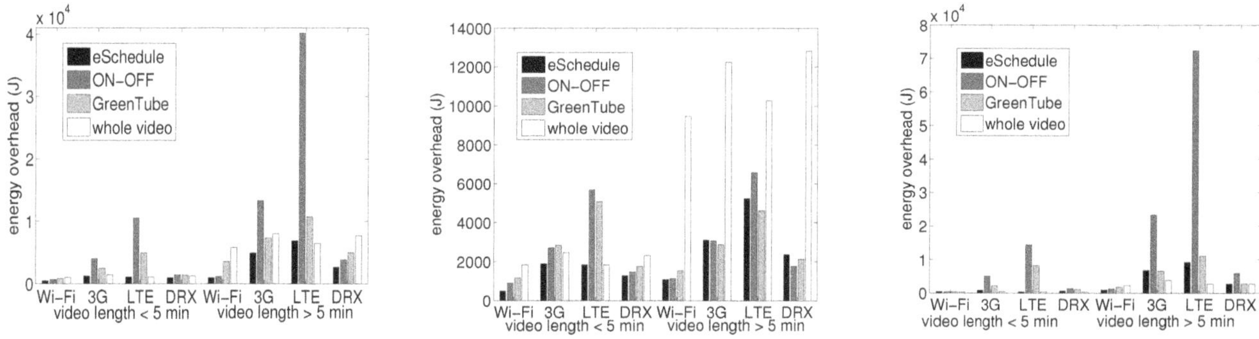


(a) average user (b) impatient user (c) patient user

**Figure 5:** Total energy overhead (J) to watch 1000 videos for three kinds of user compared to Oracle.

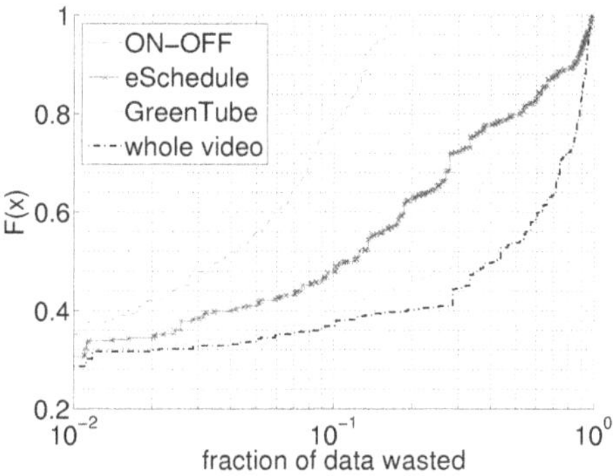


**Figure 6:** ON-OFF spends extra energy for less data waste when streaming long videos over LTE.

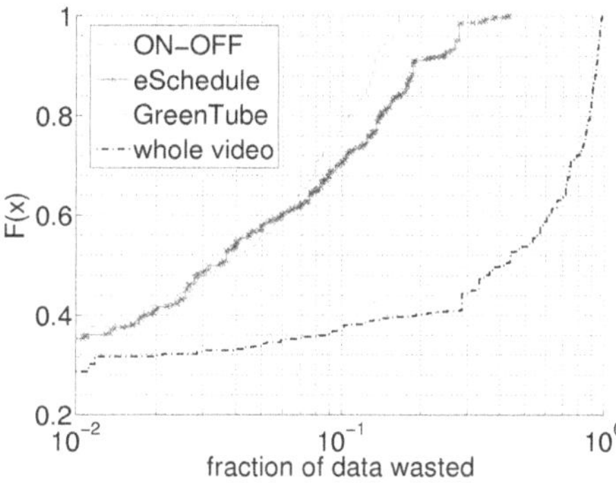


**Figure 7:** eSchedule and ON-OFF download least unnecessary data when streaming over Wi-Fi.

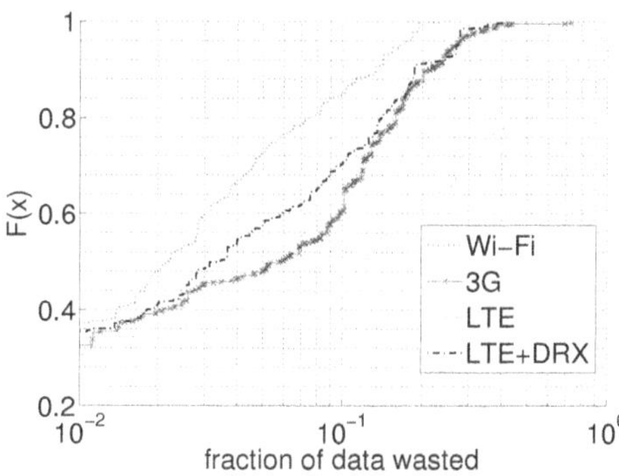


**Figure 8:** The smaller the tail energy, the less unnecessary content is downloaded when using eSchedule.

## 4.3 User Bias

To understand the resulting energy consumption when the user deviates from the average behaviour, we also simulated two different user types which we term *impatient* and *patient*. The impatient user always abandons watching a particular video before the median user did according to the audience retention, while the patient user always continues to watch at least as long as the median user did. We again randomly draw the viewing time from the probability distribution following the audience retention but this time only from the first or second part of it for the impatient and patient users, respectively, the boundary being the time where 50% of users had abandoned the session.

The overall results are shown in Figure 5(b) and 5(c). First thing to notice with respect to the "impatient" user behaviour is that downloading the whole video is a poor strategy if the video is relatively long. GreenTube does a better job with the long videos because the user behaviour is *consistently biased* in which case local viewing history helps. eSchedule performs roughly similarly with it when viewing long videos but better with the short videos. Users that continue viewing longer than the median user are most penalized by the default ON-OFF strategy because of the tail energy associated with each chunk. Downloading the whole video is a good strategy in this case. Again, eSchedule and GreenTube perform similarly with long videos but eSchedule does a better job with the short ones. We discuss in Section 6 how eSchedule can be extended to adapt to this kind of situations to provide even better performance.

## 4.4 Data Waste

A download schedule that minimizes energy consumption does not always minimize unnecessary content download. The reason is the tail energy. Indeed, the larger the tail energy, the more favorable an aggressive buffering will generally be from the energy consumption perspective. Yet, limiting the amount of unnecessarily downloaded data is important for some mobile network users who have a quota in their data plan. It is equally important, too, for ISPs, who need to provision networks based on traffic volumes.

We computed the amount of content downloaded but not watched for all the simulated scenarios. Figures 6 and 7 plot the data waste for the scenarios where videos longer than five minutes are streamed over LTE both without and with DRX. These figures illustrate the role of the amount of tail energy. The results demonstrate that downloading the whole video in one go leads to a lot of data waste: half of the sessions download roughly 40% of the content unnecessarily. Using GreenTube also leads to considerable amount of data waste: half of the sessions download approximately 30% of the content unnecessarily. Compared to these two, the data waste generated by eSchedule is on average much more reasonable: approximately 10% when streaming over LTE and only about 3% when DRX is enabled for half of the sessions. Figure 8 confirms that the amount of content unnecessar-

**Algorithm 1** StreamThrottler

```
bytes = 0, brate = 0, bwidth = 0, faststart = 40;
contentlength = 0, videodownloaded = false
audret = get_audience_retention()
while videodownloaded == false do
    pos = get_playback_pos()
    if (bitrate == 0) then chunksize = 5
    else
        chunksize = eSchedule(radio, brate, bwidth, pos, audret)
        consdown = chunksize/faststart
    for i = 1 → consdown do
        shortchunk = calculatechunk(chunksize)
        request = formatrequest(bytes, contentlength)
        response=download(shortchunk,bitrate,request)
        bytes+ = process(response)
        if (brate == 0) then
            contentlength = process(response)
            brate = process(response)
            bwidth = process(response)
    if (bytes == contentlength) then
        videodownloaded = true
    sleep(chunksize − 5)
```

ily downloaded by eSchedule depends on the size of the tail energy: the smaller it is, the smaller is also the expected data waste. It should be noted that neither GreenTube nor eSchedule were configured to specifically limit data waste in these simulations. In both solutions, it is possible to further limit the data waste by spending extra energy. In case of eSchedule, this can be achieved by specifying an upper limit for the estimated amount of unnecessarily downloaded content, i.e. the algorithm would reject all schedules where $\mathbb{E}[B_i^{waste}(T)]$ exceeds that limit in (2).

## 5. StreamThrottler: Android App

In order to show that eSchedule works also in practice, we designed and implemented a YouTube client for Android and experimented with it. This client comprises two components: the eSchedule and a downloader. We next describe both of these in turn before presenting the results obtained from testing the application.

### 5.1 eSchedule Implementation

We implemented eSchedule according to the description in Section 3. Since audience retention information is currently available only to the video owner, we used previously collected data. In addition, the algorithm requires as inputs the encoding rate of the stream, the download rate, and the wireless interface being used and their respective power models. The downloader finds the encoding rate by parsing the first few hundred bytes of the video header. It also measures the rates and determines the interface being used.

eSchedule also takes the current position of playback as input. If the user does not watch the stream continuously but instead jumps forward or backward while streaming, eSchedule simply computes the next chunk size taking into account the audience retention data when starting from the new position.

We implemented power consumption models for Wi-Fi, 3G, and LTE in the same way as we did for the Matlab evaluation (Section 3) because there are no open APIs in a mobile device to obtain information about the states of the 3G/LTE RRC protocols. We implemented the 3G power model knowing that both the testing device, Galaxy SIII, and our commercial HSPA network support Fast Dormancy having a 5 second inactivity timer. In the case of LTE, we also used a commercial network and found the RRC inactivity timer to be 10 seconds, which is commonly used.

### 5.2 Downloader

In order to start a new streaming session, StreamThrottler's downloader retrieves the YouTube HTTP video download URL and the duration of the video from the server, in the same way as a default player does. It then downloads video content from the server in chunks whose sizes are determined by the eSchedule.

The download rate and stream encoding rate are typically unknown beforehand. Therefore, the downloader uses an initial chunk of 5 seconds during which it measures the encoding and download rates and, in turn, lets eSchedule make the first scheduling decision. If the decision is to download more than 5 seconds worth of video as the first chunk, the downloader makes immediately another HTTP request and continues downloading the content after the first five seconds chunk has completely arrived. We use five seconds as the minimum chunk size.

Our traffic and power measurements in Section 2.2 suggest that the streaming services control the rate of download after the Fast Start phase, and that these methods lead to energy waste for the streaming clients. We want StreamThrottler to avoid this problem in a case where eSchedule decides to download a chunk of a size that exceeds the amount downloaded during the Fast Start phase. Therefore, we apply a maneuver to bypass the server's rate control mechanism by exploiting Fast Start. What happens is that a single TCP connection is used to download only the amount of content that the server delivers in the Fast Start phase, during which no rate limit is applied. After that phase, the connection is closed and another one is established. A new HTTP request for the subsequent range of content is sent over the new TCP connection and again the amount of content equivalent to the Fast Start phase will be downloaded without a rate limit. This behaviour continues iteratively until the amount of content equivalent to the complete chunk has been downloaded. In this way the downloader can download content at the maximum end-to-end bandwidth and can reduce the active usage time of wireless interfaces significantly. The pseudo code of the downloader is shown in Algorithm 1.

### 5.3 Dealing with Wireless Latency

eSchedule may decide to download a video in multiple chunks either when the WNI has small tail energy or when the audience retention shows little probability of viewing the whole content. Downloading content in chunks may increase the chance of letting the playback buffer run dry in between chunks. This probability is higher for a smartphone compared to a device connected to the fixed network because the mobile device spends some time accessing the wireless channel before beginning to download a chunk. This latency is not significant for Wi-Fi and LTE access. However, when using 3G access such a delay may be up to 3 seconds because of transitioning from IDLE or CELL_PCH to CELL_DCH state [19]. Therefore, it is practical to let the client to download the next chunk before the playback buffer is completely empty. StreamThrottler also does this by downloading the new chunk 5 seconds in advance. We considered this five second value based on the analysis present in [27].

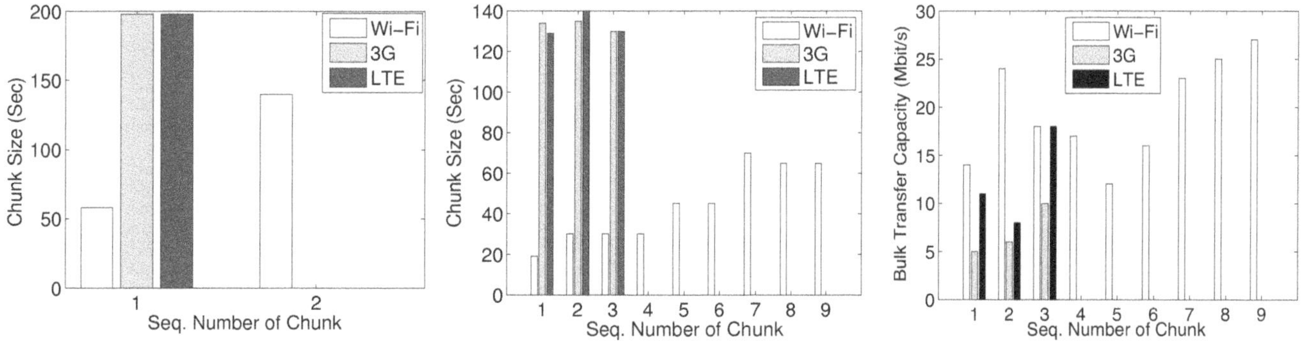


(a) 198 s (b) 399 s (c) Bulk transfer capacity (399 s)

**Figure 9:** Chunk sizes in seconds chosen by eSchedule and the downloading rates calculated by the downloader.

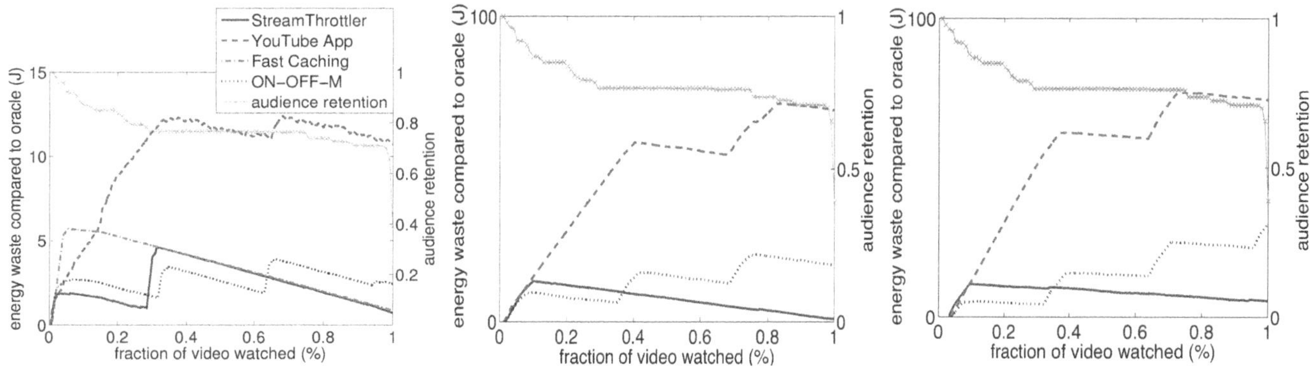


(a) Wi-Fi (b) 3G (c) LTE

**Figure 10:** Estimated energy waste compared to Oracle while streaming the 198s video using Galaxy SIII.

## 5.4 Testing and measurements

In this setup, the Wi-Fi access point was connected to the 100 Mbit/s university network and the smartphone had unlimited access to the cellular networks. We streamed two YouTube videos, a short (198s) and a long (399s) one, on Samsung Galaxy SIII 4G using (i) StreamThrottler, (ii) the default YouTube app, (iii) Fast Caching and (iv) an ON-OFF-M download strategy without throttling which downloads 65 s equivalent chunk after every 60 seconds. Both videos are of $360p$ quality. We compare these four test cases by measuring the current drawn by the smartphone using the Monsoon Power Monitor [1]. Again, as we did in Section 2.2, we subtracted the manually identified playback current from the total current consumption because of different apps and in order to compare only the current drawn by downloading.

Figure 9 shows the chunk sizes and downloading rates determined by the StreamThrottler. To illustrate the key differences in the download strategies and mechanisms, we compute the energy waste for each streaming session as a function of time. This waste is computed by subtracting the energy consumption estimate calculated for Oracle as a function of time from the cumulative energy consumption measured for above mentioned four techniques. The Oracle strategy downloads the right amount of content in each case. We assume that Oracle would on the average draw the same amount of current while downloading content and achieve the same average download rate than StreamThrottler.

The results for the short video and the corresponding audience retention for that video are plotted in Figure 10. The corresponding chunk sizes chosen by eSchedule are illustrated in Figure 9(a). What stands out first is the striking difference in overall cumulative energy consumption between StreamThrottler and the default app. This difference is mainly due to the low download rate resulting from server throttling and tail energy, in turn, due to multiple chunks (see Section 2.3), especially when streaming over 3G and LTE. Therefore, the difference becomes smaller when ON-OFF-M without throttling is used.

The second noticeable feature is that StreamThrottler, which uses eSchedule, adapts the download strategy to the audience retention and the characteristics of wireless network. When streaming over 3G and LTE, eSchedule chooses to download the whole video in one shot. The reason is the large amount of tail energy and relatively strong audience retention. Therefore, ON-OFF-M (without throttling) causes more energy waste than StreamThrottler resulting from more tail energy. As for streaming over Wi-Fi, eSchedule chooses to split the download into two chunks because the penalty arising from tail energy is clearly smaller. A careful observation reveals that the chunk sizes are chosen in such a manner that the first one is sufficient to cover

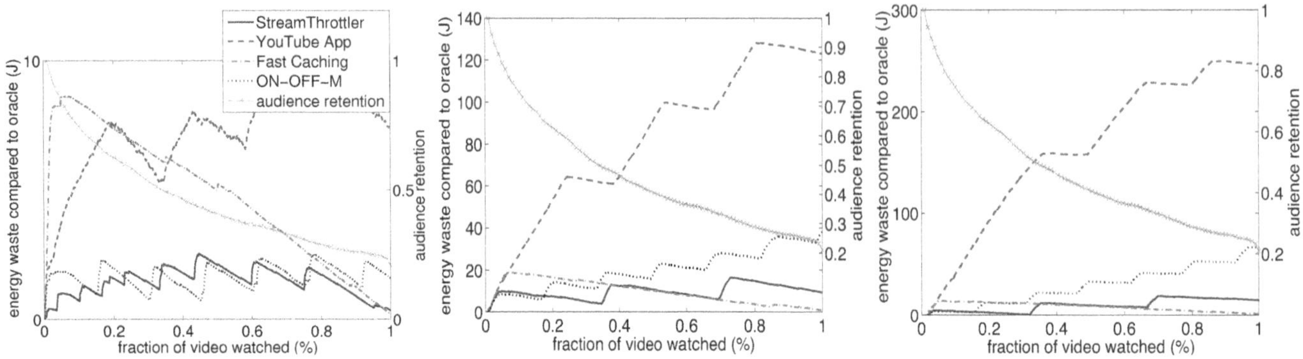


(a) Wi-Fi (b) 3G (c) LTE

**Figure 11:** Estimated energy waste compared to Oracle while streaming the 399s video using Galaxy SIII 4G.

viewing until the end of the first drop in the audience retention (first 30% of the video). The second chunk then covers the rest of the video during which almost no viewer interrupted their viewing – this is is visible as an almost flat retention curve. In this way, eSchedule does not risk a hefty energy waste caused by potential abandonment during the first 30%.

Similar results for the long video are plotted in Figure 11 and the corresponding chunk sizes eSchedule chose are shown in Figure 9(b). The viewing statistics suggest that users are continuously abandoning the viewing but the rate of abandonment is decreasing as the viewing progresses. For this reason, when streaming over Wi-Fi, eSchedule chooses chunks that are of increasing size while the viewing progresses. The much larger tail energy of 3G and LTE causes eSchedule to choose larger chunk sizes, as occurs with the short video, but this time the video is split into three chunks because the probability of a user abandoning the video is much higher than in the case of the short video. On the contrary, ON-OFF-M uses more chunks and causes more energy waste using 3G and LTE. At a first glance, it would seem that Fast Caching performs better. However, from the audience retention graph we can see that the video loses around 50% of its viewers during the first 35% of total duration and during that time there is more energy waste than the StreamThrottler.

We also measured the computational overhead of eSchedule. To do that, we measured the current consumption of the phone running StreamThrottler and computed the download schedules using eSchedule against those selecting chunk sizes from hardcoded values. No actual downloading took place. We chose to use the long video over Wi-Fi as the test case because that requires more frequent scheduling decisions than the other ones. The measured average extra power draw caused by eSchedule computation was less than 15 mW which is negligible compared to the total power draw including playback and download power.

# 6. PRACTICALITIES

A relevant question concerning the sources of energy inefficiency is why video service providers do not use encoding rate streaming or throttle the transmission rate. The answer cannot be network congestion because that is not an application level problem and it is handled by TCP. One conclusion might be the concern about "bandwidth waste", i.e. the bandwidth used to deliver content to users which is never consumed because of abandoning the session before the end. eSchedule would eliminate such concern because this download scheduler uses users' viewing statistics. Furthermore, eSchedule could be tuned to emphasize the importance of the bandwidth waste by setting an upper limit to a chunk size, as we discussed in Section 4.

Chunk size also can be limited when the device does not have enough memory to accommodate the content being downloaded. In that case, the device must spend extra energy. Although, a significant amount of YouTube videos are less than 10 minutes long [12], the size a 10 minutes long HD video (2 Mbps) can be 150 MB. However, modern smartphones have few hundred megabytes to two gigabytes of phone memory. If this memory is full then content can be downloaded to the SD card.

The design of eSchedule assumes that the amount of available bandwidth is greater than the encoding rate. However, the inverse is possible. If such situation is of persistent type, the content cannot be downloaded in time and the session is interrupted and eventually abandoned. In that case, any download schedule keeps the radio continuously on because a chunk download cannot finish before the next one should already be started. Dynamic Adaptive Streaming over HTTP (DASH) [24] is a good solution to cope with transient bandwidth fluctuations. This is because DASH allows to switch to a lower bit rate upon bandwidth degradation and it is possible to integrate eSchedule to a DASH client. In case of quality switch, a new chunk size calculation is triggered.

Concerning the audience retention information, we assume that other video services also collect crowd-sourced video viewing statistics in a similar manner to YouTube, but this data might be available only to the owner of the video in question. We can think of two ways to make such data available to eSchedule in the future. First, the video service provider opens up access to this data through an API. Should this data be deemed sensitive, however, the other option is for the video services to implement eSchedule in their own players, which then requests the viewing statistics from the server using some secure API only when playing a video. Yet another solution is to let the servers to do the scheduling.

In case a user behaves in a consistently biased way, at least for some time, it is possible to make eSchedule adapt to it. We can maintain a measure of user bias with respect to the average user by comparing the expected viewing time of a video computed from the audience retention data to the actual viewing time. This local bias measure could be used to adjust the interrupt probabilities when calculating the download schedule.

# 7. RELATED WORK

Energy consumption for multimedia streaming in mobile devices has been studied for the last decade. Most earlier studies have focused on streaming over Wi-Fi. A few recent papers consider energy consumption while streaming over cellular access network. The proposed solutions work from different vantage points and on different layers of the Internet protocol stack. In the following, we discuss the most important parts of that body of work and compare it to our work in this paper.

Anand et al. proposed adapting Wi-Fi power management in response to access patterns and application hints on data access [7]. Bagchi et al. [9] also presented a solution for streaming over Wi-Fi, one in which a player maintains a fixed playback buffer size and requests data from the server when the buffer status touches a low buffer watermark. The alternative is that the player plays from the playback buffer and ceases downloading. This solution is similar to the ON-OFF-S mechanism discussed in Section 2. Two other similar approaches [28, 25] modify TCP window-size of IP packets to trigger the TCP flow control mechanism artificially, which eventually generates bursty traffic when the TCP window-size is modified to a higher value. These solutions save energy by forcing the Wi-Fi into sleep mode, which means they avoid any potential auxiliary traffic such as TCP control packets, and, at the same time, the application layer keeps messages alive. However, these solutions do not address the problem of users abandoning the viewing of the video.

Several kinds of optimization techniques exist to reduce energy while communicating over 3G. For example, RadioJockey mines program execution in order to optimize the use of Fast Dormancy in 3G communication and in that way reduces energy consumption [8]. However, it does not actually target streaming; instead it focuses on background apps. ARO [18] and TOP [20] have similar objectives but they require active participation from application developers. Bartendr saves energy by prefetching streaming content when the signal strength is good [22]. It is in fact a complementary mechanism that could be integrated into eSchedule.

Some work has looked at scheduling of mobile traffic based on the power consumption characteristics of wireless radios. For example, CoolSpots propose to schedule low bit rate video transmission over Bluetooth and higher bit rate video over Wi-Fi [17]. Such a solution is orthogonal to what we propose in this paper. If eSchedule is used with a downloader that fetches each chunk of video over a separate TCP connection, such as StreamThrottler, CoolSpots could complement the system to save more energy by downloading chunks over Bluetooth when deemed beneficial.

There are also many papers studying measurement and characterization that touch on the subject of our work. For instance, 3G energy consumption was studied in [10] and LTE power characteristics in [15]. Trestian et al. specifically studied streaming and energy consumption in [26].

The closest one to our work is GreenTube [16] was recently proposed as a solution to optimize energy consumption while streaming YouTube videos to Android phones. The download scheduling part of GreenTube has two important differences to eSchedule: First, it is based on users' local viewing history rather than global per-video statistics that we propose to use in this work. Second, the use of expected value of viewing time as the sole input to scheduler may lead to a significant energy waste if tail energy is large (see Section 3).

# 8. CONCLUSION

We highlighted a number of sources of energy inefficiency in wireless video streaming two of which are contradictory, namely tail energy spent because of downloading content in chunks and energy spent in prefetching content that the user will never watch. Consequently, we designed a novel download scheduling algorithm, eSchedule, which uses crowd-sourced video viewing statistics and wireless communication power models to predict user behaviour and optimize the tradeoff between these two sources of energy waste. Evaluation results show that eSchedule cuts the energy waste to half compared to the next best alternatives. We also implemented an Android prototype called StreamThrottler which implements eSchedule and a chunk-based YouTube downloader that speeds up the downloads by exploiting Fast Start technique. Experiment results confirm that the prototype exhibits the desired properties of eSchedule and, furthermore, saves up to 80% of overall energy.

Our future work includes integrating eSchedule into DASH and considering other additional input for the scheduler, such as signal strength indicators and events indicating network activity of other apps in order to leverage the opportunity of simultaneous transfers to further amortize tail energy. Another extension of this work is to take into account the user's local viewing history, in addition to the crowd-sourced viewing statistics per video as described earlier. In this way, we could add a personalization component to the download scheduling in order to further enhance the prediction of user behaviour.

# 9. ACKNOWLEDGEMENTS

This work was supported by the Academy of Finland: grant number 253860 and FIGS. We would also like to thank the anonymous reviewers, and our shepherd, Dina Papagiannaki, for their feedback.

# 10. REFERENCES

[1] Power Monitor, www.msoon.com.

[2] 3GPP TS 25.331, Radio Resource Control (RRC); Protocol specification, May 1999.

[3] IEEE 802.11, Wireless LAN Medium Access Control and Physical Layer Specification, 1999.

[4] 3GPP TS 36.331, E-UTRA; Radio Resource Control (RRC) Protocol Specification, May 2008.

[5] Fast Dormancy best practices, GSM association, network efficiency task force, 2010.

[6] Audience retention,`http://support.google.com/youtube/bin/static.py?hl=en&topic=1715158&guide=1714169&page=guide.cs`.

[7] Anand, M., Nightingale, E. B., and Flinn, J. Self-tuning wireless network power management. In *Proceedings of the 9th annual international conference on Mobile computing and networking* (2003), MobiCom '03, ACM, pp. 176–189.

[8] Athivarapu, P. K., Bhagwan, R., Guha, S., Navda, V., Ramjee, R., Arora, D., Padmanabhan, V. N., and Varghese, G. RadioJockey: mining program execution to optimize cellular radio usage. In *Proceedings of the 18th annual international conference on Mobile computing and networking* (New York, NY, USA, 2012), Mobicom '12, ACM, pp. 101–112.

[9] Bagchi, S. A fuzzy algorithm for dynamically adaptive multimedia streaming. *ACM Trans. Multimedia Comput. Commun. Appl. 7* (2011), 11:1–11:26.

[10] Balasubramanian, N., Balasubramanian, A., and Venkataramani, A. Energy consumption in mobile phones: a measurement study and implications for network applications. In *Proceedings of the 9th ACM SIGCOMM conference on Internet measurement conference* (New York, NY, USA, 2009), IMC '09, ACM, pp. 280–293.

[11] Finamore, A., Mellia, M., Munafò, M. M., Torres, R., and Rao, S. G. Youtube everywhere: impact of device and infrastructure synergies on user experience. In *Proceedings of the 2011 ACM SIGCOMM conference on Internet measurement conference* (New York, NY, USA, 2011), IMC '11, ACM, pp. 345–360.

[12] Gill, P., Arlitt, M., Li, Z., and Mahanti, A. Youtube traffic characterization: a view from the edge. In *Proceedings of the 7th ACM SIGCOMM conference on Internet measurement* (New York, NY, USA, 2007), IMC '07, ACM, pp. 15–28.

[13] Guo, L., Tan, E., Chen, S., Xiao, Z., Spatscheck, O., and Zhang, X. Delving into internet streaming media delivery: a quality and resource utilization perspective. In *Proceedings of the 6th ACM SIGCOMM conference on Internet measurement* (New York, NY, USA, 2006), IMC '06, ACM, pp. 217–230.

[14] Hoque, M. A., Siekkinen, M., and Nurminen, J. K. Dissecting mobile video services: An energy consumption perspective. In *14th IEEE International Symposium on a World of Wireless, Mobile and Multimedia Networks(WoWMoM)* (2013), WoWMoM '13, IEEE.

[15] Huang, J., Qian, F., Gerber, A., Mao, Z. M., Sen, S., and Spatscheck, O. A close examination of performance and power characteristics of 4G LTE networks. In *Proceedings of the 10th international conference on Mobile systems, applications, and services* (New York, NY, USA, 2012), MobiSys '12, ACM, pp. 225–238.

[16] Li, X., Dong, M., Ma, Z., and Fernandes, F. GreenTube: Power Optimization for Mobile Video Streaming via Dynamic Cache Management. In *Proceedings of the ACM Multimedia* (New York, NY, USA, 2012), acmmm'12, ACM.

[17] Pering, T., Agarwal, Y., Gupta, R., and Want, R. CoolSpots: reducing the power consumption of wireless mobile devices with multiple radio interfaces. In *Proceedings of MobiSys 2006* (New York, NY, USA, 2006), ACM, pp. 220–232.

[18] Qian, F., Wang, Z., Gerber, A., Mao, Z., Sen, S., and Spatscheck, O. Profiling resource usage for mobile applications: a cross-layer approach. In *Proceedings of the 9th international conference on Mobile systems, applications, and services* (New York, NY, USA, 2011), MobiSys '11, ACM, pp. 321–334.

[19] Qian, F., Wang, Z., Gerber, A., Mao, Z. M., Sen, S., and Spatscheck, O. Characterizing radio resource allocation for 3G networks. In *Proceedings of the 10th ACM SIGCOMM conference on Internet measurement* (New York, NY, USA, 2010), IMC '10, ACM, pp. 137–150.

[20] Qian, F., Wang, Z., Gerber, A., Mao, Z. M., Sen, S., and Spatscheck, O. TOP: Tail Optimization Protocol For Cellular Radio Resource Allocation. In *Proceedings of the The 18th IEEE International Conference on Network Protocols* (Washington, DC, USA, 2010), ICNP '10, IEEE Computer Society, pp. 285–294.

[21] Rao, A., Legout, A., Lim, Y.-s., Towsley, D., Barakat, C., and Dabbous, W. Network characteristics of video streaming traffic. In *Proceedings of the Seventh COnference on emerging Networking EXperiments and Technologies* (New York, NY, USA, 2011), CoNEXT '11, ACM, pp. 25:1–25:12.

[22] Schulman, A., Navda, V., Ramjee, R., Spring, N., Deshpande, P., Grunewald, C., Jain, K., and Padmanabhan, V. N. Bartendr: a practical approach to energy-aware cellular data scheduling. In *Proceedings of the sixteenth annual international conference on Mobile computing and networking* (New York, NY, USA, 2010), MobiCom '10, ACM, pp. 85–96.

[23] Siekkinen, M., Hoque, M., K. Nurminen, J., and Aalto, M. Streaming over 3g and lte: How to save smartphone energy in radio access network-friendly way. In *Proceedings of the 5th ACM Workshop on Mobile Video* (2013), MoVid'13, ACM, pp. 13–18.

[24] Stockhammer, T. Dynamic adaptive streaming over HTTP –: standards and design principles. In *Proceedings of the second annual ACM conference on Multimedia systems* (New York, NY, USA, 2011), MMSys '11, ACM, pp. 133–144.

[25] Tan, E., Guo, L., Chen, S., and Zhang, X. PSM-Throttling: Minimizing energy consumption for bulk data communications in WLANs. In *Proceedings of International Conference on Network Protocols, 2007* (2007), IEEE, pp. 123–132.

[26] Trestian, R., Moldovan, A.-N., Ormond, O., and Muntean, G.-M. Energy consumption analysis of video streaming to android mobile devices. In *Network Operations and Management Symposium (NOMS), 2012 IEEE* (april 2012), pp. 444 –452.

[27] Wang, B., Kurose, J., Shenoy, P., and Towsley, D. Multimedia streaming via TCP: An analytic performance study. *ACM Trans. Multimedia Comput. Commun. Appl. 4*, 2 (May 2008), 16:1–16:22.

[28] Yan, H., Krishnan, R., Watterson, S. A., Lowenthal, D. K., Li, K., and Peterson, L. L. Client-centered energy and delay analysis for TCP downloads. In *IWQOS* (2004), IEEE, pp. 255–264.

# A Scheduling Framework for Adaptive Video Delivery over Cellular Networks

Jiasi Chen *
Princeton University
jiasic@princeton.edu

Rajesh Mahindra, Mohammad A. (Amir) Khojastepour
NEC Laboratories America, Inc.
rajesh, amir@nec-labs.com

Sampath Rangarajan
NEC Laboratories America, Inc.
sampath@nec-labs.com

Mung Chiang
Princeton University
chiangm@princeton.edu

## Abstract

*As the growth of mobile video traffic outpaces that of cellular network speed, industry is adopting HTTP-based adaptive video streaming technology which enables dynamic adaptation of video bit-rates to match changing network conditions. However, recent measurement studies have observed problems in fairness, stability, and efficiency of resource utilization when multiple adaptive video flows compete for bandwidth on a shared wired link. Through experiments and simulations, we confirm that such undesirable behavior manifests itself in cellular networks as well. To overcome these problems, we design an in-network resource management framework,* AVIS, *that schedules HTTP-based adaptive video flows on cellular networks.* AVIS *effectively manages the resources of a cellular base station across adaptive video flows.* AVIS *also provides a framework for mobile operators to achieve a desired balance between optimal resource allocation and user quality of experience.* AVIS *has three key differentiating features: (1) It optimally computes the bit-rate allocation for each user, (2) It includes a scheduler and per-flow shapers to enforce bit-rate stability of each flow and (3) It leverages the resource virtualization technique to separate resource management of adaptive video flows from regular video flows. We implement a prototype system of* AVIS *and evaluate it on both a WiMAX network testbed and a LTE system simulator to show its efficacy and scalability.*

## Categories and Subject Descriptors

C.2.1 [**Computer-Communication Networks**]: Network Architecture and Design—*Wireless Communication*

## Keywords

Cellular Networks, Adaptive Streaming, Proportional fairness, QoE

*This work was done when Jiasi Chen was an intern at NEC Labs America.


*MobiCom'13,* September 30–October 4, Miami, FL, USA.
Copyright 2013 ACM 978-1-4503-1999-7/13/09 ...$15.00.
http://dx.doi.org/10.1145/2500423.2500433

## 1. INTRODUCTION

As cellular data traffic surges and wireless spectrum becomes scarce, video quality of experience (QoE) degrades. Dynamically adaptive streaming [1] is gaining popularity for streaming video over cellular networks. Adaptive streaming is a technique of video streaming over HTTP where multiple versions of the source video are pre-encoded at different bit-rates on the video server. Adaptive streaming leverages the underlying TCP transport layer to estimate the available capacity for the flow and choose the most appropriate video bit-rate based on the estimated capacity. Hence, this technology attempts to maintain QoE for the user by dynamically adapting the video quality to the changing network conditions. Some recent measurement studies on wired networks [2–5] suggest that multiple adaptive video streaming flows experience performance problems when sharing a bottleneck link. These problems manifest as (a) unfairness in the allocation of bit-rates among the competing flows (b) instability due to unnecessary switching of the video bit-rate, and (c) inefficient utilization of the link. To understand the effect of wireless links on the performance of adaptive video streaming, we perform extensive LTE system simulations and experiments on a WiMAX base station prototype. Our experiments confirm that similar problems manifest themselves on wireless networks.

Although current cellular base stations incorporate sophisticated radio resource management techniques for flow scheduling, the framework lacks mechanisms for operators to effectively allocate resources across users who stream adaptive videos. Schedulers in cellular radio resource management are specifically designed to manage resources for traditional single-rate video streaming flows and elastic data flows; they are not directly applicable for adaptive video streaming flows. Adaptive video flows have unique properties that differ from traditional videos: (a) Adaptive videos are encoded at multiple bit-rate versions and (b) They continuously adapt their bit-rate based on the measured throughput. These characteristics of adaptive video flows places them somewhere between elastic and non-elastic traffic types. Hence, the scheduling framework for adaptive video streaming should take into account these characteristics while allocating resources across such flows.

In this paper, we design and implement AVIS, a resource management framework that addresses the above challenges effectively. Specifically, AVIS is designed to manage the radio resources of a cellular base station across multiple adaptive video flows to meet three goals: (a) optimal allocation as desired by the operator (b) stability of bit-rates allocated to a user and (c) maintain high resource utilization. Firstly, AVIS separates the resource management of adaptive video flows from regular video flows and other data flows using resource slicing techniques [6]. Secondly, AVIS's scheduler has two components: (a) an *Allocator* that optimally allocates the bit-rates to the different adaptive video flows to ensure fairness and high utilization and (b) an *Enforcer* that schedules the allocated bit-rate to each flow to ensure stability.

In the design of AVIS, we faced several challenges specific to the domain of wireless networks and adaptive video streaming: (1) The goals of the resource allocation are potentially conflicting. Allocating resources to the video flows to achieve fairness may lead to significant bit-rate switches for users, while reducing bit-rate switches may cause unfairness. An effective framework should incorporate appropriate mechanisms for network operators to achieve the desired balance between these goals. (2) The wireless link of a base station is dynamic and its capacity fluctuates depending upon user arrival/departure, locations of users and resource allocation policy. (3) The videos are encoded with multiple discrete bit-rates and for each bit-rate version the instantaneous rate of the video fluctuates significantly around the average bit-rate, complicating the scheduling problem.

AVIS is designed as a gateway level solution with minimum dependence on the specific cellular technology; hence, the design is applicable to multiple 4G wireless access networks such as WiMAX, LTE and LTE-A. To the best of our knowledge, this is the first detailed design, implementation and evaluation of a resource management framework for adaptive video flows on cellular base stations. Overall, we make the following contributions:

- We develop a novel flow management framework that jointly performs optimal scheduling of resources across multiple adaptive video streaming flows and enforces resource isolation across the flows. To avoid degrading the QoE for a user due to frequent bit-rate switching, AVIS enables an operator to effectively maintain a balance between (a) optimal bit-rate allocated to the different users and (b) the average bit-rate switches perceived by the users. Hence, AVIS strives to achieve fair allocation while ensuring good QoE for the users.

- We present the resource allocation as a utility optimization problem with both discrete and continuous optimization formulations.

- We present a detailed design, implementation and evaluation of the system. We evaluate AVIS on both a LTE system simulator and a mobile WiMAX (802.16e) network testbed containing a PicoChip WiMAX ASN (Access Service Network) gateway that runs AVIS, a PicoChip WiMAX base station [7], and Intel-based WiMAX clients [8].

- We design AVIS such that it does not require any client and server modifications, facilitating quicker deployment.

The rest of the paper is organized as follows. Section 2 discusses background on cellular networks and dynamic adaptive video flows followed by the motivation for AVIS. Section 3 presents our design in detail. Section 4 describes our simulation and prototype setup and provides results from our evaluations. We discuss the limitations and future work in Section 5. Section 6 presents related work to place AVIS in context and Section 7 concludes.

# 2. BACKGROUND AND MOTIVATION

In this section, we first provide a brief background of resource management on cellular networks and HTTP-based adaptive video streaming technology. We then highlight the drawbacks of current resource allocation techniques for adaptive video streaming followed by design considerations for AVIS.

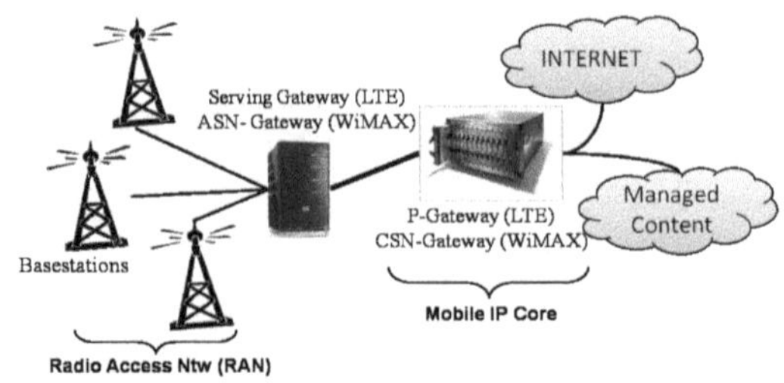


**Figure 1: A typical Cellular Network**

## 2.1 Cellular Background

Figure 1 shows a simplified 4G (e.g., LTE or WiMAX) cellular network architecture consisting of two parts: the Mobile IP Core and the Radio Access Network (RAN). For instance, in LTE, the Mobile Core includes the Serving Gateway and the PDN (Packet Data Network) gateway which provide the functionalities of IP connectivity, authentication, authorization and accounting (AAA). The serving gateway typically handles and routes traffic to and from hundreds of base stations. The RAN includes base stations or eNodeBs that perform RRM (Radio Resource Management), interference mitigation, and handover initiation. Base stations incorporate downlink and uplink MAC schedulers which achieve efficient wireless resource allocation across multiple user flows. In both LTE and WiMAX, wireless (radio) resources are OFDMA frames (or subframes) which are divided into "resource blocks or slots" in the time and frequency domain. The task of the downlink and uplink schedulers is to fill these resource blocks or slots with data packets from one or multiple user flows. To support diverse QoS requirements, flows are mapped to one of the following bearer classes: (a) **GBR bearers** which are suited for real-time applications such as VoIP and video. Each flow has an associated minimum GBR (Guaranteed Bit Rate) that defines the minimum allocation the flow desires to receive. Typically in the case of video traffic, the minimum GBR rate is set to the average bit-rate of the video. A maximum GBR rate is also defined to limit the maximum resource allocation for the flow. (b) **Non-GBR bearers** which do not receive any minimum resource allocation. These bearers are used for applications such as web browsing or FTP transfers.

Current base station schedulers allocate resources to the GBR flows by employing variations of the proportional fair (PF) scheduling policy. Such PF schedulers strive to achieve fairness of resources allocated across the users. In addition, the scheduler allocates resources to the users' flows in proportion to their GBR rate. As compared to schedulers that strive to achieve throughput fairness, PF schedulers ensure higher efficiency of the base station resources (i.e., higher base station capacity). Once all GBR flows are satisfied, the unused resources are allocated to the non-GBR flows.

## 2.2 Adaptive Video Streaming

Several proprietary solutions in the industry such as [9–12] and certain standardized solutions like Dynamic Adaptive Streaming over HTTP (DASH) [1] employ HTTP-based adaptive video streaming. The common key idea is to fragment a video into multiple segments or chunks, where each chunk is encoded using several bit-rates or resolutions. Each chunk, typically containing less than 10 seconds of video content, is stored as a regular file on the web-servers and is downloaded by the clients periodically using the standard HTTP GET requests (see Figure 2). This mechanism ensures that (a) the current web servers and CDNs do not have to be significantly modified to support adaptive streaming. (b) the video

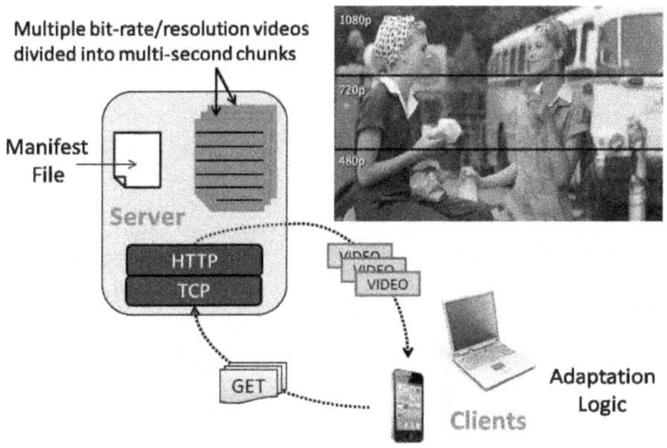


**Figure 2: How DASH works**

traffic can traverse NATs and firewalls. To enable such a framework, a file describing the list of the chunks of all the video bit-rate versions, including the corresponding HTTP link is downloaded by the client prior to streaming. For instance, the DASH standard (MPEG Dynamic Adaptive Streaming over HTTP [1]) defines a Media Presentation Description (MPD) file, an XML file that contains the HTTP URLs for each video chunk. Typically the client video player implements the adaptation algorithm that chooses the most appropriate bit-rate for the next requested chunk, based on current network and processor or memory conditions. An estimate of the TCP throughput is maintained at the client to predict the future network conditions. While most of the framework is standardized as part of the MPEG based standard DASH, the adaptation algorithm to select the most appropriate bit-rate for future chunks is left to the specific implementation. In the rest of the paper, we refer to dynamically adaptive video flows as DASH video flows.

## 2.3 Performance Metrics

To help motivate and design AVIS, we define three metrics that are critical for the performance of the network when multiple DASH video flows share the same base station. These metrics are important from the perspective of both the mobile operator and the users.

1. *Fairness*: In wireless systems, users may have different link qualities or transmission rates depending on their distance from the base station and mobility pattern. Hence, base station schedulers perform proportional fair allocation across the users with the aim of achieving fairness in terms of the resources allocated to the users. First, we define the fairness metric for each user $i$ as $F_i = r_i/C_i$ where $r_i$ is the rate allocated to the user and $C_i$ is the transmission rate of the user depending on its Signal-Noise Ration (SNR). Then, based on the above fairness metric, the fairness index is defined based on the Jain Fairness Index [13].

$$JF = (\sum_{i=1}^{N} F_i)^2/(N\sum_{i=1}^{N} F_i^2) \quad (1)$$

where $N$ is the total number of active users in the system. Hence, the above fairness index measures resource fairness across users instead of throughput fairness.

2. *Stability*: From the users' perspective, in addition to the video bit-rate, the QoE of a DASH video stream is greatly impacted by the frequency of bit-rate switches [14, 15]. To measure the stability of the system, we use the frequency of bit-rate switches perceived by the users during a video session. The frequency of bit-rate switches $S_i$ for user $i$ is defined as the total number of bit-rate switches perceived by the user in W units of time. The lower the frequency of bit-rate switches per user, the higher the stability of the system.

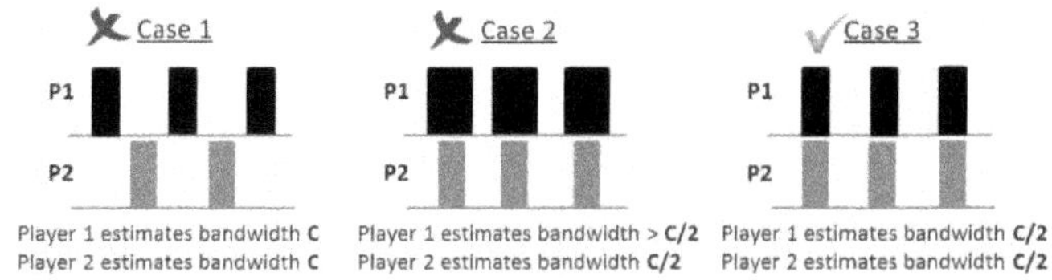


**Figure 3: Chunk overlap scenarios.**

3. *Efficiency*: Wireless resources are scarce and operators desire optimal usage of resources of their base stations. Hence we define the resource utilization as the percentage of the ratio of the total resources allocated ($R_A$) to all the active users to the total resources $R_T$ available at the base station.

$$U = 100R_A/R_T \quad (2)$$

## 2.4 Motivation

Several studies in the past [2–4] have shown that commercial players perform poorly when multiple DASH flows share a link on the Internet. Specifically, a recent study [5] confirms that most players fail to meet the above mentioned goals: (a) Fairness of resource allocation (b) Stability of bit-rate selection and (c) Efficient resource utilization. The main take-away from these measurement studies is that the fundamental problem with DASH flows is the inaccurate estimation of the network bandwidth. Since the players download chunks periodically and estimate the per-chunk throughput, the temporal overlap of the chunks of different players may cause either under-estimation or over-estimation of the underlying bandwidth (see Figure 3). These studies are performed on wired networks; the dynamic characteristics of the wireless link due to mobility of users, mobile user access patterns and channel quality fluctuations will only adversely impact the interaction between different players.

A fundamental difference between wireless links in cellular networks and wired links on the Internet is the presence of per-flow queues and a resource management scheduler at the base stations. Typical base station schedulers are designed as variants of the PF scheduler that aim to achieve fair resource allocation across the users. The schedulers also provide mobile operators with the ability to control the allocation of resources across users through appropriate configuration. In LTE, mobile operators typically leverage the GBR parameter to ensure that the users receive an allocation proportional to the requirement of their video stream. For instance, if two users stream videos with bit-rates of 1 and 2 Mbps respectively, the operator sets the GBR rates of the two users as 1 and 2 Mbps respectively to ensure that the videos are streamed smoothly. Despite providing effective resource isolation across regular video flows, current schedulers are not suited for resource management of DASH flows for the following reasons: (a) Adaptive videos are encoded at multiple bit-rates, so it is not clear how the GBR rate can be set for such flows. Hence, operators are unable to control the allocation of resources to the users that stream DASH videos. (b) Current schedulers are designed for single bit-rate videos and do not account for the bit-rate switches. (c) Current schedulers optimize resource utilization. Therefore, if certain flows do not have sufficient traffic demand to use their allocated resources, the schedulers assign the resources to other flows. Such a design is not suited for DASH flows that download small-sized chunks periodically (as

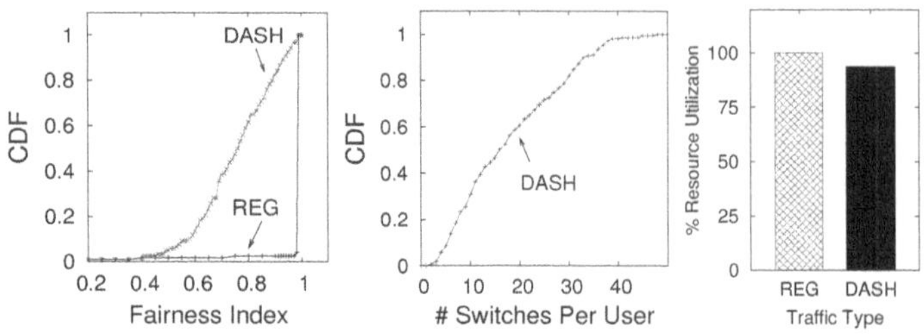


(a) Fairness (b) Stability (c) Utilization

**Figure 4: State of the Art.**

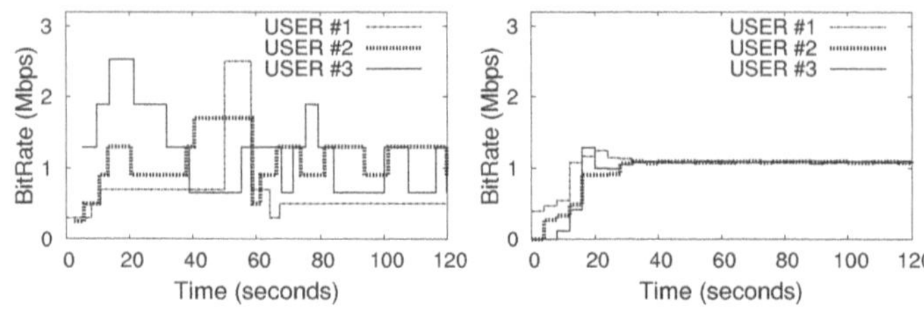


(a) Video (b) FTP (Iperf)

**Figure 5: Adobe OSMF over WiMAX.**

opposed to downloading an entire file) and estimate the network bandwidth based on the chunk download times.

To illustrate the above mentioned problems, we conduct a large-scale simulation on a 3GPP-compliant in-house LTE system-level simulator. We implemented the adaptation algorithm in the clients that keeps track of the moving average of the TCP throughput and requests chunks of the highest rate that can be supported by the estimated throughput. We set up a network of 21 base stations, with each base station serving 10 mobile users. The users at each base station are randomly placed, so that they have diverse link qualities. We experiment with 2 cases where all users stream (a) regular single-rate videos (REG) with an average bit-rate of 1Mbps (b) DASH videos (DASH) encoded at multiple bit-rates $\{0.1, 0.25, 0.5, 1, 2, 3\}$Mbps. For simplicity, we set the GBR rate of all the users to the same value to ensure that the scheduler strives to achieve a fair resource allocation. We operate each base station at just above saturation, i.e., the resources of each base station are fully utilized. We plot the Fairness Index (as defined in Equation (1)) for every base station for both the cases in Figure 4(a). From the figure, it is clear that the base station scheduler is effective in allocating resources fairly across the users streaming regular videos. However, in the case of DASH flows, the base station scheduler fails to allocate resources fairly across the flows due to the different characteristics of the DASH flows. In addition to the fairness problem, the scheduler also fails to ensure the bit-rate stability of the flows. As seen from Figure 4(b), most of the users witness significant bit-rate switching in the case of DASH flows. Although in some cases the resource utilization of a base station drops when streaming multiple DASH flows, on average the loss is not significant as shown in Figure 4(c).

To further confirm the above results on a real system, we performed an experiment on a WiMAX base station with six WiMAX mobile clients streaming DASH videos using the Adobe OSMF player [16]. As shown in Figure 5(a), the video bit-rates of three out of the six clients do not converge to their fair allocation. Moreover, the bit-rates of the video of each users frequently switch which results in poor QoE. For reference, we plot the allocation with FTP file download for the same setup in Figure 5(b); in this case the base station scheduler achieves a fair allocation. Hence, a base station supporting multiple DASH video flows fails to achieve the goals of Fairness and Stability (defined in Section 2.3), despite the presence of a sophisticated resource management framework on the base station.

## 3. AVIS DESIGN

AVIS is a resource management framework that enables mobile operators to effectively achieve (a) desired resource allocation (b) stable bit-rates and (c) high resource utilization across multiple DASH video flows. Before diving into the detailed design of the components of AVIS, we explain the considerations leading to the design of AVIS.

(1) *Network vs Client*: Designing AVIS as a network-based solution has the following advantages: (a) It is easy to deploy since client solutions require changing the players of every content or application provider. Content providers may want to use their proprietary adaptation algorithm to differentiate themselves. Moreover, with a client-level solution the operator loses control of resource allocation across the users. (b) The wireless link is extremely dynamic due to user mobility and link quality fluctuations. The adaptation algorithm in clients typically takes several seconds to react and may fail to converge with a distributed algorithm. A centralized in-network solution is more effective in converging to a fair allocation.

(2) *Gateway-level solution*: Although AVIS is designed to manage the resources of each base station independently, we design AVIS as a gateway solution for the following reasons: (a) Typically base stations have minimal computational resources since they need to be deployed at a large number of locations. Implementing AVIS on base stations would require substantial increase in computational and memory requirements of base stations. (b) Network functionality equipment like DPIs (Deep Packet Inspection) that can provide important meta-data information about video flows to AVIS are typically co-located with the Mobile Core gateways.

(3) *Independent scheduler*: One option is to design AVIS as a scheduler that jointly optimizes the resource allocation across the DASH flows, regular video flows and other data traffic. However, in our design we leverage wireless resource slicing techniques [6] to separate the resource management of DASH videos from regular video flows and data flows. Such a design framework has several benefits: (a) It allows operators to set the allocation to the different slices or traffic types based on the long-term resource usage as seen in their networks. The resource slicing technique ensures that any change in one slice due to new users or user mobility does not impact the allocation of resources to other slices. (b) The resource management techniques for DASH video flows and regular video flows can be applied independently and operators can choose their own unique combination. This enables the system to accommodate future innovations.

Drawing motivation from the above mentioned points, AVIS is designed as a gateway-level solution external to base stations (for instance as a plug-in module on serving gateways in LTE networks) as shown in Figure 6. The resource management for different traffic types is performed within individual slices, and the resource slicing technique (including the slice scheduler and the synchronizer, an adaptive downlink shaper) are borrowed from a previous work [6]. AVIS is instantiated as a separate slice as shown in Figure 6 for each base station and schedules the resources allocated to it by the slice scheduler across the DASH flows. AVIS is designed as a split architecture with two novel components: (a) an *Allocator*

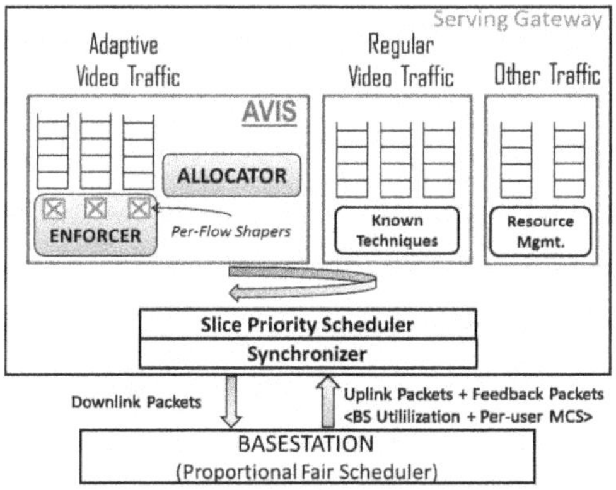


**Figure 6: AVIS Architecture.**

that allows operators to define the allocation for their users who are streaming DASH videos, much like the GBR bearer framework for regular single-rate video flows and (b) an *Enforcer* designed as a PF scheduler to ensure resource isolation across the DASH flows and enforce the appropriate bit-rate selected by the allocator for each flow. We now explain the design of each component in more detail.

## 3.1 AVIS's Allocator

The goal of the allocator is to manage the wireless resources of a base station across a set of users streaming DASH flows. Specifically, it takes as input the various available choices of video bit-rates for all the users and converts these bit-rates to their actual radio resource requirements. It then computes the optimal distribution of resources across the users by selecting the appropriate bit-rate for each user. The allocator is invoked periodically every $I$ seconds to ensure adaptability to user arrivals/departures and mobility. In what follows, we first formulate this resource allocation problem in a discrete-optimization framework and then describe the utility function in the context of achieving the two primary goals of fairness and stability. We then formulate the same problem in a continuous-optimization framework to ease computational complexity in the case of a system with large number of users.

### *3.1.1 Discrete-Optimization Framework*

Let $T$ be the total number of resource blocks assigned to the DASH flows of a base station. These resources are required to be distributed among $N$ active users. AVIS assumes that it can obtain bit-rate information about the different encoded versions of the videos of each user $i$. Such information can be obtained from DPI middleboxes that are part of existing cellular networks [17]. Let $M_i$ be the total number of the available encoded video bit-rate versions for a user $i$ and let $r_{ij}$ denote the bit-rate of version $j$ for user $i$. Since the users may have different link qualities, let $C_i$ denote the physical transmission rate depending upon the modulation and coding scheme (MCS) used by the base station for user $i$. This rate represents the maximum bits that can be transmitted to the user per resource block. Note that the base station performs coarse time-scale rate adaptation for each user depending upon the signal-to-noise ratio (SNR) for that particular user. Hence, AVIS obtains the average transmission rate $C_i$ for each user from the base station. We define the utility $u_{ij}$ for each user as a function of the video bit-rate index $j$, $x_{ij}$ as an indicator variable to represent the bit-rate selected for a user, a penalty function $f_{ij}$ to avoid frequent bit-rate switches, and $\alpha$ as a parameter to trade-off between optimal allocation and stability. We then formulate the resource allocation problem as shown below.

$$\textbf{Problem 1:} \max_{x_{ij}} \sum_{i=1}^{N}\sum_{j=1}^{M_i}(u_{ij} - \alpha f_{ij})x_{ij} \quad (3)$$

$$\text{subject to} \sum_{i=1}^{N}\sum_{j=1}^{M_i}\lceil\frac{r_{ij}}{C_i}\rceil x_{ij} \leq T \quad (4)$$

$$\sum_{j=1}^{M_i} x_{ij} = 1, x_{ij} \in \{0,1\}\ \forall\, i \quad (5)$$

The first constraint Eq (4) ensures that the video bit-rates allocated to the different users do not exceed the physical limit of the resources available at the base station (represented by $T$ resource blocks). To convert the bit-rate of the video flow of a user to actual resource blocks requirements, we scale the bit-rate for each version $j$ of the video of user $i$ by its average transmission rate $C_i$ and bound the value to the next highest integer, i.e., $\lceil\frac{r_{ij}}{C_i}\rceil$. The second constraint Eq (5) ensures that a unique version of each video must be selected for a particular user. Hence, the indicator variable $x_{ij}$ is set to 1 if bit-rate version $j$ is selected for user $i$, and 0 otherwise.

**Desired Allocation:** : Maximizing the first part of the objective function in Problem 1 (i.e., the aggregate utility $u_{ij}$ across all users) ensures that the resources of the base station are optimally allocated to the different users in accordance with the operators' policy. In our design we define the *bit-rate utility* $u_{ij}$ as follows.

$$u_{ij} = P_i \times \log r_{ij} \quad (6)$$

where $P_i$ is the relative priority of the user. This choice of the utility function has the following benefits: (a) Such a utility implies that the marginal utility of the video for a user decreases as the bit-rate of the video increases. This implies that an upgrade to the next higher bit-rate or a degrade to the next lower bit-rate for a user is visually more perceptible at lower bit-rates. (b) The *log* function is typically employed as a utility function for allocation of resources [18, 19]. The log utility ensures that AVIS strives to achieve a proportional fair allocation across the users. Although the utility $u_{ij}$ only captures the bit-rate $r_{ij}$ allocated to a user, the cost factor (that depends on the users transmission rate $C_i$) in the constraint stated in Eq (4) ensures that AVIS allocates resources proportional to both the bit-rate of the video and the link quality of the user.

**Trade-off between Fairness & Utilization:** : Due to the discrete set of bit-rates of DASH videos, allocating resources to achieve optimal fairness may result in loss in resource utilization. Optimal fairness implies that the resources are allocated equally across all users to maximize the fairness index (as defined in Equation (1)). For instance, consider 3 users with similar link quality streaming DASH videos on a base station with a capacity of 4.5 Mbps. The different bit-rates of each of the DASH videos are {0.5,1,2,3} Mbps. While allocating 1 Mbps video bit-rate to each user would be optimally fair, AVIS instead allocates the bit-rates 2, 1 and 1 Mbps to the users respectively to ensure higher resource utilization. On the contrary, a resource allocation solution that ensures optimal resource utilization may be highly unfair to users with relatively bad link qualities. For instance, in the above example an allocation of 2, 2 and 0.5 Mbps to the users respectively would utilize the link entirely. Hence, AVIS strives to achieve a balance between fair resource allocation and optimal utilization of resources.

**Trading-off Fairness and Utilization for Stability:** : While maximizing the first part of the objective function in Problem 1 (i.e., the aggregate bit-rate utility $u_{ij}$ for all users) ensures (a) that the

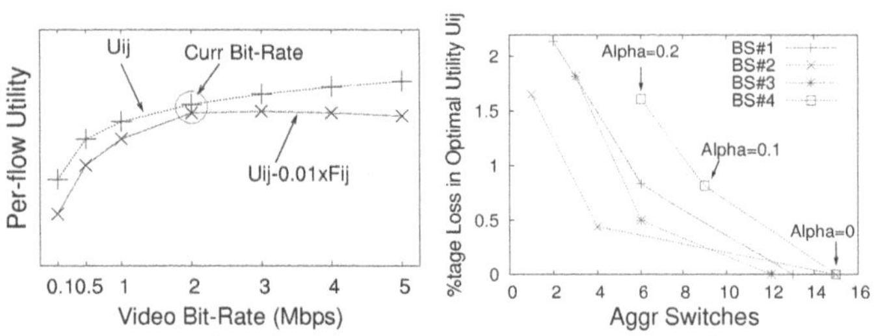


(a) Utility Functions (b) Trade-off with $\alpha$

**Figure 7: Design Consideration for AVIS.**

users receive the desired allocation according to operators policies and (b) high resource utilization, it may result in frequent bit-rate switching for users. Depending upon the rate of arrival or departure of users and user mobility, the frequency of bit-rate switching across certain users may be relatively high, causing annoyance to those users and degrading their QoE [15]. To address this issue, AVIS defines a penalty function $f_{ij}$ that is subtracted from the utility function $u_{ij}$. The function $f_{ij}$ ensures that users who experienced higher number of switches during the previous $W$ seconds are not subject to further bit-rate switching. Hence $f_{ij}$ is defined as a monotonically increasing function of $S_i$ where $S_i$ is the number of bit-rate switches that a user has perceived in the previous $W$ units of time. Furthermore, $f_{ij}$ should penalize the different bit-rates of a user depending on the user's current bit-rate. For instance, if a user's bit-rate is changed directly to 2 Mbps from 0.5 Mbps, by-passing the bit-rate version of 1 Mbps, this property ensures that AVIS counts it as two switches in the penalty function. Although there may be several possible choices for the function $f_{ij}$ that satisfy the above requirements, AVIS employs the following function definition based on inference from a simulation result discussed later. We define $j^*$ as the user's current bit-rate.

$$f_{ij} = (|j - j^*| + 1)S_i \quad (7)$$

To understand the objective function in Problem 1 conceptually, Figure 7(a) depicts a graph for both functions, i.e, the bit-rate utility $u_{ij}$ (that does not consider bit-rate switching) and the function $(u_{ij} - \alpha f_{ij})$ that does consider a penalty for bit-rate switching. The functions are plotted for specific values, in this case $\alpha = 0.01$, $S_i = 10$ and $j^* = 2$ Mbps for a video with bit-rate versions = $\{0.1, 0.5, 1, 2, 3, 4, 5\}$ Mbps.

**Setting $\alpha$:** : The parameter $\alpha$ allows an operator to balance the goals of (a) optimal bit-rate allocation by optimizing $u_{ij}$ and (b) frequency of bit-rate switching per user (stability). With $\alpha = 0$, AVIS ensures optimal bit-rate assignment (i.e., maximizes $u_{ij}$) at every execution step and hence strives to achieve proportional fair allocation and high resource utilization. On the contrary, increasing the value of $\alpha$ linearly increases the effect of the penalty function $f_{ij}$. Hence, setting higher values of $\alpha$ will ensure that AVIS stresses more on bit-rate stability and QoE rather than on optimal allocation, trading-off fairness and resource utilization for QoE. To further illustrate this trade-off, we conduct a simulation for a network of 4 base stations (BS) and plot the loss in the aggregate bit-rate utility value compared to the optimal bit-rate utility value versus the total number of switches for different values of $\alpha$ in Figure 7(b). As can be seen from the graph, increasing $\alpha$ decreases the aggregate number of bit-rate switches for users, while also increasing the loss in the aggregate bit-rate utility. The operator can set the value of $\alpha$ appropriately to balance between optimal allocation and stability of bit-rates.

**Algorithm 1** AVIS Allocator

**Variables**: $i$: User index, $j$: Bit-rate index, $N$: Number of users, $\tau$: Resources
**Inputs**: Utilities $g_{ij}$, Video Bit-rates $r_{ij}$, Transmission rates $C_i$, Total resource blocks $T$
**Output**: Selected bit-rate for each user $x_{ij}$, $x_{ij} \in [0, 1]$
**Repeat**: Every $I$ units of time

1: sort $\lceil \frac{r_{i1}}{C_i} \rceil \leq \lceil \frac{r_{i2}}{C_i} \rceil \leq \ldots \leq \lceil \frac{r_{iM_i}}{C_i} \rceil$
2: if $\sum_{i=1}^{N} \lceil \frac{r_{i1}}{C_i} \rceil \geq T$
3:   Allocate each user the lowest bit-rate and EXIT.
4: end if
5: for $\tau$ from 0 to $T$ do
6:   $V(0, \tau) := 0$
7: end for
8: for $i$ from 1 to $N$ do
9:   for $\tau$ from 0 to $T$ do
10:     $V(i, \tau) := -\infty$
11:   end for
12: end for
13: for $i$ from 1 to $N$ do
14:   for $\tau$ from 0 to $T$ do
15:     for $j$ from 1 to $NUM(r_{ij})$ do
16:       $V(i, \tau) := \max(V(i, \tau), V(i - 1, \tau - \lceil \frac{r_{ij}}{C_i} \rceil) + g_{ij})$
17:     end for
18:   end for
19: end for
20: Output the solution that gives V(N,T)

**Allocator Algorithm:** : Algorithm 1 summarizes the dynamic program for the AVIS allocator that solves Problem 1. AVIS first ensures that at least the base version of the video can be selected for each user. To achieve this feasibility check, the allocator sorts the versions of each video for all the users such that $\lceil \frac{r_{i1}}{C_i} \rceil \leq \lceil \frac{r_{i2}}{C_i} \rceil \leq \ldots \leq \lceil \frac{r_{iM_i}}{C_i} \rceil$. The solution is feasible if at least the base versions can be supported, i.e., $\sum_{i=1}^{N} \lceil \frac{r_{i1}}{C_i} \rceil \leq T$. In case this condition is not satisfied, the allocator simply selects the base version for each user (See steps 1-4).

Problem 1 falls in the category of Multi-choice Knapsack problem [20]. Each user $i$ is analogous to a *class* and the video bit-rate versions $j$ of each user are the *items* within each class. The constraint given by equation (5) in Problem 1 says that the allocator must pick exactly one item (bit-rate) from every class (user). Each item has a utility $g_{ij} = (u_{ij} - \alpha f_{ij})$ as defined in the objective function of Problem 1. The *cost* of each item is the resources required to transmit that bit-rate version defined as $\tau_{ij} = \lceil \frac{r_{ij}}{C_i} \rceil$. Let $V(i, \tau)$ denote the optimal utility of users 1 through $i$ given $\tau$ resource blocks. The initialization is done in two steps as shown in steps 5-12. The matrix $V$ is built iteratively for all the users, and for each user the problem is solved for all the capacities $0..T$ (i.e., resource blocks). The optimal utility $V(i, \tau)$ depends on which version $j$ is chosen for user $i$. So for each version $j$, the allocator checks the optimal utility obtained by $i - 1$ users given $(\tau - \tau_{ij})$ resource blocks, and adds the utility of the item $j$ for user $i$: $g_{ij}$. To obtain optimal utility $V(i, \tau)$, it picks the bit-rate version $j$ that has the highest utility (See steps 13-19). Finally, the optimal solution is obtained by back-tracking to find the combination of bit-rate versions for each user $i$ that yielded $V(N, T)$.

### 3.1.2 *Continuous Optimization Framework*

In the above, we modeled the resource allocation problem as a discrete-optimization based knapsack problem. The dynamic program has a complexity of $\mathcal{O}(NMT)$ where $N$ is the number of users, $M = \max_i M_i$ is the maximum number of versions of the video of a user, and $T$ is the total number of resource blocks. The problem is pseudo-polynomial since the complexity is proportional to the value of $T$. Hence for large values of $T$, the computational complexity grows significantly with large number of users $N$ and video bit-rate versions $M$. To get an idea of the possible values for T, in LTE the total number of resource blocks to be scheduled every second is 24000. Although the actual complexity is lower since each user is allocated its minimum bit-rate video version, in order to ease the computational complexity of the system with large number of users $N$ and video versions $M$, one alternative approach is to formulate Problem 1 as a continuous optimization problem. Specifically, we define the optimization variable $r_i$ that represents the rate allocated to each user as a continuous variable.

$$\textbf{Problem 2: } \max_{r_i} \sum_{i=1}^{N} (u_i - \alpha f_i) \tag{8}$$

$$\text{subject to } \sum_{i=1}^{N} \frac{r_i}{C_i} \leq T \tag{9}$$

$$r_{i1} < r_i \leq r_{iM_i}, \; \forall\, i \tag{10}$$

The continuous problem is defined with similar goals as those for the discrete problem (Problem 1). The first constraint Eq (9) ensures that the resource constraint of the base station is met while the second constraint Eq (10) ensures that the rate allocated to the user is at least the lowest bit-rate version of the video and is also within the maximum bit-rate version for the video. The utility for each user is defined as a log function of the allocated rate.

$$u_i = P_i \times \log r_i \tag{11}$$

The penalty function to control the frequency of bit-rate switching per user is defined similar to the discrete case.

$$f_i = (\sqrt{(r_i - r_i^*)^2} + 1)S_i \tag{12}$$

where $r_i^*$ is the current bit-rate streamed to user $i$.

Once the solution to Problem 2 is solved using well known techniques like the interior point method, the continuous optimal variables $r_i$ need to be quantized to a discrete value $r_{ij}$ among the available choices for bit-rates of user $i$. For instance, if the available video bit-rates of a DASH flow are $\{1, 2, 3\}$ Mbps and the optimal solution of the continuous resource allocation problem is $r_i = 1.45$ Mbps, then $r_i$ has to be quantized to either 1 or 2 Mbps to obtain $r_{ij}$. Although it may be possible to design an optimal quantization algorithm to return a solution that matches the solution obtained by discrete optimization (Problem 1), we found that such techniques result in similar computational complexity as the discrete optimization problem. Hence, we simplify our approach to ensure that we achieve lighter computational complexity, which trades-off with the optimality of the resource allocation. The solution is based on a greedy approach aimed at minimizing the loss in utilization of the wireless resources and contains the following steps:

1. Sort the users in increasing order of wireless resources required to upgrade their bit-rate $r_i$ to the next higher bit-rate version.

2. Round the solution $r_i$ to the next lowest bit-rate version for all users $i$.

3. Compute the amount of wireless resources that are unused after satisfying all the users with the rounded version of their optimal bit-rates (Step 2).

4. Scan through the sorted list to upgrade the maximum number of users until the resources are exhausted.

Clearly, this approach trades-off solution optimality in order to achieve a reduction in the computational complexity. As we experimentally show later, the above scheme achieves results similar to the discrete optimization solution.

The above algorithm achieves a complexity of $\mathcal{O}(N)$, although the step-wise computation time for solving the continuous problem (Problem 2) may be larger than the step-wise execution time for the dynamic program that solves the discrete optimization problem. AVIS can be deployed with the continuous optimization framework in the case of a system with large number of users $N$ and high number of video bit-rate versions $M$ for two reasons: (a) The benefit of reduction in computational complexity is higher for larger values of $N$ and $M$ for the case with the continuous optimization framework as opposed to the discrete optimization framework. (b) The error in the optimal solution obtained with the continuous optimization framework will be lower in general when $M$ is large. In our prototype, AVIS employs the discrete optimization as defined in Problem 1 by default.

## 3.2 AVIS's Enforcer

Once the allocator computes the appropriate bit-rate version $r_{ij}$ for each user $i$, it feeds this information to the enforcer. The AVIS enforcer is designed similar to the PF scheduler that is typically employed on base stations, including the ability to perform per-flow traffic shaping. The enforcer is configured to meet three key requirements: (a) It ensures isolation of resources across the DASH flows. Hence if the link quality of a user improves or degrades, the resource allocation for the other DASH flows is not affected. (b) It ensures stability by making sure that the bit-rates allocated by the allocator are enforced for every user and (c) It ensures high resource utilization.

The enforcer is designed as a weight-based packet scheduler that schedules the packets of the different DASH flows proportional to the flow's minimum rate. To ensure that each flow receives sufficient TCP throughput to support the bit-rate chosen by the allocator, the enforcer sets the minimum rate for each flow equal to the allocated bit-rate $r_{ij}$.

$$MinRate_i = r_{ij} \tag{13}$$

In addition, the enforcer considers the transmission rate of the users when scheduling the packets. This ensures that the drop of a user's transmission rate due to mobility does not affect the resource allocation for the flows of other users.

To meet the goal of stability, the enforcer employs per-flow traffic shapers. The shapers cap the rate available to a flow despite the presence of unused resources. The maximum rate for each flow is set based on the allocated bit-rates $r_{ij}$. This ensures that the TCP throughput of a flow will not exceed the allocated bit-rate of that flow. Despite availability of unused resources, the flow will not switch to a higher bit-rate, thus ensuring stability. Such a design ensures that AVIS can enforce the computed bit-rates for the users indirectly without any video server or client modifications.

To meet the final goal of high utilization, the shaper rate for each flow is set to the mean of the allocated bit-rate and the next higher bit-rate of the video for that flow. This design choice was based on an observation that most videos have VBR traffic patterns and their instantaneous rates can fluctuate around their average bit-rates. If the instantaneous requirement for a certain flow is above its average bit-rate, the enforcer can borrow resources at fine time-scales from a flow whose instantaneous rate is below its average bit-rate. Thus, setting the maximum rate for the flows above their average

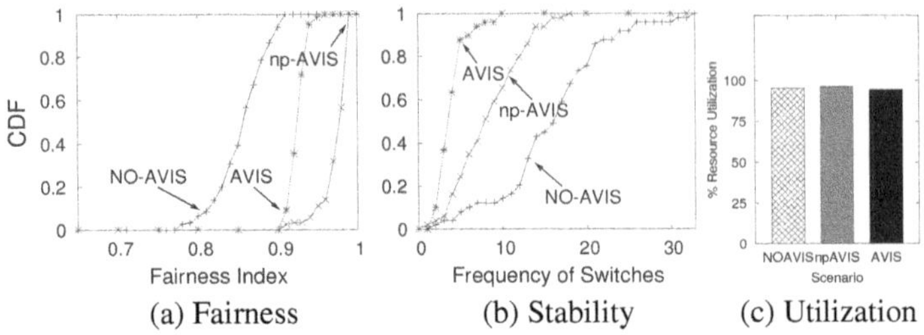


**Figure 8: Efficacy of AVIS.**

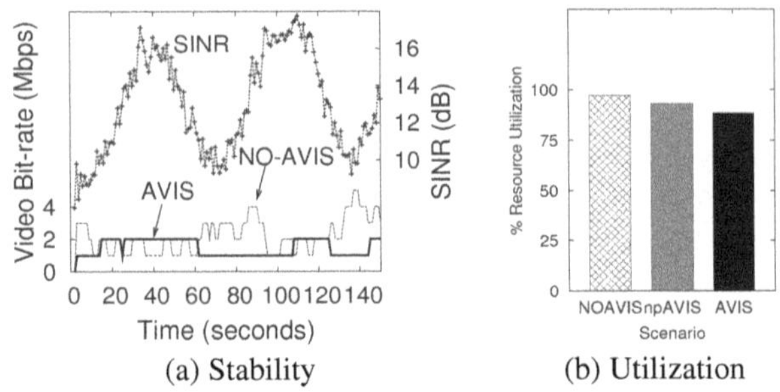


**Figure 9: User mobility.**

bit-rate ensures that the enforcer can leverage statistical multiplexing across the video flows to obtain high resource utilization. While the shaping rate could be set to higher values, AVIS sets it in the following way to ensure that the client players do not switch to higher bit-rates than those selected by the allocator.

$$MaxRate_i = \frac{r_{ij} + r_{ij+1}}{2} \tag{14}$$

While the maximum shaping rate is critical to the operation of the enforcer, the interval at which the shaping is performed is equally important. Hence while the allocator operates at coarse time-scales, the enforcer schedules the flows at much finer time-scales. For instance, in our prototype and simulations, the allocator executes every 10 seconds, while the enforcer schedules at 10 millisecond granularity with traffic shaping performed every 250 milliseconds.

# 4. EVALUATION

In this section, we evaluate AVIS extensively through simulations and a prototype implementation. In both cases, the code is written primarily in C/C++ and is around 1000 lines of code for the entire framework. We first show results from simulations, followed by the prototype description and experimental evaluations. The setup of each experiment is explained while describing the experiment. In both simulations and experiments, we set $\alpha = 0.1$ (see Problem 1). AVIS keeps track of the number of bit-rate switches for each user in the past $W$ seconds, and we set $W = 30$ seconds.

## 4.1 LTE System Simulation

We first study the efficacy of AVIS using large-scale simulations. The simulations are performed with a 3GPP-compliant LTE system-level simulator in which we implemented the allocator and the enforcer components of AVIS. The simulator is built using C++ and is capable of simulating a network of up to 57 LTE base station cells. It supports the 3GPP LTE Release 8 [21] features for both Physical layer and MAC layer stacks. The simulator supports sophisticated wireless channel models, including fast fading and user mobility, and also includes the MAC layer flow scheduling framework. At higher layers of the stack, it supports the TCP transport protocol with provisions for HTTP, FTP, and RTP-based Video and VoIP traffic for each user. We implemented DASH video streaming on top of the HTTP protocol as well as the adaptation algorithm in the clients. The adaptation algorithm keeps track of the moving average of the TCP throughput and requests chunks of the highest rate that can be supported by the estimated throughput. We implemented the AVIS functionality, including both the allocator and the enforcer, within the simulator and instantiated an instance of AVIS for each base station.

**Efficacy of AVIS:** In this simulation, we compare AVIS to a vanilla system with no AVIS. We set up a network of 21 base stations, with each base station serving 8 users. The users are randomly distributed at each base station and all the users stream DASH videos of length 5 minutes with multiple bit-rate versions: $\{0.1, 0.25, 0.5, 1, 2, 3\}$ Mbps. We compare the three performance metrics defined in Section 2.3 for the system with and without AVIS. For the case with NO-AVIS, we set the GBR rate of each flow to the same value. For AVIS, we set the same utility values for each flow according to Equation (6). This configuration ensures that the fairness of the resource allocation is comparable between the case with AVIS and the case without AVIS. We plot the fairness index (as defined by Equation (1)) for all the base stations in the network for both the cases. As seen from Figure 8(a), AVIS ensures higher fairness among the competing DASH flows than the case with NO-AVIS, despite fluctuations in the link conditions of the users. With AVIS, the fairness index is more than 0.9 for most of the video session time for all the users across all the base stations, while with NO-AVIS, the fairness index is below 0.85 for 50% of the total video session time of the users. We also plot the fairness index for the case where AVIS does not consider a penalty function for bit-rate switching, denoted by np-AVIS. As seen from the Figure 8(a), np-AVIS achieves much higher fairness as compared to AVIS since it optimizes for the aggregate bit-rate utility $u_{ij}$ across all users (Problem 1 with $\alpha = 0$) at every execution interval. However as shown in Figure 8(b), np-AVIS results in users experiencing a higher frequency of bit-rate switching. AVIS, on the other hand, employs the switch penalty function as defined by Equation (7) ensuring that users perceive more stable bit-rates, and therefore improving their QoE. In either case, AVIS achieves lower frequency of bit-rate switching among the users than the case with NO-AVIS as depicted in Figure 8(b). Finally as shown in Figure 8(c), AVIS achieves its goals while maintaining high utilization of the base station resources.

**User Mobility:** In this simulation, we show the efficacy of AVIS in presence of high user mobility. We set up a base station with 8 active users including several vehicular users. All the users stream DASH videos of length 5 minutes with multiple bit-rate versions: {0.1, 0.25, 0.5, 1, 2, 3} Mbps. To show the variation in the link quality of the vehicular clients, we plot the signal to interference-plus-noise ratio (SINR) of one of the vehicular users in Figure 9(a). We also plot the bit-rates as perceived by this user with AVIS and NO-AVIS. As seen from Figure 9(a), AVIS achieves higher stability since the user perceives lower frequency of bit-rate switches than the case with NO-AVIS. The higher stability is achieved since AVIS employs the penalty function for recent bit-rate switches perceived by the user. The stable bit-rates also shows the efficacy of the enforcer in ensuring bit-rate allocations in presence of channel fluctuations. However as seen in Figure 9(b), AVIS compromises on resource utilization to ensure higher stability for the user. In this case, the resource utilization achieved by AVIS is about 88% as compared to 97% achieved by NO-AVIS. np-AVIS achieves higher

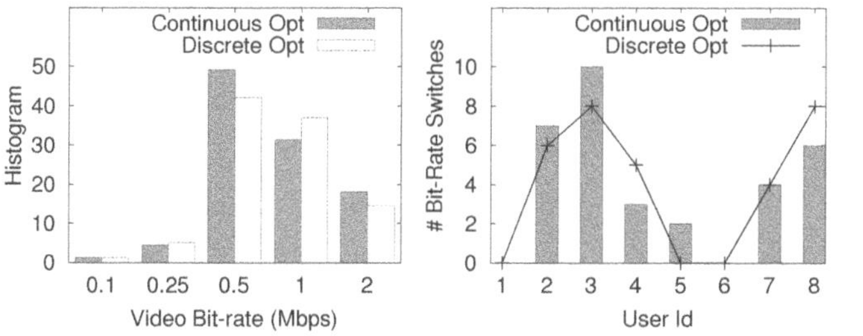


(a) Bit-Rate (b) Switches

**Figure 10: Comparison of Optimization Frameworks.**

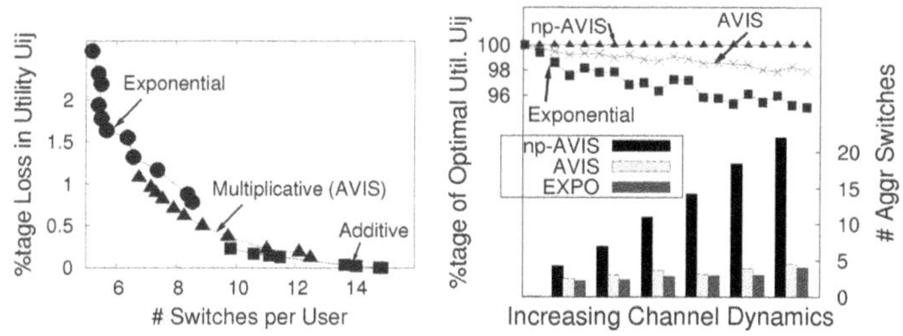


(a) Tradeoff with diff $F_{ij}$ (b) Effect of Capacity changes

**Figure 11: Penalty Functions.**

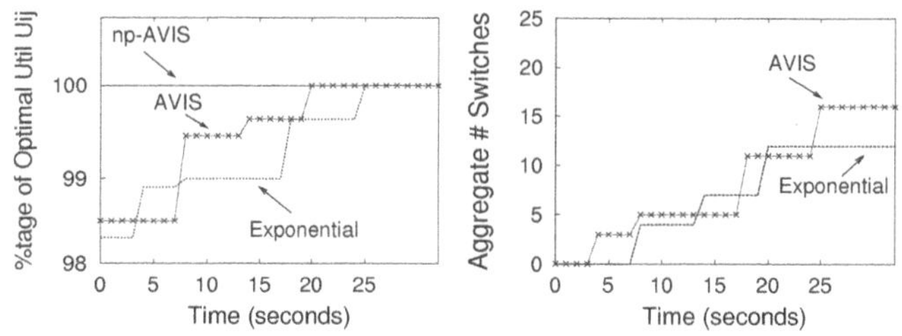


(a) Aggr. Utility (b) Aggr. Switches

**Figure 12: Convergence under Stable Conditions.**

resource utilization of 94% at the cost of lower stability (the bit-rate switches are not shown for np-AVIS for the sake of clarity).

**Continuous Optimization Framework:** To compare AVIS that employs the continuous optimization framework (as described in Section 3.1.2) with AVIS that employs the discrete optimization framework, we repeat the first simulation with AVIS employing the continuous optimization framework. In Figure 10(a), we compare the distribution of the video bit-rates allocated to all the users using both the optimization frameworks. We also plot the average number of bit-rate switches perceived by a random set of 8 users in Figure 10(b). Clearly, AVIS with continuous optimization framework is effective in emulating AVIS that employs the discrete optimization framework. We employed the non-linear optimization library OPT++ [22] to solve the continuous resource allocation problem.

**Choice of Penalty Function:** The penalty function $f_{ij}$ employed in the objective in the resource allocation problem (Problem 1) ensures that the operator can balance between optimal bit-rate allocation (which is obtained by computing the optimal value of aggregate bit-rate utility $u_{ij}$ across all users in Problem 1) and stability of bit-rates across its users. The choice of the penalty function $f_{ij}$ is an important design consideration for AVIS, as it directly impacts the effect of a user's recent bit-rate switch on the user's future bit-rate allocation. Hence, we benchmark the tradeoff between the optimal allocation and stability for the following penalty functions that we considered during our design. The functions are called additive, multiplicative and exponential respectively.

$$f_{ij}^{(1)} = |j - j^*| + 1 + S_i \quad (15)$$

$$f_{ij}^{(2)} = (|j - j^*| + 1)S_i \quad (16)$$

$$f_{ij}^{(3)} = 2^{|j-j^*|+1+S_i} \quad (17)$$

Note that if $S_i = 0$, we set $f_{ij} = 0$. We simulate a setup with several base stations for different runs of AVIS, using the above penalty functions for a range of values for $0 \leq \alpha \leq 1$ (as defined in Problem 1). Figure 11(a) shows the trade-off curves between the loss in the optimal bit-rate utility and the total number of bit-rate switches per user. Clearly, the additive function is more or less insensitive to the number of bit-rate switches and fails to lower the number of bit-rate switches even for high values of $\alpha$. On the other hand, the exponential function is too aggressive to recent bit-rate switches and is highly sensitive to $\alpha$. Hence, AVIS employs the multiplicative function since its trade-off curve lies at a sweet spot and allows the operator to further balance between the two metrics by setting $\alpha$ appropriately.

In the same experiment, we also plot the effect of increasing channel dynamics on the loss in optimal bit-rate utility and number of bit-rate switches for the users. The channel dynamics are increased by increasing the frequency of user arrivals and the mobility speed of the users. Clearly, from Figure 11(b), the loss in the bit-rate utility obtained by AVIS diverges from the optimal utility obtained by np-AVIS with increasing channel dynamics. However, AVIS ensures that the number of bit-rate switches for the users is lower than that with np-AVIS. This is because np-AVIS optimizes for the bit-rate utility $u_{ij}$ at every execution step and changes the allocated video bit-rate of the users when the effective capacity changes. On the other hand, AVIS considers the past bit-rate switches for the user before making a decision on changing its bit-rate in response to a change in the effective capacity. We also plot the result of AVIS with exponential penalty function (Equation 17). As expected, the exponential penalty function causes a further drop in the optimal allocation as compared to AVIS. However, the reduction in the number of bit-rate switches is not significant when compared to AVIS. This result further justifies our choice of the multiplicative penalty function in AVIS.

**Convergence Under Stable Channel Conditions:** As seen in the previous simulation, AVIS may not achieve the optimal bit-rate allocation as achieved by np-AVIS since AVIS employs a penalty function $f_{ij}$ for bit-rate switching. However, an interesting question to ask is whether the solution of AVIS eventually converges to that obtained by np-AVIS if the conditions of the system remain stable. Stable conditions imply that there is no new user arrival or departure and the link qualities of the users remain stable. We conduct a simulation such that the system is unstable for a certain period of time and is then kept stable. We plot the aggregate utilities obtained by AVIS, np-AVIS and AVIS with an exponential penalty function in Figure 12(a). As expected, np-AVIS converges to the optimal bit-rate allocation immediately while AVIS takes around 20 iterations. AVIS with exponential penalty function takes more iterations than AVIS to converge; however, it causes fewer bit-rate switches as shown in Figure 12(b). Although in a practical system the conditions typically do not stay stable for too long, this result confirms that the solution obtained by AVIS moves in the right direction towards the optimal bit-rate allocation even while minimizing the switches in bit-rates of the users.

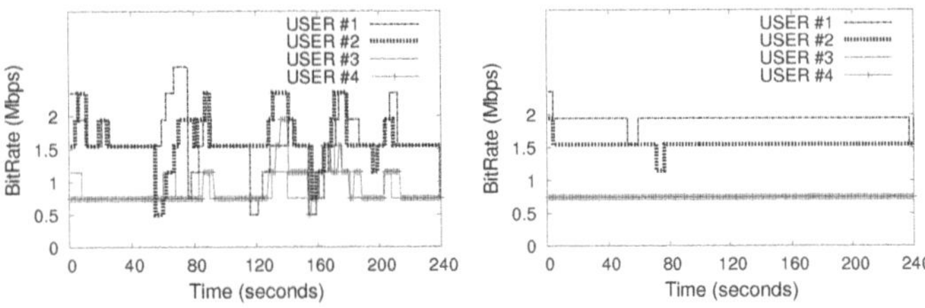


(a) No-AVIS (b) AVIS

**Figure 13: Efficacy of AVIS.**

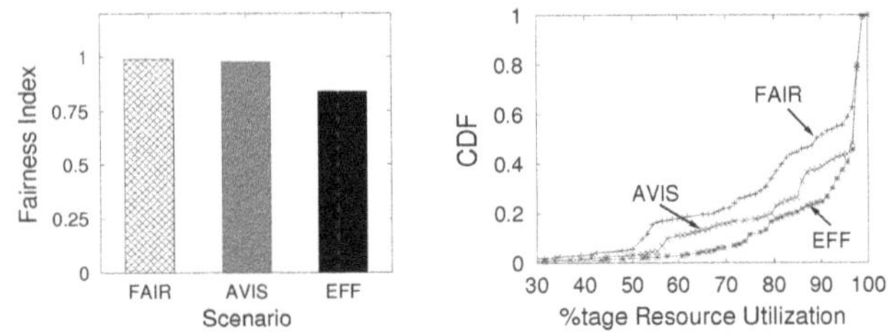


(a) Fair Allocation (b) Utilization

**Figure 14: Tradeoff between Fairness and Utilization**

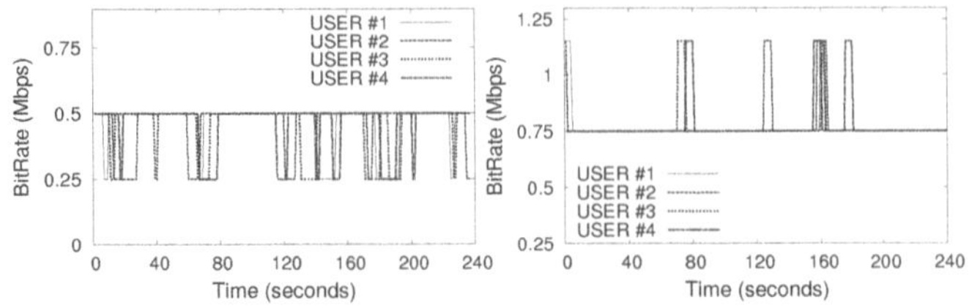


(a) Low Shaping Rate (b) High Shaping Rate

**Figure 16: Per-flow Shaping Rate**

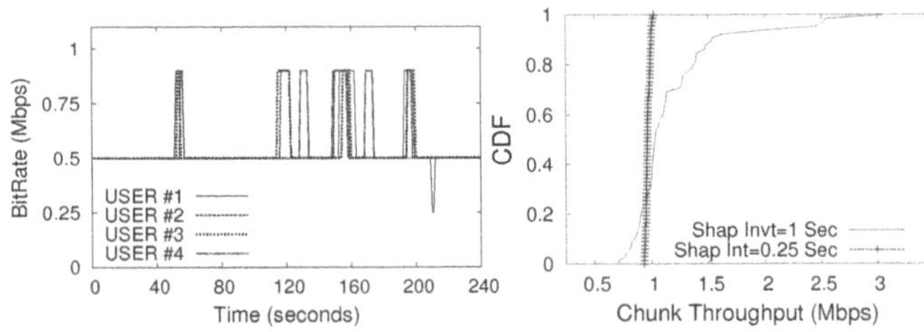


(a) Shaping Interval = 1sec (b) Estimated Throughput

**Figure 17: Effect of Shaping Interval.**

## 4.2 WiMAX Prototype Experimentation

We have developed a prototype system to validate the proposed solution on a WiMAX testbed. The testbed consists of an Access Service Network (ASN) gateway, three PicoChip [7] WiMAX femtocell base stations (IEEE 802.16e compliant), and several Intel WiMAX [8] clients (See Figure 15). The ASN gateway provides an interface to the base station for setting up service flows in the downlink and uplink directions for each client when it registers. We implement AVIS as a user-level Click module [23] in the ASN-gateway. Click intercepts all data packets from the base station in the downlink. We configure the Click classifier to route packets belonging to the DASH flows through the AVIS module. The PicoChip base station provides feedback on the average MCS per client to the AVIS scheduler every $I$ units of time. When this feedback is received, the AVIS allocator selects the video bit-rate version $j$ for each user $i$ and sets the shaper rate appropriately for each flow. AVIS maintains a separate queue for each flow and performs weighted packet scheduling and rate-shaping for each flow depending on the bit-rates selected by the allocator. On the client-side, we use Adobe OSMF [16] player that runs as a browser-plugin. We modified the player to record certain parameters such as chunk throughput, bit-rate, etc., at the clients. The videos are fetched over the Internet from an Akamai- hosted CDN server [10]. All the videos are about 4 minutes in length and are encoded to the following bit-rate versions: {0.5,0.75,1.15,1.55,1.95,2.35,2.75,3.25} Mbps.

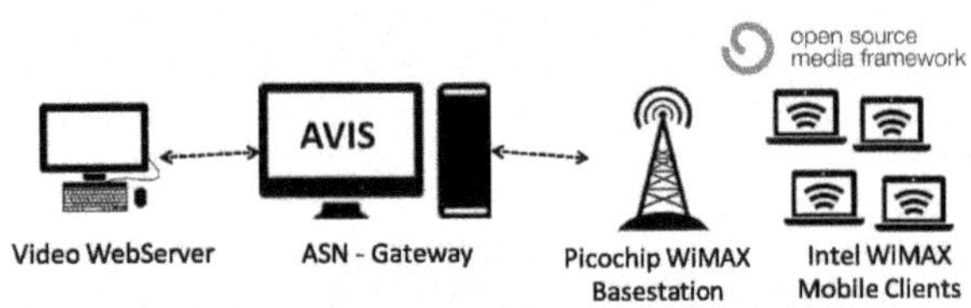


**Figure 15:** AVIS **WiMAX prototype** ***(Attribute:The Noun Project).***

**Efficacy of** AVIS**:** We conduct an end-end system evaluation of AVIS and compare it with a baseline WiMAX system without AVIS. In this scenario, we set up the base station with 4 clients placed randomly in an indoor environment. The transmission rate (or MCS) of the clients is such that Users $1, 2$ receive packets at 16QAM while Users $3, 4$ receive their packets at QPSK. In Figure 13, we show a time-series plot of the bit-rates of the videos that are streamed to the users for both AVIS and no-AVIS. AVIS allocates bit-rates of $1.95$ Mbps, $1.55$ Mbps to Users 1 and 2 respectively and $0.75$ Mbps each to Users $3, 4$; while with no-AVIS, the bit-rates of the users do not converge to any specific bit-rate.

In this experiment, we also demonstrate the efficacy of AVIS in effectively balancing the goals of fairness and optimal resource utilization. We repeat the above experiment for two other cases, one that achieves optimally fair allocation (named as FAIR) and another scheme that achieves optimal resource utilization (named as EFF). We plot the fairness index (as defined in Equation (1)) in Figure 14(a) and the CDF of resource utilization (as defined in Equation (2)) in Figure 14(b) for all 3 scenarios. Clearly, AVIS is effective in achieving a balance between optimally fair allocation and optimal resource utilization. Note that while the FAIR scheme allocated bit-rates of $1.55$ Mbps and $0.75$ Mbps to Users $1, 2$ and Users $3, 4$ respectively, the EFF scheme allocated bit-rates of $2.75$ Mbps and $1.95$ Mbps to Users 1 and 2 respectively and $0.5$ Mbps each to Users $3, 4$.

**Benchmarking the Enforcer:** Although the enforcer leverages the PF scheduler to ensure bit-rate allocation to each user, configuring the per-flow shapers is critical to its performance. We evaluate two metrics that we observed that affect the efficacy of the enforcer, in terms of bit-rate stability for the users. We set up the WiMAX base station with 4 clients placed at similar locations so that their link qualities are similar (QPSK).

*(a) Shaper Rate*: AVIS employs a shaper to ensure a maximum rate for each flow depending upon its assigned bit-rate (Equation 14). While it seems intuitive to set the shaping rate to the bit-rate assigned to a user, such a setting causes the player to switch to a lower bit-rate, mainly due to buffer underflow. In our experiment, the three flows are allocated a bit-rate of $0.5$ Mbps each by the al-

locator and the enforcer sets their shaping rates to 0.5 Mbps. As shown in Figure 16(a), the bit-rates for all the videos switch to the lower bit-rate of 0.25 Mbps frequently. While it is possible to set the shaping rate to higher values to increase stability and utilization, setting it too high causes the player to upgrade to the next higher bit-rate version. For instance, setting the shaper rate to the next higher bit-rate than the one allocated to the user causes the player to switch between the assigned bit-rate and the next higher bit-rate version. In our experiment, we set the shaping rate of the four users equal to 1.15 Mbps once the allocator assigns the bit-rate 0.75 Mbps to each user. As shown in Figure 16(b), the users occasionally switch to a higher bit-rate. Hence taking the middle-ground, we set the shaping rate as the mean of the assigned bit-rate and the next higher bit-rate as given in Equation 14.

*(b) Shaping Interval*: The shaping interval determines the time interval or granularity at which the shaping for each flow is performed. In our initial design, we set the shaping interval to 1 sec, based on the default value used by most commercial base station schedulers. In this experiment, all four users are assigned a bit-rate of 0.5 Mbps and the shaping rate is set to 0.65 Mbps with a shaping interval of 1 second. Clearly, as shown in Figure 17(a), this setting sometimes causes the players to switch to a higher bit-rate version. We observed that some video chunks (especially during static scenes) have relatively smaller size and may be downloaded within a second. A series of such chunks causes the player to over-estimate the throughput as shown in Figure 17(b). Hence, we configure AVIS with a shaping interval of 250 milliseconds.

# 5. DISCUSSION AND LIMITATIONS

AVIS is designed as a non work-conserving scheduler, which may result in resource under-utilization at certain times. However, by ensuring that the AVIS allocator is executed at short time-scales (every $I$ units of time), the operator can ensure that AVIS is adaptive to the dynamic capacity changes at a base station. However, reducing the execution time $I$ increases the amount of feedback from the base stations to the gateway. While the overhead of feedback is insignificant compared to the data traffic, the operator needs to consider this trade-off during deployment. Another point to note is that AVIS is built on a resource virtualization platform that incorporates a work-conserving slice scheduler. In the worst case that AVIS does not utilize its share of resources during certain execution periods, the slice scheduler would redistribute the unused resources to other traffic classes that have sufficient traffic. Hence, the overall base station resource utilization would not suffer.

Although we show the efficacy of AVIS in large-scale using simulations, the evaluation testbed contains a small number of clients primarily since the base station available to us is a femtocell base station that supports a maximum of 8 clients. Nevertheless, AVIS should scale to larger settings in real cellular networks, since the flow management in AVIS is done on a per-base station instance and each base station only handles a small number of flows. Since AVIS is designed as a gateway solution, the processing power for AVIS instances can be shared across base stations for better multiplexing.

To ensure stability of bit-rate allocation to the users, AVIS employs a penalty function $f_{ij}$ that is a function of $S_i$ (see Equation 7). The metric $S_i$ is simplistic in the paper as it only captures the total number of bit-rate switches that a user has perceived in the previous $W$ units of time. However, it can be extended to more sophisticated formulations: For instance $S_i$ could be defined similar to the *instability* metric in [5] that gives more weight to recent bit-rate switches and scales the number of switches by the average bit-rate achieved by the user.

There may be a few other scenarios that occur in practice, such as the presence of misbehaving clients that do not perform rate adaption according to the underlying TCP throughput. Also, for certain clients, the wired network or the computational resources at the client may be the bottleneck, forcing the client to use a bit-rate lower than that allocated by AVIS. Although AVIS is not explicitly designed to handle such scenarios, the network can either measure the TCP throughput of a flow or parse the uplink HTTP GET requests to detect clients that are not requesting the bit-rate allocated to them by AVIS. An interesting avenue for future work is to extend the allocator in AVIS to account for such cases and redistribute the resources unused by such flows to other active flows. However, the allocator must ensure that it allocates the appropriate resources to a flow once its conditions improve, such as if, for instance, the wired bandwidth increases after a short period of congestion or computational resources at the client become available.

# 6. RELATED WORK

A large number of efforts have focused on optimizing video delivery (both in the wired and wireless network domains). We cover the most relevant categories.

**Client-side adaptation:** One approach to achieve fairness and stability across multiple adaptive video flows is to employ more efficient adaptation logic like FESTIVE [5] in the video players. However, such techniques require significant changes to the video players which may not be feasible, hindering their deployment. Moreover, it is harder for players to converge to a fair bit-rate allocation efficiently in a distributed fashion, as opposed to an in-network solution like AVIS that possesses knowledge of the base station capacity. AVIS also ensures that network operators have control over the resource allocation across all their users that stream DASH videos.

**Base Station Scheduling:** There is a plethora of work, e.g., [24–28], on radio resource management for wireless networks specifically targeted at optimizing video delivery. However, these schemes are designed for single-rate video streams and are not directly applicable for DASH video flows since they do not consider client-side adaptation of the incoming video streams. In fact, such schemes are complementary to AVIS and can be employed to optimize the video delivery under heavy-load conditions where the base video bit-rate version cannot be supported for all the users. These schemes essentially rely on techniques such as intelligent frame dropping or distortion based scheduling to ensure that users receive good QoE in presence of base station congestion. Other schemes assume knowledge of the probability distribution of the wireless link conditions, and find the optimal average rate allocation region. AVIS, on the other hand, is designed as a practical solution that is not based on stochastic channel models.

**In-network Optimizers:** A recent work [29] proposes the design of an in-network per-flow proxy that resides in between the server and the client in the Internet. It performs in-line measurements to estimate the end-to-end bandwidth and guides the client player in performing bit-rate switching. AVIS, on the other hand, is an in-network optimization framework designed to perform multi-flow scheduling for DASH flows streamed over cellular networks. There are also a few approaches that involve modifying the video stream at an intermediate node in order to adapt to link capacity variations [30, 31]. However, transcoding requires significant amount of computational resources and signaling to inform the receiver of the change in coding. These techniques are less effective for DASH video flows where the original server performs adaptive bit-rate streaming anyway.

## 7. CONCLUSION

In the past, numerous research efforts have focused on efficient resource management schemes, especially on wireless access links for video streaming over unreliable transport protocols like UDP. However, industrial solutions have largely adopted TCP/HTTP as the de facto for video streaming. More recently, adaptive video streaming over HTTP (DASH) is gaining widespread popularity in commercial players to ensure smooth video streaming. Hence, there is a need to revisit resource management techniques to ensure efficient video streaming over wireless links.

In this paper, we presented the detailed design and implementation of a flow management framework for adaptive video delivery over cellular networks, namely AVIS. We demonstrated the efficacy of AVIS using both a LTE system simulator and experiments on a WiMAX prototype implementation. AVIS is effective in allocating the resources of a base station across multiple adaptive video flows and effectively balances between three important goals: (a) Fair allocation (b) Stability of a user's bit-rate and (c) Efficient resource utilization of the base station. Since the three goals are self-conflicting and quality of a video stream is highly subjective, AVIS is designed as a general framework which incorporates appropriate knobs for the mobile operators to achieve desired resource allocation across their users. To ease deployment, AVIS is designed to control the video bit-rate of each user without modifications to the video server or the client player.

## Acknowledgments

This paper benefited significantly from MobiCom 2013 reviewer comments, for which we are very thankful. We thank our shepherd, Songwu Lu, for overseeing the editing process. We would also like to thank Honghai Zhang for the initial discussion on this line of work. Jiasi Chen and Mung Chiang were supported in part by AFOSR MURI grant FA9550-09-1-0644 and by NSF NeTS grant CNS-1011962.

## 8. REFERENCES


[1] MPEG DASH standard. http://dashif.org/mpeg-dash.

[2] S. Akhshabi et al. An Experimental Evaluation of Rate-Adaptation Algorithms in Adaptive Streaming over HTTP. In *MMSys*, 2011.

[3] S. Akhshabi et al. What Happens When HTTP Adaptive Streaming Players Compete for Bandwidth? In *NOSSDAV*, 2012.

[4] C. Muller et al. An Evaluation of Dynamic Adaptive Streaming over HTTP in Vehicular Environments. In *MoVid*, 2012.

[5] J. Jiang et al. Improving Fairness, Efficiency, and Stability in HTTP-based Adaptive Video Streaming. In *CoNEXT*, 2012.

[6] R. Kokku et al. CellSlice: Cellular Wireless Resource Slicing for Active RAN Sharing. In *COMSNETS*, 2013.

[7] PicoChip Femtocell Solutions. http://www.picochip.com/.

[8] Intel WiMAX. http://tinyurl.com/73dp8wz.

[9] Adobe HTTP Dynamic Streaming. http://tinyurl.com/aqnv7y5.

[10] Akamai HD Streaming. http://tinyurl.com/yaknp7a.

[11] Microsoft Smooth Streaming. http://tinyurl.com/cyqldms.

[12] Apple http live streaming. http://tinyurl.com/cwkv9kz.

[13] R.K. Jain et al. A Quantitative Measure Of Fairness And Discrimination For Resource Allocation In Shared Computer Systems. In *Technical Report DEC*, 1984.

[14] N. Cranley et al. User perception of adapting video quality. In *Int. Journal of Human-Computer Studies*, 2006.

[15] B.Shenet et al. A Quest for an Internet Video Quality-of-Experience Metric. In *HotNets*, 2012.

[16] Adobe OSMF Player. http://www.osmf.org.

[17] Sandvine. http://www.sandvine.com.

[18] F. Kelly. Charging and rate control for elastic traffic. In *European Transactions on Telecommunications*, 1997.

[19] M. Andrew et al. Optimal Utility Based Multi-User Throughput Allocation subject to Throughput Constraints. In *Infocom*, 2005.

[20] H. Kellerer et al. *Knapsack Problems*. Springer, 2004.

[21] 3GPP Standard Rel 8. http://www.3gpp.org/Release-8.

[22] OPT++: An Object-Oriented Nonlinear Optimization Library. https://software.sandia.gov/opt++/.

[23] R. Morris et al. The click modular router. *SIGOPS Oper. Syst. Rev.*, 33(5), 1999.

[24] R. Mahindra et al. Farsighted Flow Management for Video Delivery in wireless networks. In *COMSNETS*, 2011.

[25] G. Liebl et al. Advanced Wireless Multiuser Video Streaming using the Scalable Video Coding Extensions of H.264/MPEG4-AVC. In *IEEE ICME*, 2006.

[26] M. Lu et al. Video streaming over 802.11 wlans with content-aware adaptive retry. In *Proc. IEEE Int. Conference on Multimedia and Expo*, 2007.

[27] H. Zhang et al. Cross-Layer Optimization for Streaming Scalable Video over Fading Wireless Networks. In *IEEE JSAC*, 2010.

[28] M. Burza et al. Adaptive Streaming of MPEG-based Audio/Video Content over Wireless Networks. *Multimedia*, 2007.

[29] R. Mok et al. QDASH: QoE-aware DASH system. In *MMSys*, 2012.

[30] Openwave Media Optimizer. http://www.openwave.com/solutions.

[31] B. Shen et al. Dynamic video transcoding in mobile environments. In *Proc. IEEE Multimedia*, 2008.

# An Information-Aware QoE-Centric Mobile Video Cache

Shan-Hsiang Shen and Aditya Akella
University of Wisconsin, Madison
{shan-hsi,akella}@cs.wisc.edu

## ABSTRACT

Recent years have seen a tremendous growth in the volume of video traffic in mobile settings. In this paper, we present the design of a mobile video-centric proxy cache, named iProxy, that offers improved performance in terms of both hit rates and streaming quality. Our thesis in designing iProxy is that we need to elevate the traditional view of caching from "data" to "information" in order to optimally meet the stringent requirements of video streaming in mobile settings. iProxy relies on recent advances on *information-bound references* (IBRs) to collapse multiple related cache entries into a single one, improving hitrate while lowering storage costs. iProxy incorporates a novel dynamic linear rate adaptation scheme to ensure high stream quality in face of channel diversity and device heterogeneity. Our evaluation of iProxy using realistic traffic traces shows that it can improve hitrate, but we need to use novel information-aware replacement policies for optimal performance. We show that our linear encoder can adapt well to changes in bandwidth, and yield better bit rates, lower buffering and lower start up delays than state-of-the-art schemes.

## Categories and Subject Descriptors

C.2.1 [**Computer-Communication Networks**]: Network Architecture and Design

## Keywords

Wireless Networks, Caching, Video, Quality of Experience

## 1. INTRODUCTION

This paper is motivated by two key trends: (1) video-on-demand traffic in mobile settings is seeing unprecedented growth, doubling in volume every few months [2]. Crucially, this is beginning to strain cellular network infrastructures [25]. (2) As user expectations of video quality grow, it is becoming increasingly important to improve the users' quality of experience (QoE). This is central to sustaining subscription/advertisement based revenue generation models which are the drivers behind video growth [2].


*MobiCom'13,* September 30-October 4, Miami, FL, USA.


In this paper, we focus on how cellular network providers can enhance their infrastructure to meet the goal of ensuring good end user QoE even in the face of growing traffic volumes. One option is to upgrade link capacities everywhere. However, this is expensive and can only provide a temporary solution. Another option is to rely on data offloading techniques, but this may not be universally applicable (e.g., WiFi offload may require open APs).

This paper explores a third approach: in-network caching. Caches are inexpensive, and they can be easily retrofit into an existing cellular backbone. Crucially, while the above approaches improve effective capacity, caches also improve latency which is important for good QoE.

While caching in networks is well-studied, we argue that simply adapting traditional Web cache designs to mobile video is not sufficient. First, in contrast with Web content, video content is often available in multiple different encodings and formats [43]. Not accounting for these differences leads to sub-optimal cache designs that suffer from poor hit rates (up to 20% lower compared with ideal) or need excessive storage (up to 2.4X more). Second, because of the centrality of video QoE, special measures must be adopted to orchestrate the transmission of cache contents to optimize various QoE metrics. In contrast, traditional caches can simply transmit bytes to end users. Our work presents the design, implementation, and evaluation of techniques that address both issues.

**Cache design:** We leverage the fact that the same video is often available in many different resolutions or formats and from many different content providers. This is particularly true for popular video; indeed, a recent study [43] estimated that nearly 30% of the video search results returned for 25 popular queries at various video content providers were duplicates, i.e., nearly identical to the most popular version of the video, differing only in resolution, encoding and/or the content provider hosting the video.

This insight is embodied in iProxy, our mobile video-centric cache. iProxy derives the information-bound reference (IBR) for each video, which is a collection of summaries of the frequency domain representation of the video data in multiple chunks of the video [17, 33]. We then bind videos that share "identical" IBRs into a *single* cache entry, thereby saving storage. iProxy identifies matches by comparing requested URLs against URLs that are known to have the same IBR, as opposed to looking for URL matches, or matches in content SHA-1 hashes. Because the IBR labels the information content in a video, agnostic of irrelevant details such as the source domain or host providing the content, the format of the content, the presentation, bit rate etc, iProxy enables *caching information as opposed to data.*

We argue that novel information-aware cache replacement schemes must be designed to optimize the hit rate of iProxy. We develop modifications to classical least-recently used (LRU) and least-frequently used (LFU) schemes that significantly outperform even state-of-the-art information-agnostic schemes.

**Optimizing QoE:** End-user QoE is reflected in engagement, i.e., fraction of the total video time that a user watches, and abandonment, i.e., whether a user quits a video before it starts [32]. Recent studies [32, 24] showed that a viewer who experiences buffering equal to 1% of stream duration plays 5% less of the video compared with a user with no buffering, and higher average bit rate correlated with higher video play times [24]. Furthermore, users start to abandon a video if it takes more than 2s to start up, and even 1s additional start up delay increases abandonment rate by 6% [32].

We argue that iProxy's information-aware design, coupled with the fact that it is deployed by the cellular provider, offers natural avenues for optimizing the three key quality metrics – buffering, bit rate, and start up delay – thereby improving end-user QoE. With each iProxy entry, we store the raw frequency domain data corresponding to the highest quality video observed thus far across all URLs mapping to the entry, which is needed to compute the IBR for the video any way. We then design a novel linear bit rate adapter that dynamically encodes videos directly from the raw data.

Our scheme first derives client-side constraints by parsing HTTP headers to determine what resolutions and encodings are acceptable; determining these is key to ensuring low start up times (§5). Then our scheme uses information from the mobile device's physical context – which is available to the cellular provider – to determine the baseline bit rate to use, and low-level TCP feedback to estimate network conditions and adapt the bit rate closely to fine-grained channel variations. Our bit rate adapter keeps the average bit rate as high as possible and minimizes bit rate switches, while also controlling re-buffering events. Also, by virtue of being close to clients, iProxy caches offer low RTTs, which translates to higher bit rates, compared with transfers across the network.

We implement a prototype of iProxy using a quad-core Linux desktop. We evaluate it using real traffic traces of handheld video traffic collected over the wireless network of our university over a three-day period and a public dataset of popular video queries at top content providers [6].

Our evaluation shows the following: compared with a naive conventional proxy, iProxy offers a 20% better hit rate for our university trace (60% vs 72%), and improves hit rate by a factor of 1.6X (28% vs 44%) for the public video dataset, compared with a conventional proxy. For our university traces, we find that our new information-aware cache replacement policies offer 15% better relative hit rates than even the best information-agnostic cache replacement strategies. We find that using an information-aware policy is crucial to realizing the benefits of iProxy, and that iProxy uses 2.4X less storage than conventional designs. We present an analysis of where to deploy iProxy in a cellular providers' network. We also conduct a thorough evaluation of iProxy's dynamic encoding and adaptation schemes using an Android smartphone. We show that iProxy improves start-up times by up to 13s by serving a format that is optimally suited for the phone. Some videos can simply not be played on the phone using traditional techniques, but they play almost instantly when iProxy is used. Testing against a variety of scenarios where bandwidth varies dynamically, we also find that, compared with state-of-the-art streaming techniques (specifically, MPEG DASH), iProxy's linear bit rate adaptation improves the average bit rate for a given stream by 16%, and virtually eliminates buffering.

To summarize, the contributions of this paper are as follows:

- We present the design and implementation of iProxy, a cache for mobile video that optimizes end-user QoE while alleviating load on cellular network links.
- A novel design feature of iProxy is that multiple videos containing the same underlying information but differing in format, bit rate or source are stored using a single iProxy cache entry: the index for the entry is an information-bound reference (IBR), and the value is the list of URLs that share the IBR as well as the common underlying frequency domain representation. We show that leveraging IBRs in this fashion can result in 1.2 to 1.6X better hit rates, and up to 2.4X lower storage compared with URL- or content-based approaches. But achieving these results requires careful design of information-aware cache management schemes.
- The second unique feature of iProxy, a novel bit rate adaptation scheme, builds off of the above cache design: it determines the format ideally suited for a device and further uses TCP layer feedback to encode the video directly from the stored frequency domain representation at a dynamically selected bit rate that matches network conditions as closely as possible. This design feature helps improve video start times (by up to 13s), buffering rates and average bit rates (by 16%), thereby improving end-user QoE.

# 2. MOTIVATION AND BACKGROUND

A recent study [43] analyzed similarity among video results corresponding with 25 popular queries from YouTube, Google Video, and Yahoo! Video [6] and found that on average 27% of the videos are "redundant", i.e., nearly identical to the most popular version of a video in the search results. Simply using URLs will not identify these videos as being redundant because each video has a different URL. In addition, we applied data-centric approaches [36] that identify similarities based on matching SHA-1 hashes of content chunks, but found that these approaches could identify less than a third of the redundant videos; these techniques completely missed out on videos that had minor differences due to resolution, encoding, or quality. Our analysis of requests to video content made from mobile devices traced in our campus wireless network also revealed similar qualitative results (some of these results can be found in §5).

iProxy leverages these observations. It is built on the fact that users may request the same video in different formats or encodings, potentially served by different content providers. In contrast with prior schemes, iProxy's caching scheme can identify redundancy in the face of such access to video because its use of IBRs, which we explain later in this next section, helps it match information contained in a video without being tied to the URL (i.e., the location where it is hosted) and specifics such as encoding or resolution. While we discuss iProxy in the context of caching, we argue in §4.3 that its design is also applicable to *prefetching*.

## 2.1 Design Requirements

iProxy must meet the following requirements:

**(1) Efficient caching:** While IBRs help identify matches across multiple versions of a video, we must still understand how to ensure cost-effectiveness of caching, which is reflected in bandwidth savings per unit cost. As the diversity in video formats and sources grows, it is likely that naive approaches that store all redundant versions of a video in every possible format and from every possible source may use a significant amount of storage and, as a result, be quite expensive. We seek a design whose storage cost is significantly lower than this naive alternative, but the bandwidth savings are similar. Meeting this requirement is possible if: (a) iProxy has a way of organizing the cache such that videos carrying redundant information are not stored, and (b) only those entries that correspond to the most heavily accessed information—not data—are stored in the cache.

**Good QoE:** It is nontrivial to precisely define QoE, because different users may care about different criteria, but in our paper, we focus on start-up latency, video stall time, and video quality (bit rate). Content providers today employ sophisticated mechanisms to ensure QoE, e.g., using third parties to switch downloads across multiple CDNs, and pick alternate bit rates [3]. Because iProxy interposes between content providers/CDNs and end-users, there is a danger that it may undercut content providers' QoE enhancements. To meet QoE requirements, iProxy must ensure that: (a) video is served in a resolution and encoding optimally suited to an end-device so that the start-up delay is as low as possible, minimizing the potential for abandonment [32], and (b) bit rate used stays close to the available bandwidth so that the average bit rate is high and buffering is controlled, maximizing engagement [19, 24, 32]. The use of IBRs in iProxy provides unique opportunities, enabling solutions for both.

When these requirements are met, iProxy can ensure that the effective utilization of providers' network infrastructure can be lowered for a given high aggregate mobile-video traffic load, while ensuring high end-user QoE. In what follows, we describe IBRs which form the basis for iProxy.

## 2.2 Information-Bound Referencing

Information-bound referencing (IBR) was first introduced in [17]; key details can be found in [33]. IBR derives the information from multimedia data as a "perceptual fingerprint" for the data. This fingerprint isn't tied to a specific protocol, host, file name, or multimedia format such as resolution and bit rate, but is bound only to the information it presents. Algorithms for IBRs have their basis in multimedia fingerprinting, used for copyright violation detection. In this section, we discuss how to calculate the IBR value for multimedia content and how to apply it to iProxy.

**IBR for a single frame:** We first explain the IBR calculation of a single frame. Prior work [33, 17] presents three options to retrieve fingerprint for an image: leveraging spatial structure, using color distribution, and frequency domain analysis. Of these, frequency domain analysis based on Discrete Cosine transforms (DCT) is shown to be the better choice. The main insight is that the low-frequency components provide a high-level "sketch," and the high-frequency components provide more fine-grained distinctions [16] of the underlying information content. To elaborate, the image is first scaled to a baseline resolution of $128 \times 128$ [33]. Then, the YCbCr representation of this scaled image is generated [11]. Discrete cosine transform (DCT) on the Y, Cb, and Cr matrices is then run. The IBR then consists of two parts: First, the low $9 \times 9$ frequency components are used, which capture more than 95% of the signal energy. Second, to capture more fine-grained differences, the sum of the high-frequency components of Y is computed; the lower-end $3 \times 3$ sub-matrices of Cb and Cr DCT components where most of the signal energy lies are also captured.

**IBR for a Video:** Prior work [33, 17] suggests videos be chunked and only frames at chunk boundaries be processed to compute IBRs. The way to chunk videos is using scene detection [21] which scans frames for similarity and groups together frames with similar content. The frames at chunk boundaries are called $key\ frames$, where the images change significantly due to scene changes. To identify this scene change, we need to pick a good image feature. Based on extensive experiments, [33] suggests using the variation in the amplitude of the zero-th frequency of the Y component. More specifically, the distance between frames $i$ and $i + 1$ is measured as $DistSeq(i) = \frac{|A_{i+1} - A_i|}{min(A_{i+1}, A_i)}$, where $A_i$ is the zero-th frequency of the Y-component of frame $i$. If the distance is less than $ChunkThresh$, the two frames are considered similar and grouped into the same chunk. [33] suggests that $ChunkThresh$ be set to 0.5. For each chunk, only the first and the last $ImgIBRs$ are kept. All $ImgIBR$ pairs of chunks are concatenated to form the IBR value of a video, $VideoIBR$. A 424-byte audio IBR using an existing audio fingerprinting algorithm [22] is also included.

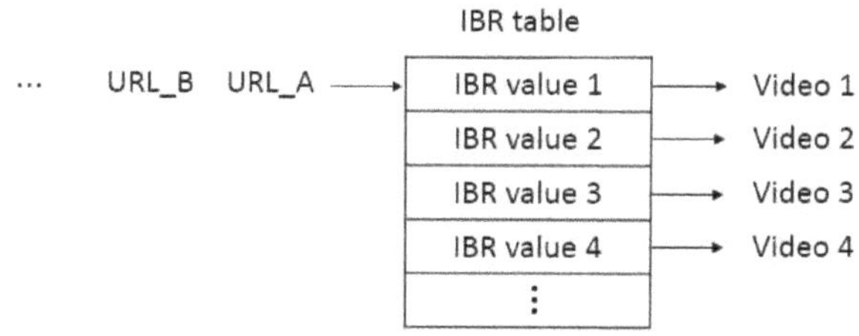


**Figure 1: In the IBR table, multiple URLs map to one IBR value, which corresponds to exactly one video.**

**IBR lookup and lookup performance:** As mentioned earlier, the same content may provide slightly different IBRs due to the random noise introduced by different encoding methods. Thus, [17] suggests using fuzzy matching based on locality sensitive hashing [18, 28] to lookup IBRs and identify videos with matching IBRs.

Analysis of IBRs over a large collection of videos in the wild shows that, using conservative match thresholds, IBRs can match related variants with a zero false positive rate. We found zero false positives in our own trace-based analysis (§5). However, false negatives are non-negligible ($\sim$5%) meaning that not all hits will be identified. In addition, [33] shows that IBRs can defend against a variety of attacks on content integrity such as the use of insets (bogus content is embedded), quantization (lower the video quality), and resizing (rescale videos); however, IBRs cannot determine differences arising due to subtitles. Luckily, many modern MPEG4 videos separate video content from subtitles.

We believe that with evolution in multimedia fingerprinting schemes, it will be possible to design even more robust IBRs with lower false negative and zero false positive rates for matching. We use the thresholds recommended in [33] for both deriving and matching IBRs in the rest of this paper.

# 3. EFFICIENT CACHING IN iProxy

iProxy is located between cellular users and video providers. No modifications are necessary at either end-user devices or video providers; so, for example, end users can still use conventional schemes such as search engines and HTTP requests to peruse and retrieve video content.

To meet the first requirement in §2 iProxy stores an *IBR table* that maps URLs to IBR values. As shown in Figure 1, each IBR value corresponds to exactly *one* video file. Multiple URLs may map to the same IBR value because these URLs represents videos with redundant information, and each IBR value associates with a single video file (no matter how many URLs map to it).

After receiving a request for a URL, iProxy checks the IBR table first (Figure 2); this table maps an URL to a particular IBR value. Three cases arise:

**The URL hits:** The URL requested by an end user can be found in the IBR table, which means that this exact URL was requested

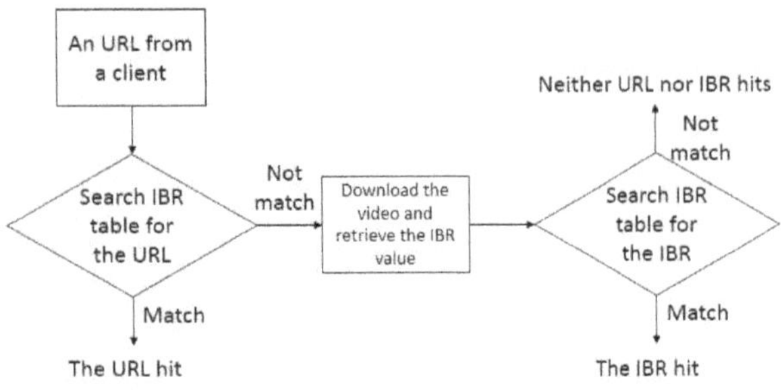


**Figure 2: The flow of cache matching.**

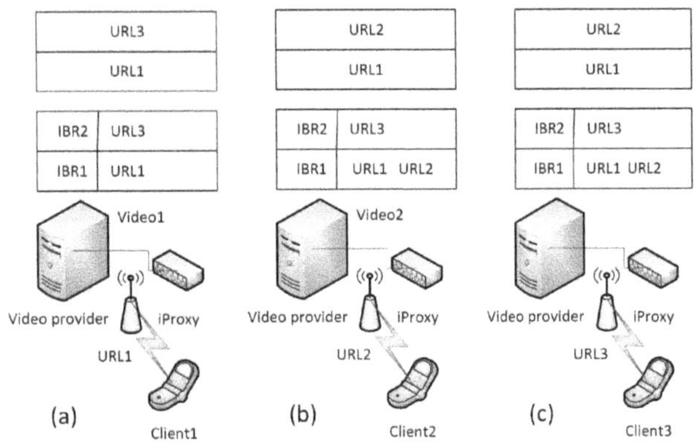


**Figure 3: iProxy vs traditional cache.**

previously. In this case, iProxy can transmit the cached video to the end user.

**The IBR (eventually) hits:** When the requested URL cannot hit any entry in the IBR table, iProxy forwards the request to the corresponding content provider. The provider transmits the requested video, and iProxy transforms it into frequency domain data. The transmission and transformation can be processed in parallel to reduce overhead. iProxy then derives the $IBR$ from this frequency domain data as described in §2.2, and the computed $IBR$ is then looked up. A match means that the same content was requested earlier, but from a different source and/or in a different format. In this case, iProxy compares the quality of the downloaded video against the in-cache video corresponding with the matching IBR. iProxy keeps the higher-quality version and drops the other (assuming the cache is full, which is iProxy's steady-state mode of operation). Finally, the IBR table is updated by inserting the new URL into the existing entry corresponding with the matching IBR. Using this approach ensures that with a limited cache size, iProxy can cover more and more URLs over time than a conventional proxy, which means its cache can satisfy more requests.

**Neither URL nor IBR hits:** After video transmission from the provider and frequency domain transformation, the computed $IBR$ may not hit any entry in the IBR table. In this case, a new entry created for the $IBR$ is inserted, the requested URL added to the entry, and the frequency domain data for the video is cached. The new entry and the corresponding video need to replace one or more IBR entries and corresponding videos in the cache (discussed in §3.1).

**Example:** Figure 3 compares iProxy to a conventional proxy. In this scenario, there are two smartphones called $Client1$, $Client2$, and $Client3$ which connect to a cellular tower. iProxy is behind the cellular tower. Assume the cache size is bound to two entries. The upper table is the cache (index) of a conventional proxy, and the lower table is the IBR table of iProxy. Both employ FIFO replacement.

In Figure 3(a), $Client1$ requests a video with $URL1$. $URL1$ is not in the IBR table, so iProxy forwards the request to the provider. After receiving a video named $Video1$, iProxy calculates its IBR value as $IBR1$, which does not exist in the IBR table. Thus, the mapping between $URL1$ and $IBR1$ is inserted, and $Video1$ (its frequency domain representation) is cached. Then, the video is forwarded to $Client1$ via dynamic video encoding. A conventional proxy works similarly, but does not employ dynamic encoding or adaptive video rate adjustment, of course.

Next, in Figure 3(b), the $URL2$ request from $Client2$ is not in the IBR table either. Thus, iProxy fetches $Video2$ from the video provider and calculates its IBR value, $IBR1$, which is close enough to the IBR value of $Video1$. Thus, we can say that $Video1$ and $Video2$ include the same underlying information. iProxy prefers to keep videos with higher quality and drops the others. In this example iProxy decides to keep the higher-quality $Video1$ and drops $Video2$. Finally, $URL2$ is inserted into the IBR table to show that $URL2$ also maps to $IBR1$. In this case, iProxy does not replace any entry and all of $URL1$, $URL2$, and $URL3$ stay in the table. However, a conventional proxy replaces potentially valuable $URL3$ content by $URL2$; it also wastes storage in caching the content for both $URL1$ and $URL2$, although they both refer to the same underlying information.

Later requests for any of $URL1$, $URL2$, or $URL3$ will hit in iProxy, but $URL3$ doesn't hit in a conventional proxy. For example, suppose $Client3$ requests videos with $URL2$ and $URL3$. Both $URL2$ and $URL3$ are in the IBR table and map to $IBR1$ and $IBR3$, respectively, so $Video1$ and $Video3$ will be forwarded to $Client3$. However, a conventional proxy can only hit $URL1$ and needs to request $Video3$ for $URL3$ from the provider.

## 3.1 Info-aware Cache Replacement

While the aforementioned design ensures that redundant videos are not stored, its FIFO cache management policy does not provide control over the usefulness of the videos stored. In this section, we consider how to design cache management schemes that work with the rest of iProxy's design, to store the most valuable data and keep hit rates high.

To optimize hit rate, our schemes prefer entries whose corresponding information shows both sufficient locality of access as well as wide-spread coverage across many URLs. In particular, we modify the least frequently used (LFU) and least recently used (LRU) schemes to result in two new schemes, as follows:

Our modification to LFU is called "LFU-based IBR-score" policy wherein we give each IBR table entry a score defined as $score_i = \frac{\sum_{u \in URLs}(\frac{C^u_{hit}}{C^u_{stay}})}{VideoSize}$. $score_i$ is the score of $entry_i$ and $\frac{C^u_{hit}}{C^u_{stay}}$ is the sub-score for individual URL $u$ which references the IBR value that $entry_i$ represents. $C^u_{hit}$ is the "hit count", i.e., the number of hits for URL $u$ and $C^u_{stay}$ is the "stay count", i.e., how long URL $u$ has been in cache in terms of the number of total requests arriving at the cache. Thus, $\sum_{u \in URLs}(\frac{C^u_{hit}}{C^u_{stay}})$ captures the contributions of different URLs $u$ to the overall "interest" in the information represented at $entry_i$. We divide the frequency by video size, so shorter videos tend to get higher score.

The policy then is to evict the item with the lowest score. This policy is better than naive LFU: unlike LFU, it does not have the "cache pollution" problem[1] because it considers how long an entry stays in cache ($C^u_{stay}$).

This scheme is better than an alternative that ignores per-URL hit and stay counts and instead computes the aggregate hit/stay counts for the IBR table entry as a whole. This alternative is a direct generalization of cost-aware cache replacement schemes such as Greedy Dual Size-Frequency (GDS) [23][2] that have been shown to be more effective than LRU and LFU. Our scheme is better because it is *information-aware*. In particular, it simultaneously prioritizes frequently referred entries as well as entries that cover more URLs. While the former (number of accesses per IBR table entry) captures the relative interest in a certain information, the latter (number of URLs for an entry) captures both the many different representations for information (i.e., different encodings/formats, which are often given different URLs at a given content provider) and ways of accessing the information (i.e., different content providers). In doing so, our scheme also better accounts for temporal locality that arises when a small number of representations or content providers are repeatedly employed when a certain piece of information is accessed. We empirically establish the superiority of our scheme in §5, especially in comparison with LFU and GDS.

We also design a modification to LRU called "LRU-based IBR-score" and it computes the following: $score_i = \frac{\sum_{URLs}(\frac{1}{C_{last}})}{VideoSize}$. $C_{last}$ means how long the last hit for a URL has been in the cache in terms of the number of total requests to the cache. $\frac{1}{C_{last}}$ is the sub-score for an individual URL. Higher $\frac{1}{C_{last}}$ means this URL is hit more recently. As the earlier scheme, this simultaneously prioritizes most recently referred entries and those that cover more URLs.

## 3.2 Cache Deployment

In a canonical cellular network architecture, there are a few potential locations to deploy iProxy, each with different trade-offs: at the radio network controller (RNC), at the serving GPRS support node (SGSN), and at gateway GPRS support node (GGSN). The RNC is closer to the user equipment (UE), so the latency between RNC and UE is lower, which can be important for QoE, discussed next. However, being low in the hierarchy, each RNC may only serve a few users, which may, in some cases (where population density is low), result in low hit rate. At the other extreme, GGSN aggregates many UEs so it can provide a higher hit rate, but this comes with much higher latency, which affects QoE.

Our design permits deployment at all three locations in the hierarchy. The "optimal" location depends on the cellular network subscriber density and the cache location relative to content servers. We evaluate these trade-offs in §5.

# 4. OPTIMIZING QOE

As mentioned earlier, iProxy must ensure good end-user QoE as it transmits videos out of the cache. There are two aspects to this: ensuring high bit rates and low buffering rates, which maximize user engagement, and ensuring low start-up times, which minimizes abandonment. We discuss these in the following two sections. In both cases, we argue that iProxy's information-aware design discussed earlier, coupled with the fact that it is deployed inside the cellular network infrastructure, provides unique opportunities.

Many cellular providers already employ transcoding proxies [20] that transform Web content to a suitable format for mobile device users to save bandwidth. For example, such proxies are employed to reduce image resolution for smartphones. However, we are not aware of any proxy that dynamically adapts video according to channel quality. That said, iProxy can work in conjunction with such proxies.

## 4.1 Bit Rate and Buffering: Handling Channel Diversity

Several prior works have measured the throughput, jitter, and loss rate of 3G networks and have found that the channel conditions and, hence, throughput performance, vary widely with location [26] and also over time at a given location [26, 38]. The dynamic range can span a few tens of Kbps to a few Mbps, and the variations can happen on sub-minute timescales [38].

Ensuring high QoE implies adapting the video stream to such rapid, arbitrary changes in bandwidth as channel conditions change and/or the mobile device moves.

In what follows, we describe a novel approach for dynamic video encoding, which drives all video transmissions out of the iProxy cache. It does not require the active participation of CDN servers or video content providers nor does it require modifications to clients.

Before describing our framework for addressing these issues, we start by providing some background on MPEG 4-based video encoding, which we use as the basis for our dynamic encoder.

**MPEG4 Video Encoding - Background:** Figure 4 presents a typical MPEG 4 video encoding process. The whole process can be divided into discrete cosine transform (DCT), scaling/quantization, motion estimation, and entropy coding.

DCT computes frequency domain data for video content [15]. More important data is located in low-frequency components and data, including more detail located in high-frequency components. DCT is widely used in lossy compression for multimedia content. Quantization determines the bit rate of the video stream. The quantization process follows DCT and compresses a range of continuous values into one discrete value. Usually we give more bits to represent low-frequency components, which are more important, and fewer bits to represent high-frequency components, which are less important. By choosing the quantization strategy, we can determine the bit rate.

Motion estimation can further reduce video size. Before compressing a video frame, we cut a video frame into multiple blocks and try to match these blocks with other blocks in the same or previous or following frames. If some blocks can be matched, we keep only their reference pointers (also called motion vectors) instead of the blocks themselves. Frames can be categorized into I-frames, P-frames, and B-frames. I-frames do not refer to any frames, P-frames refer to earlier frames (usually I-frames), and B-frames refer to earlier or following frames.

Finally, we code all data including the output from quantization and motion estimation using entropy coding. Entropy coding gathers statistics about how often each symbol appears. High-frequency symbols are given shorter codes for representation. Thus, on average the code length is reduced, which decreases the video size.

### 4.1.1 *Dynamic Video Encoding: A Linear Bit Rate Adapter*

We argue that providing high QoE in the face of cellular channel diversity implies that iProxy should provide a flexible video bit rate that is as close to the available bandwidth as possible. State-of-the-

[1] Since LFU only considers hit counts, entries that are very popular briefly tend to stick around in the cache

[2] GDS calculates a score which is the ratio of cost and size ($\frac{cost}{size}$) for each entry. The *cost* is measured in reference counts (i.e., frequency). *Size* is the data size. When the cache is full, GDS evicts the entry with lowest score.

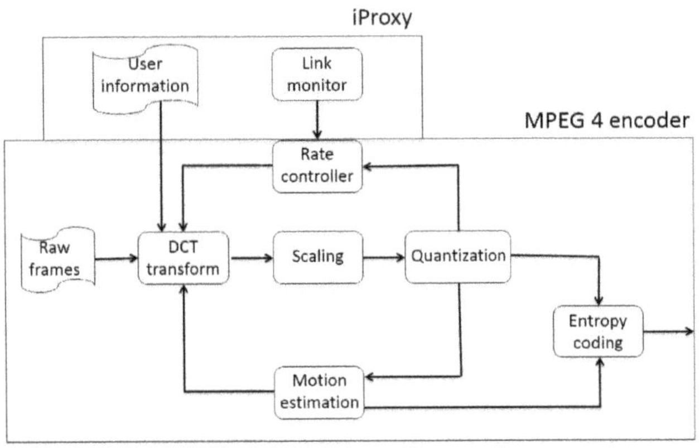


**Figure 4: MPEG4 encoding overview, and how iProxy adapts the encoder.**

art solutions, e.g., layered video encoding or MPEG DASH, are not suitable, as they cannot offer linear bit rate adaptation, e.g., MPEG DASH it employs $k$ different pre-selected versions of the video, selecting the appropriate version over time based on client-reported performance metrics. Unfortunately, these versions may differ significantly in the bit rate and the quality[3]. While using large values of $k$, where the corresponding videos are closer to each other in quality, enables smoother adaptation, it also has downsides: it needs nearly $k\times$ more storage in iProxy, and it is hard to predetermine a set of $k$ encodings that will work across all possible mobile clients. Also, the bit rate adaptation scheme in DASH works on the time-scale of several seconds [30], due to which there are multiple time-instances when the bit rate and available bandwidth differ, especially under dynamically changing conditions. As we show in §5, these attributes can cause the stream to use a lower-than-ideal bit rate or overshoot available bandwidth significantly, resulting in stalls/buffering, both of which result in poor QoE.

iProxy uses a new dynamic video encoding scheme to provide *linear bit rate adaptation.* It uses in-band schemes that provide fine-grained information on channel conditions, such that the resulting stream can gracefully fit the available bandwidth, meaning there are few buffering events, if any, and the video quality stays as high as possible. Different from other mobile video schemes, iProxy doesn't need any modification on the client and video provider side. In addition, it doesn't rely on physical layer support. Consequently, it is easier to deploy in existing infrastructures.

At a high level, the linear bit rate adapter works as follows: the original MPEG 4 encoder uses a rate controller to achieve a constant bit rate. The rate controller takes a particular bit rate and feedback from the quantization module as inputs. Then, it calculates the appropriate parameters for the quantization module to output video stream with a fixed bit rate. iProxy adds a link monitor module to monitor available bandwidth and send this information to the rate controller in the MPEG 4 encoder, as shown in the top box in Figure 4. We modify the rate controller to accept the bit rate suggested by the iProxy link monitor on-line. iProxy's link monitor uses two schemes to determine the network conditions in order to pick a bit rate, which we will describe shortly.

To enable fast dynamic video encoding based on the suggested bit rate, we cache frequency domain data and motion estimation vectors for each video instead of caching encoded videos. This allows us to skip calculating the DCT when performing dynamic video encoding. To facilitate this, when receiving a video from a video provider, iProxy transforms the video into the frequency domain data and retrieves its motion estimation vectors. As shown in §2.2, frequency domain data is also needed during IBR value calculation. Thus, caching frequency domain data and calculating the IBR value can be done in parallel.

[3]Four versions that offer 38 dB, 42 dB, 47 dB, and 50 dB in peak signal-to-noise ratio (PSNR), require 800 kbps, 1200 kbps, 1600 kbps, and 2000 kbps of bandwidth, respectively

**Baseline bit rate using in-context information:** The first scheme operates on coarse time-scales and establishes a baseline bit rate to use. The baseline is reset/chosen each time there is a significant change in the mobile device context, in particular, when the device moves to a different cell tower (known to the cellular provider), meaning that the cache-to-device network path is now different and we need to adapt the stream to it. The baseline for each cell tower can be computed by the cellular provider based on historical measurements of the average throughput mobile devices associated with the tower observe at a given time in the day.

**TCP information feedback:** Once a reasonable baseline is chosen, we must then adapt the bit rate as the achievable throughput varies on fine timescales. For this, we rely on per-packet TCP feedback information. In particular, iProxy collects current TCP-level information for a stream, such as the congestion window (CWND) and RTT (by reading off the TCP/IP stack). iProxy then estimates the current available bandwidth as: $Available\_bw = \frac{CWND \times segment\_size}{RTT}$. Finally, iProxy uses an exponentially-weighted moving average (EWMA) of $Available\_bw$ to compute the bit rate to suggest to the MPEG4 rate controller in Figure 4. Using EWMA helps avoid rapid bit-rate shifts. We set the weight to 0.9 to ensure smooth bit rate changes. Also, to account for changes in the device's cell tower, we ignore the available bandwidth reported for the first few RTTs after a device has moved and rely on the baseline bit rate instead. Finally, when the expected bit rate does not exactly match real network bandwidth, we rely on buffering at the client side to smooth out the videos.

In §5, we use extensive experiments to show that our bit rate adaptation schemes enables iProxy to keep the bit rate as high as possible, while also eliminating stalls.

## 4.2 Low Start-up Time: Accommodating Client Diversity

A recent study of handheld traffic in a campus network [27] showed that users employ devices from many vendors and with different form factors. The advent of tablets only exacerbates this diversity. The challenge is that each model typically has a different screen size and supported resolution. Thus, videos with different resolutions may be requested at iProxy. The study found a wide diversity in device OS, which means that the video decoders the devices have installed could be quite different. Finally, the study found a wide diversity in video formats requested.

A key challenge in iProxy is to stream compatible videos to clients in the face of such diversity. This is crucial to optimize start-up time: as we show in §5, transmitting a video that is encoded at a higher resolution than a device's screen resolution can inflate start up time by 2-14s; and, picking the wrong encoding can result in the video being unplayable (i.e., the start up time is infinity).

In order to stream compatible videos, client-specific information must be obtained by iProxy's dynamic video encoding module. We discuss how this can be done next.

**OS:** A majority of mobile devices employ Android, iOS, or Windows mobile. This can generally be inferred from the HTTP header, which often includes the operating system version and device type.The videos each operating system can handle are not the same; e.g., iOS

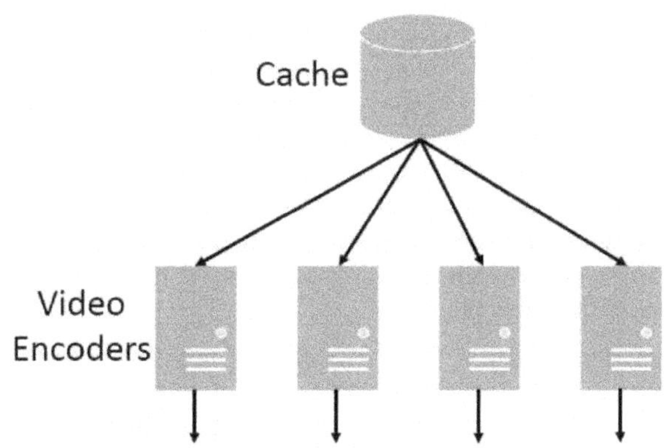


**Figure 5: Multiple dynamic video encoding nodes can be added to improve scalability.**

cannot support flash-related formats. iProxy tracks this information.

**Screen resolution:** Common screen resolutions of smartphones vary from 240x320 to 720x1280. When a smartphone is sent a video at a resolution larger than the phone can display, two problems can arise: first, the smartphone has to spend a significant amount of time buffering the high-resolution stream compared with using the optimal resolution, which inflates start-up delays (§5); second, the video cannot be displayed optimally on the screen, which further has an impact on the user experience. earlier, we can retrieve device models from the HTTP headers, and the screen resolution of any particular model is fixed. This is the upper bound of the resolution that iProxy should provide to the end user. In other words, we may reduce the resolution of a video requested by a client if her screen cannot support high-resolution videos.

**Decoder:** iProxy should ascertain what end users can decode. Some operating systems support built-in video decoders; e.g., Android 2.3.3 supports 3GPP (.3gp), MPEG-4 (.mp4), MPEG-TS (.ts), and webM (.webm) [1]. Thus, the OS can give us a hint as to what video format can be decoded. However, end users may install other decoders. To infer this, cellular providers can track requests sent to to app stores to estimate what other decoders clients have installed and, thus, the encodings/formats of videos the clients can decode and play.

## 4.3 Applicability to Prefetching

While iProxy operates as a cache, it is also applicable to prefetching which is becoming popular in the mobile video context. In particular, the cellular provider can prefetch high quality versions of videos that users are likely to access and store the corresponding frequency domain representations in iProxy, just as above. For each entry created in this manner, the provider can also obtain a list of URLs where alternate versions of the video are stored; this could be done by crawling the Web and identifying duplicates of the stored entries using the IBR matching algorithms described in §2.2. Subsequently, iProxy operates just as described above both in terms of how storage is managed and how content is streamed.

## 4.4 Scalability

A natural question that arises is whether this design is scalable: in particular, can the dynamic encoding scale with number of end-users. In §5.4.2, we show that dynamic-encoded videos are on average 42 times shorter than the original video's length, so one single machine can support multiple clients at the same time. To support even more clients simultaneously, we can leverage parallelism, as shown in Figure 5. Here, a single cache tries to match requested videos and download unmatched videos. In addition, there are multiple nodes that work on dynamic video encoding. Encoding workload can be spread among these nodes. All requests are sent to the cache first and, after obtaining the requested videos, each video is redirected to one of the dynamic video encoding nodes. The dynamic encoding nodes finally transmit videos to clients with a specific video format. Cellular network providers can provision dynamic video encoding nodes based on expected total load.

# 5. EVALUATION

Our evaluation addresses the following issues: (a) **Caching**: How do different replacement policies compare and how important is info-awareness? How much cache storage is needed? (b) **Handling diversity:** To what extent does selecting the right resolution and encoding help improve start up times? (c) **Dynamic encoding**: How well does dynamic encoding adapt to changing conditions? Does it lead to improvements in quality metrics such as buffering rate and bit rate that impact end-user QoE?

We first describe our prototype implementation.

## 5.1 Implementation

On the client's side, we use *unmodified* Android smartphones, running VPlayer [10]. VPlayer can send a request with a URL to iProxy through 3G.

We implemented iProxy in a 4-core desktop with Intel(R) Core(TM)2 Quad 2.66GHz CPU Q6700 and 8GB RAM. Our prototype proxy, written in C, can fetch videos from video providers, calculate IBRs, compare IBRs, cache raw video data, match videos, and dynamically encode videos. We modified the pHash library [7] to calculate IBRs.

For each request, our proxy iProxy checks its IBR table; we use a locality-sensitive hashing (LSH) [29] based index to aid fast lookups at scale. If the URL is not in the table, iProxy downloads the video from a original website and redirects it to the client. After the video is downloaded, we derive its IBR, and compare this IBR to others in cache (using LSH to retrieve candidates, and then obtaining nearest matches). If we find a matched IBR, we delete the copy with lower quality and update the IBR table by adding the new URL.

The video is then sent to a modified FFmpeg [4] module that supports our dynamic video encoding. It interprets requests from clients to determine client-side constraints. FFmpeg uses FFserver [9] to stream the video to VPlayer in the client's device. During streaming, the FFserver module retrieves dynamic CWND and RTT by reading the relevant network stack variables and calculates suitable video bit rates to use. It then sends this information to FFmpeg which adapts bit rate.

## 5.2 Traces

Our analysis of iProxy relies on two sets of real traffic traces. Our first trace is the Web video data set [6] we used the motivating statistics in §2. This data set had a total of 10,000 videos corresponding to the search results for the top 25 queries at three popular video content providers. This amounts to about 400 URLs per query: note that the videos corresponding to some of the URLs corresponding to a query may point to the same underlying information, whereas others may correspond to "related" videos that have entirely different information altogether. The total size of the videos is about 300GB.

In addition, we leverage packet traces collected over the University of Wisconsin's Wireless Network. The traces span three days, from April 26, 2010 (Monday) to April 28, 2010 (Wednes-

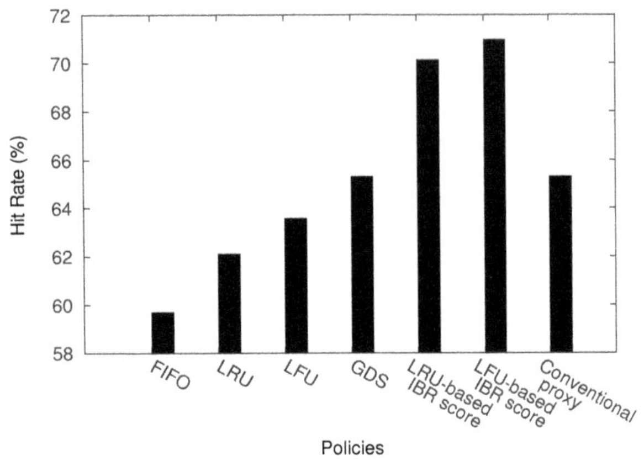


**Figure 6: Hit rates for various cache policies in iProxy.**

day). We prune the traces to only capture the subset of devices that are known to be smartphones or tablets, using the techniques identified in [27]; the techniques have known false negatives (but minimal false positives), meaning that we don't capture all handheld devices. Furthermore, we focus mainly on the trace subset containing the HTTP protocol. For each packet, we collect the first 128B, which includes the HTTP header.

We identify video traffic based on the "content type" field in the HTTP header, similar to [27]. We derive URLs from the HTTP requests for videos, and download the corresponding video files in their entirety.

## 5.3 Caching: Hit rates, Storage, Deployment

**Replacement Policies:** To evaluate the performance of our IBR specific cache replacement policies, we can compare it with other traditional cache replacement policies, including FIFO, Least Recently Used (LRU), Least Frequently Used (LFU), and Greedy Dual Size-Frequency (GDS) [23]. Unless otherwise specified, we assume that the underlying cache is IBR-based. We use hit rate (HR) as the main metric to compare the policies. All caches have the same 1GB size. We use the traces described above for the analysis.

Results from our analysis of the university data set are shown in Figure 6. As expected, FIFO offers the worst performance on HR, because it doesn't consider the importance of cache entries. The HRs of LFU and LRU are around 62%. In contrast, info-aware approaches (modified LRU or LFU) result in higher HR (70-71%), which is better than the state-of-the-art GDS scheme. The difference between GDS and our schemes is that the former only accounts for the overall interest in information, but not the number of different avenues for accessing it; both aspects must be taken into account when designing an information-aware scheme. GDS could evict large collections of URLs in bulk, which may impact future hit rates.

Interestingly, the conventional proxy offers same or better hit-rate than an iProxy that uses an info-agnostic replacement policy such as FIFO, LRU of LFU. This is because it is a sub-optimal policy that is not aware of the importance of information as captured by the hit rate across multiple related URLs. This shows that we need to use info-aware replacement policies to realize the benefits of iProxy.

The rest of the paper assumes the LFU-based IBR-score policy is employed in iProxy.

**Storage Requirement:** Recall that iProxy stores the frequency domain (DCT) data for the highest quality video in each IBR entry. What storage cost does this impose? As exemplified in Table 1,

| Video bit rate | Size |
|---|---|
| 885 kbps | 3744 KB |
| 1063 kbps | 4588 KB |
| 1277 kbps | 5403 KB |
| 1385 kbps | 5862 KB |
| DCT data | 8154 KB |

**Table 1: For a single example video, we show the size of the raw data stored with an iProxy cache entry, vs. that of different formats of the video file.**

| Population | RNC | SGSN | GGSN |
|---|---|---|---|
| 1400 | 1373.55 kbps | 1303.9 kbps | 1271.93 kbps |
| 800 | 1282.18 kbps | 1259.99 kbps | 1176.55 kbps |
| 500 | 1244.51 kbps | 1194.67 kbps | 1182.06 kbps |
| 300 | 1190.22 kbps | 1165.02 kbps | 1123.62 kbps |

**Table 2: Throughput vs. location and population.**

DCT data is larger than individual video files (we show only four different bit rates for a single example video), but: (1) the difference is not significant compared to any single video file (2.1X in the worst case) and (2) the DCT data size is 2.4X smaller than the sum of the sizes of the individual video files, meaning that iProxy outperforms the naive strategy of storing multiple versions.

**Deployment Evaluation:** As mentioned in §3.2, the performance of iProxy depends on where we deploy it and what the served population is. If we put iProxy closer to clients, the latency is lower and the performance is better. However, a less served population means less overlap in accesses which affect hit rate. We study this question using an emulation based on our traces.

To understand this, we first measure the throughput between a machine at our university and the nearest YouTube server, which determines the cost of a cache miss and the relative improvement from a hit. We calculate mean and variance and model the cost as a normal distribution. In addition, we use the data in [39] which shows the delay to RNCs, to SGSNs, and to GGSNs from UEs in a tier-1 cellular network.

We identified a total of 1400 unique users in our traces. We divide them into smaller groups and associate each group with a node in the same level of the cellular hierarchy. We compute and report the average throughput across all groups. The results are shown in Table 2. In this table, the entry corresponding to row "500" and column "SGSN," means that we divide the 1400 users randomly into three groups of 500, 500, and 400, and "assign" them to three SGSNs. We emulate requests of UEs in each group, identify cache hits/misses and compute the effective throughput observed by the clients. Each miss goes to the YouTube server, whereas a hit is served from cache.

Our goal is not to show that one location is clearly better than the other, but rather to show the trade-off between population density, iProxy location and performance, helping the cellular provider make the appropriate choices. In general, our results show that when the population density is low (e.g., 300 users per RNC, 800 or more at SGSN, and 1400 or more at GGSN), aggregating a small number of iProxy's at the SGSN and GGSN is reasonable. When the population density is high (e.g., 1400 users at an RNC), deploying at the RNCs is a good choice.

## 5.4 QoE

The setup we use to test iProxy's ability to support good QoE is shown in Figure 7. We stream videos from an iProxy located on our campus to mobile phones also located close by. However, the

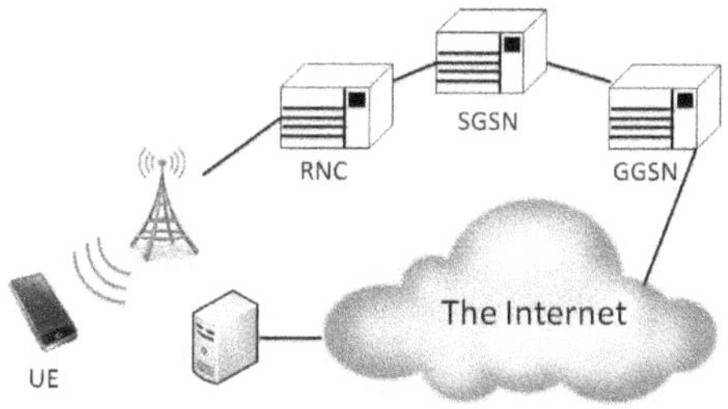


**Figure 7: Experimental scenario for video performance.**

| | Daily-motion | YouTube (HD) | Yahoo Video (.asf) |
|---|---|---|---|
| Both hit | 0s | 13s | $\infty$ |
| iProxy hit | 2s | 14s | $\infty$ |

**Table 3: Improvement in video start up latency using iProxy and a conventional proxy. $\infty$ means the client cannot play the original video format, but can play re-encoded video from iProxy.**

transfers themselves traverse the Internet and the cellular backbone before reaching the end device. In practice the proxy would be deployed a lot closer to clients; thus, our experiments below show a lower bound on the effectiveness of iProxy in ensuring QoE.

### 5.4.1 *Start up times*

We setup an experiment to show how iProxy improves start up latency. Here, we assume a set-up where users click on embedded links to videos, e.g., links in emails, blogs, etc.

In Table 3, we stream three different videos to an Android smart phone (Samsung GALAXY SII) with a 480×800 screen. The first video is in VGA (640×480 resolution, .flv) from Dailymotion, the second one is in XGA (1024×768 resolution, .flv) from YouTube, and the third one is in 360×288 (.asf) resolution from Yahoo! Video. The first column shows the improvement in video start up latency in seconds in the case where both iProxy and a conventional proxy observe a cache hit for the video request. The second column shows the improvement when only iProxy observes a cache hit.

The video from Dailymotion is in a suitable format and resolution for the client's device, so when both proxies see a cache hit, iProxy does not offer any improvement. However, when a conventional proxy does not see a cache hit, it takes two extra seconds to retrieve the video from Dailymotion, delaying start-up correspondingly.

The resolution of the second video from YouTube is much higher than the smartphone can play, causing the phone to spend time filling its cache and pre-processing the video. Furthermore, because of the resolution mismatch, the XGA video appears pixelated on the smartphone. iProxy lowers start up latency by 13s; it also converts the video into a more suitable resolution (VGA).

The smartphone simply cannot open and play the third (.asf) video file. iProxy converts the video into a suitable format (.mpg), so the smartphone can still play it.

### 5.4.2 *Bit rate and Buffering*

**Speed:** To support user video playback without lag, the time needed to dynamically encode a video from raw data should be small, otherwise users may face stalls waiting for encoded video data. To study this, we use modified ffmpeg to encode video into different bit rates to observe encoding speed compared to video length in seconds. We chose a 590s video and encode it with bit rates from 200 kbps to 1000 kbps. As shown in Table 4, encoding times are similar no matter the bit rate, and are 42 times shorter

| | |
|---|---|
| Video length | 586.98 sec |
| 200 kbps | 13.34 sec |
| 400 kbps | 13.94 sec |
| 600 kbps | 14.03 sec |
| 800 kbps | 14.36 sec |
| 1000 kbps | 14.54 sec |

**Table 4: Video length and encoding time**

than the video length. This provides evidence that dynamic video encoding can work on-line, matching real-time video playback requirements. This is further evidenced by our experiments below.

To measure the efficacy of our linear bit rate adapter in improving QoE, we experiment with scenarios where we estimate how well iProxy functions with rapid changes in network conditions. In each scenario we first send a video around 50 seconds long with a starting bit rate of 800 kbps to a smartphone over 3G. Every few seconds, a bandwidth shaper kicks in at the desktop where iProxy is running to change the available bandwidth according to a predefined pattern. Note that the available bandwidth is also affected by channel diversity; this is not in our control. We measure the average bit rate received by the smartphone and the extent of buffering, both of which impact engagement.

We compare our linear adapter against a version of iProxy that uses the state-of-the-art MPEG DASH scheme. Note that this scheme does not use cellular phone context. Also, it employs $k$ different versions of the video (§4.1). While using large values of $k$ enables greater adaptation, it also uses more storage. To strike a balance, we select $k = 4$, which uses nearly 2X more storage than iProxy with the linear adapter.

We tried out several different scenarios, each with a different way in which bandwidth gets shaped. We shows results for two randomly picked scenarios below.

Note that FFmpeg reports video bit rate of encoded video every two seconds.

Figure 8(a)shows the change in video bit rate in Scenario 1. In the beginning, the available bandwidth out of the desktop is 1000 kbps and video bit rate used by our linear adapter (Figure a) varies between 700 kbps to 1400 kbps. The variation is caused by uncontrolled background traffic. Twenty seconds later, when the bandwidth is shaped to 500 kbps, our linear adapter can detect the change and reduce the bit rate to around 400Kbps to avoid frame loss; our linear adapter keeps the bit rate at 400 kbps. Note that despite the use of EWMA, our linear adapter adjusts bit rate almost immediately after TCP detects packet loss. However, because of the use of a buffer in clients, these bursts in bit rate do not cause any perceptible impact to the user. When available bandwidth drops further to 300 kbps, it is detected by our linear adapter based on the smaller average CWND, causing the linear adapter to continue to decrease the bit rate. Because TCP CWND can reach available bandwidth more quickly when bandwidth is low, the bit rate used by the linear adapter can more closely match the available bandwidth. On the whole, the average bit rate used by our linear adapter is 490Kbps.

Figure 8(b) shows the bit rate used by MPEG DASH. While DASH can also adapt, we see that its bit rate is often significantly lower than the available bandwidth, due to the discrete choices available (e.g., between 40s and 60s). The average bit rate of DASH is about 430Kbps; our linear adapter's bit rate was 16% higher on average. Between 40s and 60s, our linear adapter's bit rate was twice as high as DASH (200Kbps vs 100Kbps).

Figures 9(a) and (b) show the results for a second scenario where the shaper causes oscillations in the bandwidth. For the linear

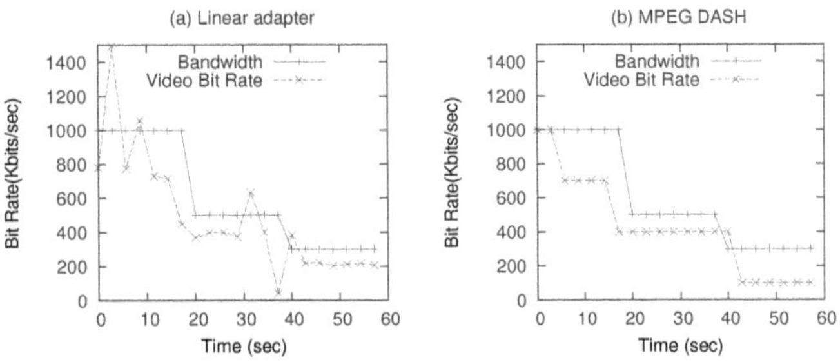


**Figure 8: Scenario 1: the available bandwidth set by the shaper falls over time. The left figure is for iProxy using the linear adapter, the right is using MPEG DASH.**

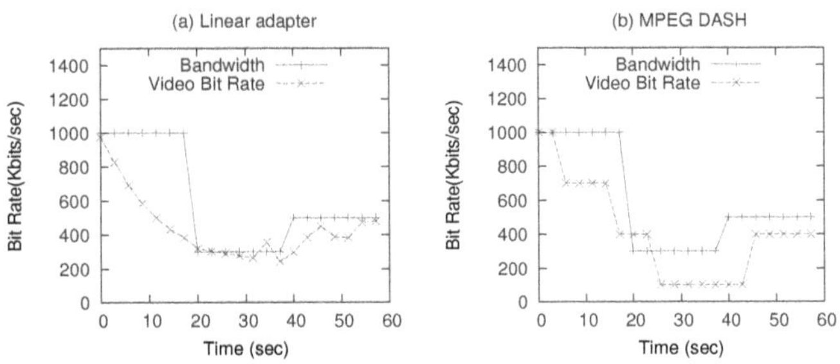


**Figure 9: Scenario 2: the available bandwidth set by the shaper oscillates. The left figure is for iProxy using the linear adapter, the right is using MPEG DASH.**

adapter, we observe that the bit rate gradually falls between 0 and 20s, perhaps because of poor channel conditions which cause the true available bandwidth to be much lower than the 1000Kbps limit set by our traffic shaper. Our scheme starts by using an statically picked initial rate of 1000Kbps; however, if the initial rate were set based on an accurate available bandwidth measure such as that inferable from the latency spread observed for TCP ACKs, we would have picked a better initial bit rate. In general, relying on direct available bandwidth estimates in this fashion could help our bit rate adapter pick better rates even during the course of streaming, compared to our current scheme of using CWND/RTT; we plan to extend our adapter to work in this fashion in the future.

At around 20s, the bit rate settles to approximately 400Kbps. After 40s, the traffic shaper sets the bandwidth to 500Kbps, and our linear adapter immediately adapts its bit rate to around 450Kbps. In contrast, MPEG DASH generally uses a lower bit rate than our linear adapter (410Kbps, on average), especially in the 20-60s time period where it is nearly 40% lower.

In both cases, our scheme suffered from *no* buffering events. In contrast, MPEG DASH saw up to 1s of buffering. While this may seem insignificant, prior studies [32] show that this lowers engagement to levels that start to matter to content providers.

**Sensitivity** Because iProxy estimates available bandwidth using simple passive measurements, there is a possibility of error, especially when the available bandwidth drops suddenly. To understand how this impacts QoE, we use the same setup as above, but shape bandwidth such that it drops suddenly from 2000 kbps to 400 kbps roughly 11s into the video (total length of 40s). We observe that the video stream suffers from around 1s of buffering in all. While this is not conclusive, it indicates that iProxy's adaptation scheme is reasonably robust against sudden variations.

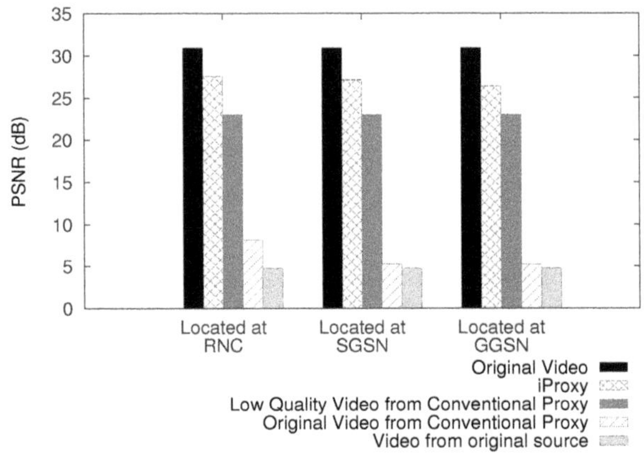


**Figure 10: Video quality evaluation**

For completeness, we also study a more traditional quality metric, namely Peak signal-to-noise ratio (PSNR). PSNR is calculated by comparing the difference in quality between raw videos and compressed videos. Higher PSNR means higher quality. There are two aspects that affect PSNR: (a) *frame loss:* if some frames are dropped, much of the information in the video will be lost, and (b) *the bit rate:* lower bit rate means we lose more information. We use an emulation-based study that also models cache deployment alternatives.

For the test video we used above, the video is compressed with 30.9dB in PSNR and 2.53Mbps in bit rate; thus, these are the maximal PSNR and bit rate we can achieve with iProxy's dynamic encoding module. We emulate three scenarios representing situations where proxies are located at the RNC, SGSN, or GGSN. We assume network bandwidth is 1.5Mbps. The average delay from the RNC to a mobile device is 90ms, from SGSN to a mobile device is 101ms, and from GGSN to a mobile device is 114ms. We measure the PSNR of the received video at the mobile device. We assume that the video player in the mobile device can buffer 10 seconds worth of video and drop any frames that pass the assigned deadline.

Figure 10 shows PSNR when different approaches are used to send the test video for each of the three deployment options. The first bar shows the original compressed video. The second bar is the PSNR of a video sent by iProxy. iProxy decreases video bit rate when available network capacity is lower. Thus, it suffers no frame loss and its PSNR is only slightly lower than the original video. In the RNC case, its PSNR is 11% lower, and in the GGSN case it is 15% lower, showing that iProxy's performance suffers with network delay.

The third bar in Figure 10 shows the case where we keep the video bit rate as low as possible instead of adapting bit rate; this options can also prevent frame loss. However, lower video bit rate means lower quality video and lower PSNR; and even though there is available network capacity, it is left unused. Since this approach suffers no frame loss and uses a fixed bit rate, the PSNR is the same in the three scenarios, but is inferior to iProxy in all three cases. Furthermore, compared to iProxy, these schemes leave 20% of the bandwidth unused in the RNC case, 18% of the bandwidth unused in the SGSN case, and 15% of the bandwidth unused in GGSN case.

The fourth bar shows a conventional proxy sending high quality video directly to mobile devices. It results in a very high frame loss rate, and consequently has a poor PSNR. In addition, the video quality is affected much more drastically by network delay than iProxy. For example, PSNR drops 55% if we move the proxy from RNC to GGSN.

The last bar shows video quality when we stream the video directly from the video source. Without any help from proxy systems, the quality of video streaming is not acceptable with very low PSNR (i.e. 4.75dB). High delay and frame loss on the long path between video sources and mobile devices hurt PSNR significantly.

### 5.5 Summary

In sum, our evaluation shows the following:

- iProxy can improve cache hit rates from 20% to up to 1.6X for the two traces we studied, compared to conventional proxies using state-of-the-art cache replacement schemes. Using information-aware schemes is crucial. iProxy uses 2.4X less storage than a naive cache design.
- iProxy improves start up delays by 2-14s compared to a proxy that is not intelligent in selecting the right video version to serve to a client when a URL is requested. In some cases, iProxy can play video that a conventional design simply cannot play.
- iProxy's linear adapter improves bit rate by 16% compared to state-of-the-art MPEG DASH scheme. Our adaption scheme gracefully changes bit rate in response to changing network conditions. Buffering is minimized, if not virtually eliminated.

## 6. RELATED WORK

**New video encoding schemes:** In recent years, there have been proposals for new video encoding schemes that allow clients to play videos even in the face of partial errors in packets. For example, in [31], the authors argue that the whole video encoding process from DCT to 16-QAM encoding should be linear. They present SoftCast which replaces non-linear entropy coding by scaling up important DCT components to provide error protection in wireless networks. FlexCast [14] provides another way to encode a video grouping equally important bits of a video using "distortion grouping." Then, they modify Raptor codes [40] to do rateless video coding to protect more important groups. While these approaches could be used by iProxy, they all require a modification of the physical layer which makes deployment difficult. Our approach is targeted toward immediate deployment.

**Video adaptation:** [12] consider network conditions to send suitable versions of videos encoded using H.264/SVC [37] in a P2P VOD system. Their work can use network resources efficiently by picking the appropriate bit rate. However, the approach cannot provide linear bit rate.

Techniques such as HLS by Apple and Smooth Streaming [5] are very similar to MPEG DASH (they can be thought of as vendor-specific realizations of DASH). They share all of DASH's drawbacks discussed earlier, making it unsuitable for iProxy. In addition, Smooth Streaming and HLS require users to install a client side program.

In [35], the authors implement a cross-layer mechanism that optimizes TCP-Friendly Rate Control protocol to stream video on wireless multi-hop mesh networks. They use feedback from the receiver as an indicator to adjust sending rate. They control the sending rate in two ways: (a) at the physical layer, they change the modulation to employ suitable bit rates on wireless links, and (b) in the application layer, they change the quantization step in video encoding to achieve the right video bit rate. However, their solution needs to modify the receiver, where as ours doesn't. In addition, they also need to coordinate with the physical layer.

Vantrix [8] transcodes and adapts videos based on user devices and available bandwidth in real time. It results in efficient bandwidth usage and a better user experience. It also provides smart caching to store popular videos and save bandwidth on Internet backhaul links. However, Vantrix still use URLs to identify videos and may cache redundant videos. In addition, it transcodes videos from the original format instead of transcoding from frequency domain data, and as such, it is more resource intensive than our scheme (which skips the DCT process).

**Video proxies:** Others have proposed video proxies (e.g., MiddleMan [13, 42]) and some have focused on caching or prefectching strategies coupled with server-side scheduling that help offer better video experience and QoS [41, 34]. However, iProxy is the first to argue for an information-centric approach that achieves better caching of important information by aggregating multiple related URLs, and co-designs an effective video adaptation scheme into the cache. We design mechanisms that help directly improve quality metrics that matter for user engagement and abandonment. We also design and evaluate information-aware cache replacement policies.

## 7. CONCLUSION

This paper presented the design of a mobile video-centric cache named iProxy that simultaneously meets three key requirements: higher video hit rates at a lower overall cost, adaptability to channel diversity, and the ability to accommodate client diversity. iProxy leverages the recently-proposed notion of IBRs to identify and club together multiple variants of the same video into a single entity. It also uses a linear bit rate adapter that directly encodes raw in-cache video data at the optimal rate given instantaneous TCP feedback about network conditions. Both of these aspects of iProxy's design are rooted in the central observation that effective mobile video-centric cache design requires us to view caching from the higher level perspective of "information" as opposed to "data." Our evaluation shows that iProxy can improve hitrate, but we need to use novel information-centric replacement policies to achieve ideal benefits. We show that our linear encoder can adapt well to changes in bandwidth, and yield better bit rates and fewer buffering events than traditional approaches. We find that our scheme is able to deliver the optimal format to clients, minimizing start up delays.

## Acknowledgements

We thank Vyas Sekar, Aaron Gember, and the anonymous MobiCom reviewers for their valuable comments on earlier versions of this paper. We also thank our shepherd Lakshmi Subramanian for his feedback. This research was supported in part by the National Science Foundation under awards CNS-1040757, CNS-0905134, and CNS-0746531.

## 8. REFERENCES

[1] android supported format. http://developer.android.com/guide/appendix/media-formats.html.

[2] Cisco visual networking index forecast, 2010. http://bit.ly/pIDtBX.

[3] Conviva. http://www.conviva.com.

[4] FFmpeg. http://ffmpeg.org/.

[5] Microsoft smooth streaming. http://www.iis.net/downloads/microsoft/smooth-streaming.
[6] Near-duplicate web video dataset. http://vireo.cs.cityu.edu.hk/webvideo/.
[7] The open source perceptual hash library. http://phash.org.
[8] Vantrix website. http://www.vantrix.com/index.html.
[9] video streaming server for ffmpeg. http://ffmpeg.org/ffserver.html.
[10] Vplayer official website. https://vplayer.net/.
[11] The ycbcr color space. http://en.wikipedia.org/wiki/YCbCr.
[12] O. Abboud, T. Zinner, K. Pussep, S. Al-Sabea, and R. Steinmetz. On the impact of quality adaptation in SVC-based P2P video-on-demand systems. In *MMSys*, New York, NY, USA, 2011.
[13] S. Acharya and B. Smith. *MiddleMan: A Video Caching Proxy Server*. NOSSDAV. 2000.
[14] S. Aditya and S. Katti. FlexCast: graceful wireless video streaming. In *MobiCom*, 2011.
[15] N. Ahmed, T. Natarajan, and K. R. Rao. Discrete cosine transform. *IEEE Transactions on Computers*, C-23(1):90–93, Jan. 1974.
[16] N. Ahmed, T. Natarajan, and K. R. Rao. Discrete cosine transforms. *IEEE Trans. Computers*, 27(1):291–301, 1974.
[17] A. Anand, A. Akella, V. Sekar, and S. Seshan. A case for information-bound referencing. In *Hotnets*, 2010.
[18] A. Andoni. Near-optimal hashing algorithms for approximate nearest neighbor in high dimensions. *FOCS*, 2006:459—468, 2006.
[19] A. Balachandran, V. Sekar, A. Akella, S. Seshan, I. Stoica, and H. Zhang. A quest for an internet video quality-of-experience metric. In *HotNets*, 2012.
[20] H. Bharadvaj, A. Joshi, and S. Auephanwiriyakul. An active transcoding proxy to support mobile web access. In *In Proceedings of the 17th IEEE Symposium on Reliable Distributed Systems*, pages 118–123, 1998.
[21] J. S. Boreczky and L. A. Rowe. Comparison of video shot boundary detection techniques. 2670:170—179, 1996.
[22] P. Cano, E. Batlle, T. Kalker, and J. Haitsma. A review of audio fingerprinting. *J. VLSI Signal Process. Syst.*, 2005.
[23] P. Cao and S. Irani. Cost-aware www proxy caching algorithms. In *USITS*, 1997.
[24] F. Dobrian, V. Sekar, A. Awan, I. Stoica, D. Joseph, A. Ganjam, J. Zhan, and H. Zhang. Understanding the impact of video quality on user engagement. In *SIGCOMM*, 2011.
[25] J. Erman, A. Gerber, K. K. Ramakrishnan, S. Sen, and O. Spatscheck. Over the top video: the gorilla in cellular networks. In *IMC*, 2011.
[26] A. Gember, A. Akella, J. Pang, A. Varshavsky, and R. Caceres. Obtaining in-context measurements of cellular network performance. In *IMC*, 2012.
[27] A. Gember, A. Anand, and A. Akella. A comparative study of handheld and non-handheld traffic in campus Wi-Fi networks. In *PAM*, 2011.
[28] A. Gionis, P. Indyk, and R. Motwani. Similarity search in high dimensions via hashing. In *VLDB*, San Francisco, CA, USA, 1999.
[29] A. Gionis, P. Indyk, and R. Motwani. Similarity search in high dimensions via hashing. In *VLDB*, 1999.
[30] T.-Y. Huang, N. Handigol, B. Heller, N. McKeown, and R. Johari. Confused, timid, and unstable: picking a video streaming rate is hard. In *IMC*, 2012.
[31] S. Jakubczak and D. Katabi. A cross-layer design for scalable mobile video. In *MobiCom*, 2011.
[32] S. Krishnan and R. Sitaraman. Video Stream Quality Impacts Viewer Behavior: Inferring Causality using Quasi-Experimental Designs. In *IMC*, 2012.
[33] A. Kumar, A. Balachandran, V. Sekar, A. Akella, and S. Seshan. Infonames: An information-based naming scheme for multimedia content. Technical Report TR1677, UW-Madison, July 2010.
[34] J. Liu and B. Li. A qos-based joint scheduling and caching algorithm for multimedia objects. *World Wide Web*, 7(3):281–296, Sept. 2004.
[35] H. Luo, D. Wu, S. Ci, H. Sharif, and H. Tang. TFRC-Based Rate Control for Real-Time Video Streaming over Wireless Multi-Hop Mesh Networks. In *ICC*, Dresden, Germany, june 2009.
[36] H. Pucha, D. G. Andersen, and M. Kaminsky. Exploiting similarity for multi-source downloads using file handprints. In *Proc. 4th USENIX NSDI*, Cambridge, MA, Apr. 2007.
[37] H. Schwarz, D. Marpe, and T. Wiegand. Overview of the scalable video coding extension of the H.264/AVC standard. *IEEE Transactions on Circuits and Systems for Video Technology*, Sept. 2007.
[38] S. Sen, J. Yoon, J. Hare, J. Ormont, and S. Banerjee. Can they hear me now?: a case for a client-assisted approach to monitoring wide-area wireless networks. In *IMC*, 2011.
[39] C. Serrano, B. Garriga, J. Velasco, J. Urbano, S. Tenorio, and M. Sierra. Latency in Broad-Band mobile networks. In *VTC*, 2009.
[40] A. Shokrollahi. Raptor codes. *IEEE Transactions on Information Theory*, 52(6):2551–2567, June 2006.
[41] O. Verscheure, C. Venkatramani, P. Frossard, and L. Amini. Joint server scheduling and proxy caching for video delivery. In *WCCD*, pages 413–423, 2001.
[42] K.-L. Wu, P. S. Yu, and J. L. Wolf. Segment-based proxy caching of multimedia streams. In *WWW*, 2001.
[43] X. Wu, A. G. Hauptmann, and C.-W. Ngo. Practical elimination of near-duplicates from web video search. In *Multimedia*, 2007.

# Panel: The Evolution of Wireless Video - Technology and Applications

Thyaga Nandagopal
National Science Foundation
thyaga.n@gmail.com

## ABSTRACT

As wireless technology has progressed from the simple GPRS-based cellular radio modems to the highly complex LTE and 802.11ac networks, users have increasingly sought a satisfactory user experience from video applications running over such networks. This panel discussion aims to look back at the progress made in this aspect, and provide guidance to researchers as to what trends to expect in improving user experience of video consumption over wireless networks.

## Categories and Subject Descriptors

C.2.m [**Computer-Communication Networks**]: Miscellaneous

## General Terms

Performance, Design, Human Factors, Standardization

## Keywords

Wireless Video; Broadcast; Multicast; Video Applications

## Panelists

This panel brings together some of the leading experts in the development and practice of wireless video technology. These experts have a wide array of expertise between them and come from academia, industry, government and the defense sector. The biographies of the panelists are given below.

### 1.1 Jill Boyce, Vidyo Inc.

Jill Boyce is Director of Algorithms at Vidyo, Inc., in Hackensack, NJ, USA, where she leads video and audio algorithm development. She represents Vidyo at the Joint Coding Team of ISO MPEG and ITU-T VCEG for the development of the HEVC video coding standard, where she is an editor of SHVC scalable coding and MV-HEVC multi-view extensions of HEVC. She was formerly VP of Research and Innovation for Technicolor in Princeton, NJ, and Associate Editor of IEEE Transactions on Circuits and Systems for Video Technology. She was an active contributor to the H.264/MPEG-4 AVC and SVC standards. She is the inventor of over 100 granted US patents, and has published more than 40 papers in peer-reviewed conferences and journals.


*MobiCom'13*, September 30–October 4, 2013, Miami, FL, USA.
ACM 978-1-4503-1999-7/13/09.

## 1.2 Dina Katabi, MIT

Dina Katabi is a Professor in the Department of Electrical Engineering and Computer Science, a member of the Computer Science and Artificial Intelligence Laboratory (CSAIL) at MIT, and the director of MIT's new wireless research center, Wireless@MIT. Katabi's work focuses on wireless networks, mobile applications, network security, and distributed resource management. She received her PhD and MS from MIT in 2003 and 1999, and her Bachelor of Science from Damascus University in 1995. She has received best paper awards from ACM SIGCOMM and Usenix NSDI. She has been awarded the ACM Murray Grace Hopper award in 2012, a Faculty Research Innovation Fellowship in 2011, the IEEE William R. Bennett prize in 2009, a Sloan Fellowship in 2006, the NBX Career Development chair in 2006, and an NSF CAREER award in 2005. Her doctoral dissertation won an ACM Honorable Mention award and a Sprowls award for academic excellence. In 2012, Prof. Katabi's and Prof. Indyk's sparse Fourier transform was selected as one of Tech Review's Top 10 Most Important Emerging Technologies.

## 1.3 Mark Rich, DARPA

Mark Rich joined DARPA in 2010, as a Program Manager for the Strategic Technology Office. Mr. Rich's program thrusts involve distributed sensor and communication systems for ISR systems and heterogeneous communication technology. Incorporation of commercial technology and development processes is a focus.

Prior to joining DARPA, Mr. Rich worked at Atheros Communications where he managed reference design and development teams for high volume commercial 802.11n semiconductor radios. Prior to Atheros, Mr. Rich developed distributed and heterogeneous communications system and protocols for military communications and sensing applications. He was cofounder and CTO of SkyPilot Networks where he developed the mesh architecture for commercial broadband wireless infrastructure services. Mr. Rich was also the laboratory director for SRI International's Communication and Signals Technology Laboratory where he contributed to satellite communications, software defined radio, terrestrial cellular communications, digital audio broadcast systems, meteor burst communications and acoustic signal processing programs.

Mr. Rich holds patents in digital audio broadcasting, polyvector modulation, mesh communications protocols and architectures and antenna systems. Mr. Rich has served on the Defense Science Board panel for tactical battlefield communications. Mr. Rich received a Bachelor of Science in electrical engineering, from Michigan Technological University, and a Master of Science in electrical engineering from Stanford University.

## 1.4 Jeffrey Foerster, Intel Inc.

Jeff Foerster is currently a Principal Engineer and manager in the Wireless Communications Lab within Intel Labs. He has led research and standards in short- and medium-range wireless technologies, which has included Ultra-wideband (UWB) technology and related regulations, 60 GHz system design, and wireless displays, and he is currently leading research in wireless mobile video services. Jeff is a Senior Member of the IEEE, has published over 15 IEEE papers including journals, magazine, and conferences, has been an invited panelist at several conferences, was lead author of a book chapter on UWB, and has contributed to several international regulatory bodies including CEPT TG3 and ITU TG1/8. He received his B.S., M.S., and Ph.D. degrees from the University of California, San Diego, where his thesis focused on adaptive interference suppression and coding techniques for CDMA systems. He is also chair of the Intel PHY Communications Research Council which reviews and approves grants to universities in the optical, RF circuits, and communications systems areas.

## 1.5 Thyaga Nandagopal, NSF

Thyaga Nandagopal is the moderator of the panel, and serves in the Directorate of Computer & Information Science and Engineering (CISE) of the National Science Foundation. He manages wireless networking and mobile computing research within the Networking Technologies and Systems (NeTS) program at NSF. He has been with the Foundation since February 2012. Dr. Nandagopal received his Ph.D. in Electrical Engineering in 2002 from the University of Illinois at Urbana-Champaign. He was at Bell Labs from 2002 to 2012. His research interests have spanned several areas over these years: wireless ad hoc/mesh networks, RFID/sensor networks, internet routing architectures and protocols, cloud computing, and energy-efficient networks.

# Indexing the Real World: Sensing, Big Data and Mobility

Henry Tirri
University of California, Berkeley
and
Nokia Corporation
200 S Mathilda Ave
Sunnyvale, CA 94086
+1-408-530-7600
henry.tirri@nokia.com

## ABSTRACT

In this presentation, Dr. Henry Tirri, EVP & CTO of Nokia and UC Berkeley will discuss insights into the social and scientific implications of the technology trends being driven by the rise of large scale multi-device cloud-based computing.

The cloud has already fundamentally transformed everyday experiences visible to consumers through their access to streaming media, social networking and location services via multiple different computing devices, from phones and tablets to connected accessories.

As bits continue to eat atoms, more elements of the physical world will turn first into code and then into code that lives in the cloud. This is driven by the enormous advantages in sharing, indexing and elasticity of computing code has with respect to physical objects. We have seen this happening to photos and videos, music and books, but this is only the beginning. Consumers will increasingly turn to connected experiences that will in turn produce a wealth of data at a at rate unprecedented in the history of mankind.

Due to the pervasiveness of this change, the next phase of the cloud era will see increased partnerships between public and private sectors around long-term technology trends in areas ranging from urban planning to health care.

It can be anticipated that connected hardware will continue to diversify, with an increased emphasis on "multi-sensing". Wearables, sensor clusters in vehicles and smart devices, and independent sensors will all become first class citizens of the cloud: both feeding data into it and drawing it back out again. We will look at one exciting example of this trend -- indexing of the real world made possible by global scale location services.

We argue that ultimately computing will totally de-centralize and live throughout a heterogeneous cloud-based architecture, but energy will continue to be the "One Ring to Rule Them All," that will define where in the cloud the execution happens.

## Categories and Subject Descriptors

CSS H H.0 [**Information Systems**]: General

## Keywords

Mobility; Cloud; Sensing; Data; Mapping; Location; Health; Infrastructure


*MobiCom'13*, September 30–October 4, 2013, Miami, FL, USA.
ACM 978-1-4503-1999-7/13/09.
http://dx.doi.org/10.1145/2500423.2500458

# SafeSlinger: Easy-to-Use and Secure Public-Key Exchange

Michael Farb
CyLab / CMU

Yue-Hsun Lin
CyLab / CMU

Tiffany Hyun-Jin Kim
CyLab / CMU

Jonathan McCune
Google Inc.

Adrian Perrig
ETH Zürich, CyLab / CMU

## ABSTRACT

Users regularly experience a crisis of confidence on the Internet. Is that email or instant message truly originating from the claimed individual? Such doubts are commonly resolved through a leap of faith, expressing the desperation and helplessness of users.

To establish a secure basis for online communication, we propose SafeSlinger, a system leveraging the proliferation of smartphones to enable people to securely and privately exchange their public keys. Through the exchanged authentic public keys, SafeSlinger establishes a secure channel offering secrecy and authenticity, which we use to support secure messaging and file exchange. SafeSlinger also provides an API for importing applications' public keys into a user's contact information. By slinging entire contact entries to others, we propose secure introductions, as the contact entry includes the SafeSlinger public keys as well as other public keys that were imported. We present the design and implementation of SafeSlinger for Android and iOS, which is available from the respective app stores. An overview video of SafeSlinger is available at: `http://www.youtube.com/watch?v=IFXL8fUqNKY`

## Categories and Subject Descriptors

C.2.0 [**Computer – Communication Networks**]: General—*security and protection*; D.2.2 [**Software Engineering**]: Design Tools and Techniques—*modules and interfaces*; H.1.2 [**Models and Principles**]: User/Machine Systems—*human factors*

## Keywords

Trust Establishment; Security & Privacy; Secure Communication.

## 1. INTRODUCTION

For many current Internet applications, users experience a crisis of confidence. Is the email or message we received from the claimed individual or did an impostor send it? Many useful protocols such as SSL/TLS or PGP have been proposed for entities that already share authentic key material. However, the drawbacks and weaknesses of the global certification process for SSL/TLS [23,28] and the usability challenges of decentralized mechanisms such as PGP [36] are well known. Furthermore, even with these protocols, the root of the problem still remains: how do we obtain the authentic public key from the intended resource or individual?

The human-centric foundation of trust establishment makes this problem universally important; protocols and interfaces need to be designed for a diverse population with varying skills, interests, ages, and cultures. We postulate that usability is one of the major barriers for widespread adoption of cryptography.

The recent proliferation of smartphones offers a promising opportunity to address these challenges, as these devices offer a general computing environment with a powerful processor, high-resolution display, several communication modalities (WiFi, 3G/4G, Bluetooth, NFC), camera, and sensors. Thus, smartphones can enable convenient, spontaneous exchanges of public keys.

We observe that individuals often have physical interactions with resources or other individuals before communicating digitally. Often, people communicate over the Internet or via SMS *after* having met in person. We leverage this *physical* encounter to bootstrap *digital* trust. People who communicate before physically meeting can bootstrap trust through a secure introduction mechanism that is rooted in physical encounters with a common acquaintance.

In this paper, we present SafeSlinger, a system for secure exchange of authentic information between two smartphones and a user interface for secure messaging while preserving secrecy. In essence, SafeSlinger exchanges contact information, containing public keys in addition to standard contact list information such as name, picture, phone numbers, email addresses, etc. Thanks to the association between the individual holding the phone and the exchanged public key, users can later associate digital communication with the previously met individual by verifying a digital signature. To make SafeSlinger usable, the cryptographic aspects are mostly hidden from the user, and we have added several mechanisms to make SafeSlinger tolerant to user error.

We envision SafeSlinger as a general approach to bootstrap secure digital communication. First, we enable groups of up to 10 individuals of physically co-located users to securely bootstrap trust by slinging keys between their devices (a one-time operation).[1] SafeSlinger can also support remote exchanges, as long as users can authenticate the other individuals, e.g., via telephone communication or live video conference. Second, SafeSlinger supports secure phone-to-phone messaging and file transfer, providing both secrecy and authenticity. Once users' devices hold each other's public keys, the SafeSlinger user experience is comparable to that of traditional SMS and MMS messaging today. Third, SafeSlinger enables *secure introductions* without physical meetings by allowing a common acquaintance to facilitate a mutual introduction

[1] For more than 10 users, Ho-Po Key [25] may be used to exchange keys among members in large groups.


*MobiCom'13,* September 30-October 4, Miami, FL, USA.

using SafeSlinger file transfer. Fourth, we enable other applications to use the SafeSlinger API to add their public key to a contact entry. Now, when a user slings its updated contact list entry to another user, each application's public key is automatically included, and the receiver's corresponding application can extract the public key. This mechanism can enable applications such as secure email, secure SMS, and encrypted file sharing to solve the problem of securely exchanging the public key without requiring a leap of faith.[2]

**Contributions.** SafeSlinger is the first complete system that provides privacy-preserving and secure group credential exchange without any external trusted parties, restricting the exchanged information to other group members only. SafeSlinger is also the first secure group credential exchange system that can be used remotely over a telephone or video conferencing line. SafeSlinger is designed to be easy to use and defend against all attacks we are aware of. We implement SafeSlinger as an open-source project and make it available for free on Android and iOS app stores.

## 2. PROBLEM SETTING

In this section, we define the problem we set out to solve, discuss our goals, present assumptions that need to hold, the adversary that we defend against, and present attacks.

### 2.1 Problem Definition

The basic primitive that we seek to accomplish is to securely exchange information that is associated with the intended individual participating in an exchange. The security properties that we seek are information secrecy (only the intended entities receive the information), and user-verifiable trustworthy association of data to an honest individual (user knows exactly the information that is associated with a specific honest individual).

Note that there are fundamental limits on the ability of an electronic protocol to protect one human against another human with the intent to deceive, hence the adjective "honest." Specifically, when the exchange involves more than two people, the group exchange should produce the exact same security properties that would result from pairwise exchanges between all members of the group. For example, if Fred, George, and Harry perform an exchange, and Harry *behaves adversarially*, we still wish for the information exchanged between Fred and George to satisfy all security properties.

Given such a secure exchange that includes a public key, all subsequent mechanisms for authentic and secret communication can be implemented using well known protocols, relying on the correct binding of the public key to the individual.

### 2.2 Goals

Our core goal is to enable groups of two or more users to spontaneously exchange their contact list information. To enable such a usable system and maintain high security, we outline four essential properties required in SafeSlinger to exchange contact data:

- **Scalable:** We emphasize groups because we wish to avoid the tedium of a group of users exchanging their information via $N(N-1)/2$ pairwise exchanges.
- **Easy to use:** We also emphasize usability while retaining the security properties described above.
- **Portability:** Another goal is to support heterogeneous platforms, thus enabling interactions among smartphones of several manufacturers and running different operating systems.
- **Authenticity:** Each user should obtain the correct contact information of other users.
- **Secrecy:** Contact information is available only to other group members after a successful completion of the exchange, and remain hidden from external adversaries.

[2] A *leap of faith* is blind trust in an initially received public key, also known as *Trust On First Use* or TOFU).

### 2.3 Assumptions

Our protocol does need to assume certain user behaviors to execute successfully. First, we assume that users are computer literate and can follow basic instructions. We also assume that users have a natural desire for security and that they do not want to deliberately disclose their private information. We also assume that users can authenticate (in the human sense, e.g., recognizing the other users' appearance, voice, etc.) the individuals that they perform information exchanges with, such that an adversary who impersonates another individual would be detected through personal identification. More specifically with respect to the SafeSlinger protocol, we assume that users perform the following security-relevant operations:

- **Exclusion of unintended participants:** Legitimate users will expel an unwanted bystander who wants to participate in the protocol.
- **Correct member count:** Users need to correctly count the number of group members who participate in an exchange.
- **Identity validation:** Users correctly validate the identity information received from the exchange. They should map the identity information to the people who participate in the exchange, and they should reject information of non-participants.
- **Impersonation detection:** Users verify that no other user has injected information that impersonates them in the current exchange. For example, a malicious user may also inject information about Alice, even though Alice is also participating in the exchange. The risk is that another user may discard the correct information and accept the wrong information.
- **Diligent comparison:** Users perform a comparison of three words with all other participants, even after executing the protocol numerous times without any attack.
- **Diligent error checking and aborting:** Users will abort the protocol and restart the protocol when suspicious or error conditions are encountered.

SafeSlinger is not limited to only smartphone users; the protocol can be implemented on laptop or desktop computers. However, we focus on participants who use their smartphones frequently since smartphones are easy to use, are more available during casual encounters, and also suitable for carrying personal information, such as an electronic business card.

We assume that the smartphone hardware and software is free of vulnerabilities and malware, as these aspects are outside the scope of this work.

### 2.4 Adversary Model

We assume that some of the legitimate users that participate in the protocol may be malicious (We call the other users honest). We consider a Dolev-Yao style network adversary that has complete control over all network messages. Furthermore, any Internet server we may use during protocol operations may be malicious. We also assume that other adversaries may be physically present in the space where information exchanges happen. We consider an adversary who wants to break the properties as described in the problem definition, i.e., violate secrecy and authenticity properties of the information exchange and subsequent communication. We consider denial-of-service attacks to be out of scope, as we assume that the users may re-start the protocol as needed.

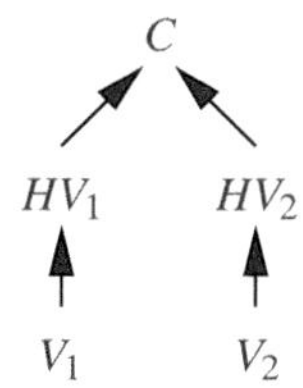


**Figure 1: Multi-value commitment structure for authenticating and disclosing either $V_1$ or $V_2$.**

## 2.5 Attacks

Secure local exchange of information is a surprisingly intricate and challenging problem. Possible attacks include:

- **Malicious bystander who participates in protocol:** A bystander can overhear conversation and attack the protocol by controlling the local wireless communication, performing a **Man-in-the-Middle (MitM) attack** on all participants.
- **Malicious group member:** A member of the group wants to violate protocol properties, such as mounting an **impersonation attack** by injecting incorrect information for another user, or performing a **Sybil attack** [12] by injecting multiple entries either for fictitious individuals or for individuals who are not present.
- **Group-in-the-Middle (GitM):** In a GitM attack [16], a malicious group member creates separate groups for the victim members and creates a sufficient number of virtual identities such that each group has the correct number of members. Each victim member believes to be part of a group with $N$ members (with the $N$-1 other members), but instead the victim is in a separate group with the adversary and $N$-2 fake members. This attack is powerful as it breaks several proposed protocols, as we briefly discuss in Section 9.
- **Malicious server:** For protocols that rely on a back-end server, the server may be controlled by a malicious administrator or become compromised.
- **Information leakage after protocol abort:** An adversary may be able to cause a protocol abort and trigger leakage of private information about a participant.
- **Collision attack on low-entropy hash:** Low-entropy hash values are vulnerable to efficient attacks unless precautions are taken [8, 17, 18, 35, 37].

# 3. CRYPTOGRAPHIC BACKGROUND

We provide background on the cryptographic mechanisms used in this paper: multi-value commitments and group Diffie-Hellman key agreement.

## 3.1 Multi-Value Commitments

A cryptographic commitment protocol is used to lock an entity to a value $V$ without disclosing $V$. Based on the commitment value, the decommitment can be validated and the protocol ensures that the correct value $V$ is disclosed. A commitment protocol for value $V$ can proceed as follows: $C = H(V,R)$, where $C$ is the commitment value, $H$ is a cryptographic hash function that is one-way, collision-free, and has pseudo-random output if $R$ is a random unpredictable nonce. Thanks to the properties of the hash function and the randomness of $R$, $V$ cannot be inferred from the commitment $C$. To open the commitment, $V$ and $R$ are disclosed. The collision resistance property of $H$ ensures that it is computationally infeasible to find another $V$ or $R$ that will result in the same commitment $C$. Note that if $V$ is unpredictable (e.g., a freshly generated ephemeral public key), the additional nonce value $R$ is not needed and we simply have $C = H(V)$.

In case we want to commit to either value $V_1$ or $V_2$ (deciding which to actually release at a future time) with a single commitment, we can employ a tree-like structure (Figure 1). $HV_1 = H(V_1)$, $HV_2 = H(V_2)$, and $C = H(HV_1 \,||\, HV_2)$, where $||$ indicates the concatenation operator. This structure enables decommitment of either $V_1$ or $V_2$ without disclosing the other. For example, to decommit $V_1$, we disclose $V_1$ and $HV_2$, and the case for $V_2$ is analogous. Note that this example is for the case when $V_1$ and $V_2$ are unpredictable to the adversary; additional use of nonces is required for well known $V_1$ or $V_2$. This type of structure is similar to one-time signatures [24].

In the SafeSlinger protocol, we further make use of hierarchical commitments, where the decommitment value is again a commitment value.

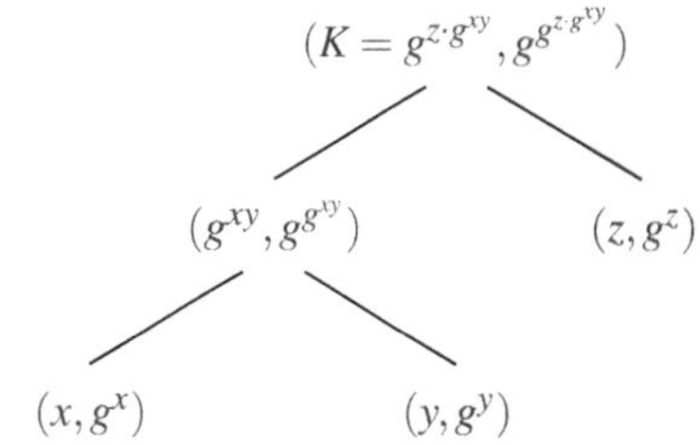


**Figure 2: Group DH key agreement tree for 3 members (*mod p* operations omitted to improve readability). The notation is (priv, pub), where the first element in the parenthesis lists the DH private key, and the second lists the DH public key. The group key is the private key $K$ at the root.**

## 3.2 Group Diffie-Hellman Key Agreement

Group Diffie-Hellman (DH) key agreement is a generalization of the two-party DH key agreement [11], where multiple parties participate to establish a common group key. The Cliques protocol is an example for group DH key establishment [31], and STR [30] and TGDH [15] protocols are tree-based group DH protocols. In the STR protocol, the tree shape is a maximally unbalanced tree (resembling a comb), and the TGDH protocol uses a balanced tree. Research has shown that total protocol latencies are lower for STR in environments where the communication latency dominates over the computation of a modular exponentiation [14], which is the case in mobile environments with smartphones. Hence, we will make use of STR, which we briefly describe in this section.

In group DH protocols, each participant is placed at a leaf node of a binary tree, where each node of the tree has a private and a public key associated with it. The value of a leaf node is the private and public DH keys of the member at that node. The value of the parent node is derived through the DH operation on the values of the two child nodes, for example if the values of the child nodes are $x$ for the private and $g^x \bmod p$ for the public key of the left child, and $y$ for the private and $g^y \bmod p$ for the public key of the right child, the parent value is $g^{xy} \bmod p$ for the private and $g^{g^{xy} \bmod p} \bmod p$ for the public value. Figure 2 illustrates a group DH key agreement with three members, where each node in the tree lists the private and public DH keys. The private key that corresponds to the root node is the shared secret of all group members.

# 4. SafeSlinger EXCHANGE PROTOCOL

## 4.1 Overview

The main purpose of SafeSlinger is to enable a set of users to exchange their contact information such that every non-malicious user receives the correct information about every other non-malicious user. Malicious users may collude and impersonate each other, for example, therefore we cannot provide any guarantees for those parties. Our main goal is to provide security and usability while preventing the attacks described in Section 2.5.

The first hurdle we need to overcome is to enable communication among the users' mobile devices. We currently target Android and iPhone devices, with an effort to make design decisions compatible with future implementations for other platforms (e.g., Windows phones). Unfortunately, current platforms do not offer consistent support for 802.11 ad-hoc mode or seamless creation of a base station to enable other devices to connect to them. Bluetooth communication is also inconvenient because of the slow discovery phase and the inability of iPhones to communicate with non-Apple devices (excepting headsets). NFC is not yet widely deployed, and such communication does not scale beyond pairwise communication. Moreover, none of these local communication mechanisms would enable remote users to exchange their contact information. As a consequence, we use Internet-based communication, where all the mobile devices connect to a cloud server via IP.

When mobile devices initially connect to the cloud server, the server does not know which devices belong to the same group. It is a challenging problem for the server to determine the grouping, especially if many concurrent exchanges are ongoing. We employ the following approach (and discuss alternatives in Section 4.4), which does not leak any sensitive information to the untrusted cloud server. The server assigns a unique ID to each mobile device, which it displays to its user. The devices prompt the users to find and enter the lowest ID. The devices then send that ID back to the server, which can thus perform the grouping. Note that the actual grouping is not security-sensitive, as an intruder can only cause denial of service.

Though the current technical limit for our protocols and implementation is much greater than 10 users, it is unclear that there is much value in scaling even this far due to human limitations. We concentrate our presentation on groups of up to 10 users, leaving it as an open question whether there is a need for protocols that scale further. As prior work shows, users can reliably count the number of participants for groups of up to 8 users, but several people start to make errors for larger groups [10]. As the SafeSlinger protocol fails to complete if only a single person miscounts, we set the threshold at 10 users. Asking users to count the number of participants rules out several attacks, as we discuss in Section 5.

As a **brief protocol description**, the mobile devices send a commitment (as described in Section 3.1) to their information to the server, which redistributes it to the other devices (the server is essentially mimicking the communication network and without performing any trustworthy operations). The users then engage in a verification of all exchanged information to ensure that they all possess an identical sets of commitments (to ensure the absence of MitM and GitM attacks) as well as the correct number of commitments based on the user-entered number of group members. For the verification, users perform a comparison of a 3-word phrase that encodes a 24-bit hash value. The words in the 3-word phrase are selected by using PGP Word List (more details are presented in Section 6.3). If the word phrases match, the devices engage in a group-DH protocol (as described in Section 3.2) to derive a group secret key that is finally used to distribute the decryption keys among group members that is used to decrypt contact information.

Two problems must be avoided: (1) users may habituate to click "Match" without performing the word phrase comparison, and (2) an attacker may compute a collision attack on the short 24-bit hash value represented by the 3-word phrase. We address (1) by presenting two decoy word phrases alongside the correct word phrase and asking users to verify which of the three word phrases match a value on other people's devices. The position of the matching phrase is drawn from a different random number generator on each device to prevent an adversary from predicting the location of the matching phrase. This forces the user to perform the comparison, as a random guess by even just a single user will cause the protocol to fail 2/3 of the time.

We address problem (2) by using Short Authentication Strings (SAS) [8, 17, 18, 35, 37]. In SAS, all devices first commit to the values that are used in the hash comparison. Once all the commitments are distributed, the devices reveal the decommitments and the short hash comparison can proceed. This approach prevents the collision attack and in Zimmermann's words [37] converts the attack from a "safe attack" into a "daring attack." The collision attack is a safe attack, because the adversary is certain that the attack will succeed as a collision has been found. However, with the commitment, the adversary cannot know ahead of time if the collision indeed will occur, and the attack only succeeds with probability of $2^{-n}$, where $n$ denotes the bit length of the authentication string, thus resulting in a "daring attack." In SafeSlinger, $n = 24$.

Another challenge that we address in SafeSlinger is to prevent the server from learning any contact information. We accomplish this by leveraging a group-DH protocol (described in Section 3.2). The group DH protocol establishes a shared secret key among all participants, which is used to encrypt the exchanged information. To prevent MitM attacks, the DH public key is included in the initial commitment and thus validated during the hash comparison. The only information leaked to the server is the IP address used by the devices. In order to provide anonymity, we could leverage other anonymous communication systems in addition to SafeSlinger, such as Tor [33]. The following section describes the intricate details of the SafeSlinger protocol.

## 4.2 SafeSlinger Exchange Protocol Details

Figure 4 describes the SafeSlinger protocol in detail. For clarity we separate our protocol into its multi-commitment tree setup and two rounds of verification.

**Multi-Commitment Generation (S1-S3).** In Step 1 (abbreviated S1), the user selects which data to share and enters the total number of protocol participants. In S2, the device computes the values needed for the group DH protocol by randomly generating the $\ell'$-bit long DH private key $n_i$ (in the current version, we use $\ell' = 512$). The device also randomly selects nonces to indicate "match" (Nonce match, $Nm_i$) and "wrong" (Nonce wrong, $Nw_i$). The device also encrypts the data $D_i$ to share with $Nm_i$ used as a symmetric encryption key (using AES with 256-bit keys): $E_i = \{D_i\}_{Nm_i}$. We use security parameter $\ell = 256$, and we use SHA-3 (256 bits) as hash function $H$. Figure 3 depicts this multi-value commitment structure for user $U_i$. Finally, in S3 the device sends the commitment $C_i$ to the server.

**Authenticity Verification Round (S4-S15).** In the next phase, the server groups the users. First, the server sends a unique ID to the device (S4) which the device displays as it prompts the user to find the lowest ID amongst all devices (S5). In S6, the user enters the lowest ID, which in S7 the device sends to the server.

The server now knows which devices belong to the same group, and distributes ID and commitment pairs $(ID_i, C_i)$ to all group members (S8). Once a device receives all commitments, in S9 it opens up the first level decommitment $HN_i, G_i, E_i$ (Figure 3). If validation of all decommitments is correct (S10), devices compute a hash over all decommitments of $C_i$, i.e., over the triplets $(HN_*, G_*, E_*)$, sorted by the value of the unique $ID_i$ assigned to each device to ensure that

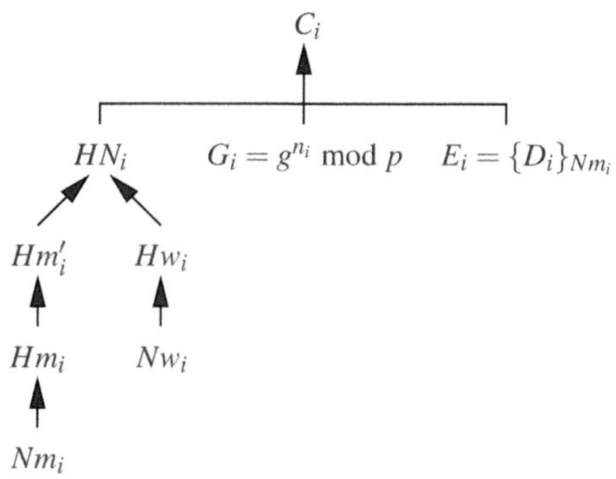


**Figure 3: Multi-value commitment structure for user $U_i$. $C_i$, $HN_i$, $Hm'_i$, $Hw_i$, $Hm_i$, $Nw_i$, $Nm_i$, are 256-bit values; $G_i$ is 512 bits, and $D_i$ varies in length.**

all devices compute the hash over the same triplet ordering. Each device then computes a 3-word phrase that represents 24 bits of the hash (S11), for which on we use the PGP Word List. The device also produces two decoy 3-word phrases, which produces two interesting challenges: (1) if the words in the decoy word phrases match words in the actual word phrase, users may get confused, and (2) if words in different users' decoy word phrases match, users may wrongly select the decoy phrase on their respective devices as a match. To avoid this, we make sure that the decoy phrases do not include any words from the actual word phrase, and we also make sure that all decoy word phrases are mutually exclusive among all devices, which is a challenge to implement. We address this by using the received decommitments as a seed to a PRNG, and having each device draw words from the word phrase for their decoy phrases without replacement. Since the word phrase only contains 512 words in total, this limits the total number of users we can support. More details on the word phrase design are presented in Section 6.4.

S12 and S13 represent the failure and success cases for user verification of 3-word phrases, respectively. If no phrase matches, the user selects "no match", causing their device to send the "wrong" nonce $Nw_i$ (along with $Hm'_i$ to enable verification) to the server (S12). This case is also triggered if the user selects one of the decoy word phrases. This approach cryptographically authenticates the "no match" message based on the commitment $C_i$ and thus prevents injection of an abort message by an adversary. If users correctly selected the matching word phrase (S13), their device reveals the pair of values indicating success $(Hm_i, Hw_i)$, which the server redistributes in S14. Each device can verify that all users selected the correct word phrase (S15). We analyze the success probability of this verification step in Section 5.

**Secret Sharing Round (S16-S20).** In S16, the devices proceed to construct the group DH tree as described in Section 3.2. The ordering in the tree is determined by the sorted order of the unique IDs $ID_*$. Since the group DH protocol is intricate, we omit the details for enhanced readability (Section 3.2 preserves more for detail).

Once the secret group key $K$ is established, the devices then proceed to send their final match nonce $Nm_i$ (which also serves as the decryption key for their data $D_i$) to the group, encrypted under key $K$ (S17). In S18, each device decrypts each received $Nm_j$ from the other devices, verifies its integrity using $C_j$, and finally uses $Nm_j$ to decrypt $E_j$ to obtain each device's data $D_j$ in S19. In S20, each user can validate the identity information from the decrypted data and save it to his/her address book.

**Multi-Commitment Generation**
Data Selection & Counting

| | |
|---|---|
| 1. $U_i \xrightarrow{UI} M_i$ | : $D_i$ (the data to be exchanged) |
| $U_i \xrightarrow{UI} M_i$ | : $\tilde{N}_i$ (number of people in the group) |

Commitment, Group DH Key Setup

| | |
|---|---|
| 2. $M_i$ | : $Nm_i \xleftarrow{R} \{0,1\}^\ell$ ("match" nonce) |
| | $Hm_i = H(Nm_i)$, $Hm'_i = H(Hm_i)$ |
| | $Nw_i \xleftarrow{R} \{0,1\}^\ell$, $Hw_i = H(Nw_i)$ ("wrong" nonce) |
| | $HN_i = H(Hm'_i \| Hw_i)$ (multi-value commitment) |
| | $n_i \xleftarrow{R} \{0,1\}^{\ell'}$, $G_i = g^{n_i} \bmod p$ (group DH key) |
| | $E_i = \{D_i\}_{Nm_i}$ (encryption of data) |
| | $C_i = H(HN_i \| G_i \| E_i)$ (commitment) |
| 3. $M_i \to S$ | : $C_i$ |

**Authenticity Verification Round**
Server Unique ID Assignment, User Grouping

| | |
|---|---|
| 4. $S \to M_i$ | : $ID_i$ (unique ID per user) |
| 5. $U_i$ | : find lowest unique ID among users $\to ID_L$ |
| 6. $U_i \xrightarrow{UI} M_i$ | : $ID_L$ (enter lowest ID) |
| 7. $M_i \to S$ | : $ID_L$ |

Collection and Distribution of Initial Decommitment

| | |
|---|---|
| 8. $S \to M_i$ | : $ID_j, C_j$ $(j \neq i)$ |
| | (other users' ID and commitment) |
| 9. $M_i \to S$ | : $HN_i, G_i, E_i$ |
| $S \to M_i$ | : $HN_j, G_j, E_j$ $(j \neq i)$ |
| | (other users' decommitments) |
| 10. $M_i$ | : $C_j \stackrel{?}{=} H(HN_j \| G_j \| E_j)$ $(j \neq i)$ (verify) |

Word Phrase Comparison of Integrity of Commitments

| | |
|---|---|
| 11. $M_i$ | : WordPhrase( $[H(HN_*, G_*, E_*)]_{24}$) (screen) |
| $U_i \xrightarrow{UI} M_i$ | : Select Matching 3-Word Phrase |
| 12. $M_i \to S$ | : **if** "no match" or wrong phrase selected: |
| | Send $Hm'_i, Nw_i$, Abort protocol. |
| 13. $M_i \to S$ | : **else if** "match" & correct phrase selected: |
| | Send $Hm_i, Hw_i$ |
| 14. $S \to M_i$ | : $Hm_j, Hw_j$ $(j \neq i)$ |
| 15. $M_i$ | : $HN_j \stackrel{?}{=} H(H(Hm_j) \| Hw_j)$ $(j \neq i)$ (verify) |
| | Abort if any verification failed |

**Secret Sharing Round**
Group DH Key Establishment

| | |
|---|---|
| 16. $M_i$ | : Computation of group DH tree |
| | $K$ = Private key of root node (see Section 3.2) |

Distribution and Verification of Data Decryption Key

| | |
|---|---|
| 17. $M_i \to S$ | : $\{Nm_i\}_K$ |
| $S \to M_i$ | : $\{Nm_j\}_K$ $(j \neq i)$ |
| 18. $M_i$ | : Decryption of $Nm_j$ $(j \neq i)$ |
| | $Hm_j \stackrel{?}{=} H(Nm_j)$ $(j \neq i)$ (verify) |

Decryption of Data and Contact Import

| | |
|---|---|
| 19. $M_i$ | : Decryption of $E_j$ with $Nm_j$ $(j \neq i) \to D_j$ |
| 20. $U_i \xrightarrow{UI} M_i$ | : Save user data $D_j$ $(j \neq i)$ |

**Figure 4: Steps for user $U_i$ $(i \in 1 \ldots N)$ to exchange data $D_i$ with the other $N-1$ users via their mobile devices. $U_i \xrightarrow{UI} M_i$ indicates input by user $U_i$ into mobile device $M_i$. $M_i \to S$ represents wireless communication from mobile device $M_i$ to server $S$. $\{X\}_K$ represents encryption of $X$ with symmetric key $K$.**

## 4.3 User Experience

Usability aspects drove many of our design considerations to make the experience convenient, efficient, and comfortable to use. SafeSlinger performs the bulk of the protocol operations without user involvement. The following list shows the required user actions in a SafeSlinger exchange, Figure 5 provides the corresponding screenshots.

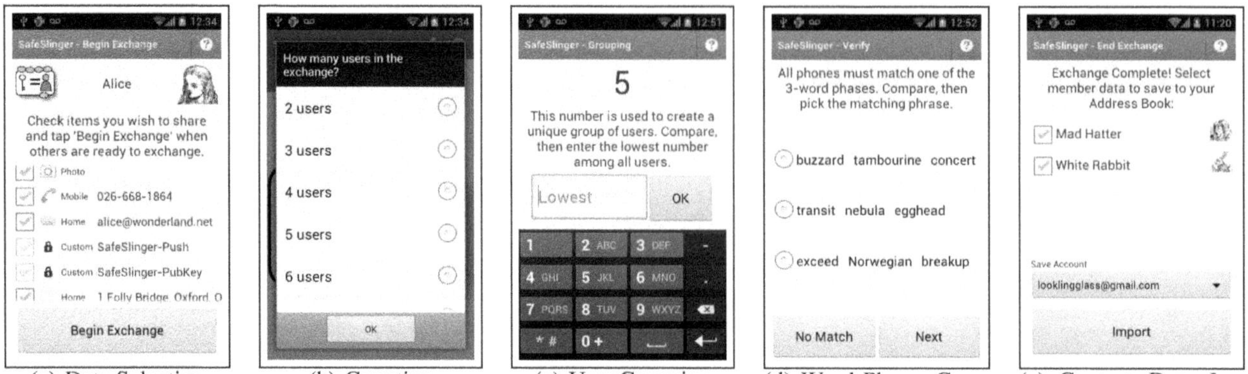


(a) Data Selection (b) Counting (c) User Grouping (d) Word Phrase Comparison (e) Contact Data Import

**Figure 5: Secure contact information exchange sequence.**

1. **Data Selection**: The user selects the items of his/her contact information to share, and presses the "Begin Exchange" button to start the protocol (Figure 5(a)).
2. **Counting**: The user counts the number of group members in the exchange, selects the group size on the dialog, and presses "OK" to continue (Figure 5(b)).
3. **User Grouping**: The user sees his/her unique ID (assigned by the server) and is prompted to enter the lowest ID of any user participating in the exchange (Figure 5(c)).
4. **Word Phrase Comparison**: The screen displays three phrases; each containing three words. The user compares the phrases with other members, selects the matching 3-word phrase, and presses "Next" if all members have the same phrase. Otherwise, (s)he selects "No Match" to abort the protocol (Figure 5(d)).
5. **Contact Data Import**: The user is prompted to select which contact entries on the list to import, and into which of his/her contact accounts (Figure 5(e)).

## 4.4 Discussion

We now discuss the rationale behind the design decisions we made. With respect to the server's grouping approach, we considered numerous alternatives. The Bump [7] application groups its members by having two users "bump" their phones together, and by measuring location, time, and acceleration the server can pair up the two phones. Although this approach is fun for the users, we did not use it for numerous reasons: (1) Bump reveals the user location to the server, which is an invasion of privacy; (2) The approach is not secure as a malicious bystander can simultaneously simulate the bump and often be paired with one of the two devices and steal the user's contact information [32]; (3) Bump does not scale to multiple users; (4) Bump cannot be performed among remote users; (5) Acquiring the device's location can be unreliable and often has a delay of 10 seconds or more; (6) Bump is often unreliable and fails to pair devices.

Another alternative for grouping we considered is to use ambient noise, but this may reveal privacy-sensitive sound to the server, and may also be unreliable in many circumstances. We finally settled on the unique *ID* assignment by the server, and having users find and enter the lowest *ID*. This approach is fast and reliable. Based on the *ID*s, all the server needs is to end up with a connected graph, where each device represents a node and an edge is formed by having one device send the *ID* of another device to the server. We considered the approach of having users simply enter an *ID* of any other intended user, but this may be confusing when multiple users are present, and it can also lead to a non-connected graph when there are more than three users. By having users enter the lowest *ID*, the resulting graph forms a star topology, which always forms a connected component with all participants.

We would like to emphasize that the group of members who perform a SafeSlinger exchange are not required to later communicate within the same group. SafeSlinger is only used for acquiring other users' information in a secure fashion. Since the contact information includes a public key, only that public key is used to subsequently establish secure communication. In particular, all cryptographic values created during the exchange (Figure 4) are erased after the exchange – the sole purpose of their brief existence is to protect a single exchange. Subsequent secure group communication can be easily established by using the exchanged public keys in conjunction with a group DH protocol, regardless of the key exchange session during which the public key was acquired. Thus, there is no mandatory relationship between the group that was used to exchange the information and subsequent membership selection for secure group communication.

# 5. SECURITY ANALYSIS

We will use the list of attacks and challenges from Section 2.5 to guide this security analysis, along with additional attacks that are specific to the operations of the SafeSlinger protocol.

We first consider attacks by malicious outsiders (who are not legitimate group members). Such adversaries can contact the server, ask for a unique ID, and attempt to join arbitrary groups by sending the server a plausible group ID to join. Since users specify the group size, legitimate clients will detect this attack, as the server will send too many commitments to the participants.

A more sophisticated version of that attack is where a local adversary jams communication of one of the local devices, and attempt to join the group in place of the jammed user. A similar attack can be performed by a malicious server, which can split the group up into different subsets of users, and fake another set of users (GitM attacks) to ensure that each device encounters the correct number of devices, even though some are virtual identities created by the malicious server. Preventing these attacks requires some amount of user diligence: the users need to ensure that they perform the hash comparison with *all other* users. If one member is singled out by a jammer or malicious server, then that user needs to inform at least one other user to abort the protocol. As long as at least one unsuppressed user is diligent, then these attacks will be prevented. If these attacks are prevented, neither the local jammer nor the malicious server learns any information about the users, as they cannot participate in the group DH protocol to discover the established group key $K$. The only way to obtain $K$ is to participate as a user and inject a commitment, which would be detected by the devices, as the number of members is larger than the user entered.

A malicious legitimate participant of the group could launch several attacks. First, attempts to infiltrate additional virtual members into the group, for example through a Sybil attack [12], will fail because the number of virtual members would be larger than the count of physical members which users enter at the beginning of the protocol. A Group-in-the-Middle (GitM) attack as described in Section 2.5 is prevented if users diligently perform the hash comparison step, as members who end up in different groups will have different hashes to compare with high probability. The adversary could also send malicious contact information for himself, e.g., it may attempt to impersonate another person who is intended to be in the group. SafeSlinger defends against this attack by enabling users to verify at the end of the protocol which of their contact entries they actually import into their address book, and if a suspicious entry exists the user can attribute that to the adversary. If the adversary impersonates a user who is present, that user can detect that someone else injected a duplicate entry for herself and inform the others.

The multi-commitment with several stages of decommitment (Figure 3), ensures that no information is revealed unless all members $M_i$ reveal their "match" nonce's hash $HNm_i$, as otherwise devices will not reveal the decryption key $Nm_i$. Hence, if any group member detects an anomaly before the hash comparison, all benign devices will abort the protocol. The multi-commitment also prevents the simple collision attack on the low-entropy hash (24 bits) that is used for the comparison, by computing the hash over the ordered triplets $(HN_*, G_*, E_*)$. Since the commitment $C_i = H(HN_i \,||\, G_i \,||\, E_i)$ locks in the value of the triplet, an adversary cannot change its triplet or predict any other triplet before the hash is pre-determined through all users' choices.

Due to the peculiarities of how the word lists are selected and to account for potentially complacent user behavior during comparison, we next analyze the success probability of a MitM attack assuming two benign users are engaging in a SafeSlinger exchange. We will consider different user behavior with respect to the 3-word phrase comparison, ranging from diligent to lazy.

If either one of the users diligently performs the word phrase comparison, the success probability is $2^{-24}$, offering sufficient deterrence against attacks since a human needs to be involved in each protocol run.

We expect that users will not be completely lazy (i.e., not perform the word phrase comparison and simply select one of the word phrases at random and click "Match") because the protocol would fail with probability 2/3 even in the absence of any adversarial action. We thus expect that some users will be "partially diligent" (or "semi-lazy"), and thus expend minimal effort for comparison to quickly complete the exchange. Assume that two "matching" word phrases $A = \{A_1, A_2, A_3\}$ and $B = \{B_1, B_2, B_3\}$ on the devices of users A and B, respectively. In the absence of a MitM attack $A = B$, otherwise $A \neq B$ with high probability.

We now compute the success probability of a MitM attack if both users are partially diligent, where we assume that the users compare by finding at least one matching word without confirming its position. We do assume that the partially diligent users would abort the exchange by selecting "no match", or select the wrong word phrase in case the match is in a decoy word phrase, which also aborts the exchange. We thus need that $A \cap B \neq \emptyset$. The probability $P[A \cap B \neq \emptyset] = 1 - P[A \cap B = \emptyset]$. All possible combinations of $A$ equals to $\binom{256}{2} \cdot \binom{256}{1}$ because two words are chosen from the "even" list and the other from the "odd" list. The number of combinations that will not result in any matching words is $\binom{254}{2} \cdot \binom{255}{1}$. Thus, $P[A \cap B \neq \emptyset] = 1 - \frac{\binom{254}{2} \cdot \binom{255}{1}}{\binom{256}{2} \cdot \binom{256}{1}} \cong 1.94\%$. This MitM success probability is optimistic, since matching words might also present in decoy word phrases, which users can "accidentally" choose, resulting in protocol failure (the attack would not succeed).

Since some partially diligent users may only compare the first words of the word phrases, we compute the probability that the first word matches, thus, $A_1 = B_1$. We obtain $P[A_1 = B_1] = \frac{1}{256} \cong 0.391\%$.

The success probability for other cases is even lower, thus, we only present these cases here. Even for the pessimistic case where both users are partially diligent, the success probability is upper bounded by 1.94%, which we believe suffices to frustrate adversaries from using this attack in practice.

# 6. IMPLEMENTATION

The current SafeSlinger implementation comprises three components: (1) a server application running on Google App Engine and written in Python, (2) a client application for Android (v2.2 or higher) written in Java, and (3) a client application for Apple iOS (v5.1.1 or higher) written in Objective-C. SafeSlinger works well over both cellular and Wi-Fi networks, and has been tested on several smartphone devices: Motorola Droid 855, Google Nexus One/S, Samsung Galaxy Nexus, Samsung Galaxy/S2/S3/S4, Apple iPod Touch, and Apple iPhone 3GS/4/4S/5.

## 6.1 Key Management using Address Book

We rely on the mobile operating systems' address book facility to manage users' contact data and public keys. It is convenient to store users' public key data in a recognizable field in the smartphone's address book, so that any existing synchronization service will seamlessly maintain backups. We have implemented this functionality by adding the name and value (base-64 encoded information) of a new instant messaging (IM) provider to the address book.

At the beginning of an exchange (Figure 5(a)), each user must identify which contact entry they wish to use as their identity, or they may create a new entry instead. During the exchange, a user's contact information is formatted in the vCard 3.0 standard format[3] to be recognizable across multiple platforms. For custom data fields in SafeSlinger (e.g., public keys), we use the IMPP field type (see IETF vCard Extensions for Instant Messaging[4] proposal) with a naming pattern so that fields do not require special handling relative to other contact fields. Our current implementation uses the labels "SafeSlinger-PubKey" for public keys and "SafeSlinger-Push" for push notification tokens.

This design offers flexibility and compatibility for mobile app developers. Other developers can include the exchange of key material (or other data made available by SafeSlinger) without the need to include dedicated support in their applications. Multiple apps can access exchanged public keys and push tokens directly from reading the user's address book without adding additional storage overhead.

## 6.2 Secrecy During Data Exchange

All exchanged data is encrypted using AES in CBC mode with PKCS#7 padding. The encryption key $K_D$ and initialization vector $IV_D$ are derived from the 256-bit "match" nonce $Nm_i$: $K_D$ = HMAC-SHA-3$_{Nm_i}(1)$, $IV_D$ = HMAC-SHA-3$_{Nm_i}(2)$. Contact data integrity is achieved through verification of the commitment $C_i$, hence, no additional Message Authentication Code (MAC) is needed.

[3]http://tools.ietf.org/html/rfc2426

[4]http://tools.ietf.org/html/rfc4770

We use SHA-3 (Keccak) [4] since previous hash algorithms, such as MD5 and SHA-1, have been successfully attacked in either theoretical or practical aspects.

Recall from Section 4 that the "match" nonce $Nm_i$ is distributed in encrypted form using $K$ (the shared secret resulting from the group DH key establishment). We use AES-CBC with PKCS#7 padding, where the AES key is derived from the group DH key $K$ as follows: $K_{CBC}$ = HMAC-SHA-$3_K(1)$. Since we can validate $Nm_i$ based on the commitment $Hm_i$, no additional MAC value is needed to ensure integrity.

## 6.3 Word Phrase Verification

Once all data has been exchanged, it must be verified to ensure the integrity of the exchange. Each device computes a hash of the ordered set of all data exchanged in the protocol. This hash is truncated and represented to the user as a 3-word phrase, with words taken from the PGP Word List. We design this phase to discourage careless comparison.

In SafeSlinger, the word phrase is constructed from the first 24 bits of the 256-bit SHA-3 hash, as indicated in Step 11 of Figure 4. We use the standard PGP approach for converting a 24-bit value into 3 words. PGP uses two word lists – an "even" and "odd" list – with 256 words each. Based on the standard PGP approach, the first 8 bits select a word in the "even" list, the second 8 bits select a word in the "odd" list, and the final 8 bits select another word from the "even" list.

We discourage careless comparison by displaying two unique decoy phrases in addition to the common phrase. In this way, users are forced to compare phrases with at least one other user and actively choose which phrase matches among them. However, to prevent attacks, all users need to validate that they all have the same word phrase. The word phrase provided in this exchange enables out-of-band verification for users in close proximity where they may view each other's screens, or via telephone or teleconference (or any other communication medium where humans can authenticate one another, e.g., by recognizing a familiar voice), where the users can read their word phrases aloud. In some social contexts, it may be considered impolite to look at or take a picture of another user's phone, and thus this protocol also enables screen privacy and comparison of phrases through comfortable conversation.

## 6.4 Word Phrase Collision Avoidance

If a word in our decoy word phrases is the same as in the actual word phrase, users may get confused and select the decoy word phrase as the match. Moreover, the words in a decoy phrase may match the words in a decoy phrase on another device, causing the user to select the decoy phrase which results in an error detected by the local device.

We thus want to select decoy phrases to prevent careless users from choosing the wrong phrase if the actual hash phrase and either of the decoy phrases contain the same word in the same position. Hence, we choose our decoy phrases deterministically such that each decoy word will be unique across all decoy phrases displayed in the group. After computing the actual word phrase, we mark those words as used. Each device will then compute the decoy phrases for all devices, such that no decoy phrase has any matches with any other decoy phrase nor with the actual word phrase.

# 7. MOBILE APPLICATIONS

We have leveraged our key exchange protocol to create a secure messaging application that supports both text and file exchange across different platforms. We now discuss these applications, and describe an application for providing secure introductions.

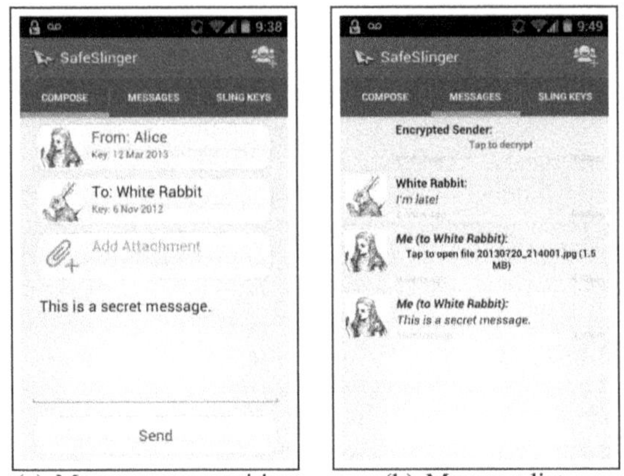


(a) Message composition (b) Message list

**Figure 6: Secure Messaging Screenshots.**

## 7.1 Secure Rich Messaging Implementation

We have implemented secure rich messaging for Android and iOS (Figure 6). Secure information and shared public keys via SafeSlinger are used to encrypt and authenticate text messages and file data. When SafeSlinger is first installed, it generates 2 RSA 2048-bit key-pairs and requests a push token to serve as that device's identity for the Push Notification service. During a SafeSlinger exchange, the push tokens of all group members are exchanged and imported to the address book alongside the public keys.

**Message Secrecy and Authenticity.** For data (simple text or files) encryption and authentication, we choose the PKCS#7 encryption format.[5] Our implementation uses the open cryptographic library PolarSSL[6] for both smartphone platforms. One alteration was to use SHA-3 as the hash algorithm for our RSA signature generation instead of SHA-1. Files to be included in a message are formatted as a separate PKCS#7 message, and downloaded independently by the receiving device.

**Push Message Notification.** To avoid text-messaging charges and conserve battery energy, we make use of smartphone operating systems' support for *push notifications* to deliver message data. Rather than requiring each application developer to implement a background task to keep a separate connection to their server to poll for updates, push notifications are an OS-provided unified update service in which the OS maintains one connection to its own service. Then, each developer can register their application with the OS' service, and the OS only needs to maintain one connection to check for updates across several applications.

We use the native push notification services offered by each smartphone's operating system. Any push notification service may change the push token of the device over time. This presents an issue similar to circumstances where a user may want to generate a new set of key-pairs and wishes to revoke older keys. In either case, we are currently testing an implementation to securely share the updated push tokens and public keys with past exchange participants to improve the user experience.

## 7.2 Secure Introduction

We leverage the secure rich messaging mechanism to enable *secure introductions*, where a common friend of two users sends those users' respective contact data (including public keys and push tokens) to each other. More concretely, consider Alice with two friends: Bob and Carol. Alice has performed direct SafeSlinger

[5]http://tools.ietf.org/html/rfc5652

[6]https://polarssl.org

exchanges with both Bob and Carol. Alice has thus received authentic SafeSlinger public keys for both Bob and Carol. Likewise, both Bob and Carol have Alice's authentic SafeSlinger public key, but do not otherwise share information.

In a secure introduction, Alice's device first encodes Bob's contact information (which includes Bob's SafeSlinger public key and push token) as a custom vCard and uses the secure message format to provide secrecy and authenticity. Alice's device then encodes Carol's information in the same way. Alice's device then sends (via SafeSlinger) the message containing Bob's information to Carol, and the message containing Carol's information to Bob. Hence, Bob and Carol can each validate that the received information indeed originates from Alice, whom they each trust not to send false information. Now that Bob and Carol have each other's public keys and push tokens, they can use SafeSlinger to securely communicate with each other directly. Bob and Carol have thus successfully built a trust relationship through secure introduction.

The above example with Alice, Bob, and Carol illustrates one-hop transitive trust: Alice is the "hop" between Bob and Carol. Presently, we only support one-hop secure introductions, and we enforce that both links used in a secure introduction were performed by direct SafeSlinger exchange. Note that these issues represent policy concerns; there is no obstacle to constructing a messaging protocol that supports an arbitrary number of transitive links.

In the SafeSlinger secure introduction implementation, each user picks any two contacts with whom they have performed a direct SafeSlinger exchange before (Figure 7(a)). When an invitee receives an invitation, his/her device verifies the message, i.e., to check that it comes from a user with whom they have performed a SafeSlinger exchange before. Finally, a dialog presents the chain of SafeSlinger exchanges to the introduced user (Figure 7(b)), and prompts for final confirmation before importing the contact.

# 8. EVALUATION

To evaluate the usability of SafeSlinger for daily usage and the willingness to use SafeSlinger for added security and privacy; we conducted a user study with 24 participants. We selected Bump as a baseline application since it is the most popular contact information exchange application available for both Android and iOS.

## 8.1 Procedure

(a) Secure Introduction feature panel for selecting recipients.

(b) Dialog displays chain of SafeSlinger exchanges from recipient to invitee.

**Figure 7: Secure Introduction Screenshots.**

We ran three instances of the same study and for each instance, we recruited 8 participants to measure the effectiveness of contact exchanges with varying group sizes. We provided a mobile device to each participant to minimize the risk of exposing the participant's privacy-sensitive data on his/her own phone. For each instance, we used 3 iPhones and 5 iPod Touch devices. We pre-installed Bump and SafeSlinger on all devices and configured them to use wireless access points for communication. For added privacy protection, we assigned a fictitious identity to each participant.

We used a within-subjects design and asked study participants to run Bump and SafeSlinger to exchange contact information. To minimize biases and learning effects, we alternated the order of the applications; i.e., in one instance, a set of 8 participants performed Bump before SafeSlinger, and in the other instance, a different set of participants performed SafeSlinger before Bump.

To evaluate the usability for group key exchanges, we asked participants to form small groups of 2 members and run the application to collect the other group member's contact information. We asked participants to repeat with a different partner once more. Then, we asked participants to form groups of 4 members, and run the application to collect all other group members' contact information. We asked them to repeat with different group members once more. Finally, we asked participants to form a large group of 8 members and run the protocol twice.

When participants finished running both Bump and SafeSlinger, we asked them to complete a brief survey. After the study, we ran a raffle to select two participants and gave iPod Nanos as prizes.

**Demographics.** We recruited participants from a university mailing list, and we selected 24 participants who have been using smartphones for at least 2 years. The participants' age range was 21–39 ($\mu = 26.9$, $\sigma = 5.3$), and 17 were male and 7 were female. Among 24 participants, 18 were students and 6 were professionals. In terms of ethnicity, 16 were Asian, 6 were Caucasian, and 2 were Hispanic. For their current phone model, 11 participants were using the iPhone and 13 were using an Android-based smartphone.

## 8.2 Results and Observations

We measured the total amount of time and bandwidth that participants consumed to complete the contact information exchanges for varying group sizes.

Figure 8 shows the timing analysis. According to this figure, participants took less time (about 50%) to exchange contact information using Bump than using SafeSlinger for the small group size (of 2). This indicates that participants found Bump easier and faster to operate for the small group size. However, as the group size increased, the execution time increased quadratically for Bump whereas SafeSlinger had linear increase. For example, four users spent more than 1 minute and eight users spent almost 4 minutes to exchange information using Bump since only two people can bump at once. Also, numerous Bump exchanges kept on failing. For SafeSlinger, on the other hand, four users spent only 27 seconds to exchange their contact information, and eight users spent only 39 seconds. These results demonstrate the efficiency and usability of SafeSlinger for exchanging contact information compared to Bump.

Figure 8 also presents the standard deviation of the execution time in Bump and SafeSlinger, and SafeSlinger resulted in a small standard deviation since participants performed SafeSlinger with very few errors; only 1 error occurred for the instance with a large group size during the entire study. For Bump, however, participants needed to repeat running the protocol due to various types of errors, such as connection failure or fetching wrong contacts. In contrast

Table 1: **Means and paired-samples T-test results from participants' feedback. The higher mean that is statistically significant from the other is highlighted in bold. For all results, $N = 24$.**

| | Easy to use min:1 max:5 | Annoyance min:1 max:5 | Security of app. min:1 max:5 | Likely to use min:1 max:5 |
|---|---|---|---|---|
| Bump | $3.3 \pm 1.4$ | $\mathbf{3.8 \pm 1.1}$ | $2.3 \pm 1.1$ | $2.4 \pm 1.1$ |
| SafeSlinger | $\mathbf{4.2 \pm 1.1}$ | $2.1 \pm 1.0$ | $\mathbf{4.3 \pm .7}$ | $\mathbf{3.6 \pm 1.1}$ |
| T-test | $t(23) = 2.6,\ p = .015$ | $t(23) = 6.1,\ p < .0001$ | $t(23) = -7.6,\ p < 0.0001$ | $t(23) = 5.1,\ p = .139$ |

with Bump, SafeSlinger led to minimal deviation even though it required more user interactions to complete the protocol.

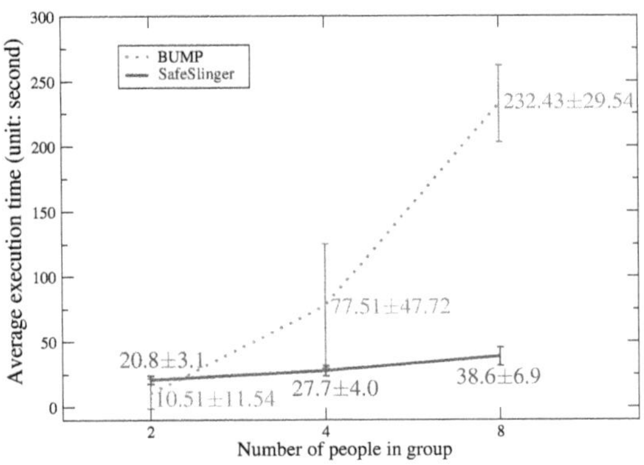


**Figure 8: Average execution time for contact exchange in various group sizes using Bump and SafeSlinger.**

Participants experienced security and privacy vulnerabilities of Bump during our study; since we conducted each instance of the study in a single room, participants experienced receiving wrong contact(s)' information if they happened to bump around the same time. Consequently, participants became noticeably frustrated during the Bump experiments. On the other hand, participants did not experience any security or privacy vulnerabilities using SafeSlinger.

Bandwidth is a limited resource given that mobile users have limited data plans. Hence, we measured the amount of data usage on each mobile device during the user study, and the results show that each device uses at most 11 KBytes for an exchange between 2 people and 65 KBytes for an exchange among 8 people. For comparison purposes, we also measured data usage for different apps on Android and iOS devices, and we found that: (1) playing a YouTube video requires over 10 MBytes per minute, (2) a voice-only Skype call requires around 0.9 MBytes per minute, and (3) reading an article (including text and images) on the Yahoo news website consumes about 350 KBytes per minute on average. Thus, SafeSlinger has modest bandwidth requirements for an exchange.

## 8.3 Feedback from Participants

At the end of the study, we asked 5-point Likert scale questions to get further feedback. For all the statistical analyses in this section, we used paired-samples T-tests and Table 1 summarizes the means and the T-test results.

We asked how easy participants found each application to use (1: very challenging to use, 5: very easy), and participants mentioned that SafeSlinger was *easier* to use than Bump with statistical significance. We also asked how annoying participants found each application to use (1: very pleasant, 5: very annoying), and participants responded that Bump was *more disturbing* to use than SafeSlinger with statistical significance. For the security measurement, we asked how secure participants felt that only the intended recipients received their contact information using Bump and SafeSlinger, and participants answered that they felt *more secure* while using SafeSlinger than while using Bump with statistical significance. In terms of likeliness to use in near future (1: very unlikely to use, 5: very likely), participants provided the answers that they are *more likely* to use SafeSlinger than Bump with statistical significance. Based on the participants' feedback, we can conclude that SafeSlinger is usable for daily use with enhanced security and privacy as compared to Bump.

# 9. RELATED WORK

Closely related research by Asokan-Ginzboorg [2], Abdalla et al. [1], Valkonen et al. [34], and Laur and Pasini [19] provides techniques for secure local establishment of a shared secret key without relying on a PKI or any prior trusted information. Unfortunately, a secret shared among nodes cannot be used to provide integrity and authenticity for exchanged messages, because any malicious group member with the key could have created that message. Therefore, a shared secret is insufficient for secure exchange of authentic information. In particular, GitM attacks are possible, exploiting the absence of message authenticity.

PGP key-signing parties [6] enable users to obtain each other's public key, but they are cumbersome for participants. SafeSlinger can be viewed as a more modern and usable approach using smartphones to securely exchange public keys.

Silent Circle [27] is a recent end-to-end secure communication system for both iOS and Android platforms, providing data encryption for different services, e.g., email, VoIP, and text messaging. Silent Circle enables key exchange between users based on DH, and adopts Short Authentication Strings (SAS) to defend against MitM attacks. Since their implementation is proprietary, one cannot verify the security of their system.

The OTR protocol [5] is a cryptographic protocol to secure communication for instant messaging services. Similar to SafeSlinger, OTR provides authentication and secrecy for messages, but in addition also provides perfect forward secrecy and repudiability. OTR requires that communicating parties initially know each other's public keys, which could be provided by SafeSlinger. Similarly, SafeSlinger could use OTR's approach to provide perfect forward secrecy and repudiability.

The most closely related works provide secure group-based exchange of contact information: GAnGS [10], SPATE [21], and Nithyanand et al. [26].

Nithyanand et al. recently studied the usability of secure group association protocols [26]. Their results with user studies conclude that the ideal group credential exchange protocol does not use a leader (i.e., is peer-based), requires users to count and input the number of participants, and requires users to verify Short Authentication Strings (SAS). Hence, their study confirms the approaches we have selected for SafeSlinger.

The GAnGS protocol [10] was designed to scale trust establishment to large groups of users. Unfortunately, GAnGS requires users to perform many operations and is thus cumbersome to use.

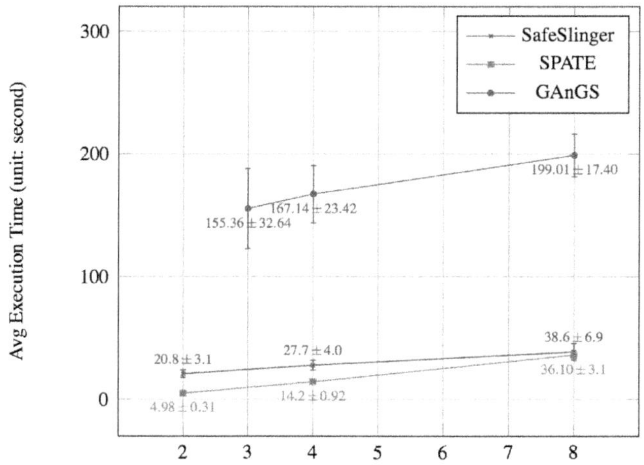


**Figure 9: Average execution time for contact exchange in various group sizes using GAnGS, SPATE, and SafeSlinger.**

SPATE [21] was designed for contact exchange in smaller groups (8 or fewer people). SafeSlinger offers numerous improvements over these prior systems: (1) GAnGS and SPATE require the acquisition of a 2D barcode displayed by another phone, which can require a significant amount of time, especially in some lighting conditions such as bright sunshine; (2) GAnGS and SPATE use a visual hash function for users to perform comparison of the hash values – such a visual hash cannot support remote execution and enables users to simply click "match" without actually performing the comparison; (3) GAnGS and SPATE require leader selection among a group of participants, which may be burdensome for people during the exchange; (4) GAnGS and SPATE enable bystanders to learn everyone's contact information, disclosing potentially sensitive private information. SafeSlinger offers significant improvements by addressing all these issues. In particular, the privacy protection achieved with the group DH protocol is critical for people who want to protect their privacy, even from a potentially malicious server.

In terms of efficiency of contact exchange (i.e., the average execution time to perform an exchange among varying group sizes), GAnGS requires significantly more time for a group exchange than SPATE or SafeSlinger: GAnGS takes over two minutes even for just 3 users as shown in Figure 9. (Note that the minimum group size supported in GAnGS is 3 instead of 2.) SPATE is markedly close to SafeSlinger's speed. For a smaller group of 2 or 4 users, SPATE is the most efficient protocol among all existing systems. SafeSlinger requires more time for the exchange because SafeSlinger's design involves more participant effort to eliminate SPATE's disadvantages as mentioned above. Figure 9 also shows the standard deviation of the execution time in all schemes. Compared to GAnGS, SafeSlinger and SPATE resulted in a small standard deviation since the SPATE and SafeSlinger protocols are more efficient and require fewer user interactions to complete.

Many researchers have studied device pairing or key setup between two devices [3, 7, 9, 13, 20, 22, 29]. These systems, however, do not generalize to more than two parties, as they would encounter the issues we describe in Section 2.5.

## 10. CONCLUSION

To realize the vision of secure online communication, we need to overcome several human challenges: some users are ambivalent about security or privacy, most users lack security expertise, and many users prefer convenience over security and may not want to expend much effort for security.

To overcome these challenges, we designed SafeSlinger as an easy-to-use application that offers many benefits to drive usage. Per Metcalfe's law, the utility of a system grows with the square of the number of users. Our goal is thus to provide immediate utility to enable epidemic growth.

We achieve immediate utility through the robust exchange of contact list information between different smartphone platforms, which does not require any location information or leakage of private information outside the participating phones. SafeSlinger also provides secure messaging and file transfer that is immediately usable. SafeSlinger supports secure local and remote exchange of contact list information, setting up a secure channel between users.

We have released the SafeSlinger application both for Android and iOS devices with the intention to provide a free and easy-to-use system that enables secure communication. We publish the full documentation and source-code to enable independent verification of all security operations. With these steps, we anticipate that SafeSlinger will help to bring secure communication to the masses, so that people can enjoy secret communication and validate the origin of messages with confidence.

## 11. ACKNOWLEDGMENTS


Numerous people helped with this project. We especially would like to thank Jason Lee, Manish Burman, and Gurtej Singh Chandok for their help with early versions of the application. We would also like to thank Virgil Gligor for his helpful suggestions. We thank Sascha Fahl, Henning Perl, and Matthew Smith for their help with analyzing the SSL certificate validation code. We also acknowledge the following students for their effort on analyzing the security of the SafeSlinger code in their class project: Ryan Caney, Yuan Tian, Sagar Medikeri, Merly Knox, Wenyao Li, Zhuangyou Xu, Shuyang Wang, Kaili Li, Pranjal Jumde, Bargav Ravikumar, Nagarathnam Muthusamy, and Sujay Jain.

We thank Moxie Marlinspike for interesting discussions and for suggesting the "sling" metaphor. We also thank Morley Mao and the anonymous reviewers for their comments and suggestions on how to improve the paper.

This research was supported by CyLab at Carnegie Mellon under grants DAAD19-02-1-0389, W911NF-09-1-0273, and MURI W 911 NF 0710287 from the Army Research Office; and by support from NSF under awards CNS-1050224, CCF-0424422, and CNS-1040801. The views and conclusions contained here are those of the authors and should not be interpreted as necessarily representing the official policies or endorsements, either expressed or implied, of ARO, CMU, NSF or the U.S. Government or any of its agencies.


## 12. REFERENCES


[1] M. Abdalla, E. Bresson, O. Chevassut, and D. Pointcheval. Password-based group key exchange in a constant number of rounds. In *Public Key Cryptography*, pages 427–442, 2006.

[2] N. Asokan and P. Ginzboorg. Key-agreement in ad-hoc networks. *Computer Communications*, 23(17):1627–1637, Nov. 2000.

[3] D. Balfanz, D. K. Smetters, P. Stewart, and H. C. Wong. Talking to strangers: Authentication in ad-hoc wireless networks. In *Proceedings of the 9th Annual Network and Distributed System Security Symposium (NDSS)*, 2002.

[4] G. Bertoni, J. Daemen, M. Peeters, and G. V. Assche. The keccak sponge function family. http://keccak.noekeon.org.

[5] N. Borisov, I. Goldberg, and E. Brewer. Off-the-record communication, or, why not to use PGP. In *Proceedings of ACM Workshop on Privacy in the Electronic Society*, pages 77–84. ACM, 2004.

[6] V. A. Brennen. The Keysigning Party HOWTO. http://rhonda.deb.at/projects/gpg-party/gpg-party.en.htmll, Jan. 2008.

[7] Bump technologies. http://bu.mp/.

[8] M. Cagalj, S. Capkun, and J.-P. Hubaux. Key agreement in peer-to-peer wireless networks. *IEEE (Special Issue on Cryptography)*, 94:467–478, 2006.

[9] C. Castelluccia and P. Mutaf. Shake Them Up! A movement-based pairing protocol for CPU-constrained devices. In *Proceedings of ACM/Usenix MobiSys*, 2005.

[10] C.-H. O. Chen, C.-W. Chen, C. Kuo, Y.-H. Lai, J. M. McCune, A. Studer, A. Perrig, B.-Y. Yang, and T.-C. Wu. GAnGS: Gather authenticate 'n group securely. In *Proceedings of ACM MobiCom*, Sept. 2008.

[11] W. Diffie and M. Hellman. New directions in cryptography. *IEEE Transactions on Information Theory*, IT-22(6):644–654, Nov. 1976.

[12] J. R. Douceur. The Sybil attack. In *First International Workshop on Peer-to-Peer Systems (IPTPS)*, Mar. 2002.

[13] L. E. Holmquist, F. Mattern, B. Schiele, P. Alahuhta, M. Beigl, and H.-W. Gellersen. Smart-its friends: A technique for users to easily establish connections between smart artefacts. In *Proceedings of Ubicomp*, 2001.

[14] Y. Kim, A. Perrig, and G. Tsudik. Group key agreement efficient in communication. *IEEE Transactions on Computers*, 53(7):905–921, July 2004.

[15] Y. Kim, A. Perrig, and G. Tsudik. Tree-based group key agreement. *ACM Transactions on Information Systems Security*, 7(1):60–96, May 2004.

[16] C. Kuo, A. Studer, and A. Perrig. Mind your manners: Socially appropriate wireless key establishment for groups. *Proceedings of First ACM WiSec*, Mar. 2008.

[17] S. Laur, N. Asokan, and K. Nyberg. Efficient mutual data authentication using manually authenticated strings. Report 2005/424, Cryptology ePrint Archive, Nov. 2005.

[18] S. Laur and K. Nyberg. Efficient mutual data authentication using manually authenticated strings. In *Cryptology and Network Security (CANS)*, pages 90–107, 2006.

[19] S. Laur and S. Pasini. Sas-based group authentication and key agreement protocols. In *Proceedings of Public Key Cryptography*, 2008.

[20] J. Lester, B. Hannaford, and B. Gaetano. Are you with me? - Using accelerometers to determine if two devices are carried by the same person. In *Proceedings of Pervasive*, 2004.

[21] Y.-H. Lin, A. Studer, H.-C. Hsiao, J. M. McCune, K.-H. Wang, M. Krohn, P.-L. Lin, A. Perrig, H.-M. Sun, and B.-Y. Yang. SPATE: Small-group PKI-less authenticated trust establishment. In *Proceedings of ACM/Usenix MobiSys*, June 2009.

[22] Linksky, J. et al. Simple Pairing Whitepaper, revision v10r00. http://www.bluetooth.com/NR/rdonlyres/0A0B3F36-D15F-4470-85A6-F2CCFA26F70F/0/SimplePairing_WP_V10r00.pdf, Aug. 2006.

[23] M. Marlinspike. Breaking SSL with null characters. In *Presented at Black Hat*, 2009.

[24] R. C. Merkle. A digital signature based on a conventional encryption function. In *Advances in Cryptology (Crypto)*, pages 369–378, 1987.

[25] G. Mezzour, A. Studer, M. Farb, J. Lee, J. McCune, H.-C. Hsiao, and A. Perrig. Ho-Po Key: Leveraging physical constraints on human motion to authentically exchange information in a group. Technical Report CMU-CyLab-11-004, CyLab, Carnegie Mellon University, Dec. 2010.

[26] R. Nithyanand, N. Saxena, G. Tsudik, and E. Uzun. Groupthink: Usability of secure group association for wireless devices. In *Proceedings of Ubicomp*, Sept. 2010.

[27] Silent Circle Co. Silent circle – global encrypted communications service. https://silentcircle.com, Sep. 2008.

[28] C. Soghoian and S. Stamm. Certified lies: Detecting and defeating government interception attacks against SSL. In *Proceedings of the Privacy Enhancing Technologies Symposium (PETS)*, July 2010.

[29] F. Stajano and R. J. Anderson. The resurrecting duckling: Security issues for ad-hoc wireless networks. In *Security Protocols Workshop*, pages 172–194, 1999.

[30] D. Steer, L. Strawczynski, W. Diffie, and M. Wiener. A Secure Audio Teleconference System. In *Advances in Cryptology (Crypto)*, 1988.

[31] M. Steiner, G. Tsudik, and M. Waidner. Key Agreement in Dynamic Peer Groups. *IEEE Transactions on Parallel and Distributed Systems*, 11(8):769–780, Aug. 2000.

[32] A. Studer, T. Passaro, and L. Bauer. Don't bump, shake on it: The exploitation of a popular accelerometer-based smart phone exchange and its secure replacement. In *Proceedings of ACSAC*, 2011.

[33] Tor Project Team. Tor: Anonymity Online. https://www.torproject.org, Dec. 2007.

[34] J. Valkonen, N. Asokan, and K. Nyberg. Ad hoc security associations for groups. In *Security and Privacy in Ad-Hoc and Sensor Networks (ESAS)*, pages 150–164, 2006.

[35] S. Vaudenay. Secure communications over insecure channels based on short authenticated strings. In *Advances in Cryptology (Crypto)*, pages 309–326, 2005.

[36] A. Whitten and J. Tygar. Why Johnny can't encrypt. In *USENIX Security*, Aug. 1999.

[37] P. R. Zimmermann. Pgpfone, pretty good privacy phone, owner's manual, version 1.0 beta 7. ftp://ftp.pgpi.org/pub/pgp/pgpfone/manual/pgpfone10b7.pdf, July 1996.

# Creating Secrets out of Erasures

Katerina Argyraki[1]*, Suhas Diggavi[2]†, Melissa Duarte[1],
Christina Fragouli[1]‡, Marios Gatzianas[1], Panagiotis Kostopoulos[1]

[1]EPFL, Switzerland [2]UCLA, USA

## ABSTRACT

Current security systems often rely on the adversary's computational limitations. Wireless networks offer the opportunity for a different, complementary kind of security, which relies on the adversary's limited network presence (i.e., that the adversary cannot be located at many different points in the network at the same time). We present a system that leverages this opportunity to enable $n$ wireless nodes to create a shared secret $\mathcal{S}$, in a way that an eavesdropper, Eve, obtains very little information on $\mathcal{S}$. Our system consists of two steps: (1) The nodes transmit packets following a special pattern, such that Eve learns very little about a given fraction of the transmitted packets. This is achieved through a combination of beam forming (from many different sources) and wiretap codes. (2) The nodes participate in a protocol that reshuffles the information known to each node, such that the nodes end up sharing a secret that Eve knows very little about. Our protocol is easily implementable in existing wireless devices and scales well with the number of nodes; these properties are achieved through a combination of public feedback, broadcasting, and network coding. We evaluate our system through a 5-node testbed. We demonstrate that a group of wireless nodes can generate thousands of new shared secret bits per second, with their secrecy being independent of the adversary's computational capabilities.

## Categories and Subject Descriptors

C.2.0 [**Computer-Communication Networks**]: General—*Security and protection*; C.2.1 [**Computer-Communication Networks**]: Network Architecture and Design—*Wireless communication*; H.1.1 [**Information Systems**]: Systems and Information Theory—*Information theory*

*Supported by ArmaSuisse.

†Supported in part by NSF award 1136174 and MURI award AFOSR FA9550-09-064.

‡Supported by ArmaSuisse and ERC Starting Grant ERC-2009-StG-240317.


*MobiCom'13,* September 30–October 4, Miami, FL, USA.
Copyright 2013 ACM 978-1-4503-1999-7/13/09 ...$15.00.
http://dx.doi.org/10.1145/2500423.2500440.

## Keywords

Physical-layer security; Group secret agreement

## 1. INTRODUCTION

To perform secret agreement in the presence of an adversary, current security systems rely on the adversary's computational limitations. Consider the scenario where a principal Alice wants to agree on a secret with a principal Bob over a communication channel, while an adversary Eve is eavesdropping on the same channel. Today, we solve this problem through algorithms like Diffie-Hellman [10] or RSA [27], which rely on the assumption that Eve cannot perform certain operations, e.g., large integer factorization, in useful time.

Wireless networks offer the opportunity for a different kind of secret agreement, which relies not on the adversary's computational limitations, but on her limited network presence (i.e., the fact that the adversary cannot be located at many different points in the network at the same time). Consider the scenario where Alice, Bob, and Eve are standing in a noisy room; when Alice whispers something, Bob hears some part of it, Eve hears another part, but, as long as Bob and Eve are not standing right next to each other, they are highly unlikely to hear exactly the same thing. Information theory tells us that Alice and Bob can agree on a secret that Eve knows nothing about, as long as they know how much information Eve has heard (e.g., they know that Eve heard half of Alice's worlds, even though they do not know which ones) [30, 21]. This result holds, even when the Alice/Bob channel is worse than the Alice/Eve channel, as long as Eve does not always hear every single bit of information that Bob does [30, 21]. So, it is theoretically possible for Alice and Bob to agree on a secret that Eve knows nothing about, even when Eve can hear Alice more clearly than Bob can.

This result has significant practical implications: It opens up the possibility of wireless nodes continuously sharing fresh secrets, simply by communicating with each other in a noisy environment. Such a "secret stream" can be used to periodically refresh the nodes' encryption and/or authentication keys [31]. This is important in light of the fact that security is most often compromised through stolen or weak keys, not vulnerabilities in the underlying algorithms [31].

But there is a second, equally important (if more academic and longer-term) reason to care for this line of work: As powerful governments and corporations amass computational power, secret agreement that makes no assumption about the adversary's computational capabilities will become a relevant problem. We do not expect this to happen tomorrow, and we are by no means advocating the replacement of existing cryptosystems that rely on the adversary's computational limitations, like RSA. But we do think that there is value in researchers starting to think about alternatives, even if these are bound to suffer, at first, from vulnerabilities and deployment hurdles.

Our goal then is to design and build a system that enables $n$ wireless nodes (we will call them "terminals") to agree on a secret $\mathcal{S}$, in a way that an eavesdropper, Eve, obtains very little information on $\mathcal{S}$. We focus on groups (as opposed to pairs) of terminals, because this scenario has received less attention by the research community, even though it is becoming increasingly relevant: Internet users are increasingly relying on their mobile phones to communicate in groups, e.g., participate in social networks and online games. There is also evidence that they like to consume online content (in particular, videos) in groups [5], and we are starting to see commercial tools that explicitly target groups of mobile users accessing the same content [4, 2].

Our system does not assume anything about Eve's computational capabilities, but it assumes limits on her network presence, e.g., that she possesses no more than a certain number of antennas. Information theory tells us that this is theoretically possible for $n = 2$ terminals, but not how to do it. In particular, the existing theoretical results (upper and lower bounds on the secrecy rate achievable between two nodes given idealized channel conditions) rely on combinatorial constructions that are not implementable in practice. More recently, researchers have started to propose implementable solutions for $n = 2$ terminals. The first proposals assumed channel reciprocity between the two nodes and required a dynamic environment [13, 7, 32, 8, 17], or else risked compromising their security. A more recent one avoids these pitfalls but requires physical-layer changes and is specifically designed for OFDM [12]. To the best of our knowledge, there exists no solution (for 2 or more terminals) that does not require physical-layer changes, has been deployed on a real testbed, and has been experimentally shown to generate high-quality secrets in the presence of an adversary.

We present such a solution that consists of two phases: In the first phase, the terminals transmit packets following a special pattern, such that Eve learns very little about a given fraction of the transmitted packets; this is achieved through a combination of beamforming (from many different sources) and wiretap codes. In the second phase, the terminals participate in a protocol that reshuffles the information known to each terminal, such that the terminals end up sharing a secret that Eve knows very little about; this is achieved through a combination of public feedback, broadcasting, and network coding.

We evaluate our system on a small testbed of 5 WARP nodes, 4 of them playing the role of the terminals and one of them playing the role of the eavesdropper Eve. We show that, for a variety of node placements (all the placements we tried), the terminals agree on thousands of new secret bits per second. We verify that these bits are perfectly secret (Eve obtains no information about them) by measuring the mutual information between the signal that reaches Eve's antenna and the signals that reach the antennas of the terminals. In other words, we ensure that Eve cannot learn anything about the shared secrets, even if she has access to corrupted packets that get discarded by the lower layers of her device.

# 2. SETUP AND OVERVIEW

In this section, we state the input and output of our system (Section 2.1), our adversary model (Sections 2.2 and 2.3), the basic elements of our approach (Section 2.4), and its limitations (Section 2.5).

## 2.1 Goal

We consider $n$ wireless nodes, $T_0, \ldots, T_{n-1}$, connected to the same broadcast channel; we will refer to these nodes as *terminals*; sometimes we will refer to terminals $T_0$, $T_1$, and $T_2$ respectively as Alice, Bob, and Calvin. We also consider an adversary node, Eve, connected to the same broadcast channel as the terminals.

The terminals can communicate with each other in two ways: (1) When we say that terminal $T_i$ *transmits* a packet, we mean that it broadcasts the packet once. (2) When we say that terminal $T_i$ *reliably broadcasts* a packet, we mean that it ensures that all other terminals $T_i$ receive it, e.g., through acknowledgments and retransmissions. To be conservative, we assume that Eve receives all reliably broadcast packets.

We design a system that enables the $n$ terminals to create a shared secret $\mathcal{S}$, in a way that Eve obtains very little information on $\mathcal{S}$. We will make no assumptions about Eve's computational capabilities, but we will make assumptions about her network presence. The input to our system is: (a) the physical locations of the terminals and certain properties of the terminals' hardware, in particular, the shape of their primary antenna lobe and the SNR range of a receiver located inside and outside the primary lobe; (b) an assumption about Eve's hardware, in particular, the minimum noise experienced by Eve's receiver relative to the noise experienced by the terminals' receivers.

## 2.2 Adversary Capabilities

The rate at which the terminals can agree on new secret bits depends on their physical locations and hardware, as well as Eve's physical location and hardware. Since we cannot know where Eve is or what kind of hardware she has, we design our system to be configurable for different adversaries. In other words, the terminals need to change the parameters of the system depending on how strong an adversary they want to be secure against. Intuitively, the stronger the adversary, the lower the rate at which the terminals can agree on new secret bits.

As mentioned above, our system takes as input certain properties of the terminals' hardware and an assumption about Eve's hardware. Based on that, it estimates: (a) what is the maximum rate at which the terminals can create new shared secret bits; (b) what is the minimum physical distance $\delta$ between any terminal and Eve for which the system is secure (i.e., Eve knows very little about the created shared secret). To be conservative, the terminals can (and should) configure for the case where Eve has a better receiver than they do. For example, a group of terminals may configure the system to be secure as long as Eve's receiver experiences at least a quarter of the noise experienced by any terminal's receiver; the system may estimate that, given this noise ratio and the terminals' hardware, the terminals can create up to 10 secret Kbps, as long as Eve is located, say, 3 m from any terminal.

We assume that Eve has access to all the layers of her device, including the physical-layer signal that reaches her receiver. So, when Eve tries to reconstruct the terminals' communication (in order to guess the secret $\mathcal{S}$), we assume that she can exploit all the data that reaches her, including data with errors that may get dropped by the higher layers of her communication device.

## 2.3 Adversary Behavior

When we say that Eve is "passive," we mean that she does not perform any transmissions, she only processes the traffic she overhears from the terminals.

When we say that Eve is "active," we mean that, on top of processing the traffic she overhears from the terminals, she transmits her own traffic. The goal of Eve's transmissions may be (1) to jam the wireless channels to prevent secret agreement from occurring in the first place, or (2) to impersonate a terminal (e.g., pretend to Bob that she is Alice).

| Attack type | Outcome | Extra mechanism |
|---|---|---|
| Passive | completes | – |
| Jamming | aborts | – |
| Impersonation | completes | bootstrap auth. |

**Table 1: Outcome of our system under attack.**

Table 1 summarizes what our system is meant to do in each case, and whether it needs any extra mechanism to do it (on top of what we describe in this paper).

In case of a passive attack, secret agreement should complete successfully. This should not require any extra knowledge or mechanism, in particular, the terminals do not need to share any bootstrap information to start the agreement. This is the main scenario that drives our design.

Our current design does not handle jamming attacks, in the sense that the terminals abort their secret agreement when they cannot establish among them communication channels of sufficient quality. At this stage of the work, we consider it acceptable that the terminals realize that they cannot agree on a secret and abort (as opposed to agreeing on a secret that is compromised by Eve).

In case of an impersonation attack, secret agreement should complete successfully, with the help of a bootstrap authentication mechanism. Once the terminals have agreed on a secret $\mathcal{S}$ using our system, they can use part of $\mathcal{S}$ to form authentication codes and authenticate each other (during subsequent uses of the system). The first time they use the system, however, they need to rely on some external authentication mechanism. For example, the terminals may share an initial secret $\sigma$ (much smaller than $\mathcal{S}$) and use it to form initial authentication codes. This is fundamentally unavoidable: the very first time Alice sends packets to Bob, she must have a way to prove that it is she (not Eve) sending the packets.

One may ask: if the terminals need to already share an initial secret $\sigma$ (to authenticate each other when they first use our system), why would they use our system at all? The answer is that our system enables the terminals to continuously create new secrets that are completely independent from $\sigma$ (and from each other), without using any out-of-band channel. So, even if the adversary at some point cracks $\sigma$, that will not give her any information on the secrets created with our system. Hence, as long as our system works as it is supposed to, the only way an adversary can compromise it is to crack $\sigma$, cancel out a terminal's transmissions, impersonate that terminal, and participate in secret agreement, *while the terminals are using our system for the first time*, i.e., before they have agreed on their first secret $\mathcal{S}$.

## 2.4 Approach

The insight we use from information theory is that, when Alice transmits, it is possible for Alice and Bob to agree on a secret, as long as Eve does not receive exactly the same information as Bob.

Our system then consists of two phases: in the first phase, the terminals exchange random packets using a special pattern, which ensures that Eve misses some fraction of the exchanged packets; in the second phase, the terminals participate in a polynomial-time protocol, which enables them to agree on a common secret $\mathcal{S}$. We would like to emphasize two points: First, we do not need to know or control which packets exactly Eve misses, it is sufficient to know that she has missed *some fraction* of the packets exchanged by the terminals in phase 1. Second, we do not assume the existence of natural erasure channels: when a terminal transmits a frame, Eve may receive only a part of that frame correctly and still extract useful information from it. This is why we use a special transmission pattern in phase 1—to ensure that, despite receiving partial frames, Eve will still completely miss some fraction of the packets exchanged by the terminals.

We now outline each phase:

First, we create channel variability, i.e., ensure that no two nodes (including Eve and any terminal) hear exactly the same information. To achieve this, in phase 1, the terminals take turns in transmitting random packets while beamforming and rotating their beams. Beamforming enables a transmitter to concentrate its power along a narrow beam, such that receivers within the beam receive a significantly stronger signal than those outside; rotating the beam keeps changing the sets of receivers that are in and out of the beam. Hence, by having the terminals take turns in beamforming while rotating, we ensure that no two nodes hear all transmissions with the same signal strength.

Next, we turn channel variability into packet erasures, i.e., ensure that any node (including Eve) completely misses some fraction of the transmitted packets. To achieve this, when the terminals transmit in phase 1, they use wiretap codes [18]. These create artificial erasure channels at the cost of extra bandwidth: they augment the packets generated by the terminals with redundant information, enough to ensure that any receiver with a signal-to-noise ratio (SNR) below a given threshold can extract zero information about any transmitted packet.

So, at the end of phase 1, the terminals share (know the contents of) some packets, while Eve has missed (knows nothing about the contents of) some fraction of these packets; the terminals know a lower bound of how many packets Eve has missed, but not which ones. This lower bound is computed based on the input to our system (the terminals' hardware properties and the assumptions about Eve's hardware properties).

In phase 2, the terminals agree on a common secret $\mathcal{S}$. To achieve this, they mostly perform simple linear combinations of the packets they share at the end of phase 1. For example, suppose we have $n = 2$ terminals, Alice and Bob; at the end of phase 1, Alice and Bob share 3 packets, $x_1$, $x_2$ and $x_3$, while Eve has missed two of these packets, $x_1$ and $x_2$. If Alice and Bob know that Eve misses two of their shared packets (but not which two), they can create a shared secret that Eve knows nothing about, by concatenating two linear combinations of their shared packets, e.g., $\langle x_1 \oplus x_2, x_2 \oplus x_3 \rangle$ (where $\oplus$ denotes the bit-wise XOR operation over the payloads of the corresponding packets). The actual protocol is more sophisticated, as it must ensure that Eve cannot guess $\mathcal{S}$ no matter which particular packets she has missed, and it must scale well with the number of terminals.

The size of the resulting common secret $\mathcal{S}$ depends on the smallest number of packets shared by any terminal pair and missed by Eve at the end of phase 1. For instance, in the above example, Eve misses 2 of the packets shared by Alice and Bob; hence, the secret $\mathcal{S}$ should have at most the size of 2 packets. If the terminals created a bigger secret, then Eve would be able to guess something about it. So, our protocol is secure, as long as we can lower-bound the number of packets missed by Eve in phase 1. We can obtain such a lower bound thanks to the combination of beamforming and wiretap codes.

## 2.5 Limitations

We have not considered yet the case where Eve has multiple receivers. Our current system takes as input the assumed level of noise at Eve's receiver; to deal with a multi-receiver Eve, it should also take as input the assumed number of receivers $R$ that Eve controls. We currently upper-bound the amount of information that Eve overhears in phase 1, by assuming that she is located in the worst possible position, e.g., in the middle of all the terminals (Section 4); to deal with a multi-receiver Eve, we would have to be more conservative, i.e., assume that Eve's $R$ receivers are located in the worst possible $R$ positions with respect to the terminals. The next question that we want to answer is how many receivers $R$ Eve must control in order to make the creation of a secret between $n$ terminals impossible.

We have experimented only with the simplest wiretap codes (two-layer codes). However, we have observed evidence that using more sophisticated wiretap codes (with more than two layers) would significantly improve the performance of our system.

Our experimental evaluation is only a first step, and we need to improve it in at least three ways:

(a) The performance of our system depends on the SNR range of a receiver located inside and outside the transmitter's primary lobe (Section 4). We need to study how sensitive these SNR ranges are to the particular environment (e.g., indoors versus outdoors, node hardware, antenna specifications) and make our system robust to environmental differences. So far, we have experimented only with one environment (outdoors, WARP wireless nodes [3], and flat-panel directional antennas [1]).

(b) The performance of our system also depends on the shape of the terminals' beam (Section 4). The antennas we are currently using have relatively poor directionality (the primary lobe opens at a 40 degree angle), which imposes a minimum physical distance of 3 meters between any terminal and Eve. We need to experiment with higher-quality antennas that can focus their beams at a smaller angle, so that we decrease this minimum physical distance to less than 1 meter.

(c) Our system relies on properties of simple wiretap codes (with two layers). We still need to experimentally validate practical implementations of such codes.

# 3. SECRET AGREEMENT

In this section, we describe phase 2, i.e., our secret-agreement protocol: the input it expects from phase 1 (Section 3.1), its two algorithms (Sections 3.2 and 3.3), and its main properties (§3.4).

At a high level: Alice first agrees on a pairwise secret $\mathcal{S}_i$ with each terminal $T_i$, such that Eve knows nothing about $\mathcal{S}_i$. Once Alice has created a pairwise secret with each terminal, she could use these pairwise secrets to communicate a group secret to all the terminals. Perhaps counter-intuitively, there exists a significantly more efficient way to agree on a group secret: Alice reliably broadcasts certain carefully chosen information, which does not increase the amount of secret information shared by Alice and each terminal, but "redistributes" it, such that all terminals share the same group secret $\mathcal{S}$.

## 3.1 Input

At the end of phase 1, the terminals have transmitted some number of packets (we will call them *$x$-packets*). Each terminal, as well as Eve, has received and knows the contents of some fraction of these $x$-packets.

The input to the secret-agreement protocol consists of:

- The identities of the $x$-packets known to each terminal.
- A lower bound on the number of $x$-packets shared by each pair of terminals and missed by Eve.
- A lower bound on the number of $x$-packets shared by at least two terminals and missed by Eve.

Obtaining this input is the topic of the next section.

## 3.2 Pairwise-Secret Algorithm

The terminals take turns playing the role of Alice and running the following algorithm:

1. Alice constructs linear combinations of the $x$-packets that she knows (we will call them *$y$-packets*), using a well-defined construction (see Appendix, Section 8.2). These $y$-packets satisfy two constraints:

   (a) Their total number is $M$.

   (b) $M_i$ of them are linear combinations of the $x$-packets that Alice shares with terminal $T_i$.

   Alice reliably broadcasts the identities of the $x$-packets she used to create each $y$-packet.

2. Each terminal $T_i$ (other than Alice) reconstructs the contents of $M_i$ $y$-packets.

At this point, Alice and terminal $T_i$ share $M_i$ $y$-packets. The pairwise secret $\mathcal{S}_i$ is their concatenation.

For example, suppose we have $n = 2$ terminals, Alice and Bob. At the end of phase 1, Alice and Bob share $x$-packets $x_1, x_2, x_3, x_4, x_5$, of which Eve knows $x_1, x_2, x_3$. The pairwise-secret algorithm works as follows: In step 1, Alice constructs $M_1 = 2$ $y$-packets that are linear combinations of the $x$-packets shared with Bob: $y_1 = x_1 \oplus x_3 \oplus x_5$ and $y_2 = x_2 \oplus x_4$. Then, Alice reliably broadcasts the identities of the $x$-packets she used to construct the $y$-packets, but not their contents. In step 2, Bob uses this information to reconstruct the contents of the $y$-packets. Eve overhears Alice's reliable broadcast, but she cannot reconstruct the contents of either $y_1$ or $y_2$, because she does not know the contents of $x_4$ or $x_5$. At this point, Alice and Bob have agreed on pairwise secret $\langle y_1, y_2 \rangle$, and Eve knows nothing about it.

It is important that Alice construct the $y$-packets using a particular construction, because not any linear combinations of $x$-packets will do. The $y$-packets that we use above happen to work for the particular example, but our protocol does not really construct so simple linear combinations, as they may leak information to Eve. For instance, suppose Alice constructed the $y$-packets as follows: $y'_1 = x_1 \oplus x_2 \oplus x_3$ and $y'_2 = x_4 \oplus x_5$. In this case, Eve would be able to reconstruct $y'_1$, hence recover half of the pairwise secret.

In this example, Eve knows nothing about the pairwise secret $\langle y_1, y_2 \rangle$, because it consists of 2 linear combinations of the $x$-packets, which is exactly the number of $x$-packets shared by Alice and Bob and missed by Eve at the end of phase 1. So, to create a perfect pairwise secret with terminal $T_i$, Alice needs to know a lower bound on the number of $x$-packets shared with $T_i$ and missed by Eve, and she must set $M_i$ (the size of the pairwise secret) to this value.

## 3.3 Group-Secret Algorithm

Next, the terminals take turns playing Alice and running a second algorithm. We first present a simplified version of it:

1. Alice constructs $M - \min\{M_1, M_2, \ldots M_{n-1}\}$ linear combinations of the $y$-packets (we will call them *$z$-packets*), using a well-defined construction (see appendix 8.2). She reliably broadcasts both the contents of each $z$-packet and the identities of the $y$-packets used to construct each $z$-packet.

2. Each terminal $T_i$ reconstructs the $(M - M_i)$ $y$-packets it is missing by combining any of the $(M - M_i)$ $z$-packets with the $M_i$ $y$-packets it reconstructed in step 2 of the pairwise algorithm.

3. Alice constructs $L = \min\{M_1, M_2, \ldots M_{n-1}\}$ linear combinations of the $y$-packets (we will call them *s-packets*), using a well-defined construction (see appendix 8.2). She reliably broadcasts the identities of the $y$-packets that she used to create each $s$-packet.

4. Each terminal is now able to reconstruct all the $s$-packets, because it has all the $y$-packets.

At this point, all terminals share the same set of $L$ $s$-packets. The group secret $\mathcal{S}$ is their concatenation.

For example, suppose we have three terminals, Alice, Bob, and Calvin. After running the pairwise algorithm, Alice has constructed $M = 3$ $y$-packets. Of these, she shares $M_1 = 2$ with Bob ($y_1$ and $y_2$) and $M_2 = 2$ with Calvin ($y_1$ and $y_3$). Eve knows nothing about any of the $y$-packets.

First, we reach a point where all terminals share all the $y$-packets: In step 1, Alice constructs $M - \min\{M_1, M_2\} = 1$ linear combination of the $y$-packets, $y_2 \oplus y_3$, and reliably broadcasts its contents. In step 2, each of Bob and Calvin uses this information to reconstruct the $y$-packet that he is missing. At this point, all terminals share $y_1, y_2, y_3$, while Eve knows the value of $y_2 \oplus y_3$.

Next, the terminals condense the $y$-packets into a group secret: In step 3, Alice constructs $L = \min\{M_1, M_2\} = 2$ $s$-packets that are linear combinations of the $y$-packets: $s_1 = y_1 \oplus y_2 \oplus y_3$ and $s_2 = y_1 \oplus y_2$. Then, Alice reliably broadcasts the identities of the $y$-packets she used to create the $s$-packets, but not their contents. In step 4, Bob and Calvin use this information to reconstruct the contents of the $s$-packets. Eve overhears Alice's reliable broadcast, but she cannot reconstruct the contents of $s_1$ or $s_2$, because she does not know the contents of $y_1$ or $y_2$. At this point, Alice, Bob, and Calvin have agreed on group secret $\langle s_1, s_2 \rangle$, and Eve knows nothing about it.

As with the $y$-packets, it is important that Alice construct the $z$-packets and $s$-packets using specific constructions, otherwise they may leak information to Eve.

The size $L$ of the final group secret is the size of the smallest pairwise secret ($\min M_i$). So, the group-secret algorithm does not increase the amount of secret information shared by Alice and any terminal, but it "redistributes" this information, such that all terminals share the same group secret.

What we presented above is a simplified version of the group secret algorithm: according to our description, each terminal plays the role of Alice and creates a separate group secret with the other terminals; in the actual algorithm, all the terminals together act as one "distributed Alice" and create a single group secret (see Appendix, Section 8.3).

## 3.4 Properties

Our secret-agreement protocol starts from the assumption that each terminal pair shares some $x$-packets that Eve has missed. It builds on this assumption to create, first pairwise secrets between terminal pairs, then a common group secret $\mathcal{S}$ among all terminals.

The protocol is secure, in the sense that Eve knows nothing about the group secret $\mathcal{S}$ (or the pairwise secrets), as long as the input to the protocol (the lower bounds on what Eve knows) are correct.

Equivalently, to ensure that Eve knows nothing about the group and pairwise secrets, we need to restrict their sizes: The size of each pairwise secret $\mathcal{S}_i$ must be no more than the number of $x$-packets $M_i$ shared by Alice and $T_i$ and missed by Eve at the end of phase 1. The group secret $\mathcal{S}$ must be no bigger than the smallest pairwise secret $\mathcal{S}_i$. So, the security of the protocol depends on our ability to lower-bound the number of $x$-packets shared by different terminal pairs and missed by Eve at the end of phase 1.

The intuition behind the security of the protocol is the following: If Alice and Bob share $N$ packets, of which Eve misses $M$ (but we do not know which ones), Alice and Bob can create exactly $M$ linear combinations of their $N$ shared packets that are perfectly secret from Eve. This is always the case, as long as $N$ is above a given threshold.

A practical question is how to pick linear combinations that are guaranteed to be unknown to Eve and linearly independent, no matter which particular $M$ packets she has missed; we do so with the help of Maximum Distance Separable (MDS) codes. MDS codes (which were created for entirely different purposes) have a convenient property: any $M$ columns of the $M \times N$ generator matrix of an $[N, M, N - M + 1]$ MDS code are linearly independent. Thus, if we use this generation matrix to create $M$ linear combinations of $N$ unknowns, and then set to zero any $N - M$ of these unknowns (i.e. remove them from the equations because Eve knows them), the $M$ equations (of the remaining $M$ unknowns) are still linearly independent.

The complexity of the protocol is polynomial in the size of the secret and comes mainly from the encoding operations that Alice has to perform. We note that there exist efficient implementations, and similar-complexity encoding operations are often performed by wireless systems today.

# 4. CREATING ERASURE CHANNELS

In this section, we describe phase 1, i.e., how the terminals create erasure channels between themselves and Eve (Section 4.1), and how they estimate the input needed for the next phase (Section 4.2).

At a high level: The terminals take turns in transmitting random packets while beamforming and rotating their beams. When they are done, they exchange information on which packets each of them received correctly, and they estimate conservative lower bounds on the number of packets missed by Eve (the input to phase 2).

## 4.1 Wiretap Coding and Beamforming

Our secret-agreement protocol assumes erasure channels between the terminals and Eve: when a terminal transmits, Eve either receives a packet correctly or not at all. This assumption is fundamental to the correctness of the protocol (if it does not hold, Eve may collect significant information about the secret).

Since erasure channels do not occur naturally, the terminals use two-layer wiretap codes to emulate them: Such a code is characterized by two parameters, $SNR_1$ and $SNR_2$. When Alice transmits using such a code, it is guaranteed that Bob will receive all her packets correctly, while Eve will receive zero information about any of them, as long as Bob hears Alice with SNR above $SNR_1$ and Eve hears Alice with SNR below $SNR_2$. Hence, as long as there is a sufficient gap between Bob's and Eve's SNRs, the wiretap code ensures that Bob will receive everything and Eve will receive nothing. In this sense, wiretap coding translates SNR differences into erasures (for a brief background on wiretap codes, please see Appendix, Section 8.1).

Our main idea is the following: Provided that Alice, Bob and Eve are physically separated by some minimum distance, when Alice transmits, as she rotates her beam, there will exist some time interval during which Bob will be inside Alice's primary lobe, while Eve will be outside (unless Alice, Bob, and Eve are located on a single line). Suppose we could guarantee that, during this time interval, Bob hears Alice with SNR above $SNR_1$, while Eve hears Alice with SNR below $SNR_2$. Then, we could also guarantee that Bob will receive correctly all the packets transmitted by Alice during this time interval, while Eve will receive zero information about any of them. To achieve this, we need to set $SNR_1$ to the minimum

SNR that Bob may experience when he is inside Alice's primary lobe and $SNR_2$ to the maximum SNR that Eve may experience when she is outside Alice's primary lobe (while also satisfying the minimum acceptable physical distance from Alice and Bob). In short, Alice transmits with a wiretap code such that: when Bob is inside her primary lobe and Eve outside, Bob receives everything and Eve nothing.

One challenge here is how to practically estimate the two thresholds, $SNR_1$ and $SNR_2$. Fortunately, we do not need to be accurate, merely conservative. One approach is to use the specifications of the terminals' antennas and plug them into an analytical model, e.g., the Friis equation, augmented with a factor that takes into account the nature of the environment, e.g., indoors versus outdoors, presence of multi-path, etc. Another approach is to rely on calibration: before starting phase 1, the terminals perform measurements in the specific environment where they plan to create a shared secret, in order to assess the behavior of their antennas and receivers within this environment. This calibration needs to happen only once for each specific environment. Since this is the approach we take in our experimental evaluation, we describe it next in more detail.

We set $SNR_1$ to the minimum SNR value experienced during calibration by any receiving terminal when it is located inside the transmitter's primary lobe. Our rationale is that, whenever a receiving terminal is inside the transmitter's primary lobe, we want the receiver to correctly decode all transmissions. The worst-case scenario related to $SNR_1$ is that, during phase 1, Bob experiences SNR below $SNR_1$, even though he is located inside Alice's primary lobe (e.g., because he is located too far from her, or there is an obstacle between them). In this case, Bob will not be able to decode Alice's transmissions, which will reduce the size of the final group secret created in phase 2. This does not affect the security of our system (Eve still knows very little about the created group secret), but, if it happened often, it would reduce the system's efficiency.

$SNR_2$ is meant to capture the best SNR that Eve may experience when she is located (a) at the minimum physical distance $\delta$ from the transmitter, but (b) still outside the transmitter's primary lobe. One approach would be to set $SNR_2$ to the maximum SNR value experienced during calibration by any receiving terminal that satisfies (a) and (b). In our experimental evaluation, we take a more conservative approach: we put a node (playing the role of Eve) in the best possible location where Eve can position herself while still satisfying (a) and (b), we let the terminals take turns transmitting, and we set $SNR_2$ to the average SNR experienced by our fictitious Eve. For instance, in our testbed (Figure 1), we place our $n = 4$ terminals at the corners of a rectangle and the fictitious Eve right in the middle, because, to the best of our current understanding, given this environment and this number of terminals, this is the best location where Eve can position herself to overhear the terminals' transmissions (she is on a perfect line with two terminal pairs).

To account for the scenario where Eve has better hardware than our terminals, we increase $SNR_2$ by multiplying it by a factor of $\frac{\nu_T}{\nu_E}$, where $\nu_T$ and $\nu_E$ denote the thermal noise power at a terminal's and Eve's receiver. For instance, $\frac{\nu_T}{\nu_E} = 2$ configures the system to be secure in the scenario where Eve's receiver introduces half the thermal noise introduced by any terminal's receiver.

## 4.2 Estimating Eve's uncertainty

At the end of phase 1, we lower-bound the amount of information that Eve has missed. More specifically, of all the transmitted packets that have been correctly received by at least one terminal, we lower-bound the number missed by Eve. For this, we rely on geometry and the same rationale that we used to estimate $SNR_2$: We assume that, when a terminal transmits, those inside the primary lobe receive everything while those outside receive nothing. We also assume that Eve has positioned herself in the best possible location to overhear the terminals' transmissions.

We illustrate with an example: Suppose we have $n = 4$ terminals, not positioned on a single line (as illustrated in Figure 1), all of them within each other's transmit range. When a transmitting terminal has positioned its beam such that one other terminal is inside the primary lobe and Eve is outside, we call this a "useful" beam position (because it allows the transmitting and receiving terminals to create secrecy). In our particular example, when a terminal transmits, there are at least two useful beam positions: the transmitting terminal will point its beam once at each of the 3 other terminals, and Eve can be inside the primary lobe in at most one of these beam positions. Hence, of all the packets transmitted by a terminal in phase 1, at least those transmitted during 2 beam positions are received by one other terminal and not Eve. Of course, we do not know which two these beam positions are (because we do not know Eve's location). And this is precisely why we need a secret-agreement protocol like the one described in Section 3, which only needs as input a lower bound on the number of packets missed by Eve, not which particular packets she missed.

The geometric approach that we use requires at least $n = 3$ terminals, not all positioned on a single line and within each other's transmit range. Otherwise, our system conservatively creates no group secret, because it is always possible for Eve to position herself so as to prevent one of the terminals from creating any secrecy with the rest.

# 5. EVALUATION

In this section, we evaluate our system in terms of the quality of the secrets it generates (how much Eve knows about them) and the rate at which it generates new secrets. We first describe our testbed (Section 5.1) and metrics (Section 5.2), then present our experimental results (Section 5.3).

## 5.1 Testbed

Our testbed consists of 5 WARP nodes [3], deployed as depicted in Figure 1, on a $7 \times 7$ m$^2$ open terrace. Each node transmits through a flat-panel directional antenna [1] with a 40-degree primary-lobe angle. The transmission power is $-19$ dBm and the transmission rate 1 Mbps. In each experiment, one node plays the role of Eve and $n = 4$ nodes play the role of the terminals that use our system to continuously create new secrets. In phase 1, all the terminals take turns in transmitting, and in phase 2 these transmissions are used to create a shared group secret. Each experiment corresponds to specific physical locations for the terminals and Eve, and it yields a stream of new secrets agreed on by the terminals.

We selected this particular placement of the nodes, because it allows us to experiment with an adversarial scenario: when the role of Eve is played by the node located in the middle. We call this adversarial for three reasons: (a) Eve is located at 3 m from any terminal, which is closer than any pair of terminals are located to each other. (b) Whenever one terminal points at another, Eve is positioned close to the peak of the main secondary lobe of the transmitter's antenna. This results in the maximum SNR that we measured in this environment for a node positioned outside the transmitter's primary lobe. (c) Eve is positioned on the lines that connect two pairs of terminals (hence prevents them from creating pairwise secrets in phase 1). This results in the maximum fraction of packets overheard by Eve that we measured in this environment. We do not have a proof that this is the worst node placement for our system given this environment, $n = 4$ terminals, and a minimum distance

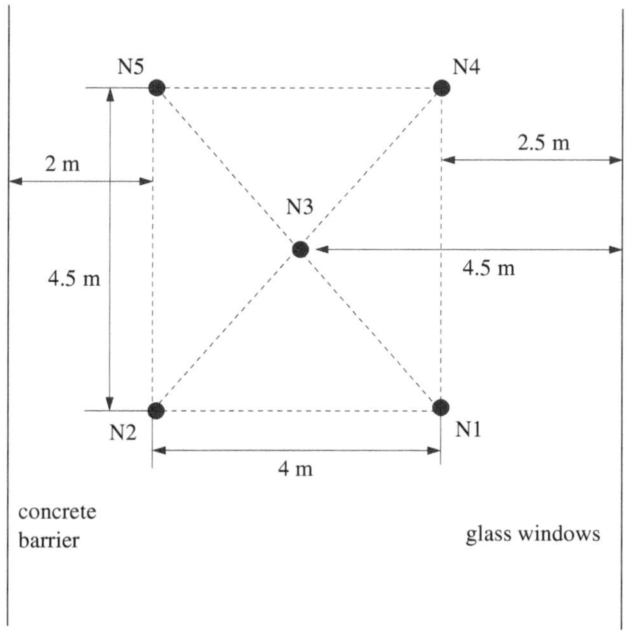


**Figure 1: Our testbed: 5 nodes (4 terminals and 1 Eve). The identity of the node that plays the role of Eve changes with each experiment.**

of $\delta = 3$ m between any terminal and Eve; but it is the worst that we were able to observe.

This testbed has the following characteristics:

(a) The minimum physical distance between the terminals and Eve is $\delta = 3$ m, which is determined by the shape of the transmitting antenna beam. If Eve can be closer than 3 m to a terminal, she manages to be inside its transmitter primary lobe all the time, and the system is not secure any more.

(b) The maximum physical distance at which the terminals can communicate with each other is about 5 m. If two terminals are further away (e.g., nodes $N_1$ and $N_5$), they do not hear each other with a sufficient SNR to decode each other's packets.

(c) We conservatively assume that each transmitting terminal achieves only one useful beam position in phase 1 (Section 4.2). E.g., consider the case where the role of Eve is played by node $N_3$: Node $N_1$ exchanges packets with $N_2$ and $N_4$ ($N_5$ is too far and cannot decode $N_1$'s packets). Since Eve's location is not known to the terminals, the system assumes that she may be located either between $N_1$ and $N_2$ or between $N_1$ and $N_4$. Hence, it conservatively assumes that Eve overheard half of the packets transmitted by $N_1$ and received by any other terminal.

## 5.2 Metrics

We consider the following metrics:

- *Reliability* represents how much Eve knows about the secret stream. Reliability $q$ means that Eve can correctly guess each secret bit with probability $2^{-q}$. The maximum reliability is 1, which means that Eve can correctly guess each secret bit with probability 0.5, i.e., knows nothing about the secret stream.
- *Efficiency* is the number of secret bits agreed on by the terminals, divided by the total number of bits transmitted by the terminals. By definition, efficiency has to be below 1 (otherwise, every bit transmitted by the terminals would automatically become a secret bit, which is infeasible).
- *Secrecy rate* is the rate at which the terminals agree on new secrets (in bits per second). This does not provide any extra information over efficiency (it is equal to efficiency times the transmission rate of the terminals). We report it only because we find "1 secret Kbps" a more intuitive piece of information than "efficiency 0.001."

We consider two variations of our system:

- *Sequential beamforming*: In phase 1, each terminal transmits in beam positions that differ by 20 degrees from each other (half the angle of the primary lobe). The reason we rotate by half the primary-lobe angle (as opposed to the exact angle) is to ensure that each receiving terminal will be located close to the vertical center of the transmitter's primary lobe in at least one beam position. We use enough beam positions to cover the area of the testbed, and each terminal transmits the same number of packets from each beam position.
- *Selective beamforming*: This is like sequential beamforming, with the difference that, in phase 1, a terminal transmits only when pointing its beam at a receiving terminal, which requires that the terminals know each other's exact position. This variation is designed to achieve better efficiency (avoid useless transmissions) in sparse topologies, where most beam positions are useless, in the sense that they do not point to any receiving terminal.

We compare our system against two non-implementable alternatives, where an oracle helps us configure our system and/or determine Eve's uncertainty:

- *Oracle-Erasures*: This alternative helps us evaluate how well we lower-bound the number of packets missed by Eve in phase 1: it works like our system, with the difference that an oracle tells us the correct number of packets missed by Eve in phase 1. I.e., this alternative achieves perfect reliability and the maximum possible efficiency that can be achieved using our beamforming and wiretap coding with the given $SNR_1$ and $SNR_2$ thresholds, and our secret-agreement protocol.
- *Oracle*: This alternative helps us evaluate how well we choose our $SNR_1$ and $SNR_2$ thresholds: it works like Oracle-Erasures, with the difference that an oracle tells us the SNR thresholds that—given the traffic exchanged during phase 1—will lead to perfect reliability and the maximum possible efficiency. I.e., this alternative achieves perfect reliability and the maximum possible efficiency that can be achieved using our beamforming and wiretap coding, and our secret-agreement protocol.

## 5.3 Results

In all experiments, we achieve perfect reliability. This is because we conservatively lower-bound the number of packets missed by Eve in phase 1. However, the more conservative we are in picking this lower bound, the smaller the size of the secret that we create given a certain number of terminal transmissions. So, the question is: how much does our conservatism cost us in terms of efficiency and secrecy rate?

We show the efficiency and secrecy rate achieved by our system and the oracle alternatives, with sequential and selective beamforming, in Figures 2 and 3, respectively. The $x$-axis corresponds to the identity of the node playing the role of Eve. We make three observations:

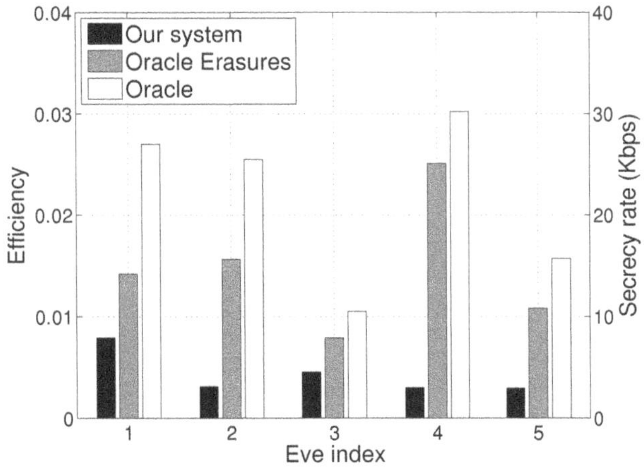


**Figure 2: Efficiency with sequential beamforming.**

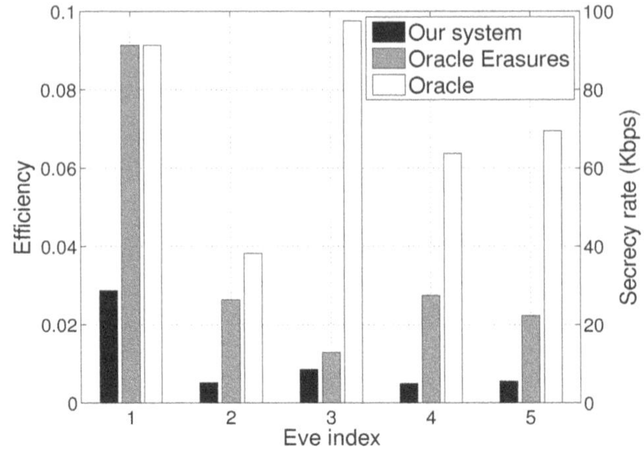


**Figure 3: Efficiency with selective beamforming.**

First, in all experiments, our system achieves a secrecy rate of several Kbps. As expected, Oracle is more efficient than Oracle-Erasures, which is more efficient than our system. This is because Oracle-Erasures knows exactly which packets Eve has successfully decoded, hence it does not need to conservatively lower-bound this number. Oracle, moreover, knows exactly which packets the terminals and Eve will successfully decode, hence it does not need to conservatively choose the SNR thresholds for the wiretap code. The gap between the efficiency achieved by these alternatives and our system shows the price we pay for being conservative.

Second, when we use sequential beamforming (Figure 2), the efficiency gap between our system and the oracle alternatives is smallest when Eve is the node in the middle. This is not surprising, given that we chose the SNR thresholds for our wiretap code based on this scenario. It illustrates why we cannot achieve high efficiency for all possible positions of Eve: if we want to account for the adversarial scenario (where Eve is in the middle), we necessarily become inefficient in the friendlier scenarios (where Eve is further away from the terminals).

Third, selective beamforming (Figure 2) can significantly improve the efficiency of our system, up to 20 secret Kbps. This is not surprising, given that it reduces useless transmissions. At the same time, selective beamforming increases the efficiency gap between our system and the Oracle alternative. This is due to the fact that Oracle chooses the SNR thresholds for its wiretap code based on a-priori knowledge of who will receive what and when; if we also allow it to leverage this knowledge to altogether avoid useless transmissions (which is what selective beamforming enables), it can pick even better SNR thresholds.

# 6. RELATED WORK

Wyner introduced the wire-tap channel, where Alice transmits information to Bob, and a "wiretapper" Eve receives a noisy version of what Bob receives; he showed that Alice and Bob can achieve non-zero secrecy rate when the Alice/Bob channel is better than the Alice/Eve channel [30]. Maurer extended the wire-tap channel with public discussion; he provided lower and upper bounds for the secrecy rate from Alice to Bob and showed that it can be non-zero even when the Alice/Bob channel is worse than the Alice/Eve channel [21]. This work proved the theoretical feasibility of perfect pairwise secrets (assuming Alice is connected to Eve through an idealized channel). This triggered a significant body of theoretical work [22, 23, 29, 24, 25, 26, 16], which also addressed the scenario of multiple terminals [9].

More recently, researchers have started to propose concrete, implementable protocols for creating pairwise shared secrets in wireless networks. Some of them rely on the time-varying nature of wireless channels and the fact that Alice and Bob can measure the (time-varying) channel between them whereas Eve cannot [13, 17, 7, 32, 8]. Of these protocols, the ones that have been implemented achieve secret generation rates up to a few tens of bps (in modified 802.11 or 802.15 environments). However, they rely on channel changes to extract secret bits, hence they are better-suited for mobile environments (in static environments, they can be vulnerable to eavesdropping) [15].

Our work is more closely related to the following proposals: Alice and Bob can create pairwise shared secrets by combining and heuristically condensing the frames that are transmitted between them only once (the assumption being that these frames are less likely to have been heard by Eve than the rest) [31]. In another proposal, Alice and Bob create pairwise shared secrets by leveraging transmissions made by Alice while pointing a directional antenna at Bob (the assumption being that Eve is not located close to the line between Alice and Bob and, even if she is, she does not always have the computational capability to decode the frames that reach her receiver) [6]. These two protocols have been implemented in an 802.11 environment, but there has not been any evaluation of the reliability or efficiency of these implementations yet. In iJam, when Alice transmits, Bob jams a part of her transmission in a special way (specific to OFDM) that prevents Eve from guessing which part was jammed. Hence, Alice and Bob share common knowledge that is secret from Eve, and they use it to create a pairwise secret [12]. iJam achieves a secret-generation rate up to 18 Kbps (in a modified 802.11 environment).

Our proposal differs from the above protocols in the following ways: First, we create group secrets, whereas the above protocols are fundamentally tied to pairwise secrets. Second, we do not require (a) the existence of quick channel changes in the wireless environment, nor (b) that Eve has limited computational capabilities, nor (c) custom physical-layer operations that are specific to OFDM (or any other transmission scheme).

We build on the idea that a conservative estimate of the number of bits missed by Eve is sufficient for creating shared secrets at Kbps rates, which we first expressed in an earlier workshop paper [28]. We have improved on that work in two ways: First, that work relied on artificial noise to create a secrecy-friendly environment; the problem with artificial noise is that (a) it requires trusted infrastructure to generate it and (b) a powerful adversary may be able to cancel at least some part of it. Instead, we are now using beam-forming, performed by the terminals themselves. Second, our earlier work assumed the existence of erasure channels between the terminals and Eve, i.e., did not account for the fact that Eve may extract useful information from partially received packets. Instead, we are now using wiretap codes to enforce this condition.

# 7. CONCLUSIONS

We have presented a system that enables $n$ wireless nodes to agree on a group secret $\mathcal{S}$ in the presence of an eavesdropper Eve, such that Eve obtains very little information on $\mathcal{S}$. The novelty of the system lies in the fact that it does not make any assumptions about Eve's computational capabilities, but instead assumes that she has limited network presence. Our system is not yet ready for deployment (we have evaluated it only on one testbed, with one adversary). However, it constitutes the first experimental evidence that it is feasible for a group of wireless nodes to agree on thousands of perfectly secret bits per second, without relying on the adversary's computational limitations.

# 8. APPENDIX

## 8.1 Background: Multi-layer Wiretap Codes

A wiretap code, first introduced by Wyner in [30], enables a Bob who has a "better" channel than Eve, to receive securely information from Alice at a rate that depends on how much better his reception SNR is. More specifically, assume that the Alice-Bob and Alice-Eve channels take the fixed values $(h_B, h_E) = (h_1, h_2)$, and thus Bob and Eve experience receive SNRs $SNR_1 = \frac{|h_1|^2}{N_0}$ and $SNR2 = \frac{|h_2|^2}{N_0}$, respectively, where assumed they experience the same thermal power $N_0$. Then the two channels become simple Gaussian channels of capacity $C_B = \log_2(1 + SNR_1)$ and $C_E = \log_2(1 + SNR_2)$. Assume Bob has a "better" channel than Eve, that is, $SNR_1 > SNR_2$ and $C_B > C_E$. Alice can use a wiretap code to securely transmit a message at any rate $0 < R < C_B - C_E$ so that Bob can decode the message with an arbitrarily small probability of error while Eve is kept totally ignorant of the message. Hence, Bob receives the message essentially "perfectly" while Eve knows nothing about it, it is erased for her. The difference in the quality of the $SNR_1$ and $SNR_2$ channels, determines the rate at which we can securely send information.

This is the simplest form of a wiretap code, that is designed specifically for the values $SNR_1$, $SNR_2$, and achieves the maximum secure rate for these channels. If we do not know what these values are, we can employ a *layered* wiretap code [19, 18] that leverages the following observation. The wiretap code we designed for the channels $SNR_1$ and $SNR_2$ will still yield perfect reception for Bob and an erasure for Eve as long as $SNR_B > SNR_1$ and $SNR_E < SNR_2$. It would not achieve the optimal rate possible, as it is designed to only exploit the $SNR_1$ and $SNR_2$ difference, but it would still guarantee erasures. Thus we can think of the $SNR_1$ and $SNR_2$ as two thresholds we can impose, that enable us to get secrecy at a fixed rate whenever Bob has a channel realization better than $SNR_1$ and Eve worse than $SNR_2$. Such a code is determined by two design parameters: the values of $SNR_1$ and $SNR_2$.

To achieve rates that more closely follow the actual differences in the channel realizations of Bob and Eve, we can use instead of two, multiple layers [19, 18]. The more layers we use, we better match the difference in the Bob-Eve realizations, but the more complex the wiretap code becomes. Moreover, the more difficult it also becomes to accurately estimate the distribution of the channel realizations of Eve. Other optimizations are possible to further increase the secrecy rates, such as power allocation optimizations.

## 8.2 Linear Combinations

### *Main approach*

Our algorithms construct the $y$-packets, the $z$-packets and the $s$-packets as linear combinations of the $x$-packets. Namely, let $X$, $Y$, $Z$, $S$, be matrices that have as rows the $x$, $y$, $z$, and $s$-packets respectively, then

$$Y = A_y X, \qquad Z = A_z Y, \qquad S = A_s Y.$$

During the first phase, Eve observes some of the $x$-packets, i.e., she observes $W = A_E X$, where the matrix $A_E$ specifies which distinct $x$-packets are known to Eve. During the second phase we assume that Eve observes all the $z$-packets, i.e., the matrix $Z$. In this appendix we provide the constructions for the matrices $A_y$, $A_z$ and $A_s$, and prove that they enable information theoretical security as we described in Section 3.

To prove that our constructions are secure, we need to prove that

$$H(S|Z, W) = H(S).$$

We achieve this in steps, by constructing $y$-packets, $z$-packets and $s$-packets that have the following properties:

- The $y$-packets are constructed to be linearly independent from Eve's observations, and thus information-theoretically secure from Eve. That is, our constructions achieve

$$H(Y|W) = H(Y). \tag{1}$$

- The $z$-packets that enable reconciliation, are a function of the $y$-packets. Thus, since the $y$-packets are linearly independent from Eve's observations, so are the $z$-packets, and we have

$$H(Z|W) = H(Z). \tag{2}$$

- We construct the $s$-packets to be linearly independent from the $z$-packets, since Eve may overhear the $z$-packets during the reconciliation. Thus, we construct the $s$-packets to satisfy

$$H(S|Z) = H(S). \tag{3}$$

  Note that since the s and $z$-packets are a function of the $y$-packets, we also have

$$H(S, Z|W) = H(S, Z). \tag{4}$$

We then have

$$\begin{aligned} & H(S|Z, W) \\ & = H(S, Z|W) - H(Z|W) \\ & \overset{(a)}{=} H(S, Z) - H(Z) \\ & = H(S|Z) \\ & \overset{(b)}{=} H(S) \end{aligned} \tag{5}$$

where (a) is due to (2) and (4), and (b) is due to (3).

### *Construction of y-packets*

Alice considers each subset of terminals $\mathcal{J}$, identifies the $N^{\mathcal{J}}$ $x$-packets that were received by all the terminals in the subset but no other terminals, and creates $M^{\mathcal{J}}$ linear combinations $y_1, \ldots, y_{M^{\mathcal{J}}}$ of these packets as

$$Y = A_y X,$$

where matrix $X$ has as rows the $N^{\mathcal{J}}$ $x$-packets, matrix $Y$ has as rows the $M^{\mathcal{J}}$ $y$-packets and $A_y$ is the generator matrix of a Maximum Distance Separable (MDS) linear code with parameters $[N^{\mathcal{J}}, M^{\mathcal{J}}, N^{\mathcal{J}} - M^{\mathcal{J}} + 1]$ (*e.g.*, a Reed-Solomon code [20]). Each terminal $T_i$ in the set $\mathcal{J}$ can also reconstruct these $y$ packets. We next prove in Lemma 1 that this construction ensures that the $y$-packets are linearly independent, and Eve has no information about any of them. Alice creates in this manner in total $M = \bigcup_{\mathcal{J}} M^{\mathcal{J}}$ $y$-packets. Each terminal $T_i$ creates $M_i = \bigcup_{T_i \in \mathcal{J}} M^{\mathcal{J}}$ $y$-packets.

LEMMA 1. *Consider a set of $N$ $x$-packets, say $x_1, \ldots, x_N$, and assume Eve has a subset of size $N - M$ of the $x$-packets. Construct $M$ $y$-packets, say $y_1, \ldots, y_M$, as*

$$Y = AX,$$

*where matrix $X$ has as rows the $N$ $x$-packets, matrix $Y$ has as rows the $M$ $y$-packets, and $A$ is the generator matrix of a Maximum Distance Separable (MDS) linear code with parameters $[N, M, N - M + 1]$ (e.g., a Reed-Solomon code [20]). Then the $M$ $y$-packets are information-theoretically secure from Eve, irrespective of which subset (of size $N - M$) of the $x$-packets Eve has.*

*Proof:* ▷Let $W$ be a matrix that has as rows the packets Eve has. To prove that the $y$-packets are information-theoretically secure from Eve, we must show that:

$$H(Y|W) = H(Y).$$

▷ We can write

$$\begin{bmatrix} Y \\ W \end{bmatrix} = \begin{bmatrix} A \\ A_E \end{bmatrix} X \stackrel{def}{=} BX,$$

where $A_E$ is a $N - M \times N$ matrix of $\text{rank}(A_E) = N - M$, which specifies the $N - M$ distinct $x$-packets that are known to Eve. $A_E$ is *not known* to us, however we know is that in each row of $A_E$ there is only one 1 and the remaining elements are zero; so all of the vectors in the row span of $A_E$ have Hamming weight (the number of nonzero elements of a vector [20]) less than or equal to $N - M$. On the other hand, from properties of MDS codes, $\text{rank}(A) = N - N_E$, and any set of $M$ columns of the matrix $A_y$ are linearly independent [20]; thus the row span of $A$ and $A_E$ are disjoint (except for the zero vector) and the matrix $B$ is full-rank, i.e. $\text{rank}\,(B) = N$.

▷ If the packets $x_i$ have length $\Lambda$, we have that:

$$\begin{aligned} &H(Y|W) = H(Y, W) - H(W) = \\ &= \text{rank}\,(B)\,\Lambda - \text{rank}(A_E)\Lambda = M\Lambda \\ &= \text{rank}(A)\Lambda = H(Y). \end{aligned}$$

■

### *Construction of z-packets*

Alice constructs the $z$-packets as linear combinations of the Y packets., i.e.,

$$Z = A_z Y,$$

so that: every terminal $T_{i \neq 0}$ can combine $M - M_i$ $z$-packets with the $M_i$ $y$-packets it already has and reconstruct all the $M$ $y$-packets; choosing the $z$-packets can be done using standard network-coding techniques [11].

### *Construction of s-packets*

Alice constructs the $L$ $s$-packets using again a linear code, i.e,

$$S = A_s Y,$$

where $A_s$ is constructed using any standard basis-extension method so that

$$\text{rank}\left(\begin{bmatrix} A_s \\ A_z \end{bmatrix}\right) = M.$$

Lemma 2 shows that the $s$-packets are secure from Eve.

LEMMA 2. *Consider a set of $M$ $y$-packets, say $y_1, \ldots, y_M$, and a set of $M - L$ $z$-packets, say $z_1, \ldots, z_{M-L}$, related as*

$$Z = A_z Y,$$

*where matrix $Y$ has as rows the $M$ $y$-packets, matrix $Z$ has as rows the $M - L$ $z$-packets, and $A_z$ is a known $M - L \times M$ full rank matrix. Assume that Eve knows all the $z$-packets. Using any standard basis-extension method [14], find an $L \times M$ matrix $A_s$, with $\text{rank}\,(A_s) = L$, such that*

$$\text{rank}\left(\begin{bmatrix} A_s \\ A_z \end{bmatrix}\right) = M.$$

*Then we can construct $L$ $s$-packets, say $s_1, \ldots, s_L$, as*

$$S = A_s Y,$$

*where matrix $S$ has as rows the $s$-packets, and satisfy $H(S|Z) = H(S)$.*

*Proof:* To prove that the $s$-packets are information-theoretically secure from Eve, we need to show that $H(S|Z) = H(S)$. Similarly to the proof of Lemma 1, if the $y$-packets have length $\Lambda$, we have that:

$$H(S|Z) = H(S, Z) - H(Z) = \text{rank}\left(\begin{bmatrix} A_s \\ A_z \end{bmatrix}\right)\Lambda -$$
$$- \text{rank}\,(A_z)\,\Lambda = L\Lambda = \text{rank}\,(A_s)\,\Lambda = H(S).$$

■

## 8.3 Coded Cooperative Data Exchange

Assume we have $n$ nodes and a set of packets; each node has a subset of the packets, and is interested in collecting the ones she misses. We want to achieve this using the minimum total number of transmissions from the nodes. We can solve this problem in *polynomial time*; for completeness, we provide in the following an Integer Linear Program (ILP).

We will use the following notation:

- $\mathcal{L}$: a subset of the nodes; there exist $2^n$ such subsets.
- $\mathcal{L}^c$: set of all nodes not in $\mathcal{L}$.
- $\mathcal{P}_i^c$: set of all packets that node $i$ does not have.
- $K_i$: total number of transmissions that source $i$ makes.

$$\begin{aligned} &\min\ K_1 + K_2 + \ldots + K_n \\ &\text{subject to} \\ &\sum_{i \in \mathcal{L}} K_i \geq |\bigcap_{i \in \mathcal{L}^c} \mathcal{P}_i^c|, \quad \forall \mathcal{L}, \\ &K_i \in \mathbf{Z}^+. \end{aligned}$$

## 9. REFERENCES


[1] DataSheet for the L-com HyperLink HG2418P Antenna. http://www.l-com.com/multimedia/datasheets/DS_HG2418P.PDF.

[2] Redbow Labs. http://vimeo.com/37679492.

[3] Rice University Wireless Open-Access Research Platform (WARP). http://warp.rice.edu.

[4] Shoelace Wireless. http://www.shoelacewireless.com/.

[5] Google Survey: The On-demand Video Consumer. http://www.youtube.com/yt/advertise/research.html, 2012.

[6] Y. Abdallah, L. A. Latif, M. Yousse, A. Sultan, and H. E. Gamal. Keys through ARQ: Theory and Practice. *IEEE Transactions on Information Forensics and Security*, 6(3):737–751, 2011.

[7] B. Azimi-Sadjadi, A. Kiayias, A. Mercado, and B. Yener. Robust Key Generation from Signal Envelopes in Wireless Networks. In *Proceedings of the ACM Conference on Computer and Communications Security (CCS)*, 2007.

[8] J. Croft, N. Patwari, and S. Kasera. Robust Uncorrelated Bit Extraction Methodologies for Wireless Sensors. In *Proceedings of the ACM/IEEE International Conference on Information Processing in Sensor Networks (IPSN)*, 2010.

[9] I. Csiszar and P. Narayan. Secrecy Capacities for Multiterminal Channels. *IEEE Transactions on Information Theory*, 54(6):2437–2452, 2008.

[10] W. Diffie and M. E. Hellman. New Directions in Cryptography. *IEEE Transactions on Information Theory*, 22(6):644–654, 1976.

[11] C. Fragouli and E. Soljanin. Network Coding Fundamentals. *Foundations and Trends in Networking*, 2007.

[12] S. Gollakota and D. Katabi. Physical Layer Wireless Security Made Fast and Channel Independent. In *Proceedings of the IEEE INFOCOM Conference*, 2011.

[13] J. Hershey, A. Hassan, and R. Yarlagadda. Unconventional Cryptographic Keying Variable Management. *IEEE Transactions on Communications*, 43(1):3–6, 1995.

[14] Horn and Johnson. Matrix Analysis. *Cambridge press*, 1985.

[15] S. Jana, S. N. Premnath, M. Clark, S. Kasera, N. Patwari, and S. Krishnamurthy. On the Effectiveness of Secret Key Extraction from Wireless Signal Strength in Real Environments. In *Proceedings of the ACM MOBICOM Conference*, 2009.

[16] B. Kanukurthi and L. Reyzin. Key Agreement from Close Secrets over Unsecured Channels. In *Proceedings of the International Conference on the Theory and Application of Cryptographic Techniques (EUROCRYPT)*, 2009.

[17] H. Koorapaty, A. Hassan, and S. Chennakeshu. Secure Information Transmission for Mobile Radio. *IEEE Communications Letters*, 4:52–55, 2000.

[18] Y. Liang, L. Lai, H. Poor, and S. Shamai. A Broadcast Approach for Fading Wiretap Channels. Submitted to IEEE Transactions on Information Theory.

[19] Y. Liang, L. Lai, H. Poor, and S. Shamai. The Broadcast Approach over Fading Gaussian Wiretap Channels. In *Proceedings of the IEEE International Symposium on Information Theory (ISIT)*, 2009.

[20] F. J. Macwilliams and N. J. A. Sloane. The Theory of Error Correcting Codes. *North-Holland*, 2006.

[21] U. Maurer. Secret-Key Agreement by Public Discussion from Common Information. *IEEE Transactions on Information Theory*, 39:733–742, 1993.

[22] U. Maurer. Information-Theoretically Secure Secret-Key Agreement by NOT Authenticated Public Discussion. In *Proceedings of the International Conference on the Theory and Application of Cryptographic Techniques (EUROCRYPT)*, 1997.

[23] U. Maurer and S. Wolf. Privacy Amplification Secure Against Active Adversaries. In *Proceedings of the International Conference on Cryptology (CRYPTO)*, 1997.

[24] U. Maurer and S. Wolf. Secret Key Agreement over Unauthenticated Public Channels Part III: Privacy Amplification. *IEEE Transactions on Information Theory*, 49(4):839–851, 2003.

[25] R. Renner and S. Wolf. Unconditional Authenticity and Privacy from an Arbitrarily Weak Secret. In *Proceedings of the International Conference on Cryptology (CRYPTO)*, 2003.

[26] R. Renner and S. Wolf. The Exact Price for Unconditionally Secure Asymmetric Cryptography. In *Proceedings of the International Conference on the Theory and Application of Cryptographic Techniques (EUROCRYPT)*, 2004.

[27] R. L. Rivest, A. Shamir, and L. Adleman. A Method for Obtaining Digital Signatures and Public-key Cryptosystems. *Communications of the ACM*, 21(2):120–126, 1978.

[28] I. Safaka, C. Fragouli, K. Argyraki, and S. Diggavi. Creating Shared Secrets Out of Thin Air. In *Proceedings of the ACM Workshop on Hot Topics in Networks (HotNets)*, 2012.

[29] S. Wolf. Strong Security Against Active Attacks in Information-Theoretic Secret-Key Agreement. In *Proceedings of the International Conference on the Theory and Application of Cryptology and Information Security (ASIACRYPT)*, 1998.

[30] A. D. Wyner. The Wire-tap Channel. *Bell System Technical Journal*, 54(8):1355–1387, 1975.

[31] S. Xiao, W. Gong, and D. Towsley. Secure Wireless Communication with Dynamic Secrets. In *Proceedings of the IEEE INFOCOM Conference*, 2010.

[32] C. Ye, S. Mathur, A. Reznik, Y. Shah, W. Trappe, and N. Mandayam. Information-Theoretically Secret Key Generation for Fading Wireless Channels. *IEEE Transactions on Information Forensics and Security*, 5:240–254, 2010.

# SecureArray: Improving WiFi Security with Fine-Grained Physical-Layer Information


Jie Xiong
Department of Computer Science
University College London
United Kingdom
j.xiong@cs.ucl.ac.uk

Kyle Jamieson
Department of Computer Science
University College London
United Kingdom
k.jamieson@cs.ucl.ac.uk



## Abstract

Despite the important role that WiFi networks play in home and enterprise networks they are relatively weak from a security standpoint. With easily available directional antennas, attackers can be physically located off-site, yet compromise WiFi security protocols such as WEP, WPA, and even to some extent WPA2 through a range of exploits specific to those protocols, or simply by running dictionary and human-factors attacks on users' poorly-chosen passwords. This presents a security risk to the entire home or enterprise network. To mitigate this ongoing problem, we propose SecureArray, a system designed to operate alongside existing wireless security protocols, adding defense in depth against active attacks. SecureArray's novel signal processing techniques leverage multi-antenna access point (AP) to profile the directions at which a client's signals arrive, using this angle-of-arrival (AoA) information to construct highly sensitive signatures that with very high probability uniquely identify each client. Upon overhearing a suspicious transmission, the client and AP initiate an AoA signature-based challenge-response protocol to confirm and mitigate the threat. We also discuss how SecureArray can mitigate direct denial-of-service attacks on the latest 802.11 wireless security protocol. We have implemented SecureArray with an eight-antenna WARP hardware radio acting as the AP. Our experimental results show that in a busy office environment, SecureArray is orders of magnitude more accurate than current techniques, mitigating 100% of WiFi spoofing attack attempts while at the same time triggering false alarms on just 0.6% of legitimate traffic. Detection rate remains high when the attacker is located only five centimeters away from the legitimate client, for AP with fewer numbers of antennas and when client is mobile.



## Categories and Subject Descriptors

C.2.3 [**Computer-Communication Networks**]: Network Operations—*Network Monitoring*

## Keywords

Wireless, AoA signature, 802.11, Antenna array system, Security, SecureArray, SecureAngle




*MobiCom'13*, September 30–October 4, Miami, FL, USA.
Copyright 2013 ACM 978-1-4503-1999-7/13/09 ...$15.00.
http://dx.doi.org/10.1145/2500423.2500444.


## 1. INTRODUCTION

WiFi networks are ubiquitous, widely deployed in both the home and enterprise, and at public hotspots. However, from a security perspective, their prevalence presents a number of well-known difficulties. Once an attacker has compromised a wireless access point (AP), she may both eavesdrop on users' traffic and inject traffic into the wireless network. Security protocols such as WPA, WPA2 (802.11i), and 802.11w have been proposed in the past few years, but they have a track record of being compromised [8, 9, 13]. Moreover, once vulnerabilities are discovered, they are slow to be fixed: Bittau *et al.* [10] report that a staggering 76% of secured APs in London had still used the older WEP security protocol six years after it was known to be insecure [31, 37]. The result is a cycle between better wireless security protocols and new protocol exploits.

Another notable trend in the design of wireless APs is the increasing number of antennas, mainly to bolster capacity with multiple-input, multiple-output (MIMO) and spatial division multiplexing techniques [6, 34, 18, 36]. Both 802.11n and the recent 802.11ac exploit MIMO extensively through the use of multiple AP antennas. Our observation is that it is possible to leverage this trend to measure the physical angles-of-arrival (AoA) at which client's transmitted signals arrive at the AP. What determines this AoA information? The multipath wireless channel between client and AP, in particular the physical propagation paths that exist between client and AP at the instant the client transmits a packet.

The dynamism of the wireless channel and the multitude of propagation paths in an indoor multipath environment present an exciting opportunity: APs can leverage this AoA information to construct an *AoA signature* that is unique to each client and extremely difficult for an attacker to forge—far more difficult to forge than previously-proposed signatures based on channel impulse response [29], received signal strength [16, 33], or other properties of the transmitter. To forge a legitimate client's AoA signature, our experiments (§4) show that an attacker's antennas would need to be co-located to within under five centimeters of the legitimate client's antennas, an unlikely event. Otherwise, even with knowledge of the legitimate client's AoA information at the AP and possession of a phased antenna array, it is still fundamentally difficult for an attacker to mimic the AoA signature, as it is highly unlikely that the set of physical paths from the attacker to the AP arrive at the same bearings as those of the legitimate client.

This paper describes the *SecureArray* system, a cross-layer approach to enhance wireless security that is designed to provide defense in depth against active attacks, those in which the attacker injects a frame into the network for the purpose of compromising the network, eliciting a denial-of-service state, or even causing a protocol deadlock and extended denial-of-service. SecureArray operates alongside and strengthens the latest protocol-based wireless security measures that establish a shared secret between the AP and legitimate client. In fact, SecureArray mitigates the most pressing current 802.11 security threats: those for which strong encryption is useless, which might be for any of the following reasons:

1. The security protocol has not yet established (in the process of establishing) a shared secret between client and AP, or
2. The 802.11 specification disallows encryption for certain protocol control messages, or
3. The shared secret has been compromised by factors outside the security protocol.

Our approach is wholly within the context of the latest 802.11 security specification for creating a "robust security network", which patches some (but not all) of the holes described above. We carefully examine the operation of the security protocol and exploit, and identify instants where the attacker must inject frames within wireless channel coherence time in order to successfully compromise the protocol. This happens with surprising frequency, often because security exploits depend on software data races with a concurrent operation at the AP that a legitimate client's transmission triggers. As an extension of this approach, we also propose *DataCheck* (§2.2.2), a new, proactive protocol that triggers a transmission within a wireless coherence time from a legitimate client when it overhears suspicious activity that may indicate ongoing spoofing.

We have implemented SecureArray with an eight-antenna Rice WARP FPGA platform acting as the AP. Our exhaustive security evaluation over one floor of a busy office space tests more than 150 sets of client and attacker locations in an active office environment with operational network traffic present in the background. Experimental results in this setting show that SecureArray achieves an overall 100% attack detection rate while simultaneously keeping the false alarm rate at 0.6% in the presence of legitimate traffic, orders of magnitude more accurate than current CSI approach [24]. Our results also show that efficacy degrades very little when we reduce the number of antennas at the AP to six and four.

The contributions of this paper are threefold: First, we propose a novel AoA signature generation scheme with random perturbations (§2.1) to increase the attack detection rate. Next, we incorporate it with, to our knowledge, the first wireless security system that uses AoA to augment existing 802.11 protocol-based security. Finally, we describe a novel proactive protocol (§2.2.2) that leverages AoA signatures to block unauthorized use of a client's security credentials, even if those credentials are compromised. We also describe solutions to two known recent 802.11 vulnerabilities, one of which results in a protocol deadlock and the other of which is a known denial-of-service issue.

In the next section, we detail SecureArray's design. Section 3 is a description of our implementation and the performance evaluation (§4) follows. The related work is in Section 5 followed by a discussion section (§6), and Section 7 concludes.

## 2. DESIGN

In this section we sketch the design of SecureArray, beginning with the threat model our system targets, followed by an explanation of what an AoA signature is, and a description of our AoA signature generation and comparison schemes. Next (§2.2), we describe how we integrate our AoA signature comparison algorithm with an 802.11 robust security network, the current state-of-the-art in WiFi security. It should thus become clear how SecureArray operates in concert with a security protocol to provide defense-in-depth against penetration or denial-of-service attacks.

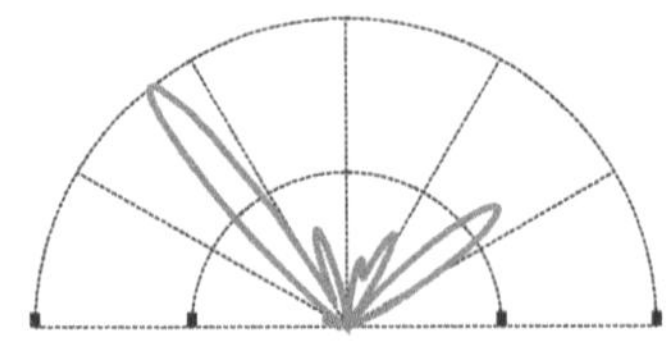


**Figure 1: The *AoA spectrum* of a client's received packet at a multi-antenna AP gives an estimate of the incoming packet's power as a function of its angle of arrival.**

The crux of SecureArray is to use the information contained within two or more AoA spectra resulting from two or more received packets to fingerprint the origin of each of those packets, testing whether a single client or multiple clients sent those packets. As we show in Section 2.2, knowledge of the underlying security protocol along with a method of comparing SecureArray's AoA signatures and bounds on the rate of change of the dynamic wireless channel can, with high probability, pinpoint a security breach.

**Threat model.** SecureArray makes no assumptions about the type of antenna that the attacker uses. In particular, the system is designed to be effective in the presence of an attacker equipped with omnidirectional antenna, directional antenna (such as the "Pringles can" antennas famously used in past high-profile WiFi security breaches [19]), or even a phased array of antennas capable of selectively beamforming and nulling transmissions to arbitrary sets of 802.11 receivers on a per-packet basis. Furthermore, our design assumes that the attacker may have breached the security protocol and may have access to the legitimate user's secret authentication credentials in the WPA2-Enterprise setup.

SecureArray offers protection only against active attacks—in particular, we do not offer any added protection against eavesdropping attacks. We do however note that in most cases to penetrate the network the attacker must transmit, and once the attacker has penetrated 802.11 protocol security, must transmit in order to send data or simply open a TCP connection.

### 2.1 AoA signatures

Our approach of computing AoA signatures is inspired by previous algorithms [30], but we propose an entirely novel signal processing technique in this paper to enhance the specificity of the AoA signature. In indoor environment, RF signals interact with objects in the environment, resulting in reflections, absorption, and diffraction. This results in multiple attenuated and summed copies of a client's transmitted signal arriving at an AP, a phenomenon known as wireless multipath propagation. An *AoA spectrum* of a client's received signals at a multi-antenna AP is an estimate of the incoming signals' power as a function of angle of arrival, as shown in Figure 1.

To convey the intuition of how SecureArray computes AoA spectra, we consider a single client transmitting near an AP with no multipath reflections. If the client is at a bearing $\theta$ to the AP as shown in Figure 2 (left), then its signal will travel an extra distance of $1/2\lambda \sin\theta$ to the second AP antenna, as compared with the first. This distance directly corresponds to a *measured baseband phase difference* $\Omega = \pi \sin\theta$ between the two signals' baseband symbol representations, as shown in the figure (right). Therefore, our estimate of the client's bearing to the AP $\hat{\theta}$ based on a measured

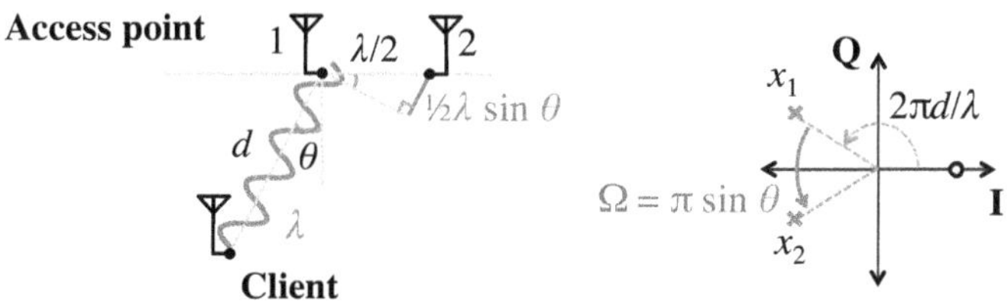


**Figure 2: Principle of SecureArray's AoA spectrum computation. *Left:* The phase of the signal goes through a $2\pi$ cycle every radio wavelength $\lambda$, and the difference in distance between the client and successive antennas on the AP is governed by the client's bearing to the access point. *Right:* The complex baseband representation of the sent signal (filled dot) and received signals at the AP (crosses) reflects this relationship.**

baseband phase difference $\Omega$ is

$$\hat{\theta} = \arcsin(\Omega/\pi). \tag{1}$$

In indoor multipath environments, Equation 1 breaks down, because multiple paths' signals sum in the I-Q plot. Prior work has shown that the above concepts generalize to compute AoA spectra using $M$ antennas in the presence of indoor multipath propagation. The best known algorithm is MUSIC [30] based on eigenstructure analysis of an $M \times M$ *array correlation matrix* $\mathbf{R_{xx}}$.

Suppose $D$ signals $s_1(t), \ldots, s_D(t)$ arrive from bearings $\theta_1, \ldots, \theta_D$ at $M$ ($M > D$) antennas. Recalling the relationship between measured phase differences and bearing discussed above, we use the *array steering vector* $\mathbf{a}(\theta)$ to characterize the phases added relative to the first antenna, as a function of the incoming signal's bearing. For a linear array:

$$\mathbf{a}(\theta) = \exp\left(\frac{-j2\pi d}{\lambda}\right) \begin{bmatrix} 1 \\ \exp(-j\pi\lambda\cos\theta) \\ \exp(-j2\pi\lambda\cos\theta) \\ \vdots \\ \exp(-j(M-1)\pi\lambda\cos\theta) \end{bmatrix} \tag{2}$$

The array correlation matrix $\mathbf{R_{xx}}$ at AP has $M$ eigenvalues associated respectively with $M$ eigenvectors $\mathbf{E} = [\mathbf{e}_1\ \mathbf{e}_2\ \cdots\ \mathbf{e}_M]$. The eigenvalues are sorted in non-decreasing order, the smallest $M - D$ eigenvalues correspond to the noise while the next $D$ eigenvalues correspond to the $D$ incoming signals. Based on this process, the corresponding eigenvectors in $\mathbf{E}$ can be classified as noise or signal:

$$\mathbf{E} = \Big[\overbrace{e_1 \ldots e_{M-D}}^{\mathbf{E}_N}\ \overbrace{e_{M-D+1} \ldots e_M}^{\mathbf{E}_S}\Big] \tag{3}$$

We refer to $\mathbf{E}_N$ as the *noise subspace* and $\mathbf{E}_S$ as the *signal subspace*. The MUSIC AoA spectrum is then computed as:

$$P(\theta) = \frac{1}{\mathbf{a}(\theta)^H \mathbf{E}_N \mathbf{E}_N^H \mathbf{a}(\theta)} \tag{4}$$

### *2.1.1 Random phase perturbation*

We note that $\hat{\theta}$ and $\Omega$ do not have a linear relationship with each other. We plot estimated client bearing in Figure 3 (upper), in units of degrees and the derivation of $\hat{\theta}$ with respect to $\Omega$ in Figure 3 (lower). Here, note that a small perturbation of $\Omega$ translates to smaller perturbations of $\hat{\theta}$ when the client is broadside to the axis of the array (*i.e.*, $\theta \approx 0$), but larger perturbations of $\hat{\theta}$ when

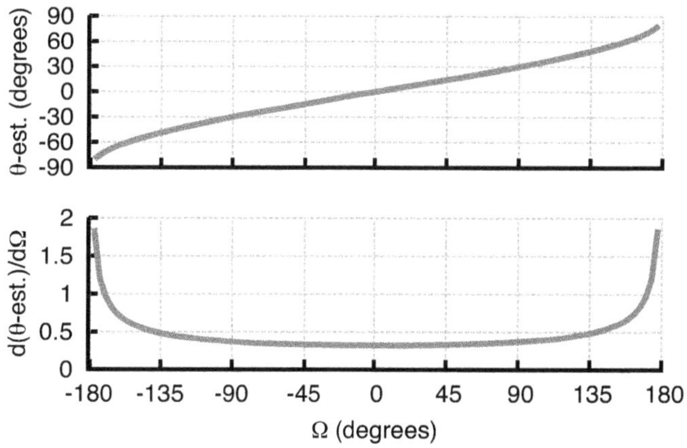


**Figure 3: *Upper:* Estimated client bearing to the AP $\hat{\theta}$ as a function of measured baseband phase difference $\Omega$, and its rate of change with respect to $\Omega$ (*lower*).**

the client is close to $\theta = \pm\pi/2$ radians (corresponding to $\Omega = \pm\pi$ radians):

$$\frac{\mathrm{d}}{\mathrm{d}\Omega}\hat{\theta} = \frac{1}{\sqrt{\pi^2 - \Omega^2}} \tag{5}$$

we see that $\mathrm{d}\hat{\theta}/\mathrm{d}\Omega$ reaches a minimum of $\pi^{-1} \approx 0.32$ when the client is broadside, and increases sharply when the client is near the array axis. The AoA computation in Equation 4 yields one AoA spectrum. But since we are trying to formulate a highly specific client signature, we wish to make the signature sensitive to slight changes at any angle. Based on the above observation of non-uniform rate of change of $\hat{\theta}$ with respect to $\Omega$, we propose a novel scheme to add a random phase offset $\zeta_2$ to $\Omega$, and compute another AoA signature. We iterate this process, adding $L - 1$ further random offsets[1], so obtaining $L$ AoA signatures $\sigma_1(\theta), \ldots, \sigma_L(\theta)$ based on $L$ random phase offsets $\zeta_1 = 0, \zeta_2, \ldots, \zeta_L$.

Note that we could have introduced a deterministic perturbation to bring the bearing $\theta$ close to $\pm\pi/2$ to make the signature most unique in order to increase the attack detection rate. However, deterministic perturbation has the following disadvantages compared with random perturbations:

1. The false alarm rate will be increased accordingly.
2. The bearings very close to $\pm\pi/2$ become unstable (sensitive to very tiny changes).
3. As there are multiple peaks on a signature, it's difficult to bring all the bearings near to $\pm\pi/2$ at the same time.

SecureArray thus employs random perturbations to spread the bearings all over the range between $-\pi/2$ and $+\pi/2$ to maintain a balance between high detection rate and low false alarm rate. The averaging process described in next section mitigates the inaccuracies caused near $\pm\pi/2$ radians and also reduces the possibility of similar peaks in coincidence.

We demonstrate how random perturbation works with Figure 4. Figure 4 (upper) shows the effect of random perturbation on two frames transmitted 100 milliseconds apart, from a legitimate client and an attacker placed five centimeter away. The signatures are similar (but not identical) under one random phase perturbation, with a rather high similarity metric $\mathcal{M} = 0.79$ (§2.1.2), but the other random phase perturbation produces relatively different sig-

[1]For more than two antennas, each offset here is an offset vector with size $M - 1$ while $M$ is the number of antennas at each AP.

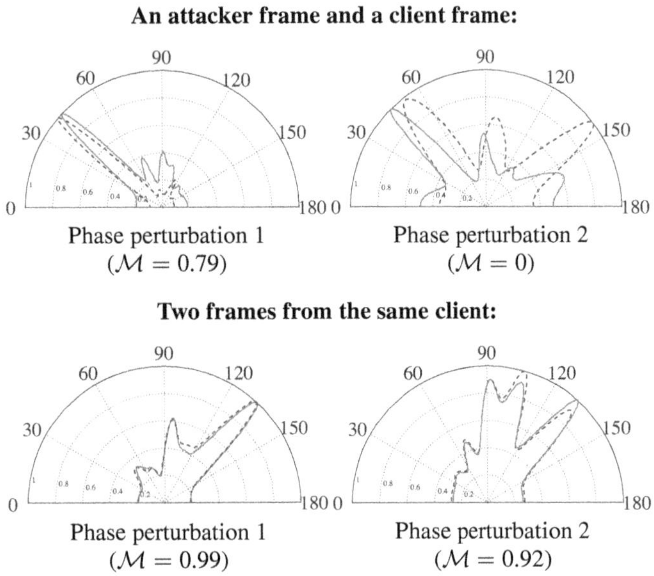


**Figure 4: The effect of random phase perturbation on AOA signatures: *Upper:* comparison between an attacker's frame and a client's frame. *Lower:* comparison between two frames from the same client. $\mathcal{M}$ is the similarity metric (§2.1.2).**

natures with a similarity metric $\mathcal{M} = 0$. So with multiple random random perturbations, we have a higher chance that the two signatures are separated with some of the perturbations introduced. Figure 4 (lower) shows that the random perturbations do not separate (which is desired) the AoA signatures of frames (also spaced 100 ms apart) from the same client, enhancing the AoA signature specificity and selectivity.

### 2.1.2 AoA signature comparison algorithm

Given two AoA signatures $\sigma^A(\theta)$ and $\sigma^B(\theta)$, we first find local maxima in each signature using standard numerical methods. We design a metric $\mathcal{M}$ that pairs local maximum $i$ from $\sigma^A$ with local maximum $j$ from $\sigma^B$. The metric takes two pseudospectra $\sigma^A$ and $\sigma^B$ as inputs, and pairs peaks only if they are positioned within a small constant angle threshold $\Theta$ of each other. The similarity metric $\mathcal{M}$ also takes the magnitudes (normalized) of paired peaks into consideration. If two peaks are paired in coincidence, their peak magnitudes may vary significantly. In order for $\mathcal{M}$ to approach one, the peaks need to be paired and at the same time, the magnitudes of paired peaks should also be close to each other.

$$
\begin{aligned}
S &= \{(i,j) : |\angle i - \angle j| < \Theta\} \\
\mathcal{M}\left(\sigma^A, \sigma^B\right) &= \frac{\sum_{(i,j)\in S} m_i \cdot m_j}{\left(\sum_i m_i^2 + \sum_j m_j^2\right)/2}. \qquad (6)
\end{aligned}
$$

To incorporate the random phase perturbation scheme described in Section 2.1.1, we obtain one similarity metric with one random phase perturbation by comparing pseudospectra $\sigma_1^A(\theta)$ and $\sigma_1^B(\theta)$. We iterate this process to obtain $L$ metrics from comparing the $L$ pseudospectra $\sigma_1^A(\theta), ..., \sigma_L^A(\theta)$ arising from random phase perturbations of $\sigma^A$ pairwise with the $L$ pseudospectra $\sigma_1^B(\theta), ..., \sigma_L^B(\theta)$ arising from $\sigma^B$ with the same random phase perturbations applied. We average the $L$ metrics obtained to achieve $\bar{\mathcal{M}}$.

Based on empirical data from our performance evaluation below, we use a binary classification threshold test, choosing a threshold $\eta$, classifying signature pairs $(\sigma_1, \sigma_2)$ as different (thus flagging an attack) if $\bar{\mathcal{M}} < \eta$, and same (thus identifying normal traffic) if $\bar{\mathcal{M}} \geq \eta$. Table 2 (page. 7) defines the full confusion matrix for the terms we use in our evaluation, and we report our choice of $\eta$ in Section 4.2.1.

| Speed | Coherence time at 2.4 GHz |
|---|---|
| Near-stationary (1 kph) | 77 ms |
| Walking (5 kph) | 15 ms |
| Running (12 kph) | 6 ms |

**Table 1: Wireless coherence times at 2.4 GHz as computed with Equation 7 for typical client motion speeds.**

**Wireless coherence time.** The wireless channel between client and AP is determined by scattering, reflection, and refraction by objects in the environment. A key design parameter is the time duration over which the wireless channel can be considered unchanging with high likelihood, as a function of the speed of the client's motion and/or motion of objects in the environment. The wireless *coherence time* $T_c$ is determined by carrier wavelength $\lambda$ and maximum client velocity $v$. If we measure $v$ in meters per second, then the coherence time is given by [35]:

$$T_c = \frac{9}{16\pi(v/\lambda)}. \qquad (7)$$

Table 1 shows wireless coherence time at 2.4 GHz as a function of typical client motion speeds indoors. Within this time, we can be confident that the AoA signatures of two transmissions from the same client will indeed be the same, making a false alarm (see Table 2) a rare event. Note that SecureArray introduces very little amount of overhead, as SecureArray is not triggered all the time but activated only when some particular control packets are received or unusual behaviors are detected.

### 2.1.3 Collision detection and attacker jamming

In many cases an attacker will have no incentive to jam a client's uplink transmission, but in some cases she may have an incentive to do so. The attacker can employ two directional antennas: one pointed towards the legitimate client and the other pointed at the AP. The attacker uses one directional antenna to jam the client's transmission at the AP and records the client's transmission with another directional antenna. The attacker then replays the recorded packet to cheat the AP. We will illustrate this jamming and reply attack in more detail in Section 2.2.4. SecureArray performs collision detection by searching for energy changes and preambles in the middle of incoming frames as is a standard practice in prior work [17, 36]. When the attacker jams the legitimate client's data frame, the AoA for the overlapping portions of the two packets will be the superposition of the two signatures $\sigma_1$ and $\sigma_2$ as shown in Figure 5, which SecureArray's classification algorithm will flag as differing from the client's signature $\sigma_1$.

## 2.2 Robust security network integration

We now explain how SecureArray can integrate with an 802.11 robust security network, mitigating attacks against the security protocol itself as well as mitigating authenticated but unauthorized spoofing of a user's stolen credentials. To integrate SecureArray with the entirety of the 802.11 protocol, we envision AP designers will follow similar reasoning, annotating their implementations with packet pairs or triplets in the security protocol exchange between client and AP where the AP should make an AoA signature comparison, and a proper corresponding action to be taken if that comparison fails.

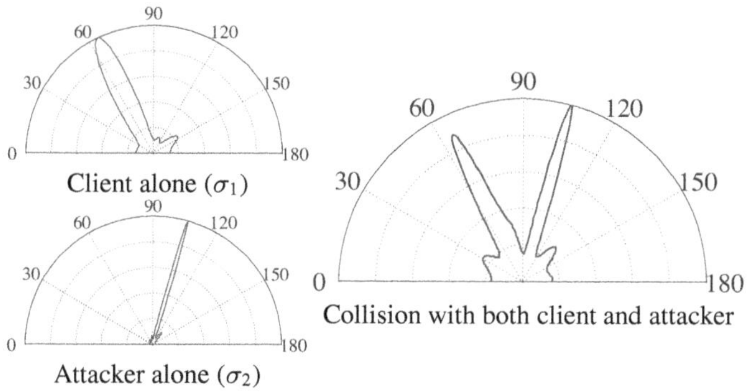


**Figure 5: The result of an attempted jamming attack on DataCheck: the attacker's jamming attempt *(right)* is discernible as the superposition of its own AoA signature atop the legitimate client's AoA signature *(left up)*.**

### 2.2.1 Deauthentication deadlock attack

WPA2 uses IEEE 802.1X and in turn the Extensible Authentication Protocol (EAP) in order to authenticate wireless clients to an authentication server. EAP messages defined by 802.1X are referred to as *EAP over LANs* (EAPOL). Recently, Eian and Mjølsnes [14] and Bertka [9] have separately observed that an attacker can inject an unauthenticated deauthentication notification after the third message of the EAPOL four-way handshake (see Figure 6) that takes place when a client connects to a WPA2 AP. Furthermore, since the attack takes place during the EAPOL four-way handshake, amendments to 802.11 (802.11w [2]) that protect management frames (and in particular deauthentication frames) do not mitigate this vulnerability [9]. A successful attack causes a deadlock, leading to denial of service for the wireless client. Note that for the attack to be successful, the attacker must inject the deauthentication packet between the client's receipt of EAPOL message three and the client's transmission of EAPOL message four.

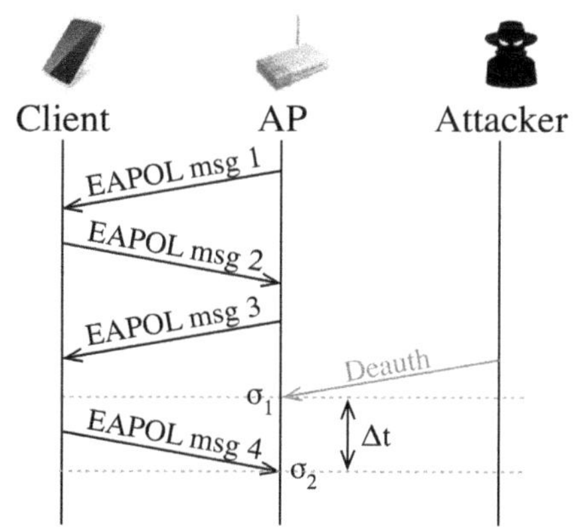


**Figure 6: *EAPOL Deauthentication deadlock attack.* The attacker sends a "deauth" message to a client whose 802.1x four-way authentication handshake is in progress. The AP makes an AoA signature comparison between the attacker's deauth packet ($\sigma_1$) and the legitimate client's subsequent EAPOL message four ($\sigma_2$).**

**Mitigating deauthentication deadlock.** Using a wireless sniffer operating in monitor mode, we measured typical interpacket spacing times for 100 EAPOL four-way handshakes on a variety of AP platforms. We find that the vulnerability gap ($\Delta t$ in Figure 6) between EAPOL message three and EAPOL message four ranges between 30–59 $\mu s$ with an average value of 36 $\mu s$, well within even a running-speed wireless coherence time (*cf.* Table 1), enabling the AP to make a rapid AoA signature comparison (§2.1.2) between the attacker's deauthentication packet and the legitimate client's subsequent EAPOL message 4, flagging an attack and dropping the attacker's frame at the link layer if the signatures do not match.

### 2.2.2 Authenticated spoofing attack

In many cases, users select easily-guessable passwords that are susceptible to dictionary or social engineering attacks, and the attacker gains access to the network using an authorized user's WPA2-Enterprise login credentials. By thus authenticating and associating with the AP, the attacker can sniff the user's MAC address and then inject packets that are completely identical to the legitimate user via the AP.

SecureArray can mitigate these types of attacks when clients overhear acknowledgment frames resulting from injected traffic. We now present *DataCheck*, a protocol that uses this mechanism in conjunction with AoA signatures to mitigate this traffic injection.

**DataCheck: Mitigating authenticated spoofing.** We propose a client-assisted protocol to mitigate authenticated spoofing that requires minimal protocol changes to 802.11 clients, focusing instead on the addition of AoA signature processing at the AP.

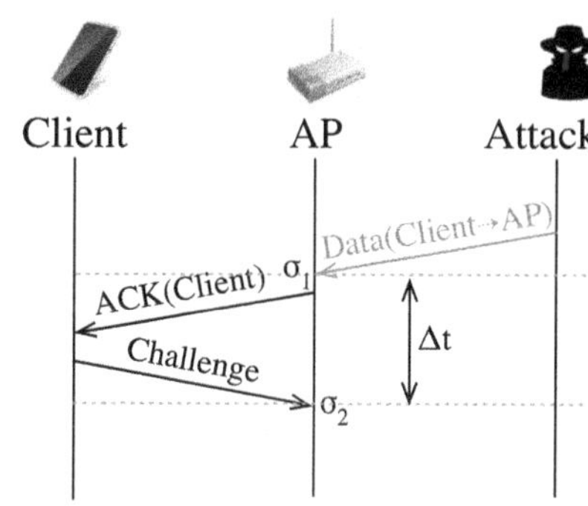


**Figure 7: *Authenticated spoofing attack and mitigation with DataCheck.* Clients send protected minimal-length data frames or normal traffic in response to unexpected ACKs from the AP. The AP makes an AoA signature comparison between the attacker's data frame ($\sigma_1$) and the legitimate client's subsequent *challenge* data frame ($\sigma_2$).**

Figure 7 outlines the protocol. As part of the 802.11 Distributed Coordination Function (DCF) medium access control, clients normally maintain a state as to whether they are awaiting an ACK from a frame they sent to the AP. DataCheck modifies the DCF so that if a client receives an ACK for a frame that it did not send (or even overhear, in the case that the attacker uses a phased array to direct the frame solely to the AP and null the client) the client sends a *challenge* (another data frame, or a zero-length data frame if it has no data outstanding) to the AP. The AP then makes a signature comparison between the attacker's data frame ($\sigma_1$) and the legitimate client's challenge frame ($\sigma_2$) and flags the exchange as suspicious if the two signatures do not match **and** both data frames are protected with 802.11 security.

If the attacker has the legitimate user's security credentials, she could trigger an alarm by injecting a (security-protected) data frame after overhearing a legitimate data-ACK exchange between client and AP, but this simply alerts network administrators that the user's account has been compromised. If the attacker doesn't have the user's security credentials, the encryption check on the DataCheck data frame ($\sigma_2$) prevents her from triggering a false alarm.

Through the application of AoA signatures and in the presence of a saturated wireless network, DataCheck incurs no additional overhead on the wireless medium. It also does not require any form of header format changes.

### 2.2.3 *Authentication deadlock attack*

In 2011, Eian *et al.* used model checking to uncover another distinct authentication-related denial-of-service vulnerability in 802.11i [13]. In this case the vulnerability appears to be based on implementation flaws in hostapd's implementation of 802.11i. As shown in Figure 8, the attack is possible when the AP and client are taking turns sending data frames to each other, each decrypting data frame as they arrive from the other. Just after the attacker overhears a data from the client to the AP, she injects an Open System authentication request frame for the same client to the AP. This causes the AP to delete its security association with the station, but internally, its security state machine transitions to the wrong state (possibly because of a race condition). Since the AP has deleted its key for the victim client, it cannot transmit or receive any frames for that client, and since the AP is in the wrong state, resynchronization mechanisms that exist in the 802.11-2012 standard are not triggered. The result, therefore, is a deadlock that typically results in client disconnection for periods of several minutes.

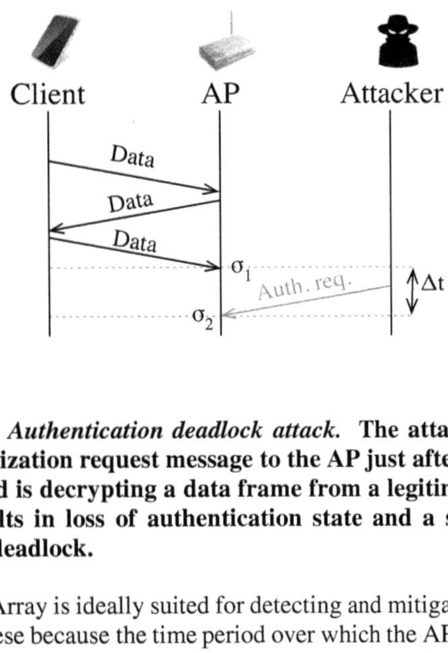


**Figure 8: *Authentication deadlock attack.* The attacker sends an authorization request message to the AP just after it has received and is decrypting a data frame from a legitimate client. This results in loss of authentication state and a subsequent protocol deadlock.**

SecureArray is ideally suited for detecting and mitigating attacks such as these because the time period over which the AP is vulnerable $\Delta t$ is the immediate few hundred microseconds after it receives a frame from the legitimate client. Indeed, the attacker needs to inject the frame in an early backoff slot after just a DIFS time spacing (from 34 $\mu s$ in 802.11a to 50 $\mu s$ 802.11b and 802.11g networks backwards compatible with 802.11b) in order to win the 802.11 MAC protocol contention. This is clearly within the coherence time, making a robust AoA signature comparison possible.

**Mitigating authentication deadlock.** If SecureArray finds a mismatch between the AoA signature of the authentication request frame $\sigma_2$ and the AoA signature of the data frame $\sigma_1$, it drops the spurious authentication request frame. Note that since the authentication request must nominally come from the legitimate client already authenticated in order for the attack to be effective, this policy will not affect other legitimate clients attempting to authenticate in the presence of heavy traffic.

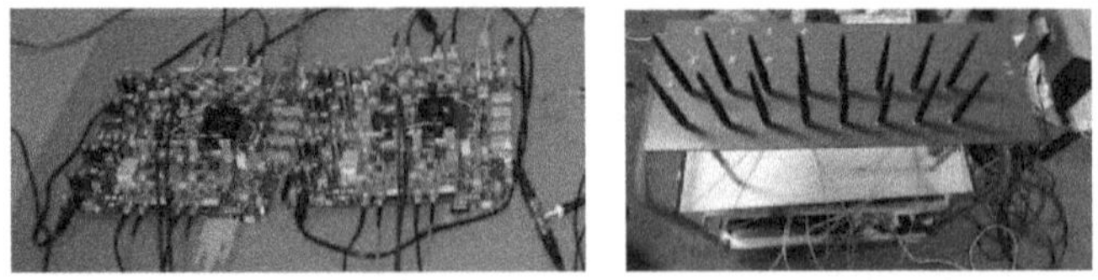

**Figure 9: *Left:* the SecureArray prototype AP is composed of two WARP radios, while a cable-connected USRP2 software-defined radio (not shown) calibrates the array. *Right:* The AP and antenna array mounted on a cart.**

### 2.2.4 *Jamming and replay attack*

Advanced attack such as *jamming and replay attack* can be initiated by attacker with two directional antennas. Take deauthentication deadlock attack as an example shown in Figure 6, the attacker jams the reception of EAPOL message four at the AP with one directional antenna, while at the same time records message four with another directional antenna. The attacker then replays the recorded message four to the AP so both deauthentication packet and message four are now from the attacker which means the AoA signatures are the same. However, when the attacker jams the reception of message four, the AoA at the AP during jamming is a superposition of bearings from both the legitimate client and attacker. This causes the AoA signature to vary significantly as shown in Figure 5, which can be easily detected.

## 3. IMPLEMENTATION

**SecureArray AP.** The prototype SecureArray AP, shown in Figure 9, uses two Rice WARP FPGA-based platforms. Each WARP has four radio front ends and four omnidirectional antennas. Digital I/O pins on one of the two WARPs output a time synchronization signal on a wire connected between the two, so that the second WARP board records and buffers the same time-indexed samples as the first. The WARPs run a custom FPGA hardware design architected with Xilinx System Generator for DSP that implements the functionality described above (§2).

We place the eight antennas attached to the WARP radios in a linear geometry (Figure 9, right). Antennas are spaced at a half wavelength distance (6.13 cm) to yield a 180 degree spectrum range. This also happens to yield maximum MIMO wireless capacity, and so is the arrangement preferred in commodity APs.

**AP phase calibration.** Equipping the AP with multiple antennas is necessary for SecureArray. Note that calibration is mandatory for AoA localization purpose as described in [39] but optional for SecureArray. As the random perturbation AoA scheme is employed, SecureArray is immune to random phase offsets introduced by oscillators and hardware imperfections. However, as calibrated version of AoA has the true signal arrival bearing information, the peak corresponds to the direct path signal is relatively stable when the client is mobile, including this calibrated version of AoA into SecureArray reduces the false alarm rate. So we still describe the calibration scheme employed for SecureArray:

*Random phase offsets introduced by WARP:* Each radio receiver has 2.4 GHz oscillator whose purpose is to *downconvert* the incoming radio frequency signal to its representation in I-Q space. This

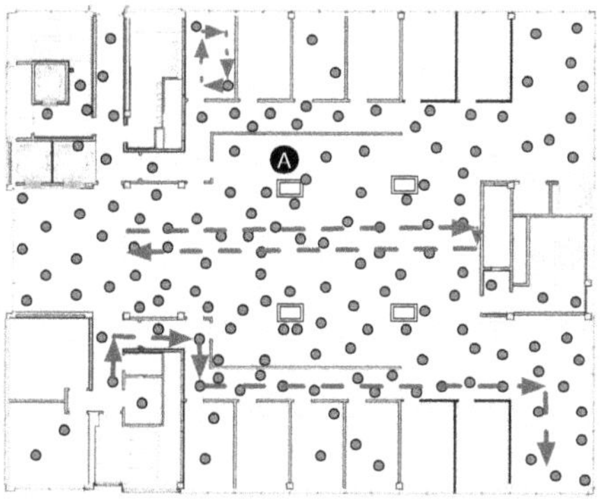

**Figure 10: Floor plan of our evaluation environment. Mobile experiment trajectories are shown by the dashed lines.**

introduces an unknown phase offset to the resulting signal. These unknown phase offsets are constant during each WARP power on/off cycle which only need to be calibrated once.

*Hardware imperfections:* Because of hardware imperfections for SMA splitters and small differences between cables of the same nominal length, we use the following one-time (run only once for a particular set of hardware) calibration scheme to handle these equipment imperfections.

To remove the hardware imperfections and obtain the unknown random phase offsets introduced by oscillators, we calibrate the array with a USRP2 generating a continuous wave tone. The signal from the USRP2 travels through splitters and cables (we call them *external* paths, giving rise to an external phase difference) before reaching the WARP radios. The phase offset $\phi^I$ we want to measure is the *internal* (due to RF downconversion) phase difference between radios one and two, $\phi_2^I - \phi_1^I$. Running cable calibration once, we obtain offset $\phi_1$:

$$\phi_1 = (\phi_2^E + \phi_2^I) - \left(\phi_1^E + \phi_1^I\right) \quad (8)$$

Because of equipment imperfections, $\phi_2^E$ is slightly different from $\phi_1^E$, so $\phi_1$ does not equal the quantity we want to measure, $\phi^I$. We then physically exchange the external cable connections and re-run cable calibration:

$$\phi_2 = \left(\phi_1^E + \phi_2^I\right) - \left(\phi_2^E + \phi_1^I\right) \quad (9)$$

Combining Equations 8 and 9, we obtain the desired quantity:

$$\phi^I = \frac{1}{2}(\phi_2 + \phi_1) \quad (10)$$

**Testbed clients.** The clients we use in our experiments are Soekris boxes equipped with Atheros 802.11g radios operating in the 2.4 GHz band.

# 4. EVALUATION

We first describe our methodology (§4.1), then evaluate SecureArray's performance when clients are static (§4.2), followed by an evaluation under mobility (§4.3). Finally, we examine system latency of SecureArray (§4.4).

## 4.1 Methodology

For static clients, we deploy them at 150 randomly-chosen positions (and then deploy the attacker randomly at a particular distance with respect to the client) in a $30 \times 40$ meter typical office environment, as shown in Figure 10. We aim to have both line-of-sight (LOS) and non-line-of-sight (NLOS) clients in our test environment. We also deliberately place the client and attacker behind and near to human, ceramic, wood, plastic and metal materials in the office to make our results more comprehensive and realistic. We also run the experiments in both daytime and night time. We evaluate SecureArray with signature comparisons from packets recorded with different time gaps from one millisecond to two seconds, and also vary the distances between the client and attacker from above three meters down to just five centimeters to challenge our system.

For mobile clients, we evaluate the challenging scenarios when both the client and attacker are moving at the same time. The experimenter holds the client and attacker in his two hands walking smoothly following the predefined routes. We evaluate SecureArray with signatures from packets recorded with different time gaps.

| | | Test: Do signatures differ? | |
|---|---|---|---|
| | | **Yes** | **No** |
| Ground truth: Are signatures from different senders? | **Yes** | TP: *Attack detected* | FN: *Missed attack* |
| | **No** | FP: *False alarm* | TN: *Normal traffic* |

**Table 2: Confusion matrix defining the terms SecureArray uses to classify signatures. *TP:* true positive, *FN:* false negative, *FP:* false positive, *TN:* true negative.**

## 4.2 Static experiments

We first show how SecureArray performs in a typical office environment when both client and attacker are static. We evaluate SecureArray with all combinations of different locations, different distances between attacker and client, and different time intervals between the packets, which is a total of 1500 comparisons.

### *4.2.1 Overall system performance*

As shown in Section 2.1.2, the similarity metric $\mathcal{M}$ obtained varies between zero and one. This metric should be compared with a carefully chosen threshold $\eta$ to reject packets from attacker and accept packets from legitimate client. Table 2 shows the confusion matrix defining the terms that we use to classify the signature comparison test described in Section 2.1.2. To choose the best threshold $\eta$, we examine the *receiver operating characteristic* (ROC) curve. This plots the attack detection rate $\frac{TP}{TP+FN}$ versus the rate of false alarms $\frac{FP}{FP+TN}$ on signature comparisons from the same sender, for varying choices of threshold $\eta$.

We show the overall ROC curves in Figure 11, averaging across different packet time gaps, and different distances for maximum generality. Besides SecureArray, we also present the curves for a *phase-calibrated* version (remove the phases introduced by WARP and hardware imperfections), and a *random phase* version (adding one group of eight random phases to each of the radio board). We see that SecureArray achieves a 100% attack detection rate at a false alarm rate as low as 0.67% with $L$ set to 15. We see clearly that SecureArray outperforms the two other versions with $L = 1$.

**Choice of $\eta$.** To maintain a balance between attack detection rate and false alarm rate, we choose $\eta = 0.7$ and evaluate with this threshold in the remainder of the evaluation.

### *4.2.2 Number of random-phase perturbations (L)*

We show the effect of number of groups of random perturbations employed on SecureArray here. As shown in Figure 12 and the zoomed in version in Figure 13, with more groups of random per-

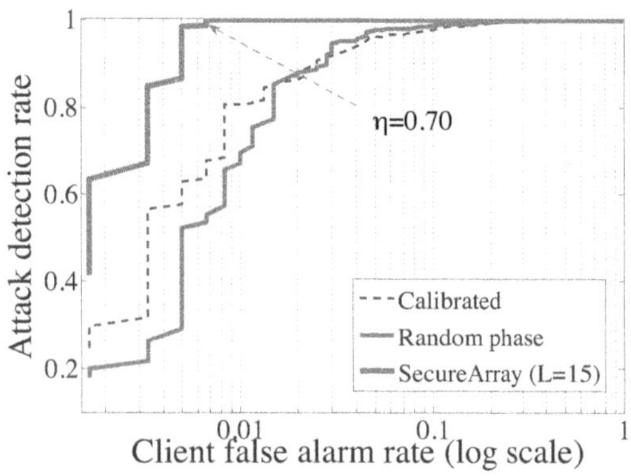


**Figure 11: Overall performance (*receiver operating characteristic* (ROC) curve) using calibrated AoA signatures, AoA signatures perturbed by one random phase, and SecureArray (with $L = 15$).**

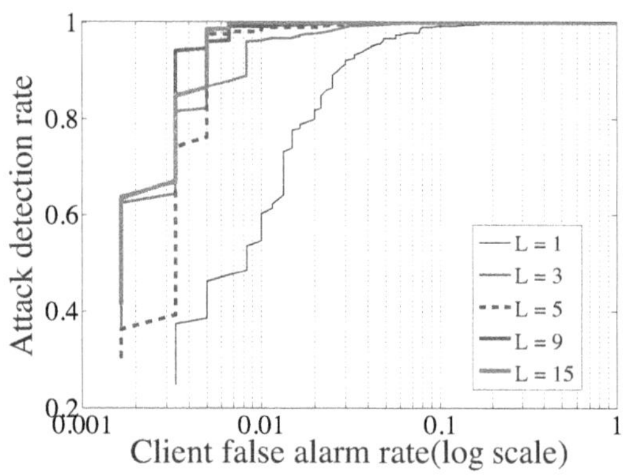


**Figure 12: ROC curves for SecureArray, varying the number of random phase perturbations attempted for each AoA signature from $L = 1$ to $L = 15$.**

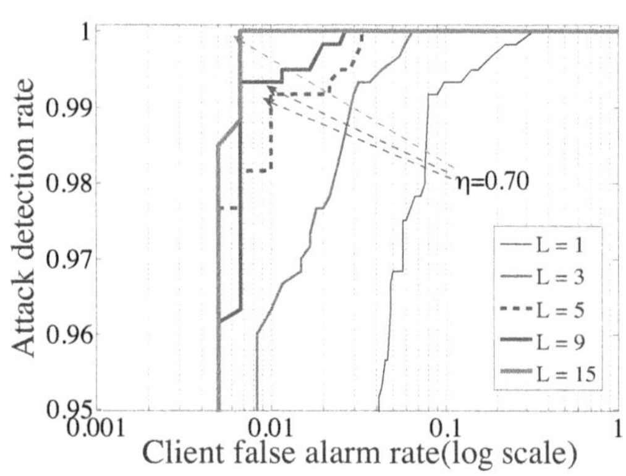


**Figure 13: Detailed view of the ROC curves in Figure 12, for high attack detection rates.**

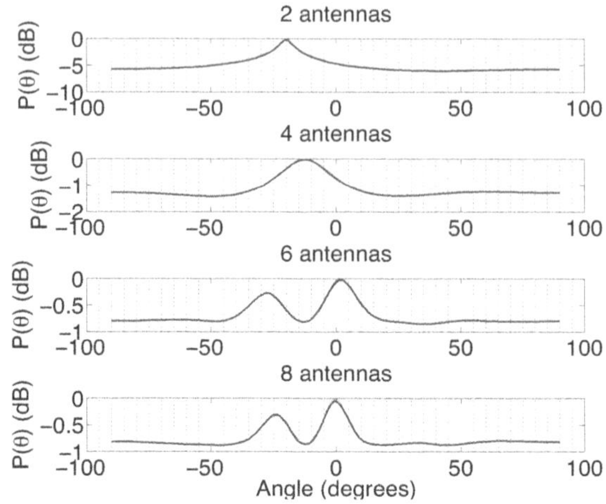


**Figure 14: Effect of the number of antennas on the AoA signature: more antennas yield more unique signatures.**

turbations employed, performance improves further. The biggest improvement gap is between $L = 1$ and $L = 3$ which demonstrates the efficiency and necessity of our random phase perturbation scheme. However, this improvement becomes insignificant when we increase $L$ past five. We should notice that this improvement is achieved at the price of more computation with a larger $L$. However, as shown later in Section 4.4, the computational load involved for SecureArray is very little and a typical desktop can complete the process within milliseconds. Furthermore, the $L$ computational processes are independent from each other which can be executed in parallel at the same time. For all subsequent results presented, if not mentioned, we employ $L = 5$ groups of randomly perturbations for averaging.

### *4.2.3 Number of AP antennas*

The number of antennas at the AP is an important factor for computing the AoA signature and accordingly for SecureArray performance as it decides the maximum number of lobes on the signature and the sharpness of the lobes. With eight antennas, we can have a maximum of seven lobes on the signatures corresponding to seven incoming signals (two signals arriving at very close bearings will merge into one lobe on the signature). With more lobes, the signature has a tendency to be more specific to each client and easier to be differentiated, as shown in Figure 14. We present the ROC curves for SecureArray with varying numbers of antennas in Figure 15. With a threshold $\eta = 0.7$ and $L = 5$, SecureArray achieves 99.2%, 99.8% and 99.3% attack detection rate and 1%, 4.7% and 11.3% false alarm rate respectively.

We observe that with our chosen threshold of $\eta = 0.7$, the attack detection rate remains high even with four antennas. However, the client false alarm rate does increase a little bit with fewer numbers of antennas. As the next generation 802.11ac supports up to eight spatial streams, eight antennas are very likely to be equipped on one single AP in the near future.

### *4.2.4 Distance between client and attacker*

In most scenarios, an attacker will be far away from the legitimate client which is the scenario most prior work [24] evaluates. However, with devices becoming smaller, it's plausible that the attacker may be very close to the legitimate client, such as when a smartphone is placed in the same bag or on the same table. We would like

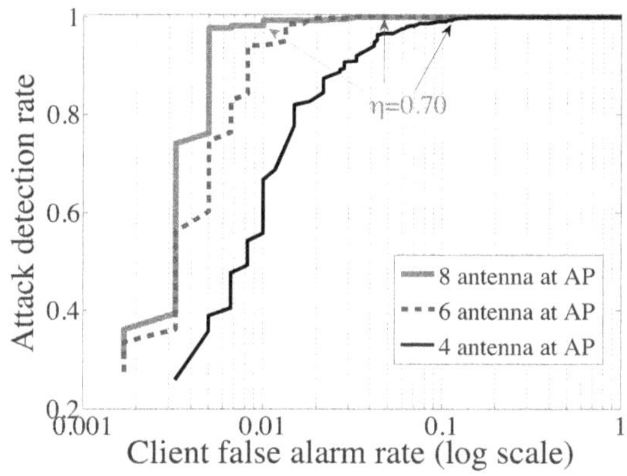


**Figure 15: Performance of SecureArray with different numbers of antennas at the AP.**

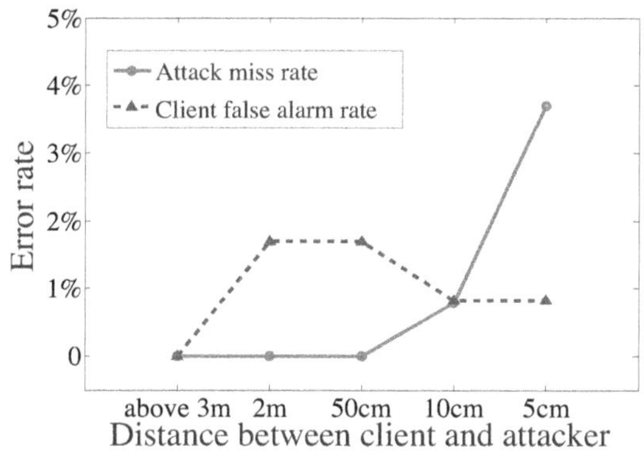


**Figure 16: Performance of SecureArray with varying distances between client and attacker.**

to evaluate SecureArray's performance for these most challenging scenarios when the attacker is very close to legitimate client.

In this section, we present results for different distances between client and attacker. We move the attacker from far away (above three meters) to a medium distance (two meters and 50 cm) to very close (10 cm and five centimeters) to see how SecureArray performs. The results presented here are averaged across different locations and different time gaps. As shown in Figure 16, we observe that when the client and attacker get closer, the client false alarm rate is more or less the same while the attack miss rate slightly increases. This is expected as the peaks on the AoA signatures reflecting the direct path signal (if not blocked) become similar when the client and attacker are very close to each other. This brings in some degree of similarity between the two AoAs and increases the similarity metric especially when the direct path signal is stronger than all the reflection path signals. We can see that the attack miss rate is zero for large and medium distances and increases slightly to 3.7%, which is still well within an acceptable level when the client and attacker are only five centimeters to each other. Please note that it's unlikely that an attacker can be placed at exactly the same location (0 cm distance) as the client when the client is static.

### *4.2.5 Inter-packet time*

The channel is dynamic between any particular antenna pair in both amplitude and phase. In terms of our AoA signature stability, the phases of most antennas at the array need to change at the same time to the same direction in order to show a obvious effect on the lobe peak positions on an AoA signature. From Figure 17, we can

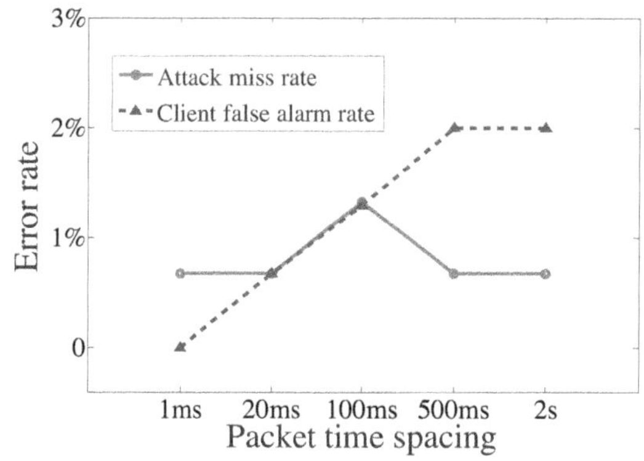


**Figure 17: Performance of SecureArray with different time gaps between the packets obtained for signature comparison from client-client and client-attacker, for static senders.**

see that in a typical working office environment when the clients are static, with the inter-packet time gap increased from one millisecond to two seconds, SecureArray still performs well, with the client false alarm rate increased slightly to around 2%, due to human movements in the environment, we believe. Note that the attack detection rate is always high because the attacker's signature does not tend to change to be similar to the legitimate client's signature with time. So the attack detection rate is not affected by the large time gaps between packets employed for comparison. However, movements in the environment do change the clients' signatures, which is reflected in the slightly increased false alarm rate.

## 4.3 Mobile experiments

In this section, we evaluate SecureArray's performance for mobile clients. The two Soekris boxes serving as the attacker and legitimate client are held by the experimenter with a separation of around 60 cm (this value varies during the walking process with natural human movements) away from each other. We test SecureArray with the experimenter walking along the three routes labeled as dashed lines in Figure 10. To measure the attack detection rate, signatures generated from packets recorded at the attacker and client with different time gaps are compared. All the packets are recorded when the experimenter is walking along the trajectories. To measure the false alarm rate, two signatures generated from packets both recorded at the client with different time gaps are employed for comparison. We choose one route to be in the same office with a strong line-of-sight to the AP and the other two routes with many non-line-of-sight portions. The experimenter walks at a speed of around 4 kph so the expected coherence time is around 12 ms.

We compare the attack detection rate and client false alarm rate with respect to different time gaps between the packets employed for signature comparison. The results are shown in Figure 18, varying the time gaps from 200 ms to one millisecond. We can see that the attack detection rate is always high, roughly 100%. However, when the time gap is 200 ms and 50 ms, the client false alarm rate is 100% and 96.7% which means the legitimate client itself is hardly ever identified with such big time gaps when client is moving. When the time gap decreases to around 20 ms, we have the false alarm rate decreased to 46.7% but still high. When the time gap becomes 5 ms below the wireless coherence time, the false alarm rate decreases dramatically to 6.7% and this value further decreases to 0% for one millisecond time gap. One point we note here is that, the phase-calibrated version is a special candidate among all the perturbation groups. The false alarm rate is lower when applying

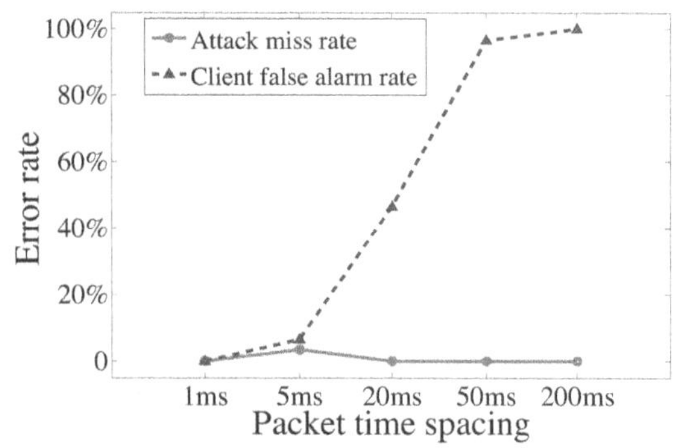


**Figure 18: Performance of SecureArray with different time gaps for mobile clients in our testbed.**

the correct calibration phases especially in line-of-sight scenarios, as the direct path is strong and relatively stable compared with reflection paths during movements, which increases our metric value and mitigates the false alarm error rate. When the AP has no idea of the mobility status of the client, the safe option is to include this perturbation group in for averaging. Nowadays, a lot of devices have a variety of different sensors built in and when a device starts moving, it can be easily detected at the client side and at the AP side. If the AP has the information of client's mobility status, it can choose intelligent random perturbation options. We will explore possible schemes to reduce the false alarm rate for mobile clients when the packets employed for comparison are not recorded within the coherence time in our future work. We believe one promising direction is to explore the stability nature of the direct path peak on the AoA signature when the client is moving.

## 4.4 System latency

System latency is an important characteristic for any real-time system. As SecureArray works with any kind of packet and any part of the packet, we choose to use the most robust preamble part for our processing. The preamble itself contains hundreds of samples when sampled at 40 MHz rate. In principle, one sample would suffice, but because of noise, it's preferable to employ multiple samples and average the correlation matrix to achieve a more stable AoA signature. As shown in prior work [39], 10 samples suffice for AoA signature stability. Once SecureArray detects the preamble and records this number of samples, it begins processing while the rest of the packet is still on the air. The components of system latency (measured from the start of the second packet in a comparison) are described below:

- $T_1$: time taken for packet detection and samples recording with WARP. If one short training symbol in the preamble is employed for packet detection, $T_1$ is 1.6 $\mu s$.

- $T_2$: time taken for samples to be transferred to the server. As we employ 10 samples for processing, we have 80 samples to be transferred with a total of eight radio boards at the transfer rate of 1 Mbps supported by the WARP second generation platform: $T_2 = \frac{(80 \text{ samples})(32 \text{ bits/sample})}{1 \text{ Mbit/s}} = 2.56$ ms.

- $T_3$: time taken for the server to compute the metric and make the decision. For an eight-antenna array, our AoA signature generation involves eigenvalue decomposition and processing of 8x8 matrices. The peak finding and comparison algorithm run very fast. More computation is needed for a larger $L$ value. However, these are independent processes and can be run in parallel. For our current Matlab implementation with an Intel Core i7 2.30 GHz CPU and 8 GB of RAM, the processing time is in the range of 10 ms to 20 ms with $L = 5$.

Therefore, the total latency that our prototype incurs starting from the start of the second packet (excluding bus latency) is around 20 ms. We expect a full FPGA implementation to operate orders of magnitude faster.

# 5. RELATED WORK

Xiong *et al.* have proposed the use of AoA signatures as a fingerprinting mechanism [38] to be used in wireless networks. SecureArray expands upon this work by proposing new signal processing techniques for enhancing AoA signature specificity, integrating AoA signature checking into the existing 802.11 security protocol framework, introducing the DataCheck (§2.2.2) protocol for mitigating authenticated spoofing in the event of user password compromise, and providing a comprehensive security evaluation measuring false alarm and miss rates (§4).

SecureArray is designed to operate alongside traditional protocol-based security, which has a history of first becoming widely-deployed and then being compromised. In the light of WEP's well-known security flaws (§1), the 802.11 specification was amended in 2004 (802.11i) to include enhanced security [1]. In 2009, the 802.11 specification was again amended (802.11w) to include protection for deauthentication, disassociation, and certain other management frames [2]. The 2012 revision of IEEE 802.11 [3] incorporates this amendment. Nonetheless, several attacks on this revision exist [9, 14, 4] and are mitigated by SecureArray as described above (§2). We again note that SecureArray only mitigates active attacks. Other MIMO-based schemes such as STROBE [5] have recently been proposed to mitigate passive eavesdropping; these schemes complement our work.

**Localization systems.** In general, an accurate localization system [39, 40] could serve as a proxy for SecureArray fingerprints, but a key advantage of SecureArray over most RF-based location systems is that it only requires the involvement of one AP. PinLoc [32] is a recent localization system that uses per-OFDM subcarrier channel measurements (CSI). This is made possible on a commodity NIC by a CSI measurement tool previously released by Halperin [21]. PinLoc uses the phase information in CSI measurements along with amplitude to fingerprint clients and then localize them in a one meter by one meter grid. One could imagine PinLoc being co-opted for security purposes, but this would in fact be undesirable from a security standpoint, because an attacks may originate centimeters away from the victim (consider, for example, an attacker surreptitiously placing a mobile phone in the victim's handbag). Like many other systems, PinLoc requires a a time-intensive environmental calibration step to learn location signatures. SecureArray requires no environmental calibration.

**PHY-layer channel fingerprinting.** The concept of fingerprinting clients based on physical layer channel information has been explored in many ways in the wireless systems literature. In one of the first such designs, Faria and Cheriton propose the use of a "signalprint" [16], the vector of received signal strengths (RSS) that a predetermined set of nearby APs observe from a wireless client's transmission. In later work, Chandrasekaran *et al.* use RSS to detect spoofing, achieving 10% false alarm and missed attack rates when the two are equalized [12]. AoA information is much more detailed than RSS, and so SecureArray can achieve orders of magnitude better specificity and selectivity over RSS-based systems with just one AP, as is common in home settings, obviating the need for multiple nearby APs or any coordination of differently-administered APs.

CSITE [24] is a recent system that is perhaps closest in spirit to SecureArray; it uses CSI magnitude measurements averaged in time over multiple frames to form a client signature. There are two main differences between SecureArray and CSITE. Firstly, SecureArray uses AoA information at the AP instead of averaged CSI magnitudes. As Patwari and Kasera observe in the context of RSS, however, approaches based on channel strength can be subverted by attackers with directional or phased-array antennas [29]. Since RSS is simply CSI magnitude information averaged across different subcarriers, per-subcarrier CSI approaches such as CSITE can be subverted by attackers with phased array software-defined radios capable of transmitting with independent beamforming weights on different subcarriers. Secondly, CSITE uses multi-packet time-averages of channel magnitude information, which yields a less selective discriminator with missed intrusion attempts of up to 5% and false alarm rates of up to 60%, depending on the traffic intensity of the legitimate client.

Other candidates for wireless channel signatures at the physical layer include time of flight [28], signal-to-noise ratio measured at an AP [15], client-AP channel impulse response [29], and combination of multi-tonal probes and channel impulse response [41]. SecureArray has an intrinsic advantage over these approaches because it is extremely difficult for an attacker to generate a signal that arrives at the AP from the same physical directions as the legitimate client without being co-located with the client to within small fractions of the RF wavelength (*i.e.*, 12 cm at 2.4 GHz).

**PHY-layer client fingerprinting.** The problem of fingerprinting 802.11 clients themselves (in contrast to fingerprinting the channel between client and AP as do SecureArray and other prior work below) has been thoroughly explored in the literature. PARADIS [11] is a prime example of this type of device fingerprinting system that achieves 99% accuracy. Though this device fingerprinting can improve security, the solution is qualitatively different because an attacker can simply acquire a legitimate client's 802.11 device to launch her attack. Other candidates for device fingerprinting include radio transmission startup transient signal envelope [7], the 802.11 probe request interarrival time distribution [26], and client CPU clock skew [25, 23].

**Link-layer client fingerprinting.** These techniques encompass examining MAC (hardware) addresses, active probe requests for cached SSIDs, and requests for a certain set of network servers from clients [20, 27]. SecureArray has an advantage over such link-layer techniques in that it is reliable even if clients take countermeasures, such as reprogramming their hardware addresses, cached SSIDs, and encrypting their network-layer traffic.

# 6. DISCUSSION

**1. SecureArray overhead:** SecureArray introduces very limited overhead because the operation is triggered only when suspicious packets are received or unusual behaviors are detected. SecureArray is not trying to update the AoA information continuously at the frequency decided by the coherence time.

**2. Forge the legitimate client's AoA signature:** It's very difficult for the attacker to forge the legitimate client's AoA signature even if it's equipped with an advanced phased array. There are multiple schemes the attacker may employ:

- The attacker is placed at exactly the same location as the legitimate client. The attacker may have a chance to be located near to the client. However, it is unlikely for the attacker to be placed at the same physical location and furthermore, the attacker usually has a preference to be located far away in order not to be discovered. A small five centimeters location difference causes a significant AoA signature change which can be easily detected.

- The attacker obtains the legitimate client's AoA signature and then employ an antenna array to mimic the client's signature while the attacker is at a different location. We argue that this is difficult to be realized. In order for the attacker to obtain the client's AoA signature at the AP, the attacker needs to have the same number of antennas and all the antenna to be at the same positions as the AP. Even we assume the AP has successfully obtained the client's AoA signature, it's still challenging for the attacker to mimic this signature at a different location. If the attacker is equipped with an antenna array, the attacker can utilize it to form different radiation patterns. However, the radiation pattern at the attacker side is not the AoA signature generated at the AP. The AoA signature at the AP is decided by both the radiation pattern and the physical prorogation paths between the attacker and AP. It's almost impossible for the attacker to create a same physical environment at a different location. The dynamic nature of the environment makes it even more challenging.

- When the client is moving, the attacker tries to predict the client's future location. We argue that it's challenging to predict a precise future location of a mobile client. A rough location estimate does not fail SecureArray as we show experimentally in Figure 16 that even a five centimeter small location difference presents a very high detection rate.

# 7. CONCLUSION

We have described SecureArray, a system that leverages multipath propagation in the wireless channel to construct highly specific client signatures, just as MIMO leverages multipath to increase capacity. Our testbed results show that in a typical office environment, SecureArray is able to mitigate 100% of WiFi spoofing attack attempts while at the same time triggering false alarms on just 0.6% of legitimate traffic. Detection rate remains high even when the attacker is located very close to the legitimate client. The performance of SecureArray degrades very little with fewer numbers of antennas on the AP and when clients are mobile.

To identify wireless protocol exploits, the security community uses model checking tools such as SPIN [22], augmented with timing information. We anticipate that the tests we describe above (§2.2) will in the future be integrated into such model checkers so that SecureArray can check all testable points (places where a legitimate client transmits two frames within a coherence time) in the protocol for attack activity.

For mobile clients, the direct path is relatively stable compared with the reflection paths. By identifying the stable direct path peak on the AoA signatures when the client is moving, heavier weight can be assigned to the direct path bearing for signature comparison. We believe with smart process, SecureArray may be able to break the coherence time constraint and work with packets recorded within a larger time interval so the application scope of SecureArray can be extended.

# 8. ACKNOWLEDGEMENT

This material is based on work supported by the European Research Council under Grant No. 279976. Jie Xiong is supported by the Google European Doctoral Fellowship in Wireless Networking. We would like to thank Prof. Sneha Kumar Kasera, as well as the anonymous reviewers, for their valuable feedback on this paper.

## 9. REFERENCES

[1] IEEE Standard 802.11i-2004: MAC Security Enhancements, June 2004.

[2] IEEE Standard 802.11w-2009: Protected Management Frames, Sept. 2009.

[3] IEEE Standard 802.11: Wireless LAN MAC and PHY Layer Specifications, Mar. 2012.

[4] M. Ahmad and S. Tadakamadla. Short paper: security evaluation of IEEE 802.11w specification. In *Proceedings of ACM WiSec*, 2011.

[5] N. Anand, S. Lee, and E. Knightly. STROBE: Actively securing wireless communications using zero-forcing beamforming. In *Proc. of IEEE Infocom*, 2012.

[6] E. Aryafar, N. Anand, T. Salonidis, and E. Knightly. Design and experimental evaluation of multi-user beamforming in wireless LANs. In *Proc. of ACM MobiCom*, 2010.

[7] M. Barbeau, J. Hall, and E. Kranakis. Detecting impersonation attacks in future wireless and mobile networks. *Springer Lecture Notes in Computer Science*, 4074(2006):80–95, Aug. 2006.

[8] M. Beck and E. Tews. Practical attacks against WEP and WPA. In *Proc. of ACM WiSec*, pages 79–86, 2009.

[9] B. Bertka. 802.11w security: DoS attacks and vulnerability controls. In *Proc. of Infocom*, 2012.

[10] A. Bittau, M. Handley, and J. Lackey. The final nail in WEP's coffin. In *Proc. of IEEE Symp. on Security and Privacy*, 2006.

[11] V. Brik, S. Banerjee, M. Gruteser, and S. Oh. Wireless device identification with radiometric signatures. In *Proc. of ACM MobiCom*, 2008.

[12] G. Chandrasekaran, J. Deymious, V. Ganapathy, M. Gruteser, and W. Trappe. Detecting identity spoofs in 802.11e wireless networks. In *Proc. of IEEE Globecom*, 2009.

[13] M. Eian and S. Mjølsnes. The modeling and comparison of wireless network denial of service attacks. In *Proc. of ACM MobiHeld*, 2011.

[14] M. Eian and S. Mjølsnes. A formal analysis of IEEE 802.11w deadlock vulnerabilities. In *Proc. of IEEE Infocom*, 2012.

[15] D. Faria and D. Cheriton. No long-term secrets: Location based security in overprovisioned wireless LANs. In *Proc. of ACM HotNets*, 2004.

[16] D. Faria and D. Cheriton. Radio-layer security: Detecting identity-based attacks in wireless networks using signalprints. In *Proc. of ACM WiSe*, 2006.

[17] S. Gollakota and D. Katabi. Zigzag decoding: Combating hidden terminals in wireless networks. In *Proc. of ACM SIGCOMM*, 2008.

[18] S. Gollakota, S. Perli, and D. Katabi. Interference alignment and cancellation. In *Proc. of ACM SIGCOMM*, Aug. 2009.

[19] D. Goodin. Lax security led to TJX breach. *The Register*, May 2007. http://www.the-register.co.uk/2007/05/04/txj_nonfeasance.

[20] M. Gruteser and D. Grunwald. Enhancing location privacy in wireless LAN through disposable interface identifiers: a quantitative analysis. In *Proc. of ACM WMASH*, 2003.

[21] D. Halperin, W. Hu, A. Sheth, and D. Wetherall. Tool release: Gathering 802.11n traces with channel state information. *SIGCOMM CCR*, 41(1):53, Jan. 2011.

[22] G. Holzmann. The model checker SPIN. *IEEE Trans. Software Eng.*, 23(5):279–295, 1997.

[23] S. Jana and S. K. Kasera. On fast and accurate detection of unauthorized wireless access points using clock skews. In *Proceedings of ACM MobiCom*, 2008.

[24] Z. Jiang, J. Zhao, X. Li, J. Han, and W. Xi. Rejecting the Attack: Source Authentication for Wi-Fi Management Frames using CSI Information. In *Proc. of IEEE Infocom*, 2013.

[25] T. Kohno, A. Broido, and K. Claffy. Remote physical device fingerprinting. In *Proc. of IEEE Symp. on Sec. and Priv.*, pages 211–225, May 2005.

[26] D. C. Loh, C. Y. Cho, C. P. Tan, and R. S. Lee. Identifying unique devices through wireless fingerprinting. In *Proc. of the ACM WiSec Conf.*, pages 46–55, Mar. 2008.

[27] J. Pang, B. Greenstein, R. Gummadi, S. Seshan, and D. Wetherall. 802.11 user fingerprinting. In *Proc. of ACM MobiCom*, 2007.

[28] P. Papadimitratos, M. Poturalski, P. Schaller, P. Lafourcade, D. Basin, S. Čapkun, and J. Hubaux. Secure neighborhood discovery: a fundamental element for mobile ad hoc networking. *IEEE Comm. M.*, 46(2):132–139, Feb. 2008.

[29] N. Patwari and S. Kasera. Robust location distinction using temporal link signatures. In *Proc. of the ACM MobiCom Conf.*, pages 111–122, Sept. 2007.

[30] R. Schmidt. Multiple emitter location and signal parameter estimation. *IEEE Trans. on Antennas and Propagation*, AP-34(3):276–280, Mar. 1986.

[31] B. Schneier, Mudge, and D. Wagner. Cryptanalysis of Microsoft's PPTP authentication mechanisms (MS-CHAPv2), Oct. 1999.

[32] S. Sen, B. Radunovic, R. Choudhury, and T. Minka. Spot localization using PHY layer information. In *Proceedings of ACM MobiSys*, 2012.

[33] Y. Sheng, G. Chen, D. Kotz, and A. Campbell. Detecting 802.11 MAC layer spoofing using received signal strength. In *Proc. of IEEE Infocom*, pages 1768–1776, Apr. 2008.

[34] C. Shepard, H. Yu, N. Anand, L. Li, T. Marzetta, R. Yang, and L. Zhong. Argos: Practical many-antenna base stations. In *Proc. of ACM MobiCom*, 2012.

[35] R. Steele. *Mobile Radio Communications*. IEEE Press, 1994.

[36] K. Tan, H. Liu, J. Fang, W. Wang, J. Zhang, M. Chen, and G. Voelker. SAM: Enabling practical spatial multiple access in wireless LAN. In *Proc. of ACM MobiCom*, 2009.

[37] E. Tews, R.-P. Weinmann, and A. Pyshkin. Breaking 104-bit WEP in less than 60 seconds. *Springer Lecture Notes in Computer Science*, 4867:188–202, Jan. 2008.

[38] J. Xiong and K. Jamieson. SecureAngle: Improving wireless security using angle-of-arrival signatures. In *Proc. of ACM HotNets*, 2010.

[39] J. Xiong and K. Jamieson. ArrayTrack: A Fine-Grained Indoor Location System. In *Proc. of NSDI*, 2013.

[40] M. Youssef and A. Agrawala. The Horus WLAN location determination system. In *Proc. of ACM MobiSys*, 2005.

[41] J. Zhang, M. H. Firooz, N. Patwari, , and S. K. Kasera. Advancing wireless link signatures for location distinction. In *Proceedings of ACM MobiCom*, 2008.

# NEMOx: Scalable Network MIMO for Wireless Networks

Xinyu Zhang
University of Wisconsin-Madison
xyzhang@ece.wisc.edu

Karthikeyan Sundaresan
Mohammad A. (Amir) Khojastepour
Sampath Rangarajan
NEC Laboratories America
{karthiks,amir,sampath}@nec-labs.com

Kang G. Shin
University of Michigan-Ann Arbor
kgshin@eecs.umich.edu

## ABSTRACT

Network MIMO (netMIMO) has potential for significantly enhancing the capacity of wireless networks with tight coordination of access points (APs) to serve multiple users concurrently. Existing schemes realize netMIMO by integrating distributed APs into one "giant" MIMO but do not scale well owing to their global synchronization requirement and overhead in sharing data between APs. To remedy this limitation, we propose a novel system, NEMOx, that realizes netMIMO downlink transmission for *large-scale* wireless networks. NEMOx organizes a network into practical-size clusters, each containing multiple distributed APs (dAPs) that opportunistically synchronize with each other for netMIMO downlink transmission. Inter-cluster interference is managed with a decentralized channel-access algorithm, which is designed to balance between the dAPs' cooperation gain and spatial reuse—a unique tradeoff in netMIMO. Within each cluster, NEMOx optimizes the power budgeting among dAPs and the set of users to serve, ensuring fairness and effective cancellation of cross-talk interference. We have implemented and evaluated a prototype of NEMOx in a software radio testbed, demonstrating its throughput scalability and multiple folds of performance gain over current wireless LAN architecture and alternative netMIMO schemes.

## Categories and Subject Descriptors

C.2.1 [**Computer-Communication Networks**]: Network Architecture and Design—*Wireless Communications*; C.2.2 [**Computer-Communication Networks**]: Network Protocols

## General Terms

Algorithms, Design, Experimentation, Performance

## Keywords

Network MIMO, multi-user MIMO networks

## 1. INTRODUCTION

Despite the well-known bit-rate enhancements via multiplexing gain, the throughput of MIMO networks has been improving at a much slower pace. *Throughput-efficiency*—defined as the ratio of network throughput to PHY bit-rate—is only around 20% in 300Mbps 802.11n MIMO networks, and below 10% in Gbps 802.11ac MU-MIMO networks [1]. One major reason for this is that the multiplexing gain does not scale to multi-cell WLANs that involve spatially-distributed transmitters. Deploying more APs does not solve this problem either, as inter-cell contention overhead may undo the intra-cell multiplexing gain from MIMO.

Network MIMO (netMIMO) [2], also referred to as *distributed MU-MIMO*, has potential for eliminating inter-cell interference, and hence eliminating contention, by allowing APs to tightly synchronize and share the transmission of data packets. An ideal netMIMO system can enable concurrent transmissions from distributed APs, thus scaling the downlink capacity linearly with the number of APs in a network. Researchers have explored the design of netMIMO by combining distributed APs into one giant MIMO transmitter [3–6]. APs are completely synchronized at the carrier-signal level by using a reference signal, and share each other's data (for cancelling cross-talk interference) via a wireline backhaul. While these schemes are promising for small-scale networks within a single contention domain, their tight synchronization requirement renders them infeasible for large-scale multi-cell wireless networks. The need for sharing data packets and channel state in real time may also deplete the backhaul capacity even if an expensive fiber backhaul connection were used [2].

We believe that the eventual means of realizing netMIMO is a hierarchical architecture that decomposes a large network into small, practical-size clusters, each containing multiple tightly coordinated APs running netMIMO. Distant clusters do not interfere with each other and can leverage spatial reuse; synchronization and data sharing are limited to within each cluster, thus eliminating the need for network-wide coordination. Realizing this vision, however, is very challenging. Interference between clusters, unless properly managed, can easily nullify the intra-cluster netMIMO gain. An extension of existing interference-avoidance protocols, which regards a cluster as one node, is feasible but insufficient—interference patterns can vary significantly over distributed APs even within one cluster, and thus coarse-grained interference avoidance may severely lower the spatial reuse.

In this paper, we design and implement a novel framework, called *NEMOx*, that realizes the potential of netMIMO for large-scale wireless networks. In NEMOx, a *cluster* contains one master AP (mAP) which coordinates a set of distributed APs (dAPs) (Figure 1) for netMIMO downlink transmission. The dAPs employ a distributed CSMA mechanism to avoid inter-cluster interference, which evades global synchronization and enables spatial reuse across clusters.

The nature of operation in netMIMO, however, poses a fundamental challenge. CSMA realizes asynchronous contention, but cannot handle the synchronous cooperation (*i.e.*, netMIMO trans-


*MobiCom'13,* September 30-October 4, Miami, FL, USA.

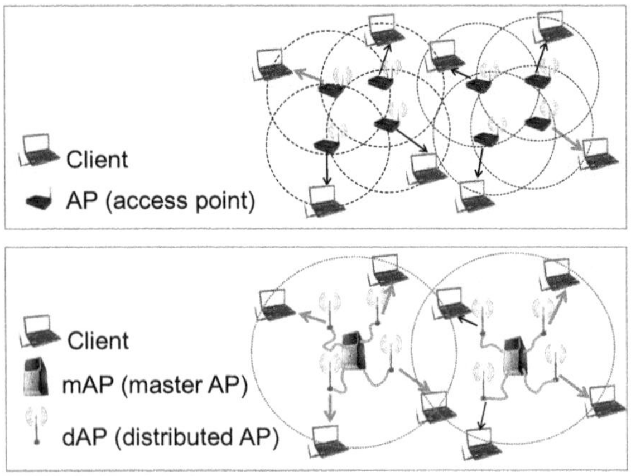


**Figure 1: Provisioning capacity and coverage using a traditional multi-cell WLAN (top) and NEMOx (bottom), respectively. Thick arrows indicate concurrent interference-free transmissions.**

mission) between distributed APs. NEMOx overcomes this difficulty via a semi-synchronized group-based contention mechanism, which prescribes subsets of dAPs as contention entities. At runtime, the mAP opportunistically schedules the subset with idle dAPs. Such a contention mechanism—contention being group-specific yet transmission being dAP-specific—is unique to netMIMO and has not been addressed in existing MAC designs. NEMOx proposes a simple, decentralized algorithm to optimize the contention between groups, and achieve proportionally fair channel access among dAPs.

While intra-cluster netMIMO transmission can be devised by migrating the 802.11ac MU-MIMO modulation algorithm that exploits multiplexing gain [5, 7], we find this could severely degrade netMIMO's performance. In particular, netMIMO may encounter unbalanced topologies where clients are concentrated near a few dAPs (which is common in, for example, conference rooms). In such cases, greedy exploitation of dAPs' multiplexing gain may result in low throughput for all clients. Further, since a client's throughput is coupled with dAPs and other clients within the same netMIMO transmission group, NEMOx meets these challenges by jointly optimizing the power budget of dAPs and opportunistically serving subsets of clients, so as to create balanced topologies and provide clients throughput fairness.

**Implementation.** We have prototyped NEMOx's MAC/PHY components on the WARP software radio platform [8]. Each cluster is built on one WARP node serving as an mAP connecting to, and controlling 4 dAPs (remote antennas). Sharing a central processing unit at the mAP, the dAPs achieve carrier-level synchronization without using an external clock, and real-time data sharing without a backhaul network, thereby making it possible to realize netMIMO transmission within a cluster. Our extensive experiments demonstrate that NEMOx effectively addresses the PHY-level challenges unique to netMIMO, allowing downlink throughput to scale linearly with the number of dAPs in a cluster. Experiments in a network testbed with multiple clusters and trace-driven emulation further verify the effectiveness of NEMOx's MAC in coordinating netMIMO clusters in large networks, yielding a multi-fold gain over current wireless LAN architecture and existing netMIMO schemes.

NEMOx confines its main operations to the mAP and requires no modification to client receivers. Further, its approach of building netMIMO preserves the signal processing modules in 802.11ac hardware, thus facilitating its deployment by simply upgrading the mAP's MAC driver and distributing its transmission points (antennas) using RF cables. Note that NEMOx's MAC/PHY components are not tied to this deployment model. Existing approaches [5, 6]

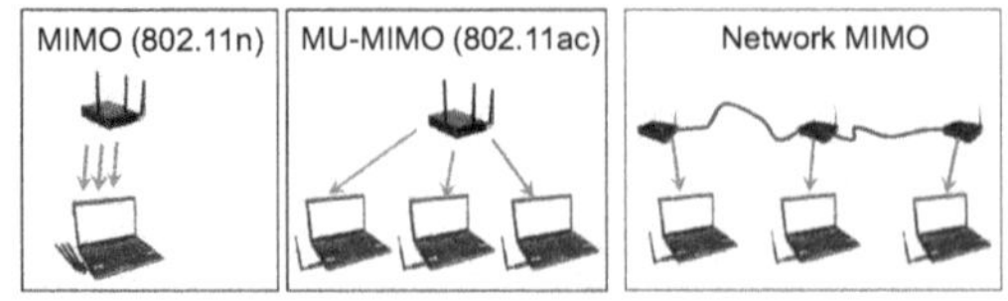


**Figure 2: Wireless LAN architecures other than SISO, and NEMOx shown in Figure 1.**

to building single-cluster netMIMO can also be used in our framework.

**Contributions.** We make several contributions via NEMOx as follows:

- Proposed a scalable, hierarchical architecture for netMIMO in wireless networks that realizes netMIMO efficiently within small clusters and employs asynchronous random access to enable spatial reuse across clusters.
- Designed a protocol to manage the synchronous cooperation and asynchronous channel access for dAPs in netMIMO. This protocol balances between multiplexing gain and spatial reuse, allowing network capacity to scale with the number of clusters.
- Optimized the netMIMO scheme that accounts for joint power control and client selection within each cluster, allowing a cluster's capacity to scale with the number of dAPs.
- Developed a simple way to build netMIMO clusters and implemented a working prototype of NEMOx in a WARP-based testbed, demonstrating NEMOx's effectiveness.

The rest of the paper is organized as follows. Sec. 2 briefly introduces MIMO-based network architectures. Sec. 3 presents an overview of the NEMOx architecture while Sec. 4 and 5 detail the design of NEMOx. Sec. 6 and 7 describe the implementation and experimental validation of NEMOx. Sec. 8 discusses NEMOx's limitations and our future work. Sec. 9 covers related work and finally, Sec. 10 concludes the paper.

## 2. BACKGROUND

Over the last several years, there has been an explosive growth of mobile traffic demand, whereas wireless spectrum remains a scarce resource, and this trend is expected to continue in future. It is, therefore, important to increase the transmission concurrency, or multiplexing gain. Ideally, a WLAN infrastructure should scale its multiplexing gain with the density of APs, while ensuring good coverage of a given area. Spatial reuse should also be exploited to scale the network capacity as its network area expands. Wireless LANs have evolved over the last decade with different architectures (Figure 2) to deal with these two levels of scalability.

Table 1 shows the capacity-scaling profiles of these WLAN architectures. For a fair comparison, they are assumed to use the same number of transmit antennas to cover the same area. Each transmit antenna has the same power budget, a practical constraint for radio hardware [2].

**SISO and MIMO.** In 802.11a/b/g SISO WLANs, neighboring APs interfere with each other and hence can only transmit alternately, *i.e.*, multiplexing gain is infeasible for transmitters in the same contention domain. However, APs in different contention domains can exploit spatial reuse to scale network capacity with network size. A MIMO AP, based on 802.11n, can send multiple streams of data to the *same client*, or beamform the same data through multiple antennas to improve SINR and link capacity, *i.e.*,

| | SISO | MIMO | CAS | netMIMO | NEMOx |
|---|---|---|---|---|---|
| Multiplexing gain | No | No | No | Yes | Yes |
| Diversity gain | No | Yes | Yes | Yes | Yes |
| Spatial reuse | Yes | Yes | Yes | No | Yes |
| Scalability, one contention domain | No | No | No | Yes | Yes |
| Scalability, multiple contention domains | Yes | Yes | Yes | No | Yes |

**Table 1: Scalability profiles for WLAN architectures. The multiplexing gain and diversity gain refer to the gains from cooperation across multiple WLAN cells.**

*diversity gain*. However, like SISO, neighboring MIMO APs are not cooperative, and hence provide no multiplexing gain among them.

**MU-MIMO or CAS.** The emerging 802.11ac multi-user MIMO (MU-MIMO) network [9] allows a multi-antenna AP to send different data streams concurrently to *multiple clients*. However, concurrency is achievable only for clients in the same cell, with all transmit antennas co-located at one AP. Like MIMO networks, such a co-located antenna system (CAS) cannot harness multiplexing gain for distributed APs, thereby not allowing the network capacity to scale with AP density.

**NetMIMO.** NetMIMO enables simultaneous transmission of different data streams through multiple dAPs that are tightly synchronized to form a "giant" multi-antenna transmitter [3–6]. The dAPs can serve their clients simultaneously by cancelling cross-talk interference, thus achieving multiplexing gain and scaling capacity with the AP density. However, existing netMIMO schemes require *full-synchronization* (*w.r.t.* transmission time, sampling clock-rate, carrier frequency and phase) and data sharing between all APs, which is not feasible for large networks with many APs spanning multiple contention domains.

NEMOx is designed as a practical solution to overcome this fundamental limitation, allowing netMIMO's downlink capacity to scale with both AP density and network size.

# 3. NEMOx: AN OVERVIEW

## 3.1 Motivation and Challenges

### *3.1.1 Why MAC for netMIMO?*

A hierarchical architecture makes it feasible to deploy netMIMO for large-scale wireless networks. But a fundamental question associated with it is: *How should a cluster contend for channel access and avoid interference with its neighbors?*

Although the intra-cluster dAPs' operations can be centralized at the mAP, they may border on dAPs of different clusters, thus experiencing asynchronous channel states or interference patterns. Unfortunately, netMIMO transmission can be realized only when all dAPs in a cluster synchronize their transmission attempts, *i.e.*, each senses an idle channel and finishes a random backoff at the same time.

To overcome this dilemma, the mAP may opt to wait for all its dAPs to become available and then trigger synchronous netMIMO transmissions from them. While this approach would provide a maximum multiplexing gain, the strict binding of dAPs can severely reduce spatial reuse opportunity of those dAPs that have less contention with dAPs in other clusters. Alternatively, dAPs in each cluster can run CSMA independently and start synchronous netMIMO transmissions if they acquire channels simultaneously. However, such opportunities are rare due to the decentralized and asynchronous nature of CSMA. Thus, this approach significantly limits multiplexing gain and reduces NEMOx to an 802.11 multi-cell WLAN.

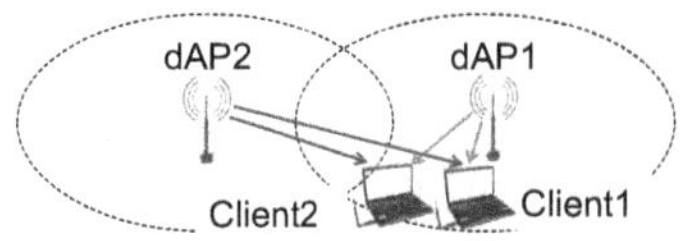


**Figure 3: In an unbalanced topology, concurrently serving two clients results in underutilization of the dAP's power budget, leading to low-rate for both.**

In arbitrating channel contention between clusters, the medium access mechanism in NEMOx must therefore *strike a balance between multiplexing gain and spatial reuse in coordinating dAPs within the same cluster.* Realizing this objective entails a new MAC design for netMIMO which (i) allows asynchronous contention across clusters to achieve scalability, (ii) employs flexible subsets of cooperating dAPs in each cluster to leverage spatial reuse, and (iii) opportunistically synchronizes dAPs within a cluster to realize netMIMO transmission and harvest multiplexing gain.

### *3.1.2 Tailoring netMIMO PHY for distributed APs*

A common approach to realizing netMIMO transmission is to migrate the 802.11ac MU-MIMO PHY, treating dAPs as multiple antennas of a giant AP [5,6], and using zero-forcing beamforming (ZFBF) to cancel cross-talk interference. ZFBF is a linear *precoding* mechanism that allows each dAP to send a weighted combination of the data symbols intended for different clients. Suppose $\boldsymbol{h}$ is the channel matrix and $\boldsymbol{x}$ the vector of symbols, then the weights, or so called the *precoding vector*, are created through a pseudo-inverse: $\boldsymbol{v} = \boldsymbol{h}'(\boldsymbol{h}\boldsymbol{h}')^{-1}$. Since $\boldsymbol{h}\boldsymbol{v}\boldsymbol{x} = \boldsymbol{I}\boldsymbol{x}$ where $\boldsymbol{I}$ is the identity matrix, each client only receives the data intended for itself. In other words, the clients' cross-talk interference is pre-cancelled by the dAPs.

However, we found ZFBF to be sub-optimal for netMIMO, especially in an unbalanced network topology. In MU-MIMO, transmit antennas are co-located and impose a similar level of cross-talk interference on each client, and hence, it is reasonable to use ZFBF which implicitly projects equal power for all clients [7]. But for netMIMO, due to the distributed nature of transmit antennas, the cross-talk interference may dominate the useful signals when clients are concentrated near one dAP.

For example, the two clients in Figure 3 are concentrated near dAP1. Since dAP2 is far away, it needs much greater power to cancel the cross-talk interference created by dAP1. However, since both dAPs have the same power budget, dAP2 should use its full power whereas dAP1 must reduce its power so that its cross-talk interference can still be cancelled by dAP2. As a result, only a small fraction of the power budget is used on useful signals, resulting in low rates for both clients. In such a case, it may be preferable to serve a single client (leveraging diversity gain) with full transmit power, or select clients that form a more balanced topology.

In addition, unlike in existing MAC/PHY protocols [10,11], where fairness can be defined *w.r.t.* a link (Tx–Rx pair), such a notion does not exist in netMIMO, where clients' rates are coupled and depend on a set of dAPs that are jointly serving them.

Therefore, *optimizing NEMOx's netMIMO operations involves not only ZFBF precoding, but also allocation of power from dAPs to clients, and the set of clients to be served on each transmission attempt.*

## 3.2 Basic Operations

NEMOx adopts a *thin AP* approach to building a netMIMO cluster. The dAPs in each cluster are simply a set of distributed anten-

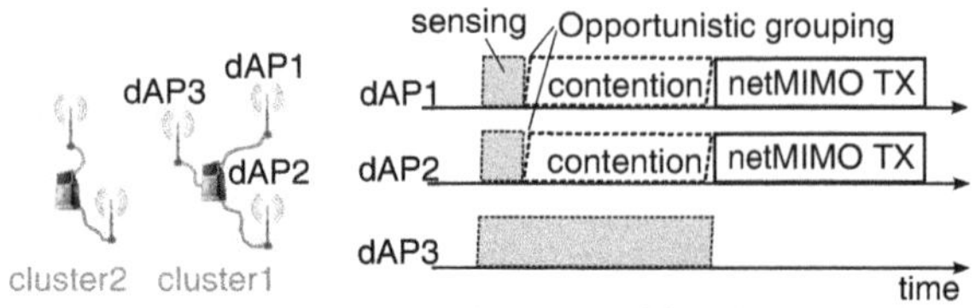


**Figure 4: Operations of an mAP controlling 3 dAPs. The mAP schedules dAPs' transmissions and modulates their data to remove cross-talk interference. The dAPs are responsible for carrier sensing and emitting modulated signals.**

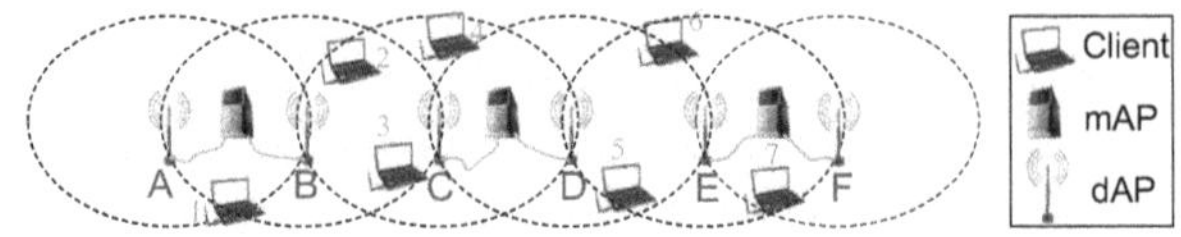


**Figure 5: An example topology in NEMOx with 3 clusters each containing 2 dAPs. The dotted circle represents a dAP's carrier sensing range.**

nas responsible for carrier sensing and emitting modulated signals. Both their PHY-layer packet modulation/demodulation and MAC-layer channel access protocols are centrally managed by the mAP. The MAC/PHY follows a modular design with a simple interface. The PHY provides each dAP's carrier sensing decision to the MAC, whereas the MAC is responsible for acquiring channel access opportunities, telling the PHY when to start netMIMO transmission and which dAPs to employ. As in existing netMIMO schemes [5,6], NEMOx primarily focuses on concurrent *downlink transmissions* from dAPs to clients.

Figure 4 illustrates a typical operation flow of an mAP controlling 3 dAPs (in cluster1). The mAP adopts a group contention algorithm in which subsets of dAPs opportunistically contend for netMIMO transmission. When dAP1 and dAP2 sense an idle channel, the mAP may choose to synchronize them into one group and then run a probabilistic contention algorithm to acquire the channel and avoid collision with external dAPs (those in different clusters). The mAP's choice between spatial reuse (schedule subset of dAPs for contention) and multiplexing gain (wait for all dAPs to become idle) is driven by a local optimization algorithm, which realizes proportionally fair channel access among all dAPs.

After a group of dAPs win channel contention, the mAP needs to match them with a set of clients. In particular, it needs to modulate their data and budget the transmit power of each dAP, so as to cancel cross-talk interference and maximize multiplexing gain. When the number of selected clients is less than the number of dAPs, the dAPs can beamform their power to the clients to improve their SINR, *i.e.*, harvesting the diversity gain. These operations are managed by the mAP's PHY module, which optimizes long-term throughput subject to proportional fairness among clients.

# 4. EFFICIENT NEMOx CHANNEL ACCESS

## 4.1 Creating virtual APs

While allowing for opportunistic grouping of dAPs strikes a balance between their multiplexing gain and spatial reuse, there still remains an important question: *how is a dAP group formed?* Recall that this problem involves a conflict between asynchronous contention and synchronized cooperation between dAPs. NEMOx resolves this tension by separating contention from dAP grouping. An mAP first prescribes all potential groups of dAPs in its cluster; each group is called a *virtual AP* (vAP). It then runs a contention algorithm that allows the vAPs to contend with each other and also with external vAPs.

A vAP decides on an idle channel only if all its dAPs sense idle channels, and switches to busy if any of its dAPs becomes busy. Upon sensing an idle channel, the vAP maintains a single back-off timer whose expiration triggers the netMIMO transmission of all dAPs contained in the vAP. As these dAPs are virtually synchronized within a vAP, but vAPs contend with each other asynchronously, we call this *semi-synchronized contention*. NEMOx's unique architecture makes it possible to realize such a contention mechanism, because *the MAC/PHY operations of all vAPs and dAPs inside each cluster are centrally executed by the mAP.*

**Dominance relation.** In its simplest form, the vAPs in a cluster are equivalent to all of its subsets of dAPs. But direct enumeration of all subsets results in an exponential number of vAPs. Since not all cooperating sets contribute equally to the cluster's capacity, NEMOx discriminates them by defining a *dominance* relation.

A vAP $S_i$ is said to *dominate* another vAP $S_j$ within the same cluster if $S_j$'s dAPs is a subset of $S_i$'s, and $S_i$'s interfering dAPs in neighboring clusters are a subset of $S_j$'s dAPs. In this case, $S_i$ has similar or fewer number of contenders than $S_j$, but it has a higher multiplexing gain. The dominated vAPs in $S_j$ are pruned to achieve higher computation and contention efficiency. For example, for the leftmost cluster in Figure 5, the vAP $\{A, B\}$ dominates $\{B\}$ because they are interfered by the same set of dAPs (*i.e.*, dAP $C$) in other clusters, and $\{B\}$ is only a subset of $\{A, B\}$.

To establish a dominance relation, vAPs simply sample the channel status, instead of decoding the identities of their interfering dAPs—which is not always feasible. If vAP $S_j$ is always busy when $S_i$ is busy, but not vice versa, then $S_i$'s interfering dAPs are a subset of $S_j$. The mAP performs such sampling and refreshes the dominance relation periodically (akin to an 802.11 beacon period), which can be done easily as all vAPs' operations are running centrally at the mAP.

## 4.2 Semi-synchronized CSMA

By constructing vAPs, an mAP translates the medium access problem of an entire cluster into channel contention between vAPs. Below we describe the channel-access protocol from the perspectives of an mAP and its vAPs.

**Client association.** If a client associated with the cluster has downlink packets to receive, then all dAPs which can deliver packets to the client will be marked as potential transmitters. Further, all vAPs that contain any potential transmitters, will trigger channel contention. Depending on the outcome of contention, a client may be served by a different vAP for each transmission attempt. Such a *soft association* mechanism is a unique feature of the NEMOx architecture, as dAPs or vAPs in a cluster are centrally controlled by the mAP, and can flexibly adjust their association with clients on a per-packet basis. This flexibility makes it possible to vary the throughput provisioning for a client by matching it with vAPs of different sizes, which will be further optimized in NEMOx's PHY component (see Sec. 5).

**State transition.** NEMOx runs a probabilistic channel-access algorithm, where each vAP adjusts its aggressiveness in contention following the state-transition diagram in Figure 6. A vAP updates its state on a per-time-slot basis. The slot duration is the same as that in 802.11 (*e.g.*, 9$\mu s$ in 802.11g). Time slots are synchronized only for vAPs within the same cluster. A vAP, $V_j$, starts with the *busy state* by default. It enters the *idle state* if all of its dAPs sense an idle channel for a fixed number of slots (the DIFS period defined in 802.11 [9]). Then, it transits to *contention state* with a *contention probability* $q_j$. With probability $(1-q_j)$, it remains in the idle state, and advances its contention probability as:

$$q_j \leftarrow q_j + \alpha \quad (1)$$

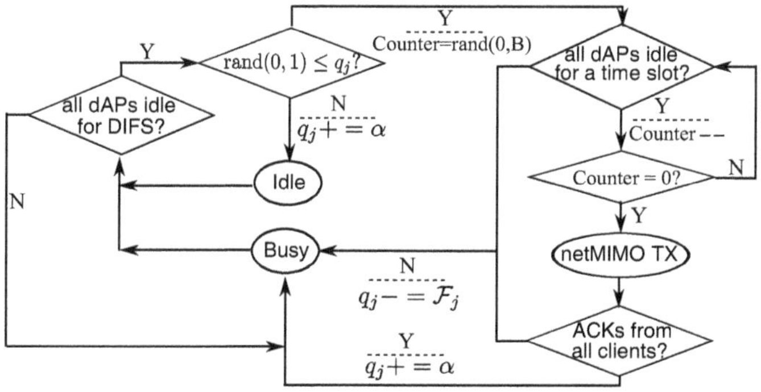


**Figure 6: State-transition diagram for a vAP.**

where $\alpha \in (0, 1)$ is a fixed parameter that determines how aggressively $V_j$ should advance its contention probability.

After entering the contention state, it starts the backoff procedure by selecting a random number between 0 and the backoff window $B$, and counting the corresponding number of idle slots. If the backoff counter expires on time, $V_j$ calls its PHY module to start netMIMO transmission. If $V_j$ senses a busy channel during backoff due to another (either internal or external) vAP acquiring the channel beforehand, then it declares a *contention failure*, switches back to busy state, and reduces its contention probability as:

$$q_j \leftarrow q_j - \mathcal{F}_j \tag{2}$$

where $\mathcal{F}_j$ is a parameter to be optimized (see Sec. 4.3.3).

Upon completing transmission and receiving ACKs from all intended clients, $V_j$ returns to its initial busy state and advances its contention probability according to Eq. (1). Otherwise, a *transmission failure* occurs and $V_j$ reduces its contention probability according to Eq. (2).

In NEMOx, collision can only occur between vAPs of different clusters. When vAPs inside the same cluster fire backoff counters simultaneously, the mAP randomly enables one of them. By migrating the medium access from node (dAP) level to group (vAP) level, NEMOx substantially reduces the number of contention domains compared to traditional 802.11 WLANs, thus lowering the collision overhead.

It is now evident that the key to NEMOx's MAC efficiency and fairness lies in how a vAP advances or regresses its contention probability $q_j$ as in Eqs. (1) and (2). In what follows, we forward-engineer these operations to achieve optimal and fair channel access among all dAPs.

## 4.3 Optimizing medium access

As clients' population is dynamic and their traffic demands are unpredictable, NEMOx opts to provision *optimal and fair channel access* for the netMIMO infrastructure, *i.e.*, the dAPs instead. Responsibility for fairness among clients is delegated to the PHY module (Sec. 5) which selectively serves clients, given the dAPs available for netMIMO transmission.

### *4.3.1 Formulation of the optimization problem*

The overarching goal of the MAC module is thus to optimize the semi-synchronized contention algorithm, run by vAPs, to ensure optimal and fair channel access for all dAPs—the actual transmitters. Suppose $r_i$ is the probability of successful transmission for dAP $i$, and $\mathcal{C}$ the set of clusters. Then, the optimization problem can be cast as:

$$\max \sum_{K \in \mathcal{C}} \sum_{i \in K} \alpha_K U(r_i). \tag{3}$$

Each dAP $i$ is associated with a utility function $U(r_i)$, which reflects the fairness objective. When $U(r_i) = \log(r_i)$, maximizing the sum utility is proven to achieve global optimality *w.r.t.* $r_i$ and proportional fairness [12]. $\alpha_K$ is the weight that can be used for prioritizing cluster $K$.

The optimization objective must be pursued subject to network resource constraints. The nature of CSMA contention allows at most one vAP to transmit in any contention domain, which can be characterized by a maximal clique—a complete graph in which there exists an edge between two vAPs if they can sense each other. In other words, the sum contention probability of all vAPs in any maximal clique should not exceed 1. Let $\mathcal{M}$ denote the set of maximal cliques in the network, then

$$\sum_{j \in m} q_j \leq 1, \quad \forall m \in \mathcal{M}. \tag{4}$$

Furthermore, the effective transmission probability, $r_i$, of dAP $i$, equals the sum transmission probability of all vAPs containing it. Let $P_j$ be the probability that vAP $j$ experiences a transmission/contention failure, then its effective transmission probability is equal to $(1 - P_j)q_j$. So, we have:

$$r_i = \sum_{i \in j} (1 - P_j) q_j \tag{5}$$

Note that $r_i$ is the probability of successful transmission and $q_j$ is the overall *contention probability*. To derive $r_i$ from $q_j$, an attrition factor $(1 - P_j)$ is multiplied, thus accounting for both transmission and contention failure.

Consequently, the semi-synchronized contention algorithm can achieve optimality and fairness if it solves the optimization problem (3) subject to constraints (4) and (5). With this formulation, the rate of each dAP would be a function of all of the vAPs it belongs to, as well as their collision probability. Moreover, with the utility defined *w.r.t.* each dAP, the above optimization implicitly favors vAPs with more dAPs and hence a higher netMIMO gain.

The solution of this optimization directly provides the channel contention probability $q_j$ for each vAP $j$. But solving the problem is non-trivial as it involves exchange of global information between all vAPs and dAPs in a network, which we strive to avoid. In what follows, we derive a decentralized solution that can be mapped to each vAP's local state transitions (Figure 6) but can still achieve the optimization objective.

### *4.3.2 Decentralized solution for each vAP*

We first obtain a decentralized solution to the optimization problem (3) by decomposing its variables into subsets, each associated with one NEMOx cluster. Observing that (3) is a concave optimization problem, we can obtain its Lagrangian as:

$$L = \sum_{K \in \mathcal{C}} \sum_{i \in K} \alpha_K U(r_i) - \sum_{m \in \mathcal{M}} \sum_{j \in m} \beta_m q_j \tag{6}$$

where $\beta_m$ is the Lagrange multiplier for maximal clique $m$. We can write $\beta_m$ as $\beta_m = \beta P_m$, where $P_m$ is the collision probability in maximal clique $m$. Since a vAP $j$ may belong to multiple maximal cliques, its collision probability is $P_j = 1 - \Pi_{m:j \in m}(1 - P_m)$. If $P_m$ is kept small, then we have:

$$P_j \approx \sum_{m:j \in m} P_m \tag{7}$$

The assumption of a small $P_m$ requires that the collision probability of any contention domain within the network be kept low. This can be satisfied by keeping a reasonably small value for $\alpha$ and a large value for $B$ (Figure 6), so that no vAP becomes overly aggressive during contention. A similar assumption has been used in traditional utility-based wireless MAC design [10].

Following the approximation in Eq. (7), the parameter $P_j$ can be approached by allowing vAP $j$ to locally keep track of its contention/transmission failure probability, without knowledge of its maximal cliques or loss probabilities in each of them. Now, substituting for $\beta_m$ and making the approximation, we have $L = \sum_{K \in C} L_K$, where

$$L_K = \sum_{i \in K} \alpha_K U(r_i) - \beta \sum_{i \in K, j: i \in j} P_j q_j. \tag{8}$$

The analysis in [10,11] has shown that the aggregate utility for a system of equations of the above form is maximized when the individual components maximize their own utilities. While the component corresponds to a single link in traditional WLANs, this corresponds to a cluster $K$ in netMIMO, thereby requiring joint adaptation of vAPs within each cluster for optimality. Applying the KKT conditions for optimality with respect to each vAP $j$, we obtain

$$\frac{\mathrm{d}L_K}{\mathrm{d}q_j} = \sum_{i \in j} \alpha_K U'(r_i)(1 - P_j) - \beta P_j = 0, \ \forall j \in m. \tag{9}$$

Since $U(r_i) = \log(r_i)$, at the optimum, for every vAP $j$ in cluster $K$, we have:

$$\frac{\mathrm{d}L_K}{\mathrm{d}q_j} = \sum_{i \in j} \alpha_K (1 - P_j) r_i^{-1} - \beta P_j = 0. \tag{10}$$

Or equivalently, $\alpha_K(1 - P_j) - \beta P_j \cdot \left(\sum_{i \in j}(1/r_i)\right)^{-1} = 0.$

While $\alpha_K$ can be used to prioritize different clusters, we set $\alpha_K = \alpha'$ for an equal bias. Given that $P_j$ can be locally inferred by each vAP $j$, the above optimality condition can be approached by adapting each vAP $j$'s contention probability in a completely decentralized manner as:

$$q_j \leftarrow q_j + \alpha' - P_j\Big(\beta(\sum_{i \in j}(1/r_i))^{-1} + \alpha'\Big). \tag{11}$$

The adaptation mechanism for each vAP follows a gradient approach based on the KKT conditions. Further, since the utility function $U(r_i) = \log(r_i)$ and the resulting Lagrangian are concave with respect to each $q_j$, there exists a unique maximum, to which the individual adaptations converge. We omit the detailed proof of convergence as it bears a spirit similar to the one in [10].

#### 4.3.3 *Mapping optimization solution to NEMOx*

We can now map the optimization solution (11) to NEMOx's channel-access algorithm shown in Figure 6. The adaptation can be done in discrete time frames, each spanning one of three states: idle, transmission success, and transmission/contention failure. At the end of each frame, a vAP $j$ advances its contention probability by $\alpha'$, so $\alpha$ in NEMOx (Eq. (1)) should be set to $\alpha'$. A large value of $\alpha'$ leads to fast adaptation, but cause oscillation of $p_j$ around its optimum. By default, we set $\alpha' = 0.05$. By using (11), a vAP should deduct its $q_j$ by $(\beta(\sum_{i \in j}(1/r_i))^{-1} + \alpha)$ whenever a transmission/contention failure occurs (with probability $P_j$). Since failure is conditioned upon a contention attempt with probability $q_j$, the actual deduction should be scaled down by $q_j$. The resulting deduction is exactly the parameter $\mathcal{F}_j$ in Figure 6:

$$\mathcal{F}_j = q_j^{-1}\Big(\beta(\sum_{i \in j}(1/r_i))^{-1} + \alpha\Big). \tag{12}$$

When following the adaptation step of (11), each vAP $j$ should truncate $q_j$ to make it fall in the range $[0, 1]$.

Note that the parameter $\beta$ represents a scalar component for the Lagrange multiplier component $\beta_m$ in Eq. (6). A larger $\beta$ incurs a larger penalty to $p_j$ when collision occurs, but larger oscillation around the optimum. By default, we use an empirical value of $\beta = 0.25$ which keeps a relatively low collision probability.

When mutually interfering vAPs advance their contention probabilities to high values, severe collision may occur which will waste channel time for corrupted packets. NEMOx reduces the risk of collision with an additional backoff, which buffers and randomizes vAP's transmissions. The backoff window size $B$ need not be adapted over time as a vAP can react to and reduce collisions by adapting its contention probability. Here $B$ is defaulted to 32.

## 5. NEMOx: NETMIMO TRANSMISSION

NEMOx's PHY module resolves a second challenge unique to netMIMO, *i.e.*, optimizing power budgeting for dAPs and ensuring fairness among clients. This section describes the PHY module from the perspective of a vAP (and its dAPs) that has won channel contention. We first introduce how the vAP budgets power for a given set of clients, and then discuss how it selects clients for fairness.

### 5.1 Optimal power budgeting for dAPs

As we observed in Sec. 3, a direct application of ZFBF precoding to netMIMO may severely degrade its performance. The fundamental reason for this is that ZFBF forces dAPs to explore multiplexing gain and implicitly allocates the same power for all clients [7]. NEMOx overcomes this limitation with optimal power budgeting. It trades multiplexing gain for diversity gain in unbalanced topologies, by beamforming multiple dAPs' power to one client, while also opportunistically scheduling clients to reduce topology imbalance. The tradeoff between diversity and multiplexing gains is made automatically via the following optimization framework that performs joint precoding and power (JPP) allocation:

$$\text{JPP:} \quad \max \quad \textstyle\sum_{i=1}^{|D|} w_i \log(1 + \frac{P_i}{N_0}) \tag{13}$$

$$\text{s.t.} \quad P_i = |\textstyle\sum_{k=1}^{|S|} h_{ik} v_{ki}|^2, \forall i \in D \tag{14}$$

$$\textstyle\sum_{i=1}^{|D|} |v_{ki}|^2 \leq P_{\max}, \forall k \in S \tag{15}$$

$$\textstyle\sum_{k=1}^{|S|} h_{jk} v_{ki} = 0, i \in D, j \neq i, \tag{16}$$

where $D$ and $S$ are the set of clients and dAPs, respectively. Eq. (14) represents client $i$'s received power under the joint effects of precoding $v_{ki}$ and channel distortion $h_{ik} (k \in S, i \in D)$ *w.r.t.* dAP $k$. Eq. (15) is the per-dAP power budget constraint. Eq. (16) represents the precoding constraint, *i.e.*, precoded data symbols intended for client $i$ should cancel each other when arriving at client $j$ ($i \neq j$) after experiencing channel distortion. The weight $w_i$ associated with client $i$ determines throughput fairness and will be discussed in Sec. 5.2.

The objective of this JPP framework is to maximize the weighted sum throughput of all clients, *by optimizing elements of the precoding matrix $v_{ki} (k \in S, i \in D)$, which in turn determines dAP $k$'s power budget for client $i$.* When the topology is unbalanced, this objective implicitly favors a few clients with high capacity, instead of fairly serving all clients with extremely low capacity. To the best of our knowledge, such a tradeoff between diversity and multiplexing gain has not been addressed in existing netMIMO system designs [5,6]. The significance of both the problem and our approach will be highlighted in Sec. 7.1 through our testbed experiments.

The JPP formulation can be easily proven to be non-convex [13] *w.r.t.* the real and imaginary components of $v_{ki}$, due to the norm operator in Eq. (14). Fortunately, by phase-shifting the vector $v_{ik}, \forall k \in S$ appropriately, we can restrict $Im(\sum_{k=1}^{|S|} h_{ik} v_{ik}) = 0$, while both constraints (15) and (16) are insensitive to the phase-shift. The resulting problem then becomes convex, and can be easily solved using standard convex optimization techniques.

**Algorithm 1** Opportunistic client scheduling.

1. **Input:** $S$: set of dAPs in a vAP who won contention; $D$: set of clients that can be served by the dAPs in $S$.
   $\mathcal{D}$: set of clients in this cluster.
2. **Initialize:** $D' \leftarrow$NULL, $O_{\max} \leftarrow 0$
3. **while** $|D'| < |S|$
4. **foreach** $i \in D \backslash D'$
5. Solve JPP, with the set of dAPs $S$ and set of clients $i \cup D'$. Obtain optimal sum capacity $O_i$.
6. **if** $O_i > O_{\max}$ **then** $O_{\max} \leftarrow O_i$; bestClient$\leftarrow i$;
7. **endif**
8. **endfor**
9. $D' \leftarrow$ bestClient $\cup D'$
10. **end while**
11. Run netMIMO transmission from $S$ to $D'$.
12. Client $i$ throughput is $R_i$ in this transmission, $i \in \mathcal{D}$
13. $\overline{R}_i \leftarrow \gamma R_i + (1-\gamma)\overline{R}_i$
14. $w_i \leftarrow 1/\overline{R}_i$

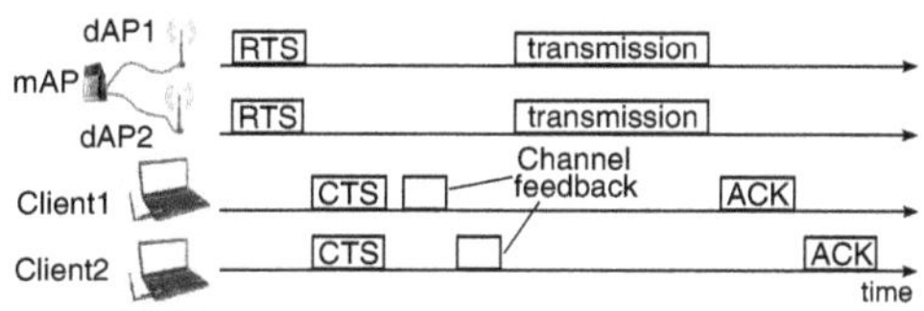


**Figure 7: Flow of operations for a netMIMO transmission in NEMOx.**

## 5.2 Opportunistic client scheduling

NEMOx adopts an opportunistic client scheduling algorithm (Algorithm 1) to restrict the set of clients to be served in each transmission attempt, and integrates client selection with the JPP precoding matrix design to achieve its fairness objective.

Client selection affects the topology pattern (balanced or unbalanced), which in turn affects the netMIMO capacity. This observation leads to an iterative client-selection algorithm for NEMOx. In each iteration, the algorithm searches for a *bestClient* that maximizes the weighted sum rate (according to JPP), when served together with those clients already selected. The selection aborts if the number of selected clients exceeds the number of dAPs, or the bestClient yields a lower sum rate than that in the previous iteration.

Then, netMIMO transmission is executed and client $i$ achieves a throughput of $R_i$. It then updates its time-averaged throughput $\overline{R}_i$ using a moving average with a smoothing factor $\gamma$ (set to 0.1 by default). Further, its throughput weight $w_i$ is adjusted to achieve a certain long-term fairness objective. For *proportional fairness*, we can configure $w_i$ to be the inverse of $\overline{R}_i$ [14].

## 5.3 Channel estimation, reservation and ACK

Figure 7 illustrates a typical flow of operations in a netMIMO transmission, which involves a set of dAPs selected by NEMOx's MAC module, and clients selected by the above opportunistic client scheduling algorithm.

Before starting the data transmission, the dAPs synchronously broadcast the same RTS packet that indicates the transmission duration and clients' addresses. Then, all selected clients return the same CTS packet. The CTS packet contains the duration of this transmission attempt, and is sent by all clients synchronously to reserve a channel from transmitters in neighboring clusters. The dAPs' RTS packets serve as a reference broadcast for all clients, so that they can synchronize their CTS responses. Since the CTS packets contain the same information, they do not collide with each other when synchronized. Such synchronized responses are shown

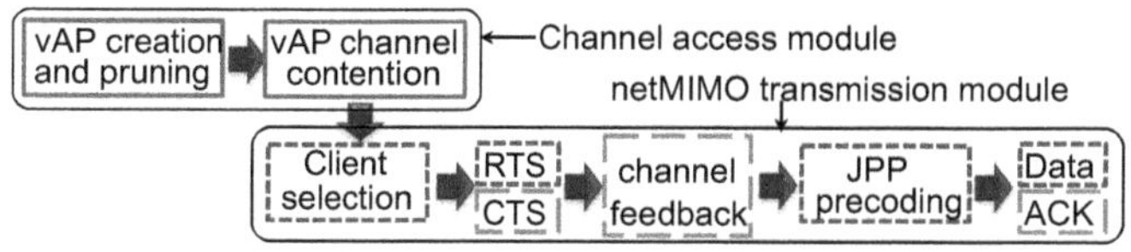


**Figure 8: Summary of NEMOx operations.**

to be effective even when COTS WiFi and ZigBee hardware are used [15, 16].

After the RTS/CTS handshake, the clients sequentially feed back the channel state information (CSI), *i.e.*, the channel vector from the dAPs to itself. Such feedback is necessary for the mAP to compute the precoding matrix following JPP. The netMIMO transmission is aborted if feedback from some clients is missing, perhaps due to a CTS channel reservation failure. In such a case, other vAPs can reuse the transmission opportunity, thanks to NEMOx's contention-based channel access protocol. If the netMIMO transmission succeeds, an ACK is also sent sequentially by each client in a similar manner to the CSI feedback.

NEMOx's CSI and ACK feedback operations are similar to those in 802.11ac, but its channel reservation mechanism is unique. In 802.11ac's MU-MIMO mode [9], an AP needs to broadcast a *TXOP* packet, which signals neighboring transmitters and reserves the channel. TXOP itself does not resolve the hidden terminal problem; NEMOx addresses it using the synchronous CTS from clients.

NEMOx's client-selection algorithm needs a channel matrix from the dAPs to all potential clients (line 5 in Algorithm 1). Estimating such a channel matrix incurs huge overhead. Observe, however, that dAPs and clients tend to spread over a large area, and small-scale fading (which causes small magnitude and phase variation) has relatively small impact on topology imbalance, compared to large-scale pathloss due mainly to transmitter/receiver distance. Therefore, without losing much accuracy, NEMOx runs client selection using the latest channel gain statistics in previous transmissions, so as to reduce the channel-estimation overhead.

# 6. IMPLEMENTATION

**Flow of Operations in NEMOx.** Figure 8 summarizes NEMOx's flow of operations throughout one channel contention and transmission attempt. An mAP periodically runs the vAP prunning algorithm (Sec. 4.1). It continuously contends for channel access on behalf of all remaining vAPs (Sec. 4.2). The vAP that wins contention in each cluster will start its netMIMO transmission attempt immediately. It first uses the client selection algorithm (Sec. 5.2) to determine the set of clients to serve, and initiates the RTS/CTS exchange with the selected clients and obtains channel matrix (Sec. 5.3). Then, it computes the precoding matrix $\boldsymbol{v}$ following the JPP framework (Sec. 5.1), precodes the data vector $\boldsymbol{x}$ into a new vector $\boldsymbol{vx}$, and sends each element of the vector through the corresponding dAP. Based on ACK feedback the clients, the vAP infers transmission success/failure, updates contention parameters and starts a new round of contention (Sec. 4.2).

**Implementation.** We have implemented a prototype of NEMOx on the WARP [8] software radio platform. We use the original WARP board as an mAP, and deploy the dAPs by extending the WARP antennas (with a radio board) by up to 30 ft using LMR-400 $50\Omega$ coaxial cables and SMA male-to-female connectors (Figure 9). Based on the WARPlab driver, we have implemented a full-fledged multi-user MIMO-OFDM modulation/demodulation library to support NEMOx. Figure 10 shows the basic components and interfaces in our implementation.

*Transmit path.* In the transmit path, we implement the NEMOx client-selection algorithm to determine the set of dAPs/clients to

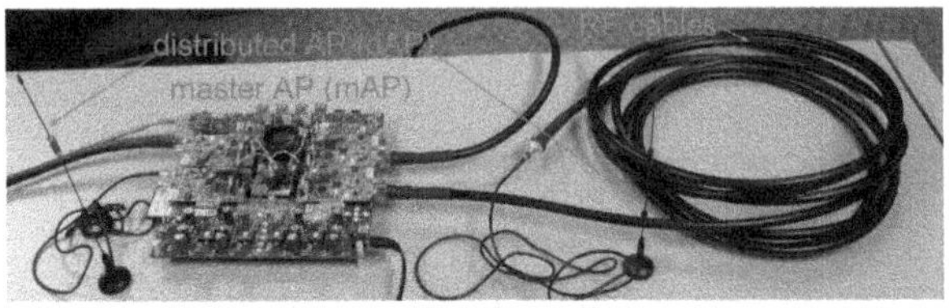


**Figure 9: Building a NEMOx cluster using WARP.**

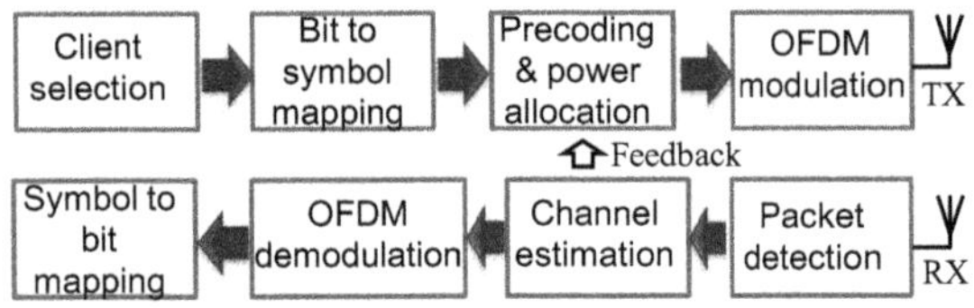


**Figure 10: The MIMO-OFDM PHY layer implementation of NEMOx on WARP.**

be used for netMIMO transmissions. Then, the digital bits of each client are mapped to symbols via BPSK. NEMOx's joint precoding and power-allocation algorithm is then performed in the frequency domain (on the symbols carried by each OFDM subcarrier). The precoded symbols for each dAP are modulated using OFDM and sent over the air.

*Receive path.* Each client runs the receiver path that detects the packets and then estimates the channel from each dAP. All packets start with a short-preamble that can be detected using a self-correlation based algorithm [17]. Due to the long interface latency between the WARP radio and its PC host, the synchronous CTS feedback from clients cannot be directly implemented. Thus, we simulate the RTS/CTS-based channel reservation with a C++ based module running on the PC host, as will be detailed below. Our implementation of channel estimation follows a similar procedure as in 802.11ac. Specifically, the dAPs first send the same short-preamble synchronously, and then sequentially send a long-preamble, which is used for each client to correct frequency offset and estimate the CSI. The CSI is estimated for each OFDM subcarrier and contains the channel phase/amplitude distortion between all dAPs and the receiver itself. CSI elements are quantized to 8-bit following 802.11ac [9] and fed back to the mAP for precoding. In our implementation, all dAPs' and clients' signal processing operations run on a PC host, so the feedback is realized directly using function calls. This alleviates the problem of CSI feedback delay, although the signal processing delay is still on the order of tens of milliseconds, much longer than an actual hardware implementation.

Following the long-preambles is an additional preamble sent by all dAPs concurrently and used by each receiver to estimate the composite channel created by channel distortion and precoding. Based on the estimation estimation results, the receiver can demodulate the OFDM symbols and decode the digital bits therein. Within each OFDM symbol, 4 pilot subcarriers (with known bits) are sent by the transmitter and used for correcting residual errors in the frequency offset estimation using long-preambles.

*Implementation of NEMOx MAC.* We implement NEMOx's MAC protocol as a C++ back-end module running on the WARP controller. Time-critical functionalities, such as backoff countdown and inter-frame timing, are realized using a virtual timer instead of wallclock time. Carrier sensing relation between dAPs are measured offline for each experimental topology and fed into the MAC module. If contention succeeds, the MAC of the winning mAP calls its PHY transmit path to realize the packet transmission. This approach circumvents the long latency of the WARP-PC interface, but preserves the contention behaviors of different mAPs, as well as the channel pathloss/fading effects.

# 7. EVALUATION

In this section, we first evaluate NEMOx's PHY components. Then, we run it in a multi-cluster testbed to evaluate its *network-level* throughput, fairness and scalability.

## 7.1 Micro-benchmark evaluation

We deployed a single cluster in an office environment (its floor map shown in Figure 11). To isolate ambient interference, all experiments were conducted at night, and over a 2.4 GHz ISM band (channel 14) unused by any other nearby devices. As a WARP board can only support up to 4 dAPs, we use trace-driven emulation for more than 4 dAPs. For emulation, each dAP broadcasts short probing packets containing only the synchronization and channel estimation preambles. Channel matrices are recorded by clients for 1 minute and then replayed in our PHY module implementation. Sampling one channel matrix takes only around 8.7 ms with the latest WARPLab driver, well below the typical coherence time for indoor radio environments (800 ms according to [18]) and ensures that the channel matrices represent a snapshot of the real channel effects. The accuracy of this emulation will be validated by comparing it with real-time experiments.

**Multiplexing gain.** We compare NEMOx with a baseline scheme in which dAPs are non-cooperative, referred to as *NonCoop*, essentially the default protocol in 802.11 WLANs. To isolate the MAC-layer effects, we first assume NonCoop can centrally schedule dAPs alternately (*w/o MAC*). By default, we run UDP transmissions with packet size 1.5KB and BPSK modulation. The SINR of *decoded* BPSK symbols is then mapped to the Shannon rate. Figure 12(a) plots NEMOx's multiplexing gain (reflected by per-client throughput gain) over NonCoop, where the number of clients increases along with that of dAPs. As dAP density rises, the number of concurrent transmissions (and hence multiplexing gain) grows almost linearly. Ideally, the gain should increase in the same order as dAP density, but the experimental results are shown to be less than ideal, *e.g.*, the average capacity gain is 6.45 with dAP density equal to 8. This is because the dAP-to-client channels are not perfectly orthogonal. Each dAP needs to reduce power to combat the channel correlation and cancel cross-talk interference. Similar observations have been made in an existing theoretical analysis [14].

Figure 12(a) also compares the trace-driven emulation (for dAP density 2—4) with real-time experiments (represented with solid symbols), which match each other very well. Our analysis of the traces show that the received signal power variation is negligible over tens of seconds to several minutes, as our experimental setting avoids ambient mobility and interference. Thus, collecting and replaying channel traces produces consistent experimental results with real-time runs.

We further enable NEMOx's MAC implementation and compare it with our implementation of 802.11 CSMA for NonCoop (*w/ MAC*). Figure 12(a) shows that NEMOx's gain grows to 3.92 and 7.91, for dAP density 4 and 8, respectively, even higher than w/o MAC. Under a realistic CSMA-based MAC, the NonCoop APs need to spend a substantial amount of time for channel contention and collision resolution. By contrast, NEMOx eliminates such overhead, and therefore, *NEMOx's multiplexing gain comes from both netMIMO cooperation at PHY layer and reduced contention overhead at MAC layer*. The combined capacity gain can be even larger than the dAP density in one cluster.

**Diversity gain.** When the client population is small, multiple dAPs can harvest diversity gain by beamforming the same data towards one client. Figure 12(b) evaluates such diversity gain for two clients: client A, located at the network edge, and client B, located near the network center (with similar distance to all dAPs). The for-

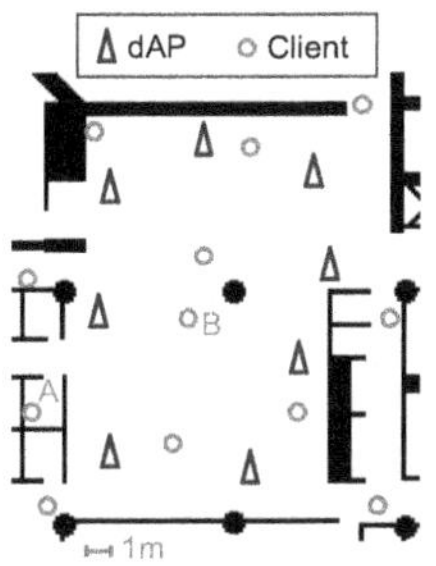


Figure 11: Single-cluster testbed. Black dots are pillars in our building.

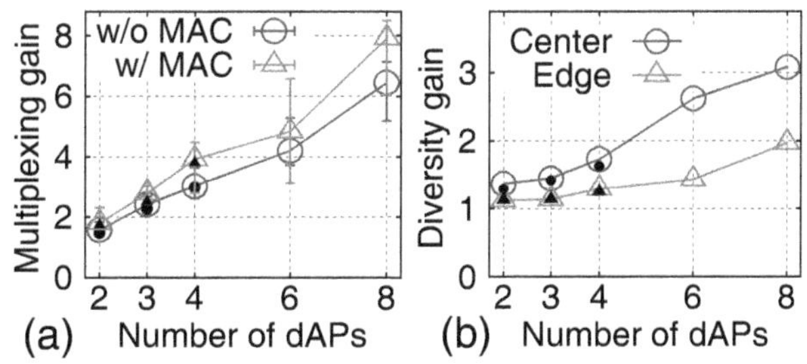


**Figure 12: NEMOx's multiplexing and diversity gains over non-cooperative multi-AP networks. Error bars represent maximum and minimum among clients.**

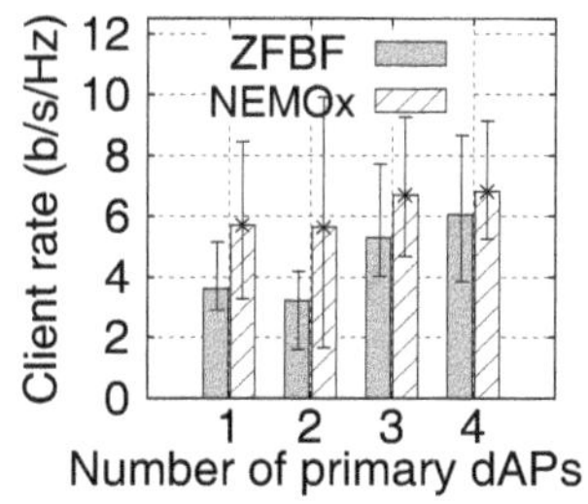


**Figure 13: Impact of power allocation: error bars show max and min of 5 topologies.**

mer benefits little from diversity, as its signal power mainly comes from the few dAPs nearby. The latter's capacity scales with the number of beamforming dAPs. With 8 dAPs, the average diversity gain is 3.08. This implies that the diversity gain scales sub-linearly with $M$ (the number of dAPs), consistent with the theoretical rule of $\log(M^2)$ scalability [14].

**Impact of power allocation.** NEMOx's JPP module is critical when the cluster's topology is unbalanced. In practice, such topologies are formed when clients are concentrated around a few dAPs, which we call *primary dAPs*. In Figure 13, we place 4 dAPs in a cluster, and vary the clients' concentrated locations to create different numbers of primary dAPs. The results show that, compared to ZFBF, NEMOx improves the mean link capacity by around 59% when the clients are concentrated near 1 or 2 dAPs. Despite its remarkable performance for co-located antenna systems [7, 19], the equal power allocation strategy in ZFBF may severely underutilize netMIMO's capacity in such topologies.

**Impact of opportunistic client selection.** An additional dimension of optimization in NEMOx is client selection. Figure 14 shows the experimental results when the number of dAPs is fixed at 4 while varying that of clients. Compared to a naive scheme that randomly selects 4 clients, NEMOx achieves a 58.9–75.6% higher average rate for clients. Even when the number of dAPs equals that of clients, the random scheme always schedules all clients. By contrast, NEMOx may partition the clients into multiple (overlapping) groups, each having a high sum-rate and served over different transmission attempts to achieve higher network capacity.

Figure 14 also plots the results from NEMOxZ, an alternative scheme that runs NEMOx's iterative client selection (Algorithm 1), but replaces the JPP component with ZFBF. The results show that NEMOxZ achieves performance comparable to NEMOx when the number of clients is much larger (*e.g.*, twice) than that of dAPs. This is because with more clients, NEMOxZ has a better chance to group clients that form a balanced topology, thus maintaining high capacity. Therefore, *when the number of clients is large, NEMOx can replace its JPP module with ZFBF to reduce its computational complexity.*

## 7.2 Scaling netMIMO with NEMOx

**Throughput optimality and fairness in benchmark topologies.** We first benchmark NEMOx's MAC-layer performance by deploying 3 clusters (top 3 ones in Figure 15), each containing 2 dAPs serving 2 clients. Every two adjacent dAPs can sense each other. The topology is essentially the same as Figure 5. It has a well-defined optimal and fair allocation of access rate for all dAPs, which can be obtained by solving the optimization problem (3). Our experiments focus on NEMOx's MAC-layer access opportunity and fairness, and isolate PHY-layer effects by forcing BPSK modulation (identical data rate) for served clients. We will later evaluate the joint MAC/PHY effects. We evaluate MAC throughput by sending saturated UDP traffic to each client, with maximum aggregated frame size of 4 KB, unless noted otherwise. We use 50ms as the CSI feedback period, assuming this is much shorter than the channel coherence time.

We compare NEMOx with 3 other schemes. The first is Oracle that directly assigns the optimal channel access probability $q_j$ to each vAP $j$. The second is FullCoop that groups all dAPs in each cluster into one vAP, *i.e.*, it greedily employs netMIMO cooperation gain without the semi-synchronized contention in NEMOx. FullCoop represents an extension of existing netMIMO proposals [5, 6] to multiple contention domains. The third is NonCoop representing the 802.11 MAC which runs CSMA among dAPs, *i.e.*, no netMIMO gain.

Figure 16 plots the throughput of each client. NEMOx achieves a similar level of total network throughput and per-client throughput compared to the Oracle MAC, implying that its distributed MAC approximates a centralized protocol well. FullCoop loses spatial reuse for dAPs 1 and 6 (which should have more transmission opportunities due to less contention), thus reducing the corresponding clients' throughput by more than 79%. Though NonCoop leverages spatial reuse, it sacrifices cooperation gain between dAPs, resulting in 32% lower network throughput than NEMOx in this benchmark topology. Note that for clients 2 to 5, FullCoop and NonCoop may achieve higher throughput than NEMOx. But this comes at the cost of proportional fairness for clients 1 and 6, which should have achieved higher throughput when served by dAPs 1 and 6.

We proceed to quantitatively verify NEMOx's fairness, *i.e.*, whether it delivers throughput gains to all clients by combining its MAC and PHY modules. As NEMOx targets proportional fairness, the fairness metric should be the log-utility function $\sum_{k=1}^{D}\log(H_k)$, where $H_k$ is the throughput of client $k$). We evaluate NEMOx with 2 clusters (involving dAPs 1–4), 4 clusters (dAPs 1–8), and 6 clusters (dAPs 1–12) in the testbed topology (Figure 15). By varying the number of clusters, we can test NEMOx under different patterns and levels of inter-cluster contention. Due to limited hardware, the 6-cluster case is evaluated using trace-driven emulation.

Figure 17(a) shows that NEMOx's network utility is substantially higher than NonCoop, *i.e.*, it delivers throughput gain without sacrificing fairness. Figure 17(b) plots the per-client throughput gain over NonCoop. The results show that NEMOx's throughput gain is strictly higher than 1 for all clients, which further verifies its MAC-level fairness. Consistent with the above benchmark evaluation, FullCoop sacrifices spatial reuse for certain clients, rendering their throughput gain below 1. Interestingly, NEMOx's median throughput increases slightly with the number of clusters, even under a fixed dAP density. A close examination reveals that in large topologies, NonCoop often starves links that fall in the middle of others (the "flow-in-the-middle" anomaly in 802.11 [20]). Through tight coordination of dAPs within each cluster, NEMOx alleviates

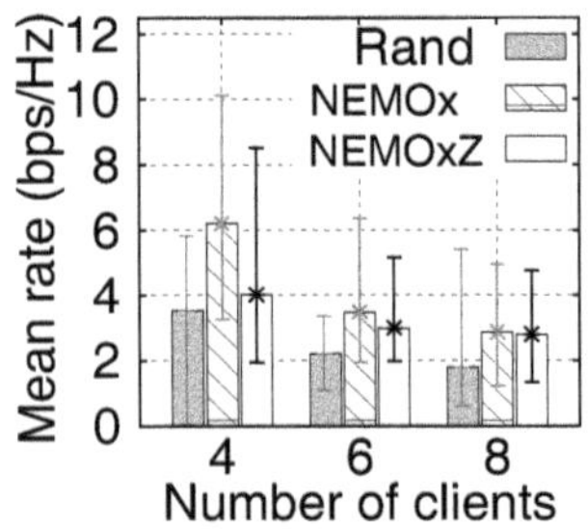


**Figure 14: Effectiveness of client selection.**

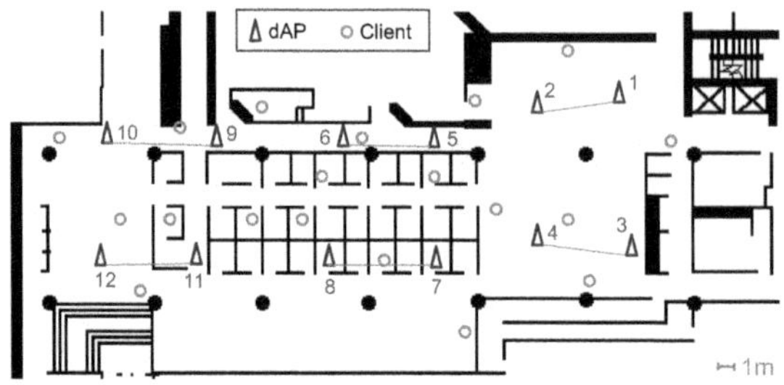


**Figure 15: Multi-cluster NEMOx testbed. Connected dAPs belong to the same cluster.**

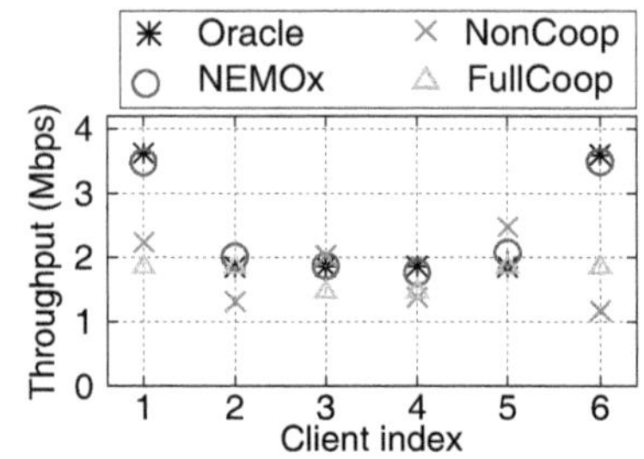


**Figure 16: Throughput optimality in a benchmark topology.**

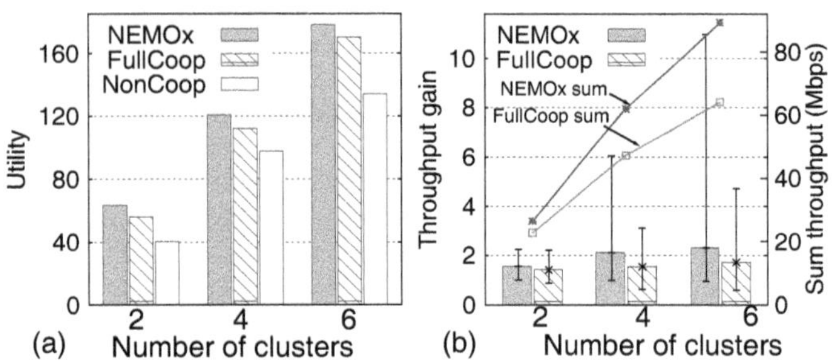


**Figure 17: Fairness evaluation. (a) Network utility; (b) Bars show the median of per-client throughput gain over non-cooperative multi-AP WLANs. Error bars show the min and max among all clients.**

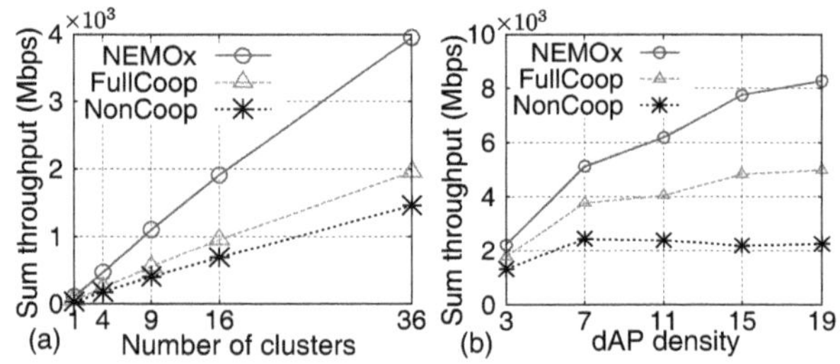


**Figure 18: Scalability with (a) network size (dAP density equals 3) and (b) dAP density (network size set to 4 clusters).**

such effects, thus substantially improving the throughput of starved clients. Figure 17(b) also implies that NEMOx's total network throughput scales as the number of clusters grows from 2 to 6.

**Scalability with network size.** We further verify the throughput scalability of NEMOx in large wireless networks with hundreds of nodes. Deploying such a network incurs formidable hardware cost. However, note that NEMOx's scalability mainly relies on its inter-cluster MAC, whose properties can be faithfully captured by the C++-based MAC implementation. We thus run the MAC together with empirical channel traces. We use a pair of WARP nodes to measure the channel magnitude and packet loss rate over 40 meters in our office building. The resulting empirical model is used to generate synthetic channel traces for given node locations, and fed into the WARPlab-based PHY and C++ based MAC modules to emulate NEMOx, FullCoop and NonCoop.

To evaluate NEMOx's scalability with network size, we increase the number of clusters from 4 to 36. Each cluster contains 3 dAPs uniformly placed around the cluster-center, and 6 clients randomly deployed within the coverage of dAPs. Each dAP uses a transmit power of 10 dBm. The dAPs' communication range *partially overlaps* with each other to ensure no dead spot, thus the network area expands with the number of clusters or dAPs. We define the communication range as the empirical distance within which a dAP can deliver at least 6 Mbps bit-rate with less than 10% loss rate. The dAPs' carrier-sensing threshold is set to -70 dBm, translating to around 1.2× the communication range under the empirical channel model. From the results in Figure 18(a), we find that all three schemes can scale their network capacity linearly with network size. However, NEMOx's scalability is higher by more than 2× (with a dAP density of only 3), as it opportunistically leverages spatial reuse and cooperation between dAPs, which are missing in FullCoop and NonCoop, respectively.

**Scalability with dAP density.** To validate NEMOx's scalability with dAPs' deployment density, we fix the number of clusters at 4, while increasing the number of dAPs per cluster from 3 to 19. Other experimental settings remain the same as above. The results in Figure 18(b) show that the capacity of both NEMOx and FullCoop increases with network density, due to more concurrency (multiplexing opportunities) brought by netMIMO. However, NEMOx's MAC can leverage the spatial reuse between dAPs, thus achieving a throughput gain of 1.33× FullCoop at a practical dAP density of 7, and 1.64× with density 19. It is clear that FullCoop, a straightforward extension of existing netMIMO schemes from single cluster (contention domain) to multiple clusters, cannot fully exploit the multiplexing gain of netMIMO. The random access MAC in NEMOx is critical to capacity scaling in this regard.

NonCoop's capacity increases initially due to higher spatial-reuse created by a denser topology. However, the gain soon plateaus when interference between links dominates. NEMOx achieves a throughput gain of 2.21× with dAP density 7, and the gain increases consistently with higher density. Thus, NEMOx makes the best balance between multiplexing within each cluster and reuse across clusters.

**Channel estimation overhead.** Like other MU-MIMO and netMIMO schemes, NEMOx's gain comes with MAC-layer overhead due to CSI feedback. In Figure 19, we evaluate the relative channel time cost of CSI feedback overhead in comparison with that of data transmissions. The results show that when the dAP density is high, more dAPs tend to be grouped for netMIMO transmission, thus raising the feedback overhead. However, even in the extreme case with an unusually high density of 19, the overhead is around 7%, negligible compared to NEMOx's throughput gain. Such overhead does not grow unbounded with dAP density, mainly because NEMOx's opportunistic MAC prevents the dAPs from greedily using large group sizes (Sec. 3.1.1). In addition, by increasing the packet size through frame aggregation, the overhead can be reduced to a minimum level (*e.g.*, below 2.2% for 4 KB packet size).

We remark that for effective precoding, the CSI feedback period must be shorter than the coherence time. Recent measurement studies of indoor radio environment [18, 21] found the channel coherence time to be on the order of several seconds for static nodes, and several hundred milliseconds for nodes moving at walking speed. These experiments were conducted under controlled settings, with

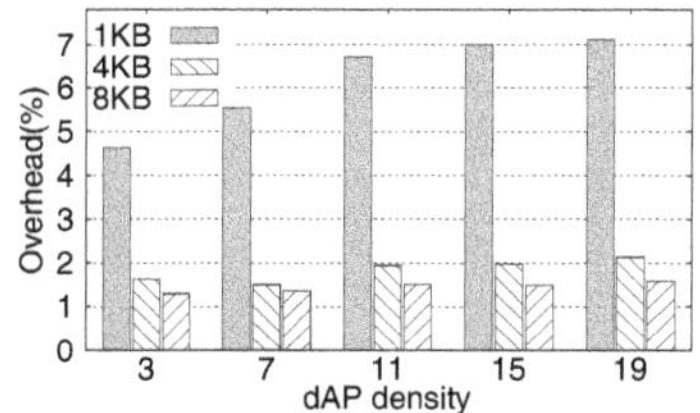

**Figure 19: Channel estimation overhead under varying dAP density and data packet size.**

short link distances and no moving objects around the links. Depending on the correlation threshold for defining coherence time, MIMO performance may be affected even when the coherence time is longer than the CSI feedback period [21]. In the above MAC-level experiments, we have used 50 ms as the CSI feedback period, which is conservative for static scenarios but may cause capacity loss for highly mobile scenarios. It has been observed in [18] that a feedback interval of 15 ms is sufficient for an indoor network environment with low-mobility and short-distance links. As we decrease the feedback interval from 50 ms to 15 ms, NEMOx's overhead would increase from around 7–23% (Figure 19). Its network throughput will be discounted by 16% accordingly, but still much higher than the above benchmark protocols.

# 8. DISCUSSIONS

**Compatibility with existing protocols.** NEMOx promotes cooperation between distributed APs. Hence, it is best applicable to managed network environments, such as conference venues, office buildings, and multi-media classrooms. Even after NEMOx is deployed in such an environment, legacy devices are unlikely to fade out anytime soon. Our main design choices for NEMOx were made with backward compatibility in mind. NEMOx' PHY layer is built on ZFBF, and its channel estimation and ACK mechanisms are consistent with the 802.11ac MU-MIMO standard. Its power allocation and client selection algorithms only customize the precoding matrix, and can be implemented in the driver. NEMOx's MAC uses a probabilistic algorithm and needs modifications to the 802.11ac AP. But it can be converted to a backoff-based algorithm by translating the contention probability into a backoff window size [11]. Moreover, NEMOx requires no modifications to clients. It can easily be degenerated to an 802.11-compatible network by regarding each dAP as the 802.11 AP and allowing the NEMOx mAP to run the 802.11 MAC for them. We plan to investigate the co-deployment of NEMOx and 802.11 networks in future.

**Uplink transmission.** In this paper, we focused on improving the downlink capacity of wireless networks using NEMOx, as downlink traffic is known to dominate wireless infrastructure networks. A simple way to accommodate uplink transmissions is to allow the clients to send RTS, and dAPs to defer the CTS, waiting for an opportunity when multiple uplink transmissions can be done simultaneously. Such uplink transmissions can exploit SIMO decoding algorithms [22] and will be utilized in our future work.

**Deployment issues.** We have built a netMIMO cluster by extending existing MIMO APs with commercial off-the-shelf RF cables (LMR-400). At 2.4 GHz, the cable causes an attenuation of 6.8 dB per 100 ft (sufficient to cover a typical indoor WLAN cell). With higher-quality cables, such as LMR-1700, the attenuation can be reduced to 1.7 dB, which is negligible and outweighed by NEMOx's cooperation gains.

**Multi-Antenna dAP and clients.** In NEMOx, each dAP or client has only one antenna. By allowing multiple antennas and integrating MU-MIMO communications algorithms, the per-client throughput can be boosted further. NEMOx's inter-cluster channel-access algorithm will still be valid in such a case, but the JPP frmmework needs to be re-designed to exploit this capability.

**Dynamic environment.** Our experiments focused on static scenarios where channel state remains relatively stable, so as to prevent experimental artifacts caused by the latency of the WARPLab framework. In practice, network dynamics affect MIMO performance, and the effects depend on a variety of factors, such as node mobility, number of antennas, link distances, and the variation of LOS/NLOS. A comprehensive study of such dynamics and the impacts on NEMOx's performance would require a full-fledged real-time implementation of NEMOx and experimentation on a large-scale testbed with high dAP density. This is a matter of our future inquiry.

# 9. RELATED WORK

Network MIMO has recently attracted significant attention from the communications and information theory communities. Using simple channel models, existing work [23, 24] has proven that the capacity of a single-cluster netMIMO can scale with the number of distributed transmitters (or antennas). Analysis and simulation of multi-cluster netMIMO also verified its advantage in large cellular networks [25, 26]. Precoding and scheduling algorithms have been migrated from MU-MIMO to deal with problems in netMIMO [27], and have also been applied across netMIMO clusters [28, 29]. This line of research commonly assumes a cellular network model, where a netMIMO cluster is deployed in isolation (*e.g.*, leveraging dedicated spectrum) or neighboring clusters are synchronized and centrally managed through TDMA/FDMA. It is, however, difficult to apply such a model to the indoor multi-cell WLANs that are decentralized and self-organized via CSMA-based protocols.

Coordinated Multi-Point Transmission (CoMP), a concept built on the theoretical foundation of network MIMO, is expected to be realized in future LTE networks [2, 30]. CoMP allows netMIMO cooperation between base stations that form a cluster, so as to remove mutual interference. It is still in a conceptual development stage and there remain many practical challenges [31], *e.g.*, synchronization and scheduling of clusters. To date, only small-scale field tests [31, 32] have been done, while focusing on a single isolated cluster.

MU-MIMO and netMIMO communications for indoor WLANs have recently been realized in experimental settings. Both downlink [7] and uplink interference cancellation algorithms for MU-MIMO have been implemented [22, 33]. Shepard *et al.* [19] pushed the limit of MU-MIMO by building a *massive antenna system* with 64 transmit antennas that can serve tens of users simultaneously. It has also been proven [34] that netMIMO only needs an order-of-magnitude smaller number of antennas to achieve the same spectrum efficiency as MU-MIMO, primarily because of much shorter distance between transmit and receive antennas. Yet netMIMO incurs extra infrastructure cost in deploying the dAPs.

Practical netMIMO systems (*e.g.*, [5]) usually share the same communication algorithm (*e.g.*, ZFBF) with MU-MIMO, except that the antennas are from distributed transmitters. However, existing netMIMO systems [5, 6] assumed a single contention domain where every transmitter can hear and synchronize with others. A primary objective of NEMOx is to enable netMIMO in large-scale multi-cell WLANs spanning multiple contention domains.

NEMOx's PHY-layer JPP framework synthesizes linear precoding and power allocation, and is integrated with opportunistic user selection. These individual problems have been explored in existing simulation and analytical studies. For example, Yoo *et al.* [35] proved the asymptotic optimality of ZFBF precoding when combined with user selection and water-filling-based power allocation, but under a sum-power constraint that is impractical for netMIMO [2]. Per-antenna power constraints were incorporated in [36], where precoding and power allocation are separated, and no user selection/scheduling is allowed. Alternative precoding schemes, *e.g.*, DPC and TH-precoding [14], can be used to replace the ZFBF in NEMOx. Evaluation of such schemes is left as our future work.

# 10. CONCLUSION

In this paper, we have proposed a novel system, called NEMOx, to exploit netMIMO gain for scalable performance in wireless networks. NEMOx organizes a network into multiple clusters, optimizes and performs netMIMO within each cluster containing distributed APs, and manages interference and reuse across clusters efficiently through a decentralized channel-access mechanism. Our prototype implementation and evaluation of NEMOx on networked WARP nodes have shown scalable netMIMO performance both within each cluster and across the network. These indicate NEMOx's potential for scaling the gains of netMIMO in wireless networks.

## Acknowledgement

We appreciate insightful comments and feedback from the shepherd, Lin Zhong, and the anonymous reviewers. The work reported in this paper was supported in part by the NSF under Grants CNS-1160775 and 1317411.

# 11. REFERENCES

[1] K. Tan, J. Fang, Y. Zhang, S. Chen, L. Shi, J. Zhang, and Y. Zhang, "Fine-Grained Channel Access in Wireless LAN," in *Proc. of ACM SIGCOMM*, 2010.

[2] D. Gesbert, S. Hanly, H. Huang, S. Shamai Shitz, O. Simeone, and W. Yu, "Multi-Cell MIMO Cooperative Networks: A New Look at Interference," *IEEE Journal on Selected Areas in Communications (JSAC)*, vol. 28, no. 9, 2010.

[3] S. Gollakota, S. D. Perli, and D. Katabi, "Interference Alignment and Cancellation," in *Proc. of ACM SIGCOMM*, 2009.

[4] K. C.-J. Lin, S. Gollakota, and D. Katabi, "Random Access Heterogeneous MIMO Networks," in *ACM SIGCOMM*, 2011.

[5] H. S. Rahul, S. Kumar, and D. Katabi, "JMB: Scaling Wireless Capacity With User Demands," in *Proc. of ACM SIGCOMM*, 2012.

[6] H. V. Balan, R. Rogalin, A. Michaloliakos, K. Psounis, and G. Caire, "Achieving High Data Rates in a Distributed MIMO System," in *Proc. of ACM MobiCom*, 2012.

[7] E. Aryafar, N. Anand, T. Salonidis, and E. W. Knightly, "Design and Experimental Evaluation of Multi-user Beamforming in Wireless LANs," in *Proc. of ACM MobiCom*, 2010.

[8] A. Khattab, J. Camp, C. Hunter, P. Murphy, A. Sabharwal, and E. W. Knightly, "WARP: a Flexible Platform for Clean-Slate Wireless Medium Access Protocol Design," *SIGMOBILE Mob. Comput. Commun. Rev.*, vol. 12, 2008.

[9] "Wireless LAN Medium Access Control (MAC) and Physical Layer (PHY) Specifications," *IEEE Std. 802.11ac Draft 3.0*, 2012.

[10] T. Nandagopal, T.E.Kim, X. Gao, and V. Bhargavan, "Achieving MAC Layer Fairness in Wireless Packet Networks," in *ACM MobiCom*, 2000.

[11] J. W. Lee, M. Chiang, and R. A. Calderbank, "Optimal MAC design based on utility maximization: Reverse and forward engineering," in *IEEE INFOCOM*, 2006.

[12] F. P. Kelly, A. K. Maulloo, and D. K. H. Tan, "Rate Control for Communication Networks: Shadow Prices, Proportional Fairness and Stability," *The Journal of the Operational Research Society*, vol. 49, no. 3, pp. 237–252, 1998.

[13] A. Wiesel, Y. Eldar, and S. Shamai, "Zero-Forcing Precoding and Generalized Inverses," *IEEE Transactions on Signal Processing*, vol. 56, no. 9, 2008.

[14] D. Tse and P. Viswanath, *Fundamentals of Wireless Communication*. Cambridge University Press, 2005.

[15] M. Kurth, A. Zubow, and J. P. Redlich, "Cooperative Opportunistic Routing Using Transmit Diversity in Wireless Mesh Networks," in *Proc. of IEEE INFOCOM*, 2008.

[16] P. Dutta, R. Musaloiu-E, I. Stoica, and A. Terzis, "Wireless ACK Collisions Not Considered Harmful," in *In HotNets-VII: The Seventh Workshop on Hot Topics in Networks*, 2008.

[17] X. Zhang and K. G. Shin, "Adaptive Subcarrier Nulling: Enabling Partial Spectrum Sharing in Wireless LANs," in *Proc. of IEEE ICNP*, 2011.

[18] R. Kudo, K. Ishihara, and Y. Takatori, "Measured Channel Variation and Coherence Time in NTT Lab," *IEEE 802.11-09/0161r1*, 2010.

[19] C. Shepard, H. Yu, N. Anand, E. Li, T. Marzetta, R. Yang, and L. Zhong, "Argos: Practical Many-Antenna Base Stations," in *Proc. of ACM MobiCom*, 2012.

[20] B. Nardelli, J. Lee, K. Lee, Y. Yi, S. Chong, E. Knightly, and M. Chiang, "Experimental Evaluation of Optimal CSMA," in *Proc. of IEEE INFOCOM*, 2011.

[21] X. Xie, X. Zhang, and K. Sundaresan, "Adaptive Feedback Compression for MIMO Networks," in *Proc. of ACM MobiCom*, 2013.

[22] K. Tan, H. Liu, J. Fang, W. Wang, J. Zhang, M. Chen, and G. M. Voelker, "SAM: Enabling Practical Spatial Multiple Access in Wireless LAN," in *Proc. of ACM MobiCom*, 2009.

[23] R. Heath, T. Wu, Y. H. Kwon, and A. Soong, "Multiuser MIMO in Distributed Antenna Systems With Out-of-Cell Interference," *IEEE Transactions on Signal Processing*, vol. 59, no. 10, 2011.

[24] J. Zhang and J. Andrews, "Distributed Antenna Systems with Randomness," *IEEE Transactions on Wireless Communications*, vol. 7, no. 9, 2008.

[25] S. A. Ramprashad, H. C. Papadopoulos, A. Benjebbour, Y. Kishiyama, N. Jindal, and G. Caire, "Cooperative Cellular Networks Using Multi-User MIMO: Trade-offs, Overheads, and Interference Control Across Architectures," *IEEE Communications Magazine*, vol. 49, no. 5, 2011.

[26] H. Huang, M. Trivellato, A. Hottinen, M. Shafi, P. Smith, and R. Valenzuela, "Increasing Downlink Cellular Throughput with Limited Network MIMO Coordination," *IEEE Transactions on Wireless Communications*, vol. 8, no. 6, 2009.

[27] H. Huh, A. M. Tulino, and G. Caire, "Network MIMO With Linear Zero-Forcing Beamforming: Large System Analysis, Impact of Channel Estimation, and Reduced-Complexity Scheduling," *IEEE Transactions on Information Theory*, vol. 58, no. 5, 2012.

[28] J. Zhang, R. Chen, J. Andrews, A. Ghosh, and R. Heath, "Networked MIMO with Clustered Linear Precoding," *IEEE Transactions on Wireless Communications*, vol. 8, no. 4, 2009.

[29] S. Kaviani and W. Krzymien, "Multicell Scheduling in Network MIMO," in *Proc. of IEEE GLOBECOM*, 2010.

[30] M. Sawahashi, Y. Kishiyama, A. Morimoto, D. Nishikawa, and M. Tanno, "Coordinated Multipoint Transmission/Reception Techniques for LTE-Advanced," *IEEE Wireless Communications*, vol. 17, no. 3, 2010.

[31] Patrick Marsch (Editor) and Gerhard P. Fettweis (Editor), *Coordinated Multi-Point in Mobile Communications: From Theory to Practice*. Cambridge University Press, 2011.

[32] R. Irmer, H. Droste, P. Marsch, M. Grieger, G. Fettweis, S. Brueck, H. P. Mayer, L. Thiele, and V. Jungnickel, "Coordinated Multipoint: Concepts, Performance, and Field Trial Results," *IEEE Communications Magazine*, vol. 49, no. 2, 2011.

[33] W.-L. Shen, Y.-C. Tung, K.-C. Lee, K. C.-J. Lin, S. Gollakota, D. Katabi, and M.-S. Chen, "Rate Adaptation for 802.11 Multiuser MIMO Networks," in *Proc. of ACM MobiCom*, 2012.

[34] H. Huh, G. Caire, H. Papadopoulos, and S. Ramprashad, "Achieving "Massive MIMO" Spectral Efficiency with a Not-So-Large Number of Antennas," *IEEE Transactions on Wireless Communications*, vol. 11, no. 9, 2012.

[35] T. Yoo and A. Goldsmith, "On the Optimality of Multiantenna Broadcast Scheduling Using Zero-Forcing Beamforming," *IEEE Journal on Selected Areas in Communications*, vol. 24, no. 3, 2006.

[36] K. Karakayali, R. Yates, G. Foschini, and R. Valenzuela, "Optimum Zero-forcing Beamforming with Per-antenna Power Constraints," in *IEEE International Symposium on Information Theory (ISIT)*, 2007.

# ZIMO: Building Cross-Technology MIMO to Harmonize ZigBee Smog with WiFi Flash without Intervention

Yubo Yan[1], Panlong Yang[1,3], Xiang-Yang Li[2,3], Yue Tao[2], Lan Zhang[3], Lizhao You[4]
[1]PLA University of Science and Technology, China
[2]Department of Computer Science, Illinois Institute of Technology, USA
[3]School of Software and TNLIST, Tsinghua University, China
[4]Department of Computer Science and Technology, Nanjing University, China
yanyub@gmail.com, panlongyang@gmail.com, xli@cs.iit.edu, nightvista@gmail.com, zhanglan03@gmail.com, youlizhao.nju@gmail.com

## ABSTRACT

Recent studies show that WiFi interference has been a major problem for low power urban sensing technology ZigBee networks. Existing approaches for dealing with such interferences often modify either the ZigBee nodes or WiFi nodes. However, massive deployment of ZigBee nodes and uncooperative WiFi users call for innovative cross-technology coexistence without intervening legacy systems.

In this work we investigate the WiFi and ZigBee coexistence when ZigBee is the interested signal. Mitigating short duration WiFi interference (called *flash*) in long duration ZigBee data (called *smog*) is challenging, especially when we cannot modify the WiFi APs and the massively deployed sensor nodes. To address these challenges, we propose ZIMO, a sink-based MIMO design for harmony coexistence of ZigBee and WiFi networks with the goal of protecting the ZigBee data packets. The key insight of ZIMO is to properly exploit opportunities resulted from differences between WiFi and ZigBee, and bridge the gap between interested data and cross technology signals. Also, extracting the channel coefficient of WiFi and ZigBee will enhance other coexistence technologies such as TIMO [1]. We implement a prototype for ZIMO in GNURadio-USRP N200. Our extensive evaluations under real wireless conditions show that ZIMO can improve up to 1.9× throughput for ZigBee network, with median gain of 1.5×, and 1.1× to 1.9× for WiFi network as byproduct in ZigBee signal recovery.

## Categories and Subject Descriptors

C.2.1 [**COMPUTER-COMMUNICATION NETWORKS**]: Network Architecture and Design—*Wireless communication*

## General Terms

Design, Experimentation, Performance



## Keywords

MIMO, Physical Layer, Sensor Networks

## 1. INTRODUCTION

Urban area wireless sensor networks are becoming vitally important for nowadays "smart city" programs. These grand engineering work heavily depend on sensor nodes and efficient network connections for monitoring environment. Most of the urban sensing systems are leveraging the COTS ZigBee, such as Urban sense [2], CitySee [3]. Unfortunately, in urban areas, WiFi interference is pervasive and possibly the primary factor leading to ZigBee throughput degradation [1, 4–7]. Meanwhile, it has been verified that the WiFi network performance can be affected by the ZigBee interference [8]. It is worth noting that, protecting ZigBee signal and extracting the interested data from the cross-technology noise is not trivial. Previous studies [1, 8] indiscriminately take the ZigBee signal as cross-technology interference, especially RF *smog*, which leaves a gap between WiFi and other cross-technologies for coexistence. Notably, ZigBee is similar to WiFi in sense of CSMA scheme, and apparently different from RF technologies without communication functionality, such as microwave oven.

In summary, existing solutions can not reasonably work in urban sensing sensor networks. There are several specific requirements in building an efficient ZigBee system coexisting with WiFi systems. Foremost, there should be no modification or intervention on the end nodes in either ZigBee or WiFi networks. For urban sensing, modifying the software and/or hardware on the sensor nodes is difficult and expensive. Furthermore, WiFi AP holders are reluctant to make any changes even when ZigBee nodes interfere them. Meanwhile, it is expected that the performance degradation caused by coexistence should be minimized. In our case, ZigBee is interested signal, but the WiFi transmission is expected to be pervasive. This is the key idea of harmony coexistence, where two systems can share the conflicted network resource, without harming each other.

Fully considering these design requirements, we propose ZIMO, a cross-technology MIMO sink design to harmonize the coexistence of ZigBee and WiFi networks. Different from previous studies, in our design, the sink node performs the coexistence work, and the end nodes in WiFi and ZigBee networks need not do any further modification. Adding a modified sink is relatively easy and more affordable than re-

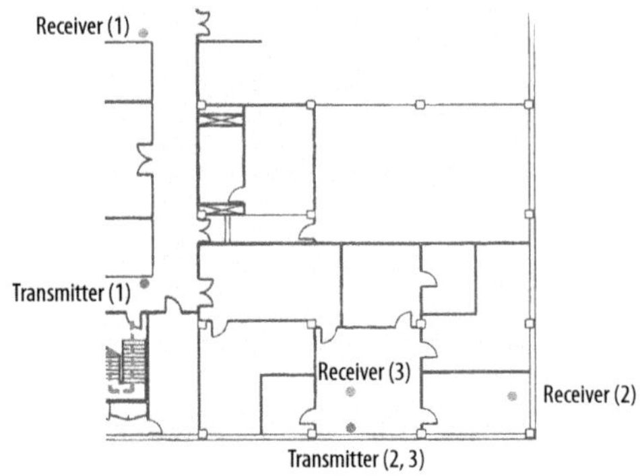


Figure 1: Indoor layout of the experiment.

programming all the deployed sensor nodes. In ZIMO, we leverage a 2-antenna MIMO system for WiFi and ZigBee interference resolution. To the best of our knowledge, ZIMO is the first implemented working system meeting the aforementioned requirements. There are several challenges that need to be addressed carefully in designing and implementing ZIMO, which are summarized as follows.

First, unpredictable and uncooperative WiFi interference will incur different interference patterns. When WiFi preamble is clear, the WiFi signal needs to be nullified first for ZigBee signal decoding. Inevitably, the WiFi channel coefficient estimation will suffer unfavorable distortions due to ZigBee interference, and will incur unsatisfiable ZigBee signal recovery.

Second, when WiFi flash is drowned in ZigBee smog, signals in two technologies are cross-affected in both time and frequency domain. For WiFi signal, there is no clear reference for accurate channel coefficient estimation. Even worse, considering the low-power ZigBee signal, more accurate and thorough interference cancelation for WiFi signal is needed. Thus, the CFO (Carrier Frequency Offset) estimation across receiving symbols are not negligible comparing with conventional interference cancelation and alignment schemes [9]. For ZigBee signal, the channel coefficient estimation should be carefully considered as the frequency offset can be possibly up to 200 KHz [10], which means accurate and fast enough synchronization should be done within ZigBee preamble time.

ZIMO addresses these challenges with two innovative techniques. For the first challenge, a blind recovery method for WiFi channel coefficient is presented, based on interpolation that exploits the continuous and steady feature in frequency domain. With this advantage, the second challenge for WiFi signal is addressed by a linear regression model used for fine frequency offset compensation across WiFi symbols. Also for ZigBee signal, an innovative ZigBee channel coefficient estimation method is proposed, where large frequency offset is estimated and compensated through modulation-independent approach.

In summary, our main contributions are as follows.

We propose ZIMO, a sink based MIMO design for harmony coexistence of WiFi and ZigBee by protecting the ZigBee data from being interfered. Our design need not modify and intervene on WiFi APs or ZigBee nodes. A key insight of the work is to properly handle the relationship between WiFi and ZigBee where opportunities in time, spectral and power domain due to cross-technology can be leveraged. The

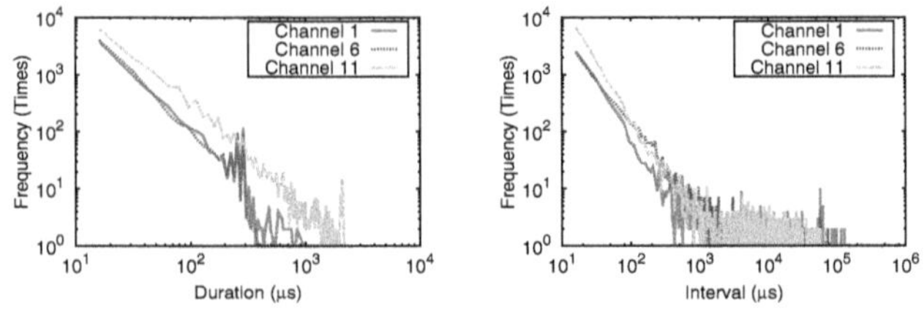


(a) Duration of Corrupted (b) Interval between Corrupted

Figure 2: Corruption of ZigBee transmission covered by different WiFi channels at site 1 with log-log plot.

ZIMO sink can also serve as a sniffer that can recover the interfered WiFi packets. Extracting accurate channel coefficients of WiFi and ZigBee will also enhance other coexistence technology such as TIMO [1].

We implement ZIMO on USRP platform and present a working system. Comparing with SAM [11], we solve the distributed cross-technology multiplexing with virtual MIMO implementation, and recover WiFi and ZigBee data at the same time. Comparing with TIMO [1], we intelligently handle the ZigBee and WiFi signal simultaneously, leveraging the channel coefficient of the cross-technologies in data domain. In power domain, we can handle the smog-like interference in TIMO scenario [1], and the flash-like interference experienced in our experimental study in Section 8 as well. Surprisingly, we find that ZIMO can help enhance WiFi and ZigBee communications. ZIMO will help recover the interfered ZigBee signals as well as WiFi signals, leading a way from coexistence to co-prosperity.

The rest of the paper is organized as follows. We conduct a comprehensive experimental study on the impacts of WiFi interference on ZigBee networks in Section 2. Section 3 provides background on ZigBee and WiFi system, as well as MIMO communication. The problem domain and system design overview are introduced in Sections 4 and 5 respectively. After describing our system design in Section 6, and implementation in Section 7, we evaluate the performance of ZIMO in Section 8. We make extensive discussions on ZIMO in Section 9, and review the related work in Section 10. Finally, we conclude the work in Section 11.

## 2. IMPACT OF WIFI ON ZIGBEE

### 2.1 Experiment Rationale and Setup

A preliminary experiment was made to investigate the interference between WiFi and ZigBee networks. Since the CSMA/CA mechanism restricts that only one pair of nodes can transmit at one time when multiple ZigBee senders are presented, in our experiment, the ZigBee networks consist only one sender and one receiver, without losing significance of the result. The transmitter repeatedly sends packets with identical content, and the interference will be represented on the received data as corrupted bytes. Note that, we've tested that, the ZigBee transmission experiences very low error rate before WiFi interference is introduced.

The experiment is conducted in a basement of the school building at IIT, with layout specified in Fig. 1. Although we are not permitted to obtain the number and locations of WiFi APs for security reasons, a scanning made on a laptop at the location of ZigBee receiver shows that more than 20 WiFi APs can be found with distinct signal strength, ranging from -65dBm to -27dBm.

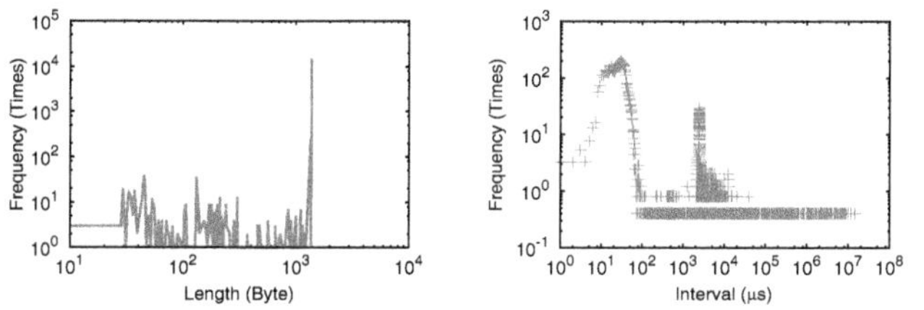


(a) Length statistics (b) Interval statistics

Figure 3: Packet length and packet interval statistics of busy WiFi connection.

Both ZigBee nodes are installed with Contiki OS [12]. The sender transmits the packet every 0.03 seconds. In order to compensate the variation of WiFi interference signal, the sender changes the transmission power every 10 seconds, looping over the scale from 1 to 31. Similarly, both the sender and receiver change their channel every 600 seconds, looping over all ZigBee channels which could be affected by WiFi communication, from channel 11 to 25.

## 2.2 Analysis of ZigBee Corruption

Our experiment shows that the results from different locations are similar. We choose the result from one site for simplicity. Since the ZigBee channels covered by the same WiFi channel show same behavior, we separate the results of different ZigBee channels into 3 groups, which are covered by the WiFi channel 1, 6, and 11 respectively.

Fig. 2a and Fig. 2b illustrate the duration and interval of corrupted symbols using log-log plot respectively. We observed that different channels have similar patterns.

The results show that the corruption durations and intervals distribute similarly and are close to power-law distribution. As short corruption durations and intervals are far more frequent than those of long corruptions, it's reasonable to conclude that most of the short durations and short intervals of corruptions occur alternately. Thus, the results suggest that *short and frequent WiFi data transmission (i.e., flash) plays the main role of WiFi interference on ZigBee. Further, the power-law like distributions indicate shorter flashes will interfere ZigBee signal with exponentially increasing probability, which is a drastic threat for ZigBee signal.*

## 2.3 Analysis of WiFi Interference Behavior

We also collect the WiFi data in the same experiment, and investigate the behavior of WiFi transmission in detail. When massive data is being transmitted over a WiFi connection, the length of the data packet could be varied, while the interval between two consecutive WiFi packets is relatively short. Fig. 3a shows that most of the WiFi packets are short and the packet length is usually less than 256 bytes. Note that, there is a peak when the packet length is larger than $10^3$ bytes, because 1500 bytes is also a typical WiFi frame length for TCP transmissions.

Fig. 3b shows that, most of the WiFi interval is less than 1ms, *i.e.*, $10^3\mu$s. Because the length of the data packet is usually with the full length of a WiFi frame, *i.e.*, 1406 bytes. When the WiFi is working on the max data rate, 56Mbps, a packet will last for $200\mu$s, and the interval between two data packets is also seldom lower than $10\mu$s. Note that, another peak shows between $10^3\mu$s and $10^5\mu$s, which shows that, even when WiFi communication is idle, the ZigBee communication can still be affected by the WiFi beacon and probe frames, because the beacon interval is typically $10^5\mu$s (*i.e.* 0.1s) long. Note that, the interval is much lower than $10^5\mu$s because there are multiple WiFi APs around (about 20), which will significantly shorten the beacon interval independently. Note that, there is a thick but extremely low line in Fig. 3b, which cannot be overlooked. This line shows that, part of the WiFi packets' intervals are evenly distributed across a wide range of values, although the frequency is low.

The results in Fig. 2 show similarity between interference intervals and durations. Also, most of the WiFi interferences are short and periodical. We conclude that *the WiFi interference is distributed across ZigBee symbols, rather than concentrated on particular positions. Hence it is not possible to avoid the interference thoroughly with MAC layer technique only. We need to resort to the signal processing techniques for fundamental solutions.*

# 3. BACKGROUND AND MOTIVATIONS

In this section we provide background on wireless communication fundamentals and single-user multiple-input multiple-output (MIMO) systems. We then describe the signal character of WiFi and ZigBee in a typical WiFi and ZigBee coexistence environment. The motivations are presented according to the technologies and observations mentioned above.

## 3.1 MIMO and Interference Nullifying

In a MIMO system, multiple antennas are coupled together and signals are transmitted over the channels, say mathematically, in a linear combinatorial manner. Here we show a $2 \times 2$ MIMO system using a simplified mathematical model, where the signal stream $s_i(t)$ is on the $i$-th antenna, $i = 1, 2$. The signal receiving model for MIMO system can be expressed as follows:

$$\begin{cases} y_1(t) = h_{11}s_1(t) + h_{21}s_2(t) \\ y_2(t) = h_{12}s_1(t) + h_{22}s_2(t) \end{cases} \tag{1}$$

Here $h_{ij}$ is a complex value for channel coefficient, where the magnitude attenuation and delay of a transmitted signal from antenna $i$ to antenna $j$ is evaluated. In each MIMO transmission, there is a previously known preamble used for channel coefficient calculation. The receiver node can compute this value according to the signal and preambles.

At the receiver side, as the 4 channel coefficient values $h_{ij}$ are known, the transmitted signals $s_1(t)$ and $s_2(t)$ can be successfully recovered from the received signals $y_1(t)$ and $y_2(t)$. It is worth noting that, this model is applied to narrow band channel communication system, such as ZigBee. However for wideband communication system such as OFDM, the channel coefficient is a series of complex values, that is, a channel coefficient vector.

To deal with the concurrent transmissions from different stations, the interference nullifying technique can be used for unaligned signals. The key idea of the interference nullifying technique is based on Eq. (1). As for the unaligned interference signals, there are *clear part* and the *interfered part*. For the interfered part, the nullifying process is used to cancel the interference signal. For example, according to Eq. (1), the interference can be mitigated by subtracting the other interference signal when $s_1(t)$ is the interested signal.

$$s_1(t) = \frac{y_1(t) - \frac{h_{21}}{h_{22}} y_2(t)}{h_{11} - h_{12}\frac{h_{21}}{h_{22}}} \tag{2}$$

## 3.2 Preliminary Observations for IEEE 802.11 and 802.15.4 Signals

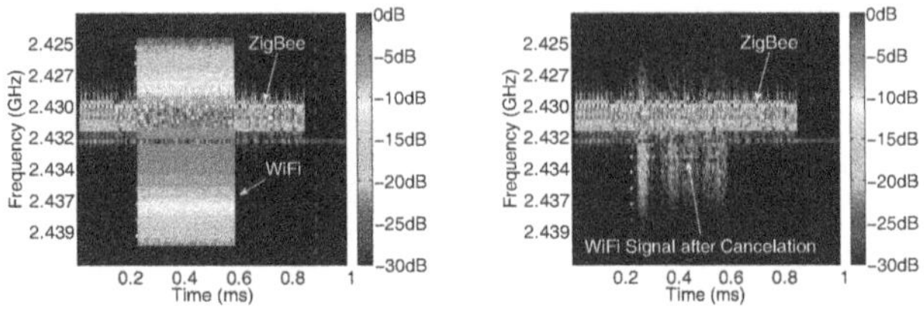


(a) Spectral and time domain (b) After WiFi Cancelation

Figure 4: Power Spectral Density (PSD) form of WiFi and ZigBee signals.

We demonstrate a particular co-channel example: In IEEE 802.11g, we use channel 5 (with 2.432GHz central frequency), and in IEEE802.15.4, we use channel 16 (2.430GHz). Fig. 4a shows the spectrum and time characteristics of WiFi and ZigBee signal in power spectral density (PSD), where WiFi's bandwidth is much larger than ZigBee, and they are in different central frequency.

Signals in Fig. 4a are sampled by USRP/GNURadio in WiFi channel, which conforms to the IEEE standards 802.11g and 802.15.4: WiFi's bandwidth is 20MHz, and ZigBee's bandwidth is 2MHz, while central frequency offset of WiFi and ZigBee is 2MHz. The payload of WiFi is 256 Bytes with TX rate 6Mbps, and the payload of ZigBee is 20 Bytes with TX rate 250kbps. As we can see, WiFi is faster than ZigBee, and WiFi signal is 5 to 10dB stronger than ZigBee. We only consider co-channel interference case.

The differences are just that they collide in different frequency. Here Fig. 4a shows collided WiFi and ZigBee signal in time domain. We can tell WiFi signal from ZigBee signals easily. First, the ZigBee signal is slower than WiFi due to its low bandwidth. Second, WiFi's signal is stronger than ZigBee due to its high-power. High-power implies high SNR reception at the same distance. Fig. 4b shows the PSD of ZigBee signal when WiFi interference is canceled. This demonstrates the feasibility of recovering ZigBee signal from WiFi interference.

## 3.3 Motivations

Basically, there are three technical points driving us to tackle the intrinsic difficulties in mitigating the WiFi flashes from the ZigBee smog.

*The cross technology interference leaves opportunities in power, spectral and time domain.* As shown in Fig. 4, there are opportunities for protecting ZigBee smog from WiFi flashes. First, in power domain, significantly different signal strengths may exist between WiFi and ZigBee. Second, in spectral domain, only portion of WiFi frequency band is interfered. Third, in time domain, not all signal duration is interfered, and referred signal can be leveraged for further interference mitigation and decoding enhancement. It should be noted that, except for the frequency domain, the power and temporal differences are dynamic and not easy for use.

*The nullifying process on coupled antennas can deal with the power and temporal uncertainty.* The MIMO design can deal with the power uncertainty easily, because signals from same node on different antennas may not have significant difference. Also, only the overlapping portion is nullified, where temporal differences can be omitted temporarily before further processing.

*Harmonize ZigBee with WiFi system is possible and feasible.* MIMO based sink will receive the WiFi and ZigBee signal at the same time. Preferable interference cancelation of WiFi signal relies on the accurate recovery of the WiFi signal. A 2-antenna MIMO system will also improve the possibility on WiFi signal recovery. The ZigBee and WiFi can work together as if they are from the same technology, and no interventions among systems are needed.

# 4. ZIMO PROBLEM DOMAIN

ZIMO deals with interference from WiFi APs and protects the ZigBee signals from being corrupted. We focus on typical situations that arise in large-scale urban sensing networks, where WiFi and ZigBee signals are severely interfering each other. In particular,

- *ZIMO tackles scenarios where the WiFi APs use antennas no more than what the ZIMO Sink has.* Typically, the WiFi transmissions use one antenna. If $n$-antenna system such as [13] is applied in WiFi AP, the ZIMO node should place $(n+1)$ antennas for transceiving packets. Such constraint also applies to other cross technology devices in ISM band.
- *ZIMO applies to scenarios where at least one preamble is clear when interference happens during data transmissions.* The preamble value, whether it comes from WiFi or ZigBee, should be clear for packet detection as well as channel coefficient estimation.
- *ZIMO applies to scenarios where the ZIMO empowered sink node can be deployed in the asymmetric area [6].* Considering the long-range coverage region by WiFi and the limited communication range of ZigBee devices for power saving, the asymmetric area is common in urban sensing networks. Also, even in symmetric area, the ZigBee sensor node and WiFi node can disable the CCA scheme, and transmit packets as they will.
- *ZIMO can address environments where the interference is wideband and the interested signals are narrow-band.* When WiFi and ZigBee technologies are coexisted, the reference signal for WiFi channel coefficient computation is often unavailable. Extracting ZigBee from WiFi and other cross-technology system is apparently different from previous study such as TIMO [1].

# 5. ZIMO DESIGN OVERVIEW

In ZIMO design, the conventional one-antenna sink node is modified to a 2-antenna MIMO system. The WiFi and ZigBee signals can be transmitted concurrently and then received by this sink.

The basic idea of ZIMO is simple. When WiFi preamble is clear, we use the interference nullification to WiFi signal directly, and leave the residual signal for ZigBee decoding. When WiFi preamble is not clear, we need to leverage the clear ZigBee preamble to nullify ZigBee signal. After that, WiFi signal can be decoded. Using the decoded data and accurate channel coefficient, we can regenerate the received WiFi signal accurately. After using the interference cancellation technique, the WiFi interference is mitigated, and the residual signal can be used for ZigBee decoding.

The working flow of ZIMO is illustrated in Fig. 5. There are basically five operation modules in ZIMO, which are

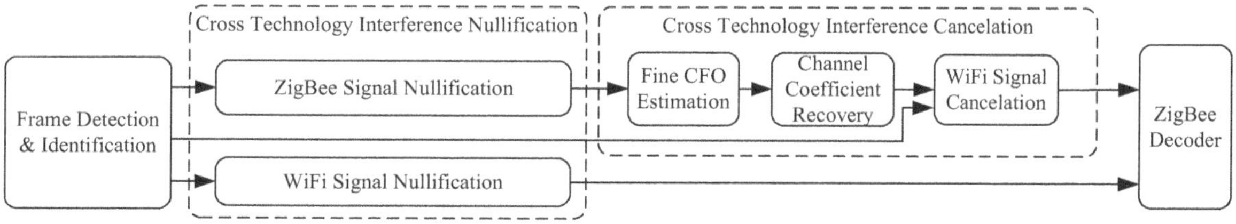


Figure 5: Working flow of ZIMO

frame detection & identification, spectrum slicing, cross technology IC (Interference Cancelation) and IN (Interference Nullification), and ZigBee decoder. When interfered signals are received, the frame detection & identification module is applied for interference pattern recognition. When WiFi preamble is clear, we first nullify the WiFi signal and send the signal to spectrum slicing module for ZigBee decoding. Specifically, when WiFi flashes (fast and short-duration WiFi transmissions) are covered by ZigBee smog (slow and long-duration ZigBee transmissions), although ZigBee signal is nullified, the estimated channel coefficient cannot be used for IC directly due to interfered WiFi signals. Thus in ZIMO, we use a linear fitting model for fine central frequency offset (CFO) estimation. After CFO is compensated, channel coefficient is recovered through blind recovery method, where missing values are interpolated by leveraging the partially interfered channel and SNR disparity in cross-technology coexistence. In summary, ZIMO extends convention MIMO system as well as virtual MIMO, such as SAM [11], from multiplexing signals in same technology to embracing cross-technology. Also, we make an extension to TIMO because ZIMO makes it possible to survive the ZigBee signal from WiFi interference. We then describe these basic functions in detail in the following sections.

# 6. DECODING IN THE PRESENCE OF WIFI INTERFERENCES

## 6.1 Spectrum Slicing and Combining

In order to incorporate ZigBee and WiFi signal for processing, ZIMO uses wideband RF frontend. However, wideband sampling means that sampled signal has wide spectrum, which cannot be used for ZigBee decoding directly. Then in ZIMO, a spectrum slicing block is used to convert the over sampled signal to appropriate signal for ZigBee decoding. In this work, we use WiFi setup (*e.g.*, WiFi channel No.5: with central frequency at $2.432GHz$, and $20Mbps$) to determine front-end parameters (complex sampling rate: at least $40Mbps$).

We take only one ZigBee transmission in our experiment study because of contention scheme in IEEE 802.15.4. The extension to multiple orthogonal ZigBee networks is possible: all we need is to add parallel reception chain with different frequency translation parameters.

## 6.2 Interfered Frame Processing

### 6.2.1 Frame Detection and IdentiŒation

The auto-correlation is a basic step for frame detection, which means a multiplication of received signal and its delayed version, and the sum of all the multiplications during the delayed period. Auto-correlation method can be used for clear header signal. However, the deferred signal can not use this method because the interference destroies the correlations among symbols.

In dealing with this difficulty, we group 80 samples for one checking window (equal to one symbol length), and make 64-point FFT for subcarrier energy detection. Once the detected energy is 5 dB (verified by our experiments in Section 8.2.3) higher than the noise, the interference signal is identified. Further, we need to identify whether the interference comes from WiFi or ZigBee. Luckily, WiFi is wideband signal and ZigBee is narrow band, we can use the occupied subcarrier number for interference identification.

### 6.2.2 Boundary Detection

Another important issue is boundary detection, *i.e.*, determining where the interference happens. Accurate 'clear preamble' identification is highly correlated with the packet detection and further interfered signal resolution. For signal detection, we take the standard auto-correlation approach that is widely used in packet detection. For WiFi signal, we exploit repeat patterns in short training symbol (STS) for detection. After compensating the frequency offset, we use the long training symbol (LTS) for accurate frame boundary detection. And for ZigBee signal, when preamble is auto-correlated, the frequency offset will be compensated. Thus the start of frame delimiter (SFD) can be detected through cross-correlation, which means the start of a ZigBee packet. Note when ZigBee header is interfered, the WiFi nullification process will ensure the preamble autocorrelation and reliable SFD recovery.

For signal detection, auto correlation is enough, and will not be affected by the frequency offset. However, boundary detection need more accuracy, which is different from signal detection with repeated patterns, e.g., the preambles. In ZIMO design, we use cross correlation instead of auto-correlation. First, we use STS for signal detection. After receiving the signal and successful frequency offset compensation, we can actually leverage the LTS, which has given and known symbols, and achieve robust boundary detection. Fig. 6 shows the effects of frequency compensation for boundary detection when WiFi signal is interfered by ZigBee. Fig. 6a shows clear WiFi and ZigBee boundary through SFD and LTS respectively. However, when frequency offset is not compensated, it is hard to identify the boundary as shown in Fig. 6b.

## 6.3 ZigBee Channel Coefficient Estimation

### 6.3.1 Frequency Offset Compensation

Compared with WiFi systems, the main challenge is that we have to use the short and simple preamble in ZigBee system with frequency bias up to $200KHz$. Thus, the key technology is frequency compensation.

The received band OQPSK signal $x(n)$ with a phase index $k$ ($k = 0, 1, 2, 3$), frequency offset $\delta_f$ and phase offset $\delta_\phi$ can

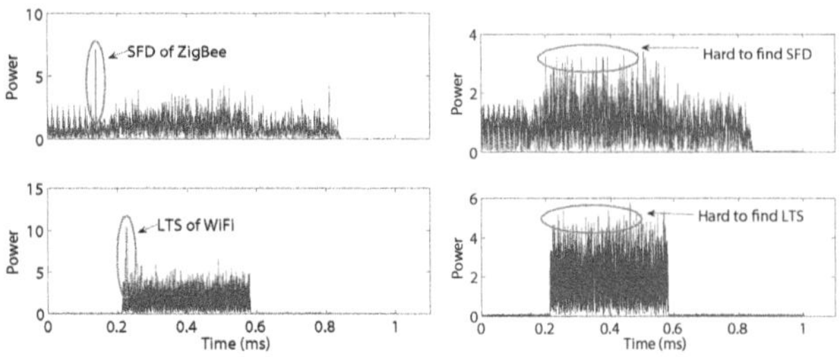


(a) Boundary detection for WiFi signal (b) Boundary detection without frequency compensation

Figure 6: Effects of frequency compensation for boundary detection

be expressed as:

$$x(n) = A_n e^{(j(k\pi/2+2\pi\delta_f n+\delta_\phi))} \tag{3}$$

According to Equ.3, there are three main factors affecting the received signal,*i.e.*, modulation, frequency offset and phase offset. To mitigate the modulation values from our equation, we raise our received signal with the power of 4. Note that only four cases can happen in modulated signal, *i.e.*, 0, $\frac{\pi}{2}, \pi, and \frac{3\pi}{2}$. When the subsystem raises the signal to the power of 4, the phases of the modulated signal have all been shifted to multiply of $2\pi$, which can be eliminated from the received signals.

Therefore, to eliminate the effect of modulation,

$$x^4(n) = A_n^4 e^{(j(2k\pi+4(2\pi\delta_f n)+4\delta_\phi))} = A_n^4 e^{(j(4(2\pi\delta_f n)+4\delta_\phi)))}$$

After that, we perform an FFT on the modulation independent signal to estimate the tone at four times the frequency offset. The received signal can be corrected by:

$$y(n) = x(n)e^{-j2\pi\delta_f n} = A_n e^{(j(k\pi/2+\delta_\phi))}, k = 0, 1, 2, 3$$

There is usually a residual frequency offset even after the coarse frequency compensation, which would cause a slow rotation of the constellation. In ZIMO implementation, the sample frequency $f_s = 2MHz$, and FFT size is 2048. The minimum frequency offset value is $\delta_f^{min} = 244.14Hz$ and the maximum offset $\delta_f^{max} = 250kHz$. Our evaluation results in real wireless environment show that the coarse frequency compensation is enough for channel coefficient estimation to nullify ZigBee signal.

#### 6.3.2 Timing Recovery

After frequency compensation, the time recovery is needed to achieve accurate channel coefficient. The timing recovery subsystem implements a PLL (Phase Locked Loop) to correct the timing error in the received signal. The input of the timing recovery subsystem is over-sampled by two for basic over-sampling processing. Four folds or higher makes no difference as two is enough. On average, the timing recovery subsystem generates one output sample for every two input samples. The NCO (Numerical Controlled Oscillator) control subsystem implements a decrementing modulo-1 counter to generate the control signal to select the interpolations of the Interpolation Filter. This control signal also enables the Timing Error Detector (TED), so that it calculates the timing errors at the correct timing instants.

The NCO Control subsystem updates the timing difference for the Interpolation Filter, generating interpolator structure. Based on the interpolations, timing errors are generated by a zero-crossing Timing Error Detector, filtered by a tunable proportional-plus-integral Loop Filter, and fed into the NCO control for a timing difference update. The Loop Bandwidth (normalized by the sample rate) and Loop Damping Factor are tunable for the Loop Filter. The default normalized loop bandwidth is set to 0.07 and the default damping factor is set to 2, such that the PLL quickly locks to the correct timing while introducing little noise.

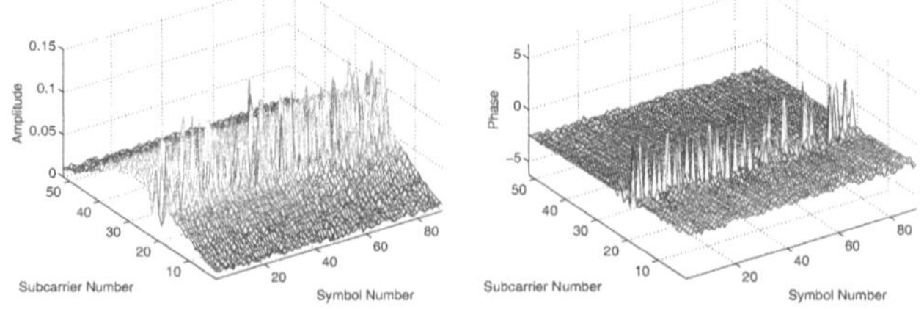


(a) Amplitude (b) Phase

Figure 7: Amplitude, phase of channel coefficient on overlapping ZigBee and WiFi

### 6.4 Interference Nullifying

In ZIMO, to remove the WiFi impact, we need to mitigate the ZigBee signal temporarily for further WiFi signal cancelation. Inspired by two antenna MIMO-based design, we use interference nullifying process for ZigBee noise mitigation. When WiFi signal is 'covered' by the ZigBee smog, we should first nullify the ZigBee smog according to Eq. (2) in Section 3.

As ZigBee signal is narrow band, for efficient computation, we estimate channel coefficient in time domain. The optimal equalizer will minimize the differences between received signal $y(t)$ and the training signal $w(t)$, where

$$\mathbf{c} = \arg\min_{\mathbf{c}} \|w(t) - \mathbf{c} * y(t)\|$$

In the time domain, $\mathbf{c} = \{c_{-L}, \cdots, c_0, \cdots, c_L\}$ is a good estimation of channel coefficient $\mathbf{H}$. For WiFi signal, we compute the channel coefficient in frequency domain, using the FFT of the received signal to divide that of transmitted signal. Then the interference nullifying technology is applied for cross-technology data decoding.

### 6.5 Interference Cancelation

If we can separate WiFi signal from the mixed signal, we can use standard ZigBee decoder to extract ZigBee packets. The overall processing is called Successive Interference Cancelation (SIC).

#### 6.5.1 Fine frequency offset estimation for WiFi

Fine carrier frequency offset (CFO) estimation is necessary to minimize the residual noise after interference cancelation (IC). Inaccurate CFO estimation will lead to increased residual noise over time. A coarse estimation in WiFi training symbols (*i.e.* STS & LTS) is not enough for IC because of limited preamble length and noise. For finer CFO estimation, we remodulate the received data, and compare the phase shifts with the received symbol. Note that, our scheme is data aided, because the remodulated symbol can be achieved after the coarse CFO estimation.

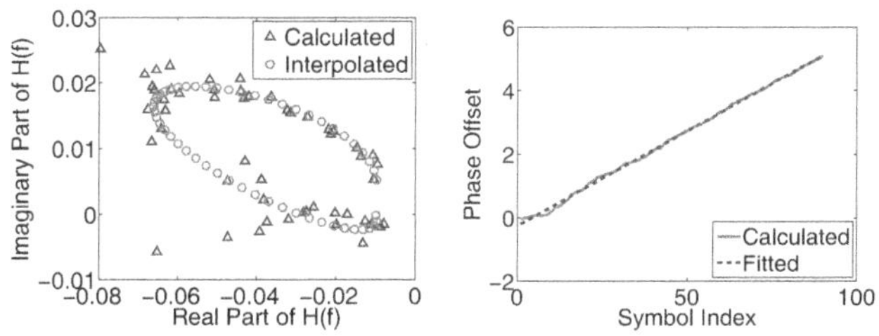


(a) Interpolation result in Real part and Imaginary part (b) Fitting line of fine frequency offset estimation for WiFi

Figure 8: Improvement methods for WiFi IC

As the synchronization process in preamble has successfully compensated the clock difference between sender and receiver, the phase shifts grow linearly with the accumulative symbols in a constant CFO estimation. Consequently, we use linear regression method across symbols in achieving the CFO estimation. The fitting model is based on minimizing the least squares of the noisy data. As shown in Fig. 8b, the fitting line is regressed from the calculated phase shifts over the symbols. There is also a merit in using this CFO estimation method, that is, the channel coefficient can be corrected during data transmission in any length.

### *6.5.2 Blind Recovery for WiFi Channel CoefŒient*

To recover the channel coefficient $\mathbf{H}_w$ for interfered WiFi signals blindly, we use the interpolation method for the missing data. Here blind means recovery channel coefficient without any additional information. The key insight is that, in cross technology coexistence of WiFi and ZigBee, the frequency occupation scheme differs. Note in frequency domain, WiFi can only *partially* overlap with the ZigBee signal as shown in Fig. 7. As ZigBee is a narrow band system while WiFi is wideband, we can reasonably recover the overlapping coefficient according to the known channel coefficient in other subcarriers. Other MIMO multiplexing schemes, *e.g.* SAM [11], can not take this advantage due to the complete frequency overlapping signals in same technology.

We interpolate the interfered parts of WiFi channel coefficient with a fourth-degree polynomial function, and the unknown fitting parameters are computed by minimizing the sum of the squares of deviations. For channel coefficient estimations, quartic-function is smooth enough. We show the interpolation result in Fig. 8a, which validates our scheme. We use the real part versus imaginary part comparison in Fig. 8a to show the relationship between calculated channel coefficient and the interpolated value. Obviously, the effect of the cross-technology interference is reduced, and a reasonably accurate channel coefficient for WiFi is recovered.

### *6.5.3 WiFi Interference Cancelation with ZigBee*

To be more accurate, let us assume the mixed (collided) signal is $y_m(t)$, and the mixed signal is down-sampled using central frequency and bandwidth of WiFi setup. Let $x_w(t)$ be the packet bits from WiFi, and $x_z(t)$ be the packet bits from ZigBee. Then we have

$$y_m(t) = \mathbf{H}_w x_w(t) + \mathbf{H}_z x_z(t) e^{j2\pi\delta_f t} + n(t)$$

where $\mathbf{H}_w$ and $\mathbf{H}_z$ are the channel coefficient of WiFi and ZigBee respectively, and $\delta_f$ is the central frequency offset between WiFi and ZigBee.

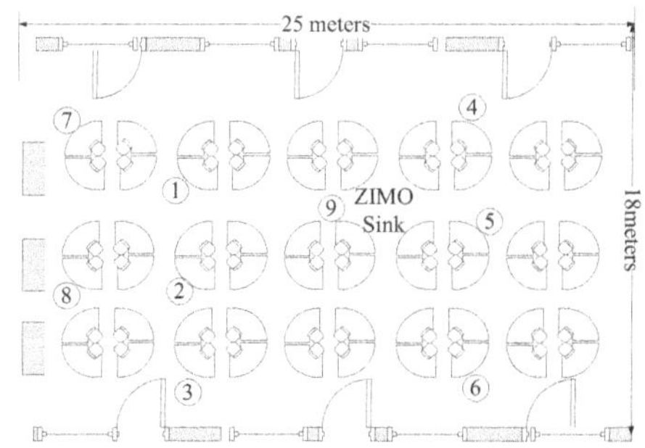


Figure 9: ZIMO test environment with 9 testing locations

Due to successful ZigBee signal nullification, we can get $x_w(t)$ using standard decoder from the WiFi signal (ZigBee signal is nullified). Then we re-modulate the WiFi signal as $S_w = \mathbf{H}_w x_w(t)$, and setup a new formula as $Y(t) = y(t) - S_w = \mathbf{H}_z x_z(t) e^{j2\pi\delta_f t} + n(t)$. Then we can process $Y(t)$ to get ZigBee packet.

## 6.6 ZigBee Data Decoding

The data decoding subsystem performs fine frequency offset compensation, phase ambiguity resolution, timing recovery, OQPSK demodulation, chip to symbol decoding and CRC calculation. Fine frequency offset compensation is achieved by a Phase Locked Loop (PLL). Next, we exploit the preamble to resolve phase ambiguity. Particularly, we calculate the cross correlation of input signal and modulated symbol zero. Then we estimate the phase of the cross correlation result. We classify the estimated phase ambiguity into 0, $\pm\frac{\pi}{2}$ and $\pi$ phase offset. The input signal for demodulation is corrected with this phase ambiguity. After timing recovery, the received signal is demodulated to chip sequence.

Once a preamble symbol is detected, we continuously search the SFD byte in the incoming signal. If SFD is found, the PHR (PHY headeR) information can be extracted and the packet can be resembled. After that, the CRC of this packet can be calculated for verifying correctness of packets.

## 7. IMPLEMENTATION

We use GNURadio/USRP N200 software radios to evaluate ZIMO performance, because ZIMO design requires total control of wireless physical layer (*e.g.*, WiFi and ZigBee signal-level control), which cannot be accomplished using commercial network interface cards and sensor nodes. However, due to the inherent unpredictable and long latency between RF frontend and hosts, software radios cannot support precise MAC timing control. We have built a prototype of ZIMO sink with GNURadio/USRP N200, including all components described in Section 6. As in the literature we use trace-driven approach. The real-time trace is collected using USRP/GNURadio, and then fed into decoder. We not only study the physical layer performance, but also conduct network level experiments.

We implement the OFDM PHY layer of WiFi and OQPSK PHY layer of ZigBee. The bandwidth of WiFi and ZigBee is 20 MHz and 2 MHz respectively. In Section 8, we will demonstrate that, our design can ensure sufficient number of processing for every interfered patterns in our random sampling collections.

Table 1: Setup for Test-bed

| No. | WiFi | | | ZigBee | | |
|---|---|---|---|---|---|---|
| | Dist (Loc) | Amp | SNR (dB) | Dist (Loc) | Amp | SNR (dB) |
| 1 | 5(1) | 0.3 | 23.6-35.6 | 5(5) | 0.15 | 14.7-24.5 |
| 2 | 5(1) | 0.25 | 11.8-34.2 | 5(5) | 0.1 | 15.8-21.8 |
| 3 | 5(1) | 0.2 | 14.2-32.1 | 5(5) | 0.05 | -0.3-7.3 |
| 4 | 7(6) | 0.2 | 4.2-23.4 | 10(7) | 0.2 | 5.6-17.3 |
| 5 | 10(8) | 0.2 | 3.4-18.4 | 10(7) | 0.2 | 0.3-15.8 |
| 6 | 10(8) | 0.3 | 10.0-23.0 | 10(7) | 0.2 | 4.1-15.9 |

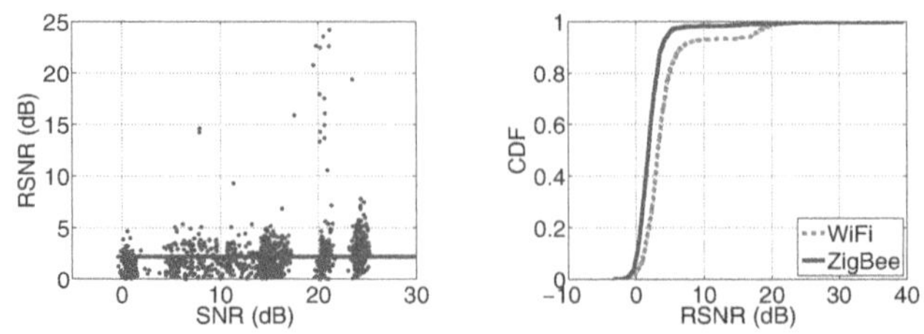


(a) RSNR across different SNR values

(b) CDF of RSNR, with ZigBee & WiFi signals

Figure 10: IN performance in RSNR, the solid line in 10a shows the linear regression of the data.

# 8. EXPERIMENTAL RESULTS

## 8.1 Experiment Setups

Fig. 9 shows the layout of our testing environment. It's a typical semi-open office floor with table and cubicles. For simplicity of explanation, both WiFi and ZigBee channels are assumed to be fixed. The channel number of WiFi and ZigBee is 5 and 16, *i.e.*, 2.432 GHz and 2.430 GHz. WiFi uses BPSK and $\frac{1}{2}$ channel coding rate (*i.e.*, 6Mbps), and ZigBee system is set to 250Kbps. We select the WiFi and ZigBee payload length to be 256 Bytes and 20 Bytes respectively. And in our system design, the transmission durations are 0.358ms and 0.8325ms respectively. In order to evaluate the ZIMO decoding performance under WiFi interference, we need to collect collision signal. However, it is non-trivial to synchronize two USRPs, since the packet collision happens in signal-level. We exploit the time stamp mechanism provided by GNURadio community to deliberately create the WiFi/ZigBee collision. For example, ZigBee packets are sent periodically every 1ms, and WiFi packets are sent periodically every 2.5ms. Because ZigBee and WiFi have different packet lengths, the overlapping pattern can change as packets accumulate, but be retained periodically.

The ZIMO sink is fixed at location 9, while WiFi and ZigBee transmissions are randomly selected from other 8 different locations in Fig. 9. ZIMO sink captures 10 traces of the channel periodically. Each trace contains around 200 ms signal data on one 20 MHz 802.11g channel, which is equivalent to collect over 1000 packets in the air. Thus over 10,000 respective WiFi and ZigBee packets are collected, which contain various interfered patterns for validated evaluation.

The experiment is evaluated in different locations with various SNR values. Table 1 shows the configurations of USRP based WiFi and ZigBee nodes. We use 6 different location pairs in total. The 'dist' column shows the distance between ZIMO sink and the configured WiFi/ZigBee node with exact number in brackets shown in Fig. 9 accordingly, and the 'Amp' column is the amplifying factor in RF end. Notably, the 'SNR' column shows the range of SNR value in respective location. In our configuration, although distances are not very long, the SNR values are dynamic with multiple choices, which would be helpful for further evaluation tests. Comparing with the larger scale experiment setups, ours could provide more SNR levels for evaluating the effects of interference handling processes comprehensively.

## 8.2 Micro Benchmark

We evaluate ZIMO using GNURadio/USRP software radio testbed. Our goal is to show ZIMO is plausible in realistic environments. We conduct micro-benchmark to evaluate the three key techniques in ZIMO, including interference nullification, interference cancelation and interference detection performance. We then show the benefit of ZIMO for coexisted networks, by measuring the end-to-end throughput gain of ZIMO over conventional wireless sensor network as well as WiFi networks.

### *8.2.1 Interference Nullify of ZigBee & WiFi Signal*

We first study the performance of interference nullification (IN) in the ZIMO implementation.

As stated in Section 6, the IN step of ZigBee signal is important for IC of WiFi signal. Only the well performed IC in WiFi will lead to ideal ZigBee data decoding. Similarly, the WiFi signal IN is also a fundamental step for ZigBee signal decoding. To evaluate how effective our IN algorithm performs, we examine the (Residual Signal+Noise) to Noise Ratio (called RSNR) after IN process under different SNR settings. This rule can here be applied to both WiFi and ZigBee signals. RSNR is defined as $\frac{R+N}{N}$, where $R$ is the residual noise after IN and $N$ is the energy of background noise. Obviously, lower RSNR in fixed background noise $N$ means better performance of IN. Also, we need to evaluate the residual noise across different background noise.

Fig. 10a shows the result of ZigBee signal nullification. The x-axis shows the average of SNR values of the ZigBee signal with clear preamble at both antennas. Observe that the majority of frames are with SNR between 0dB to 25dB, which is the usual SNR range for ZigBee system to work reliably in practice. We also observed frames with very low SNRs. This is due to the dynamic fading effects of ZigBee channel. We notice that IN has removed a significant portion of interfering energy, and the majority of RSNR is very small, with 0 to 5dB higher than the noise. The solid line is a linear regression of the data, which shows the steady performance of IN. In practice, many wireless links work at higher SNR range than this minimal requirement. For example, in our data set, most ZigBee links have a SNR higher than 10dB. Thus, this additional noise has little impact on the following decoding process. We then evaluate the residual noise level over all SNR settings. Fig. 10b plots the Cumulative Distribution Function (CDF) of the RSNR values for ZigBee signal. We can observe that over 90% cases, IN can effectively remove the interference and the resulted RSNR is less than 4dB. There are only around 5% cases that RSNR is larger than 5dB, such that, the decoding of the WiFi may be affected.

Similar results are also shown in Fig. 11a. The WiFi signals are ranging from 0dB to 35dB, and most of the signals

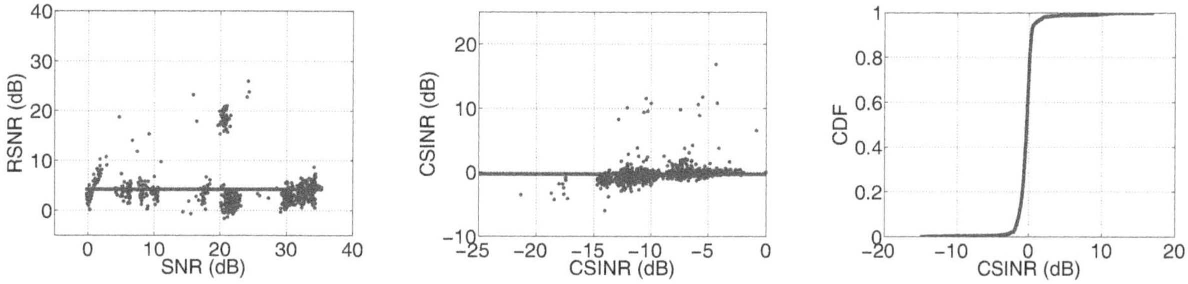


(a) RSNR of WiFi Nullification (b) CSINR of WiFi Cancelation (c) CDF of WiFi Cancelation

Figure 11: WiFi nullification and cancelation.

are nullified below 5dB. Notably, in Fig. 11a, small but significant portion of residual signals are around 15dB to 25dB when the input signal is around 20dB, because the WiFi preamble is interfered but can still be detected. Actually, the channel coefficient value is not accurate. As the interference detection module will not take this case as interference, the residual noise after IN is not satisfiable. When the signal is larger than 20dB, the ZigBee interference signal will not effectively affect the WiFi IN process.

### *8.2.2 Interference Cancelation of WiFi Signal*

Next, we evaluate the performance of interference cancelation in the ZIMO implementation. We use the same experiment setups and same data as in the previous experiment. We defined the CSINR (cancellation based signal-to-interference-and-noise) in our study, so as to show the effectiveness of interference cancellation. CSINR is defined as $\frac{S+N}{S+I+N}$, where $S$ is the signal energy of the first frame, $I$ is the energy of interference frames, and $N$ is the noise. If the interference can be successfully canceled, the ratio in our definition is 1, and the according value is 0dB. Thus, the CDF figure for IC effects will be clear. If the interference can be successfully canceled, the line will be very close to the line '$x = 0$'. Then, we evaluate how effective our IC algorithm can improve the CSINR value of the first frame and thereby enable correct decoding.

Fig. 11b shows the CSINR of the ZigBee after canceling the interference from WiFi. The x-axis is the SINR before IC. We observed the follows. First, IC effectively improves SINR of the frame by reducing the energy from interference. From Fig. 11b, we can see that SINR has been substantially improved up to $15dB$, and most of the SINR values are around 5 to 10dB. Thereby the interfered ZigBee frames can all be decoded successfully. Second, the improved SINR value reduces as the original SINR increases. This is reasonable since SINR is a ratio between the desired signal energy and the sum of interference and noise. A larger SINR usually means the interference is small. As shown in Fig. 11c, the CDF of CSINR shows that, over 95% SINR value is around 0dB, which means the successful IC process.

Fig. 12a shows the cancelation effects between our interpolation method and original method without correction for channel coefficient. The upmost sub-figure shows the interfered ZigBee signal with WiFi flash, and there is no clear WiFi signal for reference. The middle sub-figure shows the cancelation effects of the original method. The bottom sub-figure shows that, the interpolation method has provided significantly ideal cancelation effects for ZigBee signal de-

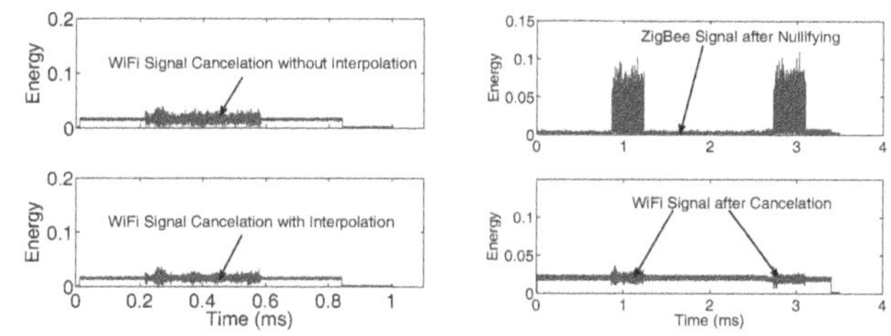


(a) Interpolation scheme for IC (b) Multiple WiFi cancelation

Figure 12: WiFi cancellation effects

coding. It will also contribute to the WiFi data recovery, which leads to co-prosperity in ZIMO.

When ZigBee smog is interfered by multiple WiFi flashes, ZIMO can still work without modification. Fig. 12b shows that, in such case, after the ZigBee signal is nullified, the WiFi flashes are significantly detectable. Whether it comes from same WiFi AP or multiple APs, the cancelation process can work independently and automatically, where the WiFi interferences can be successfully mitigated.

### *8.2.3 Frame Detection Accuracy*

We evaluate the accuracy of frame detection of ZIMO under different SNR settings. The data is generated and collected with USRP devices. Various overlapping patterns are presented, where over 1,000 WiFi and 1,000 ZigBee frames are used for accuracy evaluation of ZIMO frame detection.

Fig. 13 shows that, the false negative (FN) rate is always negligible, even in very low SNR. This result means ZIMO can reliably detect the WiFi and ZigBee frame. The false positive (FP) values in Fig. 13a, although are relatively high in low SNR, will not affect the network performance much. For ZigBee signals, it only costs unnecessary ZIMO processing. For keeping the FN low, raising the FP value a little higher is tolerable and reasonable.

## 8.3 Throughput Gain of ZIMO

We then evaluate throughput gain of ZIMO under the GNURadio-USRP implementations. We mainly compare the throughput of ZIMO to a baseline system designed for comparison. We use the following method to measure the throughput of ZIMO as our current decoder cannot run in real-time due to hardware limit. The ZIMO sink node will take 100 snapshots during 3 hours randomly. Each snapshot contains 200ms data, which is equivalent to 100 frames

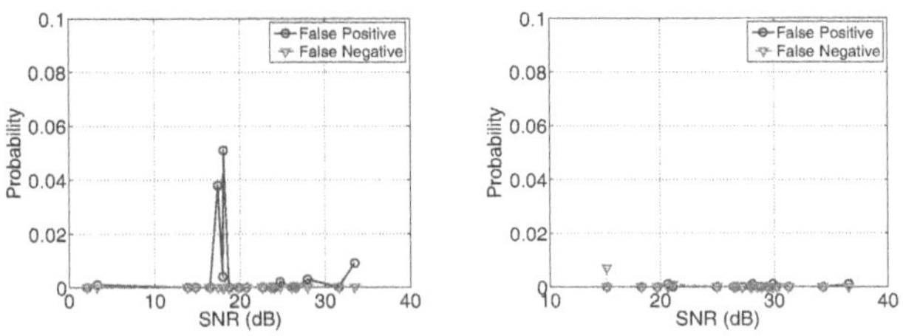


(a) ZigBee frame (b) WiFi frame

Figure 13: Frame detection accuracy in FP & FN

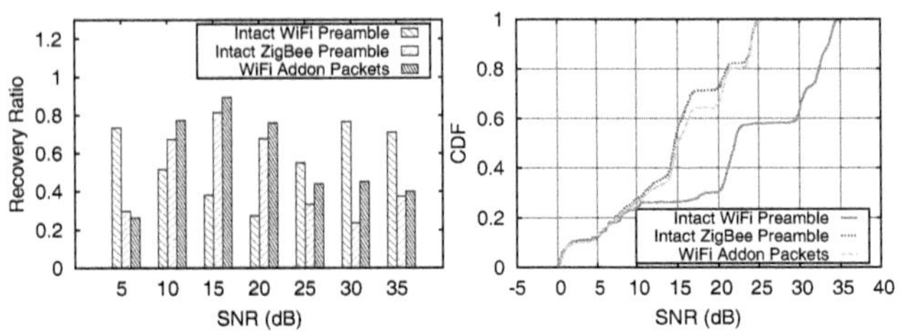


(a) Different SNR values (b) CDF versus SNR

Figure 14: Recovery ratio of ZIMO network.

in different interference patterns and 10,000 frames in total. We store the data and process it off-line. With these traces, we can estimate the throughput as well as the recovery ratio during the snapshot period.

### 8.3.1 Baseline System Design

Our baseline system is designed according to IEEE standards 802.11 and 802.15.4. The reference codings and procedures are validated, evaluated, and tested for standard conformance sufficiently. We omit the details due to page limit. In summary, the baseline system can successfully tranceive WiFi and ZigBee packets and can decode COTS WiFi and ZigBee packets as well.

### 8.3.2 Throughput Gain of ZIMO over ZigBee

Fig. 14a shows the recovery ratio of ZIMO across different levels of SNR value. In the 'x-axis', the SNR value is calculated according to the first received intact symbols. Thus, when the intact preamble is from ZigBee, the SNR value is calculated by ZigBee symbol at the receiver side. Also, SNR is accordingly computed for intact WiFi preamble. In 'y-axis', we evaluate the recovery ratio, which is the fraction of the successfully recovered ZigBee packets among all the interfered packets. Notably, for WiFi packets, we also evaluate the case where WiFi packets can be recovered when ZigBee interference exists.

The recovery ratio of ZIMO ranges from 20% to 80% when ZigBee preamble is intact, and up to 90% when WiFi preamble is intact. Note that with higher SNR value, the benefits of ZIMO degrade. For WiFi network, this degradation is due to the interference of ZigBee. Fig. 14b shows the CDF of the recovery ratio for the cases mentioned above.

Fig. 15a shows the throughput gain of ZIMO comparing with the baseline system. We observe that for all cases, ZIMO significantly improves the network throughput compared to ZigBee. It shows that coexisting WiFi and ZigBee signals with MIMO can make full use of two antennas by overlapping two concurrent transmissions from cross technology. Three cases are listed for clear evaluation and categorization. The 'intact ZigBee preamble' and 'intact WiFi preamble' means reliable detection of the packets because the preamble is not affected. These two cases are used to illustrate the performance of ZIMO in different processes. It is 'IN+IC+Decoding' comparing with the 'IN+Decoding'. Interestingly, to show the effects of the harmonizing process, where WiFi data can be recovered for the IC process, we take the 'WiFi add on packets' for evaluation, showing the recoverability of the interfered WiFi signals during ZIMO process. Note that, it is a special case of 'intact ZigBee preamble', because only in this case, the WiFi data can be recovered as a co-prosperous gain under the favorable 'IN+IC+Decoding' process.

In Fig. 15a, the 'x-axis' is location pair, which is labeled with $\langle i, j \rangle$, denoting WiFi node at location $i$, and ZigBee node at location $j$, as shown in Fig. 9. In 10 location pairs of our experiment, ZIMO makes over 3-folds throughput gain.

### 8.3.3 Throughput Gain of WiFi Network

We then evaluate the throughput gain of WiFi network, which is illustrated in Fig. 15b. There are about 200kbps to 400kbps throughput gain across location pairs. Except for location pair 2, where the gain is not significant. The main reason is, the WiFi signal (from location 1) strength is comparatively much higher than ZigBee signal (from location 2). Thus, the ZigBee will not make effective interference, *i.e.* corruptions, on WiFi signal.

We thus claim that ZIMO enables co-prosperity in coexisting cross-technology systems with only one MIMO sink node. Note that, comparing with the asymmetric regions, the ZigBee interference is relatively weak. However, the WiFi data corruptions are not negligible. In some location pairs, *e.g.*, location pairs 3, 9, 10, the throughput gain is nearly 2-folds to the baseline system.

### 8.3.4 Structural Analysis for Interference Patterns

Fig. 15c shows the throughput of ZIMO, also with the statistical result for different interference patterns (InPs). It is shown that, in most location pairs, three InPs, including intact WiFi preamble, intact ZigBee preamble and intact ZigBee frame (no interference) are well distributed, *i.e.* no significant difference on the number of interfered packets among InPs, which shows that our configurations on packet length and interval are reasonable. The structural analysis will provide us information about the InPs and help us know how the ZIMO performs. For example, if we know the InPs, there are two potential enhancements: one is for the optimal placement of ZIMO sinks, while the other is for the optimal number of ZIMO sinks. Obviously, the structural analysis is more precise than conventional spectrum sensing schemes for ensuring good throughput performance.

## 9. DISCUSSIONS

## 9.1 Fundamental Differences from TIMO

Applying TIMO technology [1] directly to Sink node will not help us solve the coexistence problem. Actually, ZIMO is fundamentally different from TIMO. The main difference is, when WiFi and ZigBee signals are interfering each other, successful WiFi decoding will not ensure successful ZigBee signal recovery. When we need to recover ZigBee signal un-

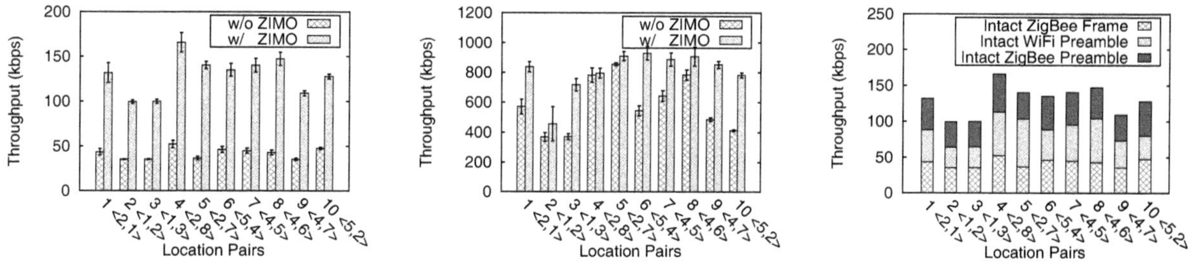


(a) ZIMO over ZigBee baseline system (b) ZIMO over WiFi baseline system (c) Fractions of interference patterns

Figure 15: Throughput gain of ZIMO network over baseline system in distinctive location pairs

der WiFi interfere, decoding WiFi is not enough, because we have to achieve a more accurate channel coefficient under the CFO (Central Frequency Offset). The main challenge is to make a finer and more accurate channel coefficient estimation for WiFi decoding, tackling the relatively large CFO and interfered channel coefficient values. Note that, in interfered signals, achieving accurate CFO evaluation directly is extremely difficult. In tackling these difficulties, we use the frequency offset estimation method and channel coefficient interpolation to recover ZigBee data from WiFi interference.

## 9.2 Coexisting with Multiple WiFi and Other Cross-technology Signals

Our concern originates from a real deployed large-scale wireless sensor network, CitySee [3], the world largest environment monitoring network based on wireless sensors. When these sensors are deployed in city scale, especially in residential area, shopping mall, and railway stations, etc, the WiFi interference became the No.1 interference source to ZigBee network transmission and forwarding. On the other hand, numerous sensor nodes (For GreenOrbs and CitySee projects in WuXi, China [3], there will be up to 4,000 wireless sensor nodes at the end of 2013, and over 10,000 ZigBee-based sensors before 2015!) make the modifications on either software or hardware extremely difficult. It is also very interesting and challenging to deal with Bluetooth and other cross technology devices. We will focus on this topic in future work.

## 9.3 Extension to Multihop Scenario

Our scheme only works in one hop away for WiFi and ZigBee transmission. Extending our solution to multi-hop network will need multiple or dynamic ZIMO sink deployment. It's similar to cellular network deployment and optimizations, which has been widely studied. Moreover, adding ZIMO sink will be easy and affordable, especially for densely deployed WSNs.

The only difficulty lies in the site survey for interference between cross technology devices. Fortunately, there are some candidate solutions in recent studies. For example, Zhou *et al.* [14] propose an instructive method for mining the practical conflict graphs for dynamic spectrum distribution, especially in outdoor scenario. Also, inspiring works are leveraging the crowdsourcing data [15] [16] to characterize the signal and interference map for indoor scenario.

# 10. RELATED WORK

In most of the previous studies, WiFi is the interested signal, and other mixed signals are eliminated as interference [1,5]. In technology independent multi-output receiver design, *e.g.*, TIMO [1], the ZigBee transmissions are treated as same band interference with microwave interference. Solutions making the WiFi network aware of the existence of ZigBee are not bandwidth efficient [7, 17], because the high speed WiFi node is suppressed by the ZigBee notification. Suppressing subcarriers will also lead to performance reduction [7, 18]. Leveraging the silent duration between WiFi transmissions is a passive method [4], where the ZigBee transmissions depend on WiFi networks. Liang *et al.* [6] proposed multi-header (for handling symmetric regions) and payload redundancy (for handling asymmetric regions) to protect the ZigBee data, but the sensor node needs to be reprogrammed. Another inspiring and creative work is Picasso [19], a full duplex wireless system with only one antenna, providing adaptive and efficient RF and spectrum slicing. Such technology can be used for efficient coexistence only when spectrum usages are not conflicting or overlapping. Such constraint makes Picasso not suitable to address our concern without intervening or modifying deployed WiFi and ZigBee systems.

Special signaler devices were introduced to improve the visibility of low-power ZigBee in [17, 20]. A special node emits strong jamming signal [20] or fake WiFi header [17] during ZigBee transmission to let WiFi backoff explicitly. Radunovic *et al.* [21] redesigned the preamble of low-power wireless technology based on a key observation that longer preamble sequence can be detected easier. In this case, WiFi will sense the presence of ZigBee, and thus backoff. The mutual visibility solutions can enhance a fair coexistence, but is not a perfect solution in urban monitoring scenario. Long-term running of mutual visibility solutions will cause WiFi performance degradation, and WiFi can also have anti-jamming capability [22] to make such solutions infeasible. Moreover, the signaler solution requires strict timing control of ZigBee's transmission, leading to severe protocol overhead in large-scale ZigBee networks.

Then several solutions [7, 18, 23] utilized OFDM subcarrier suppressing technique to vacate spectrum that ZigBee networks are using. The strong WiFi devices first find the existence of weak ZigBee devices (either by sensing [7,18] or learning [23]), decide which spectrum ZigBee networks are using, and nullify those spectrum to enable simultaneous access. The subcarrier suppressing solution requires hardware redesign of high-power nodes, *e.g.*, preamble design and packet detection algorithm, which limits the application if it is not compatible with existing devices.

Inspiring works SAM [11] and IAC [9], used interference cancelation technique in multi-user MIMO scenario. Moreover, [9,24,25] demonstrated the interference cancelation using DSSS style communication system, while we use OFDM.

WiZi-Cloud [26] proposed to use additional ZigBee radios to help WiFi clients achieve ubiquitous connectivity, high energy efficiency, and real time inter-AP handover. WiBee [27] exploited low-cost ZigBee sensor networks to build real-time WiFi radio maps.

## 11. CONCLUSIONS

We presented ZIMO, a cross-technology MIMO design to harmonize ZigBee smog with WiFi flash without modifying legacy systems. We implemented ZIMO on the GNURadio/USRP platform using commercial compatible implementations of WiFi and ZigBee. Our experiment results showed that, up to 80% interfered signals are effectively recovered by ZIMO. Moreover, 30% to 90% interfered WiFi signals are effectively recovered in the process, which demonstrates the co-prosperity goal in ZIMO design.

ZIMO enables the sink node to protect WiFi and ZigBee signal in one framework. In future design, ZIMO could be enhanced into a composite AP for both ZigBee and WiFi networks. Thus, downlink design is needed for effective communications. For large-scale wireless sensor networks, ZIMO sinks can be deployed in asymmetric areas for multi-hop support. Placement of ZIMO sinks depends on interference relationship between WiFi and WSN deployments, which makes optimal placement an interesting and challenging work for future research. Also, in symmetric area, clear carrier sensing scheme can be encouraged to be disabled for concurrent transmissions. Finally, ZIMO can be applied to other WiFi standards with slight modifications, such as IEEE 802.11n.

## 12. ACKNOWLEDGMENTS

This research is partially supported by NSF China under Grants No. 61003277, 61232018, 61272487, 61170216, 61172062, 61228202, 61273210, NSF CNS-0832120, NSF CNS-1035894, NSF EECS-1247944, China 973 Program under Grants No. 2009CB320400, 2010CB328100, 2010CB334707, 2011CB302705. We thank all the reviewers for their insightful comments and valuable suggestions, and Prof. Kannan Srinivasan for shepherding the final revision of the paper in dedication. Particularly, the research work is mainly done during the authors' scholar visiting in IOT Tech-center of TNLIST, Wuxi, China.

## 13. REFERENCES

[1] S. Gollakota, F. Adib, D. Katabi, and S. Seshan, "Clearing the RF smog: making 802.11n robust to cross-technology interference," in *Proc. of ACM SIGCOMM*, 2011.

[2] R. Murty, G. Mainland, I. Rose, and M. Welsh, "CitySense: An Urban-Scale Wireless Sensor Network and Testbed," in *Proc. of IEEE HST*, 2008.

[3] X. Mao, X. Miao, Y. He, T. Zhu, J. Wang, W. Dong, and X. Li, "CitySee: Urban CO2 Monitoring with Sensors," in *Proc. of IEEE INFOCOM*, 2012.

[4] J. Huang, G. Xing, G. Zhou, and R. Zhou, "Beyond co-existence: Exploiting WiFi white space for Zigbee performance assurance," in *Proc. of IEEE ICNP*, 2010.

[5] R. Zhou, Y. Xiong, G. Xing, L. Sun, and J. Ma, "ZiFi: Wireless LAN Discovery via ZigBee Interference," in *Proc. of ACM MobiCom*, 2010.

[6] C.-J. M. Liang, N. B. Priyantha, J. Liu, and A. Terzis, "Surviving wi-fi interference in low power ZigBee networks," in *Proc. of ACM SenSys*, 2010.

[7] X. Zhang and K. Shin, "Adaptive Subcarrier Nulling: Enabling partial spectrum sharing in wireless LANs," in *Proc. of IEEE ICNP*, 2011.

[8] S. B. S. Rayachu, A. Patro, "Airshark: Detecting Non-WiFi RF Devices using Commodity WiFi Hardware," in *Proc. of ACM IMC*, 2011.

[9] S. P. S. Gollakota and D. Katabi, "Interference alignment and cancelation," in *Proc. of ACM SIGCOMM*, 2009.

[10] IEEE Standard, "Wireless Medium Access Control (MAC) and Physical Layer (PHY) Specifications for Low-Rate Wireless Personal Area Networks (WPANs)," 2006.

[11] K. Tan, H. Liu, and J. Fang, "SAM: Enabling Practical Spatial Multiple Access in Wireless LAN," in *Proc. of ACM MobiCom*, 2009.

[12] *Contiki website*, http://www.contiki-os.org.

[13] C. Shepard, H. Yu, N. Anand, L. Li, T. Marzetta, Y. Yang, and L. Zhong, "Argos: practical base stations with many antennas," in *Proc. of ACM MobiCom*, 2012.

[14] X. Zhou, Z. Zhang, G. Wang, X. Yu, B. Y. Zhao, and H. Zheng, "Practical conflict graphs for dynamic spectrum distribution," in *Proc. of ACM Sigmetrics*, 2013.

[15] Z. Yang, C. Wu, and Y. Liu, "Locating in fingerprint space: wireless indoor localization with little human intervention," in *Proc. of ACM MobiCom*, 2012.

[16] G. Shen, Z. Chen, P. Zhang, T. Moscibroda, and Y. Zhang, "Walkie-Markie: Indoor Pathway Mapping Made Easy," in *Proc. of USENIX NSDI*, 2013.

[17] Y. Wang, Q. Wang, Z. Zeng, G. Zheng, and R. Zheng, "WiCop: Engineering WiFi Temporal White-Spaces for Safe Operations of Wireless Body Area Networks in Medical Applications," in *Proc. of IEEE RTSS*, 2011.

[18] Y. He, J. Fang, J. Zhang, H. Shen, K. Tan, and Y. Zhang, "MPAP: virtualization architecture for heterogenous wireless APs," *SIGCOMM Comput. Commun. Rev.*, vol. 41, no. 1, Jan. 2011.

[19] S. S. Hong, J. Mehlman, and S. Katti, "Picasso: flexible RF and spectrum slicing," in *Proc. of ACM SIGCOMM*, 2012.

[20] X. Zhang and K. G. Shin, "Cooperative Carrier Signaling: Harmonizing Coexisting WPAN and WLAN Devices," *IEEE Trans on Networking*, 2012.

[21] B. Radunovic, R. Chandra, and D. Gunawardena, "Weeble: Enabling low-power nodes to coexist with high-power nodes in white space networks," *ACM CoNEXT*, 2012.

[22] K. Pelechrinis, I. Broustis, S. Krishnamurthy, C. Gkantsidis, B. Radunovic, R. Chandra, and D. Gunawardena, "ARES: an anti-jamming reinforcement system for 802.11 networks," in *Proc. of CoNEXT*, 2009.

[23] H. Rahul, N. Kushman, D. Katabi, C. Sodini, and F. Edalat, "Learning to share: narrowband-friendly wideband networks," in *Proc. of ACM SIGCOMM*, 2008.

[24] D. Halperin, T. Anderson, and D. Wetherall, "Taking the sting out of carrier sense: interference cancellation for wireless LANs," in *Proc. of ACM MobiCom*, 2008.

[25] S. Gollakota and D. Katabi, "Zigzag decoding: combating hidden terminals in wireless networks," in *Proc. of ACM SIGCOMM*, 2008.

[26] T. Jin, G. Noubir, and B. Sheng, "WiZi-Cloud: Application-transparent dual ZigBee-WiFi radios for low power internet access," in *Proc. of IEEE INFOCOM*, 2011.

[27] W. Li, Y. Zhu, and T. He, "WiBee: Building WiFi radio map with ZigBee sensor networks," in *Proc. of IEEE INFOCOM*, 2012.

# Adaptive Feedback Compression for MIMO Networks

Xiufeng Xie and Xinyu Zhang
University of Wisconsin-Madison
{xiufeng,xyzhang}@ece.wisc.edu

Karthikeyan Sundaresan
NEC Laboratories America
karthiks@nec-labs.com

## ABSTRACT

MIMO beamforming technology can scale wireless data rate proportionally with the number of antennas. However, the overhead induced by receivers' CSI (channel state information) feedback scales at a higher rate. In this paper, we address this fundamental tradeoff with Adaptive Feedback Compression (AFC). AFC quantizes or compresses CSI from 3 dimensions — time, frequency and numerical values, and adapts the intensity of compression according to channel profile. This simple principle faces many practical challenges, *e.g.*, a huge search space for adaption, estimation or prediction of the impact of compression on network throughput, and the coupling of different users in multi-user MIMO networks. AFC meets these challenges using a novel cross-layer adaptation metric, a metric extracted from 802.11 packet preambles, and uses it to guide the selection of compression intensity, so as to balance the tradeoff between overhead reduction and capacity loss (due to compression). We have implemented AFC on a software radio testbed. Our experiments show that AFC can outperform alternative approaches in a variety of radio environments.

## Categories and Subject Descriptors

C.2.1 [**Computer-Communication Networks**]: Network Architecture and Design—*Wireless Communications*; C.2.2 [**Computer-Communication Networks**]: Network Protocols

## General Terms

Algorithms, Design, Theory, Performance

## Keywords

Multi-user MIMO networks, limited feedback, feedback compression



## 1. INTRODUCTION

MIMO beamforming, also referred to as *closed-loop MIMO* technology, has the potential to scale wireless data rate proportionally with the number of transmit antennas. In fact, it has become a hallmark of recent high-throughput 802.11 standards. In particular, 802.11n adopted single-user MIMO (SU-MIMO) beamforming, where multiple transmit antennas *precode* one packet, so that the precoded signals coherently combine at a receiver to enhance SNR. The ongoing 802.11ac further incorporates multi-user beamforming (MU-MIMO), which precodes different receivers' packets, so that they can be transmitted simultaneously without interference. The precoding operations in SU- and MU-MIMO are essentially a weighted combination of outgoing packets, and the weights must be carefully designed based on the channel state information (CSI), *i.e.*, the channel matrix from transmit antennas to all receive antennas. Hence, a transmitter must obtain timely CSI feedback from all receivers. As CSI is needed for different transmit antennas, frequency bands and receivers, the resulting information grows with a multiplication of all these parameters, which causes formidable overhead and may even nullify the MIMO capacity gain. Therefore, managing feedback overhead is critical to the performance of MIMO beamforming.

The 802.11n/ac standards propose to compress the CSI along three dimensions: time — sending CSI less frequently; frequency— allowing adjacent spectrum units (called *subcarriers*) to share the same CSI; and numerical values — quantizing CSI values into a small number of bits. Though promising for reducing feedback overhead, such compression comes with a loss in CSI accuracy and may adversely affect the MIMO network throughput. Therefore, it is critical to strike a balance between overhead reduction and capacity loss. But finding such a sweet spot is non-trivial as it involves sophisticated coupling of all three dimensions. Similar to the bit-rate options, the choice of compression options and levels remains vendor-specific in 802.11, and to the best of our knowledge has not been explored before.

This paper attempts to fill the gap in this space through: a comprehensive measurement study of the impact of compression on network performance, and the design of Adaptive Feedback Compression (AFC) - a feedback management mechanism for SU-/MU-MIMO networks. Our measurement study is based on a comprehensive software-radio implementation of the 802.11n SU-MIMO and 802.11ac MU-MIMO OFDM PHY layer. The results reveal that although CSI compression can save substantial overhead, it may significantly degrade link capacity if too aggressive. More importantly, a link's tolerance to CSI compression depends not only on its channel stability, but also on SNR, spectrum location, and user pairing (for MU-MIMO) — a number of factors unreported in previous works. This calls for an automatic configuration scheme that maximizes compression intensity without losing too much capacity.

AFC is designed to meet this goal with a simple principle. It quantizes or compresses CSI from 3 dimensions: time, frequency and numerical values, and adapts the intensity of compression according to channel profile. Realizing this principle involves non-trivial challenges: (1) The 3 dimensions together constitute a huge parameter space. Hence a comprehensive search algorithm is inefficient and may never converge. In fact, when searching over one dimension, the channel profile w.r.t. the other two dimensions may have already changed. (2) Compression intensity can be configured according to a certain metric that reflects channel stability over time or frequency. Coherence time/frequency is widely used for this purpose. But through experimental study, we find that there does not exist a fixed mapping between such a metric and the optimal compression intensity. (3) An efficient adaptation algorithm must be able to estimate the link capacity change due to CSI compression over a certain dimension. However, the effects of different dimensions on capacity loss are coupled.

AFC meets these challenges using *CNo*, a novel cross-layer adaptation metric that can model the information loss (or errors) due to compression. Upon each packet arrival, AFC can instantaneously extract the CNo metric from the CSI of 802.11 packet preambles, and evaluate the errors and SNR reduction caused by each dimension of compression respectively. As CNo decouples the 3 dimensions of adaptation, it substantially reduces the search space. It also helps isolate the effects of compression from channel fading, which can both result in changes in link capacity. Based on CNo, AFC can easily identify the appropriate compression level that optimizes the overall network throughput, taking into account both capacity loss and overhead reduction.

We have implemented AFC on top of the SU-/MU-MIMO OFDM module that we built on WARP. This PHY module closely follows the 802.11n/ac specifications, and realizes linear precoding based beamforming, OFDM modulation/demodulation, CSI estimation as well as symbol-level decoding. Experiments on a WARP testbed show that AFC's adaptation metric leads to fast and effective selection of compression levels along all 3 dimensions. In contrast, no single static configuration of compression intensity can fit all channel/network profiles. Overall, by balancing the capacity-overhead tradeoff, AFC's *throughput performance* is comparable with the best fixed compression scheme for any given channel profiles, and 40% to 120% higher than the non-adaptive scheme in 802.11n/ac.

In summary, we make the following contributions in this paper.

- We present the first comprehensive measurement study of the effects of feedback compression in 802.11 SU-/MU-MIMO networks.
- We propose AFC, which introduces effective cross-layer metrics to trigger the adaptation of compression levels along 3 dimensions, and strike a balance between overhead reduction and capacity loss.

To our knowledge, AFC represents the first algorithm that provides guidelines to address this tradeoff for SU-/MU-MIMO beamforming in wireless networks.

# 2. BACKGROUND

## 2.1 SU-/MU-MIMO networks

MU-MIMO systems are commonly realized use Zero-Forcing Beamforming (ZFBF), a low-complexity linear precoding scheme that is amenable for practical transceivers. Consider a network with a $n$-antenna AP and $n$ single-antenna receivers. Let $\boldsymbol{X}$ be a $n \times 1$ vector, representing the data symbols to be sent to $n$ receivers, then the vector of received symbols corresponding to the $n$ receivers is:

$$\boldsymbol{Y} = \boldsymbol{HWX} + \boldsymbol{V} \tag{1}$$

where $\boldsymbol{H}$ is the $n \times n$ channel matrix, and $\boldsymbol{V}$ the $n \times 1$ noise vector. $\boldsymbol{W}$ is the precoding matrix, with each row $W_{*k}$ corresponding to the precoding vector of transmit antenna $k$. In ZFBF, $\boldsymbol{W}$ is obtained via a pseudo-inverse of the channel matrix:

$$\boldsymbol{W} = \boldsymbol{H}^* \cdot (\boldsymbol{H} \cdot \boldsymbol{H}^*)^{-1} \tag{2}$$

where $(\cdot)^*$ is the complex conjugate operator.

With precoding, it is straightforward that the received symbols become $\boldsymbol{Y} = \boldsymbol{X} + \boldsymbol{V}$, *i.e.*, data symbols of different receivers are decoupled — each receiver only obtains its own symbol plus some noise. In practical MIMO transceivers, each antenna is accompanied by one radio back-end and has a maximum power constraint $P_m$. To satisfy this constraint, the precoding vector of each transmit antenna $k$ should be scaled by: $\arg\max_j \sqrt{P_m}/||W_{*j}||$ [1].

SU-MIMO can be considered as a MU-MIMO network with one receiver but $n$ transmit antennas. The pseudo-inverse precoding will result in $n$ copies of the receiver's symbols added up, boosting the signal power to $n^2$.

To perform precoding, however, both SU- and MU-MIMO transmitters need to know the CSI, *i.e.*, the channel matrix $\boldsymbol{H}$, which can only be obtained from receivers' feedback. In this paper, we only consider precoding for single-antenna receivers, but multi-antenna precoding is also feasible through block-diagonalization [2]. The adaptation algorithm proposed in this paper is not limited to any precoding scheme as it only leverages vanilla 802.11 preambles.

## 2.2 CSI feedback and compression in 802.11 SU-/MU-MIMO

In 802.11n/ac, before beamforming a data packet, a SU-/MU-MIMO transmitter follows a polling procedure to obtain CSI from the receiver(s). Fig. 1 illustrates an example for a MU-MIMO network with 2 transmit antennas and 2 receivers. The transmitter first sends an NDP announcement to initiate the procedure, and then polls the intended receivers one by one and obtains CSI feedback from them. Afterwards it precodes the data packets based on the CSI. CSI feedback for SU-MIMO follows the same procedure.

The accuracy of CSI determines how effectively the inter data-symbol interference can be cancelled for MU-MIMO, and whether copies of a symbol can align their phases to enhance received SNR in SU-MIMO. Hence, it is critical to the SNR and consequently network capacity.

However, accuracy comes at the cost of overhead. To bound the CSI overhead, 802.11 allows CSI to be compressed,

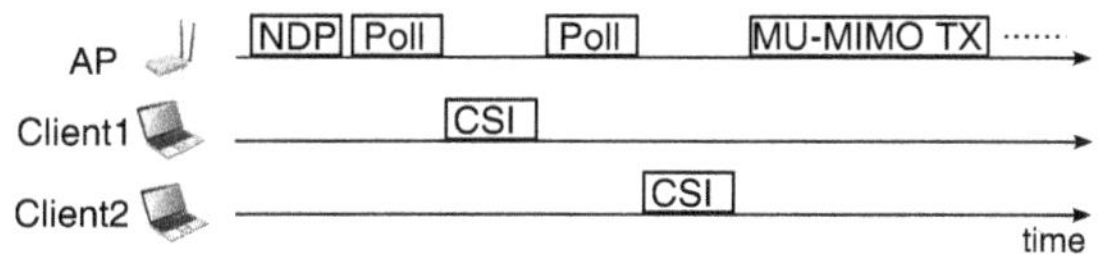


**Figure 1: CSI feedback and MU-MIMO beamforming in 802.11ac.**

with multiple levels of intensity, along three dimensions: i) Time, *i.e.*, instead of per-packet feedback, allowing CSI to be shared among multiple subsequent packets. ii) Frequency, *i.e.*, instead of collecting CSI for each subcarrier (the smallest spectrum unit in an 802.11 OFDM band), group neighboring subcarriers and use one subcarrier's CSI to represent its neighbors'. iii) Numerical values, *i.e.*, instead of sending float-point complex numbers directly, quantizing the CSI into a small number of bits.

To compress CSI in frequency-domain, 802.11 allows 1, 2, or 4 subcarriers to be grouped and share the same CSI[1]. In addition, for each CSI value, its real and imaginary components can be quantized into 4, 5, 6 or 8 bits [3]. As channel stability and inter-packet time are hard to characterize, 802.11n/ac employs per-packet CSI feedback, leaving the time-domain compression as an open option.

# 3. MOTIVATION

In this section, we use simulation and testbed measurement to evaluate the MAC-layer overhead reduction and PHY-layer capacity loss due to compression, which motivates the need for an mechanism that automatically configures compression intensity to address this tradeoff.

## 3.1 How much can compression save?

We provide an account of all factors that contribute to the CSI feedback *overhead* – defined to be the ratio between the time spent in obtaining CSI (including the NDP and polling packets) and that in data transmission. To this end, we extend the ns-2 simulator with a SU-/MU-MIMO MAC module, following the 802.11n/ac MAC specifications. We then evaluate the CSI overhead for UDP transmissions in a MIMO WLAN. By default, the simulation is configured to 20MHz bandwidth (with 52 data subcarriers), 1.5KB packet size, 4 transmit antennas and 1 receiver, 32-bit float-point CSI (for both real and imaginary components), and per-packet CSI feedback. We first isolate the PHY layer effect by configuring an intermediate data rate of 18Mbps for all receivers. Note that CSI feedback is always sent with 6Mbps data rate in 802.11. Fig. 2 plots the CSI overhead when varying each factor while keeping others to the default values.

**Bandwidth (number of subcarriers).** CSI overhead increases linearly with the spectrum width, which in turn depends on the number of subcarriers. For a typical 20MHz spectrum, the CSI feedback overhead can be 3.4× compared to data transmission, and increases linearly with bandwidth (Fig. 2(a)). Note that the NDP, polling packets, and their inter-frame spacing also contribute to the overhead. However, these are fixed, resulting in the CSI overhead dominating. By compressing CSI in frequency domain, the feedback overhead decreases sharply, on the same order as the number of subcarriers grouped together to share CSI.

[1]A 20MHz band in 802.11 contains 52 data subcarriers. The number of subcarriers increases linearly with bandwidth.

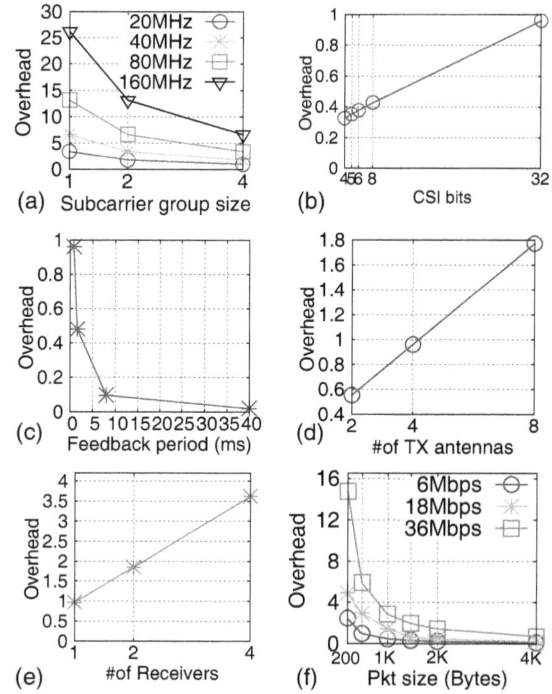


**Figure 2: Various parameters affect CSI feedback overhead. y-axis is the ratio between channel time usage of CSI feedback and that of data frames.**

**CSI bits.** Representing CSI with full-resolution float-point numbers is clearly inefficient (Fig. 2(b)) — it induces an overhead of 0.96 under the default network setting. Quantization of the numerical values can reduce the overhead almost linearly, to 0.33 with the most aggressive 4-bit quantization defined in 802.11.

**Feedback period.** Similar to the above two factors, by compressing the CSI over time, *i.e.*, increasing the feedback period, an inverse-linear reduction in overhead is achieved, as shown in Fig. 2(c). CSI feedback overhead is only 0.096 with an 8ms feedback period and 0.019 with 40ms. Note that our simulation isolates the compression along these three dimensions. As they can be done independently, a combination would achieve a multiplicative reduction.

**Number of TX antennas and receivers.** These two factors independently account for an almost linear increase of overhead (Fig. 2(d) and (e)), as the channel from each transmit antenna to each receiver needs to be estimated and fed back. Unfortunately, no CSI compression is feasible w.r.t. these two factors.

**Data rate.** For small packet sizes, CSI induces formidable overhead, *e.g.*, 2.46× for a 200B and 0.48 for a 1KB packet sent at 6Mbps (Fig. 2(f)). Increase of data rate amplifies the relative overhead, to 2.88× for a 1KB packet at 36Mbps.

From the above simulation results, we can infer that the relative overhead of CSI feedback is roughly linear w.r.t.:

$$\frac{\#\text{SubcGroups} \times \#\text{CSIbits} \times \#\text{TXantennas} \times \#\text{Receivers} \times \text{DataRate}}{\text{Feedback period} \times \text{Pkt size}}$$

Among these factors, the number of subcarrier groups, CSI bits and feedback period can be compressed. 802.11's standard linear compression over the three dimensions can contribute to a multiplicative reduction in feedback overhead. With more sophisticated compression schemes, such as a *Givens rotation* [4, Section 20.3.12] of channel matrix,

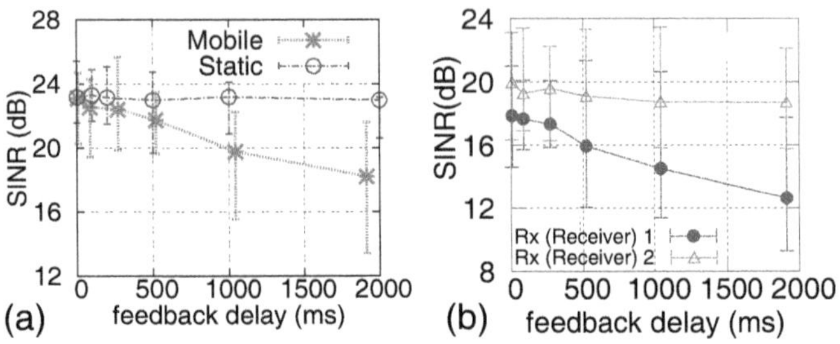


**Figure 3: Effects of time-domain compression on SNR for (a) SU-MIMO and (b) MU-MIMO. Error bars show the max and min SNR among 10 experimental runs, unless noted otherwise.**

feedback overhead can be further reduced. Besides compression, frame aggregation can also reduce the *relative overhead* of CSI by amortizing it over concatenated data frames. But large frames may incur unacceptably long buffering delay, which compromises the performance of real-time applications such as VoIP and interactive web sessions. Such effects limit the practical usage of frame aggregation.

We will now study the associated impact of feedback compression on the link capacity of MIMO networks.

## 3.2 Why adaptive compression?

Feedback compression, if too aggressive, can severely degrade the accuracy of CSI and lower the achievable SNR or bit-rate. The extent to which compression affects network performance varies with the radio environment (channel profile), which we will study through comprehensive experiments below. Our experiments are conducted on a testbed of 5 WARP MIMO software radios, located in an office building. We have implemented a full-fledged MIMO-OFDM communication module on WARP, following the 802.11n/ac specification for SU- and MU-MIMO networks (Sec. 5 provides a detailed description of our implementation). With this testbed implementation, we perform a quantitative study to identify the channel characteristics that lead to the positive and negative effects of CSI compression. These in turn contribute to the factors that AFC should monitor and react appropraitely.

**Effects of time domain compression.** The time-domain accuracy of compressed CSI depends on how frequently it is refreshed, relative to the channel variation over time. In Fig. 3, we allow a transmitter to periodically initiate CSI polling, obtain feedback from receiver(s), and send one beamforming packet. We then compute the SNR[2] by varying the feedback period.

We consider two scenarios: i) static environment: a research lab with negligible human movement. ii) mobile nodes: receiver(s) are moving around the transmitter (along a circle) at walking speed. From the results in Fig. 3(a), we see that in static environment, SU-MIMO link SNR is virtually unaffected by time-domain compression, even with a 2-second feedback period. This implies substantial space for CSI overhead saving: for each link, packets separated by within 2 seconds can share the same CSI.

The impact of stale CSI becomes pronounced as the radio environment becomes more dynamic, as reflected in the large variation of SINR. When nodes are moving at walking speed, we observed that average SINR may reduce by 1 to 2 dB when feedback period is below 300ms. But the reduction may vary significantly across different experiments. We have observed in certain experiments that even a 20ms feedback period can reduce SNR by up to 5.3dB compared with an oracle scheme with zero feedback delay.[3] Clearly, an aggressive time-domain compression will hurt the MIMO beamforming performance for mobile nodes. However, due to packet transmission delay (*e.g.*, caused by contention), inter-packet arrival time can easily reach 20ms. Hence, *per-packet feedback becomes inevitable for mobile nodes, which necessitates compression from alternative dimensions.*

Fig. 3(b) shows the performance of a MU-MIMO network with a 2-antenna AP and two receivers (one mobile, the other static). MU-MIMO is more sensitive to CSI than SU-MIMO, since the channel variation of multiple receivers are independent, and therefore their CSI errors add up and exacerbate the impact of stale CSI. Remarkably, mobility only affects the mobile receiver itself. This is because when running linear precoding, the transmitter only needs to ensure signals from all its antennas combine coherently at each intended receiver, which is only related with the channel gains between transmit antennas and that receiver. This also implies that *in MU-MIMO networks, different receivers can perform time-domain compression and adaptation independent of each other, which is critical for a scalable solution.*

**Effects of frequency domain compression.** Theoretical wireless channel models [5] have shown that neighboring subcarriers of a wide spectrum may be highly correlated with each other, hence it is sufficient to use one subcarrier's CSI to represent that of a group. Subcarrier correlation is roughly inversely proportional to multi-path delay spread, *i.e.*, the maximum separation between multiple reflected copies of a signal. In environment with rich reflections and obstacles, delay spread is small and channel may be correlated over a wide spectrum with many subcarriers, making it possible to compress CSI aggressively in frequency domain. Our experiments in Fig. 4 indeed verify this effect. In a small laboratory environment, compressing neighboring 4 subcarriers results in negligible SNR loss. A lobby – a relatively open-space environment, experiences a larger delay spread (consistent with theoretical channel models [5]) and is hence more sensitive to compression. Compressing 4 subcarriers degrades SNR by 3 dB on average and up to 3.3dB in certain cases (MU-MIMO in Fig. 4 (b)).

Interestingly, our experiments reveal several other factors governing the effectiveness of frequency-domain compression. First, different spectrum bands (with different carrier frequencies) reveal different levels of sensitivity to subcarrier grouping. A typical 2.4GHz band exhibits high sensitivity, since it may experience different level of leakage noise (interference) from neighbors across its spectrum. Even across the 5GHz bands, which are unused around our testbed, the sensitivity varies. We suspect this to be the result of imperfect radio hardware, which causes unequal RF/antenna gains across the spectrum. Finally, mobility does not affect the impact of frequency-domain compression, implying it can

[2]Our testbed implementation allows us to obtain SNR from decoded symbols. This leads to an accurate estimation, which accounts for not only ambient noise, but also receiver-induced noise due to, *e.g.*, imperfect channel estimation.

[3]We create the oracle case by collecting CSI and then replaying the channel distortion effect (Sec. 5). The transmitter is an oracle which knows the CSI without polling and feedback.

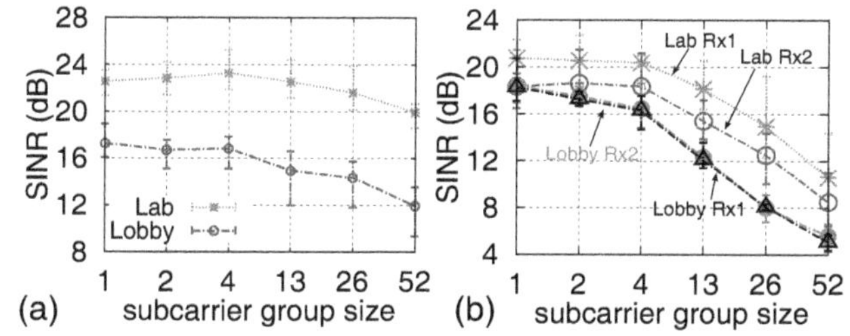


**Figure 4: Effects of subcarrier grouping on the performance of (a) SU-MIMO and (b) MU-MIMO.**

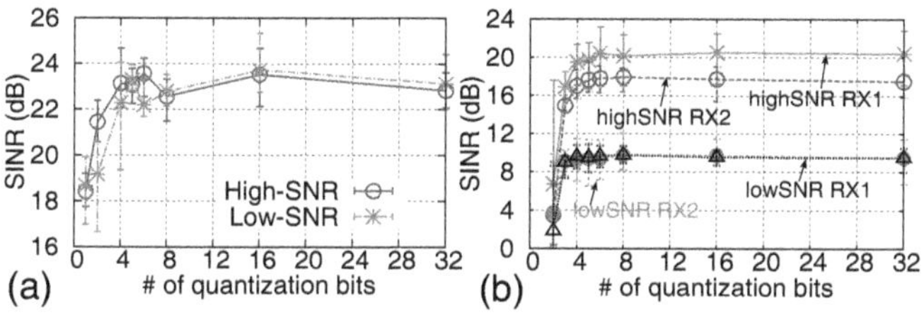


**Figure 5: Effects of CSI quantization on the performance of (a) SU-MIMO and (b) MU-MIMO.**

be decoupled from time-domain compression. MU-MIMO is more sensitive to subcarrier grouping than SU-MIMO, for the same reason as in time-domain compression.

**Effects of numerical quantization.** Fig. 5 plots the MIMO network capacity as a function of the number of quantization bits used to represent CSI[4]. It reveals a sub-linear relation: capacity grows sharply as quantization bits increases from 2 to 3, but shows marginal improvement beyond that. In addition, low SNR links are less sensitive to quantization, as channel noise dominates the quantization errors. Again, MU-MIMO is more sensitive to quantization due to the additive quantization noise of multiple receivers.

To summarize, although compression can save substantial overhead, it may come at the cost of capacity loss. This tradeoff manifests differently depending on the radio environment and network dynamics. Clearly, an autonomous algorithm is needed to guide the 3-D compression and hence balance the overhead reduction and capacity loss, thereby resulting in maximum network throughput.

# 4. ADAPTIVE FEEDBACK COMPRESSION

## 4.1 Overview

AFC is a systematic approach to balancing CSI compression intensity with SU-/MU-MIMO network capacity, thereby helping achieve optimized network throughput under various network (channel) conditions. The core component of AFC is a cross-layer adaptation algorithm that extracts the channel dynamics from 802.11 packet preambles, and approximates a throughput-optimal point by choosing an appropriate compression configuration over 3 dimensions: time, frequency and numerical values.

**Cross-layer adaptation**. Fig. 6 showcases AFC's adaptation procedure for a SU-MIMO network. CSI feedback is reactive in AFC. By default, the transmitter uses the previous (most recent) CSI feedback for beamforming precoding.

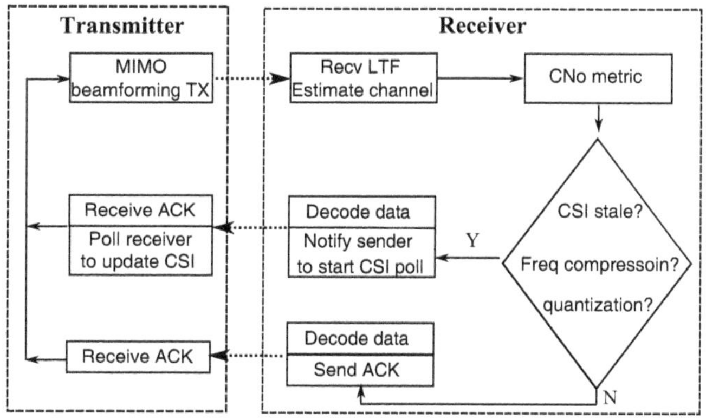


**Figure 6: Cross-layer adaptation protocol in AFC.**

It initiates the CSI polling only if the receiver indicates a need to do so. The receiver is able to refresh its channel estimation whenever it receives a new packet. It evaluates the CSI therein in comparison with its last CSI feedback to the transmitter, and, upon identifying a trend of severe CSI staleness, requests the transmitter to initiate a polling for *next* beamforming transmission. It conveys this request to the transmitter by setting the "Protected Frame" bit in the ACK for current data packet. The Protected Frame bit is an unused field in legacy 802.11 ACK packets.

For frequency-domain compression, AFC extracts per-subcarrier CSI from the 802.11 Long-Training-Field (LTF) preamble, which precedes the data portion of each packet, and is sent by each transmit antenna sequentially without beamforming. Based on the LTF, AFC designs an estimation algorithm to quantify the expected compression error and resulting capacity loss when several subcarriers are grouped to share the same CSI. The estimation of compression error induced by numerical quantization follows a similar procedure. With such estimations, AFC can select the combination of subcarrier grouping and quantization with the highest expected throughput, taking into account overhead, capacity loss as well as the time-domain feedback period. If this combination differs from the current grouping, the receiver again dictates the transmitter to reinitiate the polling for next beamforming packet. As in 802.11n/ac, information about the subcarrier group size or quantization bits are embedded in the receivers' CSI feedback packet.

For a MU-MIMO network, each receiver performs adaptation as if it forms a SU-MIMO link with the multi-antenna transmitter. Decoupling of their operations enables decentralized AFC and precludes complicated message exchanges between clients, which can be costly especially in large networks. We note, however, that the adaptation of quantization bits may be coupled among MU-MIMO receivers, and can lead to unfair power allocation. This problem will be elaborated in Sec. 4.3.2.

**A unified metric for compression.** The above adaptation mechanism entails a key question: *How does a certain level of compression affect throughput?* AFC proposes a unified metric, called *CNo* (compression noise), to evaluate the error introduced by each dimension of compression. CNo is obtained by inspecting the per-subcarrier CSI from the 802.11 LTF preamble. With CNo, AFC can instantaneously estimate the expected data-rate and weigh it against feedback overhead, to determine the optimal compression intensity. This evades the complexity of an intuitive search algorithm that attempts all combinations of compression intensities and leads to a huge search space, especially along

[4]802.11 defines three algorithms for quantizing CSI values. Without loss of generality, we adopt the direct quantization approach [4, Section 20.3.12.2.1] which compresses the real and imaginary components into a few number (4, 5, 6 or 8) of bits.

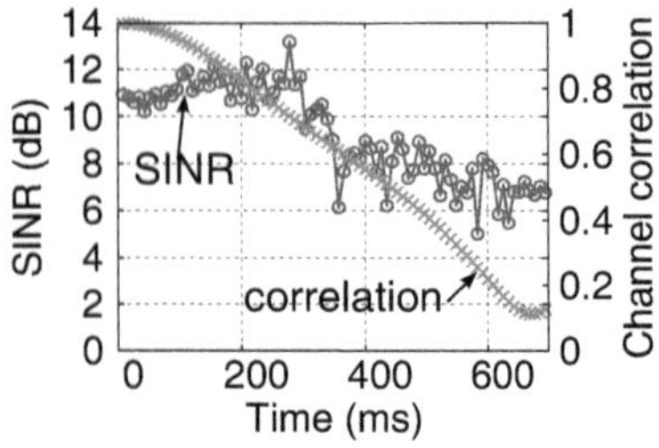

**Figure 7: Channel correlation and link SINR change over time. The receiver is moving at walking speed.**

the time dimension. In addition, CNo can be estimated separately for time, frequency and numerical values. Such isolation is important as it guarantees the total compression noise introduced by all dimensions is simply the sum of their CNo metrics.

In what follows, we detail AFC's adaptation mechanisms along three-dimensions, based on the CNo metric.

## 4.2 Time-domain adaptation

### *4.2.1 Is coherence time a good adaptation metric?*

A channel's tolerance to time-domain compression strongly depends on channel stability. A widely used stability metric is coherence time, defined as the interval within which channel gain remains highly correlated. According to the 802.11ac recommendation [6], correlation between two instances of channel estimations, separated by $T$, is defined as:

$$\mathcal{K}(T) = \frac{L}{L-T} \cdot \frac{|\sum_{t=0}^{L-T-1} h(t)h^*(t+T)|}{\sum_{t=0}^{L-1} |h(t)||h^*(t)|} \tag{3}$$

where $L$ is the total length of the sequence of sampled channel gains. Coherence time is defined as an instance $T_{0.5}$ when correlation drops to 0.5, *i.e.*, $T_{0.5} = \mathcal{K}^{-1}(0.5)$. Occasionally, $T_{0.9}$ is also used as a coherence time definition.

It is tempting to use coherence time as an update interval for CSI — CSI feedback can be initiated periodically, with a period equal to coherence time. All packets can share one CSI obtained in the beginning of each period. However, through extensive experiments, we found coherence time to be a poor gauge for predicting the effect of such CSI compression. In particular, the experiment in Fig. 7 shows that, even though channel correlation remains above 0.5 within a 400ms interval (corresponding to the $T_{0.5}$ definition for coherence time), SNR is already severely degraded before that (at around 260ms). On the other hand, the $T_{0.9}$ definition of coherence time is too conservative. Channel correlation is above 0.9 within 100ms, but SNR remains relatively stable within 200ms. Thus sending CSI at a peroid of 100ms incurs unnecessary overhead.

In addition, we found that this tradeoff manifests differently for different channel profiles (static, human moving around, or node mobility). Hence, no single definition of coherence time can be used as the period for time-domain compression.

An additional limitation of the coherence time metric is that the statistical correlation (3) is relevant only with a large number of channel gain samples, each corresponding to one packet. To adapt compression intensity, however, a responsive metric is needed that can be obtained from one or two packets. The CNo metric is designed to satisfy this requirement.

### *4.2.2 CNo metric for the time domain*

**Compression noise.** In AFC, a receiver uses a Compression Noise (CNo) metric to overcome the limitations of conventional channel stability metric. CNo gauges how current CSI (at time $t$) differs from the last CSI feedback (at time $t_0$). Suppose there are $K$ subcarriers whose CSI needs feedback and $H_k(t)$ is the channel gain for subcarrier $k$ at time $t$. Due to channel variation, $H_k(t)$ can be considered as a noisy version of $H_k(t_0)$:

$$H_k(t) = H_k(t_0) + N_k(t) \tag{4}$$

We model the noise $N_k, (k \in K)$ as complex Gaussian random variables with a similar level of variance (*i.e.*, noise power). This is reasonable as the staleness of CSI applies equally to all subcarriers. Consequently, we can model the time-domain compression-induced noise power as:

$$\mathcal{N}_T(t) = \sum_{k=1}^{K} \left| (H_k(t) - H_k(t_0)) (H_k(t) - H_k(t_0))^* \right|$$

This is exactly the CNo metric we use in time-domain. The receiver stores $H_k(t_0)$, and directly obtains $H_k(t)$, the per-subcarrier channel gain, from the 802.11 LTF preamble for each packet. Therefore, $\mathcal{N}_T(t)$ becomes an instantaneous gauge for time-domain compression error. Taking into account the signal power $P_r(t)$ and channel noise power $N_r(t)$, the expected SNR after compression becomes:

$$SNR(t) = \frac{P_r(t)}{N_r(t) + \mathcal{N}_T(t)} \tag{5}$$

An AFC receiver compares $SNR(t)$ with $SNR(t_0)$. If for any channel between a transmit antenna and a receive antenna, the difference is sufficient to cause data rate to drop from the current level to a lower level, then the receiver will request for CSI polling. Note, however, that channel fading may cause unpredictable SNR decrease/increase, which must be isolated in order to evaluate the true effect of time-domain compression.

**Isolating fading effects.** To solve this problem, the receiver also stores the nominal expected SNR (without compression noise) at $t_0$: $SNR'(t_0) = P_r(t_0)/N_r(t_0)$. It compares $SNR'(t_0)$ with $SNR'(t)$. If the difference exceeds the SNR threshold for boosting data rate to a higher level (threshold $SNR_h^{th}$), or degrading it to a lower level (threshold $SNR_l^{th}$), then the receiver will also request for a CSI polling. This helps the transmitter to select the bit-rate that fits the channel condition[5]. The SNR threshold for each data rate can be readily obtained from WiFi chip specifications (*e.g.*, [7]).

Note that a link may become idle for a long time. Without data transmission, the transmitter cannot receive any ACK or CSI update indication from the receiver, and is unaware of CSI staleness. AFC overcomes this problem by setting a maximum update interval $T_m$, which equals the average interval of the past 5 CSI update indication from the receiver. If the link becomes idle for more than $T_m$, the transmitter will initiate CSI polling without a request from the receiver.

**Signal and noise power.** So, how does AFC estimate the signal power $P_r(t)$ and noise power $N_r(t)$? We remark that such estimation should be isolated from the beamformed data portion of a packet, which mixes the channel gains from multiple transmit antennas to the receive antenna. Towards this end, we again leverage the LTF preamble which is sent by each transmit antenna sequentially. Fig. 8 illustrates the

[5]AFC's adaptation algorithm does not depend on the bit-rate adaptation mechanism.

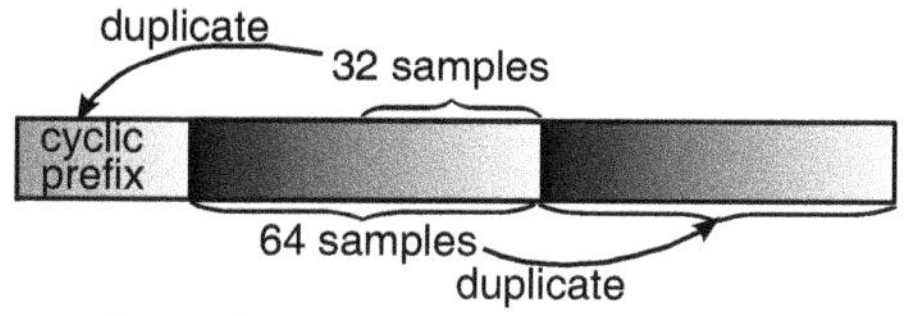


**Figure 8: Time-domain structure of the LTF preamble in an 802.11 packet.**

structure of an LTF preamble, which comprises two duplicated sequences (each containing 64 samples) and an OFDM cyclic prefix (32 samples). At the receiver side, it runs FFT over each sequence to estimate the frequency-domain channel distortion:

$$Y_k^1 = H_k X_k + N_k^1; \quad Y_k^2 = H_k X_k + N_k^2$$

$X_k$ is a known symbol carried by subcarrier $k$. Although $N_k^1$ and $N_k^2$ are instances of two random Gaussian variables, they can be considered to have the same variance, which equals the noise power per-subcarrier. Thus the channel noise power over an entire bandwidth can be estimated as:

$$N_r(t) = \sum_{k=1}^{K} |(Y_k^2 - Y_k^1) \cdot (Y_k^2 - Y_k^1)^*| \tag{6}$$

Subtracting noise power from total received power, we obtain:

$$P_r(t) = \sum_{k=1}^{K} |Y_k^1|^2 - N_r(t) \tag{7}$$

**Combating random phase offset.** Ideally, if channel is stable, the receiver should experience a similar $H_k$ for each packet. Due to the CSMA-based MAC layer, however, each transmitted packet has a random starting time and when modulated, will result in a random initial phase offset relative to the receiver. This causes a large $\mathcal{N}_T(t)$ even though the CSI does not change. We observe that transmit antennas on a MIMO radio share the same clock, and thus we use the phase of the differential channel $H_k^A/H_k^B$ between transmit antenna $A$ and $B$, instead of that of $H_k$ directly when computing $\mathcal{N}_T(t)$, which removes the random phase offset.

## 4.3 Adaptive frequency-domain compression and numerical quantization

### *4.3.1 Is coherence bandwidth a good adaptation metric?*

Coherence bandwidth is a classical metric for evaluating channel stability over frequency. Specific to 802.11 OFDM systems, it is defined as the range within which subcarriers' channel gain correlation is larger than 0.5 ($B_{0.5}$) or 0.9 ($B_{0.9}$). The correlation can be obtained in the same way as time correlation as in (3), except the separation is in frequency (number of subcarriers).

As channel gains of the subcarriers within $B_{0.5}$ or $B_{0.9}$ are highly correlated, one may wonder if they can be compressed and represented by a single subcarrier's CSI. The testbed experiments in Fig. 9 invalidate this perception. While $B_{0.9}$ is too conservative, $B_{0.5}$ is over-optimistic, incorporating more subcarriers than should be compressed, thus degrading capacity. Consistent with the experiments in Fig. 4, we found such effects to differ among different carrier frequencies and locations. In addition, correlation does not always decrease monotonically with subcarrier separation. Clearly, no single, static definition of coherence bandwidth can be used as a threshold for frequency-domain compression.

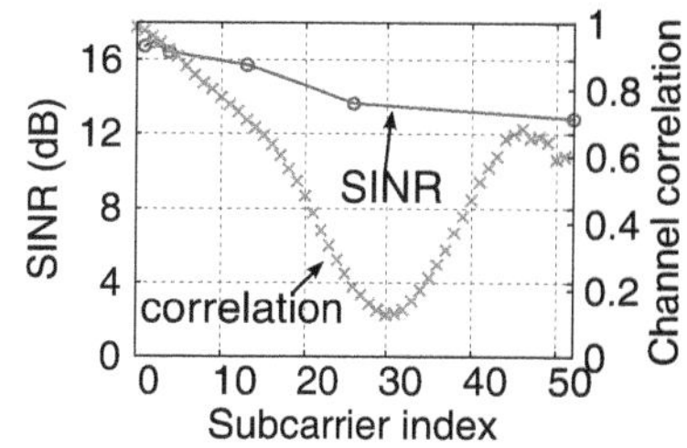


**Figure 9: Channel correlation over frequency (in a lab environment), and SU-MIMO link capacity when $K'$ subcarriers share the same CSI. PHY parameters are configured following 802.11 specification: 20MHz bandwidth, 52 data subcarriers (each occupying 312.5KHz).**

### *4.3.2 CNo metric for subcarrier grouping and numerical quantization*

We generalize the time-domain CNo metric to predict the link throughput for a certain level of frequency-domain compression and numerical quantization. Suppose $H_k(f_0, q_0)$ is the true CSI for subcarrier $k$ without compression, which is obtained from the receiver's LTF preamble. $H_k(f, q)$ is the compressed CSI for subcarrier $k$ with subcarrier group size $f$ and $q$-bit quantization. All subcarriers inside each group share the CSI of the group's first subcarrier, following the 802.11 specification. Then, given a fixed quantization level $q$, the frequency domain CNo metric is:

$$\mathcal{N}_F(f) = \sum_{k=1}^{K} |(H_k(f,q) - H_k(f_0,q))(H_k(f,q) - H_k(f_0,q))^*|$$

Similarly, given a subcarrier group size $f$, the quantization noise with $q$-bit quantization is:

$$\mathcal{N}_Q(q) = \sum_{k=1}^{K} |(H_k(f,q) - H_k(f,q_0))(H_k(f,q) - H_k(f,q_0))^*|$$

Then, the receiver estimates the effective SNR with compression intensity $f$ as $SNR'(f,q) = \frac{P_r}{N_r + \mathcal{N}_F(f) + \mathcal{N}_Q(q)}$. As $P_r$ and $N_r$ are obtained from packet preambles, they cannot reflect the power increase due to beamforming or noise increase due to multi-user cross-talk interference. Nevertheless, the receiver can estimate the true SNR based on the decoded SNR of the current packet, accounting for the SNR loss due to compression, *i.e.*,

$$SNR_{dB}(f,q) = decodedSNR_{dB} + SNR'_{dB}(f,q) - 10\log_{10}\frac{P_r}{N_r}$$

This can be mapped to data rate typically provided by WiFi vendors [7]. Then, we can estimate the increase of data packet transmission time, compared with the current compression intensity, say $(f_1, q_1)$, as:

$$\Delta T_d(f,q) = D/Rate(SNR(f,q)) - D/Rate(SNR(f_1,q_1))$$

where $D$ is the average data packet size (estimated by averaging over past 10 packets in AFC).

Owing to compression, the decrease of time in transmitting CSI, amortized over each packet, is:

$$\Delta T_o(f,q) = Kq_1 M_t(f_1 R_0 T_p)^{-1} - KqM_t(fR_0T_p)^{-1}$$

where $M_t$ is the number of transmit antennas, and $R_0$ the data rate of feedback packet (default to 6Mbps in 802.11). $T_p$ is the number of recent packets that shared one CSI over time, which reflects the current time-domain compression intensity.

AFC compares $\Delta T_o(f,q)$ with $\Delta T_d(f,q)$. A positive difference implies benefit for changing the compression intensity. This comparison is made for each possible combination of subcarrier group size and quantization level (in total there are only 12 such combinations in 802.11 as introduced in Sec. 2), and the receiver will select the combination with largest $\Delta T_o(f,q) - \Delta T_d(f,q)$. If it is positive and differs from the current one, the receiver switches to this new compression level and notifies the transmitter. Again, the above estimation is performed for each transmit antenna separately. CSI feedback will be triggered whenever one antenna passes the test.

**Isolating different users' CSI quantization.** A unique problem in MU-MIMO is that different users' CSI quantization may affect each other's performance. When users choose different quantization levels, their CSI will be scaled disproportionally. Suppose user A and B have a similar level of channel gain. If user A adopts 8-bit quantization whereas user B adopts 4-bit, then A's CSI feedback will have $2^4 = 16$ times as high magnitude as B's, causing the transmitter to think A has much better channel quality. Since zero-forcing precoding implicitly projects the same received power towards both receivers (Sec. 2), the transmitter will allocate only $\frac{1}{\sqrt{16}} = \frac{1}{4}$ as high power to user A as the case without quantization, resulting in unfair capacity loss for A.

In AFC, the transmitter solves this problem by normalizing the real and imaginary components with the maximum possible value ($2^{q-1} - 1$ for $q$-bit quantization), for each user respectively. This prevents the unfair CSI scaling and thus isolates the quantization choices of different users. Note that AFC's adaptation algorithm is immune to such an effect, as it only leverages the non-beamformed LTF preamble.

## 4.4 3-D joint adaptation

Algorithm 1 summaries AFC's adaptation over all three dimensions. Note that the CNo metric serves as a unified function for estimating compression noise for each dimension. It naturally isolates the effects of each dimension, and reduces the search space for throughput-optimal compression. It is also decentralized with respect to each user, who only needs to evaluate CNo between itself and the transmit antennas. In addition, unlike traditional metrics (*e.g.*, coherence time), it can be obtained instantaneously after receiving each packet. The complexity of AFC's adaptation depends on the number of subcarriers and transmit antennas, all of which are limited in 802.11n/ac. Thus AFC involves a constant computation time and is amenable for implementation in real WiFi drivers.

**Algorithm 1** 3-D cross-layer adaptation in AFC.

**Transmitter module:**
**if** "Protected Frame" bit in ACK equals 1 **or** link idle time exceeds $T_m$
  Initiate CSI polling and request for next packet
  Run SU-/MU-MIMO beamforming with latest CSI
**endif**

**Receiver module:**
/* Time-domain adaptation */
Compute CNo metric $\mathcal{N}_T(t)$ and $SNR(t)$
**if** $SNR(t) - SNR(t_0) > SNR_l^{th}$ **or** $SNR'(t) - SNR'(t_0) > SNR_h^{th}$ **or** $SNR'(t_0) - SNR'(t) > SNR_l^{th}$
  Request CSI update; update $T_p$
**endif**
/* Adaptive subcarrier grouping and CSI quantization*/
Compute CNo metric $\mathcal{N}_F(f)$ and $\mathcal{N}_Q(q)$
Compute expected TX time increase $\Delta T_d(f,q)$ and overhead time decrease $\Delta T_o(f,q)$
Search for $(f^*, q^*) = \arg\max_{f,q} \Delta T_o(f,q) - \Delta T_d(f,q)$
**if** $\Delta T_o(f^*, q^*) - \Delta T_d(f^*, q^*) > 0$
  Switch to new subcarrier group size $f^*$ and quantization level $q^*$
  Request CSI update; **continue** to next transmission.
**endif**

# 5. IMPLEMENTATION

## 5.1 Testbed implementation

We have implemented a full-fledged 802.11ac-compatible MU-MIMO OFDM system on the WARP [8] platform, based on the WARPLab driver which provides interfaces to the WARP software radio. Fig. 10 illustrates the main components in our system. The transmitter uses linear precoding (ZFBF, Sec. 2) to pre-cancel inter-user interference. Precoded data symbols are divided into $M_t$ streams (equal to the number of transmit antennas), each subject to OFDM modulation. The modulated data symbols are prepended with the 802.11 LTF, and STF (a preamble for synchronization). Note the SU-MIMO is a special case of MU-MIMO implementation, as introduced in Sec. 2.

The receiver uses an auto-correlation algorithm to detect the STF and identify exact starting time of each packet. It then leverages the LTF to estimate the channel matrix between itself and each transmit antenna. This channel matrix (CSI) will be compressed by the receiver using AFC and then fed back to the transmitter when needed. As inter-user interference is pre-cancelled, the receiver is able to decode the data portion of the packet using a standard OFDM demodulator.

The 3-D cross-layer adaptation algorithm is implemented at the receiver side following the description in Sec. 4. It extensively leverages the LTF to compute CNo along three dimensions, and decides if an adjustment of compression intensity is needed and in which dimensions. As the round-trip time between the PC (the central MAC/PHY processor running AFC and MU-MIMO OFDM modulation/demodulation) is several orders of magnitude longer than real WiFi hardware, we do not directly implement real-time control messages such as ACK, NDP and CSI feedback. Instead, as all WARP nodes in our testbed share the same central processor, control messages are directly realized as function calls. The exact transmission duration and inter-packet spacing (defined in 802.11) are implemented using a virtual timer. In addition, all MIMO data packets are sent through real channels by the WARP radios, and polling packets are initiated if AFC dictates a CSI refresh.

## 5.2 Trace-driven emulation

Through benchmark tests, we found it takes 127ms for a pair of WARP radios to finish an entire SU-MIMO transmission involving CSI polling, precoding, data transmission and data decoding. The latency is mainly caused by the hardware interface between WARP and its PC host. Such hardware latency is incompatible with real WiFi radios, and can-

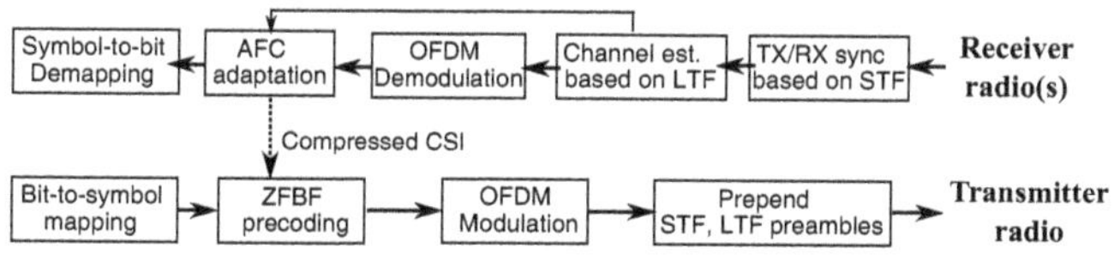


**Figure 10: Implementation of an 802.11-compatible MU-/SU-MIMO OFDM system.**

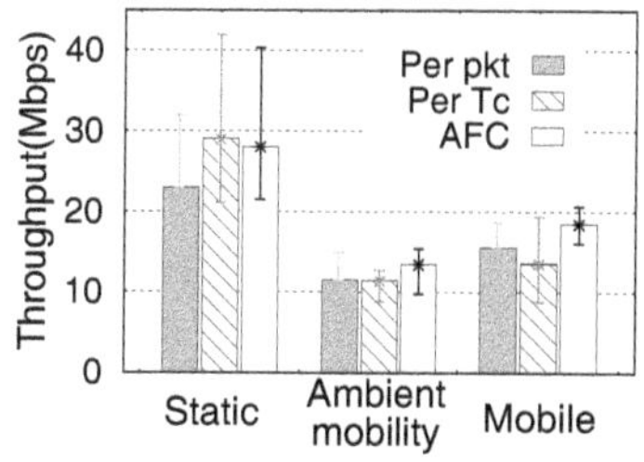


**Figure 11: Time-domain adaptation: SU-MIMO.**

not faithfully reproduce AFC's behavior in dynamic/mobile scenarios. To overcome this limitation, we adopt a trace-driven emulation approach, which is inspired by [9] but harnesses WARP's flexibility to collect raw channel traces.

We fill a WARP transmitter's transmit buffer with an 802.11 MIMO preamble (containing STF and LTF sequences), and configure it to repeatedly send the preamble over the air. The receivers log the raw digital samples to a file, and performs packet detection and channel estimation offline to obtain a sequence of channel traces. With this setting, we are able to obtain fine-grained sampling of the MIMO channel every 8.7ms, which is sufficient for evaluating mobile channels with walking speed [10].

To evaluate the feedback compression algorithms, we replace the WARPLab interface to the WARP radios with an interface to an emulated channel, whose time variation follows the collected traces. The MU-/SU-MIMO OFDM and AFC module that we implemented can run directly over this emulated channel. When a packet's arriving time does not exactly match any instances of the channel trace, the closest instance is used to represent its channel distortion. We will show in Sec. 6 that the trace-driven emulator can faithfully reproduce the results from realtime experiments.

# 6. EVALUATION

In this section, we first evaluation AFC's adaptation modules through micro-benchmark experiments. Then we integrate all the modules and validate the system-level performance under various channel conditions.

## 6.1 Micro-benchmark evaluation

### 6.1.1 *Validation of trace-driven emulation.*

Part of our experiments are conducted under mobile/dynamic channel profiles, and rely on trace-driven emulation. Thus, we first validate the accuracy of such trace-driven emulation, using real-time runs as a benchmark.

| | $T_1$ | $T_c$ | Freq 1 | Freq 52 | Qbits 2 | Qbits 8 |
|---|---|---|---|---|---|---|
| Trace | 20.206 | 20.041 | 20.262 | 16.131 | 18.662 | 20.315 |
| Real | 20.142 | 20.074 | 19.825 | 15.148 | 17.599 | 20.066 |
| Error | 0.32% | 0.16% | 2.20% | 6.49% | 6.04% | 1.24% |

**Table 1: Trace-driven emulation can faithfully reproduce the SINR results from realtime experiments. $T_1$ and $T_c$ denote per-packet and per-coherence-time CSI feedback, respectively. Freq denotes subcarrier group size 1 and 52. Qbits denote quantization bits.**

Following the steps in Sec. 5.2, we first run SU-MIMO transmission between a 2-antenna WARP transmitter and single antenna receiver, while logging the per-packet channel matrices between them. Then we replay the transmissions in the emulator based on the traces. Table 1 compares the results from real-time runs and trace-driven emulation. We create 6 traces, each lasting 1 minute and representing the case with or without compression (or with minimum compression) along three dimensions. For the majority of cases, relative error of emulation is well below 3%. When SINR is low, the relative error tends to be magnified (to around 6%). However, the absolute error remains below 1.1dB. Therefore, the trace-driven emulator can reproduce real-time experiments with a sufficient level of accuracy.

### 6.1.2 *Time-domain adaptation*

The effectiveness of AFC's time-domain compression and adaptation depends on channel stability. Thus we evaluate this component under three representative channel profiles: static, ambient mobility (human moving around the nodes) and node mobility (node moving at walking speed). All experiments run over the 2.4GHz WiFi channel 14, which is unused by nearby wireless devices. The static case runs directly on the WARP testbed. The other two cases are based on trace-driven emulation, since WARP's latency may exceed the time-resolution needed for real-time CSI feedback.

We compare AFC against two alternative CSI feedback schemes: per-packet feedback and Per-$T_c$ feedback. The former is the default scheme in 802.11n/ac. In the latter scheme, we first collect channel traces, compute the coherence time $T_{0.5}$, and then use $T_{0.5}$ as the feedback period when replaying the traces.

**SU-MIMO network.** In a typical small or medium sized network, contention overhead is much smaller compared with data transmission. Thus, without loss of generality, we first consider a single receiver SU-MIMO network[6], where the transmitter has 2 antennas and receiver 1 antenna. Fig. 11 plots the resulting network throughput.

In static case, channel variation is negligible, and thus per-packet CSI feedback incurs huge overhead. AFC only needs to opportunistically feed back CSI without affecting link capacity noticeably. Its mean throughput is 25.4% higher than that of per-packet feedback. Per-$T_c$ feedback results in a similar level of throughput as AFC.

With ambient mobility, per-packet feedback degrades even with per-$T_c$ feedback in terms of throughput, as the former maintains link capacity whereas the latter attempts to reduce feedback overhead. In contrast, AFC strikes a balance between these two objectives, improving average throughput by 17% over the other two schemes.

When receiver is mobile, Per-$T_c$ feedback underestimates channel variations, leading to even lower throughput than per-packet feedback. On the other hand, per-packet feedback incurs more overhead. AFC's time-domain adapta-

[6]Even for a single-link WLAN, contention backoff is required after each transmission attempt [4].

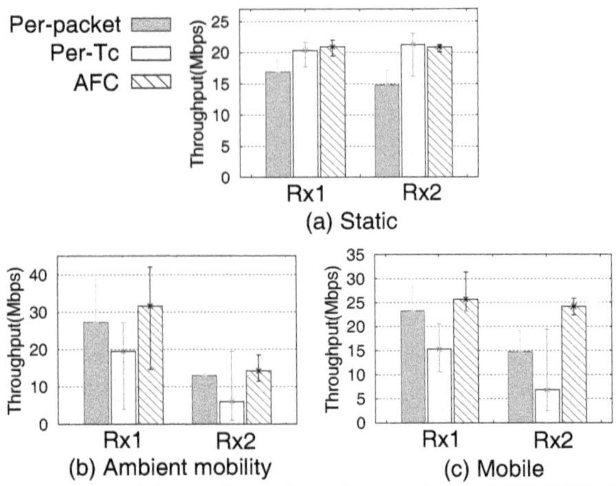


**Figure 12: Time-domain adaptation: MU-MIMO.**

tion mechanism can effectively estimate the instances when CSI feedback is needed. Its throughput is 18.2% and 38.5% higher than per-$T_c$ and per-packet, respectively.

**MU-MIMO network.** We further evaluate AFC in a MU-MIMO network with a 2-antenna AP and 2 single-antenna receivers. Fig. 12 plots the receiver's throughput under different channel profiles and feedback schemes. Similar to SU-MIMO, per-$T_c$ achieves a comparable level of throughput with AFC. However, for per-packet feedback, since the overhead doubles compared with SU-MIMO, the throughput loss is substantial. In particular, AFC can achieve 39.7% higher throughput over per-packet — a much higher gain compared with SU-MIMO case.

Under channel dynamics, MU-MIMO is expected to be more sensitive to CSI feedback errors. Fig. 12 testifies this intuition. With ambient mobility, per-$T_c$ induces long feedback delay and large CSI error, resulting in significant throughput loss. AFC can achieve 61.5% and 123% higher throughput, for receiver 1 and 2, respectively.

AFC's performance gain is most remarkable in mobile case (Fig. 12(c)). It achieves 69.1% and 269% higher throughput for the two receivers, compared with per-$T_c$; and a 13.2% and 71.3% gain compared with per-packet feedback.

In summary, none of the static CSI feedback mechanisms are appropriate for all channel profiles. On the other hand, by triggering CSI updates only when needed, AFC can achieve up to multi-folds of throughput gain over static schemes.

### *6.1.3 Frequency-domain adaptation*

We proceed to evaluate whether AFC can effectively adapt to an appropriate level of compression for the frequency domain, *i.e.*, the subcarrier group size. Our investigation of channel traces in a lab environment reveals that even for the same spectrum band, coherence bandwidth may change, *e.g.*, due to minor change of location or antenna orientation. Thus we create frequency domain dynamics by running multiple experiments with minor adjustment of transmitter's locations. We isolate the effect of the other two adaptation dimensions by assuming default configuration in 802.11n/ac (per-packet CSI feedback and 8-bit quantization).

Fig. 13 plots the throughput of AFC compared with two alternative schemes with fixed subcarrier group size 1 and 52, respectively. For SU-MIMO, AFC's throughput is 19.8% higher than Size1, implying that a fixed subcarrier group size of 1 underutilizes the channel correlation between subcarriers, which could have been harnessed to compress the CSI. In our lab environment, Size52 achieves a similar level of throughput with AFC.

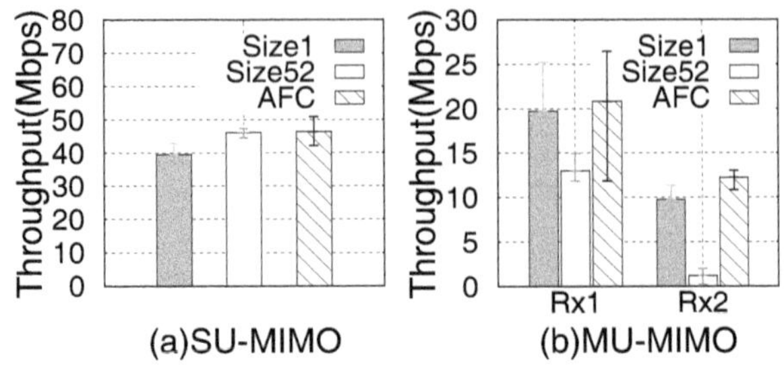


**Figure 13: Frequency-domain adaptation for (a) SU-MIMO and (b) MU-MIMO. Error bars denote maximum and minimum among 5 consecutive experiments, unless noted otherwise.**

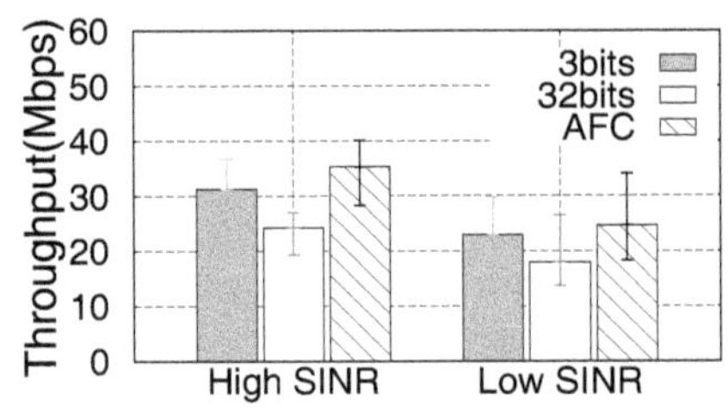


**Figure 14: Adaptive quantization: SU-MIMO.**

However, a MU-MIMO network is more sensitive to CSI compression errors, since severe inter-receiver interference can occur when CSI is noisy. In particular, Fig. 13(b) shows that for one receiver (Rx2), AFC's throughput can be 5.2× that of Size52, and 1.36× for Rx1. In this case, a fixed subcarrier group size of 1 outperforms Size52.

Therefore, from frequency domain perspective, static subcarrier grouping can be either very conservative or aggressive. AFC can effectively strike a balance, selecting the best compression level to optimize the network throughput.

### *6.1.4 Adaptive quantization*

To evaluate AFC's adaptive quantization mechanism, we compare it against static quantization algorithms with aggressive (3-bit) and conservative (32-bit, essentially no compression) quantization algorithms. Accordingly, we allow AFC to choose from these two quantization levels along with the default options in 802.11n/ac (4, 5 6 and 8 bits). Fig. 14 shows the experimental results for a SU-MIMO network. It can be seen that for both high and low SINR[7] cases, the saving of feedback overhead dominates the capacity loss, even with a very aggressive 3-bit quantization. However, there is still sufficient space for AFC to optimize the choice of quantization levels. An examination of experimental results reveals that AFC tends to choose the quantization level of 6 bits, which is close to 3-bit but avoids the capacity loss due to excessive compression.

In addition, as we noted above, in high SINR case, closed-loop MIMO transmission is more sensitive to compression, hence aggressive compression tends to suffer more from capacity loss. Indeed, Fig. 14 shows that AFC improves throughput by 15.1% over 3-bit compression in high-SNR region, and

[7]We adjust link distance to ensure the receivers' SINR level satisfy the requirement of the minimum level of modulation in 802.11, which is 9dB for BPSK modulation [7].

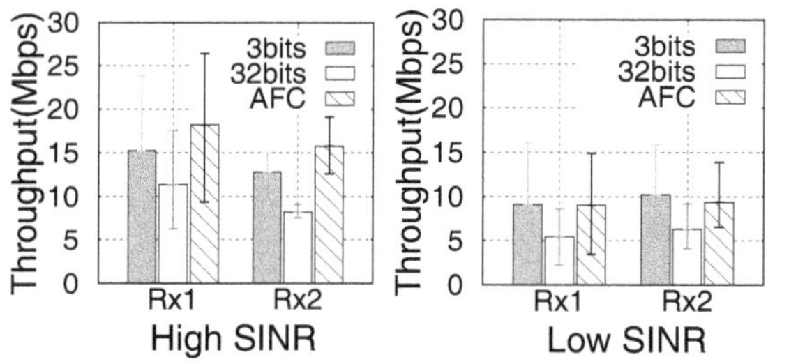


**Figure 15: Adaptive quantization: MU-MIMO.**

4.5% in low-SINR region. Owing to its intelligent overhead reduction, performance gain over fixed 32-bit reduction is more prominent (52.2% and 28.3% for high and low-SINR case, respectively).

Experimental results from a MU-MIMO network (Fig. 15) show a similar trend. In particular, for low-SINR case, channel noise dominates CSI error, and thus 3-bit quantization achieves comparable throughput as AFC. But in high SINR region, AFC achieves 18.5% higher throughput. The gain is even higher than in SU-MIMO, because aggressive quantization amplifies the effects of inter-receiver interference.

## 6.2 Field test of AFC

In this section, we integrate all three components of AFC and evaluate its network performance on our WARP radio testbed.

### 6.2.1 *AFC in action*

We first check whether AFC can react to changes in a real wireless link with unpredictable dynamics. To this end, we evaluate a 2-receiver MU-MIMO network, and vary the transmitter's location and link distance, such that a variety of channel profiles can be generated for both receivers. We collect the per-packet channel traces during this process and then replay them in our emulator.

Fig. 16 plots the throughput variation of AFC over time, in contrast with the legacy configuration in 802.11ac (per-packet feedback, subcarrier group size 1, 8-bit quantization). Throughput is calculated for each inter-packet arrival interval. The results show that AFC can react instantaneously to the change of channel state, and effectively adapt its compression levels accordingly. It consistently achieves higher throughput than 802.11ac under any channel dynamics. The throughput gain ranges from 1.4× to 2.2× in general, and varies depending on the channel profile and users. Occasionally, the fixed configuration in 802.11ac may work as well as AFC when it is appropriate for the channel state.

### 6.2.2 *Other factors*

As mentioned in Sec. 3, besides time, frequency and quantization, there are a number of other factors that determine the CSI overhead, which may in turn affect AFC's choice of compression. Below we use testbed experiments to verify such effects.

We first evaluate packet length, which affects relative overhead of CSI feedback and hence throughput. To isolate the effects of bit-rate change, we vary packet duration instead of size. Experiments in a SU-MIMO network (Fig. 17) show that for shorter packet durations, AFC achieves higher gain (*e.g.*, 2.14 × for 100 $\mu s$). In such cases, balance between overhead and capacity becomes more important, which cannot be handled by the legacy scheme.

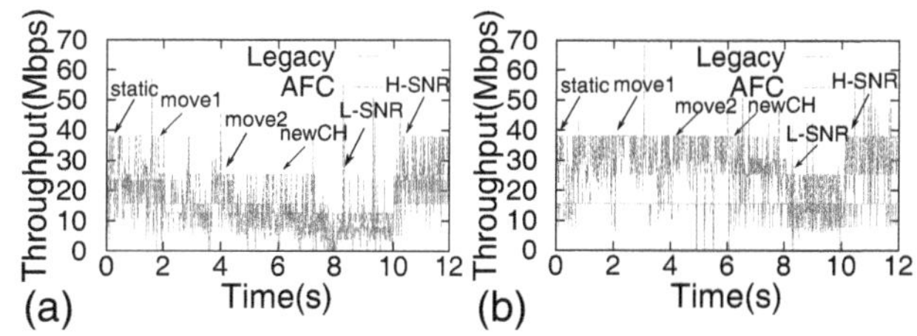


**Figure 16: Field test of AFC in a MU-MIMO network. "newCH" indicates a change of spectrum band. "L-SNR" and "H-SNR" denote low-SNR and high-SNR scenarios created by adjusting transmit power.**

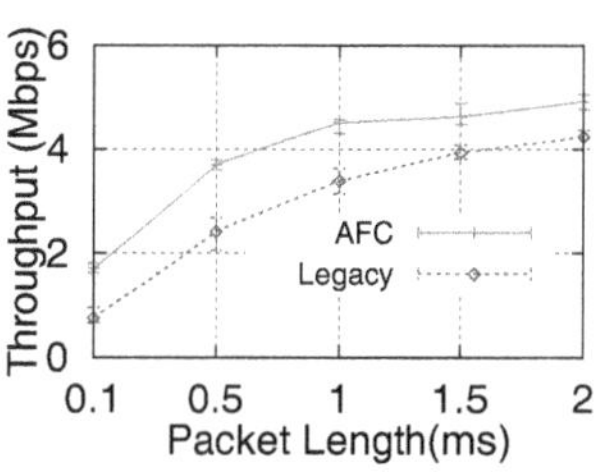


**Figure 17: Effects of packet length on MIMO network throughput.**

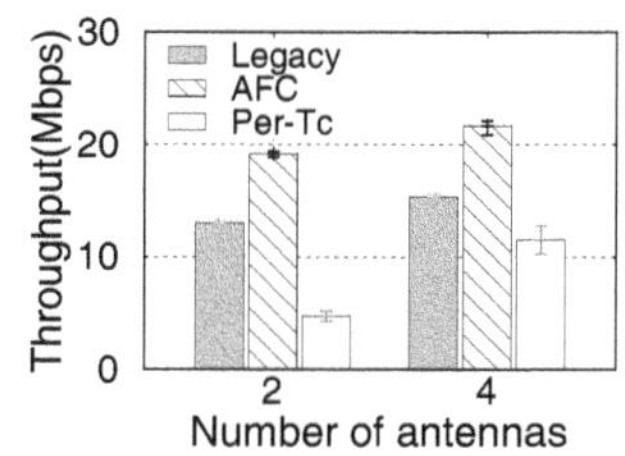


**Figure 18: SU-MIMO network throughput with 2 and 4 transmit antennas.**

Fig. 18 further shows how this balance manifests under different number of antennas. The experiment is done in a lab environment with receiver moving at walking speed. AFC's throughput gain is around 47% higher than legacy for both 2 and 4 antenna cases. Under 2 antenna case, Per-$T_c$ feedback underestimates channel variation, resulting in 72% lower throughput compared with AFC. With 4 antennas, feedback overhead plays a greater role, and thus Per-$T_c$ feedback enjoys throughput improvement due to its aggressive time-domain compression, but its throughput is still 45% lower than AFC.

# 7. RELATED WORK

CSI feedback has been a critical issue in broadband cellular networks such as LTE [11]. For CSI quantization, early generations of LTE adopt codebook based approach, which prescribes a set of precoding vectors, such that the receiver only needs to feed back an index of the best precoding vector [12]. Latest generation of LTE (Release-10) proposes quantized CSI feedback, which is shown (via simulation) to achieve comparable performance with the same number of CSI bits [13]. But even for LTE, the adaptive selection of quantization levels or feedback delay remains an open problem. There exists a vast literature of work on limited feedback MIMO communications (see [11] for a comprehensive survey), which focuses on the design of effective CSI quantization mechanisms to restrict the feedback overhead. In [14], Huang *et al.* analyzed the effect of time-domain compression, based on a theoretical model of channel correlation over time. Pohl *et al.* [15] simulated the SNR and BER of MIMO communication systems under Rayleigh fading model. However, a systematic approach is still lacking that adapts various quantization and compression mechanisms in realistic LTE channel conditions.

Relatively less work has been devoted to the CSI feedback mechanism in wireless LANs. In [16], Sun *et al.* simulated the 802.11n SU-MIMO performance in time-varying and frequency-selective channel conditions. Crepaldi *et al.* [17] proposed a sampling algorithm that can efficiently estimate the channel matrix of a MIMO link. To our knowledge, there does not exist any experimental work that addresses the tradeoff between CSI compression and capacity loss for WLANs.

Recently, there has been a number of software-radio based prototypes of multi-user MIMO [18] or distributed MIMO networks [19], which verified the practicality of theoretical MIMO communication algorithms, but ignored the CSI feedback overhead. In [20], Shepard *et al.* built a massive multi-user MIMO system, based on implicit CSI feedback — an alternative feedback mechanism defined in 802.11n, which leverages channel reciprocity of uplink/downlink to reduce CSI overhead. Implicit beamforming involves sophisticated calibration that is not amenable for handheld WiFi devices [21, 22]. In addition, it cannot be used in many practical wireless transceivers that have more receive antennas than transmit antennas [21, 23]. The new generation of 802.11ac has discarded implicit beamforming, leaving explicit CSI as the only option for CSI feedback.

# 8. CONCLUSION

In this paper, we have conducted a comprehensive measurement study that characterizes the tradeoff between feedback compression and capacity loss in SU-/MU-MIMO wireless networks. We then address this tradeoff by proposing AFC, a simple mechanism that adapts compression intensity to optimize network throughput. AFC's adaptation is steered by CNo, a unified metric that can be extracted from 802.11 packets' preambles, and used to estimate the noise effects due to compression in time, frequency and numerical values. We implemented AFC on the WARP software radio testbed and validated its performance under various channel dynamics and network scenarios. We believe AFC can be a general mechanism for other non-802.11 MIMO networks, such as those based on interference alignment [24]. Such extension is left for our future exploration.

# 9. REFERENCES


[1] F. Boccardi and H. Huang, "Zero-Forcing Precoding for the MIMO Broadcast Channel under Per-Antenna Power Constraints," in *IEEE 7th Workshop on Signal Processing Advances in Wireless Communications (SPAWC), 2006.*, 2006.

[2] D. Gesbert, M. Kountouris, R. Heath, C.-B. Chae, and T. Salzer, "Shifting the MIMO Paradigm," *Signal Processing Magazine, IEEE*, vol. 24, no. 5, 2007.

[3] "Wireless LAN Medium Access Control (MAC) and Physical Layer (PHY) Specifications," *IEEE Std. 802.11ac Draft 3.0*, 2012.

[4] "Wireless LAN Medium Access Control (MAC) and Physical Layer (PHY) Specifications," *IEEE Std. 802.11n*, 2009.

[5] D. Tse and P. Viswanath, *Fundamentals of Wireless Communication.* Cambridge University Press, 2005.

[6] G. Breit, "Coherence Time Measurement for TGac Channel Model," *IEEE 802.11-09/1173r1*, 2010.

[7] Cisco Systems Inc., "Wireless Mesh Access Points, Design and Deployment Guide," *Release 7.3*, 2012.

[8] A. Khattab, J. Camp, C. Hunter, P. Murphy, A. Sabharwal, and E. W. Knightly, "WARP: a Flexible Platform for Clean-Slate Wireless Medium Access Protocol Design," *SIGMOBILE Mob. Comput. Commun. Rev.*, vol. 12, 2008.

[9] D. Halperin, W. Hu, A. Sheth, and D. Wetherall, "Predictable 802.11 Packet Delivery From Wireless Channel Measurements," in *Proc. of ACM SIGCOMM*, 2010.

[10] R. Kudo, K. Ishihara, and Y. Takatori, "Measured Channel Variation and Coherence Time in NTT Lab," *IEEE 802.11-10/0087r0*, 2010.

[11] D. Love, R. Heath, V. Lau, D. Gesbert, B. Rao, and M. Andrews, "An Overview of Limited Feedback in Wireless Communication Systems," *IEEE Journal on Selected Areas in Communications*, vol. 26, no. 8, 2008.

[12] D. Love, R. Heath, W. Santipach, and M. Honig, "What is the Value of Limited Feedback for MIMO Channels?" *IEEE Communications Magazine*, vol. 42, no. 10, 2004.

[13] P. Frank, A. Muller, and J. Speidel, "Fair Performance Comparison Between CQI- and CSI-based MU-MIMO for the LTE Downlink," in *European Wireless Conference (EW)*, 2010.

[14] K. Huang, R. Heath, and J. Andrews, "Limited Feedback Beamforming Over Temporally-Correlated Channels," *Signal Processing, IEEE Transactions on*, vol. 57, no. 5.

[15] V. Pohl, P. Nguyen, V. Jungnickel, and C. Von Helmolt, "How Often Channel Estimation is Needed in MIMO Systems," in *Proc. of IEEE GlobeCom*, 2004.

[16] X. Sun, L. J. Cimini Jr., L. J. Greenstein, D. S. Chan, and B. Douglas, "Performance of Quantized Feedback Beamforming in MIMO-OFDM Links over Time-Varying, Frequency-Selective Channels," in *Proc. of IEEE MILCOM*, 2007.

[17] R. Crepaldi, J. Lee, R. H. Etkin, S.-J. Lee, and R. Kravets, "CSI-SF: Estimating Wireless Channel State Using CSI Sampling & Fusion," in *Proc. of IEEE INFOCOM*, 2012.

[18] H. S. Rahul, S. Kumar, and D. Katabi, "JMB: Scaling Wireless Capacity With User Demands," in *Proc. of ACM SIGCOMM*, 2012.

[19] H. V. Balan, R. Rogalin, A. Michaloliakos, K. Psounis, and G. Caire, "Achieving High Data Rates in a Distributed MIMO System," in *Proc. of ACM MobiCom*, 2012.

[20] C. Shepard, H. Yu, N. Anand, E. Li, T. Marzetta, R. Yang, and L. Zhong, "Argos: Practical Many-Antenna Base Stations," in *Proc. of ACM MobiCom*, 2012.

[21] H. Zhang et al., "802.11ac Explicit Sounding and Feedback," *IEEE 802.11-10/1105r0*, 2010.

[22] Ruckus Wireless, Inc., "All Beamforming Solutions Are Not Equal — Discussion on the Topic of Beamforming," 2013.

[23] D. Halperin, "Simplifying the Configuration of 802.11 Wireless Networks with Effective SNR," *CoRR*, vol. abs/1301.6644, 2013.

[24] S. Gollakota, S. D. Perli, and D. Katabi, "Interference Alignment and Cancellation," in *Proc. of ACM SIGCOMM*, 2009.

# Author Index

www.ingramcontent.com/pod-product-compliance
Ingram Content Group UK Ltd.
Pitfield, Milton Keynes, MK11 3LW, UK
UKHW051241300926
15471UKWH00015B/1603

9 781450 326100